# DICTIONARY OF QUOTATIONS

# DICTIONARY
# OF QUOTATIONS

This edition produced for
Bookmart 1990.

First published 1987

Printed in Great Britain by Mackays of Chatham

ISBN 1 85605 080 7

# • Contents

# • Introduction

**What is a quotation?**
A quotation can be defined as:

'a phrase or passage from a book, poem or play etc, remembered and spoken, especially to illustrate succinctly or support a point or an argument'.

This is the definition we've used in our search for interesting, amusing or revealing phrases or passages that people have written or spoken during the last 3000 years.

**Why do people consult dictionaries of quotations?**
There seem to be several possible reasons:

● To check the details about a familiar quotation, or to find a half remembered one.
Who, for example, said, 'I am dying, with the help of too many physicians'?
Didn't Churchill once say something about his troubles never happening?
● To find unfamiliar quotations about a particular topic – love, death, marriage, etc.
● To find out something about an author through their sayings or writings.
● To browse through to find unexpected and interesting quotations.

We kept all these needs in mind when compiling the *Bloomsbury Dictionary of Quotations*. The extensive index enables you to find quotations easily; it is based on key words, listed alphabetically. For example, to find the quotations mentioned above you would look up the words 'physicians' and 'troubles'. So, if you can only remember a snippet of a quotation use the index. Each key word is followed by a short identifying phrase so that you can find the quotation, or types of quotation you want. Reference is to the author's name and to the quotation number.

It's easy to find out something by or about a particular author – they are all listed in alphabetical order and each has a biographical note telling you when they lived, with a brief comment on their lives and works.

Of course, you may simply enjoy browsing through the first part of the book. The juxtaposition of quotations by authors from different periods can make for fascinating and amusing reading.

## From Confucius to Kinnock

In the *Bloomsbury Dictionary of Quotations* we have departed from established tradition in older works in that we have included both familiar quotations and perceptive or witty sayings that are less well known. We have, especially, sought quotations that reflect contemporary issues as well as those from literature and the Bible.

## How the entries are set out

In an entry under a particular author the entries are arranged according to the references. First come the subject's own works, arranged in alphabetical order (but ignoring the 'A' and 'The'). Then follow works by other people in which the subject is quoted, again listed in alphabetical order. Next come speeches, letters etc, which are generally arranged in date order. These are followed by quotations referenced as Attrib. which are sayings or remarks that are widely and generally attributed to the person involved.

We have broken these rules when it seemed logical to do so – for example by putting 'last words' at the end of the entries.

## Who said what?

There are a few cases in which problems arise in attributing quotations. Some are widely ascribed to two or more people. For these we have included explanatory notes after the quotation. Another problem is that of co-authors such as Lennon and McCartney. In these cases the quotations are included under the first named, with a cross reference from the second. This does not, of course, imply that one is in any way more important.

Mae West exemplifies another difficulty. Many of her sayings are lines from films, and the author should, strictly, be the script writer. However, remarks such as 'Come up and see me (sometime)' are so closely associated with her that it would be perverse not to include them under her name.

Yet another problem involves such quotations as those of Goldwyn and Spooner, who almost certainly never made some of the remarks attributed to them. We decided to include these, if only because they are too good to leave out. Some indication of the difficulties in attributing quotations is given by the reaction of one person we telephoned about a quotation. 'Yes,' she said, 'it is often said to be by me, but I was only repeating something I heard years ago.' And the difficulty in selection is illustrated by her next remark. 'But I have said lots of other clever things that nobody has noticed.'

We hope that you will bear with us in our solutions to these problems and will find our selection both informative and enjoyable reading.

The Editors
1987

# • Acknowledgments

**Editors**

John Daintith
Edmund Wright
Alan Isaacs
Elizabeth Martin
David Pickering

**Contributors**

Elizabeth Bonham
Sue Cope
Eve Daintith
Rosalind Fergusson
Joanna Gosling
Jock Graham
Laurence Holden
Amanda Isaacs
Valerie Illingworth
Stephen Jones
Jennifer Monk
Ruth Salomon
Jessica Scholes
Gwynneth Shaw
Mary Shields
Kate Smith
Anne Stibbs

# A

**Abbott, Berenice** (1898– ) US photographer.

1 Photography can never grow up if it imitates some other medium. It has to walk alone; it has to be itself.
*Infinity*, 'It Has to Walk Alone'

**Abel, Niels Henrik** (1809–29) Norwegian mathematician noted for his work on group theory and the theory of equations.

1 By studying the masters - not their pupils.
When asked how he had become a great mathematician so quickly
*Men of Mathematics* (E. T. Bell)

**Accius, Lucius** (170–c. 85 BC) Roman tragic playwright, who also wrote treatises on grammar, poetry, and agriculture. Of his plays, which were mostly on mythological subjects, about 700 lines survive.

1 Let them hate, so long as they fear.
*Atreus*, 'Seneca'

**Acheson, Dean Gooderham** (1893–1971) US lawyer and statesman. Noted for his strong stance against Soviet expansionism, he was prominent in the development of the Truman Doctrine, the Marshall Plan, and NATO.

1 It hasn't taken Winston long to get used to American ways. He hadn't been an American citizen for three minutes before attacking an ex-secretary of state!
At a ceremony in 1963 to make Churchill an honorary American citizen, Churchill obliquely attacked Acheson's reference to Britain losing an empire.
*Randolph Churchill* (K. Halle)

2 It is worse than immoral, it's a mistake.
Describing the Vietnam war. *See also* BOULAY DE LA MEURTHE.
Quoted by Alistair Cooke in his radio programme *Letter from America*

3 I will undoubtedly have to seek what is happily known as gainful employment, which I am glad to say does not describe holding public office.
Remark made on leaving his post as secretary of state, 1952; he subsequently returned to private legal practice

4 Great Britain has lost an Empire and has not yet found a role.
Speech, Military Academy, West Point, 5 Dec 1962

5 A memorandum is written not to inform the reader but to protect the writer.
Attrib.

**Acton, John Emerich Edward Dalberg Acton, 1st Baron** (1834–1902) British historian; planning editor of the *Cambridge Modern History*. A friend and adviser to Gladstone, he served as a Whig MP (1859–65).

1 The danger is not that a particular class is unfit to govern. Every class is unfit to govern.
Letter to Mary Gladstone, 1881

2 Power tends to corrupt, and absolute power corrupts absolutely. Great men are almost always bad men . . . There is no worse heresy than that the office sanctifies the holder of it.
Often misquoted as 'Power corrupts . . . '
Letter to Bishop Mandell Creighton, 5 Apr 1887

**Adamov, Arthur** (1908–70) Russian-born French dramatist. An exponent of the theatre of the absurd, his plays include *La Parodie* (1947), featuring a handless clock, and *Le Ping Pong* (1955) in which human destiny is controlled by a pinball machine.

1 The reason why Absurdist plays take place in No Man's Land with only two characters is primarily financial.
Said at the Edinburgh International Drama Conference, 13 Sept 1963

**Adams, Abigail** (1744–1818) US feminist campaigner and a prolific letter writer. She was the wife of the second US president, John Adams, and mother of John Quincey Adams.

1 I am more and more convinced that man is a dangerous creature and that power, whether vested in many or a few, is ever grasping, and like the grave, cries 'Give, give.'
Letter to John Adams, 27 Nov 1775

2 . . . a habit the pleasure of which increases with practise, but becomes more urksome with neglect.
Referring to letter-writing
Letter to her daughter, 8 May 1808

**Adams, F(ranklin) P(ierce)** (1881–1960) US journalist and humorist. His columns in the New York *Herald-Tribune* (1931–37) and New York *Post* (1938–41) were widely read. His books include *Tobogganing on Parnassus* (1910).

1 The rich man has his motor car,
His country and his town estate.
He smokes a fifty-cent cigar
And jeers at Fate.
*The Rich Man*

2 Yet though my lamp burns low and dim,
Though I must slave for livelihood –
Think you that I would change with him?
You bet I would!
*The Rich Man*

**Adams, John Quincy** (1767–1848) Sixth president of the USA (1825–29). As secretary of state to President James Monroe (1817–25), he formulated the Monroe Doctrine opposing foreign intervention in American affairs.

1 Think of your forefathers! Think of your posterity!
Speech, Plymouth, Massachusetts, 22 Dec 1802

2 I inhabit a weak, frail, decayed tenement; battered by the winds and broken in on by the storms, and, from all I can learn, the landlord does not intend to repair.
Said during his last illness
Attrib.

**Adams, Richard** (1920– ) British novelist. A civil servant until the success of his children's book *Watership Down* (1972), he later wrote *Shardik* (1974), *The Plague Dogs* (1977), and *The Girl in a Swing* (1980).

1 Many human beings say that they enjoy the winter, but what they really enjoy is feeling proof against it.
*Watership Down*, Ch. 50

**Adams, Samuel** (1722–1803) US revolutionary leader. A leader of the agitation known as the Boston Tea Party, he became governor of Massachusetts (1794–97).

1 A nation of shop-keepers are very seldom so disinterested.
Referring to Britain, following the Declaration of Independence, 4 July 1776
Speech, Philadelphia, 1 Aug 1776

**Adams, Sarah F(lower)** (1805–48) British poet and hymn writer.

1 Nearer, my God, to thee,
Nearer to thee!
*Nearer My God to Thee*

**Adcock, Sir Frank Ezra** (1886–1968) British classicist; coeditor of the *Cambridge Ancient History* and professor of ancient history at Cambridge University.

1 That typically English characteristic for which there is no English name – *esprit de corps*.
Presidential address

**Addams, Jane** (1860–1935) US social worker and founder of Hull House, Chicago. She won the Nobel Peace Prize in 1931.

1 Old-fashioned ways which no longer apply to changed conditions are a snare in which the feet of women have always become readily entangled.
In *Newer Ideals of Peace*, 'Utilization of Women in City Government'

2 In his own way each man must struggle, lest the moral law become a far-off abstraction utterly separated from his active life.
*Twenty Years at Hull House*

3 Civilization is a method of living, an attitude of equal respect for all men.
Speech, Honolulu, 1933

**Addison, Joseph** (1672–1719) British essayist. A Whig politician, he entered parliament in 1708. Addison contributed numerous essays to the *Tatler* and was cofounder (with Richard Steele) of *The Spectator* (1711).

1 Pray consider what a figure a man would make in the republic of letters.
*Ancient Medals*

2 'Tis not in mortals to command success,
But we'll do more, Sempronius; we'll deserve it.
*Cato*, I:2

3 And if the following day, he chance to find
A new repast, or an untasted spring,
Blesses his stars, and thinks it luxury.
*Cato*, I:4

4 The woman that deliberates is lost.
*Cato*, IV:1

5 When vice prevails, and impious men bear sway,
The post of honour is a private station.
*Cato*, IV:1

6 What pity is it
That we can die but once to serve our country!
*Cato*, IV:4

7 A reader seldom peruses a book with pleasure until he knows whether the writer of it be a black man or a fair man, of a mild or choleric disposition, married or a bachelor.
*The Spectator*, 1

8 Thus I live in the world rather as a Spectator of mankind, than as one of the species, by which means I have made myself a speculative statesman, soldier, merchant, and artisan, without ever meddling with any practical part of life.
*The Spectator*, 1

9 Nothing is capable of being well set to music that is not nonsense.
*The Spectator*, 18

10 The infusion of a China plant sweetened with the pith of an Indian cane.
*The Spectator*, 69

11 *Sir Roger* told them, with the air of a man who would not give his judgment rashly, that 'much might be said on both sides'.
Sir Roger de Coverley was a fictional archetype of the old-fashioned and eccentric country squire
*The Spectator*, 122

12 I have often thought, says Sir Roger, it happens very well that Christmas should fall out in the Middle of Winter.
*The Spectator*, 269

13 The Hand that made us is divine.
*The Spectator*, 465

14 A woman seldom asks advice until she has bought her wedding clothes.
*The Spectator*, 475

15 We are always doing something for posterity, but I would fain see posterity do something for us.
*The Spectator*, 583

16 I have but ninepence in ready money, but I can draw for a thousand pounds.
Comparing his ability to make conversation and to write
*Life of Johnson* (Boswell)

17 See in what peace a Christian can die.
Last words

**Ade, George** (1866–1944) US dramatist and humorist. Books include *Breaking into Society* (1903) and *The Old-Time Saloon* (1931); *The College Widow* (1904) and *Father and the Boys* (1907) were his best-known plays.

1 'Whom are you?' said he, for he had been to night school.
*Bang! Bang!: The Steel Box*

2 The music teacher came twice each week to bridge the awful gap between Dorothy and Chopin.
Attrib.

**Adenauer, Konrad** (1876–1967) German statesman; first chancellor of the Federal Republic (1949–63).

1 I haven't asked you to make me young again. All I want is to go on getting older.
Replying to his doctor
Attrib.

**Adler, Alfred** (1870–1937) Austrian psychiatrist. After breaking with Freud he based his work on the importance of the inferiority complex. His books include *The Neurotic Constitution* (1912) and *The Pattern of Life* (1930).

1 It is easier to fight for one's principles than to live up to them.
*Alfred Adler* (P. Bottome)

2 Against whom?
Said when he heard that an egocentric had fallen in love
*Some of My Best Friends* (J. Bishop), 'Exponent of the Soul'

**Ady, Thomas** (17th century) British poet, who wrote on the subject of witchcraft.

1 Matthew, Mark, Luke and John,
The bed be blest that I lie on.
*A Candle in the Dark*

**Aesop** (6th century BC) Reputed Greek writer of fables said by Herodotus to have been a slave from the island of Samos. Aesop's fables, popularized by the Roman poet Phaedrus (1st century AD), use animal characters to portray human frailties.

1 Beware that you do not lose the substance by grasping at the shadow.
*Fables*, 'The Dog and the Shadow'

2 I am sure the grapes are sour.
*Fables*, 'The Fox and the Grapes'

3 Thinking to get at once all the gold that the goose could give, he killed it, and opened it only to find –nothing.
*Fables*, 'The Goose with the Golden Eggs'

4 The gods help them that help themselves.
*Fables*, 'Hercules and the Waggoner'

5 It is not only fine feathers that make fine birds.
*Fables*, 'The Jay and the Peacock'

6 While I see many hoof-marks going in, I see none coming out.
*Fables*, 'The Lion, the Fox, and the Beasts'

7 I will have nothing to do with a man who can blow hot and cold with the same breath.
*Fables*, 'The Man and the Satyr'

8 Don't count your chickens before they are hatched.
*Fables*, 'The Milkmaid and her Pail'

9 The boy cried 'Wolf, wolf!' and the villagers came out to help him.
*Fables*, 'The Shepherd's Boy'

10 The lamb that belonged to the sheep whose skin the wolf was wearing began to follow the wolf in the sheep's clothing.
*Fables*, 'The Wolf in Sheep's Clothing'

**Agar, Herbert Sebastian** (1897–1980) US writer. His works include *The People's Choice* (1933), *The Pursuit of Happiness* (1938), and *A Time for Greatness* (1942).

1 The truth that makes men free is for the most part the truth which men prefer not to hear.
*A Time for Greatness*

**Agassiz, Jean Louis Rodolphe** (1807–73) Swiss naturalist.

1 I can't afford to waste my time making money.
When asked to give a lecture for a fee
Attrib.

**Agate, James (Evershed)** (1877–1947) British theatre critic. His articles and reviews were collected in his series *Ego* (1–9; 1935–47).

1 Long experience has taught me that in England nobody goes to the theatre unless he or she has bronchitis.
*See also* SCHNABEL
*Ego*, 6

2 The English instinctively admire any man who has no talent and is modest about it.
Attrib.

3 Theatre director: a person engaged by the management to conceal the fact that the players cannot act.
Attrib.

**Agathon** (c. 446–401 BC) Athenian poet and playwright.

1 Even God cannot change the past.
*Nicomachean Ethics* (Aristotle), VI

**Agnew, Spiro T(heodore)** (1918– ) US politician. Republican vice-president (1969–73), he was forced to resign as a result of a federal tax case.

1 To some extent, if you've seen one city slum you've seen them all.
Election speech, Detroit, 18 Oct 1968

**Akins, Zoë** (1886–1958) US dramatist. Among her most successful plays were the satirical comedy *The Greeks Had a Word for It* (1930) and *The Old Maid* (1935).

1 The Greeks Had a Word for It.
Play title

**Albee, Edward** (1928– ) US dramatist. Originally an exponent of the theatre of the absurd, his first success was with *Who's Afraid of Virginia Woolf?* (1962). Later plays include *A Delicate Balance* (1967) and *Seascape* (1975).

1 I have a fine sense of the ridiculous, but no sense of humour.
*Who's Afraid of Virginia Woolf?*, I

**2** You gotta have a swine to show you where the truffles are.

*Who's Afraid of Virginia Woolf?*, I

**3** Who's Afraid of Virginia Woolf?

Play title

**Albert, Prince** (1819–61) The son of Ernest, Duke of Saxe-Coburg-Gotha, and consort of Queen Victoria, whom he married in 1840. He organized the Great Exhibition of 1851 and died of typhoid ten years later.

**1** The works of art, by being publicly exhibited and offered for sale, are becoming articles of trade, following as such the unreasoning laws of markets and fashion; and public and even private patronage is swayed by their tyrannical influence.

Referring to the Great Exhibition
Speech, Royal Academy Dinner, 3 May 1851

**Alcott, Louisa May** (1832–88) US novelist. She wrote *Flower Fables* (1854) and, her most famous book, *Little Women* (1868–69).

**1** Housekeeping ain't no joke.

*Little Women*, Pt. I

**2** It takes people a long time to learn the difference between talent and genius, especially ambitious young men and women.

*Little Women*, Pt. II

**3** . . . girls are so queer you never know what they mean. They say No when they mean Yes, and drive a man out of his wits for the fun of it . . .

*Little Women*, Pt. II

**Alcuin** (c. 735–804) English theologian and scholar. Adviser to Charlemagne, he made significant contributions to the development of education.

**1** *Vox populi, vox dei.*
The voice of the people is the voice of God.

Letter to Charlemagne

**Aldiss, Brian** (1925– ) British science-fiction writer. His novels include *Hothouse, Frankenstein Unbound*, and the *Heliconia* trilogy; he has also edited many anthologies.

**1** Science fiction is no more written for scientists than ghost stories are written for ghosts.

*Penguin Science Fiction*, Introduction

**Aldrich, Dean** (1647–1710) English poet.

**1** If all be true that I do think,
There are five reasons we should drink;
Good wine – a friend – or being dry –
Or lest we should be by and by –
Or any other reason why.

*Reasons for Drinking*

**Alençon, Sophie-Charlotte, Duchesse d'** (d. 1897) Bavarian-born duchess.

**1** Because of my title, I was the first to enter here. I shall be the last to go out.

Refusing help during a fire, 4 May 1897, at a charity bazaar in Paris. She died along with 120 others.
Attrib.

**Alexander, C. F.** (1818–95) British hymn writer. Her popular hymns include *All Things Bright and Beautiful, Once in Royal David's City*, and *There is a Green Hill Far Away*.

**1** Once in royal David's city
Stood a lowly cattle shed,
Where a Mother laid her Baby
In a manger for His bed:
Mary was that Mother mild,
Jesus Christ her little Child.

*Once in Royal David's City*

**2** There is a green hill far away,
Without a city wall,
Where the dear Lord was crucified,
Who died to save us all.

*There is a Green Hill Far Away*

**Alexander (III) the Great** (356–323 BC) King of Macedon, who conquered most of the ancient world from Asia Minor to Egypt and India. He was both an outstanding general and an inspired administrator.

**1** I am dying with the help of too many physicians.

Attrib.

**Alfonso (X) the Wise** (c. 1221–84) King of Castile and Léon. His court at Toledo was a centre for Christian, Muslim, and Jewish scholars.

**1** Had I been present at the Creation, I would have given some useful hints for the better ordering of the universe.

Referring to the complicated Ptolemaic model of the universe. Often quoted as, 'Had I been consulted I would have recommended something simpler'.
Attrib.

**Ali, Muhammad** (Cassius Clay; 1942– ) US boxer noted for his extrovert personality. He was three times world heavyweight champion (1964–71, 1974–78, 1978–80).

**1** I'm the greatest!

Remark, often said after his fights

**2** Float like a butterfly
Sting like a bee

Describing his boxing style
Remark

**3** Only the nose knows
Where the nose goes
When the door close.

When asked whether a boxer should have sex before a big fight
Remark, reported by Al Silverman

**Alison, Richard** (fl. c. 1606) English poet.

**1** There cherries grow, that none can buy
Till cherry ripe themselves do cry.

*An Hour's Recreation in Music*

**2** There is a garden in her face,
Where roses and white lilies grow.
*An Hour's Recreation in Music*

**Allainval, Abbé Lénor Jean d'** (1700–53) French
dramatist.

**1** *L'embarras des richesses.*
A superfluity of good things.
Play title

**Allen, Fred** (1894–1956) US comedian.

**1** A celebrity is a person who works hard all his
life to become known, then wears dark glasses
to avoid being recognized.
*Treadmill to Oblivion*

**2** Where were you fellows when the paper was
blank?
Said to writers who heavily edited one of his scripts
Attrib.

**3** A gentleman is any man who wouldn't hit a woman with his hat on.
Attrib.

**Allen, Woody** (Allen Stewart Konigsberg; 1935–  ) US film
actor and director. His films include *Play It Again, Sam* (1972),
*Annie Hall* (1977), and *The Purple Rose of Cairo* (1985).

**1** Is sex dirty? Only if it's done right.
*All You've Ever Wanted to Know About Sex*

**2** It was the most fun I ever had without laughing.
Referring to sex
*Annie Hall*

**3** Don't knock it, it's sex with someone you love.
Referring to masturbation
*Annie Hall*

**4** I'm short enough and ugly enough to succeed on
my own.
*Play It Again Sam*

**5** I'm really a timid person – I was beaten up by
Quakers.
*Sleeper*

**6** My brain: it's my second favourite organ.
*Sleeper*

**7** It's not that I'm afraid to die. I just don't want to
be there when it happens.
*Without Feathers*, 'Death (A Play)'

**8** The lion and the calf shall lie down together but
the calf won't get much sleep.
*Without Feathers*, 'The Scrolls'

**9** And my parents finally realize that I'm kidnapped
and they snap into action immediately: they
rent out my room.
*Woody Allen and His Comedy* (E. Lax)

**10** I don't want to achieve immortality through my
work . . . I want to achieve it through not
dying.
*Woody Allen and His Comedy* (E. Lax)

**11** I want to tell you a terrific story about oral contraception. I asked this girl to sleep with me
and she said 'no'.
*Woody Allen: Clown Prince of American Humor* (Adler and
Feinman), Ch. 2

**Altman, Robert** (1922–  ) US film director. His best-known
film is *MASH* (1970).

**1** What's a cult? It just means not enough people
to make a minority.
*The Observer*, 1981

**Ambrose, St** (c. 339–97) Bishop of Milan (374–97). Born at
Trier, he settled in Milan as a provincial governor. An eloquent
preacher, he was responsible for the conversion of St Augustine.

**1** When in Rome, live as the Romans do: when
elsewhere, live as they live elsewhere.
Advice to St Augustine

**Amery, Leopold Charles Maurice Stennett** (1873–
1955) British statesman. He played an important part in the
downfall of Chamberlain's government (1940).

**1** Speak for England.
Shouted to Arthur Greenwood, Labour Party spokesman, before
he began to speak in a House of Commons debate immediately
preceding the declaration of war, 2 Sept 1939

**2** You have sat too long here for any good you
have been doing. Depart, I say, and let us have
done with you. In the name of God, *go!*
Said to Neville Chamberlain using Cromwell's words
Speech, House of Commons, May 1940

**Amis, Kingsley** (1922–  ) British novelist. He made his
name with *Lucky Jim* (1954). Subsequent novels include *I Want it
Now* (1968), *Jake's Thing* (1978), and *The Old Devils* (1986). He
has also published several volumes of verse.

**1** Outside every fat man there is an even fatter
man trying to close in.
*See also* CONNOLLY
*One Fat Englishman*, Ch. 3

**2** It was no wonder that people were so horrible
when they started life as children.
*One Fat Englishman*, Ch. 14

**3** Lucky Jim.
Title of novel

**Andersen, Hans Christian** (1805–75) Danish writer,
known for his fairy tales, including *The Snow Queen and The Ugly
Duckling*.

**1** 'But the Emperor has nothing on at all!' cried a
little child.
*The Emperor's New Clothes*

**2** The Ugly Duckling.
Story title

**3** Most of the people who will walk after me will
be children, so make the beat keep time with
short steps.
Planning the music for his funeral
*Hans Christian Andersen* (R. Godden)

**Anne, the Princess Royal** (1950–   ) The only daughter of Queen Elizabeth II, she married Mark Phillips (1948–   ) in 1973. An accomplished horsewoman, she has made a worldwide reputation as an active and resourceful President of the Save the Children Fund.

**1** When I appear in public people expect me to neigh, grind my teeth, paw the ground and swish my tail – none of which is easy.

*The Observer*, 'Sayings of the Week', 22 May 1977

**Anonymous** This includes a selection of sayings, rhymes, epitaphs, ballads, etc., for which the author is unknown. They are arranged in alphabetical order of the first line. Further anonymous quotations are given under the entries for Nursery Rhymes and Proverbs.

**1** Adieu, adieu, kind friends, adieu, adieu, adieu,
I can no longer stay with you, stay with you.
I'll hang my harp on a weeping willow-tree.
And may the world go well with thee.

*There is a Tavern in the Town*

**2** *Ad majorem Dei gloriam.*
To the greater glory of God.

Motto of the Jesuits

**3** All human beings are born free and equal in dignity and rights.

*Universal Declaration of Human Rights* (1948), Article 1

**4** All present and correct.

Report by the orderly sergeant to the officer of the day
*King's Regulations (Army).*

**5** All who come my grave to see
Avoid damp beds and think of me.

Epitaph of Lydia Eason, St Michael's, Stoke

**6** Any officer who shall behave in a scandalous manner, unbecoming the character of an officer and a gentleman shall . . . be cashiered.

The words 'conduct unbecoming the character of an officer' are a direct quotation from the Naval Discipline Act (10 Aug 1860), Article 24
*Articles of War* (1872), *Disgraceful Conduct*, 79

**7** Are we downhearted? No!

A favourite expression of the British soldiers during World War I
Attrib.

**8** As I sat on a sunny bank,
On Christmas Day in the morning,
I spied three ships come sailing by.

*As I sat on a Sunny Bank*

**9** *Ave Caesar, morituri te salutant.*
Hail Caesar; those who are about to die salute you.

Greeting to the Roman Emperor by gladiators

**10** Begone, dull care! I prithee begone from me!
Begone, dull care, you and I shall never agree.

*Begone Dull Care*

**11** Beneath this stone, in hope of Zion,
Doth lie the landlord of the 'Lion'.

His son keeps on the business still,
Resign'd unto the Heavenly will.

Epitaph, Upton-on-Severn churchyard

**12** Come landlord, fill the flowing bowl,
Until it doth run over . . .
For tonight we'll merry, merry be,
Tomorrow we'll be sober.

*Come, Landlord, Fill the Flowing Bowl*

**13** Come lasses and lads, get leave of your dads,
And away to the Maypole hie,
For every he has got him a she,
And the fiddler's standing by.

*Come Lasses and Lads*

**14** Conduct . . . to the prejudice of good order and military discipline.

Army Act, 40

**15** Dear Sir, Your astonishment's odd:
*I* am always about in the Quad.
And that's why the tree
Will continue to be,
Since observed by Yours faithfully, God.

The response to EWER's limerick

**16** Early one morning, just as the sun was rising.
I heard a maid singing in the valley below:
'Oh, don't deceive me; Oh, never leave me!
How could you use a poor maiden so?'

*Early One Morning*

**17** Everyman, I will go with thee, and be thy guide.
In thy most need to go by thy side.

*Everyman* Pt. 1

**18** Farewell and adieu to you,
Fair Spanish Ladies,
Farewell and adieu to you, Ladies of Spain.

*Spanish Ladies*

**19** From ghoulies and ghosties and long-leggety beasties
And things that go bump in the night,
Good Lord, deliver us!

Cornish

**20** God be in my head,
And in my understanding;
God be in my eyes,
And in my looking;
God be in my mouth,
And in my speaking;
God be in my heart,
And in my thinking;
God be at my end,
And at my departing.

*Sarum Missal*

**21** God rest you merry, gentlemen,
Let nothing you dismay.

*God Rest you Merry*

22 Greensleeves was all my joy,
Greensleeves was my delight,
Greensleeves was my heart of gold,
And who but Lady Greensleeves.
*Greensleeves*

23 Ha, ha, ha, you and me,
Little brown jug, don't I love thee!
*The Little Brown Jug*

24 Hail Mary, full of grace, the Lord is with thee:
Blessed art thou among women, and blessed is
the fruit of thy womb, Jesus.
*Ave Maria*, 11th century

25 Here lie I and my four daughters,
Killed by drinking Cheltenham waters.
Had we but stick to Epsom salts,
We wouldn't have been in these here vaults.
*Cheltenham Waters*

26 Here lie I by the chancel door;
They put me here because I was poor.
The further in, the more you pay,
But here lie I as snug as they.
Epitaph, Devon churchyard

27 Here lies a man who was killed by lightning;
He died when his prospects seemed to be
brightening.
He might have cut a flash in this world of
trouble,
But the flash cut him, and he lies in the stubble.
Epitaph, Torrington, Devon

28 Here lies a valiant warrior
Who never drew a sword;
Here lies a noble courtier
Who never kept his word;
Here lies the Earl of Leicester
Who governed the estates
Whom the earth could never living love,
And the just heaven now hates.
Attrib. to Ben Jonson in *Collection of Epitaphs* (Tissington), 1857

29 Here lies father and mother and sister and I,
We all died within the space of one short year;
They all be buried at Wimble, except I,
And I be buried here.
Epitaph, Staffordshire churchyard

30 Here lies Fred,
Who was alive and is dead:
Had it been his father,
I had much rather;
Had it been his brother,
Still better than another;
Had it been his sister,
No one would have missed her;
Had it been the whole generation,
Still better for the nation:
But since 'tis only Fred,
Who was alive and is dead, –
There's no more to be said.
Referring to Frederick, Prince of Wales, eldest son of George II
and father of George III.
*Memoirs of George II* (Horace Walpole)

31 Here lies my wife,
Here lies she;
Hallelujah!
Hallelujee!
Epitaph, Leeds churchyard

32 Here lies the body of Mary Ann Lowder,
She burst while drinking a seidlitz powder.
Called from the world to her heavenly rest,
She should have waited till it effervesced.
Epitaph

33 Here lies the body of Richard Hind,
Who was neither ingenious, sober, nor kind.
Epitaph

34 Here lies Will Smith – and, what's something
rarish,
He was born, bred, and hanged, all in the same
parish.
Epitaph

35 Here's a health unto his Majesty . . .
Confusion to his enemies, . . .
And he that will not drink his health,
I wish him neither wit nor wealth,
Not yet a rope to hang himself.
*Here's a Health unto his Majesty*

36 Here's tae us wha's like us?
Gey few, and they're a' deid.
Scottish toast

37 Here we come gathering nuts in May
Nuts in May,
. . .
On a cold and frosty morning.
Children's song

38 He that fights and runs away
May live to fight another day.
*Musarum Deliciae*

39 *Honi soit qui mal y pense.*
Evil be to him who evil thinks.
Motto for the Order of the Garter

40 'How different, how very different from the
home life of our own dear Queen!'
Remark about the character of Cleopatra as performed by Sarah
Bernhardt

41 I always eat peas with honey
I've done it all my life,
They do taste kind of funny,
But it keeps them on the knife.
*Peas*

42 If all the world were paper,
And all the sea were ink,
And all the trees were bread and cheese,
What should we do for drink?
*If All the World were Paper*

43 I feel no pain, dear mother, now
But oh, I am so dry!
O take me to a brewery
And leave me there to die.
Shanty

**44** I know two things about the horse,
And one of them is rather coarse.

*The Horse*

**45** I'll sing you twelve O.
*Green grow the rushes O.*
What is your twelve O?
Twelve for the twelve apostles,
Eleven for the eleven who went to heaven,
Ten for the ten commandments,
Nine for the nine bright shiners,
Eight for the eight bold rangers,
Seven for the seven stars in the sky,
Six for the six proud walkers,
Five for the symbol at your door,
Four for the Gospel makers,
Three for the rivals,
Two, two, the lily-white boys,
Clothed all in green O,
One is one and all alone
And ever more shall be so.

*The Dilly Song*

**46** I met wid Napper Tandy, and he took me by the
hand,
And he said, 'How's poor ould Ireland, and how
does she stand?'
She's the most disthressful country that iver yet
was seen,
For they're hangin' men an' women there for the
wearin' o' the Green.

*The Wearin' o' the Green*

**47** In Dublin's fair city, where the girls are so
pretty,
I first set my eyes on sweet Molly Malone,
As she wheeled her wheelbarrow, through
streets broad and narrow,
Crying, Cockles and mussels! alive, alive, O!

She was a fishmonger, but sure 'twas no
wonder,
For so were her father and mother before.

*Cockles and Mussels*

**48** In good King Charles's golden days,
When loyalty no harm meant,
A zealous High Churchman was I,
And so I got preferment.

And this is law, that I'll maintain,
Unto my dying day, Sir,
That whatsoever King shall reign,
I'll be the Vicar of Bray, Sir.

*The Vicar of Bray*

**49** In Scarlet town, where I was born,
There was a fair maid dwellin',
Made every youth cry *Well-a-way!*
Her name was Barbara Allen.

All in the merry month of May,
When green buds they were swellin',
Young Jemmy Grove on his death-bed lay,
For love of Barbara Allen.

So slowly, slowly rase she up,
And slowly she came nigh him,
And when she drew the curtain by –
'Young man, I think you're dyin'!'.

*Barbara Allen's Cruelty*

**50** John Wayne is dead
with a denial:
The hell I am

Inscription on a wall in Bermondsey Antique Market
*Evening Standard*, 1980

**51** *Liberté! Égalité! Fraternité!*
Freedom! Equality! Brotherhood!

Motto for French Revolutionaries

**52** Little Willy from his mirror
Licked the mercury right off,
Thinking in his childish error,
It would cure the whooping cough.
At the funeral his mother
Smartly said to Mrs Brown:
"Twas a chilly day for Willie
When the mercury went down'.

*Willie's Epitaph*

**53** Lizzie Borden took an axe
And gave her mother forty whacks;
When she saw what she had done
She gave her father forty-one!

On 4 Aug 1892 in Fall River, Massachusetts, Lizzie Borden was
acquitted of the murder of her stepmother and her father

**54** Lo, Hudled up, together Lye
Gray Age, Grene youth, White Infancy.
If Death doth Nature's Laws dispence,
And reconciles All Difference
Tis Fit, One Flesh, One House Should have
One Tombe, One Epitaph, One Grave:
And they that Liv'd and Lov'd Either,
Should Dye and Lye and Sleep together.

Good Reader, whether go or stay
Thou must not hence be Long Away

Epitaph, of William Bartholomew (died 1662), his wife and some
of their children, St John the Baptist, Burford

**55** Love is blind; friendship closes its eyes.

Proverb

**56** Mary Ann has gone to rest,
Safe at last on Abraham's breast;
Which may be nuts for Mary Ann,
But is certainly rough on Abraham.

Epitaph

57 Miss Buss and Miss Beale
Cupid's darts do not feel.
How different from us,
Miss Beale and Miss Buss.

*Written about the headmistresses of North London Collegiate
School and Cheltenham Ladies' College, respectively*

58 My Bonnie lies over the ocean,
My Bonnie lies over the sea,
My Bonnie lies over the ocean,
Oh, bring back my Bonnie to me.

*My Bonnie*

59 My Love in her attire doth show her wit,
It doth so well become her:
For every season she hath dressings fit,
For winter, spring, and summer.
No beauty she doth miss,
When all her robes are on;
But beauty's self she is,
When all her robes are gone.

*Madrigal*

60 My name is George Nathaniel Curzon,
I am a most superior person.
My face is pink, my hair is sleek,
I dine at Blenheim once a week.

*The Masque of Balliol*

61 My sledge and anvil lie declined
My bellows too have lost their wind
My fire's extinct, my forge decayed,
And in the Dust my Vice is laid
My coals are spent, my iron's gone
My Nails are Drove, My Work is done.

*An epitaph to William Strange, blacksmith, died 6 June 1746 and
buried in Nettlebed churchyard*

62 No one provokes me with impunity.

*Motto of the Crown of Scotland*

63 Now I am a bachelor, I live by myself and I work
at the weaving trade,
And the only only thing that I ever did wrong
Was to woo a fair young maid.

She sighed, she cried, she damned near died:
she said 'What shall I do?'
So I took her into bed and covered up her head
Just to save her from the foggy, foggy dew.

*Weaver's Song*

64 Now I lay me down to sleep,
I pray the Lord my soul to keep.
If I should die before I wake,
I pray the Lord my soul to take.

*New England Primer, 1781*

65 O Death, where is thy sting-a-ling-a-ling,
O Grave, thy victoree?
The bells of hell go ting-a-ling-a-ling
For you but not for me.

*Song of World War I*

66 O, Shenandoah, I long to hear you
Away, you rolling river.

*Shenandoah*

67 O ye'll tak' the high road, and I'll tak' the low
road,
And I'll be in Scotland afore ye,
But me and my true love will never meet again,
On the bonnie, bonnie banks o' Loch Lomon'.

*The Bonnie Banks o' Loch Lomon'*

68 *Per ardua ad astra.*
Hard and high to the stars!

*Motto of the Royal Air Force*

69 Please to remember the Fifth of November,
Gunpowder Treason and Plot.
We know no reason why gunpowder treason
Should ever be forgot.

*Traditional*

70 Sacred to the memory of
Captain Anthony Wedgwood
Accidentally shot by his gamekeeper
Whilst out shooting
"Well done thou good and faithful servant"

*Epitaph*

71 She was poor but she was honest
Victim of a rich man's game.
First he loved her, then he left her,
And she lost her maiden name.

See her on the bridge at midnight,
Saying 'Farewell, blighted love.'
Then a scream, a splash and goodness,
What is she a-doin' of?

It's the same the whole world over,
It's the poor wot gets the blame,
It's the rich wot gets the gravy.
Ain't it all a bleedin' shame?

*She was Poor but she was Honest*

72 Since wars begin in the minds of men, it is in the
minds of men that the defences of peace must
be constructed.

*Constitution of UNESCO*

73 Some talk of Alexander, and some of Hercules,
Of Hector and Lysander, and such great names
as these;
But of all the world's brave heroes there's none
that can compare
With a tow, row, row, row, row, row for the
British Grenadier.

*The British Grenadiers*

74 Stranger! Approach this spot with gravity!
John Brown is filling his last cavity.

*Epitaph of a dentist*

75 Sumer is icumen in,
Lhude sing cuccu!
Groweth sed, and bloweth med,
And springth the wude nu.

*Cuckoo Song, c. 1250*

76 Swing low sweet chariot,
Comin' for to carry me home,
I looked over Jordan an' what did I see?
A band of Angels coming after me,
Comin' for to carry me home.

*Swing Low, Sweet Chariot*

77 That this house will in no circumstances fight for
its King and country.

Motion passed at the Oxford Union, 9 Feb 1933

78 The animals went in one by one,
There's one more river to cross.

*One More River*

79 The Campbells are comin', oho, oho.

*The Campbells are Comin'*

80 The fault is great in man or woman
Who steals a goose from off a common;
But what can plead that man's excuse
Who steals a common from a goose?

*The Tickler Magazine*, 1 Feb 1821

81 The holly and the ivy,
When they are both full grown,
Of all the trees that are in the wood,
The holly bears the crown.
The rising of the sun
And the running of the deer,
The playing of the merry organ,
Sweet singing in the choir.

*The Holly and the Ivy*

82 The King over the Water.

Jacobite toast

83 The king sits in Dunfermline town
Drinking the blude-red wine.

'I saw the new moon late yestreen
Wi' the auld moon in her arm;
And if we gang to sea master,
I fear we'll come to harm.'

O lang, lang may the ladies sit,
Wi' their fans into their hand,
Before they see Sir Patrick Spens
Come sailing to the strand!

*Sir Patrick Spens*

84 The rabbit has a charming face;
Its private life is a disgrace.

*The Rabbit*, 20th century

85 There are twelve months in all the year,
As I hear many men say,
But the merriest month in all the year
Is the merry month of May.

*Robin Hood and the Widow's Three Sons*

86 There is a lady sweet and kind,
Was never face so pleased my mind;
I did but see her passing by,
And yet I love her till I die.

*Passing By*

87 There is a tavern in the town,
And there my dear love sits him down,
And drinks his wine 'mid laughter free,
And never, never thinks of me.

Fare thee well, for I must leave thee,
Do not let this parting grieve thee,
And remember that the best of friends must
part.

*There is a Tavern in the Town*

88 There is so much good in the worst of us,
And so much bad in the best of us,
That it hardly becomes any of us
To talk about the rest of us.

*Good and Bad*

89 There's a wonderful family called Stein,
There's Gert and there's Epp and there's Ein;
Gert's poems are bunk,
Epp's statues are junk,
And no one can understand Ein.

90 There was a faith-healer of Deal,
Who said, 'Although pain isn't real,
If I sit on a pin
And it punctures my skin,
I dislike what I fancy I feel.'

91 There was an old man from Darjeeling,
Who boarded a bus bound for Ealing,
He saw on the door:
'Please don't spit on the floor',
So he stood up and spat on the ceiling.

92 There was an old man of Boulogne
Who sang a most topical song.
It wasn't the words
That frightened the birds,
But the horrible double-entendre.

93 There was a young lady of Riga,
Who went for a ride on a tiger;
They returned from the ride
With the lady inside,
And a smile on the face of the tiger.

94 There was a young man of Japan
Whose limericks never would scan;
When they said it was so,
He replied, 'Yes, I know,
But I always try to get as many words into the
last line as ever I possibly can.'

95 There was a young woman called Starkie,
Who had an affair with a darky.
The result of her sins
Was quadruplets, not twins –
One black, and one white, and two khaki.

96 There were three ravens sat on a tree,
They were as black as they might be.
The one of them said to his make,
'Where shall we our breakfast take?'

*The Three Ravens*

**97** There were twa sisters sat in a bour;
*Binnorie, O Binnorie!*
There came a knight to be their wooer,
*By the bonnie milldams o' Binnorie.*
*Binnorie*

**98** The sons of the prophet were brave men and
bold,
And quite unaccustomed to fear,
But the bravest by far in the ranks of the Shah
Was Abdul the Bulbul Amir.
*Abdul the Bulbul Amir*

**99** Thirty days hath September,
April, June, and November;
All the rest have thirty-one,
Excepting February alone,
And that has twenty-eight days clear
And twenty-nine in each leap year.
*Stevins Manuscript, c. 1555*

**100** This animal is very bad; when attacked it de-
fends itself.
*La Ménagerie* (P. K. Théodore), 1828

**101** This is a rotten argument, but it should be
good enough for their lordships on a hot summer afternoon.
A note on a ministerial brief read out by mistake in the House
of Lords
*The Way the Wind Blows* (Lord Home), 1976

**102** This the grave of Mike O'Day
Who died maintaining his right of way.
His right was clear, his will was strong.
But he's just as dead as if he'd been wrong.
*Epitaph*

**103** 'Tom Pearse, Tom Pearse, lend me you grey
mare,
All along, down along, out along, lee
For I want for to go to Widdicombe Fair,
Wi' Bill Brewer, Jan Stewer, Peter Gurney,
Peter Davey, Dan'l Whiddon, Harry Hawk;
Old Uncle Tom Cobbleigh and all.
Old Uncle Tom Cobbleigh and all.'
*Widdicombe Fair*

**104** Warm summer sun shine kindly here:
Warm summer wind blow softly here:
Green sod above lie light, lie light:
Good-night, Dear Heart: good-night, good-
night.
Memorial to Clorinda Haywood, St Bartholomew's, Edgbaston

**105** What shall we do with the drunken sailor
Early in the morning?
Hoo-ray and up she rises
Early in the morning.
*What shall we do with the Drunken Sailor?*

**106** When I am dead, and laid in grave,
And all my bones are rotten,
By this may I remembered be
When I should be forgotten.
On a girl's sampler, 1736

**107** When Israel was in Egypt land,
Let my people go,
Oppressed so hard they could not stand,
Let my people go.
*Go down, Moses,*
*Way-down in Egypt land,*
*Tell old Pharaoh*
*To let my people go.*
Negro spiritual

**108** Whose Finger do you want on the Trigger
When the World Situation Is So Delicate?
Headline from the *Daily Mirror* on the day before the General
Election, Oct 1951
*Publish and Be Damned* (Hugh Cudlipp), 1953

**109** Ye Highlands and ye Lawlands,
O where hae ye been?
They hae slain the Earl of Murray,
And hae laid him on the green.

He was a braw gallant,
And he rid at the ring;
And the bonny Earl of Murray,
O he might hae been a king!

O lang will his Lady
Look owre the Castle Downe,
Ere she see the Earl of Murray
Come sounding through the town!
*The Bonny Earl of Murray*

**Anouilh, Jean** (1910- ) French dramatist, whose plays have
enjoyed considerable success on the English stage. His most
famous works include *Antigone* (1944), *Ring Round the Moon*
(1947), *The Lark* (1953), and *Becket* (1959).

**1** Oh, love is real enough, you will find it some
day, but it has one arch-enemy – and that is life.
*Ardèle*

**2** Love is, above all, the gift of oneself.
*Ardèle*

**3** Every man thinks God is on his side. The rich
and powerful know that he is.
*The Lark*

**4** The object of art is to give life a shape.
*The Rehearsal*

**5** What fun it would be to be poor, as long as one
was *excessively* poor! Anything in excess is
most exhilarating.
*Ring Round the Moon*

**Anthony, Susan B.** (1820–1906) US editor and worker for
women's suffrage.

**1** Men their rights and nothing more; women their
rights and nothing less.
*The Revolution*, Motto

**2** . . . there never will be complete equality until
women themselves help to make laws and
elect lawmakers.
In *The Arena*, (May 1897) 'The Status of Women, Past, Present
and Future'

**3** And yet, in the schoolroom more than any other place, does the difference of sex, if there is any, need to be forgotten.

*Elizabeth Cady Stanton* (ed. Theodore Stanton and Harriot Stanton Blatch), Vol. II

**4** ... and I shall earnestly and persistently continue to urge all women to the practical recognition of the old Revolutionary maxim, 'Resistance to tyranny is obedience to God.'

Speech in court, 18 June 1873
*Jailed for Freedom* (Doris Stevens)

**Antrim, Minna** (1861 – ?) US writer.

**1** A homely face and no figure have aided many women heavenward.

*Naked Truth and Veiled Allusions*

**2** A fool bolts pleasure, then complains of moral indigestion.

*Naked Truth and Veiled Allusions*

**3** Experience is a good teacher, but she sends in terrific bills.

*Naked Truth and Veiled Allusions*

**Apollinaire, Guillaume** (Wilhelm de Kostrowitzky; 1880 – 1918) Italian-born French poet. Collections of verse include *Alcools* (1913) and *Calligrammes* (1918). He also wrote the surrealist play *Les Mamelles de Tirésias* (1917).

**1** Memories are hunting horns whose sound dies on the wind.

*Cors de Chasse*

**Appius Caecus** (4th – 3rd century BC) Roman statesman (censor c. 312 BC; consul 307 and 296 BC) whose reforms benefitted the plebeians. He is regarded as the founder of Latin prose and oratory.

**1** Each man the architect of his own fate.

*De Civitate* (Sallust), Bk. I

**Appleton, Sir Edward Victor** (1892 – 1965) British physicist. He discovered the layer of ionized gas in the upper atmosphere that reflects radio waves back to earth. This is now known as the Appleton layer.

**1** I do not mind what language an opera is sung in so long as it is a language I don't understand.

*The Observer,* 'Sayings of the Week,' 28 Aug 1955

**Appleton, Thomas Gold** (1812 – 84) US writer, poet, and patron of the arts.

**1** Good Americans, when they die, go to Paris.

*Autocrat of the Breakfast Table* (O. W. Holmes), Ch. 6

**2** A Boston man is the east wind made flesh.

Attrib.

**The Arabian Nights** (c. 1500) A collection of tales from the East linked together by the story that the sultan Shahriyar decreed that all his wives should be executed on the morning after their wedding. One wife, Scheherazade, delayed her execution by telling the sultan a series of stories, promising to tell the ending the next evening. After a thousand and one nights she was reprieved.

**1** Who will change old lamps for new ones? . . . new lamps for old ones?

*The History of Aladdin*

**2** Open Sesame!

*The History of Ali Baba*

**Arabin, William** (1773 – 1841) British judge.

**1** If ever there was a case of clearer evidence than this of persons acting in concert together, this case is that case.

*Arabinesque at Law* (Sir R. Megarry)

**2** They will steal the very teeth out of your mouth as you walk through the streets. I know it from experience.

Referring to the people of Uxbridge
*Arabinesque at Law* (Sir R. Megarry)

**3** Prisoner, God has given you good abilities, instead of which you go about the country stealing ducks.

*Arabinesque at Law* (Sir R. Megarry)

**Arbuthnot, Dr John** (1667 – 1735) Scottish writer and physician. A member of the Scriblerus Club, he wrote *The History of John Bull* (1712), introducing this character.

**1** He warns the heads of parties against believing their own lies.

*The Art of Political Lying*

**Archilochus** (c. 680 – c. 640 BC) Greek poet. Only fragments of his poems survive. He became a mercenary and probably died in battle.

**1** The fox knows many things – the hedgehog one *big* one.

Attrib.

**Archimedes** (c. 287 – 212 BC) Greek mathematician, born in Sicily. He invented a number of mechanical devices, notably Archimedes' screw, and is believed to have discovered Archimedes' principle while taking a bath.

**1** Give me a firm place to stand, and I will move the earth.

*On the Lever*

**2** *Eureka!*
I have found it!

An exclamation of joy supposedly uttered as, stepping into a bath and noticing the water overflowing, he saw the answer to a problem and began the train of thought that led to his principle of buoyancy
Attrib.

**Arendt, Hannah** (1906 – 75) German-born US philosopher and historian.

**1** The defiance of established authority, religious and secular, social and political, as a world-wide phenomenon may well one day be accounted the outstanding event of the last decade.

*Crises of the Republic.* 'Civil Disobedience'

**2**  It is quite gratifying to feel guilty if you haven't done anything wrong: how noble! Whereas it is rather hard and certainly depressing to admit guilt and to repent.
*Eichmann in Jerusalem,* Ch. 15

**Ariosto, Ludovico** (1474–1533) Italian poet. He spent most of his life serving the Este family of Ferrara and is remembered for his epic poem *Orlando furioso* (1516).

**1**  Nature made him, and then broke the mould.
Referring to Charlemagne's paladin, Roland
*Orlando furioso*

**Aristotle** (384–322 BC) Greek philosopher and scientist. A former pupil of Plato and tutor to Alexander the Great, he founded a school at the Lyceum in Athens.

**1**  What we have to learn to do, we learn by doing.
*Nicomachean Ethics,* Bk. II

**2**  The man who gets angry at the right things and with the right people, and in the right way and at the right time and for the right length of time, is commended.
*Nicomachean Ethics,* Bk. IV

**3**  Obstinate people can be divided into the opinionated, the ignorant, and the boorish.
*Nicomachean Ethics,* Bk. VII

**4**  Now a whole is that which has a beginning, a middle, and an end.
Referring specifically to the dramatic form of tragedy
*Poetics,* Ch. 7

**5**  For this reason poetry is something more philosophical and more worthy of serious attention than history.
*Poetics,* Ch. 9

**6**  Man is by nature a political animal.
*Politics,* Bk. I

**7**  Either a beast or a god.
*Politics,* Bk. I

**8**  Where some people are very wealthy and others have nothing, the result will be either extreme democracy or absolute oligarchy, or despotism will come from either of those excesses.
*Politics,* Bk. IV

**9**  Inferiors revolt in order that they may be equal and equals that they may be superior. Such is the state of mind which creates revolutions.
*Politics,* Bk. V

**10**  Plato is dear to me, but dearer still is truth.
Attrib.

**Arminstead, Lewis Addison** (1817–63) US general. A brigadier general in the Confederate army, he was killed at Gettysburg.

**1**  Give them the cold steel, boys!
Exhortation given to his troops during the US Civil War
Attrib.

**Armstrong, Louis** (1900–71) US jazz trumpeter.

**1**  A lotta cats copy the Mona Lisa, but people still line up to see the original.
When asked whether he objected to people copying his style
Attrib.

**Armstrong, Neil Alden** (1930–  ) US astronaut. In July 1969, as commander of the Apollo 11 lunar mission, he became the first person to step onto the moon.

**1**  That's one small step for man, one giant leap for mankind.
Said on stepping onto the moon. Often misquoted as, 'small step for a man . . . ' (which is probably what he intended)
Remark, 21 July 1969

**Armstrong, Sir Robert (Temple)** (1913–  ) British civil servant; secretary of the cabinet (1979–87).

**1**  It contains a misleading impression, not a lie. I was being economical with the truth.
Giving evidence on behalf of the British government in an Australian court case, Nov 1986

**Arnold, George** (1834–65) US poet and humorist. His collected poems were published posthumously in 1866 and 1867.

**1**  The living need charity more than the dead.
*The Jolly Old Pedagogue*

**Arnold, Matthew** (1822–88) British poet and critic, who served for 35 years as inspector of schools.

**1**  Culture being a pursuit of our total perfection by means of getting to know, on all the matters which most concern us, the best which has been thought and said in the world.
*Culture and Anarchy,* Preface

**2**  Our society distributes itself into Barbarians, Philistines, and Populace; and America is just ourselves, with the Barbarians quite left out, and the Populace nearly.
*Culture and Anarchy,* Preface

**3**  The pursuit of perfection, then, is the pursuit of sweetness and light. . . . He who works for sweetness and light united, works to make reason and the will of God prevail.
*Culture and Anarchy,* Ch. 1

**4**  One has often wondered whether upon the whole earth there is anything so unintelligent, so unapt to perceive how the world is really going, as an ordinary young Englishman of our upper class.
*Culture and Anarchy,* Ch. 2

**5**  For this class we have a designation which now has become pretty well known, and which we may as well still keep for them, the designation of Philistines.
Referring to the middle class
*Culture and Anarchy,* Ch. 3

6 I often, therefore, when I want to distinguish
clearly the aristocratic class from the Philistines
proper, or middle class, name the former, in
my own mind *the Barbarians.*
*Culture and Anarchy,* Ch. 3

7 But that vast portion, lastly, of the working-class
which, raw and half-developed, has long lain
half-hidden amidst its poverty and squalor, and
is now issuing from its hiding-place to assert
an Englishman's heaven-born privilege of doing
as he likes, and is beginning to perplex us by
marching where it likes, meeting where it likes,
bawling what it likes, breaking what it likes –
to this vast residuum we may with great propriety give the name of Populace.
*Culture and Anarchy,* Ch. 3

8 The sea is calm to-night,
The tide is full, the moon lies fair
Upon the Straits.
*Dover Beach*

9 And we are here as on a darkling plain
Swept with confused alarms of struggle and
flight,
Where ignorant armies clash by night.
*Dover Beach*

10 Is it so small a thing
To have enjoy'd the sun,
To have lived light in the spring,
To have loved, to have thought, to have done?
*Empedocles on Etna*

11 Home of lost causes, and forsaken beliefs, and
unpopular names, and impossible loyalties!
Referring to Oxford
*Essays in Criticism,* First Series, Preface

12 I am bound by my own definition of criticism: a
disinterested endeavour to learn and propagate
the best that is known and thought in the
world.
*Essays in Criticism,* First Series, 'Functions of Criticism at the
Present Time'

13 A criticism of life under the conditions fixed for
such a criticism by the laws of poetic truth and
poetic beauty.
*Essays in Criticism,* Second Series, 'The Study of Poetry'

14 Come, dear children, let us away;
Down and away below.
*The Forsaken Merman*

15 She left lonely for ever
The kings of the sea.
*The Forsaken Merman*

16 A wanderer is man from his birth.
He was born in a ship
On the breast of the river of Time.
*The Future*

17 Wandering between two worlds, one dead,
The other powerless to be born.
*The Grande Chartreuse*

18 Years hence, perhaps, may dawn an age,
More fortunate, alas! than we,
Which without hardness will be sage,
And gay without frivolity.
*The Grande Chartreuse*

19 The great apostle of the Philistines, Lord
Macaulay.
*Joubert*

20 Culture, the acquainting ourselves with the best
that has been known and said in the world, and
thus with the history of the human spirit.
*Literature and Dogma,* Preface

21 Culture is the passion for sweetness and light,
and (what is more) the passion for making
them prevail.
*Literature and Dogma,* Preface

22 The eternal *not ourselves* that makes for
righteousness.
*Literature and Dogma,* Ch. 8

23 It always seems to me that the right sphere for
Shelley's genius was the sphere of music, not
of poetry.
*Maurice de Guérin,* Footnote

24 When Byron's eyes were shut in death,
We bow'd our head and held our breath.
He taught us little: but our soul
Had *felt* him like the thunder's roll.
*Memorial Verses*

25 He spoke, and loos'd our heart in tears.
He laid us as we lay at birth
On the cool flowery lap of earth.
Referring to Wordsworth
*Memorial Verses*

26 Time may restore us in his course
Goethe's sage mind and Byron's force:
But where will Europe's latter hour
Again find Wordsworth's healing power?
*Memorial Verses*

27 We cannot kindle when we will
The fire which in the heart resides,
The spirit bloweth and is still,
In mystery our soul abides.
*Morality*

28 Now he is dead! Far hence he lies
In the lorn Syrian town;
And on his grave, with shining eyes,
The Syrian stars look down.
*Obermann Once More*

29 He will find one English book and one only,
where, as in the *Iliad* itself, perfect plainness of
speech is allied with perfect nobleness; and that
book is the Bible.
*On Translating Homer*

30 I think it will be found that the grand style arises in poetry, when a noble nature, poetically gifted, treats with simplicity or with severity a serious subject.
Closing words
*On Translating Homer*

31 Cruel, but composed and bland,
Dumb, inscrutable and grand,
So Tiberius might have sat,
Had Tiberius been a cat.
*Poor Matthias*

32 Go, for they call you, Shepherd, from the hill.
*The Scholar Gipsy*

33 All the live murmur of a summer's day.
*The Scholar Gipsy*

34 Tired of knocking at Preferment's door.
*The Scholar Gipsy*

35 Before this strange disease of modern life,
With its sick hurry, its divided aims.
*The Scholar Gipsy*

36 Still nursing the unconquerable hope,
Still clutching the inviolable shade.
*The Scholar Gipsy*

37 Resolve to be thyself: and know, that he
Who finds himself, loses his misery.
*Self-Dependence*

38 Others abide our question, Thou art free,
We ask and ask: Thou smilest and art still,
Out-topping knowledge.
Referring to Shakespeare
*Shakespeare*

39 Truth sits upon the lips of dying men.
*Sohrab and Rustum*

40 Who saw life steadily, and saw it whole:
The mellow glory of the Attic stage.
*Sonnets to a Friend*

41 And see all sights from pole to pole,
And glance, and nod, and bustle by;
And never once possess our soul
Before we die.
*A Southern Night*

42 The difference between genuine poetry and the poetry of Dryden, Pope, and all their school, is briefly this: their poetry is conceived and composed in their wits, genuine poetry is conceived and composed in the soul.
*Thomas Gray*

43 That sweet City with her dreaming spires
She needs not June for beauty's heightening.
Referring to Oxford
*Thyrsis*

44 And sigh that one thing only has been lent
To youth and age in common – discontent.
*Youth's Agitations*

45 I am past thirty, and three parts iced over.
Letter to A. H. Clough, 12 Feb 1853

**Arnold, Thomas** (1795–1842) British educator; father of Matthew Arnold. As headmaster of Rugby school (1828–42), his reforms influenced many 19th-century public schools.

1 My object will be, if possible to form Christian men, for Christian boys I can scarcely hope to make.
Letter on appointment as Headmaster of Rugby, 1828

2 What we must look for here is, first, religious and moral principles; secondly, gentlemanly conduct; thirdly, intellectual ability.
Address to the Scholars at Rugby

**Asaf, George** (George H. Powell; 1880–1951) US songwriter.

1 What's the use of worrying?
It never was worth while,
So, pack up your troubles in your old kit-bag,
And smile, smile, smile.
*Pack up Your Troubles in Your Old Kit-bag*

**Ashburton, Baron** *See* Dunning, John.

**Asquith, Herbert Henry, 1st Earl of Oxford and Asquith** (1852–1928) British statesman; Liberal prime minister (1908–16). His government introduced old-age pensions, national insurance, and other social reforms.

1 One to mislead the public, another to mislead the Cabinet, and the third to mislead itself.
Explaining why the War Office kept three sets of figures
*The Price of Glory* (Alastair Horne), Ch. 2

2 It is fitting that we should have buried the Unknown Prime Minister by the side of the Unknown Soldier.
Said at Bonar Law's funeral, 5 Nov 1923
Attrib.

3 Wait and see.
In various speeches, 1910

**Asquith, Margot** (1865–1945) The second wife of Herbert Asquith, Earl of Oxford and Asquith. She wrote an outspoken *Autobiography* (1922).

1 To marry a man out of pity is folly; and, if you think you are going to influence the kind of fellow who has 'never had a chance, poor devil,' you are profoundly mistaken. One can only influence the strong characters in life, not the weak; and it is the height of vanity to suppose that you can make an honest man of anyone.
*The Autobiography of Margot Asquith*, Ch. 6

2 Rich men's houses are seldom beautiful, rarely comfortable, and never original. It is a constant source of surprise to people of moderate means to observe how little a big fortune contributes to Beauty.
*The Autobiography of Margot Asquith*, Ch. 17

3 If Kitchener was not a great man, he was, at least, a great poster.
*Kitchener: Portrait of an Imperialist* (Sir Philip Magnus), Ch. 14

**Astley, Jacob, Baron** (1579–1652) English Royalist general, who commanded the infantry at Edgehill during the Civil War.

**1** O Lord! thou knowest how busy I must be this day: if I forget thee, do not thou forget me.

Prayer before taking part in the Battle of Edgehill
*Memoires* (Sir Philip Warwick)

**Astor, John Jacob** (1763–1848) US fur trader and property millionaire.

**1** A man who has a million dollars is as well off as if he were rich.

Attrib.

**Astor, Nancy, Viscountess** (1879–1964) American-born British politician, the first woman to sit as an MP in the House of Commons.

**1** I married beneath me – all women do.

*Dictionary of National Biography*

**2** Take a close-up of a woman past sixty! You might as well use a picture of a relief map of Ireland!

When asked for a close-up photograph
Attrib.

**Atkinson, E. L.** (1882–1929) British naval physician, who accompanied Captain Scott on his last voyage to the Antarctic.

**1** Hereabouts died a very gallant gentleman, Captain L. E. G. Oates of the Inniskilling Dragoons. In March 1912, returning from the Pole, he walked willingly to his death in a blizzard, to try and save his comrades, beset by hardships.

Epitaph on memorial in the Antarctic

**Attlee, Clement, Earl** (1883–1967) British statesman and Labour prime minister (1945–51). As leader of the Labour Party, he was deputy prime minister in Churchill's wartime coalition government. His post-war government introduced the welfare state and granted independence to India.

**1** Democracy means government by discussion but it is only effective if you can stop people talking.

*Anatomy of Britain* (Anthony Sampson)

**Auber, David François Esprit** (1782–1871) French composer.

**1** This is the last time that I will take part as an amateur.

Said at a funeral
*Das Buch des Lachens* (W. Scholz)

**2** Aging seems to be the only available way to live a long time.

*Dictionnaire Encyclopédique* (E. Guérard)

**Aubrey, John** (1626–97) English antiquary. His *Miscellanies* (1696) was a collection of folklore, but he is best known for his *Brief Lives*, biographies which were not published in full until 1898.

**1** Sir Walter, being strangely surprised and put out of his countenance at so great a table, gives his son a damned blow over the face. His son, as rude as he was, would not strike his father, but strikes over the face the gentleman that sat next to him and said 'Box about: 'twill come to my father anon'.

*Brief Lives,* 'Sir Walter Raleigh'

**2** How these curiosities would be quite forgot, did not such idle fellows as I am put them down.

*Brief Lives,* 'Venetia Digby'

**Auden, W(ystan) H(ugh)** (1907–73) British poet; professor of poetry at Oxford University (1956–61). Auden made his name in the 1930s.

**1** Yet no one hears his own remarks as prose.

*At a Party*

**2** Political history is far too criminal and pathological to be a fit subject of study for the young. Children should acquire their heroes and villains from fiction.

*A Certain World*

**3** All sin tends to be addictive, and the terminal point of addiction is what is called damnation.

*A Certain World*

**4** Happy the hare at morning, for she cannot read
The Hunter's waking thoughts.

*The Dog Beneath the Skin* (with Christopher Isherwood)

**5** When I find myself in the company of scientists, I feel like a shabby curate who has strayed by mistake into a drawing-room full of dukes.

*The Dyer's Hand*

**6** The true men of action in our time, those who transform the world, are not the politicians and statesmen, but the scientists. Unfortunately, poetry cannot celebrate them, because their deeds are concerned with things, not persons and are, therefore, speechless.

*The Dyer's Hand*

**7** Man is a history-making creature who can neither repeat his past nor leave it behind.

*The Dyer's Hand,* 'D. H. Lawrence'

**8** Some books are undeservedly forgotten; none are undeservedly remembered.

*The Dyer's Hand,* 'Reading'

**9** No poet or novelist wishes he were the only one who ever lived, but most of them wish they were the only one alive, and quite a number fondly believe their wish has been granted.

*The Dyer's Hand,* 'Writing'

**10** Let us honour if we can
The vertical man
Though we value none
But the horizontal one.

*Epigraph for Poems*

11 To save your world you asked this man to die:
Would this man, could he see you now, ask
why?
*Epitaph for an Unknown Soldier*

12 Alone, alone, about the dreadful wood
Of conscious evil runs a lost mankind,
Dreading to find its Father.
*For the Time Being, 'Chorus'*

13 To us he is no more a person
Now but a climate of opinion
*In Memory of Sigmund Freud*

14 Now Ireland has her madness and her weather
still,
For poetry makes nothing happen.
*In Memory of W. B. Yeats, II*

15 Earth, receive an honoured guest:
William Yeats is laid to rest.
Let the Irish vessel lie
Emptied of its poetry.
*In Memory of W. B. Yeats, III*

16 It is time for the destruction of error.
The chairs are being brought in from the garden,
The summer talk stopped on that savage coast
Before the storms.
*It is time*

17 Look, stranger, at this island now
The leaping light for your delight discovers.
*Look, Stranger*

18 Lay your sleeping head, my love,
Human on my faithless arm.
*Lullaby*

19 To the man-in-the-street, who, I'm sorry to say
Is a keen observer of life,
The word Intellectual suggests straight away
A man who's untrue to his wife.
*Note on Intellectuals*

20 God bless the USA, so large,
So friendly, and so rich.
*On the Circuit*

21 Only those in the last stage of disease could believe that children are true judges of character.
*The Orators, 'Journal of an Airman'*

22 My Dear One is mine as mirrors are lonely.
*The Sea and the Mirror*

23 Their fate must always be the same as yours,
To suffer the loss they were afraid of, yes,
Holders of one position, wrong for years.
*Since you are going to begin today*

24 When it comes, will it come without warning
Just as I'm picking my nose?
Will it knock on my door in the morning,
Or tread in the bus on my toes?
Will it come like a change in the weather?
Will its greeting be courteous or rough?
Will it alter my life altogether?
O tell me the truth about love.
*Twelve Songs, XII*

25 Our researchers into Public Opinion are content
That he held the proper opinions for the time of
year;
When there was peace, he was for peace; when
there was war, he went.
*The Unknown Citizen*

26 If there are any of you at the back who do not
hear me, please don't raise your hands because
I am also nearsighted.
Starting a lecture in a large hall
In *Book of the Month Club News*, Dec 1946

27 A professor is one who talks in someone else's
sleep.
Attrib.

**Augustine of Hippo, St** (354–430) Bishop of Hippo in
north Africa (396–430). Converted to Christianity in 386, he
produced a number of influential theological works.

1 Thou hast created us for Thyself, and our heart
is not quiet until it rests in Thee.
*Confessions*, Bk. I, Ch. 1

2 Give me chastity and continence, but not yet.
*Confessions*, Bk. VIII, Ch. 7

3 There is no salvation outside the church.
*De Bapt.*, IV

4 *Roma locuta est; causa finita est.*
Rome has spoken; the case is concluded.
*Sermons*, Bk. I

5 We make ourselves a ladder out of our vices if
we trample the vices themselves underfoot.
*Sermons*, Bk. III, 'De Ascensione'

**Augustus** (63 BC–14 AD) Roman emperor, known as Octavian
until 27 BC. The adopted son of Julius Caesar, he formed a
triumvirate with Mark Antony and Lepidus in 43 BC, becoming
supreme head of the Roman Republic in 31 BC.

1 I found it brick and left it marble.
Referring to the improvements he had made to Rome
*The Lives of the Caesars* (Suetonius), 'Augustus'

**Austen, Jane** (1775–1817) British novelist. Her novels of
middle-class life combine humour with perceptive characterization.

1 One half of the world cannot understand the
pleasures of the other.
*Emma*, Ch. 9

2 Nobody is healthy in London, nobody can be.
*Emma*, Ch. 12

3 A man . . . must have a very good opinion of
himself when he asks people to leave their own
fireside, and encounter such a day as this, for
the sake of coming to see him. He must think
himself a most agreeable fellow.
*Emma*, Ch. 13

4 Human nature is so well disposed towards those
who are in interesting situations, that a young
person, who either marries or dies, is sure to
be kindly spoken of.
*Emma*, Ch. 22

5 The sooner every party breaks up the better.
*Emma*, Ch. 25

6 Business, you know, may bring money, but friendship hardly ever does.
*Emma*, Ch. 34

7 One has no great hopes from Birmingham. I always say there is something direful in the sound.
*Emma*, Ch. 36

8 One of Edward's Mistresses was Jane Shore, who has had a play written about her, but it is a tragedy and therefore not worth reading.
*The History of England*

9 She was nothing more than a mere good-tempered, civil and obliging young woman; as such we could scarcely dislike her – she was only an Object of Contempt.
*Love and Friendship*

10 Let other pens dwell on guilt and misery.
*Mansfield Park*, Ch. 48

11 But are they all horrid, are you sure they are all horrid?
*Northanger Abbey*, Ch. 6

12 Oh! who can ever be tired of Bath?
*Northanger Abbey*, Ch. 10

13 A woman, especially if she have the misfortune of knowing anything, should conceal it as well as she can.
*Northanger Abbey*, Ch. 14

14 One does not love a place the less for having suffered in it unless it has all been suffering, nothing but suffering.
*Persuasion*, Ch. 20

15 It is a truth universally acknowledged, that a single man in possession of a good fortune must be in want of a wife.
The opening words of the book
*Pride and Prejudice*, Ch. 1

16 She was a woman of mean understanding, little information, and uncertain temper.
*Pride and Prejudice*, Ch. 1

17 A lady's imagination is very rapid; it jumps from admiration to love, from love to matrimony in a moment.
*Pride and Prejudice*, Ch. 6

18 Happiness in marriage is entirely a matter of chance.
*Pride and Prejudice*, Ch. 6

19 It is happy for you that you possess the talent of flattering with delicacy. May I ask whether these pleasing attentions proceed from the impulse of the moment, or are the result of previous study?
*Pride and Prejudice*, Ch. 14

20 You have delighted us long enough.
*Pride and Prejudice*, Ch. 18

21 Next to being married, a girl likes to be crossed in love a little now and then.
*Pride and Prejudice*, Ch. 24

22 One cannot be always laughing at a man without now and then stumbling on something witty.
*Pride and Prejudice*, Ch. 40

23 For what do we live, but to make sport for our neighbours, and laugh at them in our turn?
*Pride and Prejudice*, Ch. 57

24 I have been a selfish being all my life, in practice, though not in principle.
*Pride and Prejudice*, Ch. 58

25 What dreadful hot weather we have! It keeps me in a continual state of inelegance.
Letter, 18 Sept 1796

26 Mrs Hall of Sherbourne was brought to bed yesterday of a dead child, some weeks before she expected, owing to a fright. I suppose she happened unawares to look at her husband.
Letter, 27 Oct 1798

27 I do not want people to be very agreeable, as it saves me the trouble of liking them a great deal.
Letter, 24 Dec 1798

28 We met . . . Dr Hall in such very deep mourning that either his mother, his wife, or himself must be dead.
Letter to Cassandra Austen, 17 May 1799

29 The little bit (two inches wide) of ivory on which I work with so fine a brush as produces little effect after much labour.
Letter, 16 Dec 1816

**Austin, Alfred** (1835–1913) British poet. His appointment as poet laureate in 1896 provoked widespread derision.

1 Across the wires the electric message came: 'He is no better, he is much the same.'
Generally attrib. to Austin but there is no definite evidence that he wrote it
*On the Illness of the Prince of Wales*

2 I dare not alter these things; they come to me from above.
When accused of writing ungrammatical verse
*A Number of People* (E. Marsh)

**Austin, Warren Robinson** (1877–1962) US politician and diplomat.

1 It is better for aged diplomats to be bored than for young men to die.
When asked if he got tired during long debates at the UN

2 The Jews and Arabs should sit down and settle their differences like good Christians.
Attrib.

**Avery, Oswald Theodore** (1877–1955) Canadian bacteriologist.

1 Whenever you fall, pick up something.
Attrib.

**Ayckbourn, Alan** (1939– ) British dramatist. His first success was *Relatively Speaking* (1967); subsequent plays include *Absurd Person Singular* (1973) and *The Norman Conquests* (a trilogy; 1974).

1 Few women care to be laughed at and men not at all, except for large sums of money.
*The Norman Conquests*, Preface

**Ayer, Sir Alfred Jules** (1910– ) British philosopher. His *Language, Truth and Logic* (1936) is an exposition of logical positivism.

1 No morality can be founded on authority, even if the authority were divine.
*Essay on Humanism*

2 The principles of logic and metaphysics are true simply because we never allow them to be anything else.
*Language, Truth and Logic*

# B

**Babbage, Charles** (1792–1871) British mathematician and inventor of a computing machine, which was never built but is regarded as the forerunner of the computer.

1 Every moment dies a man,
Every moment one and one sixteenth is born.
A parody of TENNYSON's *Vision of Sin*
Letter to Tennyson

**Bacon, Francis** (1909– ) British painter, born in Dublin. His pictures are characterized by strong colours and distorted human figures.

1 How can I take an interest in my work when I don't like it?
*Francis Bacon* (Sir John Rothenstein)

**Bacon, Francis, 1st Baron Verulam, Viscount St Albans** (1561–1626) English philosopher, lawyer, and politician. While lord chancellor (1618–21) he was charged with corruption and dismissed from public office. His writings include *Novum Organum* (1620), advocating the inductive method of logical reasoning.

1 For all knowledge and wonder (which is the seed of knowledge) is an impression of pleasure in itself.
*The Advancement of Learning*, Bk. I, Ch. 1

2 If a man will begin with certainties, he shall end in doubts, but if he will be content to begin with doubts, he shall end in certainties.
*The Advancement of Learning*, Bk. I, Ch. 5

3 They are ill discoverers that think there is no land, when they can see nothing but sea.
*The Advancement of Learning*, Bk. II, Ch. 7

4 Just as it is always said of slander that something always sticks when people boldly slander, so it might be said of self-praise (if it is not entirely shameful and ridiculous) that if we praise ourselves fearlessly, something will always stick.
*The Advancement of Learning*

5 One of the Seven was wont to say: 'That laws were like cobwebs; where the small flies were caught, and the great brake through.'
*Apothegms*

6 I have often thought upon death, and I find it the least of all evils.
*An Essay on Death*

7 I do not believe that any man fears to be dead, but only the stroke of death.
*An Essay on Death*

8 Prosperity doth best discover vice; but adversity doth best discover virtue.
*Essays*, 'Of Adversity'

9 God never wrought miracle to convince atheism, because his ordinary works convince it.
*Essays*, 'Of Atheism'

10 For none deny there is a God, but those for whom it maketh that there were no God.
*Essays*, 'Of Atheism'

11 Virtue is like a rich stone, best plain set.
*Essays*, 'Of Beauty'

12 There is no excellent beauty that hath not some strangeness in the proportion.
*Essays*, 'Of Beauty'

13 There is in human nature generally more of the fool than of the wise.
*Essays*, 'Of Boldness'

14 Mahomet made the people believe that he would call a hill to him . . . when the hill stood still, he was never a whit abashed, but said, 'If the hill will not come to Mahomet, Mahomet will go to the hill.'
Often misquoted as 'If the mountain will not come to Mohammed . . .'
*Essays*, 'Of Boldness'

15 Houses are built to live in and not to look on; therefore let use be preferred before uniformity, except where both may be had.
*Essays*, 'Of Building'

16 A wise man will make more opportunities than he finds.
*Essays*, 'Of Ceremonies and Respects'

17 When he wrote a letter, he would put that which was most material in the postscript, as if it had been a by-matter.
*Essays*, 'Of Cunning'

18 Men fear death, as children fear to go in the dark; and as that natural fear in children is increased with tales, so is the other.
*Essays*, 'Of Death'

19 It is natural to die as to be born; and to a little infant, perhaps, the one is as painful as the other.
*Essays*, 'Of Death'

20 To choose time is to save time.
*Essays*, 'Of Dispatch'

21 It is a miserable state of mind to have few things to desire and many things to fear.
*Essays*, 'Of Empire'

22 Nothing destroyeth authority so much as the unequal and untimely interchange of power pressed too far, and relaxed too much.
*Essays*, 'Of Empire'

23 Riches are for spending.
*Essays*, 'Of Expense'

24 Whosoever is delighted in solitude is either a wild beast or a god.
*Essays*, 'Of Friendship'

25 Cure the disease and kill the patient.
*Essays*, 'Of Friendship'

26 God Almighty first planted a garden. And indeed it is the purest of human pleasures.
*Essays*, 'Of Gardens'

27 In charity there is no excess.
*Essays*, 'Of Goodness, and Goodness of Nature'

28 If a man be gracious and courteous to strangers, it shews he is a citizen of the world.
*Essays*, 'Of Goodness and Goodness of Nature'

29 As in nature things move violently to their place and calmly in their place, so virtue in ambition is violent, in authority settled and calm.
*Essays*, 'Of Great Place'

30 He that will not apply new remedies must expect new evils: for time is the greatest innovator.
*Essays*, 'Of Innovations'

31 The place of justice is a hallowed place.
*Essays*, 'Of Judicature'

32 Nuptial love maketh mankind; friendly love perfecteth it; but wanton love corrupteth and embaseth it.
*Essays*, 'Of Love'

33 He that hath wife and children hath given hostages to fortune; for they are impediments to great enterprises, either of virtue or mischief.
*See also* LUCAN
*Essays*, 'Of Marriage and Single Life'

34 Wives are young men's mistresses, companions for middle age, and old men's nurses.
*Essays*, 'Of Marriage and Single Life'

35 He was reputed one of the wise men, that made answer to the question, when a man should marry? A young man not yet, an elder man not at all.
*Essays*, 'Of Marriage and Single Life'

36 Nature is often hidden, sometimes overcome, seldom extinguished.
*Essays*, 'Of Nature in Men'

37 A man's nature runs either to herbs, or to weeds; therefore let him seasonably water the one, and destroy the other.
*Essays*, 'Of Nature in Men'

38 The joys of parents are secret, and so are their griefs and fears.
*Essays*, 'Of Parents and Children'

39 Children sweeten labours, but they make misfortunes more bitter.
*Essays*, 'Of Parents and Children'

40 Fame is like a river, that beareth up things light and swoln, and drowns things weighty and solid.
*Essays*, 'Of Praise'

41 Dreams and predictions ought to serve but for winter talk by the fireside.
*Essays*, 'Of Prophecies'

42 Age will not be defied.
*Essays*, 'Of Regiment of Health'

43 Revenge is a kind of wild justice; which the more man's nature runs to, the more ought law to weed it out.
*Essays*, 'Of Revenge'

44 A man that studieth revenge keeps his own wounds green.
*Essays*, 'Of Revenge'

45 Money is like muck, not good except it be spread.
*Essays*, 'Of Seditions and Troubles'

46 The remedy is worse than the disease.
*Essays*, 'Of Seditions and Troubles'

47 The French are wiser than they seem, and the Spaniards seem wiser than they are.
*Essays*, 'Of Seeming Wise'

48 Nakedness is uncomely as well in mind, as body.
*Essays*, 'Of Simulation and Dissimulation'

49 Studies serve for delight, for ornament, and for ability.
*Essays*, 'Of Studies'

50 Some books are to be tasted, others to be swallowed, and some few to be chewed and digested.
*Essays*, 'Of Studies'

51 Reading maketh a full man; conference a ready man; and writing an exact man.
*Essays*, 'Of Studies'

52 It were better to have no opinion of God at all, than such an opinion as is unworthy of him.
*Essays*, 'Of Superstition'

53 Suspicions amongst thoughts are like bats amongst birds, they ever fly by twilight.
*Essays*, 'Of Suspicion'

**54** Travel, in the younger sort, is a part of education; in the elder, a part of experience.
*Essays*, 'Of Travel'

**55** Let diaries, therefore, be brought in use.
*Essays*, 'Of Travel'

**56** What is truth? said jesting Pilate, and would not stay for an answer.
*Essays*, 'Of Truth'

**57** All colours will agree in the dark.
*Essays*, 'Of Unity in Religion'

**58** It was prettily devised of Aesop, 'The fly sat upon the axletree of the chariot-wheel and said, what a dust do I raise.'
*Essays*, 'Of Vain-Glory'

**59** Be so true to thyself, as thou be not false to others.
*Essays*, 'Of Wisdom for a Man's Self'

**60** It is the wisdom of the crocodiles, that shed tears when they would devour.
*Essays*, 'Of Wisdom for a Man's Self'

**61** A man that is young in years may be old in hours, if he have lost no time.
*Essays*, 'Of Youth and Age'

**62** Nature, to be commanded, must be obeyed.
*Novum Organum*

**63** Books must follow sciences, and not sciences books.
*Proposition touching Amendment of Laws*

**64** *Nam et ipsa scientia potestas est.*
Knowledge itself is power.
*Religious Meditations*, 'Of Heresies'

**65** Universities incline wits to sophistry and affectation.
*Valerius Terminus of the Interpretation of Nature*, Ch. 26

**66** The house is well, but it is you, Your Majesty, who have made me too great for my house.
Reply when Elizabeth I remarked on the smallness of his house
*After-dinner Stories and Anecdotes* (L. Meissen)

**67** I have taken all knowledge to be my province.
Letter to Lord Burleigh, 1592

**68** For my name and memory, I leave it to men's charitable speeches, and to foreign nations, and the next ages.
Will, 19 Dec 1625

**Baedeker, Karl** (1801–59) German publisher. His guidebooks became internationally famous.

**1** Oxford is on the whole more attractive than Cambridge to the ordinary visitor; and the traveller is therefore recommended to visit Cambridge first, or to omit it altogether if he cannot visit both.
*Baedeker's Great Britain*, 'From London to Oxford'

**Bagehot, Walter** (1826–77) British economist and journalist; editor of *The Economist* (1860–77).

**1** *The Times* has made many ministries.
*The English Constitution*, 'The Cabinet'

**2** A severe though not unfriendly critic of our institutions said that 'the cure for admiring the House of Lords was to go and look at it.'
*The English Constitution*, 'The House of Lords'

**3** The best reason why Monarchy is a strong government is that it is an intelligible government. The mass of mankind understand it, and they hardly anywhere in the world understand any other.
*The English Constitution*, 'The Monarchy'

**4** It has been said that England invented the phrase, 'Her Majesty's Opposition'.
*The English Constitution*, 'The Monarchy'

**5** Women – one half the human race at least – care fifty times more for a marriage than a ministry.
*The English Constitution*, 'The Monarchy'

**6** But of all nations in the world the English are perhaps the least a nation of pure philosophers.
*The English Constitution*, 'The Monarchy'

**7** The Sovereign has, under a constitutional monarchy such as ours, three rights – the right to be consulted, the right to encourage, the right to warn.
*The English Constitution*, 'The Monarchy'

**8** Writers, like teeth, are divided into incisors and grinders.
*Estimates of some Englishmen and Scotchmen*, 'The First Edinburgh Reviewers'

**9** No man has come so near our definition of a constitutional statesman – the powers of a first-rate man and the creed of a second-rate man.
*Historical Essays*, 'The Character of Sir Robert Peel'

**10** He believes, with all his heart and soul and strength, that there *is* such a thing as truth; he has the soul of a martyr with the intellect of an advocate.
*Historical Essays*, 'Mr Gladstone'

**11** Poverty is an anomaly to rich people. It is very difficult to make out why people who want dinner do not ring the bell.
*Literary Studies*, II

**Bailly, Jean Sylvain** (1736–93) French astronomer and mayor of Paris (1789–91). He was guillotined during the French Revolution.

**1** It's time for me to enjoy another pinch of snuff. Tomorrow my hands will be bound, so as to make it impossible.
Said on the evening before his execution
*Anekdotenschatz* (H. Hoffmeister)

**Bainbridge, Kenneth** (1904– ) US physicist. He directed the first atomic-bomb tests in 1945.

**1** Now we are all sons of bitches.

After the first atomic test
*The Decision to Drop the Bomb*

**Bairnsfather, (Charles) Bruce** (1888–1959) British cartoonist, creator of the character Old Bill.

**1** Well, if you knows of a better 'ole, go to it.

*Fragments from France*

**Baker, Sir H. W.** (1821–77) British hymn writer.

**1** The King of love my Shepherd is,
Whose goodness faileth never;
I nothing lack if I am His,
And He is mine for ever.

*The King of Love My Shepherd Is*

**Baldwin, James Arthur** (1924– ) US writer. A Harlem-born black, he made his name with the novel *Go Tell It on the Mountain* (1953).

**1** If the concept of God has any validity or use, it can only be to make us larger, freer, and more loving. If God cannot do this, then it is time we got rid of Him.

*The Fire next Time*

**2** Money, it turned out, was exactly like sex, you thought of nothing else if you didn't have it and thought of other things if you did.

*Nobody Knows My Name*

**3** The price one pays for pursuing any profession or calling is an intimate knowledge of its ugly side.

*Nobody Knows My Name*

**4** Children have never been very good at listening to their elders, but they have never failed to imitate them.

*Esquire*, 1960

**5** The future is . . . black.

*The Observer*, 'Sayings of the Week', 25 Aug 1963

**Baldwin, Stanley, 1st Earl Baldwin of Bewdley** (1867–1947) British statesman; Conservative prime minister (1923–24, 1924–29, 1935–37). He was criticized for his failure to re-arm in the face of German militarism.

**1** A lot of hard-faced men who look as if they had done very well out of the war.

Referring to the first House of Commons elected after World War I (1918)
*Economic Consequences of the Peace* (J. M. Keynes), Ch. 5

**2** Then comes Winston with his hundred-horse-power mind and what can I do?

*Stanley Baldwin* (G. M. Young), Ch. 11

**3** What the proprietorship of these papers is aiming at is power, and power without responsibility – the prerogative of the harlot through the ages.

Attacking the press barons Lords Rothermere and Beaverbrook. It was first used by KIPLING. *See also* DEVONSHIRE (10th Duke)
Speech, election rally, 18 Mar 1931

**4** The only defence is in offence, which means that you have to kill more women and children more quickly than the enemy if you want to save yourselves.

Speech, Nov 1932

**5** When you think about the defence of England you no longer think of the chalk cliffs of Dover. You think of the Rhine. That is where our frontier lies to-day.

Speech, House of Commons, 30 July 1934

**6** I have seldom spoken with greater regret, for my lips are not yet unsealed. Were these troubles over I would make a case, and I guarantee that not a man would go into the Lobby against us.

Referring to the Abyssinian crisis; usually misquoted as 'My lips are sealed'
Speech, House of Commons, 10 Dec 1935

**7** I would rather be an opportunist and float than go to the bottom with my principles round my neck.

Attrib.

**8** The intelligent are to the intelligentsia what a man is to a gent.

Attrib.

**9** There are three groups that no British Prime Minister should provoke: the Vatican, the Treasury and the miners.

A similar remark is often attributed to Harold MACMILLAN
Attrib.

**10** A platitude is simply a truth repeated till people get tired of hearing it.

Attrib.

**Balfour, Arthur James, 1st Earl of** (1848–1930) British statesman; Conservative prime minister (1902–05). As foreign secretary (1916–19) he issued the Balfour Declaration supporting a Jewish national state in Palestine.

**1** I rather think of having a career of my own.

When asked whether he was going to marry Margot Tennant
*Autobiography* (Margot Asquith), Ch. 9

**2** 'Christianity, of course but why journalism?'

In reply to Frank Harris's remark, ' . . . all the faults of the age come from Christianity and journalism'
*Autobiography* (Margot Asquith), Ch. 10

**3** I thought he was a young man of promise; but it appears he was a young man of promises.

Said of Winston Churchill on his entry into politics, 1899
*Winston Churchill* (Randolph Churchill), Vol. I

**4** It is unfortunate, considering that enthusiasm moves the world, that so few enthusiasts can be trusted to speak the truth.

Letter to Mrs Drew, 1918

**5** Nothing matters very much, and very few things matter at all.

Attrib.

**Ball, John** (d. 1381) English priest and rebel; a leader of the Peasants' Revolt (1381). He was executed after the collapse of the rebellion.

**1** When Adam delved and Eve span,
Who was then the gentleman?
Text of sermon

**Balzac, Honoré de** (1799–1850) French novelist. After several popular novels written under pseudonyms, his first success came with *Les Chouans* (1829). Later novels include *Le Père Goriot* (1834) and *La Cousine Bette* (1846). His entire output – over 40 novels – was organized under the title *La Comédie humaine.*

**1** Equality may perhaps be a right, but no power on earth can ever turn it into a fact.
*La Duchesse de Langeais*

**2** There is no such thing as a great talent without great will-power.
*La Muse du département*

**3** The majority of husbands remind me of an orangutang trying to play the violin.
*La Physiologie du mariage*

**4** I am laughing to think what risks you take to try to find money in a desk by night where the legal owner can never find any by day.
Said on waking to find a burglar in the room
Attrib.

**5** I should like one of these days to be so well known, so popular, so celebrated, so famous, that it would permit me . . . to break wind in society, and society would think it a most natural thing.
Attrib.

**6** It is easier to be a lover than a husband, for the same reason that it is more difficult to show a ready wit all day long than to produce an occasional *bon mot.*
Attrib.

**Banda, Dr Hastings** (1906– ) Malawi statesman. A physician, who trained and practised in the UK and the USA, he returned to his native Nyasaland in 1958. With independence he became president (1964).

**1** I wish I could bring Stonehenge to Nyasaland to show there was a time when Britain had a savage culture.
*The Observer*, 'Sayings of the Week', 10 Mar 1963

**Bangs, Edward** (fl. 1775) US songwriter.

**1** Yankee Doodle came to town
Riding on a pony;
Stuck a feather in his cap
And called it Macaroni.
*Yankee Doodle; or Father's Return to Camp*

**Bankhead, Tallulah** (1903–68) US actress, famous for her extravagant lifestyle.

**1** I have three phobias which, could I mute them, would make my life as slick as a sonnet, but as dull as ditch water: I hate to go to bed, I hate to get up, and I hate to be alone.
*Tallulah*, Ch. 1

**2** It's one of the tragic ironies of the theatre that only one man in it can count on steady work – the night watchman.
*Tallulah*, Ch. 1

**3** I've been called many things, but never an intellectual.
*Tallulah*, Ch. 15

**4** Cocaine isn't habit-forming. I should know – I've been using it for years.
*Pentimento* (Lillian Hellman), 'Theatre'

**5** There is less in this than meets the eye.
Referring to a revival of a play by Maeterlink
*Shouts and Murmurs* (A. Woollcott), 'Capsule Criticism'

**6** Don't bother to thank me. I know what a perfectly ghastly season it's been for you Spanish dancers.
Said on dropping fifty dollars into a tambourine held out by a Salvation Army collector
*With Malice Toward All* (D. Hermann)

**7** I'm as pure as the driven slush.
*The Observer*, 'Sayings of the Week', 24 Feb 1957

**8** Only good girls keep diaries. Bad girls don't have the time.
Attrib.

**Baring, Maurice** (1874–1945) British writer and journalist. He wrote several books on Russian literature, as well as plays, novels, and some verse.

**1** If you would know what the Lord God thinks of money, you have only to look at those to whom He gives it.
*Writers at Work, First Series* (ed. Malcolm Gowley)

**Baring-Gould, Sabine** (1834–1924) British author, clergyman, and hymn writer. He wrote a 15-volume *Lives of the Saints* (1872–77), a number of novels, and many hymns.

**1** Now the day is over,
Night is drawing nigh,
Shadows of the evening
Steal across the sky.
*The Evening Hymn*

**2** Onward, Christian soldiers,
Marching as to war,
With the Cross of Jesus
Going on before.
*Onward Christian Soldiers*

**3** Through the night of doubt and sorrow
Onward goes the pilgrim band,
Singing songs of expectation,
Marching to the Promised Land.
*Through the Night of Doubt and Sorrow*

**Barker, Ronnie** (1929– ) British comedian, best known in his partnership with Ronnie Corbett ('The Two Ronnies').

**1** The marvellous thing about a joke with a double meaning is that it can only mean one thing.
*Sauce*, 'Daddie's Sauce'

**Barnard, Lady Ann** (1750–1825) British poet. Her best-known ballad is *Auld Robin Gray* (1771).

1 My father argued sair – my mother didna speak,
But she looked in my face till my heart was like to break;
They gied him my hand but my heart was in the sea;
And so auld Robin Gray, he was gudeman to me.
*Auld Robin Gray*

**Barnum, Phineas Taylor** (1810–91) US showman. After converting the American Museum into a showplace for freaks and curiosities, he created 'The Greatest Show on Earth' (1871) and finally joined his rival in founding the Barnum and Bailey Circus (1881).

1 There's a sucker born every minute.
Attrib.

2 How were the receipts today in Madison Square Garden?
Last words

**Barrie, Sir J(ames) M(atthew)** (1860–1937) British novelist and dramatist, born in Scotland; author of *Peter Pan* (1904). His other works include *The Admirable Crichton* (1902) and *Dear Brutus* (1917).

1 If it's heaven for climate, it's hell for company.
*The Little Minister*, Ch. 3

2 It's grand, and ye canna expect to be baith grand and comfortable.
*The Little Minister*, Ch. 10

3 When the first baby laughed for the first time, the laugh broke into a thousand pieces and they all went skipping about, and that was the beginning of fairies.
*Peter Pan*, I

4 Every time a child says 'I don't believe in fairies' there is a little fairy somewhere that falls down dead.
*Peter Pan*, I

5 To die will be an awfully big adventure.
*Peter Pan*, III

6 What is algebra exactly; is it those three-cornered things?
*Quality Street*, II

7 One's religion is whatever he is most interested in, and yours is Success.
*The Twelve-Pound Look*

8 It's a sort of bloom on a woman. If you have it, you don't need to have anything else; and if you don't have it, it doesn't much matter what else you have.
Referring to charm
*What Every Woman Knows*, I

9 A young Scotsman of your ability let loose upon the world with £300, what could he not do? It's almost appalling to think of; especially if he went among the English.
*What Every Woman Knows*, I

10 You've forgotten the grandest moral attribute of a Scotsman, Maggie, that he'll do nothing which might damage his career.
*What Every Woman Knows*, II

11 There are few more impressive sights in the world than a Scotsman on the make.
*What Every Woman Knows*, II

12 I have always found that the man whose second thoughts are good is worth watching.
*What Every Woman Knows*, III

13 Never ascribe to an opponent motives meaner than your own.
Speech, St Andrews, 3 May 1922

**Barth, Karl** (1886–1968) Swiss Protestant theologian. His writings include *The Epistle to the Romans* (1919) and the monumental *Church Dogmatics* (1932–67).

1 Men have never been good, they are not good, they never will be good.
*Time*, 12 Apr 1954

**Baruch, Bernard Mannes** (1870–1965) US financier and presidential adviser; he was involved in the Paris Peace Conference (1919).

2 I will never be an old man. To me, old age is always fifteen years older than I am.
*The Observer* 'Sayings of the Week', 21 Aug 1955

3 Let us not be deceived – we are today in the midst of a cold war.
Speech, South Carolina Legislature, 16 Apr 1947

**Bates, Katharine Lee** (1859–1929) US writer and poet. Collections of verse include *Sunshine and Other Verses for Children* (1890) and *America the Beautiful and Other Poems* (1911).

1 O beautiful for spacious skies,
For amber waves of grain,
For purple mountain majesties
Above the fruited plain!
America! America!
God shed His grace on thee
And crown thy good with brotherhood
From sea to shining sea!
*America the Beautiful*

**Baudelaire, Charles** (1821–67) French poet. After a dissolute life spending his inherited money, he published *La Fanfarlo* (1847), a novel, and ten years later the collection of verse for which he is best known, *Les Fleurs du mal*.

1 No task is a long one but the task on which one dare not start. It becomes a nightmare.
*My Heart Laid Bare*

2 I have more memories than if I were a thousand years old.
*Spleen*

**Bax, Sir Arnold** (1883–1953) British composer. His seven symphonies and the tone poem *Tintagel* (1917) are his best-known works. He became Master of the King's Music in 1941.

**1** One should try everything once, except incest and folk-dancing.
*Farewell to My Youth*

**Bayly, Thomas Haynes** (1797–1839) British writer of songs, ballads, plays, and novels.

**1** Absence makes the heart grow fonder, Isle of Beauty, Fare thee well!
*Isle of Beauty*

**2** It was a dream of perfect bliss, Too beautiful to last.
*It was a Dream*

**3** She wore a wreath of roses, The night that first we met.
*She Wore a Wreath of Roses*

**Beachcomber** *See* Morton, J. B.

**Beatty, David, 1st Earl** (1871–1936) British admiral. Appointed commander of the grand fleet after the Battle of Jutland in 1916, he served as first sea lord (1919–27).

**1** There's something wrong with our bloody ships today.
*Remark during Battle of Jutland, 30 May 1916*
Attrib.

**Beaumarchais, Pierre-Augustin Caron de** (1732–99) French dramatist. His comedies *Le Barbier de Séville* (1775) and *Le Mariage de Figaro* (1778) were made into operas by Rossini and Mozart, respectively.

**1** I make myself laugh at everything, so that I do not weep.
*Le Barbier de Séville*, I:2

**2** Drinking when we are not thirsty and making love all year round, madam; that is all there is to distinguish us from other animals.
*Le Mariage de Figaro*, II:21

**Beaumont, Francis** (1584–1616) English dramatist, who wrote a number of plays in collaboration with John Fletcher. These include *Philaster* (1609), and *A King and No King* (1611).

**1** You are no better than you should be.
*The Coxcomb*, IV:3

**2** But what is past my help is past my care.
With John Fletcher
*The Double Marriage*, I:1

**3** It is always good
When a man has two irons in the fire.
*The Faithful Friends*, I:2

**4** Let's meet, and either do, or die.
*The Island Princess*, II:2

**5** I'll put a spoke among your wheels.
*The Mad Lover*, III:6

**6** Those have most power to hurt us that we love.
*The Maid's Tragedy*, V:6

**7** Nothing's so dainty sweet as lovely melancholy.
*The Nice Valour*, III:3

**8** All your better deeds
Shall be in water writ, but this in marble.
*The Nice Valour*, V:3

**9** Mortality, behold and fear!
What a change of flesh is here!
*On the Tombs in Westminster Abbey*

**10** As men
Do walk a mile, women should talk an hour, After supper. 'Tis their exercise.
*Philaster*, II:4

**11** I'll have a fling.
*Rule a Wife and have a Wife*, III:5

**12** Kiss till the cow comes home.
*Scornful Lady*, II:2

**13** Whistle and she'll come to you.
*Wit Without Money*, IV:4

**Beauvoir, Simone de** (1908–86) French writer. A lifelong companion of Jean-Paul Sartre, she wrote novels on existentialist themes, notably *The Mandarins* (1954).

**1** What is an adult? A child blown up by age.
*La Femme rompue*

**2** A man would never get the notion of writing a book on the peculiar situation of the human male.
*Le Deuxième Sexe* (trans. *The Second Sex*)

**3** One is not born a woman, one becomes one.
*Le Deuxième Sexe* (trans. *The Second Sex*)

**4** If you live long enough, you'll see that every victory turns into a defeat.
*Tous les hommes sont mortels*

**Beaverbrook, Max Aitken, Baron** (1879–1964) Canadian-born British newspaper proprietor and politician. He owned the *Daily Express* and *Evening Standard*. In World War I he was minister of information and in World War II he became minister of aircraft production.

**1** He did not care in which direction the car was travelling, so long as he remained in the driver's seat.
Referring to Lloyd George
*New Statesman*, 14 June 1963

**2** Buy old masters. They fetch a better price than old mistresses.
Attrib.

**Beckett, Samuel** (1906– ) Irish novelist, dramatist, and poet. Having settled in Paris in 1937, he wrote in both English and French. His best-known work is *Waiting for Godot* (1952).

**1** CLOV. Do you believe in the life to come?
HAMM. Mine was always that.
*Endgame*

**2** Nothing happens, nobody comes, nobody goes, it's awful!
*Waiting for Godot*, I

**3** VLADIMIR. That passed the time.
ESTRAGON. It would have passed in any case.
VLADIMIR. Yes, but not so rapidly.
*Waiting for Godot*, I

**4** ESTRAGON. . . . Let's go.
VLADIMIR. We can't.
ESTRAGON. Why not?
VLADIMIR. We're waiting for Godot.
*Waiting for Godot*, I

**5** We all are born mad. Some remain so.
*Waiting for Godot*, II

**6** Habit is a great deadener.
*Waiting for Godot*, III

**Beckford, William** (1759–1844) British writer; author of the oriental novel *Vathek* (1782). He commissioned the gothic Fonthill Abbey, where he lived as a recluse until 1822.

**1** I am not over-fond of resisting temptation.
*Vathek*

**Becon, Thomas** (1512–67) English Protestant churchman and chaplain to Thomas Cranmer.

**1** For when the wine is in, the wit is out.
*Catechism*, 375

**Becque, Henry** (1837–99) French dramatist. He is best known for the plays *Les Corbeaux* (1882) and *La Parisienne* (1885).

**1** What makes equality such a difficult business is that we only want it with our superiors.
*Querelles littéraires*

**Bede, St** (The Venerable Bede; c. 673–735 AD) English churchman and historian. The author of many grammatical and historical works, his *Ecclesiastical History of the English People* (c. 731) was his major book.

**1** The present life of men on earth, O king, as compared with the whole length of time which is unknowable to us, seems to me to be like this: as if, when you are sitting at dinner with your chiefs and ministers in wintertime, . . . one of the sparrows from outside flew very quickly through the hall; as if it came in one door and soon went out through another. In that actual time it is indoors it is not touched by the winter's storm; but yet the tiny period of calm is over in a moment, and having come out of the winter it soon returns to the winter and slips out of your sight. Man's life appears to be more or less like this; and of what may follow it, or what preceded it, we are absolutely ignorant.
*Ecclesiastical History of the English People*, Bk. II, Ch. 13

**Bee, Barnard Elliot** (1824–61) US soldier. An officer in the Confederate army, he was killed at the Battle of Bull Run in 1861.

**1** Let us determine to die here, and we will conquer.
There is Jackson standing like a stone wall. Rally behind the Virginians.
Said at the First Battle of Bull Run, 1861; hence Gen Thomas Jackson's nickname, 'Stonewall Jackson'
*Reminiscences of Metropolis* (Poore), II

**Beecham, Sir Thomas** (1879–1961) British conductor. Using his inherited wealth, he popularized the works of Richard Strauss and Delius in Britain as well as founding the London Philharmonic Orchestra (1932) and the Royal Philharmonic Orchestra (1947).

**1** A musicologist is a man who can read music but can't hear it.
*Beecham Remembered* (H. Procter-Gregg)

**2** The English may not like music – but they absolutely love the noise it makes.
*The Wit of Music* (L. Ayre)

**3** Too much counterpoint; what is worse, Protestant counterpoint.
Said of J. S. Bach
*The Guardian*, 8 Mar 1971

**4** The sound of the harpsichord resembles that of a bird-cage played with toasting-forks.
Attrib.

**Beecher, Henry Ward** (1813–87) US Congregational minister and author.

**1** I have known many an instance of a man writing a letter and forgetting to sign his name, but this is the only instance I have ever known of a man signing his name and forgetting to write the letter.
Said on receiving a note containing the single word: 'Fool'
*The Best Stories in the World* (T. Masson)

**Beeching, H. C.** (1859–1919) British academic and clergyman.

**1** First come I; my name is Jowett.
There's no knowledge but I know it.
I am Master of this college:
What I don't know isn't knowledge.
Referring to Benjamin Jowett, master of Balliol College, Oxford
*The Masque of Balliol*

**Beerbohm, Sir Max** (1872–1936) British writer and caricaturist. His only novel, *Zuleika Dobson* (1911), is set in Oxford.

**1** There is always something rather absurd about the past.
*1880*

**2** To give an accurate and exhaustive account of that period would need a far less brilliant pen than mine.
*1880*

**3** Great men are but life-sized. Most of them, indeed, are rather short.
*And Even Now*

**4** I believe the twenty-four hour day has come to stay.
*A Christmas Garland*, 'Perkins and Mankind'

**5** Most women are not so young as they are painted.
*A Defence of Cosmetics*

**6** Anything that is worth doing has been done frequently. Things hitherto undone should be given, I suspect, a wide berth.
*Mainly on the Air*

**7** It is Oxford that has made me insufferable.
*More*, 'Going back to School'

**8** The lower one's vitality, the more sensitive one is to great art.
*Seven Men*, 'Enoch Soames'

**9** The dullard's envy of brilliant men is always assuaged by the suspicion that they will come to a bad end.
*Zuleika Dobson*

**10** It needs no dictionary of quotations to remind me that the eyes are the windows of the soul.
*Zuleika Dobson*, Ch. 4

**11** Women who love the same man have a kind of bitter freemasonry.
*Zuleika Dobson*, Ch. 4

**12** You will find that the woman who is really kind to dogs is always one who has failed to inspire sympathy in men.
*Zuleika Dobson*, Ch. 6

**13** Beauty and the lust for learning have yet to be allied.
*Zuleika Dobson*, Ch. 7

**14** You will think me lamentably crude: my experience of life has been drawn from life itself.
*Zuleika Dobson*, Ch. 7

**15** You cannot make a man by standing a sheep on its hind legs. But by standing a flock of sheep in that position you can make a crowd of men.
*Zuleika Dobson*, Ch. 9

**16** She was one of the people who say, 'I don't know anything about music really, but I know what I like'.
*Zuleika Dobson*, Ch. 16

**17** It's not in support of cricket but as an earnest protest against golf.
Said when giving a shilling towards W. G. Grace's testimonial
*Carr's Dictionary of Extraordinary English Cricketers*

**18** Of course we all know that Morris was a wonderful all-round man, but the act of walking round him has always tired me.
Referring to William Morris
*Conversations with Max* (S. N. Behrman)

**19** They were a tense and peculiar family, the Oedipuses, weren't they?
*Max: A Biography* (D. Cecil)

**20** What were they going to do with the Grail when they found it, Mr Rossetti?
Caption to a cartoon

**Beethoven, Ludwig van** (1770–1827) German composer. About 600 of his works survive, including such masterpieces as the nine symphonies, the opera *Fidelio* (1805–14), chamber music (particularly the piano sonatas and string quartets), and the *Missa Solemnis* (1818–23).

**1** Off with you! You're a happy fellow, for you'll give happiness and joy to many other people. There is nothing better or greater than that!
Said to Franz Liszt when Liszt, aged 11, had visited Beethoven and played for him
*Beethoven: Letters, Journals and Conversations* (M. Hamburger)

**2** When I composed that, I was conscious of being inspired by God Almighty. Do you think I can consider your puny little fiddle when He speaks to me?
Said when a violinist complained that a passage was unplayable
*Music All Around Me* (A. Hopkins)

**3** Do not let that trouble Your Excellency; perhaps the greetings are intended for me.
Said when walking with Goethe, when Goethe complained about greetings from passers-by.
*Thayer's Life of Beethoven* (E. Forbes)

**Behan, Brendan** (1923–64) Irish playwright. His best-known works are *The Quare Fellow* (1954), the autobiographical *Borstal Boy* (1958), and *The Hostage* (1958). Behan's alcoholism led to his premature death.

**1** PAT. He was an Anglo-Irishman.
MEG. In the blessed name of God, what's that?
PAT. A Protestant with a horse.
*The Hostage*, I

**2** When I came back to Dublin, I was courtmartialled in my absence and sentenced to death in my absence, so I said they could shoot me in my absence.
*The Hostage*, I

**3** He was born an Englishman and remained one for years.
*The Hostage*, I

**4** I wish I'd been a mixed infant.
*The Hostage*, II

**5** I am a sociable worker.
*The Hostage*, II

**6** I think weddings is sadder than funerals, because they remind you of your own wedding. You can't be reminded of your own funeral because it hasn't happened. But weddings always make me cry.
*Richard's Cork Leg*, I

**7** Other people have a nationality. The Irish and the Jews have a psychosis.
*Richard's Cork Leg*, I

**8** The English and Americans dislike only *some* Irish – the same Irish that the Irish themselves detest, Irish writers – the ones that *think*.
*Richard's Cork Leg*, I

9 Come in, you Anglo-Saxon swine
And drink of my Algerian wine.
'Twill turn your eyeballs black and blue,
And damn well good enough for you.

Painted as an advert on the window of a Paris café (the owner of
which could not speak English)
*My Life with Brendan* (B. Behan)

10 I am married to Beatrice Salkeld, a painter. We
have no children, except me.

Attrib.

11 Thank you, sister. May you be the mother of a
bishop!

Said to a nun nursing him on his deathbed
Attrib.

**Behn, Aphra** (1640–89) English novelist and dramatist. Her
writings include the novel *Oroonoko* (1688) and the play *The Rover*
(1677–81).

1 Love ceases to be a pleasure, when it ceases to
be a secret.

*The Lover's Watch*, 'Four o'clock'

2 Faith, Sir, we are here to-day, and gone
tomorrow.

*The Lucky Chance*, IV

**Bell, Alexander Graham** (1847–1922) Scottish scientist,
who settled in the USA in 1873 and became professor of vocal
physiology at Boston University. He patented the telephone in
1876.

1 Mr Watson, come here; I want you.

The first telephone conversation, 10 Mar 1876, in Boston
Attrib.

**Bell, (Arthur) Clive (Heward)** (1881–1964) British art
critic, who married Virginia Woolf's sister Vanessa Stephen in
1907. His books include *Art* (1914) and *Civilization* (1928).

1 It would follow that 'significant form' was form
behind which we catch a sense of ultimate
reality.

*Art*, Pt. I, Ch. 3

2 I will try to account for the degree of my aesthetic emotion. That, I conceive, is the function of the critic.

*Art*, Pt. II, Ch. 3

3 Only reason can convince us of those three fundamental truths without a recognition of which
there can be no effective liberty: that what we
believe is not necessarily true; that what we like
is not necessarily good; and that all questions
are open.

*Civilization*, Ch. 5

**Belloc, (Joseph) Hilaire (Pierre)** (1870–1953) French-
born British poet, essayist, and historian; Liberal MP for Salford
(1906–10). Publications include *Cautionary Tales* (1907) and
biographies of major historical figures. He was an ardent Roman
Catholic.

1 Child! do not throw this book about;
Refrain from the unholy pleasure
Of cutting all the pictures out!
Preserve it as your chiefest treasure.

*The Bad Child's Book of Beasts*, 'Dedication'

2 Alas! That such affected tricks
Should flourish in a child of six!

*Cautionary Tales*, 'Godolphin Horne'

3 The Chief Defect of Henry King
Was chewing little bits of String.

*Cautionary Tales*, 'Henry King'

4 'Oh, my Friends, be warned by me,
That Breakfast, Dinner, Lunch and Tea
Are all the Human Frame requires . . . '
With that the Wretched Child expires.

*Cautionary Tales*, 'Henry King'

5 A trick that everyone abhors
In little girls is slamming doors.

*Cautionary Tales*, 'Rebecca'

6 They died to save their country and they only
saved the world.

*The English Graves*

7 The accursed power which stands on Privilege
(And goes with Women, and Champagne, and
Bridge)
Broke – and Democracy resumed her reign:
(Which goes with Bridge, and Women and
Champagne).

*Epigrams*, 'On a Great Election'

8 When I am dead, I hope it may be said:
'His sins were scarlet, but his books were read.'

*Epigrams*, 'On His Books'

9 I'm tired of Love: I'm still more tired of Rhyme.
But Money gives me pleasure all the Time.

*Fatigue*

10 Whatever happens, we have got
The Maxim Gun, and they have not.

Referring to African natives
*The Modern Traveller*

11 The Microbe is so very small
You cannot make him out at all.

*More Beasts for Worse Children*, 'The Microbe'

12 Like many of the upper class
He liked the sound of broken glass.

*New Cautionary Tales*, 'About John'

13 The fleas that tease in the high Pyrenees.

*Tarantella*

14 I always like to associate with a lot of priests because it makes me understand anti-clerical
things so well.

Letter to E. S. P. Haynes, 9 Nov 1909

**15** I am a Catholic. As far as possible I go to Mass every day. As far as possible I kneel down and tell these beads every day. If you reject me on account of my religion, I shall thank God that he has spared me the indignity of being your representative.

Said in his first election campaign
Speech, Salford, 1906

**16** Candidates should not attempt more than six of these.

Suggested addition to the Ten Commandments
Attrib.

**Benchley, Robert Charles** (1889–1945) US humorist and drama critic. He published many volumes of collected essays, including *Love Conquers All* (1922) and *From Bed to Worse* (1934).

**1** Even nowadays a man can't step up and kill a woman without feeling just a bit unchivalrous.

*Chips off the Old Benchley*, 'Down in Front'

**2** A great many people have come up to me and asked how I manage to get so much work done and still keep looking so dissipated.

*Chips off the Old Benchley*, 'How to Get Things Done'

**3** I have been told by hospital authorities that more copies of my works are left behind by departing patients than those of any other author.

*Chips off the Old Benchley*, 'Why Does Nobody Collect Me?'

**4** One cubic foot less of space and it would have constituted adultery.

Describing an office shared with Dorothy Parker
Attrib.

**5** I don't trust a bank that would lend money to such a poor risk.

To a bank that granted his request for a loan. *See also* MARX, Groucho
Attrib.

**6** I do most of my work sitting down; that's where I shine.

Attrib.

**7** So who's in a hurry?

When asked whether he knew that drinking was a slow death
Attrib.

**8** Streets full of water. Please advise.

Telegram sent to his editor on arriving in Venice
Attrib.

**Benjamin, Judah Philip** (1811–84) US politician.

**1** The gentleman will please remember that when his half-civilized ancestors were hunting the wild boar in Silesia, mine were princes of the earth.

Replying to a senator of Germanic origin who had made an antisemitic remark
Attrib.

**Bennett, Alan** (1934– ) British playwright and actor in comic reviews, such as *Beyond the Fringe* (1960). His plays include *Forty Years On* (1968), *Habeas Corpus* (1973), and *An Englishman Abroad* (1982).

**1** Life is rather like a tin of sardines – we're all of us looking for the key.

*Beyond the Fringe*

**2** I have never understood this liking for war. It panders to instincts already catered for within the scope of any respectable domestic establishment.

*Forty Years On*, I

**3** It's the one species I wouldn't mind seeing vanish from the face of the earth. I wish they were like the White Rhino – six of them left in the Serengeti National Park, and all males.

Referring to dogs
*Getting On*, I

**4** Your whole life is on the other side of the glass. And there is nobody watching.

*The Old Country*, I

**5** We were put to Dickens as children but it never quite took. That unremitting humanity soon had me cheesed off.

*The Old Country*, II

**Bennett, (Enoch) Arnold** (1867–1931) British novelist. His novels, set in his native Staffordshire, include *Anna of the Five Towns* (1902) and *Clayhanger* (1910).

**1** 'Ye can call it influenza if ye like,' said Mrs Machin. 'There was no influenza in my young days. We called a cold a cold.'

*The Card*, Ch. 8

**2** The people who live in the past must yield to the people who live in the future. Otherwise the world would begin to turn the other way round.

*Milestones*

**3** Pessimism, when you get used to it, is just as agreeable as optimism.

*Things that have Interested Me*, 'The Slump in Pessimism'

**4** Well, my deliberate opinion is – it's a jolly strange world.

*The Title*, I

**5** Being a husband is a whole-time job. That is why so many husbands fail. They cannot give their entire attention to it.

*The Title*, I

**6** Journalists say a thing that they know isn't true, in the hope that if they keep on saying it long enough it will be true.

*The Title*, II

**7** Good taste is better than bad taste, but bad taste is better than no taste.

*The Observer*, 'Sayings of the Week', 24 Aug 1930

**Bennett, James Gordon** (1841–1918) US newspaper owner and editor. He became editor of the *New York Herald*, which had been founded by his father in 1867. He inherited the ownership in 1872.

**1** Deleted by French censor.

Used to fill empty spaces in his papers during World War I when news was lacking
*Americans in Paris* (B. Morton)

**2** Price of Herald three cents daily. Five cents
Sunday. Bennett.

Telegram to William Randolph Hearst, when he heard that
Hearst was trying to buy his paper
*The Life and Death of the Press Barons* (P. Brandon)

**Benny, Jack** (Benjamin Kubelsky; 1894–1974) US actor and
comedian. His many films included *Charley's Aunt* (1941) and *To
Be or Not To Be* (1942).

**1** I don't deserve this, but I have arthritis, and I
don't deserve that either.

Said when accepting an award
Attrib.

**Benson, A(rthur) C(hristopher)** (1862–1925) British
writer, schoolmaster, and master of Magdalene College,
Cambridge. He wrote the anthem *Land of Hope and Glory*, essays,
biographical studies, and works of criticism.

**1** Land of Hope and Glory, Mother of the Free,
How shall we extol thee, who are born of thee?
Wider still and wider shall thy bounds be set;
God who made thee mighty, make thee mightier
yet.

*Land of Hope and Glory*

**Bentham, Jeremy** (1748–1832) British philosopher. Works
include *Principles of Morals and Legislation* (1789), presenting his
theory of utilitarianism.

**1** The greatest happiness of the greatest number
is the foundation of morals and legislation.

*The Commonplace Book*

**2** Lawyers are the only persons in whom ignorance of the law is not punished.

Attrib.

**Bentley, Edmund Clerihew** (1875–1956) British writer
and journalist, inventor of the witty four-line verse form known as
the 'clerihew'. His writings include the detective novel *Trent's Last
Case* (1913).

**1** When their lordships asked Bacon
How many bribes he had taken
He had at least the grace
To get very red in the face.

*Baseless Biography*

**2** The Art of Biography
Is different from Geography.
Geography is about Maps,
But Biography is about Chaps.

*Biography for Beginners*

**3** What I like about Clive
Is that he is no longer alive.
There is a great deal to be said
For being dead.

*Biography for Beginners*

**4** Sir Humphry Davy
Abominated gravy.
He lived in the odium
Of having discovered Sodium.

*Biography for Beginners*

**5** John Stuart Mill
By a mighty effort of will
Overcame his natural bonhomie
And wrote 'Principles of Political Economy'.

*Biography for Beginners*

**6** Sir Christopher Wren
Said, 'I am going to dine with some men.
If anybody calls
Say I am designing St Paul's.'

*Biography for Beginners*

**Bentley, Richard** (1662–1742) English academic. He
became master of Trinity College, Cambridge, in 1700. He is
known for his critical books on classical authors.

**1** He is believed to have liked port, but to have
said of claret that 'it would be port if it could'.

*Bentley* (R. C. Jebb)

**2** I hold it as certain, that no man was ever written
out of reputation but by himself.

*The Works of Alexander Pope* (W. Warburton), Vol. IV

**Beresford, Charles William de la Poer, Baron**
(1846–1919) British naval officer and author of *The Life of Nelson
and his Times* (1898–1905).

**1** Very sorry can't come. Lie follows by post.

Reply, by telegram, to a dinner invitation at short notice from
Edward, Prince of Wales
*The World of Fashion 1837–1922* (R. Nevill), Ch. 5

**Berkeley, George, Bishop** (1685–1753) Irish churchman
and philosopher. His philosophy of idealism is set out in his
*Principles of Human Knowledge* (1710). Later works include *Siris*
(1744).

**1** It is impossible that a man who is false to his
friends and neighbours should be true to the
public.

*Maxims Concerning Patriotism*

**2** We have first raised a dust and then complain we
cannot see.

*Principles of Human Knowledge*, Introduction

**Berlin, Irving** (Israel Baline; 1888– ) US composer, born in
Russia. His works include musicals, such as *Annie Get Your Gun*
(1946), and film scores.

**1** The world would not be in such a snarl, had
Marx been Groucho instead of Karl.

Telegram to Groucho Marx on his seventy-first birthday

**Berlioz, (Louis) Hector** (1803–69) French composer. His
first success was the *Symphonie Fantastique* (1830–31); later
works include the symphony *Harold in Italy* (1834), the *Requiem*
(1837), and the opera *Les Troyens* (1856–59). He also wrote a
treatise on orchestration.

**1** Time is a great teacher, but unfortunately it kills
all its pupils.

*Almanach des lettres françaises*

**Bernard, Tristan** (1866–1947) French dramatist.

**1** In the theatre the audience want to be surprised
– but by things that they expect.

*Contes, Repliques et Bon Mots*

**Bernard, W. B.** (1807–75) British dramatist.

**1** A Storm in a Teacup.
Play title

**Bernhardt, Sarah** (Sarah Henriette Rosine Bernard; 1844–1923) French actress and theatre manager, noted especially for her passionate performances in tragedy. Among her famous roles were Cordelia, Phèdre, and Hamlet.

**1** For the theatre one needs long arms; it is better to have them too long than too short. An *artiste* with short arms can never, never make a fine gesture.
*Memories of My Life*, Ch. 6

**2** I do love cricket – it's so very English.
On seeing a game of football
*Nijinsky* (R. Buckle)

**Betjeman, Sir John** (1906–84) British poet; poet laureate (1972–84). Publications include *Collected Poems* (1958), *High and Low* (1976), and a verse autobiography, *Summoned by Bells* (1960).

**1** Spirits of well-shot woodcock, partridge, snipe
Flutter and bear him up the Norfolk sky.
*Death of King George V*

**2** You ask me what it is I do. Well actually, you know,
I'm partly a liaison man and partly P.R.O.
Essentially I integrate the current export drive
And basically I'm viable from ten o'clock till five.
*Executive*

**3** Phone for the fish knives Norman,
As Cook is a little unnerved;
You kiddies have crumpled the serviettes
And I must have things daintily served.
*How to get on in Society*

**4** I know what I wanted to ask you;
Is trifle sufficient for sweet?
*How to get on in Society*

**5** Rumbling under blackened girders, Midland, bound for Cricklewood,
Puffed its sulphur to the sunset where the Land of Laundries stood.
Rumble under, thunder over, train and tram alternate go.
*Parliament Hill Fields*

**6** Come, friendly bombs, and fall on Slough
It isn't fit for humans now.
There isn't grass to graze a cow
Swarm over, Death!
. . .
Come, friendly bombs, and fall on Slough
To get it ready for the plough.
The cabbages are coming now:
The earth exhales.
*Slough*

**7** Miss J. Hunter Dunn, Miss J. Hunter Dunn,
Furnish'd and burnish'd by Aldershot sun.
*A Subaltern's Love Song*

**Bevan, Aneurin** (1897–1960) British Labour politician and editor of the left-wing *Tribune* (1940–45). As minister of health (1945–51) he introduced the National Health Service.

**1** Its relationship to democratic institutions is that of the death watch beetle – it is not a Party, it is a conspiracy.
Referring to the Communist Party
*Tribune*

**2** The language of priorities is the religion of Socialism.
*Aneurin Bevan* (Vincent Brome), Ch. 1

**3** He is a man suffering from petrified adolescence.
Referring to Churchill
*Aneurin Bevan* (Vincent Brome), Ch. 11

**4** A dessicated calculating machine.
Referring to Hugh Gaitskell
*Hugh Gaitskell* (W. T. Rodgers)

**5** We know what happens to people who stay in the middle of the road. They get run over.
*The Observer*, 'Sayings of the Week', 9 Dec 1953

**6** I read the newspaper avidly. It is my one form of continuous fiction.
*The Observer*, 'Sayings of the Week', 3 Apr 1960

**7** This island is almost made of coal and surrounded by fish. Only an organizing genius could produce a shortage of coal and fish in Great Britain at the same time.
Speech, Blackpool, 18 May 1945

**8** No attempt at ethical or social seduction can eradicate from my heart a deep burning hatred for the Tory Party.
Speech, Manchester, 4 July 1949

**9** So far as I am concerned they are lower than vermin.
Referring to the Tory Party.
Speech, Manchester, 4 July 1949

**10** There is no reason to attack the monkey when the organ-grinder is present.
The 'monkey' was Selwyn Lloyd; the 'organ-grinder' was Harold Macmillan
Speech, House of Commons

**11** If you carry this resolution and follow out all its implications and do not run away from it, you will send a Foreign Secretary, whoever he may be, naked into the conference chamber.
Referring to unilateral disarmament
Speech, Labour Party Conference, 2 Oct 1957

**12** Fascism is not itself a new order of society. It is the future refusing to be born.
Attrib.

**Beveridge, William Henry, Baron** (1879–1963) British economist. He is best known for the so-called Beveridge Report, *The Report on Social Insurance and Allied Services* (1942), upon which the welfare state was based.

1 The object of government in peace and in war is not the glory of rulers or of races, but the happiness of the common man.
*Social Insurance*

2 The trouble in modern democracy is that men do not approach to leadership until they have lost the desire to lead anyone.
*The Observer*, 'Sayings of the Week', 15 Apr 1934

3 Scratch a pessimist, and you find often a defender of privilege.
*The Observer*, 'Sayings of the Week', 17 Dec 1943

**Bevin, Ernest** (1881–1951) British trade-union leader and politician. Elected chairman of the TUC in 1937, he became minister of labour in Churchill's wartime coalition government. In the post-war Labour government he was foreign secretary.

1 If you open that Pandora's Box you never know what Trojan 'orses will jump out.
Referring to the Council of Europe
*Ernest Bevin and the Foreign Office* (Sir Roderick Barclay)

2 My policy is to be able to take a ticket at Victoria Station and go anywhere I damn well please.
*The Spectator*, 20 Apr 1951

**Bible** Unless otherwise stated, quotations are taken from the *Authorized Version*. The books are given in their traditional order. *See also* Psalms.

GENESIS

1 In the beginning God created the heaven and the earth.
And the earth was without form, and void; and darkness was upon the face of the deep. And the Spirit of God moved upon the face of the waters.
And God said, Let there be light: and there was light.
And God saw the light, that it was good: and God divided the light from the darkness.
And God called the light Day, and the darkness he called Night. And the evening and the morning were the first day.
1:1–5

2 Fiat lux.
Vulgate 1:3

3 And God called the dry land Earth; and the gathering together of the waters called he Seas: and God saw that it was good.
And God said, Let the earth bring forth grass, the herb yielding seed, and the fruit tree yielding fruit after his kind, whose seed is in itself, upon the earth: and it was so.
1:10–11

4 And God made two great lights: the greater light to rule the day, and the lesser light to rule the night: he made the stars also.
1:16

5 And God said, Let the earth bring forth the living creature after his kind, cattle, and creeping thing, and beast of the earth after his kind: and it was so.
1:24

6 And God said, Let us make man in our image, after our likeness: and let them have dominion over the fish of the sea, and over the fowl of the air, and over the cattle, and over all the earth, and over every creeping thing that creepeth upon the earth.
So God created man in his own image, in the image of God created he him; male and female created he them.
And God blessed them, and God said unto them, Be fruitful, and multiply, and replenish the earth, and subdue it: and have dominion over the fish of the sea, and over the fowl of the air, and over every living thing that moveth upon the earth.
1:26–28

7 And on the seventh day God ended his work which he had made; and he rested on the seventh day from all his work which he had made.
2:2

8 But there went up a mist from the earth, and watered the whole face of the ground.
And the Lord God formed man of the dust of the ground, and breathed into his nostrils the breath of life; and man became a living soul.
And the Lord God planted a garden eastward in Eden; and there he put the man whom he had formed.
And out of the ground made the Lord God to grow every tree that is pleasant to the sight, and good for food; the tree of life also in the midst of the garden, and the tree of knowledge of good and evil.
And a river went out of Eden to water the garden.
2:6–10

9 And the Lord God took the man, and put him into the garden of Eden to dress it and to keep it.
And the Lord God commanded the man, saying, Of every tree of the garden thou mayest freely eat:
But of the tree of the knowledge of good and evil, thou shalt not eat of it: for in the day that thou eatest thereof thou shalt surely die.
2:15–17

10 And the Lord God said, It is not good that the man should be alone; I will make him an help meet for him.
And out of the ground the Lord God formed every beast of the field, and every fowl of the air; and brought them unto Adam to see what he would call them: and whatsoever Adam called every living creature, that was the name thereof.
2:18–19

**11** And the Lord God caused a deep sleep to fall upon Adam, and he slept: and he took one of his ribs, and closed up the flesh instead thereof;

And the rib, which the Lord God had taken from man, made he a woman, and brought her unto the man.

And Adam said, This is now bone of my bones, and flesh of my flesh: she shall be called Woman, because she was taken out of Man.

Therefore shall a man leave his father and his mother, and shall cleave unto his wife: and they shall be one flesh.

And they were both naked, the man and his wife, and were not ashamed.

2:21–25

**12** Now the serpent was more subtil than any beast of the field which the Lord God had made.

3:1

**13** God doth know that in the day ye eat thereof, then your eyes shall be opened, and ye shall be as gods, knowing good and evil.

And when the woman saw that the tree was good for food, and that it was pleasant to the eyes, and a tree to be desired to make one wise, she took of the fruit thereof, and did eat, and gave also unto her husband with her; and he did eat.

And the eyes of them both were opened, and they knew that they were naked; and they sewed fig leaves together; and made themselves aprons.

And they heard the voice of the Lord God walking in the garden in the cool of the day: and Adam and his wife hid themselves from the presence of the Lord God amongst the trees of the garden.

3:5–8

**14** And he said, I heard thy voice in the garden, and I was afraid, because I was naked; and I hid myself.

And he said, Who told thee that thou wast naked?

3:10–11

**15** And the man said, The woman whom thou gavest to be with me, she gave me of the tree, and I did eat.

And the Lord God said unto the woman, What is this that thou hast done? And the woman said, The serpent beguiled me, and I did eat.

And the Lord God said unto the serpent, Because thou hast done this, thou art cursed above all cattle, and above every beast of the field; upon thy belly shalt thou go, and dust shalt thou eat all the days of thy life:

And I will put enmity between thee and the woman, and between thy seed and her seed; it shall bruise thy head, and thou shalt bruise his heel.

Unto the woman he said, I will greatly multiply thy sorrow and thy conception; in sorrow thou shalt bring forth children; and thy desire shall be to thy husband, and he shall rule over thee.

And unto Adam he said, Because thou hast hearkened unto the voice of thy wife, and has eaten of the tree, of which I commanded thee, saying, Thou shalt not eat of it: cursed is the ground for thy sake; in sorrow shalt thou eat of it all the days of thy life.

3:12–17

**16** In the sweat of thy face shalt thou eat bread, till thou return unto the ground; for out of it wast thou taken: for dust thou art and unto dust shalt thou return.

And Adam called his wife's name Eve; because she was the mother of all living.

3:19–20

**17** Abel was a keeper of sheep, but Cain was a tiller of the ground.

4:2

**18** And the Lord said unto Cain, Where is Abel thy brother? And he said, I know not: Am I my brother's keeper?

And he said, What hast thou done? the voice of thy brother's blood crieth unto me from the ground.

4:9–10

**19** When thou tillest the ground, it shall not henceforth yield unto thee her strength; a fugitive and a vagabond shalt thou be in the earth.

And Cain said unto the Lord, My punishment is greater than I can bear.

4:12–13

**20** And the Lord said unto him, Therefore whosoever slayeth Cain, vengeance shall be taken on him sevenfold. And the Lord set a mark upon Cain, lest any finding him should kill him.

And Cain went out from the presence of the Lord, and dwelt in the land of Nod, on the east of Eden.

4:15–16

**21** And all the days of Methuselah were nine hundred sixty and nine years: and he died.

5:27

**22** The sons of God saw the daughters of men that they were fair; and they took them wives of all which they chose.

And the Lord said, My spirit shall not always strive with man, for that he also is flesh: yet his days shall be an hundred and twenty years.

There were giants in the earth in those days; and also after that, when the sons of God came in unto the daughters of men, and they bare children to them, the same became mighty men which were of old, men of renown.

6:2–4

23 And it repented the Lord that he-had made man on the earth, and it grieved him at his heart.
6:6

24 And they went in unto Noah into the ark, two and two of all flesh, wherein is the breath of life. And they that went in, went in male and female of all flesh, as God had commanded him: and the Lord shut him in.
And the flood was forty days upon the earth; and the waters increased, and bare up the ark, and it was lift up above the earth.
7:15-17

25 And the dove came in to him in the evening; and, lo, in her mouth was an olive leaf pluckt off: so Noah knew that the waters were abated from off the earth.
8:11

26 And the Lord smelled a sweet savour; and the Lord said in his heart, I will not again curse the ground any more for man's sake; for the imagination of man's heart is evil from his youth; neither will I again smite any more every thing living, as I have done.
While the earth remaineth, seedtime and harvest, and cold and heat, and summer and winter, and day and night shall not cease.
8:21-22

27 And surely your blood of your lives will I require; at the hand of every beast will I require it, and at the hand of man; at the hand of every man's brother will I require the life of man.
Whoso sheddeth man's blood, by man shall his blood be shed: for in the image of God made he man.
9:5-6

28 I do set my bow in the cloud, and it shall be for a token of a covenant between me and the earth.
9:13

29 He was a mighty hunter before the Lord: wherefore it is said, Even as Nimrod the mighty hunter before the Lord.
10:9

30 And the whole earth was of one language, and of one speech.
11:1

31 Therefore is the name of it called Babel; because the Lord did there confound the language of all the earth: and from thence did the Lord scatter them abroad upon the face of all the earth.
11:9

32 Now the Lord had said unto Abram, Get thee out of thy country, and from thy kindred, and from thy father's house, unto a land that I will shew thee:
And I will make of thee a great nation, and I will bless thee, and make thy name great; and thou shalt be a blessing:

And I will bless them that bless thee, and curse him that curseth thee: and in thee shall all families of the earth be blessed.
12:1-3

33 But the men of Sodom were wicked and sinners before the Lord exceedingly.
13:13

34 And he will be a wild man; his hand will be against every man, and every man's hand against him; and he shall dwell in the presence of all his brethren.
16:12

35 Is any thing too hard for the Lord? At the time appointed I will return unto thee, according to the time of life, and Sarah shall have a son.
18:14

36 That be far from thee to do after this manner, to slay the righteous with the wicked: and that the righteous should be as the wicked, that be far from thee: Shall not the Judge of all the earth do right?
18:25

37 Then the Lord rained upon Sodom and upon Gomorrah brimstone and fire from the Lord out of heaven.
19:24

38 But his wife looked back from behind him, and she became a pillar of salt.
19:26

39 And Abraham said, My son, God will provide himself a lamb for a burnt offering: so they went both of them together.
22:8

40 And Abraham lifted up his eyes, and looked, and behold behind him a ram caught in a thicket by his horns: and Abraham went and took the ram, and offered him up for a burnt offering in the stead of his son.
22:13

41 And Abraham was old, and well stricken in age: and the Lord had blessed Abraham in all things.
24:1

42 And Jacob said to Rebekah his mother, Behold, Esau my brother a hairy man, and I am a smooth man.
27:11

43 And he dreamed, and behold a ladder set up on the earth, and the top of it reached to heaven: and behold the angels of God ascending and descending on it.
28:12

44 And Jacob awaked out of his sleep, and he said, Surely the Lord is in this place; and I knew it not.

And he was afraid, and said, How dreadful is this place! this is none other but the house of God, and this is the gate of heaven.
28:16-17

**45** Leah was tender eyed; but Rachel was beautiful and well favoured.
29:17

**46** Now Israel loved Joseph more than all his children, because he was the son of his old age: and he made him a coat of many colours.
37:3

**47** And they said one to another, Behold, this dreamer cometh.
Come now therefore, and let us slay him, and cast him into some pit, and we will say, Some evil beast hath devoured him: and we shall see what will become of his dreams.
37:19-20

**48** And all his sons and all his daughters rose up to comfort him; but he refused to be comforted; and he said, For I will go down into the grave unto my son mourning. Thus his father wept for him.
37:35

**49** And Judah said unto Onan, Go in unto thy brother's wife, and marry her, and raise up seed to thy brother.
And Onan knew that the seed should not be his; and it came to pass, when he went in unto his brother's wife, that he spilled it on the ground, lest that he should give seed to his brother.
38:8-9

**50** And the seven thin ears devoured the seven rank and full ears. And Pharaoh awoke, and, behold, it was a dream.
41:7

**51** And the famine was sore in the land.
43:1

**52** And take your father and your households, and come unto me: and I will give you the good of the land of Egypt, and ye shall eat the fat of the land.
45:18

**53** The sceptre shall not depart from Judah, nor a lawgiver from between his feet, until Shiloh come; and unto him shall the gathering of the people be.
49:10

**54** His eyes shall be red with wine, and his teeth white with milk.
49:12

**55** Issachar is a strong ass couching down between two burdens:
And he saw that rest was good, and the land that it was pleasant; and bowed his shoulder to bear, and became a servant unto tribute.
49:14-15

**56** Dan shall be a serpent by the way, an adder in the path, that biteth the horse heels, so that his rider shall fall backward.
I have waited for thy salvation, O Lord.
49:17-18

**57** Benjamin shall ravin as a wolf: in the morning he shall devour the prey, and at night he shall divide the spoil.
49:27

EXODUS

**1** Now there arose up a new king over Egypt, which knew not Joseph.
1:8

**2** And when she could not longer hide him, she took for him an ark of bulrushes, and daubed it with slime and with pitch, and put the child therein; and she laid it in the flags by the river's brink.
2:3

**3** He called his name Gershom: for he said, I have been a stranger in a strange land.
2:22

**4** And the angel of the Lord appeared unto him in a flame of fire out of the midst of a bush: and he looked, and, behold, the bush burned with fire, and the bush was not consumed.
3:2

**5** And he said, Draw not nigh hither: put off thy shoes from off thy feet, for the place whereon thou standest is holy ground.
Moreover he said, I am the God of thy father, the God of Abraham, the God of Isaac, and the God of Jacob. And Moses hid his face; for he was afraid to look upon God.
3:5-6

**6** And I am come down to deliver them out of the hand of the Egyptians, and to bring them up out of that land unto a good land and a large, unto a land flowing with milk and honey; unto the place of the Canaanites, and the Hittites, and the Amorites, and the Perizzites, and the Hivites, and the Jebusites.
3:8

**7** And God said unto Moses, I AM THAT I AM: and he said, Thus shalt thou say unto the children of Israel, I AM hath sent me unto you.
3:14

**8** And Moses said unto the Lord, O my Lord, I am not eloquent, neither heretofore, nor since thou hast spoken unto thy servant: but I am slow of speech, and of a slow tongue.
4:10

**9** And I will harden Pharaoh's heart, and multiply my signs and my wonders in the land of Egypt.
7:3

10 For they cast down every man his rod, and they became serpents: but Aaron's rod swallowed up their rods.

7:12

11 Your lamb shall be without blemish, a male of the first year: ye shall take it out from the sheep, or from the goats.

12:5

12 And thus shall ye eat it; with your loins girded, your shoes on your feet, and your staff in your hand; and ye shall eat it in haste: it is the Lord's passover.
For I will pass through the land of Egypt this night, and will smite all the firstborn in the land of Egypt, both man and beast; and against all the gods of Egypt I will execute judgment: I am the Lord.

12:11–12

13 And the Egyptians were urgent upon the people, that they might send them out of the land in haste; for they said, We be all dead men.

12:33

14 And the Lord went before them by day in a pillar of a cloud, to lead them the way; and by night in a pillar of fire, to give them light; to go by day and night.

13:21

15 And the children of Israel went into the midst of the sea upon the dry ground: and the waters were a wall unto them on their right hand, and on their left.

14:22

16 Then sang Moses and the children of Israel this song unto the Lord, and spake, saying, I will sing unto the Lord, for he hath triumphed gloriously: the horse and his rider hath he thrown into the sea.

15:1

17 The Lord is a man of war: the Lord is his name.

15:3

18 And when the children of Israel saw it, they said one to another, It is manna: for they wist not what it was. And Moses said unto them, This is the bread which the Lord hath given you to eat.

16:15

19 And mount Sinai was altogether on a smoke, because the Lord descended upon it in fire: and the smoke thereof ascended as the smoke of a furnace, and the whole mount quaked greatly.

19:18

20 I am the Lord thy God, which have brought thee out of the land of Egypt, out of the house of bondage.
Thou shalt have no other gods before me.

Thou shalt not make unto thee any graven image, or any likeness of any thing that is in heaven above, or that is in the earth beneath, or that is in the water under the earth:
Thou shalt not bow down thyself to them, nor serve them: for I the Lord thy God am a jealous God, visiting the iniquity of the fathers upon the children unto the third and fourth generation of them that hate me;
And shewing mercy unto thousands of them that love me, and keep my commandments.
Thou shalt not take the name of the Lord thy God in vain; for the Lord will not hold him guiltless that taketh his name in vain.
Remember the sabbath day, to keep it holy.
Six days shalt thou labour, and do all thy work:
But the seventh day is the sabbath of the Lord thy God: in it thou shalt not do any work, thou, nor thy son, nor thy daughter, thy manservant, nor thy maidservant, nor thy cattle, nor thy stranger that is within thy gates:
For in six days the Lord made heaven and earth, the sea, and all that in them is, and rested the seventh day: wherefore the Lord blessed the sabbath day, and hallowed it.
Honour thy father and thy mother: that thy days may be long upon the land which the Lord thy God giveth thee.
Thou shalt not kill.
Thou shalt not commit adultery.
Thou shalt not steal.
Thou shalt not bear false witness against thy neighbour.
Thou shalt not covet thy neighbour's house, thou shalt not covet thy neighbour's wife, nor his manservant, nor his maidservant, nor his ox, nor his ass, nor any thing that is thy neighbour's.

20:2–17

21 And if any mischief follow, then thou shalt give life for life,
Eye for eye, tooth for tooth, hand for hand, foot for foot,
Burning for burning, wound for wound, stripe for stripe.

21:23–25

22 Thou shalt not suffer a witch to live.

22:18

23 The first of the firstfruits of thy land thou shalt bring into the house of the Lord thy God. Thou shalt not seethe a kid in his mother's milk.

23:19

24 And the Lord said unto Moses, Come up to me into the mount, and be there: and I will give thee tables of stone, and a law, and commandments which I have written; that thou mayest teach them.

24:12

**25** And thou shalt put in the breastplate of judgment the Urim and the Thummim; and they shall be upon Aaron's heart, when he goeth in before the Lord: and Aaron shall bear the judgment of the children of Israel upon his heart before the Lord continually.

28:30

**26** And he received them at their hand, and fashioned it with a graving tool, after he had made it a molten calf: and they said, These be thy gods, O Israel, which brought thee up out of the land of Egypt.

32:4

**27** And the Lord said unto Moses, I have seen this people, and, behold, it is a stiffnecked people.

32:9

**28** Then Moses stood in the gate of the camp, and said, Who is on the Lord's side? let him come unto me. And all the sons of Levi gathered themselves together unto him.

32:26

**29** Yet now, if thou wilt forgive their sin —; and if not, blot me, I pray thee, out of thy book which thou hast written.

32:32

**30** And he said, Thou canst not see my face: for there shall no man see me, and live.

33:20

**31** And it shall come to pass, while my glory passeth by, that I will put thee in a clift of the rock, and will cover thee with my hand while I pass by.

33:22

**NUMBERS**

**1** The Lord bless thee, and keep thee:
The Lord make his face shine upon thee, and be gracious unto thee:
The Lord lift up his countenance upon thee, and give thee peace.

6:24–26

**2** Now the man Moses was very meek, above all the men which were upon the face of the earth.

12:3

**3** Is it a small thing that thou hast brought us up out of a land that floweth with milk and honey, to kill us in the wilderness, except thou make thyself altogether a prince over us?

16:13

**4** And Moses lifted up his hand, and with his rod he smote the rock twice: and the water came out abundantly, and the congregation drank, and their beasts also.

20:11

**5** And the Lord opened the mouth of the ass, and she said unto Balaam, What have I done unto thee, that thou hast smitten me these three times?

22:28

**6** But if ye will not do so, behold, ye have sinned against the Lord: and be sure your sin will find you out.

32:23

**DEUTERONOMY**

**1** I call heaven and earth to witness against you this day, that ye shall soon utterly perish from off the land whereunto ye go over Jordan to possess it; ye shall not prolong your days upon it, but shall utterly be destroyed.

4:26

**2** For the Lord thy God bringeth thee into a good land, a land of brooks of water, of fountains and depths that spring out of valleys and hills;
A land of wheat, and barley, and vines, and fig trees, and pomegranates; a land of oil olive, and honey;
A land wherein thou shalt eat bread without scarceness, thou shalt not lack any thing in it; a land whose stones are iron, and out of whose hills thou mayest dig brass.
When thou hast eaten and art full, then thou shalt bless the Lord thy God for the good land which he hath given thee.

8:7–10

**3** Take heed to yourselves, that your heart be not deceived, and ye turn aside, and serve other gods, and worship them.

11:16

**4** Thou shalt not hearken unto the words of that prophet, or that dreamer of dreams.

13:3

**5** I call heaven and earth to record this day against you, that I have set before you life and death, blessing and cursing: therefore choose life, that both thou and thy seed may live.

30:19

**6** Be strong and of a good courage, fear not, nor be afraid of them: for the Lord thy God, he it is that doth go with thee; he will not fail thee, nor forsake thee.

31:6

**7** He found him in a desert land, and in the waste howling wilderness; he led him about, he instructed him, he kept him as the apple of his eye.

32:10

**8** And he buried him in a valley in the land of Moab, over against Beth-peor: but no man knoweth of his sepulchre unto this day.

34:6

9 And there arose not a prophet since in Israel like unto Moses, whom the Lord knew face to face.
34:10

JOSHUA

1 And the priests that bare the ark of the covenant of the Lord stood firm on dry ground in the midst of Jordan, and all the Israelites passed over on dry ground, until all the people were passed clean over Jordan.
3:17

2 So the people shouted when the priests blew with the trumpets: and it came to pass, when the people heard the sound of the trumpet, and the people shouted with a great shout, that the wall fell down flat, so that the people went up into the city, every man straight before him, and they took the city.
6:20

3 And the princes said unto them, Let them live; but let them be hewers of wood and drawers of water unto all the congregation; as the princes had promised them.
9:21

JUDGES

1 And when he shewed them the entrance into the city, they smote the city with the edge of the sword; but they let go the man and all his family.
1:25

2 They fought from heaven; the stars in their courses fought against Sisera.
5:20

3 Blessed above women shall Jael the wife of Heber the Kenite be, blessed shall she be above women in the tent.
He asked water, and she gave him milk; she brought forth butter in a lordly dish.
She put her hand to the nail, and her right hand to the workmen's hammer; and with the hammer she smote Sisera, she smote off his head, when she had pierced and stricken through his temples.
At her feet he bowed, he fell, he lay down: at her feet he bowed, he fell: where he bowed, there he fell down dead.
The mother of Sisera looked out at a window, and cried through the lattice, Why is his chariot so long in coming? why tarry the wheels of his chariots?
5:24–28

4 And the angel of the Lord appeared unto him, and said unto him, The Lord is with thee, thou mighty man of valour.
6:12

5 And he said unto them, Out of the eater came forth meat, and out of the strong came forth sweetness. And they could not in three days expound the riddle.
14:14

6 And the men of the city said unto him on the seventh day before the sun went down, What is sweeter than honey? and what is stronger than a lion? And he said unto them, If ye had not plowed with my heifer, ye had not found out my riddle.
14:18

7 And he smote them hip and thigh with a great slaughter.
15:8

8 And Samson said, With the jawbone of an ass, heaps upon heaps, with the jaw of an ass have I slain a thousand men.
15:16

9 In those days there was no king in Israel, but every man did that which was right in his own eyes.
17:6

RUTH

1 And Ruth said, Intreat me not to leave thee, or to return from following after thee: for whither thou goest, I will go; and where thou lodgest, I will lodge: thy people shall be my people, and thy God my God:
Where thou diest, will I die, and there will I be buried: the Lord do so to me, and more also, if ought but death part thee and me.
1:16–17

2 And he shall be unto thee a restorer of thy life and a nourisher of thine old age: for thy daughter in law, which loveth thee, which is better to thee than seven sons, hath born him.
4:15

I SAMUEL

1 Therefore Eli said unto Samuel, Go, lie down: and it shall be, if all thee, that thou shalt say, Speak, Lord; for thy servant heareth. So Samuel went and lay down in his place.
3:9

2 And it came to pass, when all that knew him beforetime saw that, behold, he prophesied among the prophets, then the people said one to another, What is this that is come unto the son of Kish? Is Saul also among the prophets?
10:11

3 But now thy kingdom shall not continue: the Lord hath sought him a man after his own heart, and the Lord hath commanded him to be captain over his people, because thou hast not kept that which the Lord commanded thee.
13:14

4 And the people said unto Saul, Shall Jonathan die, who hath wrought this great salvation in Israel? God forbid: as the Lord liveth, there shall not one hair of his head fall to the ground; for he hath wrought with God this day. So the people rescued Jonathan, that he died not.
14:45

5 And he took his staff in his hand, and chose him five smooth stones out of the brook, and put them in a shepherd's bag which he had, even in a scrip; and his sling was in his hand: and he drew near to the Philistine.

17:40

6 And the women answered one another as they played, and said, Saul hath slain his thousands, and David his ten thousands.

18:7

7 Then said Saul, I have sinned: return, my son David: for I will no more do thee harm, because my soul was precious in thine eyes this day: behold, I have played the fool, and have erred exceedingly.

26:21

**II SAMUEL**

1 Saul and Jonathan were lovely and pleasant in their lives, and in their death they were not divided: they were swifter than eagles, they were stronger than lions.

1:23–24

2 I am distressed for thee, my brother Jonathan: very pleasant hast thou been unto me: thy love to me was wonderful, passing the love of women.
How are the mighty fallen, and the weapons of war perished!

1:26–27

3 But the poor man had nothing, save one little ewe lamb, which he had bought and nourished up: and it grew up together with him, and with his children; it did eat of his own meat, and drank of his own cup, and lay in his bosom, and was unto him as a daughter.

12:3

4 And Nathan said to David, Thou art the man.

12:7

5 And a certain man saw it, and told Joab, and said, Behold, I saw Absalom hanged in an oak.

18:10

6 And the king was much moved, and went up to the chamber over the gate, and wept: and as he went, thus he said, O my son Absalom, my son, my son Absalom! would God I had died for thee, O Absalom, my son, my son!

18:33

**I KINGS**

1 So David slept with his fathers, and was buried in the city of David.

2:10

2 Then the king answered and said, Give her the living child, and in no wise slay it: she is the mother thereof.

And all Israel heard of the judgment which the king had judged; and they feared the king: for they saw that the wisdom of God was in him, to do judgment.

3:27–28

3 And when the queen of Sheba heard of the fame of Solomon concerning the name of the Lord, she came to prove him with hard questions.

10:1

4 But king Solomon loved many strange women, together with the daughter of Pharaoh, women of the Moabites, Ammonites, Edomites, Zidonians, and Hittites.

11:1

5 Get thee hence, and turn thee eastward, and hide thyself by the brook Cherith, that is before Jordan.
And it shall be, that thou shalt drink of the brook; and I have commanded the ravens to feed thee there.

17:3–4

6 But he himself went a day's journey into the wilderness, and came and sat down under a juniper tree: and he requested for himself that he might die; and said, It is enough; now, O Lord, take away my life; for I am not better than my fathers.

19:4

7 And he said, Go forth, and stand upon the mount before the Lord. And, behold, the Lord passed by, and a great and strong wind rent the mountains, and brake in pieces the rocks before the Lord; but the Lord was not in the wind: and after the wind an earthquake; but the Lord was not in the earthquake:
And after the earthquake a fire; but the Lord was not in the fire: and after the fire a still small voice.

19:11–12

8 And say, Thus saith the king, Put this fellow in the prison, and feed him with bread of affliction and with water of affliction, until I come in peace.

22:27

**II KINGS**

1 And it came to pass, as they still went on, and talked, that, behold, there appeared a chariot of fire, and horses of fire, and parted them both asunder; and Elijah went up by a whirlwind into heaven.
And Elisha saw it, and he cried, My father, my father, the chariot of Israel, and the horsemen thereof. And he saw him no more: and he took hold of his own clothes, and rent them in two pieces.

2:11–12

2 And when Jehu was come to Jezreel, Jezebel heard of it; and she painted her face, and tired her head, and looked out at a window.
9:30

3 And they went to bury her: but they found no more of her than the skull, and the feet, and the palms of her hands.
9:35

4 In those days was Hezekiah sick unto death. And the prophet Isaiah the son of Amoz came to him, and said unto him, Thus saith the Lord, Set thine house in order; for thou shalt die, and not live.
Then he turned his face to the wall.
20:1–2

EZRA

1 The people could not discern the noise of the shout of joy from the noise of the weeping of the people: for the people shouted with a loud shout, and the noise was heard afar off.
3:13

NEHEMIAH

1 And I said, Should such a man as I flee? and who is there, that, being as I am, would go into the temple to save his life? I will not go in.
6:11

ESTHER

1 And the king loved Esther above all the women, and she obtained grace and favour in his sight more than all the virgins; so that he set the royal crown upon her head, and made her queen instead of Vashti.
2:17

JOB

1 And the Lord said unto Satan, Whence comest thou? Then Satan answered the Lord, and said, From going to and fro in the earth, and from walking up and down in it.
And the Lord said unto Satan, Hast thou considered my servant Job, that there is none like him in the earth, a perfect and an upright man, one that feareth God, and escheweth evil?
Then Satan answered the Lord, and said, Doth Job fear God for nought?
1:7–9

2 Naked came I out of my mother's womb, and naked shall I return thither: the Lord gave, and the Lord hath taken away; blessed be the name of the Lord.
In all this Job sinned not, nor charged God foolishly.
1:21–22

3 Then said his wife unto him, Dost thou still retain thine integrity? curse God, and die.
2:9

4 Let the day perish wherein I was born, and the night in which it was said, There is a man child conceived.
3:3

5 The eye of him that hath seen me shall see me no more: thine eyes are upon me, and I am not.
7:8

6 Wherefore then hast thou brought me forth out of the womb? Oh that I had given up the ghost, and no eye had seen me!
10:18

7 With the ancient is wisdom; and in length of days understanding.
12:12

8 They grope in the dark without light, and he maketh them to stagger like a drunken man.
12:25

9 Man that is born of a woman is of few days, and full of trouble.
14:1

10 Then Job answered and said, I have heard many such things: miserable comforters are ye all.
16:1–2

11 I have said to corruption, Thou art my father: to the worm, Thou art my mother, and my sister.
17:14

12 For I know that my redeemer liveth, and that he shall stand at the latter day upon the earth:
And though after my skin worms destroy this body, yet in my flesh shall I see God.
19:25–26

13 No mention shall be made of coral, or of pearls: for the price of wisdom is above rubies.
28:18

14 I was eyes to the blind, and feet was I to the lame.
29:15

15 What man is like Job, who drinketh up scorning like water?
34:7

16 Then the Lord answered Job out of the whirlwind, and said,
Who is this that darkeneth counsel by words without knowledge?
Gird up now thy loins like a man; for I will demand of thee, and answer thou me.
Where wast thou when I laid the foundations of the earth? declare, if thou hast understanding.
Who hath laid the measures thereof, if thou knowest? or who hath stretched the line upon it?
Whereupon are the foundations thereof fastened? or who laid the corner stone thereof;
When the morning stars sang together, and all the sons of God shouted for joy?
38:1–7

**17** Hath the rain a father? or who hath begotten the drops of dew?
38:28

**18** Canst thou bind the sweet influences of Pleiades, or loose the bands of Orion?
38:31

**19** Deck thyself now with majesty and excellency; and array thyself with glory and beauty.
40:10

**20** Canst thou draw out leviathan with an hook? or his tongue with a cord which thou lettest down?
41:1

**21** So the Lord blessed the latter end of Job more than his beginning: for he had fourteen thousand sheep, and six thousand camels, and a thousand yoke of oxen, and a thousand she asses.
42:12

## PROVERBS

**1** A wise man will hear, and will increase learning; and a man of understanding shall attain unto wise counsels:
To understand a proverb, and the interpretation; the words of the wise, and their dark sayings.
The fear of the Lord is the beginning of knowledge: but fools despise wisdom and instruction.
1:5-7

**2** Wisdom is the principal thing; therefore get wisdom: and with all thy getting get understanding.
4:7

**3** But the path of the just is as the shining light, that shineth more and more unto the perfect day.
4:18

**4** For the lips of a strange woman drop as an honeycomb, and her mouth is smoother than oil:
But her end is bitter as wormwood, sharp as a two-edged sword.
5:3-4

**5** Wisdom hath builded her house, she hath hewn out her seven pillars.
9:1

**6** Stolen waters are sweet, and bread eaten in secret is pleasant.
9:17

**7** He that spareth his rod hateth his son: but he that loveth him chasteneth him betimes.
13:24

**8** Pride goeth before destruction, and an haughty spirit before a fall.
16:18

**9** He that is slow to anger is better than the mighty; and he that ruleth his spirit than he that taketh a city.
16:32

**10** Wine is a mocker, strong drink is raging: and whosoever is deceived thereby is not wise.
20:1

**11** The hearing ear, and the seeing eye, the Lord hath made even both of them.
20:12

**12** Look not thou upon the wine when it is red, when it giveth his colour in the cup, when it moveth itself aright.
At the last it biteth like a serpent, and stingeth like an adder.
23:31-32

**13** For thou shalt heap coals of fire upon his head, and the Lord shall reward thee.
25:22

**14** As cold waters to a thirsty soul, so is good news from a far country.
25:25

**15** Answer a fool according to his folly, lest he be wise in his own conceit.
26:5

**16** Boast not thyself of tomorrow; for thou knowest not what a day may bring forth.
27:1

**17** Who can find a virtuous woman? for her price is far above rubies
The heart of her husband doth safely trust in her, so that he shall have no need of spoil.
She will do him good and not evil all the days of her life.
31:10-12

## ECCLESIASTES

**1** Vanity of vanities, saith the Preacher, vanity of vanities; all is vanity.
What profit hath a man of all his labour which he taketh under the sun?
One generation passeth away, and another generation cometh: but the earth abideth for ever.
1:2-4

**2** All the rivers run into the sea; yet the sea is not full; unto the place from whence the rivers come, thither they return again.
All things are full of labour; man cannot utter it: the eye is not satisfied with seeing, nor the ear filled with hearing.
The thing that hath been, it is that which shall be; and that which is done is that which shall be done: and there is no new thing under the sun.
1:7-9

**3** There is no remembrance of former things; neither shall there be any remembrance of things that are to come with those that shall come after.
1:11

4 And I gave my heart to seek and search out by wisdom concerning all things that are done under heaven: this sore travail hath God given to the sons of man to be exercised therewith.
I have seen all the works that are done under the sun; and, behold, all is vanity and vexation of spirit.
1:13-14

5 For in much wisdom is much grief: and he that increaseth knowledge increaseth sorrow.
1:18

6 I said of laughter, It is mad: and of mirth, What doeth it?
2:2

7 Then I saw that wisdom excelleth folly, as far as light excelleth darkness.
The wise man's eyes are in his head; but the fool walketh in darkness: and I myself perceived also that one event happeneth to them all.
2:13-14

8 To every thing there is a season, and a time to every purpose under the heaven:
A time to be born, and a time to die; a time to plant, and a time to pluck up that which is planted;
A time to kill, and a time to heal; a time to break down, and a time to build up;
A time to weep, and a time to laugh; a time to mourn, and a time to dance;
A time to cast away stones, and a time to gather stones together; a time to embrace, and a time to refrain from embracing;
A time to get, and a time to lose; a time to keep, and a time to cast away;
A time to rend, and a time to sew; a time to keep silence, and a time to speak;
A time to love, and a time to hate; a time of war, and a time of peace.
3:1-8

9 Wherefore I praised the dead which are already dead more than the living which are yet alive.
Yea, better is he than both they, which hath not yet been, who hath not seen the evil work that is done under the sun.
4:2-3

10 Two are better than one; because they have a good reward for their labour.
For if they fall, the one will lift up his fellow: but woe to him that is alone when he falleth; for he hath not another to help him up.
4:9-10

11 And if one prevail against him, two shall withstand him; and a threefold cord is not quickly broken.
4:12

12 Better is a poor and a wise child than an old and foolish king, who will no more be admonished.
4:13

13 Better is it that thou shouldest not vow, than that thou shouldest vow and not pay.
5:5

14 A good name is better than precious ointment; and the day of death than the day of one's birth.
It is better to go to the house of mourning, than to go to the house of feasting: for that is the end of all men; and the living will lay it to his heart.
7:1-2

15 Then I commended mirth, because a man hath no better thing under the sun, than to eat, and to drink, and to be merry: for that shall abide with him of his labour the days of his life, which God giveth him under the sun.
8:15

16 Whatsoever thy hand findeth to do, do it with thy might; for there is no work, nor device, nor knowledge, nor wisdom, in the grave, whither thou goest.
9:10

17 I returned, and saw under the sun, that the race is not to the swift, nor the battle to the strong, neither yet bread to the wise, nor yet riches to men of understanding, nor yet favour to men of skill; but time and chance happeneth to them all.
For man also knoweth not his time: as the fishes that are taken in an evil net, and as the birds that are caught in the snare; so are the sons of men snared in an evil time, when it falleth suddenly upon them.
9:11-12

18 The words of wise men are heard in quiet more than the cry of him that ruleth among fools.
9:17

19 Dead flies cause the ointment of the apothecary to send forth a stinking savour: so doth a little folly him that is in reputation for wisdom and honour.
10:1

20 He that diggeth a pit shall fall into it; and whoso breaketh an hedge, a serpent shall bite him.
10:8

21 A feast is made for laughter, and wine maketh merry: but money answereth all things.
10:19

22 Curse not the king, no not in thy thought; and curse not the rich in thy bedchamber: for a bird of the air shall carry the voice, and that which hath wings shall tell the matter.
10:20

23 Cast thy bread upon the waters: for thou shalt find it after many days.
11:1

**24** If the clouds be full of rain, they empty themselves upon the earth: and if the tree fall toward the south, or toward the north, in the place where the tree falleth, there it shall be.

11:3

**25** And further, by these, my son, be admonished: of making many books there is no end; and much study is a weariness of the flesh.

12:12

**26** Let us hear the conclusion of the whole matter: Fear God, and keep his commandments: for this is the whole duty of man.

12:13

### SONG OF SOLOMON

**1** The song of songs, which is Solomon's.
Let him kiss me with the kisses of his mouth: for thy love is better than wine.
Because of the savour of thy good ointments thy name is as ointment poured forth, therefore do the virgins love thee.
Draw me, we will run after thee: the king hath brought me into his chambers: we will be glad and rejoice in thee, we will remember thy love more than wine: the upright love thee.
I am black, but comely, O ye daughters of Jerusalem, as the tents of Kedar, as the curtains of Solomon.
Look not upon me, because I am black, because the sun hath looked upon me: my mother's children were angry with me; they made me the keeper of the vineyards; but mine own vineyard have I not kept.
Tell me, O thou whom my soul loveth, where thou feedest, where thou makest thy flock to rest at noon: for why should I be as one that turneth aside by the flocks of thy companions?
If thou know not, O thou fairest among women, go thy way forth by the footsteps of the flock, and feed thy kids beside the shepherds' tents.
I have compared thee, O my love, to a company of horses in Pharaoh's chariots.

1:1–9

**2** I am the rose of Sharon, and the lily of the valleys.
As the lily among thorns, so is my love among the daughters.

2:1–2

**3** He brought me to the banqueting house, and his banner over me was love.
Stay me with flagons, comfort me with apples: for I am sick of love.
His left hand is under my head, and his right hand doth embrace me.

2:4–6

**4** The voice of my beloved! behold, he cometh leaping upon the mountains, skipping upon the hills.

2:8

**5** My beloved spake, and said unto me, Rise up, my love, my fair one, and come away.
For, lo, the winter is past, the rain is over and gone;
The flowers appear on the earth; the time of the singing of birds is come, and the voice of the turtle is heard in our land.

2:10–12

**6** Take us the foxes, the little foxes, that spoil the vines: for our vines have tender grapes.

2:15

**7** My beloved is mine, and I am his: he feedeth among the lilies.
Until the day break, and the shadows flee away, turn, my beloved, and be thou like a roe or a young hart upon the mountains of Bether.

2:16–17

**8** By night on my bed I sought him whom my soul loveth: I sought him, but I found him not.

3:1

**9** Behold, thou art fair, my love, behold, thou art fair; thou hast doves' eyes within thy locks; thy hair is as a flock of goats, that appear from mount Gilead.
Thy teeth are like a flock of sheep that are even shorn, which came up from the washing; whereof every one bear twins, and none is barren among them.
Thy lips are like a thread of scarlet, and thy speech is comely: thy temples are like a piece of a pomegranate within thy locks.
Thy neck is like the tower of David builded for an armoury, whereon there hang a thousand bucklers, all shields of mighty men.
Thy two breasts are like two young roes that are twins, which feed among the lilies.
Until the day break, and the shadows flee away, I will get me to the mountain of myrrh, and to the hill of frankincense.
Thou art all fair, my love; there is no spot in thee.

4:1–7

**10** A fountain of gardens, a well of living waters, and streams from Lebanon.

4:15

**11** Awake, O north wind; and come, thou south; blow upon my garden, that the spices thereof may flow out. Let my beloved come into his garden, and eat his pleasant fruits.

4:16

**12** I am come into my garden, my sister, my spouse: I have gathered my myrrh with my spice; I have eaten my honeycomb with my honey; I have drunk my wine with my milk: eat, O friends; drink, yea, drink abundantly, O beloved.

I sleep, but my heart waketh: it is the voice of my beloved that knocketh, saying, Open to me, my sister, my love, my dove, my undefiled: for my head is filled with dew, and my locks with the drops of the night.

5:1-2

**13** My beloved put in his hand by the hole of the door, and my bowels were moved for him.

5:4

**14** My beloved is gone down into his garden, to the beds of spices, to feed in the gardens, and to gather lilies.
I am my beloved's, and my beloved is mine: he feedeth among the lilies.

6:2-3

**15** Who is she that looketh forth as the morning, fair as the moon, clear as the sun, and terrible as an army with banners?

6:10

**16** Return, return, O Shulamite; return, return, that we may look upon thee. What will ye see in the Shulamite? As it were the company of two armies.

6:13

**17** How beautiful are thy feet with shoes, O prince's daughter! joints of thy thighs are like jewels, the work of the hands of a cunning workman. Thy navel is like a round goblet, which wanteth not liquor: thy belly is like an heap of wheat set about with lilies.

7:1-2

**18** How fair and how pleasant art thou, O love, for delights!

7:6

**19** I am my beloved's, and his desire is toward me.

7:10

**20** Who is this that cometh up from the wilderness, leaning upon her beloved? I raised thee up under the apple tree: there thy mother brought thee forth: there she brought thee forth that bare thee.

8:5

**21** Make haste, my beloved, and be thou like to a roe or to a young hart upon the mountains of spices.

8:14

ISAIAH

**1** Come now, and let us reason together, saith the Lord: though your sins be as scarlet, they shall be as white as snow; though they be red like crimson, they shall be as wool.

1:18

**2** How is the faithful city become an harlot! it was full of judgment; righteousness lodged in it; but now murderers.

1:21

**3** And it shall come to pass in the last days, that the mountain of the Lord's house shall be established in the top of the mountains, and shall be exalted above the hills; and all nations shall flow unto it.

2:2

**4** And he shall judge among the nations, and shall rebuke many people: and they shall beat their swords into plowshares, and their spears into pruning-hooks: nation shall not lift up sword against nation, neither shall they learn war any more.

2:4

**5** For, behold, the Lord, the Lord of hosts, doth take away from Jerusalem and from Judah the stay and the staff, the whole stay of bread, and the whole stay of water,
The mighty man, and the man of war, the judge, and the prophet, and the prudent, and the ancient,
The captain of fifty, and the honourable man, and the counsellor, and the cunning artificer, and the eloquent orator.
And I will give children to be their princes, and babes shall rule over them.
And the people shall be oppressed, every one by another, and every one by his neighbour: the child shall behave himself proudly against the ancient, and the base against the honourable.

3:1-5

**6** What mean ye that ye beat my people to pieces, and grind the faces of the poor? saith the Lord God of hosts.

3:15

**7** Woe unto them that rise up early in the morning, that they may follow strong drink; that continue until night, till wine inflame them!

5:11

**8** Woe unto them that call evil good, and good evil; that put darkness for light, and light for darkness; that put bitter for sweet, and sweet for bitter!

5:20

**9** In the year that king Uzziah died I saw also the Lord sitting upon a throne, high and lifted up, and his train filled the temple.
Above it stood the seraphims: each one had six wings; with twain he covered his face, and with twain he covered his feet, and with twain he did fly.
And one cried unto another, and said, Holy, holy, holy, is the Lord of hosts: the whole earth is full of his glory.
And the posts of the door moved at the voice of him that cried, and the house was filled with smoke.
Then said I, Woe is me! for I am undone; because I am a man of unclean lips, and I dwell in the midst of a people of unclean lips: for mine eyes have seen the King, the Lord of hosts.

Then flew one of the seraphims unto me, having a live coal in his hand, which he had taken with the tongs from off the altar:
And he laid it upon my mouth, and said, Lo, this hath touched thy lips; and thine iniquity is taken away, and thy sin purged.
Also I heard the voice of the Lord, saying, Whom shall I send, and who will go for us? Then said I, Here am I; send me.

6:1-8

10 Therefore the Lord himself shall give you a sign; Behold, a virgin shall conceive, and bear a son, and shall call his name Immanuel.
Butter and honey shall he eat, that he may know to refuse the evil, and choose the good.

7:14-15

11 And he shall be for a sanctuary; but for a stone of stumbling and for a rock of offence to both the houses of Israel, for a gin and for a snare to the inhabitants of Jerusalem.

8:14

12 The people that walked in darkness have seen a great light: they that dwell in the land of the shadow of death, upon them hath the light shined.
Thou hast multiplied the nation, and not increased the joy: they joy before thee according to the joy in harvest, and as men rejoice when they divide the spoil.
For thou hast broken the yoke of his burden, and the staff of his shoulder, the rod of his oppressor, as in the day of Midian.

9:2-4

13 For unto us a child is born, unto us a son is given: and the government shall be upon his shoulder: and his name shall be called Wonderful, Counsellor, The mighty God, The everlasting Father, The Prince of Peace.
Of the increase of his government and peace there shall be no end, upon the throne of David, and upon his kingdom, to order it, and to establish it with judgment and with justice from henceforth even for ever. The zeal of the Lord of hosts will perform this.

9:6-7

14 And there shall come forth a rod out of the stem of Jesse, and a Branch shall grow out of his roots:
And the spirit of the Lord shall rest upon him, the spirit of wisdom and understanding, the spirit of counsel and might, the spirit of knowledge and of the fear of the Lord.

11:1-2

15 The wolf also shall dwell with the lamb, and the leopard shall lie down with the kid; and the calf and the young lion and the fatling together: and a little child shall lead them.
And the cow and the bear shall feed; their young ones shall lie down together: and the lion shall eat straw like the ox.

And the sucking child shall play on the hole of the asp, and the weaned child shall put his hand on the cockatrice' den.
They shall not hurt nor destroy in all my holy mountain: for the earth shall be full of the knowledge of the Lord, as the waters cover the sea.

11:6-9

16 Therefore with joy shall ye draw water out of the wells of salvation.

12:3

17 But wild beasts of the desert shall lie there; and their houses shall be full of doleful creatures; and owls shall dwell there, and satyrs shall dance there.
And the wild beasts of the islands shall cry in their desolate houses, and dragons in their pleasant palaces: and her time is near to come, and her days shall not be prolonged.

13:21-22

18 He calleth to me out of Seir, Watchman, what of the night? Watchman, what of the night?
The watchman said, The morning cometh, and also the night: if ye will enquire, enquire ye: return, come.

21:11-12

19 And behold joy and gladness, slaying oxen, and killing sheep, eating flesh, and drinking wine: let us eat and drink; for tomorrow we shall die.

22:13

20 They shall not drink wine with a song; strong drink shall be bitter to them that drink it.

24:9

21 In that day the Lord with his sore and great and strong sword shall punish leviathan the piercing serpent, even leviathan that crooked serpent; and he shall slay the dragon that is in the sea.

27:1

22 For precept must be upon precept, precept upon precept; line upon line, line upon line; here a little, and there a little.

28:10

23 Stay yourselves, and wonder; cry ye out, and cry: they are drunken, but not with wine; they stagger, but not with strong drink.

29:9

24 And though the Lord give you the bread of adversity, and the water of affliction, yet shall not thy teachers be removed into a corner any more, but thine eyes shall see thy teachers.

30:20

25 The wilderness and the solitary place shall be glad for them; and the desert shall rejoice, and blossom as the rose.

35:1

26 Then the eyes of the blind shall be opened, and the ears of the deaf shall be unstopped.

Then shall the lame man leap as an hart, and the tongue of the dumb sing: for in the wilderness shall waters break out, and streams in the desert.

And the parched ground shall become a pool, and the thirsty land springs of water: in the habitation of dragons, where each lay, shall be grass with reeds and rushes.

35:5-7

**27** Comfort ye, comfort ye my people, saith your God.

Speak ye comfortably to Jerusalem, and cry unto her, that her warfare is accomplished, that her iniquity is pardoned: for she hath received of the Lord's hand double for all her sins.

The voice of him that crieth in the wilderness, Prepare ye the way of the Lord, make straight in the desert a highway for our God.

Every valley shall be exalted, and every mountain and hill shall be made low: and the crooked shall be made straight, and the rough places plain:

And the glory of the Lord shall be revealed, and all flesh shall see it together: for the mouth of the Lord hath spoken it.

The voice said, Cry. And he said, What shall I cry? All flesh is grass, and all the goodliness thereof is as the flower of the field:

The grass withereth, the flower fadeth: because the spirit of the Lord bloweth upon it: surely the people is grass.

The grass withereth, the flower fadeth: but the word of our God shall stand for ever.

O Zion, that bringest good tidings, get thee up into the high mountain; O Jerusalem, that bringest good tidings, lift up thy voice with strength; lift it up, be not afraid; say unto the cities of Judah, Behold your God!

40:1-9

**28** He shall feed his flock like a shepherd: he shall gather the lambs with his arm, and carry them in his bosom, and shall gently lead those that are with young.

40:11

**29** The isles saw it, and feared; the ends of the earth were afraid, drew near, and came.

They helped every one his neighbour; and every one said to his brother, Be of good courage.

41:5-6

**30** Verily thou art a God that hidest thyself, O God of Israel, the Saviour.

45:15

**31** There is no peace, saith the Lord, unto the wicked.

48:22

**32** How beautiful upon the mountains are the feet of him that bringeth good tidings, that publisheth peace; that bringeth good tidings of good, that publisheth salvation; that saith unto Zion, Thy God reigneth!

52:7

**33** All we like sheep have gone astray; we have turned every one to his own way; and the Lord hath laid on him the iniquity of us all.

He was oppressed, and he was afflicted, yet he opened not his mouth: he is brought as a lamb to the slaughter, and as a sheep before her shearers is dumb, so he openeth not his mouth.

He was taken from prison and from judgment: and who shall declare his generation? for he was cut off out of the land of the living: for the transgression of my people was he stricken.

53:6-8

**34** The righteous perisheth, and no man layeth it to heart: and merciful men are taken away, none considering that the righteous is taken away from the evil to come.

57:1

**35** Oh that thou wouldest rend the heavens, that thou wouldest come down, that the mountains might flow down at thy presence.

64:1

**36** Which say, Stand by thyself, come not near to me; for I am holier than thou. These are a smoke in my nose, a fire that burneth all the day.

65:5

**37** For, behold, I create new heavens and a new earth: and the former shall not be remembered, nor come into mind.

65:17

**JEREMIAH**

**1** They have healed also the hurt of the daughter of my people slightly, saying, Peace, peace; when there is no peace.

6:14

**2** We looked for peace, but no good came; and for a time of health, and behold trouble!

8:15

**3** Can the Ethiopian change his skin, or the leopard his spots? then may ye also do good, that are accustomed to do evil.

13:23

**4** And it shall come to pass, if they say unto thee, Whither shall we go forth? then thou shalt tell them, Thus saith the Lord; Such as are for death, to death; and such as are for the sword, to the sword; and such as are for the famine, to the famine; and such as are for the captivity, to the captivity.

15:2

5  In their heat I will make their feasts, and I will make them drunken, that they may rejoice, and sleep a perpetual sleep, and not wake, saith the Lord.

51:39

**LAMENTATIONS**

1  And I said, My strength and my hope is perished from the Lord:
Remembering mine affliction and my misery, the wormwood and the gall.

3:18–19

2  It is good for a man that he bear the yoke in his youth.

3:27

3  Waters flowed over mine head; then I said, I am cut off.

3:54

**EZEKIEL**

1  And thou, son of man, be not afraid of them, neither be afraid of their words, though briers and thorns be with thee, and thou dost dwell among scorpions: be not afraid of their words, nor be dismayed at their looks, though they be a rebellious house.

2:6

2  Son of man, thou dwellest in the midst of a rebellious house, which have eyes to see, and see not; they have ears to hear, and hear not: for they are a rebellious house.

12:2

3  Behold, every one that useth proverbs shall use this proverb against thee, saying, As is the mother, so is her daughter.

16:44–45

4  What mean ye, that ye use this proverb concerning the land of Israel, saying, The fathers have eaten sour grapes, and the children's teeth are set on edge?

18:2

5  Again, when the wicked man turneth away from his wickedness that he hath committed, and doeth that which is lawful and right, he shall save his soul alive.

18:27

6  And he said unto me, Son of man, can these bones live? And I answered, O Lord God, thou knowest.
Again he said unto me, Prophesy upon these bones, and say unto them, O ye dry bones, hear the word of the Lord.

37:3–4

7  So I prophesied as I was commanded: and as I prophesied, there was a noise, and behold a shaking, and the bones came together, bone to his bone.

37:7

8  And the man said unto me, Son of man, behold with thine eyes, and hear with thine ears, and set thine heart upon all that I shall shew thee; for to the intent that I might shew them unto thee art thou brought hither: declare all that thou seest to the house of Israel.

40:4

**DANIEL**

1  And he changeth the times and the seasons: he removeth kings, and setteth up kings: he giveth wisdom unto the wise, and knowledge to them that know understanding:
He revealeth the deep and secret things: he knoweth what is in the darkness, and the light dwelleth with him.

2:21–22

2  That at what time ye hear the sound of the cornet, flute, harp, sackbut, psaltery, dulcimer, and all kinds of musick, ye fall down and worship the golden image that Nebuchadnezzar the king hath set up:
And whoso falleth not down and worshippeth shall the same hour be cast into the midst of a burning fiery furnace.

3:5–6

3  Shadrach, Meshach, and Abed-nego, answered and said to the king, O Nebuchadnezzar, we are not careful to answer thee in this matter.

3:16

4  Then was Nebuchadnezzar full of fury, and the form of his visage was changed against Shadrach, Meshach, and Abed-nego: therefore he spake, and commanded that they should heat the furnace one seven times more than it was wont to be heated.

3:19

5  He answered and said, Lo, I see four men loose, walking in the midst of the fire, and they have no hurt; and the form of the fourth is like the Son of God.

3:25

6  The same hour was the thing fulfilled upon Nebuchadnezzar: and he was driven from men, and did eat grass as oxen, and his body was wet with the dew of heaven, till his hairs were grown like eagles' feathers, and his nails like birds' claws.

4:33

7  In the same hour came forth fingers of a man's hand, and wrote over against the candlestick upon the plaister of the wall of the king's palace: and the king saw the part of the hand that wrote.

5:5

8  And this is the writing that was written, MENE, MENE, TEKEL, UPHARSIN.
This is the interpretation of the thing: MENE; God hath numbered thy kingdom, and finished it.

TEKEL; Thou art weighed in the balances, and art found wanting.
PERES; Thy kingdom is divided, and given to the Medes and Persians.

5:25–28

9 Then the king commanded, and they brought Daniel, and cast him into the den of lions. Now the king spake and said unto Daniel, Thy God whom thou servest continually, he will deliver thee.

6:16

## HOSEA

1 For they have sown the wind, and they shall reap the whirlwind: it hath no stalk: the bud shall yield no meal: if so be it yield, the strangers shall swallow it up.

8:7

2 Sow to yourselves in righteousness, reap in mercy; break up your fallow ground: for it is time to seek the Lord, till he come an rain righteousness upon you.
Ye have plowed wickedness, ye have reaped iniquity; ye have eaten the fruit of lies: because thou didst trust in thy way, in the multitude of thy mighty men.

10:12–13

## AMOS

1 Seek him that maketh the seven stars and Orion, and turneth the shadow of death into the morning, and maketh the day dark with night: that calleth for the waters of the sea, and poureth them out upon the face of the earth: The Lord is his name.

5:8

## JONAH

1 So the shipmaster came to him, and said unto him, What meanest thou, O sleeper? arise, call upon thy God, if so be that God will think upon us, that we perish not.
And they said every one to his fellow, Come, and let us cast lots, that we may know for whose cause this evil is upon us. So they cast lots, and the lot fell upon Jonah.

1:6–7

2 Now the Lord had prepared a great fish to swallow up Jonah. And Jonah was in the belly of the fish three days and three nights.

1:17

## MICAH

1 Trust ye not in a friend, put ye not confidence in a guide: keep the doors of thy mouth from her that lieth in thy bosom.

7:5

## HABAKKUK

1 But the Lord is in his holy temple: let all the earth keep silence before him.

2:20

## HAGGAI

1 Now therefore thus saith the Lord of hosts; Consider your ways.
Ye have sown much, and bring in little; ye eat, but ye have not enough; ye drink, but ye are not filled with drink; ye clothe you, but there is none warm; and he that earneth wages earneth wages to put it into a bag with holes.

1:5–6

## MALACHI

1 Have we not all one father? hath not one God created us? why do we deal treacherously every man against his brother, by profaning the covenant of our fathers?

2:10

2 Behold, I will send my messenger, and he shall prepare the way before me: and the Lord, whom ye seek, shall suddenly come to his temple, even the messenger of the covenant, whom ye delight in: behold, he shall come, saith the Lord of hosts.
But who may abide the day of his coming? and who shall stand when he appeareth? for he is like a refiner's fire, and like fullers' soap.

3:1–2

3 But unto you that fear my name shall the Sun of righteousness arise with healing in his wings; and ye shall go forth, and grow up as calves of the stall.

4:2

## II ESDRAS

1 Then had I pity upon your mournings, and gave you manna to eat; so ye did eat angels' bread.

1:19

2 He answered and said unto me, These be they that have put off the mortal clothing, and put on the immortal, and have confessed the name of God: now are they crowned, and receive palms.
Then said I unto the angel, What young person is it that crowneth them, and giveth them palms in their hands?
So he answered and said unto me, It is the Son of God, whom they have confessed in the world. Then began I greatly to commend them that stood so stiffly for the name of the Lord.

2:45–47

3 And he said unto me, If I should ask thee how great dwellings are in the midst of the sea, or how many springs are in the beginning of the deep, or how many springs are above the firmament, or which are the outgoings of paradise: Peradventure thou wouldest say unto me, I never went down into the deep, nor as yet into hell, neither did I ever climb up into heaven.

4:7–8

4 He answered me, and said, I went into a forest into a plain, and the trees took counsel,

And said, Come, let us go and make war against the sea, that it may depart away before us, and that we may make us more woods.

The floods of the sea also in like manner took counsel, and said, Come, let us go up and subdue the woods of the plain, that there also we may make us another country.

The thought of the wood was in vain, for the fire came and consumed it.

The thought of the floods of the sea came likewise to nought, for the sand stood up and stopped them.

4:13–17

5 Then were the entrances of this world made narrow, full of sorrow and travail: they are but few and evil, full of perils, and very painful.

For the entrances of the elder world were wide and sure, and brought immortal fruit.

7:12–13

6 For the world hath lost his youth, and the times begin to wax old.

14:10

7 And come hither, and I shall light a candle of understanding in thine heart, which shall not be put out, till the things be performed which thou shalt begin to write.

14:25

TOBIT

1 Be not greedy to add money to money: but let it be as refuse in respect of our child.

5:18

2 Be of good comfort, my daughter; the Lord of heaven and earth give thee joy for this thy sorrow: be of good comfort, my daughter.

7:18

WISDOM

1 For the ear of jealousy heareth all things: and the noise of murmurings is not hid.

1:10

2 For the bewitching of naughtiness doth obscure things that are honest; and the wandering of concupiscence doth undermine the simple mind.

He, being made perfect in a short time, fulfilled a long time.

4:12–13

3 For all men have one entrance into life, and the like going out.

7:6

4 For wisdom is more moving than any motion: she passeth and go through all things by reason of her pureness.

For she is the breath of the power of God, and a pure influence flowing from the glory of the Almighty: therefore can no defiled thing fall into her.

For she is the brightness of the everlasting light, the unspotted mirror of the power of God, and the image of his goodness.

And being but one, she can do all things: and remaining in herself, she maketh all things new: and in all ages entering into holy souls, she maketh them friends of God, and prophets.

For God loveth none but him that dwelleth with wisdom.

7:24–28

5 Wisdom reacheth from one end to another mightily: and sweetly doth she order all things.

8:1

6 For thou hast power of life and death: thou leadest to the gates of hell, and bringest up again.

ECCLESIASTICUS

1 My son, if thou come to serve the Lord, prepare thy soul for temptation.

2:1

2 Be not curious in unnecessary matters: for more things are shewed unto thee than men understand

3:23

3 Winnow not with every wind, and go not into every way: for so the sinner that hath a double tongue.

5:9

4 Miss not the discourse of the elders: for they also learned of their fathers, and of them thou shalt learn understanding, and to give answer as need requireth.

8:9

5 Forsake not an old friend; for the new is not comparable to him: a new friend is as new wine; when it is old, thou shalt drink it with pleasure.

9:10

6 The physician cutteth off a long disease; and he that is today a king tomorrow shall die.

10:10

7 Desire not a multitude of unprofitable children, neither delight in ungodly sons.

16:1

8 Be not made a beggar by banqueting upon borrowing, when thou hast nothing in thy purse: for thou shalt lie in wait for thine own life, and be talked on.

18:33

9 If thou hast heard a word, let it die with thee; and be bold, it will not burst thee.

19:10

10 If thou hast gathered nothing in thy youth, how canst thou find any thing in thine age?

25:3

11 Leave off first for manners' sake: and be not unsatiable, lest thou offend.

31:17

**12** Let thy speech be short, comprehending much in few words; be as one that knoweth and yet holdeth his tongue.

32:8

**13** The wisdom of a learned man cometh by opportunity of leisure: and he that hath little business shall become wise.
How can he get wisdom that holdeth the plough, and that glorieth in the goad, that driveth oxen, and is occupied in their labours, and whose talk is of bullocks?

38:24-25

**14** Let us now praise famous men, and our fathers that begat us.

44:1

**15** Such as did bear rule in their kingdoms, men renowned for their power, giving counsel by their understanding, and declaring prophecies:
Leaders of the people by their counsels, and by their knowledge of learning meet for the people, wise and eloquent in their instructions:
Such as found out musical tunes and recited verses in writing:
Rich men furnished with ability living peaceably in their habitations:
All these were honoured in their generations, and were the glory of their times.
There be of them, that have left a name behind them, that their praises might be reported.
And some there be, which have no memorial; who are perished, as though they had never been; and are become as though they had never been born; and their children after them.

44:3-9

**16** Their bodies are buried in peace; but their name liveth for evermore.

44:14

**I MACCABEES**

**1** I perceive therefore that for this cause these troubles are come upon me, and, behold, I perish through great grief in a strange land.

6:13

**MATTHEW**

**1** Now when Jesus was born in Bethlehem of Judaea in the days of Herod the king, behold, there came wise men from the east to Jerusalem,
Saying, Where is he that is born King of the Jews? for we have seen his star in the east, and are come to worship him.
When Herod the king had heard these things, he was troubled, and all Jerusalem with him.

2:1-3

**2** And when they were come into the house, they saw the young child with Mary his mother, and fell down, and worshipped him: and when they had opened their treasures, they presented unto him gifts; gold, and frankincense, and myrrh.

And being warned of God in a dream that they should not return to Herod, they departed into their own country another way.

2:11-12

**3** For this is he that was spoken of by the prophet Esaias, saying, The voice of one crying in the wilderness, Prepare ye the way of the Lord, make his paths straight.
And the same John had his raiment of camel's hair, and a leathern girdle about his loins; and his meat was locusts and wild honey.

3:3-4

**4** But when he saw many of the Pharisees and Sadducees come to his baptism, he said unto them, O generation of vipers, who hath warned you to flee from the wrath to come?

3:7

**5** And Jesus answering said unto him, Suffer it to be so now: for thus it becometh us to fulfil all righteousness. Then he suffered him.
And Jesus, when he was baptized, went up straightway out of the water: and, lo, the heavens were opened unto him, and he saw the Spirit of God descending like a dove, and lighting upon him:
And lo a voice from heaven, saying, This is my beloved Son, in whom I am well pleased.

3:15-17

**6** Then was Jesus led up of the Spirit into the wilderness to be tempted of the devil.
And when he had fasted forty days and forty nights, he was afterward an hungred.
And when the tempter came to him, he said, If thou be the Son of God, command that these stones be made bread.
But he answered and said, It is written, Man shall not live by bread alone, but by every word that proceedeth out of the mouth of God.

4:1-4

**7** Jesus said unto him, It is written again, Thou shalt not tempt the Lord thy God.
Again, the devil taketh him up into an exceeding high mountain, and sheweth him all the kingdoms of the world, and the glory of them.

4:7-8

**8** From that time Jesus began to preach, and to say, Repent: for the kingdom of heaven is at hand.

4:17

**9** And he saith unto them, Follow me, and I will make you fishers of men.

4:19

**10** Blessed are the poor in spirit: for theirs is the kingdom of heaven.
Blessed are they that mourn: for they shall be comforted.
Blessed are the meek: for they shall inherit the earth.

Blessed are they which do hunger and thirst after righteousness: for they shall be filled.
Blessed are the merciful: for they shall obtain mercy.
Blessed are the pure in heart: for they shall see God.
Blessed are the peacemakers: for they shall be called the children of God.
Blessed are they which are persecuted for righteousness' sake: for theirs is the kingdom of heaven.
5:3-10

11 Ye are the salt of the earth: but if the salt have lost his savour, wherewith shall it be salted? it is thenceforth good for nothing, but to be cast out, and to be trodden under foot of men.
Ye are the light of the world. A city that is set on an hill cannot be hid.
Neither do men light a candle, and put it under a bushel, but on a candlestick; and it giveth light unto all that are in the house.
Let your light so shine before men, that they may see your good works, and glorify your Father which is in heaven.
5:13-16

12 For verily I say unto you, Till heaven and earth pass, one jot or one tittle shall in no wise pass from the law, till all be fulfilled.
5:18

13 For I say unto you, That except your righteousness shall exceed the righteousness of the scribes and Pharisees, ye shall in no case enter into the kingdom of heaven.
5:20

14 And if thy right eye offend thee, pluck it out, and cast it from thee: for it is profitable for thee that one of thy members should perish, and not that thy whole body should be cast into hell.
5:29

15 But I say unto you, That ye resist not evil: but whosoever shall smite thee on thy right cheek, turn to him the other also.
And if any man will sue thee at the law, and take away thy coat, let him have thy cloke also.
And whosoever shall compel thee to go a mile, go with him twain.
5:39-41

16 But I say unto you, Love your enemies, bless them that curse you, do good to them that hate you, and pray for them which despitefully use you, and persecute you;
That ye may be the children of your Father which is in heaven: for he maketh his sun to rise on the evil and on the good, and sendeth rain on the just and on the unjust.
For if ye love them which love you, what reward have ye? do not even the publicans the same?
5:44-46

17 Be ye therefore perfect, even as your Father which is in heaven is perfect.
5:48

18 But when ye pray, use not vain repetitions, as the heathen do: for they think that they shall be heard for their much speaking.
Be not ye therefore like unto them: for your Father knoweth what things ye have need of, before ye ask him.
After this manner therefore pray ye: Our Father which art in heaven, Hallowed be thy name.
Thy kingdom come. Thy will be done in earth, as it is in heaven.
Give us this day our daily bread.
And forgive us our debts, as we forgive our debtors.
And lead us not into temptation, but deliver us from evil: For thine is the kingdom, and the power, and the glory, for ever. Amen.
6:7-13

19 Lay not up for yourselves treasures upon earth, where moth and rust doth corrupt, and where thieves break through and steal:
But lay up for yourselves treasures in heaven, where neither moth nor rust doth corrupt, and where thieves do not break through nor steal:
For where your treasure is, there will your heart be also.
6:19-21

20 No man can serve two masters: for either he will hate the one, and love the other; or else he will hold to the one, and despise the other. Ye cannot serve God and mammon.
Therefore I say unto you, Take no thought for your life, what ye shall eat, or what ye shall drink; nor yet for your body, what ye shall put on. Is not the life more than meat, and the body than raiment?
6:24-25

21 Behold the fowls of the air: for they sow not, neither do they reap, nor gather into barns; yet your heavenly Father feedeth them. Are ye not much better than they?
Which of you by taking thought can add one cubit unto his stature?
And why take ye thought for raiment? Consider the lilies of the field, how they grow; they toil not, neither do they spin:
And yet I say unto you, That even Solomon in all his glory was not arrayed like one of these.
Wherefore, if God so clothe the grass of the field, which today is, and tomorrow is cast into the oven, shall he not much more clothe you, O ye of little faith?
Therefore take no thought, saying, What shall we eat? or, What shall we drink? or, Wherewithal shall we be clothed?
6:26-31

22 But seek ye first the kingdom of God, and his righteousness; and all these things shall be added unto you.

Take therefore no thought for the morrow: for the morrow shall take thought for the things of itself. Sufficient unto the day is the evil thereof.
6:33–34

23 Judge not, that ye be not judged.
7:1

24 And why beholdest thou the mote that is in thy brother's eye, but considerest not the beam that is in thine own eye?
7:3

25 Give not that which is holy unto the dogs, neither cast ye your pearls before swine, lest they trample them under their feet, and turn again and rend you.
7:6

26 Ask, and it shall be given you; seek, and ye shall find; knock, and it shall be opened unto you: For every one that asketh receiveth; and he that seeketh findeth; and to him that knocketh it shall be opened.
7:7–8

27 Or what man is there of you, whom if his son ask bread, will he give him a stone?
7:9

28 Enter ye in at the strait gate: for wide is the gate, and broad is the way, that leadeth to destruction, and many there be which go in thereat:
Because strait is the gate, and narrow is the way, which leadeth unto life, and few there be that find it.
7:13–14

29 Beware of false prophets, which come to you in sheep's clothing, but inwardly they are ravening wolves.
7:15

30 Ye shall know them by their fruits. Do men gather grapes of thorns, or figs of thistles?
Even so every good tree bringeth forth good fruit; but a corrupt tree bringeth forth evil fruit. A good tree cannot bring forth evil fruit, neither can a corrupt tree bring forth good fruit.
Every tree that bringeth not forth good fruit is hewn down, and cast into the fire.
Wherefore by their fruits ye shall know them.
7:16–20

31 Therefore whosoever heareth these sayings of mine, and doeth them, I will liken him unto a wise man, which built his house upon a rock:
And the rain descended, and the floods came, and the winds blew, and beat upon that house; and it fell not: for it was founded upon a rock.
And every one that heareth these sayings of mine, and doeth them not, shall be likened unto a foolish man, which built his house upon the sand:

And the rain descended, and the floods came, and the winds blew, and beat upon that house; and it fell: and great was the fall of it.
7:24–27

32 But the children of the kingdom shall be cast out into outer darkness: there shall be weeping and gnashing of teeth.
8:12

33 And Jesus saith unto him, The foxes have holes, and the birds of the air have nests; but the Son of man hath not where to lay his head.
8:20

34 But Jesus said unto him, Follow me; and let the dead bury their dead.
8:22

35 And his disciples came to him, and awoke him, saying, Lord, save us: we perish.
And he saith unto them, Why are ye fearful, O ye of little faith? Then he arose, and rebuked the winds and the sea; and there was a great calm.
But the men marvelled, saying, What manner of man is this, that even the winds and the sea obey him!
8:25–27

36 Neither do men put new wine into old bottles: else the bottles break, and the wine runneth out, and the bottles perish: but they put new wine into new bottles, and both are preserved.
9:17

37 Heal the sick, cleanse the lepers, raise the dead, cast out devils: freely ye have received, freely give.
10:8

38 And ye shall be hated of all men for my name's sake: but he that endureth to the end shall be saved.
10:22

39 Think not that I am come to send peace on earth: I came not to send peace, but a sword.
10:34

40 He that hath ears to hear, let him hear.
11:15

41 Come unto me, all ye that labour and are heavy laden, and I will give you rest.
Take my yoke upon you, and learn of me; for I am meek and lowly in heart: and ye shall find rest unto your souls.
For my yoke is easy, and my burden is light.
11:28–30

42 O generation of vipers, how can ye, being evil, speak good things? for out of the abundance of the heart the mouth speaketh.
12:34

**43** For whosoever shall do the will of my Father which is in heaven, the same is my brother, and sister, and mother.
12:50

**44** And he spake many things unto them in parables, saying, Behold, a sower went forth to sow; And when he sowed, some seeds fell by the way side, and the fowls came and devoured them up:
Some fell upon stony places, where they had not much earth: and forthwith they sprung up, because they had no deepness of earth:
And when the sun was up, they were scorched; and because they had no root, they withered away.
And some fell among thorns; and the thorns sprung up, and choked them:
But other fell into good ground, and brought forth fruit, some an hundredfold, some sixtyfold, some thirtyfold.
13:3–8

**45** And they were offended in him. But Jesus said unto them, A prophet is not without honour, save in his own country, and in his own house.
13:57

**46** But when Herod's birthday was kept, the daughter of Herodias danced before them, and pleased Herod.
Whereupon he promised with an oath to give her whatsoever she would ask.
And she, being before instructed of her mother, said, Give me John Baptist's head in a charger.
14:6–8

**47** And in the fourth watch of the night Jesus went unto them, walking on the sea.
And when the disciples saw him walking on the sea, they were troubled, saying, It is a spirit; and they cried out for fear.
But straightway Jesus spake unto them, saying, Be of good cheer; it is I; be not afraid.
14:25–27

**48** And immediately Jesus stretched forth his hand, and caught him, and said unto him, O thou of little faith, wherefore didst thou doubt?
14:31

**49** And besought him that they might only touch the hem of his garment: and as many as touched were made perfectly whole.
14:36

**50** And I say also unto thee, That thou art Peter, and upon this rock I will build my church; and the gates of hell shall not prevail against it.
And I will give unto thee the keys of the kingdom of heaven: and whatsoever thou shalt bind on earth shall be bound in heaven: and whatsoever thou shalt loose on earth shall be loosed in heaven.
16:18–19

**51** Then said Jesus unto his disciples, If any man will come after me, let him deny himself, and take up his cross, and follow me.
16:24

**52** And said, Verily I say unto you, Except ye be converted, and become as little children, ye shall not enter into the kingdom of heaven.
18:3

**53** And whoso shall receive one such little child in my name receiveth me.
But whoso shall offend one of these little ones which believe in me, it were better for him that a millstone were hanged about his neck, and that he were drowned in the depth of the sea.
18:5–6

**54** For where two or three are gathered together in my name, there am I in the midst of them.
18:20

**55** Then came Peter to him, and said, Lord, how oft shall my brother sin against me, and I forgive him? till seven times?
Jesus saith unto him, I say not unto thee, Until seven times: but, Until seventy times seven.
18:21–22

**56** Wherefore they are no more twain, but one flesh. What therefore God hath joined together, let not man put asunder.
19:6

**57** Jesus said unto him, If thou wilt be perfect, go and sell that thou hast, and give to the poor, and thou shalt have treasure in heaven: and come and follow me.
But when the young man heard that saying, he went away sorrowful: for he had great possessions.
19:21–22

**58** Then said Jesus unto his disciples, Verily I say unto you, That a rich man shall hardly enter into the kingdom of heaven.
And again I say unto you, It is easier for a camel to go through the eye of a needle, than for a rich man to enter into the kingdom of God.
19:23–24

**59** But many that are first shall be last; and the last shall be first.
19:30

**60** And a very great multitude spread their garments in the way; others cut down branches from the trees, and strawed them in the way.
And the multitudes that went before, and that followed, cried, saying, Hosanna to the Son of David: Blessed is he that cometh in the name of the Lord; Hosanna in the highest.
21:8–9

**61** And said unto them, It is written, My house shall be called the house of prayer; but ye have made it a den of thieves.
21:13

**62** For many are called, but few are chosen.

22:14

**63** And he saith unto them, Whose is this image and superscription?
They say unto him, Caesar's. Then saith he unto them, Render therefore unto Caesar the things which are Caesar's; and unto God the things that are God's.

22:20-21

**64** Jesus said unto him, Thou shalt love the Lord thy God with all thy heart, and with all thy soul, and with all thy mind.
This is the first and great commandment.
And the second is like unto it, Thou shalt love thy neighbour as thyself.
On these two commandments hang all the law and the prophets.

22:37-40

**65** Woe unto you, scribes and Pharisees, hypocrites! for ye are like unto whited sepulchres, which indeed appear beautiful outward, but are within full of dead men's bones, and of all uncleanness.

23:27

**66** And Jesus said unto them, See ye not all these things? verily I say unto you, There shall not be left here one stone upon another, that shall not be thrown down.

24:2

**67** And ye shall hear of wars and rumours of wars: see that ye be not troubled: for all these things must come to pass, but the end is not yet.
For nation shall rise against nation, and kingdom against kingdom: and there shall be famines, and pestilences, and earthquakes, in divers places.
All these are the beginning of sorrows.

24:6-8

**68** Immediately after the tribulation of those days shall the sun be darkened, and the moon shall not give her light, and the stars shall fall from heaven, and the powers of the heavens shall be shaken:
And then shall appear the sign of the Son of man in heaven: and then shall all the tribes of the earth mourn, and they shall see the Son of man coming in the clouds of heaven with power and great glory.
And he shall send his angels with a great sound of a trumpet, and they shall gather together his elect from the four winds, from one end of heaven to the other.

24:29-31

**69** Heaven and earth shall pass away, but my words shall not pass away.

24:35

**70** And at midnight there was a cry made, Behold, the bridegroom cometh; go ye out to meet him.

Then all those virgins arose, and trimmed their lamps.
And the foolish said unto the wise, Give us of your oil; for our lamps are gone out.

25:6-8

**71** And unto one he gave five talents, to another two, and to another one; to every man according to his several ability; and straightway took his journey.

25:15

**72** His lord said unto him, Well done, thou good and faithful servant: thou hast been faithful over a few things, I will make thee ruler over many things: enter thou into the joy of thy lord.

25:21

**73** For unto every one that hath shall be given, and he shall have abundance: but from him that hath not shall be taken away even that which he hath.
And cast ye the unprofitable servant into outer darkness: there shall be weeping and gnashing of teeth.

25:29-30

**74** And before him shall be gathered all nations: and he shall separate them one from another, as a shepherd divideth his sheep from the goats:
And he shall set the sheep on his right hand, but the goats on the left.

25:32-33

**75** Then shall the King say unto them on his right hand, Come, ye blessed of my Father, inherit the kingdom prepared for you from the foundation of the world:
For I was an hungred, and ye gave me meat: I was thirsty, and ye gave me drink: I was a stranger, and ye took me in:
Naked, and ye clothed me: I was sick, and ye visited me: I was in prison, and ye came unto me.

25:34-36

**76** And the King shall answer and say unto them, Verily I say unto you, Inasmuch as ye have done it unto one of the least of these my brethren, ye have done it unto me.

25:40

**77** And he answered and said, He that dippeth his hand with me in the dish, the same shall betray me.
The Son of man goeth as it is written of him: but woe unto that man by whom the Son of man is betrayed! it had been good for that man if he had not been born.
Then Judas, which betrayed him, answered and said, Master, is it I? He said unto him, Thou hast said.

26:23-25

**78** And as they were eating, Jesus took bread, and blessed it, and brake it, and gave it to the disciples, and said, Take, eat; this is my body.

And he took the cup, and gave thanks, and gave it to them, saying, Drink ye all of it;
For this is my blood of the new testament, which is shed for many for the remission of sins.
26:26–28

**79** Jesus said unto him, Verily I say unto thee, That this night, before the cock crow, thou shalt deny me thrice.
Peter said unto him, Though I should die with thee, yet will I not deny thee. Likewise also said all the disciples.
26:34–35

**80** Then saith he unto them, My soul is exceeding sorrowful, even unto death: tarry ye here, and watch with me.
26:38

**81** Watch and pray, that ye enter not into temptation: the spirit indeed is willing, but the flesh is weak.
26:41

**82** And forthwith he came to Jesus, and said, Hail, master; and kissed him.
And Jesus said unto him, Friend, wherefore art thou come? Then came they, and laid hands on Jesus, and took him.
26:49–50

**83** Then said Jesus unto him, Put up again thy sword into his place: for all they that take the sword shall perish with the sword.
26:52

**84** Then Judas, which had betrayed him, when he saw that he was condemned, repented himself, and brought again the thirty pieces of silver to the chief priests and elders,
Saying, I have sinned in that I have betrayed the innocent blood. And they said, What is that to us? see thou to that.
27:3–4

**85** When Pilate saw that he could prevail nothing, but that rather a tumult was made, he took water, and washed his hands before the multitude, saying, I am innocent of the blood of this just person: see ye to it.
Then answered all the people, and said, His blood be on us, and on our children.
27:24–25

**86** And about the ninth hour Jesus cried with a loud voice, saying, Eli, Eli, lama sabachthani? that is to say, My God, my God, why hast thou forsaken me?
27:46

**87** Jesus, when he had cried again with a loud voice, yielded up the ghost.
And, behold, the veil of the temple was rent in twain from the top to the bottom; and the earth did quake, and the rocks rent;
And the graves were opened; and many bodies of the saints which slept arose.
27:50–52

**88** Teaching them to observe all things whatsoever I have commanded you: and, lo, I am with you alway, even unto the end of the world. Amen.
28:20

**MARK**

**1** And he said unto them, The sabbath was made for man, and not man for the sabbath: Therefore the Son of man is Lord also of the sabbath.
2:27–28

**2** And he asked him, What is thy name? And he answered, saying, My name is Legion: for we are many.
5:9

**3** And forthwith Jesus gave them leave. And the unclean spirits went out, and entered into the swine: and the herd ran violently down a steep place into the sea, (they were about two thousand;) and were choked in the sea.
5:13

**4** For what shall it profit a man, if he sahll gain the whole world, and lose his own soul? Or what shall a man give in exchange for his soul?
8:36–37

**5** But when Jesus saw it, he was much displeased, and said unto them. Suffer the little children to come unto me, and forbid them not: for of such is the kingdom of God.
10:14

**6** And there came a certain poor widow, and she threw in two mites, which make a farthing.
And he called unto him his disciples, and saith unto them, Verily I say unto you, That this poor widow hath cast more in, than all they which have cast into the treasury: For all they did cast in of their abundance; but she of her want did cast in all that she had, even all her living.
12:42–44

**7** And he said unto them, Go ye into all the world, and preach the gospel to every creature.
16:15

**LUKE**

**1** And the angel came in unto her, and said, Hail, thou that art highly favoured, the Lord is with thee: blessed art thou among women.
And when she saw him, she was troubled at his saying, and cast in her mind what manner of salutation this should be.
1:28–29

**2** And Mary said, My soul doth magnify the Lord, And my spirit hath rejoiced in God my Saviour.
For he hath regarded the low estate of his handmaiden: for, behold, from henceforth all generations shall call me blessed.
1:46–48

**3** He hath shewed strength with his arm; he hath scattered the proud in the imagination of their hearts.

He hath put down the mighty from their seats, and exalted them of low degree.
He hath filled the hungry with good things; and the rich he hath sent empty away.
1:51–53

4 Blessed be the Lord God of Israel; for he hath visited and redeemed his people.
1:68

5 And the child grew, and waxed strong in spirit, and was in the deserts till the day of his shewing unto Israel.
1:80

6 And it came to pass in those days, that there went out a decree from Caesar Augustus, that all the world should be taxed.
2:1

7 And she brought forth her firstborn son, and wrapped him in swaddling clothes, and laid him in a manger; because there was no room for them in the inn.
2:7

8 And there were in the same country shepherds abiding in the field, keeping watch over their flock by night.
And, lo, the angel of the Lord came upon them, and the glory of the Lord shone round about them: and they were sore afraid.
And the angel said unto them, Fear not: for, behold, I bring you good tidings of great joy, which shall be to all people.
2:8–10

9 Glory to God in the highest, and on earth peace, good will toward men.
2:14

10 But Mary kept all these things, and pondered them in her heart.
2:19

11 Lord, now lettest thou thy servant depart in peace, according to thy word:
For mine eyes have seen thy salvation,
Which thou hast prepared before the face of all people;
A light to lighten the Gentiles, and the glory of thy people Israel.
2:29–32

12 And it came to pass, that after three days they found him in the temple, sitting in the midst of the doctors, both hearing them, and asking them questions.
And all that heard him were astonished at his understanding and answers.
2:46–47

13 And the devil, taking him up into an high mountain, shewed unto him all the kingdoms of the world in a moment of time.
4:5

14 And he said unto them, Ye will surely say unto me this proverb, Physician, heal thyself: whatsoever we have heard done in Capernaum, do also here in thy country.
4:23

15 No man also having drunk old wine straightway desireth new: for he saith, The old is better.
5:39

16 And stood at his feet behind him weeping, and began to wash his feet with tears, and did wipe them with the hairs of her head, and kissed his feet, and anointed them with the ointment.
7:38

17 Wherefore I say unto thee, Her sins, which are many, are forgiven; for she loved much: but to whom little is forgiven, the same loveth little.
7:47

18 And he said to the woman, Thy faith hath saved thee; go in peace.
7:50

19 Go your ways: behold, I send you forth as lambs among wolves.
Carry neither purse, nor scrip, nor shoes: and salute no man by the way.
And into whatsoever house ye enter, first say, Peace be to this house.
And if the son of peace be there, your peace shall rest upon it: if not, it shall turn to you again.
And in the same house remain, eating and drinking such things as they give: for the labourer is worthy of his hire. Go not from house to house.
10:3–7

20 And he said unto them, I beheld Satan as lightning fall from heaven.
10:18

21 And Jesus answering said, A certain man went down from Jerusalem to Jericho, and fell among thieves, which stripped him of his raiment, and wounded him, and departed, leaving him half dead.
And by chance there came down a certain priest that way: and when he saw him, he passed by on the other side.
10:30–31

22 But a certain Samaritan, as he journeyed, came where he was: and when he saw him, he had compassion on him,
And went to him, and bound up his wounds, pouring in oil and wine, and set him on his own beast, and brought him to an inn, and took care of him.
And on the morrow when he departed, he took out two pence, and gave them to the host, and said unto him, Take care of him; and whatsoever thou spendest more, when I come again, I will repay thee.
10:33–35

**23** And he said, He that shewed mercy on him. Then said Jesus unto him, Go, and do thou likewise.

10:37

**24** Woe unto you, lawyers! for ye have taken away the key of knowledge: ye entered not in yourselves, and them that were entering in ye hindered.

11:52

**25** Are not five sparrows sold for two farthings, and not one of them is forgotten before God?

12:6

**26** And they all with one consent began to make excuse. The first said unto him, I have bought a piece of ground, and I must needs go and see it: I pray thee have me excused.
And another said, I have bought five yoke of oxen, and I go to prove them: I pray thee have me excused.
And another said, I have married a wife, and therefore I cannot come.
So that servant came, and shewed his lord these things. Then the master of the house being angry said to his servant, Go out quickly into the streets and lanes of the city, and bring in hither the poor, and the maimed, and the halt, and the blind.

14:18–21

**27** What man of you, having an hundred sheep, if he lose one of them, doth not leave the ninety and nine in the wilderness, and go after that which is lost until he find it?
And when he hath found it, he layeth it on his shoulders, rejoicing.
And when he cometh home, he calleth together his friends and neighbours, saying unto them, Rejoice with me; for I have found my sheep which was lost.
I say unto you, that likewise joy shall be in heaven over one sinner that repenteth, more than over ninety and nine just persons, which need no repentance.

15:4–7

**28** And he would fain have filled his belly with the husks that the swine did eat: and no man gave unto him.
And when he came to himself, he said, How many hired servants of my father's have bread enough and to spare, and I perish with hunger!
I will arise and go to my father, and will say unto him, Father, I have sinned against heaven, and before thee,
And am no more worthy to be called thy son: make me as one of thy hired servants.
And he arose, and came to his father. But when he was yet a great way off, his father saw him, and had compassion, and ran, and fell on his neck, and kissed him.

15:16–20

**29** And bring hither the fatted calf, and kill it; and let us eat, and be merry:
For this my son was dead, and is alive again; he was lost, and is found. And they began to be merry.

15:23–24

**30** There was a certain rich man, which was clothed in purple and fine linen, and fared sumptuously every day:
And there was a certain beggar named Lazarus, which was laid at his gate, full of sores,
And desiring to be fed with the crumbs which fell from the rich man's table: moreover the dogs came and licked his sores.
And it came to pass, that the beggar died, and was carried by the angels into Abraham's bosom: the rich man also died, and was buried;

16:19–22

**31** And when he was demanded of the Pharisees, when the kingdom of God should come, he answered them and said, The kingdom of God cometh not with observation:
Neither shall they say, Lo here! or, lo there! for, behold, the kingdom of God is within you.

17:20–21

**32** Remember Lot's wife.

17:32

**33** And he saith unto him, Out of thine own mouth will I judge thee, thou wicked servant. Thou knewest that I was an austere man, taking up that I laid not down, and reaping that I did not sow.

19:22

**34** And he answered and said unto them, I tell you that, if these should hold their peace, the stones would immediately cry out.

19:40

**35** And when they were come to the place, which is called Calvary, there they crucified him, and the malefactors, one on the right hand, and the other on the left.

23:33

**36** Then said Jesus, Father, forgive them; for they know not what they do. And they parted his raiment, and cast lots.

23:34

**37** But the other answering rebuked him, saying, Dost not thou fear God, seeing thou art in the same condemnation?
And we indeed justly; for we receive the due reward of our deeds: but this man hath done nothing amiss.
And he said unto Jesus, Lord, remember me when thou comest into thy kingdom.
And Jesus said unto him, Verily I say unto thee, Today shalt thou be with me in paradise.

23:40–43

38 And when Jesus had cried with a loud voice, he said, Father, into thy hands I commend my spirit: and having said thus, he gave up the ghost.

23:46

39 And as they were afraid, and bowed down their faces to the earth, they said unto them, Why seek ye the living among the dead?

24:5

40 Saying, The Lord is risen indeed, and hath appeared to Simon.
And they told what things were done in the way, and how he was known of them in breaking of bread.

24:34-35

JOHN

1 In the beginning was the Word, and the Word was with God, and the Word was God.
The same was in the beginning with God.
All things were made by him; and without him was not any thing made that was made.
In him was life; and the life was the light of men.
And the light shineth in darkness; and the darkness comprehended it not.
There was a man sent from God, whose name was John.
The same came for a witness, to bear witness of the Light, that all men through him might believe.
He was not that Light, but was sent to bear witness of that Light.
That was the true Light, which lighteth every man that cometh into the world.
He was in the world, and the world was made by him, and the world knew him not.
He came unto his own, and his own received him not.
But as many as received him, to them gave he power to become the sons of God, even to them that believe on his name:
Which were born, not of blood, nor of the will of the flesh, the will of man, but of God.
And the Word was made flesh, and dwelt among us, (and we beheld his glory, the glory as of the only begotten of the Father,) full of grace and truth.

1:1-14

2 He it is, who coming after me is preferred before me, whose shoe's latchet I am not worthy to unloose.

1:27

3 The next day John seeth Jesus coming unto him, and saith, Behold the Lamb of God, which taketh away the sin of the world.

1:29

4 Jesus saith unto her, Woman, what have I to do with thee? mine hour is not yet come.

2:4

5 When the ruler of the feast had tasted the water that was made wine, and knew not whence it was: (but the servants which drew the water knew;) the governor of the feast called the bridegroom,
And saith unto him, Every man at the beginning doth set forth good wine; and when men have well drunk, then that which is worse: but thou hast kept the good wine until now.

2:9-10

6 Jesus answered and said unto him, Verily, verily, I say unto thee, Except a man be born again, he cannot see the kingdom of God.

3:3

7 Jesus answered, Verily, verily, I say unto thee, Except a man be born of water and of the Spirit, he cannot enter into the kingdom of God.
That which is born of the flesh is flesh; and that which is born of the Spirit is spirit.

3:5-6

8 The wind bloweth where it listeth, and thou hearest the sound thereof, but canst not tell whence it cometh, and whither it goeth: so is every one that is born of the Spirit.

3:8

9 For God so loved the world, that he gave his only begotten Son, that whosoever believeth in him should not perish, but have everlasting life.

3:16

10 And this is the condemnation, that light is come into the world, and men loved darkness rather than light, because their deeds were evil.

3:19

11 He that hath the bride is the bridegroom: but the friend of the bridegroom, which standeth and heareth him, rejoiceth greatly because of the bridegroom's voice: this my joy therefore is fulfilled.
He must increase, but I must decrease.

3:29-30

12 Jesus answered and said unto her, Whosoever drinketh of this water shall thirst again:
But whosoever drinketh of the water that I shall give him shall never thirst; but the water that I shall give him shall be in him a well of water springing up into everlasting life.

4:13-14

13 Afterward Jesus findeth him in the temple, and said unto him, Behold, thou art made whole: sin no more, lest a worse thing come unto thee.

5:14

14 Verily, verily, I say unto you, He that heareth my word, and believeth on him that sent me, hath everlasting life, and shall not come into condemnation; but is passed from death unto life.

Verily, verily, I say unto you, The hour is coming, and now is, when the dead shall hear the voice of the Son of God: and they that hear shall live.

5:24-25

**15** There is a lad here, which hath five barley loaves, and two small fishes: but what are they among so many?
And Jesus said, Make the men sit down. Now there was much grass in the place. So the men sat down, in number about five thousand.

6:9-10

**16** And Jesus said unto them, I am the bread of life: he that cometh to me shall never hunger; and he that believeth on me shall never thirst.

6:35

**17** All that the Father giveth me shall come to me; and him that cometh to me I will in no wise cast out.

6:37

**18** Your fathers did eat manna in the wilderness, and are dead.
This is the bread which cometh down from heaven, that a man may eat thereof, and not die.
I am the living bread which came down from heaven: if any man eat of this bread, he shall live for ever: and the bread that I will give is my flesh, which I will give for the life of the world.

6:49-51

**19** So when they continued asking him, he lifted up himself, and said unto them, He that is without sin among you, let him first cast a stone at her.

8:7

**20** She said, No man, Lord. And Jesus said unto her, Neither do I condemn thee: go, and sin no more.

8:11

**21** Then spake Jesus again unto them, saying, I am the light of the world: he that followeth me shall not walk in darkness, but shall have the light of life.

8:12

**22** And ye shall know the truth, and the truth shall make you free.

8:32

**23** He answered and said, Whether he be a sinner or no, I know not: one thing I know, that, whereas I was blind, now I see.

9:25

**24** Verily, verily, I say unto you, He that entereth not by the door into the sheepfold, but climbeth up some other way, the same is a thief and a robber.
But he that entereth in by the door is the shepherd of the sheep.

To him the porter openeth, and the sheep hear his voice: and he calleth his own sheep by name, and leadeth them out.
And when he putteth forth his own sheep, he goeth before them, and the sheep follow him: for they know his voice.

10:1-4

**25** I am the door: by me if any man enter in, he shall be saved, and shall go in and out, and find pasture.

10:9

**26** I am the good shepherd: the good shepherd giveth his life for the sheep.
But he that is an hireling, and not the shepherd, whose own the sheep are not, seeth the wolf coming, and leaveth the sheep, and fleeth: and the wolf catcheth them, and scattereth the sheep.
The hireling fleeth, because he is an hireling, and careth not for the sheep.

10:11-13

**27** Jesus said unto her, I am the resurrection, and the life: he that believeth in me, though he were dead, yet shall he live.

11:25

**28** When Jesus therefore saw her weeping, and the Jews also weeping which came with her, he groaned in the spirit, and was troubled,
And said, Where have ye laid him? They said unto him, Lord, come and see.
Jesus wept.

11:33-35

**29** Now is the judgment of this world: now shall the prince of this world be cast out.
And I, if I be lifted up from the earth, will draw all men unto me.

12:31-32

**30** Now there was leaning on Jesus' bosom one of his disciples, whom Jesus loved.

13:23

**31** In my Father's house are many mansions: if it were not so, I would have told you. I go to prepare a place for you.

14:2

**32** Jesus saith unto him, I am the way, the truth, and the life: no man cometh unto the Father, but by me.

14:6

**33** If ye love me, keep my commandments.
And I will pray the Father, and he shall give you another Comforter, that he may abide with you for ever;
Even the Spirit of truth; whom the world cannot receive, because it seeth him not, neither knoweth him: but ye know him; for he dwelleth with you, and shall be in you.

14:15-17

**34** Peace I leave with you, my peace I give unto you: not as the world giveth, give I unto you. Let not your heart be troubled, neither let it be afraid.
14:27

**35** I am the true vine, and my Father is the husbandman.
15:1

**36** Greater love hath no man than this, that a man lay down his life for his friends.
15:13

**37** Ye have not chosen me, but I have chosen you, and ordained you, that ye should go and bring forth fruit, and that your fruit should remain: that whatsoever ye shall ask of the Father in my name, he may give it you.
15:16

**38** But now I go my way to him that sent me; and none of you asketh me, Whither goest thou?
16:5

**39** Quo vadis?
Vulgate 16:5

**40** Nevertheless I tell you the truth; It is expedient for you that I go away: for if I go not away, the Comforter will not come unto you; but if I depart, I will send him unto you.
16:7

**41** A woman when she is in travail hath sorrow, because her hour is come: but as soon as she is delivered of the child, she remembereth no more the anguish, for joy that a man is born into the world.
16:21

**42** These things I have spoken unto you, that in me ye might have peace. In the world ye shall have tribulation: but be of good cheer; I have overcome the world.
16:33

**43** Now Caiaphas was he, which gave counsel to the Jews, that it was expedient that one man should die for the people.
18:14

**44** Pilate saith unto him, What is truth? And when he had said this, he went out again unto the Jews, and saith unto them, I find in him no fault at all.
18:38

**45** Then cried they all again, saying, Not this man, but Barabbas. Now Barabbas was a robber.
18:40

**46** Then came Jesus forth, wearing the crown of thorns, and the purple robe. And Pilate saith unto them, Behold the man!
19:5

**47** Ecce homo.
Vulgate 19:5

**48** Pilate answered, What I have written I have written.
19:22

**49** When Jesus therefore saw his mother, and the disciple standing by, whom he loved, he saith unto his mother, Woman, behold thy son! Then saith he to the disciple, Behold thy mother! And from that hour that disciple took her unto his own home.
19:26–27

**50** When Jesus therefore had received the vinegar, he said, It is finished: and he bowed his head, and gave up the ghost.
19:30

**51** Consummatum est.
Vulgate 19:30

**52** Now in the place where he was crucified there was a garden; and in the garden a new sepulchre, wherein was never man yet laid.
19:41

**53** The first day of the week cometh Mary Magdalene early, when it was yet dark, unto the sepulchre, and seeth the stone taken away from the sepulchre.
Then she runneth, and cometh to Simon Peter, and to the other disciple, whom Jesus loved, and saith unto them, They have taken the Lord out of the sepulchre, and we know not where they have laid him.
20:1–2

**54** Jesus saith unto her, Woman, why weepest thou? whom seekest thou? She, supposing him to be the gardener, saith unto him, Sir, if thou have borne him hence, tell me where thou hast laid him, and I will take him away.
Jesus saith unto her, Mary. She turned herself, and saith unto him, Rabboni; which is to say, Master.
Jesus saith unto her, Touch me not; for I am not yet ascended to my Father: but go to my brethren, and say unto them, I ascend unto my Father, and your Father; and to my God, and your God.
20:15–17

**55** Noli me tangere.
Vulgate 20:17

**56** The other disciples therefore said unto him, We have seen the Lord. But he said unto them, Except I shall see in his hands the print of the nails, and put my finger into the print of the nails, and thrust my hand into his side, I will not believe.
20:25

**57** Then saith he to Thomas, Reach hither thy finger, and behold my hands; and reach hither thy hand, and thrust it into my side: and be not faithless, but believing.
And Thomas answered and said unto him, My Lord and my God.

Jesus saith unto him, Thomas, because thou hast seen me, thou hast believed: blessed are they that have not seen, and yet have believed.

20:27–29

**58** So when they had dined, Jesus saith to Simon Peter, Simon, son of Jonas, lovest thou me more than these? He saith unto him, Yea, Lord; thou knowest that I love thee. He saith unto him, Feed my lambs.

21:15

**59** He saith unto him the third time, Simon, son of Jonas, lovest thou me? Peter was grieved because he said unto him the third time, Lovest thou me? And he said unto him, Lord, thou knowest all things; thou knowest that I love thee. Jesus saith unto him, Feed my sheep.

21:17

**60** Peter seeing him saith to Jesus, Lord, and what shall this man do?
Jesus saith unto him, If I will that he tarry till I come, what is that to thee? follow thou me.

21:21–22

ACTS

**1** And when he had spoken these things, while they beheld, he was taken up; and a cloud received him out of their sight.

1:9

**2** And when the day of Pentecost was fully come, they were all with one accord in one place.
And suddenly there came a sound from heaven as of a rushing mighty wind, and it filled all the house where they were sitting.
And there appeared unto them cloven tongues like as of fire, and it sat upon each of them.
And they were all filled with the Holy Ghost, and began to speak with other tongues, as the Spirit gave them utterance.

2:1–4

**3** Others mocking said, These men are full of new wine.

2:13

**4** Then Peter said, Silver and gold have I none; but such as I have give I thee: In the name of Jesus Christ of Nazareth rise up and walk.

3:6

**5** When they heard these things, they were cut to the heart, and they gnashed on him with their teeth.

7:54

**6** And as he journeyed, he came near Damascus: and suddenly there shined round about him a light from heaven:
And he fell to the earth, and heard a voice saying unto him, Saul, Saul, why persecutest thou me?
And he said, Who art thou, Lord? And the Lord said, I am Jesus whom thou persecutest: it is hard for thee to kick against the pricks.

9:3–5

**7** And the Lord said unto him, Arise, and go into the street which is called Straight, and enquire in the house of Judas for one called Saul, of Tarsus: for, behold, he prayeth.

9:11

**8** But the Lord said unto him, Go thy way: for he is a chosen vessel unto me, to bear my name before the Gentiles, and kings, and the children of Israel.

9:15

**9** But Peter took him up, saying, Stand up; I myself also am a man.

10:26

**10** Then Peter opened his mouth, and said, Of a truth I perceive that God is no respecter of persons.

10:34

**11** And the people gave a shout, saying, It is the voice of a god, and not of a man.
And immediately the angel of the Lord smote him, because he gave not God the glory: and he was eaten of worms, and gave up the ghost.

12:22–23

**12** (For all the Athenians and strangers which were there spent their time in nothing else, but either to tell, or to hear some new thing.)
Then Paul stood in the midst of Mars' hill, and said, Ye men of Athens, I perceive that in all things ye are too superstitious.
For as I passed by, and beheld your devotions, I found an altar with this inscription, TO THE UNKNOWN GOD. Whom therefore ye ignorantly worship, him declare I unto you.
God that made the world and all things therein, seeing that he is Lord of heaven and earth, dwelleth not in temples made with hands

17:21–24

**13** For in him we live, and move, and have our being; as certain also of your own poets have said, For we are also his offspring.

17:28

**14** And the evil spirit answered and said, Jesus I know, and Paul I know; but who are ye?

19:15

**15** And when they heard these sayings, they were full of wrath, and cried out, saying, Great is Diana of the Ephesians.

19:28

**16** And now, behold, I go bound in the spirit unto Jerusalem, not knowing the things that shall befall me there.

20:22

**17** And the chief captain answered, With a great sum obtained I this freedom. And Paul said, But I was free born.

22:28

18 Then said Paul unto him, God shall smite thee, thou whited wall: for sittest thou to judge me after the law, and commandest me to be smitten contrary to the law?
23:3

19 Then Festus, when he had conferred with the council, answered, Hast thou appealed unto Caesar? Unto Caesar shalt thou go.
25:12

I CORINTHIANS

1 For after that in the wisdom of God the world by wisdom knew not God, it pleased God by the foolishness of preaching to save them that believe.
For the Jews require a sign, and the Greeks seek after wisdom:
But we preach Christ crucified, unto the Jews a stumblingblock, and unto the Greeks foolishness.
1:21–23

2 But God hath chosen the foolish things of the world to confound the wise; and God hath chosen the weak things of the world to confound the things which are mighty.
1:27

3 But as it is written, Eye hath not seen, nor ear heard, neither have entered into the heart of man, the things which God hath prepared for them that love him.
2:9

4 For the kingdom of God is not in word, but in power.
4:20

5 Meats for the belly, and the belly for meats: but God shall destroy both it and them. Now the body is not for fornication, but for the Lord; and the Lord for the body.
6:13

6 What? know ye not that your body is the temple of the Holy Ghost which is in you, which ye have of God, and ye are not your own?
6:19

7 Let the husband render unto the wife due benevolence: and likewise also the wife unto the husband.
7:3

8 But if they cannot contain, let them marry: for it is better to marry than to burn.
7:9

9 And they that use this world, as not abusing it: for the fashion of this world passeth away.
7:31

10 But he that is married careth for the things that are of the world, how he may please his wife.
7:33

11 Now as touching things offered unto idols, we know that we all have knowledge. Knowledge puffeth up, but charity edifieth.
8:1

12 Who goeth a warfare any time at his own charges? who planteth a vineyard, and eateth not of the fruit thereof? or who feedeth a flock, and eateth not of the milk of the flock?
9:7

13 Know ye not that they which run in a race run all, but one receiveth the prize? So run, that ye may obtain.
And every man that striveth for the mastery is temperate in all things. Now they do it to obtain a corruptible crown; but we an incorruptible.
I therefore so run, not as uncertainly; so fight I, not as one that beateth the air:
But I keep under my body, and bring it into subjection: lest that by any means, when I have preached to others, I myself should be a castaway.
9:24–27

14 All things are lawful for me, but all things are not expedient: all things are lawful for me, but all things edify not.
10:23

15 For the earth is the Lord's, and the fulness thereof.
10:26

16 Conscience, I say, not thine own, but of the other: for why is my liberty judged of another man's conscience?
10:29

17 But if a woman have long hair, it is a glory to her: for her hair is given her for a covering.
11:15

18 Though I speak with the tongues of men and of angels, and have not charity, I am become as sounding brass, or a tinkling cymbal.
And though I have the gift of prophecy, and understand all mysteries, and all knowledge; and though I have all faith, so that I could remove mountains, and have not charity, I am nothing.
And though I bestow all my goods to feed the poor, and though I give my body to be burned, and have not charity, it profiteth me nothing.
Charity suffereth long, and is kind; charity envieth not; charity vaunteth not itself, is not puffed up,
Doth not behave itself unseemly, seeketh not her own, is not easily provoked, thinketh no evil;
Rejoiceth not in iniquity, but rejoiceth in the truth;
Beareth all things, believeth all things, hopeth all things, endureth all things.
Charity never faileth: but whether there be prophecies, they shall fail; whether there be tongues, they shall cease; whether there be knowledge, it shall vanish away.

For we know in part, and we prophesy in part. But when that which is perfect is come, then that which is in part shall be done away.
When I was a child, I spake as a child, I understood as a child, I thought as a child: but when I became a man, I put away childish things.
For now we see through a glass, darkly; but then face to face: now I know in part; but then shall I know even as also I am known.
And now abideth faith, hope, charity, these three; but the greatest of these is charity.
13:1-13

**19** Let all things be done decently and in order.
14:40

**20** Then cometh the end, when he shall have delivered up the kingdom to God, even the Father; when he shall have put down all rule and all authority and power.
For he must reign, till he hath put all enemies under his feet.
The last enemy that shall be destroyed is death.
15:24-26

**21** If after the manner of men I have fought with beasts at Ephesus, what advantageth it me, if the dead rise not? let us eat and drink; for tomorrow we die.
Be not deceived: evil communications corrupt good manners.
15:32-33

**22** There is one glory of the sun, and another glory of the moon, and another glory of the stars: for one star differeth from another star in glory.
So also is the resurrection of the dead. It is sown in corruption; it is raised in incorruption.
15:41-42

**23** Behold, I shew you a mystery; We shall not all sleep, but we shall all be changed,
In a moment, in the twinkling of an eye, at the last trump: for the trumpet shall sound, and the dead shall be raised incorruptible, and we shall be changed.
For this corruptible must put on incorruption, and this mortal must put on immortality.
So when this corruptible shall have put on incorruption, and this mortal shall have put on immortality, then shall be brought to pass the saying that is written, Death is swallowed up in victory.
O death, where is thy sting? O grave, where is thy victory?
15:51-55

**24** If any man love not the Lord Jesus Christ, let him be Anathema Maranatha.
The grace of our Lord Jesus Christ be with you.
16:22-23

**II CORINTHIANS**

**1** For we walk by faith, not by sight.
5:7

**2** Every man according as he purposeth in his heart, so let him give; not grudgingly, or of necessity: for God loveth a cheerful giver.
9:7

**3** For though we walk in the flesh, we do not war after the flesh:
For the weapons of our warfare are not carnal, but mighty through God to the pulling down of strong holds.
10:3-4

**4** For ye suffer fools gladly, seeing ye yourselves are wise.
11:19

**5** And lest I should be exalted above measure through the abundance of the revelations, there was given to me a thorn in the flesh, the messenger of Satan to buffet me, lest I should be exalted above measure.
12:7

**GALATIANS**

**1** O foolish Galatians, who hath bewitched you, that ye should not obey the truth, before whose eyes Jesus Christ hath been evidently set forth, crucified among you?
3:1

**2** There is neither Jew nor Greek, there is neither bond nor free, there is neither male nor female: for ye are all one in Christ Jesus.
3:28

**3** But Jerusalem which is above is free, which is the mother of us all.
4:26

**4** For the flesh lusteth against the Spirit, and the Spirit against the flesh: and these are contrary the one to the other: so that ye cannot do the things that ye would.
5:17

**5** But the fruit of the Spirit is love, joy, peace, longsuffering, gentleness, goodness, faith,
Meekness, temperance: against such there is no law.
5:22-23

**6** Be not deceived: God is not mocked: for whatsoever a man soweth, that shall he also reap.
For he that soweth to his flesh shall of the flesh reap corruption; but he that soweth to the Spirit shall of the Spirit reap life everlasting.
And let us not be weary in well doing: for in due season we shall reap, if we faint not.
6:7-9

**EPHESIANS**

**1** That he would grant you, according to the riches of his glory, to be strengthened with might by his Spirit in the inner man;
That Christ may dwell in your hearts by faith; that ye, being rooted and grounded in love,

May be able to comprehend with all saints what is the breadth, and length, and depth, and height;

And to know the love of Christ, which passeth knowledge, that ye might be filled with all the fulness of God.

Now unto him that is able to do exceeding abundantly above all that we ask or think, according to the power that worketh in us,

Unto him be glory in the church by Christ Jesus throughout all ages, world without end. Amen.

3:16–21

2 Wherefore putting away lying, speak every man truth with his neighbour: for we are members one of another.

Be ye angry, and sin not: let not the sun go down upon your wrath:

Neither give place to the devil.

Let him that stole steal no more: but rather let him labour, working with his hands the thing which is good, that he may have to give to him that needeth.

4:25–28

3 Children, obey your parents in the Lord: for this is right.

6:1

4 Finally, my brethren, be strong in the Lord, and in the power of his might.

Put on the whole armour of God, that ye may be able to stand against the wiles of the devil.

For we wrestle not against flesh and blood, but against principalities, against powers, against the rulers of the darkness of his world, against spiritual wickedness in high places.

Wherefore take unto you the whole armour of God, that ye may be able to withstand in the evil day, and having done all, to stand.

Stand therefore, having your loins girt about with truth, and having on the breastplate of righteousness;

And your feet shod with the preparation of the gospel of peace;

Above all, taking the shield of faith, wherewith ye shall be able to quench all the fiery darts of the wicked.

And take the helmet of salvation, and the sword of the Spirit, which is the word of God.

6:10–17

PHILIPPIANS

1 But made himself of no reputation, and took upon him the form of a servant, and was made in the likeness of men:

And being found in fashion as a man, he humbled himself, and became obedient unto death, even the death of the cross.

Wherefore God also hath highly exalted him, and given him a name which is above every name:

That at the name of Jesus every knee should bow, of things in heaven, and things in earth, and things under the earth.

2:7–10

2 Rejoice in the Lord alway: and again I say, Rejoice.

4:4

3 And the peace of God, which passeth all understanding, shall keep your hearts and minds through Christ Jesus.

4:7

4 Finally, brethren, whatsoever things are true, whatsoever things are honest, whatsoever things are just, whatsoever things are pure, whatsoever things are lovely, whatsoever things are of good report; if there be any virtue; and if there be any praise, think on these things.

4:8

COLOSSIANS

1 Beware lest any man spoil you through philosophy and vain deceit, after the tradition of men, after the rudiments of the world, and not after Christ.

2:8

2 Touch not; taste not; handle not.

2:21

3 Where there is neither Greek nor Jew, circumcision nor uncircumcision, Barbarian, Scythian, bond nor free; but Christ is all, and in all.

3:11

4 Husbands, love your wives, and be not bitter against them.

3:19

5 Fathers, provoke not your children to anger, lest they be discouraged.

3:21

6 Let your speech be alway with grace, seasoned with salt, that ye may know how ye ought to answer every man.

4:6

I THESSALONIANS

1 Remembering without ceasing your work of faith, and labour of love, and patience of hope in our Lord Jesus Christ, in the sight of God and our Father.

1:3

2 For yourselves know perfectly that the day of the Lord so cometh as a thief in the night.

5:2

**3** Prove all things; hold fast that which is good.
5:21

**II Thessalonians**

**1** For even when we were with you, this we commanded you, that if any would not work, neither should he eat.
3:10

**I Timothy**

**1** This is a faithful saying, and worthy of all acceptation, that Christ Jesus came into the world to save sinners; of whom I am chief.
1:15

**2** This is a true saying, If a man desire the office of a bishop, he desireth a good work.
A bishop then must be blameless, the husband of one wife, vigilant, sober, of good behaviour, given to hospitality, apt to teach;
Not given to wine, no striker, not greedy of filthy lucre; but patient, not a brawler, not covetous.
3:1–3

**3** For every creature of God is good, and nothing to be refused, if it be received with thanksgiving.
4:4

**4** Drink no longer water, but use a little wine for thy stomach's sake and thine often infirmities.
5:23

**5** For we brought nothing into this world, and it is certain we carry nothing out.
6:7

**6** For the love of money is the root of all evil: which while some coveted after, they have erred from the faith, and pierced themselves through with many sorrows.
6:10

**7** Fight the good fight of faith, lay hold on eternal life, whereunto thou art also called, and hast professed a good profession before many witnesses.
6:12

**8** O Timothy, keep that which is committed to thy trust, avoiding profane and vain babblings, and oppositions of science falsely so called.
6:20

**II Timothy**

**1** For God hath not given us the spirit of fear; but of power, and of love, and of a sound mind.
1:7

**2** But evil men and seducers shall wax worse and worse, deceiving, and being deceived.
3:13

**3** For I am now ready to be offered, and the time of my departure is at hand.
I have fought a good fight, I have finished my course, I have kept the faith:

Henceforth there is laid up for me a crown of righteousness, which the Lord, the righteous judge, shall give me at that day: and not to me only, but unto all them also that love his appearing.
4:6–8

**Titus**

**1** One of themselves, even a prophet of their own, said, The Cretians are alway liars, evil beasts, slow bellies.
1:12

**Hebrews**

**1** God, who at sundry times and in divers manners spake in time past unto the fathers by the prophets,
Hath in these last days spoken unto us by his Son, whom he hath appointed heir of all things, by whom also he made the worlds;
Who being the brightness of his glory, and the express image of his person, and upholding all things by the word of his power, when he had by himself purged our sins, sat down on the right hand of the Majesty on high;
Being made so much better than the angels, as he hath by inheritance obtained a more excellent name than they.
1:1–4

**2** For the word of God is quick, and powerful, and sharper than any two-edged sword, piercing even to the dividing asunder of soul and spirit, and of the joints and marrow, and is a discerner of the thoughts and intents of the heart.
4:12

**3** By faith the walls of Jericho fell down, after they were compassed about seven days.
11:30

**4** (Of whom the world was not worthy:) they wandered in deserts, and in mountains, and in dens and caves of the earth.
11:38

**5** Let brotherly love continue.
Be not forgetful to entertain strangers: for thereby some have entertained angels unawares.
13:1–2

**6** And almost all things are by the law purged with blood; and without shedding of blood is no remission.
9:22

**7** Now faith is the substance of things hoped for, the evidence of things not seen.
11:1

**8** These all died in faith, not having received the promises, but having seen them afar off, and were persuaded of them, and embraced them, and confessed that they were strangers and pilgrims on the earth.
11:13

**9** Esteeming the reproach of Christ greater riches than the treasures in Egypt: for he had respect unto the recompence of the reward.

11:26

JAMES

**1** Blessed is the man that endureth temptation: for when he is tried, he shall receive the crown of life, which the Lord hath promised to them that love him.

1:12

**2** Every good gift and every perfect gift is from above, and cometh down from the Father of lights, with whom is no variableness, neither shadow of turning.

1:17

**3** Wherefore, my beloved brethren, let every man be swift to hear, slow to speak, slow to wrath:
For the wrath of man worketh not the righteousness of God.
Wherefore lay apart all filthiness and superfluity of naughtiness, and receive with meekness the engrafted word, which is able to save your souls.
But be ye doers of the word, and not hearers only, deceiving your own selves.
For if any be a hearer of the word, and not a doer, he is like unto a man beholding his natural face in a glass:
For he beholdeth himself, and goeth his way, and straightway forgetteth what manner of man he was.
But whoso looketh into the perfect law of liberty, and continueth therein, he being not a forgetful hearer, but a doer of the work, this man shall be blessed in his deed.

1:19-25

**4** Even so faith, if it hath not works, is dead, being alone.

2:17

**5** Even so the tongue is a little member, and boasteth great things. Behold, how great a matter a little fire kindleth!

3:5

**6** But the tongue can no man tame; it is an unruly evil, full of deadly poison.

3:8

**7** Submit yourselves therefore to God. Resist the devil, and he will flee from you.
Draw nigh to God, and he will draw nigh to you. Cleanse your hands, ye sinners; and purify your hearts, ye double minded.

4:7-8

**8** Grudge not one against another, brethren, lest ye be condemned: behold, the judge standeth before the door.

5:9

**9** Let him know, that he which converteth the sinner from the error of his way shall save a soul from death, and shall hide a multitude of sins.

5:20

I PETER

**1** Whom having not seen, ye love; in whom, though now ye see him not, yet believing, ye rejoice with joy unspeakable and full of glory.

1:8

**2** Being born again, not of corruptible seed, but of incorruptible, by the word of God, which liveth and abideth for ever.
For all flesh is as grass, and all the glory of man as the flower of grass. The grass withereth, and the flower thereof falleth away.

1:23-24

**3** Honour all men. Love the brotherhood. Fear God. Honour the king.

2:17

**4** Even as Sara obeyed Abraham, calling him lord: whose daughters ye are, as long as ye do well, and are not afraid with any amazement.
Likewise, ye husbands, dwell with them according to knowledge, giving honour unto the wife, as unto the weaker vessel, and as being heirs together of the grace of life; that your prayers be not hindered.

3:6-7

I JOHN

**1** If we say that we have no sin, we deceive ourselves, and the truth is not in us.
If we confess our sins, he is faithful and just to forgive us our sins, and to cleanse us from all unrighteousness.

1:8-9

**2** For all that is in the world, the lust of the flesh, and the lust of the eyes, and the pride of life, is not of the Father, but is of the world.

2:16

**3** Beloved, let us love one another: for love is of God; and every one that loveth is born of God, and knoweth God.
He that loveth not knoweth not God; for God is love.

4:7-8

**4** There is no fear in love; but perfect love casteth out fear: because fear hath torment. He that feareth is not made perfect in love.

4:18

**5** If a man say, I love God, and hateth his brother, he is a liar: for he that loveth not his brother whom he hath seen, how can he love God whom he hath not seen?

4:20

**6** Little children, keep yourselves from idols.

5:21

JUDE

**1** Mercy unto you, and peace, and love, be multiplied.

2

REVELATIONS

**1** Behold, he cometh with clouds; and every eye shall see him, and they also which pierced him: and all kindreds of the earth shall wail because of him. Even so, Amen.

I am Alpha and Omega, the beginning and the ending, saith the Lord, which is, and which was, and which is to come, the Almighty.

I John, who also am your brother, and companion in tribulation, and in the kingdom and patience of Jesus Christ, was in the isle that is called Patmos, for the word of God, and for the testimony of Jesus Christ.

I was in the Spirit on the Lord's day, and heard behind me a great voice, as of a trumpet,

Saying, I am Alpha and Omega, the first and the last: and, What thou seest, write in a book, and send it unto the seven churches which are in Asia; unto Ephesus, and unto Smyrna, and unto Pergamos, and unto Thyatira, and unto Sardis, and unto Philadelphia, and unto Laodicea.

And I turned to see the voice that spake with me. And being turned, I saw seven golden candlesticks;

And in the midst of the seven candlesticks one like unto the Son of man, clothed with a garment down to the foot, and girt about the paps with a golden girdle.

His head and his hairs were white like wool, as white as snow; and his eyes were as a flame of fire;

And his feet like unto fine brass, as if they burned in a furnace; and his voice as the sound of many waters.

And he had in his right hand seven stars: and out of his mouth went a sharp twoedged sword: and his countenance was as the sun shineth in his strength.

1:7–16

**2** And he shall rule them with a rod of iron; as the vessels of a potter shall they be broken to shivers: even as I received of my Father.

2:27

**3** And I saw in the right hand of him that sat on the throne a book written within and on the backside, sealed with seven seals.

And I saw a strong angel proclaiming with a loud voice, Who is worthy to open the book, and to loose the seals thereof?

5:1–2

**4** And I beheld, and, lo, in the midst of the throne and of the four beasts, and in the midst of the elders, stood a Lamb as it had been slain, having seven horns and seven eyes, which are the seven Spirits of God sent forth into all the earth.

5:6

**5** Saying with a loud voice, Worthy is the Lamb that was slain to receive power, and riches, and wisdom, and strength, and honour, and glory, and blessing.

5:12

**6** And I looked, and behold a pale horse: and his name that sat on him was Death, and Hell followed with him. And power was given unto them over the fourth part of the earth, to kill with sword, and with hunger, and with death, and with the beasts of the earth.

6:8

**7** And one of the elders answered, saying unto me, What are these which are arrayed in white robes? and whence came they?

And I said unto him, Sir, thou knowest. And he said to me, These are they which came out of great tribulation, and have washed their robes, and made them white in the blood of the Lamb.

Therefore are they before the throne of God, and serve him day and night in his temple: and he that sitteth on the throne shall dwell among them.

They shall hunger no more, neither thirst any more; neither shall the sun light on them, nor any heat.

For the Lamb which is in the midst of the throne shall feed them, and shall lead them unto living fountains of waters: and God shall wipe away all tears from their eyes.

7:13–17

**8** And the name of the star is called Wormwood: and the third part of the waters became wormwood; and many men died of the waters, because they were made bitter.

8:11

**9** And there was war in heaven: Michael and his angels fought against the dragon; and the dragon fought and his angels,

And prevailed not; neither was their place found any more in heaven.

And the great dragon was cast out, that old serpent, called the Devil, and Satan, which deceiveth the whole world: he was cast out into the earth, and his angels were cast out with him.

12:7–9

**10** And that no man might buy or sell, save he that had the mark, or the name of the beast, or the number of his name.

Here is wisdom. Let him that hath understanding count the number of the beast: for it is the number of a man; and his number is Six hundred threescore and six.

13:17–18

11 Behold, I come as a thief. Blessed is he that watcheth, and keepeth his garments, lest he walk naked, and they see his shame.
And he gathered them together into a place called in the Hebrew tongue Armageddon.

16:15–16

12 And there came one of the seven angels which had the seven vials, and talked with me, saying unto me, Come hither; I will shew unto thee the judgment of the great whore that sitteth upon many waters.

17:1

13 And the woman was arrayed in purple and scarlet colour, and decked with gold and precious stones and pearls, having a golden cup in her hand full of abominations and filthiness of her fornication:
And upon her forehead was a name written, MYSTERY, BABYLON THE GREAT, THE MOTHER OF HARLOTS AND ABOMINATIONS OF THE EARTH.
And I saw the woman drunken with the blood of the saints, and with the blood of the martyrs of Jesus: and when I saw her, I wondered with great admiration.

17:4–6

14 And I saw heaven opened, and behold a white horse; and he that sat upon him was called Faithful and True, and in righteousness he doth judge and make war.

19:11

15 And he hath on his vesture and on his thigh a name written, KING OF KINGS, AND LORD OF LORDS.

19:16

16 Blessed and holy is he that hath part in the first resurrection: on such the second death hath no power, but they shall be priests of God and of Christ, and shall reign with him a thousand years.
And when the thousand years are expired, Satan shall be loosed out of his prison,
And shall go out to deceive the nations which are in the four quarters of the earth, Gog and Magog, to gather them together to battle: the number of whom is as the sand of the sea.

20:6–8

17 And I saw a great white throne, and him that sat on it, from whose face the earth and the heaven fled away; and there was found no place for them.

And I saw the dead, small and great, stand before God; and the books were opened: and another book was opened, which is the book of life: and the dead were judged out of those things which were written in the books, according to their works.
And the sea gave up the dead which were in it; and death and hell delivered up the dead which were in them: and they were judged every man according to their works.

20:11–13

18 And I saw a new heaven and a new earth: for the first heaven and the first earth were passed away; and there was no more sea.
And I John saw the holy city, new Jerusalem, coming down from God out of heaven, prepared as a bride adorned for her husband.
And I heard a great voice out of heaven saying, Behold, the tabernacle of God is with men, and he will dwell with them, and they shall be his people, and God himself shall be with them, and be their God.
And God shall wipe away all tears from their eyes; and there shall be no more death, neither sorrow, nor crying, neither shall there be any more pain: for the former things are passed away.
And he that sat upon the throne said, Behold, I make all things new. And he said unto me, Write: for these words are true and faithful.

21:1–5

19 And he carried me away in the spirit to a great and high mountain, and shewed me that great city, the holy Jerusalem, descending out of heaven from God.
Having the glory of God: and her light was like unto a stone most precious, even like a jasper stone, clear as crystal.

21:10–11

20 And the building of the wall of it was of jasper: and the city was pure gold, like unto clear glass.
And the foundations of the wall of the city were garnished with all manner of precious stones. The first foundation was jasper; the second, sapphire; the third, a chalcedony; the fourth, an emerald;
The fifth, sardonyx; the sixth, sardius; the seventh, chrysolite; the eighth, beryl; the ninth, a topaz; the tenth, a chrysoprasus; the eleventh, a jacinth; the twelfth, an amethyst.
And the twelve gates were twelve pearls; every several gate was of one pearl: and the street of the city was pure gold, as it were transparent glass.
And I saw no temple therein: for the Lord God Almighty and the Lamb are the temple of it.
And the city had no need of the sun, neither of the moon, to shine in it: for the glory of God did lighten it, and the Lamb is the light thereof.

21:18–23

**21** And he shewed me a pure river of water of life, clear as crystal, proceeding out of the throne of God and of the Lamb.

In the midst of the street of it, and on either side of the river, was there the tree of life, which bare twelve manner of fruits, and yielded her fruit every month: and the leaves of the tree were for the healing of the nations.

*22:1-2*

**22** He that is unjust, let him be unjust still: and he which is filthy, let him be filthy still: and he that is righteous, let him be righteous still: and he that is holy, let him be holy still.

And, behold, I come quickly; and my reward is with me, to give every man according as his work shall be.

*22:11-12*

**Bickerstaffe, Isaac** (c. 1735 - c. 1812) Irish dramatist, especially of comedies and comic operas.

**1** There was a jolly miller once,
Lived on the river Dee;
He worked and sang from morn till night;
No lark more blithe than he.
*Love in a Village, I*

**2** And this the burthen of his song,
For ever us'd to be,
I care for nobody, not I,
If no one cares for me.
*Love in a Village, I*

**Bidault, Georges** (1899 - 1983) French statesman. A leader of the resistance during World War II, he was twice prime minister (1946, 1949 - 50).

**1** The weak have one weapon: the errors of those who think they are strong.
*The Observer, 1962*

**Bierce, Ambrose Gwinnett** (1842 - ?1914) US writer and journalist. His short stories were published in such collections as *In the Midst of Life* (1892). He also compiled *The Devil's Dictionary* (1906).

**1** *Bore*, n. A person who talks when you wish him to listen.
*The Devil's Dictionary*

**2** *Brain*, n. An apparatus with which we think that we think.
*The Devil's Dictionary*

**3** *Debauchee*, n. One who has so earnestly pursued pleasure that he has had the misfortune to overtake it.
*The Devil's Dictionary*

**4** *Egotist*, n. A person of low taste, more interested in himself than in me.
*The Devil's Dictionary*

**5** *Future*, n. That period of time in which our affairs prosper, our friends are true and our happiness is assured.
*The Devil's Dictionary*

**6** *Marriage*, n. The state or condition of a community consisting of a master, a mistress and two slaves, making in all two.
*The Devil's Dictionary*

**7** *Patience*, n. A minor form of despair, disguised as a virtue.
*The Devil's Dictionary*

**8** *Peace*, n. In international affairs, a period of cheating between two periods of fighting.
*The Devil's Dictionary*

**8** *Peace*, n. In international affairs, a period of cheating between two periods of fighting.
*The Devil's Dictionary*

**Binyon (Robert) Laurence** (1869 - 1943) British poet and dramatist. His poetic works include *The Sirens* (1924), *The Idols* (1928), and the wartime elegy 'For the Fallen' (1914).

**1** Now is the time for the burning of the leaves.
*The Burning of the Leaves*

**2** With proud thanksgiving, a mother for her children,
England mourns for her dead across the sea.
In response to the slaughter of World War I
*Poems For the Fallen*

**3** They shall grow not old, as we that are left grow old:
Age shall not weary them, nor the years condemn.
At the going down of the sun and in the morning
We will remember them.
*Poems For the Fallen*

**Birkenhead, F(rederick) E(lwin) Smith, Earl of** (1872 - 1930) British lawyer and politician. As attorney general (1915 - 19), he prosecuted Roger Casement; he was lord chancellor from 1919 to 1922.

**1** We have the highest authority for believing that the meek shall inherit the Earth; though I have never found any particular corroboration of this aphorism in the records of Somerset House.
*Contemporary Personalities*, 'Marquess Curzon'

**2** JUDGE WILLIS. You are extremely offensive, young man.
F. E. SMITH. As a matter of fact, we both are, and the only difference between us is that I am trying to be, and you can't help it.
*Frederick Elwin, Earl of Birkenhead* (Lord Birkenhead), Vol. I, Ch. 9

**3** JUDGE WILLIS. What do you suppose I am on the Bench for, Mr Smith?
SMITH. It is not for me to attempt to fathom the inscrutable workings of Providence.
*Frederick Elwin, Earl of Birkenhead* (Lord Birkenhead), Vol. I, Ch. 9

**4** The world continues to offer glittering prizes to those who have stout hearts and sharp swords.
Speech, Glasgow University, 7 Nov 1923

## Bismarck, Otto Eduard Leopold, Prince von
(1815–98) German statesman. As prime minister of Prussia (1862–90), he played a major role in the creation (1871) of the German Empire, which he then dominated as chancellor (1871–90).

**1** The great questions of our day cannot be solved by speeches and majority votes . . . but by iron and blood.

Usually misquoted as 'blood and iron' – a form Bismarck himself used in 1886
Speech, Prussian Chamber, 30 Sept 1862

**2** Politics is not an exact science.

Speech, Prussian Chamber, 18 Dec 1863

**3** Politics is the art of the possible.

Said to Meyer von Waldeck, 11 Aug 1867

**4** We will not go to Canossa.

A declaration of his anti-Roman Catholic policy; the Emperor Henry IV had submitted to Pope Gregory VII at Canossa, N. Italy, in 1077
Speech, Reichstag, 14 May 1872

**5** The healthy bones of a single Pomeranian grenadier.

A price too high for Germany to pay regarding the Eastern Question
Speech, Reichstag, 5 Dec 1876

**6** An honest broker.

His professed role in the diplomacy of 1878, including the Congress of Berlin
Speech, Reichstag, 19 Feb 1878

**7** Politics is not a science . . . but an art.

Speech, Reichstag, 15 Mar 1884

**8** If there is ever another war in Europe, it will come out of some damned silly thing in the Balkans.

Remark to Ballen, shortly before Bismarck's death

## Blacker, Valentine (1778–1823) British soldier, who served in India.

**1** Put your trust in God, my boys, and keep your powder dry.

*Oliver Cromwell's Advice*

## Blackstone, Sir William (1723–80) British jurist; author of the classic Commentaries on the Laws of England (1765–69).

**1** Man was formed for society.

*Commentaries on the Laws of England*, Introduction

**2** The king never dies.

*Commentaries on the Laws of England*, Bk. I, Ch. 7

**3** Time whereof the memory of man runneth not to the contrary.

*Commentaries on the Laws of England*, Bk. I, Ch. 18

**4** That the king can do no wrong, is a necessary and fundamental principle of the English constitution.

*Commentaries on the Laws of England*, Bk. III, Ch. 17

**5** It is better that ten guilty persons escape than one innocent suffer.

*Commentaries on the Laws of England*, Bk. IV, Ch. 27

## Blackwell, Antoinette Brown (1825–1921) US feminist writer and minister.

**1** Mr. Darwin . . . has failed to hold definitely before his mind the principle that the difference of sex, whatever it may consist in, must itself be subject to natural selection and to evolution.

*The Sexes Throughout Nature*

## Blackwood, Helen Selina, Countess of Dufferin
(1807–67) British poet. As Impulsia Gushington she wrote humorous ballads.

**1** I'm sitting on the stile, Mary,
Where we sat, side by side.

*Lament of the Irish Emigrant*

**2** They say there's bread and work for all,
And the sun shines always there:
But I'll not forget old Ireland,
Were it fifty times as fair.

*Lament of the Irish Emigrant*

## Blair, Eric See Orwell, George.

## Blair, Robert (1699–1746) Scottish poet and churchman. He is best remembered for the poem The Grave (1743), which was later illustrated by William Blake.

**1** The schoolboy, with his satchel in his hand,
Whistling aloud to bear his courage up.

*The Grave*

**2** Its visits,
Like those of angels, short, and far between.

*The Grave*

## Blake, Charles Dupee (1846–1903) British writer of nursery rhymes.

**1** Rock-a-bye baby on the tree top,
When the wind blows the cradle will rock,
When the bough bends the cradle will fall,
Down comes the baby, cradle and all.

Attrib.

## Blake, William (1757–1827) British poet, painter, engraver, and visionary. Blake's mystical engravings and watercolours illustrate such works as Songs of Innocence (1789) and the poem Jerusalem (1804–20).

**1** For everything that lives is holy, life delights in life.

*America*

**2** The strongest poison ever known
Came from Caesar's laurel crown.

*Auguries of Innocence*

**3** Every wolf's and lion's howl
Raises from Hell a human soul.

*Auguries of Innocence*

**4** A truth that's told with bad intent
Beats all the lies you can invent.

*Auguries of Innocence*

5 Every tear from every eye
Becomes a babe in Eternity.
*Auguries of Innocence*

6 He who shall teach the child to doubt
The rotting grave shall ne'er get out.
*Auguries of Innocence*

7 To see a World in a grain of sand,
And a Heaven in a wild flower,
Hold Infinity in the palm of your hand,
And Eternity in an hour.
*Auguries of Innocence*

8. A robin redbreast in a cage
Puts all Heaven in a rage.
*Auguries of Innocence*

9 Does the Eagle know what is in the pit
Or wilt thou go ask the Mole?
Can Wisdom be put in a silver rod,
Or love in a golden bowl?
*The Book of Thel, 'Thel's Motto'*

10 "What," it will be questioned, "when the sun
rises, do you not see a round disc of fire somewhat like a guinea?" "O no, no, I see an innumerable company of the heavenly host crying,
'Holy, Holy, Holy is the Lord God Almighty!'"
*Descriptive Catalogue, 'The Vision of Judgment'*

11 Humility is only doubt,
And does the sun and moon blot out.
*The Everlasting Gospel*

12 Great things are done when men and mountains
meet;
This is not done by jostling in the street.
*Gnomic Verses*

13 He who bends to himself a Joy
Doth the wingèd life destroy;
But he who kisses the Joy as it flies
Lives in Eternity's sunrise.
*Gnomic Verses*

14 He who would do good to another must do it in
Minute Particulars.
General Good is the plea of the scoundrel, hypo-
crite, and flatterer.
*Jerusalem*

15 I care not whether a man is Good or Evil; all that
I care
Is whether he is a Wise Man or a Fool. Go! put
off Holiness,
And put on Intellect.
*Jerusalem*

16 Without Contraries is no progression. Attraction
and Repulsion, Reason and Energy, Love and
Hate, are necessary to Human existence.
*The Marriage of Heaven and Hell, 'The Argument'*

17 If the doors of perception were cleansed everything would appear to man as it is, infinite.
*The Marriage of Heaven and Hell, 'A Memorable Fancy'*

18 Prisons are built with stones of Law, brothels
with bricks of Religion.
*The Marriage of Heaven and Hell, 'Proverbs of Hell'*

19 Sooner murder an infant in its cradle than nurse
unacted desires.
*The Marriage of Heaven and Hell, 'Proverbs of Hell'*

20 In seed time learn, in harvest teach, in winter
enjoy.
*The Marriage of Heaven and Hell, 'Proverbs of Hell'*

21 The cut worm forgives the plough.
*The Marriage of Heaven and Hell, 'Proverbs of Hell'*

22 What is now proved was once only imagined.
*The Marriage of Heaven and Hell, 'Proverbs of Hell'*

23 The road of excess leads to the palace of
Wisdom.
*The Marriage of Heaven and Hell, 'Proverbs of Hell'*

24 He who desires but acts not, breeds pestilence.
*The Marriage of Heaven and Hell, 'Proverbs of Hell'*

25 A fool sees not the same tree that a wise man
sees.
*The Marriage of Heaven and Hell, 'Proverbs of Hell'*

26 Damn braces. Bless relaxes.
*The Marriage of Heaven and Hell, 'Proverbs of Hell'*

27 Exuberance is Beauty.
*The Marriage of Heaven and Hell, 'Proverbs of Hell'*

28 Those who restrain Desire, do so because theirs
is weak enough to be restrained.
*The Marriage of Heaven and Hell, 'Those who restrain Desire
. . .'*

29 Man has no Body distinct from his Soul; for that
called Body is a portion of Soul discerned by
the five Senses, the chief inlets of Soul in this
age.
*The Marriage of Heaven and Hell, 'The Voice of the Devil'*

30 Energy is Eternal Delight.
*The Marriage of Heaven and Hell, 'The Voice of the Devil'*

31 And did those feet in ancient time
Walk upon England's mountains green?
And was the holy lamb of God
On England's pleasant pastures seen?
. . .
I will not cease from mental fight,
Nor shall my sword sleep in my hand,
Till we have built Jerusalem
In England's green and pleasant land.
Better known as the hymn 'Jerusalem', with music by Sir Hubert
Parry; not to be confused with Blake's longer poem *Jerusalem*.
*Milton*, Preface

32 Mock on, mock on, Voltaire, Rousseau;
Mock on, mock on; 'tis all in vain!
You throw the sand against the wind,
And the wind blows it back again.
*Mock on, mock on, Voltaire, Rousseau*

33 When Sir Joshua Reynolds died
All Nature was degraded;
The King dropped a tear in the Queen's ear,
And all his pictures faded.
*On Art and Artists*

34 Love seeketh not itself to please,
Nor for itself hath any care,
But for another gives its ease,
And builds a Heaven in Hell's despair.
*Songs of Experience*, 'The Clod and the Pebble'

35 Love seeketh only Self to please,
To bind another to its delight,
Joys in another's loss of ease,
And builds a Hell in Heaven's despite.
*Songs of Experience*, 'The Clod and the Pebble'

36 My mother groan'd, my father wept,
Into the dangerous world I leapt;
Helpless, naked, piping loud,
Like a fiend hid in a cloud.
*Songs of Experience*, 'Infant Sorrow'

37 Tiger! Tiger! burning bright
In the forests of the night,
What immortal hand or eye
Could frame thy fearful symmetry?
*Songs of Experience*, 'The Tiger'

38 When the stars threw down their spears,
And watered heaven with their tears,
Did he smile his work to see?
Did he who made the Lamb make thee?
*Songs of Experience*, 'The Tiger'

39 Piping down the valleys wild,
Piping songs of pleasant glee,
On a cloud I saw a child.
*Songs of Innocence*, Introduction

40 'Pipe a song about a Lamb!'
So I piped with merry cheer.
*Songs of Innocence*, Introduction

41 To Mercy, Pity, Peace, and Love
All pray in their distress.
*Songs of Innocence*, 'The Divine Image'

42 For Mercy has a human heart,
Pity a human face,
And Love, the human form divine,
And Peace, the human dress.
*Songs of Innocence*, 'The Divine Image'

43 'Twas on a Holy Thursday, their innocent faces
clean,
The children walking two and two, in red and
blue and green.
*Songs of Innocence*, 'Holy Thursday'

44 Little Lamb, who made thee?
Dost thou know who made thee?
*Songs of Innocence*, 'The Lamb'

45 When the green woods laugh with
the voice of joy.
*Songs of Innocence*, 'Laughing song'

46 My mother bore me in the southern wild.
And I am black, but O! my soul is white;
White as an angel is the English child,
But I am black, as if bereav'd of light.
*Songs of Innocence*, 'The Little Black Boy'

47 Man's Desires are limited by his Perceptions;
none can desire what he has not perceived.
*There is no Natural Religion*

48 The Desire of Man being Infinite, the possession
is Infinite, and himself Infinite.
*There is no Natural Religion*

49 I mock thee not, though I by thee am mockèd;
Thou call'st me madman, but I call thee
blockhead.
*To Flaxman*

50 To generalize is to be an idiot.
*Life of Blake* (Gilchrist)

**Boethius, Anicius Manlius Severinus** (c. 480–524)
Roman statesman, philosopher, and scholar. His writings include
translations of Aristotle, treatises on theology, music, and
mathematics, and philosophical works, notably *The Consolation of
Philosophy*.

1 In every adversity of fortune, to have been happy is the most unhappy kind of misfortune.
*The Consolation of Philosophy*

**Bogart, Humphrey** (1899–1957) US film star. His films
incude *Casablanca* (1942), *The African Queen* (1951), and a host
of others in which he played tough gangsters.

1 Here's looking at you, kid.
*Casablanca*

2 Play it, Sam. Play 'As Time Goes By'.
Often misquoted as 'Play it again, Sam'.
*Casablanca*

**Bogart, John B.** (1845–1920) US journalist.

1 When a dog bites a man that is not news, but
when a man bites a dog that is news.
Sometimes attributed to Charles Dana and Amos Cummings
Attrib.

**Bohr, Niels Henrik David** (1885–1962) Danish physicist.
He made great contributions to the theory of atomic structure. His
laboratory in Copenhagen was a haven for many Jewish scientists
expelled by Hitler and he took to America the news that an atom
bomb had become possible.

1 Of course I don't believe in it. But I understand
that it brings you luck whether you believe in it
or not.
When asked why he had a horseshoe on his wall
Attrib.

2 An expert is a man who has made all the mistakes, which can be made, in a very narrow
field.
Attrib.

**Boileau, Nicolas** (1636–1711) French writer and poet. His
*L'Art poétique* (1674) was widely read in Europe. *Le Lutrin* (1674)
was a mock epic poem.

1 No one who cannot limit himself has ever been able to write.
*L'Art poétique*, I

2 Often the fear of one evil leads us into a worse.
*L'Art poétique*, I

3 A fool always finds a greater fool to admire him.
*L'Art poétique*, I

4 The dreadful burden of having nothing to do.
*Épitres*, XI

**Boleyn, Anne** (1507–36) Second wife (1533–36) of King Henry VIII of England. She was the mother of Elizabeth I, but failed to produce the male heir that Henry wanted. When he tired of her, she was accused of treason through adultery and executed.

1 The king has been very good to me. He promoted me from a simple maid to be a marchioness. Then he raised me to be a queen. Now he will raise me to be a martyr.
*Notable Women in History* (W. Abbot)

**Bolt, Robert** (1924– ) British playwright. His plays include *A Man for All Seasons* (1960).

1 Morality's not practical. Morality's a gesture. A complicated gesture learnt from books.
*A Man for All Seasons*

**Bone, Sir David** (1874–1959) British sea captain and writer, especially of seafaring novels.

1 It's 'Damn you, Jack – I'm all right!' with you chaps.
*The Brassbounder*, Ch. 3

**Bone, James** (1872–1962) British journalist.

1 He made righteousness readable.
Referring to C. P. Scott, former editor of *The Manchester Guardian*
Attrib.

**Bonhoeffer, Dietrich** (1906–45) German theologian. An anti-Nazi, he was imprisoned and hanged in Buchenwald. His posthumous *Letters and Papers from Prison* (1953) were widely read.

1 Man has learned to cope with all questions of importance without recourse to God as a working hypothesis.
See also LAPLACE
*Letters and Papers from Prison*, 8 June 1944

2 A God who let us prove his existence would be an idol.
*No Rusty Swords*

**Bono, Edward de** (1933– ) British physician and writer. His books include *The Use of Lateral Thinking* (1967), *The Mechanism of Mind* (1969), and *Beyond Yes and No* (1972).

1 Unhappiness is best defined as the difference between our talents and our expectations.
*The Observer*, 'Sayings of the Week', 12 June 1977

**Book of Common Prayer, The**

1 Read, mark, learn and inwardly digest.
*Collect, 2nd Sunday in Advent*

2 All our doings without charity are nothing worth.
*Collect, Quinquagesima Sunday*

3 We have erred, and strayed from thy ways like lost sheep.
*Morning Prayer, General Confession*

4 We have left undone those things which we ought to have done; and we have done those things we ought not to have done.
*Morning Prayer, General Confession*

5 As it was in the beginning, is now, and ever shall be: world without end.
*Morning Prayer, Gloria*

6 When two or three are gathered together in thy Name thou wilt grant their requests.
*Morning Prayer, Prayer of St Chrysostom*

7 Defend us from all perils and dangers of this night.
*Morning Prayer, Prayer of St Chrysostom*

8 All the deceits of the world, the flesh, and the devil.
*Morning Prayer, Prayer of St Chrysostom*

9 In the hour of death, and in the day of judgement.
*Morning Prayer, Prayer of St Chrysostom*

10 Give peace in our time, O Lord.
*Morning Prayer, Versicles*

11 Being now come to the years of discretion.
*Order of Confirmation*

12 Renounce the devil and all his works.
*Publick Baptism of Infants*

13 If any of you know cause, or just impediment.
*Solemnization of Matrimony*

14 Let him now speak, or else hereafter for ever hold his peace.
*Solemnization of Matrimony*

15 To have and to hold from this day forward, for better for worse, for richer for poorer, in sickness and in health, to love and to cherish, till death us do part.
*Solemnization of Matrimony*

**Boone, Daniel** (1734–1820) US pioneeer, who led the settlement of Kentucky.

1 I can't say I was ever lost, but I was bewildered once for three days.
Reply when asked if he had ever been lost
Attrib.

**Boorstin, Daniel J.** (1914– ) US writer. His books include *The Image* (1961).

1 The celebrity is a person who is known for his well-knownness.

*The Image*, 'From Hero to Celebrity: The Human Pseudo-event'

2 A best-seller was a book which somehow sold well simply because it was selling well.

*The Image*, 'From Shapes to Shadows: Dissolving Forms'

**Borges, Jorge Luis** (1899–1986) Argentinian writer. *A Universal History of Infamy* (1935) was the first of his several volumes of short stories; he also wrote poetry, especially in the blindness of his later life.

1 I have known uncertainty: a state unknown to the Greeks.

*Ficciones*, 'The Babylonian Lottery'

2 The visible universe was an illusion or, more precisely, a sophism. Mirrors and fatherhood are abominable because they multiply it and extend it.

*Ficciones*, 'Tlön, Uqbar, Orbis Tertius'

3 The original is unfaithful to the translation.

Referring to Henley's translation of Beckford's *Vathek*
*Sobre el 'Vathek' de William Beckford*

**Borrow, George Henry** (1803–81) British writer. His extensive travels in Britain and Europe inspired such works as *Lavengro* (1851) and *The Romany Rye* (1857).

1 There are no countries in the world less known by the British than these selfsame British Islands.

*Lavengro*, Preface

2 Youth will be served, every dog has his day, and mine has been a fine one.

*Lavengro*, Ch. 92

**Bosquet, Pierre** (1810–61) French marshal, who served with distinction during the Crimean War, especially at the Battle of Alma.

1 *C'est magnifique, mais ce n'est pas la guerre.*
It is magnificent, but it is not war.

Referring to the Charge of the Light Brigade at the Battle of Balaclava, 25 Oct 1854
Attrib.

**Bossidy, John Collins** (1860–1928) US writer.

1 And this is good old Boston,
The home of the bean and the cod,
Where the Lowells talk only to Cabots,
And the Cabots talk only to God.

Toast at Holy Cross Alumni dinner, 1910

**Boswell, James** (1740–95) Scottish lawyer and writer. His biography of Dr Johnson, published in 1791, is still widely read.

1 JOHNSON. Well, we had a good talk.
BOSWELL. Yes, Sir; you tossed and gored several persons.

*Life of Johnson*, Vol. II

2 A man, indeed, is not genteel when he gets drunk; but most vices may be committed very genteelly: a man may debauch his friend's wife genteelly: he may cheat at cards genteelly.

*Life of Johnson*, Vol. II

**Bottomley, Horatio William** (1860–1933) British newspaper editor and proprietor. An MP, he was imprisoned for misappropriation of funds held in trust.

1 VISITOR. Ah, Bottomley, sewing?
BOTTOMLEY. No, reaping.

When found sewing mail bags
*Horatio Bottomley* (Julian Symons)

**Boucicault, Dion** (Dionysius Lardner Boursiquot; 1820–90) Irish-born US actor and dramatist. His plays include *The Octoroon* (1859) and *The Jilt* (1886).

1 Men talk of killing time, while time quietly kills them.

*London Assurance*, II:1

**Boulay de la Meurthe, Antoine** (1761–1840) French politician. A member of the Council of Five Hundred, he was banished by Louis XVIII.

1 It is worse than a crime, it is a blunder.

*See also* ACHESON. Referring to the summary execution of the Duc d'Enghien by Napoleon, 1804
Attrib.

**Boulton, Sir H. E.** (1859–1935) Scottish songwriter.

1 Speed, bonny boat, like a bird on the wing;
'Onward', the sailors cry;
Carry the lad that's born to be king
Over the sea to Skye.

*Skye Boat Song*

**Bowen, Charles Synge Christopher, Baron** (1835–94) British judge.

1 The rain it raineth on the just
And also on the unjust fella:
But chiefly on the just, because
The unjust steals the just's umbrella.

*Sands of Time* (Walter Sichel)

2 A blind man in a dark room – looking for a black hat – which isn't there.

Characterization of a metaphysician
Attrib.

**Bowen, E. E.** (1836–1901) British writer.

1 Forty years on, when afar and asunder
Parted are those who are singing to-day.

*Forty Years On* (the Harrow school song)

2 Follow up! Follow up! Follow up! Follow up! Follow up!
Till the field ring again and again,
With the tramp of the twenty-two men,
Follow up!

*Forty Years On* (the Harrow school song)

**Bowen, Elizabeth** (1899–1973) Irish novelist. Her books include *The Hotel* (1927), *The Death of the Heart* (1938), and *The Heat of the Day* (1949).

1  Experience isn't interesting till it begins to repeat itself – in fact, till it does that, it hardly *is* experience.
*The Death of the Heart*, Pt. I, Ch. 1

2  Art is the only thing that can go on mattering once it has stopped hurting.
*The Heat of the Day*, Ch. 16

3  Nobody speaks the truth when there's something they must have.
*The House in Paris*, Ch. 5

4  No, it is not only our fate but our business to lose innocence, and once we have lost that, it is futile to attempt a picnic in Eden.
In *Orion III*, 'Out of a Book'

**Bowra, Sir Maurice** (1898–1971) British scholar and classicist. His books include *The Heritage of Symbolism* (1943) and *The Creative Experiment* (1949).

1  I'm a man
More dined against than dining.
*Summoned by Bells* (J. Betjeman)

2  Any amusing deaths lately?
Attrib.

**Brabazon of Tara, Derek Charles Moore-Brabazon, Baron** (1910–74) British businessman and Conservative politician.

1  I take the view, and always have done, that if you cannot say what you have to say in twenty minutes, you should go away and write a book about it.
Attrib.

**Bracken, Brendan, 1st Viscount** (1901–58) British newspaper publisher and politician. He served as parliamentary private secretary to Winston Churchill (1940–41), minister of information (1941–45), and first lord of the Admiralty (1945).

1  It's a good deed to forget a poor joke.
*The Observer*, 'Sayings of the Week', 17 Oct 1943

**Bradbury, Malcolm** (1932– ) British academic, novelist, and critic. Novels include *Eating People is Wrong* (1954) and *Rates of Exchange* (1983). His *The Social Context of Modern English Literature* (1972) is widely read.

1  Sympathy – for all these people, for being foreigners – lay over the gathering like a woolly blanket; and no one was enjoying it at all.
*Eating People is Wrong*, Ch. 2

2  I like the English. They have the most rigid code of immorality in the world.
*Eating People is Wrong*, Ch. 5

3  'We stay together, but we distrust one another.' 'Ah, yes . . . but isn't that a definition of marriage?'
*The History Man*, Ch. 3

4  I've noticed your hostility towards him . . . I ought to have guessed you were friends.
*The History Man*, Ch. 7

5  Reading someone else's newspaper is like sleeping with someone else's wife. Nothing seems to be precisely in the right place, and when you find what you are looking for, it is not clear then how to respond to it.
*Stepping Westward*, Bk. I, Ch. 1

6  The English are polite by telling lies. The Americans are polite by telling the truth.
*Stepping Westward*, Bk. II, Ch. 5

7  If God had meant us to have group sex, I guess he'd have given us all more organs.
*Who Do You Think You Are?*, 'A Very Hospitable Person'

**Bradford, John** (?1510–55) English Protestant martyr. Chaplain to King Edward VI and popular preacher, he was burned as a heretic after the accession of Queen Mary.

1  There, but for the grace of God, goes John Bradford.
Said on seeing some criminals being led to execution
Remark

**Bradley, F(rancis) H(erbert)** (1846–1924) British philosopher. *Appearance and Reality* (1893) outlined his idealist metaphysics.

1  The hunter for aphorisms on human nature has to fish in muddy water, and he is even condemned to find much of his own mind.
*Aphorisms*

2  This is the temple of Providence where disciples still hourly mark its ways and note the system of its mysteries. Here is the one God whose worshippers prove their faith by their works and in their destruction still trust in Him.
Referring to Monte Carlo
*Aphorisms*

3  It is good to know what a man is, and also what the world takes him for. But you do not understand him until you have learnt how he understands himself.
*Aphorisms*

4  The propriety of some persons seems to consist in having improper thoughts about their neighbours.
*Aphorisms*

5  Metaphysics is the finding of bad reasons for what we believe upon instinct; but to find these reasons is no less an instinct.
*Appearance and Reality*, Preface

6  His mind is open; yes, it is so open that nothing is retained; ideas simply pass through him.
Attrib.

**Bradley, Omar Nelson** (1893–1981) US general. He was responsible for successful campaigns in North Africa, Sicily, and France during World War II.

1 The way to win an atomic war is to make certain it never starts.
*The Observer*, 'Sayings of the Week', 20 Apr 1952

2 The wrong war, at the wrong place, at the wrong time, and with the wrong enemy.
Said in evidence to a Senate inquiry, May 1951, over a proposal by MacArthur that the Korean war should be extended into China

**Brahms, Johannes** (1833–97) German composer, who worked in Vienna after 1863. A musical conservative, his works include four symphonies, two piano concertos, and *A German Requiem* (1868).

1 If there is anyone here whom I have not insulted, I beg his pardon.
Said on leaving a gathering of friends
*Brahms* (P. Latham)

2 A master is dead. Today we sing no more.
Stopping a choral rehearsal on hearing of the death of Wagner
*Brahms* (P. Latham)

**Brancusi, Constantin** (1876–1957) Romanian sculptor.

1 Nothing grows well in the shade of a big tree.
Refusing Rodin's invitation to work in his studio
*Compton's Encyclopedia*

**Brando, Marlon** (1924– ) US film star. Originally a 'method' actor, he made many successful films, including *A Streetcar Named Desire* (1951), *On the Waterfront* (1954), and *The Godfather* (1972).

1 An actor's a guy who, if you ain't talking about him, ain't listening.
*The Observer*, 'Sayings of the Year', Jan 1956

**Braun, Wernher von** (1912–77) German rocket engineer who designed the V-2 rocket that was used to bomb London in World War II. After the war he was taken to the USA, where he worked on US space rockets.

1 It was very successful, but it fell on the wrong planet.
Referring to the first V2 rocket to hit London during World War II
Attrib.

**Brecht, Bertolt** (1898–1956) German dramatist and poet. A Marxist, he lived in exile from 1933 to 1949. His best-known works are *The Threepenny Opera* (1928), in collaboration with Kurt Weil, *Mother Courage* (1941), and *The Caucasian Chalk Circle* (1948).

1 Those who have had no share in the good fortunes of the mighty often have a share in their misfortunes.
*The Caucasian Chalk Circle*

2 ANDREA. Unhappy the land that has no heroes.
GALILEO. No, unhappy the land that needs heroes.
*Galileo*, 13

3 What they could do with round here is a good war.
*Mother Courage*, I

4 When he told men to love their neighbour, their bellies were full. Nowadays things are different.
*Mother Courage*, II

5 I don't trust him. We're friends.
*Mother Courage*, III

6 The finest plans have always been spoiled by the littleness of those that should carry them out. Even emperors can't do it all by themselves.
*Mother Courage*, VI

7 A war of which we could say it left nothing to be desired will probably never exist.
*Mother Courage*, VI

8 What happens to the hole when the cheese is gone?
*Mother Courage*, VI

9 War is like love, it always finds a way.
*Mother Courage*, VI

10 Don't tell me peace has broken out.
*Mother Courage*, VIII

11 The wickedness of the world is so great you have to run your legs off to avoid having them stolen from under you.
*The Threepenny Opera*, I:3

**Brenan, Gerald** (Edward Fitzgerald Brenan; 1894– ) British writer. His works include *The Face of Spain* (1950), *A Holiday by the Sea* (1961), and *Thoughts in a Dry Season* (1978).

1 When we attend the funerals of our friends we grieve for them, but when we go to those of other people it is chiefly our own deaths that we mourn for.
*Thoughts in a Dry Season*, 'Death'

2 Intellectuals are people who believe that ideas are of more importance than values. That is to say, their own ideas and other people's values.
*Thoughts in a Dry Season*, 'Life'

3 Old age takes away from us what we have inherited and gives us what we have earned.
*Thoughts in a Dry Season*, 'Life'

4 The cliché is dead poetry. English, being the language of an imaginative race, abounds in clichés, so that English literature is always in danger of being poisoned by its own secretions.
*Thoughts in a Dry Season*, 'Literature'

5 Miller is not really a writer but a non-stop talker to whom someone has given a typewriter.
Referring to Henry Miller
*Thoughts in a Dry Season*, 'Literature'

6 Poets and painters are outside the class system, or rather they constitute a special class of their own, like the circus people and the gipsies.
*Thoughts in a Dry Season*, 'Writing'

**Bridges, Robert Seymour** (1844–1930) British poet and physician. He gave up medicine in 1882 and published several verse collections as well as an edition of the verse of his friend, Gerard Manley Hopkins. His own books include *Eros and Psyche* (1885), *The Spirit of Man* (1916), and *The Testament of Beauty* (1926). He was poet laureate from 1913.

1 For beauty being the best of all we know
Sums up the unsearchable and secret aims
Of nature.

*The Growth of Love*

2 Beauty sat with me all the summer day,
Awaiting the sure triumph of her eye;
Nor mark'd I till we parted, how, hard by,
Love in her train stood ready for his prey.

*The Growth of Love*

3 The day begins to droop, –
Its course is done:
But nothing tells the place
Of the setting sun.

*Winter Nightfall*

**Brien, Alan** (1925– ) British critic and journalist. Books include *Domes of Fortune* (1979) and various collections of his articles.

1 I have done almost every human activity inside a taxi which does not require main drainage.

*Punch*, 5 July 1972

**Bright, John** (1811–89) British radical politician and orator. With Richard Cobden he campaigned successfully for the abolition of the Corn Laws.

1 The Angel of Death has been abroad throughout the land: you may almost hear the beating of his wings.

Referring to the Crimean War
Speech, House of Commons, 23 Feb 1855

2 England is the mother of parliaments.

Speech, Birmingham, 18 Jan 1865

3 Force is not a remedy.

Speech, Birmingham, 16 Nov 1880

4 And he adores his maker.

Comment when informed that Disraeli should be admired for being a self-made man
Attrib.

**Brittain, Vera (Mary)** (1893–1970) British writer and feminist. Her best-known book, *Testament of Youth* (1933), relates her experiences as an army nurse in World War I.

1 It is probably true to say that the largest scope for change still lies in men's attitude to women, and in women's attitude to themselves.

*Lady into Woman*, Ch. 15

2 The idea that it is necessary to go to a university in order to become a successful writer, or even a man or woman of letters (which is by no means the same thing), is one of those phantasies that surround authorship.

*On Being an Author*, Ch. 2

3 Politics are usually the executive expression of human immaturity.

*The Rebel Passion*

**Bronowski, Jacob** (1908–74) British scientist and writer, born in Poland. His television series *The Ascent of Man* (1973) was highly successful. His critical works on William Blake are also well-known.

1 Every animal leaves traces of what it was; man alone leaves traces of what he created.

*The Ascent of Man*, Ch. 1

2 That is the essence of science: ask an impertinent question, and you are on the way to the pertinent answer.

*The Ascent of Man*, Ch. 4

3 Physics becomes in those years the greatest collective work of science – no, more than that, the great collective work of art of the twentieth century.

Referring to the period around the turn of the century marked by the elucidation of atomic structure and the development of the quantum theory
*The Ascent of Man*, Ch. 10

4 The wish to hurt, the momentary intoxication with pain, is the loophole through which the pervert climbs into the minds of ordinary men.

*The Face of Violence*, Ch. 5

5 The world is made of people who never quite get into the first team and who just miss the prizes at the flower show.

*The Face of Violence*, Ch. 6

**Brontë, Emily (Jane)** (1818–48) British novelist and poet. With her sisters Charlotte and Anne she published *Poems by Currer, Ellis and Acton Bell* in 1846. Her most famous work is the novel *Wuthering Heights* (1847).

1 No coward soul is mine,
No trembler in the world's storm-troubled sphere:
I see Heaven's glories shine,
And faith shines equal, arming me from fear.

*Last Lines*

2 Vain are the thousand creeds
That move men's hearts: unutterably vain;
Worthless as wither'd weeds.

*Last Lines*

3 O! dreadful is the check – intense the agony –
When the ear begins to hear, and the eye begins to see;
When the pulse begins to throb – the brain to think again –
The soul to feel the flesh, and the flesh to feel the chain.

*The Prisoner*

4 Once drinking deep of that divinest anguish,
How could I seek the empty world again?

*Remembrance*

**Brooke, Rupert (Chawner)** (1887–1915) British poet, who became a national hero after the publication of his war poems *1914 and Other Poems* (1915). He died of blood poisoning in the Aegean before seeing action.

1 For England's the one land, I know,
  Where men with Splendid Hearts may go;
  And Cambridgeshire, of all England,
  The shire for Men who Understand.
  *The Old Vicarage, Grantchester*

2 Just now the lilac is in bloom
  All before my little room.
  *The Old Vicarage, Grantchester*

3 Stands the Church clock at ten to three?
  And is there honey still for tea?
  *The Old Vicarage, Grantchester*

4 War knows no power. Safe shall be my going,
  Secretly armed against all death's endeavour;
  Safe though all safety's lost; safe where men fall;
  And if these poor limbs die, safest of all.
  *Safety*

5 If I should die, think only this of me:
  That there's some corner of a foreign field
  That is forever England.
  *The Soldier*

**Brooks, Mel** (Melvyn Kaminsky; 1926– ) US film actor and director. His films include *The Producers* (1968), *Blazing Saddles* (1974), and *High Anxiety* (1977).

1 That's it, baby, if you've got it, flaunt it.
  *The Producers*

2 Tragedy is if I cut my finger. Comedy is if I walk into an open sewer and die.
  *New Yorker*, 30 Oct 1978

**Brooks, Phillips** (1835–93) US Episcopal bishop and evangelist. His books include *New Starts in Life* (1896) and he wrote the hymn *O Little Town of Bethlehem*.

1 O little town of Bethlehem,
  How still we see thee lie;
  Above thy deep and dreamless sleep
  The silent stars go by.
  *O Little Town of Bethlehem*

**Brougham, Henry Peter, Baron** (1778–1868) Scottish lawyer and politician. He advocated the abolition of slavery and defended Queen Caroline at her trial (1820). He was also a founder of London University and the designer of the horse-drawn carriage that bears his name.

1 The great Unwashed.
  *Attrib.*

**Brown, Thomas** (1663–1704) English satirist and translator; author of numerous lampoons and epigrams.

1 I do not love thee, Doctor Fell,
  The reason why I cannot tell;
  But this alone I know full well,
  I do not love thee, Doctor Fell.
  *Translation of Martial's Epigrams*

**Brown, Thomas Edward** (1830–97) British poet. Born in the Isle of Man, he produced a number of works in the Manx dialect, notably *Foc's'le Yarns* (1881).

1 A rich man's joke is always funny.
  *The Doctor*

2 A garden is a lovesome thing, God wot!
  *My Garden*

**Browne, Charles Farrar** *See* Ward, Artemus.

**Browne, Sir Thomas** (1605–82) English physician and writer. The reflective *Religio Medici* (1642), not originally intended for publication, established his reputation as a writer. Later works included *Pseudodoxia Epidemia* (1646).

1 He who discommendeth others obliquely commendeth himself.
  *Christian Morals*, Pt. I

2 They do most by Books, who could do much without them, and he that chiefly owes himself unto himself, is the substantial Man.
  *Christian Morals*, Pt. II

3 All things are artificial, for nature is the art of God.
  *Religio Medici*, Pt. I

4 Thus the devil played at chess with me, and yielding a pawn, thought to gain a queen of me, taking advantage of my honest endeavours.
  *Religio Medici*, Pt. I

5 For my part, I have ever believed, and do now know, that there are witches.
  *Religio Medici*, Pt. I

6 It is the common wonder of all men, how among so many million of faces, there should be none alike.
  *Religio Medici*, Pt. II

7 No man can justly censure or condemn another, because indeed no man truly knows another.
  *Religio Medici*, Pt. II

8 Charity begins at home, is the voice of the world.
  *Religio Medici*, Pt. II

9 Lord, deliver me from myself.
  *Religio Medici*, Pt. II

10 For the world, I count it not an inn, but an hospital, and a place, not to live, but to die in.
  *Religio Medici*, Pt. II

11 There is surely a piece of divinity in us, something that was before the elements, and owes no homage unto the sun.
  *Religio Medici*, Pt. II

12 Man is a noble animal, splendid in ashes, and pompous in the grave.
  *Urn Burial*, Ch. 5

**Browning, Elizabeth Barrett** (1806–61) British poet. A semi-invalid, she married the poet Robert Browning in 1846 and lived with him in Italy. Her books include *Sonnets from the Portuguese* (1850), *Aurora Leigh* (1856), and *Poems Before Congress* (1860).

1 Since when was genius found respectable?
*Aurora Leigh*, Bk. VI

2 Do you hear the children weeping, O my brothers,
Ere the sorrow comes with years?
*The Cry of the Children*

3 God's gifts put man's best gifts to shame.
*Sonnets from the Portuguese*, XXVI

4 I love thee with a love I seemed to lose
With my lost saints – I love thee with the breath,
Smiles, tears, of all my life! – and, if God choose,
I shall but love thee better after death.
*Sonnets from the Portuguese*, XLIII

**Browning, Robert** (1812–89) British poet. *Men and Women* (1855), *Dramatis Personae* (1864), and *The Ring and the Book* (1868–69), were written after his marriage to the poet Elizabeth Barrett, with whom he eloped to Italy in 1846.

1 So free we seem, so fettered fast we are!
*Andrea del Sarto*

2 Ah, but a man's reach should exceed his grasp,
Or what's a heaven for?
*Andrea del Sarto*

3 Why need the other women know so much?
*Any Wife to any Husband*

4 My sun sets to rise again.
*At the 'Mermaid'*

5 Best be yourself, imperial, plain and true!
*Bishop Blougram's Apology*

6 We mortals cross the ocean of this world
Each in his average cabin of a life.
*Bishop Blougram's Apology*

7 Just when we are safest, there's a sunset-touch,
A fancy from a flower-bell, some one's death,
A chorus-ending from Euripides, –
And that's enough for fifty hopes and fears
As old and new at once as Nature's self,
To rap and knock and enter in our soul.
*Bishop Blougram's Apology*

8 The grand Perhaps!
*Bishop Blougram's Apology*

9 All we have gained then by our unbelief
Is a life of doubt diversified by faith,
For one of faith diversified by doubt:
We called the chess-board white, – we call it black.
*Bishop Blougram's Apology*

10 No, when the fight begins within himself,
A man's worth something.
*Bishop Blougram's Apology*

11 He said true things, but called them by wrong names.
*Bishop Blougram's Apology*

12 'Tis the Last Judgment's fire must cure this place,
Calcine its clods and set my prisoners free.
*Childe Roland to the Dark Tower Came*, XI

13 As for the grass, it grew as scant as hair
In leprosy.
*Childe Roland to the Dark Tower Came*, XIII

14 I never saw a brute I hated so;
He must be wicked to deserve such pain.
*Childe Roland to the Dark Tower Came*, XIV

15 Dauntless the slug-horn to my lips I set,
And blew. *Childe Roland to the Dark Tower came*.
*Childe Roland to the Dark Tower Came*, XXXIV

16 Though Rome's gross yoke
Drops off, no more to be endured,
Her teaching is not so obscured
By errors and perversities,
That no truth shines athwart the lies.
*Christmas Eve*, XI

17 Such ever was love's way; to rise, it stoops.
*A Death in the Desert*

18 For I say, this is death, and the sole death,
When a man's loss comes to him from his gain,
Darkness from light, from knowledge ignorance,
And lack of love from love made manifest.
*A Death in the Desert*

19 Man partly is and wholly hopes to be.
*A Death in the Desert*

20 How very hard it is
To be a Christian!
*Easter-Day*, I

21 At last awake
From life, that insane dream we take
For waking now.
*Easter-Day*, XIV

22 No, at noonday in the bustle of man's worktime
Greet the unseen with a cheer!
*Epilogue to Asolando*

23 Oh, to be in England
Now that April's there.
*Home Thoughts from Abroad*

24 And after April, when May follows,
And the whitethroat builds, and all the swallows!
*Home Thoughts from Abroad*

25 That's the wise thrush; he sings each song twice over,
Lest you should think he never could recapture
The first fine careless rapture!
*Home Thoughts from Abroad*

26 I sprang to the stirrup, and Joris, and he;
I galloped, Dirck galloped, we galloped all three.
*How they brought the Good News from Ghent to Aix*

27 Oh, good gigantic smile o' the brown old earth.
*James Lee's Wife*, VII

28 And, Robert Browning, you writer of plays,
Here's a subject made to your hand!
*A Light Woman*, XIV

29 Just for a handful of silver he left us,
Just for a riband to stick in his coat.
*The Lost Leader*

30 Blot out his name, then, record one lost soul
more,
One task more declined, one more footpath
untrod,
One more devils'-triumph and sorrow for angels,
One wrong more to man, one more insult to
God!
*The Lost Leader*

31 Then let him receive the new knowledge and
wait us,
Pardoned in heaven, the first by the throne!
*The Lost Leader*

32 Where the quiet-coloured end of evening smiles,
Miles and miles.
*Love among the Ruins*, I

33 She had
A heart – how shall I say? – too soon made
glad,
Too easily impressed.
*My Last Duchess*

34 Never the time and the place
And the loved one all together!
*Never the Time and the Place*

35 What's come to perfection perishes.
Things learned on earth, we shall practise in
heaven.
Works done least rapidly, Art most cherishes.
*Old Pictures in Florence*, XVII

36 There remaineth a rest for the people of God:
And I have had troubles enough, for one.
*Old Pictures in Florence*, XVII

37 Suddenly, as rare things will, it vanished.
*One Word More*, IV

38 God be thanked, the meanest of his creatures
Boasts two soul-sides, one to face the world
with,
One to show a woman when he loves her!
*One Word More*, XVII

39 Hamelin Town's in Brunswick,
By famous Hanover city;
The river Weser, deep and wide,
Washes its wall on the southern side;
A pleasanter spot you never spied.
*The Pied Piper of Hamelin*

40 Rats!
They fought the dogs and killed the cats,
And bit the babies in the cradles.
*The Pied Piper of Hamelin*

41 And the muttering grew to a grumbling;
And the grumbling grew to a mighty rumbling;
And out of the houses the rats came tumbling.
*The Pied Piper of Hamelin*

42 'You threaten us, fellow? Do your worst,
Blow your pipe there till you burst!'
*The Pied Piper of Hamelin*

43 The year's at the spring,
And day's at the morn;
Morning's at seven;
The hill-side's dew-pearled;
The lark's on the wing;
The snail's on the thorn;
God's in His heaven –
All's right with the world.
*Pippa Passes*, Pt. I

44 A king lived long ago,
In the morning of the world,
When earth was nigher heaven than now.
*Pippa Passes*, Pt. I

45 Such grace had kings when the world begun!
*Pippa Passes*, Pt. I

46 All service ranks the same with God –
With God, whose puppets, best and worst,
Are we: there is no last or first.
*Pippa Passes*, Pt. I

47 Therefore I summon age
To grant youth's heritage.
*Rabbi ben Ezra*, XIII

48 How good is man's life, the mere living! how fit
to employ
All the heart and the soul and the senses for
ever in joy!
*Saul*, IX

49 Leave the flesh to the fate it was fit for! the
spirit be thine!
*Saul*, XIII

50 Gr-r-r- there go, my heart's abhorrence!
Water your damned flower-pots, do!
*Soliloquy of the Spanish Cloister*

51 I the Trinity illustrate,
Drinking watered orange-pulp –
In three sips the Arian frustrate;
While he drains his at one gulp.
*Soliloquy of the Spanish Cloister*

52 There's a great text in Galatians,
Once you trip on it, entails
Twenty-nine distinct damnations,
One sure, if another fails.
*Soliloquy of the Spanish Cloister*

53 My scrofulous French novel
On grey paper with blunt type!
*Soliloquy of the Spanish Cloister*

54 She looked at him, as one who awakes:
The past was a sleep, and her life began.
*The Statue and the Bust*

**55** What of soul was left, I wonder, when the kissing had to stop?
*A Toccata of Galuppi's*

**56** What's become of Waring
Since he gave us all the slip?
*Waring*

**Bruce, Lenny** (1925–66) US comedian.

**1** Every day people are straying away from the church and going back to God. Really.
*The Essential Lenny Bruce* (ed. J. Cohen), 'Religions Inc.'

**2** It was just one of those parties which got out of hand.
Referring to the Crucifixion
*The Guardian*, 10 May 1979

**Brummel, 'Beau'** (George Bryan Brummell; 1778–1840) British dandy and friend of George IV.

**1** Who's your fat friend?
Referring to George, Prince of Wales
*Reminiscences* (Gronow)

**Bruno, Giordano** (1548–1600) Italian philosopher. A Dominican, his determination to discuss philosophical views, regardless of their religious orthodoxy, eventually caused his execution for heresy.

**1** Perhaps your fear in passing judgement is greater than mine in receiving it.
Said to the cardinals who excommunicated him, 8 Feb 1600
Attrib.

**Buchanan, Robert Williams** (1841–1901) British poet, novelist, and dramatist, famous for his criticism of the Pre-Raphaelites.

**1** She just wore
Enough for modesty – no more.
*White Rose and Red*, I

**2** The Fleshly School of Poetry.
Referring to Swinburne, William Morris, D. G. Rossetti, etc.
Title of article in the *Contemporary Review*, Oct 1871

**Buck, Pearl S(ydenstricker)** (1892–1973) US novelist. Winner of the Nobel Prize in 1938, her novels include *The Good Earth* (1931) and *The Three Daughters of Madame Liang* (1969).

**1** Euthanasia is a long, smooth-sounding word, and it conceals its danger as long, smooth words do, but the danger is there, nevertheless.
*The Child Who Never Grew*, Ch. 2

**2** Nothing and no one can destroy the Chinese people. They are relentless survivors. They are the oldest civilized people on earth. Their civilization passes through phases but its basic characteristics remain the same. They yield, they bend to the wind, but they never break.
*China, Past and Present*, Ch. 1

**3** Ah well, perhaps one has to be very old before one learns how to be amused rather than shocked.
*China, Past and Present*, Ch. 6

**4** No one really understood music unless he was a scientist, her father had declared, and not just a scientist, either, oh, no, only the real ones, the theoreticians, whose language was mathematics.
*The Goddess Abides*, Pt. I

**5** It is better to be first with an ugly woman than the hundredth with a beauty.
*The Good Earth*, Ch. 1

**6** I feel no need for any other faith than my faith in human beings.
*I Believe*

**Buckingham, George Villiers, 2nd Duke of** (1628–87) English politician; a member of the Cabal. He also wrote poetry and satirical works, notably the comedy *The Rehearsal* (1671).

**1** Ay, now the plot thickens very much upon us.
*The Rehearsal*, III:1

**2** The world is made up for the most part of fools and knaves.
*To Mr Clifford, on his Humane Reason*

**Buddha** (Gautama Siddhartha; c. 563–c. 483 BC) Indian prince, who at the age of about 20 renounced his family and his rich indolent life to search for enlightenment, which he traditionally achieved beneath a banyan tree. The rest of his life was spent teaching his findings and formulating the principles of Buddhism.

**1** All things, oh priests, are on fire . . . The eye is on fire; forms are on fire; eye-consciousness is on fire; impressions received by the eye are on fire.
*The Fire Sermon*

**2** This Ariyan Eightfold Path, that is to say: Right view, right aim, right speech, right action, right living, right effort, right mindfulness, right contemplation.
*Some Sayings of the Buddha* (F. L. Woodward)

**3** Ye must leave righteous ways behind, not to speak of unrighteous ways.
*Some Sayings of the Buddha* (F. L. Woodward)

**Buffon, Georges-Louis Leclerc, Comte de** (1707–88) French naturalist. In his monumental *Histoire naturelle* (1749–89), he formulated an early theory of evolution.

**1** Style is the man himself.
*Discours sur le style*

**Buller, Arthur Henry Reginald** (1874–1944) British botanist and mycologist, who worked at the Royal Botanic Gardens, Kew.

**1** There was a young lady named Bright,
Whose speed was far faster than light;
She set out one day
In a relative way,
And returned home the previous night.
*Limerick*

**Bullock, Alan, Baron** (1914– ) British academic and historian. His books include *Hitler, A Study in Tyranny* (1952), *The Liberal Tradition* (1956), and *The Life and Times of Ernest Bevin* (1960–83).

**1** The people Hitler never understood, and whose actions continued to exasperate him to the end of his life, were the British.
*Hitler, A Study in Tyranny*, Ch. 8

**2** Hitler showed surprising loyalty to Mussolini, but it never extended to trusting him.
*Hitler, A Study in Tyranny*, Ch. 11

**Bulmer-Thomas, Ivor** (1905– ) British writer and politician. His books include *The Socialist Tragedy* (1949) and *The Growth of the British Party System* (1965).

**1** If ever he went to school without any boots it was because he was too big for them.
Referring to Harold Wilson
Remark, Conservative Party Conference, 1949

**Bulwer-Lytton, Edward George Earle, 1st Baron Lytton** (1803–73) British novelist and politician, who served in parliament first as a Liberal member, then as a Tory. He wrote many historical novels, including *The Last Days of Pompeii* (1834).

**1** Beneath the rule of men entirely great,
The pen is mightier than the sword.
*Richelieu*, II:2

**Buñuel, Luis** (1900–83) Spanish film director, who made his name with the surrealist *Un Chien andalou* (1928) and *L'Âge d'or* (1930). Many of his later films were produced in Mexico, where he settled in 1947.

**1** I am an atheist still, thank God.
*Luis Buñuel: an Introduction* (Ado Kyrou)

**Bunyan, John** (1628–88) English writer and preacher. During imprisonment for illegal preaching (1660–72) he wrote the autobiographical *Grace Abounding* (1666) and began work on his allegory *The Pilgrim's Progress* (1684).

**1** As I walked through the wilderness of this world.
*The Pilgrim's Progress*, Pt. I

**2** The name of the slough was Despond.
*The Pilgrim's Progress*, Pt. I

**3** The gentleman's name that met him was Mr Worldly Wiseman.
*The Pilgrim's Progress*, Pt. I

**4** A very stately palace before him, the name of which was Beautiful.
*The Pilgrim's Progress*, Pt. I

**5** It beareth the name of Vanity Fair, because the town where 'tis kept is lighter than vanity.
*The Pilgrim's Progress*, Pt. I

**6** So soon as the man overtook me, he was but a word and a blow.
*The Pilgrim's Progress*, Pt. I

**7** A castle called Doubting Castle, the owner whereof was Giant Despair.
*The Pilgrim's Progress*, Pt. I

**8** So I awoke, and behold it was a dream.
*The Pilgrim's Progress*, Pt. I

**9** One Great-heart.
*The Pilgrim's Progress*, Pt. II

**10** He that is down needs fear no fall;
He that is low, no pride.
*The Pilgrim's Progress*, 'Shepherd Boy's Song'

**Burgess, Anthony** (John Burgess Wilson; 1917– ) British novelist and critic. His books include *A Clockwork Orange* (1962), *Earthly Powers* (1980), and *The Kingdom of the Wicked* (1985).

**1** Not a future. At least not in Europe. America's different, of course, but America's really only a kind of Russia. You've no idea how pleasant it is not to have any future. It's like having a totally efficient contraceptive.
*Honey for the Bears*, Pt. II, Ch. 6

**2** Bath twice a day to be really clean, once a day to be passably clean, once a week to avoid being a public menace.
*Mr Enderby*, Pt. I, Ch. 2

**3** Rome's just a city like anywhere else. A vastly overrated city, I'd say. It trades on belief just as Stratford trades on Shakespeare.
*Mr Enderby*, Pt. II, Ch. 2

**4** The possession of a book becomes a substitute for reading it.
*New York Times Book Review*

**Burke, Edmund** (1729–97) British politician and political philosopher. He entered parliament as a Whig in 1765. In *Reflections on the Revolution in France* (1790) he condemned the French Revolution.

**1** Example is the school of mankind, and they will learn at no other.
*Letters on a Regicide Peace*, letter 1

**2** The only infallible criterion of wisdom to vulgar minds – success.
*Letter to a Member of the National Assembly*

**3** There is, however, a limit at which forbearance ceases to be a virtue.
*Observations on a Publication, 'The Present State of the Nation'*

**4** I am convinced that we have a degree of delight, and that no small one, in the real misfortunes and pains of others.
*On the Sublime and Beautiful*, Pt. I

**5** Beauty in distress is much the most affecting beauty.
*On the Sublime and Beautiful*, Pt. III

**6** Vice itself lost half its evil, by losing all its grossness.
*Reflections on the Revolution in France*

**7** But the age of chivalry is gone. That of sophisters, economists, and calculators, has succeeded; and the glory of Europe is extinguished for ever.
*Reflections on the Revolution in France*

**8** That chastity of honour, that felt a stain like a wound.
*Reflections on the Revolution in France*

**9** Man is by his constitution a religious animal.
*Reflections on the Revolution in France*

**10** Superstition is the religion of feeble minds.
*Reflections on the Revolution in France*

**11** The concessions of the weak are the concessions of fear.
*Speech on Conciliation with America* (House of Commons, 22 Mar 1775)

**12** All government, indeed every human benefit and enjoyment, every virtue, and every prudent act, is founded on compromise and barter.
*Speech on Conciliation with America* (House of Commons, 22 Mar 1775)

**13** The use of force alone is but *temporary*. It may subdue for a moment; but it does not remove the necessity of subduing again: and a nation is not governed, which is perpetually to be conquered.
*Speech on Conciliation with America* (House of Commons, 22 Mar 1775)

**14** I do not know the method of drawing up an indictment against an whole people.
*Speech on Conciliation with America* (House of Commons, 22 Mar 1775)

**15** Kings are naturally lovers of low company.
*Speech on the Economical Reform* (House of Commons, 11 Feb 1780)

**16** The people are the masters.
*Speech on the Economical Reform* (House of Commons, 11 Feb 1780)

**17** And having looked to government for bread, on the very first scarcity they will turn and bite the hand that fed them.
*Thoughts and Details on Scarcity*

**18** When bad men combine, the good must associate; else they will fall one by one, an unpitied sacrifice in a contemptible struggle.
*Thoughts on the Cause of the Present Discontents*

**19** Liberty, too, must be limited in order to be possessed.
*Letter to the Sherrifs of Bristol, 1777*

**20** Among a people generally corrupt, liberty cannot long exist.
*Letter to the Sherrifs of Bristol, 1777*

**21** Nothing is so fatal to religion as indifference, which is, at least, half infidelity.
*Letter to William Smith, 29 Jan 1795*

**22** Somebody has said, that a king may make a nobleman, but he cannot make a gentleman.
*Letter to William Smith, 29 Jan 1795*

**23** The greater the power, the more dangerous the abuse.
*Speech, House of Commons, 7 Feb 1771*

**24** Your representative owes you, not his industry only, but his judgement; and he betrays instead of serving you if he sacrifices it to your opinion.
*Speech to the electors of Bristol, 3 Nov 1774*

**25** He was not merely a chip of the old block, but the old block itself.
Referring to William Pitt the Younger's first speech in the House of Commons, 26 Feb 1781
Remark

**26** A thing may look specious in theory, and yet be ruinous in practice; a thing may look evil in theory, and yet be in practice excellent.
Impeachment of Warren Hastings, 19 Feb 1788

**27** Dangers by being despised grow great.
*Speech, House of Commons, 11 May 1792*

**Burke, Johnny** (1908–64) US songwriter.

**1** Don't you know each cloud contains Pennies from Heaven?
*Pennies from Heaven*

**Burnet, Gilbert** (1643–1715) English bishop and historian, born in Scotland. He was appointed Bishop of Salisbury in 1689. His autobiographical *History of His Own Times* was published posthumously.

**1** He had said that he had known many kicked downstairs, but he never knew any kicked upstairs before.
Recalling Halifax's observation
*Original Memoirs*

**Burney, Fanny** (Frances Burney D'Arblay; 1752–1840) British novelist. Her novels include *Evelina* (1778), *Camilla* (1796), and *The Wanderer* (1814). From 1802 to 1812 she lived in Paris with her French husband, General D'Arblay.

**1** Now I am ashamed of confessing that I have nothing to confess.
*Evelina*, Letter 59

**Burns, George** (1896– ) US comedian.

**1** Too bad all the people who know how to run the country are busy driving cabs and cutting hair.

**Burns, Robert** (1759–96) Scottish poet. A farmer's son, Burns established his reputation with *Poems, Chiefly in the Scottish Dialect* (1786). He subsequently wrote many songs, notably *Auld Lang Syne*, and the narrative poem *Tam o' Shanter*, all of which made him the national poet of Scotland.

**1** O Thou! Whatever title suit thee –
Auld Hornie, Satan, Nick, or Clootie.
*Address to the Devil*

**2** Should auld acquaintance be forgot,
And never brought to min'?
*Auld Lang Syne*

**3** We'll tak a cup o' kindness yet,
For auld lang syne.
*Auld Lang Syne*

4 Gin a body meet a body
  Coming through the rye;
  Gin a body kiss a body,
  Need a body cry?
  *Coming through the Rye*

5 I wasna fou, but just had plenty.
  *Death and Doctor Hornbrook*

6 On ev'ry hand it will allow'd be,
  He's just – nae better than he should be.
  *A Dedication to Gavin Hamilton*

7 Here lie Willie Michie's banes;
  O Satan, when ye tak him,
  Gie him the schoolin' of your weans,
  For clever deils he'll mak them!
  *Epitaph on a Schoolmaster*

8 A man's a man for a' that.
  *For a' that and a' that*

9 Green grow the rashes O,
  Green grow the rashes O,
  The sweetest hours that e'er I spend,
  Are spent amang the lasses O!
  *Green Grow the Rashes*

10 John Anderson my jo, John,
   When we were first acquent,
   Your locks were like the raven,
   Your bonnie brow was brent.
   *John Anderson My Jo*

11 Let them cant about decorum
   Who have characters to lose.
   *The Jolly Beggars*

12 Man's inhumanity to man
   Makes countless thousands mourn!
   *Man was Made to Mourn*

13 My heart's in the Highlands, my heart is not
   here;
   My heart's in the Highlands a-chasing the deer;
   Chasing the wild deer, and following the roe,
   My heart's in the Highlands, wherever I go.
   *My Heart's in the Highlands*

14 My love is like a red red rose
   That's newly sprung in June:
   My love is like the melodie
   That's sweetly play'd in tune.
   *A Red, Red Rose*

15 Scots, wha hae wi' Wallace bled,
   Scots, wham Bruce has aften led,
   Welcome to your gory bed,
   Or to victorie.
   *Scots, Wha Hae*

16 Liberty's in every blow!
   Let us do or die!
   *Scots, Wha Hae*

17 Some hae meat, and canna eat,
   And some wad eat that want it,
   But we hae meat and we can eat,
   And sae the Lord be thankit.
   *The Selkirk Grace*

18 Ah, gentle dames! It gars me greet
   To think how mony counsels sweet,
   How mony lengthen'd sage advices,
   The husband frae the wife despises!
   *Tam o' Shanter*

19 Wee, sleekit, cow'rin', tim'rous beastie,
   O what a panic's in thy breastie!
   *To a Mouse*

20 The best laid schemes o' mice an' men
   Gang aft a-gley,
   An' lea'e us nought but grief an' pain
   For promis'd joy.
   *To a Mouse*

21 But yet the light that led astray
   Was light from Heaven.
   *The Vision*

22 Ye banks and braes o' bonnie Doon,
   How can ye bloom sae fresh and fair?
   How can ye chant, ye little birds,
   And I sae weary fu' o' care?
   *Ye Banks and Braes*

**Burroughs, Edgar Rice** (1875–1950) US novelist. He
became famous with *Tarzan of the Apes* (1914), which has been
the basis of many films.

1 Me Tarzan.
  The line 'Me Tarzan, you Jane' comes from the films and does
  not appear in the books
  *Tarzan of the Apes*

**Burton, Robert** (1577–1640) English scholar and churchman.
He is remembered for *Anatomy of Melancholy* (1621).

1 All my joys to this are folly,
  Naught so sweet as Melancholy.
  *Anatomy of Melancholy*, Abstract

2 If there is a hell upon earth, it is to be found in a
  melancholy man's heart.
  *Anatomy of Melancholy*, Pt. I

3 From this it is clear how much more cruel the
  pen is than the sword.
  *Anatomy of Melancholy*, Pt. I

4 England is a paradise for women, and hell for
  horses: Italy a paradise for horses, hell for
  women.
  *Anatomy of Melancholy*, Pt. III

5 One religion is as true as another.
  *Anatomy of Melancholy*, Pt. III

**Bussy-Rabutin** (Roger de Rabutin, Comte de Bussy; 1618–
93) French soldier and writer. His scandalous *Histoire amoureuse
des Gaules* (1665) led to imprisonment and exile.

1 Absence is to love what wind is to fire; it extin-
  guishes the small, it inflames the great.
  *Histoire amoureuse des Gaules*

**Butler, Joseph** (1692–1752) British churchman. He became
Bishop of Durham in 1750. *The Analogy of Religion* (1736) is his
best-known work.

1 That which is the foundation of all our hopes and of all our fears; all our hopes and fears which are of any consideration: I mean a Future Life.
*The Analogy of Religion,* Introduction

**Butler, R(ichard) A(usten), Baron** (1902–82) British Conservative politician. A successful minister of education and chancellor of the exchequer, he twice failed to become prime minister. *The Art of the Possible* (1971) is his autobiography.

1 Politics is the art of the possible.
Often attrib. to Butler but used earlier by others, including Bismarck
*The Art of the Possible,* Epigraph

2 Mr Macmillan is the best prime minister we have.
Often quoted in the form above. In fact, Butler simply answered 'Yes' to the question 'Would you say that this is the best prime minister we have?'
Interview, London Airport

**Butler, Samuel** (1612–80) English satirist, secretary to George Villiers, 2nd Duke of Buckingham. The satirical poem *Hudibras* (1663–78), a mock romance, is his most famous work.

1 When civil fury first grew high,
And men fell out they knew not why.
*Hudibras,* Pt. I

2 For every why he had a wherefore.
*Hudibras,* Pt. I

3 To swallow gudgeons ere they're catched,
And count their chickens ere they're hatched.
*Hudibras,* Pt. II

4 Love is a boy, by poets styl'd,
Then spare the rod, and spoil the child.
*Hudibras,* Pt. II

5 Through perils both of wind and limb,
Through thick and thin she follow'd him.
*Hudibras,* Pt. II

6 Oaths are but words, and words but wind.
*Hudibras,* Pt. II

7 What makes all doctrines plain and clear?
About two hundred pounds a year.
*Hudibras,* Pt. III

8 He that complies against his will,
Is of his own opinion still.
*Hudibras,* Pt. III

9 The souls of women are so small,
That some believe they've none at all.
*Miscellaneous Thoughts*

**Butler, Samuel** (1835–1902) British writer. *Erewhon,* a satirical novel published anonymously in 1872, established his reputation; subsequent works include the autobiographical *The Way of All Flesh* (1903).

1 Some who had received a liberal education at the Colleges of Unreason, and taken the highest degrees in hypothetics, which are their principal study.
*Erewhon,* Ch. 9

2 Straighteners, managers and cashiers of the Musical Banks.
*Erewhon,* Ch. 9

3 While to deny the existence of an unseen kingdom is bad, to pretend that we know more about it than its bare existence is no better.
*Erewhon,* Ch. 15

4 The wish to spread those opinions that we hold conducive to our own welfare is so deeply rooted in the English character that few of us can escape its influence.
*Erewhon,* Ch. 20

5 An art can only be learned in the workshop of those who are winning their bread by it.
*Erewhon,* Ch. 20

6 It has been said that the love of money is the root of all evil. The want of money is so quite as truly.
*Erewhon,* Ch. 20

7 Spontaneity is only a term for man's ignorance of the gods.
*Erewhon,* Ch. 25

8 I keep my books at the British Museum and at Mudie's.
*The Humour of Homer,* 'Ramblings in Cheapside'

9 Life is one long process of getting tired.
*Notebooks*

10 Life is the art of drawing sufficient conclusions from insufficient premises.
*Notebooks*

11 All progress is based upon a universal innate desire on the part of every organism to live beyond its income.
*Notebooks*

12 When a man is in doubt about this or that in his writing, it will often guide him if he asks himself how it will tell a hundred years hence.
*Notebooks*

13 An apology for the Devil – it must be remembered that we have only heard one side of the case. God has written all the books.
*Notebooks*

14 God is Love – I dare say. But what a mischievous devil Love is!
*Notebooks*

15 The public buys its opinions as it buys its meat, or takes in its milk, on the principle that it is cheaper to do this than to keep a cow. So it is, but the milk is more likely to be watered.
*Notebooks*

16 The healthy stomach is nothing if not conservative. Few radicals have good digestions.
*Notebooks*

17 Though analogy is often misleading, it is the least misleading thing we have.
*Notebooks*

18 Some men love truth so much that they seem to be in continual fear lest she should catch a cold on overexposure.
*Notebooks*

19 Marriage is distinctly and repeatedly excluded from heaven. Is this because it is thought likely to mar the general felicity?

*Notebooks*

20 Man is the only animal that can remain on friendly terms with the victims he intends to eat until he eats them.

*Notebooks*

21 To be at all is to be religious more or less.

*Notebooks*

22 A client is fain to hire a lawyer to keep from the injury of other lawyers – as Christians that travel in Turkey are forced to hire Janissaries, to protect them from the insolencies of other Turks.

*Prose Observations*

23 Every man's work, whether it be literature or music or pictures or architecture or anything else, is always a portrait of himself.

*The Way of All Flesh*, Ch. 14

24 That vice pays homage to virtue is notorious; we call it hypocrisy.

*The Way of All Flesh*, Ch. 19

25 Pleasure after all is a safer guide than either right or duty.

*The Way of All Flesh*, Ch. 19

26 The advantage of doing one's praising for oneself is that one can lay it on so thick and exactly in the right places.

*The Way of All Flesh*, Ch. 34

27 'Tis better to have loved and lost than never to have lost at all.

*The Way of All Flesh*, Ch. 77

28 When you have told anyone you have left him a legacy the only decent thing to do is to die at once.

*Samuel Butler: A Memoir* (Festing Jones), Vol. 2

29 Brigands demand your money or your life; women require both.

*Attrib.*

**Byrom, John** (1692–1763) British poet and hymn writer. His collected poems were published in 1773 and a diary was published in the 19th century.

1 Christians awake, salute the happy morn, Whereon the Saviour of the world was born.

*Hymn for Christmas Day*

**Byron, George Gordon, 6th Baron** (1788–1824) British poet. The melancholy *Childe Harold's Pilgrimage* (1812) brought him to the attention of literary society. After scandalizing London with his sexual exploits he lived abroad, largely in Italy; his later works include the poetic drama *Manfred* (1817) and the epic satire *Don Juan* (1819–24).

1 The 'good old times' – all times when old are good – Are gone.

*The Age of Bronze*, I

2 The land self-interest groans from shore to shore, For fear that plenty should attain the poor.

*The Age of Bronze*, XIV

3 In short, he was a perfect cavaliero, And to his very valet seem'd a hero.

*Beppo*

4 I like the weather, when it is not rainy, That is, I like two months of every year.

*Beppo*

5 Maidens, like moths, are ever caught by glare, And Mammon wins his way where Seraphs might despair.

*Childe Harold's Pilgrimage*, I

6 Adieu, adieu! my native shore Fades o'er the waters blue.

*Childe Harold's Pilgrimage*, I

7 My native Land – Good Night!

*Childe Harold's Pilgrimage*, I

8 War, war is still the cry, 'War even to the knife!'

*Childe Harold's Pilgrimage*, I

9 Hereditary bondsmen! know ye not Who would be free themselves must strike the blow?

*Childe Harold's Pilgrimage*, I

10 There was a sound of revelry by night, And Belgium's capital had gather'd then Her Beauty and her Chivalry, and bright The lamps shone o'er fair women and brave men.

*Childe Harold's Pilgrimage*, III

11 On with the dance! let joy be unconfined; No sleep till morn, when Youth and Pleasure meet To chase the glowing Hours with flying feet.

*Childe Harold's Pilgrimage*, III

12 While stands the Coliseum, Rome shall stand; When falls the Coliseum, Rome shall fall; And when Rome falls – the World.

*Childe Harold's Pilgrimage*, IV

13 There is a pleasure in the pathless woods, There is a rapture on the lonely shore, There is society, where none intrudes, By the deep Sea, and music in its roar: I love not Man the less, but Nature more.

*Childe Harold's Pilgrimage*, IV

14 The spirit burning but unbent, May writhe, rebel – the weak alone repent!

*The Corsair*, II

15 'Tis sweet to hear the watch-dog's honest bark Bay deep-mouthed welcome as we draw near home; 'Tis sweet to know there is an eye will mark Our coming, and look brighter when we come.

*Don Juan*, I

16 What men call gallantry, and gods adultery, Is much more common where the climate's sultry.

*Don Juan*, I

17 Man's love is of man's life a thing apart,
'Tis woman's whole existence.
*Don Juan, I*

18 Man, being reasonable, must get drunk;
The best of life is but intoxication.
*Don Juan, II*

19 All tragedies are finish'd by a death,
All comedies are ended by a marriage.
*Don Juan, III*

20 Cost his enemies a long repentance,
And made him a good friend, but bad
acquaintance.
*Don Juan, III*

21 Though sages may pour out their wisdom's
treasure,
There is no sterner moralist than Pleasure.
*Don Juan, III*

22 Agree to a short armistice with truth.
*Don Juan, III*

23 The isles of Greece, the isles of Greece!
Where burning Sappho loved and sung,
Where grew the arts of war and peace,
Where Delos rose, and Phoebus sprung!
Eternal summer gilds them yet,
But all, except their sun, is set.
*Don Juan, III*

24 The mountains look on Marathon –
And Marathon looks on the sea:
And musing there an hour alone,
I dream'd that Greece might still be free.
*Don Juan, III*

25 Nothing so difficult as a beginning
In poesy, unless perhaps the end.
*Don Juan, IV*

26 I thought it would appear
That there had been a lady in the case.
*Don Juan, V*

27 The women pardoned all except her face.
*Don Juan, V*

28 There is a tide in the affairs of women,
Which, taken at the flood, leads – God knows
where.
*Don Juan, VI*

29 A lady of a 'certain age', which means
Certainly aged.
*Don Juan, VI*

30 Now hatred is by far the longest pleasure;
Men love in haste, but they detest at leisure.
*Don Juan, XIII*

31 Society is now one polish'd horde,
Form'd of two mighty tribes, the *Bores* and
*Bored*.
*Don Juan, XIII*

32 'Tis strange – but true; for truth is always
strange;
Stranger than fiction: if it could be told,
How much would novels gain by the exchange!
*Don Juan, XIV*

33 I'll publish, right or wrong:
Fools are my theme, let satire be my song.
*English Bards and Scotch Reviewers*

34 'Tis pleasant, sure, to see one's name in print;
A book's a book, although there's nothing in't.
*English Bards and Scotch Reviewers*

35 A man must serve his time to every trade
Save censure – critics all are ready made.
*English Bards and Scotch Reviewers*

36 With death doomed to grapple,
Beneath this cold slab, he
Who lied in the chapel
Now lies in the Abbey.
*Epitaph for William Pitt*

37 She walks in beauty, like the night
Of cloudless climes and starry skies;
And all that's best of dark and bright
Meet in her aspect and her eyes.
*She Walks in Beauty*

38 So, we'll go no more a roving
So late into the night,
Though the heart be still as loving,
And the moon be still as bright.
*So, we'll go no more a roving*

39 Though the night was made for loving,
And the day returns too soon,
Yet we'll go no more a roving
By the light of the moon.
*So, we'll go no more a roving*

40 A better farmer ne'er brushed dew from lawn,
A worse king never left a realm undone!
Referring to George III
*The Vision of Judgment, VIII*

41 If I should meet thee
After long years,
How should I greet thee? –
With silence and tears.
*When we two parted*

42 I awoke one morning and found myself famous.
Remark made after the publication of *Childe Harold's Pilgrimage*
(1812)
Entry in Memoranda

**Byron, Henry James** (1834–84) British dramatist and
actor. He wrote numerous comedies and farces, notably *Cyril's
Success* (1868) and *Our Boys* (1875).

1 Life's too short for chess.
*Our Boys, I*

# C

**Cabell, James Branch** (1879–1958) US novelist and journalist. He was editor of the *American Spectator* (1932–35). His novels include *The Rivet in Grandfather's Neck* (1915), *Jurgen* (1919), *The Silver Stallion* (1926), and *The First Gentleman of America* (1942).

1 I am willing to taste any drink once.
*Jurgen*, Ch. 1

2 The optimist proclaims we live in the best of all possible worlds; and the pessimist fears this is true.
*The Silver Stallion*

**Caesar, (Gaius) Julius** (100–44 BC) Roman general and statesman. A member of the first Triumvirate (60 BC) with Pompey and Crassus, his military campaigns in Gaul and Britain won adulation. After the death of Crassus, conflict with Pompey led to civil war, from which Caesar emerged as dictator of Rome. He was assassinated by republican conspirators.

1 All Gaul is divided into three parts.
*De Bello Gallico*, Vol. I, Ch. 1

2 Caesar's wife must be above suspicion.
Said in justification of his divorce from Pompeia, after she was unwittingly involved in a scandal
*Lives*, 'Julius Caesar' (Plutarch)

3 The die is cast.
Said on crossing the Rubicon (49 BC) at the start of his campaign against Pompey
Remark

4 *Veni, vidi, vici.*
I came, I saw, I conquered.
*The Twelve Caesars* (Suetonius)

5 *Et tu, Brute?.*
You too, Brutus?
Last words

**Cage, John** (1912– ) US composer of avant garde music. His book *Silence* (1961) gives an account of his indeterminist philosophy.

1 I have nothing to say, I am saying it, and that is poetry.
In *The Sunday Times* (quoted by Cyril Connolly), 10 Sep 1972

**Cahn, Sammy** ((Samuel Cohen; 1913– )) US songwriter. Many of his songs, including *Three Coins in the Fountain* and *Call Me Irresponsible* were featured in Hollywood films.

1 Love and marriage, love and marriage,
Go together like a horse and carriage.
*Our Town*, 'Love and Marriage'

**Calderón de la Barca, Pedro** (1600–81) Spanish dramatist and poet. He became chaplain to Philip IV and wrote many plays, including *La Vida Es Sueño* and *Astrólogo Fingido*.

1 For man's greatest crime is to have been born.
*La Vida es Sueño*, I

2 For I see now that I am asleep that I dream when I am awake.
*La Vida es Sueño*, II

**Caligula** (Gaius Caesar; 12–41 AD) Roman Emperor. His tyrannical and extravagant behaviour led to accusations of madness and eventually to his assassination.

1 Would that the Roman people had but one neck!
*Life of Caligula* (Suetonius), Ch. 30

**Callaghan, Sir (Leonard) James** (1912– ) British statesman. He was Labour prime minister (1976–79).

1 A lie can be half-way round the world before the truth has got its boots on.
Speech, 1 Nov 1976

2 Either back us or sack us.
Speech, Labour Party Conference, Brighton, 5 Oct 1977

**Calverley, C(harles) S(tuart)** (1831–84) British poet. He is remembered for his humorous collections *Verses and Translations* (1862) and *Fly Leaves* (1872).

1 The heart which grief hath cankered
Hath one unfailing remedy – the Tankard.
*Beer*

2 Jones – (who, I'm glad to say,
Asked leave of Mrs J. – )
Daily absorbs a clay
After his labours.
*Ode to Tobacco*

3 Yet it is better to drop thy friends, O my daughter, than to drop thy 'H's'.
*Proverbial Philosophy*, 'Of Friendship'

**Camden, William** (1551–1623) English antiquary and historian. His *Britannia*, a topographical and historical survey of the British Isles, was first published (in Latin) in 1586 and translated in 1610.

1 Betwixt the stirrup and the ground
Mercy I asked, mercy I found.
*Epitaph for a Man killed by falling from his Horse*

**Campbell, Jane Montgomery** (1817–78) British hymn writer.

1 We plough the fields, and scatter
The good seed on the land,
But it is fed and watered
By God's Almighty Hand.
He sends the snow in winter,
The warmth to swell the grain,
The breezes and the sunshine,
And soft refreshing rain.
*Hymn*

**Campbell, Joseph** (1879–1944) Irish poet. His works include *The Rushlight* (1906) and *The Mountainy Singer* (1909).

1 As a white candle
In a holy place,
So is the beauty
Of an aged face.
*The Old Woman*

**Campbell, Mrs Patrick** (Beatrice Stella Tanner; 1865–1940) British actress. She appeared in several plays by her friend G. B. Shaw.

1 It doesn't matter what you do in the bedroom as long as you don't do it in the street and frighten the horses.

*The Duchess of Jermyn Street* (Daphne Fielding), Ch. 2

2 Wedlock – the deep, deep peace of the double bed after the hurly-burly of the chaise-longue.

*Jennie* (Ralph G. Martin), Vol. II

**Campbell, (Ignatius) Roy(ston Dunnachie)** (1901–57) South African poet. His works include *The Flaming Terrapin* (1924); *The Georgiad* (1931), satirizing the Bloomsbury group; and the autobiographical *Broken Record* (1934) and *Light on a Dark Horse* (1951).

1 Now Spring, sweet laxative of Georgian strains, Quickens the ink in literary veins, The Stately Homes of England ope their doors To piping Nancy-boys and Crashing Bores.

*The Georgiad*

2 Translations (like wives) are seldom faithful if they are in the least attractive.

*Poetry Review*

**Campbell, Thomas** (1777–1844) British poet, who made his name with *The Pleasures of Hope* (1799).

1 O leave this barren spot to me! Spare, woodman, spare the beechen tree.

*The Beech-Tree's Petition*

2 On Linden, when the sun was low, All bloodless lay the untrodden snow, And dark as Winter was the flow of Iser, rolling rapidly.

*Hohenlinden*

3 'Tis distance lends enchantment to the view, And robes the mountain in its azure hue.

*Pleasures of Hope*, I

4 The proud, the cold untroubled heart of stone, That never mused on sorrow but its own.

*Pleasures of Hope*, I

5 What millions died – that Caesar might be great!

*Pleasures of Hope*, II

6 Ye Mariners of England That guard our native seas, Whose flag has braved, a thousand years, The battle and the breeze – Your glorious standard launch again To match another foe! And sweep through the deep, While the stormy winds do blow, – While the battle rages loud and long, And the stormy winds do blow.

*Ye Mariners of England*

7 Gentlemen, you must not mistake me. I admit that he is the sworn foe of our nation, and, if you will, of the whole human race. But, gentlemen, we must be just to our enemy. We must not forget that he once shot a bookseller.

Excusing himself in proposing a toast to Napoleon at a literary dinner

*The Life and Letters of Lord Macaulay* (G. O. Trevelyan)

8 Now Barabbas was a publisher.

Attrib.

**Campion, Thomas** (1567–1620) English poet, composer, and physician. In *Observations in the Art of English Poesie* (1602) he attacked the use of rhyme.

1 Follow thy fair sun, unhappy shadow.

*Follow Thy Fair Sun*

2 There is a garden in her face, Where roses and white lilies grow; A heav'nly paradise is that place, Wherein all pleasant fruits do flow. There cherries grow, which none may buy Till 'Cherry ripe' themselves do cry.

See also HERRICK
*Fourth Book of Airs*

3 The man of life upright, Whose guiltless heart is free From all dishonest deeds Or thought of vanity.

*The Man of Life Upright*

4 Good thoughts his only friends, His wealth a well-spent age, The earth his sober inn And quiet pilgrimage

*The Man of Life Upright*

5 The Summer hath his joys, And Winter his delights. Though Love and all his pleasures are but toys, They shorten tedious nights.

*Now Winter Nights Enlarge*

**Camus, Albert** (1913–60) French existentialist novelist, essayist, and dramatist, born in Algiers. His works include the novels *The Outsider* (1942) and *The Plague* (1947); the play *Caligula* (1944); and *The Myth of Sisyphus* (1942), an essay on the absurd.

1 Alas, after a certain age every man is responsible for his face.

*The Fall*

2 Style, like sheer silk, too often hides eczema.

*The Fall*

3 A single sentence will suffice for modern man: he fornicated and read the papers.

*The Fall*

4 How many crimes committed merely because their authors could not endure being wrong!

*The Fall*

5 No man is a hypocrite in his pleasures.

*The Fall*

**6** Don't wait for the Last Judgement. It takes place every day.
*The Fall*

**7** Politics and the fate of mankind are shaped by men without ideals and without greatness. Men who have greatness within them don't go in for politics.
*Notebooks, 1935–42*

**8** An intellectual is someone whose mind watches itself.
*Notebooks, 1935–42*

**9** The future is the only kind of property that the masters willingly concede to slaves.
*The Rebel*

**10** One cannot be a part-time nihilist.
*The Rebel*

**11** What is a rebel? A man who says no.
*The Rebel*

**12** All modern revolutions have ended in a reinforcement of the power of the State.
*The Rebel*

**13** He who despairs over an event is a coward, but he who holds hopes for the human condition is a fool.
*The Rebel*

**Canetti, Elias** (1905– ) Bulgarian born novelist. His books, all written in German, include *Auto da Fé* and *Crowds and Power*. He won the Nobel Prize for Literature in 1981.

**1** Whenever you observe an animal closely, you feel as if a human being sitting inside were making fun of you.
*The Human Province*

**2** It is important what a man still plans at the end. It shows the measure of injustice in his death.
*The Human Province*

**3** The great writers of aphorisms read as if they had all known each other well.
*The Human Province*

**Canning, George** (1770–1827) British statesman. He was Tory foreign secretary (1807–09, 1822–27) and prime minister for the four months preceding his death.

**1** But of all plagues, good Heaven, thy wrath can send,
Save me, oh, save me, from the candid friend.
*New Morality*

**2** Pitt is to Addington
As London is to Paddington.
*The Oracle*

**3** I called the New World into existence to redress the balance the Old.
*Speech, 12 Dec 1826*

**Capone, Al** (1899–1947) Italian-born US gangster. His gang terrorized the underworld of Chicago until his imprisonment (1931) for tax evasion.

**1** I've been accused of every death except the casualty list of the World War.
*The Bootleggers* (Kenneth Allsop), Ch. 11

**2** This is virgin territory for whorehouses.
Talking about suburban Chicago
*The Bootleggers* (Kenneth Allsop), Ch. 16

**3** They can't collect legal taxes from illegal money.
Objecting to the US Bureau of Internal Revenue claiming large sums in unpaid back tax
*Capone* (J. Kobler)

**Capote, Truman** (1924–84) US novelist. He made his name with *Other Voices, Other Rooms* (1948). Subsequent books include *Breakfast at Tiffany's* (1958) and *Music for Chameleons* (1980).

**1** Venice is like eating an entire box of chocolate liqueurs at one go.
*The Observer*, 'Sayings of the Week', 26 Nov 1961

**Caracciolo, Domenico, Marquis** (1715–89) Governor of Sicily (1781, 1786).

**1** In England there are sixty different religions, and only one sauce.
Attrib.

**Carew, Thomas** (c. 1595–1640) English poet. A diplomat for much of his life, he is remembered for his *Elegy on the Death of Dr Donne* and his love lyrics.

**1** Here lies a King that ruled, as he thought fit, The universal monarchy of wit.
Referring to John Donne
*Elegy on the Death of Dr Donne*

**Carey, Henry** (c. 1690–1743) English poet, musician, and writer of burlesques and farces. *Sally in our Alley* is his best-known work; the words and music of *God Save the King* have also been attributed to him.

**1** God save our Gracious King,
Long live our noble King,
God save the King.
Send him victorious,
Happy and glorious.
*God Save the King*

**2** Of all the days that's in the week
I dearly love but one day –
And that's the day that comes betwixt
A Saturday and Monday.
*Sally in our Alley*

**3** Of all the girls that are so smart
There's none like pretty Sally;
She is the darling of my heart
And she lives in our alley.
*Sally in our Alley*

**Carlyle, Jane Welsh** (1801–66) The wife of Thomas Carlyle. Clearly a writer of some talent, her output was restricted by her difficult life with her husband. Her letters and journal are often witty and stringent.

**1** When one has been threatened with a great injustice, one accepts a smaller as a favour.
*Journal, 21 Nov 1855*

**2** He has his talents, his vast and cultivated mind, his vivid imagination, his independence of soul and his high-souled principles of honour. But then – ah, these Buts! Saint Preux never kicked the fireirons, nor made puddings in his tea cup.
Referring to her husband, Thomas Carlyle
Letter to a friend, July 1821

**3** If they had said the sun and the moon was gone out of the heavens it could not have struck me with the idea of a more awful and dreary blank in the creation than the words: Byron is dead.
Referring to the death of Byron
Letter to Thomas Carlyle, 1824

**4** Medical men all over the world having merely entered into a tacit agreement to call all sorts of maladies people are liable to, in cold weather, by one name; so that one sort of treatment may serve for all, and their practice thereby be greatly simplified.
Letter to John Welsh, 4 Mar 1837

**Carlyle, Thomas** (1795–1881) Scottish historian and essayist. *Sartor Resartus*, a philosophical work, appeared in 1836; his subsequent writings include *The French Revolution* (1837) and *Heroes, Hero-Worship and the Heroic in History* (1841).

**1** A poet without love were a physical and metaphysical impossibility.
*Critical and Miscellaneous Essays*, 'Burns'

**2** A witty statesman said, you might prove anything by figures.
*Critical and Miscellaneous Essays*, 'Chartism'

**3** All reform except a moral one will prove unavailing.
*Critical and Miscellaneous Essays*, 'Corn Law Rhymes'

**4** History is the essence of innumerable biographies.
*Critical and Miscellaneous Essays*, 'History'

**5** A well-written Life is almost as rare as a well-spent one.
*Critical and Miscellaneous Essays*, 'Richter'

**6** Literary men are . . . a perpetual priesthood.
*Critical and Miscellaneous Essays*, 'The State of German Literature'

**7** The three great elements of modern civilization, Gunpowder, Printing, and the Protestant Religion.
*Critical and Miscellaneous Essays*, 'The State of German Literature'

**8** Genius (which means transcendent capacity of taking trouble, first of all).
*Frederick the Great*, Vol. IV, Ch. 3

**9** No great man lives in vain. The history of the world is but the biography of great men.
*Heroes and Hero-Worship*, 'The Hero as Divinity'

**10** The true University of these days is a collection of books.
*Heroes and Hero-Worship*, 'The Hero as Man of Letters'

**11** Burke said that there were Three Estates in Parliament; but, in the Reporters' Gallery yonder, there sat a *Fourth Estate*, more important far than they all.
*Heroes and Hero-Worship*, 'The Hero as Man of Letters'

**12** France was a long despotism tempered by epigrams.
*History of the French Revolution*, Pt. I, Bk. I, Ch. 1

**13** To a shower of gold most things are penetrable.
*History of the French Revolution*, Pt. I, Bk. III, Ch. 7

**14** A whiff of grapeshot.
Describing how Napoleon, early in his career, quelled a minor riot in Paris
*History of the French Revolution*, Pt. I, Bk. V, Ch. 3

**15** The difference between Orthodoxy or My-doxy and Heterodoxy or Thy-doxy.
*History of the French Revolution*, Pt. II, Bk. IV, Ch. 2

**16** The seagreen Incorruptible.
Referring to Robespierre
*History of the French Revolution*, Pt. II, Bk. IV, Ch. 4

**17** The Public is an old woman. Let her maunder and mumble.
*Journal*, 1835

**18** Respectable Professors of the Dismal Science.
Referring to economics
*Latter-Day Pamphlets*, 1

**19** Nature admits no lie.
*Latter-Day Pamphlets*, 5

**20** Captains of industry.
*Past and Present*, Bk. IV, Ch. 4

**21** No man who has once heartily and wholly laughed can be altogether irreclaimably bad.
*Sartor Resartus*, Bk. I, Ch. 4

**22** Be not the slave of Words.
*Sartor Resartus*, Bk I, Ch. 8

**23** Lives there the man that can figure a naked Duke of Windlestraw addressing a naked House of Lords?
*Sartor Resartus*, Bk. I, Ch. 9

**24** Sarcasm I now see to be, in general, the language of the devil.
*Sartor Resartus*, Bk. II, Ch. 4

**25** A good book is the purest essence of a human soul.
Speech made in support of the London Library
*Carlyle and the London Library* (F. Harrison)

**26** If Jesus Christ were to come to-day, people would not even crucify him. They would ask him to dinner, and hear what he had to say, and make fun of it.
*Carlyle at his Zenith* (D. A. Wilson)

**27** Macaulay is well for a while, but one wouldn't *live* under Niagara.
*Notebook* (R. M. Milnes)

**28** The crash of the whole solar and stellar systems could only kill you once.
Letter to John Carlyle, 1831

**29** Work is the grand cure of all the maladies and miseries that ever beset mankind.
Speech, Edinburgh, 2 Apr 1886

**30** I never heard tell of any clever man that came of entirely stupid people.
Speech, Edinburgh, 2 Apr 1886

**31** I don't pretend to understand the Universe – it's a great deal bigger than I am . . . People ought to be modester.
Attrib.

**32** There they are cutting each other's throats, because one half of them prefer hiring their servants for life, and the other by the hour.
Referring to the American Civil War
Attrib.

**33** MARGARET FULLER. I accept the universe.
CARLYLE. Gad! she'd better!
Attrib.

**34** Thirty millions, mostly fools.
When asked what the population of England was
Attrib.

**Carnegie, Dale** (1888–1955) US lecturer and writer. A teacher of public speaking, he also produced a number of books and broadcasts on this and related subjects.

**1** How to Win Friends and Influence People.
Book title

**Carroll, Lewis** (Charles Lutwidge Dodgson; 1832–98) British writer and mathematician; author of the children's classics *Alice's Adventures in Wonderland* (1865) and *Through the Looking-Glass* (1872).

**1** 'What is the use of a book,' thought Alice, 'without pictures or conversation?'
*Alice's Adventures in Wonderland*, Ch. 1

**2** 'Curiouser and curiouser!' cried Alice.
*Alice's Adventures in Wonderland*, Ch. 2

**3** 'You are old, Father William,' the young man said,
'And your hair has become very white;
And yet you incessantly stand on your head –
Do you think at your age, it is right?'
*Alice's Adventures in Wonderland*, Ch. 5

**4** 'If everybody minded their own business,' the Duchess said in a hoarse growl, 'the world would go round a deal faster than it does.'
*Alice's Adventures in Wonderland*, Ch. 6

**5** This time it vanished quite slowly, beginning with the end of the tail, and ending with the grin, which remained some time after the rest of it had gone.
Describing the Cheshire Cat
*Alice's Adventures in Wonderland*, Ch. 6

**6** 'Then you should say what you mean,' the March Hare went on. 'I do,' Alice hastily replied; 'at least – at least I mean what I say – that's the same thing, you know.'
'Not the same thing a bit!' said the Hatter. 'Why, you might just as well say that 'I see what I eat' is the same thing as 'I eat what I see!"
*Alice's Adventures in Wonderland*, Ch. 7

**7** Twinkle, twinkle, little bat!
How I wonder what you're at!
Up above the world you fly!
Like a teatray in the sky.
*Alice's Adventures in Wonderland*, Ch. 7

**8** 'Take some more tea,' the March Hare said to Alice, very earnestly.
'I've had nothing yet,' Alice replied in an offended tone, 'so I can't take more.'
'You mean you can't take *less*,' said the Hatter: 'it's very easy to take *more* than nothing.'
*Alice's Adventures in Wonderland*, Ch. 7

**9** 'Off with his head!'
*Alice's Adventures in Wonderland*, Ch. 8

**10** Everything's got a moral, if only you can find it.
*Alice's Adventures in Wonderland*, Ch. 9

**11** Take care of the sense, and the sounds will take care of themselves.
*Alice's Adventures in Wonderland*, Ch. 9

**12** 'Reeling and Writhing, of course, to begin with,' the Mock Turtle replied; 'and then the different branches of Arithmetic – Ambition, Distraction, Uglification, and Derision.'
*Alice's Adventures in Wonderland*, Ch. 9

**13** 'Will you walk a little faster?' said a whiting to a snail,
'There's a porpoise close behind us, and he's treading on my tail.'
*Alice's Adventures in Wonderland*, Ch. 10

**14** Will you, won't you, will you, won't you, will you join the dance?
*Alice's Adventures in Wonderland*, Ch. 10

**15** Soup of the evening, beautiful Soup!
Said by the Mock Turtle
*Alice's Adventures in Wonderland*, Ch. 10

**16** The Queen of Hearts, she made some tarts,
All on a summer day:
The Knave of Hearts, he stole those tarts,
And took them quite away!
*Alice's Adventures in Wonderland*, Ch. 11

**17** 'Where shall I begin, please your Majesty?' he asked.
'Begin at the beginning' the King said, gravely, 'and go on till you come to the end: then stop.'
*Alice's Adventures in Wonderland*, Ch. 11

**18** 'No, no!' said the Queen. 'Sentence first – verdict afterwards.'
*Alice's Adventures in Wonderland*, Ch. 12

19 For the Snark *was* a Boojum, you see.
*The Hunting of the Snark*

20 'Twas brillig, and the slithy toves
Did gyre and gimble in the wabe;
All mimsy were the borogoves,
And the mome raths outgrabe.
*Through the Looking-Glass,* Ch. 1

21 Now, *here,* you see, it takes all the running *you* can do, to keep in the same place. If you want to get somewhere else, you must run at least twice as fast as that!
*Through the Looking-Glass,* Ch. 2

22 Tweedledum and Tweedledee
Agreed to have a battle;
For Tweedledum said Tweedledee
Had spoiled his nice new rattle.
*Through the Looking-Glass,* Ch. 4

23 'Contrariwise,' continued Tweedledee, 'if it was so, it might be; and if it were so, it would be: but as it isn't, it ain't. That's logic.'
*Through the Looking-Glass,* Ch. 4

24 The Walrus and the Carpenter
Were walking close at hand;
They wept like anything to see
Such quantities of sand:
'If this were only cleared away,'
They said, 'it *would* be grand!'
*Through the Looking-Glass,* Ch. 4

25 'The time has come,' the Walrus said,
'To talk of many things:
Of shoes – and ships – and`sealing-wax –
Of cabbages – and kings –
And why the sea is boiling hot –
And whether pigs have wings.'
*Through the Looking-Glass,* Ch. 4

26 But answer came there none –
And this was scarcely odd because
They'd eaten every one.
*Through the Looking-Glass,* Ch. 4

27 The rule is, jam tomorrow and jam yesterday – but never jam today.
*Through the Looking-Glass,* Ch. 5

28 'They gave it me,' Humpty Dumpty continued thoughtfully, . . . 'for an un-birthday present.'
*Through the Looking-Glass,* Ch. 6

29 'When *I* use a word,' Humpty Dumpty said in rather a scornful tone, 'it means just what I choose it to mean – neither more nor less.'
*Through the Looking-Glass,* Ch. 6

30 He's an Anglo-Saxon Messenger – and those are Anglo-Saxon attitudes.
*Through the Looking-Glass,* Ch. 7

31 It's as large as life, and twice as natural!
*Through the Looking-Glass,* Ch. 7

32 The Lion looked at Alice wearily. 'Are you animal – or vegetable – or mineral?' he said, yawning at every other word.
*Through the Looking-Glass,* Ch. 7

33 'Speak when you're spoken to!' the Red Queen sharply interrupted her.
*Through the Looking-Glass,* Ch. 9

34 'You look a little shy; let me introduce you to that leg of mutton,' said the Red Queen. 'Alice – Mutton; Mutton – Alice.'
*Through the Looking-Glass,* Ch. 9

**Carson, Rachel Louise** (1907–64) US biologist. *The Sea Around Us* (1951) and *Silent Spring* (1962) warned of the dangers of polluting the environment.

1 For all at last return to the sea – to Oceanus, the ocean river, like the ever-flowing stream of time, the beginning and the end.
The closing words of the book
*The Sea Around Us*

2 As cruel a weapon as the cave man's club, the chemical barrage has been hurled against the fabric of life.
*The Silent Spring*

3 Over increasingly large areas of the United States, spring now comes unheralded by the return of the birds, and the early mornings are strangely silent where once they were filled with the beauty of bird song.
*The Silent Spring*

**Carter, Jimmy** (1924– ) US statesman; governor of Georgia (1970–74) and president (1977–81).

1 I'm surprised that a government organization could do it that quickly.
Visiting Egypt, when told that it took twenty years to build the Great Pyramid
*Presidential Anecdotes* (P. Boller)

**Carter, ('Miz') Lillian** (1902– ) The mother of Jimmy Carter (US president, 1977–81).

1 I love all my children, but some of them I don't like.
In *Woman,* 9 Apr 1977

**Cartland, Barbara** (1902– ) British romantic novelist.

1 Of course they have, or I wouldn't be sitting here talking to someone like you.
When asked in a radio interview whether she thought that British class barriers had broken down
*Class* (J. Cooper)

**Cartwright, John** (1740–1824) British writer and supporter of American colonists. He was also a parliamentary reformer and agitated for the abolition of slavery.

1 One man shall have one vote.
*People's Barrier Against Undue Influence*

**Caruso, Enrico** (1873–1921) Italian tenor noted for his singing in the operas of Verdi and Puccini.

1 You know whatta you do when you shit? Singing,
it's the same thing, only up!
*Whose Little Boy Are You?* (H. Brown)

**Cary, (Arthur) Joyce (Lunel)** (1888–1957) British
novelist. *Mister Johnson* (1939), set in West Africa, was followed
by a trilogy about artists, which included his best-known book, *The
Horse's Mouth* (1944).

1 Sara could commit adultery at one end and weep
for her sins at the other, and enjoy both operations at once.
*The Horse's Mouth*, Ch. 8

2 Remember I'm an artist. And you know what
that means in a court of law. Next worst to an
actress.
*The Horse's Mouth*, Ch. 14

**Cary, Phoebe** (1824–71) US poet. Her verse collections
include *Poems of Alice and Phoebe Cary* (1850), compiled in
collaboration with her sister Alice (1820–71).

1 And though hard be the task,
'Keep a stiff upper lip.'
*Keep a Stiff Upper Lip*

**Case, Phila Henrietta** (fl. 1864) British poet.

1 Oh! why does the wind blow upon me so wild? –
It is because I'm nobody's child?
*Nobody's Child*

**Casson, Sir Hugh** (1910– ) British architect. Director of
architecture for the Festival of Britain (1951), his books include
*Victorian Architecture* (1948).

1 The British love permanence more than they
love beauty.
*The Observer*, 'Sayings of the Week', 14 June 1964

**Castling, Harry** (19th cent.) British songwriter.

1 Let's all go down the Strand.
*Song title*

**Caswall, Edward** (1814–78) British hymn writer.

1 Days and moments quickly flying,
Blend the living with the dead;
Soon will you and I be lying
Each within our narrow bed.
*Hymn*

**Cather, Willa (Siebert)** (1873–1947) US writer and poet.

1 The history of every country begins in the heart
of a man or woman.
*O Pioneers!*, Pt. II, Ch. 4

**Catherwood, Mary (Hartwell)** (1847–1901) US writer.

1 Two may talk together under the same roof for
many years, yet never really meet; and two
others at first speech are old friends.
*Mackinac and Lake Stories*, 'Marianson'

**Cato the Elder** (Marcius Porcius C; 234–149 BC) Roman
statesman, orator, and writer. Elected censor in 184 BC, he wrote
on a variety of subjects, notably agriculture and Roman history.

1 Carthage must be destroyed.
*Life of Cato* (Plutarch)

**Catullus, Gaius Valerius** (c. 84–c. 54 BC) Roman poet,
remembered for his love poems addressed to Lesbia and his
satirical attacks on Julius Caesar.

1 For the godly poet must be chaste himself, but
there is no need for his verses to be so.
*Carmina*, XVI

2 *Odi et amo.*
I hate and love.
*Carmina*, LXXXV

3 *Atque in perpetuum, frater, ave atque vale.*
And for ever, brother, hail and farewell!
*Carmina*, CI

**Causley, Charles** (1917– ) British poet and broadcaster.
Publications include *Hands to Dance* (1951), *Johnny Alleluia*
(1961), and *Collected Poems 1951–1975* (1975).

1 Ears like bombs and teeth like splinters:
A blitz of a boy is Timothy Winters.
*Timothy Winters*

**Cavell, Edith (Louisa)** (1865–1915) British nurse. During
World War I she became involved in the escape of Allied soldiers
from Belgium, which led to her execution by the Germans in 1915.

1 I realize that patriotism is not enough. I must
have no hatred or bitterness towards anyone.
*Last words*

**Cawein, Madison Julius** (1865–1914) US poet. Verse
collections include *Lyrics and Idyls* (1890), *Poems of Nature and
Love* (1893), and *Kentucky Poems* (1902).

1 An old Spanish saying is that 'a kiss without a
moustache is like an egg without salt'.
*Nature-Notes*

**Cecil, Lord David** (1902–86) British writer and critic. The
author of biographies of Jane Austen, Thomas Hardy, and Max
Beerbohm, he also wrote *A Portrait of Charles Lamb* (1983).

1 It does not matter that Dickens' world is not life-
like; it is alive.
*Early Victorian Novelists*

**Cervantes (Saavedra), Miguel de** (1547–1616)
Spanish novelist and dramatist; creator of *Don Quixote* (1605;
1615), a satirical romance of chivalry.

1 A silly remark can be made in Latin as well as in
Spanish.
*The Dialogue of the Dogs*

2 Take care, your worship, those things over
there are not giants but windmills.
*Don Quixote*, Pt. I, Ch. 8

3 Didn't I tell you, Don Quixote, sir, to turn back,
for they were not armies you were going to attack, but flocks of sheep?
*Don Quixote*, Pt. I, Ch. 18

**4** The Knight of the Doleful Countenance.

*Sancho Panza describing Don Quixote; sometimes translated as 'knight of the sad countenance'*
*Don Quixote, Pt. I, Ch. 19*

**5** Fear has many eyes and can see things underground.

*Don Quixote, Pt. I, Ch. 20*

**6** A leap over the hedge is better than good men's prayers.

*Don Quixote, Pt. I, Ch. 21*

**7** I have always heard, Sancho, that doing good to base fellows is like throwing water into the sea.

*Don Quixote, Pt. I, Ch. 23*

**8** Let them eat the lie and swallow it with their bread. Whether the two were lovers or no, they'll have accounted to God for it by now. I have my own fish to fry.

*Don Quixote, Pt. I, Ch. 25*

**9** A knight errant who turns mad for a reason deserves neither merit nor thanks. The thing is to do it without cause.

*Don Quixote, Pt. I, Ch. 25*

**10** One shouldn't talk of halters in the hanged man's house.

*Don Quixote, Pt. I, Ch. 25*

**11** She isn't a bad bit of goods, the Queen! I wish all the fleas in my bed were as good.

*Don Quixote, Pt. I, Ch. 30*

**12** In me the need to talk is a primary impulse, and I can't help saying right off what comes to my tongue.

*Don Quixote, Pt. I, Ch. 30*

**13** Every man is as Heaven made him, and sometimes a great deal worse.

*Don Quixote, Pt. II, Ch. 4*

**14** The best sauce in the world is hunger.

*Don Quixote, Pt. II, Ch. 5*

**15** Well, now, there's a remedy for everything except death.

*Don Quixote, Pt. II, Ch. 10*

**16** Never meddle with play-actors, for they're a favoured race.

*Don Quixote, Pt. II, Ch. 11*

**17** He's a muddle-headed fool, with frequent lucid intervals.

*Sancho Panza describing Don Quixote*
*Don Quixote, Pt. II, Ch. 18*

**18** There are only two families in the world, my old grandmother used to say, The *Haves* and the *Have-Nots*.

*Don Quixote, Pt. II, Ch. 20*

**19** A private sin is not so prejudicial in the world as a public indecency.

*Don Quixote, Pt. II, Ch. 22*

**20** Tell me what company thou keepest, and I'll tell thee what thou art.

*Don Quixote, Pt. II, Ch. 23*

**21** Good painters imitate nature, bad ones spew it up.

*El Licenciado Vidriera*

**Chalmers, Patrick Reginald** (1872–1942) British banker and novelist. His novels include *The Golden Bee* and *Prior's Mead*.

**1** What's lost upon the roundabouts we pulls up on the swings!

*Green Days and Blue Days: Roundabouts and Swings*

**Chamberlain, Joseph** (1836–1914) British politician. Having entered parliament as a Liberal in 1876, he came into conflict with Gladstone over Irish Home Rule and transferred his support to the Conservatives.

**1** Provided that the City of London remains as at present, the Clearing-house of the World.

*Speech, Guildhall, London, 19 Jan 1904*

**2** The day of small nations has long passed away. The day of Empires has come.

*Speech, Birmingham, 12 May 1904*

**Chamberlain, (Arthur) Neville** (1869–1940) British statesman; son of Joseph Chamberlain. As Conservative prime minister (1937–40) his negotiations with Hitler preceding World War II led him finally to abandon his policy of appeasement and to declare war on Germany. He died shortly after resigning in favour of Churchill.

**1** In war, whichever side may call itself the victor, there are no winners, but all are losers.

*Speech, Kettering, 3 July 1938*

**2** How horrible, fantastic, incredible, it is that we should be digging trenches and trying on gas-masks here because of a quarrel in a far-away country between people of whom we know nothing.

*Referring to Germany's annexation of the Sudetenland*
*Radio broadcast, 27 Sept 1938*

**3** I believe it is peace for our time . . . peace with honour.

*Broadcast after Munich Agreement, 1 Oct 1938*

**4** Hitler has missed the bus.

*Speech, House of Commons, 4 Apr 1940*

**Chamfort, Nicolas** (1741–94) French writer. He wrote many comedies, essays, and poems, but is best known for his *Maximes et pensées*.

**1** Someone said of a very great egotist: 'He would burn your house down to cook himself a couple of eggs.'

*Caractères et anecdotes*

**2** The most wasted of all days is that on which one has not laughed.

*Maximes et pensées*

**3** Our gratitude to most benefactors is the same as our feeling for dentists who have pulled our teeth. We acknowledge the good they have done and the evil from which they have delivered us, but we remember the pain they occasioned and do not love them very much.
*Maximes et pensées*

**Chandler, John** (1806–76) British clergyman, writer, and translator of Latin hymns. His works include *The Hymns of the Primitive Church* (1837) and *Life of William of Wykeham* (1842).

**1** Conquering kings their titles take.
Poem title

**Chandler, Raymond** (1888–1959) US novelist, famous for his detective stories and thrillers. His detective, Philip Marlowe, first appeared in *The Big Sleep* (1939).

**1** It was a blonde. A blonde to make a bishop kick a hole in a stained-glass window.
*Farewell, My Lovely*, Ch. 13

**2** She gave me a smile I could feel in my hip pocket.
*Farewell, My Lovely*, Ch. 18

**3** Alcohol is like love: the first kiss is magic, the second is intimate, the third is routine. After that you just take the girl's clothes off.
*The Long Good-bye*

**4** Down these mean streets a man must go who is not himself mean; who is neither tarnished nor afraid.
*The Simple Art of Murder*

**5** If my books had been any worse I should not have been invited to Hollywood, and if they had been any better I should not have come.
*The Life of Raymond Chandler* (F. MacShane)

**6** When I split an infinitive, god damn it, I split it so it stays split.
Letter to his English publisher

**Chanel, Coco** (1883–1971) French dress designer.

**1** There goes a woman who knows all the things that can be taught and none of the things that cannot be taught.
*Coco Chanel, Her Life, Her Secrets* (Marcel Haedrich)

**2** Youth is something very new: twenty years ago no one mentioned it.
*Coco Chanel, Her Life, Her Secrets* (Marcel Haedrich)

**3** Wherever one wants to be kissed.
When asked where one should wear perfume
*Coco Chanel, Her Life, Her Secrets* (Marcel Haedrich)

**4** Fashion is architecture: it is a matter of proportions.
*Coco Chanel, Her Life, Her Secrets* (Marcel Haedrich)

**Chaplin, Charlie** (Sir Charles Spencer C.; 1889–1977) British film actor. He developed the character of the pathetic tramp – with baggy trousers, bowler hat, and walking stick – in such films as *The Kid* (1921), *The Gold Rush* (1925), and *Modern Times* (1936).

**1** All I need to make a comedy is a park, a policeman and a pretty girl.
*My Autobiography*

**2** I am for people. I can't help it.
*The Observer*, 'Sayings of the week', 28 Sept 1952

**3** I remain just one thing, and one thing only – and that is a clown.
It places me on a far higher plane than any politician
*The Observer*, 'Sayings of the Week', 17 June 1960

**4** Life is a tragedy when seen in close-up, but a comedy in long-shot.
In *The Guardian*, Obituary, 28 Dec 1977

**Charles, Elizabeth (Rundle)** (1828–96) British writer.

**1** To know how to say what others only know how to think is what makes men poets or sages; and to dare to say what others only dare to think makes men martyrs or reformers – or both.
*Chronicle of the Schönberg-Cotta Family*

**Charles, Hughie** See Parker, Ross.

**Charles Francis Joseph** (1887–1922) Emperor of Austria.

**1** What should I do? I think the best thing is to order a new stamp to be made with my face on it.
On hearing of his accession to emperor
*Anekdotenschatz* (H. Hoffmeister)

**Charles I** (1600–49) King of England, Scotland, and Ireland (1625–49); son of James I. Charles' early reign was marked by conflict with parliament; from 1629 to 1640 he ruled without it. This caused widespread unrest and led finally to the Civil War (1642), culminating in the king's execution.

**1** Never make a defence or apology before you be accused.
Letter to Lord Wentworth, 3 Sept 1636

**2** I die a Christian, according to the Profession of the Church of England, as I found it left me by my Father.
Speech on the scaffold, 30 Jan 1649

**Charles II** (1630–85) King of England, Scotland, and Ireland (1660–85); son of Charles I. Exiled during Cromwell's Protectorate (1653–59), he returned to England at the Restoration of the monarchy in 1660. Charles' Roman Catholic sympathies led to conflict with parliament; anti-Catholic feeling intensified after the Popish Plot of 1678.

**1** Brother, I am too old to go again to my travels.
Referring to his exile, 1651–60
*History of Great Britain (Hume)*, Vol. II, Ch. 7

**2** Not a religion for gentlemen.
Referring to Presbyterianism
*History of My Own Time* (Burnet), Vol. I, Bk. II, Ch. 2

**3** This is very true: for my words are my own, and my actions are my ministers'.
Replying to Lord ROCHESTER's suggested epitaph
*King Charles II* (A. Bryant)

**4** I am sure no man in England will take away my life to make you King.
To his brother James following revelation of Popish Plot fabricated by Titus Oates
Attrib.

**5** Better than a play.
Referring to House of Lords debate on the Divorce Bill
Attrib.

**6** Let not poor Nelly starve.
Referring to Nell Gwynne
Said on his death bed

**7** He had been, he said, a most unconscionable time dying; but he hoped that they would excuse it.
*History of England* (Macaulay), Vol. I, Ch. 4

**Charles V** (1500–58) Holy Roman Emperor (1519–56). Warfare with France and the Turks dominated much of his reign, which also saw the religious struggles of the Reformation: Charles presided at the Diet of Worms (1521) where Luther was condemned.

**1** My cousin Francis and I are in perfect accord – he wants Milan, and so do I.
Referring to his dispute with Francis I of France over Italian territory
*The Story of Civilization* (W. Durant), Vol. 5

**2** I make war on the living, not on the dead.
After the death of Martin Luther, when it was suggested that he hang the corpse on a gallows
Attrib.

**3** I speak Spanish to God, Italian to women, French to men, and German to my horse.
Attrib.

**Charles X** (1757–1836) King of France (1824–30). After the French Revolution, he lived abroad, returning in 1815 with the restoration of the Bourbons. Following his overthrow, he went into exile in England.

**1** I would rather hew wood than be a king under the conditions of the King of England.
*Encyclopaedia Britannica*

**2** There is no middle course between the throne and the scaffold.
Said to Talleyrand, who is said to have replied 'You are forgetting the postchaise'.
Attrib.

**Charles, Prince of Wales** (1948– ) Eldest son of Elizabeth II and heir to the throne of the United Kingdom.

**1** All the faces here this evening seem to be bloody Poms.
Remark at Australia Day dinner, 1973

**2** British management doesn't seem to understand the importance of the human factor.
Speech, Parliamentary and Scientific Committee lunch, 21 Feb 1979

**3** Like a carbuncle on the face of an old and valued friend.
Referring to a proposed modern extension to the National Gallery
Speech, 1986

**Chateaubriand, Vicomte François-René de** (1768–1848) French diplomat and writer. His publications include *Le Génie du Christianisme* (1802) and *Mémoires d'Outre-tombe* (1849).

**1** An original writer is not one who imitates nobody, but one whom nobody can imitate.
*Génie du Christianisme*

**2** One is not superior merely because one sees the world in an odious light.
Attrib.

**Chaucer, Geoffrey** (c. 1342–1400) English poet. *The Canterbury Tales* is a collection of stories told by pilgrims on their way to Canterbury. His other works include the poem *The Book of the Duchess* and *Troilus and Criseyde*.

**1** Whan that Aprille with his shoures sote
The droghte of Marche hath perced to the rote.
*The Canterbury Tales*, Prologue

**2** He was a verray parfit gentil knight.
Referring to the knight
*The Canterbury Tales*, Prologue

**3** He was as fresh as is the month of May.
Referring to the squire
*The Canterbury Tales*, Prologue

**4** Ful wel she song the service divyne,
Entuned in hir nose ful semely.
Referring to the prioress
*The Canterbury Tales*, Prologue

**5** A Clerk ther was of Oxenford also,
That un-to logik hadde longe y-go.
*The Canterbury Tales*, Prologue

**6** As lene was his hors as is a rake.
*The Canterbury Tales*, Prologue

**7** Souninge in moral vertu was his speche,
And gladly wolde he lerne, and gladly teche.
Referring to the clerk
*The Canterbury Tales*, Prologue

**8** No-wher so bisy a man as he ther nas,
And yet he semed bisier than he was.
Referring to the man of law
*The Canterbury Tales*, Prologue

**9** For gold in phisik is a cordial,
Therfore he lovede gold in special.
Referring to the doctor
*The Canterbury Tales*, Prologue

**10** She was a worthy womman al hir lyve,
Housbondes at chirche-dore she hadde fyve,
Withouten other companye in youthe.
Referring to the wife of Bath
*The Canterbury Tales*, Prologue

**11** The smyler with the knyf under the cloke.
*The Canterbury Tales*, 'The Knight's Tale'

**12** This world nis but a thurghfare ful of wo,
And we ben pilgrimes, passinge to and fro;
Deeth is an ende of every worldly sore.
*The Canterbury Tales*, 'The Knight's Tale'

**13** Tragedie is to seyn a certeyn storie,
As olde bokes maken us memorie,
Of him that stood in greet prosperitee
And is y-fallen out of heigh degree
Into miserie, and endeth wrecchedly.

*The Canterbury Tales*, 'The Monk's Prologue'

**14** Whan that the month in which the world bigan,
That highte March, whan God first maked man.

*The Canterbury Tales*, 'The Nun's Priest's Tale'

**15** Mordre wol out, that see we day by day.

*The Canterbury Tales*, 'The Nun's Priest's Tale'

**16** So was hir joly whistle wel y-wet.

*The Canterbury Tales*, 'The Reve's Tale'

**17** That lyf so short, the craft so long to lerne,
Th' assay so hard, so sharp the conquerynge.

*See also* HIPPOCRATES
*The Parliament of Fowls*

**18** For of fortunes sharp adversitee
The worst kinde of infortune is this,
A man to have ben in prosperitee,
And it remembren, what is passed is.

*Troilus and Criseyde*, 3

**19** Go, litel book, go litel myn tragedie.
O moral Gower, this book I directe To thee.

*Troilus and Criseyde*, 5

**Chekhov, Anton Pavlovich** (1860–1904) Russian
dramatist and writer. Plays include *The Seagull* (1896), *Uncle
Vanya* (1897), *The Three Sisters* (1901), and *The Cherry Orchard*
(1904).

**1** LIBOV ANDREEVNA. Are you still a student?
TROFIMOV. I expect I shall be a student to the
end of my days.

*The Cherry Orchard*, I

**2** When a lot of remedies are suggested for a disease, that means it can't be cured.

*The Cherry Orchard*, II

**3** Before the cherry orchard was sold everybody
was worried and upset, but as soon as it was
all settled finally and once for all, everybody
calmed down, and felt quite cheerful.

*The Cherry Orchard*, IV

**4** MEDVEDENKO. Why do you wear black all the
time?
MASHA. I'm in mourning for my life, I'm
unhappy.

*The Seagull*, I

**5** NINA. Your play's hard to act, there are no living
people in it.
TREPLEV. Living people! We should show life
neither as it is nor as it ought to be, but as we
see it in our dreams.

*The Seagull*, I

**6** The time's come: there's a terrific thunder-cloud
advancing upon us, a mighty storm is coming to
freshen us up. . . . It's going to blow away all
this idleness and indifference, and prejudice
against work. . . . I'm going to work, and in
twenty-five or thirty years' time every man and
woman will be working.

*Three Sisters*, I

**7** Man has been endowed with reason, with the
power to create, so that he can add to what he's
been given. But up to now he hasn't been a
creator, only a destroyer. Forests keep disap-
pearing, rivers dry up, wild life's become extinct, the climate's ruined and the land grows
poorer and uglier every day.

*Uncle Vanya*, I

**8** A woman can become a man's friend only in the
following stages – first an acquaintance, next a
mistress, and only then a friend.

*Uncle Vanya*, II

**9** SONYA. I'm not beautiful.
HELEN. You have lovely hair.
SONYA. No, when a woman isn't beautiful, people always say, 'You have lovely eyes, you
have lovely hair.'

*Uncle Vanya*, III

**10** When all is said and done, no literature can outdo the cynicism of real life; you won't intoxicate
with one glass someone who has already
drunk up a whole barrel.

*Letter*, 1887

**Chesterfield, Philip Dormer Stanhope, 4th Earl
of** (1694–1773) English statesman and diplomat; author of the
famous *Letters* (1774) to his illegitimate son. Appointed ambassador
to The Hague in 1728, he subsequently served in Ireland and as
secretary of state (1746–48).

**1** Be wiser than other people if you can, but do not
tell them so.

*Letter to his son, 19 Nov 1745*

**2** Whatever is worth doing at all is worth doing
well.

*Letter to his son, 10 Mar 1746*

**3** An injury is much sooner forgotten than an
insult.

*Letter to his son, 9 Oct 1746*

**4** Take the tone of the company you are in.

*Letter to his son, 9 Oct 1747*

**5** Do as you would be done by is the surest
method that I know of pleasing.

*Letter to his son, 16 Oct 1747*

**6** I knew once a very covetous, sordid fellow, who
used to say, 'Take care of the pence, for the
pounds will take care of themselves.'

Possibly referring to William Lowndes
*Letter to his son, 6 Nov 1747*

7 I recommend you to take care of the minutes: for hours will take care of themselves.

Letter to his son, 6 Nov 1747

8 Advice is seldom welcome; and those who want it the most always like it the least.

Letter to his son, 29 Jan 1748

9 It must be owned, that the Graces do not seem to be natives of Great Britain; and I doubt, the best of us here have more of rough than polished diamond.

Letter to his son, 18 Nov 1748

10 Due attention to the inside of books, and due contempt for the outside, is the proper relation between a man of sense and his books.

Letter to his son, 10 Jan 1749

11 Idleness is only the refuge of weak minds.

Letter to his son, 20 July 1749

12 Women are much more like each other than men: they have, in truth, but two passions, vanity and love; these are their universal characteristics.

Letter to his son, 19 Dec 1749

13 Every woman is infallibly to be gained by every sort of flattery, and every man by one sort or other.

Letter to his son, 16 Mar 1752

14 A chapter of accidents.

Letter to his son, 16 Feb 1753

15 Religion is by no means a proper subject of conversation in a mixed company.

Letter to his godson

16 We, my lords, may thank heaven that we have something better than our brains to depend upon.

Speech, House of Lords
The Story of Civilization (W. Durant), Vol. 9

17 Make him a bishop, and you will silence him at once.

When asked what steps might be taken to control the evangelical preacher George Whitefield
Attrib.

18 When your ladyship's faith has removed them, I will go thither with all my heart.

Said to his sister, Lady Gertrude Hotham, when she suggested he go to a Methodist seminary in Wales to recuperate, recommending the views
Attrib.

19 Give Dayrolles a chair.

Said on his deathbed when visited by his godson, Solomon Dayrolles
Last words

**Chesterton, G(ilbert) K(eith)** (1874–1936) British essayist, novelist, and poet. His detective stories feature the priest Father Brown and his novels include *The Napoleon of Notting Hill* (1904). After conversion to Roman Catholicism (1933) much of his writing was religious.

1 A great deal of contemporary criticism reads to me like a man saying: 'Of course I do not like green cheese: I am very fond of brown sherry.'

All I Survey

2 The modern world . . . has no notion except that of simplifying something by destroying nearly everything.

All I Survey

3 Talk about the pews and steeples
And the cash that goes therewith!
But the souls of Christian peoples . . .
Chuck it, Smith!

Antichrist, or the Reunion of Christendom

4 The strangest whim has seized me . . . After all I think I will not hang myself today.

A Ballade of Suicide

5 'My country, right or wrong' is a thing that no patriot would thing of saying, except in a desperate case. It is like saying 'My mother, drunk or sober.'

The Defendant

6 There is a road from the eye to the heart that does not go through the intellect.

The Defendant

7 The one stream of poetry which is continually flowing is slang.

The Defendant

8 All slang is metaphor, and all metaphor is poetry.

The Defendant

9 The devil's walking parody
On all four-footed things.

The Donkey

10 Fools! For I also had my hour;
One far fierce hour and sweet;
There was a shout about my ears,
And palms before my feet.

The Donkey

11 The rich are the scum of the earth in every country.

The Flying Inn

12 One sees great things from the valley; only small things from the peak.

The Hammer of God

13 The word 'orthodoxy' not only no longer means being right; it practically means being wrong.

Heretics, Ch. 1

14 There is no such thing on earth as an uninteresting subject; the only thing that can exist is an uninterested person.

Heretics, Ch. 1

15 As enunciated today, 'progress' is simply a comparative of which we have not settled the superlative.

Heretics, Ch. 2

**16** We ought to see far enough into a hypocrite to see even his sincerity.
*Heretics*, Ch. 5

**17** Happiness is a mystery like religion, and should never be rationalized.
*Heretics*, Ch. 7

**18** Charity is the power of defending that which we know to be indefensible. Hope is the power of being cheerful in circumstances which we know to be desperate.
*Heretics*, Ch. 12

**19** Carlyle said that men were mostly fools. Christianity, with a surer and more reverend realism, says that they are all fools.
*Heretics*, Ch. 12

**20** A good novel tells us the truth about its hero; but a bad novel tells us the truth about its author.
*Heretics*, Ch. 15

**21** The artistic temperament is a disease that afflicts amateurs.
*Heretics*, Ch. 17

**22** To be clever enough to get all that money, one must be stupid enough to want it.
*The Innocence of Father Brown*

**23** Evil comes at leisure like the disease; good comes in a hurry like the doctor.
*The Man who was Orthodox*

**24** You can only find truth with logic if you have already found truth without it.
*The Man who was Orthodox*

**25** The human race, to which so many of my readers belong.
*The Napoleon of Notting Hill*, Vol. I, Ch. 1

**26** The madman is not the man who has lost his reason. The madman is the man who has lost everything except his reason.
*Orthodoxy*, Ch. 1

**27** The cosmos is about the smallest hole that a man can hide his head in.
*Orthodoxy*, Ch. 1

**28** Reason is itself a matter of faith. It is an act of faith to assert that our thoughts have any relation to reality at all.
*Orthodoxy*, Ch. 3

**29** Mr Shaw is (I suspect) the only man on earth who has never written any poetry.
Referring to George Bernard Shaw
*Orthodoxy*, Ch. 3

**30** All conservatism is based upon the idea that if you leave things alone you leave them as they are. But you do not. If you leave a thing alone you leave it to a torrent of change.
*Orthodoxy*, Ch. 7

**31** Angels can fly because they take themselves lightly.
*Orthodoxy*, Ch. 7

**32** Before the Roman came to Rye or out to Severn strode,
The rolling English drunkard made the rolling English road.
*The Rolling English Road*

**33** Smile at us, pay us, pass us; but do not quite forget.
For we are the people of England, that never have spoken yet.
*The Secret People*

**34** Is ditchwater dull? Naturalists with microscopes have told me that it teems with quiet fun.
*The Spice of Life*

**35** He could not think up to the height of his own towering style.
Speaking of Tennyson
*The Victorian Age in Literature*, Ch. 3

**36** Compromise used to mean that half a loaf was better than no bread. Among modern statesmen it really seems to mean that half a loaf is better than a whole loaf.
*What's Wrong with the World*

**37** Mankind is not a tribe of animals to which we owe compassion. Mankind is a club to which we owe our subscription.
*Daily News*, 10 Apr 1906

**38** Just the other day in the Underground I enjoyed the pleasure of offering my seat to three ladies.
Suggesting that fatness had its consolations
*Das Buch des Lachens* (W. Scholz)

**39** There is nothing the matter with Americans except their ideals. The real American is all right; it is the ideal American who is all wrong.
*New York Times*, 1 Feb 1931

**40** Democracy means government by the uneducated, while aristocracy means government by the badly educated.
*New York Times*, 1 Feb 1931

**41** Education is simply the soul of a society as it passes from one generation to another.
*The Observer*, 'Sayings of the Week', 6 July 1924

**42** I want to reassure you I am not this size, really – dear me no, I'm being amplified by the mike.
At a lecture in Pittsburgh
*The Outline of Sanity: A Life of G. K. Chesterton* (S. D. Dale)

**43** Am in Birmingham. Where ought I to be?
Telegram to his wife during a lecture tour
*Portrait of Barrie* (C. Asquith)

**44** The only way to be sure of catching a train is to miss the one before it.
*Vacances à tous prix*, 'Le Supplice de l'heure' (P. Daninos)

**45** How beautiful it would be for someone who could not read.
Referring to the lights on Broadway
Attrib.

**46** A puritan's a person who pours righteous indignation into the wrong things.
Attrib.

**47** New roads: new ruts.
Attrib.

**Chevalier, Albert** (1861–1923) British music-hall artist. He introduced many popular songs, such as *The Future Mrs. 'Awkins* and *My Old Dutch*.

**1** There ain't a lady livin' in the land
As I'd swop for my dear old Dutch!
*My Old Dutch*

**2** Laugh! I though I should 'ave died,
Knocked 'em in the Old Kent Road.
*Wot Cher* or *Knocked 'em in the Old Kent Road*

**Chevalier, Maurice** (1888–1972) French singer, actor, and entertainer. His films include *Love Me Tonight* (1932) and *Gigi* (1958).

**1** Many a man has fallen in love with a girl in a light so dim he would not have chosen a suit by it.
Attrib.

**2** I prefer old age to the alternative.
Attrib.

**Child, Lydia M.** (1802–80) US abolitionist campaigner.

**1** But men never violate the laws of God without suffering the consequences, sooner or later.
*The Freedmen's Book*, 'Toussaint L'Ouverture'

**2** Not in vain is Ireland pouring itself all over the earth . . . The Irish, with their glowing hearts and reverent credulity, are needed in this cold age of intellect and skepticism.
*Letters from New York*, Vol. I, No. 33, 8 Dec 1842

**3** England may as well dam up the waters from the Nile with bulrushes as to fetter the step of Freedom, more proud and firm in this youthful land.
*The Rebels*, Ch. 4

**Chomsky, Noam** (1928– ) US academic linguist. His *Syntactic Structures* (1957) and *Aspects of the Theory of Syntax* (1965) set out his development of transformational grammar.

**1** Colourless green ideas sleep furiously.
Used by Chomsky to demonstrate that an utterance can be grammatical without having meaning
*Syntactic Structures*

**Chopin, Kate** (1851–1904) US writer.

**1** The voice of the sea speaks to the soul. The touch of the sea is sensuous, enfolding the body in its soft, close embrace.
*The Awakening*, Ch. 6

**2** The past was nothing to her; offered no lesson which she was willing to heed. The future was a mystery which she never attempted to penetrate. The present alone was significant . . .
*The Awakening*, Ch. 15

**3** There are some people who leave impressions not so lasting as the imprint of an oar upon the water.
*The Awakening*, Ch. 34

**Chou En Lai** (1898–1976) Chinese statesman. He became political commissar to the Red Army in 1932. He was prime minister of the People's Republic of China (1949–76) and foreign minister (1949–58).

**1** All diplomacy is a continuation of war by other means.
*Compare* CLAUSEWITZ

**Christie, Dame Agatha** (1891–1976) British detective-story writer. Her detective Hercule Poirot first appeared in *The Mysterious Affair at Styles* (1920). Among her 50 or so other stories are *Murder on the Orient Express* (1934) and *Death on the Nile* (1937). Her play *The Mousetrap* (1952) has had the longest run of any London play (over 35 years).

**1** One doesn't recognize in one's life the really important moments – not until it's too late.
*Endless Night*, Bk. II, Ch. 14

**2** Where large sums of money are concerned, it is advisable to trust nobody.
*Endless Night*, Bk. II, Ch. 15

**3** If one sticks too rigidly to one's principles one would hardly see anybody.
*Toward's Zero*, I

**4** Curious things, habits. People themselves never knew they had them.
*Witness for the Prosecution*

**5** An archaeologist is the best husband any woman can have: the older she gets, the more interested he is in her.
Attrib.

**Chuang Tse** (or Zhuangzi; c. 369–286 BC) Chinese philosopher. The book to which he gave his name has influenced the development of Buddhism.

**1** I do not know whether I was then a man dreaming I was a butterfly, or whether I am now a butterfly dreaming I am a man.
*Chuang Tse* (H. A. Giles), Ch. 2

**Churchill, Charles** (1731–64) British poet. His satirical verse includes *The Rosciad* (1761) and *The Prophecy of Famine* (1763), an attack on the government.

**1** The danger chiefly lies in acting well,
No crime's so great as daring to excel.
*Epistle to William Hogarth*

**2** Be England what she will,
With all her faults, she is my country still.
*The Farewell*

**3** A joke's a very serious thing.
*The Ghost*, Bk. IV

4 Old-age, a second child, by Nature curs'd
With more and greater evils than the first,
Weak, sickly, full of pains; in ev'ry breath
Railing at life, and yet afraid of death.
*Gotham, I*

5 Keep up appearances; their lies the test
The world will give thee credit for the rest.
*Night*

**Churchill, Jennie Jerome** (1854–1921) US-born British
hostess and writer, who married Lord Randolph Churchill in 1874.
She was the mother of Sir Winston Churchill.

1 ALMA. I rather suspect her of being in love with
him.
MARTIN. Her own husband? Monstrous! What a
selfish woman!
*His Borrowed Plumes*

2 ... we owe something to extravagance, for
thrift and adventure seldom go hand in hand. ...

*Pearson's, 'Extravagance'*

3 You seem to have no real purpose in life and
won't realize at the age of twenty-two that for a
man life means work, and hard work if you
mean to succeed. ...
Letter to Winston Churchill, 26 Feb 1897
*Jennie (Ralph G. Martin), Vol. II*

**Churchill, Lord Randolph Henry Spencer** (1849–
95) British Conservative politician; father of Sir Winston Churchill.
He was appointed secretary for India in 1885 and served for a few
months as chancellor of the exchequer (1886).

1 The duty of an opposition is to oppose.
*Lord Randolph Churchill (W. S. Churchill)*

2 I never could make out what those damned dots
meant.
Referring to decimal points
*Lord Randolph Churchill (W. S. Churchill)*

3 Ulster will fight; Ulster will be right.
Letter, 7 May 1886

4 An old man in a hurry.
Referring to Gladstone
Speech, June 1886

**Churchill, Sir Winston Leonard Spencer** (1874–
1965) British statesman and writer, prime minister (1940–45,
1951–55). After service as a war correspondent in the Boer War,
he became first Lord of the Admiralty in World War I and led a
coalition government in World War II. He was celebrated for his
skill as an orator and was the author of several historical books.

1 Well, the principle seems the same. The water
still keeps falling over.
When asked whether the Niagara Falls looked the same as when
he first saw them
*Closing the Ring, Ch. 5*

2 I said that the world must be made safe for at
least fifty years. If it was only for fifteen to

twenty years then we should have betrayed our
soldiers.
*Closing the Ring, Ch. 20*

3 We must have a better word than 'prefabricat-
ed'. Why not 'ready-made'?
*Closing the Ring, Appendix C*

4 The redress of the grievances of the vanquished
should precede the disarmament of the victors.
*The Gathering Storm, Ch. 3*

5 I felt as if I were walking with destiny, and that
all my past life had been but a preparation for
this hour and this trial.
*The Gathering Storm, Ch. 38*

6 I have only one purpose, the destruction of
Hitler, and my life is much simplified thereby. If
Hitler invaded Hell I would make at least a fa-
vourable reference to the Devil in the House
of Commons.
*The Grand Alliance*

7 When you have to kill a man it costs nothing to
be polite.
Justifying the fact that the declaration of war against Japan was
made in the usual diplomatic language
*The Grand Alliance*

8 Before Alamein we never had a victory. After
Alamein we never had a defeat.
*The Hinge of Fate, Ch. 33*

9 By being so long in the lowest form I gained an
immense advantage over the cleverest boys
... I got into my bones the essential structure
of the normal British sentence – which is a noble thing.
*My Early Life, Ch. 2*

10 Headmasters have powers at their disposal with
which Prime Ministers have never yet been
invested.
*My Early Life, Ch. 2*

11 So they told me how Mr Gladstone read Homer
for fun, which I thought served him right.
*My Early Life, Ch. 2*

12 Which brings me to my conclusion upon Free
Will and Predestination, namely – let the reader
mark it – that they are identical.
*My Early Life, Ch. 3*

13 It is a good thing for an uneducated man to read
books of quotations.
*My Early Life, Ch. 9*

14 Everyone threw the blame on me. I have noticed
that they nearly always do. I suppose it is because they think I shall be able to bear it best.
*My Early Life, Ch. 17*

15 Those who can win a war well can rarely make a
good peace and those who could make a good
peace would never have won the war.
*My Early Life, Ch. 26*

**16** I have never seen a human being who more perfectly represented the modern conception of a robot.
Referring to the Soviet statesman Molotov
*The Second World War*

**17** I must point out that my rule of life prescribed as an absolutely sacred rite smoking cigars and also the drinking of alcohol before, after, and if need be during all meals and in the intervals between them.
Said during a lunch with the Arab leader Ibn Saud, when he heard that the king's religion forbade smoking and alcohol
*The Second World War*

**18** In Franklin Roosevelt there died the greatest American friend we have ever known and the greatest champion of freedom who has ever brought help and comfort from the New World to the Old.
*The Second World War*

**19** In war, resolution; in defeat, defiance; in victory, magnanimity; in peace, goodwill.
Epigram used by Sir Edward Marsh after World War II; used as 'a moral of the work' in Churchill's book
*The Second World War*

**20** No one can guarantee success in war, but only deserve it.
*Their Finest Hour*

**21** Wars are not won by evacuations.
Referring to Dunkirk
*Their Finest Hour*

**22** When I look back on all these worries I remember the story of the old man who said on his deathbed that he had had a lot of trouble in his life, most of which had never happened.
*Their Finest Hour*

**23** Peace with Germany and Japan on our terms will not bring much rest. . . . As I observed last time, when the war of the giants is over the wars of the pygmies will begin.
*Triumph and Tragedy*, Ch. 25

**24** Dictators ride to and fro upon tigers which they dare not dismount. And the tigers are getting hungry.
*While England Slept*

**25** In defeat unbeatable; in victory unbearable.
Referring to Viscount Montgomery
*Ambrosia and Small Beer* (E. Marsh), Ch. 5

**26** You may take the most gallant sailor, the most intrepid airman, or the most audacious soldier, put them at a table together – what do you get? *The sum of their fears*.
Talking about the Chiefs of Staffs system, 16 Nov 1943
*The Blast of War* (H. Macmillan), Ch. 16

**27** Don't talk to me about naval tradition. It's nothing but rum, sodomy, and the lash.
*Former Naval Person* (Sir Peter Gretton), Ch. 1

**28** Jellicoe was the only man on either side who could lose the war in an afternoon.
*The Observer*, 'Sayings of the Week', 13 Feb 1927

**29** Everybody has a right to pronounce foreign names as he chooses.
*The Observer*, 'Sayings of the Week', 5 Aug 1951

**30** This is the sort of English up with which I will not put.
The story is that Churchill wrote the comment in the margin of a report in which a Civil Servant had used an awkward construction to avoid ending a sentence with a preposition. An alternative version substitutes 'bloody nonsense' for 'English'.
*Plain Words* (E. Gowers), Ch. 9

**31** Men will forgive a man anything except bad prose.
Election speech, Manchester, 1906

**32** It cannot in the opinion of His Majesty's Government be classified as slavery in the extreme acceptance of the word without some risk of terminological inexactitude.
Speech, House of Commons, 22 Feb 1906

**33** *The Times* is speechless and takes three columns to express its speechlessness.
Referring to Irish Home Rule
Speech, Dundee, 14 May 1908

**34** He is one of those orators of whom it was well said, 'Before they get up they do not know what they are going to say; when they are speaking, they do not know what they are saying; and when they sit down, they do not know what they have said'.
Referring to Lord Charles Beresford
Speech, House of Commons, 20 Dec 1912

**35** The maxim of the British people is 'Business as usual'.
Speech, Guildhall, 9 Nov 1914

**36** Labour is not fit to govern.
Election speech, 1920

**37** I remember, when I was a child, being taken to the celebrated Barnum's circus, which contained an exhibition of freaks and monstrosities, but the exhibit . . . which I most desired to see was the one described as 'The Boneless Wonder'. My parents judged that that spectacle would be too revolting and demoralising for my youthful eyes, and I have waited 50 years to see the boneless wonder sitting on the Treasury Bench.
Referring to Ramsey MacDonald
Speech, House of Commons, 28 Jan 1931

**38** India is a geographical term. It is no more a united nation than the Equator.
Speech, Royal Albert Hall, 18 Mar 1931

**39** We have sustained a defeat without a war.
Speech, House of Commons, 5 Oct 1938

**40** I cannot forecast to you the action of Russia. It is a riddle wrapped in a mystery inside an enigma.
Broadcast talk, 1 Oct 1939

**41** I have nothing to offer but blood, toil, tears and sweat.
On becoming prime minister
Speech, House of Commons, 13 May 1940

**42** Victory at all costs, victory in spite of all terror, victory however long and hard the road may be; for without victory there is no survival.
Speech, House of Commons, 13 May 1940

**43** We shall not flag or fail. We shall fight in France, we shall fight on the seas and oceans, we shall fight with growing confidence and growing strength in the air, we shall defend our island, whatever the cost may be, we shall fight on the beaches, we shall fight on the landing grounds, we shall fight in the fields and in the streets, we shall fight in the hills; we shall never surrender.
Speech, House of Commons, 4 June 1940

**44** This was their finest hour.
Referring to the Dunkirk evacuation
Speech, House of Commons, 18 June 1940

**45** The battle of Britain is about to begin.
Speech, House of Commons, 1 July 1940

**46** Never in the field of human conflict was so much owed by so many to so few.
Referring to the Battle of Britain pilots
Speech, House of Commons, 20 Aug 1940

**47** We are waiting for the long-promised invasion. So are the fishes.
Radio broadcast to the French people, 21 Oct 1940

**48** Give us the tools, and we will finish the job.
Referring to Lend-lease, which was being legislated in the USA
Radio Broadcast, 9 Feb 1941

**49** You do your worst, and we will do our best.
Addressed to Hitler
Speech, 14 July 1941

**50** Do not let us speak of darker days; let us rather speak of sterner days. These are not dark days: these are great days – the greatest days our country has ever lived.
Address, Harrow School, 29 Oct 1941

**51** When I warned them that Britain would fight on alone whatever they did, their Generals told their Prime Minister and his divided Cabinet: 'In three weeks England will have her neck wrung like a chicken.'
Some chicken! Some neck!
Referring to the French Government
Speech, Canadian Parliament, 30 Dec 1941

**52** This is not the end. It is not even the beginning of the end. But it is, perhaps, the end of the beginning.
Referring to the Battle of Egypt
Speech, Mansion House, 10 Nov 1942

**53** I have not become the King's First Minister in order to preside over the liquidation of the British Empire.
Speech, Mansion House, 10 Nov 1942

**54** The Almighty in His infinite wisdom did not see fit to create Frenchmen in the image of Englishmen.
Speech, House of Commons, 10 Dec 1942

**55** There is no finer investment for any community than putting milk into babies.
Radio Broadcast, 21 Mar 1943

**56** There are few virtues which the Poles do nòt possess and there are few errors they have ever avoided.
Speech, House of Commons, 1945

**57** An iron curtain has descended across the Continent.
Address, Westminster College, Fulton, USA, 5 Mar 1946

**58** We must build a kind of United States of Europe.
Speech, Zurich, 19 Sept 1946

**59** Perhaps it is better to be irresponsible and right than to be responsible and wrong.
Party Political Broadcast, London, 26 Aug 1950

**60** To jaw-jaw is better than to war-war.
Speech, Washington, 26 June 1954

**61** They are the only people who like to be told how bad things are – who like to be told the worst.
Referring to the British
Speech, 1921

**62** An appeaser is one who feeds a crocodile – hoping that it will eat him last.
Attrib.

**63** The nation had the lion's heart. I had the luck to give the roar.
Said on his 80th birthday

**Cibber, Colley** (1671–1757) British actor and dramatist. His plays include the comedies *Love's Last Shift* (1696) and *The Careless Husband* (1704).

**1** One had as good be out of the world, as out of the fashion.
*Love's Last Shift*, II

**2** Stolen sweets are best.
*The Rival Fools*, I

**Cicero, Marcus Tullius** (106–43 BC) Roman orator and statesman. Elected consul in 63 BC, he was exiled (58–57 BC) and subsequently opposed Caesar in the civil war. After Caesar's assassination he delivered a famous series of speeches (the *Philippics*) against Mark Antony.

**1** There is nothing so absurd but some philosopher has said it.
*De Divinatione*, II

**2** The good of the people is the chief law.
*De Legibus*, III

**3** *Summum bonum.*
The greatest good.
*De Officiis*, I

**4** *O tempora! O mores!*
What times! What customs!
*In Catilinam,* I

**5** *Cui bono.*
To whose profit.
*Pro Milone,* IV

**Clarke, Arthur C.** (1917– ) British science-fiction writer. His novels include *Childhood's End* (1953) and *2001: A space odyssey* (1968).

**1** When a distinguished but elderly scientist states that something is possible, he is almost certainly right. When he states that something is impossible, he is very probably wrong.
*Profiles of the Future*

**Clarke, John** (fl. 1639) English scholar; author of *Paroemiologia Anglo-Latina* (1639), a collection of English and Latin proverbs.

**1** Home is home, though it be never so homely.
*Paroemiologia Anglo-Latina*

**Clausewitz, Karl von** (1780–1831) Prussian general. His military writings include *Vom Kriege*, which influenced strategy in World War I.

**1** War is the continuation of politics by other means.
The usual misquotation of 'War is nothing but a continuation of politics with the admixture of other means'; *compare* CHOU EN LAI
*Vom Kriege*

**Clay, Henry** (1777–1852) US politician, nicknamed 'the great compromiser (or pacificator)'. He was secretary of state to the Republican president John Quincy Adams (1825–29).

**1** I had rather be right than be President.
*Speech, 1850*

**Clemenceau, Georges** (1841–1929) French statesman. Prime minister (1906–09, 1917–20), he led France to victory at the end of World War I.

**1** America is the only nation in history which miraculously has gone directly from barbarism to degeneration without the usual interval of civilization.
*Attrib.*

**2** War is too important to be left to the generals.
*Attrib.*

**Clemens, Samuel Langhorne** *See* Twain, Mark

**Clive of Plassey, Robert, Baron** (1725–74) British soldier and governor of Bengal. He went to Madras with the East India Company in 1743 and distinguished himself in the Anglo-French conflict: his victory at the Battle of Plassey (1757) helped to establish British supremacy.

**1** By God, Mr Chairman, at this moment I stand astonished at my own moderation!
*Reply during Parliamentary Inquiry, 1773*

**Clough, Arthur Hugh** (1819–61) British poet. His works include *The Bothie of Tober-na-Vuolich* (1848), 'Amours de Voyage' (1858), and 'The Latest Decalogue' (1862).

**1** *Action will furnish belief,* – but will that belief be the true one?
This is the point, you know.
*Amours de voyage,* V

**2** A world where nothing is had for nothing.
*The Bothie of Tober-na-Vuolich,* Bk. VIII, Ch. 5

**3** How pleasant it is to have money.
*Dipsychus,* Bk. I

**4** This world is very odd we see,
We do not comprehend it;
But in one fact we all agree,
God won't, and we can't mend it.
*Dipsychus,* Bk. II

**5** Thou shalt have one God only; who
Would be at the expense of two?
*The Latest Decalogue,* 1

**6** Thou shalt not kill; but needst not strive
Officiously to keep alive.
*The Latest Decalogue,* 11

**7** 'Tis better to have fought and lost,
Than never to have fought at all.
*Peschiera*

**Cobbett, William** (1763–1835) British journalist and writer, editor of the *Political Register* (1802–35). His controversial articles led to imprisonment and temporary exile; on returning to England he compiled his famous *Rural Rides* (1830).

**1** To be poor and independent is very nearly an impossibility.
*Advice to Young Men*

**2** From a very early age, I had imbibed the opinion, that it was every man's duty to do all that lay in his power to leave his country as good as he had found it.
*Political Register,* 22 Dec 1832

**3** But what is to be the fate of the great wen of all?
Referring to London
*Rural Rides*

**Cobden, Richard** (1804–65) British politician. An outstanding orator, he was an advocate of free trade. With John Bright he formed the Anti-Corn Law League.

**1** I believe it has been said that one copy of *The Times* contains more useful information than the whole of the historical works of Thucydides.
*Speech, Manchester, 27 Dec 1850*

**Coborn, Charles** (1852–1945) US songwriter.

**1** Two lovely black eyes,
Oh, what a surprise!
Only for telling a man he was wrong.
Two lovely black eyes!
*Two Lovely Black Eyes*

**Cocks, Sir (Thomas George) Barnett** (1907-  )
British political writer, clerk of the House of Commons 1962-73.

1 A committee is a cul-de-sac down which ideas
are lured and then quietly strangled.

*New Scientist*, 1973

**Cocteau, Jean** (1889-1963) French poet and artist. He
made his name with *Les Enfants terribles* (1929), which he later
(1950) made into a film. His poetry included *L'Ange Heurtebise*
(1925) and he also wrote *Orphée* (1926), a play.

1 A true poet does not bother to be poetical. Nor
does a nursery gardener scent his roses.

*Professional Secrets*

2 Tact consists in knowing how far we may go too
far.

In *Treasury of Humorous Quotations*

**Coke, Desmond** (1879-1931) British writer. His works
include *Sandford of Merton* (1903), *The Golden Key* (1909), and
*The Worm* (1927).

1 All rowed fast but none so fast as stroke.

Popular misquotation, derived from the passage: 'His blade
struck the water a full second before any other ... until ... as
the boats began to near the winning post, his own was dipping
into the water *twice* as often as any other.')
*Sandford of Merton*

**Coke, Sir Edward** (1552-1634) English lawyer and
politician. A lifelong rival of Francis Bacon, he became attorney
general in 1594 and served as chief justice of the King's Bench
under James I (1613-16).

1 The house of every one is to him as his castle
and fortress.

*Semayne's Case*

2 Magna Charta is such a fellow, that he will have
no sovereign.

Speaking on the Lords Amendment to the Petition of Right, 17
May 1628
*Hist. Coll.* (Rushworth), I

**Colby, Frank More** (1865-1925) US editor. His works
included *The New International Encyclopedia* (1900-03).

1 Men will confess to treason, murder, arson,
false teeth, or a wig. How many of them will
own up to a lack of humour?

*Essays*, I

2 I have found some of the best reasons I ever had
for remaining at the bottom simply by looking at
the men at the top.

*Essays*, II

**Coleridge, (David) Hartley** (1796-1849) British poet.
The son of Samuel Taylor Coleridge, he wrote many sonnets and
songs.

1 But what is Freedom? Rightly understood,
A universal licence to be good.

*Liberty*

**Coleridge, Samuel Taylor** (1772-1834) British poet,
chiefly remembered for such works as 'Kubla Khan' (composed in
1797, under the influence of opium) and *The Rime of the Ancient
Mariner* (1798). His *Lyrical Ballads* (1798), written with William
Wordsworth, was extremely influential.

1 He who begins by loving Christianity better than
Truth will proceed by loving his own sect or
church better than Christianity, and end by loving himself better than all.

*Aids to Reflection: Moral and Religious Aphorisms*,

2 If a man could pass through Paradise in a dream,
and have a flower presented to him as a pledge
that his soul had really been there, and if he
found that flower in his hand when he awoke -
Aye, and what then?

*Anima Poetae*

3 The primary imagination I hold to be the living
power and prime agent of all human perception, and as a repetition in the finite mind of the
eternal act of creation in the infinite I AM.

*Biographia Literaria*, Ch. 13

4 The Fancy is indeed no other than a mode of
memory emancipated from the order of time and
space.

*Biographia Literaria*, Ch. 13

5 Nothing can permanently please, which does not
contain in itself the reason why it is so, and not
otherwise.

*Biographia Literaria*, Ch. 14

6 That willing suspension of disbelief for the moment, which constitutes poetic faith.

*Biographia Literaria*, Ch. 14

7 Our myriad-minded Shakespeare.

*Biographia Literaria*, Ch. 15

8 A sight to dream of, not to tell!

*Christabel*, I

9 I may not hope from outward forms to win
The passion and the life, whose fountains are
within.

*Dejection: An Ode*

10 Swans sing before they die - 'twere no bad
thing,
Did certain persons die before they sing.

*Epigram on a Volunteer Singer*

11 On awaking he ... instantly and eagerly wrote
down the lines that are here preserved. At this
moment he was unfortunately called out by a
person on business from Porlock.

*Kubla Khan* (preliminary note)

12 In Xanadu did Kubla Khan
A stately pleasure-dome decree:
Where Alph, the sacred river, ran
Through caverns measureless to man
Down to a sunless sea.

*Kubla Khan*

**13** It was a miracle of rare device,
A sunny pleasure-dome with caves of ice!
*Kubla Khan*

**14** A savage place! as holy and enchanted
As e'er beneath a waning moon was haunted
By woman wailing for her demon-lover!
*Kubla Khan*

**15** And all should cry, Beware! Beware!
His flashing eyes, his floating hair!
Weave a circle round him thrice,
And close your eyes with holy dread,
For he on honey-dew hath fed,
And drunk the milk of Paradise.
*Kubla Khan*

**16** Poetry is not the proper antithesis to prose, but
to science. Poetry is opposed to science, and
prose to metre.
*Lectures and Notes of 1818,* I

**17** Reviewers are usually people who would have
been poets, historians, biographers, . . . if they
could; they have tried their talents at one or at
the other, and have failed; therefore they turn
critics.
*Lectures on Shakespeare and Milton,* I

**18** The faults of great authors are generally excel-
lences carried to an excess.
*Miscellanies,* 149

**19** With Donne, whose muse on dromedary trots,
Wreathe iron pokers into true-love knots.
*On Donne's Poetry*

**20** The most happy marriage I can picture or imagine to myself would be the union of a deaf man
to a blind woman.
*Recollections* (Allsop)

**21** If men could learn from history, what lessons it
might teach us! But passion and party blind our
eyes and the light which experience gives is a
lantern on the stern, which shines only on the
waves behind us!
*Recollections* (Allsop)

**22** It is an ancient Mariner,
And he stoppeth one of three.
'By thy long grey beard and glittering eye,
Now wherefore stopp'st thou me?'
*The Rime of the Ancient Mariner,* I

**23** The Sun came up upon the left,
Out of the sea came he!
And he shone bright, and on the right
Went down into the sea.
*The Rime of the Ancient Mariner,* I

**24** The ice was here, the ice was there,
The ice was all around:
It cracked and growled, and roared and howled,
Like noises in a swound!
*The Rime of the Ancient Mariner,* I

**25** With my cross-bow
I shot the albatross.
*The Rime of the Ancient Mariner,* I

**26** As idle as a painted ship
Upon a painted ocean.
*The Rime of the Ancient Mariner,* I

**27** The fair breeze blew, the white foam flew,
The furrow followed free;
We were the first that ever burst
Into that silent sea.
*The Rime of the Ancient Mariner,* II

**28** Water, water, every where,
And all the boards did shrink;
Water, water, every where,
Nor any drop to drink.
*The Rime of the Ancient Mariner,* II

**29** Alone, alone, all, all alone,
Alone on a wide wide sea!
And never a saint took pity on
My soul in agony.
*The Rime of the Ancient Mariner,* IV

**30** The many men, so beautiful!
And they all dead did lie:
And a thousand thousand slimy things
Lived on; and so did I.
*The Rime of the Ancient Mariner,* IV

**31** The moving Moon went up the sky,
And no where did abide:
Softly she was going up,
And a star or two beside.
*The Rime of the Ancient Mariner,* IV

**32** Oh sleep! it is a gentle thing,
Beloved from pole to pole!
*The Rime of the Ancient Mariner,* V

**33** Quoth he, 'The man hath penance done,
And penance more will do.'
*The Rime of the Ancient Mariner,* V

**34** Like one, that on a lonesome road
Doth walk in fear and dread,
And having once turned round walks on,
And turns no more his head;
Because he knows, a frightful fiend
Doth close behind him tread.
*The Rime of the Ancient Mariner,* VI

**35** No voice; but oh! the silence sank
Like music on my heart.
*The Rime of the Ancient Mariner,* VI

**36** He prayeth well, who loveth well
Both man and bird and beast.
*The Rime of the Ancient Mariner,* VII

**37** He prayeth best, who loveth best
All things both great and small;
For the dear God who loveth us,
He made and loveth all.
*The Rime of the Ancient Mariner,* VII

**38** A sadder and a wiser man,
He rose the morrow morn.
*The Rime of the Ancient Mariner*, VII

**39** I wish our clever young poets would remember
my homely definitions of prose and poetry; that
is, prose = words in their best order; – poetry = the best words in the best order.
*Table Talk*

**40** No mind is thoroughly well organized that is deficient in a sense of humour.
*Table Talk*

**41** What comes from the heart, goes to the heart.
*Table Talk*

**42** The misfortune is, that he has begun to write
verses without very well understanding what
metre is.
Referring to Tennyson
*Table Talk*

**43** To see him act, is like reading Shakespeare by
flashes of lightning.
Referring to Kean
*Table Talk*

**44** Summer has set in with its usual severity.
Quoted in Lamb's letter to V. Novello, 9 May 1826

**45** I believe the souls of five hundred Sir Isaac
Newtons would go to the making up of a Shake-
speare or a Milton.
Letter to Thomas Poole, 23 Mar 1801

**Colette, Sidonie Gabrielle** (1873–1954) French novelist.
Colette's early works, the 'Claudine' stories, were published under
her first husband's pen-name; her later independent novels include
*La Vagabonde* (1910), *Chéri* (1920), and *Gigi* (1944).

**1** Total absence of humour renders life impossible.
*Chance Acquaintances*

**2** When she raises her eyelids it's as if she were
taking off all her clothes.
*Claudine and Annie*

**3** My virtue's still far too small, I don't trot it out
and about yet.
*Claudine at School*

**4** Don't ever wear artistic jewellery; it wrecks a
woman's reputation.
*Gigi*

**5** Don't eat too many almonds; they add weight to
the breasts
*Gigi*

**Collingbourne, William** (d. 1484) English landowner.

**1** The Cat, the Rat, and Lovell our dog
Rule all England under a hog.
The cat was Sir William Catesby; the rat Sir Richard Ratcliffe;
the dog Lord Lovell who had a dog on his chest. The hog refers
to the emblem of Richard III, a wild boar
*Chronicles* (R. Holinshed), III

**Collings, Jesse** (1831–1920) British politician. He was an
active agitator for land reform and later became undersecretary to
the Home Office.

**1** Three acres and a cow.
Slogan used in his land-reform propaganda

**Collingwood, Cuthbert, Baron** (1750–1810) British
admiral. He blockaded Cádiz under Nelson, and took command at
Trafalgar after Nelson's death.

**1** Now, gentlemen, let us do something today
which the world may talk of hereafter.
Said before Trafalgar, 21 Oct 1805
*Correspondence and Memoir of Lord Collingwood* (G. L. Newn-
ham; ed. Collingwood)

**Collingwood, Robin George** (1889–1943) British
philosopher and archaeologist. His books include *The New
Leviathan* (1946) and *The Idea of History* (1946).

**1** So, perhaps, I may escape otherwise than by
death the last humiliation of an aged scholar,
when his juniors conspire to print a volume of
essays and offer it to him as a sign that they now
consider him senile.
*Autobiography*

**Collins, Michael** (1890–1922) Irish nationalist. Imprisoned
for his part in the Easter Rising (1916), he later became finance
minister in the Republican government. He played an important
part in setting up the Irish Free State, but was shot by
republicans who opposed the Anglo-Irish Treaty.

**1** I am signing my death warrant.
Said on signing the agreement with Great Britain, 1921, that es-
tablished some months later.
*Peace by Ordeal* (Longford), Pt. 6, Ch. 1

**Collins, Mortimer** (1827–76) British writer. His novels
include *Sweet Anne Page* (1868); he also wrote poems and a
collection of essays, *The Secret of Long Life* (1871).

**1** A man is as old as he's feeling,
A woman as old as she looks.
*The Unknown Quantity*

**Colman, George, The Elder** (1732–94) British
dramatist. He became famous with his play *The Clandestine
Marriage* (1766).

**1** Love and a cottage! Eh, Fanny! Ah, give me indifference and a coach and six!
*The Clandestine Marriage*, I:2

**Colman, George, The Younger** (1762–1836) British
dramatist and manager of the Haymarket Theatre (1789–1820).
His plays include *The Battle of Hexham* (1789), *The Heir-at-Law*
(1797); and *John Bull* (1803).

**1** Mum's the word.
*The Battle of Hexham*, II:1

**2** Lord help you! Tell'em Queen Anne's dead.
*Heir-at-Law*, I:1

**3** Not to be sneezed at.
*Heir-at-Law*, II:1

**Colton, Charles Caleb** (?1780–1832) British clergyman and writer. *Lacon* (1820), his most famous work, is a collection of aphorisms; he also wrote essays and poems.

1 Men will wrangle for religion; write for it; fight for it; anything but – live for it.
*Lacon, Vol. I*

2 When you have nothing to say, say nothing.
*Lacon, Vol. I*

3 Imitation is the sincerest of flattery.
*Lacon, Vol. I*

4 Examinations are formidable even to the best prepared, for the greatest fool may ask more than the wisest man can answer.
*Lacon, Vol. II*

5 The debt which cancels all others.
*Lacon, Vol. II*

**Compton-Burnett, Dame Ivy** (1892–1969) British novelist. *Pastors and Masters* (1925) was her first successful novel. This was followed by some 16 others, including *Brothers and Sisters* (1929) and *Mother and Son* (1955).

1 Appearances are not held to be a clue to the truth. But we seem to have no other.
*Manservant and Maidservant*

2 There is more difference within the sexes than between them.
*Mother and Son*

3 'She still seems to me in her own way a person born to command,' said Luce . . .
'I wonder if anyone is born to obey,' said Isabel.
'That may be why people command rather badly, that
they have no suitable material to work on.'
*Parents and Children, Ch. 3*

**Confucius** (K'ung Fu-tzu; 551–479 BC) Chinese philosopher, whose sayings are collected in the *Analects*.

1 When you meet someone better than yourself, turn your thoughts to becoming his equal. When you meet someone not as good as you are, look within and examine your own self.
*Analects*

2 Chi Wen Tzu always thought three times before taking action. Twice would have been quite enough.
*Analects*

3 Men's natures are alike; it is their habits that carry them far apart.
*Analects*

4 Study the past, if you would divine the future.
*Analects*

5 Learning without thought is labour lost; thought without learning is perilous.
*Analects*

6 Fine words and an insinuating appearance are seldom associated with true virtue.
*Analects*

7 Have no friends not equal to yourself.
*Analects*

8 When you have faults, do not fear to abandon them.
*Analects*

9 To be able to practise five things everywhere under heaven constitutes perfect virtue . . . gravity, generosity of soul, sincerity, earnestness, and kindness.
*Analects*

10 The superior man is satisfied and composed; the mean man is always full of distress.
*Analects*

11 The people may be made to follow a course of action, but they may not be made to understand it.
*Analects*

12 Recompense injury with justice, and recompense kindness with kindness.
*Analects*

13 The superior man is distressed by his want of ability.
*Analects*

14 What you do not want done to yourself, do not do to others.
*Analects*

**Congreve, William** (1670–1729) British Restoration dramatist, whose comedies include *Love for Love* (1695) and *The Way of the World* (1700). He also wrote a tragedy, *The Mourning Bride* (1697).

1 She lays it on with a trowel.
*The Double Dealer, III:10*

2 See how love and murder will out.
*The Double Dealer, IV:6*

3 I am always of the opinion with the learned, if they speak first.
*Incognita*

4 O fie miss, you must not kiss and tell.
*Love for Love, II:10*

5 I know that's a secret, for it's whispered every where.
*Love for Love, III:3*

6 Music has charms to soothe a savage breast.
*The Mourning Bride, I*

7 Heaven has no rage like love to hatred turned, Nor hell a fury like a woman scorned.
*The Mourning Bride, III*

8 SHARPER. Thus grief still treads upon the heels of pleasure:
Marry'd in haste, we may repent at leisure.
SETTER. Some by experience find those words mis-plac'd:
At leisure marry'd, they repent in haste.
*The Old Bachelor, V:8*

9 Courtship to marriage, as a very witty prologue to a very dull Play.
*The Old Bachelor*, V:10

10 Alack he's gone the way of all flesh.
*Squire Bickerstaff Detected*, attrib.

11 Say what you will, 'tis better to be left than never to have been loved.
*The Way of the World*, II:1

12 Lord, what is a lover that it can give? Why one makes lovers as fast as one pleases, and they live as long as one pleases, and they die as soon as one pleases: and then if one pleases one makes more.
*The Way of the World*, II:4

13 I nauseate walking; 'tis a country diversion, I loathe the country and everything that relates to it.
*The Way of the World*, IV:4

14 I hope you do not think me prone to any iteration of nuptials.
*The Way of the World*, IV:12

15 O, she is the antidote to desire.
*The Way of the World*, IV:14

**Connell, James** (1852–1929) British socialist; author of *The Red Flag* and other socialist songs and poems.

1 The people's flag is deepest red;
It shrouded oft our martyred dead,
And ere their limbs grew stiff and cold,
Their heart's blood dyed its every fold.
Then raise the scarlet standard high!
Within its shade we'll live or die.
Tho' cowards flinch and traitors sneer,
We'll keep the red flag flying here.
Traditionally sung at the close of annual conferences of the British Labour Party
*The Red Flag*, in *Songs that made History* (H. E. Piggot), Ch. 6

**Connolly, Cyril (Vernon)** (1903–74) British journalist and writer. A contributor to the *New Statesman*, the *Sunday Times*, and other papers, he published several collections of essays, such as *Enemies of Promise* (1938).

1 It is closing time in the gardens of the West.
*The Condemned Playground*

2 A great writer creates a world of his own and his readers are proud to live in it. A lesser writer may entice them in for a moment, but soon he will watch them filing out.
*Enemies of Promise*, Ch. 1

3 The ape-like virtues without which no one can enjoy a public school.
*Enemies of Promise*, Ch. 1

4 Literature is the art of writing something that will be read twice; journalism what will be grasped at once.
*Enemies of Promise*, Ch. 3

5 An author arrives at a good style when his language performs what is required of it without shyness.
*Enemies of Promise*, Ch. 3

6 As repressed sadists are supposed to become policemen or butchers so those with irrational fear of life become publishers.
*Enemies of Promise*, Ch. 3

7 Whom the gods wish to destroy they first call promising.
*Enemies of Promise*, Ch. 3

8 There is no more sombre enemy of good art than the pram in the hall.
*Enemies of Promise*, Ch. 3

9 All charming people have something to conceal, usually their total dependence on the appreciation of others.
*Enemies of Promise*, Ch. 16

10 I have always disliked myself at any given moment; the total of such moments is my life.
*Enemies of Promise*, Ch. 18

11 Boys do not grow up gradually. They move forward in spurts like the hands of clocks in railway stations.
*Enemies of Promise*, Ch. 18

12 The only way for writers to meet is to share a quick pee over a common lamp-post.
*The Unquiet Grave*

13 Life is a maze in which we take the wrong turning before we have learnt to walk.
*The Unquiet Grave*

14 In the sex-war thoughtlessness is the weapon of the male, vindictiveness of the female.
*The Unquiet Grave*

15 There is no fury like an ex-wife searching for a new lover.
*The Unquiet Grave*

16 Imprisoned in every fat man a thin one is wildly signalling to be let out.
Similar sentiments have been stated by others. *See* AMIS, ORWELL.
*The Unquiet Grave*

17 Better to write for yourself and have no public, than write for the public and have no self.
*Turnstile One* (ed. V. S. Pritchett)

18 The man who is master of his passions is Reason's slave.
*Turnstile One* (ed. V. S. Pritchett)

**Conrad, Joseph** (Teodor Josef Konrad Korzeniowski; 1857–1924) Polish-born British novelist. His 20 years at sea provided the background for most of his novels and stories, notably *The Nigger of the Narcissus* (1897) and *Lord Jim* (1900).

1 Exterminate all brutes.
*Heart of Darkness*

2 The horror! The horror!
*Heart of Darkness*

**3** Mistah Kurtz – he dead.

*Heart of Darkness*

**4** You shall judge of a man by his foes as well as by his friends.

*Lord Jim*, Ch. 34

**5** A work that aspires, however humbly, to the condition of art should carry its justification in every line.

*The Nigger of the Narcissus*, Preface

**6** The terrorist and the policeman both come from the same basket.

*The Secret Agent*, Ch. 4

**7** The belief in a supernatural source of evil is not necessary; men alone are quite capable of every wickedness.

*Under Western Eyes*, Part 2

**8** I remember my youth and the feeling that will never come back any more – the feeling that I could last for ever, outlast the sea, the earth, and all men; the deceitful feeling that lures us on to perils, to love, to vain effort – to death . . .

*Youth*

**9** This could have occurred nowhere but in England, where men and sea interpenetrate, so to speak.

*Youth*

**Conran, Shirley** (1932– ) Designer and journalist. Formerly married (1955–62) to Sir Terence Conran, her books include *Superwoman* (1975), *Action Woman* (1979), and the novel *Lace* (1982).

**1** Our motto: Life is too short to stuff a mushroom.

*Superwoman*, Epigraph

**2** I make no secret of the fact that I would rather lie on a sofa than sweep beneath it. But you have to be efficient if you're going to be lazy.

*Superwoman*, 'The Reason Why'

**Constable, John** (1776–1837) British landscape painter, who specialized in paintings of the Suffolk countryside.

**1** There is nothing ugly; *I never saw an ugly thing in my life:* for let the form of an object be what it may, – light, shade, and perspective will always make it beautiful.

Letter to John Fisher, 23 Oct 1821

**Cook, A(rthur) J(ames)** (1885–1931) British trade-union leader. He was influential in bringing the miners out on strike in 1926, which led to the General Strike.

**1** Not a penny off the pay; not a minute on the day.

Slogan used in the miners' strike, 1925

**Cook, Peter** (1937– ) British writer and entertainer. He made his name in the revue *Beyond The Fringe* (1959) and has since appeared in many plays and revues, especially with Dudley Moore.

**1** I am very interested in the Universe – I am specializing in the universe and all that surrounds it.

*Beyond the Fringe*

**2** You know, I go to the theatre to be entertained . . . I don't want to see plays about rape, sodomy and drug addiction . . . I can get all that at home.

*The Observer*, caption to cartoon, 8 July 1962

**Coolidge, (John) Calvin** (1872–1933) 30th president of the USA (1923–29). A Republican, he served as governor of Massachusetts and as vice-president to Warren G. Harding before succeeding to the presidency.

**1** The business of America is business.

Speech, Washington, 17 Jan 1925

**2** There is no right to strike against the public safety by anybody, anywhere, any time.

Referring to the Boston police strike
Remark, 14 Sept 1919

**3** He said he was against it.

Reply when asked what a clergyman had said regarding sin in his sermon
Attrib.

**Cooper, James Fenimore** (1789–1851) US novelist. His works include *The Pioneers* (1823), *The Last of the Mohicans* (1826), and *The Pathfinder* (1840).

**1** The Last of the Mohicans.

Title of Novel

**Corbusier, Le.** *See* Le Corbusier.

**Coren, Alan** (1938– ) British humorist and writer. He has been editor of *Punch* and columnist in a number of national papers. Books include *All Except The Bastard* (1969), *Golfing for Cats* (1975), and *The Lady from Stalingrad Mansions* (1977).

**1** No visit to Dove Cottage, Grasmere, is complete without examining the outhouse where Hazlitt's father, a Unitarian minister of strong liberal views, attempted to put his hand up Dorothy Wordsworth's skirt.

*All Except the Bastard*, 'Bohemia'

**2** The Act of God designation on all insurance policies; which means, roughly, that you cannot be insured for the accidents that are most likely to happen to you.

*The Lady from Stalingrad Mansions*, 'A Short History of Insurance'

**3** They are short, blue-vested people who carry their own onions when cycling abroad, and have a yard which is 3.37 inches longer than other people's.

*The Sanity Inspector*, 'All You Need to Know about Europe'

**4** Apart from cheese and tulips, the main product of the country is advocaat, a drink made from lawyers.

Referring to Holland
*The Sanity Inspector*, 'All You Need to Know about Europe'

5 Since both its national products, snow and chocolate, melt, the cuckoo clock was invented solely in order to give tourists something solid to remember it by.
Referring to Switzerland
*The Sanity Inspector,* 'And Though They Do Their Best'

6 Television is more interesting than people. If it were not, we should have people standing in the corners of our rooms.
In *The Times*

**Corneille, Pierre** (1606–84) French dramatist; a pioneer of such French tragedies as *Le Cid* (1636–37), *Horace* (1640), *Cinna* (1641), and *Polyeucte* (1641–42).

1 Do your duty and leave the rest to the Gods.
*Horace,* II:8

2 We triumph without glory when we conquer without danger.
*Le Cid,* II:2

3 The manner of giving is worth more than the gift.
*Le Menteur,* I:1

4 A good memory is needed after one has lied.
*Le Menteur,* IV:5

5 One often calms one's grief by recounting it.
*Polyeucte,* I:3

**Cornford, F. M.** (1886–1960) British poet, best known for the poem 'To a Fat Lady Seen from a Train'.

1 O fat white woman whom nobody loves,
Why do you walk through the fields in gloves . . .
Missing so much and so much?
*To a Fat Lady Seen from a Train*

2 Propaganda is that branch of the art of lying which consists in nearly deceiving your friends without quite deceiving your enemies.
*New Statesman,* 15 Sept 1978

**Cornuel, Anne-Marie Bigot de** (1605–94) French society hostess and courtier of Louis XIV. Her salon was frequented by the most influential people in France.

1 No man is a hero to his valet.
*Lettres de Mlle Aïssé,* 13 Aug 1728

**Cory, William Johnson** (1823–92) British schoolmaster and poet. His verse collections include *Ionica* (1858).

1 Jolly boating weather,
And a hay harvest breeze,
Blade on the feather,
Shade off the trees
Swing, swing together
With your body between your knees.
*Eton Boating Song*

**Coubertin, Pierre de, Baron** (1863–1937) French educator and sportsman. He revived the Olympic Games in 1894 and was president of the International Olympic Committee (1894–1925). The first modern Games were held in 1896 at Athens.

1 The most important thing in the Olympic Games is not winning but taking part . . . The essential thing in life is not conquering but fighting well.
Speech, Banquet to Officials of Olympic Games, London, 24 July 1908

**Coué, Émile** (1857–1920) French doctor and advocate of autosuggestion. Originally a pharmacist, he studied hypnotism and developed the psychotherapy known as Couéism.

1 Every day, in every way, I am getting better and better.
Formula for a cure by autosuggestion

**Cousin, Victor** (1792–1867) French philosopher. He was director of the École Normale and minister of public instruction (from 1840); his books include studies of Pascal and Kant.

1 Art for art's sake.
Lecture, Sorbonne, 1818

**Coward, Sir Noël** (1899–1973) British actor, dramatist, and songwriter. After his first success, *The Vortex* (1924), he wrote a number of comedies, including *Blithe Spirit* (1941) and *Brief Encounter* (1946), both made into films. His songs include *Mad Dogs and Englishmen*.

1 We have no reliable guarantee that the afterlife will be any less exasperating than this one, have we?
*Blithe Spirit,* I

2 Never mind, dear, we're all made the same, though some more than others.
*The Café de la Paix*

3 There's always something fishy about the French.
*Conversation Piece,* I:6

4 Dance, dance, dance little lady.
*Title of song*

5 Don't let's be beastly to the Germans.
*Title of song*

6 Don't put your daughter on the stage, Mrs Worthington.
*Title of song*

7 Everybody was up to something, especially, of course, those who were up to nothing.
*Future Indefinite*

8 Sunburn is very becoming – but only when it is even – one must be careful not to look like a mixed grill.
*The Lido Beach*

9 Mad about the boy.
*Title of song*

10 Mad dogs and Englishmen go out in the mid-day sun.
*Title of song*

11 And though the Van Dycks have to go
And we pawn the Bechstein grand,
We'll stand by the Stately Homes of England.
*Operette,* 'The Stately Homes of England'

12 The Stately Homes of England
How beautiful they stand,
To prove the upper classes
Have still the upper hand.
*Operette, 'The Stately Homes of England'*

13 Poor Little Rich Girl.
*Title of song*

14 Very flat, Norfolk.
*Private Lives*

15 Strange how potent cheap music is.
*Private Lives*

16 Certain women should be struck regularly, like gongs.
*Private Lives* ·

17 She refused to begin the 'Beguine'
Tho' they besought her to
And with language profane and obscene
She curs'd the man who taught her to
She curs'd Cole Porter too!
*Sigh No More, 'Nina'*

18 Twentieth-Century Blues.
*Title of song*

19 I've over-educated myself in all the things I shouldn't have known at all.
*Wild Oats*

20 Work is much more fun than fun.
*The Observer, 'Sayings of the Week', 21 June 1963*

21 Dear 338171 (May I call you 338?).
Starting a letter to T. E. Lawrence who had retired from public life to become Aircraftsman Brown, 338171
*Letters to T. E. Lawrence*

22 I never realized before that Albert married beneath him.
After seeing a certain actress in the role of Queen Victoria
*Tynan on Theatre* (K. Tynan)

**Cowley, Abraham** (1618–67) English poet. A royalist secret agent in England, he wrote a metaphysical verse, which was published in *The Mistress* (1647) and other collections. He also published *Pindaric Odes* (1656).

1 God the first garden made, and the first city Cain.
*The Garden*

2 Life is an incurable disease.
*To Dr Scarborough*

**Cowper, William** (1731–1800) British poet. A lawyer and commissioner of bankrupts, his life was dogged by depression, bouts of insanity, and suicide attempts. His ballad *John Gilpin's Ride* (1783) and the long poem *The Task* (1785) established his reputation; he also translated Homer.

1 Regions Caesar never knew
Thy posterity shall sway,
Where his eagles never flew,
None invincible as they.
*Boadicea*

2 When the British warrior queen,
Bleeding from the Roman rods,
Sought, with an indignant mien,
Counsel of her country's gods.
*Boadicea*

3 Rome shall perish – write that word
In the blood that she has spilt.
*Boadicea*

4 We perish'd, each alone:
But I beneath a rougher sea,
And whelm'd in deeper gulphs than he.
*The Castaway*

5 He found it inconvenient to be poor.
*Charity*

6 Absence from whom we love is worse than death.
*Hope, like the Short-lived Ray*

7 John Gilpin was a citizen
Of credit and renown,
A train-band captain eke was he
Of famous London town.
*John Gilpin*

8 To-morrow is our wedding-day,
And we will then repair
Unto the Bell at Edmonton,
All in a chaise and pair.
*John Gilpin*

9 Now let us sing, Long live the king,
And Gilpin, long live he;
And when he next doth ride abroad,
May I be there to see!
*John Gilpin*

10 My hat and wig will soon be here,
They are upon the road.
*John Gilpin*

11 Says John, It is my wedding-day,
And all the world would stare,
If wife should dine at Edmonton,
And I should dine at Ware.
*John Gilpin*

12 What peaceful hours I once enjoyed!
How sweet their memory still!
But they have left an aching void
The world can never fill.
*Olney Hymns, 1*

13 Prayer makes the Christian's armour bright;
And Satan trembles when he sees
The weakest saint upon his knees.
*Olney Hymns, 29*

14 I seem forsaken and alone,
I hear the lion roar;
And every door is shut but one,
And that is Mercy's door.
*Olney Hymns, 33*

15 God moves in a mysterious way
His wonders to perform;
He plants his footsteps in the sea,
And rides upon the storm.
*Olney Hymns, 35*

16 The bud may have a bitter taste,
But sweet will be the flower.
*Olney Hymns, 35*

17 The poplars are felled, farewell to the shade,
And the whispering sound of the cool colonnade!
*The Poplar Field*

18 Mortals, whose pleasures are their only care,
First wish to be imposed on, and then are.
*The Progress of Error*

19 For 'tis a truth well known to most,
That whatsoever thing is lost –
We seek it, ere it come to light,
In every cranny but the right.
*The Retired Cat*

20 God made the country, and man made the town.
*The Task*

21 England, with all thy faults, I love thee still,
My country.
*The Task*

22 Variety's the very spice of life
That gives it all its flavour.
*The Task*

23 While the bubbling and loud-hissing urn
Throws up a steamy column, and the cups,
That cheer but not inebriate, wait on each,
So let us welcome peaceful evening in.
*The Task*

24 Nature is but a name for an effect
Whose cause is God.
*The Task*

25 Oh for a lodge in some vast wilderness,
Some boundless contiguity of shade,
Where rumour of oppression and deceit,
Of unsuccessful or successful war,
Might never reach me more!
*The Task*

26 Mountains interposed
Make enemies of nations, who had else,
Like kindred drops, been mingled into one.
*The Task*

27 Slaves cannot breathe in England; if their lungs
Receive our air, that moment they are free;
They touch our country, and their shackles fall.
A situation resulting from a judicial decision in 1772
*The Task*

28 Riches have wings, and grandeur is a dream.
*The Task*

29 Detested sport,
That owes its pleasures to another's pain.
*The Task*

30 Knowledge dwells
In heads replete with thoughts of other men;
Wisdom in minds attentive to their own.
*The Task*

31 Society, friendship, and love,
Divinely bestowed upon man,
Oh, had I the wings of a dove,
How soon would I taste you again!
*Verses supposed to be written by Alexander Selkirk*

32 I am monarch of all I survey,
My right there is none to dispute;
From the centre all round to the sea
I am lord of the fowl and the brute.
Oh, solitude! where are the charms
That sages have seen in thy face?
Better dwell in the midst of alarms,
Than reign in this horrible place.
*Verses supposed to be written by Alexander Selkirk*

**Crabbe, George** (1754 – 1832) British poet and clergyman.
His reputation was established by *The Village* (1783); other
writings, include *The Borough* (1810).

1 Books cannot always please, however good;
Minds are not ever craving for their food.
*The Borough,* 'Schools'

2 The ring so worn, as you behold,
So thin, so pale, is yet of gold.
*His Mother's Wedding Ring*

3 Oh! rather give me commentators plain,
Who with no deep researches vex the brain;
Who from the dark and doubtful love to run,
And hold their glimmering tapers to the sun.
*The Parish Register,* 'Baptisms'

**Craig, Sir (Edward Henry) Gordon** (1872 – 1966)
British actor and stage designer. The son of Ellen Terry, he
joined Henry Irving's company at the Lyceum as a child actor. He
opened an acting school in Florence and founded the theatrical
magazine *The Mask.*

1 Farce is the essential theatre. Farce refined becomes high comedy: farce brutalized becomes
tragedy.
*The Story of my Days, Index*

**Crane, Stephen** (1871 – 1900) US writer. His *Maggie, A Girl
of the Streets* (1893) was followed by the successful war novel *The
Red Badge of Courage* (1895).

1 The Red Badge of Courage.
*Title of novel*

**Cranmer, Thomas** (1489 – 1556) English churchman. For
supporting Henry VIII in his divorce dispute with the pope, he was
made Archbishop of Canterbury, in which position he introduced an
English Bible (1538) and two Prayer Books (1549 and 1552).
However, under Queen Mary he was burnt at the stake as a
heretic.

1 This hand hath offended.
*Memorials of Cranmer* (Strype)

**Creighton, Mandell** (1843 – 1901) British churchman. First
editor of the *English Historical Review* (1886 – 91), he became
Bishop of Peterborough (1891) and then of London (1897).

1 No people do so much harm as those who go about doing good.
*Life*

**Crisp, Quentin** (?1910– ) Model, publicist, and writer. He first attracted attention with his book *The Naked Civil Servant* (1968).

1 If any reader of this book is in the grip of some habit of which he is deeply ashamed, I advise him not to give way to it in secret but to do it on television. No-one will pass him with averted gaze on the other side of the street. People will cross the road at the risk of losing their own lives in order to say 'We saw you on the telly'.
*How to Become a Virgin*

2 The young always have the same problem – how to rebel and conform at the same time. They have now solved this by defying their parents and copying one another.
*The Naked Civil Servant*

3 Keeping up with the Joneses was a full-time job with my mother and father. It was not until many years later when I lived alone that I realized how much cheaper it was to drag the Joneses down to my level.
*The Naked Civil Servant*

4 There was no need to do any housework at all. After the first four years the dirt doesn't get any worse.
*The Naked Civil Servant*

5 Tears were to me what glass beads are to African traders.
*The Naked Civil Servant*

6 Vice is its own reward.
*The Naked Civil Servant*

7 I became one of the stately homos of England.
*The Naked Civil Servant*

8 I don't hold with abroad and think that foreigners speak English when our backs are turned.
*The Naked Civil Servant*

9 The . . . problem which confronts homosexuals is that they set out to win the love of a 'real' man. If they succeed, they fail. A man who 'goes with' other men is not what they would call a real man.
*The Naked Civil Servant*

10 The idea that He would take his attention away from the universe in order to give me a bicycle with three speeds is just so unlikely I can't go along with it.
*The Sunday Times*, 18 Dec 1977

**Croce, Benedetto** (1866–1952) Italian philospher. His system was published in *Philosophy of Mind* (1910) and several other books. He became minister of public instruction (1920–21).

1 Art is ruled uniquely by the imagination.
*Esthetic*, Ch. 1

**Croker, John Wilson** (1780–1857) British Tory politician, born in Ireland. He attacked Keats' *Endymion* in the *Quarterly Review* and edited Boswell's *Life of Johnson* (1831).

1 A game which a sharper once played with a dupe, entitled 'Heads I win, tails you lose.'
*Croker Papers*

2 We now are, as we always have been, decidedly and conscientiously attached to what is called the Tory, and which might with more propriety be called the Conservative, party.
The first use of the term 'Conservative Party'
In *Quarterly Review*, Jan 1830

**Crompton, Richmal** ((Richmal Crompton Lamburn; 1890–1969)) British writer of children's books. Her first of many William books, *Just William*, appeared in 1922.

1 Violet Elizabeth dried her tears. She saw that they were useless and she did not believe in wasting her effects. 'All right,' she said calmly, 'I'll thcream then. I'll thcream, an' thcream, an' thcream till I'm thick.'
Violet Elizabeth Bott, a minor character in the *William* books, had both a lisp and an exceptional ability to get her own way
*Just William*

**Cromwell, Oliver** (1599–1658) English soldier and statesman. As a leader of the parliamentary army, he was largely responsible for Charles I's defeat in the Civil War. After the king's execution, as Lord Protector of England (1653–58) he failed to find a constitutional basis for ruling the country.

1 Mr Lely, I desire you would use all your skill to paint my picture truly like me, and not flatter me at all; but remark all these roughnesses, pimples, warts, and everything as you see me, otherwise I will never pay a farthing for it.
The origin of the expression 'warts and all'
*Anecdotes of Painting* (Horace Walpole), Ch. 12

2 I beseech you, in the bowels of Christ, think it possible you may be mistaken.
Letter to the General Assembly of the Church of Scotland, 3 Aug 1650

3 What shall we do with this bauble? There, take it away.
Speech dismissing Parliament, 20 Apr 1653

4 It is not fit that you should sit here any longer! . . . you shall now give place to better men.
Speech to the Rump Parliament, 22 Jan 1655

5 The State, in choosing men to serve it, takes no notice of their opinions. If they be willing faithfully to serve it, that satisfies.
Said before the Battle of Marston Moor, 2 July 1644

6 The people would be just as noisy if they were going to see me hanged.
Referring to a cheering crowd

**Crosby, Bing** ((Harry Lillis Crosby; 1904–77)) US singer and crooner. Immensely popular, he made many films, often with Bob Hope.

**1** There is nothing in the world I wouldn't do for Hope, and there is nothing he wouldn't do for me . . . We spend our lives doing nothing for each other.
Referring to Bob Hope
*The Observer*, 'Sayings of the Week', 7 May 1950

**cummings, e(dward) e(stlin)** (1894–1962) US poet. His verse relied to some extent on typographical devices. Collections include *Tulips and Chimneys* (1923) and *Eimi* (1933).

**1** who knows if the moon's
a balloon, coming out of a keen city
in the sky – filled with pretty people?
Used for the title and epigraph of David Niven's first volume of autobiography, *The Moon's a Balloon*, about his experiences in the film industry
&

**2** a pretty girl who naked is
is worth a million statues.
*Collected Poems*, 133

**3** a politician is an arse upon which everyone has sat except a man
*A Politician*

**Curie, Marie** (1867–1934) Polish chemist, who emigrated to France in 1891 and pioneered research into radioactivity. With her husband Pierre Curie she also discovered radium and polonium; she won the Nobel Prize in 1903 and 1911.

**1** After all, science is essentially international, and it is only through lack of the historical sense that national qualities have been attributed to it.
*Memorandum*, 'Intellectual Co-operation'

**2** All my life through, the new sights of Nature made me rejoice like a child.
*Pierre Curie*

**3** I have no dress except the one I wear every day. If you are going to be kind enough to give me one, please let it be practical and dark so that I can put it on afterwards to go to the laboratory.
Referring to a wedding dress
Letter to a friend, 1849

**4** One never notices what has been done; one can only see what remains to be done. . . .
Letter to her brother, 18 Mar 1894

**Curran, John Philpot** (1750–1817) Irish judge. A Protestant, he sought Catholic emancipation and defended the leaders of the insurrection of 1798.

**1** The condition upon which God hath given liberty to man is eternal vigilance.
Speech on the Right of Election of Lord Mayor of Dublin, 10 July 1790

**Curtiz, Michael** (1888–1962) Hungarian-born US film director. He made many films in Europe before settling in Hollywood, where he made a string of films ranging from *Mammy* (1930) to *Casablanca* (1942).

**1** Bring on the empty horses!
Said during the filming of *The Charge of the Light Brigade*. Curtiz, who was not noted for his command of English grammar, meant 'riderless horses'. When people laughed at his order he became very angry, shouting, 'You think I know fuck-nothing, when I know fuck-all!' David Niven used the remark as the title of his second volume of autobiography about his experiences in the film industry.
*Bring on the Empty Horses* (David Niven)

**Curzon, George Nathaniel, Marquess** (1859–1925) British politician. He was viceroy of India (1898–1905) and became Lord Privy Seal in World War I. After the war he was foreign secretary (1919–20).

**1** Not even a public figure. A man of no experience. And of the utmost insignificance.
Referring to Stanley Baldwin on his appointment as Prime Minister
*Curzon: The Last Phase* (Harold Nicolson)

**2** Better send them a Papal Bull.
Written in the margin of a Foreign Office document. The phrase 'the monks of Mount Athos were violating their vows' had been misprinted as ' . . . violating their cows'.
*Life of Lord Curzon* (Ronaldshay), Vol. III, Ch. 15

**3** I hesitate to say what the functions of the modern journalist may be; but I imagine that they do not exclude the intelligent anticipation of facts even before they occur.
Speech, House of Commons, 29 Mar 1898

**Cuvier, Georges Léopold, Baron** (1769–1832) French zoologist, who pioneered the study of comparative anatomy and palaeontology.

**1** Nurse, it was I who discovered that leeches have red blood.
On his deathbed when the nurse came to apply leeches
*The Oxford Book of Death* (D. Enright)

**Cyrano de Bergerac, Savinien** (1619–55) French writer and dramatist. Noted for his extraordinary nose and as a fighter of duels, he wrote a number of plays, including the comedy *Le Pédant Joué* (1654) and the tragedy *La Mort d'Agrippine* (1654).

**1** Perish the Universe, provided I have my revenge.
*La Mort d'Agrippine*, IV

# D

**Dacre, Harry** (19th century) British songwriter.

1 Daisy, Daisy, give me your answer, do!
I'm half crazy, all for the love of you!
It won't be a stylish marriage,
I can't afford a carriage,
But you'll look sweet upon the seat
Of a bicycle made for two!
*Daisy Bell*

**Dahl, Roald** (1916– ) British writer. His collections of short stories include *Kiss Kiss* (1959), *Switch Bitch* (1974), and *Tales of the Unexpected* (1979). He has written several books for children, including *Charlie and the Chocolate Factory* (1964).

1 Do you *know* what breakfast cereal is made of? It's made of all those little curly wooden shavings you find in pencil sharpeners!
*Charlie and the Chocolate Factory*, Ch. 27

**Dali, Salvador** (1904– ) Spanish painter. From 1929 he produced startling works based on subconscious imagery and executed with photographic realism. After settling in New York (1940), he adopted other styles and also developed his talent for self-publicity.

1 It's either easy or impossible.
*Reply when asked if he found it hard to paint a picture*
*Attrib.*

**Dalton, John** (1766–1844) British scientist. His experiments with gases led him to formulate Dalton's law of partial pressures and the foundations of modern atomic theory (1803).

1 This paper will no doubt be found interesting by those who take an interest in it.
*Said on many occasions when chairing scientific meetings*
*Attrib.*

**Daly, Dan** (20th century) Sergeant in the US Marines.

1 Come on, you sons of bitches! Do you want to live for ever?
*Remark during Allied resistance at Belleau Wood, June 1918. See also* FREDERICK THE GREAT
*Attrib.*

**Damien, Father** (Joseph de Veuster; 1840–89) Belgian Roman Catholic missionary, who died from leprosy after working in a leper colony in Hawaii.

1 What would you do with it? It is full of leprosy.
*When asked on his deathbed whether he would leave another priest his mantle, like Elijah*
*Memoirs of an Aesthete* (H. Acton)

**Dana, Charles Anderson** (1819–97) US newspaper editor, who both owned and edited the New York *Sun* (1868–97).

1 When a dog bites a man that is not news, but when a man bites a dog, that is news.
*New York Sun*, 1882

**Daniel, Samuel** (c. 1562–1619) English poet and dramatist. He is best known for his sonnet *Delia* (1592) and his verse history *The Civil Wars* (1609).

1 Love is a sickness full of woes,
All remedies refusing;
A plant that with most cutting grows,
Most barren with best using.
Why so?
More we enjoy it, more it dies;
If not enjoyed, it sighing cries,
Hey ho.
*Hymen's Triumph*, I

**Dante, Alighieri** (1265–1321) Italian poet. Born a Guelf, he was involved in the political struggles of the time, which forced him to leave his native Florence; he finally settled in Ravenna. His major works include *La vita nuova* (c. 1292) and *The Divine Comedy* (1307).

1 Abandon hope, all ye who enter here.
*The inscription at the entrance to Hell*
*Divine Comedy, Inferno*, III

2 There is no greater sorrow than to recall a time of happiness when in misery.
*Divine Comedy, Inferno*, V

**Danton, Georges Jacques** (1759–94) French political activist and leader of the Cordeliers (a revolutionary club). He became minister of justice in the new republic but lost power in the Reign of Terror and was guillotined.

1 Boldness, and again boldness, and always boldness!
*Speech, French Legislative Committee, 2 Sept 1792*

2 Thou wilt show my head to the people: it is worth showing.
*Said as he mounted the scaffold, 5 Apr 1794*
*French Revolution* (Carlyle), Bk. VI, Ch. 2

**Darling, Charles John, Baron** (1849–1936) British judge and writer.

1 If a man stays away from his wife for seven years, the law presumes the separation to have killed him; yet according to our daily experience, it might well prolong his life.
*Scintillae Juris*

2 A timid question will always receive a confident answer.
*Scintillae Juris*

3 Much truth is spoken, that more may be concealed.
*Scintillae Juris*

4 Perjury is often bold and open. It is truth that is shamefaced – as, indeed, in many cases is no more than decent.
*Scintillae Juris*

5 The Law of England is a very strange one; it cannot compel anyone to tell the truth.... But what the Law can do is to give you seven years for not telling the truth.
*Lord Darling* (D. Walker-Smith), Ch. 27

6 The law-courts of England are open to all men, like the doors of the Ritz Hotel.
Attrib.

## Darrow, Clarence Seward (1857–1938) US lawyer.

1 I go to a better tailor than any of you and pay more for my clothes. The only difference is that you probably don't sleep in yours.
Reply when teased by reporters about his appearance
2500 Anecdotes (E. Fuller)

2 I do not consider it an insult but rather a compliment to be called an agnostic. I do not pretend to know where many ignorant men are sure.
Remark during the trial (1925) of John Scopes for teaching the theory of evolution in school

## Darwin, Charles Galton (1887–1962) British life scientist and great-grandson of the originator of the theory of evolution.

1 The evolution of the human race will not be accomplished in the ten thousand years of tame animals, but in the million years of wild animals, because man is and will always be a wild animal.
The Next Ten Million Years, Ch. 4

## Darwin, Charles Robert (1809–82) British life scientist, who originated the theory of evolution based on natural selection. The publication of his Origin of Species by Means of Natural Selection (1859) caused great controversy because it conflicted with the biblical account of creation. In The Descent of Man (1871), Darwin applied his theory to mankind.

1 I have tried lately to read Shakespeare, and found it so intolerably dull that it nauseated me.
Autobiography

2 The highest possible stage in moral culture is when we recognize that we ought to control our thoughts.
Descent of Man, Ch. 4

3 We must, however, acknowledge, as it seems to me, that man with all his noble qualities, still bears in his bodily frame the indelible stamp of his lowly origin.
Closing words
Descent of Man, Ch. 21

4 I have called this principle, by which each slight variation, if useful, is preserved, by the term of Natural Selection.
Origin of Species, Ch. 3

5 We will now discuss in a little more detail the struggle for existence.
Origin of Species, Ch. 3

6 The expression often used by Mr Herbert Spencer of the Survival of the Fittest is more accurate, and is sometimes equally convenient.
Origin of Species, Ch. 3

## Darwin, Erasmus (1731–1802) British physician, biologist, and poet. The grandfather of Charles Darwin, his view of evolution was based on a concept later expounded by Lamarck. His books include Economy of Vegetation.

1 No, Sir, because I have time to think before I speak, and don't ask impertinent questions.
Reply when asked whether he found his stammer inconvenient
Reminiscences of My Father's Everyday Life (Sir Francis Darwin)

## Davies, Sir John (1569–1626) English jurist and poet. The speaker of the Irish parliament, he was appointed lord chief justice of England but died before taking office. His verse includes Orchestra (1594) and Hymns to Astraea (1599).

1 Judge not the play before the play be done.
Respice Finem

## Davies, W(illiam) H(enry) (1871–1940) British poet. For many years a tramp in both England and America, he first published his verse in 1905. His Autobiography of a Super-Tramp (1907) had a preface by G. B. Shaw.

1 It was the Rainbow gave thee birth,
And left thee all her lovely hues.
The Kingfisher

2 What is this life if, full of care,
We have no time to stand and stare?
Leisure

3 Sweet Stay-at-Home, sweet Well-content.
Sweet Stay-at-Home

4 I love thee for a heart that's kind –
Not for the knowledge in thy mind,
Sweet Stay-at-Home

## Davis, Bette (Ruth Elizabeth Davis; 1908– ) US film star. Her films include Of Human Bondage (1934), The Little Foxes (1941), and All About Eve (1950).

1 With the newspaper strike on I wouldn't consider it.
When told that a rumour was spreading that she had died
Book of Lists (I. Wallace)

2 I see – she's the original good time that was had by all.
Referring to a starlet of the time
The Filmgoer's Book of Quotes (Leslie Halliwell)

3 Pray to God and say the lines.
Advice to the actress Celeste Holm
Attrib.

## Davis, Sammy, Jnr (1925– ) Black US singer and entertainer. He has appeared in many films including Porgy and Bess (1959), A Man Called Adam (1966), and The Cannonball Run (1981).

1 Being a star has made it possible for me to get insulted in places where the average Negro could never hope to get insulted.
Yes I Can

2 I'm a coloured, one-eyed Jew.
When asked what his handicap was during a game of golf
Attrib.

## Davy, Sir Humphry (1778–1829) British chemist. Best known as the inventor (1815) of the miner's safety lamp, he also discovered the use of nitrous oxide as an anaesthetic and identified several metallic elements.

1 The finest collection of frames I ever saw.

When asked what he thought of the Paris art galleries
Attrib.

**Day, Clarence Shepard** (1874–1935) US writer. His
books include *This Simian World* (1920), *Life with Father* (1935)
and *Life with Mother* (1937).

1 Imagine the Lord talking French! Aside from a
few odd words in Hebrew, I took it completely
for granted that God had never spoken anything
but the most dignified English.

*Life With Father*, 'Father interferes'

2 'If you don't go to other men's funerals,' he told
Father stiffly, 'they won't go to yours.'

*Life With Father*, 'Father plans'

**Dayan, Moshe** (1915–81) Israeli general and archaeologist.
Chief of Israel's general staff (1953–58), he later became defence
minister (1967; 1969–74), resigning after criticism that Israel was
taken by surprise in the Yom Kippur War (1973–74).

1 Whenever you accept our views we shall be in
full agreement with you.

Said to Cyrus Vance during Arab-Israeli negotiations
*The Observer*, 'Sayings of the Week', 14 Aug 1977

2 If we lose this war, I'll start another in my wife's
name.

Attrib.

**Day Lewis, C(ecil)** (1904–72) British poet. A left-wing poet
of the 1930s, his collections include *The Magnetic Mountain* (1933)
and *Time to Dance* (1935). He was poet laureate (1968–72) and
wrote detective stories as **Nicholas Blake**.

1 Now the peak of summer's past, the sky is
overcast
And the love we swore would last for an age
seems deceit.

*Hornpipe*

2 It is the logic of our times,
No subject for immortal verse –
That we who lived by honest dreams
Defend the bad against the worse.

*Where are the War Poets?*

**de Blank, Joost** (1908–68) Dutch-born British churchman.
He became Bishop of Stepney and later Archbishop of Capetown.
In this capacity his opposition to apartheid made him unpopular
with the South African government.

1 Christ in this country would quite likely have
been arrested under the Suppression of Communism Act.

Referring to South Africa
*The Observer*, 'Sayings of the Week', 27 Oct 1963

2 I suffer from an incurable disease – colour
blindness.

Attrib.

**Debs, Eugene Victor** (1855–1926) US trade unionist,
socialist, and pacifist.

1 It is the government that should ask me for a
pardon.

When released from prison (1921) on the orders of President
Harding after being jailed for sedition (1918)
*The People's Almanac* (D. Wallechinsky)

**Debussy, Claude Achille** (1862–1918) French composer.
His opera *Pelléas et Mélisande* (1892–1902) and the three
symphonic sketches *La Mer* (1903–05) are his best-known works.
He also wrote much music for piano and for chamber ensembles.

1 Music is the arithmetic of sounds as optics is the
geometry of light.

Attrib.

**Decatur, Stephen** (1779–1820) US naval officer. He
commanded the *United States* in the War of 1812, defeating the
British *Macedonia*. He commanded the squadron which imposed
peace on Algeria on American terms.

1 Our country! In her intercourse with foreign nations, may she always be in the right; but our
country, right or wrong.

Speech, Norfolk, Virginia, Apr 1816

**Deffand, Marquise du** (Marie de Vichy-Chamrond; 1697–
1780) French noblewoman whose friends included Voltaire and
Walpole, with whom she corresponded.

1 The distance doesn't matter; it is only the first
step that is difficult.

Referring to the legend of St Denis, who is traditionally believed
to have carried his severed head for six miles after his
execution
Letter to d'Alembert, 7 July 1763

**Defoe, Daniel** (1660–1731) British journalist and writer.
Imprisoned for writing seditious pamphlets, he turned late in his
life to fiction, achieving success with *Robinson Crusoe* (1719) and
*Moll Flanders* (1722).

1 The good die early, and the bad die late.

*Character of the late Dr. Annesley*

2 Nature has left this tincture in the blood,
That all men would be tyrants if they could.

*The Kentish Petition*, Addenda

3 He bade me observe it, and I should always find,
that the calamities of life were shared among
the upper and lower part of mankind; but that
the middle station had the fewest disasters.

*Robinson Crusoe*, Pt. I

4 I takes my man Friday with me.

*Robinson Crusoe*, Pt. I

5 Wherever God erects a house of prayer,
The Devil always builds a chapel there;
And 'twill be found, upon examination,
The latter has the largest congregation.

*The True-Born Englishman*, Pt. I

6 And of all plagues with which mankind are curst,
Ecclesiastic tyranny's the worst.

*The True-Born Englishman*, Pt. II

**Degas, (Hilaire Germain) Edgar** (1834–1917) French
artist. A master of the human figure in movement, some of his
best-known works are scenes of race meetings and ballet.

1 I feel as a horse must feel when the beautiful cup is given to the jockey.

On seeing one of his pictures sold at auction
Attrib.

**De Gaulle, Charles André Joseph Marie** (1890–1970) French general and statesman. President (1958–69), he became an international figure after World War II. He advocated mechanized warfare in the 1930s, and became leader of the Free French in London after the fall of France, taking over as head of the provisional government after Germany's defeat.

1 Deliberation is the work of many men. Action, of one alone.

War Memoirs, Vol. 2

2 I myself have become a Gaullist only little by little.

The Observer, 'Sayings of the Year', 29 Dec 1963

3 Now at last our child is just like all children.

On the death of his retarded daughter Anne
Ten First Ladies of the World (Pauline Frederick)

4 They really are bad shots.

Remark after narrowly escaping death in an assassination attempt
Ten First Ladies of the World (Pauline Frederick)

5 The French will only be united under the threat of danger. Nobody can simply bring together a country that has 265 kinds of cheese.

Speech, 1951

6 *Changez vos amis.*
Change your friends

Replying to the complaint by Jacques Soustelle that he was being attacked by his own friends
Attrib.

7 One does not arrest Voltaire.

Explaining why he had not arrested Jean-Paul Sartre for urging French soldiers in Algeria to desert
Attrib.

8 Since a politician never believes what he says, he is surprised when others believe him.

Attrib.

9 Treaties are like roses and young girls – they last while they last.

Attrib.

10 In order to become the master, the politician poses as the servant.

Attrib.

11 I have come to the conclusion that politics are too serious a matter to be left to the politicians.

Attrib.

**Dekker, Thomas** (c. 1572–1632) English dramatist, his best-known play being *The Shoemaker's Holiday* (1600). His pamphlets, including *The Seven Deadly Sins of London* (1606), were widely read.

1 Golden slumbers kiss your eyes,
Smiles awake you when you rise.

*Patient Grissil*, IV:2

**De La Mare, Walter** (1873–1956) British poet and novelist. His verse collections include *Songs of Childhood* (1902) and his novel *Memoirs of a Midget* (1921) is his best-known fiction work.

1 It's a very odd thing –
As odd as can be –
That whatever Miss T eats
Turns into Miss T.

*Miss T*

2 Until we learn the use of living words we shall continue to be waxworks inhabited by gramophones.

The Observer, 'Sayings of the Week', 12 May 1929

3 Too late for fruit, too soon for flowers.

On being asked, as he lay seriously ill, whether he would like some fruit or flowers
Attrib.

**Delaney, Shelagh** (1939– ) British dramatist. Her first success was *A Taste of Honey* (1958), which was followed by *The Lion in Love* (1960). She has also written for radio and TV.

1 I'm not frightened of the darkness outside. It's the darkness inside houses I don't like.

*A Taste of Honey*, I:1

2 Women never have young minds. They are born three thousand years old.

*A Taste of Honey*, I:1

**Delille, Jacques** (1738–1813) French abbé and poet. He is remembered for his verse *Les Jardins* and his translations of Virgil and Milton.

1 Fate chooses your relations, you choose your friends.

*Malheur et pitié*, I

**Denman, Thomas, Baron** (1779–1854) British judge. Attorney general (1830) and lord chief justice (1832–50), he defended Queen Caroline before the House of Lords.

1 Trial by jury itself, instead of being a security to persons who are accused, will be a delusion, a mockery, and a snare.

Judgment in O'Connell v The Queen, 4 Sept 1844

**Dennis, John** (1657–1734) British critic and dramatist. His plays, including *Liberty Asserted* (1704), were less influential than his *Advancement and Reformation of Modern Poetry* (1701).

1 A man who could make so vile a pun would not scruple to pick a pocket.

The Gentleman's Magazine, 1781

**Dennis, Nigel (Forbes)** (1912– ) British writer and dramatist. *Cards of Identity* (1955) and *The Making of Moo* established him as a playwright. He has also been a drama critic and columnist.

1 This man, she reasons, as she looks at her husband, is a poor fish. But he is the nearest I can get to the big one that got away.

*Cards of Identity*

2 · But then one is always excited by descriptions of money changing hands. It's much more fundamental than sex.

*Cards of Identity*

**De Quincey, Thomas** (1785–1859) British writer. A friend of Wordsworth and Coleridge, he became addicted to opium as a consequence of taking it for toothache. His *Confessions of an Opium Eater* appeared in 1822.

1 Books, we are told, propose to *instruct* or to *amuse*. Indeed! . . . The true antithesis to knowledge, in this case, is not *pleasure*, but *power*. All that is literature seeks to communicate power; all that is not literature, to communicate knowledge.

*Letters to a Young Man*

2 Murder considered as one of the Fine Arts.

Essay title

3 Even imperfection itself may have its ideal or perfect state.

*Murder Considered as one of the Fine Arts*

**Descartes, René** (1596–1650) French philosopher and mathematician. His *Le Discours de la Méthode* (1637) introduced his technique of analysis, while his work on analytical geometry resulted in the Cartesian system of coordinates.

1 *Cogito, ergo sum.*
I think, therefore I am.

*Le Discours de la méthode*

2 The reading of all good books is like a conversation with the finest men of past centuries.

*Le Discours de la méthode*

3 Travelling is almost like talking with men of other centuries.

*Le Discours de la méthode*

**Deschamps, Eustache** (c. 1340–c. 1407) French poet. He wrote many ballads and the poem *Le Miroir de Mariage*.

1 Who will bell the cat?

*Ballade: Le Chat et les souris*

**De Sica, Vittorio** (1901–74) Italian film director. His films include *Shoeshine* (1946) and *Umberto D* (1952).

1 Moral indignation is in most cases 2 percent moral, 48 percent indignation and 50 percent envy.

*The Observer*, 1961

**de Valois, Dame Ninette** (Edris Stannus; 1898– ) British ballet dancer and choreographer. She founded the Sadler's Wells (later Royal) Ballet in 1931, and directed it until 1963.

1 Ladies and gentleman, it takes more than one to make a ballet.

*New Yorker*

**Devonshire, Spencer Compton Cavendish, 8th Duke of** (1833–1908) Conservative politician. War secretary (1866) and secretary of state for India (1880–82).

1 I dreamt that I was making a speech in the House. I woke up, and by Jove I was!

*Thought and Adventures* (W. S. Churchill)

**Devonshire, Edward William Spencer Cavendish, 10th Duke of** (1895–1950) Conservative politician. He was an MP before inheriting his title and later a parliamentary undersecretary.

1 Good God, that's done it. He's lost us the tarts' vote.

Referring to Stanley BALDWIN's attack on newspaper proprietors; recalled by Harold Macmillan
Attrib.

**De Vries, Peter** (1910– ) US novelist. His novels include *No But I Saw the Movie* (1952), *Comfort me with Apples* (1956), *The Mackerel Plaza* (1958), and *The Glory of the Hummingbird* (1975).

1 We know the human brain is a device to keep the ears from grating on one another.

*Comfort me with Apples*, Ch. 1

2 Gluttony is an emotional escape, a sign something is eating us.

*Comfort me with Apples*, Ch. 7

3 Probably a fear we have of facing up to the real issues. Could you say we were guilty of Noel Cowardice?

*Comfort me with Apples*, Ch. 8

4 I wanted to be bored to death, as good a way to go as any.

*Comfort me with Apples*, Ch. 17

5 Anyone informed that the universe is expanding and contracting in pulsations of eighty billion years has a right to ask, 'What's in it for me?'

*The Glory of the Hummingbird*, Ch. 1

6 It is the final proof of God's omnipotence that he need not exist in order to save us.

*The Mackerel Plaza*, Ch. 2

7 Let us hope . . . that a kind of Providence will put a speedy end to the acts of God under which we have been labouring.

*The Mackerel Plaza*, Ch. 3

8 Everybody hates me because I'm so universally liked.

*The Vale of Laughter*, Pt. I

**De Wolfe, Elsie** (1865–1950) US designer and leader of fashion.

1 It's beige! My color!

On first sighting the Acropolis
*Elsie de Wolfe* (J. Smith)

**Díaz, Porfirio** (1830–1915) Mexican general and statesman. He was President for seven terms but was finally forced to abdicate and he died in Paris in exile.

1 Poor Mexico, so far from God and so near to the United States!

Attrib.

**Dibdin, Charles** (1745–1814) British actor and dramatist. He wrote many plays including *The Waterman* (1774) and *The Quaker* (1775), as well as many songs for the theatre.

1 What argufies pride and ambition?
Soon or late death will take us in tow:
Each bullet has got its commission,
And when our time's come we must go.
*Each Bullet has its Commission*

2 Then trust me, there's nothing like drinking
So pleasant on this side the grave;
It keeps the unhappy from thinking,
And makes e'en the valiant more brave.
*Nothing like Grog*

**Dickens, Charles** (1812–70) British novelist. His career began with contributions to magazines using the pen name Boz, *Pickwick Papers* (1837) bringing him sudden fame. His many subsequent novels, all appearing in monthly instalments and depicting the poverty of the working classes in Victorian England, have remained immensely popular.

1 'There are strings', said Mr Tappertit, 'in the human heart that had better not be wibrated.'
*Barnaby Rudge*, Ch. 22

2 This is a London particular . . . A fog, miss.
*Bleak House*, Ch. 3

3 I expect a judgment. Shortly.
*Bleak House*, Ch. 3

4 'Old girl,' said Mr Bagnet, 'give him my opinion. You know it.'
*Bleak House*, Ch. 27

5 It is a melancholy truth that even great men have their poor relations.
*Bleak House*, Ch. 28

6 O let us love our occupations,
Bless the squire and his relations,
Live upon our daily rations,
And always know our proper stations.
*The Chimes*, '2nd Quarter'

7 'God bless us every one!' said Tiny Tim, the last of all.
*A Christmas Carol*

8 'I am a lone lorn creetur,' were Mrs Gummidge's words . . . 'and everythink goes contrairy with me.'
*David Copperfield*, Ch. 3

9 Barkis is willin'.
*David Copperfield*, Ch. 5

10 Annual income twenty pounds, annual expenditure nineteen nineteen six, result happiness. Annual income twenty pounds, annual expenditure twenty pounds ought and six, result misery.
*David Copperfield*, Ch. 12

11 I am well aware that I am the 'umblest person going . . . . My mother is likewise a very 'umble person. We live in a numble abode.
Said by Uriah Heep
*David Copperfield*, Ch. 16

12 We are so very 'umble.
*David Copperfield*, Ch. 17

13 Uriah, with his long hands slowly twining over one another, made a ghastly writhe from the waist upwards.
*David Copperfield*, Ch. 17

14 Accidents will occur in the best-regulated families.
*David Copperfield*, Ch. 28

15 I'm Gormed – and I can't say no fairer than that.
*David Copperfield*, Ch. 63

16 When found, make a note of.
*Dombey and Son*, Ch. 15

17 There's a young man hid with me, in comparison with which young man I am a Angel. That young man hears the words I speak. That young man has a secret way pecooliar to himself, of getting at a boy, and at his heart, and at his liver.
Said by Magwitch
*Great Expectations*, Ch. 1

18 Now, what I want is Facts . . . Facts alone are wanted in life.
*Hard Times*, Bk. I, Ch. 1

19 Whatever was required to be done, the Circumlocution Office was beforehand with all the public departments in the art of perceiving – HOW NOT TO DO IT.
*Little Dorrit*, Bk. I, Ch. 10

20 In company with several other old ladies of both sexes.
Said by Mr Meagles
*Little Dorrit*, Bk. I, Ch. 17

21 It was not a bosom to repose upon, but it was a capital bosom to hang jewels upon.
Describing Mrs Merdle
*Little Dorrit*, Bk. I, Ch. 21

22 As she frequently remarked when she made any such mistake, it would be all the same a hundred years hence.
Said by Mrs Squeers
*Martin Chuzzlewit*, Ch. 9

23 Let us be moral. Let us contemplate existence.
*Martin Chuzzlewit*, Ch. 10

24 Here's the rule for bargains: 'Do other men, for they would do you.' That's the true business precept.
*Martin Chuzzlewit*, Ch. 11

25 Buy an annuity cheap, and make your life interesting to yourself and everybody else that watches the speculation.
*Martin Chuzzlewit*, Ch. 18

26 He'd make a lovely corpse.
*Martin Chuzzlewit*, Ch. 25

27 'She's the sort of woman now,' said Mould, . . .
'one would almost feel disposed to bury for
nothing: and do it neatly, too!'
*Martin Chuzzlewit*, Ch. 25

28 He had but one eye, and the popular prejudice
runs in favour of two.
Said by Mr Squeers
*Nicholas Nickleby*, Ch. 4

29 When he has learnt that bottinney means a
knowledge of plants, he goes and knows 'em.
That's our system, Nickleby; what do you think
of it?
Said by Mr Squeers
*Nicholas Nickleby*, Ch. 8

30 Every baby born into the world is a finer one
than the last.
*Nicholas Nickleby*, Ch. 36

31 All is gas and gaiters.
*Nicholas Nickleby*, Ch. 49

32 'Did you ever taste beer?' 'I had a sip of it once,'
said the small servant. 'Here's a state of
things!' cried Mr Swiveller. . . . 'She *never* tasted it—it can't be tasted in a sip!'
*The Old Curiosity Shop*, Ch. 57

33 Oliver Twist has asked for more.
*Oliver Twist*, Ch. 2

34 Known by the *sobriquet* of 'The artful Dodger.'
*Oliver Twist*, Ch. 8

35 'If the law supposes that,' said Mr Bumble . . . ,
'the law is a ass - a idiot.'
*Oliver Twist*, Ch. 51

36 The question about everything was, would it
bring a blush to the cheek of a young person?
Pondered by Mr Podsnap
*Our Mutual Friend*, Bk. I, Ch. 11

37 I think . . . that it is the best club in London.
Mr Tremlow describing the House of Commons
*Our Mutual Friend*, Bk. II, Ch. 3

38 He'd be sharper than a serpent's tooth, if he
wasn't as dull as ditch water.
*Our Mutual Friend*, Bk. III, Ch. 10

39 Kent, sir – everybody knows Kent – apples,
cherries, hops and women.
*Pickwick Papers*, Ch. 2

40 I wants to make your flesh creep.
*Pickwick Papers*, Ch. 8

41 'It's always best on these occasions to do what
the mob do.'
'But suppose there are two mobs?' suggested
Mr Snodgrass.
'Shout with the largest,' replied Mr Pickwick.
*Pickwick Papers*, Ch. 13

42 Take example by your father, my boy, and be
very careful o' vidders all your life.
*Pickwick Papers*, Ch. 13

43 Poverty and oysters always seem to go
together.
*Pickwick Papers*, Ch. 22

44 Wery glad to see you indeed, and hope our acquaintance may be a long 'un, as the gen'l'm'n
said to the fi' pun' note.
*Pickwick Papers*, Ch. 25

45 Poetry's unnat'ral; no man ever talked poetry
'cept a beadle on boxin' day.
*Pickwick Papers*, Ch. 33

46 It's my opinion, sir, that this meeting is drunk.
*Pickwick Papers*, Ch. 33

47 I am afeered that werges on the poetical,
Sammy.
Said by Sam Weller
*Pickwick Papers*, Ch. 33

48 Never sign a walentine with your own name.
Said by Sam Weller
*Pickwick Papers*, Ch. 33

49 Put it down a we, my lord, put it down a we!
*Pickwick Papers*, Ch. 34

50 Miss Bolo rose from the table considerably agitated, and went straight home, in a flood of
tears and a Sedan chair.
*Pickwick Papers*, Ch. 35

51 Anythin' for a quiet life, as the man said wen he
took the sitivation at the lighthouse.
*Pickwick Papers*, Ch. 43

52 A smattering of everything, and a knowledge of
nothing.
*Sketches by Boz*, 'Tales', Ch. 3

53 It was the best of times, it was the worst of
times, it was the age of wisdom, it was the age
of foolishness, it was the epoch of belief, it was
the epoch of incredulity, it was the season of
Light, it was the season of Darkness, it was the
spring of hope, it was the winter of despair, we
had everything before us, we had nothing
before us, we were all going direct to Heaven,
we were all going direct the other way.
The opening words of the book
*A Tale of Two Cities*, Bk. I, Ch. 1

54 It is a far, far, better thing that I do, than I have
ever done; it is a far, far, better rest that I go
to, than I have ever known.
*A Tale of Two Cities*, Bk. II, Ch. 15

**Dickinson, Emily** (1830–86) US poet. Of her 1700 poems,
only 7 were published during her lifetime. Six volumes were
published posthumously.

1 Because I could not stop for Death,
He kindly stopped for me;
The carriage held but just ourselves
And Immortality.
*The Chariot*

2 Parting is all we know of heaven,
And all we need of hell.
*My Life Closed Twice Before its Close*

3 Our journey had advanced;
  Our feet were almost come
  To that odd fork in Being's road,
  Eternity by term.
  *Our Journey had Advanced*

4 Success is counted sweetest
  By those who ne'er succeed.
  *Success is Counted Sweetest*

**Diderot, Denis** (1713–84) French writer and editor. With Voltaire he created the *Encyclopédie*, which was responsible for the Enlightenment.

1 Wandering in a vast forest at night, I have only a faint light to guide me. A stranger appears and says to me: 'My friend, you should blow out your candle in order to find your way more clearly.' This stranger is a theologian.
  *Addition aux Pensées philosophiques*

2 It has been said that love robs those who have it of their wit, and gives it to those who have none.
  *Paradoxe sur le comédien*

3 What a fine comedy this world would be if one did not play a part in it!
  *Letters to Sophie Volland*

**Dietrich, Marlene** (Maria Magdalene von Losch; 1904– ) German-born film star and singer. She made her name in the German version of *The Blue Angel* (1930); subsequently she went to Hollywood, where she made many films including *Destry Rides Again* (1939), and *A Foreign Affair* (1948).

1 Once a woman has forgiven her man, she must not reheat his sins for breakfast.
  *Marlene Dietrich's ABC*

2 Latins are tenderly enthusiastic. In Brazil they throw flowers at you. In Argentina they throw themselves.
  *Newsweek*, 24 Aug 1959

3 The average man is more interested in a woman who is interested in him than he is in a woman – any woman – with beautiful legs.
  News Item, 13 Dec 1954

4 Most women set out to try to change a man, and when they have changed him they do not like him.
  Attrib.

**Diller, Phyllis** (1917– ) US writer, comedienne, and pianist.

1 Cleaning your house while your kids are still growing
  Is like shoveling the walk before it stops snowing.
  *Phyllis Diller's Housekeeping Hints*

2 Never go to bed mad. Stay up and fight.
  *Phyllis Diller's Housekeeping Hints*

**Dillingham, Charles Bancroft** (1868–1934) US theatrical manager and producer. He managed the Globe Theatre in York, amongst others.

1 I bet you a hundred bucks he ain't in here.
  Referring to the escapologist Harry Houdini; said at his funeral, while carrying his coffin
  Attrib.

**Diogenes** (412–322 BC) Greek philosopher, who founded the Cynics. He is reputed to have lived in a tub in Athens and to have wandered the streets with a lamp, seeking an honest man.

1 Stand a little less between me and the sun.
  When Alexander the Great asked if there was anything he wanted
  *Life of Alexander* (Plutarch)

2 If only it were as easy to banish hunger by rubbing the belly as it is to masturbate.
  *Lives and Opinions of Eminent Philosophers* (Diogenes Laertius)

3 I am a citizen of the world.
  Replying to a question concerning his nationality
  Attrib.

**Dionysius of Halicarnassus** (40–8 BC) Greek historian. He taught in Rome from 30 BC and compiled a 20-volume history of Rome.

1 History is philosophy teaching by examples.
  *Ars rhetorica*, XI:2

**Disraeli, Benjamin, 1st Earl of Beaconsfield** (1804–81) British statesman of Italian-Jewish descent, who became Conservative prime minister (1868; 1874–80). He was supported by Queen Victoria, who he made Empress of India. He also wrote novels including *Coningsby* (1844) and *Sybil* (1845).

1 Youth is a blunder; manhood a struggle; old age a regret.
  *Coningsby*, Bk. III, Ch. 1

2 Almost everything that is great has been done by youth.
  *Coningsby*, Bk. III, Ch. 1

3 His Christianity was muscular.
  *Endymion*, Bk. I, Ch. 14

4 'Sensible men are all of the same religion.' 'And pray what is that?' inquired the prince. 'Sensible men never tell.'
  *Endymion*, Bk. I, Ch. 81

5 The blue ribbon of the turf.
  Describing the Derby
  *Life of Lord George Bentinck*, Ch. 26

6 When a man fell into his anecdotage it was a sign for him to retire from the world.
  *Lothair*, Ch. 28

7 Every woman should marry – and no man.
  *Lothair*, Ch. 30

8 'My idea of an agreeable person,' said Hugo Bohun, 'is a person who agrees with me.'
  *Lothair*, Ch. 35

9 'Two nations; between whom there is no intercourse and no sympathy; who are as ignorant of each other's habits, thoughts, and feelings, as if they were dwellers in different zones, or inhabitants of different planets; who are formed by a different breeding, are fed by a different food, are ordered by different manners, and are not governed by the same laws.'
'You speak of –' said Egremont, hesitatingly.
'THE RICH AND THE POOR.'
*Sybil*, Bk. II, Ch. 5

10 Little things affect little minds.
*Sybil*, Bk. III, Ch. 2

11 A majority is always the best repartee.
*Tancred*, Bk. II, Ch. 14

12 It destroys one's nerves to be amiable every day to the same human being.
*The Young Duke*

13 There are three kinds of lies: lies, damned lies and statistics.
*Autobiography* (Mark Twain)

14 I will not go down to posterity talking bad grammar.
Remark made when correcting proofs of his last parliamentary speech, 31 Mar 1881
*Disraeli* (Blake), Ch. 32

15 I know he is, and he adores his maker.
Replying to a remark made in defence of John Bright that he was a self-made man
*The Fine Art of Political Wit* (L. Harris)

16 Thank you for the manuscript; I shall lose no time in reading it.
His customary reply to those who sent him unsolicited manuscripts
*Irreverent Social History* (F. Muir)

17 I will sit down now, but the time will come when you will hear me.
Maiden Speech, House of Commons, 7 Dec 1837

18 The Continent will not suffer England to be the workshop of the world.
Speech, House of Commons, 15 Mar 1838

19 Thus you have a starving population, an absentee aristocracy, and an alien Church, and in addition the weakest executive in the world. That is the Irish Question.
Speech, House of Commons, 16 Feb 1844

20 The right honourable gentleman caught the Whigs bathing, and walked away with their clothes.
Referring to Sir Robert Peel
Speech, House of Commons, 28 Feb 1845

21 A Conservative government is an organized hypocrisy.
Speech, 17 Mar 1845

22 A precedent embalms a principle.
Speech, House of Commons, 22 Feb 1848

23 He has to learn that petulance is not sarcasm, and that insolence is not invective.
Said of Sir C. Wood
Speech, House of Commons, 16 Dec 1852

24 I am myself a gentleman of the Press, and I bear no other scutcheon.
Speech, House of Commons, 18 Feb 1863

25 The question is this: Is man an ape or an angel? I, my lord, am on the side of the angels.
Speech, 25 Nov 1864

26 Assassination has never changed the history of the world.
Speech, House of Commons, 1 May 1865

27 An author who speaks about his own books is almost as bad as a mother who talks about her own children.
Speech in Glasgow, 19 Nov 1873

28 Lord Salisbury and myself have brought you back peace – but a peace I hope with honour.
Speech, House of Commons, 16 July 1878

29 A sophistical rhetorician inebriated with the exuberance of his own verbosity.
Referring to Gladstone
Speech, 27 July 1878

30 Your dexterity seems a happy compound of the smartness of an attorney's clerk and the intrigue of a Greek of the lower empire.
Speaking to Lord Palmerston
Attrib.

31 If a traveller were informed that such a man was leader of the House of Commons, he may well begin to comprehend how the Egyptians worshipped an insect.
Referring to Lord John Russell
Attrib.

32 Pray remember, Mr Dean, no dogma, no Dean.
Attrib.

33 Nobody is forgotten when it is convenient to remember him.
Attrib.

34 Her Majesty is not a subject.
Responding to Gladstone's taunt that Disraeli could make a joke out of any subject, including Queen Victoria
Attrib.

35 When I meet a man whose name I can't remember, I give myself two minutes; then, if it is a hopeless case, I aways say, And how is the old complaint?
Attrib.

36 She is an excellent creature, but she never can remember which came first, the Greeks or the Romans.
Referring to his wife
Attrib.

37 When I want to read a novel I write one.
Attrib.

**38** I am dead: dead, but in the Elysian fields.

Said on his move to the House of Lords
Attrib.

**39** No, it is better not. She will only ask me to take a message to Albert.

On his deathbed, declining an offer of a visit from Queen Victoria
Attrib.

**Dix, Dom Gregory** (1901–52) British monk. He was prior of Nashdom Abbey (1926–52). His books include *The Question of Anglican Orders* (1943).

**1** It is no accident that the symbol of a bishop is a crook, and the sign of an archbishop is a double-cross.

Letter to *The Times*, 3 Dec 1977 (Francis Bown)

**Dix, Dorothy** (Elizabeth Meriwether Gilmer; 1861–1951) US journalist and writer. She wrote an agony aunt column for many years. Her books include *How to Win and Hold a Husband* (1939).

**1** It is only the women whose eyes have been washed clear with tears who get the broad vision that makes them little sisters to all the world.

*Dorothy Dix, Her Book*, Introduction

**2** I have learned to live each day as it comes, and not to borrow trouble by dreading tomorrow. It is the dark menace of the future that makes cowards of us.

*Dorothy Dix, Her Book*, Introduction

**3** Now one of the great reasons why so many husbands and wives make shipwreck of their lives together is because a man is always seeking for happiness, while a woman is on a perpetual still hunt for trouble.

*Dorothy Dix, Her Book*, Ch. 1

**4** The reason that husbands and wives do not understand each other is because they belong to different sexes.

News item

**Dobrée, Bonamy** (1891– ) British scholar and writer. An authority on Restoration drama, his books include *Restoration Tragedy* (1929).

**1** It is difficult to be humble. Even if you aim at humility, there is no guarantee that when you have attained the state you will not be proud of the feat.

*John Wesley*

**Dodd, Ken** (1931– ) British comedian and entertainer.

**1** The trouble with Freud is that he never played the Glasgow Empire Saturday night.

TV interview, 1965

**Dodgson, Charles Lutwidge** *See* Carroll, Lewis.

**Donleavy, J(ames) P(atrick)** (1926– ) US novelist now living in Ireland. He made his name with *The Ginger Man* (1956). Other books include *The Onion Eaters* (1971) and *Leila* (1983).

**1** I got disappointed in human nature as well and gave it up because I found it too much like my own.

*Fairy Tales of New York*

**Donne, John** (1573–1631) English poet of the metaphysical school. He was ordained at the age of 43 and was appointed Dean of St Pauls (1621). His verse includes *Divine Poems* (1607) and *Epithalamium* (1613).

**1** And new Philosophy calls all in doubt,
The Element of fire is quite put out;
The Sun is lost, and th' earth, and no man's wit
Can well direct him where to look for it.

*An Anatomy of the World*, 205

**2** Come live with me, and be my love,
And we will some new pleasures prove
Of golden sands, and crystal brooks,
With silken lines, and silver hooks.

*The Bait*

**3** For God's sake hold your tongue and let me love.

*The Canonization*

**4** But I do nothing upon myself, and yet I am mine own Executioner.

*Devotions*, 12

**5** No man is an Island, entire of itself; every man is a piece of the Continent, a part of the main.

*Devotions*, 17

**6** Any man's death diminishes me, because I am involved in Mankind; And therefore never send to know for whom the bell tolls; it tolls for thee.

*Devotions*, 17

**7** Love built on beauty, soon as beauty, dies.

*Elegies*, 2, 'The Anagram'

**8** She, and comparisons are odious.

*Elegies*, 8, 'The Comparison'

**9** Licence my roving hands, and let them go,
Before, behind, between, above, below.

*Elegies*, 18, 'Love's Progress'

**10** O my America! my new-found-land,
My Kingdom, safeliest when with one man man'd.

*Elegies*, 19, 'Going To Bed'

**11** Go, and catch a falling star,
Get with child a mandrake root,
Tell me, where all past years are,
Or who cleft the Devil's foot.

*Go and Catch a Falling Star*

**12** Death be not proud, though some have called thee
Mighty and dreadful, for, thou art not so.

*Holy Sonnets*, 10

**13** It comes equally to us all, and makes us all equal when it comes. The ashes of an Oak in the Chimney, are no epitaph of that Oak, to tell me how high or how large that was; It tells me not what flocks it sheltered while it stood, nor what men it hurt when it fell. The dust of great persons' graves is speechless too, it says nothing, it distinguishes nothing.

*Speaking of Death*
*Sermons, XV*

**14** Busy old fool, unruly Sun,
Why dost thou thus,
Through windows and through curtains call on us?

*The Sun Rising*

**15** I am two fools, I know,
For loving, and for saying so
In whining Poetry.

*The Triple Fool*

**Dostoevsky, Anna** (1846–1918) Russian diarist and writer. She was the wife of Fedor Dostoevsky.

**1** From a timid, shy girl I had become a woman of resolute character, who could not longer be frightened by the struggle with troubles.

*Dostoevsky Portrayed by His Wife*

**2** It seems to me that he has never loved, that he has only imagined that he has loved, that there has been no real love on his part. I even think that he is incapable of love; he is too much occupied with other thoughts and ideas to become strongly attached to anyone earthly.

*Dostoevsky Portrayed by His Wife*

**Dostoevsky, Fedor Mikhailovich** (1821–81) Russian novelist. His major works are *Crime and Punishment* (1866), *The Idiot* (1868–69), *The Possessed* (1869–72) and *The Brothers Karamazov* (1879–80).

**1** The formula 'Two and two make five' is not without its attractions.

*Notes from the Underground*

**Douglas, Lord Alfred (Bruce)** (1870–1945) British writer and poet. At the centre of the Oscar Wilde scandal, he wrote *The City of the Soul* (1899) and a verse collection *Sonnets and Lyrics* (1935).

**1** I am the Love that dare not speak its name.

*Poem about homosexual love*
*Two Loves*

**Douglas, Archibald, 5th Earl of Angus** (1449–1514) Scottish nobleman. He led the rebellion against James III. He was known as the 'Great Earl' and as 'Bell-the-Cat'.

**1** I'll bell the cat.

*Of his proposed capture of Robert Cochrane (executed 1482)*

**Douglas, James, 4th Earl of Morton** (1525–81) Scottish nobleman. He was Lord High Chancellor of Scotland (1563) and helped to secure the abdication of Mary, Queen of Scots. He was regent in 1572 but was ousted and finally executed.

**1** Here lies he who neither feared nor flattered any flesh.

*Said of John Knox at his funeral, 26 Nov 1572*
*Life of John Knox (G. R. Preedy), VII*

**Douglas, Norman** (1868–1952) British novelist. His novels include *South Wind* (1917); his travel books *Siren Land* (1911) and *Old Calabria* (1915) were also popular.

**1** It is the drawback of all sea-side places that half the landscape is unavailable for purposes of human locomotion, being covered by useless water.

*Alone, 'Mentone'*

**2** Bouillabaisse is only good because cooked by the French, who, if they cared to try, could produce an excellent and nutritious substitute out of cigar stumps and empty matchboxes.

*Siren Land, 'Rain on the Hills'*

**3** Many a man who thinks to found a home discovers that he has merely opened a tavern for his friends.

*South Wind, Ch. 24*

**Douglas, William** (1672–1748) Scottish poet. He is remembered for his poem written for Anne, daughter of Sir Robert Laurie, called *Annie Laurie*.

**1** And for bonnie Annie Laurie
I'll lay me doun and dee.

*Annie Laurie*

**Douglas-Home, Sir Alec, Baron Home of the Hirsel** (1903– ) British statesman. Prime minister (1963–64). He was an MP before inheriting the Earldom of Home. He was then foreign secretary (1960–63) and renounced his title to succeed Macmillan as prime minister. He was made a life peer in 1974.

**1** As far as the 14th Earl is concerned, I suppose Mr Wilson, when you come to think of it, is the 14th Mr Wilson.

*On renouncing his peerage (as 14th Earl of Home) to become prime minister*
*TV interview, 21 Oct 1963*

**2** There are two problems in my life. The political ones are insoluble and the economic ones are incomprehensible.

*Speech, Jan 1964*

**Douglas-Home, Lady Caroline** (1937– ) Daughter of Lord Home of the Hirsel. She has been a lady-in-waiting to the Duchess of Kent.

**1** He is used to dealing with estate workers. I cannot see how anyone can say he is out of touch.

*Referring to her father's suitability for his new role as prime minister*
*Daily Herald, 21 Oct 1963*

**Dow, Lorenzo** (1777–1834) British churchman, who wrote *Reflections on the Love of God* (1836).

**1** You will be damned if you do – And you will be damned if you don't.

*Speaking of Calvinism*
*Reflections on the Love of God*

**Dowson, Ernest (Christopher)** (1867–1900) British lyric poet. From 1894 he lived in France, where he died of tuberculosis and absinthe addiction.

1  I have been faithful to thee, Cynara! in my fashion.

*Non Sum Qualis Eram Bonae Sub Regno Cynarae*

2  I have forgot much, Cynara! gone with the wind, Flung roses, roses riotously with the throng.

*Non Sum Qualis Eram Bonae Sub Regno Cynarae*

3  And I was desolate and sick of an old passion.

*Non Sum Qualis Eram Bonae Sub Regno Cynarae*

4  They are not long, the days of wine and roses.

*Vitae Summa Brevis Spem Nos Vetat Incohare Longam*

**Doyle, Sir Arthur Conan** (1856–1930) British writer and creator of the detective Sherlock Holmes. Originally a doctor, he ceased to practise in 1890, devoting himself entirely to his writing. He also wrote books on spiritualism.

1  It is an old maxim of mine that when you have excluded the impossible, whatever remains, however improbable, must be the truth.

*The Beryl Coronet*

2  You know my method. It is founded upon the observance of trifles.

*The Boscombe Valley Mystery*

3  The husband was a teetotaller, there was no other woman, and the conduct complained of was that he had drifted into the habit of winding up every meal by taking out his false teeth and hurling them at his wife.

*A Case of Identity*

4  It has long been an axiom of mine that the little things are infinitely the most important.

*A Case of Identity*

5  Depend upon it, there is nothing so unnatural as the commonplace.

*A Case of Identity*

6  It is my belief, Watson, founded upon my experience, that the lowest and vilest alleys of London do not present a more dreadful record of sin than does the smiling and beautiful countryside.

*Copper Beeches*

7  'Excellent!' I cried. 'Elementary,' said he.

Watson talking to Sherlock Holmes; Holmes's reply is often misquoted as 'Elementary my dear Watson'
*The Crooked Man*

8  'It is my duty to warn you that it will be used against you,' cried the Inspector, with the magnificent fair play of the British criminal law.

*The Dancing Men*

9  He is the Napoleon of crime.

Referring to Professor Moriarty
*The Final Problem*

10  A man should keep his little brain attic stocked with all the furniture that he is likely to use, and the rest he can put away in the lumber room of his library, where he can get it if he wants it.

*Five Orange Pips*

11  It is quite a three-pipe problem.

*The Red-Headed League*

12  An experience of women which extends over many nations and three continents.

*The Sign of Four*

13  'Is there any point to which you would wish to draw my attention?'
'To the curious incident of the dog in the night-time.'
'The dog did nothing in the night-time.'
'That was the curious incident,' remarked Sherlock Holmes.

*The Silver Blaze*

14  London, that great cesspool into which all the loungers of the Empire are irresistibly drained.

*A Study in Scarlet*

15  Mediocrity knows nothing higher than itself, but talent instantly recognizes genius.

*The Valley of Fear*

**Drake, Sir Francis** (1540–96) British navigator and admiral, who was the first Englishman to circumnavigate the globe, bringing back potatoes and tobacco from Virginia. He later helped to defeat the Spanish Armada.

1  I have singed the Spanish king's beard.

Referring to the raid on Cadiz harbour, 1587
Attrib.

2  There is plenty of time to win this game, and to thrash the Spaniards too.

Referring to the sighting of the Armada during a game of bowls, 20 July 1588
Attrib.

**Drayton, Michael** (1563–1631) English poet, whose *England's Heroical Epistles* (1597) and *Polyolbion* (1612–22), sang the praises of England.

1  Fair stood the wind for France
When we our sails advance.

*Agincourt*

2  Since there's no help, come let us kiss and part –
Nay, I have done, you get no more of me;
And I am glad, yea glad with all my heart
That thus so cleanly I myself can free.

*Sonnets, 61*

**Dreiser, Theodore** (1871–1945) US novelist. He made his reputation with *Sister Carrie* (1900). Subsequent successes included *An American Tragedy* (1925).

1  Shakespeare, I come!

His intended last words
*The Constant Circle* (S. Mayfield)

**Drummond, Thomas** (1797–1840) British engineer and statesman, whose limelight apparatus facilitated the 1820s survey of Britain. He was later appointed undersecretary of state for Ireland.

**1** Property has its duties as well as its rights.

Letter to the Earl of Donoughmore, 22 May 1838

**Dryden, John** (1631–1700) British poet and dramatist. His play *Marriage à la Mode* (1673) and the verse satire *Absalom and Achitophel* (1681) were highly regarded. He was made poet laureate by Charles II in 1668, but having become a Catholic in 1685, he was deprived of the office by William of Orange on his accession.

**1** In pious times, e'r Priest-craft did begin,
Before Polygamy was made a Sin.

*Absalom and Achitophel,* I

**2** What e'r he did was done with so much ease,
In him alone, 'twas Natural to please.

*Absalom and Achitophel,* I

**3** Great Wits are sure to Madness near alli'd
And thin Partitions do their Bounds divide.

*Absalom and Achitophel,* I

**4** Bankrupt of Life, yet Prodigal of Ease.

*Absalom and Achitophel,* I

**5** For Politicians neither love nor hate.

*Absalom and Achitophel,* I

**6** But far more numerous was the Herd of such,
Who think too little, and who talk too much.

*Absalom and Achitophel,* I

**7** A man so various, that he seem'd to be
Not one, but all Mankind's Epitome.
Stiff in Opinions, always in the wrong;
Was Everything by starts, and Nothing long.

*Absalom and Achitophel,* I

**8** Did wisely from Expensive Sins refrain,
And never broke the Sabbath, but for Gain.

*Absalom and Achitophel,* I

**9** During his Office, Treason was no Crime.
The Sons of Belial had a Glorious Time.

*Absalom and Achitophel,* I

**10** Nor is the Peoples Judgment always true:
The Most may err as grosly as the Few.

*Absalom and Achitophel,* I

**11** Beware the Fury of a Patient Man.

*Absalom and Achitophel,* I

**12** The people's prayer, the glad diviner's theme,
The young men's vision, and the old men's dream!

*Absalom and Achitophel,* I

**13** To die for faction is a common evil,
But to be hanged for nonsense is the Devil.

*Absalom and Achitophel,* II

**14** None but the Brave deserves the Fair.

*Alexander's Feast*

**15** Errors, like Straws, upon the surface flow;
He who would search for Pearls must dive below.

*All for Love,* Prologue

**16** Men are but children of a larger growth;
Our appetites as apt to change as theirs,
And full as craving too, and full as vain.

*All for Love,* IV

**17** So sicken waning moons too near the sun,
And blunt their crescents on the edge of day.

*Annus Mirabilis*

**18** By viewing Nature, Nature's handmaid, art,
Makes mighty things from small beginnings grow.

*Annus Mirabilis*

**19** Here lies my wife; here let her lie!
Now she's at rest, and so am I.

*Epitaph Intended for Dryden's Wife*

**20** He was the man who of all modern, and perhaps ancient poets had the largest and most comprehensive soul.

Referring to Shakespeare
*Essay of Dramatic Poesy*

**21** He was naturally learned; he needed not the spectacles of books to read nature; he looked inwards, and found her there.

Referring to Shakespeare
*Essay of Dramatic Poesy*

**22** If by the people you understand the multitude, the *hoi polloi,* 'tis no matter what they think; they are sometimes in the right, sometimes in the wrong; their judgement is a mere lottery.

*Essay of Dramatic Poesy*

**23** For present joys are more to flesh and blood
Than a dull prospect of a distant good.

*The Hind and the Panther,* III

**24** All humane things are subject to decay,
And, when Fate summons, Monarchs must obey.

*Mac Flecknoe*

**25** I am resolved to grow fat and look young till forty, and then slip out of the world with the first wrinkle and the reputation of five-and-twenty.

*The Maiden Queen,* III

**26** I am to be married within these three days; married past redemption.

*Marriage à la Mode,* I

**27** For, Heaven be thanked, we live is such an age,
When no man dies for love, but on the stage.

*Mithridates,* Epilogue

**28** A man is to be cheated into passion, but to be reasoned into truth.

*Religio Laici,* Preface

**29** Happy the Man, and happy he alone,
He who can call today his own:
He who, secure within, can say,
Tomorrow do thy worst, for I have liv'd today.
*Translation of Horace*, III

**Dubček, Alexander** (1921– ) Czech statesman. A resistance fighter in World War II, he became leader of the Communist Party in 1968. His liberal reforms led to the Soviet invasion in 1968, shortly after which he was ousted from power.

**1** Communism with a human face.
Popular attribution, describing Dubček's aims and policies in the short-lived 'Prague Spring' of 1968.
Attrib.

**Dublin, Al** (20th century) US songwriter.

**1** Tiptoe through the tulips with me.
From the musical, *Gold Diggers of Broadway*
*Tiptoe Through the Tulips*

**2** You may not be an angel
'Cause angels are so few,
But until the day that one comes along
I'll string along with you.
*Twenty Million Sweethearts*

**Duhamel, Georges** (1884–1966) French writer and physician. His books include *Des Légendes, des Batailles* (verse; 1907), *La Lumière* (play; 1911), *Civilisation* (war experiences; 1918), and many others.

**1** Courtesy is not dead – it has merely taken refuge in Great Britain.
*The Observer*, 'Sayings of Our Times', 31 May 1953

**Dulles, John Foster** (1888–1959) US politician and diplomat. Eisenhower made him secretary of state (1953–59) and he was delegate to the UN, which he helped to form.

**1** Yes, once – many, many years ago. I thought I had made a wrong decision. Of course, it turned out that I had been right all along. But I was wrong to have *thought* that I was wrong.
On being asked whether he had ever been wrong
*Facing the Music* (H. Temianka)

**Dumas, Alexandre, Fils** (1824–95) French writer. The illegitimate son of Dumas (Père), he is best known for *La Dame aux camélias* (1848), which Verdi used as the basis of his opera *La Traviata*. His plays include *Le Demi-monde* (1853) and *Le Fils naturel* (1858).

**1** If God were suddenly condemned to live the life which he has inflicted on men, He would kill Himself.
*Pensées d'album*

**2** All generalizations are dangerous, even this one.
Attrib.

**3** It is only rarely that one can see in a little boy the promise of a man, but one can almost always see in a little girl the threat of a woman.
Attrib.

**Dumas, Alexandre, Père** (1802–70) French novelist and dramatist. His early melodramas were less successful than such novels as *The Three Musketeers* (1844) and *The Count of Monte Cristo* (1845).

**1** All for one, and one for all.
*The Three Musketeers*

**Du Maurier, Daphne** (1907– ) British novelist. Her books, often set in her native Cornwall, include *Rebecca* (1938) and *The Flight of the Falcon* (1965).

**1** Last night I dreamt I went to Manderley again.
*Rebecca*, Ch. 1

**2** It . . . was full of dry rot. An unkind visitor said the only reason Menabilly still stood was that the woodworm obligingly held hands.
Interview – referring to her own house in Cornwall upon which Manderley in *Rebecca* was based

**Duncan, Isadora** (1878–1927) US dancer, who lived in Europe for most of her life. Her innovative dancing and her flamboyant lifestyle attracted considerable attention.

**1** I have discovered the dance. I have discovered the art which has been lost for two thousand years.
*My Life*

**2** People do not live nowadays – they get about ten percent of life.
*This Quarter Autumn*, 'Memoirs'

**3** America has all that Russia has not. Russia has things America has not. Why will America not reach out a hand to Russia, as I have given my hand?
Speaking in support of Russia following the 1917 Revolution
Speech, Symphony Hall, Boston, 1922

**4** So that ends my first experience with matrimony, which I always thought a highly overrated performance.
*The New York Times*, 1923

**Dunning, John, Baron Ashburton** (1731–83) British lawyer and politician, who is remembered for his defence of The East India Company.

**1** The influence of the Crown has increased, is increasing, and ought to be diminished.
Motion passed by the House of Commons, 1780

**Duport, James** (1606–79) English classicist. He is remembered for his collection of aphorisms *Homeri Gnomologia* (1660).

**1** Whom God would destroy He first sends mad.
*Homeri Gnomologia*

**Durocher, Leo** (1905– ) US baseball player and manager of the Brooklyn team (1951–54).

**1** Nice guys finish last.
Attrib.

**Durrell, Lawrence** (1912– ) British novelist and poet. His *Alexandria Quartet – Justine* (1957), *Balthazar* (1958), *Mountolive* (1958), and *Clea* (1960) – established his reputation. Later books include *Tunc* (1968) and *Nunquam* (1970).

**1** No one can go on being a rebel too long without turning into an autocrat.
*Balthazar, II*

**2** No more about sex, it's too boring.
*Tunc*

**3** History is an endless repetition of the wrong way of living.
*The Listener, 1978*

**Dyer, John** (1700–58) British poet. He is remembered for *Grongar Hill* (1726) and *The Fleece* (1757).

**1** Ever charming, ever new,
When will the landscape tire the view?
*Grongar Hill*

**2** A little rule, a little sway,
A sunbeam in a winter's day,
Is all the proud and mighty have
Between the cradle and the grave.
*Grongar Hill*

**Dylan, Bob** (Robert Allen Zimmerman; 1941– ) US popular singer and songwriter. Originally a member of the 1960s protest movement, producing such albums as *The Times They Are A-changin'* (1964), in the late 1970s his conversion to Christianity led to such religious albums as *Saved* (1980).

**1** How many roads must a man walk down
Before you call him a man?
*Blowin' in the Wind*

**2** Yes, 'n' how many years can some people exist
Before they're allowed to be free?
Yes, 'n' how many times can a man turn his head,

Pretending he just doesn't see?
The answer, my friend, is blowin' in the wind.
*Blowin' in the Wind*

**3** She takes just like a woman, yes, she does
She makes love just like a woman, yes, she does
And she aches just like a woman
But she breaks just like a little girl.
*Just Like a Woman*

**5** She knows, there's no success like failure
And that failure's no success at all.
*Love Minus Zero/No Limit*

**4** How does it feel
To be without a home
Like a complete unknown
Like a rolling stone?
*Like a Rolling Stone*

**6** Hey! Mr Tambourine Man, play a song for me.
I'm not sleepy and there is no place I'm going to.
*Mr Tambourine Man*

**7** Come mothers and fathers
Throughout the land
And don't criticize
What you can't understand
*The Times They Are A-Changin'*

**8** Yeah, some of them are about ten minutes long, others five or six.
On being asked, during an interview, if he would say something about his songs

**9** A Hard Rain's A-Gonna Fall.
*Song title*

---

# E

**Eames, Emma** (1865–1952) US opera singer. She wrote an autobiography *Some Memoirs and Reflections*.

**1** I would rather be a brilliant memory than a curiosity.
Referring to her retirement at the age of 47
*The Elephant that Swallowed a Nightingale* (C. Galtey)

**Earhart, Amelia** (1898–1937) US flyer; the first woman to fly solo over both the Atlantic (1932) and Pacific (1935).

**1** Courage is the price that Life exacts for granting peace.
*Courage*

**2** Of course I realized there was a measure of danger. Obviously I faced the possibility of not returning when first I considered going. Once faced and settled there really wasn't any good reason to refer to it.
Referring to her flight in the 'Friendship'
*20 Hours: 40 Minutes – Our Flight in the Friendship*, Ch. 5

**Eccles, David McAdam, Viscount** (1904– ) British politician. An MP (1943–62), he became minister of education (1954–57; 1959–62) and paymaster general (1970–73).

**1** A small acquaintance with history shows that all Governments are selfish and the French Governments more selfish than most.
*The Observer*, 'Sayings of the Year', 29 Dec 1962

**Eddington, Sir Arthur** (1882–1944) British astronomer and popularizer of science. His books include *The Nature of the Physical World* (1928) and *The Expanding Universe* (1933).

**1** Electrical force is defined as something which causes motion of electrical charge; an electrical charge is something which exerts electric force.
*The Nature of the Physical World*

**2** We used to think that if we knew one, we knew two, because one and one are two. We are finding that we must learn a great deal more about 'and'.
*The Harvest of a Quiet Eye* (A. L. Mackay)

**Eddy, Mary Baker** (1821–1910) US religious leader who founded the Church of Christ, Scientist, in Boston (1879).

1 The prayer that reforms the sinner and heals the sick is an absolute faith that all things are possible to God – a spiritual understanding of Him, an unselfed love.
*Science and Health, with Key to the Scriptures*

2 Christian Science explains all cause and effect as mental, not physical.
*Science and Health, with Key to the Scriptures*

3 Sin brought death, and death will disappear with the disappearance of sin.
*Science and Health, with Key to the Scriptures*

4 Sickness, sin and death, being inharmonious, do not originate in God, nor belong to His government.
*Science and Health, with Key to the Scriptures*

**Eden, Sir (Robert) Anthony, 1st Earl of Avon**
(1897–1977) British statesman. He resigned as foreign secretary in 1938 in protest against Chamberlain's policy of appeasement, but was reappointed by Churchill, whom he succeeded as prime minister in 1955. He resigned in 1957 after the Suez debacle.

1 REPORTER. If Mr Stalin dies, what will be the effect on international affairs?
EDEN. That is a good question for you to ask, not a wise question for me to answer.
Interview on board the *Queen Elizabeth*, 4 Mar 1953

2 Everybody is always in favour of general economy and particular expenditure.
*The Observer*, 'Sayings of the Week', 17 June 1956

3 We are not at war with Egypt. We are in an armed conflict.
Speech, House of Commons, 4 Nov 1956

**Eden, Clarissa, Countess of Avon** (1920–85) Wife of the Earl of Avon (Sir Anthony Eden).

1 During the last few weeks I have felt that the Suez Canal was flowing through my drawing room.
Said during the Suez crisis of 1956
Attrib.

**Edison, Thomas Alva** (1847–1931) US inventor. A very prolific inventor, he produced the filament light bulb, the microphone, the gramophone, the alkaline accumulator, and some thousand other devices.

1 Genius is one per cent inspiration and ninety-nine per cent perspiration.
Attrib.

**Edward III** (1312–77) King of England (1327–77). Through his mother, Isabella of France, he claimed the French throne, thus starting the Hundred Years' War.

1 Let the boy win his spurs.
Replying to a suggestion that he should send reinforcements to his son, the Black Prince, during the Battle of Crécy, 1346
Attrib.

**Edward VII** (1841–1910) King of the United Kingdom (1901–10).

1 My good man, I'm not a strawberry.
Rebuking a footman who had spilt cream on him
*The Last Country Houses* (C. Aslat)

**Edward VIII** (1894–1972) King of the United Kingdom who abdicated in 1936 because of his relationship with the American divorcée Wallis Simpson, whom he subsequently married. He became the Duke of Windsor.

1 I have found it impossible to carry the heavy burden of responsibility and to discharge my duties as King as I would wish to do without the help and support of the woman I love.
Radio broadcast, 11 Dec 1936

2 Now what do I do with *this*?
On being handed the bill after a lengthy stay in a luxury hotel
Attrib.

3 Something must be done.
Said while visiting areas of high unemployment in South Wales during the 1930s
Attrib.

4 Of course, I do have a slight advantage over the rest of you. It helps in a pinch to be able to remind your bride that you gave up a throne for her.
Discussing the maintenance of happy marital relations
Attrib.

**Einstein, Albert** (1879–1955) German physicist who became a Swiss citizen (1901) and later a US citizen (1940). His theory of relativity revolutionized scientific thought. He was persuaded to write to President Roosevelt to warn him that Germany could possibly make an atomic bomb.

1 Science without religion is lame, religion without science is blind.
*Out of My Later Years*

2 If you want to find out anything from the theoretical physicists about the methods they use, I advise you to stick closely to one principle: Don't listen to their words, fix your attention on their deeds.
*The World As I See It*

3 God is subtle but he is not malicious.
Inscribed over the fireplace in the Mathematical Institute, Princeton. It refers to Einstein's objection to the quantum theory.
*Albert Einstein* (Carl Seelig), Ch. 8

4 God does not play dice.
Einstein's objection to the quantum theory, in which physical events can only be known in terms of probabilities. It is sometimes quoted as 'God does not play dice with the Universe'.
*Albert Einstein, Creator and Rebel* (B. Hoffman), Ch. 10

5 If only I had known, I should have become a watchmaker.
Reflecting on his role in the development of the atom bomb
*New Statesman*, 16 Apr 1965

6 Common sense is the collection of prejudices acquired by age eighteen.
*Scientific American*, Feb 1976

**7** A theory can be proved by experiment; but no path leads from experiment to the birth of a theory.

*The Sunday Times,* 18 July 1976

**8** As far as the laws of mathematics refer to reality, they are not certain, and as far as they are certain, they do not refer to reality.

*The Tao of Physics* (F. Capra), Ch. 2

**9** I never think of the future. It comes soon enough.

Interview, 1930

**Eisenhower, Dwight D(avid)** (1890–1969) US general and statesman. President (1953–61) during the Cold War and the period of anticommunist witch hunts led by Senator McCarthy. In World War II he became supreme commander and was responsible for the D-day invasion of Europe.

**1** Whatever America hopes to bring to pass in this world must first come to pass in the heart of America.

Inaugural address, 1953

**2** There is one thing about being President – nobody can tell you when to sit down.

*The Observer,* 'Sayings of the Week', 9 Aug 1953

**3** Your business is to put me out of business

Addressing a graduating class at a university
*Procession* (J. Gunther)

**Eliot, George** (Mary Ann Evans; 1819–80) British woman novelist who concealed her identity behind a man's name. Her novels, including *Adam Bede* (1854), *The Mill on the Floss* (1860), and *Silas Marner* (1861), were highly acclaimed.

**1** A patronizing disposition always has its meaner side.

*Adam Bede*

**2** It's but little good you'll do a-watering the last year's crop.

*Adam Bede*

**3** He was like a cock who thought the sun had risen to hear him crow.

*Adam Bede*

**4** A different taste in jokes is a great strain on the affections.

*Daniel Deronda*

**5** Errors look so very ugly in persons of small means – one feels they are taking quite a liberty in going astray; whereas people of fortune may naturally indulge in a few delinquencies.

*Janet's Repentance,* Ch. 25

**6** I should like to know what is the proper function of women, if it is not to make reasons for husbands to stay at home, and still stronger reasons for bachelors to go out.

*The Mill on the Floss,* Ch. 6

**7** Animals are such agreeable friends – they ask no questions, they pass no criticisms.

*Scenes of Clerical Life,* 'Mr Gilfil's Love Story', Ch. 7

**Eliot, T(homas) S(tearns)** (1888–1965) US-born British poet and dramatist. He worked as a bank clerk before publication of his *Prufrock and Other Observations* (1917). *The Waste Land* (1922) established his reputation, which was confirmed by his *Four Quartets* (1935–41). His verse dramas include *Murder in the Cathedral* (1935) and *The Cocktail Party* (1949).

**1** Because I do not hope to turn again
Because I do not hope
Because I do not hope to turn.

*Ash-Wednesday*

**2** We can say of Shakespeare, that never has a man turned so little knowledge to such great account.

*The Classics and the Man of Letters* (lecture)

**3** Hell is oneself;
Hell is alone, the other figures in it
Merely projections. There is nothing to escape from
And nothing to escape to. One is always alone.

*The Cocktail Party,* I:3

**4** Time present and time past
Are both perhaps present in time future,
And time future contained in time past.

*Four Quartets,* 'Burnt Norton'

**5** Human kind
Cannot bear very much reality.

*Four Quartets,* 'Burnt Norton'

**6** Here I am, an old man in a dry month,
Being read to by a boy, waiting for rain.

*Gerontion*

**7** We are the hollow men
We are the stuffed men
Leaning together
Headpiece filled with straw.

*The Hollow Men*

**8** This is the way the world ends
Not with a bang but a whimper.

*The Hollow Men*

**9** Let us go then, you and I,
When the evening is spread out against the sky
Like a patient etherized upon a table.

*The Love Song of J. Alfred Prufrock*

**10** In the room the women come and go
Talking of Michelangelo.

*The Love Song of J. Alfred Prufrock*

**11** I have measured out my life with coffee spoons.

*The Love Song of J. Alfred Prufrock*

**12** I grow old . . . I grow old . . .
I shall wear the bottoms of my trousers rolled.

*The Love Song of J. Alfred Prufrock*

**13** Shall I part my hair behind? Do I dare to eat a peach?
I shall wear white flannel trousers, and walk upon the beach.
I have heard the mermaids singing, each to each.

*The Love Song of J. Alfred Prufrock*

**14** Macavity, Macavity, there's no one like
Macavity,
There never was a Cat of such deceitfulness and
suavity.
He always has an alibi, and one or two to spare:
At whatever time the deed took place – MA-
CAVITY WASN'T THERE!

*Macavity: The Mystery Cat*

**15** I am aware of the damp souls of the housemaids
Sprouting despondently at area gates.

*Morning at the Window*

**16** The last temptation is the greatest treason:
To do the right deed for the wrong reason.

*Murder in the Cathedral*, 1

**17** The winter evening settles down
With smell of steaks in passageways.

*Preludes*

**18** 'Put your shoes at the door, sleep, prepare for
life.'
The last twist of the knife.

*Rhapsody on a Windy Night*

**19** Birth, and copulation, and death.
That's all the facts when you come to brass
tacks.

*Sweeney Agonistes*, 'Fragment of an Agon'

**20** The host with someone indistinct
Converses at the door apart,
The nightingales are singing near
The Convent of the Sacred Heart.

*Sweeney among the Nightingales*

**21** No poet, no artist of any sort, has his complete
meaning alone. His significance, his appreciation
is the appreciation of his relation to the dead
poets and artists.

*Tradition and the Individual Talent*

**22** Poetry is not a turning loose of emotion, but an
escape from emotion; it is not the expression of
personality, but an escape from personality.

*Tradition and the Individual Talent*

**23** April is the cruellest month, breeding
Lilacs out of the dead land, mixing
Memory and desire, stirring
Dull roots with spring rain.

*The Waste Land*, 'The Burial of the Dead'

**24** I read, much of the night, and go south in the
winter.

*The Waste Land*, 'The Burial of the Dead'

**25** And I will show you something different from
either
Your shadow at morning striding behind you,
Or your shadow at evening rising to meet you
I will show you fear in a handful of dust.

*The Waste Land*, 'The Burial of the Dead'

**Elizabeth I** (1533–1603) Queen of England. The daughter of
Henry VIII and Anne Boleyn, she established the Protestant
Church in England and had her Catholic cousin, Mary, Queen of
Scots, beheaded. The Elizabethan age was one of greatness for
England.

**1** Though God hath raised me high, yet this I
count the glory of my crown: that I have reigned
with your loves.

*The Golden Speech*, 1601

**2** Madam I may not call you; mistress I am
ashamed to call you; and so I know not what to
call you; but howsoever, I thank you.

Writing to the wife of the Archbishop of Canterbury, expressing
her disapproval of married clergy
*Brief View of the State of the Church* (Harington)

**3** God may pardon you, but I never can.

To the Countess of Nottingham
*History of England under the House of Tudor* (Hume), Vol. II,
Ch. 7

**4** Good-morning, gentlemen both.

When addressing a group of eighteen tailors
*Sayings of Queen Elizabeth* (Chamberlin)

**5** I will make you shorter by a head.

*Sayings of Queen Elizabeth* (Chamberlin)

**6** Must! Is *must* a word to be addressed to
princes? Little man, little man! thy father, if he
had been alive, durst not have used that word.

Said to Robert Cecil, on her death bed
*A Short History of the English People* (J. R. Green), Ch. 7

**7** If thy heart fails thee, climb not at all.

Written on a window in reply to Sir Walter RALEIGH's line.
*Worthies of England* (Fuller), Vol. I

**8** I know I have the body of a weak and feeble
woman, but I have the heart and stomach of a
King, and of a King of England too.

Speech at Tilbury on the approach of the Spanish Armada

**9** All my possessions for a moment of time.

Last words

**Elizabeth II** (1926– ) Queen of the United Kingdom (since
1952) and head of the British Commonwealth. She married Prince
Philip (1947).

**1** I should like to be a horse.

When asked about her ambitions when a child.
Attrib.

**2** I think that everyone will conceed that – today
of all days – I should begin by saying, 'My husband and I'.

On her silver-wedding
Speech, Guildhall, 1972

**Elizabeth the Queen Mother** (1900– ) The wife of
King George VI and mother of Elizabeth II. Formerly Lady
Elizabeth Bowes-Lyon.

**1** Now we can look the East End in the face.

Surveying the damage caused to Buckingham Palace by a bomb
during the Blitz in World War II
Attrib.

**Ellerton, John** (1826–93) British churchman. He is
remembered for his *Liturgy for Missionary Meetings*.

1 The day Thou gavest, Lord, is ended,
The darkness falls at Thy behest.
*A Liturgy for Missionary Meetings*

**Ellis, (Henry) Havelock** (1859–1939) British sexologist.
His seven-volume *Studies in the Psychology of Sex* was a landmark
in the open discussion of sexual problems.

1 What we call progress is the exchange of one
nuisance for another nuisance.
Attrib.

**Eluard, Paul** (Eugène Grindel; 1895–1952) French surrealist
poet. After becoming a communist in 1942 he adopted a more
realistic style and his poetry was circulated secretly among
Resistance fighters in World War II.

1 *Adieu tristesse*
*Bonjour tristesse*
*Tu es inscrite dans les lignes du plafond.*
Farewell sadness
Good day sadness
You are written in the lines of the ceiling.
*La Vie immédiate*

**Emerson, Ralph Waldo** (1803–82) US poet and essayist.
Ordained in 1829, his book *Nature* (1836) contained his
transcendental philosophy. He expressed his optimistic humanism
in *Representative Men* (1850) and the *Conduct of Life* (1860).

1 A person seldom falls sick, but the bystanders
are animated with a faint hope that he will die.
*Conduct of Life*, 'Considerations by the Way'

2 Art is a jealous mistress.
*Conduct of Life*, 'Wealth'

3 The louder he talked of his honour, the faster
we counted our spoons.
*Conduct of Life*, 'Worship'

4 The religions we call false were once true.
*Essays*, 'Character'

5 Nothing great was ever achieved without
enthusiasm.
*Essays*, 'Circles'

6 A Friend may well be reckoned the masterpiece
of Nature.
*Essays*, 'Friendship'

7 There is properly no history; only biography.
*Essays*, 'History'

8 All mankind love a lover.
*Essays*, 'Love'

9 The reward of a thing well done is to have done
it.
*Essays*, 'New England Reformers'

10 Every man is wanted, and no man is wanted
much.
*Essays*, 'Nominalist and Realist'

11 In skating over thin ice, our safety is in our
speed.
*Essays*, 'Prudence'

12 Whoso would be a man must be a nonconformist.
*Essays*, 'Self-Reliance'

13 A foolish consistency is the hobgoblin of little
minds, adored by little statesmen and philosophers and divines. With consistency a great soul
has simply nothing to do.
*Essays*, 'Self-reliance'

14 To be great is to be misunderstood.
*Essays*, 'Self-Reliance'

15 What is a weed? A plant whose virtues have not
been discovered.
*Fortune of the Republic*

16 Talent alone cannot make a writer. There must
be a man behind the book.
*Goethe*

17 I pay the schoolmaster, but 'tis the schoolboys
that educate my son.
*Journal*

18 The book written against fame and learning has
the author's name on the title-page.
*Journal*

19 Old age brings along with its uglinesses the comfort that you will soon be out of it, – which
ought to be a substantial relief to such discontented pendulums as we are.
*Journal*

20 Every hero becomes a bore at last.
*Representative Men*, 'Uses of Great Men'

21 Hitch your wagon to a star.
*Society and Solitude*, 'Civilization'

22 We boil at different degrees.
*Society and Solitude*, 'Eloquence'

23 America is a country of young men.
*Society and Solitude*, 'Old Age'

24 If a man make a better mouse-trap than his
neighbour, though he build his house in the
woods, the world will make a beaten path to his
door.
Attrib.

**English, Thomas Dunn** (1819–1902) US lawyer,
physician, and writer. He wrote many novels, plays, and songs,
including the well-known *Ben Bolt*.

1 Oh! don't you remember sweet Alice, Ben Bolt,
Sweet Alice, whose hair was so brown,
Who wept with delight when you gave her a
smile,
And trembled with fear at your frown?
*Ben Bolt*

**Epictetus** (c. 60–110 AD) Stoic philosopher. His teaching was
recorded by his pupil Arrian in *Discourses* and in the *Enchiridion*.

1 If you hear that someone is speaking ill of you,
instead of trying to defend yourself you should
say: 'He obviously does not know me very
well, since there are so many other faults he
could have mentioned'.
*Enchiridion*

**Epicurus** (341–270 BC) Greek philosopher who established the school of epicureanism in Athens, teaching that the greatest good was pleasure attained by tranquility and detachment.

1 It is not so much our friends' help that helps us as the confident knowledge that they will help us.

**Erasmus, Desiderius** (1466–1536) Dutch humanist, scholar, and writer, one of the leading Renaissance thinkers. His works include *The Praise of Folly* (1511) and a translation of the Greek New Testament.

1 I have a Catholic soul, but a Lutheran stomach.
Replying to criticism of his failure to fast during Lent
*Dictionnaire Encyclopédique*

**Eschenbach, Marie Ebner von** (1830–1916) Austrian writer.

1 Whenever two good people argue over principles, they are both right.
*Aphorism*

2 We don't believe in rheumatism and true love until after the first attack.
*Aphorism*

3 We are so vain that we even care for the opinion of those we don't care for.
*Aphorism*

4 'Good heavens!' said he, 'if it be our clothes alone which fit us for society, how highly we should esteem those who make them.'
*The Two Countesses*

**Estienne, Henri** (1528–98) French scholar and printer. He ran the family printing business in Geneva, where he compiled the *Thesaurus Linguae Graecae* (1572).

1 *Si jeunesse savait; si vieillesse pouvait.*
If only youth knew, if only age could.
*Les Prémices*

**Euclid** (c. 300 BC) Greek mathematician who compiled his book *Elements*, containing all the geometry then known, from a few basic axioms.

1 *Quod erat demonstrandum.*
Which was to be proved.
Hence, of course, Q.E.D.
*Elements*, I:5

2 There is no 'royal road' to geometry.
Said to Ptolemy I when asked if there were an easier way to solve theorems
*Comment on Euclid* (Proclus)

**Euripides** (c. 480–406 BC) Greek dramatist. Of his 90 plays, only 19 survive, including *Medea* (431), *Hippolytus* (428), and *Electra* (415).

1 Those whom God wishes to destroy, he first makes mad.
*Fragment*

**Evans, Abel** (1679–1737) English writer.

1 Under this stone, Reader, survey
Dead Sir John Vanbrugh's house of clay.
Lie heavy on him, Earth! for he
Laid many heavy loads on thee!
*Epitaph on Sir John Vanbrugh, Architect of Blenheim Palace*

**Evans, Dame Edith** (1888–1976) British actress. She is remembered for her many Shakespearian roles, as well as her classic performance as Lady Bracknell in *The Importance of Being Earnest*.

1 When a woman behaves like a man, why doesn't she behave like a nice man?
*The Observer*, 'Sayings of the Week', 30 Sept 1956

2 Death is my neighbour now.
Said a week before her death
BBC radio interview, 14 Oct 1976

**Evans, Harold** (1928– ) British journalist; a former editor of *The Sunday Times*.

1 The camera cannot lie. But it can be an accessory to untruth.
*Pictures on a Page*

**Evarts, William M(axwell)** (1818–1901) US lawyer and statesman; secretary of state (1877–81).

1 It was a brilliant affair; water flowed like champagne.
Describing a dinner given by US President Rutherford B. Hayes (1877–81), an advocate of temperance
Attrib.

**Ewer, William Norman** (1885–1976) British writer and humorist.

1 How odd
Of God
To choose
The Jews.
For a reply, *see* ANONYMOUS
*How Odd*

## F

**Fadiman, Clifton** (1904– ) US writer and broadcaster.

1 We prefer to believe that the absence of inverted commas guarantees the originality of a thought, whereas it may be merely that the utterer has forgotten its source.
*Any Number Can Play*

2 Experience teaches you that the man who looks you straight in the eye, particularly if he adds a firm handshake, is hiding something.
*Enter, Conversing*

**Faraday, Michael** (1791–1867) British scientist. He discovered the laws of electrolysis and the connection between electricity and magnetism. He also showed how electromagnetic induction could be used in the generator and transformer.

1 Tyndall, I must remain plain Michael Faraday to the last; and let me now tell you, that if I accepted the honour which the Royal Society desires to confer upon me, I would not answer for the integrity of my intellect for a single year.

Said when Faraday was offered the Presidency of the Royal Society
*Faraday as a Discoverer* (J. Tyndall), 'Illustrations of Character'

**Farjeon, Herbert** (1887–1945) British writer and dramatist. With his sister, Eleanor Farjeon, he wrote the plays *Kings and Queens* (1932) and *An Elephant in Arcady* (1938).

1 I've danced with a man, who's danced with a girl, who's danced with the Prince of Wales.
*Picnic*

**Farmer, Edward** (1809–76) British writer.

1 I have no pain, dear mother, now;
But oh! I am so dry:
Just moisten poor Jim's lips once more;
And, mother, do not cry!

A typical sentimental verse of the time. For a typical parody, *see* ANONYMOUS
*The Collier's Dying Child*

**Farouk I** (1920–65) The last king of Egypt. After the first Arab–Israeli War (1948–49) he was ousted and went into exile in Monaco.

1 There will soon be only five kings left – the Kings of England, Diamonds, Hearts, Spades and Clubs.

Remark made to Lord Boyd-Orr

**Farquhar, George** (1678–1707) Irish dramatist. He achieved fame in London with his first play, *Love and a Bottle* (1699). *The Recruiting Officer* (1706) and *The Beaux' Stratagem* (1707) were subsequent successes.

1 There's no scandal like rags, nor any crime so shameful as poverty.
*The Beaux' Stratagem*, I:1

2 Lady Bountiful.
*The Beaux' Stratagem*, I:1

3 Spare all I have, and take my life.
*The Beaux' Stratagem*, V:2

**Faulkner, William** (1897–1962) US novelist. His first verse collection *The Marble Faun* (1924) was followed by the novels *Sartoris* (1929), *The Sound and the Fury* (1929), *Absalom, Absalom!* (1936), and *The Rivers* (1966).

1 The Swiss who are not a people so much as a neat clean quite solvent business.
*Intruder in the Dust*, Ch. 7

2 He has never been known to use a word that might send the reader to the dictionary.
Referring to Ernest HEMINGWAY
Attrib.

**Feather, Vic, Baron** (1908–76) British trade-union leader. He was general secretary of the TUC (1969–73).

1 Industrial relations are like sexual relations. It's better between two consenting parties.
*Guardian Weekly*, 8 Aug 1976

**Feiffer, Jules** (1929– ) US writer, cartoonist, and humorist.

1 At sixteen I was stupid, confused, insecure and indecisive. At twenty-five I was wise, self-confident, prepossessing and assertive. At forty-five I am stupid, confused, insecure and indecisive. Who would have supposed that maturity is only a short break in adolescence?
*The Observer*, 3 Feb 1974

**Feldman, Marty** (1933–83) British comedian. He was originally a scriptwriter, but became a TV comedian and made a number of films, including *High Anxiety* (1978) and *Sex with a Smile* (1979).

1 Comedy, like sodomy, is an unnatural act.
*The Times*, 9 June 1969

**Fénelon, François de Salignac de La Mothe** (1651–1715) French writer and prelate. Archbishop of Cambrai, he wrote *Maximes des Saints*, which was condemned by the Pope.

1 Nothing is more despicable than a professional talker who uses his words as a quack uses his remedies.
Letter to M. Dacier

2 A good historian is timeless; although he is a patriot, he will never flatter his country in any respect.
Letter to M. Dacier

**Ferber, Edna** (1887–1968) US writer. She wrote such novels as *Gigolo* (1922), *Show Boat* (1926), and *Come and Get It* (1935), many of which were filmed.

1 Being an old maid is like death by drowning, a really delightful sensation after you cease to struggle.
*Wit's End* (R. E. Drennan), 'Completing the Circle'

**Ferdinand I** (1503–64) Holy Roman Emperor (1558–64). In 1526 he became King of Bohemia and of Hungary.

1 Let justice be done, though the world perish.
Attrib.

**Ferdinand I** (1793–1875) Emperor of Austria (1835–48). Of unsound mind, he abdicated during the 1848 revolution.

1 I am the emperor, and I want dumplings.
*The Fall of the House of Habsburg* (E. Crankshaw)

**Fern, Fanny** (1811–72) US writer.

1 The way to a man's heart is through his stomach.
*Willis Parton*

**Ferrier, Kathleen** (1912–53) British contralto, who died of cancer at the peak of her career.

1 Now I'll have *eine kleine Pause*.
Said shortly before her death
*Am I Too Loud?* (Gerald Moore)

**Field, Eugene** (1850-95) US poet and journalist. His work consisted mainly of verses for children and humorous articles. Books include *Trumpet and Drum* (1892) and *Echoes from the Sabine Farm* (1892).

1 He played the King as though under momentary apprehension that someone else was about to play the ace.
Referring to Creston Clarke's performance in the role of King Lear
Attrib.

**Fielding, Henry** (1707-54) British novelist and dramatist. He wrote some 25 plays and the novels *Joseph Andrews* (1742), *Jonathan Wild* (1743), and *Tom Jones* (1749).

1 It hath been often said, that it is not death, but dying, which is terrible.
*Amelia*, Bk. III, Ch. 4

2 These are called the pious frauds of friendship.
*Amelia*, Bk. III, Ch. 4

3 When widows exclaim loudly against second marriages, I would always lay a wager, that the man, if not the wedding-day, is absolutely fixed on.
*Amelia*, Bk. VI, Ch. 8

4 One fool at least in every married couple.
*Amelia*, Bk. IX, Ch. 4

5 I am as sober as a Judge.
*Don Quixote in England*, III:14

6 Oh! The roast beef of England.
And old England's roast beef.
*The Grub Street Opera*, III:3

7 Never trust the man who hath reason to suspect that you know he hath injured you.
*Jonathan Wild*, Bk. III, Ch. 4

8 He in a few minutes ravished this fair creature, or at least would have ravished her, if she had not, by a timely compliance, prevented him.
*Jonathan Wild*, Bk. III, Ch. 7

9 For clergy are men as well as other folks.
*Joseph Andrews*, Bk. II, Ch. 6

10 Public schools are the nurseries of all vice and immorality.
*Joseph Andrews*, Bk. III, Ch. 5

11 What is commonly called love, namely the desire of satisfying a voracious appetite with a certain quantity of delicate white human flesh.
*Tom Jones*, Bk. VI, Ch. 1

12 His designs were strictly honourable, as the phrase is; that is, to rob a lady of her fortune by way of marriage.
*Tom Jones*, Bk. XI, Ch. 4

13 Composed that monstrous animal a husband and wife.
*Tom Jones*, Bk. XV, Ch. 9

14 All Nature wears one universal grin.
*Tom Thumb the Great*, I:1

**Fields, W(illiam) C(laude)** (1880-1946) US actor. After starting in vaudeville, he began making film comedies in the 1920s.

1 It ain't a fit night out for man or beast.
*The Fatal Glass of Beer*

2 Fish fuck in it.
His reason for not drinking water
Attrib.

3 Anybody who hates children and dogs can't be all bad.
Attrib.

4 I am free of all prejudice. I hate everyone equally.
Attrib.

**Firbank, Ronald** (1886-1926) British novelist. Best-known novels were *Caprice* (1917), *Valmouth* (1919), and *The Flower Beneath the Foot* (1922).

1 It is said, I believe, that to behold the Englishman at his *best* one should watch him play tip-and-run.
*The Flower Beneath the Foot*, Ch. 14

2 The world is disgracefully managed, one hardly knows to whom to complain.
*Vainglory*

3 To be sympathetic without discrimination is so very debilitating.
*Vainglory*

**Firmont, Abbé Edgeworth de** (1745-1807) Irish-born confessor to Louis XVI. He later became chaplain to the future Louis XVIII.

1 Son of Saint Louis, ascend to heaven.
Said to Louis XVI as he climbed up to the guillotine
Attrib.

**Fitzgerald, Edward** (1809-83) British poet and translator. His translation of *The Rubáiyát of Omar Khayyám* was a free adaption of the 12th-century Persian original.

1 Taste is the feminine of genius.
Letter to J. R. Lowell, Oct 1877

2 Awake! for Morning in the Bowl of Night
Has flung the Stone that puts the Stars to Flight:
And Lo! the Hunter of the East has caught
The Sultan's Turret in a Noose of Light.
*The Rubáiyát of Omar Khayyám* (1st edn.), I

3 Come, fill the Cup, and in the Fire of Spring
The Winter Garment of Repentance fling:
The Bird of Time has but a little way
To fly — and Lo! the Bird is on the Wing.
*The Rubáiyát of Omar Khayyám* (1st edn.), VII

4 The Wine of Life keeps oozing drop by drop,
The Leaves of Life keep falling one by one.
*The Rubáiyát of Omar Khayyám* (4th edn.), VIII

5 Here with a Loaf of Bread beneath the Bough,
A Flask of Wine, a Book of Verse — and Thou
Beside me singing in the Wilderness —
And Wilderness is Paradise enow.
*The Rubáiyát of Omar Khayyám* (1st edn.), XI

6 Ah, take the Cash in hand and waive the Rest;
Oh, the brave Music of a *distant* Drum!
*The Rubáiyát of Omar Khayyám* (1st edn.), XII

7 The Worldly Hope men set their Hearts upon
Turns Ashes – or it prospers; and anon,
Like Snow upon the Desert's dusty face,
Lighting a little Hour or two – is gone.
*The Rubáiyát of Omar Khayyám* (1st edn.), XIV

8 I sometimes think that never blows so red
The Rose as where some buried Caesar bled;
That every Hyacinth the Garden wears
Dropt in her Lap from some once lovely Head.
*The Rubáiyát of Omar Khayyám* (1st edn.), XVIII

9 Ah, my Belovéd, fill the Cup that clears
TO-DAY of past Regrets and Future Fears:
*To-morrow!* – Why, To-morrow I may be
Myself with Yesterday's Sev'n thousand Years.
*The Rubáiyát of Omar Khayyám* (1st edn.), XX

10 One thing is certain, that Life flies;
One thing is certain, and the Rest is Lies;
The Flower that once has blown for ever dies.
*The Rubáiyát of Omar Khayyám* (1st edn.), XXVI

11 I came like Water, and like Wind I go.
*The Rubáiyát of Omar Khayyám* (1st edn.), XXVIII

12 Ah, fill the Cup: – what boots it to repeat
How Time is slipping underneath our Feet:
Unborn TOMORROW, and dead YESTERDAY,
Why fret about them if TODAY be sweet!
*The Rubáiyát of Omar Khayyám* (1st edn.), XXXVII

13 'Tis all a Chequer-board of Nights and Days
Where Destiny with Men for Pieces plays:
Hither and thither moves, and mates, and slays,
And one by one back in the Closet lays.
*The Rubáiyát of Omar Khayyám* (1st edn.), XLIX

14 The Moving Finger writes; and, having writ,
Moves on: nor all thy Piety nor Wit
Shall lure it back to cancel half a Line,
Nor all thy Tears wash out a Word of it.
*The Rubáiyát of Omar Khayyám* (1st edn.), LI

15 And that inverted Bowl we call The Sky,
Whereunder crawling coop't we live and die,
Lift not thy hands to *It* for help – for It
Rolls impotently on as Thou or I.
*The Rubáiyát of Omar Khayyám* (1st edn.), LII

16 'Who *is* the Potter, pray, and who the Pot?'
*The Rubáiyát of Omar Khayyám* (1st edn.), LX

17 Strange, is it not? that of the myriads who
Before us pass'd the door of Darkness through,
Not one returns to tell us of the Road,
Which to discover we must travel too.
*The Rubáiyát of Omar Khayyám* (4th edn.), LXIV

18 Drink! for you know not whence you came, nor
why:
Drink! for you know not why you go, nor where.
*The Rubáiyát of Omar Khayyám* (4th edn.), LXXIV

**Fitzgerald, F(rancis) Scott (Key)** (1896–1940) US novelist. His first successful novel was the autobiographical *This Side of Paradise* (1920). This was followed by *The Great Gatsby* (1925) and *Tender is the Night* (1934) before he declined into alcoholism.

1 In the real dark night of the soul it is always
three o'clock in the morning.
*See* ST JOHN OF THE CROSS
*The Crack-Up*

2 Though the Jazz Age continued, it became less
and less an affair of youth. The sequel was like
a children's party taken over by the elders.
*The Crack-Up*

3 FITZGERALD. The rich are different from us.
HEMINGWAY. Yes, they have more money.
*The Crack-Up*, 'Notebooks, E'

4 I entertained on a cruising trip that was so much
fun that I had to sink my yacht to make my
guests go home.
*The Crack-Up*, 'Notebooks, K'

5 One of those men who reach such an acute limited excellence at twenty-one that everything afterward savours of anti-climax.
*The Great Gatsby*, Ch. 1

6 I was one of the few guests who had actually
been invited. People were not invited – they
went there.
*The Great Gatsby*, Ch. 3

7 One girl can be pretty – but a dozen are only a
chorus.
*The Last Tycoon*

8 He differed from the healthy type that was essentially middle-class – he never seemed to
perspire.
*This Side of Paradise*, Bk. I, Ch. 2

9 Beware of the artist who's an intellectual also.
The artist who doesn't fit.
*This Side of Paradise*, Bk. II, Ch. 5

10 'I know myself,' he cried, 'but that is all.'
*This Side of Paradise*, Bk. II, Ch. 5

11 A big man has no time really to do anything but
just sit and be big.
*This Side of Paradise*, Bk. III, Ch. 2

12 First you take a drink, then the drink takes a
drink, then the drink takes you.
*Ackroyd* (Jules Feiffer), '1964, May 7'

13 Sometimes I don't know whether Zelda and I are
real or whether we are characters in one of my
novels.
Said of himself and his wife
*A Second Flowering* (Malcolm Cowley)

14 All good writing is *swimming under water* and
holding your breath.
Letter to Frances Scott Fitzgerald

**Fitzgerald, Zelda** (1900–48) US writer. The wife of F. Scott Fitzgerald, she suffered increasingly from schizophrenia and was confined to an asylum from 1930.

1  I don't want to live – I want to love first,
and live incidentally.
Letter to F. Scott Fitzgerald, 1919

2  Don't you think I was made for you? I feel like
you had me ordered – and I was delivered to
you – to be worn – I want you to wear me,
like a watch-charm or a button hole boquet – to
the world.
Letter to F. Scott Fitzgerald, 1919

3  A vacuum can only exist, I imagine, by the
things which enclose it.
Journal, 1932

**Fitzsimmons, Bob** (Robert Prometheus Fitzsimmons; 1862–
1917) British-born New Zealand boxer, who was world
heavyweight champion (1897–99).

1  The bigger they come the harder they fall.
Remark before a fight, San Francisco, 9 June 1899

**Flanagan, Bud** (Robert Winthrop; 1896–1968) British
comedian who formed part of a double act with Chesney Allen,
within the six-strong Crazy Gang. His songs include *Hometown*,
*Underneath the Arches*, and *Umbrella Man*.

1  Underneath the arches
We dream our dreams away.
*Underneath the Arches*

**Flanders, Michael** (1922–75) British comedian and
songwriter. Confined to a wheelchair by polio, he performed in a
double-act with Donald Swann. *At the Drop of a Hat* (1956) was
the forerunner of many other similar revues. He also wrote a
number of songs.

1  Eating people is wrong.
*The Reluctant Cannibal*

**Flaubert, Gustave** (1821–80) French novelist. He made his
name with *Madame Bovary* (1856), which was followed by
*Salammbô* (1862), and *La Tentation de Saint Antoine* (1874).

1  All one's inventions are true, you can be sure of
that. Poetry is as exact a science as geometry.
Letter to Louise Colet, 14 Aug 1853

2  Books are made not like children but like pyra-
mids . . . and they're just as useless! and they
stay in the desert! . . . Jackals piss at their
foot and the bourgeois climb up on them.
Letter to Ernest Feydeau, 1857

**Flecker, James Elroy** (1884–1915) British poet, best
known for his poem *The Golden Journey to Samarkand* (1913) and
the verse drama *Hassan*, produced posthumously in 1922 with
music by Delius.

1  For lust of knowing what should not be known,
We take the Golden Road to Samarkand.
*Hassan*, V:2

**Fletcher, John** (1579–1625) English dramatist, who
collaborated with Francis Beaumont, Philip Massinger, and others
on many plays.

1  Best while you have it use your breath,
There is no drinking after death.
With Jonson and others
*The Bloody Brother*, II:2

2  And he that will go to bed sober,
Falls with the leaf still in October.
*The Bloody Brother*, II:2

3  Death hath so many doors to let out life.
With Massinger
*The Custom of the Country*, II:2

**Florian, Jean-Pierre Claris de** (1755–94) French writer
of fables.

1  *Plaisir d'amour ne dure qu'un moment,*
*Chagrin d'amour dure toute la vie.*
Love's pleasure lasts but a moment; love's sor-
row lasts all through life.
*Celestine*

**Florio, John** (c. 1553–1625) English lexicographer and
translator, who published an Italian–English dictionary (1598) and
an English translation of Montaigne's *Essays* (1603).

1  England is the paradise of women, the purgatory
of men, and the hell of horses.
*Second Fruits*

**Foch, Ferdinand, Marshal** (1851–1929) French soldier.
He played a dominant part in World War I, being appointed
supreme commander of all allied forces in 1918.

1  My centre is giving way, my right is in retreat;
situation excellent. I shall attack.
Message sent during the second battle of the Marne, 1918
*Biography of Foch* (Aston), Ch. 13

2  What a marvellous place to drop one's mother-
in-law!
Remark on being shown the Grand Canyon
Attrib.

3  None but a coward dares to boast that he has
never known fear.
Attrib.

**Fontenelle, Bernard de** (1657–1757) French philosopher,
whose writings helped to popularize the theories of Descartes and
Newton.

1  It is high time for me to depart, for at my age I
now begin to see things as they really are.
Remark on his deathbed, at the age of 99
*Anekdotenschatz* (H. Hoffmeister)

2  I feel nothing, apart from a certain difficulty in
continuing to exist.
Remark made on his deathbed, at the age of 99
*Famous Last Words* (B. Conrad)

**Foot, Michael (Mackintosh)** (1913– ) British Labour
politician and journalist. Leader of the Labour Party (1980–83).
He has been editor of *Tribune* and political columnist in the *Daily
Herald*. His many books include *Trial of Mussolini* (1943),
*Parliament in Danger* (1959), and a two-volume biography of
Aneurin Bevan (1962–73).

1  A Royal Commission is a broody hen sitting on a
china egg.
Speech, House of Commons, 1964

**Foote, Samuel** (1720–77) British actor and dramatist. He built the Haymarket Theatre, where he presented some of his own plays, including *The Englishman in Paris* (1753) and *The Nabob* (1772).

1 So she went into the garden to cut a cabbage-leaf; to make an apple-pie; and at the same time a great she-bear, coming up the street, pops its head into the shop. 'What! no soap?' So he died, and she very imprudently married the barber; and there were present the Picninnies, and the Joblillies, and the Garyalies, and the grand Panjandrum himself, with the little round button at top, and they all fell to playing the game of catch as catch can, till the gun powder ran out at the heels of their boots.

*Nonsense composed to test the actor Charles Macklin's claim that he could memorize anything*

2 He is not only dull in himself, but the cause of dullness in others.

*Parody of a line from Shakespeare's Henry IV, Part 2*
*Life of Johnson (J. Boswell)*

**Forbes, C. F.** (1817–1911) British writer.

1 The sense of being well-dressed gives a feeling of inward tranquillity which religion is powerless to bestow.

*Social Aims (Emerson)*

**Ford, Gerald R(udolph)** (1913– ) US statesman. Following Nixon's resignation, he became the first President of the USA not to have been elected to the office.

1 I guess it proves that in America anyone can be President.

*Referring to his own appointment as president*
*A Ford Not a Lincoln (Richard Reeves), Ch. 4*

**Ford, Henry** (1863–1947) US car manufacturer, who founded the Ford Motor Company in 1903 and introduced assembly-line production.

1 History is more or less bunk. It's tradition. We don't want tradition. We want to live in the present and the only history that is worth a tinker's damn is the history we make today.

*Chicago Tribune, 25 May 1916*

2 Exercise is bunk. If you are healthy, you don't need it: if you are sick, you shouldn't take it.

*Attrib.*

3 Any colour, so long as it's black.

*Referring to the colour options offered for the Model-T Ford car*
*Attrib.*

**Ford, John** (c. 1586–c. 1640) English dramatist. The tragedies *The Broken Heart* (1630) and *'Tis Pity She's a Whore* (1632) are still performed.

1 Tempt not the stars, young man, thou canst not play
With the severity of fate.

*The Broken Heart, I:3*

2 He hath shook hands with time.

*The Broken Heart, V:2*

3 'Tis Pity She's a Whore.

*Play title*

**Ford, John** (Sean O'Feeney; 1895–1973) US film director. Best known for westerns, including *Stagecoach* (1939) and *How The West Was Won* (1962), his other films include *The Grapes of Wrath* (1940).

1 It is easier to get an actor to be a cowboy than to get a cowboy to be an actor.

*Attrib.*

**Forgy, Howell Maurice** (1908– ) US naval captain.

1 Praise the Lord and pass the ammunition!

*Remark made during the Japanese attack on Pearl Harbor, 7 Dec 1941*
*Attrib. in The Los Angeles Times*

**Formby, George** (1905–61) British comedian. He was popular in music halls and in such films as *Keep Your Seats Please* (1936) and *Let George Do It* (1940), invariably featuring his comic songs accompanied by his ukelele.

1 I'm leaning on a lamp-post at the corner of the street,
In case a certain little lady walks by.

*Leaning on a Lamp-post*

2 With my little stick of Blackpool rock,
Along the Promenade I stroll.
It may be sticky but I never complain,
It's nice to have a nibble at it now and again

*With My Little Stick of Blackpool Rock*

**Forrest, Nathan Bedford** (1821–77) Confederate general in the US Civil War.

1 I got there fustest with the mostest.

*Popular misquotation of his explanation of his success in capturing Murfreesboro; his actual words were, 'I just took the short cut and got there first with the most men'*
*A Civil War Treasury (B. Botkin)*

2 Ah, colonel, all's fair in love and war, you know.

*Remark to a captured enemy officer who had been tricked into surrendering*
*A Civil War Treasury (B. Botkin)*

**Forster, E(dward) M(organ)** (1879–1970) British novelist. His books include *Where Angels Fear to Tread* (1905), *A Room with a View* (1908), *Howard's End* (1910), and *A Passage to India* (1924).

1 The historian must have . . . some conception of how men who are not historians behave. Otherwise he will move in a world of the dead.

*Abinger Harvest, 'Captain Edward Gibbon'*

2 It is not that the Englishman can't feel – it is that he is afraid to feel. He has been taught at his public school that feeling is bad form. He must not express great joy or sorrow, or even open his mouth too wide when he talks – his pipe might fall out if he did.

*Abinger Harvest, 'Notes on the English Character'*

**3** They go forth into it with well-developed bodies, fairly developed minds, and undeveloped hearts.

Referring to public schoolboys going into the world
*Abinger Harvest*, 'Notes on the English Character'

**4** Works of art, in my opinion, are the only objects in the material universe to possess internal order, and that is why, though I don't believe that only art matters, I do believe in Art for Art's sake.

*Art for Art's Sake*

**5** Yes – oh dear, yes – the novel tells a story.

*Aspects of the Novel*, Ch. 2

**6** Creative writers are always greater than the causes that they represent.

*Gide and George*

**7** Beethoven's Fifth Symphony is the most sublime noise that has ever penetrated into the ear of man.

*Howards End*, Ch. 5

**8** Death destroys a man, the idea of Death saves him.

*Howards End*, Ch. 27

**9** Only connect!

*Howards End*, Epigraph

**10** The so-called white races are really pinko-gray.

*A Passage to India*, Ch. 7

**11** I hate the idea of causes, and if I had to choose between betraying my country and betraying my friend, I hope I should have the guts to betray my country.

*Two Cheers for Democracy*, 'What I Believe'

**12** Spoon feeding in the long run teaches us nothing but the shape of the spoon.

*The Observer*, 'Sayings of the Week', 7 Oct 1951

**Fosdick, Harry Emerson** (1878–1969) US baptist minister. His books include *The Second Mile* (1908) and *On Being a Real Person* (1943).

**1** An atheist is a man who has no invisible means of support.

Attrib.

**Foster, S(tephen) C(ollins)** (1826–64) US composer of popular songs, including *My Old Kentucky Home*, *The Old Folks at Home*, and *O, Susanna*. A big earner, but a bigger spender, he died in poverty.

**1** Gwine to run all night!
Gwine to run all day!
I bet my money on the bob-tail nag.
Somebody bet on the bay.

*Camptown Races*

**2** Weep no more, my lady,
Oh! weep no more today!
We will sing one song for the old Kentucky Home,
For the old Kentucky Home far away.

*My Old Kentucky Home*

**3** 'Way down upon de Swanee Ribber,
Far, far away,
Dere's where my heart is turning ebber:
Dere's where de old folks stay.
All up and down de whole creation
Sadly I roam,
Still longing for de old plantation,
And for de old folks at home.

*The Old Folks at Home*

**4** O, Susanna! O, don't you cry for me,
I've come from Alabama, wid my banjo on my knee.

*O, Susanna*

**5** I'm coming, I'm coming,
For my head is bending low
I hear their gentle voices calling, 'Poor old Joe'

*Poor Old Joe*

**6** Dere's no more work for poor old Ned,
He's gone whar de good niggers go.

*Uncle Ned*

**Fourier, (François Marie) Charles** (1772–1837) French social scientist. His *Théorie des Quatre Mouvements* (1808) advocated a reorganization of society known as Fourierism.

**1** The extension of women's rights is the basic principle of all social progress.

*Théorie des Quatre Mouvements*

**Fowles, John** (1926– ) British novelist. He made his name with *The Collector* (1963), *The Magus* (1966), and *The French Lieutenant's Woman* (1969), all of which have been filmed. Later books include *A Maggot* (1985).

**1** In essence the Renaissance was simply the green end of one of civilization's hardest winters.

*The French Lieutenant's Woman*, Ch. 10

**2** We all write poems; it is simply that poets are the ones who write in words.

*The French Lieutenant's Woman*, Ch. 19

**3** There are many reasons why novelists write, but they all have one thing in common – a need to create an alternative world.

*The Sunday Times Magazine*, 2 Oct 1977

**Fox, Charles James** (1749–1806) British Whig politician. He became foreign secretary twice (1782; 1806); a supporter of the French Revolution, he was dismissed from the privy council for opposing war with France after the Revolution.

**1** He was uniformly of an opinion which, though not a popular one, he was ready to aver, that the right of governing was not property but a trust.

Referring to William Pitt's plans for parliamentary reform
*C.J. Fox* (J. L. Hammond)

**2** No man could be so wise as Thurlow looked.

*Lives of the Lord Chancellors* (Campbell), Vol. V

**3** How much the greatest event it is that ever happened in the world! and how much the best!

Referring to the fall of the Bastille, 14 July 1789
Letter to Fitzpatrick, 30 July 1789

**4** Kings govern by means of popular assemblies only when they cannot do without them.
Attrib.

**5** I die happy.
His last words
*Life and Times of C. J. Fox* (Russell), Vol. III

**Fox, George** (1624–91) English religious leader, who founded the Quakers. He was frequently imprisoned for his beliefs; his best-known work is his *Journal* (1674).

**1** When the Lord sent me forth into the world, He forbade me to put off my hat to any high or low.
*Journal*

**Fox, Henry Stephen** (1791–1846) British diplomat.

**1** I am so changed that my oldest creditors would hardly know me.
Remark after an illness.
Letter from Byron to John Murray, 8 May 1817

**France, Anatole** (Jacques Anatole François Thibault; 1844–1924) French poet, novelist, and critic. His verse collection *Poèmes Dorés* (1873) was followed by a number of novels, including *La Révolte des Anges* (1914). His *Histoire Contemporaine* comprises a series of books ending with *La Vie en Fleur* (1922).

**1** It is only the poor who are forbidden to beg.
*Crainquebille*

**2** To disarm the strong and arm the weak would be to change the social order which it's my job to preserve. Justice is the means by which established injustices are sanctioned.
*Crainquebille*

**3** Man is so made that he can only find relaxation from one kind of labour by taking up another.
*The Crime of Sylvestre Bonnard*

**4** The Arab who builds himself a hut out of the marble fragments of a temple in Palmyra is more philosophical than all the curators of the museums in London, Munich or Paris.
*The Crime of Sylvestre Bonnard*

**5** The wonder is, not that the field of the stars is so vast, but that man has measured it.
*The Garden of Epicurus*

**6** Christianity has done a great deal for love by making a sin of it.
*The Garden of Epicurus*

**7** A good critic is one who narrates the adventures of his mind among masterpieces.
*The Literary Life*, Preface

**8** It was in the barbarous, gothic times when words had a meaning; in those days, writers expressed thoughts.
*The Literary Life*, 'M. Charles Morice'

**9** The majestic egalitarianism of the law, which forbids rich and poor alike to sleep under bridges, to beg in the streets, and to steal bread.
*The Red Lily*, Ch. 7

**10** It is only the poor who pay cash, and that not from virtue, but because they are refused credit.
*A Cynic's Breviary* (J. R. Solly)

**Francis I** (1494–1547) King of France (1515–47). His reign was dominated by conflict with Charles V, Holy Roman Emperor. At Pavia (1525) he was defeated by Charles and taken prisoner. He was released after agreeing to give up Burgundy and his claims to other lands – promises that he did not keep.

**1** Of all I had, only honour and life have been spared.
Referring to his defeat at the Battle of Pavia, 24 Feb 1525; usually misquoted as 'All is lost save honour.'
Letter to Louise of Savoy (his mother), 1525

**Franklin, Benjamin** (1706–90) US scientist and statesman. His experiments with a kite established the electrical nature of thunderstorms and enabled him to invent lightning conductors. As a diplomat in Paris he negotiated peace with Britain in 1783.

**1** Remember that time is money.
*Advice to a Young Tradesman*

**2** No nation was ever ruined by trade.
*Essays*, 'Thoughts on Commercial Subjects'

**3** A little neglect may breed mischief, . . . for want of a nail, the shoe was lost; for want of a shoe the horse was lost; and for want of a horse the rider was lost.
*Poor Richard's Almanack*

**4** Some are weather-wise, some are otherwise.
*Poor Richard's Almanack*

**5** Three may keep a secret, if two of them are dead.
*Poor Richard's Almanack*

**6** At twenty years of age, the will reigns; at thirty, the wit; and at forty, the judgement.
*Poor Richard's Almanack*

**7** Dost thou love life? Then do not squander time, for that's the stuff life is made of.
*Poor Richard's Almanack*

**8** Many a long dispute among divines may be thus abridged: It is so. It is not so. It is so. It is not so.
*Poor Richard's Almanack*

**9** What is the use of a new-born child?
Response when asked the same question of a new invention
*Life and Times of Benjamin Franklin* (J. Parton), Pt. IV

**10** Man is a tool-making animal.
*Life of Johnson* (J. Boswell), 7 Apr 1778

**11** A lonesome man on a rainy day who does not know how to read.
On being asked what condition of man he considered the most pitiable
*Wit, Wisdom, and Foibles of the Great* (C. Shriner)

**12** Here Skugg
  Lies snug
  As a bug
  In a rug.

An epitaph for a squirrel, 'skug' being a dialect name for the animal
Letter to Georgiana Shipley, 26 Sept 1772

**13** We must indeed all hang together, or most assuredly, we shall all hang separately.

Remark on signing the Declaration of Independence, 4 July 1776

**14** There never was a good war or a bad peace.

Letter to Josiah Quincy, 11 Sept 1783

**15** In this world nothing is certain but death and taxes.

Letter to Jean-Baptiste Leroy, 13 Nov 1789

**16** The body of
  Benjamin Franklin, printer,
  (Like the cover of an old book,
  Its contents worn out,
  And stript of its lettering and gilding)
  Lies here, food for worms!
  Yet the work itself shall not be lost,
  For it will, as he believed, appear once more
  In a new
  And more beautiful edition,
  Corrected and amended
  By its Author!

Suggestion for his own epitaph

**Franks, Oliver, Baron** (1905– ) British philosopher and administrator. British ambassador to the USA (1948–52), he was Provost of Worcester College, Oxford (1962–76), and has held many other academic offices.

**1** It is a secret in the Oxford sense: you may tell it to only one person at a time.

*Sunday Telegraph*, 30 Jan 1977

**Frayn, Michael** (1933– ) British journalist, novelist, and dramatist. His plays include *The Sandboy* (1971) and *Noises Off* (1982). *The Tin Men* (1965) is his best-known novel.

**1** No woman so naked as one you can see to be naked underneath her clothes.

*Constructions*

**2** For hundreds of pages the closely-reasoned arguments unroll, axioms and theorems interlock. And what remains with us in the end? A general sense that the world can be expressed in closely-reasoned arguments, in interlocking axioms and theorems.

*Constructions*

**3** To be absolutely honest, what I feel really bad about is that I don't feel worse. There's the ineffectual liberal's problem in a nutshell.

*The Observer*, 8 Aug 1965

**Frederick the Great** (1712–86) King of Prussia. A writer and composer himself, he gathered a distinguished circle of writers and musicians at his palace of Sans Souci near Potsdam.

**1** Rascals, would you live for ever?

Addressed to reluctant soldiers at the Battle of Kolin, 18 June 1757. *See also* DALY

**2** My people and I have come to an agreement which satisfies us both. They are to say what they please, and I am to do what I please.

Attrib.

**Freed, Arthur** (1894–1973) US film producer and songwriter. He made several musicals featuring his own lyrics.

**1** I'm singing in the rain, just singing in the rain;
  What a wonderful feeling, I'm happy again.

From the musical, *Hollywood Revue of 1929*
*Singing in the Rain*

**Freud, Clement** (1924– ) British Liberal politician, writer, broadcaster, and caterer. His books include *Freud on Food* (1978) and *The Book of Hangovers* (1981).

**1** If you resolve to give up smoking, drinking and loving, you don't actually live longer; it just seems longer.

*The Observer*, 27 Dec 1964

**2** I find it hard to say, because when I was there it seemed to be shut.

On being asked for his opinion of New Zealand. Similar remarks have been attributed to others
BBC radio, 12 Apr 1978

**Freud, Sigmund** (1856–1939) Austrian psychoanalyst. As a physician in Vienna he studied hypnosis but moved on to develop psychoanalysis and the theory that many neuroses were caused by suppressed sexual desires. His works include *The Interpretation of Dreams* (1899) and *Totem and Taboo* (1913).

**1** The voice of the intellect is a soft one, but it does not rest till it has gained a hearing.

*The Future of an Illusion*

**2** The psychic development of the individual is a short repetition of the course of development of the race.

*Leonardo da Vinci*

**3** Religion is an illusion and it derives its strength from the fact that it falls in with our instinctual desires.

*New Introductory Lectures on Psychoanalysis*, 'A Philosophy of Life'

**4** Conscience is the internal perception of the rejection of a particular wish operating within us.

*Totem and Taboo*

**5** At bottom God is nothing more than an exalted father.

*Totem and Taboo*

**6** The great question . . . which I have not been able to answer, despite my thirty years of research into the feminine soul, is 'What does a woman want'?

*Psychiatry in American Life* (Charles Rolo)

**Frisch, Max** (1911– ) Swiss dramatist and novelist. His plays include *The Fire Raisers* (1958) and *Andorra* (1961), and his novels *Stiller* (1954) and *Homo Faber* (1957).

**1** He cannot bear old men's jokes. That is not new. But now he begins to think of them himself.
*Sketchbook 1966–71*

**Frost, David** (1939– ) British television personality.

**1** Television is an invention that permits you to be entertained in your living room by people you wouldn't have in your home.
Remark, CBS television, 1971

**Frost, Robert Lee** (1875–1963) US poet, whose collections *Boy's Will* (1913) and *North of Boston* (1914) brought him considerable acclaim.

**1** Most of the change we think we see in life
Is due to truths being in and out of favour.
*The Black Cottage*

**2** No tears in the writer, no tears in the reader.
*Collected Poems*, Preface

**3** Home is the place where, when you have to go there,
They have to take you in.
*The Death of the Hired Man*

**4** Forgive, O Lord, my little jokes on Thee
And I'll forgive Thy great big one on me.
*In the Clearing*, 'Cluster of Faith'

**5** Something there is that doesn't love a wall.
*North of Boston*, 'Mending Wall'

**6** My apple trees will never get across
And eat the cones under his pines, I tell him.
He only says, 'Good fences make good neighbours.'
*North of Boston*, 'Mending Wall'

**7** Two roads diverged in a wood, and I –
I took the one less traveled by,
And that has made all the difference.
*The Road Not Taken*

**8** The woods are lovely, dark, and deep,
But I have promises to keep,
And miles to go before I sleep,
And miles to go before I sleep.
*Stopping by Woods on a Snowy Evening*

**9** Writing free verse is like playing tennis with the net down.
Speech, Milton Academy, 17 May 1935

**10** A diplomat is a man who always remembers a woman's birthday but never remembers her age.
Attrib.

**11** Poetry is what gets lost in translation.
Attrib.

**Froude, J(ames) A(nthony)** (1818–94) British historian. His *History of England* (1856–70) established his reputation.

**1** Wild animals never kill for sport. Man is the only one to whom the torture and death of his fellow-creatures is amusing in itself.
*Oceana*, Ch. 5

**2** Men are made by nature unequal. It is vain, therefore, to treat them as if they were equal.
*Short Studies on Great Subjects*, 'Party Politics'

**3** Fear is the parent of cruelty.
*Short Studies on Great Subjects*, 'Party Politics'

**Fry, Christopher** (1907– ) British dramatist. His verse drama *The Lady's Not for Burning* (1948) brought him considerable popularity. Other plays include *Venus Observed* (1950) and *A Sleep of Prisoners* (1951).

**1** Why so shy, my pretty Thomasina?
Thomasin, O Thomasin,
Once you were so promisin'.
*The Dark Is Light Enough*, II

**2** I sometimes think
His critical judgement is so exquisite
It leaves us nothing to admire except his opinion.
*The Dark is Light Enough*, II

**3** Religion
Has made an honest woman of the supernatural,
And we won't have it kicking over the traces again.
*The Lady's Not for Burning*, II

**4** Where in this small-talking world can I find
A longitude with no platitude?
*The Lady's Not for Burning*, III

**5** Try thinking of love, or something.
*Amor vincit insomnia.*
*A Sleep of Prisoners*

**Fuller, Richard Buckminster** (1895–1983) US architect and inventor. His Dymaxion house (1928) never achieved success but his geodesic dome is widely used. Writings include *Operating Manual for Spaceship Earth* (1969).

**1** I am a passenger on the spaceship, Earth.
*Operating Manual for Spaceship Earth*

**Fuller, Thomas** (1608–61) English historian. His best-known work is the *History of Worthies of England* (1662) – a biographical dictionary.

**1** There is a great difference between painting a face and not washing it.
*Church History*, Bk. VII

**2** A proverb is much matter decorated into few words.
*The History of the Worthies of England*, Ch. 2

**3** Fame is sometimes like unto a kind of mushroom, which Pliny recounts to be the greatest miracle in nature, because growing and having no root.
*The Holy State and the Profane State*

**4** Many have been the wise speeches of fools, though not so many as the foolish speeches of wise men.
*The Holy State and the Profane State*

**5** Anger is one of the sinews of the soul.
*The Holy State and the Profane State*

6 Learning hath gained most by those books by which the printers have lost.
*The Holy State and the Profane State*

**Furber, Douglas** (1885–1961) British songwriter; author and co-author of many musicals and songs.

1 Any time you're Lambeth way,
Any evening, any day,

You'll find us all doin' the Lambeth walk.
*Doin' the Lambeth Walk*

**Fyleman, Rose** (1877–1957) British writer of children's books.

1 There are fairies at the bottom of our garden.
*Fairies and Chimneys*

# G

**Gabor, Zsa Zsa** (1919– ) Hungarian-born US film star. In 1961 she published her autobiography *My Story.*

1 Husbands are like fires. They go out when unattended.
*Newsweek*, 28 Mar 1960

2 A man in love is incomplete until he has married. Then he's finished.
*Newsweek*, 28 Mar 1960

3 I never hated a man enough to give him diamonds back.
*The Observer*, 'Sayings of the Week', 28 Aug 1957

**Gainsborough, Thomas** (1727–88) British portrait and landscape painter.

1 We are all going to Heaven, and Vandyke is of the company.
Last words
*Thomas Gainsborough* (Boulton), Ch. 9

**Gaisford, Thomas** (1799–1855) British classicist and clergyman. He was dean of Christ Church, Oxford and edited many classical texts.

1 Nor can I do better, in conclusion, than impress upon you the study of Greek literature which not only elevates above the vulgar herd, but leads not infrequently to positions of considerable emolument.
Christmas Day Sermon at Oxford
*Reminiscences of Oxford* (Revd W. Tuckwell)

**Gaitskell, Hugh** (1906–63) British Labour politician. He was chancellor of the exchequer (1950–51) in Attlee's government and succeeded him as party leader. He reunited the party before his untimely death.

1 Surely the right course is to test the Russians, not the bombs.
*Observer*, 'Sayings of the Week', 23 June 1957

2 All terrorists, at the invitation of the Government, end up with drinks at the Dorchester.
Letter to *The Guardian*, 23 Aug 1977 (Dora Gaitskell)

3 There are some of us . . . who will fight, fight, fight, and fight again to save the party we love.
After his policy for a nuclear deterrent had been defeated. Speech, Labour Party conference, Scarborough, 3 Oct 1960

**Galbraith, John Kenneth** (1908– ) US economist in the Keynesian tradition; he was US ambassador (1961–63) to India and adviser to President Kennedy. His books include *The Affluent Society* (1958) and *Economics and the Public Purpose* (1973).

1 Wealth is not without its advantages, and the case to the contrary, although it has often been made, has never proved widely persuasive.
*The Affluent Society*, Ch. 1

2 Wealth has never been a sufficient source of honour in itself. It must be advertised, and the normal medium is obtrusively expensive goods.
*The Affluent Society*, Ch. 7

3 Few things are as immutable as the addiction of political groups to the ideas by which they have once won office.
*The Affluent Society*, Ch. 13

4 In the affluent society no useful distinction can be made between luxuries and necessaries.
*The Affluent Society*, Ch. 21

5 All races have produced notable economists, with the exception of the Irish who doubtless can protest their devotion to higher arts.
*The Age of Uncertainty*, Ch. 1

6 Much of the world's work, it has been said, is done by men who do not feel quite well. Marx is a case in point.
*The Age of Uncertainty*, Ch. 3

7 Money differs from an automobile, a mistress or cancer in being equally important to those who have it and those who do not.
Attrib.

8 The salary of the chief executive of the large corporation is not a market award for achievement. It is frequently in the nature of a warm personal gesture by the individual to himself.
*Annals of an Abiding Liberal*

**Galilei, Galileo** (1564–1642) Italian scientist. He made a number of major discoveries in mechanics and astronomy. Using the newly invented telescope he showed that Copernicus' heliocentric model of the universe was vastly superior to the Ptolomaic system favoured by the Roman Catholic Church. The Inquisition, however, forced him to recant and held him under house arrest for some 25 years.

1 *Eppur si muove*
Yet it moves

Referring to the Earth. Remark supposedly made after his recantation (1632) of belief in the Copernican system.
Attrib.

**Galsworthy, John** (1867–1933) British novelist and dramatist. His series of novels, *The Forsyte Saga*, made his name. Plays include *The Silver Box* (1906).

1 Oh, your precious 'lame ducks'!
*The Man of Property*, Pt. II, Ch. 12

**Gandhi, Indira** (1917–84) Indian stateswoman. The daughter of Jawaharla Nehru, she was prime minister twice (1966–67; 1980–84). She was assassinated by Sikh extremists.

1 To bear many children is considered not only a religious blessing but also an investment. The greater their number, some Indians reason, the more alms they can beg.
*New York Review of Books*, 'Indira's Coup' (Oriana Fallaci)

2 There exists no politician in India daring enough to attempt to explain to the masses that cows can be eaten.
*New York Review of Books*, 'Indira's Coup' (Oriana Fallaci)

3 You cannot shake hands with a clenched fist.
Remark at a press conference, New Delhi, 19 Oct 1971

4 There are moments in history when brooding tragedy and its dark shadows can be lightened by recalling great moments of the past.
Letter to Richard Nixon, 16 Dec 1971

**Gandhi, Mahatma** (Mohandas Karamchand Gandhi; 1869–1948) Indian national leader who used civil disobedience to achieve political aims. He became leader of the Indian National Congress and was treated as a saint in his own country. He was influential in the achievement of Indian independence, but his advocacy of cooperation between Hindus and Muslims led to his assassination by a Hindu fanatic.

1 I think it would be a good idea.
On being asked for his view on Western civilization
Attrib.

**Garbo, Greta** (1905–  ) Swedish-born US film star, whose films include *Grand Hotel* (1932), *Camille* (1936), and *Ninotchka* (1939). She retired in 1941 into an enigmatic private life.

1 I want to be alone.
Words spoken by Garbo in the film *Grand Hotel*, and associated with her for the rest of her career. *See below.*

2 I never said, 'I want to be alone.' I only said, 'I want to be *left* alone.' There is all the difference.
*Garbo* (John Bainbridge)

**Garfield, James A(bram)** (1831–81) US statesman. He became Republican President (1881) after a military career. He was assassinated.

1 My fellow citizens, the President is dead, but the Government lives and God Omnipotent reigns.
Speech following the assassination of Lincoln

**Garibaldi, Giuseppe** (1807–82) Italian general and political leader, who was active in the campaign for Italian unification.

1 Anyone who wants to carry on the war against the outsiders, come with me. I can't offer you either honours or wages; I offer you hunger, thirst, forced marches, battles and death. Anyone who loves his country, follow me.
*Garibaldi* (Guerzoni)

**Garland, Judy** (Frances Gumm; 1922–69) US film star and singer. She established herself as a child star in *The Wizard of Oz* (1939). Later films, such as *Easter Parade* (1948) and *A Star Is Born* (1954) also brought success, but addiction caused her premature death.

1 I was born at the age of twelve on a Metro-Goldwyn-Mayer lot.
*The Observer*, 'Sayings of the Week', 18 Feb 1951

**Garrick, David** (1717–79) British actor and manager, who ran the Drury Lane Theatre (1747–76), where he introduced many innovations.

1 Prologues precede the piece – in mournful verse;
As undertakers – walk before the hearse.
*Apprentice*, Prologue

2 Come cheer up, my lads! 'tis to glory we steer,
To add something more to this wonderful year;
To honour we call you, not press you like slaves,
For who are so free as the sons of the waves?
Heart of oak are our ships,
Heart of oak are our men:
We always are ready;
Steady, boys, steady;
We'll fight and we'll conquer again and again.
*Heart of Oak*

**Garrison, William Lloyd** (1805–79) US abolitionist. He founded *The Liberator* (1831), the antislavery journal.

1 Our country is the world – our countrymen are all mankind.
*The Liberator*, 15 Dec 1837

2 The compact which exists between the North and the South is a covenant with death and an agreement with hell.
Resolution, Massachusetts Anti-Slavery Society, 27 Jan 1843

**Garrod, Heathcote William** (1878–1960) British classical scholar and literary critic.

1 Madam, I am the civilization they are fighting to defend.
Replying to criticism that he was not fighting to defend civilization, during World War I
*Oxford Now and Then* (D. Balsdon)

**Gaskell, Elizabeth Cleghorn** (1810–65) British novelist. Her novels include *Mary Barton* (1848) and *Cranford* (1853).

1 A man . . . is *so* in the way in the house!
*Cranford*, Ch. 1

2 'It is very pleasant dining with a bachelor,' said Miss Matty, softly, as we settled ourselves in the counting-house. 'I only hope it is not improper; so many pleasant things are!'
*Cranford*, Ch. 4

3 That kind of patriotism which consists in hating all other nations.
*Sylvia's Lovers*, Ch. 1

**Gautier, Théophile** (1811–72) French poet and critic. Verse collections include *Poésies* (1830) and *Émaux et camées* (1852).

1 I am a man for whom the outside world exists.
*Journal des Goncourt*, 1 May 1857

2 Yes, the work comes out more beautiful from a material that resists the process, verse, marble, onyx, or enamel.
*L'Art*

**Gavarni, Paul** (1801–66) French illustrator best known for his sketches of Parisian life.

1 *Les enfants terribles.*
The embarrassing young.
Title of a series of prints

**Gay, John** (1685–1732) English poet and dramatist. A member of the Scriblerus Club with Pope and Swift, his *Fables* (1727) were his best-known poems but he is now remembered for his ballad opera *The Beggar's Opera* (1728).

1 A moment of time may make us unhappy for ever.
*The Beggar's Opera*

2 How, like a moth, the simple maid
Still plays about the flame!
*The Beggar's Opera*

3 If with me you'd fondly stray,
Over the hills and far away.
*The Beggar's Opera*

4 Do you think your mother and I should have liv'd comfortably so long together, if ever we had been married?
*The Beggar's Opera*

5 She who has never loved has never lived.
*Captives*

6 In every age and clime we see,
Two of a trade can ne'er agree.
*Fables*

7 While there is life, there's hope,' he cried;
'Then why such haste?' so groaned and died.
*Fables*

8 'Tis a gross error, held in schools,
That Fortune always favours fools.
*Fables*

9 Fools may our scorn, not envy raise,
For envy is a kind of praise.
*Fables*

10 Life is a jest; and all things show it.
I thought so once; but now I know it.
*My Own Epitaph*

11 No sir, tho' I was born and bred in England, I can dare to be poor, which is the only thing now-a-days men are asham'd of.
*Polly*

12 We only part to meet again.
Change, as ye list, ye winds; my heart shall be
The faithful compass that still points to thee.
*Sweet William's Farewell*

**Geddes, Sir Eric Campbell** (1875–1937) British politician. First Lord of the Admiralty (1917–18), he later became minister of transport (1919–21).

1 The Germans, if this Government is returned, are going to pay every penny; they are going to be squeezed, as a lemon is squeezed – until the pips squeak. My only doubt is not whether we can squeeze hard enough, but whether there is enough juice.
Speech, Cambridge, 10 Dec 1918

**George, Dan** (1899–1982) Canadian Indian chief, who acted in a number of films, including *Little Big Man* (1970).

1 When the white man came we had the land and they had the Bibles; now they have the land and we have the Bibles.
Attrib.

**George II** (1683–1760) King of Britain and Elector of Hanover. He was a considerable patron of music.

1 No, I shall have mistresses.
Reply to Queen Caroline's suggestion, as she lay on her deathbed, that he should marry again after her death.
*Memoirs of George the Second* (Hervey), Vol. II

2 Oh! he is mad, is he? Then I wish he would bite some other of my generals.
Replying to advisors who told him that General James Wolfe was mad
Attrib.

**George IV** (1762–1830) King of the United Kingdom and Hanover (1820–30). His treatment of Queen Caroline and secret marriage to Maria Fitzherbert undermined his authority.

1 Harris, I am not well; pray get me a glass of brandy.
On seeing Caroline of Brunswick for the first time
*Diaries* (Earl of Malmesbury)

**George V** (1865–1936) King of the United Kingdom (1910–36), who, with his consort, Mary of Teck, reigned throughout World War I and during the preparations for World War II.

1 I have many times asked myself whether there can be more potent advocates of peace upon earth through the years to come than this massed multitude of silent witnesses to the desolation of war.
Referring to the massed World War I graves in Flanders, 1922
*Silent Cities* (ed. Gavin Stamp)

**2** Is it possible that my people live in such awful conditions? . . . I tell you, Mr Wheatley, that if I had to live in conditions like that I would be a revolutionary myself.

On being told Mr Wheatley's life story
*The Tragedy of Ramsay MacDonald* (L. MacNeill Weir), Ch. 16

**3** How is the Empire?

Last words.
*The Times*, 21 Jan 1936

**4** Bugger Bognor

His alleged last words, when his doctor promised him he would soon be well enough to visit Bognor Regis
Attrib.

**Getty, J(ean) Paul** (1892–1976) US oil magnate, who retired to live in England and founded an art museum in California.

**1** If you can actually count your money you are not really a rich man.

*Gossip* (A. Barrow)

**Gibbon, Edward** (1737–94) British historian whose monumental *The History of the Decline and Fall of the Roman Empire* (1776–88) caused considerable controversy for its treatment of Christianity.

**1** To the University of Oxford I acknowledge no obligation; and she will as cheerfully renounce me for a son, as I am willing to disclaim her for a mother. I spent fourteen months at Magdalen College: they proved the fourteen months the most idle and unprofitable of my whole life.

*Autobiography*

**2** Crowds without company, and dissipation without pleasure.

Referring to London
*Autobiography*

**3** The romance of *Tom Jones*, that exquisite picture of human manners, will outlive the palace of the Escurial and the imperial eagle of the house of Austria.

*Autobiography*

**4** The various modes of worship, which prevailed in the Roman world, were all considered by the people as equally true; by the philosopher, as equally false; and by the magistrate, as equally useful. And thus toleration produced not only mutual indulgence, but even religious concord.

*Decline and Fall of the Roman Empire*, Ch. 2

**5** The principles of a free constitution are irrecoverably lost, when the legislative power is nominated by the executive.

*Decline and Fall of the Roman Empire*, Ch. 3

**6** His reign is marked by the rare advantage of furnishing very few materials for history; which is, indeed, little more than the register of the crimes, follies, and misfortunes of mankind.

Referring to the reign of Antoninus Pius
*Decline and Fall of the Roman Empire*, Ch. 3

**7** Corruption, the most infallible symptom of constitutional liberty.

*Decline and Fall of the Roman Empire*, Ch. 21

**8** All that is human must retrograde if it does not advance.

*Decline and Fall of the Roman Empire*, Ch. 71

**Gibbons, Stella** (1902– ) British poet and novelist, whose books include *The Mountain Beast* (poetry; 1930) and *Cold Comfort Farm* (novel; 1932).

**1** Something nasty in the woodshed.

*Cold Comfort Farm*

**Gide, André** (1869–1951) French novelist and critic. Novels include *Fruits of the Earth* (1897), *The Vatican Cellars* (1914), and *The Counterfeiters* (1926).

**1** *L'acte gratuite.*
The unmotivated action.

*Les Caves du Vatican*

**2** Fish die belly-upward and rise to the surface; it is their way of falling.

*Journals*

**3** *Hugo – hélas!*

Replying to an inquiry as to whom he considered the finest poet of the 19th century.
*André Gide–Paul Valéry Correspondence 1890–1942*

**Gilbert, Fred** (1850–1903) British songwriter.

**1** As I walk along the Bois Bou-long,
With an independent air,
You can hear the girls declare,
'He must be a millionaire',
You can hear them sigh and wish to die,
You can see them wink the other eye
At the man who broke the Bank at Monte Carlo.

The Bois de Boulogne was a fashionable recreational area on the outskirts of Paris
*The Man who Broke the Bank at Monte Carlo* (song)

**Gilbert, Sir Humphrey** (c. 1539–83) English navigator. Half-brother of Sir Walter Raleigh, he failed to reach America on his first voyage, but on his second (1583) reached Newfoundland, which he claimed for Britain.

**1** We are as near to heaven by sea as by land.

Remark made shortly before he went down with his ship *Squirrel*
*A Book of Anecdotes* (D. George)

**Gilbert, Sir William Schwenk** (1836–1911) British dramatist and comic writer. His comic verse published as *Bab Ballads* (1896) preceded his libretti for 14 comic operas written for Arthur Sullivan's music.

**1** He led his regiment from behind
He found it less exciting.

*The Gondoliers*, I

**2** Of that there is no manner of doubt –
No probable, possible shadow of doubt –
No possible doubt whatever.

*The Gondoliers*, I

**3** A taste for drink, combined with gout,
Had doubled him up for ever.

*The Gondoliers*, I

4 All shall equal be.
The Earl, the Marquis, and the Dook,
The Groom, the Butler, and the Cook,
The Aristocrat who banks with Coutts,
The Aristocrat who cleans the boots.
*The Gondoliers,* I

5 When every blessed thing you hold
Is made of silver, or of gold,
You long for simple pewter.
When you have nothing else to wear
But cloth of gold and satins rare,
For cloth of gold you cease to care –
Up goes the price of shoddy.
*The Gondoliers,* I

6 I'm called Little Buttercup – dear Little
Buttercup,
Though I could never tell why.
*HMS Pinafore,* I

7 I am the Captain of the *Pinafore*;
And a right good captain too!
*HMS Pinafore,* I

8 CAPTAIN. I'm never, never sick at sea!
ALL. What never?
CAPTAIN. No, never!
ALL. What, *never?*
CAPTAIN. Hardly ever!
*HMS Pinafore,* I

9 And so do his sisters, and his cousins and his
aunts!
His sisters and his cousins,
Whom he reckons up by dozens,
And his aunts!
*HMS Pinafore,* I

10 I always voted at my party's call,
And I never thought of thinking for myself at all.
*HMS Pinafore,* I

11 Stick close to your desks and never go to sea,
And you all may be Rulers of the Queen's
Navee!
*HMS Pinafore,* I

12 When I was a lad I served a term
As office boy to an Attorney's firm.
I cleaned the windows and I swept the floor,
And I polished up the handle of the big front
door.
I polished up that handle so carefullee
That now I am the Ruler of the Queen's Navee!
*HMS Pinafore,* I

13 For he might have been a Roosian,
A French, or Turk, or Proosian,
Or perhaps Ital-ian!
But in spite of all temptations
To belong to other nations,
He remains an Englishman!
*HMS Pinafore,* II

14 I see no objection to stoutness, in moderation.
*Iolanthe,* I

15 Bow, bow, ye lower middle classes!
Bow, bow, ye tradesmen, bow, ye masses!
*Iolanthe,* I

16 When I went to the Bar as a very young man,
(Said I to myself – said I),
I'll work on a new and original plan,
(Said I to myself – said I).
*Iolanthe,* I

17 The prospect of a lot
Of dull MPs in close proximity,
All thinking for themselves is what
No man can face with equanimity.
*Iolanthe,* I

18 The Law is the true embodiment
Of everything that's excellent.
It has no kind of fault or flaw,
And I, my lords, embody the Law.
*Iolanthe,* I

19 I often think it's comical
How Nature always does contrive
That every boy and every gal
That's born into the world alive
Is either a little Liberal
Or else a little Conservative!
*Iolanthe,* II

20 The House of Peers, throughout the war,
Did nothing in particular,
And did it very well.
*Iolanthe,* II

21 For you dream you are crossing the Channel,
and tossing about in a steamer from Harwich –
Which is something between a large bathing machine and a very small second-class carriage.
*Iolanthe,* II

22 Pooh-Bah (Lord High Everything Else)
*The Mikado, Dramatis Personae*

23 A wandering minstrel I –
A thing of shreds and patches,
Of ballads, songs and snatches,
And dreamy lullaby!
*The Mikado,* I

24 I can trace my ancestry back to a protoplasmal
primordial atomic globule. Consequently, my
family pride is something in-conceivable. I can't
help it. I was born sneering.
*The Mikado,* I

25 As some day it may happen that a victim must
be found
I've got a little list – I've got a little list
Of society offenders who might well be
underground,
And who never would be missed – who never
would be missed!
*The Mikado,* I

26 The idiot who praises, with enthusiastic tone,
All centuries but this, and every country but his
own.
*The Mikado,* I

27 Three little maids from school are we,
Pert as a school-girl well can be,
Filled to the brim with girlish glee.
*The Mikado*, I

28 Ah, pray make no mistake,
We are not shy;
We're very wide awake,
The moon and I.
*The Mikado*, II

29 My object all sublime
I shall achieve in time –
To let the punishment fit the crime –
The punishment fit the crime.
*The Mikado*, II

30 The billiard sharp whom any one catches,
His doom's extremely hard –
He's made to dwell –
In a dungeon cell
On a spot that's always barred.
And there he plays extravagant matches
In fitless finger-stalls
On a cloth untrue
With a twisted cue
And elliptical billiard balls.
*The Mikado*, II

31 I have a left shoulder-blade that is a miracle of loveliness. People come miles to see it. My right elbow has a fascination that few can resist.
*The Mikado*, IJ

32 Something lingering, with boiling oil in it, I fancy.
*The Mikado*, II

33 The flowers that bloom in the spring,
Tra la,
Have nothing to do with the case.
I've got to take under my wing,
Tra la,
A most unattractive old thing,
Tra la,
With a caricature of a face.
*The Mikado*, II

34 On a tree by a river a little tom-tit
Sang 'Willow, titwillow, titwillow!'
*The Mikado*, II

35 If this young man expresses himself in terms too deep for *me*,
Why, what a very singularly deep young man this deep young man must be!
*Patience*, I

36 Poor wandering one!
Though thou hast surely strayed,
Take heart of grace,
Thy steps retrace,
Poor wandering one!
*The Pirates of Penzance*, I

37 I am the very model of a modern Major-General,
I've information vegetable, animal and mineral,
I know the kings of England, and I quote the fights historical,
From Marathon to Waterloo, in order categorical.
*The Pirates of Penzance*, I

38 About binomial theorems I'm teeming with a lot of news,
With many cheerful facts about the square on the hypoteneuse.
*The Pirates of Penzance*, I

39 When the foeman bares his steel,
Tarantara! tarantara!
We uncomfortable feel.
*The Pirates of Penzance*, II

40 When constabulary duty's to be done –
A policeman's lot is not a happy one.
*The Pirates of Penzance*, II

41 He combines the manners of a Marquis with the morals of a Methodist.
*Ruddigore*, I

42 Is life a boon?
If so, it must befall
That Death, whene'er he call,
Must call too soon.
The lines are written on Arthur Sullivan's memorial in the Embankment gardens
*The Yeoman of the Guard*, I

43 I have a song to sing O!
Sing me your song, O!
*The Yeoman of the Guard*, I

44 It's a song of a merryman, moping mum,
Whose soul was sad, and whose glance was glum,
Who sipped no sup, and who craved no crumb,
As he sighed for the love of a ladye.
*The Yeoman of the Guard*, I

45 She may very well pass for forty-three
In the dusk, with a light behind her!
*Trial by Jury*

46 Sir, I view the proposal to hold an international exhibition at San Francisco with an equanimity bordering on indifference.
*Gilbert, His Life and Strife* (Hesketh Pearson)

47 My dear chap! Good isn't the word!
Speaking to an actor after he had given a poor performance
Attrib.

48 Funny without being vulgar.
Referring to Sir Henry Irving's *Hamlet*
Attrib.

**Gilman, Charlotte Perkins** (1860–1935) US writer and lecturer on sociology, economics, and feminism.

1 However, one cannot put a quart in a pint cup.
*The Living of Charlotte Perkins Gilman*

2 . . . New York . . . that unnatural city where every one is an exile, none more so than the American.
*The Living of Charlotte Perkins Gilman*

3 Where young boys plan for what they will achieve and attain, young girls plan for whom they will achieve and attain.
*Women and Economics*, Ch. 5

**Giraudoux, Jean** (1882–1944) French dramatist and writer. His novels, including *Elpénor* (1919), and *Adorable Clio* (1920), established his reputation. His later plays include *Ondine* (1939) and *The Madwoman of Chaillot* (1949).

1 It's odd how people waiting for you stand out far less clearly than people you are waiting for.
*Tiger at the Gates*, I

2 There's no better way of exercising the imagination than the study of law. No poet ever interpreted nature as freely as a lawyer interprets truth.
*Tiger at the Gates*, I

**Gladstone, William Ewart** (1809–98) British statesman. He became Liberal prime minister (1868–74; 1880–85; 1886; 1892–94), dominating British politics in opposition to Disraeli for much of the second half of the 19th century.

1 You cannot fight against the future. Time is on our side.
*Advocating parliamentary reform*
Speech, 1866

2 All the world over, I will back the masses against the classes.
Speech, Liverpool, 28 June 1886

3 We are part of the community of Europe, and we must do our duty as such.
Speech, Caenarvon, 10 Apr 1888

**Glasse, Hannah** (18th century) English writer, especially on cookery.

1 Take your hare when it is cased . . .
The saying 'First catch your hare' has often been attributed incorrectly to Mrs Glasse.
*The Art of Cookery Made Plain and Easy*, Ch. 1

**Gloucester, William, Duke of** (1743–1805) The brother of George III.

1 Another damned, thick, square book! Always scribble, scribble, scribble! Eh! Mr Gibbon?
*Literary Memorials* (Best)

**Glover-Kind, John A.** (19th century) US songwriter.

1 I do Like to be Beside the Seaside.
Song title

**Godard, Jean-Luc** (1930– ) French film director. His new wave films include *Week-End* (1967) and *Tout va bien* (1972).

1 Photography is truth. And cinema is truth twenty-four times a second.
*Le Petit Soldat*

2 I like a film to have a beginning, a middle and an end, but not necessarily in that order.
Attrib.

**Goebbels, Joseph** (1897–1945) German politician. As Hitler's minister of propaganda he established a system for disseminating whatever 'information' the Nazis considered appropriate. Having murdered his six children, he committed suicide after the German collapse.

1 The Iron Curtain.
*Das Reich*

2 This was the Angel of History! We felt its wings flutter through the room. Was that not the fortune we awaited so anxiously?
*Referring to Roosevelt's death*
*Diary*

**Goering, Hermann** (1893–1946) German leader, who commanded the Brownshirts (1922) and established the Gestapo (1933). He developed the air force and became Hitler's successor in 1939. He committed suicide after being condemned to hang at the Nuremburg trials.

1 They entered the war to prevent us from going into the East, not to have the East come to the Atlantic.
*Referring to the war aims of the British in World War II*
*Nuremberg Diary* (G. M. Gilbert)

2 I herewith commission you to carry out all preparations with regard to . . . a *total solution* of the Jewish question, in those territories of Europe which are under German influence.
*The Rise and Fall of the Third Reich* (William Shirer)

3 Guns will make us powerful; butter will only make us fat.
Radio broadcast, 1936

4 When I hear anyone talk of Culture, I reach for my revolver.
Attrib. to Goering but probably said by Hanns JOHST

**Goethe, Johann Wolfgang von** (1749–1832) German poet, dramatist, and scientist. His novel *The Sorrows of Young Werther* (1774) brought him international fame, which was enhanced by *Faust* (1808), a poetic drama.

1 I do not know myself, and God forbid that I should.
*Conversations with Eckermann*, 10 Apr 1829

2 Dear friend, theory is all grey,
And the golden tree of life is green.
*Faust*, Pt. I

3 Two souls dwell, alas! in my breast.
*Faust*, Pt. I

4 I am the spirit that always denies.
*Faust*, Pt. I

5 A useless life is an early death.
*Iphegenie*, I:2

6 Superstition is the poetry of life.
*Sprüche in Prosa*, III

7 Talent develops in quiet places, character in the full current of human life.

*Torquato Tasso, I*

8 God could cause us considerable embarrassment by revealing all the secrets of nature to us: we should not know what to do for sheer apathy and boredom.

*Memoirs (Riemer)*

9 From today and from this place there begins a new epoch in the history of the world.

On witnessing the victory of the French at the battle of Valmy
*The Story of Civilization* (W. Durant), Vol. II

10 I was not unaware that I had begotten a mortal.

On learning of his son's death
*The Story of Civilization* (W. Durant), Vol. X

11 *Mehr Licht!*
More light!

Attrib. last words. In fact he asked for the second shutter to be opened, to allow more light in

**Golding, William** (1911– ) British novelist. He made his name with *Lord of the Flies* (1954). Subsequent books include *Free Fall* (1959), *Rites of Passage* (1980), and *The Paper Men* (1984).

1 Philip is a living example of natural selection. He was as fitted to survive in this modern world as a tapeworm in an intestine.

*Free Fall,* Ch. 2

2 Ralph wept for the end of innocence, the darkness of man's heart, and the fall through the air of the true, wise friend called Piggy.

*Lord of the Flies,* Ch. 12

**Goldsmith, Oliver** (1728–74) Irish-born British writer, dramatist, and poet. He is remembered for his novel *The Vicar of Wakefield* (1776) and the play *She Stoops to Conquer* (1773) in addition to a considerable amount of verse.

1 True genius walks along a line, and, perhaps, our greatest pleasure is in seeing it so often near falling, without being ever actually down.

*The Bee,* 'The Characteristics of Greatness'

2 As writers become more numerous, it is natural for readers to become more indolent.

*The Bee,* 'Upon Unfortunate Merit'

3 To a philosopher no circumstance, however trifling, is too minute.

*The Citizen of the World*

4 Ill fares the land, to hast'ning ills a prey,
Where wealth accumulates, and men decay;
Princes and lords may flourish, or may fade;
A breath can make them, as a breath has made;
But a bold peasantry, their country's pride,
When once destroy'd, can never be supplied.

*The Deserted Village*

5 In arguing too, the parson own'd his skill,
For e'en though vanquish'd, he could argue still;
While words of learned length, and thund'ring sound
Amazed the gazing rustics rang'd around,
And still they gaz'd, and still the wonder grew,
That one small head could carry all he knew.

*The Deserted Village*

6 Man wants but little here below,
Nor wants that little long.

*Edwin and Angelina, or the Hermit*

7 The doctor found, when she was dead,
Her last disorder mortal.

*Elegy on Mrs. Mary Blaize*

8 The dog, to gain some private ends,
Went mad and bit the man.

*Elegy on the Death of a Mad Dog*

9 The man recovered of the bite,
The dog it was that died.

*Elegy on the Death of a Mad Dog*

10 I hate the French because they are all slaves, and wear wooden shoes.

*Essays,* 'Distresses of a Common Soldier'

11 The true use of speech is not so much to express our wants as to conceal them.

*Essays,* 'The Use of Language'

12 Friendship is a disinterested commerce between equals; love, an abject intercourse between tyrants and slaves.

*The Good-Natured Man, I*

13 We must touch his weaknesses with a delicate hand. There are some faults so nearly allied to excellence, that we can scarce weed out the fault without eradicating the virtue.

*The Good-Natured Man, I*

14 LEONTINE. An only son, sir, might expect more indulgence.
CROAKER. An only father, sir, might expect more obedience.

*The Good-Natured Man, I*

15 I am told he makes a very handsome corpse, and becomes his coffin prodigiously.

*The Good-Natured Man, I*

16 Silence is become his mother tongue.

*The Good-Natured Man, II*

17 I love everything that's old: old friends, old times, old manners, old books, old wine.

*She Stoops to Conquer, I*

18 In my time, the follies of the town crept slowly among us, but now they travel faster than a stagecoach.

*She Stoops to Conquer, I*

**19** Let schoolmasters puzzle their brain,
With grammar, and nonsense, and learning,
Good liquor, I stoutly maintain,
Gives genius a better discerning.
*She Stoops to Conquer,* I

**20** This is Liberty-Hall, gentlemen.
*She Stoops to Conquer,* II

**21** Where wealth and freedom reign, contentment fails,
And honour sinks where commerce long prevails.
*The Traveller*

**22** Laws grind the poor, and rich men rule the law.
*The Traveller*

**23** A book may be amusing with numerous errors, or it may be very dull without a single absurdity.
*The Vicar of Wakefield,* Advertisement

**24** I . . . chose my wife, as she did her wedding gown, not for a fine glossy surface, but such qualities as would wear well.
*The Vicar of Wakefield,* Preface

**25** I was ever of opinion, that the honest man who married and brought up a large family, did more service than he who continued single and only talked of population.
*The Vicar of Wakefield,* Ch. 1

**26** Let us draw upon content for the deficiencies of fortune.
*The Vicar of Wakefield,* Ch. 3

**27** When lovely woman stoops to folly,
And finds too late that men betray,
What charm can soothe her melancholy,
What art can wash her guilt away?
*The Vicar of Wakefield,* Ch. 9

**28** Conscience is a coward, and those faults it has not strength enough to prevent it seldom has justice enough to accuse.
*The Vicar of Wakefield,* Ch. 13

**29** There is no arguing with Johnson; for when his pistol misses fire, he knocks you down with the butt end of it.
*Life of Johnson* (J. Boswell)

**30** As I take my shoes from the shoemaker, and my coat from the tailor, so I take my religion from the priest.
*Life of Johnson* (J. Boswell)

**Goldwater, Barry** (1904– ) US politician. An unsuccessful Republican candidate for the presidency, he is Senator from Arizona.

**1** A government that is big enough to give you all you want is big enough to take it all away.
*Bachman's Book of Freedom Quotations* (M. Ivens and R. Dunstan)

**2** I would remind you that extremism in the defence of liberty is no vice. And let me remind you also that moderation in the pursuit of justice is no virtue!
Speech, San Francisco, 17 July 1964

**3** You've got to forget about this civilian. Whenever you drop bombs, you're going to hit civilians.
Speech, New York, 23 Jan 1967

**Goldwyn, Samuel** (Samuel Goldfish; 1882–1974) Polish-born US film producer, whose own company merged with others to form Metro-Goldwyn-Mayer (MGM) in 1924 –a company that made many Hollywood successes. He is noted for his so-called 'Goldwynisms', most of which are apocryphal.

**1** Let's have some new clichés.
*The Observer,* 'Sayings of the Week', 24 Oct 1948

**2** Why should people go out and pay money to see bad films when they can stay at home and see bad television for nothing?
*The Observer,* 'Sayings of the Week', 9 Sept 1956

**3** Too caustic? To hell with cost; we'll make the picture anyway.
Attrib.

**4** We're overpaying him but he's worth it.
Attrib.

**5** What we want is a story that starts with an earthquake and works its way up to a climax.
Attrib.

**6** I am willing to admit that I may not always be right, but I am never wrong.
Attrib.

**7** Chaplin is no business man – all he knows is that he can't take anything less.
Attrib.

**8** I don't care if doesn't make a nickel, I just want every man, woman, and child in America to see it!
Referring to his film *The Best Years of Our Lives*
Attrib.

**9** A wide screen just makes a bad film twice as bad.
Attrib.

**10** For years I have been known for saying 'Include me out'; but today I am giving it up for ever.
Address, Balliol College, Oxford, 1 Mar 1945

**11** In two words: im - possible.
Attrib.

**12** Anybody who goes to see a psychiatrist ought to have his head examined.
Attrib.

**13** Every director bites the hand that lays the golden egg.
Attrib.

**14** I'll give you a definite maybe.
Attrib.

**15** A verbal contract isn't worth the paper it's written on.
Attrib.

**16** You ought to take the bull between the teeth.
Attrib.

**17** We have all passed a lot of water since then.
Attrib.

**18** I read part of it all the way through.
Attrib.

**19** If Roosevelt were alive he'd turn in his grave.
Attrib.

**20** It's more than magnificent – it's mediocre.
Attrib.

**21** 'Why only twelve?' 'That's the original number.' 'Well, go out and get thousands.'
Referring to the number of disciples whilst filming a scene for *The Last Supper*
Attrib.

**22** Yes, I'm going to have a bust made of them.
Replying to an admiring comment about his wife's hands
Attrib.

**23** Tell me, how did you love my picture?
Attrib. in *Colombo's Hollywood* (J. R. Colombo)

**Goncourt, Edmond de** (1822–96) French novelist who collaborated with his brother, **Jules de Goncourt** (1830–70), in such books as *Sœur Philomène* (1861). He left his money to found the coveted Prix Goncourt.

**1** Historians tell the story of the past, novelists the story of the present.
*Journal*

**Gordon, Adam Lindsay** (1833–70) Australian poet. Collections include *Sea Spray and Smoke Drift* (1867) and *Bush Ballads and Galloping Rhymes* (1870).

**1** Life is mostly froth and bubble;
Two things stand like stone,
Kindness in another's trouble,
Courage in your own.
*Ye Wearie Wayfarer*, Fytte 8

**Gorky, Maxim** (Aleksei Maksimovich Peshkov; 1868–1936) Russian novelist, dramatist, and short-story writer. Novels include *Mother* (1907); *The Lower Depths* (1903) is his best-known play. Autobiographical writings include *Fragments from My Diary* (1924) and *Reminiscences of My Youth* (1924).

**1** You must write for children in the same way as you do for adults, only better.
Attrib.

**Gosse, Sir Edmund** (1849–1928) British writer and critic. Best known for his translations and biography of Ibsen and his autobiographical *Father and Son* (1907).

**1** We were as nearly bored as enthusiasm would permit.
Referring to a play by Swinburne
*Biography of Edward Marsh* (C. Hassall)

**2** A sheep in sheep's clothing.
Referring to T. Sturge Moore. Sometimes attributed to Winston Churchill, referring to Clement Attlee.
*Under the Bridge* (Ferris Greenslet), Ch. 12

**Gournay, Jean Claude Vincent de** (1712–59) French economist and advocate of free trade.

**1** *Laissez faire, laissez passer.*
Liberty of action, liberty of movement.
Speech, Sept 1758

**Grace, W(illiam) G(ilbert)** (1848–1915) British doctor and cricketer. He was captain of Gloucestershire (1871–98) and England in 13 Test matches. He is regarded as England's greatest cricketer.

**1** They came to see me bat not to see you bowl.
Refusing to leave the crease after being bowled first ball in front of a large crowd
Attrib.

**Gracián, Baltasar** (1601–58) Spanish writer and Jesuit. He is remembered for his philosophical novel *El Criticón* (1651–57).

**1** Good things, when short, are twice as good.
*The Art of Worldly Wisdom*

**Grade, Lew, Baron** (Lewis Winogradsky; 1906– ) British film and TV producer and impressario. Films include *The Legend of the Lone Ranger* (1980), *Raise the Titanic* (1980), and *On Golden Pond* (1981).

**1** All my shows are great. Some of them are bad. But they are all great.
*The Observer*, 'Sayings of the Week', 14 Sept 1975

**2** What about it? Do you want to crucify the boy?
Referring to the revelation that an actor portraying Christ on television was living with a woman to whom he was not married
Attrib.

**Grafton, Richard** (d. c. 1572) English chronicler and printer. Printed the *Great Bible* (1539) and *Book of Common Prayer* (1549). Also compiled two sets of historical chronicles (1562, 1568).

**1** Thirty days hath November,
April, June and September,
February hath twenty-eight alone,
And all the rest have thirty-one.
*Abridgement of the Chronicles of England*, Introduction

**Graham, Clementina Stirling** (1782–1877) British writer.

**1** The best way to get the better of temptation is just to yield to it.
*Mystifications*, 'Soirée at Mrs Russel's'

**Graham, Harry** (1874–1936) British writer, poet, and dramatist. Verse collections include *Ruthless Rhymes for Heartless Homes* (1899).

**1** 'There's been an accident' they said,
'Your servant's cut in half; he's dead!'
'Indeed!' said Mr Jones, 'and please
Send me the half that's got my keys.'
*Ruthless Rhymes for Heartless Homes*, 'Mr. Jones'

2 Billy, in one of his nice new sashes,
Fell in the fire and was burnt to ashes;
Now, although the room grows chilly,
I haven't the heart to poke poor Billy.

*Ruthless Rhymes for Heartless Homes*, 'Tender-Heartedness'

## Graham, James, Marquis of Montrose (1612–50)
Scottish general. He fought for Charles I in the Civil War but his army of highlanders was defeated (1645). He returned from exile on the continent in 1650 but was captured and executed by the parliamentarians.

1 Let them bestow on every airth a limb;
Then open all my veins, that I may swim
To thee, my Maker! in that crimson lake;
Then place my parboiled head upon a stake –
Scatter my ashes – strew them in the air; –
Lord! since thou know'st where all these atoms
are,
I'm hopeful thou'lt recover once my dust,
And confident thou'lt raise me with the just.

*Lines written on the Window of his Jail the Night before his Execution*

## Grahame, Kenneth (1859–1932) Scottish writer of
children's books, including *The Wind in the Willows* (1908), which was later adapted by A. A. Milne as the play *Toad of Toad Hall* (1929).

1 There is nothing – absolutely nothing – half so much worth doing as simply messing about in boats.

*The Wind in the Willows*, Ch. 1

2 The clever men at Oxford
Know all that there is to be known.
But they none of them know one half as much
As intelligent Mr Toad.

*The Wind in the Willows*, Ch. 10

## Grandma Moses (Anna Mary Robertson Moses; 1860–
1961) US primitive painter. A farmer's wife, she took up painting aged 67 and was entirely self-taught.

1 What a strange thing is memory, and hope; one looks backward, the other forward. The one is of today, the other is the Tomorrow. Memory is history recorded in our brain, memory is a painter, it paints pictures of the past and of the day.

*Grandma Moses, My Life's History* (ed. Aotto Kallir), Ch. 1

2 If I didn't start painting, I would have raised chickens.

*Grandma Moses, My Life's History* (ed. Aotto Kallir), Ch. 3

3 I don't advise any one to take it up as a business proposition, unless they really have talent, and are crippled so as to deprive them of physical labor.

Referring to painting
*The New York Times* 'How Do I Paint?', 11 May 1947

## Grant, Cary (Archibald Leach; 1904–86) British-born US film
star. Films include *Born to be Bad* (1934), *Topper* (1937), *The Philadelphia Story* (1940), *To Catch a Thief* (1955), and *Indiscreet* (1958).

1 'Old Cary Grant fine. How you?'

Replying to a telegram sent to his agent inquiring: 'How old Cary Grant?'
*The Filmgoer's Book of Quotes* (Leslie Halliwell)

## Grant, Sir Robert (1779–1838) British hymn writer.

1 O worship the King, all glorious above!
O gratefully sing his power and his love!
Our Shield and Defender – the Ancient of Days,
Pavilioned in splendour, and girded with praise.

Hymn

## Grant, Ulysses Simpson (1822–85) US general who
became a Republican President (1869–77). As supreme commander of the Federal armies he defeated the Confederates.

1 No terms except unconditional and immediate surrender can be accepted. I propose to move immediately upon your works.

Message to opposing commander, Simon Bolivar Buckner, during siege of Fort Donelson, 16 Feb 1862

2 I purpose to fight it out on this line, if it takes all summer.

Dispatch to Washington, 11 May 1864

3 Let us have peace.

On accepting nomination
Letter, 29 May 1868

4 I know no method to secure the repeal of bad or obnoxious laws so effective as their stringent execution.

Inaugural address, 4 Mar 1869

5 Let no guilty man escape, if it can be avoided
... No personal considerations should stand in the way of performing a public duty.

Referring to the Whiskey Ring
Indorsement of a letter, 29 July 1875

## Granville-Barker, Harley (1877–1946) British actor and
dramatist. As co-manager of the Royal Court Theatre in London he was responsible for the first productions of several of Shaw's plays. His own plays included *The Madras House* (1910).

1 Rightly thought of there is poetry in peaches ...
even when they are canned.

*The Madras House*, I

2 But oh, the farmyard world of sex!

*The Madras House*, IV

3 What is the prose for God?

*Waste*, I

## Graves, John Woodcock (1795–1886) British poet,
huntsman, and songwriter, who is best remembered for his song 'D'ye Ken John Peel', about his Cumberland friend of this name, who was master of foxhounds at Caldbeck for nearly 50 years.

1 D'ye ken John Peel with his coat so gay?
  D'ye ken John Peel at the break of the day?
  D'ye ken John Peel when he's far far away
  With his hounds and his horn in the morning?

  'Twas the sound of his horn called me from my
  bed,
  And the cry of his hounds has me oft-times led;
  For Peel's view-hollo would waken the dead,
  Or a fox from his lair in the morning.

  *John Peel*

**Graves, Robert** (1895–1985) British poet and novelist. His World War I autobiography *Goodbye to All That* (1929) made his name and enabled him to publish several editions of his collected poems. His historical novels included *I Claudius* (1934) and *Claudius the God* (1934).

1 Goodbye to All That.

  Book title

2 As for the Freudian, it is a very low, Central European sort of humour.

  *Occupation: Writer*

3 In love as in sport, the amateur status must be strictly maintained.

  *Occupation: Writer*

4 To be a poet is a condition rather than a profession.

  *Horizon*

5 The remarkable thing about Shakespeare is that he is really very good – in spite of all the people who say he is very good.

  *The Observer*, 'Sayings of the Week', 6 Dec 1964

**Gray, Thomas** (1716–71) British poet. He published several odes but is best known for his *Elegy Written in a Country Churchyard* (1751), written at Stoke Poges in Buckinghamshire.

1 The Curfew tolls the knell of parting day,
  The lowing herd winds slowly o'er the lea,
  The plowman homeward plods his weary way,
  And leaves the world to darkness and to me.

  *Elegy Written in a Country Churchyard*

2 Let not Ambition mock their useful toil,
  Their homely joys, and destiny obscure;
  Nor Grandeur hear with a disdainful smile,
  The short and simple annals of the poor.

  *Elegy Written in a Country Churchyard*

3 The boast of heraldry, the pomp of pow'r,
  And all that beauty, all that wealth e'er gave,
  Awaits alike th' inevitable hour,
  The paths of glory lead but to the grave.

  *Elegy Written in a Country Churchyard*

4 Can storied urn or animated bust
  Back to its mansion call the fleeting breath?
  Can honour's voice provoke the silent dust,
  Or flatt'ry soothe the dull cold ear of death?

  *Elegy Written in a Country Churchyard*

5 Full many a gem of purest ray serene,
  The dark unfathom'd caves of ocean bear:
  Full many a flower is born to blush unseen,
  And waste its sweetness on the desert air.

  *Elegy Written in a Country Churchyard*

6 Some village-Hampden, that with dauntless
  breast
  The little Tyrant of his fields withstood;
  Some mute inglorious Milton here may rest,
  Some Cromwell guiltless of his country's blood.

  *Elegy Written in a Country Churchyard*

7 Far from the madding crowd's ignoble strife,
  Their sober wishes never learn'd to stray;
  Along the cool sequester'd vale of life
  They kept the noiseless tenor of their way.

  *Elegy Written in a Country Churchyard*

8 Here rests his head upon the lap of Earth
  A youth to fortune and to fame unknown.
  Fair Science frown'd not on his humble birth,
  And Melancholy mark'd him for her own.

  *Elegy Written in a Country Churchyard*

9 Alas, regardless of their doom,
  The little victims play!

  *Ode on a Distant Prospect of Eton College*

10 To each his suff'rings, all are men,
   Condemn'd alike to groan;
   The tender for another's pain,
   Th' unfeeling for his own.
   Yet ah! why should they know their fate?
   Since sorrow never comes too late,
   And happiness too swiftly flies.
   Thought would destroy their paradise.
   No more; where ignorance is bliss,
   'Tis folly to be wise.

   *Ode on a Distant Prospect of Eton College*

11 What female heart can gold despise?
   What cat's averse to fish?

   *Ode on the Death of a Favourite Cat*

12 A fav'rite has no friend.

   *Ode on the Death of a Favourite Cat*

13 Not all that tempts your wand'ring eyes
   And heedless hearts, is lawful prize;
   Nor all, that glisters, gold.

   *Ode on the Death of a Favourite Cat*

**Greeley, Horace** (1811–72) US politician and journalist. He founded the *New Yorker* (1834) and the *Tribune* (1841). He later became an unsuccessful presidential candidate.

1 Go West, young man, and grow up with the country.

  *Hints toward Reform*

**Greene, Graham** (1904–  ) British novelist. After the success of *The Man Within* (1929), he subsequently published *Brighton Rock* (1938), *The Power and the Glory* (1940), *The Heart of the Matter* (1948), *The Human Factor* (1978), and others. His 'entertainments' (literary thrillers) include *The Third Man* (1950) and *Our Man in Havana* (1958).

1 Those who marry God . . . can become domesticated too – it's just as humdrum a marriage as all the others.
*A Burnt-Out Case*, Ch. 1

2 I have often noticed that a bribe . . . has that effect – it changes a relation. The man who offers a bribe gives away a little of his own importance; the bribe once accepted, he becomes the inferior, like a man who has paid for a woman.
*The Comedians*, Pt. I, Ch. 4

3 Catholics and Communists have committed great crimes, but at least they have not stood aside, like an established society, and been indifferent. I would rather have blood on my hands than water like Pilate.
*The Comedians*, Pt. III, Ch. 4

4 He gave the impression that very many cities had rubbed him smooth.
*A Gun for Sale*, Ch. 4

5 Against the beautiful and the clever and the successful, one can wage a pitiless war, but not against the unattractive.
*The Heart of the Matter*

6 They had been corrupted by money, and he had been corrupted by sentiment. Sentiment was the more dangerous, because you couldn't name its price. A man open to bribes was to be relied upon below a certain figure, but sentiment might uncoil in the heart at a name, a photograph, even a smell remembered.
*The Heart of the Matter*

7 That whisky priest, I wish we had never had him in the house.
*The Power and the Glory*, Pt. I

8 Of course, before we *know* he is a saint, there will have to be miracles.
*The Power and the Glory*, Pt. IV

9 Perhaps if I wanted to be understood or to understand I would bamboozle myself into belief, but I am a reporter; God exists only for leader-writers.
*The Quiet American*

10 Fame is a powerful aphrodisiac.
*Radio Times*, 10 Sept 1964

**Greer, Germaine** (1939– ) Australian-born British writer and feminist. She made her reputation with *The Female Eunuch* (1970). Subsequent books include *Sex and Destiny* (1984).

1 Probably the only place where a man can feel really secure is in a maximum security prison, except for the imminent threat of release.
*The Female Eunuch*

2 Mother is the dead heart of the family, spending father's earnings on consumer goods to enhance the environment in which he eats, sleeps and watches the television.
*The Female Eunuch*

3 Love, love, love – all the wretched cant of it, masking egotism, lust, masochism, fantasy under a mythology of sentimental postures, a welter of self-induced miseries and joys, blinding and masking the essential personalities in the frozen gestures of courtship, in the kissing and the dating and the desire, the compliments and the quarrels which vivify its barrenness.
*The Female Eunuch*

**Gregory I** (540–604) Pope and saint. He sponsored Augustine's mission to England and introduced the Gregorian plainchant into the Catholic liturgy.

1 *Non Angli sed Angeli*
Not Angles, but angels.
Attrib.

**Grellet, Stephen** (1773–1855) French-born US missionary, who was responsible for many prison and almshouse reforms.

1 I expect to pass through this world but once; any good thing therefore that I can do, or any kindness that I can show to any fellow-creature, let me do it now; let me not defer or neglect it, for I shall not pass this way again.
Attrib.
*Treasure Trove* (John o'London)

**Greville, Fulke, Baron Brooke** (1554–1628) English poet and politician, who was chancellor of the exchequer (1614–22). His sonnets *Caelica* (1633) and biography *The Life of the Renowned Sir Philip Sidney* (1652) were widely read.

1 Oh wearisome condition of humanity!
Born under one law, to another bound.
*Mustapha*, V:6

**Grey, Edward, Viscount** (1862–1933) British statesman. He was Liberal foreign secretary (1905–16).

1 The United States is like a gigantic boiler. Once the fire is lighted under it there is no limit to the power it can generate.
*Their Finest Hour* (Winston S. Churchill), Ch. 32

2 The lamps are going out over all Europe; we shall not see them lit again in our lifetime.
Remark made on 3 Aug 1914, the eve of World War I

**Griffith-Jones, Mervyn** (1909–78) British lawyer. A prosecuting counsel at the Nuremberg War Trials (1945–46), he became a counsel to the Crown and later Common Serjeant in the City of London.

1 Would you allow your wife or your servant to read this book?
As counsel for the prosecution in the *Lady Chatterley's Lover* trial

**Grimké, Angelina** (1805–79) US writer, abolitionist, and reformer.

1 I know you do not make the laws but I also know that you are the wives and mothers, the sisters and daughters of those who do . . .
*The Anti-Slavery Examiner* (Sep 1836), 'Appeal to the Christian Women of the South'

**Grossmith, George** (1847–1912) British singer and comedian. With his brother Walter Weedon Grossmith (1854–1919) he wrote the highly successful *Diary of a Nobody* (1892).

1 What's the good of a home, if you are never in it?
*The Diary of a Nobody*, Ch. 1

**Grossmith the Younger, George** (1874–1935) British singer, actor, and songwriter. The son of George Grossmith, he appeared in many musical comedies and a few films.

1 If you were the only girl in the world, And I were the only boy.
*The Bing Boys*, 'If you were the Only Girl' (with Fred Thompson; 1884–1949)

**Guedalla, Philip** (1889–1944) British writer. His books include *The Second Empire* (1922), *Conquistador* (1927), and *Argentine Tango* (1932).

1 The work of Henry James has always seemed divisible by a simple dynastic arrangement into three reigns: James I, James II, and the Old Pretender.
*Collected Essays*, 'Men of Letters: Mr. Henry James'

2 The little ships, the unforgotten Homeric catalogue of *Mary Jane* and *Peggy IV*, of *Folkestone Belle*, *Boy Billy*, and *Ethel Maud*, of *Lady Haig* and *Skylark* . . . the little ships of England

brought the Army home.
*Referring to the evacuation of Dunkirk*
*Mr. Churchill*

3 Any stigma will do to beat a dogma.
*Attrib.*

**Guitry, Sacha** (1885–1957) French actor and dramatist. He wrote several light comedies and appeared in numerous films, including *Napoléon* (1955).

1 The others were only my wives. But you, my dear, will be my widow.
*Allaying his fifth wife's jealousy of his previous wives*
*Speaker's and Toastmaster's Handbook* (J. Brawle)

**Gurney, Dorothy** (1858–1932) British poet.

1 The kiss of sun for pardon, The song of the birds for mirth – One is nearer God's Heart in a garden Than anywhere else on earth.
*The Lord God Planted a Garden*

**Gwyn, Nell** (1650–87) English actress. Originally an orange seller in Drury Lane, she became the mistress of Charles II.

1 Pray, good people, be civil. I am the Protestant whore.
*On being surrounded in her coach by an angry mob in Oxford at the time of the Popish Terror*
*Nell Gwyn* (Bevan), Ch. 13

# H

**Haggard, Sir Henry Rider** (1856–1925) British novelist. *King Solomon's Mines* (1885) was his best-known work. His later books include *She* (1887).

1 She-who-must-be-obeyed.
*She*

**Haig, Douglas, Earl** (1861–1928) British general. He commanded the British Expeditionary Force in World War I; under Foch, he directed the assault on the Hindenberg Line.

1 Every position must be held to the last man: there must be no retirement. With our backs to the wall, and believing in the justice of our cause, each one of us must fight on to the end.
*Order to the British Army, 12 Apr 1918*

**Haile Selassie** (1892–1975) Emperor of Ethiopia (1930–36; 1941–74). After the Italian invasion (1936) he fled to Britain, but returned in 1941 with the authority of the Allies. He was deposed by a military coup and died shortly afterwards.

1 We have finished the job, what shall we do with the tools?
*Telegram sent to Winston Churchill, mimicking his 'Give us the tools, and we will finish the job'*
*Ambrosia and Small Beer*, Ch. 4 (Edward Marsh)

**Hailsham, Quintin Hogg, Baron** (1907– ) British Conservative politician. He relinquished his hereditary peerage to contest (1963), unsuccessfully, the leadership of the Conservative party. He became lord chancellor (1970–74; 1979–87).

1 A great party is not to be brought down because of a scandal by a woman of easy virtue and a proved liar.
*Referring to the Profumo affair, in BBC interview, 13 June 1963*
*The Pendulum Years*, Ch. 3 (Bernard Levin)

2 If the British public falls for this, I say it will be stark, staring bonkers.
*Referring to Labour policy in the 1964 general-election campaign*
*Press conference, Conservative Central Office, 12 Oct 1964*

**Haldane, J(ohn) B(urdon) S(anderson)** (1892–1964) British geneticist. A Marxist, he edited the *Daily Worker* in the 1930s. In 1957 he emigrated to India. His books include *Science and Ethics* (1928), *The Inequality of Man* (1932), and *Science and Everyday Life* (1939).

1 Einstein – the greatest Jew since Jesus. I have no doubt that Einstein's name will still be remembered and revered when Lloyd George, Foch and William Hohenzollern share with Charlie Chaplin that ineluctable oblivion which awaits the uncreative mind.
*Daedalus or Science and the Future*

2 Shelley and Keats were the last English poets who were at all up to date in their chemical knowledge.
*Daedalus or Science and the Future*

3 If human beings could be propagated by cutting, like apple trees, aristocracy would be biologically sound.

*The Inequality of Man*, title essay

4 My own suspicion is that the universe is not only queerer than we suppose, but queerer than we *can* suppose.

*Possible Worlds*, 'On Being the Right Size'

5 An inordinate fondness for beetles.

Reply when asked what inferences could be drawn about the nature of God from a study of his works.
*Reader's Digest*, Feb 1979

**Hale, Edward Everett** (1822–1909) US author and clergyman. His books include *A New England Boyhood* (1893).

1 'Do you pray for the senators, Dr Hale?' 'No, I look at the senators and I pray for the country.'

*New England Indian Summer* (Van Wyck Brooks)

**Hale, Sir Matthew** (1609–76) English judge. He became lord chief justice (1671); his *History of the Common Law of England* (1713) was an important reference work.

1 Christianity is part of the Common Law of England.

*Historia Placitorum Coronae* (ed. Sollom Emlyn)

**Hale, Nathan** (1755–76) US revolutionary hero. Captured by the British as a spy, he was subsequently hanged.

1 I only regret that I have but one life to lose for my country.

Speech before his execution, 22 Sept 1776

**Hale, Sarah Josepha** (1788–1879) US writer and editor. Her books include *Poems for our Children* (1830).

1 Mary had a little lamb,
Its fleece was white as snow,
And everywhere that Mary went
The lamb was sure to go.

*Poems for Our Children*, 'Mary's Little Lamb'

**Halifax, George Saville, Marquis of** (1633–95) English statesman. Dismissed from offices he had held by James II, he supported the Glorious Revolution.

1 Men are not hanged for stealing horses, but that horses may not be stolen.

*Political, Moral and Miscellaneous Thoughts and Reflections*

2 It is a general mistake to think the men we like are good for everything, and those we do not, good for nothing.

*Political, Moral and Miscellaneous Thoughts and Reflections*

3 It is flattering some men to endure them.

*Political, Moral and Miscellaneous Thoughts and Reflections*

4 Our virtues and vices couple with one another, and get children that resemble both their parents.

*Political, Moral and Miscellaneous Thoughts and Reflections*

5 Popularity is a crime from the moment it is sought; it is only a virtue where men have it whether they will or no.

*Political, Moral and Miscellaneous Thoughts and Reflections*

6 When the People contend for their Liberty, they seldom get anything by their Victory but new masters.

*Political, Moral, and Miscellaneous Thoughts and Reflections*

7 Power is so apt to be insolent and Liberty to be saucy, that they are seldom upon good Terms.

*Political, Moral, and Miscellaneous Thoughts and Reflections*

8 Most men make little use of their speech than to give evidence against their own understanding.

*Political, Moral, and Miscellaneous Thoughts and Reflections*

9 He had said he had known many kicked down stairs, but he never knew any kicked up stairs before.

*Original Memoirs* (Burnet)

**Hall, Charles Sprague** (19th century) US songwriter.

1 John Brown's body lies a-mouldering in the grave,
His soul is marching on!

The song commemorates the American hero who died in the cause of abolishing slavery
*John Brown's Body*

**Halsey, Margaret** (1910– ) US writer.

1 . . . it takes a great deal to produce ennui in an Englishman and if you do, he only takes it as convincing proof that you are well-bred.

*With Malice Toward Some*

2 The attitude of the English . . . toward English history reminds one a good deal of the attitude of a Hollywood director toward love.

*With Malice Toward Some*

3 Living in England, provincial England, must be like being married to a stupid but exquisitely beautiful wife.

*With Malice Toward Some*

4 . . . the English think of an opinion as something which a decent person, if he has the misfortune to have one, does all he can to hide.

*With Malice Toward Some*

5 All of Stratford, in fact, suggests powdered history – add hot water and stir and you have a delicious, nourishing Shakespeare.

*With Malice Toward Some*

**Hamilton, Sir William** (1788–1856) Scottish philosopher. His books include edited lectures on metaphysics and logic.

1 Truth, like a torch, the more it's shook it shines.

*Discussions on Philosophy*, title page

2 On earth there is nothing great but man; in man there is nothing great but mind.

*Lectures on Metaphysics*

**Hamilton, William (Willie) Winter** (1917- ) Scottish MP and Labour politician. An active antimonarchist, his publications include *My Queen and I* (1975).

1 The tourists who come to our island take in the Monarchy along with feeding the pigeons in Trafalgar Square.
*My Queen and I*, Ch. 9

2 Britain is not a country that is easily rocked by revolution . . . In Britain our institutions evolve. We are a Fabian Society writ large.
*My Queen and I*, Ch. 9

**Hammarskjöld, Dag** (1905-61) Swedish diplomat, who became secretary general of the UN. He was killed in a plane crash. His diaries, *Markings*, were published in 1964.

1 Pray that your loneliness may spur you into finding something to live for, great enough to die for.
*Diaries*, 1951

**Hammerstein, Oscar** (1895-1960) US lyricist and librettist. With Richard Rogers he wrote many successful musicals, including *Oklahoma* (1943), *South Pacific* (1949), and *The Sound of Music* (1959).

1 Hello, Young Lovers, Wherever You Are.
From the musical *The King and I*
Song title

2 I Whistle a Happy Tune.
From the musical *The King and I*
Song title

3 Oh, what a beautiful morning!
Oh, what a beautiful day!
From the musical *Oklahoma*
*Oh, What a Beautiful Morning*

4 Ol' man river, dat ol' man river,
He must know sumpin', but don't say nothin',
He just keeps rollin', he keeps on rollin' along.
From the musical *Show Boat*
*Ol' Man River*

5 The hills are alive with the sound of music
With the songs they have sung
For a thousand years.
*The Sound of Music*, title song

**Hampton, Christopher** (1946- ) British writer and dramatist. Plays include *The Philanthropist* (1970), *Savages* (1973), and *Treats* (1976).

1 You know very well that unless you're a scientist, it's much more important for a theory to be shapely, than for it to be true.
*The Philanthropist*, Sc. 1

2 You see, I always divide people into two groups. Those who live by what they know to be a lie, and those who live by what they believe, falsely, to be the truth.
*The Philanthropist*, Sc. 6

3 If I had to give a definition of capitalism I would say: the process whereby American girls turn into American women.
*Savages*, Sc. 16

4 It's possible to disagree with someone about the ethics of non-violence without wanting to kick his face in.
*Treats*, Sc. 4

5 Asking a working writer what he thinks about critics is like asking a lamp-post how it feels about dogs.
*The Sunday Times Magazine*, 16 Oct 1977

**Hancock, John** (1737-93) US revolutionary. President of congress (1775-77), and the first to sign the Declaration of Independence, he became governor of Massachusetts (1780-85; 1787-93).

1 There, I guess King George will be able to read that.
Referring to his signature, written in a bold hand, on the US Declaration of Independence.
*The American Treasury* (C. Fadiman)

**Hankey, Katherine** (1834-1911) British hymn writer.

1 Tell me the old, old story
Of unseen things above,
Of Jesus and His glory
Of Jesus and His love.
*Tell Me the Old, Old Story*

**Harback, Otto** (1873-1963) US dramatist and librettist. His musical comedies included *Girl of My Dreams* (1910), *No! No! Nannette* (with Frank Mandel; 1924), and *The Desert Song* (1926).

1 Tea for Two, and Two for Tea.
From the musical *No! No! Nanette*
Song title

**Harbord, James Guthrie** (1866-1947) US general. He rose from the ranks to become chief of staff of the American Expeditionary Force in France during World War I.

1 I met the great little man, the man who can be silent in several languages.
Referring to Colonel House
*Mr Wilson's War* (John Dos Passos), Ch. 3

**Harburg, E(dgar) Y(ip)** (1896-1981) US songwriter.

1 Someday I'll wish upon a star.
From the musical *The Wizard of Oz*
*Over the Rainbow*

2 Somewhere over the rainbow,
Way up high:
There's a land that I heard of
Once in a lullaby.
From the musical *The Wizard of Oz*
*Over the Rainbow*

**Harcourt, Sir William** (1827-1904) British statesman. He was home secretary (1880-85) and later chancellor of the exchequer (1886; 1892-95).

1 We are all Socialists now.
Attrib.

**Hardwicke, Philip Yorke, Earl of** (1690-1764) English judge. He became attorney general (1724) and lord chancellor (1737).

**1** His doubts are better than most people's
certainties.
Referring to Dirleton's *Doubts*
*Life of Johnson* (J. Boswell)

**Hardy, Thomas** (1840–1928) British novelist and poet. His
novels include *The Mayor of Casterbridge* (1886), *Tess of the
D'Urbervilles* (1891), and *Jude the Obscure* (1895). His poetry was
collected in *Wessex Poems* (1898) and he wrote an epic drama *The
Dynasts* (1903–08).

**1** A local cult called Christianity.
*The Dynasts*, I:6

**2** My argument is that War makes rattling good
history; but Peace is poor reading.
*The Dynasts*, II:5

**3** A lover without indiscretion is no lover at all.
*The Hand of Ethelberta*, Ch. 20

**4** Life's Little Ironies.
Title of book of stories

**5** Dialect words – those terrible marks of the
beast to the truly genteel.
*The Mayor of Casterbridge*, Ch. 20

**6** Good, but not religious-good.
*Under the Greenwood Tree*, Ch. 2

**7** That man's silence is wonderful to listen to.
*Under the Greenwood Tree*, Ch. 14

**8** This is the weather the cuckoo likes,
And so do I;
When showers betumble the chestnut spikes,
And nestlings fly:
And the little brown nightingale bills his best,
And they sit outside at 'The Travellers' Rest'.
*Weathers*

**9** This is the weather the shepherd shuns,
And so do I.
*Weathers*

**10** If Galileo had said in verse that the world
moved, the Inquisition might have let him alone.
*The Later Years of Thomas Hardy* (F. E. Hardy)

**Hargreaves, W. F.** (1846–1919) British songwriter.

**1** I'm Burlington Bertie:
I rise at ten-thirty.
*Burlington Bertie*

**2** I walk down the Strand
With my gloves on my hand,
And I walk down again
With them off.
*Burlington Bertie*

**Harington, Sir John** (1561–1612) English writer. He
translated Ariosto's *Orlando Furioso* and his own collected
epigrams were published in 1618.

**1** Treason doth never prosper: what's the reason?
For if it prosper, none dare call it treason.
*Epigrams*, 'Of Treason'

**Harris, George** (1844–1922) US congressman; president of
Amherst college (1899–1912).

**1** I intended to give you some advice but now I
remember how much is left over from last year
unused.
Said when addressing students at the start of a new academic
year
*Braude's Second Encyclopedia* (J. Braude)

**Hart, Lorenz** (1895–1943) US songwriter. He wrote the
lyrics for many musicals, including *Babes in Arms* (1937) and *The
Boys from Syracuse* (1938), for which Richard Rogers wrote the
music.

**1** Bewitched, Bothered and Bewildered.
From the musical *Babes in Arms*
Song title

**2** That's Why the Lady Is a Tramp.
From the musical *Babes in Arms*
Song title

**Hartley, L(esley) P(oles)** (1895–1972) British novelist.
His early trilogy, starting with *The Shrimp and the Anemone*
(1944), established his reputation. Later books include *The Boat*
(1949) and *The Go-Between* (1953).

**1** The past is a foreign country: they do things differently there.
*The Go-Between*

**Haskell, Arnold** (1903–80) English writer on ballet.

**1** Unlike so many who find success, she remained
a 'dinkum hard-swearing Aussie' to the end.
Referring to Dame Nellie Melba
*Waltzing Matilda*

**Haskins, Minnie Louise** (1875–1957) US writer.

**1** And I said to the man who stood at the gate of
the year: 'Give me a light that I may tread safely into the unknown'. And he replied: 'Go out
into the darkness and put your hand into the
hand of God. That shall be to you better than
light and safer than a known way.'
Remembered because it was quoted by George VI in his Christmas broadcast, 1939
*The Desert*, Introduction

**Hastings, Lady Flora** (1806–39) British poet.

**1** Grieve not that I die young. Is it not well
To pass away ere life hath lost its brightness?
*Swan Song*

**Hawker, R(obert) S(tephen)** (1803–75) British poet. An
Anglican clergyman, he later became a Roman Catholic priest. His
verse collections include *Cornish Ballads and Other Poems* (1864).

**1** And have they fixed the where and when?
And shall Trelawny die?
Here's twenty thousand Cornish men
Will know the reason why!
Referring to the imprisonment (1688) of Trelawny, Bishop of
Bristol, by James II
*Song of the Western Men*

**Hawthorne, Nathaniel** (1804–64) US novelist and writer. His best-known novels, *The Scarlet Letter* (1850) and *The House of Seven Gables* (1851), were followed by a period in England as US consul in Liverpool, after which he lived in Italy.

1  We sometimes congratulate ourselves at the moment of waking from a troubled dream; it may be so the moment after death.
*American Notebooks*

2  Dr Johnson's morality was as English an article as a beefsteak.
*Our Old Home*, 'Lichfield and Uttoxeter'

**Hay, Lord Charles** (d. 1760) British soldier.

1  Gentlemen of the French Guard, fire first!
Said at the Battle of Fontenoy, 1745
Attrib.

**Hay, Ian** (John Hay Beith; 1876–1952) British novelist and dramatist. His novels include *Pip* (1907), *The Last Million* (1918), and *Paid, With Thanks* (1925). He also wrote the successful play *The Housemaster* (1930).

1  Funny peculiar, or funny ha-ha?
*The Housemaster*, III

**Hay, Will** (1888–1949) British comedian. After years in the music halls, he made a number of films, including *Oh, Mr Porter!* (1937).

1  MASTER. They split the atom by firing particles at it, at 5,500 miles a second.
BOY. Good heavens. And they only split it?
*The Fourth Form at St Michael's*

**Hayes, J. Milton** (1884–1940) British writer.

1  There's a one-eyed yellow idol to the north of Khatmandu,
There's a little marble cross below the town;
There's a broken-hearted woman tends the grave of Mad Carew
And the Yellow God forever gazes down.
*The Green Eye of the Yellow God*

**Hazlitt, William** (1778–1830) British essayist and journalist. His collections of writings include *Lectures on the English Poets* (1818) and *The Spirit of the Age* (1825).

1  The least pain in our little finger gives us more concern and uneasiness than the destruction of millions of our fellow-beings.
*American Literature*, 'Dr Channing'

2  If the world were good for nothing else, it is a fine subject for speculation.
*Characteristics*

3  Man is an intellectual animal, and therefore an everlasting contradiction to himself. His senses centre in himself, his ideas reach to the ends of the universe; so that he is torn in pieces between the two, without a possibility of its ever being otherwise.
*Characteristics*

4  His sayings are generally like women's letters; all the pith is in the postscript.
Referring to Charles Lamb
*Conversations of Northcote*

5  He writes as fast as they can read, and he does not write himself down.
*English Literature*, Ch. XIV, 'Sir Walter Scott'

6  His worst is better than any other person's best.
*English Literature*, Ch. XIV, 'Sir Walter Scott'

7  So have I loitered my life away, reading books, looking at pictures, going to plays, hearing, thinking, writing on what pleased me best. I have wanted only one thing to make me happy, but wanting that have wanted everything.
*English Literature*, Ch. XVII, 'My First Acquaintance with Poets'

8  You will hear more good things on the outside of a stagecoach from London to Oxford than if you were to pass a twelvemonth with the undergraduates, or heads of colleges, of that famous university.
*The Ignorance of the Learned*

9  He talked on for ever; and you wished him to talk on for ever.
Referring to Coleridge
*Lectures on the English Poets*, Lecture VIII, 'On the Living Poets'

10  A nickname is the heaviest stone that the devil can throw at a man.
*Nicknames*

11  There is nothing good to be had in the country, or, if there is, they will not let you have it.
*Observations on Wordsworth's 'Excursion'*

12  The greatest offence against virtue is to speak ill of it.
*On Cant and Hypocrisy*

13  Those who make their dress a principal part of themselves, will, in general, become of no more value than their dress.
*On the Clerical Character*

14  The English (it must be owned) are rather a foul-mouthed nation
*On Criticism*

15  We can scarcely hate any one that we know.
*On Criticism*

16  There is an unseemly exposure of the mind, as well as of the body.
*On Disagreeable People*

17  No young man believes he shall ever die.
*On the Feeling of Immortality in Youth*

18  One of the pleasantest things in the world is going on a journey; but I like to go by myself.
*On Going a Journey*

19  When I am in the country I wish to vegetate like the country.
*On Going a Journey*

**20** To great evils we submit; we resent little provocations.
*On Great and Little Things*

**21** There is not a more mean, stupid, dastardly, pitiful, selfish, spiteful, envious, ungrateful animal than the public. It is the greatest of cowards, for it is afraid of itself.
*On Living to Oneself*

**22** The art of pleasing consists in being pleased.
*On Manner*

**23** A person may be indebted for a nose or an eye, for a graceful carriage or a voluble discourse, to a great-aunt or uncle, whose existence he has scarcely heard of.
*On Personal Character*

**24** The dupe of friendship, and the fool of love; have I not reason to hate and to despise myself? Indeed I do; and chiefly for not having hated and despised the world enough.
*On the Pleasure of Hating*

**25** We never do anything well till we cease to think about the manner of doing it.
*On Prejudice*

**26** The most fluent talkers or most plausible reasoners are not always the justest thinkers.
*On Prejudice*

**27** Rules and models destroy genius and art.
*On Taste*

**28** The love of liberty is the love of others; the love of power is the love of ourselves.
*The Times*, 1819

**29** Spleen can subsist on any kind of food.
*On Wit and Humour*

**30** Well, I've had a happy life.
Last words

**Healey, Denis Winston** (1917– ) British Labour politician. He became chancellor of the exchequer (1974–79) and opposition spokesman on foreign affairs (1980– ). His books include *The Curtain Falls* (1951) and *Labour Britain and the World* (1963).

**1** Like being savaged by a dead sheep.
Referring to the attack launched by Geoffrey Howe upon his Budget proposals
*The Listener*, 21 Dec 1978

**2** Their Europeanism is nothing but imperialism with an inferiority complex.
Referring to the policies of the Conservative party
*The Observer*, 'Sayings of the Week', 7 Oct 1962

**3** I am the Gromyko of the Labour party.
Alluding to Andrei Gromyko (1909– ), Soviet statesman who was foreign minister from 1957 to 1985
Attrib.

**Hearst, William Randolph** (1863–1951) US newspaper owner, who built up the vast newspaper empire that inspired Orson Welles' film *Citizen Kane* (1941).

**1** Stop running those dogs on your page. I wouldn't have them peeing on my cheapest rug.
Referring to the publication of Thurber's drawings by one of his editors
*The Years with Ross* (James Thurber)

**Heath, Edward** (1916– ) British statesman. He was Conservative prime minister (1970–74) when the UK joined the EEC. After losing two elections in 1975 he resigned the party leadership and was succeeded by Margaret Thatcher.

**1** It is the unpleasant and unacceptable face of capitalism but one should not suggest that the whole of British industry consists of practices of this kind.
Referring to the Lonrho Affair
Speech, House of Commons, 15 May 1973

**Heber, Reginald** (1783–1826) British bishop and hymn writer.

**1** From Greenland's icy mountains,
From India's coral strand,
Where Afric's sunny fountains
Roll down their golden sand.
*From Greenland's Icy Mountains*

**2** What though the spicy breezes
Blow soft o'er Ceylon's isle;
Though every prospect pleases,
And only man is vile . . .
*From Greenland's Icy Mountains*

**3** Holy, holy, holy, Lord God Almighty!
Early in the morning our song shall rise to thee.
*Holy, Holy, Holy*

**Hegel, Georg Wilhelm Friedrich** (1770–1831) German philosopher. His works include *The Phenomenology of Mind* (1807) and the *Encyclopedia of the Philosophical Sciences* (1817).

**1** What experience and history teach is this – that people and governments never have learned anything from history, or acted on principles deduced from it.
*Philosophy of History*, Introduction

**2** Only one man ever understood me. . . . And he didn't understand me.
Said on his deathbed
*Famous Last Words* (B. Conrad)

**Heifetz, Jascha** (1901– ) Russian-born US violinist.

**1** If the Almighty himself played the violin, the credits would still read 'Rubinstein, God, and Piatigorsky', in that order.
Whenever Heifitz played in trios with Arthur Rubinstein (piano) and Gregor Piatigorsky (cello), Rubinstein always got top billing
*Los Angeles Times*, 29 Aug 1982

**Heine, Heinrich** (1797–1856) German poet and writer. His early collection *Buch der Lieder* (1827) preceded his move to Paris (1831), where he remained until his death.

**1** Whenever books are burned men also in the end are burned.
*Almansor*

2 Sleep is good, death is better; but of course, the best thing would be never to have been born at all.
*Morphine*

3 I just met X in the street, I stopped for a moment to exchange ideas, and now I feel like a complete idiot.
*Autant en apportent les mots* (Pedrazzini)

4 It is extremely difficult for a Jew to be converted, for how can he bring himself to believe in the divinity of – another Jew?
Attrib.

5 God will pardon me. It is His trade.
Last words
*Journal* (Edmond and Charles Goncourt), 23 Feb 1863

**Heisenberg, Werner** (1901–76) German physicist, who made great contributions to quantum theory and discovered the uncertainty principle. He was one of the few physicists to remain in Germany during the Nazi period.

1 An expert is someone who knows some of the worst mistakes that can be made in his subject, and how to avoid them.
*Physics and Beyond*

2 Natural science does not simply describe and explain nature, it is part of the interplay between nature and ourselves.
*Physics and Philosophy*

**Heller, Joseph** (1923– ) US novelist. He made his name with the war novel *Catch-22* (1961); subsequent books include *Good as Gold* (1979) and *God Knows* (1984).

1 He was a self-made man who owed his lack of success to nobody.
*Catch-22*, Ch. 3

2 He had decided to live for ever or die in the attempt.
*Catch-22*, Ch. 3

3 There was only one catch and that was Catch-22, which specified that a concern for one's own safety in the face of dangers that were real and immediate was the process of a rational mind.
*Catch-22*, Ch. 5

4 He knew everything about literature except how to enjoy it.
*Catch-22*, Ch. 8

5 Some men are born mediocre, some men achieve mediocrity, and some men have mediocrity thrust upon them. With Major Major it had been all three.
*Catch-22*, Ch. 9

6 Hungry Joe collected lists of fatal diseases and arranged them in alphabetical order so that he could put his finger without delay on any one he wanted to worry about.
*Catch-22*, Ch. 17

7 Prostitution gives her an opportunity to meet people. It provides fresh air and wholesome exercise, and it keeps her out of trouble.
*Catch-22*, Ch. 33

**Hellman, Lillian** (1905–84) US dramatist. Her plays include *The Little Foxes* (1939) and *Watch on the Rhine* (1941), which were made into films using her own screenplays. She also wrote several books of memoirs.

1 Cynicism is an unpleasant way of saying the truth.
*The Little Foxes*, I

2 I cannot and will not cut my conscience to fit this year's fashions, even though I long ago came to the conclusion that I was not a political person and could have no comfortable place in any political group.
Letter to the US House of Representatives Committee on Un-American Activities, *The Nation*, 31 May 1952

3 It makes me feel masculine to tell you that I do not answer questions like this without being paid for answering them.
When asked by *Harper's* magazine when she felt most masculine; this question had already been asked of several famous men *Reader's Digest*, July 1977

**Helps, Sir Arthur** (1813–75) British historian. Works include *Conquerors of the New World* (1848) and *Friends in Council* (1847–53).

1 Reading is sometimes an ingenious device for avoiding thought.
*Friends in Council*

2 What a blessing this smoking is! perhaps the greatest that we owe to the discovery of America.
*Friends in Council*

3 There is one statesman of the present day, of whom I always say that he would have escaped making the blunders that he has made if he had only ridden more in omnibuses.
*Friends in Council*

**Helvétius, Claude-Adrien** (1715–71) French philosopher. *De l'esprit* (1758), his major work, was publicly denounced by the Sorbonne.

1 Education made us what we are.
*Discours XXX*, Ch. 30

**Hemans, Felicia Dorothea** (1793–1835) British poet. Her lyrics include *Casabianca* and *The Homes of England*.

1 The boy stood on the burning deck
Whence all but he had fled;
The flame that lit the battle's wreck
Shone round him o'er the dead.
*Casabianca*

2 The stately homes of England,
How beautiful they stand!
Amidst their tall ancestral trees,
O'er all the pleasant land.
*The Homes of England*

**Hemingway, Ernest** (1898–1961) US novelist, who lived for much of his life in Paris. His first successful novel was *The Sun Also Rises* (1926); subsequent novels include *A Farewell to Arms* (1929) and *For Whom the Bell Tolls* (1940). He was a keen sportsman and admirer of bullfighting.

1 Bullfighting is the only art in which the artist is in danger of death and in which the degree of brilliance in the performance is left to the fighter's honour.
*Death in the Afternoon*, Ch. 9

2 But did thee feel the earth move?
*For Whom the Bell Tolls*, Ch. 13

3 If you are lucky enough to have lived in Paris as a young man, then wherever you go for the rest of your life, it stays with you, for Paris is a moveable feast.
*A Moveable Feast*, Epigraph

4 A man can be destroyed but not defeated.
*The Old Man and the Sea*

5 Because I am a bastard.
When asked why he had deserted his wife for another woman
*Americans in Paris* (B. Morton)

6 Poor Faulkner. Does he really think big emotions come from big words? He thinks I don't know the ten-dollar words. I know them all right. But there are older and simpler and better words, and those are the ones I use.
In response to a jibe by William FAULKNER
Attrib.

**Henley, William Ernest** (1849–1903) British writer. An editor of various weekly journals, his verse collections include *Book of Verses* (1888) and *For England's Sake* (1900). He collaborated with Robert Louis Stevenson on several plays.

1 In the fell clutch of circumstance,
I have not winced nor cried aloud;
Under the bludgeonings of chance
My head is bloody, but unbowed.
*Echoes*, IV, 'Invictus. In Mem. R.T.H.B.'

2 It matters not how strait the gate,
How charged with punishments the scroll,
I am the master of my fate:
I am the captain of my soul.
*Echoes*, IV, 'Invictus. In Mem. R.T.H.B.'

**Henri IV** (1553–1610) The first Bourbon King of France. In 1594 he became a Roman Catholic, granting Huguenots freedom of worship by the Edict of Nantes (1598).

1 I want there to be no peasant in my kingdom so poor that he is unable to have a chicken in his pot every Sunday.
*Hist. de Henry le Grand* (Hardouin de Péréfixe)

2 Paris is worth a mass.
Said on entering Paris (March 1594), having secured its submission to his authority by becoming a Roman Catholic
Attrib.

3 The wisest fool in Christendom.
Referring to James I of England
Attrib.

**Henry, Matthew** (1662–1714) English nonconformist minister. His *Exposition of the Old and New Testaments* was completed by thirteen of his colleagues.

1 The better day, the worse deed.
*Exposition of the Old and New Testaments*

2 They that die by famine die by inches.
*Exposition of the Old and New Testaments*

3 All this and heaven too.
*Life of Philip Henry*

**Henry, O.** (William Sidney Porter; 1862–1910) US short-story writer. His pseudonym was invented while serving a prison sentence for embezzlement. His first collection, *Cabbages and Kings*, was published in 1904.

1 If men knew how women pass the time when they are alone, they'd never marry.
*Memoirs of a Yellow Dog*

2 Turn up the lights, I don't want to go home in the dark.
His last words, quoting a popular song of the time
*O. Henry* (C. A. Smith), Ch. 9

**Henry, Patrick** (1736–99) US statesman. The first governor of Virginia, he mobilized a Virginia militia on the eve of the American Revolution.

1 Caesar had his Brutus – Charles the First, his Cromwell – and George the Third – ('Treason,' cried the Speaker) . . . *may profit by their example. If this* be treason, make the most of it.
Speech, Virginia Convention, May 1765

2 I know not what course others may take; but as for me, give me liberty or give me death.
Speech, Virginia Convention, 23 Mar 1775

**Henry II** (1133–89) King of England. Married to Eleanor of Aquitaine, his empire stretched to the Pyrenees. He was unintentionally responsible for the murder of Thomas Becket.

1 Will no one rid me of this turbulent priest?
Referring to Thomas Becket, Archbishop of Canterbury; four of Henry's household knights took these words literally, hurried to Canterbury, and killed Becket in the cathedral (Dec 1170)
Attrib.

**Henry VIII** (1491–1547) King of England. Six times married, his divorce from his first wife, Catherine of Aragon, on her failure to produce a male heir, precipitated the Reformation in England.

1 You have sent me a Flanders mare.
Said on meeting his fourth wife, Anne of Cleves, for the first time
Attrib.

**Hepworth, Dame Barbara** (1903–75) British sculptor, whose typical works were massive abstract shapes in stone or wood, pierced by holes.

1 . . . I rarely draw what I see. I draw what I feel in my body.
*World of Art Series* (A. M. Hammersmith)

**Heraclitus** (c. 535 – c. 475 BC) Greek philosopher. An early metaphysician, his major work was *On Nature*.

1 Everything flows and nothing stays.

*Cratylus* (Plato), 402a

2 You can't step into the same river twice.

*Cratylus* (Plato), 402a

**Herbert, Sir A(lan) P(atrick)** (1890–1971) British writer and politician. His novels include *The Secret Battle* (1919) and *Holy Deadlock* (1934). He also wrote the libretti for a number of musical comedies, of which the most successful was *Bless the Bride* (1947). As an MP, he helped to reform the divorce law and was the prime mover in the act to pay royalties to authors on library books.

1 Other people's babies –
That's my life!
Mother to dozens,
And nobody's wife.

*A Book of Ballads*, 'Other People's Babies'

2 Let's find out what everyone is doing,
And then stop everyone from doing it.

*Let's Stop Somebody*

3 The Common Law of England has been laboriously built about a mythical figure – the figure of 'The Reasonable Man'.

*Uncommon Law*

4 People must not do things for fun. We are not here for fun. There is no reference to fun in any Act of Parliament.

*Uncommon Law*

5 The critical period in matrimony is breakfast-time.

*Uncommon Law*

6 The Englishman never enjoys himself except for a noble purpose.

*Uncommon Law*

7 For any ceremonial purposes the otherwise excellent liquid, water, is unsuitable in colour and other respects.

*Uncommon Law*

8 An Act of God was defined as *something which no reasonable man could have expected.*

*Uncommon Law*

**Herbert, George** (1593–1633) English poet. His religious lyrics were collected in *The Temple* (1633).

1 I struck the board, and cried, 'No more;
I will abroad.'
What, shall I ever sigh and pine?
My lines and life are free; free as the road,
Loose as the wind, as large as store.

*The Collar*

2 But as I rav'd and grew more fierce and wild
At every word,
Methought I heard one calling, 'Child';
And I replied, 'My Lord.'

*The Collar*

3 Oh that I were an orange-tree,
That busy plant!
Then I should ever laden be,
And never want
Some fruit for Him that dressed me.

*Employment*

4 And now in age I bud again,
After so many deaths I live and write;
I once more smell the dew and rain,
And relish versing; O, my only Light,
It cannot be
That I am he
On whom Thy tempests fell all night.

*The Flower*

5 Death is still working like a mole,
And digs my grave at each remove.

*Grace*

6 Love bade me welcome; yet my soul drew back,
Guilty of dust and sin.

*Love*

7 'You must sit down,' says Love, 'and taste My meat,'
So I did sit and eat.

*Love*

8 He that makes a good war makes a good peace.

*Outlandish Proverbs*, 420

9 Sweet day, so cool, so calm, so bright,
The bridal of the earth and sky.

*Virtue*

10 Only a sweet and virtuous soul,
Like season'd timber, never gives;
But though the whole world turn to coal,
Then chiefly lives.

*Virtue*

**Herford, Oliver** (1863–1935) British-born US humorist, writer, and illustrator.

1 I would like to throw an egg into an electric fan.

When asked if he really had no ambition beyond making people laugh
Attrib.

**Herrick, Robert** (1591–1674) English poet. Ordained in 1623, his religious and secular verse is collected in *Hesperides* (1648).

1 Cherry ripe, ripe, ripe, I cry.
Full and fair ones; come and buy.

*See also* CAMPION
*Hesperides*, 'Cherry Ripe'

2 A sweet disorder in the dress
Kindles in clothes a wantonness.

*Hesperides*, 'Delight in Disorder'

3 'Twixt kings and tyrants there's this difference known;
Kings seek their subjects' good: tyrants their own.

*Hesperides*, 'Kings and Tyrants'

4 Fair daffodils, we weep to see
You haste away so soon:
As yet the early-rising sun
Has not attain'd his noon.
Stay, stay,
Until the hasting day
Has run
But to the even-song;
And, having pray'd together, we
Will go with you along.

We have short time to stay, as you,
We have as short a Spring;
As quick a growth to meet decay,
As you or any thing.

*Hesperides*, 'To Daffodils'

5 Gather ye rosebuds while ye may,
Old time is still a-flying:
And this same flower that smiles today
Tomorrow will be dying.

*Hesperides*, 'To the Virgins, to Make Much of Time'

6 Then be not coy, but use your time;
And while ye may, go marry:
For having lost but once your prime,
You may for ever tarry.

*Hesperides*, 'To the Virgins, to Make Much of Time'

7 Whenas in silks my Julia goes
Then, then (methinks) how sweetly flows
That liquefaction of her clothes.

*Hesperides*, 'Upon Julia's Clothes'

**Hesse, Hermann** (1877–1962) German novelist and poet.
His novels include *Peter Camenzind* (1904) and *Steppenwolf* (1927).
He lived in Switzerland from 1911.

1 If you hate a person, you hate something in him
that is part of yourself. What isn't part of ourselves doesn't disturb us.

*Demian*, Ch. 6

**Hewart, Gordon, Baron** (1870–1943) British lawyer and
politician. He became attorney general (1919–22) and lord chief
justice (1922–40).

1 Justice should not only be done, but should manifestly and undoubtedly be seen to be done.

*The Chief* (R. Jackson)

**Heywood, Thomas** (c. 1574–1641) English dramatist and
actor. He wrote numerous comedies and tragedies.

1 Seven cities warr'd for Homer, being dead,
Who, living, had no roof to shroud his head.

*The Hierarchy of the Blessed Angels*

2 A Woman Killed with Kindness.

Play title

**Hicks, Sir (Edward) Seymour** (1871–1949) British
actor-manager. He was a comedian in the Gaiety company and
specialized in musical comedies.

1 You will recognize, my boy, the first sign of old
age: it is when you go out into the streets of
London and realize for the first time how young
the policemen look.

*They Were Singing* (C. Pulling)

**Hickson, William Edward** (1803–70) British
educationalist and writer.

1 If at first you don't succeed,
Try, try again.

*Try and Try Again*

**Higley, Brewster** (19th century) US songwriter.

1 Oh give me a home where the buffalo roam,
Where the deer and the antelope play,
Where seldom is heard a discouraging word
And the skies are not cloudy all day.

*Home on the Range*

**Hill, Aaron** (1685–1750) British poet and dramatist. He wrote
the words for Handel's *Rinaldo* and translated Voltaire's plays.

1 Tender-handed stroke a nettle,
And it stings you for your pains;
Grasp it like a man of mettle,
And it soft as silk remains.

*Verses Written on Window*

**Hill, Rowland** (1744–1833) British clergyman.

1 I do not see any reason why the devil should
have all the good tunes.

Attrib.

**Hillary, Sir Edmund** (1919– ) New Zealand mountaineer.
With the Sherpa, Tenzing Norgay, he was the first to climb
Everest. He became New Zealand's High Commissioner to India in
1984.

1 As far as I knew, he had never taken a photograph before, and the summit of Everest was
hardly the place to show him how.

Referring to Tenzing Norgay, his companion on the conquest of
Mt Everest (1953)
*High Adventure*

2 There is precious little in civilization to appeal to
a Yeti.

*The Observer*, 'Sayings of the Week', 3 June 1960

**Hilton, James** (1900–54) British novelist. His novels *Lost
Horizon* (1933) and *Good-bye, Mr Chips* (1934) were made into
films and he subsequently worked as a scriptwriter in Hollywood.

1 Anno domini – that's the most fatal complaint of
all in the end.

*Good-bye, Mr Chips*, Ch. 1

**Hippocrates** (c. 460–c. 377 BC) Greek physician, who
founded the Hippocratic school of medicine, where students were
required to take an oath (the Hippocratic oath) to observe a code
of practice putting the patient's interest above all others.

1 The life so short, the craft so long to learn.

Describing medicine. It is often quoted in Latin as *Ars longa, vita
brevis*, and interpreted as 'Art lasts, life is short'. *See also*
CHAUCER
*Aphorisms*, I

**2** Extreme remedies are most appropriate for extreme diseases.

*Aphorisms, I*

**Hitchcock, Sir Alfred** (1889–1980) British film director, working mainly in the USA from 1940. His films – mostly sophisticated thrillers – include *Vertigo* (1958), *North by Northwest* (1959), *Psycho* (1960), and *The Birds* (1963).

**1** Actors should be treated like cattle.

Said in clarification of a remark attributed to him, 'Actors are like cattle'
*Quote, Unquote* (N. Rees)

**Hitler, Adolf** (1889–1945) German dictator, who became president of the Nazi party in 1921 and chancellor of Germany in 1933. His campaign of world conquest led to World War II, defeat and disgrace for Germany, and his own suicide.

**1** All those who are not racially pure are mere chaff.

*Mein Kampf,* Ch. 2

**2** Only constant repetition will finally succeed in imprinting an idea on the memory of the crowd.

*Mein Kampf,* Ch. 6

**3** The broad mass of a nation . . . will more easily fall victim to a big lie than to a small one.

*Mein Kampf,* Ch. 10

**4** Germany will be either a world power or will not be at all.

*Mein Kampf,* Ch. 14

**5** In starting and waging a war it is not right that matters, but victory.

*The Rise and Fall of the Third Reich* (W. L. Shirer), Ch. 16

**6** The essential thing is the formation of the political will of the nation: that is the starting point for political action.

Speech, Düsseldorf, 27 Jan 1932

**7** I go the way that Providence dictates with the assurance of a sleepwalker.

Referring to his successful re-occupation of the Rhineland, despite advice against the attempt
Speech, Munich, 15 Mar 1936

**8** When Barbarossa commences, the world will hold its breath and make no comment.

Referring to the planned invasion of the USSR, Operation Barbarossa, which began on 22 June 1941
Attrib.

**9** Is Paris burning?

Referring to the liberation of Paris, 1944

**Hobbes, Thomas** (1588–1679) English philosopher and political thinker. His *Leviathan* (1651) set out his political philosophy.

**1** The condition of man . . . is a condition of war of everyone against everyone.

*Leviathan,* Pt. I, Ch. 4

**2** True and False are attributes of speech, not of things. And where speech is not, there is neither Truth nor Falsehood.

*Leviathan,* Pt. I, Ch. 4

**3** They that approve a private opinion, call it opinion; but they that mislike it, heresy: and yet heresy signifies no more than private opinion.

*Leviathan,* Pt. I, Ch. 11

**4** No arts; no letters; no society; and which is worst of all, continual fear and danger of violent death; and the life of man, solitary, poor, nasty, brutish, and short.

*Leviathan,* Pt. I, Ch. 13

**5** The only way to erect such a common power, as may be able to defend them from the invasion of foreigners, and the injuries of one another . . . is, to confer all their power and strength upon one man, or upon one assembly of men, that may reduce all their wills, by plurality of voices, unto one will . . . This is the generation of that great Leviathan, or rather (to speak more reverently) of that *Mortal God,* to which we owe under the *Immortal God,* our peace and defence.

*Leviathan,* Pt. II, Ch. 17

**6** They that are discontented under *monarchy,* call it *tyranny;* and they that are displeased with *aristocracy,* call it *oligarchy:* so also, they which find themselves grieved under a *democracy,* call it *anarchy,* which signifies the want of government; and yet I think no man believes, that want of government, is any new kind of government.

*Leviathan,* Pt. II, Ch. 19

**7** The Papacy is not other than the Ghost of the deceased Roman Empire, sitting crowned upon the grave thereof.

*Leviathan,* Pt. IV, Ch. 37

**8** I am about to take my last voyage, a great leap in the dark.

Last words

**Hobhouse, John Cam, Baron Broughton de Gyfford** (1786–1869) British politician. He became secretary of war (1832–33) and secretary for Ireland (1833). He was a friend of Byron, advising that his *Memoirs* be destroyed. His own autobiography, *Recollections of a Long Life,* were published in 1865.

**1** When I invented the phrase 'His Majesty's Opposition' he paid me a compliment on the fortunate hit.

Speaking about Canning
*Recollections of a Long Life,* II, Ch. 12

**Hobson, Sir Harold** (1904– ) British theatre critic and writer. His books include *The Theatre Now* (1953) and the autobiography *Indirect Journey* (1978).

**1** The United States, I believe, are under the impression that they are twenty years in advance of this country; whilst, as a matter of actual verifiable fact, of course, they are just about six hours behind it.

*The Devil in Woodford Wells,* Ch. 8

**Hodgson, Ralph** (1871–1962) British poet. His poems include *The Bells of Heaven*, *The Bull*, *Eve*, and *Last Blackbird*.

1   'Twould ring the bells of Heaven
The wildest peal for years,
If Parson lost his senses
And people came to theirs,
And he and they together
Knelt down with angry prayers
For tamed and shabby tigers
And dancing dogs and bears,
And wretched, blind, pit ponies,
And little hunted hares.
*The Bells of Heaven*

**Hoffer, Eric** (1902–   ) US writer. Working as a docker on the Pacific Coast for many years, he is the author of several philosophical works.

1   When people are free to do as they please, they usually imitate each other.
*The Passionate State of Mind*

**Hoffman, Heinrich** (1809–74) German writer and illustrator.

1   But one day, one cold winter's day,
He screamed out, 'Take the soup away!'
*Struwwelpeter*, 'Augustus'

2   Look at little Johnny there,
Little Johnny Head-in-Air.
*Struwwelpeter*, 'Johnny Head-in-Air'

3   The door flew open, in he ran,
The great, long, red-legged scissor-man.
*Struwwelpeter*, 'The Little Suck-a-Thumb'

4   Anything to me is sweeter
Than to see Shock-headed Peter.
*Struwwelpeter*, 'Shock-headed Peter'

**Hoffmann, Ernst Theodor Amadeus** (1776–1822) German composer. His opera *Undine* (1816) was the basis for Offenbach's *Tales of Hoffmann*. He also wrote many romantic novels and stories.

1   He's a wicked man that comes after children when they won't go to bed and throws handfuls of sand in their eyes.
*The Sandman*

**Hoffmann, Max** (1869–1927) German general, who in World War I succeeded Ludendorff as chief of the general staff (1916).

1   LUDENDORFF. The English soldiers fight like lions.
HOFFMANN. True. But don't we know that they are lions led by donkeys.
Referring to the performance of the British army in World War I
*The Donkeys* (A. Clark)

**Hoffmann von Fallersleben, Heinrich** (1798–1876) German poet and scholar, author of the patriotic poem (1841) that was adopted as the German national anthem after World War I.

1   *Deutschland, Deutschland über alles.*
Germany, Germany before all else.
German national anthem

**Hogg, James** (1770–1835) Scottish poet and writer. Originally a shepherd (known as 'The Ettrick Shepherd'), he wrote many ballads and the novel *The Confessions of a Justified Sinner* (1824).

1   Will you no come back again?
Better lo'ed you'll never be,
And will ye no come back again?
*Jacobite Relics of Scotland*, 'Will Ye No Come Back Again?'

2   My love she's but a lassie yet.
Title of song

**Hokusai** (1760–1849) Japanese painter and book illustrator, famous for his ukiyo-e colour prints. His best-known work is *Views of Mount Fuji* (1835).

1   If heaven had granted me five more years, I could have become a real painter.
Said on his deathbed
*Famous Last Words* (B. Conrad)

**Holberg, Ludwig, Baron** (1684–1754) Danish dramatist, poet, and historian, claimed as the founder of modern Danish and Norwegian literature. His works include the satirical epic poem *Peder Paas* (1719) and the comic play *The Political Tinker*.

1   Do you call that thing under your hat a head?
Reply to the jibe, 'Do you call that thing on your head a hat?'
*Anekdotenschatz* (H. Hoffmeister)

**Holland, Henry Fox, Baron** (1705–74) British politician. A Royalist, he accompanied Charles II to Holland. He became an MP, secretary of war (1746–54), and leader of the Commons (1755–56).

1   If Mr Selwyn calls again, shew him up: if I am alive I shall be delighted to see him; and if I am dead he would like to see me.
Said during his last illness. George Selwyn was known for his morbid fascination for dead bodies.
*George Selwyn and his Contemporaries* (J. H. Jesse), Vol. III

**Holmes, John Haynes** (1879–1964) US clergyman. His books include *Religion for Today* (1917) and *A Sensible Man's View of Religion* (1933).

1   The universe is not hostile, nor yet is it friendly. It is simply indifferent.
*A Sensible Man's View of Religion*

**Holmes, Oliver Wendell** (1809–94) US writer and physician. The dean of Harvard Medical School, he wrote several medical books as well as collections of verse and essays, including *Old Ironsides* (verse; 1830) and *The Autocrat of the Breakfast Table* (essays; 1857).

1   Man has his will, – but woman has her way.
*The Autocrat of the Breakfast Table*, Prologue

2   A thought is often original, though you have uttered it a hundred times.
*The Autocrat of the Breakfast Table*, Ch. 1

3   The world's great men have not commonly been great scholars, nor great scholars great men.
*The Autocrat of the Breakfast Table*, Ch. 6

4   The axis of the earth sticks out visibly through the centre of each and every town or city.
*The Autocrat of the Breakfast Table*, Ch. 6

5 Wisdom has taught us to be calm and meek,
To take one blow, and turn the other cheek;
It is not written what a man shall do
If the rude caitiff smite the other too!

*Non-Resistance*

6 It is the province of knowledge to speak and it is
the privilege of wisdom to listen.

*The Poet at the Breakfast Table,* Ch. 10

7 A moment's insight is sometimes worth a life's
experience.

*The Professor at the Breakfast Table,* Ch. 10

8 It's giggle – gabble – gobble – 'n' git.

Referring to afternoon tea
Attrib.

**Holmes, Oliver Wendell, Jr.** (1841–1935) US jurist. As
a judge in the Supreme Court of Massachusetts and the US
Supreme Court, he was known for his support of the individual
rights of the private citizen. His best-known book is *The Common
Law* (1881).

1 War? War is an organized bore.

*Yankee from Olympus* (C. Bowen)

2 Many ideas grow better when transplanted into
another mind than in the one where they
sprang up.

3 Oh, to be seventy again!

Said in his eighty-seventh year, while watching a pretty girl
*The American Treasury* (C. Fadiman)

**Holst, Gustav** (1874–1934) British composer. His best-
known works are the choral *Hymn of Jesus* (1917) and the suite
*The Planets.*

1 Never compose anything unless the not composing of it becomes a positive nuisance to you.

Letter to W. G. Whittaker

**Hood, Thomas** (1799–1845) British poet. His collection *Odes
and Addresses* (1825) was followed by several volumes of
humorous verse and such political poems as *The Story of the Shirt*
(1843).

1 The sedate, sober, silent, serious, sad-coloured
sect.

Referring to the Quakers
*The Doves and the Crows*

2 Ben Battle was a soldier bold,
And used to war's alarms:
But a cannon-ball took off his legs,
So he laid down his arms!

*Faithless Nelly Gray*

3 For here I leave my second leg,
And the Forty-second Foot!

*Faithless Nelly Gray*

4 The love that loves a scarlet coat
Should be more uniform.

*Faithless Nelly Gray*

5 His death, which happen'd in his berth,
At forty-odd befell:
They went and told the sexton, and
The sexton toll'd the bell.

*Faithless Sally Brown*

6 I remember, I remember,
The house where I was born,
The little window where the sun
Came peeping in at morn;
He never came a wink too soon,
Nor brought too long a day,
But now, I often wish the night
Had borne my breath away!

*I Remember*

7 I remember, I remember,
The fir trees dark and high;
I used to think their slender tops
Were close against the sky:
It was a childish ignorance,
But now 'tis little joy
To know I'm farther off from heav'n
Than when I was a boy.

*I Remember*

8 But evil is wrought by want of thought,
As well as want of heart!

*The Lady's Dream*

9 For that old enemy the gout
Had taken him in toe!

*Lieutenant Luff*

10 No warmth, no cheerfulness, no healthful ease,
No comfortable feel in any member –
No shade, no shine, no butterflies, no bees,
No fruits, no flowers, no leaves, no birds, –
November!

*No!*

11 O! men with sisters dear,
O! men with mothers and wives!
It is not linen you're wearing out,
But human creatures' lives!

*The Song of the Shirt*

12 Oh! God! that bread should be so dear,
And flesh and blood so cheap!

*The Song of the Shirt*

13 Holland . . . lies so low they're only saved by being dammed.

*Up the Rhine*

14 What is a modern poet's fate?
To write his thoughts upon a slate;
The critic spits on what is done,
*Gives it a wipe* – and all is gone.

*Alfred Lord Tennyson, A Memoir* (Hallam Tennyson), Vol. II,
Ch. 3

15 There are three things which the public will always clamour for, sooner or later: namely,
Novelty, novelty, novelty.

Announcement of *Comic Annual*, 1836

**Hooker, Richard** (c. 1554–1600) English theologian. His *On the Laws of Ecclesiastical Polity* (1594) influenced Anglican thought for several generations.

1 Change is not made without inconvenience, even from worse to better.

*English Dictionary* (Johnson), Preface

**Hoover, Herbert Clark** (1874–1964) US statesman and Republican President (1929–33).

1 The American system of rugged individualism.

Speech, New York, 22 Oct 1928

2 Older men declare war. But it is youth that must fight and die.

Speech, Republican National Convention, Chicago, 27 June 1944

**Hope, Anthony** (Sir Anthony Hope Hawkins; 1863–1933) British novelist. After the success of *The Prisoner of Zenda* (1894), which was made into a film three times (1922, 1937, and 1952), he wrote many similar romances.

1 Unless one is a genius, it is best to aim at being intelligible.

*The Dolly Dialogues*

2 He is very fond of making things which he does not want, and then giving them to people who have no use for them.

*The Dolly Dialogues*

3 Economy is going without something you do want in case you should, some day, want something you probably won't want.

*The Dolly Dialogues*

4 'You oughtn't to yield to temptation.'
'Well, somebody must, or the thing becomes absurd.'

*The Dolly Dialogues*

5 Boys will be boys – '
'And even that . . . wouldn't matter if we could only prevent girls from being girls.'

*The Dolly Dialogues*

6 '*Bourgeois*,' I observed, 'is an epithet which the riff-raff apply to what is respectable, and the aristocracy to what is decent'.

*The Dolly Dialogues*

7 I wish you would read a little poetry sometimes. Your ignorance cramps my conversation.

*The Dolly Dialogues*

8 Good families are generally worse than any others.

*The Prisoner of Zenda*, Ch. 1

9 His foe was folly and his weapon wit.

Written for the inscription on the memorial to W. S. Gilbert, Victoria Embankment, London

**Hope, Laurence** (Mrs M. H. Nicolson; 1804–1905) British poet and songwriter. A member of the British Raj, she wrote *The Garden of Kama and other Love Lyrics from India* (1901) under a male pseudonym. It contained the immensely popular song 'Pale Hands I Loved'.

1 Less than the dust beneath thy chariot wheel,
Less than the weed that grows beside thy door,
Less than the rust that never stained thy sword,
Less than the need thou hast in life of me,
Even less am I.

*The Garden of Kama and other Love Lyrics from India*, 'Less than the Dust'

2 Pale hands I loved beside the Shalimar,
Where are you now? Who lies beneath your spell?

*The Garden of Kama and other Love Lyrics from India*, 'Pale Hands I Loved'

**Hopkins, Gerard Manley** (1844–99) British Jesuit and poet. An innovator in poetry, he is remembered for his *Wreck of the Deutschland* and other verse.

1 Not, I'll not, carrion comfort, Despair, not feast on thee;
Not untwist – slack they may be – these last strands of man
In me or, most weary, cry *I can no more*. I can;
Can something, hope, wish day come, not choose not to be.

*Carrion Comfort*

2 That night, that year
Of now done darkness I wretch lay wrestling with (my God!) my God.

*Carrion Comfort*

3 The world is charged with the grandeur of God.

*God's Grandeur*

4 Glory be to God for dappled things –
For skies of couple-colour as a brinded cow;
For rose-moles all in stipple upon trout that swim.

*Pied Beauty*

5 Look at the stars! look, look up at the skies!
O look at all the fire-folk sitting in the air!
The bright boroughs, the circle-citadels there!

*The Starlight Night*

**Hopper, Hedda** (1890–1966) US writer. Originally an actress, she later became well known as a Hollywood gossip columnist.

1 At one time I thought he wanted to be an actor. He had certain qualifications, including no money and a total lack of responsibility.

*From Under My Hat*

**Horace** (Quintus Horatius Flaccus; 65–8 BC) Roman poet. His *Odes* and *Epistles* portray Roman life in considerable detail.

1 'Painters and poets alike have always had licence to dare anything.' We know that, and we both claim and allow to others in their turn this indulgence.

*Ars Poetica*

2 I strive to be brief, and I become obscure.

*Ars Poetica*

3 You will have written exceptionally well if, by skilful arrangement of your words, you have made an ordinary one seem original.
*Ars Poetica*

4 Many terms which have now dropped out of favour, will be revived, and those that are at present respectable will drop out, if usage so choose, with whom resides the decision and the judgement and the code of speech.
*Ars Poetica*

5 Scholars dispute, and the case is still before the courts.
*Ars Poetica*

6 Mountains will heave in childbirth, and a silly little mouse will be born.
*Ars Poetica*

7 He always hurries to the main event and whisks his audience into the middle of things as though they knew already.
*Ars Poetica*

8 To the Greeks the Muse gave native wit, to the Greeks the gift of graceful eloquence.
*Ars Poetica*

9 I'm aggrieved when sometimes even excellent Homer nods.
*Ars Poetica*

10 Not gods, nor men, nor even booksellers have put up with poets' being second-rate.
*Ars Poetica*

11 Let it be kept till the ninth year, the manuscript put away at home: you may destroy whatever you haven't published; once out, what you've said can't be stopped.
*Ars Poetica*

12 To save a man's life against his will is the same as killing him.
*Ars Poetica*

13 *Nullius addictus iurare in verba magistri, Quo me cumque rapit tempestas, deferor hospes.*
Not bound to swear allegiance to any master, wherever the wind takes me I travel as a visitor.
*Nullius in verba* is the motto of the Royal Society
*Epistles, I*

14 The happy state of getting the victor's palm without the dust of racing.
*Epistles, I*

15 If possible honestly, if not, somehow, make money.
*Epistles, I*

16 Let me remind you what the wary fox said once upon a time to the sick lion: 'Because those footprints scare me, all directed your way, none coming back.'
*Epistles, I*

17 We are just statistics, born to consume resources.
*Epistles, I*

18 Believe each day that has dawned is your last. Some hour to which you have not been looking forward will prove lovely. As for me, if you want a good laugh, you will come and find me fat and sleek, in excellent condition, one of Epicurus' herd of pigs.
*Epistles, I*

19 To marvel at nothing is just about the one and only thing, Numicius, that can make a man happy and keep him that way.
*Epistles, I*

20 You may drive out nature with a pitchfork, yet she'll be constantly running back.
*Epistles, I*

21 They change their clime, not their frame of mind, who rush across the sea. We work hard at doing nothing: we look for happiness in boats and carriage rides. What you are looking for is here, is at Ulubrae, if only peace of mind doesn't desert you.
*Epistles, I*

22 For it is your business, when the wall next door catches fire.
*Epistles, I*

23 If you believe Cratinus from days of old, Maecenas, (as you must know) no verse can give pleasure for long, nor last, that is written by drinkers of water.
*Epistles, I*

24 And seek for truth in the groves of Academe.
*Epistles, II*

25 Hard to train to accept being poor.
*Odes, I*

26 And if you include me among the lyric poets, I'll hold my head so high it'll strike the stars.
*Odes, I*

27 Pale Death kicks his way equally into the cottages of the poor and the castles of kings.
*Odes, I*

28 Life's short span forbids us to enter on far-reaching hopes.
*Odes, I*

29 Drop the question what tomorrow may bring, and count as profit every day that Fate allows you.
*Odes, I*

30 Do not try to find out – we're forbidden to know –what end the gods have in store for me, or for you.
*Odes, I*

**31** While we're talking, time will have meanly run on: pick today's fruits, not relying on the future in the slightest.
*Odes*, I

**32** *Carpe diem*
Seize the day.
*Odes*, I

**33** When things are steep, remember to stay level-headed.
*Odes*, II

**34** *Dulce et decorum est pro patria mori.*
It is a sweet and seemly thing to die for one's country.
*Odes*, III

**35** Force, if unassisted by judgement, collapses through its own mass.
*Odes*, III

**36** Undeservedly you will atone for the sins of your fathers.
*Odes*, III

**37** What do the ravages of time not injure? Our parents' age (worse than our grandparents') has produced us, more worthless still, who will soon give rise to a yet more vicious generation.
*Odes*, III

**38** My life with girls has ended, though till lately I was up to it and soldiered on not ingloriously; now on this wall will hang my weapons and my lyre, discharged from the war.
*Odes*, III

**39** I have executed a memorial longer lasting than bronze.
*Odes*, III

**40** That I make poetry and give pleasure (if I give pleasure) are because of you.
*Odes*, IV

**41** Not to hope for things to last for ever, is what the year teaches and even the hour which snatches a nice day away.
*Odes*, IV

**42** Many brave men lived before Agamemnon's time; but they are all, unmourned and unknown, covered by the long night, because they lack their sacred poet.
*Odes*, IV

**43** Not the owner of many possessions will you be right to call happy: he more rightly deserves the name of happy who knows how to use the gods' gifts wisely and to put up with rough poverty, and who fears dishonour more than death.
*Odes*, IV

**44** Mix a little foolishness with your serious plans: it's lovely to be silly at the right moment.
*Odes*, IV

**45** How is it, Maecenas, that no one lives contented with his lot, whether he has planned it for himself or fate has flung him into it, but yet he praises those who follow different paths?
*Satires*, I

**46** An accomplished man to his finger-tips.
*Satires*, I

**47** Strong enough to answer back to desires, to despise distinctions, and a whole man in himself, polished and well-rounded.
*Satires*, II

**Horne, Richard Henry** (*or* **Hengist**) (1803–84) English writer. A magistrate in Australia, his verse includes *Orion* (1843) and *Ballad Romances* (1846).

**1** 'Tis always morning somewhere in the world.
*Orion*, Bk III, Ch. 2

**Horsley, Bishop Samuel** (1733–1806) British bishop, who edited Newton's works.

**1** In *this* country, my Lords, . . . the individual subject . . . 'has nothing to do with the laws but to obey them.'
House of Lords, 13 Nov 1795

**Household, Geoffrey (Edward West)** (1900– ) British writer and novelist. His novels include *Rogue Male* (1939), *A Time to Kill* (1952), and *Red Anger* (1975).

**1** I have noticed that what cats most appreciate in a human being is not the ability to produce food which they take for granted – but his or her entertainment value.
*Rogue Male*

**2** It's easy to make a man confess the lies he tells to himself; it's far harder to make him confess the truth.
*Rogue Male*

**Housman, A(lfred) E(dward)** (1859–1936) British scholar and poet. His own verse collections include *A Shropshire Lad* (1896) and *Last Poems* (1922).

**1** We'll to the woods no more,
The laurels all are cut.
*Last Poems*, Introductory

**2** The candles burn their sockets,
The blinds let through the day,
The young man feels his pockets
And wonders what's to pay.
*Last Poems*, 'Eight O'Clock'

**3** They say my verse is sad: no wonder;
Its narrow measure spans
Tears of eternity, and sorrow,
Not mine, but man's.
*Last Poems*, 'Fancy's Knell'

**4** Even when poetry has a meaning, as it usually has, it may be inadvisable to draw it out . . . Perfect understanding will sometimes almost extinguish pleasure.
*The Name and Nature of Poetry*

5 Loveliest of trees, the cherry now
Is hung with bloom along the bough,
And stands about the woodland ride
Wearing white for Eastertide.
*A Shropshire Lad*, '1887'

6 They hang us now in Shrewsbury jail:
The whistles blow forlorn,
And trains all night groan on the rail
To men that die at morn.
*A Shropshire Lad*, 'Reveillé'

7 Look not in my eyes, for fear
They mirror true the sight I see,
And there you find your face too clear
And love it and be lost like me.
*A Shropshire Lad*, 'March'

8 Here of a Sunday morning,
My love and I would lie,
And see the coloured counties,
And hear the larks so high
About us in the sky.
*A Shropshire Lad*, 'Bredon Hill'

9 Is my team ploughing,
That I was used to drive?
*A Shropshire Lad*, 'Bredon Hill'

10 The goal stands up, the keeper
Stands up to keep the goal.
*A Shropshire Lad*, 'Bredon Hill'

11 On Wenlock Edge the wood's in trouble;
His forest fleece the Wrekin heaves;
The gale, it plies the saplings double,
And thick on Severn snow the leaves.
*A Shropshire Lad*, 'The Welsh Marches'

12 East and west on fields forgotten
Bleach the bones of comrades slain,
Lovely lads and dead and rotten;
None that go return again.
*A Shropshire Lad*, 'The Welsh Marches'

13 Into my heart an air that kills
From yon far country blows:
What are those blue remembered hills,
What spires, what farms are those?
*A Shropshire Lad*, 'The Welsh Marches'

14 With rue my heart is laden
For golden friends I had,
For many a rose-lipt maiden
And many a lightfoot lad.
*A Shropshire Lad*, 'The Welsh Marches'

15 Malt does more than Milton can
To justify God's ways to man.
*A Shropshire Lad*, 'The Welsh Marches'

**Howe, Julia Ward** (1819–1910) US feminist and peace worker. She composed and published the *Battle Hymn of the Republic* (1862) and several books, including *Modern Society* (1881) and *At Sunset* (1910).

1 Mine eyes have seen the glory of the coming of the Lord:
He is trampling out the vintage where the grapes of wrath are stored.
*Battle Hymn of the American Republic*

**Howitt, Mary** (1799–1888) British writer. Her books, written with her husband William Howitt (1792–1879), include *The Literature and Romances of Northern Europe* (1852). She also wrote some verse.

1 'Will you walk into my parlour?' said a spider to a fly:
'Tis the prettiest little parlour that ever you did spy.'
*The Spider and the Fly*

**Hoyle, Edmond** (1672–1769) English writer on card games.

1 When in doubt, win the trick.
*Hoyle's Games*, 'Whist, Twenty-four Short Rules for Learners'

**Hubbard, Elbert** (1856–1915) US writer and editor.

1 One machine can do the work of fifty ordinary men. No machine can do the work of one extraordinary man.
*Roycroft Dictionary and Book of Epigrams*

2 Little minds are interested in the extraordinary; great minds in the commonplace.
*Roycroft Dictionary and Book of Epigrams*

3 Life is just one damned thing after another.
*A Thousand and One Epigrams*

**Hughes, Thomas** (1822–96) British novelist. A Liberal MP, he is remembered for his novel *Tom Brown's Schooldays* (1857) based on Rugby School.

1 Life isn't all beer and skittles.
*Tom Brown's Schooldays*, Pt. I, Ch. 2

2 It's more than a game. It's an institution.
Referring to cricket
*Tom Brown's Schooldays*, Pt. II, Ch. 7

**Hughes, William Morris** (1864–1952) Australian statesman. He was prime minister first as leader of the Labour party (1915–16) and then as leader of the Nationalist Party (1916–23).

1 I'm waiting for the cock to crow.
Said in parliament, after being viciously criticed by a member of his own party
*The Fine Art of Political Wit* (L. Harris)

**Hugo, Victor** (1802–85) French poet, novelist, and dramatist. His novels include *Notre Dame de Paris* (1831), *Le Roi s'amuse* (1832), and *Les Misérables* (1862). Verse collections include *Les Contemplations* (1856); at the age of 80 he wrote the play *Torquemada* (1882). He was regarded as a national hero and the foremost writer of 19th-century France.

1 If suffer we must, let's suffer on the heights.
*Contemplations*, 'Les Malheureux'

2 A stand can be made against invasion by an army; no stand can be made against invasion by an idea.
*Histoire d'un Crime*, 'La Chute'

**3** Symmetry is tedious, and tedium is the very basis of mourning. Despair yawns.
*Les Misérables*, Vol. II, Bk. IV, Ch. 1

**4** Popularity? It's glory's small change.
*Ruy Blas*, III

**5** ?

The entire contents of a telegram sent to his publishers asking how *Les Misérables* was selling; the reply was '!'
*The Literary Life* (R. Hendrickson)

**Hume, David** (1711–76) Scottish philosopher. His major works were *A Treatise of Human Nature* (1739) and *An Enquiry Concerning Human Understanding* (1748). He also wrote a *History of England* (1754–62).

**1** Custom, then, is the great guide of human life.
*An Enquiry Concerning Human Understanding*

**2** If we take in our hand any volume; of divinity or school metaphysics, for instance; let us ask, *Does it contain any abstract reasoning concerning quantity or number?* No. *Does it contain any experimental reasoning, concerning matter of fact and existence?* No. Commit it then to the flames: for it can contain nothing but sophistry and illusion.
*An Enquiry Concerning Human Understanding*

**3** The Christian religion not only was at first attended with miracles, but even at this day cannot be believed by any reasonable person without one. Mere reason is insufficient to convince us of its veracity: and whoever is moved by faith to assent to it, is conscious of a continued miracle in his own person, which subverts all the principles of his understanding, and gives him a determination to believe what is most contrary to custom and experience.
*Essays*, 'Of Miracles'

**4** Beauty in things exists in the mind which contemplates them.
*Essays*, 'Of Tragedy'

**5** We never remark any passion or principle in others, of which, in some degree or other, we may not find a parallel in ourselves.
*A Treatise of Human Nature*

**6** Everyone has observed how much more dogs are animated when they hunt in a pack, than when they pursue their game apart. We might, perhaps; be at a loss to explain this phenomenon, if we had not experience of a similar in ourselves.
*A Treatise of Human Nature*

**7** Grief and disappointment give rise to anger, anger to envy, envy to malice, and malice to grief again, till the whole circle be completed.
*A Treatise of Human Nature*

**8** Philosophers never balance between profit and honesty, because their decisions are general, and neither their passions nor imaginations are interested in the objects.
*A Treatise of Human Nature*

**Hungerford, Margaret Wolfe** (c. 1855–97) Irish novelist. Her best-known book is *Molly Bawn* (1878).

**1** Beauty is altogether in the eye of the beholder.
*Molly Bawn*

**Hunt, George William** (c. 1829–1904) British writer and composer of music-hall songs.

**1** We don't want to fight, but, by jingo if we do,
We've got the ships, we've got the men, we've got the money too.
We've fought the Bear before, and while Britons shall be true,
The Russians shall not have Constantinople.
*We Don't Want to Fight*

**Hunt, (James Henry) Leigh** (1784–1859) British poet and journalist. A friend and supporter of Keats and other romantic poets, he was imprisoned (1813) for attacks on the Prince Regent. His books include *Imagination and Fancy* (1844) and *Autobiography* (1850).

**1** Abou Ben Adhem (may his tribe increase!)
Awoke one night from a deep dream of peace,
And saw, within the moonlight in his room,
Making it rich, and like a lily in bloom,
An angel writing in a book of gold: – . . .
*Abou Ben Adhem and the Angel*

**2** 'I pray thee then,
Write me as one that loves his fellow-men.'
*Abou Ben Adhem and the Angel*

**3** And lo! Ben Adhem's name led all the rest.
*Abou Ben Adhem and the Angel*

**4** Jenny kissed me when we met,
Jumping from the chair she sat in;
Time, you thief, who love to get
Sweets into your list, put that in:
Say I'm weary, say I'm sad,
Say that health and wealth have missed me,
Say I'm growing old, but add,
Jenny kissed me.
Writing about Jane Carlyle
*Rondeau*

**5** Stolen sweets are always sweeter,
Stolen kisses much completer,
Stolen looks are nice in chapels,
Stolen, stolen, be your apples.
*Song of Fairies Robbing an Orchard*

**Hupfeld, Herman** (20th century) US songwriter.

**1** You must remember this;
A kiss is just a kiss,
A sigh is just a sigh –
The fundamental things apply
As time goes by.
From the film *Casablanca*
*As Time Goes By*

**Hurst, Sir Gerald** (1877–1957) British writer and judge. His books include *Closed Chapters* (1942) and *Lincoln's Inn Essays* (1949).

1 One of the mysteries of human conduct is why adult men and women all over England are ready to sign documents which they do not read, at the behest of canvassers whom they do not know, binding them to pay for articles which they do not want, with money which they have not got.
*Closed Chapters*

**Huss, John** (Jan Hus; c. 1369–1415) Bohemian religious reformer and priest. He was excommunicated (1410) for his support of Wycliffe, tried for heresy, and burnt at the stake, which led to the Hussite War (1419–34).

1 O holy simplicity!
On noticing a peasant adding a faggot to the pile at his execution.
*Apophthegmata* (Zincgreff-Weidner), Pt. III

**Hutcheson, Francis** (1694–1746) Scottish philosopher. His various philosophical treatises include the posthumous *System of Moral Philosophy* (1755).

1 That action is best, which procures the greatest happiness for the greatest numbers.
*Inquiry into the Original of our Ideas of Beauty and Virtue*, Treatise II, 'Concerning Moral Good and Evil'

**Huxley, Aldous** (1894–1964) British novelist and essayist. His novels include *Antic Hay* (1923), *Point Counter Point* (1928), *Brave New World* (1932), and *Eyeless in Gaza* (1936). His nonfiction includes *The Doors of Perception* (1954).

1 Thanks to words, we have been able to rise above the brutes; and thanks to words, we have often sunk to the level of the demons.
*Adonis and the Alphabet*

2 Since Mozart's day composers have learned the art of making music throatily and palpitatingly sexual.
*Along the Road*, 'Popular music'

3 Christlike in my behaviour,
Like every good believer,
I imitate the Saviour,
And cultivate a beaver.
*Antic Hay*, Ch. 4

4 He was only the Mild and Melancholy one foolishly disguised as a complete Man.
*Antic Hay*, Ch. 9

5 There are few who would not rather be taken in adultery than in provincialism.
*Antic Hay*, Ch. 10

6 Mr Mercaptan went on to preach a brilliant sermon on that melancholy sexual perversion known as continence.
*Antic Hay*, Ch. 18

7 Lady Capricorn, he understood, was still keeping open bed.
*Antic Hay*, Ch. 21

8 Official dignity tends to increase in inverse ratio to the importance of the country in which the office is held.
*Beyond the Mexique Bay*

9 The time of our Ford.
*Brave New World*, Ch. 3

10 The proper study of mankind is books.
*Chrome Yellow*

11 We participate in a tragedy; at a comedy we only look.
*The Devils of Loudon*, Ch. 11

12 Consistency is contrary to nature, contrary to life. The only completely consistent people are the dead.
*Do What you Will*

13 Thought must be divided against itself before it can come to any knowledge of itself.
*Do What You Will*

14 People will insist . . . on treating the *mons Veneris* as though it were Mount Everest.
*Eyeless in Gaza*, Ch. 30

15 Death . . . It's the only thing we haven't succeeded in completely vulgarizing.
*Eyeless in Gaza*, Ch. 31

16 A million million spermatozoa,
All of them alive:
Out of their cataclysm but one poor Noah
Dare hope to survive.
*Fifth Philosopher's Song*

17 Christianity accepted as given a metaphysical system derived from several already existing and mutually incompatible systems.
*Grey Eminence*, Ch. 3

18 The quality of moral behaviour varies in inverse ratio to the number of human beings involved.
*Grey Eminence*, Ch. 10

19 'Bed,' as the Italian proverb succinctly puts it, 'is the poor man's opera.'
*Heaven and Hell*

20 I can sympathize with people's pains, but not with their pleasures. There is something curiously boring about somebody else's happiness.
*Limbo*, 'Cynthia'

21 She was a machine-gun riddling her hostess with sympathy.
*Mortal Coils*, 'The Gioconda Smile'

22 Most of one's life . . . is one prolonged effort to prevent oneself thinking.
*Mortal Coils*, 'Green Tunnels'

23 She was one of those indispensables of whom one makes the discovery, when they are gone, that one can get on quite as well without them.
*Mortal Coils*, 'Nuns at Luncheon'

24 Happiness is like coke - something you get as a by-product in the process of making something else.
*Point Counter Point*

25 There is no substitute for talent. Industry and all the virtues are of no avail.
*Point Counter Point*

26 Silence is as full of potential wisdom and wit as the unhewn marble of great sculpture.
*Point Counter Point*

27 A bad book is as much a labour to write as a good one; it comes as sincerely from the author's soul.
*Point Counter Point*

28 That all men are equal is a proposition to which, at ordinary times, no sane individual has ever given his assent.
*Proper Studies*

29 Those who believe that they are exclusively in the right are generally those who achieve something.
*Proper Studies*

30 Facts do not cease to exist because they are ignored.
*Proper Studies*

31 Most human beings have an almost infinite capacity for taking things for granted.
*Themes and Variations*

32 I'm afraid of losing my obscurity. Genuineness only thrives in the dark. Like celery.
*Those Barren Leaves*, Pt. I, Ch. 1

33 'It's like the question of the authorship of the *Iliad*,' said Mr Cardan. 'The author of that poem is either Homer or, if not Homer, somebody else of the same name.'
*Those Barren Leaves*, Pt. V, Ch. 4

34 How appallingly thorough these Germans always managed to be, how emphatic! In sex no less than in war – in scholarship, in science. Diving deeper than anyone else and coming up muddier.

35 Knowledge is proportionate to being. . . . You know in virtue of what you are.
*Time Must Have a Stop*, Ch. 26

36 The aristocratic pleasure of displeasing is not the only delight that bad taste can yield. One can love a certain kind of vulgarity for its own sake.
*Vulgarity in Literature*, Ch. 4

37 Defined in psychological terms, a fanatic is a man who consciously over-compensates a secret doubt.
*Vulgarity in Literature*, Ch. 4

**Huxley, Sir Julian** (1887–1975) British biologist. The first director general of UNESCO (1946–48), his books include *Essays of a Biologist* (1923) and *Evolution Restated* (1940).

1 We all know how the size of sums of money appears to vary in a remarkable way according as they are being paid in or paid out.
*Essays of a Biologist*, 5

2 Operationally, God is beginning to resemble not a ruler but the last fading smile of a cosmic Cheshire cat.
*Religion without Revelation*

**Huxley, T(homas) H(enry)** (1825–95) British biologist. A supporter of Darwin's theory of evolution, his books include *Science and Culture* (1881) and *Evolution and Ethics* (1893).

1 The great tragedy of Science – the slaying of a beautiful hypothesis by an ugly fact.
*Collected Essays*, 'Biogenesis and Abiogenesis'

2 Science is nothing but trained and organized common sense, differing from the latter only as a veteran may differ from a raw recruit: and its methods differ from those of common sense only as far as the guardsman's cut and thrust differ from the manner in which a savage wields his club.
*Collected Essays*, 'The Method of Zadig'

3 It is the customary fate of new truths to begin as heresies and to end as superstitions.
*The Coming of Age of the Origin of Species*

4 One of the unpardonable sins, in the eyes of most people, is for a man to go about unlabelled. The world regards such a person as the police do an unmuzzled dog, not under proper control.
*Evolution and Ethics*

5 I doubt if the philosopher lives, or ever has lived, who could know himself to be heartily despised by a street boy without some irritation.
*Evolution and Ethics*

6 The chess-board is the world; the pieces are the phenomena of the universe; the rules of the game are what we call the laws of Nature. The player on the other side is hidden from us. We know that his play is always fair, just, and patient. But also we know, to our cost, that he never overlooks a mistake, or makes the smallest allowance for ignorance.
*Lay Sermons*, 'A Liberal Education'

7 Some experience of popular lecturing had convinced me that the necessity of making things plain to uninstructed people was one of the very best means of clearing up the obscure corners in one's own mind.
*Man's Place in Nature*, Preface

8 If a little knowledge is dangerous, where is the man who has so much as to be out of danger?
*On Elementary Instruction in Physiology*

9 Logical consequences are the scarecrows of fools and the beacons of wise men.
*Science and Culture*, 'On the Hypothesis that Animals are Automata'

10 I am too much of a sceptic to deny the possibility of anything.
*Letter to Herbert Spencer, 22 Mar 1886*

**11** I asserted – and I repeat – that a man has no reason to be ashamed of having an ape for his grandfather. If there were an ancestor whom I should feel shame in recalling it would rather be a *man* – a man of restless and versatile intellect – who, not content with an equivocal success in his own sphere of activity, plunges into scientific questions with which he has no real acquaintance, only to obscure them by an aimless rhetoric, and distract the attention of his hearers from the real point at issue by eloquent digressions and skilled appeals to religious prejudice.

Replying to Bishop WILBERFORCE in the debate on Darwin's theory of evolution at the meeting of the British Association at Oxford. No transcript was taken at the time; the version above is commonly quoted. After hearing Wilberforce's speech, and before rising himself, Huxley is said to have remarked, 'The Lord has delivered him into my hands!'
Speech, 30 June 1860

---

# I

**Ibarruri, Dolores** (1895– ) Spanish politician. A leading communist, known as 'La Pasionaria', she lived in the Soviet Union (1939–77), returning to Spain after the Communist party became legal.

**1** They shall not pass!
*The Spanish Civil War* (H. Thomas), Ch. 16

**2** It is better to die on your feet than to live on your knees.
Speech, Paris, 1936

**3** It is better to be the widow of a hero than the wife of a coward.
Speech, Valencia, 1936

**Ibsen, Henrik** (1828–1906) Norwegian dramatist and poet. His initial successes came with *Brand* (1865) and *Peer Gynt* (1867). Subsequent works, such as *A Doll's House* (1879), *Ghosts* (1881), *An Enemy of the People* (1882), and *Hedda Gabler* (1890) established him a Europe's leading 19th-century playwright.

**1** Fools are in a terrible, overwhelming majority, all the wide world over.
*An Enemy of the People,* IV

**2** The majority has the might – more's the pity – but it hasn't right . . . The minority is always right.
*An Enemy of the People,* IV

**3** The worst enemy of truth and freedom in our society is the compact majority. Yes, the damned, compact, liberal majority.
*An Enemy of the People,* IV

**4** A man should never put on his best trousers when he goes out to battle for freedom and truth.
*An Enemy of the People,* V

**5** Ten o'clock . . . and back he'll come. I can just see him.
With vine leaves in his hair. Flushed and confident.
*Hedda Gabler,* II

**6** Youth will come here and beat on my door, and force its way in.
*The Master Builder,* I

**7** Castles in the air – they're so easy to take refuge in. So easy to build, too.
*The Master Builder,* III

**8** What's a man's first duty? The answer's brief: To be himself.
*Peer Gynt,* IV:1

**9** Take the life-lie away from the average man and straight away you take away his happiness.
*The Wild Duck,* V

**10** On the contrary!
Ibsen's last words; his nurse had just remarked that he was feeling a little better
*True Remarkable Occurrences* (J. Train)

**Ickes, Harold L(e Clair)** (1874–1952) US Republican politician. He became Secretary of the Interior (1933–46).

**1** I am against government by crony.
Comment on his resignation as Secretary of the Interior (1946) after a dispute with President Truman

**2** The trouble with Senator Long is that he is suffering from halitosis of the intellect. That's presuming Emperor Long has an intellect.
*The Politics of Upheaval* (A. M. Schlesinger Jnr), Pt. II, Ch. 14

**Illich, Ivan** (1926– ) Austrian sociologist. A former Catholic priest, he is critical of the consumer society. His books include *Deschooling Society* (1971) and *Tools for Conviviality* (1973).

**1** Any attempt to reform the university without attending to the system of which it is an integral part is like trying to do urban renewal in New York City from the twelfth storey up.
*Deschooling Society,* Ch. 3

**2** Man must choose whether to be rich in things or in the freedom to use them.
*Deschooling Society,* Ch. 4

**3** We must rediscover the distinction between hope and expectation.
*Deschooling Society,* Ch. 7

**4** In a consumer society there are inevitably two kinds of slaves: the prisoners of addiction and the prisoners of envy.
*Tools for Conviviality*

**Inge, William Ralph** (1860–1954) British churchman, who became Dean of St Pauls (1911–34) and wrote a number of books, including *Christian Mysticism* (1899).

1 What we know of the past is mostly not worth knowing. What is worth knowing is mostly uncertain. Events in the past may roughly be divided into those which probably never happened and those which do not matter.
*Assessments and Anticipations*, 'Prognostications'

2 The enemies of Freedom do not argue; they shout and they shoot.
*The End of an Age*, Ch. 4

3 The effect of boredom on a large scale in history is underestimated. It is a main cause of revolutions, and would soon bring to an end all the static Utopias and the farmyard civilization of the Fabians.
*The End of an Age*, Ch. 6

4 Many people believe that they are attracted by God, or by Nature, when they are only repelled by man.
*More Lay Thoughts of a Dean*

5 To become a popular religion, it is only necessary for a superstition to enslave a philosophy.
*Outspoken Essays*

6 It takes in reality only one to make a quarrel. It is useless for the sheep to pass resolutions in favour of vegetarianism while the wolf remains of a different opinion.
*Outspoken Essays*

7 Democracy is only an experiment in government, and it has the obvious disadvantage of merely counting votes instead of weighing them.
*Possible Recovery?*

8 Literature flourishes best when it is half a trade and half an art.
*The Victorian Age*

9 The proper time to influence the character of a child is about a hundred years before he is born.
*The Observer*, 21 June, 1929

10 A nation is a society united by a delusion about its ancestry and by a common hatred of its neighbours.
*The Perpetual Pessimist* (Sagittarius and George)

11 A man may build himself a throne of bayonets, but he cannot sit on it.
*Wit and Wisdom of Dean Inge* (ed. Marchant)

12 The nations which have put mankind and posterity most in their debt have been small states – Israel, Athens, Florence, Elizabethan England.
*Wit and Wisdom of Dean Inge* (ed. Marchant)

**Ingersoll, Robert G(reen)** (1833–99) US lawyer and agnostic. His books include *The Gods* (1876) and *Why I am an Agnostic* (1896).

1 An honest God is the noblest work of man.
*The Gods*

2 In nature there are neither rewards nor punishments – there are consequences.
*Lectures & Essays*, 'Some Reasons Why'

**Ingrams, Richard** (1937– ) British editor and writer. Former editor of *Private Eye*, he has written a number of books, including *God's Apology* (1977), and *Mrs Wilson's Diary* (with John Wells; 1965).

1 I have come to regard the law courts not as a cathedral but rather as a casino.
*The Guardian*, 30 July 1977

2 My own motto is publish and be sued.
Referring to his editorship of *Private Eye*
BBC radio broadcast, 4 May 1977

**Ionesco, Eugène** (1912– ) French dramatist. His 'theatre-of-the-absurd' plays include *The Bald Prima Donna* (1950), *Chairs* (1951), and *Rhinoceros* (1961).

1 Many people have delusions of grandeur but you're deluded by triviality.
*Exit the King*

**Iphicrates** (d. 353 BC) Athenian general who fought against Sparta during the Corinthian war (394–387 BC).

1 The difference between us is that my family begins with me, whereas yours ends with you.
Reply to a descendant of Harmodius (an Athenian hero), who had derided Iphicrates for being the son of a cobbler
Attrib.

**Irving, Washington** (1783–1859) US writer. His collection of short stories, *The Sketch Book* (1819), established his reputation, which was reinforced by his five-volume biography of George Washington.

1 Whenever a man's friends begin to compliment him about looking young, he may be sure that they think he is growing old.
*Bracebridge Hall*, 'Bachelors'

2 A tart temper never mellows with age, and a sharp tongue is the only edged tool that grows keener with constant use.
*The Sketch Book*, 'Rip Van Winkle'

3 There is a certain relief in change, even though it be from bad to worse; as I have found in travelling in a stage-coach, that it is often a comfort to shift one's position and be bruised in a new place.
*Tales of a Traveller*, 'To the Reader'

4 The almighty dollar, that great object of universal devotion throughout our land, seems to have no genuine devotees in these peculiar villages.
*Wolfert's Roost*, 'The Creole Village'

**Isherwood, Christopher** (1904–86) British novelist. He described pre-war Berlin in *Mr Norris Changes Trains* (1935) and *Goodbye to Berlin* (1939). Other books include *A Single Man* (1964) and the autobiographical *Christopher and His Kind* (1977).

1 I am a camera with its shutter open, quite passive, recording, not thinking.
*Goodbye to Berlin*

2 We live in stirring times – tea-stirring times.
*Mr Norris Changes Trains*

# J

**Jackson, Andrew** (1767–1845) US statesman and soldier. A hero of the War of 1812, he served as US president from 1829 to 1837.

1 Elevate them guns a little lower.
Order given whilst watching the effect of the US artillery upon the British lines at the battle of New Orleans
Attrib.

**Jackson, F. J. Foakes** (1855–1941) British academic.

1 It's no use trying to be *clever* – we are all clever here; just try to be *kind* – a little kind.
Advice given to a new don at Jesus College, Cambridge
Noted in A. C. Benson's Commonplace Book

**Jacobi, Karl Gustav Jacob** (1804–51) German mathematician who made important discoveries in function theory, the theory of determinants, and mechanics.

1 Pardon me, madam, but *I* am my brother.
On being mistaken by a lady for his brother
*Men of Mathematics* (M. H. Jacobi)

**Jacobs, Joe** (1896–1940) US boxing manager.

1 We was robbed!
Complaining to the audience when the heavyweight title of Max Schmeling, whom he managed, was passed to Jack Sharkey
Attrib.

**James, Alice** (1848–92) US diarist; the sister of William and Henry James.

1 It is so comic to hear oneself called old, even at ninety I suppose!
Letter to William James, 14 June 1889
*The Diary of Alice James* (ed. Leon Edel)

2 Notwithstanding the poverty of my outside experience, I have always had a significance for myself, and every chance to stumble along my straight and narrow little path, and to worship at the feet of my Deity, and what more can a human soul ask for?
*The Diary of Alice James* (ed. Leon Edel)

3 I suppose one has a greater sense of intellectual degradation after an interview with a doctor than from any human experience.
*The Diary of Alice James* (ed. Leon Edel), 27 Sept 1890

**James, Henry** (1843–1916) US novelist, who spent much of his life in Europe (from 1876 in England). *Roderick Hudson* (1875), his first successful novel, was followed by *Washington Square* (1881), *The Bostonians* (1886), *The Turn of the Screw* (1898), *The Ambassadors* (1903), and several others.

1 Live all you can; it's a mistake not to. It doesn't so much matter what you do in particular, so long as you have your life. If you haven't had that what *have* you had?
*The Ambassadors*, Bk. V, Ch. 2

2 Experience was to be taken as showing that one might get a five-pound note as one got a light for a cigarette; but one had to check the friendly impulse to ask for it in the same way.
*The Awkward Age*

3 It takes a great deal of history to produce a little literature.
*Life of Nathaniel Hawthorne*, Ch. 1

4 He was unperfect, unfinished, inartistic; he was worse than provincial – he was parochial.
Referring to Thoreau
*Life of Nathaniel Hawthorne*, Ch. 4

5 To kill a human being is, after all, the least injury you can do him.
*My Friend Bingham*

6 The only obligation to which in advance we may hold a novel, without incurring the accusation of being arbitrary, is that it be interesting.
*Partial Portraits*, 'The Art of Fiction'

7 Experience is never limited, and it is never complete; it is an immense sensibility, a kind of huge spider-web of the finest silken threads suspended in the chamber of consciousness, and catching every air-borne particle in its tissue.
*Partial Portraits*, 'The Art of Fiction'

8 What is character but the determination of incident? What is incident but the illustration of character?
*Partial Portraits*, 'The Art of Fiction'

9 The superiority of one man's opinion over another's is never so great as when the opinion is about a woman.
*The Tragic Muse*, Ch. 9

10 Nurse, take away the candle and spare my blushes.
On being informed, whilst confined to his bed, that he had been awarded the Order of Merit
*The American Treasury* (C. Fadiman)

11 Summer afternoon – summer afternoon; to me those have always been the two most beautiful words in the English language.
*A Backward Glance* (Edith Wharton), Ch. 10

12 So it has come at last, the distinguished thing.
Referring to his own death
*A Backward Glance* (Edith Wharton), Ch. 14

**James, William** (1842–1910) US psychologist and philosopher. His most acclaimed works were *Varieties of Religious Experience* (1902) and *The Meaning of Truth* (1909).

1 Our civilization is founded on the shambles, and every individual existence goes out in a lonely spasm of helpless agony.
*Varieties of Religious Experience*

2 If merely 'feeling good' could decide, drunkenness would be the supremely valid human experience.
*Varieties of Religious Experience*

3 We are thinking beings, and we cannot exclude the intellect from participating in any of our functions.
*Varieties of Religious Experience*

4 The moral flabbiness born of the bitch-goddess Success.
Letter to H. G. Wells, 11 Sept 1906

**James I** (1566–1625) The first Stuart King of England and Ireland and, as James VI, King of Scotland. One of the achievements of his reign was the publication of the King James (Authorized) version of the Bible.

1 A custom loathsome to the eye, hateful to the nose, harmful to the brain, dangerous to the lungs, and in the black, stinking fume thereof, nearest resembling the horrible Stygian smoke of the pit that is bottomless.
Referring to smoking
*A Counterblast to Tobacco*

2 A branch of the sin of drunkenness, which is the root of all sins.
*A Counterblast to Tobacco*

3 I will govern according to the common weal, but not according to the common will.
*History of the English People* (J. R. Green)

4 These are rare attainments for a damsel, but pray tell me, can she spin?
On being introduced to a young girl proficient in Latin, Greek, and Hebrew
Attrib.

5 Dr Donne's verses are like the peace of God; they pass all understanding.
Attrib.

**Jarrell, Randall** (1914–65) US author and poet.

1 President Robbins was so well adjusted to his environment that sometimes you could not tell which was the environment and which was President Robbins.
*Pictures from an Institution*, Pt. I, Ch. 4

2 To Americans English manners are far more frightening than none at all.
*Pictures from an Institution*, Pt. I, Ch. 5

**Jarry, Alfred** (1873–1907) French surrealist dramatist. His *Ubu Roi* is a satire on bourgeois conventions.

1 Madame, I would have given you another!
On being reprimanded by a woman for firing his pistol in the vicinity of her child, who might have been killed
*Recollections of a Picture Dealer* (A. Vollard)

**Jay, Peter** (1937– ) British economist and broadcaster. He is the son-in-law of the former Labour prime minister, James Callaghan.

1 As the Prime Minister put it to me . . . he saw his role as being that of Moses.
Referring to a conversation with James Callaghan
*Guardian Weekly*, 18 Sept 1977

**Jeans, Sir James Hopwood** (1877–1946) British scientist. He worked on the kinetic theory of gases but is best remembered for his books popularizing science, including *The Universe Around Us* (1930), *Through Space and Time* (1934), and *Science and Music* (1937).

1 Life exists in the universe only because the carbon atom possesses certain exceptional properties.
*The Mysterious Universe*, Ch. 1

2 Science should leave off making pronouncements: the river of knowledge has too often turned back on itself.
*The Mysterious Universe*, Ch. 5

**Jefferson, Thomas** (1743–1826) US statesman; the third President (1801–09). He was the chief author of the Declaration of Independence.

1 When in the course of human events, it becomes necessary for one people to dissolve the political bonds which have connected them with another, and to assume among the powers of the earth the separate and equal station to which the laws of nature and of Nature's God entitle them, a decent respect to the opinions of mankind requires that they should declare the causes which impel them to the separation.
Declaration of Independence, Preamble

2 We hold these truths to be sacred and undeniable; that all men are created equal and independent, that from that equal creation they derive rights inherent and inalienable, among which are the preservation of life, and liberty, and the pursuit of happiness.
Declaration of Independence (original draft)

3 We hold these truths to be self-evident: that all men are created equal; that they are endowed by their Creator with certain unalienable rights; that among these are life, liberty, and the pursuit of happiness.
Declaration of Independence, 4 July 1776

4 A little rebellion now and then is a good thing.
Letter to James Madison, 30 Jan 1787

5 The tree of liberty must be refreshed from time to time with the blood of patriots and tyrants. It is its natural manure.
Letter to W. S. Smith, 13 Nov 1787

**Jellicoe, John Rushworth, Earl** (1859–1935) British admiral. He was commander of the grand fleet in World War I.

1 I had always to remember that I could have lost the war in an afternoon.
   Referring to the battle of Jutland

**Jenkins, Roy (Harris)** (1920– ) British statesman and historian. He was chancellor of the exchequer (1967–70), home secretary (1974–76), and president of the EEC commission (1977–81). Originally a member of the Labour Party he was one of the founders of the Social Democratic Party (1981).

1 There are always great dangers in letting the best be the enemy of the good.
   Speech, House of Commons, 1975

**Jennings, Elizabeth** (1926– ) British poet and writer. Her collections include *Poems* (1953), *Song for a Birth or a Death* (1961), and *Moments of Grace* (1980).

1 Now deep in my bed I turn
   And the world turns on the other side.
   *In the Night*

**Jennings, Paul** (1918– ) British humorous writer.

1 Of all musicians, flautists are most obviously the ones who know something we don't know.
   *The Jenguin Pennings*, 'Flautists Flaunt Afflatus'

2 Wembley, adj. Suffering from a vague *malaise*. 'I feel a bit w. this morning.'
   *The Jenguin Pennings*, 'Ware, Wye, Watford'

**Jerome, Jerome K(lapka)** (1859–1927) British dramatist and humorist. His books include *The Idle Thoughts of an Idle Fellow* (1889), *Three Men in a Boat* (1889), and *The Passing of the Third Floor Back* (1908).

1 Love is like the measles; we all have to go through with it.
   *Idle Thoughts of an Idle Fellow*

2 Conceit is the finest armour a man can wear.
   *Idle Thoughts of an Idle Fellow*

3 It is easy enough to say that poverty is no crime. No; if it were men wouldn't be ashamed of it. It is a blunder, though, and is punished as such. A poor man is despised the whole world over.
   *Idle Thoughts of an Idle Fellow*

4 If you are foolish enough to be contented, don't show it, but grumble with the rest.
   *Idle Thoughts of an Idle Fellow*

5 It is impossible to enjoy idling thoroughly unless one has plenty of work to do.
   *Idle Thoughts of an Idle Fellow*

6 But there, everything has its drawbacks, as the man said when his mother-in-law died, and they came down upon him for the funeral expenses.
   *Three Men in a Boat*, Ch. 3

7 I like work; it fascinates me. I can sit and look at it for hours. I love to keep it by me; the idea of getting rid of it nearly breaks my heart.
   *Three Men in a Boat*, Ch. 15

**Jerrold, Douglas William** (1803–57) British dramatist. His plays include *Black-eyed Susan* (1829) and *Time Works Wonders* (1845).

1 Religion's in the heart, not in the knees.
   *The Devil's Ducat*, I.2

2 The best thing I know between France and England is – the sea.
   *Wit and Opinions of Douglas Jerrold*, 'The Anglo-French Alliance'

3 That fellow would vulgarize the day of judgment.
   *Wit and Opinions of Douglas Jerrold*, 'A Comic Author'

4 Talk to him of Jacob's ladder, and he would ask the number of the steps.
   *Wit and Opinions of Douglas Jerrold*, 'A Matter-of-fact Man'

5 Love's like the measles – all the worse when it comes late in life.
   *Wit and Opinions of Douglas Jerrold*, 'A Philanthropist'

6 The ugliest of trades have their moments of pleasure. Now, if I were a grave-digger, or even a hangman, there are some people I could work for with a great deal of enjoyment.
   *Wit and Opinions of Douglas Jerrold*, 'Ugly Trades'

7 The only athletic sport I ever mastered was backgammon.
   *Douglas Jerrold* (W. Jerrold), Vol. I, Ch. 1

8 Sir, you are like a pin, but without either its head or its point.
   Speaking to a small thin man who was boring him
   Attrib.

**Jewel, John** (1522–71) English bishop. His *Apologia pro Ecclesia Anglicana* (1562) was the first formal statement of Anglican theology.

1 In old time we had treen chalices and golden priests, but now we have treen priests and golden chalices.
   *Certain Sermons Preached Before the Queen's Majesty*

**Joad, Cyril (Edwin Mitchinson)** (1891–1953) British writer and broadcaster.

1 Whenever I look inside myself I am afraid.
   *The Observer*, 'Sayings of the Week', 8 Nov 1942

2 There was never an age in which useless knowledge was more important than in our own.
   *The Observer*, 'Sayings of the Week', 30 Sept 1951

3 It will be said of this generation that it found England a land of beauty and left it a land of beauty spots.
   *The Observer*, 'Sayings of Our Times', 31 May 1953

**John III Sobieski** (1624–96) King of Poland (1674–96).

1 I came; I saw; God conquered.
   Announcing his victory over the Turks at Vienna to the pope (paraphrasing Caesar's 'veni, vidi, vici')
   Attrib.

**John XXIII** (Angelo Roncalli; 1881–1963) Italian churchman, who was Pope (1958–63) and called the 1962 Vatican Council. His diary, *The Journal of a Soul*, was published in 1965.

1 I am able to follow my own death step by step. Now I move softly towards the end.

Remark made two days before he died
*The Guardian*, 3 June 1963

**John of the Cross, St** (Juan de Yepes y Alvarez; 1542–91) Spanish churchman and poet. His mystical poems include *Noche oscura del alma.*

1 I die because I do not die.

*Coplas del alma que pena por ver a dios*

2 The dark night of the soul.

English translation of *Noche oscura del alma*, the title of a poem; *see also* FITZGERALD, F. Scott

**John Paul II** (Karol Wojtyta; 1920– ) Polish pope (1978– ); the first non-Italian pope since 1952.

1 It is unbecoming for a cardinal to ski badly.

Replying to the suggestion that it was inappropriate for him, a cardinal, to ski
*John Paul II*

**Johnson, Amy** (1903–41) British flyer; she made record solo flights to Australia (1930), Tokyo (1932), and the Cape of Good Hope (1936). She flew the Atlantic in 1936 with her husband. She was killed in an air crash.

1 Had I been a man I might have explored the Poles or climbed Mount Everest, but as it was my spirit found outlet in the air. . . .

*Myself When Young* (ed. Margot Asquith)

**Johnson, Hiram Warren** (1866–1945) US politician. He was governor of California (1911–17) and a senator (1917).

1 The first casualty when war comes is truth.

Speech, US Senate, 1917

**Johnson, Lyndon B(aines)** (1908–73) US statesman. He became Democratic President from 1963 to 1969. His increased involvement in the Vietnam war made him unpopular.

1 Jerry Ford is so dumb that he can't fart and chew gum at the same time.

Sometimes quoted as '. . . can't walk and chew gum'
*A Ford, Not a Lincoln* (R. Reeves), Ch. 1

2 If you're in politics and you can't tell when you walk into a room who's for you and who's against you, then you're in the wrong line of work.

*The Lyndon Johnson Story* (B. Mooney)

3 I am going to build the kind of nation that President Roosevelt hoped for, President Truman worked for and President Kennedy died for.

*The Sunday Times*, 27 Dec 1964

4 I'd much rather have that fellow inside my tent pissing out, than outside my tent pissing in.

When asked why he retained J. Edgar Hoover at the FBI
*Guardian Weekly*, 18 Dec 1971

**Johnson, Paul** (1928– ) British editor and writer. He was editor of the *New Statesman* (1965–70); his books include *The Suez War* (1957), *A History of Christianity* (1976), and *Ireland: Land of Troubles* (1980).

1 For me this is a vital litmus test: no intellectual society can flourish where a Jew feels even slightly uneasy.

*The Sunday Times Magazine*, 6 Feb 1977

**Johnson, Samuel** (1709–84) British lexicographer and writer. His *Dictionary of the English Language* appeared in 1755. The moral fable *Rasselas* (1759) was followed by *The Lives of the English Poets* (1781). His close friend James Boswell wrote his celebrated biography, *Boswell's Life of Johnson* (1791).

1 Every quotation contributes something to the stability or enlargement of the language.

*Dictionary of the English Language*

2 But these were the dreams of a poet doomed at last to wake a lexicographer.

*Dictionary of the English Language*

3 I am not yet so lost in lexicography, as to forget that words are the daughters of earth, and that things are the sons of heaven. Language is only the instrument of science, and words are but the signs of ideas: I wish, however, that the instrument might be less apt to decay, and that signs might be permanent, like the things which they denote.

*Dictionary of the English Language*

4 I have protracted my work till most of those whom I wished to please have sunk into the grave; and success and miscarriage are empty sounds.

*Dictionary of the English Language*

5 *Dull.* 8. To make dictionaries is dull work.

*Dictionary of the English Language*

6 *Excise.* A hateful tax levied upon commodities.

*Dictionary of the English Language*

7 *Lexicographer.* A writer of dictionaries, a harmless drudge.

*Dictionary of the English Language*

8 *Net.* Anything reticulated or decussated at equal distances, with interstices between the intersections.

*Dictionary of the English Language*

9 *Oats.* A grain, which in England is generally given to horses, but in Scotland supports the people.

*Dictionary of the English Language*

10 *Patron.* Commonly a wretch who supports with insolence, and is paid with flattery.

*Dictionary of the English Language*

11 When the messenger who carried the last sheet to Millar returned, Johnson asked him, 'Well, what did he say?' – 'Sir (answered the messenger), he said, thank God I have done with him.' – 'I am glad (replied Johnson, with a smile) that he thanks God for anything.'

After the final page of his *Dictionary* had been delivered

12 When two Englishmen meet, their first talk is of the weather.
*The Idler*

13 Pleasure is very seldom found where it is sought; our brightest blazes of gladness are commonly kindled by unexpected sparks.
*The Idler*

14 We are inclined to believe those whom we do not know because they have never deceived us.
*The Idler*

15 A Scotchman must be a very sturdy moralist who does not love Scotland better than truth.
*Journey to the Western Islands of Scotland, 'Col'*

16 The reciprocal civility of authors is one of the most risible scenes in the farce of life.
*Life of Sir Thomas Browne*

17 The true genius is a mind of large general powers, accidentally determined to some particular direction.
*Lives of the English Poets, 'Cowley'*

18 I am disappointed by that stroke of death, which has eclipsed the gaiety of nations and impoverished the public stock of harmless pleasure.
Epitaph on David Garrick
*Lives of the English Poets, 'Edmund Smith'*

19 We are perpetually moralists, but we are geometricians only by chance. Our intercourse with intellectual nature is necessary; our speculations upon matter are voluntary, and at leisure.
*Lives of the English Poets, 'Milton'*

20 There are minds so impatient of inferiority that their gratitude is a species of revenge, and they return benefits, not because recompense is a pleasure, but because obligation is a pain.
*The Rambler*

21 I have laboured to refine our language to grammatical purity, and to clear it from colloquial barbarisms, licentious idioms, and irregular combinations.
*The Rambler*

22 The love of life is necessary to the vigorous prosecution of any undertaking.
*The Rambler*

23 Almost every man wastes part of his life in attempts to display qualities which he does not possess, and to gain applause which he cannot keep.
*The Rambler*

24 There is a certain race of men that either imagine it their duty, or make it their amusement, to hinder the reception of every work of learning or genius, who stand as sentinels in the avenues of fame, and value themselves upon giving Ignorance and Envy the first notice of a prey.
*The Rambler*

25 Human life is everywhere a state in which much is to be endured, and little to be enjoyed.
*Rasselas, Ch. 11*

26 Marriage has many pains, but celibacy has no pleasures.
*Rasselas, Ch. 26*

27 Integrity without knowledge is weak and useless, and knowledge without integrity is dangerous and dreadful.
*Rasselas, Ch. 41*

28 Madam, before you flatter a man so grossly to his face, you should consider whether or not your flattery is worth his having.
*Diary and Letters (Mme D'Arblay), Vol. I, Ch. 2*

29 Every man has, some time in his life, an ambition to be a wag.
*Diary and Letters (Mme D'Arblay), Vol. III, Ch. 46*

30 If the man who turnips cries,
Cry not when his father dies,
'Tis a proof that he had rather
Have a turnip than his father.
*Johnsonian Miscellanies (ed. G. B. Hill), Vol. I*

31 GOLDSMITH. Here's such a stir about a fellow that has written one book, and I have written many.
JOHNSON. Ah, Doctor, there go two-and-forty sixpences you know to one guinea.
Referring to Beattie's *Essay on Truth*
*Johnsonian Miscellanies (ed. G. B. Hill), Vol. I*

32 It is very strange, and very melancholy, that the paucity of human pleasures should persuade us ever to call hunting one of them.
*Johnsonian Miscellanies (ed. G. B. Hill), Vol. I*

33 Was there ever yet anything written by mere man that was wished longer by its readers, excepting *Don Quixote, Robinson Crusoe,* and the *Pilgrim's Progress?*
*Johnsonian Miscellanies (ed. G. B. Hill), Vol. I*

34 A man is in general better pleased when he has a good dinner upon his table, than when his wife talks Greek.
*Johnsonian Miscellanies (ed. G. B. Hill), Vol. II*

35 A tavern chair is the throne of human felicity.
*Johnsonian Miscellanies (ed. G. B. Hill), Vol. II*

36 The only sensual pleasure without vice.
Referring to music
*Johnsonian Miscellanies (ed. G. B. Hill), Vol. II*

37 Difficult do you call it, Sir? I wish it were impossible.
On hearing a famous violinist
*Johnsonian Miscellanies (ed. G. B. Hill), Vol. II*

38 What is written without effort is in general read without pleasure.
*Johnsonian Miscellanies (ed. G. B. Hill), Vol. II*

**39** Love is the wisdom of the fool and the folly of the wise.
*Johnsonian Miscellanies* (ed. G. B. Hill), Vol. II

**40** In my early years I read very hard. It is a sad reflection, but a true one, that I knew almost as much at eighteen as I do now.
*Life of Johnson* (J. Boswell), Vol. I

**41** It is incident to physicians, I am afraid, beyond all other men, to mistake subsequence for consequence.
*Life of Johnson* (J. Boswell), Vol. I

**42** He was a vicious man, but very kind to me. If you call a dog *Hervey*, I shall love him.
*Life of Johnson* (J. Boswell), Vol. I

**43** I'll come no more behind your scenes, David; for the silk stockings and white bosoms of your actresses excite my amorous propensities.
Said to the actor-manager David Garrick
*Life of Johnson* (J. Boswell), Vol. I

**44** A man may write at any time, if he will set himself doggedly to it.
*Life of Johnson* (J. Boswell), Vol. I

**45** Is not a Patron, my Lord, one who looks with unconcern on a man struggling for life in the water, and, when he has reached ground, encumbers him with help? The notice which you have been pleased to take of my labours, had it been early, had been kind; but it has been delayed till I am indifferent, and cannot enjoy it; till I am solitary, and cannot impart it; till I am known, and do not want it.
Letter to Lord Chesterfield, 7 Feb 1755
*Life of Johnson* (J. Boswell), Vol. I

**46** A fly, Sir, may sting a stately horse and make him wince; but one is but an insect, and the other is a horse still.
Referring to critics
*Life of Johnson* (J. Boswell), Vol. I

**47** This man I thought had been a Lord among wits; but, I find, he is only a wit among Lords.
Referring to Lord Chesterfield
*Life of Johnson* (J. Boswell), Vol. I

**48** They teach the morals of a whore, and the manners of a dancing master.
Referring to Lord Chesterfield's *Letters*
*Life of Johnson* (J. Boswell), Vol. I

**49** There are two things which I am confident I can do very well: one is an introduction to any literary work, stating what it is to contain, and how it should be executed in the most perfect manner; the other is a conclusion, shewing from various causes why the execution has not been equal to what the author promised to himself and to the public.
*Life of Johnson* (J. Boswell), Vol. I

**50** Ignorance, madam, pure ignorance.
His reply on being questioned, by a lady reader of his *Dictionary*, why he had defined 'pastern' as the 'knee' of a horse
*Life of Johnson* (J. Boswell), Vol. I

**51** If a man does not make new acquaintance as he advances through life, he will soon find himself left alone. A man, Sir, should keep his friendship in constant repair.
*Life of Johnson* (J. Boswell), Vol. I

**52** The booksellers are generous liberal-minded men.
*Life of Johnson* (J. Boswell), Vol. I

**53** No man will be a sailor who has contrivance enough to get himself into a jail; for being in a ship is being in a jail, with the chance of being drowned . . . A man in a jail has more room, better food, and commonly better company.
*Life of Johnson* (J. Boswell), Vol. I

**54** BOSWELL. I do indeed come from Scotland, but I cannot help it . . .
JOHNSON. That, Sir, I find, is what a very great many of your countrymen cannot help.
*Life of Johnson* (J. Boswell), Vol. I

**55** Yes, Sir, many men, many women, and many children.
When asked by Dr Blair whether any man of their own time could have written the poems of Ossian
*Life of Johnson* (J. Boswell), Vol. I

**56** You *may* abuse a tragedy, though you cannot write one. You may scold a carpenter who has made you a bad table, though you cannot make a table. It is not your trade to make tables.
Referring to the qualifications needed to indulge in literary criticism
*Life of Johnson* (J. Boswell), Vol. I

**57** He is the richest author that ever grazed the common of literature.
Referring to Dr John Campbell
*Life of Johnson* (J. Boswell), Vol. I

**58** Great abilities are not requisite for an Historian . . . Imagination is not required in any high degree.
*Life of Johnson* (J. Boswell), Vol. I

**59** Norway, too, has noble wild prospects; and Lapland is remarkable for prodigious noble wild prospects. But, Sir, let me tell you, the noblest prospect which a Scotchman ever sees, is the high road that leads him to England!
*Life of Johnson* (J. Boswell), Vol. I

**60** A man ought to read just as inclination leads him; for what he reads as a task will do him little good.
*Life of Johnson* (J. Boswell), Vol. I

**61** But if he does really think that there is no distinction between virtue and vice, why, Sir, when he leaves our houses let us count our spoons.
*Life of Johnson* (J. Boswell), Vol. I

**62** Truth, Sir, is a cow, which will yield such people no more milk, and so they are gone to milk the bull.
Referring to sceptics
*Life of Johnson* (J. Boswell), Vol. I

63 Your levellers wish to level *down* as far as themselves; but they cannot bear levelling *up* to themselves.
*Life of Johnson* (J. Boswell), Vol. I

64 It is no matter what you teach them first, any more than what leg you shall put into your breeches first.
Referring to the education of children
*Life of Johnson* (J. Boswell), Vol. I

65 It is burning a farthing candle at Dover, to shew light at Calais.
Referring to the impact of Sheridan's works upon the English language
*Life of Johnson* (J. Boswell), Vol. I

66 A woman's preaching is like a dog's walking on his hinder legs. It is not done well; but you are surprised to find it done at all.
*Life of Johnson* (J. Boswell), Vol. I

67 This was a good dinner enough, to be sure; but it was not a dinner to *ask* a man to.
*Life of Johnson* (J. Boswell), Vol. I

68 I refute it *thus*.
Replying to Boswell's contention that they were unable to refute Bishop Berkeley's theory of matter, by kicking a large stone with his foot
*Life of Johnson* (J. Boswell), Vol. I

69 A very unclubable man.
Referring to Sir John Hawkins
*Life of Johnson* (J. Boswell), Vol. I

70 That all who are happy, are equally happy, is not true. A peasant and a philosopher may be equally *satisfied*, but not equally *happy*. Happiness consists in the multiplicity of agreeable consciousness.
*Life of Johnson* (J. Boswell), Vol. II

71 Our tastes greatly alter. The lad does not care for the child's rattle, and the old man does not care for the young man's whore.
*Life of Johnson* (J. Boswell), Vol. II

72 Shakespeare never had six lines together without a fault. Perhaps you may find seven, but this does not refute my general assertion.
*Life of Johnson* (J. Boswell), Vol. II

73 Why, Sir, most schemes of political improvement are very laughable things.
*Life of Johnson* (J. Boswell), Vol. II

74 There is no idolatry in the Mass. They believe God to be there, and they adore him.
*Life of Johnson* (J. Boswell), Vol. II

75 It matters not how a man dies, but how he lives. The act of dying is not of importance, it lasts so short a time.
*Life of Johnson* (J. Boswell), Vol. II

76 That fellow seems to me to possess but one idea, and that is a wrong one.
*Life of Johnson* (J. Boswell), Vol. II

77 I do not care to speak ill of any man behind his back, but I believe the gentleman is an *attorney*.
*Life of Johnson* (J. Boswell), Vol. II

78 The triumph of hope over experience.
Referring to the hasty remarriage of an acquaintance following the death of his first wife, with whom he had been most unhappy
*Life of Johnson* (J. Boswell), Vol. II

79 Every man has a lurking wish to appear considerable in his native place.
Letter to Sir Joshua Reynolds
*Life of Johnson* (J. Boswell), Vol. II

80 I would not give half a guinea to live under one form of government rather than another. It is of no moment to the happiness of an individual.
*Life of Johnson* (J. Boswell), Vol. II

81 Sir, I perceive you are a vile Whig.
Speaking to Sir Adam Fergusson
*Life of Johnson* (J. Boswell), Vol. II

82 A man who is good enough to go to heaven, is good enough to be a clergyman.
*Life of Johnson* (J. Boswell), Vol. II

83 Much may be made of a Scotchman, if he be *caught* young.
Referring to Lord Mansfield
*Life of Johnson* (J. Boswell), Vol. II

84 ELPHINSTON. What, have you not read it through? . . .
JOHNSON. No, Sir, do *you* read books *through*?
*Life of Johnson* (J. Boswell), Vol. II

85 Read over your compositions, and where ever you meet with a passage which you think is particularly fine, strike it out.
Recalling the advice of a college tutor
*Life of Johnson* (J. Boswell), Vol. II

86 The woman's a whore, and there's an end on't.
Referring to Lady Diana Beauclerk
*Life of Johnson* (J. Boswell), Vol. II

87 The Irish are a fair people; – they never speak well of one another.
*Life of Johnson* (J. Boswell), Vol. II

88 There are few ways in which a man can be more innocently employed than in getting money.
*Life of Johnson* (J. Boswell), Vol. II

89 He was dull in a new way, and that made many people think him *great*.
Referring to the poet Thomas Gray
*Life of Johnson* (J. Boswell), Vol. II

90 I think the full tide of human existence is at Charing-Cross.
*Life of Johnson* (J. Boswell), Vol. II

91 A man will turn over half a library to make one book.
*Life of Johnson* (J. Boswell), Vol. II

92 Patriotism is the last refuge of a scoundrel.
*Life of Johnson* (J. Boswell), Vol. II

93 Their learning is like bread in a besieged town: every man gets a little, but no man gets a full meal.

Referring to education in Scotland
*Life of Johnson* (J. Boswell), Vol. II

94 Knowledge is of two kinds. We know a subject ourselves, or we know where we can find information upon it.

*Life of Johnson* (J. Boswell), Vol. II

95 Politics are now nothing more than a means of rising in the world.

*Life of Johnson* (J. Boswell), Vol. II

96 In lapidary inscriptions a man is not upon oath.

*Life of Johnson* (J. Boswell), Vol. II

97 There is now less flogging in our great schools than formerly, but then less is learned there; so that what the boys get at one end they lose at the other.

*Life of Johnson* (J. Boswell), Vol. II

98 When men come to like a sea-life, they are not fit to live on land.

*Life of Johnson* (J. Boswell), Vol. II

99 There is nothing which has yet been contrived by man, by which so much happiness is produced as by a good tavern or inn.

*Life of Johnson* (J. Boswell), Vol. II

100 Questioning is not the mode of conversation among gentlemen.

*Life of Johnson* (J. Boswell), Vol. II

101 Fine clothes are good only as they supply the want of other means of procuring respect.

*Life of Johnson* (J. Boswell), Vol. II

102 If a madman were to come into this room with a stick in his hand, no doubt we should pity the state of his mind; but our primary consideration would be to take care of ourselves. We should knock him down first, and pity him afterwards.

*Life of Johnson* (J. Boswell), Vol. III

103 Consider, Sir, how should you like, though conscious of your innocence, to be tried before a jury for a capital crime, once a week.

*Life of Johnson* (J. Boswell), Vol. III

104 We would all be idle if we could.

*Life of Johnson* (J. Boswell), Vol. III

105 No man but a blockhead ever wrote, except for money.

*Life of Johnson* (J. Boswell), Vol. III

106 It is better that some should be unhappy than that none should be happy, which would be the case in a general state of equality.

*Life of Johnson* (J. Boswell), Vol. III

107 A man who has not been in Italy, is always conscious of an inferiority, from his not having seen what it is expected a man should see. The grand object of travelling is to see the shores of the Mediterranean.

*Life of Johnson* (J. Boswell), Vol. III

108 'Why Sir, it is much easier to say what it is not. We all *know* what light is; but it is not easy to *tell* what it is.'

When asked, 'What is poetry'
*Life of Johnson* (J. Boswell), Vol. III

109 Nay, Madam, when you are declaiming, declaim; and when you are calculating, calculate.

Commenting on Mrs Thrales's discourse on the price of children's clothes
*Life of Johnson* (J. Boswell), Vol. III

110 Sir, it is not so much to be lamented that Old England is lost, as that the Scotch have found it.

*Life of Johnson* (J. Boswell), Vol. III

111 To Oliver Goldsmith, A Poet, Naturalist, and Historian, who left scarcely any style of writing untouched, and touched none that he did not adorn.

Epitaph on Goldsmith
*Life of Johnson* (J. Boswell), Vol. III

112 If I had no duties, and no reference to futurity, I would spend my life in driving briskly in a post-chaise with a pretty woman.

*Life of Johnson* (J. Boswell), Vol. III

113 Depend upon it, Sir, when a man knows he is to be hanged in a fortnight, it concentrates his mind wonderfully.

*Life of Johnson* (J. Boswell), Vol. III

114 When a man is tired of London, he is tired of life; for there is in London all that life can afford.

*Life of Johnson* (J. Boswell), Vol. III

115 He who praises everybody praises nobody.

*Life of Johnson* (J. Boswell), Vol. III

116 Round numbers are always false.

*Life of Johnson* (J. Boswell), Vol. III

117 All argument is against it; but all belief is for it.

Of the ghost of a dead person
*Life of Johnson* (J. Boswell), Vol. III

118 Seeing Scotland, Madam, is only seeing a worse England.

*Life of Johnson* (J. Boswell), Vol. III

119 A country governed by a despot is an inverted cone.

*Life of Johnson* (J. Boswell), Vol. III

120 I am willing to love all mankind, *except an American.*

*Life of Johnson* (J. Boswell), Vol. III

121 Sir, the insolence of wealth will creep out.

*Life of Johnson* (J. Boswell), Vol. III

122 All censure of a man's self is oblique praise. It
is in order to shew how much he can spare.
*Life of Johnson* (J. Boswell), Vol. III

123 Were it not for imagination, Sir, a man would
be as happy in the arms of a chambermaid as
of a Duchess.
*Life of Johnson* (J. Boswell), Vol. III

124 There are innumerable questions to which the
inquisitive mind can in this state receive no
answer: Why do you and I exist? Why was
this world created? Since it was to be created,
why was it not created sooner?
*Life of Johnson* (J. Boswell), Vol. III

125 Claret is the liquor for boys; port for men; but
he who aspires to be a hero must drink
brandy.
*Life of Johnson* (J. Boswell), Vol. III

126 A man who exposes himself when he is intoxicated, has not the art of getting drunk.
*Life of Johnson* (J. Boswell), Vol. III

127 Worth seeing? yes; but not worth going to
see.
Referring to the Giant's Causeway
*Life of Johnson* (J. Boswell), Vol. III

128 I have got no further than this: Every man has
a right to utter what he thinks truth, and every other man has a right to knock him down
for it. Martyrdom is the test.
*Life of Johnson* (J. Boswell), Vol. IV

129 They are forced plants, raised in a hot-bed;
and they are poor plants; they are but cucum-
bers after all.
Referring to Gray's *Odes*
*Life of Johnson* (J. Boswell), Vol. IV

130 A Frenchman must be always talking, whether
he knows anything of the matter or not; an
Englishman is content to say nothing, when he
has nothing to say.
*Life of Johnson* (J. Boswell), Vol. IV

131 Sir, your wife, under pretence of keeping a
bawdy-house, is a receiver of stolen goods.
An example of the customary badinage between travellers on
the Thames
*Life of Johnson* (J. Boswell), Vol. IV

132 Depend upon it that if a man talks of his misfortunes there is something in them that is
not disagreeable to him; for where there is
nothing but pure misery there never is any recourse to the mention of it.
*Life of Johnson* (J. Boswell), Vol. IV

133 Mrs Montagu has dropt me. Now, Sir, there
are people whom one should like very well
to drop, but would not wish to be dropped by.
*Life of Johnson* (J. Boswell), Vol. IV

134 Classical quotation is the *parole* of literary men
all over the world.
*Life of Johnson* (J. Boswell), Vol. IV

135 I have two very cogent reasons for not printing
any list of subscribers; – one, that I have lost
all the names, – the other, that I have spent
all the money.
Referring to subscribers to his *Dictionary of the English
Language*
*Life of Johnson* (J. Boswell), Vol. IV

136 Always, Sir, set a high value on spontaneous
kindness. He whose inclination prompts him
to cultivate your friendship of his own accord,
will love you more than one whom you have
been at pains to attach to you.
*Life of Johnson* (J. Boswell), Vol. IV

137 Resolve not to be poor: whatever you have,
spend less. Poverty is a great enemy to human
happiness; it certainly destroys liberty, and it
makes some virtues impracticable and others
extremely difficult.
*Life of Johnson* (J. Boswell), Vol. IV

138 I hate a fellow whom pride, or cowardice, or
laziness drives into a corner, and who does
nothing when he is there but sit and *growl*; let
him come out as I do, and *bark*.
*Life of Johnson* (J. Boswell), Vol. IV

139 How few of his friends' houses would a man
choose to be at when he is sick.
*Life of Johnson* (J. Boswell), Vol. IV

140 There is a wicked inclination in most people to
suppose an old man decayed in his intellects.
If a young or middle-aged man, when leaving
a company, does not recollect where he laid
his hat, it is nothing; but if the same inat-
tention is discovered in an old man, people will
shrug up their shoulders, and say, 'His memory is going.'
*Life of Johnson* (J. Boswell), Vol. IV

141 Sir, there is no settling the point of precedency
between a louse and a flea.
When Maurice Morgann asked him who he considered to be
the better poet – Smart or Derrick
*Life of Johnson* (J. Boswell), Vol. IV

142 When I observed he was a fine cat, saying,
'why yes, Sir, but I have had cats whom I liked
better than this'; and then as if perceiving
Hodge to be out of countenance, adding, 'but
he is a very fine cat, a very fine cat indeed.'
*Life of Johnson* (J. Boswell), Vol. IV

143 My dear friend, clear your *mind* of cant . . .
You may *talk* in this manner; it is a mode of
talking in Society: but don't *think* foolishly.
*Life of Johnson* (J. Boswell), Vol. IV

144 As I know more of mankind I expect less of
them, and am ready now to call a man *a good
man*, upon easier terms than I was formerly.
*Life of Johnson* (J. Boswell), Vol. IV

145 If a man were to go by chance at the same time with Burke under a shed, to shun a shower, he would say – 'this is an extraordinary man.'
Referring to Edmund Burke
*Life of Johnson* (J. Boswell), Vol. IV

146 It is as bad as bad can be: it is ill-fed, ill-killed, ill-kept, and ill-drest.
About the roast mutton at an inn
*Life of Johnson* (J. Boswell), Vol. IV

147 Milton, Madam, was a genius that could cut a Colossus from a rock; but could not carve heads upon cherry-stones.
When Miss Hannah More had wondered why Milton could write the epic *Paradise Lost* but only very poor sonnets
*Life of Johnson* (J. Boswell), Vol. IV

148 Sir, I have found you an argument; but I am not obliged to find you an understanding.
*Life of Johnson* (J. Boswell), Vol. IV

149 No man is a hypocrite in his pleasures.
*Life of Johnson* (J. Boswell), Vol. IV

150 Dublin, though a place much worse than London, is not so bad as Iceland.
Letter to Mrs Christopher Smart
*Life of Johnson* (J. Boswell), Vol. IV

151 Sir, I look upon every day to be lost, in which I do not make a new acquaintance.
*Life of Johnson* (J. Boswell), Vol. IV

152 I will be conquered; I will not capitulate.
Referring to his illness
*Life of Johnson* (J. Boswell), Vol. IV

153 A cow is a very good animal in the field; but we turn her out of a garden.
Responding to Boswell's objections to the expulsion of six Methodists from Oxford University
*The Personal History of Samuel Johnson* (C. Hibbert)

154 A lawyer has no business with the justice or injustice of the cause which he undertakes, unless his client asks his opinion, and then he is bound to give it honestly. The justice or injustice of the cause is to be decided by the judge.
*Tour to the Hebrides* (J. Boswell)

155 I have, all my life long, been lying till noon; yet I tell all young men, and tell them with great sincerity, that nobody who does not rise early will ever do any good.
*Tour to the Hebrides* (J. Boswell)

156 I am always sorry when any language is lost, because languages are the pedigree of nations.
*Tour to the Hebrides* (J. Boswell)

157 No, Sir; there were people who died of dropsies, which they contracted in trying to get drunk.
Scornfully criticizing the strength of the wine in Scotland before the Act of Union in response to Boswell's claim that there had been a lot of drunkenness
*Tour to the Hebrides* (J. Boswell)

158 A cucumber should be well sliced, and dressed with pepper and vinegar, and then thrown out, as good for nothing.
*Tour to the Hebrides* (J. Boswell)

159 Come, let me know what it is that makes a Scotchman happy!
Ordering for himself a glass of whisky
*Tour to the Hebrides* (J. Boswell)

160 I am sorry I have not learned to play at cards. It is very useful in life: it generates kindness and consolidates society.
*Tour to the Hebrides* (J. Boswell)

161 Fly fishing may be a very pleasant amusement; but angling or float fishing I can only compare to a stick and a string, with a worm at one end and a fool at the other.
Attrib. in *Instructions to Young Sportsmen* (Hawker)

**Johst, Hanns** (1890– ) German novelist and dramatist.

1 Whenever I hear the word 'culture' . . . I reach for my gun.
Popularly attrib. to Herman GOERING
*Schlageter*, I:1

**Joliot-Curie, Iréne** (1897–1956) French scientist. The daughter of Marie Curie, she worked with her husband Frédéric Joliot (1900–59). They were the first to produce artificial radioactivity and received the Nobel Chemistry prize in 1935.

1 That one must do some work seriously and must be independent and not merely amuse oneself in life – this our mother has told us always, but never that science was the only career worth following.
Recalling the advice of her mother, Marie Curie
*A Long Way from Missouri* (Mary Margaret McBride), Ch. 10

**Jolson, Al** (Asa Yoelson; 1886–1950) US actor and singer, born in Russia. A vaudeville singer, he became famous for his blacked-up face and the song *Mammy*. He appeared in the first full-length talkie *The Jazz Singer* (1927).

1 You ain't heard nothin' yet, folks.
In the film *The Jazz Singer*, July 1927; later adopted as a catch phrase by President Ronald Reagan
*The Jazz Singer*

**Jones, John Paul** (1747–92) Scottish-born US naval commander. He commanded the flagship *Bonhomme Richard* in the naval battle against the British in 1779 and later served in the Russian navy.

1 I have not yet begun to fight.
Retort when informed his ship was sinking
*Life and Letters of J. P. Jones* (De Koven), Vol. I

**Jonson, Ben** (1573–1637) English dramatist and poet. His plays include *Volpone* (1606), *The Alchemist* (1610), and *Bartholomew Fair* (1614); he published two collections of verse.

1 Fortune, that favours fools.
*The Alchemist*, Prologue

2 Neither do thou lust after that tawney weed tobacco.
*Bartholomew Fair*, II:6

3 Alas, all the castles I have, are built with air,
thou know'st.

*Eastward Ho*, II:2

4 Ods me, I marvel what pleasure or felicity they
have in taking their roguish tobacco. It is good
for nothing but to choke a man, and fill him full
of smoke and embers.

*Every Man in His Humour*, III:5

5 Drink to me only with thine eyes,
And I will pledge with mine;
Or leave a kiss but in the cup,
And I'll not look for wine.
The thirst that from the soul doth rise
Doth ask a drink divine;
But might I of Jove's nectar sup,
I would not change for thine.

I sent thee late a rosy wreath,
Not so much honouring thee,
As giving it a hope that there
It could not wither'd be.

*The Forest*, IX, 'To Celia'

6 They say princes learn no art truly, 'but the art
of horsemanship. The reason is, the brave
beast is no flatterer. He will throw a prince as
soon as his groom.

*Timber, or Discoveries made upon Men and Matter*

7 Talking and eloquence are not the same: to
speak, and to speak well, are two things.

*Timber, or Discoveries made upon Men and Matter*

8 Thou hadst small Latin, and less Greek.

*To the Memory of William Shakespeare*

9 He was not of an age, but for all time!

*To the Memory of William Shakespeare*

10 Sweet Swan of Avon!

*To the Memory of William Shakespeare*

11 She is Venus when she smiles;
But she's Juno when she walks,
And Minerva when she talks.

*The Underwood*, 'Celebration of Charis, V. His Discourse with
Cupid'

12 Good morning to the day: and, next, my gold! –
Open the shrine, that I may see my saint.

*Volpone*, I:1

13 Calumnies are answered best with silence.

*Volpone*, II:2

14 Come, my Celia, let us prove,
While we can, the sports of love,
Time will not be ours for ever,
He, at length, our good will sever.

*Volpone*, III:6

15 O rare Ben Jonson.

Epitaph in Westminster Abbey

**Joseph, Michael** (1897–1958) British publisher.

1 Authors are easy to get on with – if you're fond
of children.

*The Observer*, 1949

**Joseph II** (1741–90) Holy Roman Emperor (1765–90).

1 Here lies Joseph, who failed in everything he
undertook.

Suggesting his own epitaph when reflecting upon the disappointment of his hopes for reform
Attrib.

**Jowett, Benjamin** (1817–93) British theologian and
classicist. His *Epistles of St Paul* (1855) caused considerable
protest. As Master of Balliol College, Oxford, he was known for
his care of students.

1 My dear child, you must believe in God in spite
of what the clergy tell you.

*Autobiography* (Asquith), Ch. 8

2 One man is as good as another until he has written a book.

*Letters of B. Jowett* (Abbott and Campbell)

3 Nowhere probably is there more true feeling,
and nowhere worse taste, than in a churchyard
– both as regards the monuments and the inscriptions. Scarcely a word of true poetry
anywhere.

*Letters of B. Jowett* (Abbott and Campbell)

4 Young men make great mistakes in life; for one
thing, they idealize love too much.

*Letters of B. Jowett* (Abbott and Campbell)

5 Research! A mere excuse for idleness; it has
never achieved, and will never achieve any re-
sults of the slightest value.

*Unforgotten Years* (Logan Pearsall Smith)

6 The way to get things done is not to mind who
gets the credit of doing them.

Attrib.

7 If you don't find a God by five o'clock this afternoon you must leave the college.

Responding to a conceited young student's assertion that he
could find no evidence for a God
Attrib.

**Joyce, James** (1882–1941) Irish novelist and poet. His short
stories *The Dubliners* (1914) brought him to public notice, but it
was his controversial stream-of-consciousness novel *Ulysses* (1922)
that made him famous. *Finnegans Wake* (1939) was his last book.

1 Three quarks for Muster Mark!

The word quark has since been adopted by physicists for hypo-
thetical elementary particles
*Finnegans Wake*

2 Ireland is the old sow that eats her farrow.

*A Portrait of the Artist as a Young Man*, Ch. 5

3 'When I makes tea I makes tea,' as old mother
Grogan said. 'And when I makes water I makes
water'.

*Ulysses*

4 'History', Stephen said, 'is a nightmare from which I am trying to awake'.
*Ulysses*

5 Greater love than this, he said, no man hath that a man lay down his wife for a friend. Go thou and do likewise. Thus, or words to that effect, saith Zarathustra, sometime regius professor of French letters to the University of Oxtail.
*Ulysses*

6 The snotgreen sea. The scrotumtightening sea.
*Ulysses*

7 It is a symbol of Irish art. The cracked looking glass of a servant.
*Ulysses*

8 The desire of the moth for the star.
Commenting on the interruption of a music recital when a moth flew into the singer's mouth
*James Joyce* (R. Ellmann)

9 Never mind about my soul, just make sure you get my tie right.
Responding to the painter Patrick Tuohy's assertion that he wished to capture Joyce's soul in his portrait of him
*James Joyce* (R. Ellmann)

10 We have met too late. You are too old for me to have any effect on you.
On meeting W. B. Yeats
*James Joyce* (R. Ellmann)

**Juang-zu** (4th century BC) Chinese Taoist philosopher.

1 Above ground I shall be food for kites; below I shall be food for mole-crickets and ants. Why rob one to feed the other?
Deciding against interment when asked on his deathbed what his wishes were regarding the disposal of his body
*Famous Last Words* (B. Conrad)

**Julia** (39 BC–AD 14) Daughter of Augustus. She was notorious for her extravagance and licentious behaviour.

1 Today I dressed to meet my father's eyes; yesterday it was for my husband's.
On being complimented by her father, the emperor Augustus, on her choice of a more modest dress than the one she had worn the previous day
*Saturnalia* (Macrobius)

2 He sometimes forgets that he is Caesar, but I always remember that I am Caesar's daughter.
Replying to suggestions that she should live in the simple style of her father, which contrasted with her own extravagance
*Saturnalia* (Macrobius)

**Jung, Carl Gustav** (1875–1961) Swiss psychoanalyst. He collaborated with Freud until 1912, subsequently elaborated his own theory of analysis, described in such books as *The Psychology of the Unconscious* (1916) and *Modern Man in Search of a Soul* (1933).

1 Fortunately, in her kindness and patience, Nature has never put the fatal question as to the meaning of their lives into the mouths of most people. And where no one asks, no one needs to answer.
*The Development of Personality*

2 The pendulum of the mind oscillates between sense and nonsense, not between right and wrong.
*Memories, Dreams, Reflections,* Ch. 5

3 A man who has not passed through the inferno of his passions has never overcome them.
*Memories, Dreams, Reflections,* Ch. 9

4 As far as we can discern, the sole purpose of human existence is to kindle a light in the darkness of mere being.
*Memories, Dreams, Reflections,* Ch. 11

5 Every form of addiction is bad, no matter whether the narcotic be alcohol or morphine or idealism.
*Memories, Dreams, Reflections,* Ch. 12

6 Among all my patients in the second half of life . . . there has not been one whose problem in the last resort was not that of finding a religious outlook on life.
*Modern Man in Search of a Soul*

7 The least of things with a meaning is worth more in life than the greatest of things without it.
*Modern Man in Search of a Soul*

8 Sentimentality is a superstructure covering brutality.
*Reflections*

9 Show me a sane man and I will cure him for you.
*The Observer,* 19 July 1975

10 Wherever an inferiority complex exists, there is a good reason for it. There is always something inferior there, although not just where we persuade ourselves that it is.
Interview, 1943

11 We need more understanding of human nature, because the only real danger that exists is man himself . . . We know nothing of man, far too little. His psyche should be studied because we are the origin of all coming evil.
BBC television interview

**Junius** An unidentified writer of letters (1769–72) to the *London Public Advertiser,* criticizing the government of George III. Sir Philip Francis (1740–1818) was possibly the author.

1 The Liberty of the press is the *Palladium* of all the civil, political and religious rights of an Englishman.
*Letters,* 'Dedication'

2 There is a holy, mistaken zeal in politics, as well as religion. By persuading others we convince ourselves.
Letter, 19 Dec 1769

**Junot, Andoche, Duc d'Abrantes** (1771–1813) French general. He served under Napoleon and became governor of Paris (1806). Having captured Lisbon (1807), he was defeated by Wellesley and had to evacuate Portugal.

1 I am my own ancestor.
Said on being made a duke
Attrib.

**Justinian I** (482–565 AD) Byzantine emperor. He codified Roman Law in the Justinian Code and, as a Christian, built the church of St Sophia in Constantinople.

1 Justice is the constant and perpetual wish to render to every one his due.
*Institutes*, I

**Juvenal** (Decimus Junius Juvenalis; 60–130 AD) Roman satirist. His *Satires* (c. 100 AD) savagely attack Roman society.

1 It's hard not to write satire.
*Satires*, I

2 No one ever suddenly became depraved.
*Satires*, II

3 The misfortunes of poverty carry with them nothing harder to bear than that it exposes men to ridicule.
*Satires*, III

4 It's not easy for people to rise out of obscurity when they have to face straitened circumstances at home.
*Satires*, III

5 *Quis custodiet ipsos custodes?*
Who is to guard the guards themselves?
*Satires*, VI

6 I will have this done, so I order it done; let my will replace reasoned judgement.
*Satires*, VI

7 Many suffer from the incurable disease of writing, and it becomes chronic in their sick minds.
*Satires*, VII

8 The people long eagerly for just two things – bread and circuses.
*Satires*, X

9 Travel light and you can sing in the robber's face.
*Satires*, X

10 *Orandum est ut sit mens sana in corpore sano.*
Your prayer must be for a sound mind in a sound body.
*Satires*, X

11 No one delights more in vengeance than a woman.
*Satires*, XIII

12 A child deserves the maximum respect; if you ever have something disgraceful in mind, don't ignore your son's tender years.
*Satires*, XIV

## K

**Kafka, Franz** (1883–1924) Czech novelist, many of whose books were published posthumously against his wish by Max Brod, his literary executor. His novels include *Metamorphosis* (1912), *The Trial* (1925), and *The Castle* (1926).

1 Don't despair, not even over the fact that you don't despair.
*Diary*

2 It's often safer to be in chains than to be free.
*The Trial*, Ch. 8

3 Let me remind you of the old maxim: people under suspicion are better moving than at rest, since at rest they may be sitting in the balance without knowing it, being weighed together with their sins
*The Trial*, Ch. 8

**Kant, Immanuel** (1724–1804) German philosopher. His *Critique of Pure Reason* (1781), *Critique of Practical Reason* (1788), and *Critique of Judgment* (1790) summarize his powerful theories.

1 Two things fill the mind with ever new and increasing wonder and awe, the more often and the more seriously reflection concentrates upon them: the starry heaven above me and the moral law within me.
*Critique of Practical Reason*, Conclusion

2 Finally, there is an imperative which commands a certain conduct immediately . . . This imperative is Categorical . . . This imperative may be called that of Morality.
*Grundlegung zur Metaphysik der Sitten*, II

3 . . . because happiness is not an ideal of reason but of imagination.
*Grundlegung zur Metaphysik der Sitten*, II

4 Out of the crooked timber of humanity no straight thing can ever be made.
*Idee zu einer allgemeinen Geschichte in weltbürgerlicher Absicht*

**Karr, Alphonse** (1808–90) French writer and editor of *Figaro* (1839). He founded the satirical review *Les Guêpes*. His books include *Voyage autour de mon Jardin* (1845) and *Le Credo du Jardinier* (1875).

1 *Plus ça change, plus c'est la même chose.*
The more things change, the more they stay the same.
*Les Guêpes*, Jan 1849

2 If we are to abolish the death penalty, I should like to see the first step taken by our friends the murderers.
*Les Guêpes*, Jan 1849

**Kaufman, George S(imon)** (1889–1961) US dramatist and journalist. He collaborated with Moss Hart on *Bandwagon* (1931) and many other Broadway comedies and with George Gershwin on *Of Thee I Sing* (1932).

1 Over my dead body!
   On being asked to suggest his own epitaph
   *The Algonquin Wits* (R. Drennan)

**Kavanagh, Ted** (1892–1958) British radio scriptwriter, mainly remembered for his wartime radio comedy series, *ITMA*.

1 Can I do you now, sir?
   Said by Mrs Mop
   *ITMA*, BBC Radio

2 I don't mind if I do.
   Said by Colonel Chinstrap
   *ITMA*, BBC Radio

3 It's that man again.
   *ITMA*, BBC Radio

**Kearney, Denis** (1847–1907) US Labor leader.

1 Horny-handed sons of toil.
   Speech, San Francisco, c. 1878

**Keats, John** (1795–1821) British poet. Trained as a doctor, he devoted most of his short life to poetry. *Endymion* (1818) was attacked by the critics but he eventually established his reputation with *La Belle Dame Sans Merci* (1820), *Ode to a Nightingale* (1820), and other works. He died in Rome of tuberculosis.

1 Bright star, would I were steadfast as thou art.
   *Bright Star*

2 A thing of beauty is a joy for ever:
   Its loveliness increases; it will never
   Pass into nothingness; but still will keep
   A bower quiet for us, and a sleep
   Full of sweet dreams, and health, and quiet
   breathing.
   *Endymion*, I

3 Their smiles,
   Wan as primroses gather'd at midnight
   By chilly finger'd spring.
   *Endymion*, IV

4 St Agnes' Eve – Ah, bitter chill it was!
   The owl, for all his feathers, was a-cold;
   The hare limp'd trembling through the frozen
   grass,
   And silent was the flock in woolly fold.
   *The Eve of Saint Agnes*, I

5 The Beadsman, after thousand aves told,
   For aye unsought-for slept among his ashes cold.
   *The Eve of Saint Agnes*, I

6 Soft adorings from their loves receive
   Upon the honey'd middle of the night.
   *The Eve of Saint Agnes*, VI

7 The music, yearning like a God in pain.
   *The Eve of Saint Agnes*, VII

8 He play'd an ancient ditty, long since mute,
   In Provence call'd, 'La belle dame sans mercy'.
   *The Eve of Saint Agnes*, XXXIII

9 And they are gone: aye, ages long ago
   These lovers fled away into the storm.
   *The Eve of Saint Agnes*, XLII

10 Fanatics have their dreams, wherewith they
   weave
   A paradise for a sect.
   *The Fall of Hyperion*, I

11 The poet and the dreamer are distinct,
   Diverse, sheer opposite, antipodes.
   The one pours out a balm upon the world,
   The other vexes it.
   *The Fall of Hyperion*, I

12 Ever let the fancy roam,
   Pleasure never is at home.
   *Fancy*, I

13 Where's the cheek that doth not fade,
   Too much gaz'd at? Where's the maid
   Whose lip mature is ever new?
   *Fancy*, I

14 Four seasons fill the measure of the year;
   There are four seasons in the mind of men.
   *Four Seasons*

15 O aching time! O moments big as years!
   *Hyperion*, I

16 As when, upon a trancèd summer-night,
   Those green-rob'd senators of mighty woods,
   Tall oaks, branch-charmèd by the earnest stars,
   Dream, and so dream all night without a stir.
   *Hyperion*, I

17 Oh what can ail thee, knight at arms
   Alone and palely loitering;
   The sedge has wither'd from the lake,
   And no birds sing.
   *La Belle Dame Sans Merci*

18 'La belle Dame sans Merci
   Hath thee in thrall!'
   *La Belle Dame Sans Merci*

19 Love in a hut, with water and a crust,
   Is – Love, forgive us! – cinders, ashes, dust;
   Love in a palace is perhaps at last
   More grievous torment than a hermit's fast.
   *Lamia*, II

20 Do not all charms fly
   At the mere touch of cold philosophy?
   *Lamia*, II

21 Souls of poets dead and gone,
   What Elysium have ye known,
   Happy field or mossy cavern,
   Choicer than the Mermaid Tavern?
   Have ye tippled drink more fine
   Than mine host's Canary wine?
   *Lines on the Mermaid Tavern*

22 Thou still unravish'd bride of quietness,
   Thou foster-child of silence and slow time.
   *Ode on a Grecian Urn*

23 Heard melodies are sweet, but those unheard
Are sweeter; therefore, ye soft pipes, play on.
*Ode on a Grecian Urn*

24 Thou, silent form, dost tease us out of thought
As doth eternity: Cold Pastoral!
*Ode on a Grecian Urn*

25 'Beauty is truth, truth beauty,' – that is all
Ye know on earth, and all ye need to know.
*Ode on a Grecian Urn*

26 For ever warm and still to be enjoy'd,
For ever panting and for ever young;
All breathing human passion far above,
That leaves a heart high-sorrowful and cloy'd,
A burning forehead, and a parching tongue.
*Ode on a Grecian Urn*

27 No, no, go not to Lethe, neither twist
Wolf's-bane, tight-rooted, for its poisonous wine.
*Ode on Melancholy*

28 Nor let the beetle, nor the death-moth be
Your mournful Psyche.
*Ode on Melancholy*

29 Ay, in the very temple of delight
Veil'd Melancholy has her sovran shrine.
Though seen of none save him whose strenuous tongue
Can burst Joy's grape against his palate fine.
*Ode on Melancholy*

30 My heart aches, and a drowsy numbness pains
My sense.
*Ode to a Nightingale*

31 O, for a draught of vintage! that hath been
Cool'd a long age in the deep-delved earth.
*Ode to a Nightingale*

32 O for a beaker full of the warm South,
Full of the true, the blushful Hippocrene,
With beaded bubbles winking at the brim,
And purple-stained mouth.
*Ode to a Nightingale*

33 Fade far away, dissolve, and quite forget
What thou among the leaves hast never known,
The weariness, the fever, and the fret,
Here, where men sit and hear each other groan.
*Ode to a Nightingale*

34 Thou wast not born for death, immortal Bird!
No hungry generations tread thee down;
The voice I hear this passing night was heard
In ancient days by emperor and clown:
Perhaps the self-same song that found a path
Through the sad heart of Ruth, when sick for home,
She stood in tears amid the alien corn;
The same that oft-times hath
Charm'd magic casements, opening on the foam
Of perilous seas, in faery lands forlorn.
*Ode to a Nightingale*

35 Darkling I listen; and, for many a time
I have been half in love with easeful Death,
Call'd him soft names in many a mused rhyme,
To take into the air my quiet breath;
Now more than ever seems it rich to die,
To cease upon the midnight with no pain,
While thou art pouring forth thy soul abroad
In such an ecstasy!
*Ode to a Nightingale*

36 Much have I travell'd in the realms of gold,
And many goodly states and kingdoms seen.
*On first looking into Chapman's Homer*

37 Then felt I like some watcher of the skies
When a new planet swims into his ken;
Or like stout Cortez when with eagle eyes
He star'd at the Pacific – and all his men
Look'd at each other with a wild surmise –
Silent, upon a peak in Darien.
*On first looking into Chapman's Homer*

38 It keeps eternal whisperings around
Desolate shores, and with its mighty swell
Gluts twice ten thousand Caverns.
*On the Sea*

39 A drainless shower
Of light is poesy; 'tis the supreme of power;
'Tis might half slumb'ring on its own right arm.
*Sleep and Poetry*

40 Season of mists and mellow fruitfulness,
Close bosom-friend of the maturing sun;
Conspiring with him how to load and bless
With fruit the vines that round the thatch-eaves run.
*To Autumn*

41 Where are the songs of Spring? Ay, where are they?
*To Autumn*

42 O soft embalmer of the still midnight.
*To Sleep*

43 Turn the key deftly in the oiled wards,
And seal the hushed casket of my soul.
*To Sleep*

44 Here lies one whose name was writ in water.
Suggesting his own epitaph (recalling a line from *Philaster* by Beaumont and Fletcher)
*Life of Keats* (Lord Houghton), Ch. 2

45 A long poem is a test of invention which I take to be the Polar star of poetry, as fancy is the sails, and imagination the rudder.
Letter to Benjamin Bailey, 8 Oct 1817

46 I am certain of nothing but the holiness of the heart's affections and the truth of imagination – what the imagination seizes as beauty must be truth – whether it existed before or not.
Letter to Benjamin Bailey, 22 Nov 1817

47 O for a life of sensations rather than of thoughts!
Letter to Benjamin Bailey, 22 Nov 1817

**48** Negative Capability, that is, when a man is capable of being in uncertainties, mysteries, doubts, without any irritable reaching after fact and reason.

Letter to G. and T. Keats, 21 Dec 1817

**49** The excellence of every art is its intensity, capable of making all disagreeables evaporate, from their being in close relationship with beauty and truth.

Letter to G. and T. Keats, 21 Dec 1817

**50** There is an old saying 'well begun is half done' – 'tis a bad one. I would use instead – Not begun at all until half done.

Letter, 1817

**51** We hate poetry that has a palpable design upon us – and if we do not agree, seems to put its hand in its breeches pocket. Poetry should be great and unobtrusive, a thing which enters into one's soul, and does not startle or amaze it with itself, but with its subject.

Letter to J. H. Reynolds, 3 Feb 1818

**52** If poetry comes not as naturally as leaves to a tree it had better not come at all.

Letter to John Taylor, 27 Feb 1818

**53** Scenery is fine – but human nature is finer.

Letter to Benjamin Bailey, 13 Mar 1818

**54** Axioms in philosophy are not axioms until they are proved upon our pulses; we read fine things but never feel them to the full until we have gone the same steps as the author.

Letter to J. H. Reynolds, 3 May 1818

**55** I am in that temper that if I were under water I would scarcely kick to come to the top.

Letter to Benjamin Bailey, 21 May 1818

**56** I do think better of womankind than to suppose they care whether Mister John Keats five feet high likes them or not.

Letter to Benjamin Bailey, 18 July 1818

**57** I think I shall be among the English Poets after my death.

Letter to George and Georgiana Keats, 14 Oct 1818

**58** I never can feel certain of any truth but from a clear perception of its beauty.

Letter to George and Georgiana Keats, 16 Dec 1818–4 Jan 1819

**59** Nothing ever becomes real till it is experienced –even a proverb is no proverb to you till your life has illustrated it.

Letter to George and Georgiana Keats, 19 Mar 1819

**60** My friends should drink a dozen of Claret on my Tomb.

Letter to Benjamin Bailey, 14 Aug 1819

**61** Give me books, fruit, French wine and fine weather and a little music out of doors, played by somebody I do not know.

Letter to Fanny Keats, 29 Aug 1819

**62** Love is my religion – I could die for that.

Letter to Fanny Brawne, 13 Oct 1819

**63** Though a quarrel in the streets is a thing to be hated, the energies displayed in it are fine; the commonest man shows a grace in his quarrel.

Letter

**64** I go among the fields and catch a glimpse of a stoat or a fieldmouse peeping out of the withered grass – the creature hath a purpose and its eyes are bright with it. I go amongst the buildings of a city and I see a man hurrying along – to what? the Creature has a purpose and his eyes are bright with it.

Letter, 1819

**65** Upon the whole I dislike mankind: whatever people on the other side of the question may advance, they cannot deny that they are always surprised at hearing of a good action and never of a bad one.

Letter, 1820

**66** Is there another life? Shall I awake and find all this a dream? There must be, we cannot be created for this sort of suffering.

Letter, 1820

**67** I shall soon be laid in the quiet grave – thank God for the quiet grave – O! I can feel the cold earth upon me – the daisies growing over me – O for this quiet –it will be my first.

In a letter to John Taylor by Joseph Severn, 6 Mar 1821

**Keble, John** (1792–1866) British poet and clergyman. His sermon on national apostasy (1833) led to the formation of the Oxford Movement. His hymns were published as *The Christian Year* (1827).

**1** The trivial round, the common task,
Would furnish all we ought to ask;
Room to deny ourselves; a road
To bring us, daily, nearer God.

*The Christian Year*, 'Morning'

**Keller, Helen (Adams)** (1880–1968) US writer and lecturer. Blind and deaf from infancy, she learnt to speak, read, and write, graduating from Radcliffe College in 1904. Her lectures raised money for educating the handicapped, and her books include the autobiographical *The Story of My Life* (1902).

**1** . . . militarism . . . is one of the chief bulwarks of capitalism, and the day that militarism is undermined, capitalism will fail.

*The Story of My Life*

**2** . . . we could never learn to be brave and patient, if there were only joy in the world.

*Atlantic Monthly* (May 1890)

**3** How reconcile this world of fact with the bright world of my imagining? My darkness has been filled with the light of intelligence, and behold, the outer day-light world was stumbling and groping in social blindness.

*The Cry for Justice* (ed. Upton Sinclair)

**Kelvin, William Thomson, 1st Baron** (1824–1907) British physicist, famous for his work in thermodynamics. He devised the Kelvin temperature scale, with a zero point of absolute zero. The unit of thermodynamic temperature is named after him.

1 At what time does the dissipation of energy begin?

On realizing that his wife was planning an afternoon excursion
*Memories of a Scientific Life* (A. Fleming)

**Kemble, Charles** (1775–1854) British actor, specializing in comic roles. Father of the actress Fanny Kemble and brother of Sarah Siddons, he managed the Covent Garden Theatre from 1822.

1 Sir, I now pay you this exorbitant charge, but I must ask you to explain to her Majesty that she must not in future look upon me as a source of income.

On being obliged to hand over his income tax to the tax collector
*Humour in the Theatre* (J. Aye)

**Kemble, John Philip** (1757–1823) British tragic actor, brother of Charles Kemble. He managed the Drury Land and Covent Garden theatres.

1 Ladies and gentlemen, unless the play is stopped, the child cannot possibly go on.

Announcement to the audience when the play he was in was continually interrupted by a child crying
*A Book of Anecdotes* (D. George)

**Kempis, Thomas à** (Thomas Hemmerken; c. 1380–1471) German monk and writer. He is reputed to be the author of the religious treatise *The Imitation of Christ*.

1 *Sic transit gloria mundi.*
Thus the glory of the world passes away.
*The Imitation of Christ*, I

2 It is much safer to obey than to rule.
*The Imitation of Christ*, I

3 If you cannot mould yourself as you would wish, how can you expect other people to be entirely to your liking?
*The Imitation of Christ*, I

4 Man proposes but God disposes.
*The Imitation of Christ*, I

5 Would to God that we might spend a single day really well!
*The Imitation of Christ*, I

**Ken, Thomas** (1637–1711) English bishop. He was deprived of his see after refusing to take the oath of allegiance to William and Mary. He was also the author of many hymns.

1 Teach me to live, that I may dread
The grave as little as my bed.
*An Evening Hymn*

2 Redeem thy mis-spent time that's past;
Live this day, as if 'twere thy last.
*A Morning Hymn*

**Keneally, Thomas** (1935– ) Australian novelist. His books include *The Chant of Jimmie Blacksmith* (1972), the award-winning *Schindler's Ark* (1982), and *A Family Madness* (1985).

1 Pass a law to give every single wingeing bloody Pommie his fare home to England. Back to the smoke and the sun shining ten days a year and shit in the streets. Yer can have it.
*The Chant of Jimmy Blacksmith*

**Kennedy, John Fitzgerald** (1917–63) US statesman; the first Roman Catholic President (1961–63). His liberal New Frontier policies were cut short by his assassination.

1 It was involuntary. They sank my boat.

Responding to praise for his courage whilst serving in the US navy against the Japanese in World War II
*Nobody Said It Better* (M. Ringo)

2 I can't see that it's wrong to give him a little legal experience before he goes out to practice law.

On being criticized for making his brother Robert attorney general
*Nobody Said It Better* (M. Ringo)

3 I guess this is the week I earn my salary.

Comment made during the Cuban missile crisis
*Nobody Said It Better* (M. Ringo)

4 We must use time as a tool, not as a couch.
*The Observer*, 'Sayings of the Week', 10 Dec 1961

5 The United States has to move very fast to even stand still.
*The Observer*, 'Sayings of the Week', 21 July 1963

6 The worse I do, the more popular I get.

Referring to his popularity following the failure of the US invasion of Cuba
*The People's Almanac* (D. Wallechinsky)

7 Do you realize the responsibility I carry? I'm the only person standing between Nixon and the White House.

Said to Arthur Schlesinger, 13 Oct 1960; Richard Nixon was the Republican candidate in the 1960 US Presidential election
*A Thousand Days* (Arthur M. Schlesinger, Jnr)

8 We stand today on the edge of a new frontier.

Said on his nomination as Presidential candidate
Speech, Democratic Party Convention, 15 July 1960

9 And so, my fellow Americans: ask not what your country can do for you – ask what you can do for your country. My fellow citizens of the world: ask not what America will do for you, but what together we can do for the freedom of man.

Inaugural address, 20 Jan 1961

10 I think it's the most extraordinary collection of talent, of human knowledge, that has ever been gathered together at the White House – with the possible exception of when Thomas Jefferson dined alone.

Said at a dinner for Nobel Prizewinners, 29 Apr 1962

11 The war against hunger is truly mankind's war of liberation.

Speech, World Food Congress, 4 June 1963

12 If we cannot now end our differences, at least we can help make the world safe for diversity.

Speech, American University (Washington, DC), 10 June 1963

**13** All free men, wherever they may live, are citizens of Berlin. And therefore, as a free man, I take pride in the words *Ich bin ein Berliner*.
Speech, City Hall, West Berlin, 26 June 1963

**14** When power narrows the areas of man's concern, poetry reminds him of the richness and diversity of his existence.
Address at Dedication of the Robert Frost Library, 26 Oct 1963

**15** In free society art is not a weapon . . . Artists are not engineers of the soul.
Address at Dedication of the Robert Frost Library, 26 Oct 1963

**16** Victory has a thousand fathers but defeat is an orphan.
Attrib.

**Kennedy, Robert** (1925–68) US politician. Attorney general (1961–64) in his brother's administration, he became a senator in 1965 and was campaigning for the Democratic presidential nomination in 1968 when he was assassinated.

**1** One fifth of the people are against everything all the time.
*The Observer*, 'Sayings of the Week', 10 May 1964

**Kerouac, Jack** (1922–69) US novelist. His novel *On the Road* (1957) introduced the beat movement; subsequent books include *Big Sur* (1962) and *Desolation Angels* (1965).

**1** You can't teach the old maestro a new tune.
*On the Road*, Pt. I

**2** We're really all of us bottomly broke. I haven't had time to work in weeks.
*On the Road*, Pt. I

**3** I had nothing to offer anybody except my own confusion.
*On the Road*, Pt. II

**4** The beat generation.
Expression

**Kerr, Jean** (1923– ) US dramatist, screenwriter, and humorist. Her works include the screenplay for *Please Don't Eat the Daisies*.

**1** Man is the only animal that learns by being hypocritical. He pretends to be polite and then, eventually, he *becomes* polite.
*Finishing Touches*

**2** You don't seem to realize that a poor person who is unhappy is in a better position than a rich person who is unhappy. Because the poor person has hope. He thinks money would help.
*Poor Richard*

**3** Even though a number of people have tried, no one has yet found a way to drink for a living.
*Poor Richard*

**4** I feel about airplanes the way I feel about diets. It seems to me that they are wonderful things for other people to go on.
*The Snake Has All the Lines*, 'Mirror, Mirror, on the Wall'

**Key, Ellen** (Karolina Sofia Key; 1849–1926) Swedish writer and feminist. After teaching and lecturing in Sweden, she made a number of lecture tours abroad.

**1** . . . the emancipation of women is practically the greatest egoistic movement of the nineteenth century, and the most intense affirmation of the right of the self that history has yet seen . . .
*The Century of the Child*, Ch. 2

**2** At every step the child should be allowed to meet the real experiences of life; the thorns should never be plucked from his roses.
*The Century of the Child*, Ch. 3

**3** Nothing would more effectively further the development of education than for all flogging pedagogues to learn to educate with the head instead of with the hand.
*The Century of the Child*, Ch. 3

**4** Corporal punishment is as humiliating for him who gives it as for him who receives it; it is ineffective besides. Neither shame nor physical pain have any other effect than a hardening one . . .
*The Century of the Child*, Ch. 8

**5** Love is moral even without legal marriage, but marriage is immoral without love.
*The Morality of Woman and Other Essays*, 'The Morality of Woman'

**6** Formerly, a nation that broke the peace did not trouble to try and prove to the world that it was done solely from higher motives . . . *Now war has a bad conscience*. Now every nation assures us that it is bleeding for a human cause, the fate of which hangs in the balance of its victory. . . . No nation dares to admit the guilt of blood before the world.
*War, Peace, and the Future*, Preface

**7** Everything, everything in war is barbaric . . . But the worst barbarity of war is that it forces men collectively to commit acts against which individually they would revolt with their whole being.
*War, Peace, and the Future*, Ch. 6

**Key, Francis Scott** (1779–1843) US lawyer and writer of *The Star Spangled Banner*, first published in the Baltimore paper *American* in 1814.

**1** 'Tis the star-spangled banner; O long may it wave
O'er the land of the free, and the home of the brave!
*The Star-Spangled Banner*

**Keynes, John Maynard, Baron** (1883–1946) British economist. His *General Theory of Employment, Interest and Money* (1936), which supports increased public spending as a means of reducing unemployment, still has its advocates.

**1** In the long run we are all dead.
*Collected Writings*, 'A Tract on Monetary Reform'

2 I do not know which makes a man more conservative – to know nothing but the present, or nothing but the past.
*The End of Laisser-Faire,* I

3 Marxian Socialism must always remain a portent to the historians of Opinion – how a doctrine so illogical and so dull can have exercised so powerful and enduring an influence over the minds of men, and, through them, the events of history.
*The End of Laisser-Faire,* III

4 This goat-footed bard, this half-human visitor to our age from the hag-ridden magic and enchanted woods of Celtic antiquity.
Referring to Lloyd George
*Essays and Sketches in Biography*

5 Worldly wisdom teaches that it is better for the reputation to fail conventionally than to succeed unconventionally.
*The General Theory of Employment, Interest and Money,* Bk. IV, Ch. 12

6 It is better that a man should tyrannize over his bank balance than over his fellow citizens.
*The General Theory of Employment, Interest and Money,* Bk. VI, Ch. 24

7 Practical men, who believe themselves to be quite exempt from any intellectual influences, are usually the slaves of some defunct economist. Madmen in authority, who hear voices in the air, are distilling their frenzy from some academic scribbler of a few years back.
*The General Theory of Employment, Interest and Money,* Bk. VI, Ch. 24

8 I will not be a party to debasing the currency.
On refusing to pay more than a small tip on having his shoes polished, whilst on a visit to Africa
*John Maynard Keynes* (C. Hession)

9 Does that mean that because Americans won't listen to sense, you intend to talk nonsense to them?
Said before a monetary conference, 1944 or 1945

10 No, I don't know his telephone number. But it was up in the high numbers.
Attrib.

11 The avoidance of taxes is the only pursuit that still carries any reward.
Attrib.

**Khayyam, Omar** see Fitzgerald, Edward

**Khrushchev, Nikita** (1894–1971) Soviet statesman. Stalin's successor, he became prime minister (1958–64). As a result of his unsuccessful confrontation with Kennedy over the attempted installation of missiles in Cuba he was ousted from office.

1 We had no use for the policy of the Gospels: if someone slaps you, just turn the other cheek. We had shown that anyone who slapped us on our cheek would get his head kicked off.
*Khrushchev Remembers,* Vol. II

2 When you are skinning your customers, you should leave some skin on to grow so that you can skin them again.
Said to British businessmen
*The Observer,* 'Sayings of the Week', 28 May 1961

3 They talk about who won and who lost. Human reason won. Mankind won.
Referring to the Cuban missiles crisis
*The Observer,* 'Sayings of the Week', 11 Nov 1962

4 If you start throwing hedgehogs under me, I shall throw two porcupines under you.
*The Observer,* 'Sayings of the Week', 10 Nov 1963

5 Every year humanity takes a step towards Communism. Maybe not you, but at all events your grandson will surely be a Communist.
Said to Sir William Hayter, June 1956

6 We will bury you.
Said at a reception at the Kremlin, 26 Nov 1956

7 Politicians are the same all over. They promise to build a bridge even where there's no river.
Said to journalists while visiting the USA, Oct 1960

8 If you feed people just with revolutionary slogans they will listen today, they will listen tomorrow, they will listen the day after tomorrow, but on the fourth day they will say 'To hell with you!'
Attrib.

**Kierkegaard, Soren** (1813–55) Danish philosopher. His books, *The Concept of Irony* (1841), *Either-Or* (1843), and *Works of Love* (1847), influenced existentialism.

1 Job endured everything – until his friends came to comfort him, then he grew impatient.
*Journal*

2 That is the road we all have to take – over the Bridge of Sighs into eternity.
*Kierkegaard Anthology* (Auden)

**Kilmer, Alfred Joyce** (1886–1918) US poet, who was killed in action in World War I. His verse collections include *Summer of Love* (1911) and *Trees and Other Poems* (1914).

1 I think that I shall never see
A poem lovely as a tree.
*Trees*

2 Poems are made by fools like me,
But only God can make a tree.
*Trees*

**Kilvert, Francis** (1840–79) British diarist and clergyman. His diary, written in the Welsh marches in the 1870s, was published in 1938.

1 Of all noxious animals, too, the most noxious is a tourist. And of all tourists the most vulgar, ill-bred, offensive and loathsome is the British tourist.
*Diary,* 5 Apr 1870

2 It is a fine thing to be out on the hills alone. A man can hardly be a beast or a fool alone on a great mountain.
*Diary,* 29 May 1871

**King, Benjamin Franklin** (1857–94) American humorist.

**1** Nothing to do but work,
Nothing to eat but food,
Nothing to wear but clothes,
To keep one from going nude.

*The Pessimist*

**King, Martin Luther** (1929–68) US Black clergyman and
civil-rights leader. His nonviolent demonstrations led to the Civil
Rights Act (1964). He was awarded the Nobel Peace Prize in 1964
and assassinated four years later.

**1** A riot is at bottom the language of the unheard.

*Chaos or Community*, Ch. 4

**2** I want to be the white man's brother, not his
brother-in-law.

*New York Journal-American*, 10 Sept 1962

**3** I have a dream that one day this nation will rise
up, live out the true meaning of its creed: we
hold these truths to be self-evident, that all
men are created equal.

He used the words 'I have a dream' in a number of speeches
Speech, Washington, 27 Aug 1963

**Kingsley, Charles** (1819–75) British writer and clergyman.
A chaplain to Queen Victoria, he is remembered for his novels,
including *Westward Ho!* (1855) and the children's book *The Water
Babies* (1863).

**1** Be good, sweet maid, and let who can be clever;
Do lovely things, not dream them, all day long;
And so make Life, and Death, and that For
Ever,
One grand sweet song.

*A Farewell. To C. E. G.*

**2** To be discontented with the divine discontent,
and to be ashamed with the noble shame, is the
very germ and first upgrowth of all virtue.

*Health and Education*

**3** We have used the Bible as if it was a constable's
handbook – an opium-dose for keeping beasts
of burden patient while they are being
overloaded.

*Letters to the Chartists*, 2

**4** 'O Mary, go and call the cattle home,
And call the cattle home,
And call the cattle home,
Across the sands of Dee.'
The western wind was wild and dank with foam,
And all alone went she.

*The Sands of Dee*

**5** The western tide crept up along the sand,
And o'er and o'er the sand,
And round and round the sand,
As far as eye could see.
The rolling mist came down and hid the land:
And never home came she.

*The Sands of Dee*

**6** When all the world is young, lad,
And all the trees are green;
And every goose a swan, lad,
And every lass a queen;
Then hey for boot and horse, lad,
And round the world away:
Young blood must have its course, lad,
And every dog his day.

*Songs from The Water Babies*, 'Young and Old'

**7** For men must work, and women must weep,
And there's little to earn, and many to keep,
Though the harbour bar be moaning.

*The Three Fishers*

**8** He did not know that a keeper is only a poacher
turned outside in, and a poacher a keeper
turned inside out.

*The Water Babies*, Ch. 1

**9** More ways of killing a cat than choking her with
cream.

*Westward Ho!*, Ch. 20

**10** Some say that the age of chivalry is past, that
the spirit of romance is dead. The age of chivalry
is never past, so long as there is a wrong left
unredressed on earth.

*Life* (Mrs C. Kingsley), Vol. II, Ch. 28

**Kinnock, Neil** (1942– ) British politician; leader of the
Labour Party since 1983.

**1** It is inconceivable that we could transform this
society without a major extension of public
ownership.

*Marxism Today*, 1983 ownership

**2** Proportional Representation, I think, is fundamentally counter-democratic.

*Marxism Today*, 1983

**3** You cannot fashion a wit out of two half-wits.

*The Times*, 1983

**4** We cannot remove the evils of capitalism without
taking its source of power: ownership.

*Tribune*, 1975

**5** I'm prepared to take advice on leisure from
Prince Philip. He's a world expert on leisure.
He's been practising for most of his adult life.

*Western Mail*, 1981

**6** Compassion is not a sloppy, sentimental feeling
for people who are underprivileged or sick . . .
it is an absolutely practical belief that, regardless of a person's background, ability or ability to
pay, he should be provided with the best that
society has to offer.

Maiden speech, House of Commons, 1970

**7** Like Brighton pier, all right as far as it goes, but
inadequate for getting to France.

Speech, House of Commons, 1981

8 Those who prate about Blimpish patriotism in the mode of Margaret Thatcher are also the ones who will take millions off the caring services of this country.
Speech, Labour Party Conference, Brighton, 1983

9 The grotesque chaos of a Labour council – a *Labour* council – hiring taxis to scuttle around a city handing out redundancy notices to its own workers.
Attacking militant members in Liverpool
Speech, Labour Party Conference, Bournemouth, 1985

10 Political renegades always start their career of treachery as 'the best men of all parties' and end up in the Tory knackery.
Speech, Welsh Labour Party Conference, 1985

11 The idea that there is a model Labour voter, a blue-collar council house tenant who belongs to a union and has 2.4 children, a five-year-old car and a holiday in Blackpool, is patronizing and politically immature.
Speech, 1986

12 I would die for my country . . . but I would not let my country die for me.
Speech on nuclear disarmament, 1987

**Kipling, (Joseph) Rudyard** (1865–1936) Indian-born British writer and poet. His verse collection *Barrack Room Ballads and Other Verses* (1892) included the well-known poems 'If' and 'Gunga Din'. Other works were the *Jungle Books* (1894, 1895), *Kim* (1901) and the children's books *Just So Stories* (1902) and *Puck of Pook's Hill* (1906).

1 Oh, East is East, and West is West, and never the twain shall meet.
*The Ballad of East and West*

2 And a woman is only a woman, but a good cigar is a smoke.
*The Betrothed*

3 Teach us delight in simple things,
And mirth that has no bitter springs;
Forgiveness free of evil done,
And love to all men 'neath the sun!
*The Children's Song*

4 But the Devil whoops, as he whooped of old:
'It's clever, but is it art?'
*The Conundrum of the Workshops*

5 'For they're hangin' Danny Deever, you can hear the Dead March play,
The Regiment's in 'ollow square – they're hangin' 'im to-day;
They've taken of 'is buttons off an' cut 'is stripes away,
An' they're hangin' Danny Deever in the mornin'.'
*Danny Deever*

6 Winds of the World, give answer! They are whimpering to and fro –
And what should they know of England who only England know?
*The English Flag*

7 When the Himalayan peasant meets the he-bear in his pride,
He shouts to scare the monster, who will often turn aside.
But the she-bear thus accosted rends the peasant tooth and nail
For the female of the species is more deadly than the male.
*The Female of the Species*

8 So 'ere's to you, Fuzzy-Wuzzy, at your 'ome in the Soudan;
You're a pore benighted 'eathen but a first-class fightin' man;
An' 'ere's to you, Fuzzy-Wuzzy, with your 'ayrick 'ead of 'air –
You big black boundin' beggar – for you broke a British square!
*Fuzzy-Wuzzy*

9 We're poor little lambs who've lost our way,
Baa! Baa! Baa!
We're little black sheep who've gone astray,
Baa-aa-aa!
Gentleman-rankers out on the spree,
Damned from here to Eternity,
God ha' mercy on such as we,
Baa! Yah! Bah!
*Gentleman-Rankers*

10 Oh, Adam was a gardener, and God who made him sees
That half a proper gardener's work is done upon his knees,
So when your work is finished, you can wash your hands and pray
For the Glory of the Garden, that it may not pass away!
*The Glory of the Garden*

11 The uniform 'e wore
Was nothin' much before,
An' rather less than 'arf o' that be'ind.
*Gunga Din*

12 An' for all 'is dirty 'ide
'E was white, clear white, inside
When 'e went to tend the wounded under fire!
*Gunga Din*

13 Though I've belted you an' flayed you,
By the livin' Gawd that made you,
You're a better man than I am, Gunga Din!
*Gunga Din*

14 If you can keep your head when all about you
Are losing theirs and blaming it on you.
*If*

**15** If you can talk with crowds and keep your
virtue,
Or walk with Kings – nor lose the common
touch,
If neither foes nor loving friends can hurt you,
If all men count with you, but none too much;
If you can fill the unforgiving minute
With sixty seconds' worth of distance run,
Yours is the Earth and everything that's in it,
And – which is more – you'll be a Man my son!
*If*

**16** Asia is not going to be civilized after the methods of the West. There is too much Asia and
she is too old.
*Life's Handicap*, 'The Man Who Was'

**17** The Light that Failed.
Novel title

**18** The Saxon is not like us Normans. His manners
are not so polite.
But he never means anything serious till he talks
about justice and right,
When he stands like an ox in the furrow with his
sullen set eyes on your own,
And grumbles, 'This isn't fair dealing,' my son,
leave the Saxon alone.
*Norman and Saxon*

**19** The silliest woman can manage a clever man; but
it needs a very clever woman to manage a fool.
*Plain Tales from the Hills*, 'Three and – an Extra'

**20** If, drunk with sight of power, we loose
Wild tongues that have not Thee in awe,
Such boastings as the Gentiles use,
Or lesser breeds without the Law.
*Recessional*

**21** On the road to Mandalay
Where the flyin'-fishes play.
*The Road to Mandalay*

**22** I am sick o' wastin' leather on these gritty
pavin'-stones,
An' the blasted English drizzle wakes the fever
in my bones;
Tho' I walks with fifty 'ousemaids outer Chelsea
to the Strand,
An' they talks a lot o' lovin', but wot do they
understand?
Beefy face an' grubby 'and –
Law! Wot do they understand?
I've a neater, sweeter maiden in a cleaner,
greener land!
*The Road to Mandalay*

**23** Ship me somewheres east of Suez, where the
best is like the worst,
Where there aren't no Ten Commandments, an'
a man can raise a thirst:
For the temple-bells are callin', an' it's there that
I would be –
By the old Moulmein Pagoda, looking lazy at the
sea.
*The Road to Mandalay*

**24** Being kissed by a man who didn't wax his moustache was – like eating an egg without salt.
*Soldiers Three*, 'The Gadsbys, Poor Dear Mamma'

**25** No one thinks of winter when the grass is green!
*A St Helena Lullaby*

**26** Oh, it's Tommy this, an' Tommy that, an' 'Tommy, go away';
But it's 'Thank you, Mister Atkins,' when the
band begins to play.
*Tommy*

**27** It's Tommy this, an' Tommy that, an' 'Chuck
him out, the brute!'
But it's 'Saviour of 'is country' when the guns
begin to shoot.
*Tommy*

**28** They shut the road through the woods
Seventy years ago.
Weather and rain have undone it again,
And now you would never know
There was once a road through the woods.
*The Way Through the Woods*

**29** Take up the White Man's burden –
And reap his old reward:
The blame of those ye better,
The hate of those ye guard.
*The White Man's Burden*

**30** I've just read that I am dead. Don't forget to de-
lete me from your list of subscribers.
Writing to a magazine that had mistakenly published an announcement of his death
*Anekdotenschatz* (H. Hoffmeister)

**31** A Soldier of the Great War Known unto God.
The words he selected to be inscribed on the headstones of the
graves of unknown soldiers when he was literary adviser for
the Imperial War Graves Commission, 1919
*Silent Cities* (ed. Gavin Stamp)

**32** Words are, of course, the most powerful drug
used by mankind.
Speech, 14 Feb 1923

**33** Power without responsibility – the prerogative
of the harlot throughout the ages.
Better known for its subsequent use by BALDWIN
Attrib.

**Kissinger, Henry** (1923– ) German-born US politician and
diplomat. Secretary of State (1973–76), he helped to negotiate an
end to the Vietnam war and, with his shuttle diplomacy, a truce
between Syria and Israel (1974). His books include *Nuclear
Weapons and Foreign Policy* (1956) and *Years of Upheaval* (1982).

**1** The conventional army loses if it does not win.
The guerrilla wins if he does not lose.
*Foreign Affairs*, XIII (Jan 1969), 'The Vietnam Negotiations'

**2** Power is the ultimate aphrodisiac.
*The Guardian*, 28 Nov 1976

**3** We are all the President's men.
Said regarding the invasion of Cambodia, 1970
*The Sunday Times Magazine*, 4 May 1975

**4** Even a paranoid can have enemies.
*Time*, 24 Jan 1977

**Kitchener (of Khartoum), Horatio Herbert, Earl** (1850–1916) British field marshal. He reconquered the Sudan (1898) and became its governor general (1899). In World War I he became war secretary; he initiated a successful recruitment campaign but did not achieve effective power.

1 I don't mind your being killed, but I object to your being taken prisoner.

Said to the Prince of Wales (later Edward VIII) when he asked to go to the Front
*Journal* (Viscount Esher), 18 Dec 1914

**Klinger, Friedrich Maximilian von** (1752–1831) German dramatist and novelist. His best-known play is *Sturm und Drang* (1776).

1 *Sturm und Drang.*
Storm and stress.

Used to designate a late 18th-century literary movement in Germany
Play title

**Knox, John** (c. 1514–72) Scottish religious reformer. A Protestant, he became chaplain to Edward VI of England. After Mary I's accession he returned to Scotland and became the leading Protestant reformer there.

1 A man with God is always in the majority.

Inscription, Reformation Monument, Geneva, Switzerland

2 The First Blast of the Trumpet Against the Monstrous Regiment of Women.

Title of Pamphlet, 1558

**Knox, Philander Chase** (1853–1921) US lawyer and politician. He served as attorney general (1901–04) and secretary of state (1909–13).

1 Oh, Mr. President, do not let so great an achievement suffer from any taint of legality.

Responding to Theodore Roosevelt's request for legal justification of his acquisition of the Panama Canal Zone
*Violent Neighbours* (T. Buckley)

**Knox, Ronald (Arbuthnot)** (1888–1957) British Roman Catholic priest and writer. He is remembered for his translation of the Vulgate (1945–49) and *A Spiritual Aeneid* (1918).

1 It is so stupid of modern civilization to have given up believing in the devil when he is the only explanation of it.

*Let Dons Delight*

2 The baby doesn't understand English and the Devil knows Latin.

Said when asked to conduct a baptism service in English
*Ronald Knox* (Evelyn Waugh), Pt. I, Ch. 5

3 A loud noise at one end and no sense of responsibility at the other.

Definition of a baby
Attrib.

4 There once was a man who said 'God
Must think it exceedingly odd
If he find that this tree
Continues to be
When there's no one about in the Quad.'

For a reply, see ANONYMOUS
Attrib.

**Knox, Vicesimus** (1752–1821) British essayist and supporter of feminism.

1 Can anything be more absurd than keeping women in a state of ignorance, and yet so vehemently to insist on their resisting temptation?

*Liberal Education*, Vol. I, 'On the Literary Education of Women'

**Koestler, Arthur** (1905–83) Hungarian-born British writer and novelist. His novels include *Darkness at Noon* (1940), *Thieves in the Night* (1946), and *The Call Girls* (1972). Nonfiction concerned politics, as in *The Yogi and the Commissar* (1945), or scientific creativity, as in *The Act of Creation* (1964) and *The Ghost in the Machine* (1967). He and his wife committed suicide when his Parkinson's disease became intolerable.

1 One may not regard the world as a sort of metaphysical brothel for emotions.

*Darkness at Noon*, 'The Second Hearing'

2 If the creator had a purpose in equipping us with a neck, he surely meant us to stick it out.

*Encounter*, May 1970

3 Two half-truths do not make a truth, and two half-cultures do not make a culture.

*The Ghost in the Machine*, Preface

4 The most persistent sound which reverberates through men's history is the beating of war drums.

*Janus: A Summing Up*, Prologue

5 A writer's ambition should be to trade a hundred contemporary readers for ten readers in ten years' time and for one reader in a hundred years' time.

*New York Times Book Review*, 1 Apr 1951

6 Hitherto man had to live with the idea of death as an individual; from now onward mankind will have to live with the idea of its death as a species.

Referring to the development of the atomic bomb
*Peter's Quotations* (Laurence J. Peter)

**Kollwitz, Käthe** (1867–1945) German sculptor and graphic artist. Deeply concerned about social injustice, many of her works depicted victims of urban poverty, war, and fascism.

1 I do not want to die . . . until I have faithfully made the most of my talent and cultivated the seed that was placed in me until the last small twig has grown.

*Diaries and Letters*, 15 Feb 1915

**Korda, Sir Alexander** (Sandor Kellner; 1893–1956) Hungarian-born British film director and producer. His successes include *The Scarlet Pimpernel* (1934) and *Anna Karenina* (1948).

1 It's not enough to be Hungarian, you must have talent too.

*Alexander Korda* (K. Kulik)

**Kristofferson, Kris** (1936– ) US film actor and former folk musician.

1 Freedom's just another word for nothing left to lose.

*Me and Bobby McGee*

**Kubrick, Stanley** (1928– ) US film director and writer. His leading films include *Dr Strangelove* (1963), *2001: A Space Odyssey* (1968), and *A Clockwork Orange* (1971).

1 The great nations have always acted like gangsters, and the small nations like prostitutes.
*The Guardian*, 5 June 1963

## L

**Labouchère, Henry, Baron Taunton** (1798–1869) British statesman. He was president of the Board of Trade (1839–41; 1847–52) and colonial secretary (1855–58).

1 I do not object to Gladstone's always having the ace of trumps up his sleeve, but only to his pretence that God had put it there.
Attrib.

**La Bruyère, Jean de** (1645–96) French satirist. He served in the household of Louis II and wrote one book of lasting merit *Les Caractères de Théophraste* (1688).

1 A pious man is one who would be an atheist if the king were.
*Les Caractères*

2 The majority of men devote the greater part of their lives to making their remaining years unhappy.
*Les Caractères*

3 There are some who speak one moment before they think.
*Les Caractères*

4 The pleasure of criticizing robs us of the pleasure of being moved by some very fine things.
*Les Caractères*

5 Liberality lies less in giving liberally than in the timeliness of the gift.
*Les Caractères*

6 There are only three events in a man's life; birth, life, and death; he is not conscious of being born, he dies in pain, and he forgets to live.
*Les Caractères*

7 Women run to extremes; they are either better or worse than men.
*Les Caractères*

8 One must laugh before one is happy, or one may die without ever laughing at all.
*Les Caractères*

9 Party loyalty lowers the greatest of men to the petty level of the masses.
*Les Caractères*

10 There exist some evils so terrible and some misfortunes so horrible that we dare not think of them, whilst their very aspect makes us shudder; but if they happen to fall on us, we find ourselves stronger than we imagined, we grapple with our ill luck, and behave better than we expected we should.
*Les Caractères*

11 If poverty is the mother of crime, stupidity is its father.
*Les Caractères*

12 'There is a report that Piso is dead; it is a great loss; he was an honest man, who deserved to live longer; he was intelligent and agreeable, resolute and courageous, to be depended upon, generous and faithful.' Add: 'provided he is really dead'.
*Les Caractères*

13 If we heard it said of Orientals that they habitually drank a liquor which went to their heads, deprived them of reason and made them vomit, we should say: 'How very barbarous!'
*Les Caractères*

14 To endeavour to forget anyone is a certain way of thinking of nothing else.
*Les Caractères*

15 A slave has but one master; an ambitious man has as many masters as there are people who may be useful in bettering his position.
*Les Caractères*

16 The shortest and best way to make your fortune is to let people see clearly that it is in their interests to promote yours.
*Les Caractères*

**La Fontaine, Jean de** (1621–95) French poet. His *Fables* (1668–94) was his major work. He repudiated his somewhat bawdy *Contes* (1664) after his religious conversion in 1692.

1 Rather suffer than die is man's motto.
*Fables*, I, 'La Mort et le Bûcheron'

2 Be advised that all flatterers live at the expense of those who listen to them.
*Fables*, I, 'Le Corbeau et le Renard'

3 One should oblige everyone to the extent of one's ability. One often needs someone smaller than oneself.
*Fables*, II, 'Le Lion et le Rat'

4 Patience and passage of time do more than strength and fury.
*Fables*, II, 'Le Lion et le Rat'

5 This fellow did not see further than his own nose.
*Fables*, III, 'Le Renard et le Bouc'

6 A mountain in labour shouted so loud that everyone, summoned by the noise, ran up expecting that she would be delivered of a city bigger than Paris; she brought forth a mouse.
*Fables*, V, 'La Montagne qui accouche'

7 He told me never to sell the bear's skin before one has killed the beast.
*Fables*, V, 'L'Ours et les deux Compagnons'

**8** People must help one another; it is nature's law.

*Fables*, VIII, 'L'Âne et le Chien'

**9** A hungry stomach has no ears.

*Fables*, IX, 'Le Milan et le Rossignol'

**10** What God does, He does well.

*Fables*, IX, 'Le Gland et la Citrouille'

**11** But the shortest works are always the best.

*Fables*, X, 'Les Lapins'

**Laing, R(onald) D(avid)** (1927–  ) British psychiatrist. His radical views on schizophrenia are set out in his books *The Divided Self* (1960), *The Politics of Experience* (1967), and *The Politics of the Family* (1971). *Knots* (1970) is a collection of his poetry.

**1** The statesmen of the world who boast and threaten that they have Doomsday weapons are far more dangerous, and far more estranged from 'reality', than many of the people on whom the label 'psychotic' is affixed.

*The Divided Self*, Preface

**2** Schizophrenia cannot be understood without understanding despair.

*The Divided Self*, Ch. 2

**3** Few books today are forgivable.

*The Politics of Experience*, Introduction

**4** We are effectively destroying ourselves by violence masquerading as love.

*The Politics of Experience*, Ch. 13

**5** Madness need not be all breakdown. It may also be break-through. It is potential liberation and renewal as well as enslavement and existential death.

*The Politics of Experience*, Ch. 16

**Lamb, A. J.** (1870–1928) British songwriter.

**1** She's only a bird in a gilded cage.

*Song title*

**Lamb, Lady Caroline** (1785–1828) The wife of William Lamb (who became the Whig prime minister, Viscount Melbourne). She had a much publicized affair with Lord Byron and wrote a novel, *Glenavon* (1816), containing idealized portraits of herself and Byron. She died insane.

**1** Mad, bad, and dangerous to know.

*Said of Byron*
*Journal*

**Lamb, Charles** (1775–1834) British essayist. He is best remembered for his *Essays of Elia* (1822).

**1** Nothing is to me more distasteful than that entire complacency and satisfaction which beam in the countenances of a new-married couple.

*Essays of Elia*, 'A Bachelor's Complaint of Married People'

**2** We are nothing; less than nothing, and dreams. We are only what might have been, and must wait upon the tedious shores of Lethe millions of ages before we have existence, and a name.

In Greek mythology, Lethe was a river in the underworld, whose waters were drunk by souls about to be reborn in order to forget their past lives
*Essays of Elia*, 'Dream Children'

**3** I hate a man who swallows it, affecting not to know what he is eating. I suspect his taste in higher matters.

Referring to food
*Essays of Elia*, 'Grace before Meat'

**4** I have been trying all my life to like Scotchmen, and am obliged to desist from the experiment in despair.

*Essays of Elia*, 'Imperfect Sympathies'

**5** Man is a gaming animal. He must always be trying to get the better in something or other.

*Essays of Elia*, 'Mrs Battle's Opinions on Whist'

**6** In everything that relates to science, I am a whole Encyclopaedia behind the rest of the world.

*Essays of Elia*, 'The Old and the New Schoolmaster'

**7** Boys are capital fellows in their own way, among their mates; but they are unwholesome companions for grown people.

*Essays of Elia*, 'The Old and the New Schoolmaster'

**8** The human species, according to the best theory I can form of it, is composed of two distinct races, the men who borrow, and the men who lend.

*Essays of Elia*, 'The Two Races of Men'

**9** Borrowers of books – those mutilators of collections, spoilers of the symmetry of shelves, and creators of odd volumes.

*Essays of Elia*, 'The Two Races of Men'

**10** Credulity is the man's weakness, but the child's strength.

*Essays of Elia*, 'Witches and other Night Fears'

**11** I love to lose myself in other men's minds. When I am not walking, I am reading; I cannot sit and think. Books think for me.

*Last Essays of Elia*, 'Detached Thoughts on Books and Reading'

**12** Newspapers always excite curiosity. No one ever lays one down without a feeling of disappointment.

*Last Essays of Elia*, 'Detached Thoughts on Books and Reading'

**13** A poor relation – is the most irrelevant thing in nature.

*Last Essays of Elia*, 'Poor Relations'

**14** It is a pistol let off at the ear; not a feather to tickle the intellect.

Referring to the nature of a pun
*Last Essays of Elia*, 'Popular Fallacies'

15 How sickness enlarges the dimensions of a man's self to himself.

*Last Essays of Elia, 'The Convalescent'*

16 The greatest pleasure I know, is to do a good action by stealth, and to have it found out by accident.

*The Athenaeum, 'Table Talk by the late Elia', 4 Jan 1834*

17 I have had playmates, I have had companions
In my days of childhood, in my joyful schooldays
—
All, all are gone, the old familiar faces.

*The Old Familiar Faces*

18 Riddle of destiny, who can show
What thy short visit meant, or know
What thy errand here below?

*On an Infant Dying as soon as Born*

19 Damn the age. I'll write for antiquity.

Referring to his lack of payment for the *Essays of Elia*
*English Wits* (L. Russell)

20 Dr Parr . . . asked him, how he had acquired his power of smoking at such a rate? Lamb replied, 'I toiled after it, sir, as some men toil after virtue.'

*Memoirs of Charles Lamb* (Talfourd)

21 I came home . . . hungry as a hunter.

Letter to Coleridge, Apr 1800

22 Separate from the pleasure of your company, I don't much care if I never see another mountain in my life.

Letter to William Wordsworth, 30 Jan 1801

23 A little thin, flowery border, round, neat, not gaudy.

Letter to Wordsworth, June 1806

24 This very night I am going to leave off tobacco! Surely there must be some other world in which this unconquerable purpose shall be realized. The soul hath not her generous aspirings implanted in her in vain.

Letter to Thomas Manning, 26 Dec 1815

**Lamb, Mary** (1764–1847) Sister of Charles Lamb. She killed her mother in a fit of insanity and was looked after by her brother until he, himself, became insane.

1 A child's a plaything for an hour.

*Parental Recollections*

**Lampton, William James** (1859–1917) British writer.

1 Same old slippers,
Same old rice,
Same old glimpse of
Paradise.

*June Weddings*

**Lancaster, Osbert** (1908–86) British cartoonist and writer of many books on architecture, including *Pillar to Post* (1938).

1 'Fan vaulting' . . . an architectural device which arouses enormous enthusiasm on account of the difficulties it has all too obviously involved but which from an aesthetic standpoint frequently belongs to the 'Last-supper-carved-on-a-peach-stone' class of masterpiece.

*Pillar to Post, 'Perpendicular'*

2 A hundred and fifty accurate reproductions of Anne Hathaway's cottage, each complete with central heating and garage.

*Pillar to Post, 'Stockbrokers Tudor'*

**Lanchester, Elsa** (1902–86) British-born US actress, married to Charles Laughton. Her many films include *The Bride of Frankenstein* (1935), *Bell, Book, and Candle* (1957), and *Mary Poppins* (1964).

1 She looked as though butter wouldn't melt in her mouth – or anywhere else.

Referring to Maureen O'Hara
Attrib.

**Landon, Letitia** (1802–38) British poet and novelist. She sometimes used the initials L.E.L. as a pen name. Her verse collections include *The Venetian Bracelet* (1829); her best-known novel is *Ethel Churchill* (1837).

1 Were it not better to forget
Than but remember and regret?

*Despondency*

2 Few, save the poor, feel for the poor.

*The Poor*

3 We might have been – These are but common words,
And yet they make the sum of life's bewailing.

*Three Extracts from the Diary of a Week*

**Landor, Walter Savage** (1775–1864) British poet and writer. His collections include *Imaginary Conversations of Literary Men and Statesmen* (1824–29), *Hellenics* (1847), and *Dry Sticks, Fagoted* (1858).

1 Stand close around, ye Stygian set,
With Dirce in one boat conveyed!
Or Charon, seeing, may forget
That he is old and she a shade.

In Greek mythology, Dirce, a follower of Dionysius, was killed by her great-nephews Amphion and Zethus because of her mistreatment of their mother Antiope; Charon was the ferryman who transported dead souls across the River Styx to the underworld
*Dirce*

2 Prose on certain occasions can bear a great deal of poetry: on the other hand, poetry sinks and swoons under a moderate weight of prose.

*Imaginary Conversations, 'Archdeacon Hare and Walter Landor'*

3 Goodness does not more certainly make men happy than happiness makes them good.

*Imaginary Conversations, 'Lord Brooke and Sir Philip Sidney'*

4 States, like men, have their growth, their manhood, their decrepitude, their decay.

*Imaginary Conversations, 'Pollio and Calvus'*

**5** Clear writers, like clear fountains, do not seem so deep as they are; the turbid look the most profound.
*Imaginary Conversations*, 'Southey and Porson'

**6** Fleas know not whether they are upon the body of a giant or upon one of ordinary size.
*Imaginary Conversations*, 'Southey and Porson'

**7** I strove with none; for none was worth my strife;
Nature I loved, and, next to Nature, Art;
I warmed both hands before the fire of life;
It sinks, and I am ready to depart.
*I Strove with None*

**8** Good God, I forgot the violets!
Having thrown his cook out of an open window onto the flowerbed below
*Irreverent Social History* (F. Muir)

**Landseer, Sir Edwin Henry** (1802–73) British painter and sculptor. His Highland paintings were popular with Queen Victoria; his four bronze lions stand at the foot of Nelson's column in Trafalgar Square, London.

**1** If people only knew as much about painting as I do, they would never buy my pictures.
Said to W. P. Frith
*Landseer the Victorian Paragon* (Campbell Lennie), Ch. 12

**Lang, Andrew** (1844–1912) Scottish writer and poet. His historical writings include *A History of Scotland* (1900–07) and *John Knox and the Reformation* (1905). His *Custom and Myth* (1884) was an important work of literary mythology and his poetry included the popular collection *Grass of Parnassus* (1888).

**1** He uses statistics as a drunken man uses lampposts – for support rather than illumination.
*Treasury of Humorous Quotations*

**Lang, Julia S.** (1921– ) British broadcaster who presented the BBC children's radio series *Listen With Mother*.

**1** Are you sitting comfortably? Then I'll begin.
Introduction to the story in *Listen with Mother*

**Langbridge, Frederick** (1849–1923) British religious writer.

**1** Two men look out through the same bars:
One sees the mud, and one the stars.
*A Cluster of Quiet Thoughts*

**Langland, William** (c. 1330–c. 1400) English poet. He was the reputed author of the allegorical poem *The Vision of Piers Plowman*.

**1** In a somer season, when soft was the sonne.
*The Vision of Piers Plowman*, Prologue

**2** Dowel, Dobet and Dobest.
Do well, Do better, and Do Best: three concepts central to the search for Truth in *Piers Plowman*, in which they appear as allegorical characters
*The Vision of Piers Plowman*

**Laplace, Pierre-Simon, Marquis de** (1749–1827) French mathematician and astronomer. His major work *Mécanique céleste* (1799–1825) reported work he did with Lagrange (although Lagrange was not credited).

**1** I have no need of that hypothesis.
On being asked by Napoleon why he had made no mention of God in his book about the universe, *Mécanique céleste*. See also BONHOEFFER
*Men of Mathematics* (E. Bell)

**Lardner, Ring, Jnr** (1885–1933) American humorist and writer of short stories. His books include *Gullible's Travels* (1917), *The Big Town* (1921), and *What of It?* (1925).

**1** He looked at me as if I was a side dish he hadn't ordered.
Referring to W. H. Taft, US president (1909–13)
*The Home Book of Humorous Quotations* (A. K. Adams)

**2** How do you look when I'm sober?
Speaking to a flamboyantly dressed stranger who walked into the club where he was drinking
*Ring* (J. Yardley)

**3** Frenchmen drink wine just like we used to drink water before Prohibition.
*Wit's End* (R. E. Drennan)

**Larkin, Philip** (1922–85) British poet. Collections include *The Whitsun Weddings* (1964) and *High Windows* (1974). He also edited *The Oxford Book of Twentieth Century Verse* (1973) and wrote two novels.

**1** Clearly money has something to do with life
– In fact, they've a lot in common, if you enquire:
You can't put off being young until you retire.
*Money*

**2** Perhaps being old is having lighted rooms
Inside your head, and people in them, acting.
People you know, yet can't quite name.
*The Old Fools*

**3** Get stewed:
Books are a load of crap.
*A Study of Reading Habits*

**4** They fuck you up, your mum and dad.
They may not mean to, but they do.
They fill you with the faults they had
And add some extra, just for you.
*This be the Verse*

**5** Far too many relied on the classic formula of a beginning, a muddle, and an end.
Referring to modern novels
*New Fiction*, 15 (January 1978)

**Laski, H(arold) J(oseph)** (1893–1950) British political theorist. A socialist and teacher at the London School of Economics, he became leader of the Labour Party during Attlee's administration, although his Marxist leanings failed to influence the parliamentary party.

**1** The meek do not inherit the earth unless they are prepared to fight for their meekness.
Attrib.

**Latimer, Hugh** (1485–1555) English churchman, who became an advisor to Henry VIII after showing his Protestant inclinations. On the accession of the Roman Catholic Queen Mary, he was imprisoned and burnt at the stake with Nicholas Ridley for refusing to acknowledge Catholic doctrines.

1 The drop of rain maketh a hole in the stone, not by violence, but by oft falling.
*See also* LUCRETIUS; OVID
Sermon preached before Edward VI

2 Be of good comfort, Master Ridley, and play the man; we shall this day light such a candle, by God's grace, in England as I trust shall never be put out.
Said to Nicholas Ridley as they were about to be burnt at the stake for heresy
*Famous Last Words* (B. Conrad)

**Lauder, Sir Harry** (Hugh MacLennon; 1870–1950) Scottish music-hall artist. His famous songs included 'I Love a Lassie' and 'Roamin' in the Gloamin".

1 Just a wee deoch-an-duoris
Before we gang awa' . . .
If y' can say
It's a braw brecht moonlecht necht,
Yer a' recht, that's a'.
Song

2 O! it's nice to get up in the mornin',
But it's nicer to stay in bed.
Song

3 Roamin' in the gloamin',
By the bonny banks of Clyde.
Song

4 I love a lassie.
Song title

5 Keep right on to the end of the road.
Song title

**Laurence, William L.** (1888–1977) US journalist.

1 At first it was a giant column that soon took the shape of a supramundane mushroom.
Referring to the explosion of the first atomic bomb, over Hiroshima, 6 Aug 1945
*The New York Times*, 26 Sept 1945

**Law, (Andrew) Bonar** (1858–1923) British statesman. He became Conservative prime minister (1922–23) after Lloyd George's resignation from the coalition, in which Bonar Law had been chancellor of the exchequer.

1 I must follow them; I am their leader.
*Mr Balfour* (E. T. Raymond), Ch. 15

2 If, therefore, war should ever come between these two countries, which Heaven forbid! it will not, I think, be due to irresistible natural laws, it will be due to the want of human wisdom.
Referring to the UK and Germany
Speech, House of Commons, 27 Nov 1911

3 We have heard of people being thrown to the wolves, but never before have we heard of a man being thrown to the wolves with a bargain on the part of the wolves that they would not eat him.
Referring to the fact that the then war minister, Col Seely, had offered his resignation
Speech, House of Commons, Mar 1914

4 If I am a great man, then a good many of the great men of history are frauds.
Attrib.

5 Look at that man's eyes. You will hear more of him later.
Referring to Mussolini
Attrib.

**Lawrence, D(avid) H(erbert)** (1885–1930) British novelist. The son of a coalminer, he earned his reputation with the autobiographical *Sons and Lovers* (1913). Subsequent novels include *Women in Love* (1921), *Kangaroo* (1923), and *Lady Chatterley's Lover* (1928).

1 You must always be a-waggle with LOVE.
*Bibbles*

2 The English people on the whole are surely the *nicest* people in the world, and everyone makes everything so easy for everybody else, that there is almost nothing to resist at all.
*Dull London*

3 To the Puritan all things are impure, as somebody says.
*Etruscan Places*, 'Cerveteri'

4 The Romans and Greeks found everything human. Everything had a face, and a human voice. Men spoke, and their fountains piped an answer.
*Fantasia of the Unconscious*, Ch. 4

5 The refined punishments of the spiritual mode are usually much more indecent and dangerous than a good smack.
*Fantasia of the Unconscious*, Ch. 4

6 Morality which is based on ideas, or on an ideal, is an unmitigated evil.
*Fantasia of the Unconscious*, Ch. 7

7 When Eve ate this particular apple, she became aware of her own womanhood, mentally. And mentally she began to experiment with it. She has been experimenting ever since. So has man. To the rage and horror of both of them.
*Fantasia of the Unconscious*, Ch. 7

8 O pity the dead that are dead, but cannot make the journey, still they moan and beat against the silvery adamant walls of life's exclusive city.
*The Houseless Dead*

9 How beastly the bourgeois is especially the male of the species.
*How beastly the bourgeois is*

10 You may be the most liberal Liberal Englishman, and yet you cannot fail to see the categorical difference between the responsible and the irresponsible classes.
*Kangaroo*, Ch. 1

11 And all lying mysteriously within the Australian underdark, that peculiar, lost weary aloofness of Australia. There was the vast town of Sydney. And it didn't seem to be real, it seemed to be sprinkled on the surface of a darkness into which it never penetrated.
*Kangaroo*, Ch. 1

12 The very best that is in the Jewish blood: a faculty for pure disinterestedness, and warm, physically warm love, that seems to make the corpuscles of the blood glow.
*Kangaroo*, Ch. 6

13 We have all lost the war. All Europe.
*The Ladybird*, 'The Ladybird'

14 The young Cambridge group, the group that stood for 'freedom' and flannel trousers and flannel shirts open at the neck, and a well-bred sort of emotional anarchy, and a whispering, murmuring sort of voice, and an ultra-sensitive sort of manner.
*Lady Chatterley's Lover*, Ch. 1

15 It's all this cold-hearted fucking that is death and idiocy.
*Lady Chatterley's Lover*, Ch. 14

16 But tha mun dress thysen, an' go back to thy stately homes of England, how beautiful they stand. Time's up! Time's up for Sir John, an' for little Lady Jane! Put thy shimmy on, Lady Chatterley!
*Lady Chatterley's Lover*, Ch. 15

17 Water is $H_2O$, hydrogen two parts, oxygen one, but there is also a third thing, that makes it water
and nobody knows what that is.
*Pansies*, 'The Third Thing'

18 It always seemed to me that men wore their beards, like they wear their neckties, for show. I shall always remember Lewis for saying his beard was part of him.
*St Mawr*

19 The modern pantheist not only sees the god in everything, he takes photographs of it.
*St Mawr*

20 It was one of those places where the spirit of aboriginal England still lingers, the old savage England, whose last blood flows still in a few Englishmen, Welshmen, Cornishmen.
*St Mawr*

21 Ideal mankind would abolish death, multiply itself million upon million, rear up city upon city, save every parasite alive, until the accumulation of mere existence is swollen to a horror.
*St Mawr*

22 And suddenly she craved again for the more absolute silence of America. English stillness was so soft, like an inaudible murmur of voices, of presences.
*St Mawr*

23 You may have my husband, but not my horse. My husband won't need emasculating, and my horse I won't have you meddle with. I'll preserve one last male thing in the museum of this world, if I can.
*St Mawr*

24 There's nothing so artificial as sinning nowadays. I suppose it once was real.
*St Mawr*

25 One realizes with horror, that the race of men is almost extinct in Europe. Only Christ-like heroes and woman-worshipping Don Juans, and rabid equality-mongrels.
*Sea and Sardinia*, Ch. 3

26 A snake came to my water-trough
On a hot, hot day, and I in pyjamas for the heat,
To drink there.
*Snake*

27 And so, I missed my chance with one of the lords
Of life.
And I have something to expiate;
A pettiness.
*Snake*

28 When I read Shakespeare I am struck with wonder
That such trivial people should muse and thunder
In such lovely language.
*When I Read Shakespeare*

29 Be a good animal, true to your animal instincts.
*The White Peacock*, Pt. II, Ch. 2

30 No absolute is going to make the lion lie down with the lamb unless the lamb is inside.
*The Later D. H. Lawrence*

31 Away with all ideals. Let each individual act spontaneously from the for ever incalculable prompting of the creative wellhead within him. There is no universal law.
*Phoenix*, Preface to 'All Things are Possible' by Leo Shostov

32 Russia will certainly inherit the future. What we already call the greatness of Russia is only her pre-natal struggling.
*Phoenix*, Preface to 'All Things are Possible' by Leo Shostov

33 Pornography is the attempt to insult sex, to do dirt on it.
*Phoenix*, 'Pornography and Obscenity',

34 It is no good casting out devils. They belong to us, we must accept them and be at peace with them.
*Phoenix*, 'The Reality of Peace'

35 Neither can you expect a revolution, because there is no new baby in the womb of our society. Russia is a collapse, not a revolution.
*Phoenix*, 'The Good Man'

**36** I am a man, and alive . . . For this reason I am a novelist. And being a novelist, I consider myself superior to the saint, the scientist, the philosopher, and the poet, who are all great masters of different bits of man alive, but never get the whole hog.

*Phoenix*, 'Why the Novel Matters'

**37** We know these new English Catholics. They are the last words in Protest. They are Protestants protesting against Protestantism.

*Phoenix*, 'Review of Eric Gill, *Art Nonsense*'

**38** To every man who struggles with his own soul in mystery, a book that is a book flowers once, and seeds, and is gone.

*Phoenix*, 'A Bibliography of D.H.L.'

**39** I like to write when I feel spiteful: it's like having a good sneeze.

Letter to Lady Cynthia Asquith, Nov 1913

**40** They are great parables, the novels, but false art. They are only parables. All the people are *fallen angels* – even the dirtiest scrubs. This I cannot stomach. People are not fallen angels, they are merely people.

Referring to the novels of Dostoyevsky
Letter to J. Middleton Murry and Katherine Mansfield, 17 Feb 1916

**41** I am only half there when I am ill, and so there is only half a man to suffer. To suffer in one's whole self is so great a violation, that it is not to be endured.

Letter to Catherine Carswell, 16 Apr 1916

**42** The dead don't die. They look on and help.

Letter

**43** I'm not sure if a mental relation with a woman doesn't make it impossible to love her. To know the *mind* of a woman is to end in hating her. Love means the pre-cognitive flow . . . it is the honest state before the apple.

Letter to Dr Trigant Burrow, 3 Aug 1927

**Lawrence, James** (1781–1813) US naval officer. He commanded the *Hornet* on its raids against British shipping and was later transferred to the *Chesapeake*.

**1** Don't give up the ship.

Last words as he lay dying in his ship, the US frigate *Chesapeake*, during the battle with the British frigate *Shannon*
Attrib.

**Lawrence, T(homas) E(dward)** (1888–1935) British soldier and writer, known as Lawrence of Arabia. He became famous after leading a successful Arab revolt against the Turks (1917–18). He wrote *The Seven Pillars of Wisdom* (1926) and *The Mint* (1955).

**1** Many men would take the death-sentence without a whimper to escape the life-sentence which fate carries in her other hand.

*The Mint*, Pt. I, Ch. 4

**2** All men dream: but not equally. Those who dream by night in the dusty recesses of their minds wake in the day to find that it was vanity: but the dreamers of the day are dangerous men, for they may act their dream with open eyes, to make it possible.

*Seven Pillars of Wisdom*, Ch. 1

**3** I fancy, for myself, that they are rather out of touch with reality; by reality I mean shops like Selfridges, and motor buses, and the *Daily Express*.

Referring to expatriate authors living in Paris, such as James Joyce
Letter to W. Hurley, 1 Apr 1929

**4** I'm re-reading it with a slow deliberate carelessness.

Letter to Edward Marsh, 18 Apr 1929

**Lazarus, Emma** (1849–87) US poet and philanthropist. Her collections include *Admetus and Other Poems* (1871) and *Songs of a Semite* (1882). She organized relief for Jews persecuted in Russia (1879–83).

**1** Give me your tired, your poor,
Your huddled masses yearning to breathe free,
The wretched refuse of your teeming shore,
Send these, the homeless, tempest-tossed to me,
I lift my lamp beside the golden door!

Used as an inscription on the Statue of Liberty
*The New Colossus*

**Leach, Sir Edmund** (1910– ) British social anthropologist and author of *Rethinking Anthropology* (1961), *Genesis as Myth* (1970), *Social Anthropology* (1982), and many other books and articles.

**1** Far from being the basis of the good society, the family, with its narrow privacy and tawdry secrets, is the source of all our discontents.

In the BBC Reith Lectures for 1967. Lecture reprinted in *The Listener*

**Leacock, Stephen (Butler)** (1869–1944) English-born Canadian economist and humorist. His *Literary Lapses* (1910) and *Nonsense Novels* (1911) were two of some 30 humorous books.

**1** If every day in the life of a school could be the last day but one, there would be little fault to find with it.

*College Days*, 'Memories and Miseries of a Schoolmaster'

**2** The classics are only primitive literature. They belong in the same class as primitive machinery and primitive music and primitive medicine.

*Homer and Humbug*

**3** I detest life-insurance agents; they always argue that I shall some day die, which is not so.

*Literary Lapses*, 'Insurance. Up to Date'

**4** Get your room full of good air, then shut up the windows and keep it. It will keep for years. Anyway, don't keep using your lungs all the time. Let them rest.

*Literary Lapses*, 'How to Live to be 200'

5 Astronomy teaches the correct use of the sun and the planets.
*Literary Lapses*, 'A Manual of Education'

6 The landlady of a boarding-house is a parallelogram – that is, an oblong angular figure, which cannot be described, but which is equal to anything.
*Literary Lapses*, 'Boarding-House Geometry'

7 Any two meals at a boarding-house are together less than two square meals.
*Literary Lapses*, 'Boarding-House Geometry'

8 It takes a good deal of physical courage to ride a horse. This, however, I have. I get it at about forty cents a flask, and take it as required.
*Literary Lapses*, 'Reflections on Riding'

9 The great man . . . walks across his century and leaves the marks of his feet all over it, ripping out the dates on his goloshes as he passes.
*Literary Lapses*, 'The Life of John Smith'

10 Lord Ronald said nothing; he flung himself from the room, flung himself upon his horse and rode madly off in all directions.
*Nonsense Novels*, 'Gertrude the Governess'

11 Golf may be played on Sunday, not being a game within the view of the law, but being a form of moral effort.
*Other Fancies*, 'Why I refuse to play Golf'

12 A 'Grand Old Man'. That means on our continent any one with snow white hair who has kept out of jail till eighty.
*The Score and Ten*

13 The general idea, of course, in any first-class laundry is to see that no shirt or collar ever comes back twice.
*Winnowed Wisdom*, Ch. 6

**Lear, Edward** (1812–88) British artist and writer. His *Book of Nonsense* (1846) was the forerunner of several others, such as *Laughable Lyrics* (1876).

1 There was an Old Man with a beard,
Who said, 'It is just as I feared! –
Two Owls and a Hen,
Four Larks and a Wren,
Have all built their nests in my beard!'
*Book of Nonsense*

2 On the Coast of Coromandel
Where the early pumpkins blow,
In the middle of the woods
Lived the Yonghy-Bonghy-Bò.
*The Courtship of the Yonghy-Bonghy-Bò*

3 The Dong! – the Dong!
The wandering Dong through the forest goes!
The Dong! – the Dong!
The Dong with a luminous Nose!
*The Dong with a Luminous Nose*

4 They went to sea in a sieve, they did
In a sieve they went to sea.
*The Jumblies*

5 Far and few, far and few,
Are the lands where the Jumblies live;
Their heads are green, and their hands are blue,
And they went to sea in a sieve.
*The Jumblies*

6 Serve up in a clean dish, and throw the whole out of the window as fast as possible.
*To make an Amblongus Pie*

7 He has many friends, laymen and clerical.
Old Foss is the name of his cat:
His body is perfectly spherical,
He weareth a runcible hat.
*Nonsense Songs*, Preface

8 The Owl and the Pussy-Cat went to sea
In a beautiful pea-green boat,
They took some honey, and plenty of money,
Wrapped up in a five-pound note.
*The Owl and the Pussy-Cat*

9 They dined on mince, and slices of quince,
Which they ate with a runcible spoon;
And hand in hand, on the edge of the sand,
They danced by the light of the moon.
*The Owl and the Pussy-Cat*

**Leavis, F(rank) R(aymond)** (1895–1978) British literary critic, who stressed the moral value of the study of literature. He edited the journal *Scrutiny* (1932–53) and wrote *The Great Tradition* (1948), as well as studies of Dickens and D. H. Lawrence.

1 His verse exhibits . . . something that is rather like Keats's vulgarity with a Public School accent.
Referring to Rupert Brooke
*New Bearings in English Poetry*, Ch. 2

**Lebowitz, Fran** (1950– ) US writer and columnist. Her collected essays *Metropolitan Life* (1978) established her reputation as a humorous writer.

1 Never judge a cover by its book.
*Metropolitan Life*

2 Food is an important part of a balanced diet.
*Metropolitan Life*, 'Food for Thought and Vice Versa'

**Le Corbusier** (Charles-Édouard Jeanneret; 1887–1965) Swiss-born French architect. He progressed from cubist-style houses to more innovative ideas, such as the *unité d'habitation* at Marseilles. The city of Chandigarh was his most ambitious town-planning project.

1 A house is a machine for living in.
*Towards an Architecture*

**Ledru-Rollin, Alexandre Auguste** (1807–74) French lawyer and politician. An advocate of universal suffrage, he was largely responsible for its adoption in France.

1 Let me pass, I have to follow them, I am their leader.
Trying to force his way through a mob during the Revolution of 1848, of which he was one of the chief instigators
*The Fine Art of Political Wit* (L. Harris)

**Lee, Harper** (1926– ) US writer. Her only novel *To Kill a Mockingbird* (1960) was made into a film in 1963.

**1** Being Southerners, it was a source of shame to some members of the family that we had no recorded ancestors on either side of the Battle of Hastings.

*To Kill a Mockingbird*, Pt. I, Ch. 1

**2** Shoot all the bluejays you want, if you can hit 'em, but remember it's a sin to kill a mockingbird.

*To Kill a Mockingbird*, Pt. II, Ch. 10

**Lee, Robert E(dward)** (1807–70) US general. An outstanding leader, he was a Confederate commander in the US Civil War and defended Virginia against Federal attacks.

**1** It is well that war is so terrible; else we would grow too fond of it.

Speaking to another general during the battle of Fredericksburg
*The American Treasury* (C. Fadiman)

**2** I should be trading on the blood of my men.

Refusing to write his memoirs
*Nobody Said It Better* (M. Ringo)

**Lefèvre, Théo** (1914–73) Belgian prime minister (1961–65). A lawyer, he became a member of the underground after the German occupation in 1940. He entered parliament as a Christian Democrat in 1946.

**1** In Western Europe there are now only small countries – those that know it and those that don't know it yet.

*The Observer*, 'Sayings of the Year', 1963

**Lehman, Ernest** (1920– ) US screenwriter and author.

**1** Sweet Smell of Success.

Novel and film title

**Lehrer, Tom** (1928– ) US university teacher and songwriter. He has taught physics, business administration, and psychology. His humorous songs are collected in *Tom Lehrer's Song Book* (1954) and others.

**1** It is sobering to consider that when Mozart was my age he had already been dead for a year.

*An Encyclopedia of Quotations about Music* (N. Shapiro)

**Leigh, Fred W.** (19th century) British songwriter.

**1** There was I, waiting at the church,
Waiting at the church, waiting at the church,
When I found he'd left me in the lurch,
Lor', how it did upset me! . . .
Can't get away to marry you today –
My wife won't let me.

*Waiting at the Church*

**Lenclos, Ninon de** (1620–1705) French courtesan whose salon was popular with many writers and politicians, including her lovers La Rochefoucauld and Sévigné.

**1** Old age is woman's hell.

Attrib.

**Lenin, Vladimir Ilich** (Vladimir Ilich Ulyanov; 1870–1924) Russian revolutionary leader, who led the Bolsheviks to victory, establishing the Soviet of People's Commissars and the Third International. He died after a series of strokes resulting from an assassination attempt; his embalmed body is on permanent exhibition in Moscow.

**1** If it were necessary to give the briefest possible definition of imperialism we should have to say that imperialism is the monopoly stage of capitalism.

*Imperialism, the Highest Stage of Capitalism*, Ch. 7

**2** One step forward, two steps back . . . It happens in the lives of individuals, and it happens in the history of nations and in the development of parties.

*One Step Forward, Two Steps Back*

**3** Under capitalism we have a state in the proper sense of the word, that is, a special machine for the suppression of one class by another.

*The State and Revolution*, Ch. 5

**4** So long as the state exists there is no freedom. When there is freedom there will be no state.

*The State and Revolution*, Ch. 5

**5** Under socialism *all* will govern in turn and will soon become accustomed to no one governing.

*The State and Revolution*, Ch. 6

**6** A Social-Democrat must never forget that the proletariat will inevitably have to wage a class struggle for Socialism even against the most democratic and republican bourgeoisie and petty bourgeoisie.

*The State and Revolution*, Ch. 10

**7** Any cook should be able to run the country.

*The First Circle* (Alexander Solzhenitsyn)

**8** When a liberal is abused, he says: Thank God they didn't beat me. When he is beaten, he thanks God they didn't kill him. When he is killed, he will thank God that his immortal soul has been delivered from its mortal clay.

Lenin heard this characterisation at a meeting, and repeated it with approval
*The Government's Falsification of the Duma and the Tasks of the Social-Democrats*, 'Proletary', Dec 1906

**9** Communism is Soviet power plus the electrification of the whole country.

Political slogan of 1920, promoting the programme of electrification

**10** A good man fallen among Fabians.

Referring to Bernard Shaw
Attrib.

**11** It is true that liberty is precious – so precious that it must be rationed.

Attrib.

**Lennon, John** (1940–80) British rock musician and member of the Beatles. His most distinctive solo recording was *Imagine* (1971). He was assassinated in 1980.

1 Life is what happens to you while you're busy making other plans.

*Beautiful Boy*

2 For I don't care too much for money,
For money can't buy me love,

*Can't Buy Me Love* (with Paul McCartney)

3 Waits at the window, wearing the face that she keeps in a jar by the door
Who is it for? All the lonely people, where do they all come from?
All the lonely people, where do they all belong?

*Eleanor Rigby* (with Paul McCartney)

4 If there's anything that you want,
If there's anything I can do,
Just call on me,
And I'll send it along with love from me to you.

*From Me to You* (with Paul McCartney)

5 I've got to admit it's getting better.
It's a little better all the time.

*Getting Better* (with Paul McCartney)

6 It's been a hard day's night.

*A Hard Day's Night* (with Paul McCartney)

7 Picture yourself in a boat on a river with tangerine trees and marmalade skies.
Somebody calls you, you answer quite slowly a girl with kaleidoscope eyes.

*Lucy in the Sky with Diamonds* (with Paul McCartney)

8 He's a real Nowhere Man,
Sitting in his Nowhere Land,
Making all his nowhere plans for nobody.
Doesn't have a point of view,
Knows not where he's going to,
Isn't he a bit like you and me?

*Nowhere Man* (with Paul McCartney)

9 Sergeant Pepper's Lonely Hearts Club Band.

Song title (with Paul McCartney)

10 She loves you, yeh, yeh, yeh,
And with a love like that you know you should be glad.

*She Loves You* (with Paul McCartney)

11 She's leaving home after living alone for so many years.

*She's Leaving Home* (with Paul McCartney)

12 I get by with a little help from my friends.

*With a Little Help from My Friends* (with Paul McCartney)

13 We're more popular than Jesus Christ now. I don't know which will go first. Rock and roll or Christianity.

*The Beatles Illustrated Lyrics*

**Lenthall, William** (1591–1662) English parliamentarian and speaker of the Long Parliament.

1 I have neither eye to see, nor tongue to speak here, but as the House is pleased to direct me.

Said on 4 Jan 1642 in the House of Commons when asked by Charles I if he had seen five MPs whom the King wished to arrest. It was a succinct restatement of the Speaker's traditional role
*Historical Collections* (Rushworth)

**Leo X** (Giovanni de' Medici; 1475–1521) Pope (1513–21). The son of Lorenzo the Magnificent, he was a lavish patron of the arts. He gave France control over its own church appointments (Concordat of Boulogne; 1516).

1 Since God has given us the papacy, let us enjoy it.

*Men of Art* (T. Craven)

**Léon, Luis Ponce de** (1527–91) Spanish monk, Thomist theologian, and vicar-general of the Augustinian order. His works include lyrics and translations of classical and biblical texts.

1 As I was saying the other day.

Said on resuming a lecture interrupted by five years' imprisonment

**Leonard, Hugh** (1926– ) Irish dramatist whose plays include *A Leap in the Dark* (1957) and *Da* (1973). He has also written plays for television.

1 The problem with Ireland is that it's a country full of genius, but with absolutely no talent.

Said during an interview
*The Times*, Aug 1977

**Leonardo da Vinci** 1452–1519) Italian artist, engineer, and scientist. His best-known paintings are the *Last Supper* and the *Mona Lisa*. His *Notebooks* (1508–18) cover a wide range of subjects.

1 While I thought that I was learning how to live, I have been learning how to die.

*Notebooks*

**Leonidas** (died 480 BC) King of Sparta (490–480 BC). He defended the pass of Thermopylae, against an enormous Persian army, with a small force all of which was lost.

1 Go, stranger, and tell the Lacedaemonians that here we lie, obedient to their commands.

Epitaph over the tomb in which he and his followers were buried after their defeat at Thermopylae

**Leopold II** (1835–1909) King of the Belgians (1865–1909). He sponsored Stanley's exploration of the Congo and obtained Belgian sovereignty over it in 1885.

1 A constitutional king must learn to stoop.

Instructing Prince Albert, the heir apparent, to pick up some papers that had fallen onto the floor
*The Mistress* (Betty Kelen)

**Lerner, Alan Jay** (1918–86) US songwriter and librettist, who collaborated with Frederick Loewe in such musicals as *My Fair Lady* (1956) and *Camelot* (1960).

1 An Englishman's way of speaking absolutely classifies him
The moment he talks he makes some other Englishman despise him.

*My Fair Lady*, I:1

2  All I want is a room somewhere,
Far away from the cold night air;
With one enormous chair . . .
Oh, wouldn't it be loverly?
*My Fair Lady*, I:1

3  I'd be equally as willing
For a dentist to be drilling
Than to ever let a woman in my life.
*My Fair Lady*, I:2

4  Oozing charm from every pore,
He oiled his way around the floor.
*My Fair Lady*, II:1

5  I'm getting married in the morning!
Ding dong! the bells are gonna chime.
Pull out the stopper!
Let's have a whopper!
But get me to the church on time!
*My Fair Lady*, II:3

6  Why can't a woman be more like a man?
Men are so honest, so thoroughly square;
Eternally noble, historically fair.
*My Fair Lady*, II:4

7  I've grown accustomed to the trace
Of something in the air,
Accustomed to her face.
*My Fair Lady*, II:6

**Lesage, Alain-René** (1668–1747) French writer. He is remembered for his novel *Gil Blas* (1715–35), *Le Diable boiteux* (1707), and the play *Crispin rival de son maître* (1707).

1  Justice is such a fine thing that we cannot pay too dearly for it.
*Crispin rival de son maître*, IX

2  They made peace between us; we embraced, and we have been mortal enemies ever since.
*Le Diable boiteux*, Ch. 3

**Lessing, Doris** (1919–  ) British novelist, brought up in Rhodesia. The five-novel sequence *Children of Violence* (1952–69) was followed by *The Golden Notebook* (1962), *Memoirs of a Survivor* (1974), and *The Good Terrorist* (1985).

1  . . . that is what learning is. You suddenly understand something you've understood all your life, but in a new way.
*The Four-Gated City*

2  When old settlers say 'One has to understand the country', what they mean is, 'You have to get used to our ideas about the native.' They are saying, in effect, 'Learn our ideas, or otherwise get out; we don't want you.'
Referring specifically to South Africa
*The Grass is Singing*, Ch. 1

3  When a white man in Africa by accident looks into the eyes of a native and sees the human being (which it is his chief preoccupation to avoid), his sense of guilt, which he denies, fumes up in resentment and he brings down the whip.
*The Grass is Singing*, Ch. 8

4  If people dug up the remains of this civilization a thousand years hence, and found Epstein's statues and that man Ellis, they would think we were just savages.
*Martha Quest*, Pt. I, Ch. 1

5  In university they don't tell you that the greater part of the law is learning to tolerate fools.
*Martha Quest*, Pt. III, Ch. 2

6  If a fish is the movement of water embodied, given shape, then cat is a diagram and pattern of subtle air.
*Particularly Cats*, Ch. 2

**Lessing, Gotthold Ephraim** (1729–81) German dramatist. His plays include *Minna von Barnhelm* (1763), *Miss Sara Sampson* (1755), and *Emilia Galotti* (1772). In his *Hamburgische Dramaturgie* (1767–69) he expounded his theories of drama.

1  A man who does not lose his reason over certain things has none to lose.
*Emilia Galotti*, IV:7

**L'Estrange, Sir Roger** (1616–1704) English journalist and writer. His writings include the *Observator* (1681–87) and translations of Seneca, Cicero, and Josephus, as well as *Aesop's Fables* (1692).

1  It is with our passions as it is with fire and water, they are good servants, but bad masters.
*Aesop's Fables*, 38

2  Though this may be play to you, 'tis death to us.
*Aesop's Fables*, 398

**Lethaby, W(illiam) R(ichard)** (1857–1931) British architect whose work was characteristic of the Arts and Crafts movement at the beginning of the 20th century.

1  Art is not a special sauce applied to ordinary cooking; it is the cooking itself if it is good.
*Form in Civilization*, 'Art and Workmanship'

**Leverson, Ada Beddington** (1862–1933) British writer.

1  It is an infallible sign of the second-rate in nature and intellect to make use of everything and everyone.
*The Limit*

2  Thou canst not serve both cod and salmon.
Reply when offered a choice of fish at dinner
*The Times*, 7 Nov 1970

3  The last gentleman in Europe.
Said of Oscar Wilde
*Letters to the Sphinx* (Wilde), 'Reminiscences', 2

4  I'm sure he had a fork in the other.
Reply when told by Oscar Wilde of a devoted *apache* (Parisian gangster) who used to follow him with a knife in one hand
Attrib.

**Levin, Bernard** (1928–  ) British journalist and author. A columnist in *The Times*, television personality, and music critic, he has written several books including *Taking Sides* (1979) and *Enthusiasms* (1983).

1 Inflation in the Sixties was a nuisance to be endured, like varicose veins or French foreign policy.
*The Pendulum Years*, 'Epilogue'

2 Once, when a British Prime Minister sneezed, men half a world away would blow their noses. Now when a British Prime Minister sneezes nobody will even say 'Bless You'.
*The Times*, 1976

3 What has happened to architecture since the second world war that the only passers-by who can contemplate it without pain are those equipped with a white stick and a dog?
*The Times*, 1983

**Lévis, Gaston Pierre Marc, Duc de** (1764–1830) French writer and soldier. His books include *Maximes et Réflexions* (1808).

1 *Noblesse oblige.*
Nobility has its own obligations.
*Maximes et Réflexions*

**Lévi-Strauss, Claude** (1908– ) French anthropologist and leading exponent of structuralism. His works include *The Elementary Structures of Kinship* (1949) and *Structural Anthropology* (1958).

1 The anthropologist respects history, but he does not accord it a special value. He conceives it as a study complementary to his own: one of them unfurls the range of human societies in time, the other in space.
*The Savage Mind*

**Lewes, G(eorge) H(enry)** (1817–78) British philosopher and writer. He was the common-law husband of Marian Evans (George Eliot). His books include a *Life of Goethe* (1855), *The History of Philosophy from Thales to Comte* (1845–46), *Physiology of Common Life* (1859), and *The Problems of Life and Mind* (1874–79).

1 Murder, like talent, seems occasionally to run in families.
*The Physiology of Common Life*, Ch. 12

**Lewis, C(live) S(taples)** (1898–1963) British academic and writer. An Oxford professor, his books on Christianity include *The Problem of Pain* (1940) and *The Screwtape Letters* (1942). He also wrote children's books and science fiction.

1 Friendship is unnecessary, like philosophy, like art. . . . It has no survival value; rather it is one of those things that give value to survival.
*The Four Loves, Friendship*

2 The coarse joke proclaims that we have here an animal which finds its own animality either objectionable or funny.
*Miracles*

3 There is wishful thinking in Hell as well as on earth.
*The Screwtape Letters*, Preface

4 There must be several young women who would render the Christian life intensely difficult to him if only you could persuade him to marry one of them.
*The Screwtape Letters*

5 The Future is something which everyone reaches at the rate of sixty minutes an hour, whatever he does, whoever he is.
*The Screwtape Letters*

6 She's the sort of woman who lives for others – you can always tell the others by their hunted expression.
*The Screwtape Letters*

**Lewis, D(ominic) B(evan) Wyndham** (1891–1969) British journalist and writer, especially of biographies. He wrote *François Villon* (1928) and *Emperor of the West, Charles V* (1932) among others.

1 I am one of those unfortunates to whom death is less hideous than explanations.
*Welcome to All This*

**Lewis, Sir George Cornewall** (1806–63) British statesman and writer. He became chancellor of the exchequer (1855–58), home secretary under Lord Palmerston (1859–61), and secretary for war (1861–63).

1 Life would be tolerable, were it not for its amusements.
*The Perpetual Pessimist* (Sagittarius and George)

**Lewis, John Llewellyn** (1880–1969) US labour leader and president of the United Mine Workers of America for 40 years; he organized mass-production workers into industrial unions.

1 I'm not interested in classes . . . Far be it from me to foster inferiority complexes among the workers by trying to make them think they belong to some special class. That has happened in Europe but it hasn't happened here yet.
*The Coming of the New Deal* (A. M. Schlesinger, Jnr), Pt. 7, Ch. 25·

**Lewis, (Percy) Wyndham** (1882–1957) British novelist and painter. He helped to found the Vorticist movement in 1913; his novels include *The Apes of God* (1930) and the trilogy *The Human Age* (1928–55).

1 The soul started at the knee-cap and ended at the navel.
*The Apes of God*, Pt. XII

2 'Dying for an idea,' again, sounds well enough, but why not let the idea die instead of you?
*The Art of Being Ruled*, Pt. I, Ch. 1

3 I believe that (in one form or another) castration may be the solution. And the feminization of the white European and American is already far advanced, coming in the wake of the war.
*The Art of Being Ruled*, Pt. II, Ch. 2

4 The 'homo' is the legitimate child of the 'suffragette'.
*The Art of Being Ruled*, Pt. VIII, Ch. 4

**5** You persisted for a certain number of years like a stammer. You were a *stammer*, if you like, of Space-Time.

*The Human Age*, 'The Childermass'

**6** The revolutionary simpleton is everywhere.

*Time and Western Man*, Bk. I, Ch. 6

**Lewis, Sinclair** (1885–1951) US novelist. The first US writer to win the Nobel prize (1930), he is remembered for *Main Street* (1920), *Babbitt* (1922), and *Elmer Gantry* (1927).

**1** In fact there was but one thing wrong with the Babbitt house; it was not a home.

*Babbitt*, Ch. 2

**2** In other countries, art and literature are left to a lot of shabby bums living in attics and feeding on booze and spaghetti, but in America the successful writer or picture-painter is indistinguishable from any other decent business man.

*Babbitt*, Ch. 14

**3** She did her work with the thoroughness of a mind that reveres details and never quite understands them.

*Babbitt*, Ch. 18

**4** Our American professors like their literature clear and cold and pure and very dead.

Speech, on receiving the Nobel Prize, 1930

**Ley, Robert** (1890–1945) German Nazi. He was head of the Labour Front (from 1933) and committed suicide awaiting trial as a war criminal.

**1** *Kraft durch Freude.*
Strength through joy.

German Labour Front slogan

**Leybourne, George** (?–1884) British songwriter.

**1** O, he flies through the air with the greatest of ease,
This daring young man on the flying trapeze.

*The Man on the Flying Trapeze*

**Liberace** (Wladzin Valentino Liberace; 1919–87) US pianist and showman. He made a number of films and was highly successful on TV.

**1** I cried all the way to the bank.

Said when asked whether he minded being criticized
*Liberace: An Autobiography*, Ch. 2

**Lichtenberg, Georg Christoph** (1742–99) German physicist and writer. He wrote satirical books on several subjects and published a collection of *Aphorisms* (1764–99).

**1** Probably no invention came more easily to man than Heaven.

*Aphorisms*

**2** There can hardly be a stranger commodity in the world than books. Printed by people who don't understand them; sold by people who don't understand them; bound, criticized and read by people who don't understand them; and now even written by people who don't understand them.

*Aphorisms*

**3** Just as the meanest and most vicious deeds require spirit and talent, so even the greatest deeds require a certain insensitiveness which on other occasions is called stupidity.

*Aphorisms*

**Lie, Trygve** (1896–1968) Norwegian lawyer, who became the first secretary-general of the United Nations (1946–53). Formerly foreign minister of Norway, he presided over the commission that drafted the UN charter.

**1** Now we are in a period which I can characterize as a period of cold peace.

*The Observer*, 'Sayings of the Week', 21 Aug 1949

**Liebermann, Max** (1847–1935) German painter and etcher, who specialized in portraits and genre scenes, such as *Women Plucking Geese* (1872) and *The Flax Spinners* (1887).

**1** I can piss the old boy in the snow.

Remark to an artist who said he could not draw General Paul von Hindenburg's face
*Conversations with Stravinsky* (Igor Stravinsky and Robert Craft)

**Lillie, Beatrice** (Constance Sylvia Muston, Lady Peel; 1898– ) Canadian-born British actress, who was a star of revues between the wars. She also made a few films, including *Exit Smiling* (1926) and *On Approval* (1943).

**1** I'll simply say here that I was born Beatrice Gladys Lillie at an extremely tender age because my mother needed a fourth at meals.

*Every Other Inch a Lady*, Ch. 1

**2** Heard there was a party. Came.

On arriving breathlessly at a friend's house seeking help after a car crash
Attrib.

**Lillo, George** (1693–1739) English dramatist. His plays include *The Christian Hero* (1735) and *Fatal Curiosity* (1736), as well as the ballad opera *Silvia, or the Country Burial* (1730).

**1** There's sure no passion in the human soul,
But finds its food in music.

*Fatal Curiosity*, I:2

**Lincoln, Abraham** (1809–65) US statesman and Republican president (1861–65). He achieved freedom for slaves and the prohibition of slavery. He was assassinated a few days after the surrender of the South in the Civil War.

**1** So you're the little woman who wrote the book that made this great war!

Said on meeting Harriet Beecher Stowe, the author of *Uncle Tom's Cabin* (1852), which stimulated opposition to slavery before the US Civil War
*Abraham Lincoln: The War Years* (Carl Sandburg), Vol. II, Ch. 39

**2** The Lord prefers common-looking people. That is why he makes so many of them.
*Our President* (James Morgan), Ch. 6

**3** Die when I may, I want it said of me by those who know me best, that I have always plucked a thistle and planted a flower where I thought a flower would grow.
*Presidential Anecdotes* (P. Boller)

**4** I intend no modification of my oft-expressed personal wish that all men everywhere could be free.
Letter to Horace Greeley, 22 Aug 1862

**5** If you don't want to use the army, I should like to borrow it for a while. Yours respectfully, A. Lincoln.
Letter to General George B. McClellan, whose lack of activity during the US Civil War irritated Lincoln

**6** No man is good enough to govern another man without that other's consent.
Speech, 1854

**7** The ballot is stronger than the bullet.
Speech, 19 May 1856

**8** Those who deny freedom to others, deserve it not for themselves.
Speech, 19 May 1856

**9** What is conservatism? Is it not adherence to the old and tried, against the new and untried?
Speech, 27 Feb 1860

**10** This country, with its institutions, belongs to the people who inhabit it. Whenever they shall grow weary of the existing government, they can exercise their constitutional right of amending it, or their revolutionary right to dismember or overthrow it.
First Inaugural Address, 4 Mar 1861

**11** An old Dutch farmer, who remarked to a companion once that it was not best to swap horses in mid-stream.
Speech, 9 June 1864

**12** In a larger sense we cannot dedicate, we cannot consecrate, we cannot hallow this ground. The brave men, living and dead, who struggled here, have consecrated it far above our power to add or detract. The world will little note, nor long remember, what we say here, but it can never forget what they did here. It is for us, the living, rather to be dedicated here to the unfinished work which they who fought here have thus far so nobly advanced. It is rather for us to be here dedicated to the great task remaining before us . . . that we here highly resolve that the dead shall not have died in vain, that this nation, under God, shall have a new birth of freedom; and that government of the people, by the people, and for the people, shall not perish from the earth.
Report of Lincoln's address at the dedication (19 Nov 1863) of the national cemetery on the site of the Battle of Gettysburg

**13** You can fool some of the people all the time and all the people some of the time; but you can't fool all the people all the time.
Attrib.

**14** People who like this sort of thing will find this is the sort of thing they like.
A comment on a book
Attrib.

**15** I can't spare this man; he fights.
Resisting demands for the dismissal of Ulysses Grant
Attrib.

**16** Well, he looks like a man.
On catching sight of Walt Whitman for the first time
Attrib.

**17** I don't know who my grandfather was; I am much more concerned to know what his grandson will be.
Taking part in a discussion on ancestry
Attrib.

**Lindsay, (Nicholas) Vachel** (1879–1931) US poet, who recited his poetry before audiences in return for food and shelter. His best-known volumes are *General Booth Enters into Heaven and Other Poems* (1913) and *The Congo and Other Poems* (1914).

**1** And who will bring white peace
That he may sleep upon his hill again?
*Abraham Lincoln Walks at Midnight*

**2** Booth died blind and still by faith he trod,
Eyes still dazzled by the ways of God.
*General William Booth Enters Heaven*

**Linklater, Eric** (1889–1974) Scottish novelist, who lived in the USA for many years. His books include *Juan in America* (1931) and *Judas* (1939).

**1** With a heavy step Sir Matthew left the room and spent the morning designing mausoleums for his enemies.
*Juan in America*, Prologue

**2** I've been married six months. She looks like a million dollars, but she only knows a hundred and twenty words and she's only got two ideas in her head. The other one's hats.
*Juan in America*, Pt. II, Ch. 5

**3** There won't be any revolution in America . . . The people are too clean. They spend all their time changing their shirts and washing themselves. You can't feel fierce and revolutionary in a bathroom.
*Juan in America*, Pt. V, Ch. 3

**4** All I've got against it is that it takes you so far from the club house.
Referring to golf
*Poet's Pub*, Ch. 3

**Linton, W(illiam) J(ames)** (1812–97) British writer and wood engraver. An active Chartist, his books include *To the Future* (1848), *The Plaint of Freedom* (1852), and *Claribel and Other Poems* (1865).

**1** For he's one of Nature's Gentlemen, the best of every time.

*Nature's Gentleman*

**Lippman, Walter** (1889–1974) US editor and writer. A columnist in the *New York Herald-Tribune*, he wrote the influential book *Public Opinion* (1922).

**1** In a free society the state does not administer the affairs of men. It administers justice among men who conduct their own affairs.

*An Enquiry into the Principles of a Good Society*

**Livermore, Mary Ashton** (c. 1820–1905) US writer, lecturer, feminist, and social reformer. Her most popular book was *What Shall We Do with Our Daughters* (1883).

**1** Other books have been written by men physicians . . . One would suppose in reading them that women possess but one class of physical organs, and that these are always diseased. Such teaching is pestiferous, and tends to cause and perpetuate the very evils it professes to remedy.

*What Shall We Do with Our Daughters?*, Ch. 2

**2** Above the titles of wife and mother, which, although dear, are transitory and accidental, there is the title human being, which precedes and out-ranks every other.

*What Shall We Do with Our Daughters?*, Ch. 7

**Livy** (Titus Livius; 59 BC–17 AD) Roman historian. Of his monumental 142-volume history of Rome, only 35 books survive.

**1** Woe to the vanquished.

*History*, V:48

**Lloyd, Harold** (1893–1971) US silent-film comedian. He usually took the part of a bespectacled little man who ultimately triumphed over adversity.

**1** I am just turning forty and taking my time about it.

*Reply when, aged 77, he was asked his age*
*The Times*, 23 Sept 1970

**Lloyd, Marie** (1870–1922) British music-hall singer, who specialized in cockney humour.

**1** Oh, mister porter, what shall I do?
I wanted to go to Birmingham, but they've carried me on to Crewe.

*Oh, Mister Porter*

**2** A little of what you fancy does you good.

*Song title*

**3** I'm one of the ruins that Cromwell knocked about a bit.

*Song title*

**Lloyd, Robert** (1733–64) British poet. His books include *The Actor* (1760) and a comic opera *Capricious Lovers* (1764).

**1** Slow and steady wins the race.

*The Hare and the Tortoise*

**Lloyd George, David, Earl of Dwyfor** (1863–1945) British Liberal statesman. As prime minister (1916–22), he replaced Asquith as leader of a coalition government during World War I and for four years after it.

**1** He saw foreign policy through the wrong end of a municipal drainpipe.

*Referring to Neville Chamberlain*
*The Fine Art of Political Wit* (Harris), Ch. 6

**2** Poor Bonar can't bear being called a liar. Now I don't mind.

*Referring to Bonar Law, prime minister 1922–23*
*Stanley Baldwin* (G. M. Young)

**3** You cannot feed the hungry on statistics.

*Advocating Tariff Reform*
*Speech, 1904*

**4** Mr Balfour's Poodle.

*Referring to the House of Lords and its in-built Conservative majority; said in reply to a claim that it was 'the watchdog of the nation'*
*Remark, House of Commons, 26 June 1907*

**5** A fully equipped Duke costs as much to keep up as two Dreadnoughts, and Dukes are just as great a terror, and they last longer.

*Speech, Limehouse, 30 July 1909*

**6** What is our task? To make Britain a fit country for heroes to live in.

*Speech, 24 Nov 1918*

**7** Every man has a House of Lords in his own head. Fears, prejudices, misconceptions – those are the peers, and they are hereditary.

*Speech, Cambridge, 1927*

**8** If we are going in without the help of Russia we are walking into a trap.

*Speech, House of Commons, 3 Apr 1939*

**9** The Right Hon. gentleman has sat so long on the fence that the iron has entered his soul.

*Referring to Sir John Simon*
*Attrib.*

**10** When they circumcised Herbert Samuel they threw away the wrong bit.

*Attrib. in The Listener*, 7 Sept 1978

**11** Like a cushion, he always bore the impress of the last man who sat on him.

*Referring to Lord Derby*
*Attrib. in The Listener*, 7 Sept 1978. This remark is also credited to Earl Haig

**12** Well, I find that a change of nuisances is as good as a vacation.

*On being asked how he maintained his cheerfulness when beset by numerous political obstacles*
*Attrib.*

**13** This war, like the next war, is a war to end war.

*Referring to the popular opinion that World War I would be the last major war*

**14** The world is becoming like a lunatic asylum run by lunatics.

*The Observer*, 'Sayings of Our Times', 31 May 1953

**Locke, John** (1632–1704) English philosopher. His best-known work was the *Essay Concerning Human Understanding* (1690). His book *Of Government* (1690) was also influential.

1 New opinions are always suspected, and usually opposed, without any other reason but because they are not already common.

*An Essay Concerning Human Understanding*, dedicatory epistle

2 It is one thing to show a man that he is in an error, and another to put him in possession of truth.

*An Essay Concerning Human Understanding*, Bk. IV, Ch. 7

**Lockier, Francis** (1667–1740) English writer.

1 In all my travels I never met with any one Scotchman but what was a man of sense. I believe everybody of that country that has any, leaves it as fast as they can.

*Anecdotes* (Joseph Spence)

**Lodge, David John** (1935–  ) British author and critic whose novels include *The British Museum is Falling Down* (1965) and *Changing Places* (1975).

1 Literature is mostly about having sex and not much about having children; life is the other way round.

*The British Museum is Falling Down*, Ch. 4

2 Rummidge . . . had lately suffered the mortifying fate of most English universities of its type (civic redbrick): having competed strenuously for fifty years with two universities chiefly valued for being old, it was, at the moment of drawing level, rudely overtaken in popularity and prestige by a batch of universities chiefly valued for being new.

*Changing Places*, Ch. 1

3 Four times, under our educational rules, the human pack is shuffled and cut – at eleven-plus, sixteen-plus, eighteen-plus and twenty-plus – and happy is he who comes top of the deck on each occasion, but especially the last. This is called Finals, the very name of which implies that nothing of importance can happen after it. The British postgraduate student is a lonely forlorn soul . . . for whom nothing has been real since the Big Push.

*Changing Places*, Ch. 1

4 The British, he thought, must be gluttons for satire: even the weather forecast seemed to be some kind of spoof, predicting every possible combination of weather for the next twenty-four hours without actually committing itself to anything specific.

*Changing Places*, Ch. 2

5 Walt Whitman who laid end to end words never seen in each other's company before outside of a dictionary.

*Changing Places*, Ch. 5

**Loesser, Frank** (1910–69) US songwriter. His film scores included *Hans Christian Andersen* (1952) and *Guys and Dolls* (1955).

1 I'd like to get you
On a slow boat to China.

*Slow Boat to China*

**Logau, Friedrich von, Baron** (1604–55) German poet and writer. His best-known collection is *Deutscher Sinngedichte Dreitausend* (1654).

1 Though the mills of God grind slowly, yet they grind exceeding small;
Though with patience He stands waiting, with exactness grinds He all.

*Sinngedichte*, III

**Logue, Christopher** (1926–  ) British poet, journalist, dramatist, and actor. His verse collections include *Songs* (1959) and *Twelve Cards* (1972). His play *The Lilywhite Boys* (with Hugo Claus; 1959) was successful and he has written several screenplays.

1 Said Marx: 'Don't be snobbish, we seek to abolish
The 3rd Class, not the 1st.'

*Christopher Logue's ABC*, 'M'

**Lombardi, Vince** (1913–70) US football coach.

1 Winning isn't everything, but wanting to win is.

**Lombroso, Cesare** (1853–1909) Italian criminologist. His book *L'uomo delinquente* (1876) put forward the view that there is a criminal type.

1 The ignorant man always adores what he cannot understand.

*The Man of Genius*, Pt. III, Ch. 3

**London, Jack** (1876–1916) US novelist. *The Call of the Wild* (1903) was written after his experience of the Klondike gold rush (1897). Other books include *The Sea Wolf* (1902) and *Martin Eden* (1909).

1 In an English ship, they say, it is poor grub, poor pay, and easy work; in an American ship, good grub, good pay, and hard work. And this is applicable to the working populations of both countries.

*The People of the Abyss*, Ch. 20

**Longfellow, Henry Wadsworth** (1807–82) US poet. A professor of modern languages, he travelled widely in Europe. His narrative poems, including *Evangeline* (1847) and *The Song of Hiawatha* (1855), achieved great popularity.

1 I shot an arrow into the air,
It fell to earth, I knew not where.

*The Arrow and the Song*

2 I stood on the bridge at midnight,
As the clocks were striking the hour.

*The Bridge*

3 If you would hit the mark, you must aim a little
above it;
Every arrow that flies feels the attraction of
earth.
*Elegiac Verse*

4 Sorrow and silence are strong, and patient endurance is godlike.
*Evangeline*

5 The shades of night were falling fast,
As through an Alpine village passed
A youth, who bore, 'mid snow and ice,
A banner with the strange device,
Excelsior!
Opening of a poem best known as a Victorian drawing-room bal-
lad, and the butt of many music hall jokes. Excelsior means
'higher' (Latin)
*Excelsior*

6 Know how sublime a thing it is
To suffer and be strong.
*The Light of Stars*

7 You would attain to the divine perfection,
And yet not turn your back upon the world.
*Michael Angelo*

8 Art is long, and Time is fleeting,
And our hearts, though stout and brave,
Still, like muffled drums, are beating
Funeral marches to the grave.
See also HIPPOCRATES
*A Psalm of Life*

9 There is a Reaper whose name is Death,
And, with his sickle keen,
He reaps the bearded grain at a breath,
And the flowers that grow between.
*The Reaper and the Flowers*

10 'Wouldst thou' – so the helmsman answered –
'Learn the secret of the sea?
Only those who brave its dangers
Comprehend its mystery!'
*The Secret of the Sea*

11 Onaway! Awake, beloved!
Opening of the song sung by Chibiabos at Hiawatha's wedding
feast; best known in the setting by Coleridge-Taylor
*The Song of Hiawatha*, XI, 'Hiawatha's Wedding-feast'

12 Our ingress into the world
Was naked and bare;
Our progress through the world
Is trouble and care.
*Tales of A Wayside Inn*, 'The Student's Tale'

13 Ships that pass in the night, and speak each
other in passing;
Only a signal shown and a distant voice in the
darkness;
So on the ocean of life we pass and speak one
another,
Only a look and a voice; then darkness again and
a silence.
*Tales of a Wayside Inn*, 'The Theologian's Tale. Elizabeth'

14 Under the spreading chestnut tree
The village smithy stands;
The smith, a mighty man is he,
With large and sinewy hands;
And the muscles of his brawny arms
Are strong as iron bands.
*The Village Blacksmith*

15 Looks the whole world in the face,
For he owes not any man.
*The Village Blacksmith*

16 It was the schooner Hesperus,
That sailed the wintry sea;
And the skipper had taken his little daughter,
To bear him company.
*The Wreck of the Hesperus*

**Longford, Francis Aungier Pakenham, Earl of**
(1905– ) British politician and social reformer. His books include
*Born to Believe* (1953) and *The Idea of Punishment* (1961) as well
as several biographies.

1 No sex without responsibility.
*The Observer*, 'Sayings of the Week', 3 May 1954

2 On the whole I would not say that our Press is
obscene. I would say that it trembles on the
brink of obscenity.
*The Observer*, 'Sayings of the Year', 1963

**Longworth, Alice Roosevelt** (1884–1980) US hostess.
She was a daughter of Theodore Roosevelt.

1 He looks as if he had been weaned on a pickle.
Referring to John Calvin Coolidge, US President 1923–29
*Crowded Hours*

**Loos, Anita** (1891–1981) US novelist and scriptwriter. She
worked in Hollywood for many years and is best remembered for
*Gentlemen Prefer Blondes* (1928).

1 Gentlemen always seem to remember blondes.
*Gentlemen Prefer Blondes*, Ch. 1

2 So this gentleman said a girl with brains ought to
do something else with them besides think.
*Gentlemen Prefer Blondes*, Ch. 1

3 Kissing your hand may make you feel very very
good but a diamond and safire bracelet lasts
forever.
*Gentlemen Prefer Blondes*, Ch. 4

4 Any girl who was a lady would not even think of
having such a good time that she did not remember to hang on to her jewelry.
*Gentlemen Prefer Blondes*, Ch. 4

5 I'm furious about the Women's Liberationists.
They keep getting up on soapboxes and pro-
claiming that women are brighter than men.
That's true, but it should be kept very quiet or it
ruins the whole racket.
*The Observer*, 'Sayings of the Year', 30 Dec 1973

**Lorenz, Konrad** (1903– ) Austrian zoologist and pioneer of
ethology. His books include *King Solomon's Ring* (1949), *Man
Meets Dog* (1950), and *On Aggression* (1963).

1 It is a good morning exercise for a research scientist to discard a pet hypothesis every day before breakfast. It keeps him young.

*On Aggression*, Ch. 2

**Louis, Joe** (Joseph Louis Barrow; 1914–81) US boxer. He has been regarded as one of the best boxers of all time, having been world heavyweight champion from 1937 to 1948.

1 He can run, but he can't hide.

Referring to the speed for which his coming opponent, Billy Conn, was renowned
Attrib.

**Louis Philippe** (1773–1850) King of the French (1830–48), described as the 'Citizen King'. He supported the French Revolution until 1793, when he deserted to Austria. Returning to France after the Restoration, he became king after the July Revolution had ousted Charles X. He abdicated in the 1848 Revolution and died in exile in England.

1 *La cordiale entente qui existe entre mon gouvernement et le sien.*
   The friendly understanding that exists between my government and hers.

Queen Victoria's: referring to an informal understanding reached between Britain and France in 1843. The more familiar phrase, 'entente cordiale', was first used in 1844
Speech, 27 Dec 1843

**Louis XIV** (1638–1715) French king. He believed in the divine right of kings, held a lavish court at Versailles, and was a generous patron of the arts.

1 How could God do this to me after all I have done for him?

On receiving news of the French army's defeat at the battle of Blenheim
*Saint-Simon at Versailles* (L. Norton)

2 Has God then forgotten what I have done for him?

Reportedly said after Marlborough's pyrrhic victory over the French at the Battle of Malplaquet, 11 Sept 1709

3 First feelings are always the most natural.

Recorded by Mme de Sévigné, 1709

4 *L'État c'est moi.*
   I am the State.

Attrib.

5 The Pyrenees have ceased to exist.

On the accession of his grandson to the Spanish throne (1700); attributed by Voltaire

6 Ah, if I were not king, I should lose my temper.

Attrib.

7 Why are you weeping? Did you imagine that I was immortal?

Noticing as he lay on his deathbed that his attendants were crying
*Louis XIV* (V. Cronin)

**Louis XVIII** (1755–1824) French king, who ruled after Napoleon's overthrow, fled from Paris when Napoleon returned from Elba, and ruled again with diminished prestige after Waterloo.

1 Punctuality is the politeness of kings.

Attrib.

**Lovelace, Richard** (1618–58) English poet. Twice imprisoned during the Civil War as a royalist, he wrote his famous poem 'To Althea, from Prison'. His best poems are collected in *Lucasta* (1649).

1 Stone walls do not a prison make,
   Nor iron bars a cage.

*To Althea, from Prison*

**Lovell, Maria** (1803–77) British actress and dramatist.

1 Two souls with but a single thought,
   Two hearts that beat as one.

*Ingomar the Barbarian*, II (transl. of Friedrich Halm)

**Lover, Samuel** (1797–1868) Irish novelist and portrait painter. Novels include *Rory O'More* (1837) and *Handy Andy* (1842).

1 When once the itch of literature comes over a man, nothing can cure it but the scratching of a pen.

*Handy Andy*, Ch. 36

**Low, David (Alexander Cecil)** (1871–1963) New-Zealand-born newspaper cartoonist. Working in *The Star, Evening Standard*, and *The Guardian*, he created world-famous characters, notably Colonel Blimp.

1 I do not know whether he draws a line himself. But I assume that his is the direction . . . It makes Disney the most significant figure in graphic art since Leonardo.

*Walt Disney* (R. Schickel), Ch. 20

**Lowe, Robert, Viscount Sherbrooke** (1811–92) British lawyer and politician. He became chancellor of the exchequer (1868–73) and home secretary (1873–74) under Gladstone.

1 The Chancellor of the Exchequer is a man whose duties make him more or less of a taxing machine. He is intrusted with a certain amount of misery which it is his duty to distribute as fairly as he can.

Speech, House of Commons, 11 Apr 1870

**Lowell, Robert** (1917–77) US poet. Imprisoned as a conscientious objector (1943), he became involved in left-wing politics in the 1960s. His last book was *Day by Day* (1977).

1 The man is killing time – there's nothing else.

*The Drinker*

2 The monument sticks like a fishbone
   in the city's throat.

*For the Union Dead*

3 But I suppose even God was born
   too late to trust the old religion –
   all those setting out
   that never left the ground,
   beginning in wisdom, dying in doubt.

*Tenth Muse*

**Lowry, Malcolm** (1909–57) British novelist, who lived in Canada from 1940. *Ultramarine* (1933) was based on his experiences as a sailor and *Under the Volcano* (1947) reflects his stay in Mexico.

1 Where are the children I might have had? You may suppose I might have wanted them. Drowned to the accompaniment of the rattling of a thousand douche bags.
*Under the Volcano*, Ch. 10

2 How alike are the groans of love to those of the dying.
*Under the Volcano*, Ch. 12

**Loyola, St Ignatius** (1491–1556) Spanish priest, who founded the Society of Jesus (Jesuits) in 1540. His *Spiritual Exercises* (1548) is still highly regarded.

1 To give and not to count the cost;
To fight and not to heed the wounds;
To toil and not to seek for rest;
To labour and not ask for any reward
Save that of knowing that we do Thy will.
*Prayer for Generosity*

**Lucan** (Marcus Annaeus Lucanus; 39–65 AD) Roman poet. The nephew of Seneca, he committed suicide after his plot against Nero was discovered. *Pharsalia*, an epic poem about the civil war between Pompey and Caesar, is his main surviving work.

1 I have a wife, I have sons: all of them hostages given to fate.
*See also* BACON (1521–1626)
*Works*, VII

**Lucas, George** (1945– ) US film director whose films include *American Graffiti* (1973) and *Star Wars* (1977).

1 May the Force be with you.
*Star Wars*

**Lucretius** (Titus Lucretius Carus; c. 99–55 BC) Roman philosopher and poet. His six-volume *On the Nature of the Universe* gives a complete account of the philosophy of Epicurus.

1 Nothing can be created out of nothing.
*On the Nature of the Universe*, I

2 Constant dripping hollows out a stone.
*On the Nature of the Universe*, I. *See also* LATIMER; OVID

3 *Inque brevi spatio mutantur saecla animantum*
*Et quasi cursores vitai lampada tradunt.*
The generations of living things pass in a short time, and like runners hand on the torch of life.
*On the Nature of the Universe*, II

4 What is food to one man is bitter poison to others.
*On the Nature of the Universe*, IV

**Luther, Martin** (1483–1546) German Protestant and founder of Lutheranism. Incensed by the sale of indulgences to swell papal funds, he nailed his thesis to the door of the Wittenberg church, and was subsequently excommunicated. After the Augsburg Confession (1530) he gave up his hope of reforming the church and set up the separate Protestant church.

1 Here stand I. I can do no other. God help me. Amen.
Speech at the Diet of Worms, 18 Apr 1521

2 Who loves not wine, woman and song,
Remains a fool his whole life long.
Attrib.

**Lutyens, Sir Edwin Landseer** (1869–1944) British architect who was responsible for the viceregal palace in New Delhi (1912–30).

1 The answer is in the plural and they bounce.
Attrib.

2 This piece of cod passes all understanding.
Comment made in a restaurant
Attrib.

**Lyndhurst, John Singleton Copley, Baron** (1772–1863) US-born British lawyer who became lord chancellor (1827–30; 1834–35; 1841–46).

1 Campbell has added another terror to death.
Referring to Lord Campbell's controversial *Lives of the Lord Chancellors* (1845–47), from which Lyndhurst was excluded because he was still alive

**Lyte, Henry Francis** (1793–1847) British hymn writer and Anglican clergyman.

1 Abide with me; fast falls the eventide;
The darkness deepens; Lord, with me abide;
When other helpers fail, and comforts flee,
Help of the helpless, O, abide with me.
*Abide with Me*

**Lytton, Lady Constance** (1869–1923) British suffragette, daughter of the Earl of Lytton. She was imprisoned, went on a hunger strike, and was released – but was rearrested posing as a working-class woman. As home secretary, Churchill refused a public enquiry into the difference in her treatment on these occasions.

1 The first time you meet Winston you see all his faults and the rest of your life you spend in discovering his virtues.
Referring to Churchill
*Edward Marsh* (Christopher Hassall), Ch. 7

**Lytton, 1st Earl of** *See* Meredith, Owen

# M

**Macarthur, Douglas** (1880–1964) US general. As allied commander, he recaptured the south-west Pacific in World War II and commanded the occupation of Japan. The commander of UN forces in the Korean War, he advocated active operations against China, for which he was dismissed by Truman.

**1** I shall return.

Message (11 Mar 1942) on leaving Corregidor in the Philippines after being dismissed by Truman

**Macaulay, Dame Rose** (1889–1958) British writer. She wrote many novels, including *Dangerous Ages* (1921) and *The Towers of Trebizond* (1956).

**1** Gentlemen-know that fresh air should be kept in its proper place – out of doors – and that, God having given us indoors and out-of-doors, we should not attempt to do away with this distinction.

*Crewe Train*, Pt. I, Ch. 5

**2** Decades have a delusive edge to them. They are not, of course, really periods at all, except as any other ten years would be. But we, looking at them, are caught by the different name each bears, and give them different attributes, and tie labels on them, as if they were flowers in a border.

*Told by an Idiot*, Pt. II, Ch. 1

**3** A group of closely related persons living under one roof; it is a convenience, often a necessity, sometimes a pleasure, sometimes the reverse; but who first exalted it as admirable, an almost religious ideal?

*The World My Wilderness*, Ch. 20

**4** Poem me no poems.

*Poetry Review*, Autumn 1963

**5** The great and recurrent question about abroad is, is it worth getting there?

Attrib.

**6** It was a book to kill time for those who like it better dead.

Attrib.

**Macaulay, Thomas Babington, Baron** (1800–59) British historian and writer. An MP for many years, he is remembered for his five-volume *History of England* (1849–61).

**1** The English Bible, a book which, if everything else in our language should perish, would alone suffice to show the whole extent of its beauty and power.

*Essays and Biographies*, 'John Dryden'. *Edinburgh Review*

**2** His imagination resembled the wings of an ostrich. It enabled him to run, though not to soar.

*Essays and Biographies*, 'John Dryden'. *Edinburgh Review*

**3** Knowledge advances by steps, and not by leaps.

*Essays and Biographies*, 'History'. *Edinburgh Review*

**4** The gallery in which the reporters sit has become a fourth estate of the realm.

Referring to the press gallery in the House of Commons
*Historical Essays Contributed to the 'Edinburgh Review'*, 'Hallam's 'Constitutional History''

**5** The reluctant obedience of distant provinces generally costs more than it is worth.

*Historical Essays Contributed to the 'Edinburgh Review'*, 'Lord Mahon's War of the Succession'

**6** The highest intellects, like the tops of mountains, are the first to catch and to reflect the dawn.

*Historical Essays Contributed to the 'Edinburgh Review'*, 'Sir James Mackintosh'

**7** He . . . felt towards those whom he had deserted that peculiar malignity which has, in all ages, been characteristic of apostates.

*History of England*, Vol. I, Ch. 1

**8** The Puritan hated bear-baiting, not because it gave pain to the bear, but because it gave pleasure to the spectators.

*History of England*, Vol. I, Ch. 2

**9** There were gentlemen and there were seamen in the navy of Charles the Second. But the seamen were not gentlemen; and the gentlemen were not seamen.

*History of England*, Vol. I, Ch. 3

**10** In every age the vilest specimens of human nature are to be found among demagogues.

*History of England*, Vol. I, Ch. 5

**11** Then out spake brave Horatius,
The Captain of the Gate:
'To every man upon this earth
Death cometh soon or late.
And how can man die better
Than facing fearful odds,
For the ashes of his fathers,
And the temples of his Gods?'

*Lays of Ancient Rome*, 'Horatius', 27

**12** The dust and silence of the upper shelf.

*Literary Essays Contributed to the 'Edinburgh Review'*, 'Milton'

**13** As civilization advances, poetry almost necessarily declines.

*Literary Essays Contributed to the 'Edinburgh Review'*, 'Milton'

**14** Perhaps no person can be a poet, or can even enjoy poetry, without a certain unsoundness of mind.

*Literary Essays Contributed to the 'Edinburgh Review'*, 'Milton'

**15** Many politicians of our time are in the habit of laying it down as a self-evident proposition, that no people ought to be free till they are fit to use their freedom. The maxim is worthy of the fool in the old story, who resolved not to go into the water till he had learnt to swim. If men are to wait for liberty till they become wise and good in slavery, they may indeed wait for ever.

*Literary Essays Contributed to the 'Edinburgh Review', 'Milton'*

**16** We know no spectacle so ridiculous as the British public in one of its periodical fits of morality.

*Literary Essays Contributed to the 'Edinburgh Review', 'Moore's 'Life of Lord Byron'*

**17** His writing bears the same relation to poetry which a Turkey carpet bears to a picture. There are colours in the Turkey carpet out of which a picture might be made. There are words in Mr Montgomery's writing which, when disposed in certain orders and combinations, have made, and will make again, good poetry. But, as they now stand, they seem to be put together on principle in such a manner as to give no image of anything 'in the heavens above, or in the earth beneath, or in the waters under the earth'.

*Literary Essays Contributed to the 'Edinburgh Review', 'Mr. Robert Montgomery's Poems'*

**18** Thank you, madam, the agony is abated.

*Replying, aged four, to a lady who asked if he had hurt himself
Life and Letters of Macaulay* (Trevelyan), Ch. 1

**19** Ye diners-out from whom we guard our spoons.

*Letter to Hannah Macaulay, 29 June 1831*

**20** I shall not be satisfied unless I produce something that shall for a few days supersede the last fashionable novel on the tables of young ladies.

*Letter to Macvey Napier, 5 Nov 1841*

**21** A broken head in Cold Bath Fields produces a greater sensation among us than three pitched battles in India.

*Speech, 10 July 1833*

**MacCarthy, Sir Desmond** (1878–1952) British writer and theatre critic.

**1** When I meet those remarkable people whose company is coveted, I often wish they would show off a little more.

*Theatre, 'Good Talk'*

**2** You understand *Epipsychidion* best when you are in love; *Don Juan* when anger is subsiding into indifference. Why not Strindberg when you have a temperature?

*Theatre, 'Miss Julie and the Pariah'*

**3** The whole of art is an appeal to a reality which is not without us but in our minds.

*Theatre, 'Modern Drama'*

**MacDiarmid, Hugh** (Christopher Murray Grieve; 1892–1978) Scottish poet. A Marxist and Scottish nationalist, he wrote his early verse, such as *A Drunken Man Looks at the Thistle* (1926), in a Scots language but later used English.

**1** Killing
Is the ultimate simplification of life.
*England's Double Knavery*

**2** It is very rarely that a man loves
And when he does it is nearly always fatal.
*The International Brigade*

**3** Our principal·writers have nearly all been fortunate in escaping regular education.
*The Observer, 'Sayings of the Week', 29 Mar 1953*

**MacDonald, Betty** (1908–58) US writer. Her books include *The Egg and I* (1945).

**1** In high school and college my sister Mary was very popular with the boys, but I had braces on my teeth and got high marks.
*The Egg and I, Ch. 2*

**MacDonald, (James) Ramsey** (1866–1937) British statesman. He was the first Labour prime minister (1924; 1929–31; 1931–35). His first (minority) administration was defeated after a vote of no confidence. His second administration was broadened into a coalition in which he was replaced by Baldwin in 1935.

**1** Let them especially put their demands in such a way that Great Britain could say that she supported both sides.
*Referring to France and Germany
The Origins of the Second Word War* (A. J. P. Taylor), Ch. 3

**2** Society goes on and on and on. It is the same with ideas.
*Speech, 1935*

**Machiavelli, Niccolò** (1469–1527) Italian statesman, diplomat, and political theorist. In his best-known book, *The Prince* (1532; written 1513), he argues that all means are justified in achieving a stable political state.

**1** It is the nature of men to be bound by the benefits they confer as much as by those they receive.
*The Prince*

**MacInnes, Colin** (1914–76) British novelist and journalist. His best-known novels are *City of Spades* (1957) and *Absolute Beginners* (1957).

**1** In England, pop art and fine art stand resolutely back to back.
*England, Half English, 'Pop Songs and Teenagers'*

**2** England is . . . a country infested with people who love to tell us what to do, but who very rarely seem to know what's going on.
*England, Half English, 'Pop Songs and Teenagers'*

**3** A coloured man can tell, in five seconds dead, whether a white man likes him or not. If the white man *says* he does, he is instantly – and usually quite rightly – mistrusted.
*England, Half English, 'A Short Guide for Jumbles'*

**Mackenzie, Sir Compton** (1883–1972) British writer. He made his reputation with the semiautobiographical *Sinister Street* (1913). Later novels include *The Parson's Progress* (1923) and *Whisky Galore* (1947). He also wrote some verse and several plays.

**1** Women do not find it difficult nowadays to behave like men; but they often find it extremely difficult to behave like gentlemen.

*On Moral Courage*

**Mackintosh, Sir James** (1765–1832) Scottish lawyer, philosopher, and historian, who became a judge in India. His best-known philosophical work is the *Dissertation on the Progress of Ethical Philosophy* (1830); he also wrote a number of historical books and articles.

**1** The Commons, faithful to their system, remained in a wise and masterly inactivity.

*Vindiciae Gallicae*

**MacLeish, Archibald** (1892–1982) US poet and dramatist. *Collected Poems* (1952) was followed by the plays *JB* (1958) and *Six Plays* (1980).

**1** We have learned the answers, all the answers:
It is the question that we do not know.

*The Hamlet of A. Macleish*

**Macleod, Fiona** (William Sharp; 1856–1905) Scottish poet and writer. He published several collections of verse under his own name, including *Earth's Voices* (1884) and *Romantic Ballads and Poems of Fantasy* (1888). As Fiona Macleod he published a number of works on the Celtic world, including *Green Fire* (1896), *The Immortal Hour* (1900), and *Deirdre* (1903).

**1** My heart is a lonely hunter that hunts on a lonely hill.

*The Lonely Hunter*

**Macleod, Iain** (1913–70) British politician. After various ministerial posts in the 1950s and 1960s, he became chancellor of the exchequer in 1970, but died in office. He was also a bridge theorist who, with Jack Marx, invented the Acol system.

**1** History is too serious to be left to historians.

*The Observer*, 'Sayings of the Week', 16 July 1961

**Macmillan, (Maurice) Harold, Earl of Stockton** (1894–1986) British statesman and publisher; Conservative prime minister (1957–63). His last year in office was notorious for the Profumo scandal.

**1** Most of our people have never had it so good.

Speech, Bedford Football Ground, 20 July 1957

**2** I thought the best thing to do was to settle up these little local difficulties, and then turn to the wider vision of the Commonwealth.

Referring to resignation of ministers
Remark, London Airport, 7 Jan 1958

**3** When you're abroad you're a statesman: when you're at home you're just a politician.

Speech, 1958

**4** The wind of change is blowing through the continent. Whether we like it or not, this growth of national consciousness is a political fact.

Speech, South African Parliament, 3 Feb 1960

**5** There are three groups that no prime minister should provoke: the Treasury, the Vatican, and the National Union of Mineworkers.

First used by Stanley BALDWIN
Attrib.

**6** Selling the family silver.

Referring to privatization of profitable nationalized industries
Speech, House of Lords, 1986

**MacNally, Leonard** (1752–1820) Irish dramatist, poet, and political informer. He betrayed the revolutionaries, whom he had supposedly joined, to the government. His work includes the song *The Lass of Richmond Hill*.

**1** On Richmond Hill there lives a lass,
More sweet than May day morn,
Whose charms all other maids surpass,
A rose without a thorn.

*The Lass of Richmond Hill*

**MacNeice, Louis** (1907–63) Irish-born British poet. His verse publications include *Blind Fireworks* (1929), *Autumn Journal* (1939), and *The Burning Perch* (1963). He also wrote radio plays and worked for the BBC.

**1** It's no go the picture palace, it's no go the stadium,
It's no go the country cot with a pot of pink geraniums,
It's no go the Government grants, it's no go the elections,
Sit on your arse for fifty years and hang your hat on a pension.

*Bagpipe Music*

**2** Time was away and somewhere else,
There were two glasses and two chairs
And two people with one pulse.

*Meeting Point*

**Madariaga y Rogo, Salvador de** (1886–1978) Spanish diplomat and writer. The Spanish ambassador to the USA (1931) and France (1932–34), he also wrote a number of historical books and biographies.

**1** First the sweetheart of the nation, then the aunt, woman governs America because America is a land of boys who refuse to grow up.

*The Perpetual Pessimist* (Sagitarius and George)

**2** In politics, as in grammar, one should be able to tell the substantives from the adjectives. Hitler was a substantive; Mussolini only an adjective. Hitler was a nuisance. Mussolini was bloody. Together a bloody nuisance.

Attrib.

**Madden, Samuel** (1686–1765) Irish writer, best remembered for his poem *Boulter's Monument* (1745).

**1** Words are men's daughters, but God's sons are things.

*See also* Samuel JOHNSON
*Boulter's Monument*

**Magee, William Connor** (1821–91) British clergyman. He became Bishop of Peterborough (1868–91) and Archbishop of York (1891).

1 It would be better that England should be free than that England should be compulsorily sober.
Speech on the Intoxicating Liquor Bill, House of Lords, 2 May 1872

**Magidson, Herb** (20th century) US songwriter.

1 Music, Maestro, Please.
Song title

**Mailer, Norman** (1923– ) US writer. His books include the novels *The Naked and the Dead* (1948), *The American Dream* (1965), and *The Executioner's Song* (1979).

1 Growth is a greater mystery than death. All of us can understand failure, we all contain failure and death within us, but not even the successful man can begin to describe the impalpable elations and apprehensions of growth.
*Advertisements for Myself*

2 Once a newspaper touches a story, the facts are lost forever, even to the protagonists.
*The Presidential Papers*

**Maistre, Joseph de** (1753–1821) French monarchist, who opposed the Revolution. He had faith in the divine right of kings and a belief, expressed in *Du pape* (1819), in the infallibility of the pope.

1 Every country has the government it deserves.
*Lettres et Opuscules Inédits*, 15 Aug 1811

2 Scratch the Russian and you will find the Tartar.
Attributed also to Napoleon and Prince de Ligne

**Malamud, Bernard** (1914– ) US novelist. A writer using Jewish themes, he has written *The Assistant* (1957), *Pictures of Fidelman* (1969), *The Tenants* (1971), and *God's Grace* (1982).

1 Levin wanted friendship and got friendliness; he wanted steak and they offered spam.
*A New Life*, VI

**Malcolm X** See X, Malcolm.

**Malesherbes, Chrétien Guillaume de Lamoignonde** (1721–94) French statesman, noted for his liberalism as director of censorship. Banned from court in 1771 for criticizing the monarchy, he was nevertheless executed as a royalist during the Revolution.

1 A new maxim is often a brilliant error.
*Pensées et maximes*

**Malherbe, François de** (1555–1628) French poet. Court poet to Henry IV, his poetry is mostly devoted to religious and political themes.

1 But she was of the world where the fairest things have the worst fate. Like a rose, she has lived as long as roses live, the space of one morning.
*Consolation à M. du Périer*

**Mallaby, Sir (Howard) George** (1902–78) British diplomat and writer. His books include memoirs and literary criticism.

1 Never descend to the ways of those above you.
*From My Level*

**Mallet, Robert** (1915– ) French writer and academic. Rector of the University of Paris (1969–80), he is the author of poetry, plays, and novels.

1 How many pessimists end up by desiring the things they fear, in order to prove that they are right.
*Apostilles*

**Mallory, George Leigh** (1886–1924) British mountaineer.

1 Because it is there.
Answer to the question 'Why do you want to climb Mt. Everest?'
*George Mallory* (D. Robertson)

**Malory, Sir Thomas** (1400–71) English writer. Probably a Warwickshire knight and MP, he is remembered as the author of *Morte d'Arthur*, an account of the legendary court of King Arthur, based on French sources.

1 For, as I suppose, no man in this world hath lived better than I have done, to achieve that I have done.
*Morte d'Arthur*, Bk. XVII, Ch. 16

2 For love that time was not as love is nowadays.
*Morte d'Arthur*, Bk. XX, Ch. 3

3 And much more am I sorrier for my good knights' loss than for the loss of my fair queen; for queens I might have enough, but such a fellowship of good knights shall never be together in no company.
*Morte d'Arthur*, Bk. XX, Ch. 9

4 Then Sir Launcelot saw her visage, but he wept not greatly, but sighed!
*Morte d'Arthur*, Bk. XXI, Ch. 11

**Malthus, Thomas Robert** (1766–1834) British clergyman and economist. His *Essays on the Principle of Population* (1798–1803) warns that the geometrical increase in population, if unrestrained, will quickly outstrip the arithmetical growth of food production.

1 Population, when unchecked, increases in a geometrical ratio. Subsistence only increases in an arithmetical ratio.
*Essays on the Principle of Population*

2 The perpetual struggle for room and food.
*Essays on the Principle of Population*

**Mancroft, Stormont Samuel, Baron** (1917– ) British businessman and writer. A well-known after-dinner speaker, he also wrote *Booking the Cooks* (1969) and *Bees in Some Bonnets* (1979).

1 Happy is the man with a wife to tell him what to do and a secretary to do it.
*The Observer*, 'Sayings of the Week', 18 Dec 1966

**Mandela, Nelson** (1918– ) South African lawyer and politician. A Black and an active member of the African National Congress, he was charged with treason, acquitted in 1961, retried in 1963–64, and sentenced to life imprisonment. His wife has campaigned ceaselessly for his release.

MAP · 227

1 I cannot and will not give any undertaking at a time when I, and you, the people, are not free. Your freedom and mine cannot be separated.

Message read by his daughter to a rally in Soweto, 10 Feb 1985

**Mandelstam, Osip** (1891–1938) Russian poet. His verse collections include *Tristia* (1922). He was arrested as a political dissident (1934) and is presumed to have died in a labour camp.

1 No, I am no one's contemporary – ever.
That would have been above my station . . .
How I loathe that other with my name.
He certainly never was me.

*Poems*, No. 141

2 Now I'm dead in the grave with my lips moving
And every schoolboy repeating my words by heart.

*Poems*, No. 306

**Manikan, Ruby** (20th century) Indian Church leader.

1 If you educate a man you educate a person, but if you educate a woman you educate a family.

*The Observer*, 'Sayings of the Week', 30 Mar 1947

**Mankeiwicz, Herman J.** (1897–1953) US journalist, screenwriter, and wit. His films include *Citizen Kane* (with Orson Welles; 1941), *Christmas Holiday* (1944), and *Pride of St Louis* (1952).

1 It is the only disease you don't look forward to being cured of.

Referring to death
*Citizen Kane*

2 There, but for the Grace of God, goes God.

Said of Orson Welles in the making of *Citizen Kane*. Also attributed to others
*The Citizen Kane Book*

3 You know it's hard to hear what a bearded man is saying. He can't speak above a whisker.

*Wit's End* (R. E. Drennan)

**Mann, Thomas** (1875–1955) German novelist. His books include *Buddenbrooks* (1901), *The Magic Mountain* (1924), *Doctor Faustus* (1947), and the four novels *Joseph and His Brothers* (1933–44). His novella *Death in Venice* (1912) became a film and an opera. He went to the USA in the 1930s to escape the Nazis.

1 What we call mourning for our dead is perhaps not so much grief at not being able to call them back as it is grief at not being able to want to do so.

*The Magic Mountain*

2 Every intellectual attitude is latently political.

*The Observer*, 11 Aug 1974

**Mansfield, Katherine** (1888–1923) New-Zealand-born British short-story writer and poet. She married (1918) John Middleton Murry and lived abroad on account of her tuberculosis. Her collections include *In a German Pension* (1911), *Bliss* (1920), and *The Garden Party* (1922). Her *Poems* (1923), *Journal* (1927), and *Letters* (1928) were published after her premature death.

1 How idiotic civilization is! Why be given a body if you have to keep it shut up in a case like a rare, rare fiddle?

*Bliss and Other Stories*, 'Bliss'

2 Whenever I prepare for a journey I prepare as though for death. Should I never return, all is in order. This is what life has taught me.

*The Journal of Katherine Mansfield*, 1922

**Mansfield, William Murray, Earl of** (1705–93) British judge and politician. He was chief justice of the Kings Bench (1756–88).

1 Consider what you think justice requires, and decide accordingly. But never give your reasons; for your judgement will probably be right, but your reasons will certainly be wrong.

Advice given to a new colonial governor
*Lives of the Chief Justices* (Campbell), Ch. 40

**Mao Tse-Tung** (1893–1976) Chinese communist leader. As chairman of the Communist Party, in 1949 he proclaimed the People's Republic of China and in 1966–68 launched the Cultural Revolution. He developed the form of communism known as Maoism.

1 'War is the continuation of politics'. In this sense war is politics and war itself is a political action.

*See also* CHOU EN-LAI; CLAUSEWITZ
*Quotations from Chairman Mao Tse-Tung*, Ch. 5

2 We are advocates of the abolition of war, we do not want war; but war can only be abolished through war, and in order to get rid of the gun it is necessary to take up the gun.

*Quotations from Chairman Mao Tse-Tung*, Ch. 5

3 All reactionaries are paper tigers.

*Quotations from Chairman Mao Tse-Tung*, Ch. 6

4 Letting a hundred flowers blossom and a hundred schools of thought contend is the policy for promoting the progress of the arts and the sciences.

*Quotations from Chairman Mao Tse-Tung*, Ch. 32

5 Every Communist must grasp the truth, 'Political power grows out of the barrel of a gun.'

*Selected Works*, Vol II, 'Problems of War and Strategy', 6 Nov 1938

6 To read too many books is harmful.

*The New Yorker*, 7 Mar 1977

7 The atom bomb is a paper tiger which the United States reactionaries use to scare people.

Interview, Aug 1946

8 The government burns down whole cities while the people are forbidden to light lamps.

Attrib.

**Map, Walter** (c. 1140–c. 1209) Welsh clergyman and writer. He became Archdeacon of Oxford (from 1197). His *De Nugis Curialium* (c. 1182) is a miscellany of gossip, theological argument, diary, etc. He was also involved in the formulation of parts of the Arthurian legend.

1 If die I must, let me die drinking in an inn.

*De Nugis Curialium*

**Marco Polo** (c. 1254–1324) Venetian traveller. Having spent many years in the service of the Mongol emperor Kublai Khan, he fought for the Venetians against the Genoese and was captured. In prison he dictated an account of his travels.

1 I have not told half of what I saw.

Last words
*The Story of Civilization* (W. Durant), Vol. I

**Marcus Aurelius Antoninus** (121–180 AD) Roman emperor (161–180). He is remembered for his *Meditations*, 12 books of Stoic aphorisms.

1 Whatever this is that I am, it is a little flesh and breath, and the ruling part.

*Meditations*, Bk. II, Ch. 2

2 And thou wilt give thyself relief, if thou doest every act of thy life as if it were the last.

*Meditations*, Bk. II, Ch. 5

3 Remember that no man loses any other life than this which he now lives, nor lives any other than this which he now loses.

*Meditations*, Bk. II, Ch. 14

4 All things from eternity are of like forms and come round in a circle.

*Meditations*, Bk. II, Ch. 14

5 The universe is transformation; our life is what our thoughts make it.

*Meditations*, Bk. IV, Ch. 3

6 Everything that happens happens as it should, and if you observe carefully, you will find this to be so.

*Meditations*, Bk. IV, Ch. 10

7 Everything is only for a day, both that which remembers and that which is remembered.

*Meditations*, Bk. IV, Ch. 35

8 Time is like a river made up of the events which happen, and its current is strong; no sooner does anything appear than it is swept away, and another comes in its place, and will be swept away too.

*Meditations*, Bk. IV, Ch. 43

9 Nothing happens to any man that he is not formed by nature to bear.

*Meditations*, Bk. V, Ch. 18

10 Live with the gods. And he does so who constantly shows them that his soul is satisfied with what is assigned to him.

*Meditations*, Bk. V, Ch. 27

11 Remember that to change your mind and follow him who sets you right is to be none the less free than you were before.

*Meditations*, Bk. VIII, Ch. 16

12 Whatever may happen to you was prepared for you from all eternity; and the implication of causes was from eternity spinning the thread of your being.

*Meditations*, Bk. X, Ch. 5

**Marcuse, Herbert** (1898–1979) German-born US philosopher, noted for his radical anti-authoritarian views. His books include *The Ethics of Revolution* (1966).

1 Not every problem someone has with his girlfriend is necessarily due to the capitalist mode of production.

*The Listener*

**Marie-Antoinette** (1755–93) Queen of France, as wife of Louis XVI. Her extravagance contributed to the unpopularity of the monarchy and after the Revolution, like her husband, she was guillotined.

1 Let them eat cake.

On being told that the people had no bread to eat; in fact she was repeating a much older saying
Attrib.

**Marlborough, Sarah, Duchess of** (1660–1744) Wife of John Churchill, 1st Duke of Marlborough. A trusted friend of Princess (later Queen) Anne, she exercised control over the Whig ministry after Anne's accession. However, she eventually fell from favour and lived in retirement.

1 The Duke returned from the wars today and did pleasure me in his top-boots.

Attributed to her in various forms; a more ambitious version goes '... pleasure me three times in his top-boots'
Attrib.

**Marlowe, Christopher** (1564–93) English dramatist and poet. His plays include *Tamburlaine the Great* (1587), *The Jew of Malta* (1590), *Doctor Faustus* (1592), and *Edward II* (1592). He was killed in a fight in a Deptford tavern.

1 When all the world dissolves,
And every creature shall be purified,
All place shall be hell that is not heaven.

*Doctor Faustus*, II:1

2 Was this the face that launch'd a thousand ships
And burnt the topless towers of Ilium?
Sweet Helen, make me immortal with a kiss.

*Doctor Faustus*, V:1

3 Oh, thou art fairer than the evening air
Clad in the beauty of a thousand stars.

*Doctor Faustus*, V:1

4 Now hast thou but one bare hour to live,
And then thou must be damn'd perpetually!
Stand still, you ever-moving spheres of heaven,
That time may cease, and midnight never come.

*Doctor Faustus*, V:2

5 Ugly hell, gape not! come not, Lucifer!
I'll burn my books!

*Doctor Faustus*, V:2

6 Cut is the branch that might have grown full straight,
And burned is Apollo's laurel-bough,
That sometime grew within this learned man.

*Doctor Faustus*, Epilogue

7 My men, like satyrs grazing on the lawns,
Shall with their goat-feet dance an antic hay.

*Edward the Second*, I:1

**8** Who ever loved, that loved not at first sight?

*Hero and Leander*, I

**9** I count religion but a childish toy,
And hold there is no sin but ignorance.

*The Jew of Malta*, Prologue

**10** And, as their wealth increaseth, so inclose
Infinite riches in a little room.

*The Jew of Malta*, I:1

**11** FRIAR BARNARDINE. Thou hast committed –
BARABAS. Fornication: but that was in another
country;
And beside the wench is dead.

*The Jew of Malta*, IV:1

**12** I'm arm'd with more than complete steel –
The justice of my quarrel.

Play also attributed to others
*Lust's Dominion*, IV:3

**13** Come live with me, and be my love;
And we will all the pleasures prove
That hills and valleys, dales and fields,
Woods or steepy mountain yields.

*The Passionate Shepherd to his Love*

**14** And I will make thee beds of roses
And a thousand fragrant posies.

*The Passionate Shepherd to his Love*

**Marquis, Don(ald Robert)** (1878–1937) US journalist
and writer. His column in the *New York Sun* (1912–22)
introduced mehitabel (a cat) and archy (a cockroach). Books
include *archy and mehitabel* (1927) and *The Old Soak* (1921).

**1** An idea isn't responsible for the people who believe in it.

*New York Sun*

**2** To stroke a platitude until it purrs like an
epigram.

*New York Sun*

**Marryat, Captain Frederick** (1792–1848) British
novelist. His books deriving from his experience in the navy
include *Mr. Midshipman Easy* (1836) and *Masterman Ready* (1841).

**1** If you please, ma'am, it was a very little one.

Said by the nurse to excuse the fact that she had had an illegitimate baby
*Mr. Midshipman Easy*, Ch. 3

**2** I never knows the children. It's just six of one
and half-a-dozen of the other.

*The Pirate*, Ch. 4

**3** I think it much better that . . . every man paddle
his own canoe.

*Settlers in Canada*, Ch. 8

**Marsh, Sir Edward Howard** (1872–1953) British civil
servant, writer, and wit. Private secretary to Winston Churchill
(1917–22; 1924–29) and others, he wrote several books including
*Minima* (1947).

**1** Dear Roger Fry whom I love as a man but detest as a movement.

Roger Fry (1866–1934) was an artist and art critic, who champi-
oned the postimpressionists
*Edward Marsh* (Christopher Hassall), Ch. 11

**Martineau, Harriet** (1802–76) British writer. She wrote
novels and books on history, religion, and economics.

**1** I am in truth very thankful for not having married at all.

*Harriet Martineau's Autobiography*, Vol. I

**2** If there is any country on earth where the
course of true love may be expected to run
smooth, it is America.

*Society in America*, Vol. III, 'Marriage'

**3** . . . the early marriages of silly children . . .
where . . . every woman is married before she
well knows how serious a matter human life is.

*Society in America*, Vol. III, 'Marriage'

**4** In no country, I believe, are the marriage laws
so iniquitous as in England, and the conjugal
relation, in consequence, so impaired.

*Society in America*, Vol. III, 'Marriage'

**5** Any one must see at a glance that if men and
women marry those whom they do not love,
they must love those whom they do not marry.

*Society in America*, Vol. III, 'Marriage'

**6** . . . is it to be understood that the principles of
the Declaration of Independence bear no relation to half of the human race?

*Society in America*, Vol. III, 'Marriage'

**Marvell, Andrew** (1621–78) English poet. MP for Hull for
nearly 20 years, he published many pamphlets attacking corruption
in the government. His poetry, much of which was published
posthumously, includes 'To His Coy Mistress' and 'The Garden'.

**1** How vainly men themselves amaze
To win the palm, the oak, or bays.

*The Garden*

**2** Annihilating all that's made
To a green thought in a green shade.

*The Garden*

**3** So restless Cromwell could not cease
In the inglorious arts of peace.

*An Horatian Ode upon Cromwell's Return from Ireland*

**4** He nothing common did or mean
Upon that memorable scene,
But with his keener eye
The axe's edge did try.

Referring to the execution of Charles I
*An Horatian Ode upon Cromwell's Return from Ireland*

**5** Ye living lamps, by whose dear light
The nightingale does sit so late,
And studying all the summer night,
Her matchless songs does meditate.

*The Mower to the Glow-worms*

6 I have a garden of my own,
But so with roses overgrown,
And lilies, that you would it guess
To be a little wilderness.
*The Nymph Complaining for the Death of her Fawn*

7 Who can foretell for what high cause
This darling of the Gods was born?
*The Picture of Little T.C. in a Prospect of Flowers*

8 Gather the flowers, but spare the buds.
*The Picture of Little T.C. in a Prospect of Flowers*

9 Had we but world enough, and time,
This coyness, lady, were no crime.
*To His Coy Mistress*

10 But at my back I always hear
Time's winged chariot hurrying near;
And yonder all before us lie
Deserts of vast eternity.
*To His Coy Mistress*

11 Let us roll all our strength and all
Our sweetness up into one ball,
And tear our pleasures with rough strife
Thorough the iron gates of life:
Thus, though we cannot make our sun
Stand still, yet we will make him run.
*To His Coy Mistress*

12 The grave's a fine and private place,
But none, I think, do there embrace.
*To His Coy Mistress*

**Marx, Groucho** (Julius Marx; 1895–1977) US comedian and
film actor; the member of the Marx brothers team who specialized
in wisecracks. Their films included *Monkey Business* (1931), *Horse
Feathers* (1932), *A Night at the Opera* (1935), and *A Night in
Casablanca* (1945).

1 You're the most beautiful woman I've ever seen,
which doesn't say much for you.
*Animal Crackers*

2 One morning I shot an elephant in my pajamas.
How he got into my pajamas I'll never know.
*Animal Crackers*

3 What's a thousand dollars? Mere chicken feed. A
poultry matter.
*The Cocoanuts*

4 Your eyes shine like the pants of my blue serge
suit.
*The Cocoanuts*

5 Either he's dead or my watch has stopped.
*A Day at the Races*

6 A child of five would understand this.
Send somebody to fetch a child of five.
*Duck Soup*

7 My husband is dead.
– I'll bet he's just using that as an excuse.
I was with him to the end.
– No wonder he passed away.
I held him in my arms and kissed him.
– So it was murder!
*Duck Soup*

8 Go, and never darken my towels again!
*Duck Soup*

9 Remember, men, we're fighting for this woman's
honour; which is probably more than she ever
did.
*Duck Soup*

10 There's a man outside with a big black
moustache.
– Tell him I've got one.
*Horse Feathers*

11 You're a disgrace to our family name of Wagstaff, if such a thing is possible.
*Horse Feathers*

12 You've got the brain of a four-year-old boy, and I
bet he was glad to get rid of it.
*Horse Feathers*

13 Look at me: I worked my way up from nothing
to a state of extreme poverty.
*Monkey Business*

14 I want to register a complaint. Do you know who
sneaked into my room at three o'clock this
morning? . . .
– Who? . . .
Nobody, and that's my complaint.
*Monkey Business*

15 Do you suppose I could buy back my introduction to you?
*Monkey Business*

16 Sir, you have the advantage of me.
– Not yet I haven't, but wait till I get you
outside.
*Monkey Business*

17 Do they allow tipping on the boat?
– Yes, sir.
Have you got two fives?
– Oh, yes, sir.
Then you won't need the ten cents I was going
to give you.
*A Night at the Opera*

18 The strains of Verdi will come back to you tonight, and Mrs Claypool's cheque will come
back to you in the morning.
*A Night at the Opera*

19 Send two dozen roses to Room 424 and put
'Emily, I love you' on the back of the bill.
*A Night in Casablanca*

20 I never forget a face, but I'll make an exception
in your case.
*The Guardian, 18 June 1965*

**21** I was so long writing my review that I never got around to reading the book.
Attrib.

**22** Time wounds all heels.
Attrib.

**23** Please accept my resignation. I don't want to belong to any club that will accept me as a member.
Resigning from the Friar's Club in Hollywood; *see also* BENCHLEY
Attrib.

**24** No, Groucho is not my real name. I'm breaking it in for a friend.
Attrib.

**25** Whoever named it necking was a poor judge of anatomy.
Attrib.

**26** A man is only as old as the woman he feels.
Attrib.

**Marx, Karl** (1818–83) German philosopher and revolutionary. *The Communist Manifesto* (1848), *A Contribution to the Critique of Political Economy* (1859), and *Das Kapital* (1867) are some of his books on the theory of communism. He became leader of the First International and lived abroad (in London from 1849) for much of his life.

**1** The history of all hitherto existing society is the history of class struggles.
*The Communist Manifesto*, 1

**2** The workers have nothing to lose but their chains. They have a world to gain. Workers of the world, unite.
*The Communist Manifesto*, 4

**3** From each according to his abilities, to each according to his needs.
*Criticism of the Gotha Programme*

**4** Religion . . . is the opium of the people.
*Criticism of the Hegelian Philosophy of Right*, Introduction

**5** Capitalist production begets, with the inexorability of a law of nature, its own negation.
*Das Kapital*, Ch. 15

**6** Hegel says somewhere that all great events and personalities in world history reappear in one fashion or another. He forgot to add: the first time as tragedy, the second as farce.
*The Eighteenth Brumaire of Louis Napoleon*

**7** The dictatorship of the proletariat.
Attrib.

**Mary I** (1516–58) Queen of England, the daughter of Henry VIII and Catharine of Aragon. Resolutely attempting to reestablish Catholicism in England, she had nearly 300 citizens burnt at the stake, which earned her the nickname 'Bloody Mary'.

**1** When I am dead and opened, you shall find 'Calais' lying in my heart.
*Chronicles* (Holinshed), III

**Maschwitz, Eric** (20th century) British songwriter.

**1** A Nightingale Sang in Berkeley Square.
Song title

**Masefield, John** (1878–1967) British poet. His poetry includes *Salt-Water Ballads* (1902) and *Reynard the Fox* (1919). He also wrote several novels of which *Sard Harker* (1924) is the best known. He was poet laureate from 1930 to 1967.

**1** He was one of those born neither to obey nor to command, but to be evil to the commander and the obeyer alike. Perhaps there was nothing in life that he had much wanted to do, except to shoot rabbits and hit his father on the jaw, and both these things he had done.
*The Bird of Dawning*

**2** Quinquireme of Nineveh from distant Ophir
Rowing home to haven in sunny Palestine,
With a cargo of ivory,
And apes and peacocks,
Sandalwood, cedarwood, and sweet white wine.
*Cargoes*

**3** Dirty British coaster with a salt-caked smoke stack,
Butting through the Channel in the mad March days,
With a cargo of Tyne coal,
Road-rail, pig-lead,
Firewood, iron-ware, and cheap tin trays.
*Cargoes*

**4** The stars grew bright in the winter sky,
The wind came keen with a tang of frost,
The brook was troubled for new things lost,
The copse was happy for old things found,
The fox came home and he went to ground.
*Reynard the Fox*

**5** I must down to the seas again, to the lonely sea and the sky,
And all I ask is a tall ship and a star to steer her by,
And the wheel's kick and the wind's song and the white sail's shaking,
And a grey mist on the sea's face and a grey dawn breaking.
Often quoted using 'sea' rather than 'seas'
*Sea Fever*

**Mason, Walt** (1862–1939) Canadian poet and humorous writer. His books include *Uncle Walt* (1910) and *Terse Verse* (1917).

**1** He's the Man Who Delivers the Goods.
*The Man Who Delivers the Goods*

**Massinger, Philip** (1583–1640) English dramatist. His most popular plays were *A New Way to Pay Old Debts* (1621) and *The City Madam* (1632). In 1625 he became chief dramatist for the King's Men.

**1** He that would govern others, first should be The master of himself.
*The Bondman*, I

**Mathew, Sir James** (1830–1908) British judge, who became a Lord Justice of Appeal.

1 In England, Justice is open to all, like the Ritz hotel.
*Miscellany-at-Law* (R. E. Megarry)

**Matthews, Brander** (1852–1929) US writer and professor of literature. His plays include *On Probation* and he wrote several books on drama.

1 A gentleman need not know Latin, but he should at least have forgotten it.
Attrib.

**Maudling, Reginald** (1917–77) British politician. He became Conservative chancellor of the exchequer (1962–64) and home secretary (1970–72).

1 There comes a time in every man's life when he must make way for an older man.
Remark made on being replaced in the shadow cabinet by John Davies, his elder by four years
*The Guardian*, 20 Nov 1976

**Maugham, W(illiam) Somerset** (1874–1965) British novelist and doctor. After practicing medicine, he became a full-time writer with the success of *Liza of Lambeth* (1896). *Of Human Bondage* (1915), *The Moon and Sixpence* (1919), and *The Razor's Edge* (1944) were among his most successful books.

1 You know, of course, that the Tasmanians, who never committed adultery, are now extinct.
*The Bread-Winner*

2 Hypocrisy is the most difficult and nerve-racking vice that any man can pursue; it needs an unceasing vigilance and a rare detachment of spirit. It cannot, like adultery or gluttony, be practised at spare moments; it is a whole-time job.
*Cakes and Ale*, Ch. 1

3 From the earliest times the old have rubbed it into the young that they are wiser than they, and before the young had discovered what nonsense this was they were old too, and it profited them to carry on the imposture.
*Cakes and Ale*, Ch. 9

4 You can't learn too soon that the most useful thing about a principle is that it can always be sacrificed to expediency.
*The Circle*, III

5 A woman will always sacrifice herself if you give her the opportunity. It is her favourite form of self-indulgence.
*The Circle*, III

6 When married people don't get on they can separate, but if they're not married it's impossible. It's a tie that only death can sever.
*The Circle*, III

7 She's too crafty a woman to invent a new lie when an old one will serve.
*The Constant Wife*, II

8 The mystic sees the ineffable, and the psychopathologist the unspeakable.
*The Moon and Sixpence*, Ch. 1

9 Impropriety is the soul of wit.
*The Moon and Sixpence*, Ch. 4

10 Because women can do nothing except love, they've given it a ridiculous importance.
*The Moon and Sixpence*, Ch. 41

11 Like all weak men he laid an exaggerated stress on not changing one's mind.
*Of Human Bondage*, Ch. 37

12 People ask you for criticism, but they only want praise.
*Of Human Bondage*, Ch. 50

13 Money is like a sixth sense without which you cannot make a complete use of the other five.
*Of Human Bondage*, Ch. 51

14 The degree of a nation's civilization is marked by its disregard for the necessities of existence.
*Our Betters*, I

15 The right people are rude. They can afford to be.
*Our Betters*, II

16 It was such a lovely day I thought it was a pity to get up.
*Our Betters*, II

17 For to write good prose is an affair of good manners. It is, unlike verse, a civil art . . . . Poetry is baroque.
*The Summing Up*

18 I would sooner read a time-table or a catalogue than nothing at all. They are much more entertaining than half the novels that are written.
*The Summing Up*

19 Life is too short to do anything for oneself that one can pay others to do for one.
*The Summing Up*

20 There is an impression abroad that everyone has it in him to write one book; but if by this is implied a good book the impression is false.
*The Summing Up*

21 I'll give you my opinion of the human race . . . Their heart's in the right place, but their head is a thoroughly inefficient organ.
*The Summing Up*

22 Casting my mind's eye over the whole of fiction, the only absolutely original creation I can think of is Don Quixote.
*10 Novels and Their Authors*, Ch. 1

23 Music-hall songs provide the dull with wit, just as proverbs provide them with wisdom.
*A Writer's Notebook*

**24** I recognize that I am made up of several persons and that the person that at the moment has the upper hand will inevitably give place to another. But which is the real one? All of them or none?

*A Writer's Notebook*

**25** Sentimentality is only sentiment that rubs you up the wrong way.

*A Writer's Notebook*

**26** Dying is a very dull, dreary affair. And my advice to you is to have nothing whatever to do with it.

*Escape from the Shadows* (Robin Maugham)

**27** I am sick of this way of life. The weariness and sadness of old age make it intolerable. I have walked with death in hand, and death's own hand is warmer than my own. I don't wish to live any longer.

Said on his ninetieth birthday
*Familiar Medical Quotations* (M. B. Strauss)

**28** I've always been interested in people, but I've never liked them.

*The Observer*, 'Sayings of the Week', 28 Aug 1949

**29** The trouble with our younger authors is that they are all in the sixties.

*The Observer*, 'Sayings of the Week', 14 Oct 1951

**Maurois, André** (Émile Herzog; 1885–1967) French writer. Having served in the British army in World War I he wrote several biographies of British people, including Disraeli, Shelley, and Byron. He also wrote biographies of Voltaire, Proust, and Victor Hugo.

**1** In England there is only silence or scandal.

Attrib.

**Maxton, James** (1885–1946) Scottish Labour leader. He became an MP in 1922. His books include *Lenin* (1932) and *If I were Dictator* (1935).

**1** Sit down, man. You're a bloody tragedy.

Said to Ramsay MacDonald when he made his last speech in Parliament
Attrib.

**Mayakovsky, Vladimir** (1893–1930) Soviet poet. His collections include *Mystery Bouffe* (1918) and *150 Million* (1920). An active member of the Bolsheviks, he committed suicide.

**1** Art is not a mirror to reflect the world, but a hammer with which to shape it.

*The Guardian*, 11 Dec 1974

**Mayer, Louis B(urt)** (1885–1957) Russian-born US film producer. With Samuel Goldwyn he founded Metro-Goldwyn-Mayer, which perpetuated the star system in Hollywood.

**1** The number one book of the ages was written by a committee, and it was called The Bible.

Comment to writers who had objected to changes in their work
*The Filmgoer's Book of Quotes* (Leslie Halliwell)

**Maynard, Sir John** (1602–90) English judge and politician. He was imprisoned briefly (1655) for criticizing Cromwell's government.

**1** I have forgotten more law than you ever knew, but allow me to say, I have not forgotten much.

Replying to Judge Jeffreys' suggestion that he was so old he had forgotten the law

**Mayo, William James** (1861–1934) US surgeon, who, with his brother Charles, founded the Mayo Clinic.

**1** Specialist – A man who knows more and more about less and less.

Also attributed to Nicholas Butler

**McCarthy, Joseph** (20th century) US lyricist, who usually worked with composer Harry Tierney.

**1** In my sweet little Alice blue gown, When I first wandered out in the town.

*Alice Blue Gown*

**McCarthy, Joseph R(aymond)** (1908–57) US senator, notorious as the instigator of investigations of supposed communists (1950–54).

**1** McCarthyism is Americanism with its sleeves rolled.

Speech, 1952

**McCarthy, Mary** (1912– ) US novelist. Her books include *Groves of Academe* (1952), *The Group* (1963), and *Cannibals and Missionaries* (1974).

**1** If someone tells you he is going to make 'a realistic decision', you immediately understand that he has resolved to do something bad.

*On the Contrary*

**2** There are no new truths, but only truths that have not been recognized by those who have perceived them without noticing.

*On the Contrary*

**3** When an American heiress wants to buy a man, she at once crosses the Atlantic. The only really materialistic people I have ever met have been Europeans.

*On the Contrary*

**4** The immense popularity of American movies abroad demonstrates that Europe is the unfinished negative of which America is the proof.

*On the Contrary*

**5** An interviewer asked me what book I thought best represented the modern American woman. All I could think of to answer was: *Madame Bovary*.

*On the Contrary*

**6** And I don't feel the attraction of the Kennedys at all . . . I don't think they are Christians; they may be Catholics but they are not Christians, in my belief anyway.

*The Observer*, 14 Oct 1979

**McCartney, Paul** (1943– ) British rock musician and composer. Formerly a member of the Beatles, he wrote many songs with John Lennon. He launched his solo career with 'Maybe I'm Amazed' (1970). He later formed the band Wings. *See* Lenon, John.

1 The issues are the same. We wanted peace on earth, love, and understanding between everyone around the world. We have learned that change comes slowly.

*The Observer*, 'Sayings of the Week', 7 June 1987

**McCrae, John** (1872–1918) Canadian poet and doctor. He was killed at the end of World War I, in which he worked as a medical officer. He is remembered for his war poem *In Flanders Fields*.

1 In Flanders fields the poppies blow
Between the crosses, row on row,
That mark our place.

*In Flanders Fields*, 'Ypres Salient', 3 May 1915

**McGonagall, William** (1830–1902) Scottish poet. His naive doggerel has earned him the title of the world's worst poet. His *Poetic Gems* were published in 1890, including the unbelievable 'The Tay Bridge Disaster'.

1 Alas! Lord and Lady Dalhousie are dead, and buried at last,
Which causes many people to feel a little downcast.

*The Death of Lord and Lady Dalhousie*

2 Beautiful Railway Bridge of the Silv'ry Tay!
Alas, I am very sorry to say
That ninety lives have been taken away
On the last Sabbath day of 1879,
Which will be remember'd for a very long time.

*The Tay Bridge Disaster*

**McGough, Roger** (1937– ) British poet. Publications include *Watchword* (1969), *Gig* (1972), *Waving at Trains* (1982), and *Sky in the Pie* (1983).

1 You will put on a dress of guilt
and shoes with broken high ideals.

*Comeclose and Sleepnow*

**McLuhan, Marshall** (1911–81) Canadian sociologist and writer on the impact of technology on society. His books include *The Medium is the Message* (1967) and *The City as Classroom* (1977).

1 The new electronic interdependence recreates the world in the image of a global village.

*The Gutenberg Galaxy*

2 For tribal man space was the uncontrollable mystery. For technological man it is time that occupies the same role.

*The Mechanical Bride*, 'Magic that Changes Mood'

3 If the nineteenth century was the age of the editorial chair, ours is the century of the psychiatrist's couch.

*Understanding Media*, Introduction

4 The medium is the message. This is merely to say that the personal and social consequences of any medium . . . result from the new scale that is introduced into our affairs by each extension of ourselves or by any new technology.

*Understanding Media*, Ch. 1

5 The car has become the carapace, the protective and aggressive shell, of urban and suburban man.

*Understanding Media*, Ch. 22

6 Television brought the brutality of war into the comfort of the living room. Vietnam was lost in the living rooms of America – not on the battlefields of Vietnam.

Montreal *Gazette*, 16 May 1975

**Mead, Margaret** (1901–78) US anthropologist, working mainly in New Guinea and the Pacific Islands. Her books include *Coming of Age in Samoa* (1929) and various works on education and science.

1 We are living beyond our means. As a people we have developed a life-style that is draining the earth of its priceless and irreplaceable resources without regard for the future of our children and people all around the world.

*Redbook*, 'The Energy Crisis – Why Our World Will Never Again Be the Same.'

2 Women want mediocre men, and men are working to be as mediocre as possible.

*Quote Magazine*, 15 May 1958

**Mearns, Hughes** (1875–1965) US writer and educationalist. His books include *Creative Power* (1929) and *Creative Adult* (1940), as well as several novels.

1 As I was going up the stair
I met a man who wasn't there.
He wasn't there again to-day.
I wish, I wish he'd stay away.

*The Psychoed*

**Medawar, Sir Peter Bruin** (1915– ) British immunologist, who shared a Nobel Prize with Sir Macfarlane Burnet for his work on the immune system. His general books include *The Art of the Soluble* (1967), *Induction and Intuition* (1969) and *The Limits of Science* (1984).

1 Scientific discovery is a private event, and the delight that accompanies it, or the despair of finding it illusory does not travel.

*Hypothesis and Imagination*

**Meir, Golda** (1898–1978) Russian-born Israeli stateswoman, who was brought up in the USA. A founder of the Israeli Workers' Party, she became minister of Labour (1949–56) and foreign minister (1956–66), before becoming prime minister (1969–74).

1 A leader who doesn't hesitate before he sends his nation into battle is not fit to be a leader.

*As Good as Golda* (ed. Israel and Mary Shenker)

2 I can honestly say that I was never affected by the question of the success of an undertaking. If I felt it was the right thing to do, I was for it regardless of the possible outcome.

*Golda Meir: Woman with a Cause* (Marie Syrkin)

3 . . . there's no difference between one's killing and making decisions that will send others to kill. It's exactly the same thing, or even worse.

*L'Europeo* (Oriana Fallaci)

**4** Pessimism is a luxury that a Jew never can allow himself.

*The Observer*, 'Sayings of the Year', 29 Dec 1974

**5** Being seventy is not a sin.

*Reader's Digest* (July 1971), 'The Indestructible Golda Meir'

**6** We intend to remain alive. Our neighbors want to see us dead. This is not a question that leaves much room for compromise.

*Reader's Digest* (July 1971), 'The Indestructible Golda Meir'

**7** There are not enough prisons and concentration camps in Palestine to hold all the Jews who are ready to defend their lives and property.

Speech, 2 May 1940

**Melba, Dame Nellie** (Helen Porter Mitchell; 1861–1931) Australian soprano.

**1** The first rule in opera is the first rule in life: see to everything yourself.

*Melodies and Memories*

**2** Music is not written in red, white and blue. It is written in the heart's blood of the composer.

*Melodies and Memories*

**3** One of the drawbacks of Fame is that one can never escape from it.

*Melodies and Memories*

**4** So you're going to Australia! Well, I made twenty thousand pounds on my tour there, but of course *that* will never be done again. Still, it's a wonderful country, and you'll have a good time. What are you going to sing? All I can say is – sing 'em muck! It's all they can understand!

Speaking to Clara Butt
*Clara Butt: Her Life Story* (W. H. Ponder)

**Melbourne, William Lamb, Viscount** (1779–1848) British statesman. Whig prime minister (1934; 1835–41). His marriage to Lady Caroline Ponsonby (1805) ended in divorce after her affair with Lord Byron.

**1** Now, is it to lower the price of corn, or isn't it? It is not much matter which we say, but mind, we must all say *the same*.

Said at a cabinet meeting
*The English Constitution* (Bagehot), Ch. 1

**2** What I want is men who will support me when I am in the wrong.

Replying to someone who said he would support Melbourne as long as he was in the right
*Lord M.* (Lord David Cecil)

**3** For God's sake, ma'am, let's have no more of that. If you get the English people into the way of making kings, you'll get them into the way of *un*making them.

Advising Queen Victoria against granting Prince Albert the title of King Consort
*Lord M.* (Lord David Cecil)

**4** I like the Garter; there is no damned merit in it.

*Lord Melbourne* (H. Dunckley), 'On the Order of the Garter'

**5** I wish I was as cocksure of anything as Tom Macaulay is of everything.

*Preface to Lord Melbourne's Papers* (Earl Cowper)

**6** Nobody ever did anything very foolish except from some strong principle.

*The Young Melbourne* (Lord David Cecil)

**7** Damn it all, another Bishop dead, – I verily believe they die to vex me.

Attrib.

**8** While I cannot be regarded as a pillar, I must be regarded as a buttress of the church, because I support it from the outside.

Attrib.

**9** Things have come to a pretty pass when religion is allowed to invade the sphere of private life.

Attrib.

**Mellon, Andrew William** (1855–1937) US financier and art collector. Ambassador to the UK (1932–33), he donated his art collection to the National Gallery of Art in Washington, DC.

**1** A nation is not in danger of financial disaster merely because it owes itself money.

Attrib.

**Melville, Herman** (1819–91) US novelist. After sailing in a whaler to the South Seas, he wrote *Typee* (1846), *Redburn* (1849), and his best known book, *Moby Dick* (1851). His *Billy Budd*, posthumously published in 1924, was used by Benjamin Britten as the libretto of an opera.

**1** Better sleep with a sober cannibal than a drunken Christian.

*Moby Dick*, Ch. 3

**2** A whale ship was my Yale College and my Harvard.

*Moby Dick*, Ch. 24

**Menander** (c. 341–c. 290 BC) Greek dramatist. He wrote many comedies, of which *Dyscolus* is the only one to survive, although others are known from their Roman adaptations.

**1** Whom the gods love dies young.

*Dis Exapaton*

**Mencken, H(enry) L(ouis)** (1880–1956) US journalist and editor. His collected essays were published in *Prejudices* (6 vols; 1919–27).

**1** Puritanism – The haunting fear that someone, somewhere, may be happy.

*A Book of Burlesques*

**2** Conscience is the inner voice that warns us somebody may be looking.

*A Mencken Chrestomathy*

**3** We must respect the other fellow's religion, but only in the sense and to the extent that we respect his theory that his wife is beautiful and his children smart.

*Notebooks*, 'Minority Report'

4 It is now quite lawful for a Catholic woman to avoid pregnancy by a resort to mathematics, though she is still forbidden to resort to physics and chemistry.
*Notebooks*, 'Minority Report'

5 War will never cease until babies begin to come into the world with larger cerebrums and smaller adrenal glands.
*Notebooks*, 'Minority Report'

6 One of the things that makes a Negro unpleasant to white folk is the fact that he suffers from their injustice. He is thus a standing rebuke to them.
*Notebooks*, 'Minority Report'

7 The chief contribution of Protestantism to human thought is its massive proof that God is a bore.
*Notebooks*, 'Minority Report'

8 The worst government is the most moral. One composed of cynics is often very tolerant and human. But when fanatics are on top there is no limit to oppression.
*Notebooks*, 'Minority Report'

9 God is the immemorial refuge of the incompetent, the helpless, the miserable. They find not only sanctuary in His arms, but also a kind of superiority, soothing to their macerated egos; He will set them above their betters.
*Notebooks*, 'Minority Report'

10 It takes a long while for a naturally trustful person to reconcile himself to the idea that after all God will not help him.
*Notebooks*, 'Minority Report'

11 A society made up of individuals who were all capable of original thought would probably be unendurable. The pressure of ideas would simply drive it frantic.
*Notebooks*, 'Minority Report'

12 Poetry is a comforting piece of fiction set to more or less lascivious music.
*Prejudices*, 'The Poet and his Art'

13 No man is genuinely happy, married, who has to drink worse gin than he used to drink when he was single.
*Prejudices*, 'Reflections on Monogamy'

14 Faith may be defined briefly as an illogical belief in the occurrence of the improbable.
*Prejudices*, 'Types of Men'

15 He is the only man who is for ever apologizing for his occupation.
Referring to businessmen
*Prejudices*, 'Types of Men'

16 An idealist is one who, on noticing that a rose smells better than a cabbage, concludes that it will also make better soup.
*Sententiae*

17 Opera in English, is, in the main, just about as sensible as baseball in Italian.
*The Frank Muir Book* (Frank Muir)

18 I've made it a rule never to drink by daylight and never to refuse a drink after dark.
*New York Post*, 18 Sept 1945

**Menuhin, Sir Yehudi** (1916– ) US-born British violinist of Russian-Jewish parents. A former director of the Bath Festival, he founded a school for musically gifted children.

1 Music creates order out of chaos; for rhythm imposes unanimity upon the divergent, melody imposes continuity upon the disjointed, and harmony imposes compatibility upon the incongruous.
*The Sunday Times*, 10 Oct 1976

**Mercer, Johnny** (1909–76) US lyricist and composer, who wrote many hit tunes in Hollywood in the 1930s.

1 Jeepers Creepers – where'd you get them peepers?
*Jeepers Creepers*

2 That old black magic has me in its spell.
*That Old Black Magic*

**Meredith, George** (1828–1909) British novelist and poet. His poem *Modern Love* (1862) was partly based on his own unhappy marriage; his novels included *The Egoist* (1879) and *The Tragic Comedians* (1880).

1 I expect that Woman will be the last thing civilized by Man.
*The Ordeal of Richard Feverel*, Ch. 1

2 Kissing don't last: cookery do!
*The Ordeal of Richard Feverel*, Ch. 28

3 Much benevolence of the passive order may be traced to a disinclination to inflict pain upon oneself.
*Vittoria*, Ch. 42

**Meredith, Owen** (Robert Bulmer-Lytton, 1st Earl of Lytton; 1831–91) British statesman and poet. He became Viceroy of India in 1876. As Owen Meredith he published several volumes of poetry.

1 Genius does what it must, and Talent does what it can.
*Last Words of a Sensitive Second-rate Poet*

**Merrill, Bob** (Robert Merrill; 1890–1977) US lyricist and composer. His chief film score was for *Funny Girl* (1968).

1 People who need people are the luckiest people in the world.
*People Who Need People*

**Meynell, Alice** (1847–1922) British poet and literary critic.

1 My heart shall be thy garden.
*The Garden*

**Michelet, Jules** (1798–1874) French historian. His main works are his 17-volume *History of France* (1833–67) and *The French Revolution* (1847–53).

**1** You are one of the forces of nature.
From a letter received by Dumas
*Memoirs*, Vol. VI, Ch. 138 (Alexandre Dumas)

**Middleton, Thomas** (1580–1627) English dramatist. His best-known plays are *A Game at Chess* (1624), *Women Beware Women* (c. 1621), and *The Changeling* (in collaboration with William Rowley; 1622).

**1** Though I be poor, I'm honest.
*The Witch*, III:2

**Midlane, Albert** (1825–1909) British hymn writer.

**1** There's a Friend for little children
Above the bright blue sky,
A Friend who never changes,
Whose love will never die.
Hymn

**Mikes, George** (1912– ) Hungarian-born British writer and humorist.

**1** On the Continent people have good food; in England people have good table manners.
*How to be an Alien*

**2** An Englishman, even if he is alone, forms an orderly queue of one.
*How to be an Alien*

**3** Continental people have sex life; the English have hot-water bottles.
*How to be an Alien*

**4** It was twenty-one years ago that England and I first set foot on each other. I came for a fortnight; I have stayed ever since.
*How to be Inimitable*

**5** The one class you do *not* belong to and are not proud of at all is the lower-middle class. No one ever describes himself as belonging to the lower-middle class.
*How to be Inimitable*

**Mill, John Stuart** (1806–73) British philosopher and social reformer. His works include *On Liberty* (1859), *Utilitarianism* (1863), and *Subjection of Women* (1869).

**1** Ask yourself whether you are happy, and you cease to be so.
*Autobiography*, Ch. 5

**2** He who knows only his own side of the case knows little of that.
*On Liberty*, Ch. 2

**3** All good things which exist are the fruits of originality.
*On Liberty*, Ch. 3

**4** The liberty of the individual must be thus far limited; he must not make himself a nuisance to other people.
*On Liberty*, Ch. 3

**5** The worth of a State in the long run is the worth of the individuals composing it.
*On Liberty*, Ch. 5

**6** The most important thing women have to do is to stir up the zeal of women themselves.
Letter to Alexander Bain, 14 July 1869

**Millard, Emma** (1787–1870) British songwriter.

**1** Rocked in the cradle of the deep.
Song

**Millay, Edna St Vincent** (1892–1950) US poet. Her verse collections include *A Few Figs from Thistles* (1920), *The Buck in the Snow* (1928), and *Huntsman, What Quarry?* (1939). She also wrote the play *The Lamp and the Bell* (1921) and an opera libretto.

**1** My candle burns at both ends;
It will not last the night;
But ah, my foes, and oh my friends –
It gives a lovely light!
*A Few Figs from Thistles*, 'First Fig'

**Miller, Arthur** (1915– ) US dramatist. His plays include *Death of a Salesman* (1947), *The Crucible* (1953), and *After the Fall* (1964), based on the life of his late wife, Marilyn Monroe.

**1** There are many who stay away from church these days because you hardly ever mention God any more.
*The Crucible*, I

**2** He's liked, but he's not well liked.
*Death of a Salesman*, I

**3** Years ago a person, he was unhappy, didn't know what to do with himself – he'd go to church, start a revolution – *something*. Today you're unhappy? Can't figure it out? What is the salvation? Go shopping.
*The Price*, I

**4** I am inclined to notice the ruin in things, perhaps because I was born in Italy.
*A View from the Bridge*, I

**5** A good newspaper, I suppose, is a nation talking to itself.
*The Observer*, 'Sayings of the Week', 26 Nov 1961

**6** Why should I go? She won't be there.
When asked if he would attend Marilyn Monroe's funeral
Attrib.

**Miller, Henry** (1891–1980) US novelist. He lived in Paris in the 1930s and established his reputation with the sexually explicit novels *Tropic of Cancer* (1934) and *Tropic of Capricorn* (1939). His later books include *My Life and Times* (1972).

**1** Sex is one of the nine reasons for reincarnation . . . The other eight are unimportant.
*Big Sur and the Oranges of Hieronymus Bosch*

**2** Every man with a belly full of the classics is an enemy of the human race.
*Tropic of Cancer*, 'Dijon'

**Miller, Jonathan** (1934– ) British doctor and television and stage director. Co-author of *Beyond the Fringe* (1961–64), he has produced plays, operas, and the television series *The Body in Question* (1978).

1 I'm not really a Jew; just Jew-ish, not the whole hog.
*Beyond the Fringe*

2 They do those little personal things people sometimes do when they think they are alone in railway carriages; things like smelling their own armpits.
*Beyond the Fringe*

**Miller, Max** (Harold Sargent; 1895–1963) British music-hall comedian, known for his vulgar clothes and suggestive act.

1 There was a little girl
Who had a little curl
Right in the middle of her forehead,
When she was good she was very very good
And when she was bad she was very very popular.
*The Max Miller Blue Book*

**Milligan, Spike** (1918–  ) British comic actor and author, best known as co-author of and performer in the BBC radio series *The Goon Show*.

1 I shook hands with a friendly Arab . . . I still have my right hand to prove it.
*A Dustbin of Milligan*, 'Letters to Harry Secombe'

2 I have for instance among my purchases . . . several original Mona Lisas and all painted (according to the Signature) by the great artist Kodak.
*A Dustbin of Milligan*, 'Letters to Harry Secombe'

3 – 'Do you come here often?'
'Only in the mating season.'
*The Goon Show*

4 I don't like this game.
*The Goon Show*

5 I'm walking backwards till Christmas
*The Goon Show*

6 MORIARTY. How are you at Mathematics?
HARRY SECOMBE. I speak it like a native.
*The Goon Show*

7 You silly twisted boy.
*The Goon Show*

8 Contraceptives should be used on every conceivable occasion.
*The Last Goon Show of All*

9 Policemen are numbered in case they get lost.
*The Last Goon Show of All*

10 Money can't buy friends, but you can get a better class of enemy.
*Puckoon*, Ch. 6

11 One day the don't-knows will get in, and then where will we be?
Attributed remark made about a pre-election poll

**Mills, Hugh** (1913–71) British screenwriter. His films include *Knave of Hearts* (1952) and *Prudence and the Pill* (1968).

1 Nothing unites the English like war. Nothing divides them like Picasso.
*Prudence and the Pill*

**Milman, Henry Hart** (1791–1868) British poet and historian. As dean of St Paul's he is known for his historical works, including *History of the Jews* (1830) and *History of Latin Christianity* (1854–55). He also wrote poetry, including *Samor* (1818) and the tragedy *Fazio* (1815).

1 Ride on! ride on in majesty!
In lowly pomp ride on to die.
*Ride On*

**Milne, A(lan) A(lexander)** (1882–1956) British writer, best known for his books for and about his son Christopher Robin, including *When We Were Very Young* (1924), *Winnie-the-Pooh* (1926), and *Now We Are Six* (1927).

1 I am old enough to be – in fact am – your mother.
*Belinda*

2 If the English language had been properly organized . . . then there would be a word which meant both 'he' and 'she', and I could write, 'If John or Mary comes heesh will want to play tennis,' which would save us a lot of trouble.
*The Christopher Robin Birthday Book*

3 For one person who dreams of making fifty thousand pounds, a hundred people dream of being left fifty thousand pounds.
*If I May*, 'The Future'

4 They're changing guard at Buckingham Palace –
Christopher Robin went down with Alice.
Alice is marrying one of the guard.
'A soldier's life is terrible hard,'
Says Alice.
*When We Were Very Young*, 'Buckingham Palace'

5 And some of the bigger bears try to pretend
That they came round the corner to look for a friend;
And they'll try to pretend that nobody cares
Whether you walk on the lines or the squares.
*When We Were Young*, 'Lines and Squares'

6 I am a Bear of Very Little Brain, and long words Bother me.
*Winnie-the-Pooh*, Ch. 4

7 Time for a little something.
*Winnie-the-Pooh*, Ch. 6

**Milton, John** (1608–74) English poet. His poems include *L'Allegro* and *Il Penseroso* (1632) and the great epics *Paradise Lost* (1667) and *Paradise Regained* (1671).

1 Who kills a man kills a reasonable creature, God's image; but he who destroys a good book, kills reason itself, kills the image of God, as it were in the eye.
*Areopagitica*

2 A good book is the precious life-blood of a master spirit, embalmed and treasured up on purpose to a life beyond life.
*Areopagitica*

3 Let her and Falsehood grapple; who ever knew
Truth put to the worse, in a free and open
encounter?
*Areopagitica*

4 Blest pair of Sirens, pledges of Heaven's joy,
Sphere-born harmonious sisters, Voice and
Verse.
*At a Solemn Music*

5 Wrapt in a pleasing fit of melancholy.
*Comus*

6 Hence, vain deluding Joys,
The brood of Folly without father bred!
*Il Penseroso*

7 And looks commercing with the skies,
Thy rapt soul sitting in thine eyes.
*Il Penseroso*

8 Sweet bird, that shunn'st the noise of folly,
Most musical, most melancholy!
Referring to the nightingale
*Il Penseroso*

9 Where glowing embers through the room
Teach light to counterfeit a gloom,
Far from all resort of mirth,
Save the cricket on the hearth.
*Il Penseroso*

10 Where more is meant than meets the ear.
*Il Penseroso*

11 Come, and trip it as you go
On the light fantastic toe.
*L'Allegro*

12 To hear the lark begin his flight,
And singing startle the dull night,
From his watch-tower in the skies,
Till the dappled dawn doth rise.
*L'Allegro*

13 Then to the spicy nut-brown ale.
*L'Allegro*

14 Or sweetest Shakespeare, Fancy's child,
Warble his native wood-notes wild.
*L'Allegro*

15 The melting voice through mazes running;
Untwisting all the chains that tie
The hidden soul of harmony.
*L'Allegro*

16 Yet once more, O ye laurels, and once more,
Ye myrtles brown, with ivy never sere,
I come to pluck your berries harsh and crude,
And with forced fingers rude
Shatter your leaves before the mellowing year.
*Lycidas*

17 Under the opening eye-lids of the morn.
*Lycidas*

18 As killing as the canker to the rose.
*Lycidas*

19 To sport with Amaryllis in the shade,
Or with the tangles of Neaera's hair.
*Lycidas*

20 Fame is the spur that the clear spirit doth raise
(That last infirmity of noble mind)
To scorn delights, and live laborious days.
*Lycidas*

21 The hungry sheep look up, and are not fed,
But, swoln with wind and the rank mist they
draw,
Rot inwardly, and foul contagion spread.
*Lycidas*

22 At last he rose, and twitched his mantle blue:
To-morrow to fresh woods, and pastures new.
*Lycidas*

23 Rhyme being no necessary adjunct or true ornament of poem or good verse, in longer works
especially, but the invention of a barbarous age,
to set off wretched matter and lame metre.
*Paradise Lost, The Verse. Preface to 1668 ed.*

24 The troublesome and modern bondage of
Rhyming.
*Paradise Lost, The Verse. Preface to 1668 ed.*

25 Of Man's first disobedience, and the fruit
Of that forbidden tree, whose mortal taste
Brought death into the World, and all our woe
. . .
*Paradise Lost, Bk. I*

26 What in me is dark
Illumine, what is low raise and support;
That, to the height of this great argument,
I may assert Eternal Providence,
And justify the ways of God to men.
*Paradise Lost, Bk. I*

27 What though the field be lost?
All is not lost – the unconquerable will,
And study of revenge, immortal hate,
And courage never to submit or yield:
And what is else not to be overcome?
*Paradise Lost, Bk. I*

28 A mind not to be changed by place or time.
The mind is its own place, and in itself
Can make a Heaven of Hell, a Hell of Heaven.
*Paradise Lost, Bk. I*

29 To reign is worth ambition, though in Hell:
Better to reign in Hell than serve in Heaven.
*Paradise Lost, Bk. I*

30 Care
Sat on his faded cheek.
*Paradise Lost, Bk. I*

31 Tears such as angels weep, burst forth.
*Paradise Lost, Bk. I*

32 Who overcomes
By force, hath overcome but half his foe.
*Paradise Lost, Bk. I*

**33** From morn
To noon he fell, from noon to dewy eve,
A summer's day, and with the setting sun
Dropped from the zenith, like a falling star.
*Paradise Lost*, Bk. I

**34** High on a throne of royal state, which far
Outshone the wealth of Ormus and of Ind,
Or where the gorgeous East with richest hand
Showers on her kings barbaric pearl and gold,
Satan exalted sat, by merit raised
To that bad eminence.
*Paradise Lost*, Bk. II

**35** Long is the way
And hard, that out of hell leads up to light.
*Paradise Lost*, Bk. II

**36** Vain wisdom all, and false philosophy.
*Paradise Lost*, Bk. II

**37** For neither man nor angel can discern
Hypocrisy, the only evil that walks
Invisible, except to God alone.
*Paradise Lost*, Bk. III

**38** Which way I fly is Hell; myself am Hell;
And, in the lowest deep, a lower deep
Still threat'ning to devour me opens wide,
To which the Hell I suffer seems a Heaven.
*Paradise Lost*, Bk. IV

**39** Farewell remorse! All good to me is lost;
Evil, be thou my Good.
*Paradise Lost*, Bk. IV

**40** A heav'n on earth.
*Paradise Lost*, Bk. IV

**41** Now came still Evening on, and Twilight grey
Had in her sober livery all things clad.
*Paradise Lost*, Bk. IV

**42** Abashed the devil stood,
And felt how awful goodness is.
*Paradise Lost*, Bk. IV

**43** Midnight brought on the dusky hour
Friendliest to sleep and silence.
*Paradise Lost*, Bk. V

**44** In solitude
What happiness? who can enjoy alone,
Or, all enjoying, what contentment find?
*Paradise Lost*, Bk. VIII

**45** Accuse not Nature, she hath done her part;
Do thou but thine.
*Paradise Lost*, Bk. VIII

**46** Revenge, at first though sweet,
Bitter ere long back on itself recoils.
*Paradise Lost*, Bk. IX

**47** The world was all before them, where to choose
Their place of rest, and Providence their guide:
They, hand in hand, with wandering steps and
slow,
Through Eden took their solitary way.
*Paradise Lost*, Bk. XII

**48** Most men admire
Virtue, who follow not her lore.
*Paradise Regained*, Bk. I

**49** Beauty stands
In the admiration only of weak minds
Led captive.
*Paradise Regained*, Bk. II

**50** Let us with a gladsome mind
Praise the Lord, for he is kind,
For his mercies ay endure,
Ever faithful, ever sure.
*Psalm*

**51** A little onward lend thy guiding hand
To these dark steps, a little further on.
*Samson Agonistes*

**52** Ask for this great deliverer now, and find him
Eyeless in Gaza at the mill with slaves.
*Samson Agonistes*

**53** O dark, dark, dark, amid the blaze of noon,
Irrecoverably dark, total eclipse,
Without all hope of day!
*Samson Agonistes*

**54** How soon hath Time, the subtle thief of youth,
Stolen on his wing my three-and-twentieth year!
*Sonnet: 'On Being Arrived at the Age of Twenty-three'*

**55** When I consider how my light is spent
Ere half my days in this dark world and wide,
And that one talent which is death to hide
Lodged with me useless.
*Sonnet: 'On his Blindness'*

**56** God doth not need
Either man's work or his own gifts. Who best
Bear his mild yoke, they serve him best: his
state
Is kingly; thousands at his bidding speed,
And post o'er land and ocean without rest;
They also serve who only stand and wait.
*Sonnet: 'On his Blindness'*

**57** New Presbyter is but old Priest writ large.
*Sonnet: 'On the New Forcers of Conscience under the Long Parliament'*

**58** Peace hath her victories
No less renowned than war.
*Sonnet: 'To the Lord General Cromwell, May 1652'*

**59** None can love freedom heartily, but good men;
the rest love not freedom, but licence.
*Tenure of Kings and Magistrates*

**60** One tongue is sufficient for a woman.
On being asked whether he would allow his daughters to learn foreign languages
*Attrib.*

**Mirabeau, Honoré Gabriel Riquetti, Comte de**
(1749–91) French statesman. A revolutionary leader, who visited England and Germany, he wrote *De la monarchie prussienne sous Frédéric le Grand* (1788). An influential speaker in the National Assembly, he argued for a constitutional monarchy. He was elected president of the Assembly but died before taking office.

**1** War is the national industry of Prussia.
Attrib.

**Mitchell, Adrian** (1932– ) British writer and dramatist. Plays include *Tyger* (1971), *The White Deer* (1978), and *The Wild Animal Song Contest* (1983). Novels include *The Bodyguard* (1970) and *Wartime* (1973). He has also written several verse collections.

**1** I want to be a movement
But there's no one on my side.
*Loose Leaf Poem*

**Mitchell, Joni** (1945– ) Singer and songwriter.

**1** I've looked at life from both sides now
From win and lose and still somehow
It's life's illusions I recall
I really don't know life at all.
*Both Sides Now*

**Mitchell, Julian** (1935– ) British writer and dramatist. His novels include *As Far as You Can Go* (1963) and *The Undiscovered Country* (1968). The plays *Half-Life* (1977) and *Another Country* (1981) have been successful.

**1** The sink is the great symbol of the bloodiness of family life. All life is bad, but family life is worse.
*As Far as You Can Go*, Pt. I, Ch. 1

**Mitchell, Margaret** (1909–49) US novelist, whose single success was *Gone with the Wind* (1936, filmed 1939).

**1** Until you've lost your reputation, you never realize what a burden it was or what freedom really is.
*Gone with the Wind*

**2** Fighting is like champagne. It goes to the heads of cowards as quickly as of heroes. Any fool can be brave on a battle field when it's be brave or else be killed.
*Gone with the Wind*

**3** Death and taxes and childbirth! There's never any convenient time for any of them!
*Gone with the Wind*

**4** After all, tomorrow is another day.
The closing words of the book
*Gone with the Wind*

**Mitford, Jessica Lucy** (1917– ) British writer, sister of Nancy Mitford, who settled in the USA. *Hons and Rebels* (1960) gives an account of her eccentric family.

**1** I have nothing against undertakers personally. It's just that I wouldn't want one to bury my sister.
Attrib. in *Saturday Review*, 1 Feb 1964

**Mitford, Nancy** (1904–73) British writer, sister of Jessica Mitford. Her best-known novels are *The Pursuit of Love* (1945), *Love in a Cold Climate* (1949), and *The Blessing* (1951). She has also written historical biographies.

**1** An aristocracy in a republic is like a chicken whose head has been cut off: it may run about in a lively way, but in fact it is dead.
*Noblesse Oblige*

**2** English women are elegant until they are ten years old, and perfect on grand occasions.
*The Wit of Women* (L. and M. Cowan)

**Mizner, Wilson** (1876–1933) US writer and wit.

**1** Be nice to people on your way up because you'll meet 'em on your way down.
Also attributed to Jimmy Durante
*A Dictionary of Catch-Phrases* (Eric Partridge)

**Molière** (Jean Baptiste Poquelin; 1622–73) French dramatist. In his plays, such as *Tartuffe* (1664), *Le Bourgeois Gentilhomme* (1670), and *Le Malade Imaginaire* (1673), he satirized contemporary society.

**1** He who lives without tobacco is not worthy to live.
*Don Juan*, I:1

**2** One should eat to live, not live to eat.
*L'Avare*, III:2

**3** Good heavens! I have been talking prose for over forty years without realizing it.
*Le Bourgeois Gentilhomme*, II:4

**4** One dies only once, and it's for such a long time!
*Le Dépit amoureux*, V:3

**5** He must have killed a lot of men to have made so much money.
*Le Malade imaginaire*, I:5

**6** It is a stupidity second to none, to busy oneself with the correction of the world.
*Le Misanthrope*, I:1

**7** One should examine oneself for a very long time before thinking of condemning others.
*Le Misanthrope*, III:4

**8** Age will bring all things, and everyone knows, Madame, that twenty is no age to be a prude.
*Le Misanthrope*, III:4

**9** Grammar, which can govern even kings.
*Les Femmes savantes*, II:6

**10** It is a public scandal that gives offence, and it is no sin to sin in secret.
*Tartuffe*, IV:5

**Monmouth, James Scott, Duke of** (1649–85) An illegitimate son of Charles II, and the focus of the Protestant opposition to the Catholic James II. After James' accession he landed at Lyme Regis from exile in France to raise a rebellion, but was defeated at Sedgemoor and beheaded.

**1** Do not hack me as you did my Lord Russell.
Said to the headsman before his execution
*History of England* (Macaulay), Vol. I, Ch. 5

**Monroe, Harriet** (1860–1936) US poet and editor.

**1** . . . poetry, "The Cinderella of the Arts."
*Famous American Women* (Hope Stoddard), 'Harriet Monroe'

**Monroe, Marilyn** (Norma-Jean Baker; 1926–62) US film star. A comedienne and sex symbol, her films include *Gentlemen Prefer Blondes* (1953) and *The Misfits* (1961), written by her third husband, Arthur Miller. She died of a barbiturate overdose.

1 JOURNALIST. Didn't you have anything on?
M. M. I had the radio on.
Attrib.

**Monsell, John** (1811–75) British hymn writer.

1 Fight the good fight with all thy might,
Christ is thy strength and Christ thy right,
Lay hold on life, and it shall be
Thy joy and crown eternally.
Hymn

**Montagu, Lady Mary Wortley** (1689–1762) English writer. The wife of the English ambassador to Turkey, she is remembered especially for her letters written from Constantinople, published as *Letters from the East*.

1 Satire should, like a polished razor keen,
Wound with a touch that's scarcely felt or seen.
*To the Imitator of the First Satire of Horace*, Bk. II

**Montague, C(harles) E(dward)** (1867–1928) British editor, writer, and critic. His novels include *Rough Justice* (1926); he also wrote *Disenchantment* (1922) about his experiences in World War I.

1 War hath no fury like a non-combatant.
*Disenchantment*, Ch. 15

2 To be amused at what you read – that is the great spring of happy quotation
*A Writer's Notes on his Trade*

**Montaigne, Michel de** (1533–92) French essayist. His *Essais* (1580 and 1588) started a new literary genre, in which he expressed his philosophy of humanism.

1 The greatest thing in the world is to know how to be self-sufficient.
*Essais*, I

2 A man must keep a little back shop where he can be himself without reserve. In solitude alone can he know true freedom.
*Essais*, I

3 Unless a man feels he has a good enough memory, he should never venture to lie.
*Essais*, I

4 The daughter-in-law of Pythagoras said that a woman who goes to bed with a man ought to lay aside her modesty with her skirt, and put it on again with her petticoat.
*Essais*, I

5 When I play with my cat, who knows whether she is not amusing herself with me more than I with her?
*Essais*, II

6 Man is quite insane. He wouldn't know how to create a maggot and he creates Gods by the dozen.
*Essais*, II

7 Marriage is like a cage; one sees the birds outside desperate to get in, and those inside equally desperate to get out.
*Essais*, III

8 Many a man has been a wonder to the world, whose wife and valet have seen nothing in him that was even remarkable. Few men have been admired by their servants.
*Essais*, III

9 The world is but a school of inquiry.
*Essais*, III

10 Poverty of goods is easily cured; poverty of soul, impossible.
*Essais*, III

11 A man who fears suffering is already suffering from what he fears.
*Essais*, III

**Montesquieu, Charles Louis de Secondat, Baron de** (1688–1755) French writer and historian. He is remembered for his influential *Considérations sur les causes de la grandeur et de la décadence des romains* (1734) and *Esprit des lois* (1748).

1 An empire founded by war has to maintain itself by war.
*Considérations sur les causes de la grandeur et de la décadence des romains*, Ch. 8

2 A really intelligent man feels what other men only know.
*Essai sur les causes qui peuvent affecter les esprits et les caractères*

3 Liberty is the right to do everything which the laws allow.
*L'Esprit des lois*

4 There is a very good saying that if triangles invented a god, they would make him three-sided.
*Lettres persanes*

5 No kingdom has ever had as many civil wars as the kingdom of Christ.
*Lettres persanes*

6 Great lords have their pleasures, but the people have fun.
*Pensées diverses*

7 The English are busy; they don't have time to be polite.
*Pensées diverses*

8 I suffer from the disease of writing books and being ashamed of them when they are finished.
*Pensées diverses*

**Montessori, Maria** (1870–1952) Italian doctor and educationalist. She devised the Montessori system for educating young children.

1 And if education is always to be conceived along the same antiquated lines of a mere transmission of knowledge, there is little to be hoped from it in the bettering of man's future. For what is the use of transmitting knowledge if the individual's total development lags behind?
*The Absorbent Mind*

**2** We teachers can only help the work going on, as servants wait upon a master.

*The Absorbent Mind*

### Montgomery of Alamein, Bernard Law, Viscount
(1887–1976) British field marshal, who commanded the Eighth Army in Africa in World War II, which defeated Rommel. He became chief of the land forces in the Normandy invasion and after victory over Germany was deputy commander of NATO forces (1951–58).

**1** The U.S. has broken the second rule of war. That is, don't go fighting with your land army on the mainland of Asia. Rule One is don't march on Moscow. I developed these two rules myself.

Referring to the Vietnam war
*Montgomery of Alamein* (Chalfont)

**2** This sort of thing may be tolerated by the French, but we are British – thank God.

Comment on a bill to relax the laws against homosexuals
*Daily Mail*, 27 May 1965

### Montherlant, Henry de
(1896–1972) French novelist and dramatist. His work includes the four-novel cycle, *Les Jeunes Filles* (1936), *Pitié pour les femmes* (1936), *Le Démon du bien* (1937), and *Les Lépreuses* (1939).

**1** A lot of people, on the verge of death, utter famous last words or stiffen into attitudes, as if the final stiffening in three days' time were not enough; they will have ceased to exist three days' hence, yet they still want to arouse admiration and adopt a prose and tell a lie with their last gasp.

*Explicit Mysterium*

**2** Stupidity does not consist in being without ideas. Such stupidity would be the sweet, blissful stupidity of animals, molluscs and the gods. Human Stupidity consists in having lots of ideas, but stupid ones.

*Notebooks*

### Montrose, Percy
(19th century) US songwriter.

**1** In a cavern, in a canyon,
Excavating for a mine
Dwelt a miner, Forty-niner,
And his daughter, Clementine.
Oh, my darling, Oh, my darling, Oh, my darling Clementine!
Thou art lost and gone for ever, dreadful sorry,
Clementine.

*Clementine*

**2** But I kissed her little sister,
And forgot my Clementine.

*Clementine*

### Moore, Clement Clarke
(1779–1863) US writer. He is remembered for his Hebrew lexicon and the ballad 'A Visit from St. Nicholas'.

**1** 'Twas the night before Christmas, when all through the house
Not a creature was stirring, not even a mouse;
The stockings were hung by the chimney with care,
In hopes that St Nicholas soon would be there.

In *Troy Sentinel*. 23 Dec 1823, 'A Visit from St. Nicholas'

### Moore, Edward
(1712–57) British dramatist. His works include *Fables of the Female Sex* (1744) as well as the tragedies *The Foundling* (1747–48) and *The Gamester* (1753).

**1** This is adding insult to injuries.

*The Foundling*, V

**2** I am rich beyond the dreams of avarice.

*The Gamester*, II

### Moore, George
(1852–1933) Irish writer and art critic. His best-known works are the novels *Esther Waters* (1894) and *The Brook Kerith* (1916). He also wrote plays, poetry, short stories, and an autobiography.

**1** A man travels the world over in search of what he needs and returns home to find it.

*The Brook Kerith*, Ch. 11

**2** Acting is therefore the lowest of the arts, if it is an art at all.

*Mummer-Worship*

**3** To be aristocratic in Art one must avoid polite society.

*Enemies of Promise* (Cyril Connolly), Ch. 15

### Moore, Thomas
(1779–1852) Irish poet. His most popular works are the collection *Irish Melodies* (1807–34) and the oriental romance *Lalla Rookh* (1817).

**1** Yet, who can help loving the land that has taught us
Six hundred and eighty-five ways to dress eggs?

*The Fudge Family in Paris*

**2** The harp that once through Tara's halls
The soul of music shed,
Now hangs as mute on Tara's walls
As if that soul were fled. –
So sleeps the pride of former days,
So glory's thrill is o'er;
And hearts, that once beat high for praise,
Now feel that pulse no more.

*Irish Melodies*, 'The Harp that Once'

**3** The Minstrel Boy to the war has gone,
In the ranks of death you'll find him;
His father's sword he has girded on,
And his wild harp slung behind him.

*Irish Melodies*, 'The Minstrel Boy'

**4** She is far from the land where her young hero sleeps,
And lovers are round her, sighing:
But coldly she turns from their gaze, and weeps,
For her heart in his grave is lying.

*Irish Melodies*, 'She is Far'

5 'Tis the last rose of summer
Left blooming alone;
All her lovely companions
Are faded and gone.

*Irish Melodies*, 'Tis the Last Rose'

6 I never nurs'd a dear gazelle,
To glad me with its soft black eye
But when it came to know me well,
And love me, it was sure to die!

*See also* PAYN
*Lalla Rookh*

7 Oft in the stilly night,
Ere Slumber's chain has bound me,
Fond Memory brings the light
Of other days around me;
The smiles, the tears,
Of boyhood's years,
The words of love then spoken;
The eyes that shone,
Now dimmed and gone,
The cheerful hearts now broken!

*National Airs*, 'Oft in the Stilly Night'

**Moravia, Alberto** (Alberto Pincherle; 1907– ) Italian
novelist. His books include *The Time of Indifference* (1929), *Roman
Tales* (1954), and *The Lie* (1966).

1 The ratio of literacy to illiteracy is constant, but
nowadays the illiterates can read and write.

*The Observer*, 14 Oct 1979

**More, Sir Thomas** (1478–1535) English lawyer, scholar,
and saint. As chancellor to Henry VIII (1529–32), he opposed the
king's assumption of the headship of the English Church; he was
subsequently imprisoned, tried, and beheaded for treason.

1 Yea, marry, now it is somewhat, for now it is
rhyme; before, it was neither rhyme nor reason.

On reading an unremarkable book recently rendered into verse
by a friend of his
*Apophthegms* (Bacon), 287

2 I cumber you goode Margaret muche, but I
woulde be sorye, if it shoulde be any lenger than
to morrowe, for it is S. Thomas evin and the
vtas of Sainte Peter and therefore to morowe
longe I to goe to God, it were a daye very
meete and conveniente for me. I neuer liked
your maner towarde me better then when you
kissed me laste for I loue when doughterly loue
and deere charitie hathe no laisor to looke to
worldely curtesye. Fare well my deere childe
and praye for me, and I shall for you and all your
friendes that we maie merily meete in heaven.

Last letter to Margaret Roper, his daughter, on the eve of his
execution on 6 July 1535

3 I pray you, Master Lieutenant, see me safe up,
and for coming down let me shift for myself.

On climbing onto the scaffold prior to his execution
*Life of Sir Thomas More* (William Roper)

4 Pluck up thy spirits, man, and be not afraid to do
thine office; my neck is very short; take heed
therefore thou strike not awry, for saving of
thine honesty.

Said to the headsman at his execution
*Life of Sir Thomas More* (Roper)

5 This hath not offended the king.

Said as he drew his beard aside before putting his head on the
block

**Morell, Thomas** (1703–84) British classicist, who edited the
works of Chaucer and Spenser. He wrote the librettos for
Handel's oratorios *Judas Maccabaeus* (1746) and *Joshua* (1748).

1 See, the conquering hero comes!
Sound the trumpets, beat the drums!

The libretto for Handel's oratorio
*Joshua*, Pt. III

**Morgan, Augustus de** (1806–71) British mathematician
and logician. He developed a new system of nomenclature for
logical expression, formulated 'de Morgan's theorem', and
advocated decimal coinage.

1 Great fleas have little fleas upon their backs to
bite 'em,
And little fleas have lesser fleas, and so *ad
infinitum*.

*A Budget of Paradoxes*

**Morgan, Elaine** (1920– ) British writer and educator. She
has written a number of plays and television scripts.

1 The trouble with specialists is that they tend to
think in grooves.

*The Descent of Woman*, Ch. 1

2 . . . the rumblings of women's liberation are only
one pointer to the fact that you already have a
discontented work force. And if conditions
continue to lag so far behind the industrial norm
and the discomfort increases, you will find . . .
that you will end up with an inferior product.

*The Descent of Woman*, Ch. 11

**Morgenstern, Christian** (1871–1914) German poet. His
collections include *Ich und die Welt* (1898) and *Ich und Du* (1911).

1 There is a ghost
That eats handkerchiefs;
It keeps you company
On all your travels.

*Der Gingganz*, 'Gespenst'

**Morley, Christopher Darlington** (1890–1957) US
writer and journalist. His books include *Parnassus on Wheels*
(1917), *Kathleen* (1920), *Where The Blue Begins* (1922) and
*Thunder on the Left* (1925).

1 There are three ingredients in the good life:
learning, earning and yearning.

*Parnassus on Wheels*, Ch. 10

2 Why do they put the Gideon Bibles only in the
bedrooms where it's usually too late?

*Quotations for Speakers and Writers*

**Morley, Robert** (1908– ) British actor. His many films include *Major Barbara* (1940), *Oscar Wilde* (1960), and *The Blue Bird* (1976).

**1** Beware of the conversationalist who adds 'in other words'. He is merely starting afresh.

*The Observer*, 'Sayings of the Week', 6 Dec 1964

**2** There's no such thing in Communist countries as a load of old cod's wallop, the cod's wallop is always fresh made.

*Punch*, 20 Feb 1974

**Morpurgo, J(ack) E(ric)** (1918– ) British writer and academic. Professor of American Literature at Sussex University (1969–83), he has written books on history, travel, and literary criticism.

**1** Austria is Switzerland speaking pure German and with history added.

*The Road to Athens*

**Morris, Desmond** (1928– ) British biologist and writer. His books, including *The Naked Ape* (1967) and *Manwatching* (1977), draw parallels between human and animal behaviour.

**1** Clearly, then, the city is not a concrete jungle, it is a human zoo.

*The Human Zoo*, Introduction

**2** There are one hundred and ninety-three living species of monkeys and apes. One hundred and ninety-two of them are covered with hair. The exception is a naked ape self-named *Homo sapiens*.

*The Naked Ape*, Introduction

**Morris, George Pope** (1802–64) US journalist. He edited several papers and published a volume of collected verse containing the poems 'Woodman, Spare That Tree' and 'My Mother's Bible'.

**1** Woodman, spare that tree!
Touch not a single bough!
In youth it sheltered me,
And I'll protect it now.

*Woodman, Spare That Tree*

**Mortimer, John Clifford** (1923– ) British lawyer and dramatist. Best-known for his TV series about Horace Rumpole, a fictional barrister, his plays include *The Dock Brief* (1958).

**1** Eddy was a tremendously tolerant person, but he wouldn't put up with the Welsh. He always said, surely there's enough English to go round.

*Two Stars for Comfort*, I:2

**2** No brilliance is needed in the law. Nothing but common sense, and relatively clean finger nails.

*A Voyage Round My Father*, I

**Morton, J. B.** (1893–1979) British journalist and story writer, who for many years wrote a newspaper column under the name 'Beachcomber'.

**1** She has a Rolls body and a Balham mind.

*The Best of Beachcomber*, 'A Foul Innuendo'

**2** Sixty Horses Wedged in a Chimney
The story to fit this sensational headline has not turned up yet.

*The Best of Beachcomber*, 'Mr Justice Cocklecarrot: Home Life'

**3** Vegetarians have wicked, shifty eyes, and laugh in a cold and calculating manner. They pinch little children, steal stamps, drink water, favour beards . . . wheeze, squeak, drawl and maunder.

*By the Way*, '4 June'

**4** Dr Strabismus (Whom God Preserve) of Utrecht is carrying out research work with a view to crossing salmon with mosquitoes. He says it will mean a bite every time for fishermen.

*By the Way*, 'January Tail-piece'

**5** Wagner is the Puccini of music.

Attrib.

**Mosley, Sir Oswald** (1896–1980) British politician and founder of the British Union of Fascists (1932). His second wife (from 1936) was Diana Mitford.

**1** Before the organization of the Blackshirt movement free speech did not exist in this country.

Selections from the *New Statesman*, *This England*, Pt. I

**2** I am not and never have been, a man of the right. My position was on the left and is now in the centre of politics.

*The Times*, 26 Apr 1968

**3** 'Can't' will be the epitaph of the British Empire – unless we wake up in time.

Speech, Manchester, 9 Dec 1937

**Motley, John Lothrop** (1814–77) US historian and diplomat. His particular interest was the history of the Netherlands from 1847. He served as ambassador to Austria (1861–67) and Great Britain (1869–70).

**1** Give us the luxuries of life, and we will dispense with its necessities.

*The Autocrat of the Breakfast Table* (O. W. Holmes), Ch. 6

**Muggeridge, Malcolm** (1903– ) British writer and editor. The editor of *Punch* (1953–57), he has written a number of books including *The Thirties* (1940), *Affairs of the Heart* (1949), and *Jesus Rediscovered* (1969), as well as an autobiography and diaries.

**1** An orgy looks particularly alluring seen through the mists of righteous indignation.

*The Most of Malcolm Muggeridge*, 'Dolce Vita in a Cold Climate'

**2** The orgasm has replaced the Cross as the focus of longing and the image of fulfilment.

*The Most of Malcolm Muggeridge*, 'Down with Sex'

**3** Macmillan seemed, in his very person, to embody the national decay he supposed himself to be confuting. He exuded a flavour of mothballs.

*Tread Softly For You Tread on My Jokes*, 'England, whose England'

**4** He is not only a bore but he bores for England.

Referring to Sir Anthony Eden
In *Newstatesmanship* (E. Hyams), 'Boring for England'.

**Muir, Frank** (1920– ) British writer and broadcaster. With Dennis Norden he wrote many well-known comedy scripts. His books include *Frank Muir on Children* (1980) and *A Book at Bathtime* (1982).

1  I've examined your son's head, Mr Glum, and there's nothing there.

*Take It from Here* (Frank Muir and Dennis Norden), 1957

2  It has been said that a bride's attitude towards her betrothed can be summed up in three words: Aisle. Altar. Hymn.

*Upon My Word!* (Frank Muir and Dennis Norden), 'A Jug of Wine'

3  Another fact of life that will not have escaped you is that, in this country, the twenty-four-hour strike is like the twenty-four-hour flu. You have to reckon on it lasting at least five days.

*You Can't Have Your Kayak and Heat It* (Frank Muir and Dennis Norden), 'Great Expectations'

4  Dogs, like horses, are quadrupeds. That is to say, they have four rupeds, one at each corner, on which they walk.

*You Can't Have Your Kayak and Heat It* (Frank Muir and Denis Norden), 'Ta-ra-ra-boom-de-ay!'

**Munro, Hector Hugh** *See* Saki.

**Münster, Ernst Friedrich Herbert** (1766–1839) Hanovarian statesman. Ambassador to Russia (1801–04) and minister in London (1805–31), he was partly responsible for the entente between Russia and England.

1  Absolutism tempered by assassination.

Referring to the Russian Constitution
Letter

**Murdoch, Dame Iris** (1919– ) Irish-born British novelist and philosophy teacher. Her novels include *The Bell* (1958), *A Severed Head* (1961), *The Sea, The Sea* (1978), and *The Good Apprentice* (1985).

1  All art deals with the absurd and aims at the simple. Good art speaks truth, indeed *is* truth, perhaps the only truth.

*The Black Prince*, 'Bradley Pearson's Foreword'

2  Writing is like getting married. One should never commit oneself until one is amazed at one's luck.

*The Black Prince*, 'Bradley Pearson's Foreword'

3  "What are you famous *for*?"
"For nothing. I am just famous."

*The Flight from the Enchanter*

4  He led a double life. Did that make him a liar? He did not feel a liar. He was a man of two truths.

*The Sacred and Profane Love Machine*

5  Only lies and evil come from letting people off.
. . .

*A Severed Head*

**Murphy, Arthur** (1727–1805) Irish dramatist, writer, and actor. His plays include *The Apprentice* (1756) and *The Upholsterer* (1757). He also translated Sallust and Tacitus.

1  Above the vulgar flight of common souls.

*Zenobia*, V

**Murphy, C. W.** (19th century) British songwriter.

1  Has anybody here seen Kelly?
Kelly from the Isle of Man?

*Has Anybody Here Seen Kelly?*

**Murray, David** (1888–1962) British journalist and writer, editor of the *Times Literary Supplement* (1938–44).

1  A reporter is a man who has renounced everything in life but the world, the flesh, and the devil.

*The Observer*, 'Sayings of the Week', 5 July 1931

**Musset, Alfred de** (1810–57) French dramatist and poet. His *Contes d'Espagne et d'Italie* (1830) established his reputation; subsequent poems included 'La Nuit de mai' and 'L'Espoir en dieu'. *Barberine* (1835) and *Un Caprice* (1837) are his best-remembered plays. He had an affair with George Sand.

1  I cannot help it; – in spite of myself, infinity torments me.

*L'Espoir en Dieu*

2  Great artists have no country.

*Lorenzaccio*, I:5

**Mussolini, Benito** (1883–1945) Italian dictator, responsible for the organization and spread of fascism in Italy. In World War II he formed the Axis with Germany (1940); after the Allied invasion of Italy, he was deposed (1943) and murdered.

1  I should be pleased, I suppose, that Hitler has carried out a revolution on our lines. But they are Germans. So they will end by ruining our idea.

*Benito Mussolini* (C. Hibbert), Pt. II, Ch. 1

2  The Italians will laugh at me; every time Hitler occupies a country he sends me a message.

*Hitler* (Alan Bullock), Ch. 8

3  We cannot change our policy now. After all, we are not political whores.

*Hitler* (Alan Bullock), Ch. 8

4  Fascism is a religion; the twentieth century will be known in history as the century of Fascism.

On Hitler's seizing power
*Sawdust Caesar* (George Seldes), Ch. 24

5  Fascism is not an article for export.

Report in the German press, 1932

# N

**Nabokov, Vladimir** (1899–1977) Russian-born US novelist. He was educated at Cambridge but emigrated to the USA in 1945. Of his many novels *Lolita* (1955) is the best known.

1 Lolita, light of my life, fire of my loins. My sin, my Soul.
*Lolita*

2 Like so many ageing college people, Pnin had long ceased to notice the existence of students on the campus.
*Pnin*, Ch. 3

3 Discussion in class, which means letting twenty young blockheads and two cocky neurotics discuss something that neither their teacher nor they know.
*Pnin*, Ch. 6

4 Poor Knight! he really had two periods, the first – a dull man writing broken English, the second – a broken man writing dull English.
*The Real Life of Sebastian Knight*, Ch. 1

5 Spring and summer did happen in Cambridge almost every year.
*The Real Life of Sebastian Knight*, Ch. 5

6 A novelist is, like all mortals, more fully at home on the surface of the present than in the ooze of the past.
*Strong Opinions*, Ch. 20

7 Literature and butterflies are the two sweetest passions known to man.
*Radio Times*, Oct 1962

**Nairne, Carolina, Baroness** (1766–1845) Scottish songwriter.

1 Better lo'ed ye canna be,
Will ye no come back again?
Referring to Bonnie Prince Charlie
*Bonnie Charlie's now awa!*

2 Charlie is my darling, my darling, my darling,
Charlie is my darling, the young Chevalier.
Referring to Bonnie Prince Charlie
*Charlie is my Darling*

3 Wi' a hundred pipers an' a', an' a'.
A romantic glorification of the 1745 Jacobite Rebellion
*The Hundred Pipers*

**Napoleon I** (Napoleon Bonaparte; 1769–1821) French emperor. Having extended his power into most of Europe, the disastrous invasion of Russia (1812) marked a turning point; after his defeat at Waterloo (1815) he was exiled to St Helena, where he died.

1 I still love you, but in politics there is no heart, only head.
Referring to his divorce, for reasons of state, from the Empress Josephine (1809)
*Bonaparte* (C. Barnett)

2 Maybe it would have been better if neither of us had been born.
Said while looking at the tomb of the philosopher Jean-Jacques Rousseau, whose theories had influenced the French Revolution
*The Story of Civilization* (W. Durant), Vol. II

3 There rises the sun of Austerlitz.
Said at the Battle of Borodino (7 Sept 1812), near Moscow; the Battle of Austerlitz (2 Dec 1805) was Napoleon's great victory over the Russians and Austrians

4 It's the most beautiful battlefield I've ever seen.
Referring to carnage on the field of Borodino, near Moscow, after the battle (7 Sept 1812)
Attrib.

5 It is only a step from the sublime to the ridiculous.
Remark following the retreat from Moscow, 1812
Attrib.

6 The bullet that is to kill me has not yet been moulded.
In reply to his brother Joseph, King of Spain, who had asked whether he had ever been hit by a cannonball
Attrib.

7 Oh well, no matter what happens, there's always death.
Attrib.

8 England is a nation of shopkeepers.
Attrib.

9 An army marches on its stomach.
Attrib.

10 *Tête d'Armée.*
Chief of the Army.
Last words
Attrib.

**Napoleon III** (1808–73) French emperor. The nephew of Napoleon I, he ruled for 20 years before being driven into exile during the Franco-Prussian War.

1 This vice brings in one hundred million francs in taxes every year. I will certainly forbid it at once – as soon as you can name a virtue that brings in as much revenue.
Reply when asked to ban smoking
*Anekdotenschatz* (H. Hoffmeister)

2 I don't care for war, there's far too much luck in it for my liking.
Said after the narrow but bloody French victory at Solferino (24 June 1859)
*The Fall of the House of Habsburg* (E. Crankshaw)

**Narváez, Ramón María** (1800–68) Spanish general and political leader, several times prime minister under Isabella II.

1 I do not have to forgive my enemies, I have had them all shot.
Said on his deathbed, when asked by a priest if he forgave his enemies.
*Famous Last Words* (B. Conrad)

**Nash, Ogden** (1902–71) US poet. He wrote many books of satirical verse, including *I'm a Stranger Here Myself* (1938) and *Collected Verse* (1961).

**1** The cow is of the bovine ilk;
One end is moo, the other, milk.
*The Cow*

**2** A door is what a dog is perpetually on the wrong side of.
*A Dog's Best Friend Is His Illiteracy*

**3** To be an Englishman is to belong to the most exclusive club there is.
*England Expects*

**4** Women would rather be right than reasonable.
*Frailty, Thy Name Is a Misnomer*

**5** Home is heaven and orgies are vile
But you need an orgy, once in a while.
*Home, 99.44100% Sweet Home*

**6** Beneath this slab
John Brown is stowed.
He watched the ads
And not the road.
*Lather as You Go*

**7** Do you think my mind is maturing late,
Or simply rotted early?
*Lines on Facing Forty*

**8** Children aren't happy with nothing to ignore,
And that's what parents were created for.
*The Parents*

**9** I prefer to forget both pairs of glasses and pass my declining years saluting strange women and grandfather clocks.
*Peekaboo, I Almost See You*

**10** I think that I shall never see
A billboard lovely as a tree.
Perhaps unless the billboards fall,
I'll never see a tree at all.
*Song of the Open Road*

**Neale, John Mason** (1818–66) British churchman and hymn writer. His *Introduction to the History of the Holy Eastern Church* (1850) is less well-known than his hymn 'Jerusalem the Golden' and his carol 'Good King Wenceslas'.

**1** Art thou weary, art thou languid,
Art thou sore distressed?
*Art thou Weary?*

**2** Good King Wenceslas looked out,
On the Feast of Stephen;
When the snow lay round about,
Deep and crisp and even.
*Good King Wenceslas*

**3** Jerusalem the golden,
With milk and honey blest,
Beneath thy contemplation
Sink heart and voice opprest.
*Jerusalem the Golden*

**Needham, Joseph** (1900– ) British biochemist, who lived and worked in China. His books include *The Sceptical Biologist* (1929), *Science and Civilisation in China* (1954– ), and *Celestial Lancets* (1980).

**1** *Laboratorium est oratorium.* The place where we do our scientific work is a place of prayer.
*The Harvest of a Quiet Eye* (A. L. Mackay)

**Nelson, Horatio, Viscount** (1758–1805) British admiral. Hero of many naval battles, he defeated the French at Trafalgar (1805) but was killed during the battle. His affair with Lady Hamilton caused a considerable scandal.

**1** The Nelson touch.
*Diary, 9 Oct 1805*

**2** You must hate a Frenchman as you hate the devil.
*Life of Nelson* (Southey), Ch. 3

**3** England expects every man will do his duty.
*Signal hoisted prior to the Battle of Trafalgar, 1805*

**4** Kiss me, Hardy.
*Last words, spoken to Sir Thomas Hardy, captain of the Victory, during the Battle of Trafalgar, 1805*

**Nevins, Allan** (1890–1971) US historian. His books include *Grover Cleveland – A Study in Courage* (1932) and *The Gateway to History* (1938).

**1** The former allies had blundered in the past by offering Germany too little, and offering even that too late, until finally Nazi Germany had become a menace to all mankind.
*Current History, May 1935*

**Newbolt, Sir Henry John** (1862–1938) British poet. An authority on the British navy, many of his poems are about the sea and his *Songs of the Sea* (1904) and *Songs of the Fleet* (1910) were set to music by Stanford.

**1** He clapped the glass to his sightless eye,
And 'I'm damned if I see it', he said.
*Referring to Lord Nelson at the battle of Copenhagen*
*Admirals All*

**2** 'Take my drum to England, hang et by the shore,
Strike et when your powder's runnin' low;
If the Dons sight Devon, I'll quit the port o' Heaven,
An' drum them up the Channel as we drummed them long ago.'
*Drake's Drum*

**3** Drake he's in his hammock till the great Armadas come.
(Capten, art tha sleepin' there below?)
Slung atween the round shot, listenin' for the drum,
An dreamin' arl the time o' Plymouth Hoe.
*Drake's Drum*

**4** Now the sunset breezes shiver,
And she's fading down the river,
But in England's song for ever
She's the Fighting Téméraire.
*The Fighting Téméraire*

5 But cared greatly to serve God and the King,
And keep the Nelson touch.
*See* NELSON
*Minora Sidera*

6 There's a breathless hush in the Close tonight –
Ten to make and the match to win – –
A bumping pitch and a blinding light,
An hour to play and the last man in.
*Vitaï Lampada*

7 The sand of the desert is sodden red, –
Red with the wreck of a square that broke; –
The gatling's jammed and the colonel dead,
And the regiment blind with the dust and smoke.
The river of death has brimmed its banks
And England's far and honour a name.
But the voice of a schoolboy rallies the ranks:
'Play up! play up! and play the game!'
*Vitaï Lampada*

**Newcastle, Margaret, Duchess of** (1624–74) Second wife of William Cavendish, 1st Duke of Newcastle, the Royalist leader and patron of the arts. She wrote several volumes of poems, letters, and plays.

1 For all the Brothers were valiant, and all the Sisters virtuous.
*Epitaph, in Westminster Abbey*

**Newley, Anthony** (1931– ) British actor, composer, singer, and comedian.

1 Stop the World, I Want to Get Off.
*With Leslie Bricusse*
*Title of musical*

**Newman, Ernest** (1868–1959) British music critic and writer. He wrote studies of several composers, including Wagner and Elgar.

1 I sometimes wonder which would be nicer – an opera without an interval, or an interval without an opera.
*Berlioz, Romantic and Classic,* (ed. Peter Heyworth)

2 The higher the voice the smaller the intellect.
*Attrib.*

**Newman, John Henry, Cardinal** (1801–90) British theologian. His *Tracts for the Times* (from 1833) gave their name to the Tractarian Movement. He published many theological works, including the hymn *Lead, Kindly Light* (1833).

1 It is very difficult to get up resentment towards persons whom one has never seen.
*Apologia pro Vita Sua* (1864), 'Mr Kingsley's Method of Disputation'

2 It is almost a definition of a gentleman to say that he is one who never inflicts pain.
*The Idea of a University,* 'Knowledge and Religious Duty'

3 Lead, kindly Light, amid the encircling gloom,
Lead thou me on;
The night is dark, and I am far from home,
Lead thou me on.
*Lead Kindly Light*

4 She holds that it were better for sun and moon to drop from heaven, for the earth to fail, and for all the many millions who are upon it to die of starvation in extremest agony, as far as temporal affliction goes, than that one soul, I will not say, should be lost, but should commit one single venial sin, should tell one wilful untruth, . . . or steal one poor farthing without excuse.
Referring to the Roman Catholic Church
*Lectures on Anglican Difficulties,* VIII

5 *We can believe what we choose.* We are answerable for what we choose to believe.
*Letter to Mrs Froude, 27 June 1848*

6 When men understand what each other mean, they see, for the most part, that controversy is either superfluous or hopeless.
*Sermon, Oxford, Epiphany 1839*

**Newton, Sir Isaac** (1642–1727) British scientist, one of the greatest of all time, who discovered gravitation, recognized that white light is a mixture of coloured lights, invented calculus, and laid the foundations of dynamics with his laws of motion. His principal publications were the *Principia Mathematica* (1686–87) and *Optiks* (1704).

1 Nature is very consonant and conformable with herself.
*Opticks,* Bk. III

2 I do not know what I may appear to the world, but to myself I seem to have been only like a boy playing on the sea-shore, and diverting myself in now and then finding a smoother pebble or a prettier shell than ordinary, whilst the great ocean of truth lay all undiscovered before me.
*Isaac Newton* (L. T. More)

3 O Diamond! Diamond! thou little knowest the mischief done!
Said to a dog that set fire to some papers, representing several years' work, by knocking over a candle
*Wensley-Dale . . . a Poem* (Thomas Maude)

4 If I have seen further it is by standing on the shoulders of giants.
*Letter to Robert Hooke, 5 Feb 1675*

**Newton, John** (1725–1807) British hymn writer and clergyman. After several years as a naval midshipman, and then a slave trader, he was ordained and became a curate at Olney. He became friendly with Cowper and joint writer with him of the *Olney Hymns* (1779).

1 Glorious things of thee are spoken,
Zion, city of our God.
*Glorious Things*

2 How sweet the name of Jesus sounds.
In a believer's ear!
*The Name of Jesus*

**Nicholas I** (1796–1855) Tsar of Russia. A notorious autocrat, his attempts to take Constantinople instigated war with Turkey, which led to the Crimean War.

**1** We have on our hands a sick man – a very sick man.

Referring to Turkey, the 'sick man of Europe'; said to Sir G. H. Seymour, British envoy to St Petersburg, Jan 1853
Attrib.

**2** Russia has two generals in whom she can confide – Generals Janvier and Février.

Referring to the Russian winter. Nicholas himself succumbed to a February cold in 1855 – the subject of the famous *Punch* Cartoon, 'General Février turned traitor', 10 Mar 1855
Attrib.

**Niebuhr, Reinhold** (1892– ) US churchman. He wrote a number of books, including *Does Civilization Need Religion* (1927) and *Beyond Tragedy* (1937).

**1** Man's capacity for evil makes democracy necessary and man's capacity for good makes democracy possible.

Quoted by Anthony Wedgwood Benn in *The Times*, 18 July 1977

**Niemöller, Martin** (1892–1984) German pastor. He was a U-boat commander in World War I, ordained in 1924, dismissed from his post by the Nazis in 1934, and sent to a concentration camp in 1937. He survived to become a bishop in the Evangelical Church.

**1** In Germany, the Nazis came for the Communists and I didn't speak up because I was not a Communist. Then they came for the Jews and I didn't speak up because I was not a Jew. Then they came for the trade unionists and I didn't speak up because I was not a trade unionist. Then they came for the Catholics and I was a Protestant so I didn't speak up. Then they came for me . . . By that time there was no one to speak up for anyone.

*Concise Dictionary of Religious Quotations* (W. Neil)

**Nietzsche, Friedrich Wilhelm** (1844–1900) German philosopher. His rejection of all religion and his glorification of the superman in *Thus Spake Zarathustra* (1883–92) influenced Nazi philosophy in Germany.

**1** When a man is in love he endures more than at other times; he submits to everything.

*The Antichrist*

**2** God created woman. And boredom did indeed cease from that moment – but many other things ceased as well! Woman was God's *second* mistake.

*The Antichrist*

**3** I call Christianity the one great curse, the one enormous and innermost perversion, the one great instinct of revenge, for which no means are too venomous, too underhand, too underground and too petty – I call it the one immortal blemish of mankind.

*The Antichrist*

**4** God is dead: but considering the state the species Man is in, there will perhaps be caves, for ages yet, in which his shadow will be shown.

*Die Fröhliche Wissenschaft*, Bk. III

**5** Believe me! The secret of reaping the greatest fruitfulness and the greatest enjoyment from life is to *live dangerously!*

*Die Fröhliche Wissenschaft*, Bk. IV

**6** As an artist, a man has no home in Europe save in Paris.

*Ecce Homo*

**7** My time has not yet come either; some are born posthumously.

*Ecce Homo*

**8** My doctrine is: Live that thou mayest desire to live again – that is thy duty – for in any case thou wilt live again!

*Eternal Recurrence*

**9** Do you really believe that the sciences would ever have originated and grown if the way had not been prepared by magicians, alchemists, astrologers and witches whose promises and pretensions first had to create a thirst, a hunger, a taste for *hidden* and *forbidden* powers? Indeed, infinitely more had to be *promised* than could ever be fulfilled in order that anything at all might be fulfilled in the realms of knowledge.

*The Gay Science*

**10** The thought of suicide is a great source of comfort: with it a calm passage is to be made across many a bad night.

*Jenseits von Gut und Böse*

**11** Morality in Europe today is herd-morality.

*Jenseits von Gut und Böse*

**12** Is not life a hundred times too short for us to bore ourselves?

*Jenseits von Gut und Böse*

**13** In the philosopher there is nothing whatever impersonal; and, above all, his morality bears decided and decisive testimony to *who he is* – that is to say, to the order of rank in which the innermost drives of his nature stand in relation to one another.

*Jenseits von Gut und Böse*

**14** Insects sting, not from malice, but because they want to live. It is the same with critics – they desire our blood, not our pain.

*Miscellaneous Maxims and Reflections*

**15** He who does not need to lie is proud of not being a liar.

*Nachgelassene Fragmente*

**16** I teach you the Superman. Man is something that is to be surpassed.

*Thus Spake Zarathustra*

**17** To show pity is felt as a sign of contempt because one has clearly ceased to be an object of *fear* as soon as one is pitied.

*The Wanderer and His Shadow*

**Nightingale, Florence** (1820–1910) British nurse. She worked under appalling conditions in the Crimean War, becoming known as 'The Lady with the Lamp'. Later she founded the Nightingale School of Nurses at St Thomas's Hospital, London.

1 No *man*, not even a doctor, ever gives any other definition of what a nurse should be than this – "devoted and obedient." This definition would do just as well for a porter. It might even do for a horse. It would not do for a policeman.
*Notes on Nursing*

2 To understand God's thoughts we must study statistics, for these are the measure of his purpose.
*Life . . . of Francis Galton* (K. Pearson), Vol. II, Ch. 13

**Niven, Larry** (1938– ) US science-fiction writer. His works include *Ringworld* (1970) and, with Jerry Pournelle, *The Mote in God's Eye* (1974), *Lucifer's Hammer* (1977), and *Footfall* (1985).

1 On my twenty-first birthday my father said, 'Son, here's a million dollars. Don't lose it.'
When asked 'What is the best advice you have ever been given?'
Attrib.

**Nixon, Richard Milhous** (1913– ) US president. A republican, he became president in 1969 and was responsible for ending the US commitment in Vietnam (1973). He was forced to resign after the Watergate scandal (1974), but was pardoned by his successor, President Ford.

1 There can be no whitewash at the White House.
Referring to the Watergate scandal
*The Observer*, 'Sayings of the Week', 30 Dec 1973

2 I let down my friends, I let down my country. I let down our system of government.
*The Observer*, 'Sayings of the Week', 8 May 1977

3 You won't have Nixon to kick around any more, gentlemen. This is my last Press Conference.
Press conference for governorship of California, 2 Nov 1962

4 Let us begin by committing ourselves to the truth, to see it like it is and to tell it like it is, to find the truth, to speak the truth and live with the truth. That's what we'll do.
Nomination acceptance speech, Miami, 8 Aug 1968

5 It is time for the great silent majority of Americans to stand up and be counted.
Election speech, Oct 1970

6 This is the greatest week in the history of the world since the creation.
Said when men first landed on the moon
Attrib., 24 July 1969

7 I am not a crook.
Attrib., 17 Nov 1973

**Norden, Dennis** (1922– ) British scriptwriter and broadcaster. With Frank Muir he wrote many comedy radio scripts. His books include *Upon My Word* (1974) and *Oh, My Word!* (1980). *See* Muir, Frank.

**Norman, Barry** (1933– ) British cinema critic and broadcaster.

1 Perhaps at fourteen every boy should be in love with some ideal woman to put on a pedestal and worship. As he grows up, of course, he will put her on a pedestal the better to view her legs.
*The Listener*

**Norman, Frank** (1931– ) British dramatist and novelist. His low-life musicals include *Fings Ain't Wot They Used T'Be* (1959) and *A Kayf Up West* (1964).

1 Fings Ain't Wot They Used T'Be.
Title of musical

**North, Christopher** (John Wilson; 1785–1854) Scottish poet, essayist, and critic. His works include poetry, fiction, and *Noctes Ambrosianae* (1822–35), a collection of articles on literature, politics, and philosophy.

1 His Majesty's dominions, on which the sun never sets.
*Noctes Ambrosianae*, 20 Apr 1829

2 Laws were made to be broken.
*Noctes Ambrosianae*, 24 May 1830

**Northcliffe, Alfred Charles William Harmsworth, Viscount** (1865–1922) Irish-born British newspaper proprietor, who, with his brother, who became Lord Rothermere, bought the *Evening News* (1894). He later founded the *Daily Mail* and the *Daily Mirror* and acquired control of *The Times*.

1 They are only ten.
Rumoured to have been a notice to remind his staff of his opinion of the mental age of the general public.
Attrib.

2 When I want a peerage, I shall buy one like an honest man.
Attrib.

**Northcote, Sir Stafford, 1st Earl of Iddesleigh** (1818–87) British statesman. An MP, he became chancellor of the exchequer (1874–80) in Disraeli's administration and foreign secretary (1886) under Gladstone.

1 Argue as you please, you are nowhere, that grand old man, the Prime Minister, insists on the other thing.
Referring to Gladstone; the phrase, and its acronym GOM, became his nickname – temporarily reversed to MOG ('Murderer of Gordon') in 1885, after the death of General Gordon at Khartoum
Speech, Liverpool, 12 Apr 1882

**Norton, Caroline Elizabeth Sarah** (1808–77) British poet and writer. She wrote a pamphlet on divorce reform but is remembered for her poetry.

1 I do not love thee! – no! I do not love thee!
And yet when thou art absent I am sad.
*I do Not Love Thee*

**Norworth, Jack** (1879–1959) US vaudeville comedian and songwriter.

1 Oh! shine on, shine on, harvest moon
Up in the sky.
I ain't had no lovin'
Since April, January, June or July.
*Shine On, Harvest Moon* (song)

**Novello, Ivor** (David Ivor Davies; 1893–1951) British actor, composer, and dramatist. In World War I he wrote 'Keep the Home Fires Burning' and later wrote a number of musicals, including *Careless Rapture* (1936) and *The Dancing Years* (1939).

1   And Her Mother Came Too.

*Title of song*

2   There's something Vichy about the French.

*Ambrosia and Small Beer* (Edward Marsh), Ch. 4

**Noyes, Alfred** (1880–1958) British poet. His epic narrative poems include *Drake* (1906–08) and *The Torchbearers* (1922–30).

1   The wind was a torrent of darkness among the
    gusty trees,
    The moon was a ghostly galleon tossed upon
    cloudy seas,
    The road was a ribbon of moonlight over the
    purple moor,
    And the highwayman came riding –
    Riding – riding –
    The highwayman came riding, up to the old inn-
    door.

*The Highwayman*

2   Look for me by moonlight;
    Watch for me by moonlight;
    I'll come to thee by moonlight, though hell
    should bar the way!

*The Highwayman*

**Nursery Rhymes** A selection of nursery rhymes is given here. The wording used is the one most commonly used today; not the form in the form in the original publication.

1   A frog he would a-wooing go,
    Heigh ho! says Rowley,
    A frog he would a-wooing go,
    Whether his mother would let him or no.
    With a rowley, powley, gammon and spinach,
    Heigh ho! says Anthony Rowley.

*Melismata* (Thomas Ravenscroft)

2   All the birds of the air
    Fell a-sighing and a-sobbing,
    When they heard the bell toll
    For poor Cock Robin.

*Tommy Thumb's Pretty Song Book*

3   As I was going to St Ives,
    I met a man with seven wives.
    Each wife had seven sacks
    Each sack had seven cats,
    Each cat had seven kits,
    How many were going to St Ives?

*Mother Goose's Quarto*

4   Baa, baa, black sheep,
    Have you any wool?
    Yes, sir, yes, sir,
    Three bags full;
    One for the master,
    And one for the dame,
    And one for the little boy
    Who lives down the lane.

*Tommy Thumb's Pretty Song Book*

5   Bobby Shafto's gone to sea,
    Silver buckles on his knee;
    He'll come back and marry me,
    Bonny Bobby Shafto!

*Songs for the Nursery*

6   Boys and girls come out to play,
    The moon doth shine as bright as day.

*Useful Transactions in Philosophy* (William King)

7   Come, let's to bed
    Says Sleepy-head;
    Tarry a while, says Slow;
    Put on the pan;
    Says Greedy Nan,
    Let's sup before we go.

*Gammer Gurton's Garland* (R. Christopher)

8   Curly locks, Curly locks,
    Wilt thou be mine?
    Thou shalt not wash dishes
    Nor yet feed the swine,
    But sit on a cushion
    And sew a fine seam,
    And feed upon strawberries,
    Sugar and cream

*Infant Institutes*

9   Ding dong, bell,
    Pussy's in the well.
    Who put her in?
    Little Johnny Green.
    Who pulled her out?
    Little Tommy Stout.

*Mother Goose's Melody*

10  Doctor Foster went to Gloucester
    In a shower of rain:
    He stepped in a puddle,
    Right up to his middle,
    And never went there again.

*The Nursery Rhymes of England* (J. O. Halliwell)

11  Eena, meena, mina, mo,
    Catch a nigger by his toe;
    If he hollers, let him go,
    Eena, meena, mina, mo.

*Games and Songs of American Children* (Newell)

12  Georgie Porgie, pudding and pie,
    Kissed the girls and made them cry;
    When the boys came out to play,
    Georgie Porgie ran away.

*The Nursery Rhymes of England* (J. O. Halliwell)

13  Goosey, goosey gander,
    Whither shall I wander?
    Upstairs and downstairs
    And in my lady's chamber.

*Gammer Gurton' Garland*

14  Hey diddle diddle,
    The cat and the fiddle,
    The cow jumped over the moon;
    The little dog laughed
    To see such sport,
    And the dish ran away with the spoon.

*Mother Goose's Melody*

**15** Hickory, dickory, dock,
The mouse ran up the clock.
The clock struck one,
The mouse ran down,
Hickory, dickory, dock.

*Tommy Thumb's Pretty Song Book*

**16** Hot cross buns!
Hot cross buns!
One a penny, two a penny,
Hot cross buns!

*Christmas Box*

**17** How many miles to Babylon?
Three score miles and ten.
Can I get there by candle-light?
Yes, and back again.
If your heels are nimble and light,
You may get there by candle-light.

*Songs for the Nursery*

**18** Humpty Dumpty sat on a wall,
Humpty Dumpty had a great fall.
All the king's horses,
And all the king's men,
Couldn't put Humpty together again.

*Gammer Gurton's Garland*

**19** Hush-a-bye, baby, on the tree top,
When the wind blows the cradle will rock;
When the bough breaks the cradle will fall,
Down will come baby, cradle, and all.

*Mother Goose's Melody*

**20** I had a little nut tree,
Nothing would it bear
But a silver nutmeg
And a golden pear;
The King of Spain's daughter
Came to visit me,
And all for the sake
Of my little nut tree.

*Newest Christmas Box*

**21** I had a little pony,
His name was Dapple Grey;
I lent him to a lady
To ride a mile away.
She whipped him, she lashed him,
She rode him through the mire;
I would not lend my pony now,
For all the lady's hire.

*Poetical Alphabet*

**22** I love sixpence, jolly little sixpence,
I love sixpence better than my life;
I spent a penny of it, I lent a penny of it,
And I took fourpence home to my wife.

*Gammer Gurton's Garland*

**23** I'm the king of the castle,
Get down you dirty rascal.

*Brand's Popular Antiquities*

**24** I see the moon,
And the moon sees me;
God bless the moon,
And God bless me.

*Gammer Gurton's Garland*

**25** Jack and Jill went up the hill
To fetch a pail of water;
Jack fell down and broke his crown,
And Jill came tumbling after.

*Mother Goose's Melody*

**26** Jack Sprat could eat no fat,
His wife could eat no lean,
And so between them both you see,
They licked the platter clean.

*Paroemiologia Anglo-Latina* (John Clark)

**27** Ladybird, ladybird,
Fly away home,
Your house is on fire
And your children all gone.

*Tommy Thumb's Pretty Song Book*

**28** Little Bo-peep has lost her sheep,
And can't tell where to find them;
Leave them alone, and they'll come home,
Bringing their tails behind them.

*Gammer Gurton's Garland*

**29** Little Boy Blue,
Come blow your horn,
The sheep's in the meadow,
The cow's in the corn.

*Famous Tommy Thumb's Little Story Book*

**30** Little Jack Horner
Sat in the corner,
Eating a Christmas pie;
He put in his thumb,
And pulled out a plum,
And said, What a good boy am I!

*Namby Pamby* (Henry Carey)

**31** Little Miss Muffet
Sat on a tuffet,
Eating her curds and whey;
There came a big spider,
Who sat down beside her
And frightened Miss Muffet away.

*Songs for the Nursery*

**32** Little Tommy Tucker,
Sings for his supper:
What shall we give him?
White bread and butter
How shall he cut it
Without a knife?
How will be be married
Without a wife?

*Tommy Thumb's Pretty Song Book*

**33** London Bridge is broken down,
My fair lady.

*Namby Pamby* (Henry Carey)

34 Mary, Mary, quite contrary,
How does your garden grow?
With silver bells and cockle shells,
And pretty maids all in a row.

*Tommy Thumb's Pretty Song Book*

35 Monday's child is fair of face,
Tuesday's child is full of grace,
Wednesday's child is full of woe,
Thursday's child has far to go,
Friday's child is loving and giving,
Saturday's child works hard for his living,
And the child that is born on the Sabbath day
Is bonny and blithe, and good and gay.

*Traditions of Devonshire* (A. E. Bray)

36 My mother said that I never should
Play with the gypsies in the wood;
If I did, she would say,
Naughty girl to disobey.

*Come Hither* (Walter de la Mare)

37 Oh! the grand old Duke of York
He had ten thousand men;
He marched them up to the top of the hill,
And he marched them down again.
And when they were up they were up,
And when they were down they were down,
And when they were only half way up,
They were neither up nor down.

*Traditional*

38 Old King Cole
Was a merry old soul,
And a merry old soul was he;
He called for his pipe,
And he called for his bowl,
And he called for his fiddlers three.

*Useful Transactions in Philosophy* (William King)

39 Old Mother Hubbard
Went to the cupboard,
To fetch her poor dog a bone;
But when she got there
The cupboard was bare
And so the poor dog had none.

*The Comic Adventures of Old Mother Hubbard and Her Dog*

40 One, two,
Buckle my shoe;
Three, four,
Knock at the door.

*Songs for the Nursery*

41 Oranges and lemons,
Say the bell of St Clement's.
You owe me five farthings,
Say the bells of St Martin's.
When will you pay me?
Say the bells of Old Bailey.
When I grow rich,
Say the bells of Shoreditch.
When will that be?
Say the bells of Stepney.

I'm sure I don't know,
Says the great bell at Bow.
Here comes a candle to light you to bed,
Here comes a chopper to chop off your head.

*Tommy Thumb's Pretty Song Book*

42 Pat-a-cake, pat-a-cake, baker's man,
Bake me a cake as fast as you can;
Pat it and prick it, and mark it with B,
Put it in the oven for baby and me.

*The Campaigners* (Tom D'Urfey)

43 Peter Piper picked a peck of pickled pepper;
A peck of pickled pepper Peter Piper picked;
If Peter Piper picked a peck of pickled pepper,
Where's the peck of pickled pepper Peter Piper picked?

*Peter Piper's Practical Principles of Plain and Perfect Pronunciation*

44 Polly put the kettle on,
Polly put the kettle on,
Polly put the kettle on,
We'll all have tea.

Sukey take it off again,
Sukey take it off again,
Sukey take it off again,
They've all gone away.

*Traditional*

45 Pussy cat, pussy cat, where have you been?
I've been to London to look at the queen.
Pussy cat, pussy cat, what did you there?
I frightened a little mouse under her chair.

*Songs for the Nursery*

46 Ride a cock-horse to Banbury Cross,
To see a fine lady upon a white horse;
Rings on her fingers and bells on her toes,
And she shall have music wherever she goes.

*Gammer Gurton's Garland*

47 Ring-a-ring o'roses,
A pocket full of posies,
A-tishoo! A-tishoo!
We all fall down.

*Mother Goose* (Kate Greenway)

48 Round and round the garden
Like a teddy bear;
One step, two step,
Tickle you under there!

*Traditional*

49 Rub-a-dub-dub,
Three men in a tub,
And who do you think they be?
The butcher, the baker,
The candlestick-maker,
And they all sailed out to sea.

*Christmas Box*

50 See-saw, Margery Daw,
Jacky shall have a new master;
Jacky shall have put a penny a day,
Because he can't work any faster.

*Mother Goose's Melody*

51 Simple Simon met a pieman,
Going to the fair;
Says Simple Simon to the pieman,
Let me taste your ware.
Says the pieman to Simple Simon,
Show me first your penny;
Says Simple Simon to the pieman,
Indeed I have not any.

*Simple Simon (Chapbook Advertisement)*

52 Sing a song of sixpence,
A pocket full of rye;
Four and twenty blackbirds,
Baked in a pie.
When the pie was opened,
The birds began to sing;
Was not that a dainty dish,
To set before the king?

The king was in his counting-house,
Counting out his money;
The queen was in the parlour,
Eating bread and honey.
The maid was in the garden,
Hanging out the clothes,
When down came a blackbird,
And pecked off her nose.

*Tommy Thumb's Pretty Song Book*

53 Solomon Grundy,
Born on a Monday,
Christened on Tuesday,
Married on Wednesday,
Took ill on Thursday,
Worse on Friday,
Died on Saturday,
Buried on Sunday.
This is the end
Of Solomon Grundy.

*The Nursery Rhymes of England (J. O. Halliwell)*

54 The first day of Christmas,
My true love sent to me
A partridge in a pear tree.

*Mirth without Mischief*

55 The lion and the unicorn
Were fighting for the crown;
The lion beat the unicorn
All round about the town.

*Useful Transactions in Philosophy (William King)*

56 The Queen of Hearts
She made some tarts,
All on a summer's day;
The Knave of Hearts
He stole the tarts,
And took them clean away.

*The European Magazine*

57 There was a crooked man, and he walked a
crooked mile,
He found a crooked sixpence against a crooked
stile:
He bought a crooked cat, which caught a crooked mouse,
And they all lived together in a little crooked
house.

*The Nursery Rhymes of England (J. O. Halliwell)*

58 There was an old woman
Lived under a hill,
And if she's not gone
She lives there still.

*Academy of Complements*

59 There was an old woman who lived in a shoe,
She had so many children she didn't know what
to do;
She gave them some broth without any bread;
She whipped them all soundly and put them to
bed.

*Gammer Gurton's Garland*

60 The twelfth day of Christmas,
My true love sent to me
Twelve lords a-leaping,
Eleven ladies dancing,
Ten pipers piping,
Nine drummers drumming,
Eight maids a-milking,
Seven swans a-swimming,
Six geese a-laying,
Five gold rings,
Four colly birds,
Three French hens,
Two turtle doves, and
A partridge in a pear tree.

*Mirth without Mischief*

61 Thirty days hath September,
April, June, and November;
All the rest have thirty-one,
Excepting February alone
And that has twenty-eight days clear
And twenty-nine in each leap year.

*Abridgement of the Chronicles of England (Richard Grafton)*

62 This is the farmer sowing his corn,
That kept the cock that crowed in the morn,
That waked the priest all shaven and shorn,
That married the man all tattered and torn,
That kissed the maiden all forlorn,
That milked the cow with the crumpled horn,
That tossed the dog,
That worried the cat,
That killed the rat,
That ate the corn,
That lay in the house that Jack built.

*Nurse Truelove's New-Year-Gift*

63 This little piggy went to market,
This little piggy stayed at home,
This little piggy had roast beef,
This little piggy had none,
And this little piggy cried, Wee-wee-wee-wee-
wee,
I can't find my way home.
*The Famous Tommy Thumb's Little Story Book*

64 Three blind mice, see how they run!
They all run after the farmer's wife,
Who cut off their tails with a carving knife,
Did you ever see such a thing in your life,
As three blind mice?
*Deuteromelia* (Thomas Ravenscroft)

65 Tinker,
Tailor,
Soldier,
Sailor,
Rich man,
Poor man,
Beggarman,
Thief.
*Popular Rhymes and Nursery Tales* (J. O. Halliwell)

66 Tom, he was a piper's son,
He learnt to play when he was young,
And all the tune that he could play
Was 'Over the hills and far away'.
*Tom, The Piper's Son*

67 Tom, Tom, the piper's son,
Stole a pig and away he run;
The pig was eat
And Tom was beat,
And Tom went howling down the street.
*Tom, The Piper's Son*

68 Two little dicky birds,
Sitting on a wall;
One named Peter,
The other named Paul,
Fly away, Peter!
Fly away, Paul!
Come back, Peter!
Come back, Paul!
*Mother Goose's Melody*

69 Wee Willie Winkie runs through the town
upstairs and downstairs and in his nightgown,
Rapping at the window, crying through the lock,
Are the children all in bed? It's past eight
o'clock.
In *Whistle-Binkie* (W. Miller)

70 What are little boys made of?
Frogs and snails
And puppy-dogs' tails,
That's what little boys are made of.
What are little girls made of?
Sugar and spice
And all that's nice,
That's what little girls are made of.
*Nursery Rhymes* (J. O. Halliwell)

71 What is your fortune, my pretty maid?
My face is my fortune, sir, she said.
Then I can't marry you, my pretty maid.
Nobody asked you, sir, she said.
*Archaeologia Cornu-Britannica* (William Pryce)

72 Where are you going to, my pretty maid?
I'm going a-milking, sir, she said.
*Archaeologia Cornu-Britannica* (William Pryce)

73 Who killed Cock Robin?
I, said the Sparrow,
With my bow and arrow,
I killed Cock Robin.
Who saw him die?
I, said the Fly,
With my little eye,
I saw him die.
*Tommy Thumb's Pretty Song Book*

74 Yankee Doodle came to town,
Riding on a pony;
He stuck a feather in his cap
And called it macaroni.
*Gammer Gurton's Garland*

# O

**Oakeley, Frederick** (1802–80) British churchman, who became Roman Catholic canon of Westminster. He translated the Latin hymn *Adeste Fideles* (1841).

1 O come all ye faithful,
Joyful and triumphant,
O come ye, O come ye to Bethlehem.
Translated from the Latin hymn, *Adeste Fideles*
*O Come All Ye Faithful*

**Oates, Lawrence Edward Grace** (1880–1912) British soldier and explorer. He was a member of Scott's expedition to the Antarctic (1910–12) and reached the South Pole. Afraid that his lameness on the return journey would slow down the others, he heroically walked out into the blizzard to die.

1 I am just going outside and may be some time.
Last words before leaving the tent and vanishing into the blizzard.
*Journal* (R. F. Scott), 17 Mar 1912

**O'Brien, Conor Cruise** (1917– ) Irish diplomat and writer. He became UN representative in the Congo (1961) and later a minister (1973–77) in the Irish government. He was then a senator (1977–79) before becoming editor (1979–81) of *The Observer* newspaper in London. His books include *United Nation: Sacred Drama* (1967), *Camus* (1969), and *States of Ireland* (1972).

1 It is a city where you can see a sparrow fall to the ground, and God watching it.
Referring to Dublin
Attrib.

**O'Brien, Edna** (1936– ) Irish novelist. Her books include *The Country Girls* (1960), *Night* (1972), and *Returning* (1982). She has also written plays and filmscripts.

**1** To Crystal, hair was the most important thing on earth. She would never get married because you couldn't wear curlers in bed.
*Winter's Tales*, 8, 'Come into the Drawing Room, Doris'

**2** The vote, I thought, means nothing to women. We should be armed.
Quoted as epigraph to *Fear of Flying* (Erica Jong), Ch. 16

**O'Brien, Flann** (Brian O'Nolan; 1911–66) Irish novelist and journalist. His books include *At Swim-Two-Birds* (1939) and *The Third Policeman* (1967). As "Myles na Gopaleen" he wrote a satirical column in the *Irish Times*.

**1** A thing of duty is a boy for ever.
About policemen always seeming to be young-looking.
*The Listener*, 24 Feb 1977

**O'Casey, Sean** (1884–1964) Irish dramatist. Formerly a labourer, his plays give a starkly realistic picture of Irish life. They include *Juno and the Paycock* (1924) and *The Silver Tassie* (1928).

**1** I ofen looked up at the sky an' assed meself the question – what is the stars, what is the stars?
*Juno and the Paycock*, I

**2** He's an oul' butty o' mine – oh, he's a darlin' man, a daarlin' man.
*Juno and the Paycock*, I

**3** There's no reason to bring religion into it. I think we ought to have as great a regard for religion as we can, so as to keep it out of as many things as possible.
*The Plough and the Stars*, I

**4** English literature's performing flea.
Referring to P. G. Wodehouse
Attrib.

**Ochs, Adolph Simon** (1858–1935) US newspaper publisher. His newspapers included the Chattanooga, New York, and Philadelphia *Times*.

**1** All the news that's fit to print.
The motto of the *New York Times*

**O'Connell, Daniel** (1775–1847) Irish politician. A Roman Catholic, he succeeded in forcing Catholic emancipation, becoming an MP at Westminster himself. He agitated for repeal of the union of Ireland and Britain and became Lord Mayor of Dublin (1841).

**1** Peel's smile: like the silver plate on a coffin.
Referring to Sir Robert Peel; quoting J. P. Curran (1750–1817)
*Hansard*, 26 Feb 1835

**O'Hara, Geoffrey** (1882–1967) Canadian-born US songwriter and composer. His operettas include *Riding Down the Sky* (1928) and *Harmony Hall* (1933).

**1** K-K-Katy, beautiful Katy,
You're the only g-g-g-girl that I adore,
When the m-m-m-moon shines over the cowshed,
I'll be waiting at the k-k-k-kitchen door.
*K-K-Katy* (song)

**O'Keefe, Patrick** (1872–1934) US advertising agent.

**1** Say it with flowers.
Slogan for Society of American Florists

**Okham, William of** (c. 1280–1349) English philosopher. A pupil of Duns Scotus, he is remembered for the proposition known as 'Okham's Razor'.

**1** Entities should not be multiplied unnecessarily. No more things should be presumed to exist than are absolutely necessary.
'Okham's Razor'. Despite its attribution to William of Okham, it was in fact a repetition of an ancient philosophical maxim

**Olivier, Laurence, Baron** (1907– ) British actor and manager. With the Old Vic Theatre he played many leading Shakespearean roles and later made several films of Shakespeare's plays. He was director of the National Theatre Company (1961–73). The Olivier Theatre at the National Theatre is named after him.

**1** Shakespeare – the nearest thing in incarnation to the eye of God.
*Kenneth Harris Talking To:* 'Sir Laurence Olivier'

**O'Neill, Eugene** (1888–1953) US dramatist. His plays include *Emperor Jones* (1920), *Mourning Becomes Electra* (1931), *The Iceman Cometh* (1946), and *Long Day's Journey into Night* (1956).

**1** Our lives are merely strange dark interludes in the electric display of God the Father.
*Strange Interlude*

**Opie, John** (1761–1807) British painter, known as the 'Cornish Wonder'. He painted many portraits of writers, including Dr Johnson, Burke, and Southey.

**1** I mix them with my brains, sir.
When asked what he mixed his colours with
*Self-Help* (Samuel Smiles), Ch. 4

**Oppenheimer, J. Robert** (1904–67) US physicist. He contributed to quantum mechanics and was in charge of the development of the atom bomb at Los Alamos. His opposition to the H-bomb resulted in his dismissal as chairman of the Atomic Energy Commission and his investigation as a security risk.

**1** We knew the world would not be the same.
After the first atomic test
*The Decision to Drop the Bomb*

**2** The physicists have known sin; and this is a knowledge which they cannot lose.
Lecture, Massachusetts Institute of Technology, 25 Nov 1947

**Orczy, Emmusca, Baroness** (1865–1947) British novelist, born in Hungary. Her books include *The Scarlet Pimpernel* (1905).

**1** We seek him here, we seek him there, Those Frenchies seek him everywhere. Is he in heaven? – Is he in hell? That damned elusive Pimpernel?
*The Scarlet Pimpernel*, Ch. 12

**2** The weariest nights, the longest days, sooner or later must perforce come to an end.
*The Scarlet Pimpernel*, Ch. 22

**Ortega y Gasset, José** (1883–1955) Spanish philosopher and writer. His best-known book is *The Revolt of the Masses* (1930).

**1** The uprising of the masses implies a fabulous increase of vital possibilities; quite the contrary of what we hear so often about the decadence of Europe.

*The Revolt of the Masses,* Ch. 2

**2** Revolution is not the uprising against pre-existing order, but the setting-up of a new order contradictory to the traditional one.

*The Revolt of the Masses,* Ch. 6

**Orton, Joe** (1933–67) British dramatist. His black comedies include *Entertaining Mr Sloane* (1964), *Loot* (1965), and *What the Butler Saw* (1969). He was battered to death by his homosexual lover.

**1** I'd the upbringing a nun would envy and that's the truth. Until I was fifteen I was more familiar with Africa than my own body.

*Entertaining Mr Sloane,* I

**2** It's all any reasonable child can expect if the dad is present at the conception.

*Entertaining Mr Sloane,* III

**3** The humble and meek are thirsting for blood.

*Funeral Games,* I

**4** Every luxury was lavished on you – atheism, breast-feeding, circumcision. I had to make my own way.

*Loot,* I

**5** Reading isn't an occupation we encourage among police officers. We try to keep the paper work down to a minimum.

*Loot,* II

**6** God is a gentleman. He prefers blondes.

*Loot,* II

**7** You were born with your legs apart. They'll send you to the grave in a Y-shaped coffin.

*What the Butler Saw,* I

**Orwell, George** (Eric Blair; 1903–50) British novelist. His books include *The Road to Wigan Pier* (1937), *Animal Farm* (1945), and *Nineteen Eighty-Four* (1949).

**1** Man is the only creature that consumes without producing.

An allegory of the Marxist analysis of capitalism, with man representing the capitalist

*Animal Farm,* Ch. 1

**2** Four legs good, two legs bad.

*Animal Farm,* Ch. 3

**3** War is war. The only good human being is a dead one.

*Animal Farm,* Ch. 4

**4** He intended, he said, to devote the rest of his life to learning the remaining twenty-two letters of the alphabet.

*Animal Farm,* Ch. 9

**5** All animals are equal but some animals are more equal than others.

*Animal Farm,* Ch. 10

**6** The high sentiments always win in the end, the leaders who offer blood, toil, tears and sweat always get more out of their followers than those who offer safety and a good time. When it comes to the pinch, human beings are heroic.

*The Art of Donald McGill*

**7** I'm fat, but I'm thin inside. Has it ever struck you that there's a thin man inside every fat man, just as they say there's a statue inside every block of stone?

*Coming Up For Air,* Pt. I, Ch. 3

**8** Before the war, and especially before the Boer War, it was summer all the year round.

*Coming Up for Air,* Pt. II, Ch. 1

**9** Prolonged, indiscriminate reviewing of books involves constantly *inventing* reactions towards books about which one has no spontaneous feelings whatever.

*Confessions of a Book Reviewer*

**10** He was an embittered atheist (the sort of atheist who does not so much disbelieve in God as personally dislike Him).

*Down and Out in Paris and London,* Ch. 30

**11** Probably the Battle of Waterloo *was* won on the playing-fields of Eton, but the opening battles of all subsequent wars have been lost there.

*The Lion and the Unicorn,* 'England, Your England'

**12** A family with the wrong members in control – that, perhaps, is as near as one can come to describing England in a phrase.

*The Lion and the Unicorn,* 'The Ruling Class'

**13** Who controls the past controls the future. Who controls the present controls the past.

*Nineteen Eighty-Four*

**14** If you want a picture of the future, imagine a boot stamping on a human face – for ever.

*Nineteen Eighty-Four*

**15** Big Brother is watching you.

*Nineteen Eighty-Four*

**16** War is Peace, Freedom is Slavery, Ignorance is Strength.

*Nineteen Eighty-Four*

**17** Doublethink means the power of holding two contradictory beliefs in one's mind simultaneously, and accepting both of them.

*Nineteen Eighty-Four*

**18** In our time, political speech and writing are largely the defence of the indefensible.

*Politics and the English Language*

**19** The books one reads in childhood, and perhaps most of all the bad and good bad books, create in one's mind a sort of false map of the world, a series of fabulous countries into which one can retreat at odd moments throughout the rest of life, and which in some cases can even survive a visit to the real countries which they are supposed to represent.
*Riding Down from Bangor*

**20** It is brought home to you . . . that it is only because miners sweat their guts out that superior persons can remain superior.
*The Road to Wigan Pier, Ch. 2*

**21** I sometimes think that the price of liberty is not so much eternal vigilance as eternal dirt.
*The Road to Wigan Pier, Ch. 4*

**22** We may find in the long run that tinned food is a deadlier weapon than the machine-gun.
*The Road to Wigan Pier, Ch. 6*

**23** There can hardly be a town in the South of England where you could throw a brick without hitting the niece of a bishop.
*The Road to Wigan Pier, Ch. 7*

**24** As with the Christian religion, the worst advertisement for Socialism is its adherents.
*The Road to Wigan Pier, Ch. 11*

**25** To the ordinary working man, the sort you would meet in any pub on Saturday night, Socialism does not mean much more than better wages and shorter hours and nobody bossing you about.
*The Road to Wigan Pier, Ch. 11*

**26** The higher-water mark, so to speak, of Socialist literature is W. H. Auden, a sort of gutless Kipling.
*The Road to Wigan Pier, Ch. 11*

**27** We have nothing to lose but our aitches.
Referring to the middle classes
*The Road to Wigan Pier, Ch. 13*

**28** The quickest way of ending a war is to lose it.
*Second Thoughts on James Burnham*

**29** Most people get a fair amount of fun out of their lives, but on balance life is suffering and only the very young or the very foolish imagine otherwise.
*Shooting an Elephant*

**30** Serious sport has nothing to do with fair play. It is bound up with hatred, jealousy, boastfulness, disregard of all rules and sadistic pleasure in witnessing violence; in other words it is war minus the shooting.
*The Sporting Spirit*

**31** To a surprising extent the war-lords in shining armour, the apostles of the martial virtues, tend not to die fighting when the time comes. History is full of ignominious getaways by the great and famous.
*Who Are the War Criminals?*

**32** He is pretty certain to come back into favour. One of the surest signs of his genius is that women dislike his books.
Referring to Conrad
*New English Weekly, 23 July 1936*

**33** Each generation imagines itself to be more intelligent than the one that went before it, and wiser than the one that comes after it.
Book Review

**34** At 50, everyone has the face he deserves.
Last words in his manuscript notebook, 17 Apr 1949

**Osborne, John** (1929– ) British dramatist. He made his reputation as one of the Angry Young Men with *Look Back in Anger* (1956). His subsequent plays include *The Entertainer* (1957), *Luther* (1960), and *Inadmissible Evidence* (1964).

**1** Don't clap too hard – it's a very old building.
*The Entertainer*

**2** Well, there are only two posh papers on a Sunday – the one you're reading and this one.
*Look Back in Anger, I*

**3** He really deserves some sort of decoration . . . a medal inscribed 'For Vaguery in the Field'.
*Look Back in Anger, I*

**4** I don't think one 'comes down' from Jimmy's university. According to him, it's not even red brick, but white tile.
*Look Back in Anger, II:1*

**5** They spend their time mostly looking forward to the past.
*Look Back in Anger, II:1*

**6** Poor old Daddy – just one of those sturdy old plants left over from the Edwardian Wilderness, that can't understand why the sun isn't shining any more.
*Look Back in Anger, II.2*

**7** She's like the old line about justice – not only must be done but must be seen to be done.
*Time Present, I*

**O'Sullivan, John L.** (1813–95) US writer.

**1** A torchlight procession marching down your throat.
Referring to whisky
*Collections and Recollections* (G. W. E. Russell), Ch. 19

**Otis, James** (1725–83) US political activist, who defended the legal rights of American colonists.

**1** Taxation without representation is tyranny.
As 'No taxation without representation' this became the principal slogan of the American Revolution
Generally attributed to Otis

**Ouida** (Marie Louise de la Ramée; 1839–1908) British novelist. Her adventure stories included *Under Two Flags* (1867).

1 Christianity has made of death a terror which was unknown to the gay calmness of the Pagan.
*The Failure of Christianity*

2 ... with peaches and women, it's only the side next the sun that's tempting.
*Strathmore*

3 The song that we hear with our ears is only the song that is sung in our hearts.
*Wisdom, Wit and Pathos*, 'Ariadne'

4 A cruel story runs on wheels, and every hand oils the wheels as they run.
*Wisdom, Wit and Pathos*, 'Moths'

**Ouspensky, P. D.** (1878–1947) Russian-born occultist. His writings include *Tertium Organum* (1912) and *A New Model of the Universe* (1914).

1 Man, as he is, is not a genuine article. He is an imitation of something, and a very bad imitation.
*The Psychology of Man's Possible Evolution*, Ch. 2

**Overbury, Sir Thomas** (1581–1613) English poet. Imprisoned in the Tower for disrespect to the monarch, he was poisoned by the agents of Lady Essex, whose marriage to Viscount Rochester he had opposed. His best-known poem is *A Wife* (1614).

1 He disdains all things above his reach, and preferreth all countries before his own.
*Miscellaneous Works*, 'An Affectate Traveller'

**Ovid** (Publius Ovidius Naso; 43 BC–17 AD) Roman poet. He is remembered for his love poems, including the *Amores* and *Heroides*, and his *Metamorphoses*, a collection of mythical and historical tales.

1 Whether a pretty woman grants or withholds her favours, she always likes to be asked for them.
*Ars Amatoria*

2 Dripping water hollows out a stone, a ring is worn away by use.
*See also* LATIMER; LUCRETIUS
*Epistulae Ex Ponto*, Bk. IV

3 Now there are fields where Troy once was.
*Heroides*, Bk. I

4 *Tu quoque.*
You also.
*Tristia*

**Owen, David** (1938– ) British doctor and politician. He became Labour foreign secretary (1977–79) but resigned from the Labour party in 1983 to cofound the Social Democratic Party. With David Steel he headed the SDP-Liberal Alliance.

1 It was on this issue, the nuclear defence of Britain, on which I left the Labour Party, and on this issue I am prepared to stake my entire political career.
*The Observer*, 'Sayings of the Week', 9 Nov 1986

2 No general in the midst of battle has a great discussion about what he is going to do if defeated.
*The Observer*, 'Sayings of the Week', 6 June 1987

**Owen, Robert** (1771–1858) British social reformer. He advocated 'villages of cooperation' run on Socialist lines, modelled on the New Lanark mill, which he managed. He was also active in the trades-union movement.

1 All the world is queer save thee and me, and even thou art a little queer.
Referring to William Allen, his partner in business
Attrib., 1828

**Owen, Wilfred** (1893–1918) British poet. Written during World War I, his poetry expresses the horror of war and includes 'Strange Meeting' and 'Anthem for Doomed Youth'. He was killed in action.

1 The pallor of girls' brows shall be their pall;
Their flowers the tenderness of patient minds,
And each slow dusk a drawing-down of blinds.
*Anthem for Doomed Youth*

2 And in the happy no-time of his sleeping
Death took him by the heart.
*Asleep*

3 The old Lie: *Dulce et decorum est*
*Pro patria mori.*
*Dulce et decorum est*

4 Red lips are not so red
As the stained stones kissed by the English dead.
*Greater Love*

5 Above all I am not concerned with Poetry. My subject is War, and the pity of War. The Poetry is in the pity.
*Poems*, Preface

**Oxenstierna, Axel, Count** (1583–1654) Swedish statesman, who was chancellor of Sweden (1612–54). After the death of Gustavus II Adolphus, he led Sweden into the Thirty Years' War.

1 Do you not know, my son, with how little wisdom the world is governed?
Letter to his son, 1648

# P

**Paine, Thomas** (1737–1809) British writer and political philosopher. His pamphlets include *Common Sense* (1776), which influenced the move towards American Independence.

1 ·It is necessary to the happiness of man that he be mentally faithful to himself. Infidelity does not consist in believing, or in disbelieving, it consists in professing to believe what one does not believe.

*The Age of Reason*, Pt. 1

2 The sublime and the ridiculous are often so nearly related that it is difficult to class them separately. One step above the sublime makes the ridiculous; and one step above the ridiculous makes the sublime again.

*The Age of Reason*, Pt. 2

3 Government, even in its best state, is but a necessary evil; in its worst state, an intolerable one.

*Common Sense*, Ch. 1

4 As to religion, I hold it to be the indispensable duty of government to protect all conscientious professors thereof, and I know of no other business which government hath to do therewith.

*Common Sense*, Ch. 4

5 The summer soldier and the sunshine patriot will, in this crisis, shrink from the service of their country.

*Pennsylvania Journal*, 'The American Crisis'

**Palmer, Samuel** (1805–81) British landscape painter. He was influenced by William Blake in his early mystical paintings, but became more conventional as he grew older and more successful.

1 A picture has been said to be something between a thing and a thought.

*Life of Blake* (Arthur Symons)

**Palmerston, Henry John Temple, Viscount** (1784–1865) British statesman. Changing from Tory to Whig (1830), he became prime minister (1855–58; 1859–65).

1 Accidental and fortuitous concurrence of atoms.

Speech, House of Commons, 1857

2 Die, my dear Doctor, that's the last thing I shall do!

Last words
Attrib.

**Pankhurst, Dame Christabel** (1880–1958) British suffragette. The daughter of Emmeline Pankhurst, she was arrested for assaulting the policeman who removed her from an election meeting.

1 Never lose your temper with the Press or the public is a major rule of political life.

*Unshackled*

2 We are not ashamed of what we have done, because, when you have a great cause to fight for, the moment of greatest humiliation is the moment when the spirit is proudest.

Speech, Albert Hall, London, 19 Mar 1908

3 We are here to claim our rights as women, not only to be free, but to fight for freedom. It is our privilege, as well as our pride and our joy, to take some part in this militant movement, which, as we believe, means the regeneration of all humanity.

Speech, 23 Mar 1911

4 What we suffragettes aspire to be when we are enfranchised is ambassadors of freedom to women in other parts of the world, who are not so free as we are.

Speech, Carnegie Hall, New York, 25 Oct 1915

**Pankhurst, Emmeline** (1858–1928) British suffragette. She founded, in Manchester, the Women's Social and Political Union (1903). She was frequently imprisoned for destroying property, but during World War I abandoned her campaign and encouraged women to do industrial war work.

1 . . . if civilisation is to advance at all in the future, it must be through the help of women, women freed of their political shackles, women with full power to work their will in society. It was rapidly becoming clear to my mind that men regarded women as a servant class in the community, and that women were going to remain in the servant class until they lifted themselves out of it.

*My Own Story*

2 Women had always fought for men, and for their children. Now they were ready to fight for their own human rights. Our militant movement was established.

*My Own Story*

3 I have no sense of guilt. I look upon myself as a prisoner of war. I am under no moral obligation to conform to, or in any way accept, the sentence imposed upon me.

Speech in court, Apr 1913
*The Fighting Pankhursts* (David Mitchell)

4 We have taken this action, because as women . . . we realize that the condition of our sex is so deplorable that it is our duty even to break the law in order to call attention to the reasons why we do so.

Speech in court, 21 Oct 1908
*Shoulder to Shoulder* (ed. Midge Mackenzie)

**Pankhurst, Sylvia** (1882–1960) British suffragette. The daughter of Emmeline Pankhurst, she wrote a biography of her mother.

1 I could not give my name to aid the slaughter in this war, fought on both sides for grossly material ends, which did not justify the sacrifice of a single mother's son. Clearly I must continue to oppose it, and expose it, to all whom I could reach with voice or pen.
*The Home Front*, Ch. 25

2 I have gone to war too ... I am going to fight capitalism even if it kills me. It is wrong that people like you should be comfortable and well fed while all around you people are starving.
*The Fighting Pankhursts* (David Mitchell)

**Park, Mungo** (1771-1806) Scottish explorer. He twice explored the River Niger and wrote *Travels in the Interior Districts of Africa* (1797). In a subsequent expedition his party was attacked by Africans and he died.

1 The sight of it gave me infinite pleasure, as it proved that I was in a civilized society.
Remark on finding a gibbet in an unexplored part of Africa
Attrib.

**Parker, Charlie (Christopher)** (1920-55) US black jazz saxophonist and composer, at the peak of his fame during the 1950s. He was known as 'Bird' or 'Yardbird'.

1 Music is your own experience, your thoughts, your wisdom. If you don't live it, it won't come out of your horn.
*Hear Me Talkin' to Ya* (Nat Shapiro and Nat Hentoff)

**Parker, Clarke Ross** (1914-74) British songwriter, who with Hughie Charles (1907- ) wrote 'There'll Always Be an England'.

1 There'll always be an England
While there's a country lane,
Wherever there's a cottage small
Beside a field of grain.
*There'll Always Be an England*

**Parker, Dorothy (Rothschild)** (1893-1967) US writer and wit. Her New York circle in the 1920s included Ogden Nash and James Thurber. She is best known for her short stories, sketches, and poems; her books include *Not So Deep As a Well* (1936).

1 Razors pain you
Rivers are damp;
Acids stain you;
And drugs cause cramp.
Guns aren't lawful;
Nooses give;
Gas smells awful;
You might as well live.
*Enough Rope*, 'Resumé'

2 He lies below, correct in cypress wood,
And entertains the most exclusive worms.
*Epitaph for a Very Rich Man*

3 All I say is, nobody has any business to go around looking like a horse and behaving as if it were all right. You don't catch horses going around looking like people, do you?
*Horsie*

4 How do people go to sleep? I'm afraid I've lost the knack. I might try busting myself smartly over the temple with the nightlight. I might repeat to myself, slowly and soothingly, a list of quotations beautiful from minds profound; if I can remember any of the damn things.
*The Little Hours*

5 I'm never going to be famous ... I don't do anything. Not one single thing. I used to bite my nails, but I don't even do that any more.
*The Little Hours*

6 I might repeat to myself ... a list of quotations from minds profound - if I can remember any of the damn things.
*The Little Hours*

7 Why is it no one ever sent me yet
One perfect limousine, do you suppose?
Ah no, it's always just my luck to get
One perfect rose.
*One Perfect Rose*

8 Sorrow is tranquillity remembered in emotion.
*Sentiment*

9 It costs me never a stab nor squirm
To tread by chance upon a worm.
"Aha, my little dear," I say,
"Your clan will pay me back one day."
*Sunset Gun*, 'Thought for a Sunshiny Morning'

10 By the time you swear you're his,
Shivering and sighing,
And he vows his passion is
Infinite, undying -
Lady, make a note of this:
One of you is lying.
*Unfortunate Coincidence*

11 That should assure us of at least forty-five minutes of undisturbed privacy.
Pressing a button marked NURSE during a stay in hospital
*The Algonquin Wits* (R. Drennan)

12 The poor son-of-a-bitch!
Quoting from *The Great Gatsby* on paying her last respects to F. Scott Fitzgerald
*Thalberg: Life and Legend* (B. Thomas)

13 If all the young ladies who attended the Yale promenade dance were laid end to end, no one would be the least surprised.
*While Rome Burns* (Alexander Woollcott)

14 Brevity is the soul of lingerie.
*While Rome Burns* (Alexander Woollcott)

15 This is not a novel to be tossed aside lightly. It should be thrown with great force.
Book review
*Wit's End* (R. E. Dremman)

16 A list of authors who have made themselves most beloved and therefore, most comfortable financially, shows that it is our national joy to mistake for the first-rate, the fecund rate.
*Wit's End* (R. E. Drennan)

**17** You can't teach an old dogma new tricks.

*Wit's End* (R. E. Drennan)

**18** I was fired from there, finally, for a lot of things, among them my insistence that the Immaculate Conception was spontaneous combustion.

*Writers at Work, First Series* (Malcolm Cowley)

**19** This is on me.

Suggesting words for tombstone
*You Might As Well Live* (J. Keats), Pt. I, Ch. 5

**20** It serves me right for putting all my eggs in one bastard.

Said on going into hospital to get an abortion
*You Might as Well Live* (J. Keats), Pt. II, Ch. 3

**21** Oh, don't worry about Alan . . . Alan will always land on somebody's feet.

Said of her husband on the day their divorce became final
*You Might As Well Live* (J. Keats), Pt. IV, Ch. 1

**22** How could they tell?

Reaction to news of the death of Calvin Coolidge, US President
1923–29; also attributed to H. L. Mencken
*You Might As Well Live* (J. Keats)

**23** Dear Mary, We all knew you had it in you.

Telegram sent to a friend on the successful outcome of her
much-publicized pregnancy

**24** You can lead a whore to culture but you can't make her think.

Speech to American Horticultural Society

**25** You know, she speaks eighteen languages. And she can't say 'No' in any of them.

Speaking of an acquaintance
Attrib.

**26** Men seldom make passes
At girls who wear glasses.

Attrib.

**27** Check enclosed.

Giving her version of the two most beautiful words in the English
language
Attrib.

**28** She ran the whole gamut of the emotions from A to B.

Referring to a performance by Katharine Hepburn on Broadway
Attrib.

**29** Excuse my dust.

Her own epitaph

**Parker, Henry Taylor** (1867–1934) US music critic.

**1** Those people on the stage are making such a noise I can't hear a word you're saying.

Rebuking some talkative members of an audience, near whom he
was sitting
*The Humor of Music* (L. Humphrey)

**Parker, Hubert Lister** (1900–72) Lord Chief Justice of England (1958–71).

**1** A judge is not supposed to know anything about the facts of life until they have been presented in evidence and explained to him at least three times.

*The Observer*, 'Sayings of the Week', 12 Mar 1961

**Parker, John** (1729–75) US general. In the American Revolution he commanded the Minutemen at Lexington.

**1** Stand your ground. Don't fire unless fired upon, but if they mean to have a war, let it begin here!

Command given at the start of the Battle of Lexington
*Familiar Quotations* (J. Bartlett)

**Parkinson, Cyril Northcote** (1919– ) British historian and writer. He is best known for his book *Parkinson's Law* (1958), a study of business administration.

**1** Work expands so as to fill the time available for its completion.

*Parkinson's Law*, Ch. 1

**2** The rise in the total of those employed is governed by Parkinson's Law and would be much the same whether the volume of work were to increase, diminish or even disappear.

*Parkinson's Law*, Ch. 1

**3** The British, being brought up on team games, enter their House of Commons in the spirit of those who would rather be doing something else. If they cannot be playing golf or tennis, they can at least pretend that politics is a game with very similar rules.

*Parkinson's Law*, Ch. 2

**4** It is now known . . . that men enter local politics solely as a result of being unhappily married.

*Parkinson's Law*, Ch. 10

**Parr, Samuel** (1747–1825) British writer and scholar. A learned but querulous man, he published *Characters of Fox* in 1809.

**1** Now that the old lion is dead, every ass thinks he may kick at him.

Referring to Dr Johnson
*Life of Johnson* (J. Boswell)

**Pascal, Blaise** (1623–62) French philosopher and mathematician. At the age of 18 he invented the first calculating machine. His works include *Lettres provinciales* (1656), a defence of Jansenist doctrine, and *Pensées sur la religion* (1669).

**1** I have made this letter longer than usual, only because I have not had the time to make it shorter.

*Lettres provinciales*, XVI

**2** Not to care for philosophy is to be a true philosopher.

*Pensées*, I

**3** The more intelligence one has the more people one finds original. Commonplace people see no difference between men.

*Pensées*, I

**4** If you want people to think well of you, do not speak well of yourself.

*Pensées*, I

**5** I cannot forgive Descartes; in all his philosophy he did his best to dispense with God. But he could not avoid making Him set the world in motion with a flip of His thumb; after that he had no more use for God.

*Pensées*, II

**6** Had Cleopatra's nose been shorter, the whole face of the world would have changed.

*Pensées*, II

**7** The heart has its reasons which reason does not know.

*Pensées*, IV

**Pasternak, Boris** (1890–1960) Russian Jewish poet and novelist. His book *Dr Zhivago* was banned in Russia, but was an international success after its publication in Italy in 1957.

**1** And yet the order of the acts is planned,
The way's end destinate and unconcealed.
Alone. Now is the time of Pharisees.
*To live is not like walking through a field.*

*Hamlet* (trans. Henry Kamen)

**Pasteur, Louis** (1822–95) French scientist. He developed the process of pasteurization to kill microorganisms in milk and invented vaccination to induce immunity against viral diseases. He founded, and was first director of, the Pasteur Institute in Paris.

**1** There are no such things as applied sciences, only applications of science.

Address, 11 Sept 1872

**Pater, Walter (Horatio)** (1839–94) British critic. His books include *Studies in the History of the Renaissance* (1873) and *Marius the Epicurean* (1885), in which he supported 'art for art's sake'.

**1** She is older than the rocks among which she sits.

Referring to the *Mona Lisa*
*The Renaissance*, 'Leonardo da Vinci'

**2** All art constantly aspires towards the condition of music.

*The Renaissance*, 'The School of Giorgione'

**Paterson, Andrew Barton** (1864–1941) Australian journalist and poet. His books include a verse collection, *The Animals Noah Forgot* (1933), the personal recollections *Happy Despatches* (1934), and the racing story *The Shearer's Colt* (1936). He also wrote the words of Australia's national song *Waltzing Matilda*.

**1** Once a jolly swagman camped by a billy-bong,
Under the shade of a coolibah tree,
And he sang as he sat and waited for his billy-boil,
'You'll come a-waltzing, Matilda, with me.'

*Waltzing Matilda*

**Patmore, Coventry** (1823–96) British poet. An associate of the Pre-Raphaelite Brotherhood, he wrote a poetic treatment of marriage in four volumes, *The Angel in the House* (1854–62). After becoming a Catholic in 1864 he wrote primarily on religious themes.

**1** Love's perfect blossom only blows
Where noble manners veil defect.
Angels may be familiar; those
Who err each other must respect.

*The Angel in the House*, Bk. I, Prelude 2

**2** It was not like your great and gracious ways!
Do you, that have nought other to lament,
Never, my Love, repent
Of how, that July afternoon,
You went,
With sudden, unintelligible phrase, – And frightened eye,
Upon your journey of so many days,
Without a single kiss or a good-bye?

*The Unknown Eros*, Bk. I, 'Departure'

**Patton, George Smith, Jr.** (1885–1945) US general. In World War II he commanded the Third Army in France, in its spectacular defeat of the Germans.

**1** Dear Ike, Today I spat in the Seine.

Message sent to Eisenhower reporting his crossing of the Seine in World War II
*The American Treasury* (C. Fadiman)

**Paul, Leslie (Allen)** (1905– ) British writer. His books include *Annihilation of Man* (1944), *Son of Man* (1961), and *First Love* (1971).

**1** Angry Young Man.

Book title

**Pavese, Cesare** (1908–50) Italian novelist and poet. His books include *Il Compagno* (1947) and *La Luna e i Salò* (1950). His diaries were published after his suicide as *The Business of Living* (1952).

**1** One stops being a child when one realizes that telling one's trouble does not make it better.

*The Business of Living: Diaries 1935–50*

**Pavlova, Anna** (1881–1931) Russian ballet dancer. She joined Diaghilev's company in Paris in 1909 and later formed her own company.

**1** ... although one may fail to find happiness in theatrical life, one never wishes to give it up after having once tasted its fruits. To enter the School of the Imperial Ballet is to enter a convent whence frivolity is banned, and where merciless discipline reigns.

*Pavlova: A Biography* (ed. A. H. Franks), 'Pages of My Life'

**2** As is the case in all branches of art, success depends in a very large measure upon individual initiative and exertion, and cannot be achieved except by dint of hard work.

*Pavlova: A Biography* (ed. A. H. Franks), 'Pages of My Life'

**3** When a small child . . . I thought that success spelled happiness. I was wrong. Happiness is like a butterfly which appears and delights us for one brief moment, but soon flits away.

*Pavlova: A Biography* (ed. A. H. Franks), 'Pages of My Life'

**Payn, James** (1830–98) British writer and editor. He was editor of *Chambers's Journal* (1859–74) and the *Cornhill Magazine* (1883–96). His novels include *Carlyon's Year* (1868) and *Another's Burden* (1897).

**1** I had never had a piece of toast
Particularly long and wide,
But fell upon the sanded floor,
And always on the buttered side.

*See also* Thomas MOORE
*Chambers's Journal*, 2 Feb 1884

**Payne, John Howard** (1791–1852) US actor and dramatist. His play *Brutus, or the Fall of Tarquin* (1818) was a success in New York but failed in London and he was imprisoned for debt. His opera *Clari, or the Maid of Milan* (1823) contains 'Home, Sweet Home', the song for which he is remembered.

**1** Mid pleasures and palaces though we may roam,
Be it ever so humble, there's no place like home;

. . .

Home, home, sweet, sweet home!
There's no place like home! there's no place like home!

*Clari, or the Maid of Milan*

**Peabody, Elizabeth** (1804–94) US educationalist. She opened the first American kindergarten.

**1** I saw it, but I did not realize it.

Giving a Transcendentalist explanation for her accidentally walking into a tree
*The Peabody Sisters of Salem* (L. Tharp)

**Peacock, Thomas Love** (1785–1866) British novelist. His satirical novels include *Nightmare Abbey* (1818) and *Gryll Grange* (1860).

**1** Respectable means rich, and decent means poor. I should die if I heard my family called decent.

*Crotchet Castle*, Ch. 3

**2** Ancient sculpture is the true school of modesty. But where the Greeks had modesty, we have cant; where they had poetry, we have cant; where they had patriotism, we have cant; where they had anything that exalts, delights, or adorns humanity, we have nothing but cant, cant, cant.

*Crotchet Castle*, Ch. 7

**3** A book that furnishes no quotations is, *me judice*, no book – it is a plaything.

*Crotchet Castle*, Ch. 9

**4** Nothing can be more obvious than that all animals were created solely and exclusively for the use of man.

*Headlong Hall*, Ch. 2

**5** Marriage may often be a stormy lake, but celibacy is almost always a muddy horse-pond.

*Melincourt*

**6** There are two reasons for drinking; one is, when you are thirsty, to cure it; the other, when you are not thirsty, to prevent it . . . Prevention is better than cure.

*Melincourt*

**7** The mountain sheep are sweeter,
But the valley sheep are fatter;
We therefore deemed it meeter
To carry off the latter.

*The Misfortunes of Elphin*, Ch. 11, 'The War-Song of Dinas Vawr'

**8** He was sent, as usual, to a public school, where a little learning was painfully beaten into him, and from thence to the university, where it was carefully taken out of him.

*Nightmare Abbey*, Ch. 1

**9** Laughter is pleasant, but the exertion is too much for me.

Said by the Hon. Mr Listless
*Nightmare Abbey*, Ch. 5

**10** Sir, I have quarrelled with my wife; and a man who has quarrelled with his wife is absolved from all duty to his country.

*Nightmare Abbey*, Ch. 11

**Peary, Robert Edwin** (1856–1920) US explorer, who was the first man to reach the North Pole (1909).

**1** The Eskimo had his own explanation. Said he: 'The devil is asleep or having trouble with his wife, or we should never have come back so easily.'

*The North Pole*

**2** Nothing easier. One step beyond the pole, you see, and the north wind becomes a south one.

Explaining how he knew he had reached the North Pole
Attrib.

**Peck, Gregory** (1916– ) US film star. His films include *The Keys of the Kingdom* (1944), *Twelve O'Clock High* (1949), *Mirage* (1965), and *Shootout* (1971).

**1** If you have to tell them who you are, you aren't anybody.

Remarking upon the failure of anyone in a crowded restaurant to recognize him
*Pieces of Eight* (S. Harris)

**Peel, Arthur Wellesley, Viscount** (1829–1912) British politician and son of Sir Robert Peel, who created the Irish constabulary. Arthur Peel became Speaker of the House of Commons (1884–95).

**1** My father didn't create you to arrest me.

Protesting against his arrest by the police, recently established by his father
Attrib.

**Pegler, (James) Westbrook** (1894–1969) US journalist who was a war correspondent and later a sports commentator.

**1** He will go from resort to resort getting more tanned and móre tired.

On the abdication of Edward VIII
*Six Men* (Alistair Cooke), Pt. II

**Péguy, Charles Pierre** (1873–1914) French writer. He wrote several biographies of such notable Frenchmen as Victor Hugo and Henri Bergson. He was killed in World War I.

**1** It is impossible to write ancient history because we do not have enough sources, and impossible to write modern history because we have far too many.

*Clio* ·

**Peirce, C. S.** (1839–1914) US physicist and logician. He founded pragmatism and wrote many papers on mathematics and logic.

**1** The universe ought to be presumed too vast to have any character.

*Collected Papers*, VI

**Pembroke, Henry Herbert, 10th Earl of** (1734–94) British general.

**1** Dr Johnson's sayings would not appear so extraordinary, were it not for his *bow-wow way*.

*Life of Johnson* (J. Boswell)

**Penn, William** (1644–1718) English preacher and campaigner. He joined the Society of Friends in 1664 and was imprisoned in the Tower for his political writings in 1668. Here he wrote *No Cross, No Crown* (1669) outlining Quaker practices. In 1682 he went to America to set up Quaker settlements, and founded and drew up the constitution for Pennsylvania.

**1** No pain, no palm; no thorns, no throne; no gall, no glory; no cross, no crown.

*No Cross, No Crown*

**2** Men are generally more careful of the breed of their horses and dogs than of their children.

*Some Fruits of Solitude, in Reflections and Maxims relating to the conduct of Humane Life*, Pt. I, No 52

**Pepys, Samuel** (1633–1703) English diarist. His *Diary* (1660–1669) includes detailed descriptions of the Plague and the Fire of London.

**1** And so to bed.

*Diary*, 6 May 1660 and *passim*

**2** I went out to Charing Cross, to see Major-general Harrison hanged, drawn, and quartered; which was done there, he looking as cheerful as any man could do in that condition.

*Diary*, 13 Oct 1660

**3** But Lord! to see the absurd nature of Englishmen, that cannot forbear laughing and jeering at everything that looks strange.

*Diary*, 27 Nov 1662

**4** My wife, who, poor wretch, is troubled with her lonely life.

*Diary*, 19 Dec 1662

**5** Went to hear Mrs Turner's daughter . . . play on the harpsichon; but, Lord! it was enough to make any man sick to hear her; yet was I forced to commend her highly.

*Diary*, 1 May 1663

**6** Most of their discourse was about hunting, in a dialect I understand very little.

*Diary*, 22 Nov 1663

**7** Pretty witty Nell.

Referring to Nell Gwynne
*Diary*, 3 Apr 1665

**8** Strange to say what delight we married people have to see these poor fools decoyed into our condition.

*Diary*, 25 Dec 1665

**9** Music and women I cannot but give way to, whatever my business is.

*Diary*, 9 Mar 1666

**10** To church; and with my mourning, very handsome, and new periwig, make a great show.

*Diary*, 31 Mar 1667

**11** My wife hath something in her gizzard, that only waits an opportunity of being provoked to bring up.

*Diary*, 17 June 1668

**12** And so I betake myself to that course, which is almost as much as to see myself go into my grave – for which, and all the discomforts that will accompany my being blind, the good God prepare me!

The closing words of Pepys's *Diary*; he lived another 34 years and did not go blind
*Diary*, 31 May 1669

**Perelman, S(idney) J(oseph)** (1904–79) US humorous writer, who began contributing to the *New Yorker* in the 1930s. He published numerous collections, including *Crazy Like a Fox* (1944) and *Baby, It's Cold Inside* (1970).

**1** For years I have let dentists ride roughshod over my teeth: I have been sawed, hacked, chopped, whittled, bewitched, bewildered, tattooed, and signed on again; but this is cuspid's last stand.

*Crazy Like a Fox*, 'Nothing but the Tooth'

**2** I'll dispose of my teeth as I see fit, and after they've gone, I'll get along. I started off living on gruel, and by God, I can always go back to it again.

*Crazy Like a Fox*, 'Nothing but the Tooth'

**3** I tried to resist his overtures, but he plied me with symphonies, quartettes, chamber music and cantatas.

*Crazy Like a Fox*, 'The Love Decoy'

**4** He bit his lip in a manner which immediately awakened my maternal sympathy, and I helped him bite it.

*Crazy Like a Fox*, 'The Love Decoy'

**5** A case of the tail dogging the wag.

Having escaped with some difficulty from the persistent attentions of some prostitutes in the street
*Another Almanac of Words at Play* (W. Epsy)

**6** Love is not the dying moan of a distant violin –
it's the triumphant twang of a bedspring.

*Quotations for Speakers and Writers* (A. Andrews)

**Pericles** (c. 495–429 BC) Greek statesman, who dominated
Athens during its golden age by means of his oratory and honesty.
He built the Parthenon and encouraged Sophocles, Anaxagoras, and
Phidias in their various arts. He lost office due to his unsuccessful
strategy in the Peloponnesian War.

**1** Our love of what is beautiful does not lead to extravagance; our love of the things of the mind
does not make us soft.

Part of the funeral oration, 430 BC, for the dead of the first year
of the Peloponnesian War
Attrib. in *Histories* Bk. II, Ch. 40 (Thucydides)

**Perkins, Frances** (1882–1965) US social worker and
politician. She became secretary of labor (1933–45).

**1** Call me madame.

Deciding the term of address she would prefer when made the
first woman to hold a cabinet office in the USA
*Familiar Quotations* (J. Bartlett)

**Perlman, Itzhak** (1945– ) Israeli violinist. He lost the use
of his legs through polio at the age of four and plays from a
wheelchair.

**1** You see, our fingers are circumcised, which
gives it a very good dexterity, you know, particularly in the pinky.

Responding to an observation that many great violinists are
Jewish
*Close Encounters* (M. Wallace)

**Perón, Juan Domingo** (1895–1974) Argentine statesman.
He rose to power by a military coup in 1943 and was elected
president in 1946. His wife Eva (known as 'Evita'; 1919–52) was
idolized by the poor and Perón lost popularity after her death.
However, he returned to power in 1973, died in office, and was
succeeded by his third wife Isabel (1930– ).

**1** If I had not been born Perón, I would have liked
to be Perón.

*The Observer*, 'Sayings of the Week', 21 Feb 1960

**Perronet, Edward** (1726–92) British hymn writer.

**1** All hail, the power of Jesus' name!
Let angels prostrate fall.

Hymn

**Perry, Oliver Hazard** (1785–1819) US naval officer. In the
War of 1812 he contested British control of Lake Erie.

**1** We have met the enemy, and they are ours.

Message sent reporting his victory in a naval battle on Lake Erie
*Familiar Quotations* (J. Bartlett)

**Perugino, Pietro** (1446–1523) Italian painter. He painted
the fresco *Delivery of the Keys to St Peter* in the Sistine Chapel and
*Entombment* in the Pitti Palace.

**1** I am curious to see what happens in the next
world to one who dies unshriven.

Giving his reasons for refusing to see a priest as he lay dying
Attrib.

**Pétain, Henri Philippe** (1856–1951) French marshal. He
became prime minister in 1940, signed an armistice with Germany,
and moved his government to Vichy. After the war he was
accused of collaboration with the Germans and died in prison.

**1** To make a union with Great Britain would be fu-
sion with a corpse.

On hearing Churchill's suggestion for an Anglo-French union,
1940
*Their Finest Hour* (Winston S. Churchill), Ch. 10

**2** *Ils ne passeront pas.*
They shall not pass.

Attrib; probably derived from General R.-G. Nivelle's Order of
the Day, 'Vous ne les laisserez pas passer' (June 1916)

**Peter, Laurence J.** (1919– ) Canadian writer. He is best
known for his book *The Peter Principle*.

**1** *Papyromania* – compulsive accumulation of papers . . .
*Papyrophobia* – abnormal desire for 'a clean
desk'.

*The Peter Principle*, Glossary

**2** Work is accomplished by those employees who
have not yet reached their level of
incompetence.

*The Peter Principle*

**3** A pessimist is a man who looks both ways
before crossing a one-way street.

*Peter's Quotations*

**Peterborough, Charles Mordaunt, 3rd Earl of**
(1658–1735) English military and naval commander. On the
accession of William III he became first lord of the treasury
(1689). Under George I he was appointed chief of the navy.

**1** In the first place, I have only five guineas in my
pocket; and in the second, they are very much
at your service.

Persuading an angry mob that he was not the Duke of Marlborough, notorious for his meanness
*Dictionary of National Biography*

**Petronius Arbiter** (1st century AD) Roman satirist. A
companion of Nero, he wrote the *Satyricon*, a licentious and
satirical romance.

**1** A huge dog, tied by a chain, was painted on the
wall and over it was written in capital letters
'Beware of the dog.'

Latin, *Cave canem*
*Satyricon: Cena Trimalchionis*, 29

**2** He's gone to join the majority.

Referring to a dead man
*Satyricon: Cena Trimalchionis*, 42

**Pevsner, Sir Nikolaus** (Bernhard Leon; 1902–83)
German-born British art historian. His best-known works are *An
Outline of European Architecture* (1942) and *The Buildings of
England* (1951–74).

1 No part of the walls is left undecorated. From
everywhere the praise of the Lord is drummed
into you.
*London, except the Cities of London and Westminster*

**Phelps, Edward John** (1822–1900) US lawyer and
diplomat. He was US minister to Great Britain (1855–89).

1 The man who makes no mistakes does not usually make anything.
Speech, Mansion House, London, 24 Jan 1899

**Philip, John Woodward** (1840–1900) US naval officer.
He commanded the *Texas* in the battle off Santiago in 1898.

1 Don't cheer, boys; the poor devils are dying.
Restraining his victorious crew during the naval battle off Santia-
go in the Spanish-American War.
Attrib.

**Philip, Prince, Duke of Edinburgh** (1921– ) The
consort of Queen Elizabeth II. The son of Prince Andrew of
Greece, he assumed his uncle's name, Mountbatten, when he
became a British citizen.

1 I include 'pidgin-English'. . . even though I am
referred to in that splendid language as 'Fella belong Mrs Queen'.
Speech, English-Speaking Union Conference, Ottawa, 29 Oct
1958

2 The biggest waste of water in the country by
far. You spend half a pint and flush two gallons.
Speech, 1965

3 I'm self-employed.
Answering a query as to what nature of work he did
Attrib.

4 I declare this thing open – whatever it is.
Opening a new annex at Vancouver City Hall
Attrib.

5 A man can be forgiven a lot if he can quote
Shakespeare in an economic crisis.
Attrib.

**Philippe, Charles-Louis** (1874–1909) French novelist.
His books include *Bubu de Montparnasse* (1901).

1 One always has the air of someone who is lying
when one speaks to a policeman.
*Les Chroniques du canard sauvage*

**Phillips, Wendell** (1811–84) US reformer. He advocated
the abolition of slavery, prohibition, and women's suffrage.

1 We live under a government of men and morning
newspapers.
*Address: The Press*

2 One on God's side is a majority.
Speech, Brooklyn, 1 Nov 1859

3 Every man meets his Waterloo at last.
Speech, Brooklyn, 1 Nov 1859

**Phillpotts, Eden** (1862–1960) British novelist and dramatist.
His novels include *Lying Prophets* (1896) and *Widecombe Fair*
(1913). *The Farmer's Wife* (1917) was his first play.

1 His father's sister had bats in the belfry and was
put away.
*Peacock House,* 'My First Murder'

**Picasso, Pablo** (1881–1973) Spanish painter, sculptor, and
stage designer. An exceptionally versatile artist, his work was
influenced by cubism, surrealism, African sculpture, and classicism.

1 There's no such thing as a bad Picasso, but
some are less good than others.
*Come to Judgment* (A. Whitman)

2 Painting is a blind man's profession. He paints
not what he sees, but what he feels, what he
tells himself about what he has seen.
*Journals* (Jean Cocteau), 'Childhood'

3 God is really only another artist. He invented the
giraffe, the elephant, and the cat. He has no
real style, He just goes on trying other things.
*Life with Picasso* (Françoise Gilot and Carlton Lake), Ch. 1

4 I hate that aesthetic game of the eye and the
mind, played by these connoisseurs, these mandarins who 'appreciate' beauty. What *is* beauty,
anyway? There's no such thing. I never 'appreciate', any more than I 'like'. I love or I hate.
*Life with Picasso* (Françoise Gilot and Carlton Lake), Ch. 2

5 Age only matters when one is ageing. Now that
I have arrived at a great age, I might just as
well be twenty.
*The Observer, Shouts and Murmurs,* 'Picasso in Private' (John
Richardson)

6 When I was their age, I could draw like Raphael,
but it took me a lifetime to learn to draw like
them.
Visiting an exhibition of drawings by children
*Picasso: His Life and Work* (Ronald Penrose)

7 It's better like that, if you want to kill a picture
all you have to do is to hang it beautifully on a
nail and soon you will see nothing of it but the
frame. When it's out of place you see it better.
Explaining why a Renoir in his apartment was hung crooked
*Picasso: His Life and Work* (Ronald Penrose)

**Pickles, Wilfred** (1904–78) British radio personality and
character actor. He presented the series *Have a Go* with his wife
Mabel in the 1940s and 1950s.

1 Give him the money, Barney.
Said to Barney Colehan
*Have a Go* (BBC radio programme), *passim*

**Pinero, Sir Arthur** (1855–1934) British dramatist. His early
farces included *The Magistrate* (1885) and *Dandy Dick* (1887). *The
Second Mrs Tanqueray* (1893) dealt with serious social problems.

1 From forty to fifty a man is at heart either a stoic or a satyr.
*The Second Mrs Tanqueray,* I

**Pinter, Harold** (1930– ) British dramatist. His well-known
plays include *The Birthday Party* (1958), *The Caretaker* (1960), and
*Family Voices* (1981). He has also written film scripts and directed
plays.

1 If only I could get down to Sidcup! I've been waiting for the weather to break. He's got my papers, this man I left them with, it's got it all down there, I could prove everything.
*The Caretaker*, I

2 In other words, apart from the known and the unknown, what else is there?
*The Homecoming*, II

**Piron, Alexis** (1689–1773) French poet and dramatist. He is also known for his epigrams.

1 I think you would have been very glad if I had written it.
Discussing Voltaire's *Sémiramis* with him after its poor reception on the first night
*Cyclopaedia of Anecdotes* (K. Arvine)

**Pirsig, Robert T.** (1928–  ) US writer, best-known for his book *Zen and the Art of Motorcycle Maintenance* (1974).

1 You are never dedicated to something you have complete confidence in. No one is fanatically shouting that the sun is going to rise tomorrow. They *know* it's going to rise tomorrow. When people are fanatically dedicated to political or religious faiths or any other kind of dogmas or goals, it's always because these dogmas or goals are in doubt.
*Zen and the Art of Motorcycle Maintenance*, Pt. II, Ch. 13

2 One geometry cannot be more true than another; it can only be more convenient. Geometry is not true, it is advantageous.
*Zen and the Art of Motorcycle Maintenance*, Pt. III, Ch. 22

3 Traditional scientific method has always been at the very *best*, 20-20 hindsight. It's good for seeing where you've been.
*Zen and the Art of Motorcycle Maintenance*, Pt. III, Ch. 24

4 We keep passing unseen through little moments of other people's lives.
*Zen and the Art of Motorcycle Maintenance*, Pt. III, Ch. 24

5 That's the classical mind at work, runs fine inside but looks dingy on the surface.
*Zen and the Art of Motorcycle Maintenance*, Pt. III, Ch. 25

**Pitter, Ruth** (1897–  ) British poet. Her published works include *A Trophy of Arms* (1936), *The Ermine* (1953), and *End of Drought* (1975).

1 The seldom female in a world of males!
*The Kitten's Eclogue*, IV

**Pitts, William Ewart** (1900–  ) Chief Constable, Derbyshire County Police (1953–67).

1 It is the overtakers who keep the undertakers busy.
*The Observer*, 'Sayings of the Week', 22 Dec 1963

**Pitt the Elder, William, 1st Earl of Chatham**
(1708–78) British statesman. An outstanding orator, he entered parliament in 1735, becoming paymaster general (1746–55) and secretary of state in 1756. He was in charge of foreign affairs during the Seven Years' War. Pitt resigned in 1761, returning to form a new ministry (1766–68) as Earl of Chatham.

1 The poorest man may in his cottage bid defiance to all the forces of the Crown. It may be frail – its roof may shake – the wind may blow through it – the storm may enter – the rain may enter – but the King of England cannot enter! – all his force dares not cross the threshold of the ruined tenement!
*Statesmen in the Time of George III* (Lord Brougham), Vol. I

2 The atrocious crime of being a young man . . . I shall neither attempt to palliate nor deny.
Speech, House of Commons, 27 Jan 1741

3 Unlimited power is apt to corrupt the minds of those who possess it.
*See also* Lord ACTON
Speech, House of Lords, 9 Jan 1770

4 Where laws end, tyranny begins.
Speech, House of Lords, referring to the Wilkes case, 9 Jan 1770

5 There is something behind the throne greater than the King himself.
Speech, House of Lords, 2 Mar 1770

6 If I were an American, as I am an Englishman, while a foreign troop was landed in my country, I never would lay down my arms, – never – never – never!
Speech, House of Lords, 18 Nov 1777

**Pitt the Younger, William** (1759–1806) British statesman, Britain's youngest prime minister at the age of 24 (1783–1801). He resigned following George III's refusal to accept Catholic emancipation, but returned to office (1804–06) for a second administration.

1 Necessity is the plea for every infringement of human freedom. It is the argument of tyrants; it is the creed of slaves.
Speech, House of Commons, 18 Nov 1783

2 Roll up that map: it will not be wanted these ten years.
On learning that Napoleon had won the Battle of Austerlitz
Attrib.

3 I think I could eat one of Bellamy's veal pies.
Last words
Attrib.

4 Oh, my country! How I leave my country!
Last words
Attrib.

**Plato** (429–347 BC) Greek philosopher. A disciple of Socrates and teacher of Aristotle, he founded the first university (the Academy) in Athens. His works include the *Phaedo* (on immortality), *Symposium* (on love), and *Republic* (on government).

1 The good is the beautiful.
*Lysis*

2 Our object in the construction of the state is the greatest happiness of the whole, and not that of any one class.
*Republic*, Bk. 4

**3** I wonder if we could contrive . . . some magnificent myth that would in itself carry conviction to our whole community.
*Republic*, Bk. 5

**4** There will be no end to the troubles of states, or indeed, my dear Glaucon, of humanity itself, till philosophers become kings in this world, or till those we now call kings and rulers really and truly become philosophers.
*Republic*, Bk. 5

**5** Democracy passes into despotism.
*Republic*, Bk. 8

**6** Let no one ignorant of mathematics enter here.
Inscription written over the entrance to the Academy
*Biographical Encyclopedia* (I. Asimov)

**Plautus, Titus Macclus** (254–184 BC) Roman dramatist. His 21 surviving plays were adapted from Greek New Comedy writers and have influenced both Shakespeare and Moliere.

**1** He whom the gods favour dies young.
*Bacchides* IV

**Pliny the Elder** (Gaius Plinius Secundus; 23–79 AD) Roman scholar. His *Natural History* was a major source of knowledge until the 17th century. He died while closely observing an eruption of Vesuvius.

**1** Attic wit.
*Natural History*, II

**2** It is far from easy to determine whether she has proved a kind parent to man or a merciless step-mother.
Referring to Nature
*Natural History*, VII

**3** There is always something new out of Africa.
*Natural History*, VIII

**4** *In vino veritas.*
Truth comes out in wine.
*Natural History*, XIV

**Plomer, William** (1903–73) South African poet and novelist. His published works include *Taste and Remember* (1966) and *Celebrations* (1972). He also wrote several libretti for operas by Benjamin Britten.

**1** A pleasant old buffer, nephew to a lord,
Who believed that the bank was mightier than the sword,
And that an umbrella might pacify barbarians abroad:
Just like an old liberal
Between the wars.
*Father and Son: 1939*

**2** With first-rate sherry flowing into second-rate whores,
And third-rate conversation without one single pause:
Just like a couple
Between the wars.
*Father and Son: 1939*

**3** On a sofa upholstered in panther skin
Mona did researches in original sin.
*Mews Flat Mona*

**Plotinus** (205–270 AD) Egpytian-born Greek philosopher. He developed Plato's mysticism and founded neoplatonism.

**1** It is bad enough to be condemned to drag around this image in which nature has imprisoned me. Why should I consent to the perpetuation of the image of this image?
Refusing to have his portrait painted
Attrib.

**Poe, Edgar Allan** (1809–49) US poet and writer. His many prose tales and horror stories include *The Fall of the House of Usher* (1839) and the first detective story, *The Murders in the Rue Morgue* (1841).

**1** Once upon a midnight dreary, while I pondered, weak and weary,
Over many a quaint and curious volume of forgotten lore,
While I nodded, nearly napping, suddenly there came a tapping,
As of some one gently rapping, rapping at my chamber door.
*The Raven*

**2** Take thy beak from out my heart, and take thy form from off my door!
Quoth the Raven, 'Nevermore.'
*The Raven*

**Pompadour, Madame de** (1721–64) The mistress of Louis XV of France. She exerted great influence in political affairs and was blamed for the Seven Years' War.

**1** *Après nous le déluge.*
After us the deluge.
After the Battle of Rossbach, 1757

**Pompidou, Georges (Jean Raymond)** (1911–74) French statesman. He was four times prime minister, and followed de Gaulle as president (1969–74).

**1** A statesman is a politician who places himself at the service of the nation. A politician is a statesman who places the nation at his service.
*The Observer*, 'Sayings of the Year', 30 Dec 1973

**Pope, Alexander** (1688–1744) British poet. His witty and satirical poems include the mock-heroic *The Rape of the Lock* (1712), the mock epic *The Dunciad* (1728), and the philosophical *An Essay on Man* (1733).

**1** Ye gods! annihilate but space and time.
And make two lovers happy.
*The Art of Sinking in Poetry*, 11

**2** The right divine of kings to govern wrong.
*The Dunciad*, IV

**3** When man's whole frame is obvious to a flea
*The Dunciad*, IV

**4** I mount! I fly!
O grave! where is thy victory?
O death! where is thy sting?
*The Dying Christian to his Soul*

5 A heap of dust alone remains of thee;
'Tis all thou art, and all the proud shall be!
*Elegy to the Memory of an Unfortunate Lady*

6 Line after line my gushing eyes o'erflow,
led through a sad variety of woe.
*Eloisa to Abelard*

7 You beat your pate, and fancy wit will come;
Knock as you please, there's nobody at home.
*Epigram*

8 Do good by stealth, and blush to find it fame.
*Epilogue to the Satires*, Dialogue I

9 Ask you what provocation I have had?
The strong antipathy of good to bad.
*Epilogue to the Satires*, Dialogue II

10 Yes; I am proud, I must be proud to see
Men not afraid of God, afraid of me.
*Epilogue to the Satires*, Dialogue II

11 The Muse but serv'd to ease some friend, not
Wife,
To help me through this long disease, my life.
*Epistle to Dr. Arbuthnot*

12 Damn with faint praise, assent with civil leer,
And, without sneering, teach the rest to sneer.
*Epistle to Dr. Arbuthnot*

13 Curst be the verse, how well so'er it flow,
That tends to make one worthy man my foe.
*Epistle to Dr. Arbuthnot*

14 Wit that can creep, and pride that licks the dust.
*Epistle to Dr. Arbuthnot*

15 No creature smarts so little as a fool.
*Epistle to Dr. Arbuthnot*

16 In wit a man; simplicity a child.
*Epitaph on Mr. Gay*

17 Nature, and Nature's laws lay hid in night:
God said, *Let Newton be!* and all was light.
For a reply, *see* SQUIRE
*Epitaphs*, 'Intended for Sir Isaac Newton'

18 'Tis hard to say, if greater want of skill
Appear in writing or in judging ill.
*An Essay on Criticism*

19 'Tis with our judgments as our watches, none
Go just alike, yet each believes his own.
*An Essay on Criticism*

20 Of all the causes which conspire to blind
Man's erring judgment, and misguide the mind,
What the weak head with strongest bias rules,
Is Pride, the never-failing vice of fools.
*An Essay on Criticism*

21 A little learning is a dangerous thing;
Drink deep, or taste not the Pierian spring:
There shallow draughts intoxicate the brain,
And drinking largely sobers us again.
*An Essay on Criticism*

22 Whoever thinks a faultless piece to see,
Thinks what ne'er was, nor is, nor e'er shall be.
*An Essay on Criticism*

23 True wit is nature to advantage dress'd;
What oft was thought, but ne'er so well
express'd.
*An Essay on Criticism*

24 True ease in writing comes from art, not chance,
As those move easiest who have learn'd to
dance.
'Tis not enough no harshness gives offence,
The sound must seem an echo to the sense.
*An Essay on Criticism*

25 Fondly we think we honour merit then,
When we but praise ourselves in other men.
*An Essay on Criticism*

26 To err is human, to forgive, divine.
*An Essay on Criticism*

27 For fools rush in where angels fear to tread.
*An Essay on Criticism*

28 Words are like leaves; and where they most
abound,
Much fruit of sense beneath is rarely found.
*An Essay on Criticism*

29 Nor in the critic let the man be lost.
*An Essay on Criticism*

30 Hope springs eternal in the human breast;
Man never is, but always to be blest.
*An Essay on Man*, I

31 Created half to rise, and half to fall;
Great lord of all things, yet a prey to all;
Sole judge of truth, in endless error hurl'd;
The glory, jest, and riddle of the world!
*An Essay on Man*, II

32 Know then thyself, presume not God to scan,
The proper study of Mankind is Man.
*An Essay on Man*, II

33 And hence one master-passion in the breast,
Like Aaron's serpent,
swallows up the rest.
*An Essay on Man*, II

34 That true self-love and social are the same;
That virtue only makes our bliss below;
And all our knowledge is, ourselves to know.
*An Essay on Man*, IV

35 Order is heaven's first law.
*An Essay on Man*, IV

36 Not to admire, is all the art I know
To make men happy, and to keep them so.
*Imitations of Horace*, 'To Mr. Murray'

37 To observations which ourselves we make.
We grow more partial for th' observer's sake.
*Moral Essays*, I

38 'Tis education forms the common mind,
Just as the twig is bent, the tree's inclined.
*Moral Essays*, I

39 Most women have no characters at all.
*Moral Essays*, II

40 Men, some to business, some to pleasure take;
But every woman is at heart a rake.
*Moral Essays*, II

41 Woman's at best a contradiction still.
*Moral Essays*, II

42 See how the world its veterans rewards!
A youth of frolics, an old age of cards.
*Moral Essays*, II

43 The ruling passion, be it what it will
The ruling passion conquers reason still.
*Moral Essays*, III

44 Who shall decide when doctors disagree?
*Moral Essays*, III

45 Where'er you walk, cool gales shall fan the
glade,
Trees, where you sit, shall crowd into a shade:
Where'er you tread, the blushing flow'rs shall
rise,
And all things flourish where you turn your eyes.
*Pastorals, 'Summer'*

46 What dire offence from am'rous causes springs,
What mighty contests rise from trivial things.
*The Rape of the Lock*, I

47 Here thou great Anna! whom three realms obey,
Dost sometimes counsel take – and sometimes
Tea.
*The Rape of the Lock*, III

48 Not louder shrieks to pitying heav'n are cast,
When husbands, or when lap-dogs breathe their
last.
*The Rape of the Lock*, III

49 The hungry judges soon the sentence sign,
And wretches hang that jury-men may dine.
*The Rape of the Lock*, III

50 Coffee which makes the politician wise,
And see through all things with his half-shut
eyes.
*The Rape of the Lock*, III

51 The vulgar boil, the learned roast an egg.
*Satires and Epistles of Horace Imitated*, Bk II

52 A man should never be ashamed to own he has
been in the wrong, which is but saying, in other
words, that he is wiser to-day than he was
yesterday.
*Thoughts on Various Subjects*

53 It is with narrow-souled people as with narrow-
necked bottles: the less they have in them, the
more noise they make in pouring it out.
*Thoughts on Various Subjects*

54 When men grow virtuous in their old age, they
only make a sacrifice to God of the devil's
leavings.
*Thoughts on Various Subjects*

55 I never knew any man in my life who could not
bear another's misfortunes perfectly like a
Christian.
*Thoughts on Various Subjects*

56 The vanity of human life is like a river, constantly passing away, and yet constantly coming on.
*Thoughts on Various Subjects*

57 Here am I, dying of a hundred good symptoms.
*Anecdotes by and about Alexander Pope* (Joseph Spence)

58 'Blessed is the man who expects nothing, for he
shall never be disappointed' was the ninth
beatitude.
*Letter to Fortescue*, 23 Sept 1725

59 How often are we to die before we go quite off
this stage? In every friend we lose a part of
ourselves, and the best part.
*Letter to Jonathan Swift*, 5 Dec 1732

60 I am His Highness' dog at Kew;
Pray tell me sir, whose dog are you?
*On the collar of a dog given to Frederick, Prince of Wales*

**Popper, Sir Karl** (1902– ) Austrian-born British
philosopher. Interested in science and politics, he has written *The
Logic of Scientific Discovery* (1935), *The Open Society and its
Enemies* (1945), and *The Poverty of Historicism* (1957).

1 Our knowledge can only be finite, while our ignorance must necessarily be infinite.
*Conjectures and Refutations*

2 Our civilization . . . has not yet fully recovered
from the shock of its birth – the transition from
the tribal or 'closed society', with its submission to magical forces, to the 'open society'
which sets free the critical powers of man.
*The Open Society and Its Enemies*

3 There is no history of mankind, there are only
many histories of all kinds of aspects of human
life. And one of these is the history of political
power. This is elevated into the history of the
world.
*The Open Society and Its Enemies*

4 We must plan for freedom, and not only for security, if for no other reason than that only
freedom can make security secure.
*The Open Society and Its Enemies*

5 Science must begin with myths, and with the
criticism of myths.
*British Philosophy in the Mid-Century* (ed. C. A. Mace)

6 We may become the makers of our fate when
we have ceased to pose as its prophets.
*The Observer*, 28 Dec 1975

**Porson, Richard** (1759–1808) British classicist. He edited
many classical plays and became known for his *Letters to
Archdeacon Travis* (1788–89).

**1** Life is too short to learn German.
*Gryll Grange* (T. L. Peacock), Ch. 3

**2** Your works will be read after Shakespeare and Milton are forgotten – and not till then.
Giving his opinion of the poems of Robert Southey
*Quotable Anecdotes* (L. Meissen)

**Porter, Cole** (1893–1964) American songwriter and composer, noted for his witty lyrics. He wrote scores for such musicals as *Kiss Me Kate* (1953), *High Society* (1956), and *Can-Can* (1959).

**1** Now: heaven knows, anything goes.
*Anything Goes*, title song

**2** I've Got You Under My Skin.
*Born to Dance*, song title

**3** I love Paris in the springtime.
*Can-Can*, 'I Love Paris'

**4** Night and day, you are the one,
Only you beneath the moon and under the sun.
*The Gay Divorcee*, 'Night and Day'

**5** Miss Otis regrets she's unable to lunch today.
*Hi Diddle Diddle*, Miss Otis Regrets

**6** HE. Have you heard it's in the stars
Next July we collide with Mars?
SHE. Well, did you evah! What a swell party this is.
*High Society* 'Well, Did You Evah!'

**7** And we suddenly know, what heaven we're in,
When they begin the beguine.
*Jubilee*, 'Begin the Beguine'

**8** But I'm always true to you, darlin', in my fashion,
Yes, I'm always true to you, darlin', in my way.
*Kiss Me, Kate*, 'Always True to You in My Fashion'

**9** Let's Do It; Let's Fall in Love.
*Paris*, song title

**10** Who Wants to Be a Millionaire? I don't.
*Who Wants to be a Millionaire?*, title song

**Porter, Sir George** (1920– ) British chemist who developed the technique of flash photolysis. He won the Nobel prize for chemistry in 1967.

**1** Should we force science down the throats of those that have no taste for it? Is it our duty to drag them kicking and screaming into the twenty-first century? I am afraid that it is.
Speech, Sept 1986

**Portland, William John Arthur Charles James Cavendish-Bentinck, 6th Duke of** (1857–1943) British peer.

**1** What! Can't a fellow even enjoy a biscuit any more?
On being informed that as one of several measures to reduce his own expenses he would have to dispense with one of his two Italian pastry cooks
*Their Noble Lordships* (S. Winchester)

**Post, Emily** (1873–1960) US writer and columnist. She is remembered for her book *Etiquette* (1922).

**1** Ideal conversation must be an exchange of thought, and not, as many of those who worry most about their shortcomings believe, an eloquent exhibition of wit or oratory.
*Etiquette*, Ch. 6

**2** To the old saying that man built the house but woman made of it a "home" might be added the modern supplement that woman accepted cooking as a chore but man has made of it a recreation.
*Etiquette*, Ch. 34

**Potter, Beatrix** (1866–1943) British children's writer and illustrator. *The Tale of Peter Rabbit* (1900) was the first of many books.

**1** I shall tell you a tale of four little rabbits whose names were Flopsy, Mopsy, Cottontail and Peter.
*The Tale of Peter Rabbit*

**2** Don't go into Mr McGregor's garden: your Father had an accident there; he was put in a pie by Mrs McGregor.
*The Tale of Peter Rabbit*

**Potter, Stephen** (1900–70) British writer and critic. He is best known for his humorous studies on how to outwit an opponent, including *Gamesmanship* (1947), *Lifemanship* (1950), and *One-Upmanship* (1952).

**1** Gamesmanship or The Art of Winning Games Without Actually Cheating.
Book title

**2** *How to be one up* – how to make the other man feel that something has gone wrong, however slightly.
*Lifemanship*, Introduction

**3** It is an important general rule always to refer to your friend's country establishment as a 'cottage'.
*Lifemanship*, Ch. 2

**4** There is no doubt that basic weekendmanship should contain some reference to Important Person Play.
*Lifemanship*, Ch. 2

**5** Donsmanship . . . 'the art of criticizing without actually listening'.
*Lifemanship*, Ch. 6

**6** It is WRONG to do what everyone else does – namely, to hold the wine list just out of sight, look for the second cheapest claret on the list, and say, 'Number 22, please'.
*One-Upmanship*, Ch. 14

**7** A good general rule is to state that the bouquet is better than the taste, and vice versa.
*One-Upmanship*, Ch. 14

**Pound, Ezra** (1885–1972) US poet and critic. His poetry includes *Hugh Selwyn Mauberly* (1920) and *The Pisan Cantos* (1925–69). His support for Mussolini led to his confinement in a US mental hospital (1946–58).

1 Music begins to atrophy when it departs too far from the dance; . . . poetry begins to atrophy when it gets too far from music.
*ABC of Reading*, 'Warning'

2 One of the pleasures of middle age is to *find out* that one WAS right, and that one was much righter than one knew at say 17 or 23.
*ABC of Reading*, Ch. 1

3 Literature is news that STAYS news.
*ABC of Reading*, Ch. 2

4 Any general statement is like a cheque drawn on a bank. Its value depends on what is there to meet it.
*ABC of Reading*, Ch. 2

5 Winter is icummen in,
Lhude sing Goddamm,
Raineth drop and staineth slop
And how the wind doth ramm!
Sing: Goddamm.
*Ancient Music*

6 And even I can remember
A day when the historians left blanks in their writings,
I mean for things they didn't know.
*Cantos*, XIII

7 Bah! I have sung women in three cities,
But it is all the same;
And I will sing of the sun.
*Cino*

8 The difference between a gun and a tree is a difference of tempo. The tree explodes every spring.
*Criterion*, July 1937

9 Great Literature is simply language charged with meaning to the utmost possible degree.
*How to Read*

10 For three years, out of key with his time,
He strove to resuscitate the dead art
Of poetry to maintain 'the sublime'
In the old sense. Wrong from the start.
*Pour l'élection de son sépulcre*

**Powell, Anthony** (1905– ) British novelist. His satirical *A Dance to the Music of Time* comprises twelve volumes published between 1951 and 1975.

1 He fell in love with himself at first sight and it is a passion to which he has always remained faithful. Self-love seems so often unrequited.
*A Dance to the Music of Time: The Acceptance World*, Ch. 1

2 Dinner at the Huntercombes' possessed 'only two dramatic features – the wine was a farce and the food a tragedy'.
*A Dance to the Music of Time: The Acceptance World*, Ch. 4

3 All men are brothers, but, thank God, they aren't all brothers-in-law.
*A Dance to the Music of Time: At Lady Molly's*, Ch. 4

4 It must be generations since anyone but highbrows lived in this cottage . . . I imagine most of the agricultural labourers round here commute from London.
*A Dance to the Music of Time: The Kindly Ones*, Ch. 2

5 One of the worst things about life is not how nasty the nasty people are. You know that already. It is how nasty the nice people can be.
*A Dance to the Music of Time: The Kindly Ones*, Ch. 4

6 Growing old is like being increasingly penalized for a crime you haven't committed.
*A Dance to the Music of Time: Temporary Kings*, Ch. 1

7 People think that because a novel's invented, it isn't true. Exactly the reverse is the case. Biography and memoirs can never be wholly true, since they cannot include every conceivable circumstance of what happened. The novel can do that.
*A Dance to the Music of Time: Hearing Secret Harmonies*, Ch. 3

**Powell, (John) Enoch** (1912– ) British politician. In 1974 he left the Conservative Party after his dismissal from the shadow cabinet, following a controversial speech on immigration, which he has always opposed.

1 As I look ahead, I am filled with foreboding. Like the Roman, I seem to see 'the River Tiber foaming with much blood'.
Talking about immigration
Speech in Birmingham, 20 Apr 1968

2 Above any other position of eminence, that of Prime Minister is filled by fluke.
*The Observer*, 'Sayings of the Week', 8 Mar 1987

**Powell, Sir John** (1645–1713) English judge.

1 Let us consider the reason of the case. For nothing is law that is not reason.
Coggs v. Bernard, 2 Lord Raymond, 911

**Powys, John Cowper** (1872–1963) British novelist best-known for such West-Country stories as *Wolf Solent* (1929) and *A Glastonbury Romance* (1932).

1 He combined scepticism of everything with credulity about everything . . . and I am convinced this is the true Shakespearean way wherewith to take life.
*Autobiography*

**Prescott, William** (1726–95) US revolutionary soldier. He was colonel of a regiment in the War of Independence (1775) and fought in the battle of Bunker Hill.

1 Don't fire until you see the whites of their eyes.
Command given at the Battle of Bunker Hill

**Previn, André** (1929– ) German-born conductor, pianist, and composer who has become a US citizen. He was conductor of the London Symphony Orchestra (1969–79) and music director of the Royal Philharmonic Orchestra (1985– ).

**1** The basic difference between classical music and jazz is that in the former the music is always greater than its performance – whereas the way jazz is performed is always more important than what is being played.
*An Encyclopedia of Quotations about Music* (Nat Shapiro)

**Priestley, J(ohn) B(oynton)** (1894–1984) British novelist and dramatist, who also published books of criticism and memoirs. His many successful works include *The Good Companions* (1929) and *Dangerous Corner* (1932). He was a popular radio broadcaster during World War II.

**1** Comedy, we may say, is society protecting itself – with a smile.
*George Meredith*

**2** They will review a book by a writer much older than themselves as if it were an over-ambitious essay by a second-year student . . . It is the little dons I complain about, like so many corgis trotting up, hoping to nip your ankles.
*Outcries and Asides*

**3** A number of anxious dwarfs trying to grill a whale.
Referring to politicians
*Outcries and Asides*

**4** If there was a little room somewhere in the British Museum that contained only about twenty exhibits and good lighting, easy chairs, and a notice imploring you to smoke, I believe I should become a museum man.
*Self-Selected Essays*, 'In the British Museum'

**5** Our trouble is that we drink too much tea. I see in this the slow revenge of the Orient, which has diverted the Yellow River down our throats.
*The Observer*, 'Sayings of the Week', 15 May 1949

**6** It is hard to tell where MCC ends and the Church of England begins.
*New Statesman*, 20 July 1962, 'Topside Schools'

**7** God can stand being told by Professor Ayer and Marghanita Laski that He doesn't exist.
*The Listener*, 1 July 1965, 'The BBC's Duty to Society'

**8** Our great-grandchildren, when they learn how we began this war by snatching glory out of defeat . . . may also learn how the little holiday steamers made an excursion to hell and came back glorious.
Referring to the British Expeditionary Force's evacuation from Dunkirk
Broadcast, 5 June 1940

**Prior, Matthew** (1664–1721) British poet and politician. He served as a diplomat in France and Holland; on the death of Queen Anne he was imprisoned and while in prison wrote *Alma, or the Progress of the Mind* (1718). Many of his brief epigrammatic poems are collected in *Poems on Several Occasions* (1709).

**1** Cur'd yesterday of my disease,
I died last night of my physician.
*The Remedy Worse than the Disease*

**2** For hope is but the dream of those that wake.
*Solomon*, II

**3** From ignorance our comfort flows,
The only wretched are the wise.
*To the Hon. Charles Montague*

**Pritchett, V(ictor) S(awden)** (1900– ) British short-story writer and critic, who has also written frequently about Spain. His books include two acclaimed autobiographical works, *A Cab at the Door* (1968) and *Midnight Oil* (1971).

**1** The detective novel is the art-for-art's-sake of yawning Philistinism.
*Books in General*, 'The Roots of Detection'

**Procter, Adelaide Anne** (1825–64) British poet and writer. She wrote *Legends and Lyrics* (1858), which included 'The Lost Chord', and several hymns. She also wrote verse under the pseudonym 'Mary Berwick'.

**1** Seated one day at the organ,
I was weary and ill at ease,
And my fingers wandered idly
Over the noisy keys.
. . .
But I struck one chord of music,
Like the sound of a great Amen.
Better known in the setting by Sir Arthur Sullivan
*Legends and Lyrics*, 'A Lost Chord'

**Proudhon, Pierre Joseph** (1809–65) French socialist. Founder and editor of radical journals, he played an active part in the socialist movement in Paris (1848) and is regarded as the father of anarchism.

**1** Property is theft.
*Qu'est-ce que la Propriété?*, Ch. 1

**Proust, Marcel** (1871–1922) French novelist. His masterpiece was a series of partly autobiographical novels, *À la recherche du temps perdu* (1913–27), which give a detailed portrait of the life of his time.

**1** The taste was that of the little crumb of madeleine which on Sunday mornings at Combray . . ., when I used to say good-day to her in her bedroom, my aunt Léonie used to give me, dipping it first in her own cup of real or of lime-flower tea.
*À la recherche du temps perdu: Du côté de chez Swann*

**2** People often say that, by pointing out to a man the faults of his mistress, you succeed only in strengthening his attachment to her, because he does not believe you; yet how much more so if he does!
*À la recherche du temps perdu: Du côté de chez Swann*

**3** The human face is indeed, like the face of the God of some Oriental theogony, a whole cluster of faces, crowded together but on different surfaces so that one does not see them all at once.
*À la recherche du temps perdu: À l'ombre des jeunes filles en fleurs*

**4** There can be no peace of mind in love, since the advantage one has secured is never anything but a fresh starting-point for further desires.
*À la recherche du temps perdu: À l'ombre des jeunes filles en fleurs*

5 As soon as one is unhappy one becomes moral.
*À la recherche du temps perdu: À l'ombre des jeunes filles en fleurs*

6 A PUSHING LADY. What are your views on love? MME LEROI. Love? I make it constantly but I never talk about it.
*À la recherche du temps perdu: Le Côté de Guermantes*

7 It has been said that the highest praise of God consists in the denial of Him by the atheist, who finds creation so perfect that he can dispense with a creator.
*À la recherche du temps perdu: Le Côté de Guermantes*

8 A doctor who doesn't say too many foolish things is a patient half-cured, just as a critic is a poet who has stopped writing verse and a policeman a burglar who has retired from practice.
*À la recherche du temps perdu: Le Côté de Guermantes*

9 Neurosis has an absolute genius for malingering. There is no illness which it cannot counterfeit perfectly . . . If it is capable of deceiving the doctor, how should it fail to deceive the patient?
*À la recherche du temps perdu: Le Côté de Guermantes*

10 As soon as he ceased to be mad he became merely stupid. There are maladies we must not seek to cure because they alone protect us from others that are more serious.
*À la recherche du temps perdu: Le Côté de Guermantes*

11 His hatred of snobs was a derivative of his snobbishness, but made the simpletons (in other words, everyone) believe that he was immune from snobbishness.
*À la recherche du temps perdu: Le Côté de Guermantes*

12 There is nothing like desire for preventing the thing one says from bearing any resemblance to what one has in mind.
*À la recherche du temps perdu: Le Côté de Guermantes*

13 Good-bye, I've barely said a word to you, it is always like that at parties, we never see the people, we never say the things we should like to say, but it is the same everywhere in this life. Let us hope that when we are dead things will be better arranged.
*À la recherche du temps perdu: Sodome et Gomorrhe*

14 I have sometimes regretted living so close to Marie . . . because I may be very fond of her, but I am not quite so fond of her company.
*À la recherche du temps perdu: Sodome et Gomorrhe*

15 I have a horror of sunsets, they're so romantic, so operatic.
*À la recherche du temps perdu: Sodome et Gomorrhe*

16 It is seldom indeed that one parts on good terms, because if one were on good terms one would not part.
*À la recherche du temps perdu: La Prisonnière*

17 One of those telegrams of which M. de Guermantes had wittily fixed the formula: 'Cannot come, lie follows'.
*À la recherche du temps perdu: Le Temps retrouvé*

18 Happiness is beneficial for the body, but it is grief that develops the powers of the mind.
*À la recherche du temps perdu: Le Temps retrouvé*

19 Everything great in the world is done by neurotics; they alone founded our religions and created our masterpieces.
*The Perpetual Pessimist* (Sagittarius and George)

**Proverbs** A selection of the commonest proverbs and other sayings is given here. The proverbs are arranged in alphabetical order.

1 A bad penny always turns up.

2 A bad workman always blames his tools.

3 A bird in the hand is worth two in the bush.

4 Absence makes the heart grow fonder.

5 A cask of wine works more miracles than a church full of saints.
Italian proverb

6 A cat has nine lives.

7 A cat may look at a king.

8 Accidents will happen in the best regulated families.

9 A chain is no stronger than its weakest link.

10 A constant guest is never welcome.

11 Actions speak louder than words.

12 Adam's ale is the best brew.

13 A dimple in the chin, a devil within.

14 A drowning man will clutch at a straw.

15 A fool and his money are soon parted.

16 A fool at forty is a fool indeed.

17 A fool believes everything.

18 A friend in need is a friend indeed.

19 After a storm comes a calm.

20 After shaking hands with a Greek, count your fingers.

21 A good dog deserves a good bone.

22 A good drink makes the old young.

23 A good face is a letter of recommendation.

24 A good friend is my nearest relation.

25 A good scare is worth more than good advice.

26 A hedge between keeps friendship green.

27 A judge knows nothing unless it has been explained to him three times.

28 A lawyer never goes to law himself.

29 A lawyer's opinion is worth nothing unless paid for.

30 A liar is worse than a thief.

31 All are not saints that go to church.

32 All cats are grey in the dark.

33 All good things must come to an end.

34 All is fair in love and war.

35 All men are mortal.

36 All roads lead to Rome.

37 All's grist that comes to the mill.

38 All's well that ends well.

39 All that glitters is not gold.

40 All the world loves a lover.

41 All work and no play makes Jack a dull boy.

42 Although there exist many thousand subjects for elegant conversation, there are persons who cannot meet a cripple without talking about feet.
Chinese proverb

43 A man can die but once.

44 A man is as old as he feels, and a woman as old as she looks.

45 A man of straw is worth a woman of gold.

46 A meal without flesh is like feeding on grass.
Indian proverb

47 A miss is as good as a mile.

48 An apple a day keeps the doctor away.

49 An apple-pie without some cheese is like a kiss without a squeeze.

50 An atheist is one point beyond the devil.

51 An Englishman's home is his castle.

52 An Englishman's word is his bond.

53 An honest man's word is as good as his bond.

54 An hour in the morning is worth two in the evening.

55 A nod is as good as a wink to a blind horse.

56 Any port in a storm.

57 Any publicity is good publicity.

58 A penny saved is a penny earned.

59 A piece of churchyard fits everybody.

60 Appearances are deceptive.

61 A priest sees people at their best, a lawyer at their worst, but a doctor sees them as they really are.

62 A rainbow in the morning is the shepherd's warning; a rainbow at night is the shepherd's delight.

63 Ask a silly question and you'll get a silly answer.

64 Ask no questions and hear no lies.

65 A spur in the head is worth two in the heel.

66 As soon as man is born he begins to die.

67 A still tongue makes a wise head.

68 A stitch in time saves nine.

69 A tale never loses in the telling.

70 A trouble shared is a trouble halved.

71 A truly great man never puts away the simplicity of a child.
Chinese proverb

72 Attack is the best form of defence.

73 A watched pot never boils.

74 A woman's place is in the home.

75 A woman's work is never done.

76 A young physician fattens the churchyard.

77 Bad news travels fast.

78 Barking dogs seldom bite.

79 Beauty is in the eye of the beholder.

80 Beauty is only skin-deep.

81 Beauty is potent but money is omnipotent.

82 Beggars can't be choosers.

83 Believe nothing of what you hear, and only half of what you see.

84 Benefits make a man a slave.
Arabic proverb

85 Better a lie that heals than a truth that wounds.

86 Better an egg today than a hen tomorrow.

87 Better a thousand enemies outside the house than one inside.
Arabic proverb

88 Better be a fool than a knave.

89 Better be an old man's darling than a young man's slave.

90 Better be envied than pitied.

91 Better be safe than sorry.

92 Better late than never.

93 Birds of a feather flock together.

94 Blood is thicker than water.

95 Books and friends should be few but good.

96 Borrowed garments never fit well.

97 Bread is the staff of life.

98 Caesar's wife must be above suspicion.

99 Charity begins at home.

100 Christmas comes but once a year.

101 Civility costs nothing.

102 Cold hands, warm heart.

103 Constant dripping wears away the stone.

104 Curiosity killed the cat.

105 Cut your coat according to your cloth.

106 Dead men tell no tales.

107 Death defies the doctor.

108 Death is the great leveller.

109 Desperate cuts must have desperate cures.

110 Divide and rule.

111 Do as I say, not as I do.

112 Do as you would be done by.

113 Dog does not eat dog.

114 Doing is better than saying.

115 Don't count your chickens before they are hatched.

116 Don't cross the bridge till you get to it.

117 Don't cut off your nose to spite your face.

118 Don't meet troubles half-way.

119 Don't put all your eggs in one basket.

120 Don't spoil the ship for a ha'porth of tar.

121 Don't teach your grandmother to suck eggs.

122 Don't throw the baby out with the bathwater.

123 Don't wash your dirty linen in public.

124 Early to bed and early to rise, makes a man healthy, wealthy and wise.

125 Easier said than done.

126 East, west, home's best.

127 Easy come, easy go.

128 Eat to live and not live to eat.

129 Empty vessels make the greatest sound.

130 Even a worm will turn.

131 Every book must be chewed to get out its juice.
Chinese proverb

132 Every cloud has a silver lining.

133 Every dog has his day.

134 Every dog is allowed one bite.

135 Every family has a skeleton in the cupboard.

136 Every little helps.

137 Every man after his fashion.

138 Every man for himself, and the devil take the hindmost.

139 Every man is his own worst enemy.

140 Every man to his trade.

141 Every one is innocent until he is proved guilty.

142 Every one to his taste.

143 Every picture tells a story.

144 Everything comes to him who waits.

145 Experience is the best teacher.

146 Experience is the mother of wisdom.

147 Faith will move mountains.

148 Familiarity breeds contempt.

149 Fear of death is worse than death itself.

150 Fight fire with fire.

151 Finders keepers, losers seekers.

152 Fine feathers make fine birds.

153 Fine words butter no parsnips.

154 Fingers were made before forks, and hands before knives.

155 First come, first served.

156 First impressions are the most lasting.

157 First things first.

158 Fish and guests smell in three days.

159 Fools build houses, and wise men buy them.

160 Fools live poor to die rich.

161 Footprints on the sands of time are not made by sitting down.

162 Forbidden fruit is sweet.

163 Forewarned is forearmed.

164 Forgive and forget.

165 Fortune favours fools.

166 For want of a nail the shoe was lost; for want of a shoe the horse was lost; for want of a horse the rider was lost.

167 From clogs to clogs is only three generations.

168 From small beginnings come great things.

169 From the sublime to the ridiculous is only a step.

170 Garbage in, garbage out.

171 Genius is an infinite capacity for taking pains.

172 Give a dog a bad name and hang him.

173 Give a thief enough rope and he'll hang himself.

174 Give him an inch and he'll take a yard.

175 Give me a child for the first seven years, and you may do what you like with him afterwards.

176 God defend me from my friends; from my enemies I can defend myself.

177 God helps them that help themselves.

178 God is always on the side of the big battalions.

179 Good fences make good neighbours.

180 Go to bed with the lamb, and rise with the lark.

181 Great minds think alike.

182 Great oaks from little acorns grow.

183 Grey hairs are death's blossoms.

184 Half a loaf is better than no bread.

185 Handsome is as handsome does.

186 Haste makes waste.

187 Health is better than wealth.

188 He helps little that helps not himself.

189 He that fights and runs away, may live to fight another day.

190 He that has no children brings them up well.

191 He that has no wife, beats her oft.

192 He that is his own lawyer has a fool for a client.

193 He that knows little, often repeats it.

194 He that knows nothing, doubts nothing.

195 He that lives long suffers much.

196 He travels fastest who travels alone.

197 He was a bold man that first ate an oyster.

198 He who drinks a little too much drinks much too much.

199 He who hesitates is lost.

200 He who lives by the sword dies by the sword.

201 He who pays the piper calls the tune.

202 He who rides a tiger is afraid to dismount.

203 He who sups with the devil should have a long spoon.

204 History repeats itself.

205 Hoist your sail when the wind is fair.

206 Home is home, though it be never so homely.

207 Home is where the heart is.

208 Honesty is the best policy.

209 Hope for the best.

210 Hunger is the best sauce.

211 If a job's worth doing, it's worth doing well.

212 If anything can go wrong, it will.

213 If at first you don't succeed, try, try, try again.

214 If ifs and ans were pots and pans, there'd be no trade for tinkers.

215 If the mountain will not come to Mahomet, Mahomet must go to the mountain.

216 If wishes were horses, beggars would ride.

217 If you can't be good, be careful.

218 If you don't like the heat, get out of the kitchen.

219 If you play with fire you get burnt.

220 If you trust before you try, you may repent before you die.

221 If you want a thing well done, do it yourself.

222 Imitation is the sincerest form of flattery.

223 In for a penny, in for a pound.

224 In the country of the blind, the one-eyed man is king.

225 It is a long lane that has no turning.

226 It is better to be born lucky than rich.

227 It is easy to bear the misfortunes of others.

228 It is easy to be wise after the event.

229 It is no use crying over spilt milk.

230 It never rains but it pours.

231 It's an ill wind that blows nobody any good.

232 It's a small world.

233 It's too late to shut the stable door after the horse has bolted.

234 It takes all sorts to make a world.

235 It takes two to make a quarrel.

236 It takes two to tango.

237 It will all come right in the wash.

238 It will be all the same a hundred years.

239 Jack of all trades, master of none.

240 Keep something for a rainy day.

241 Keep your mouth shut and your eyes open.

242 Keep your weather-eye open.

243 Kill not the goose that lays the golden egg.

244 Knowledge is power.

245 Knowledge is the mother of all virtue; all vice proceeds from ignorance.

246 Know thyself.

247 Laugh and grow fat.

248 Laugh before breakfast, you'll cry before supper.

249 Laughter is the best medicine.

250 Learning is a treasure which accompanies its owner everywhere.
Chinese proverb

251 Least said soonest mended.

252 Leave well alone.

253 Lend only that which you can afford to lose.

254 Let bygones be bygones.

255 Let sleeping dogs lie.

256 Let the cobbler stick to his last.

257 Life begins at forty.

258 Life is just a bowl of cherries.

259 Life is not all beer and skittles.

260 Life is sweet.

261 Like breeds like.

262 Like father, like son.

263 Listeners never hear good of themselves.

264 Live and learn.

265 Long absent, soon forgotten.

266 Look after number one.

267 Look before you leap.

268 Look on the bright side.

269 Love conquers all.

270 Love is blind.

271 Love laughs at locksmiths.

272 Love makes the world go round.

273 Love me, love my dog.

274 Love will find a way.

275 Love your neighbour, yet pull not down your hedge.

276 Lucky at cards, unlucky in love.

277 Mackerel sky and mares' tails make lofty ships carry low sails.

278 Make hay while the sun shines.

279 Manners maketh man.

280 Man proposes, God disposes.

281 Many a mickle makes a muckle.

282 Many a true word is spoken in jest.

283 Many hands make light work.

284 Many irons in the fire, some must cool.

285 March comes in like a lion and goes out like a lamb.

286 March winds and April showers bring forth May flowers.

287 Marriages are made in heaven.

288 Marry in haste, and repent at leisure.

289 Marry in Lent, and you'll live to repent.

290 Marry in May, rue for aye.

291 Meet on the stairs and you won't meet in heaven.

292 Mind your own business.

293 Moderation in all things.

294 Monday's child is fair of face, Tuesday's child is full of grace; Wednesday's child is full of woe, Thursday's child has far to go; Friday's child is loving and giving, Saturday's child works hard for its living; and the child that's born on the Sabbath day, is fair and wise and good and gay.

295 More haste, less speed.

296 Music helps not the toothache.

297 Music is the food of love.

298 Necessity is the mother of invention.

299 Needs must when the devil drives.

300 Ne'er cast a clout till May be out.

301 Never do things by halves.

302 Never judge from appearances.

303 Never look a gift horse in the mouth.

304 Never put off till tomorrow what you can do today.

305 Never say die.

306 Never speak ill of the dead.

307 Never too late to learn.

308 Ninety per cent of inspiration is perspiration.

309 No bees, no honey; no work, no money.

310 No love like the first love.

311 No man is a hero to his valet.

312 No man is infallible.

313 No names, no pack-drill.

314 No news is good news.

315 No pleasure without pain.

316 Nothing is certain but death and taxes.

317 Nothing so bad but it might have been worse.

318 Nothing succeeds like success.

319 Nothing ventured, nothing gained.

320 No time like the present.

321 Old habits die hard.

322 Old sins cast long shadows.

323 Old soldiers never die, they simply fade away.

324 Once a parson always a parson.

325 One for sorrow, two for mirth; three for a wedding, four for a birth; five for silver, six for gold; seven for a secret, not to be told; eight for heaven, nine for hell; and ten for the devil's own sel.
Referring to magpies or crows; there are numerous variants

326 One good turn deserves another.

327 One hour's sleep before midnight, is worth two after.

328 One joy scatters a hundred griefs.
Chinese proverb

329 One man's meat is another man's poison.

330 One swallow does not make a summer.

331 Opportunity seldom knocks twice.

332 Out of debt, out of danger.

333 Out of sight, out of mind.

334 Patience is a virtue.

335 Penny wise, pound foolish.

336 Pigs might fly, if they had wings.

337 Possession is nine points of the law.

338 Poverty is not a crime.

339 Practice makes perfect.

340 Practise what you preach.

341 Prevention is better than cure.

342 Promises are like pie-crust, made to be broken.

343 Punctuality is the politeness of princes.

344 Put an Irishman on the spit, and you can always get another Irishman to baste him.

345 Put off the evil hour as long as you can.

346 Rain before seven: fine before eleven.

347 Rain, rain, go away, come again another day.

348 Red sky at night, shepherd's delight; red sky in the morning, shepherd's warning.

349 Revenge is a dish that tastes better cold.

350 Revenge is sweet.

351 Rome was not built in a day.

352 Sailors have a port in every storm.

353 Salt water and absence wash away love.

354 Save your breath to cool your porridge.

355 Saying is one thing, and doing another.

356 Scratch my back and I'll scratch yours.

357 See a pin and pick it up, all the day you'll have good luck; see a pin and let it lie, you'll want a pin before you die.

358 Seeing is believing.

359 See Naples and die.

360 Self-praise is no recommendation.

361 Send a fool to the market and a fool he will return again.

362 Silence is golden.

363 Slow but sure wins the race.

364 Small is beautiful.

365 Soon learnt, soon forgotten.

366 Spare the rod and spoil the child.

367 Speak when you are spoken to.

368 Speech is silver, silence is golden.

369 Sticks and stones may break my bones, but words will never hurt me.

370 Still waters run deep.

371 Strike while the iron is hot.

372 St. Swithin's Day, if thou dost rain, for forty days it will remain; St. Swithin's Day, if thou be fair, for forty days 'twill rain no more.

373 Take a hair of the dog that bit you.

374 Take care of the pence, and the pounds will take care of themselves.

375 Take things as they come.

376 Talk of the devil, and he is bound to appear.

377 Tell the truth and shame the devil.

378 The best of friends must part.

379 The best things come in small parcels.

380 The best things in life are free.

381 The better the day, the better the deed.

382 The cuckoo comes in April, and stays the month of May; sings a song at midsummer, and then goes away.

383 The darkest hour is just before the dawn.

384 The devil finds work for idle hands to do.

385 The devil is not so black as he is painted.

386 The devil looks after his own.

387 The early bird catches the worm.

388 The end justifies the means.

389 The exception proves the rule.

390 The eye is bigger than the belly.

391 The eyes are the window of the soul.

392 The family that prays together stays together.

393 The first day a guest, the second day a guest, the third day a calamity.
Indian proverb

394 The first step is the hardest.

395 The first wife is matrimony, the second company, the third heresy.

396 The good die young.

397 The guest who outstays his fellow-guests loses his overcoat.
Chinese proverb

398 The hand that rocks the cradle rules the world.

399 The last straw breaks the camel's back.

400 The law does not concern itself about trifles.

401 The more the merrier; the fewer the better fare.

402 The nearer the bone, the sweeter the flesh.

403 The north wind does blow, and we shall have snow.

404 The old man has his death before his eyes; the young man behind his back.

405 There are more old drunkards than old doctors.

406 There are only twenty-four hours in the day.

407 There is a time and place for everything.

408 There is honour among thieves.

409 There is more than one way to skin a cat.

410 There is no accounting for tastes.

411 There is safety in numbers.

412 There's a black sheep in every flock.

413 There's always room at the top.

414 There's many a good tune played on an old fiddle.

415 There's many a slip 'twixt the cup and the lip.

416 There's no fool like an old fool.

417 There's no place like home.

418 There's no smoke without fire.

419 There's nowt so queer as folk.

420 There's one law for the rich, and another for the poor.

421 There's only one pretty child in the world, and every mother has it.

422 There will be sleeping enough in the grave.

423 The road to hell is paved with good intentions.

424 The shoemaker's son always goes barefoot.

425 The streets of London are paved with gold.

426 The style is the man.

427 The way to a man's heart is through his stomach.

428 The weakest goes to the wall.

429 Things are not always what they seem.

430 Third time lucky.

431 Throw dirt enough, and some will stick.

432 Throw out a sprat to catch a mackerel.

433 Time and tide wait for no man.

434 Time is a great healer.

435 Time will tell.

436 To deceive oneself is very easy.

437 To err is human.

438 Tomorrow is another day.

439 Tomorrow never comes.

440 Too many cooks spoil the broth.

441 Travel broadens the mind.

442 True love never grows old.

443 Truth fears no trial.

444 Truth is stranger than fiction.

445 Truth will out.

446 Two heads are better than one.

447 Two wrongs do not make a right.

448 Union is strength.

449 United we stand, divided we fall.

450 Vice is often clothed in virtue's habit.

451 Walls have ears.

452 Waste not, want not.

453 We must learn to walk before we can run.

454 What can't be cured, must be endured.

455 What must be, must be.

456 What's done cannot be undone.

457 What you don't know can't hurt you.

458 What you lose on the swings you gain on the roundabouts.

459 When one door shuts, another opens.

460 When poverty comes in at the door, love flies out of the window.

461 When the cat's away, the mice will play.

462 When the wine is in, the wit is out.

463 Where there's a will there's a way.

464 While there's life there's hope.

465 Whom the gods love dies young.

466 Who spits against the wind, it falls in his face.

467 Why buy a cow when milk is so cheap?

468 Why keep a dog and bark yourself?

469 You can have too much of a good thing.

470 You can lead a horse to the water, but you can't make him drink.

471 You cannot run with the hare and hunt with the hounds.

472 You can't get a quart into a pint pot.

473 You can't get blood out of a stone.

474 You can't make an omelette without breaking eggs.

**475** You can't make bricks without straw.

**476** You can't please everyone.

**477** You can't take it with you when you go.

**478** You can't teach an old dog new tricks.

**479** You can't tell a book by its cover.

**Pryce-Jones, David** (1936– ) British author and critic. His novels include *Owls and Satyrs* (1960), *The Sands of Summer* (1963), and *Quondam* (1965).

**1** When you're bored with yourself, marry and be bored with someone else.

*Owls and Satyrs*

**Psalms** Unless stated in the reference, the psalms given are in Coverdale's translation, which is used in the Book of Common Prayer.

**1** Blessed is the man that hath not walked in the counsel of the ungodly, nor stood in the way of sinners, and hath not sat in the seat of the scornful.
But his delight is in the law of the Lord; and in his law will he exercise himself day and night.
And he shall be like a tree planted by the water-side, that will bring forth his fruit in due season.
His leaf also shall not wither; and look, whatso-ever he doeth shall prosper.

1:1–4

**2** All mine enemies shall be confounded, and sore vexed: they shall be turned back, and put to shame suddenly.

6:10

**3** Out of the mouth of very babes and sucklings hast thou ordained strength, because of thine en-emies, that thou mightest still the enemy, and the avenger.
For I will consider thy heavens, even the works of thy fingers, the moon and the stars, which thou hast ordained.
What is man, that thou art mindful of him? and the son of man, that thou visitest him?
Thou madest him lower than the angels, to crown him with glory and worship.

8:2–5

**4** In the Lord put I my trust: how say ye then to my soul, that she should flee as a bird unto the hill?
For lo, the ungodly bend their bow, and make ready their arrows within the quiver that they may privily shoot at them which are true of heart.

11:1–2

**5** Upon the ungodly he shall rain snares, fire and brimstone, storm and tempest: this shall be their portion to drink.

11:7

**6** Keep me as the apple of an eye; hide me under the shadow of thy wings.

17:8

**7** Thou also shalt light my candle: the Lord my God shall make my darkness to be light.
For in thee I shall discomfit an host of men; and with the help of my God I shall leap over the wall.

18:28–29

**8** In them hath he set a tabernacle for the sun, which cometh forth as a bridegroom out of his chamber, and rejoiceth as a giant to run his course.

19:5

**9** The fear of the Lord is clean, and endureth for ever: the judgments of the Lord are true, and righteous altogether.
More to be desired are they than gold, yea, than much fine gold: sweeter also than honey, and the honey-comb.

19:9–10

**10** Let the words of my mouth, and the meditation of my heart, be alway acceptable in thy sight, O Lord, my strength, and my redeemer.

19:14–15

**11** Some put their trust in chariots, and some in horses: but we remember the Name of the Lord our God.
They are brought down, and fallen: but we are risen, and stand upright.

20:7–8

**12** The Lord is my shepherd; therefore can I lack nothing.
He shall feed me in a green pasture: and lead me forth beside the waters of comfort.
He shall convert my soul: and bring me forth in the paths of righteousness, for his Name's sake.
Yea, though I walk through the valley of the shadow of death, I will fear no evil: for thou art with me; thy rod and thy staff comfort me.
Thou shalt prepare a table before me against them that trouble me: thou hast anointed my head with oil, and my cup shall be full.
But thy loving-kindness and mercy shall follow me all the days of my life: and I will dwell in the house of the Lord for ever.

23:1–6

**13** The Lord is my shepherd; I shall not want.
He maketh me to lie down in green pastures: he leadeth me beside the still waters.

*Authorised Version,* 23:1–2

**14** Thou preparest a table before me in the pres-ence of mine enemies: thou anointest my head with oil; my cup runneth over.
Surely goodness and mercy shall follow me all the days of my life: and I will dwell in the house of the Lord for ever.

*Authorised Version,* 23:5–6

**15** The earth is the Lord's, and all that therein is; the compass of the world, and they that dwell therein.
24:1

**16** Lift up your heads, O ye gates, and be ye lift up, ye everlasting doors; and the King of glory shall come in.
Who is the King of glory? it is the Lord strong and mighty, even the Lord mighty in battle.
24:7-8

**17** The Lord is my light, and my salvation; whom then shall I fear? the Lord is the strength of my life; of whom then shall I be afraid?
27:1

**18** The voice of the Lord breaketh the cedar-trees; yea, the Lord breaketh the cedars of Libanus.
29:5

**19** For his wrath endureth but the twinkling of an eye, and in his pleasure is life: heaviness may endure for a night, but joy cometh in the morning.
And in my prosperity I said, I shall never be removed; thou, Lord, of thy goodness hast made my hill so strong.
30:5-6

**20** In thee, O Lord, have I put my trust: let me never be put to confusion; deliver me in thy righteousness.
31:1

**21** Into thy hands I commend my spirit: for thou hast redeemed me, O Lord, thou God of truth.
31:6

**22** I am clean forgotten, as a dead man out of mind: I am become like a broken vessel.
31:14

**23** Rejoice in the Lord, O ye righteous: for it becometh well the just to be thankful.
Praise the Lord with harp; sing praises unto him with the lute, and instrument of ten strings.
Sing unto the Lord a new song; sing praises lustily unto him with a good courage.
33:1-3

**24** He loveth righteousness and judgment: the earth is full of the goodness of the Lord.
33:5

**25** I will alway give thanks unto the Lord: his praise shall ever be in my mouth.
34:1

**26** I have been young, and now am old; and yet saw I never the righteous forsaken, nor his seed begging their bread.
37:25

**27** When thou with rebukes dost chasten man for sin, thou makest his beauty to consume away, like as it were a moth fretting a garment: every man therefore is but vanity.
39:12

**28** As for me, I am poor and needy; but the Lord careth for me.
Thou art my helper and redeemer; make no long tarrying, O my God.
40:20-21

**29** Yea, even mine own familiar friend, whom I trusted, who did also eat of my bread, hath laid great wait for me.
41:9

**30** Like as the hart desireth the water-brooks, so longeth my soul after thee, O God.
My soul is athirst for God, yea, even for the living God: when shall I come to appear before the presence of God?
42:1-2

**31** God is in the midst of her, therefore shall she not be removed God shall help her, and that right early.
The heathen make much ado, and the kingdoms are moved: but God hath shewed his voice, and the earth shall melt away.
46:5-6

**32** He maketh wars to cease in all the world; he breaketh the bow, and knappeth the spear in sunder, and burneth the chariots in the fire.
Be still then, and know that I am God: I will be exalted among the heathen, and I will be exalted in the earth.
The Lord of hosts is with us; the God of Jacob is our refuge.
46:9-11

**33** Man being in honour hath no understanding: but is compared unto the beasts that perish.
49:20

**34** Wash me throughly from my wickedness, and cleanse me from my sin.
For I acknowledge my faults: and my sin is ever before me.
51:2-3

**35** Behold, I was shapen in wickedness: and in sin hath my mother conceived me.
But lo, thou requirest truth in the inward parts: and shalt make me to understand wisdom secretly.
Thou shalt purge me with hyssop, and I shall be clean: thou shalt wash me, and I shall be whiter than snow.
Thou shalt make me hear of joy and gladness: that the bones which thou hast broken may rejoice.
Turn thy face from my sins: and put out all my misdeeds.
Make me a clean heart, O God: and renew a right spirit within me.
51:5-10

36 For thou desirest no sacrifice, else would I give it thee: but thou delightest not in burnt-offerings.
The sacrifice of God is a troubled spirit: a broken and contrite heart, O God, shalt thou not despise.
51:16-17

37 And I said, O that I had wings like a dove: for then would I flee away, and be at rest.
55:6

38 We took sweet counsel together, and walked in the house of God as friends.
55:15

39 For thou hast delivered my soul from death, and my feet from falling, that I may walk before God in the light of the living.
56:13

40 God shall send forth his mercy and truth: my soul is among lions.
And I lie even among the children of men, that are set on fire: whose teeth are spears and arrows, and their tongue a sharp sword.
57:4-5

41 O set me up upon the rock that is higher than I: for thou hast been my hope, and a strong tower for me against the enemy.
I will dwell in thy tabernacle for ever; and my trust shall be under the covering of thy wings.
61:3-4

42 Thou, O God, art praised in Sion: and unto thee shall the vow be performed in Jerusalem.
Thou that hearest the prayer, unto thee shall all flesh come.
65:1-2

43 Then shall the earth bring forth her increase; and God, even our own God, shall give us his blessing.
67:6

44 Let them be wiped out of the book of the living, and not be written among the righteous.
69:29

45 Let them for their reward be soon brought to shame, that cry over me, There, there.
70:3

46 They that dwell in the wilderness shall kneel before him; his enemies shall lick the dust.
72:9

47 So man did eat angels' food: for he sent them meat enough.
78:26

48 So the Lord awaked as one out of sleep, and like a giant refreshed with wine.
78:66

49 Thou feedest them with the bread of tears; and givest them plenteousness of tears to drink.
80:5

50 O how amiable are thy dwellings, thou Lord of hosts!
My soul hath a desire and longing to enter into the courts of the Lord: my heart and my flesh rejoice in the living God.
Yea, the sparrow hath found her an house, and the swallow a nest where she may lay her young, even thy altars, O Lord of hosts, my King and my God.
84:1-3

51 For one day in thy courts is better than a thousand.
I had rather be a door-keeper in the house of my God, than to dwell in the tents of ungodliness.
84:10-11

52 Mercy and truth are met together; righteousness and peace have kissed each other.
Truth shall flourish out of the earth; and righteousness hath looked down from heaven.
85:10-11

53 Her foundations are upon the holy hills; the Lord loveth the gates of Sion more than all the dwellings of Jacob.
Very excellent things are spoken of thee, thou city of God.
87:1-2

54 Lord, thou hast been our refuge from one generation to another.
Before the mountains were brought forth, or ever the earth and the world were made, thou art God from everlasting, and world without end.
90:1-2

55 For a thousand years in thy sight are but as yesterday, seeing that is past as a watch in the night.
As soon as thou scatterest them they are even as a sleep; and fade away suddenly like the grass.
In the morning it is green, and groweth up; but in the evening it is cut down, dried up, and withered.
90:4-6

56 For when thou art angry all our days are gone: we bring our years to an end, as it were a tale that is told.
The days of our age are threescore years and ten; and though men be so strong that they come to fourscore years, yet is their strength then but labour and sorrow; so soon passeth it away, and we are gone.
90:9-10

57 For he shall deliver thee from the snare of the hunter, and from the noisome pestilence.

He shall defend thee under his wings, and thou shalt be safe under his feathers: his faithfulness and truth shall be thy shield and buckler.

Thou shalt not be afraid for any terror by night; nor for the arrow that flieth by day;

For the pestilence that walketh in darkness; nor for the sickness that destroyeth in the noon-day.

A thousand shall fall beside thee, and ten thousand at thy right hand; but it shall not come nigh thee.

91:3-7

58 The righteous shall flourish like a palm-tree: and shall spread abroad like a cedar in Libanus.

92:11

59 He that planted the ear, shall he not hear? or he that made the eye, shall he not see?

94:9

60 O come, let us sing unto the Lord: let us heartily rejoice in the strength of our salvation.

Let us come before his presence with thanksgiving, and shew ourselves glad in him with psalms.

For the Lord is a great God, and a great King above all gods.

In his hand are all the corners of the earth: and the strength of the hills is his also.

The sea is his, and he made it: and his hands prepared the dry land.

95:1-5

61 Venite, exultemus

Vulgate 95:1

62 For he is the Lord our God; and we are the people of his pasture, and the sheep of his hand.

To-day if ye will hear his voice, harden not your hearts; as in the provocation, and as in the day of temptation in the wilderness.

95:7-8

63 Whoso hath also a proud look and high stomach, I will not suffer him.

101:7

64 The days of man are but as grass: for he flourisheth as a flower of the field.

For as soon as the wind goeth over it, it is gone; and the place thereof shall know it no more.

103:15-16

65 O give thanks unto the Lord, for he is gracious: and his mercy endureth for ever.

106:1

66 They that go down to the sea in ships, and occupy their business in great waters;

These men see the works of the Lord, and his wonders in the deep.

For at his word the stormy wind ariseth, which lifteth up the waves thereof.

They are carried up to the heaven, and down again to the deep: their soul melteth away because of the trouble.

They reel to and fro, and stagger like a drunken man, and are at their wit's end.

107:23-27

67 Then are they glad, because they are at rest: and so he bringeth them unto the haven where they would be.

107:30

68 The Lord said unto my Lord, Sit thou on my right hand, until make thine enemies thy footstool.

110:1

69 The fear of the Lord is the beginning of wisdom; a good understanding have all they that do thereafter; the praise of it endureth for ever.

111:10

70 The sea saw that, and fled: Jordan was driven back.

The mountains skipped like rams, and the little hills like young sheep.

114:3-4

71 Their idols are silver and gold, even the work of men's hands.

They have mouths, and speak not; eyes have they, and see not.

They have ears, and hear not; noses have they, and smell not.

They have hands, and handle not; feet have they, and walk not neither speak they through their throat.

115:4-7

72 The snares of death compassed me round about; and the pains of hell gat hold upon me.

116:3

73 And why? thou hast delivered my soul from death, mine eyes from tears; and my feet from falling.

I will walk before the Lord in the land of the living.

I believed, and therefore will I speak; but I was sore troubled: I said in my haste, All men are liars.

116:8-10

74 Blessed be he that cometh in the Name of the Lord: we have wished you good luck, ye that are of the house of the Lord.

118:26

75 I will lift up mine eyes unto the hills, from whence cometh my help.

121:1

76 He will not suffer thy foot to be moved: and he
that keepeth thee will not sleep.

121:3

77 The Lord himself is thy keeper: the Lord is thy
defence upon thy right hand;
So that the sun shall not burn thee by day,
neither the moon by night.
The Lord shall preserve thee from all evil: yea,
it is even he that shall keep thy soul.
The Lord shall preserve thy going out, and thy
coming in, from this time forth for evermore.

121:5-8

78 I was glad when they said unto me, We will go
into the house of the Lord.

122:1

79 Turn our captivity, O Lord, as the rivers in the
south.
They that sow in tears shall reap in joy.
He that now goeth on his way weeping, and
beareth forth good seed, shall doubtless come
again with joy, and bring his sheaves with him.

126:5-7

80 Thy wife shall be as the fruitful vine upon the
walls of thine house.
Thy children like the olive-branches round about
thy table.

128:3-4

81 Yea, that thou shalt see thy children's children,
and peace upon Israel.

128:7

82 Out of the deep have I called unto thee, O Lord:
Lord, hear my voice.
O let thine ears consider well the voice of my
complaint.
If thou, Lord, wilt be extreme to mark what is
done amiss, O Lord, who may abide it?

130:1-3

83 By the waters of Babylon we sat down and
wept, when we remembered thee, O Sion.
As for our harps, we hanged them up upon the
trees that are therein.
For they that led us away captive required of us
then a song, and melody, in our heaviness: Sing
us one of the songs of Sion.
How shall we sing the Lord's song in a strange
land?
If I forget thee, O Jerusalem, let my right hand
forget her cunning.
If I do not remember thee, let my tongue cleave
to the roof of my mouth; yea, if I prefer not
Jerusalem in my mirth.

137:1-6

84 O Lord, thou hast searched me out, and known
me; thou knowest my down-sitting, and mine
up-rising; thou understandest my thoughts long
before.
Thou art about my path, and about my bed, and
spiest out all my ways.
For lo, there is not a word in my tongue, but
thou, O Lord, knowest it altogether.

139:1-3

85 Such knowledge is too wonderful and excellent
for me: I cannot attain unto it.

139:5

86 Yea, the darkness is no darkness with thee, but
the night is as clear as the day: the darkness
and light to thee are both alike.

139:7

87 Thine eyes did see my substance, yet being imperfect, and in thy book were all my members
written.

139:15

88 Man is like a thing of nought: his time passeth
away like a shadow.

144:4

89 O put not your trust in princes, nor in any child
of man; for there is no help in them.
For when the breath of man goeth forth he shall
turn again to his earth; and then all his thoughts
perish.

146:2-3

90 The Lord looseth men out of prison: the Lord
giveth sight to the blind.
The Lord helpeth them that are fallen: the Lord
careth for the righteous.
The Lord careth for the strangers: he defendeth
the fatherless and widow; as for the way of the
ungodly, he turneth it upside down.

146:7-9

91 The Lord doth build up Jerusalem, and gather together the out-casts of Israel.
He healeth those that are broken in heart, and
giveth medicine to heal their sickness.
He telleth the number of the stars, and calleth
them all by their names.

147:2-4

92 He hath no pleasure in the strength of an horse:
neither delighteth he in any man's legs.

147:10

93 Let the saints be joyful with glory: let them
rejoice in their beds.
Let the praises of God be in their mouth, and a
two-edged sword in their hands.

149:5-6

94 Praise him in the cymbals and dances: praise him
upon the strings and pipe.
Praise him upon the well-tuned cymbals: praise
him upon the loud cymbals.

150:4-5

**95** Not unto us, O Lord, not unto us, but unto thy
Name give the praise; for thy loving mercy, and
for thy truth's sake.
115:1

**Pudney, John Sleigh** (1909–77) British poet and writer.
His poetry collections include *Ten Summers* (1944) and *Collected
Poems* (1957); novels include *Jacobson's Ladder* (1938), *The Net*
(1952), and *Thin Air* (1961). He has written many other books,
plays, and film scripts.

**1** Do not despair
For Johnny head-in-air;
He sleeps as sound
As Johnny underground.
*For Johnny*

**2** Better by far
For Johnny-the-bright-star,
To keep your head
And see his children fed.
*For Johnny*

**Pyrrhus** (319–272 BC) King of Epirus. An expansionist, he built
an empire that was based on victories incurring heavy loss of life,
especially at Asculum. Hence the expression 'Pyrrhic victory'.

**1** Such another victory and we are ruined.
Commenting upon the costliness of his victory at the Battle of
Asculum, 279 BC
*Life of Pyrrhus* (Plutarch)

# Q

**Quarles, Francis** (1592–1644) English poet. A Royalist, he
wrote pamphlets in defence of Charles I. His verse collections
include *Divine Poems* (1633) and *Emblems* (1635).

**1** I wish thee as much pleasure in the reading, as I
had in the writing.
*Emblems,* 'To the Reader'

**2** My soul; sit thou a patient looker-on;
Judge not the play before the play is done:
Her plot hath many changes, every day
Speaks a new scene; the last act crowns the
play.
*Epigram, Respice Finem*

**Queensberry, William Douglas, 4th Duke of**
(1724–1810) British peer, known for his extravagance. Known as
'Old Q', he became vice-admiral of Scotland (1767–76).

**1** What is there to make so much of in the
Thames? I am quite tired of it. Flow, flow, flow,

always the same.
*Century of Anecdote* (J. Timbs)

**Quesnay, François** (1694–1774) French economist.
Originally physician to Louis XV, he concentrated on economics
after 1756; his books include *Tableau économique* (1758).

**1** *Laissez faire, laissez passer.*
Let it be, let it pass.
Attrib.

**Quincy, Josiah** (1772–1864) US statesman and lawyer. A
member of the House of Representatives (1805–13), he became
mayor of Boston (1823–29) and president of Harvard (1829–45).
His books include *A History of Harvard University* (1840).

**1** As it will be the right of all, so it will be the duty
of some, definitely to prepare for a separation,
amicably if they can, violently if they must.
*Abridgement of Debates of Congress,* Vol. IV, 14 Jan 1811

# R

**Rabelais, François** (1483–1553) French humanist and
satirist. He is best known for his *Pantagruel* (1532) and *Gargantua*
(1534), which are renowned for their bawdiness.

**1** I drink for the thirst to come.
*Gargantua,* Bk. I, Ch. 5

**2** Appetite comes with eating.
*Gargantua,* Bk. I, Ch. 5

**3** In their rules there was only one clause: Do
what you will.
Referring to the fictional Abbey of Thélème
*Gargantua,* Bk. I, Ch. 57

**4** Man never found the deities so kindly
As to assure him that he'd live tomorrow.
*Pantagruel,* Bk. III, Ch. 2

**5** Not everyone is a debtor who wishes to be; not
everyone who wishes makes creditors.
*Pantagruel,* Bk. III, Ch. 3

**6** Nature abhors a vacuum.
Attrib.

**7** I owe much; I have nothing; the rest I leave to
the poor.
Last words
Attrib.

**8** Ring down the curtain, the farce is over.
Last words
Attrib.

**9** I am going in search of a great perhaps.
Last words
Attrib.

**Rachmaninov, Sergei** (1873–1943) Russian composer,
pianist, and conductor, living mostly in the USA after 1917. His
works include operas, symphonies, and piano concertos.

**1** My dear hands. Farewell, my poor hands.
On being informed that he was dying from cancer
*The Great Pianists* (H. Schonberg)

**Racine, Jean** (1639–99) French dramatist. His classical verse tragedies include *Andromaque* (1667), *Bérénice* (1670), and *Phèdre* (1677). His last religious dramas were *Esther* (1689) and *Athalie* (1691).

1 Oh, I have loved him too much to feel no hate for him.
*Andromaque*, II:1

2 Now my innocence begins to weigh me down.
*Andromaque*, III:1

3 I loved you when you were inconstant. What should I have done if you had been faithful?
*Andromaque*, IV:5

4 Crime, like virtue, has its degrees.
*Phèdre*, IV:2

**Rae, John** (1931– ) British schoolmaster and writer. His books include *The Custard Boys* (1960), *Christmas is Coming* (1976), and *The Public School Revolution 1964–79* (1981).

1 War is, after all, the universal perversion. We are all tainted: if we cannot experience our perversion at first hand we spend our time reading war stories, the pornography of war; or seeing war films, the blue films of war; or titillating our senses ·with the imagination of great deeds, the masturbation of war.
*The Custard Boys*, Ch. 6

**Raglan, FitzRoy James Henry Somerset, 1st Baron** (1788–1855) British field marshal. He served with distinction in the Napoleonic Wars but was criticized for his strategy as commander in the Crimean War.

1 Don't carry away that arm till I have taken off my ring.
Request immediately after his arm had been amputated following the battle of Waterloo
*Dictionary of National Biography*

**Raleigh, Sir Walter** (1554–1618) English explorer and writer. A favourite of Elizabeth I, he introduced the potato and tobacco plant from America into England. Under James I he was imprisoned for treason and eventually executed.

1 If all the world and love were young,
And truth in every shepherd's tongue,
These pretty pleasures might me move
To live with thee, and be thy love.
*Answer to Marlow*

2 Fain would I climb, yet fear I to fall.
Written on a window pane. For the reply *see* ELIZABETH I
Attrib.

3 Even such is Time, that takes in trust
Our youth, our joys, our all we have,
And pays us but with age and dust;
Who in the dark and silent grave,
When we have wandered all our ways,
Shuts up the story of our days;
But from this earth, this grave, this dust,
My God shall raise me up, I trust.
Written on the night before his execution
Attrib.

4 The world itself is but a large prison, out of which some are daily led to execution.
Said after his trial for treason, 1603
Attrib.

5 'Tis a sharp remedy, but a sure one for all ills.
Referring to the executioner's axe just before he was beheaded
Attrib.

6 So the heart be right, it is no matter which way the head lies.
On laying his head on the executioner's block
Attrib.

7 I have a long journey to take, and must bid the company farewell.
Last words
*Sir Walter Raleigh* (Edward Thompson), Ch. 26

**Raleigh, Sir Walter Alexander** (1861–1922) British scholar and critic. He wrote several books on English literature and the first volume of a history of the RAF (1922).

1 We could not lead a pleasant life,
And 'twould be finished soon,
If peas were eaten with the knife,
And gravy with the spoon.
Eat slowly: only men in rags
And gluttons old in sin
Mistake themselves for carpet bags
And tumble victuals in.
*Laughter from a Cloud*, 'Stans puer ad mensam'

1 I wish I loved the Human Race;
I wish I loved its silly face;
I wish I liked the way it walks;
I wish I liked the way it talks;
And when I'm introduced to one
I wish I thought *What Jolly Fun!*
*Laughter from a Cloud*, 'Wishes of an Elderly Man'

2 An anthology is like all the plums and orange peel picked out of a cake.
Letter to Mrs Robert Bridges, 15 Jan 1915

**Ramanujan, Srinivasa** (1887–1920) Indian mathematician, who went to England in 1914 to carry out research. He is known for his theories of numbers and continued fractions.

1 No, it is a very interesting number, it is the smallest number expressible as a sum of two cubes in two different ways.
The mathematician G. H. Hardy had referred to the number – 1729 – on the back of a taxi cab, as 'dull'. The two ways are $1^3 + 12^3$ and $9^3 + 10^3$.
*Collected Papers of Srinivasa Ramanujan*

**Raphael, Frederic** (1931– ) British author of novels, short stories, and screenplays. His books include *A Wild Surmise* (1961) and *The Glittering Prizes* (1976); he wrote the screenplays for *Darling* (1965), *Far From the Madding Crowd* (1967), and *Rogue Male* (1976).

1 This is the city of perspiring dreams.
Referring to Cambridge
*The Glittering Prizes: An Early Life*, III

**2** We thought philosophy ought to be patient and unravel people's mental blocks. Trouble with doing that is, once you've unravelled them, their heads fall off.

*The Glittering Prizes: A Double Life*, III:2

**3** I come from suburbia, Dan, personally, I don't ever want to go back. It's the one place in the world that's further away than anywhere else.

*The Glittering Prizes: A Sex Life*, I:3

**4** Great restaurants are, of course, nothing but mouth-brothels. There is no point in going to them if one intends to keep one's belt buckled.

*The Sunday Times Magazine*, 25 Sep 1977

**Rattigan, Sir Terence** (1911–77) British dramatist. His popular plays include *French Without Tears* (1936), *The Deep Blue Sea* (1952), and *Ross* (1960).

**1** A nice respectable, middle-class, middle-aged maiden lady, with time on her hands and the money to help her pass it . . . Let us call her Aunt Edna . . . Aunt Edna is universal, and to those who feel that all the problems of the modern theatre might be saved by her liquidation, let me add that . . . She is also immortal.

*Collected Plays*, Vol II, Preface

**2** You can be in the Horse Guards and still be common, dear.

*Separate Tables*: 'Table Number Seven'

**Reade, Charles** British novelist and dramatist. Of his many novels the best known is *The Cloister and the Hearth* (1861), a historical romance.

**1** Make 'em laugh; make 'em cry; make 'em wait.

Advice to an aspiring writer
Attrib.

**Reagan, Ronald** (1911– ) US Republican president (1981– ). He entered politics as governor of California (1966–74) after a career as a film actor.

**1** Please assure me that you are all Republicans!

Addressing the surgeons on being wheeled into the operating theatre for an emergency operation after an assassination attempt
*Presidential Anecdotes* (P. Boller)

**2** No one can kill Americans and brag about it. No one.

*The Observer*, 'Sayings of the Week', 27 Apr 1986

**3** You know, by the time you reach my age, you've made plenty of mistakes if you've lived your life properly

*The Observer*, 'Sayings of the Week', 8 Mar 1987

**4** They say hard work never hurt anybody, but I figure why take the chance.

Attrib.

**Reed, Henry** (1914– ) British poet and radio dramatist. His collected poems appeared in *A Map of Verona* (1946) and *The Lessons of the War* (1970). He also wrote many plays for radio.

**1** And the various holds and rolls and throws and breakfalls
Somehow or other I always seemed to put
In the wrong place. And as for war, my wars
Were global from the start.

*A Map of Verona*, 'Lessons of the War', III

**2** Today we have naming of parts. Yesterday,
We had daily cleaning. And tomorrow morning
We shall have what to do after firing. But today,
Today we have naming of parts.

*Naming of Parts*

**3** They call it easing the Spring: it is perfectly easy
If you have any strength in your thumb: like the bolt,
And the breech, and the cocking-piece, and the point of balance,
Which in our case we have not got.

*Naming of Parts*

**4** In a civil war, a general must know – and I'm afraid it's a thing rather of instinct than of practice – he must know exactly when to move over to the other side.

*Not a Drum was Heard: The War Memoirs of General Gland*

**5** If one doesn't get birthday presents it can remobilize very painfully the persecutory anxiety which usually follows birth.

*The Primal Scene, as it were*

**6** I have known her pass the whole evening without mentioning a single book, or *in fact anything unpleasant* at all.

*A Very Great Man Indeed*

**Reed, Rex** (1938– ) US columnist and actor. He appeared in the film of *Myra Breckinridge* and also wrote a showbiz column. His collections include *Do You Really Sleep in the Nude?*

**1** In Hollywood, if you don't have happiness you send out for it.

*Colombo's Hollywood* (J. R. Colombo), 'Hollywood the Bad'

**Reedy, George Edward** (1917– ) US government official and writer. He held various appointments as aide and consultant to President Lyndon Johnson. His books include *The Twilight of the Presidency* (1970).

**1** You know that nobody is strongminded around a President . . . it is always: 'yes sir', 'no sir' (the 'no sir' comes when he asks whether you're dissatisfied).

*The White House* (ed. R. Gordon Hoxie)

**Reich, Wilhelm** (1897–1957) Austrian-born US psychiatrist, who became known for his theory that a universal energy is released during sexual intercourse.

**1** The few bad poems which occasionally are created during abstinence are of no great interest.

*The Sexual Revolution*

**Reinhardt, Gottfried** (1911– ) Austrian film producer, living in the USA. His films include *The Red Badge of Courage* (1951) and *Town without Pity* (1961).

1 Money is good for bribing yourself through the inconveniences of life.

*Picture* (Lillian Ross), 'Looks Like We're Still in Business'

**Reith, John Charles Walsham, Baron** (1889–1971) British administrator. He became the first general manager of the BBC and subsequently director general (1927–38). The annual Reith lectures were named after him.

1 You can't think rationally on an empty stomach, and a whole lot of people can't do it on a full one either.

Attrib.

**Remarque, Erich Maria** (1898–1970) German novelist. After being wounded in World War I he wrote *All Quiet on the Western Front* (1929), which became a bestseller. It was banned by the Nazis, and he lived abroad after 1932, eventually becoming a US citizen. Other books include *Three Comrades* (1937) and *Flotsam* (1941).

1 All Quiet on the Western Front

Title of novel

**Renard, Jules** (1894–1910) French writer. His works include the autobiographical *Poil de carotte* (1894) and *Journal* (1925–27) as well as accounts of animal and rural life.

1 Be modest! It is the kind of pride least likely to offend.

*Journal*

2 The profession of letters is, after all, the only one in which one can make no money without being ridiculous.

*Journal*

3 There is false modesty, but there is no false pride.

*Journal*

**Rendall, Montague John** (1862–1950) British schoolmaster. He became headmaster of Winchester College (1911–24) and then vice-president of the BBC (1927–33).

1 Nation shall speak peace unto nation.

Motto of BBC, 1927

**Renoir, Pierre Auguste** (1841–1919) French impressionist painter. An influential figure in the early years of the movement, he abandoned impressionism after 1882, his later paintings being mostly of nudes.

1 The pain passes, but the beauty remains.

Explaining why he still painted when his hands were twisted with arthritis
Attrib.

2 I just keep painting till I feel like pinching. Then I know it's right.

Explaining how he achieved such lifelike flesh tones in his nudes
Attrib.

**Revson, Charles** (1906–75) US business tycoon, cofounder and president of the cosmetic firm Revlon.

1 In the factory we make cosmetics. In the store we sell hope.

*Fire and Ice* (A. Tobias)

**Rexford, Eben** (1848–1916) British songwriter.

1 Darling, I am growing old,
Silver threads among the gold.

*Silver Threads Among the Gold*

**Reynolds, Sir Joshua** (1723–92) British portrait painter. The most fashionable portraitist of his day, he painted Dr Johnson, Gibbon, Garrick, and the Duchess of Devonshire.

1 If you have great talents, industry will improve them: if you have but moderate abilities, industry will supply their deficiency.

Discourse to Students of the Royal Academy, 11 Dec 1769

2 A mere copier of nature can never produce anything great.

Discourse to Students of the Royal Academy, 14 Dec 1770

3 He who resolves never to ransack any mind but his own, will be soon reduced, from mere barrenness, to the poorest of all imitations; he will be obliged to imitate himself, and to repeat what he has before often repeated.

Discourse to Students of the Royal Academy, 10 Dec 1774

4 I should desire that the last words which I should pronounce in this Academy, and from this place, might be the name of – Michael Angelo.

Discourse to Students of the Royal Academy, 10 Dec 1790

**Reynolds, Malvina** (1900–78) US folksinger and songwriter.

1 They're all made out of ticky-tacky, and they all look just the same.

*Little Boxes*, song describing a housing scheme built in the hills south of San Francisco.

**Rhodes, Cecil John** (1853–1902) South African financier and statesman. Prime minister of Cape Colony (1890–96), he helped to found Rhodesia, which was named in his honour.

1 The real fact is that I could no longer stand their eternal cold mutton.

Explaining why he had left his friends in England and come to South Africa
*Cecil Rhodes* (G. le Sueur)

2 Remember that you are an Englishman, and have consequently won first prize in the lottery of life.

*Dear Me* (Peter Ustinov), Ch. 4

3 How can I possibly dislike a sex to which Your Majesty belongs?

Replying to Queen Victoria's suggestion that he disliked women
*Rhodes* (Lockhart)

4 So little done, so much to do.

Last words

**Rhys, Jean** (1894–1979) Dominican-born British novelist. Her books include *Voyage in the Dark* (1934), *Good Morning, Midnight* (1939), and *The Wide Sargasso Sea* (1966).

**1** Next week, or next month, or next year I'll kill myself. But I might as well last out my month's rent, which has been paid up, and my credit for breakfast in the morning.

*Good Morning, Midnight*, Pt. II

**2** I often want to cry. That is the only advantage women have over men – at least they can cry.

*Good Morning, Midnight*, Pt. II

**3** The feeling of Sunday is the same everywhere, heavy, melancholy, standing still. Like when they say, 'As it was in the beginning, is now, and ever shall be, world without end.'

*Voyage in the Dark*, Ch. 4

**Rice, Grantland** (1880–1954) US sportswriter, known widely as 'Granny'.

**1** For when the One Great Scorer comes
To write against your name,
He marks – not that you won or lost –
But how you played the game.

*Alumnus Football*

**Rice, Sir Stephen** (1637–1715) English politician.

**1** I will drive a coach and six horses through the Act of Settlement.

*State of the Protestants of Ireland* (W. King), Ch. 3

**Rice-Davies, Mandy** (1944– ) British call girl, who was involved, with Christine Keeler, in the Profumo scandal and the trial of Dr Stephen Ward.

**1** He would, wouldn't he?

Of Lord Astor, when told that he had repudiated her evidence at the trial of Stephen Ward, 29 June 1963

**Richards, Sir Gordon** (1904–86) British champion jockey and later horse trainer.

**1** Mother always told me my day was coming, but I never realized that I'd end up being the shortest knight of the year.

Referring to his diminutive size, on learning of his knighthood
Attrib.

**Richards, I(vor) A(rmstrong)** (1893–1979) British critic, linguist, and poet. His publications include *Principles of Literary Criticism* (1924) and *Tomorrow Morning Faustus!* (1962).

**1** It is a perfectly possible means of overcoming chaos.

Referring to poetry
*Science and Poetry*

**Richardson, Sir Ralph** (1902–83) British actor who rose to fame during the 1930s. He appeared in many Shakespearean and classical roles as well as in films.

**1** The art of acting consists in keeping people from coughing.

*The Observer*

**2** In music, the punctuation is absolutely strict, the bars and the rests are absolutely defined. But our punctuation cannot be quite strict, because we have to relate it to the audience. In other words, we are continually changing the score.

*The Observer Magazine*, 'Tynan on Richardson', 18 Dec 1977

**3** The most precious things in speech are pauses.

Attrib.

**Richelieu, Armand Jean du Plessis, Cardinal de** (1585–1642) French statesman. He was advisor to Louis XIII's mother and became the king's chief minister in 1629. He suppressed the Huguenots and planned France's strategy in the Thirty Years' War.

**1** If you give me six lines written by the most honest man, I will find something in them to hang him.

Exact wording uncertain
Attrib.

**Richelieu, Armand-Emmanuel du Plessis, Duc de** (1766–1822) French statesman. A monarchist, he fled to Russia during the French Revolution, returning in 1815 to become prime minister under Louis XVIII.

**1** Madame, you must really be more careful. Suppose it had been someone else who found you like this.

Discovering his wife with her lover
*The Book of Lists* (D. Wallechinsky)

**Richler, Mordecai** (1931– ) Canadian novelist now living in England. His novels include *The Apprenticeship of Buddy Kravitz* (1959), *St Urbain's Horseman* (1971), and *Joshua Now and Then* (1981).

**1** Remember this, Griffin. The revolution eats its own. Capitalism re-creates itself.

*Cocksure*, Ch. 22

**2** And furthermore did you know that behind the discovery of America there was a Jewish financier?

*Cocksure*, Ch. 24

**Richter, Jean Paul** (Johann Paul Friedrich Richter; 1763–1825) German novelist. His novels include *Hesperus* (1795), *Titan* (1800–03), and *Der Komet* (1820–22). He used the pseudonym 'Jean Paul'.

**1** Providence has given to the French the empire of the land, to the English that of the sea, and to the Germans that of the air.

Quoted by Thomas Carlyle

**Ridge, William Pett** (1860–1930) British novelist and dramatist. His novels include *Love at Paddington Green* and *Aunt Bertha*.

**1** When you take the bull by the horns . . . what happens is a toss up.

*Love at Paddington Green*, Ch. 4

**2** 'How did you think I managed at dinner, Clarence?' 'Capitally!' 'I had a knife and two forks left at the end,' she said regretfully.

*Love at Paddington Green*, Ch. 6

**Rilke, Rainer Maria** (1875–1926) Austrian poet. His collections include *Das Stunden Buch* (1905), *Duineser Elegien* (1923), and *Die Sonette an Orpheus* (1923).

1　Spring has returned. The earth is like a child that knows poems.
*Die Sonette an Orpheus*, I, 21

2　The machine threatens all achievement.
*Die Sonette an Orpheus*, II, 10

3　The hero is strangely akin to those who die young.
*Duineser Elegien*, VI

4　Stuck with placards for 'Deathless', that bitter beer that tastes sweet to its drinkers.
*Duineser Elegien*, X

**Rimsky-Korsakov, Nikolai** (1844–1908) Russian composer. One of the 'Mighty Five' nationalist composers, his works include the tone poem *Scheherazade* (1880) and the operas *The Snow Maiden* (1880) and *The Golden Cockerel* (1906).

1　I have already heard it. I had better not go: I will start to get accustomed to it and finally like it.
Referring to music by Debussy
*Conversations with Stravinsky* (Robert Craft and Igor Stravinsky)

**Ripley, R. L.** (1893–1949) US writer and journalist.

1　Believe it or not.
Title of newspaper column

**Rivarol, Antoine de** (1753–1801) French writer and wit.

1　Very good, but it has its *longueurs*.
Giving his opinion of a couplet by a mediocre poet
*Das Buch des Lachens* (W. Scholz)

**Rivera, Antonio** (d. 1936) Spanish Nationalist hero.

1　Fire – without hatred.
Giving the order to open fire at the siege of the Alcázar
*The Siege of the Alcázar* (C. Eby)

**Robbins, Tom** (1936– ) US novelist and short-story writer. His books include *Another Roadside Attraction* (1971) and *Still Life with Woodpecker* (1980).

1　Human beings were invented by water as a device for transporting itself from one place to another.
*Another Roadside Attraction*

**Robespierre, Maximilien François Marie Isidore de** (1758–94) French lawyer and revolutionary. He became a leader of the Jacobins at the beginning of the French Revolution; after Louis XVI's execution he wielded total power on the Committee of Public Safety. Public opinion turned against his Reign of Terror, however, and he was guillotined.

1　Any institution which does not suppose the people good, and the magistrate corruptible, is evil.
*Déclaration des Droits de l'homme*, 24 Apr 1793

**Robin, Leo** (1899– ) US songwriter and lyricist.

1　Thanks For the Memory.
Song title

2　Diamonds Are A Girl's Best Friend.
Song title

**Robinson, Edwin Arlington** (1869–1935) US poet. He made his name with the verse novel *Captain Craig* (1902). Other poems include *Man Against the Sky* (1916) and *Tristam* (1927).

1　I shall have more to say when I am dead.
*John Brown*

**Robinson, James Harvey** (1863–1936) US historian and educator. A pioneer in new teaching methods, his books include *The Development of Modern Europe* (1907) and *The Ordeal of Civilization* (1926).

1　Partisanship is our great curse. We too readily assume that everything has two sides and that it is our duty to be on one or the other.
*The Mind in the Making*

**Robinson, Robert** (1927– ) British writer and broadcaster. His books include *Landscape with Dead Dons* (1956) and *Robinson Country* (1983).

1　The national dish of America is menus.
BBC TV programme, *Robinson's Travels*, Aug 1977

2　Certain people are born with natural false teeth.
BBC radio programme, *Stop the Week*, 1977

**Roche, Sir Boyle** (1743–1807) British politician.

1　What has posterity done for us?
Speech, Irish Parliament, 1780

2　Mr Speaker, I smell a rat; I see him forming in the air and darkening the sky; but I'll nip him in the bud.
Attrib.

**Rochefort, (Victor) Henri, Marquis de Rochefort-Luçay** (1830–1913) French journalist, noted for his radical views.

1　My scribbling pays me zero francs per line – not including the white spaces.
Referring to his salary as a writer
*Autant en apportent les mots* (Pedrazzini)

**Rochefoucauld, François, Duc de la** (1613–80) French writer. His literary circle included Mme de Sévigné and the Comtesse de La Fayette. He is best known for his *Maximes*, published in five editions between 1665 and 1678.

1　Self-love is the greatest of all flatterers.
*Maximes*, 2

2　We are all strong enough to bear the misfortunes of others.
*Maximes*, 19

3　We need greater virtues to sustain good fortune than bad.
*Maximes*, 25

4　If we had no faults of our own, we would not take so much pleasure in noticing those of others.
*Maximes*, 31

5   Self-interest speaks all sorts of tongues, and plays all sorts of roles, even that of disinterestedness.
*Maximes*, 39

6   We are never so happy nor so unhappy as we imagine.
*Maximes*, 49

7   To succeed in the world, we do everything we can to appear successful.
*Maximes*, 50

8   There are very few people who are not ashamed of having been in love when they no longer love each other.
*Maximes*, 71

9   If one judges love by its visible effects, it looks more like hatred than like friendship.
*Maximes*, 72

10  The love of justice in most men is simply the fear of suffering injustice.
*Maximes*, 78

11  Silence is the best tactic for him who distrusts himself.
*Maximes*, 79

12  It is more shameful to distrust one's friends than to be deceived by them.
*Maximes*, 84

13  Everyone complains of his memory, but no one complains of his judgement.
*Maximes*, 89

14  In the misfortune of our best friends, we always find something which is not displeasing to us.
*Maximes*, 99

15  The intellect is always fooled by the heart.
*Maximes*, 102

16  One gives nothing so freely as advice.
*Maximes*, 110

17  One had rather malign oneself than not speak of oneself at all.
*Maximes*, 138

18  To refuse praise reveals a desire to be praised twice over.
*Maximes*, 149

19  Hypocrisy is the homage paid by vice to virtue.
*Maximes*, 218

20  The height of cleverness is to be able to conceal it.
*Maximes*, 245

21  There is scarcely a single man sufficiently aware to know all the evil he does.
*Maximes*, 269

22  We only confess our little faults to persuade people that we have no large ones.
*Maximes*, 327

23  The accent of one's birthplace lingers in the mind and in the heart as it does in one's speech.
*Maximes*, 342

24  We seldom attribute common sense except to those who agree with us.
*Maximes*, 347

25  Nothing prevents us from being natural so much as the desire to appear so.
*Maximes*, 431

26  Quarrels would not last so long if the fault were on only one side.
*Maximes*, 496

27  Most usually our virtues are only vices in disguise.
*Maximes*, added to the 4th edition

**Rochester, John Wilmot, Earl of** (1647–80) English courtier and poet. One of the most dissolute companions of Charles II, he wrote many short love poems and longer satirical poems, such as *A Satire against Mankind*.

1   Here lies our sovereign lord the King,
Whose word no man relies on;
He never said a foolish thing,
Nor ever did a wise one.
*See* CHARLES II for a reply
Epitaph on Charles II

**Rogers, Samuel** (1763–1855) British poet. He established his reputation with *The Pleasures of Memory* (1792), later collections including *Human Life* (1819). He declined to become poet laureate on Wordsworth's death.

1   It doesn't much signify whom one marries, for one is sure to find next morning that it was someone else.
*Table Talk* (ed. Alexander Dyce)

2   When a new book is published, read an old one.
Attrib.

**Rogers, Will** (1879–1935) US actor and humorist. He starred in many films and contributed daily articles to the *New York Times* (from 1926). He also wrote several books.

1   You can't say civilization don't advance, however, for in every war they kill you a new way.
*Autobiography*, Ch. 12

2   England elects a Labour Government. When a man goes in for politics over here, he has no time to labour, and any man that labours has no time to fool with politics. Over there politics is an obligation; over here it's a business.
*Autobiography*, Ch. 14

3   Communism is like prohibition, it's a good idea but it won't work.
*Autobiography*, Nov 1927

4   Everything is funny, as long as it's happening to somebody else.
*The Illiterate Digest*

5   Being a hero is about the shortest-lived profession on earth.
*Saturday Review*, 'A Rogers Thesaurus', 25 Aug 1962

**6** Coolidge is a better example of evolution than either Bryan or Darrow, for he knows when not to talk, which is the biggèst asset the monkey possesses over the human.
*Saturday Review*, 'A Rogers Thesaurus', 25 Aug 1962

**7** I don't make jokes – I just watch the government and report the facts.
*Saturday Review*, 'A Rogers Thesaurus', 25 Aug 1962

**8** It has made more liars out of the American people than Golf.
Referring to income tax
*Saturday Review*, 'A Rogers Thesaurus', 25 Aug 1962

**9** The more you read about politics, you got to admit that each party is worse than the other.
*Saturday Review*, 'A Rogers Thesaurus', 25 Aug 1962

**10** A comedian can only last till he either takes himself serious or his audience takes him serious.
Newspaper article, 1931

**11** See what will happen to you if you don't stop biting your fingernails.
Message written on a postcard of the Venus de Milo that he sent to his young niece

**12** So live that you wouldn't be ashamed to sell the family parrot to the town gossip.
Attrib.

**Roland, Madame Marie Jeanne Philipon** (1754– 93) French revolutionary. Her Paris salon was the meeting place for the Girondists (1791–93). After their fall she was tried and guillotined.

**1** *"O liberté! O liberté! Que de crimes on commet en ton nom!"*
Oh liberty! Oh liberty! What crimes are committed in thy name!
Said as she mounted the steps of the guillotine at her execution
Attrib.

**Rolleston, Sir Humphrey** (1862–1944) British physician and medical writer.

**1** First they get *on*, then they get *honour*, then they get *honest*.
Referring to physicians
*Confessions of an Advertising Man* (David Ogilvy)

**Rolmaz, James** (19th century) British songwriter.

**1** Where did you get that hat?
Where did you get that tile?
*Where Did You Get That Hat?*

**Roosevelt, Eleanor** (1884–1962) US writer and lecturer, wife of Franklin D. Roosevelt.

**1** No one can make you feel inferior without your consent.
*This is My Story*

**2** I think if the people of this country can be reached with the truth, their judgment will be in favor of the many, as against the privileged few.
*Ladies' Home Journal*

**3** I used to tell my husband that, if he could make *me* understand something, it would be clear to all the other people in the country.
Newspaper column, 'My Day', 12 Feb 1947

**4** I have spent many years of my life in opposition and I rather like the role.
Letter to Bernard Baruch, 18 Nov 1952

**Roosevelt, Franklin D(elano)** (1882–1945) US Democratic president. Although partially paralysed by polio (from 1921), he was re-elected three times and became an effective war leader.

**1** I murdered my grandmother this morning.
His habitual greeting to any guest at the White House he suspected of paying no attention to what he said
*Ear on Washington* (D. McClellan)

**2** It is fun to be in the same decade with you.
After Churchill had congratulated him on his 60th birthday
*The Hinge of Fate* (Winston S. Churchill), Ch. 4

**3** Stalin hates the guts of all your top people. He thinks he likes me better, and I hope he will continue to do so.
*The Hinge of Fate* (Winston S. Churchill), Ch. 11

**4** Defeat of Germany means the defeat of Japan, probably without firing a shot or losing a life.
*The Hinge of Fate* (Winston S. Churchill), Ch. 25

**5** The best immediate defence of the United States is the success of Great Britain defending itself.
At press conference, 17 Dec 1940.
*Their Finest Hour* (Winston S. Churchill), Ch. 28

**6** The forgotten man at the bottom of the economic pyramid.
Speech on radio, 7 Apr 1932

**7** I pledge you, I pledge myself, to a new deal for the American people.
Speech accepting nomination for presidency, Chicago, 2 July 1932

**8** Let me assert my firm belief that the only thing we have to fear is fear itself.
First Inaugural Address, 4 Mar 1933

**9** In the field of world policy; I would dedicate this nation to the policy of the good neighbor.
First Inaugural Address, 4 Mar 1933

**10** A radical is a man with both feet firmly planted in air.
Broadcast, 26 Oct 1939

**11** We must be the great arsenal of democracy.
Broadcast address to Forum on Current Problems, 29 Dec 1940

**12** We look forward to a world founded upon four essential human freedoms. The first is freedom of speech and expression – everywhere in the world. The second is freedom of every person to worship God in his own way – everywhere in the world. The third is freedom from want . . . everywhere in the world. The fourth is freedom from fear . . . anywhere in the world.
Speech to Congress, 6 Jan 1941

13 Never before have we had so little time in which to do so much.

Radio address, 23 Feb 1942

14 We all know that books burn – yet we have the greater knowledge that books cannot be killed by fire. People die, but books never die. No man and no force can abolish memory . . . In this war, we know, books are weapons.

Message to American Booksellers Association, 23 Apr 1942

15 More than an end to war, we want an end to the beginnings of all wars.

Speech broadcast on the day after his death (13 Apr 1945)

**Roosevelt, Theodore** (1858–1919) US Republican president. His presidency (1901–09) is remembered for his Square Deal programme for social reform and the construction of the Panama Canal.

1 No man is justified in doing evil on the ground of expediency.

*The Strenuous Life*

2 Kings and such like are just as funny as politicians.

*Mr Wilson's War* (John Dos Passos), Ch. 1

3 A man who will steal *for* me will steal *from* me

Firing a cowboy who had applied Roosevelt's brand to a steer belonging to a neighbouring ranch
*Roosevelt in the Bad Lands* (Herman Hagedorn)

4 I wish to preach, not the doctrine of ignoble ease, but the doctrine of the strenuous life.

Speech, Chicago, 10 Apr 1899

5 There is a homely adage which runs 'Speak softly and carry a big stick, you will go far'.

Speech, Minnesota State Fair, 2 Sept 1901

6 A man who is good enough to shed his blood for the country is good enough to be given a square deal afterwards. More than that no man is entitled to, and less than that no man shall have.

Speech at the Lincoln Monument, Springfield, Illinois, 4 June 1903

7 There is no room in this country for hyphenated Americanism.

Speech, New York, 12 Oct 1915

8 There can be no fifty-fifty Americanism in this country. There is room here for only one hundred per cent Americanism.

Speech, Saratoga, 19 July 1918

**Roscommon, Wentworth Dillon, Earl of** (1633–85) Irish-born English poet. His reputation rests on his translation of Horace's *Ars Poetica* (1680) and an *Essay on Translated Verse* (1684).

1 But words once spoke can never be recall'd.

*Art of Poetry*

2 The multitude is always in the wrong.

*Essay on Translated Verse*

**Rose, Billy** (1899–1966) US songwriter and nightclub owner.

1 Does the Spearmint Lose Its Flavour on the Bedpost Overnight?

Title of song

2 Me and My Shadow.

Title of song

**Rosebery, Archibald Philip Primrose, Earl of** (1847–1929) British statesman. Liberal prime minister after Gladstone (1894–95), he was also a well-known racehorse owner and biographer.

1 The Empire is a Commonwealth of Nations.

Speech, Adelaide, 18 Jan 1884

2 Before Irish Home Rule is conceded by the Imperial Parliament, England as the predominant member of the three kingdoms will have to be convinced of its justice and equity.

Speech, House of Lords, 11 Mar 1894

3 It is beginning to be hinted that we are a nation of amateurs.

Rectorial Address, Glasgow, 16 Nov 1900

4 You have to clean your plate.

Said to the Liberal Party
Speech, Chesterfield, 16 Dec 1901

**Ross, Alan Strode Campbell** (1907–78) British professor of linguistics. His books include *Noblesse Oblige* and *What are U.*

1 U and Non-U, An Essay in Sociological Linguistics.

Essay title, *Noblesse Oblige*, 1956

**Ross, Harold W.** (1892–1951) US journalist. He founded, and for many years edited, *The New Yorker.*

1 I've never been in there . . . but there are only three things to see, and I've seen colour reproductions of all of them.

Referring to the Louvre
*A Farewell to Arms* (Ernest Hemingway)

2 I don't want you to think I'm not incoherent.

*The Years with Ross* (James Thurber)

**Rossetti, Christina** (1830–74) British poet and supporter of the Pre-Raphaelite Brotherhood founded by her brother, Dante Gabriel Rossetti. Her collections include *Goblin Market* (1862), *The Prince's Progress* (1866), and *New Poems* (1896). Twice refusing offers of marriage, she lived a solitary, sickly, and religious life.

1 Come to me in the silence of the night;
Come in the speaking silence of a dream;
Come with soft rounded cheeks and eyes as bright
As sunlight on a stream;
Come back in tears,
O memory, hope, love of finished years.

*Echo*

2 For there is no friend like a sister
In calm or stormy weather;
To cheer one on the tedious way,
To fetch one if one goes astray,
To lift one if one totters down,
To strengthen whilst one stands.

*Goblin Market*

3 In the bleak mid-winter
Frosty wind made moan,
Earth stood hard as iron,
Water like a stone;
Snow had fallen, snow on snow,
Snow on snow,
In the bleak mid-winter,
Long ago.

*Mid-Winter*

4 Remember me when I am gone away,
Gone far away into the silent land.

*Remember*

5 Better by far you should forget and smile
Than that you should remember and be sad.

*Remember*

6 Does the road wind up-hill all the way?
Yes, to the very end.
Will the day's journey take the whole long day?
From morn to night, my friend.

*Up-Hill*

7 Will there be beds for me and all who seek?
Yea, beds for all who come.

*Up-Hill*

8 When I am dead, my dearest,
Sing no sad songs for me;
Plant thou no roses at my head,
Nor shady cypress tree:
Be the green grass above me
With showers and dewdrops wet;
And if thou wilt, remember,
And if thou wilt, forget.

*When I am Dead*

9 Who has seen the wind?
Neither you nor I:
But when the trees bow down their heads,
The wind is passing by.

*Who Has Seen the Wind?*

**Rossetti, Dante Gabriel** (1828–82) British painter and poet. With Millais and Holman Hunt he founded the Pre-Raphaelite Brotherhood. His poetic works include *Poems* (1870) and *Ballads and Sonnets* (1881).

1 A sonnet is a moment's monument, –
Memorial from the Soul's eternity
To one dead deathless hour.

*The House of Life*, Introduction

2 Look in my face; my name is Might-have-been.
I am also called No-more, Too-late, Farewell.

*The House of Life*, 'A Superscription'

3 I have been here before.
But when or how I cannot tell:
I know the grass beyond the door,
The sweet keen smell,
The sighing sound, the lights around the shore.

*Sudden Light*

4 The Stealthy School of Criticism.

Letter to the *Athenaeum*, 1871

**Rossini, Gioacchino** (1792–1868) Italian operatic composer. His works include *Tancredi* (1813), *The Barber of Seville* (1816), *The Thieving Magpie* (1817), and *William Tell* (1829).

1 Wagner has lovely moments but awful quarters of an hour.

Remark made to Emile Naumann, April 1867
*Italienische Tondichter* (Naumann)

2 Give me a laundry-list and I'll set it to music.

Attrib.

**Rostand, Edmond** (1868–1918) French poet and dramatist. His verse collection *Les Musardises* (1890) established his reputation as a poet but he then wrote for the theatre, his plays including *La Samaritaine* (1897), *Cyrano de Bergerac* (1898), *L'Aiglon* (1900), and *Chantecler* (1910).

1 My nose is huge! Vile snub-nose, flat-nosed ass, flat-head, let me inform you that I am proud of such an appendage, since a big nose is the proper sign of a friendly, good, courteous, witty, liberal, and brave man, such as I am.

*Cyrano de Bergerac*, I:1

**Rostand, Jean** (1894–1977) French biologist and writer, son of Edmond Rostand. His books include *Pensées d'un biologiste* (1955).

1 A married couple are well suited when both partners usually feel the need for a quarrel at the same time.

*Le Mariage*

2 Never feel remorse for what you have thought about your wife; she has thought much worse things about you.

*Le Mariage*

3 Kill a man, and you are a murderer. Kill millions of men, and you are a conqueror. Kill everyone, and you are a god.

*Pensées d'un biologiste*

**Roth, Philip** (1933– ) US novelist. His books include *Goodbye, Columbus* (1959), *Portnoy's Complaint* (1969), *The Ghost Writer* (1979), and *The Anatomy Lesson* (1983).

1 Doctor, my doctor, what do you say – let's put the id back in yid!

*Portnoy's Complaint*

2 A Jewish man with parents alive is a fifteen-year-old boy, and will remain a fifteen-year-old boy till they die.

*Portnoy's Complaint*

**Rouget de Lisle, Claude Joseph** (1760–1836) French military engineer and composer. He wrote the words and music of *La Marseillaise* in 1792.

1 *Allons, enfants, de la patrie,*
*Le jour de gloire est arrivé.*
Come, children of our native land,
The day of glory has arrived.
*La Marseillaise* (French national anthem)

**Rourke, M. E.** (20th century) US songwriter and lyricist.

1 And when I told them how beautiful you are
They didn't believe me! They didn't believe me!
*They Didn't Believe Me*

**Rousseau, Jean Jacques** (1712–78) French philosopher and writer. His most influential work was *Discours sur les arts et sciences* (1750). Other works include *La Nouvelle Héloïse* (1760) and *Émile* (1762).

1 Man was born free and everywhere he is in chains.
*Du contrat social,* Ch. 1

2 Everything is good when it leaves the Creator's hands; everything degenerates in the hands of man.
*Attrib.*

**Routh, Martin Joseph** (1755–1854) British scholar. He edited a collection of ecclesiastical writings from the second and third centuries in his *Reliquiae Sacrae* (1814–48).

1 Always verify your references.
*Attrib.*

**Rowe, Nicholas** (1674–1718) English dramatist. His plays include *The Fair Penitent* (1703) and *The Tragedy of Jane Shore* (1714). He became poet laureate in 1715.

1 At length the morn and cold indifference came.
*The Fair Penitent,* I:1

**Rowland, Edward** (20th century) British songwriter, known as 'Red Rowley'.

1 A mademoiselle from Armenteers,
She hasn't been kissed for forty years,
Hinky, dinky, par-lee-voo.
Armentières was completely destroyed (1918) in World War I
*Mademoiselle from Armentières*

**Rowland, Helen** (1876–1950) US writer, journalist, and humorist.

1 When you see what some girls marry, you realize how they must hate to work for a living.
*Reflections of a Bachelor Girl*

2 The follies which a man regrets most in his life are those which he didn't commit when he had the opportunity.
*Reflections of a Bachelor Girl*

3 It takes à woman twenty years to make a man of her son, and another woman twenty minutes to make a fool of him.
*Reflections of a Bachelor Girl*

4 Never trust a husband too far, nor a bachelor too near.
*The Rubaiyat of a Bachelor*

**Rowse, A(lfred) L(eslie)** (1903–   ) British historian and critic. *The Elizabethan Renaissance* (1971) is his best-known book. He has identified The Dark Lady of Shakespeare's sonnets.

1 Burnings of people and (what was more valuable) works of art.
*Historical Essays* (H. R. Trevor-Roper)

**Rubens, Paul Alfred** (1875–1917) British dramatist and songwriter.

1 We Don't Want To Lose You But We Think You Ought To Go.
Title of song

**Rubinstein, Helena** (1882–1965) Polish-born US cosmetics manufacturer and business woman, whose products are famous throughout the world.

1 I have always felt that a woman has the right to treat the subject of her age with ambiguity until, perhaps, she passes into the realm of over ninety. Then it is better she be candid with herself and with the world.
*My Life for Beauty,* Pt. I, Ch. 1

2 There are no ugly women, only lazy ones.
*My Life for Beauty,* Pt. II, Ch. 1

**Rue, Danny La** (Daniel Patrick Carroll; 1928–   ) British entertainer and female impersonator.

1 The essence of any blue material is timing. If you sit on it, it becomes vulgar.
*Attrib.*

**Runciman, Sir Steven** (1903–   ) British academic and diplomat. His books include *Byzantine Civilization* (1933) and *A History of the Crusades* (1951–54).

1 Unlike Christianity, which preached a peace that it never achieved, Islam unashamedly came with a sword.
*A History of the Crusades,* 'The First Crusade'

**Runyon, (Alfred) Damon** (1884–1946) US writer and journalist. His works include *Rhymes of the Firing Line* (1912), the collection of short stories *Guys and Dolls* (1932), and the play *A Slight Case of Murder* (1935).

1 All she has to do is to walk around and about Georgie White's stage with only a few light bandages on, and everybody considers her very beautiful, especially from the neck down.
*Furthermore,* 'A Very Honourable Guy'

2 My boy . . . always try to rub up against money, for if you rub up against money long enough, some of it may rub off on you.
*Furthermore,* 'A Very Honourable Guy'

3 More than Somewhat.
Title of a collection of stories

**4** And you cannot tell by the way a party looks or how he lives in this town, if he has any scratch, because many a party who is around in automobiles, and wearing good clothes, and chucking quite a swell is nothing but a phonus bolonus and does not have any real scratch whatever.
*More than Somewhat, 'The Snatching of Bookie Bob'*

**5** She is a smart old broad. It is a pity she is so nefarious.
*Runyon à la carte, 'Broadway Incident'*

**6** At such an hour the sinners are still in bed resting up from their sinning of the night before, so they will be in good shape for more sinning a little later on.
*Runyon à la carte, 'The Idyll of Miss Sarah Brown'*

**7** I once knew a chap who had a system of just hanging the baby on the clothes line to dry and he was greatly admired by his fellow citizens for having discovered a wonderful innovation on changing a diaper.
*Short Takes, 'Diaper Dexterity'*

**8** A free-loader is a confirmed guest. He is the man who is always willing to come to dinner.
*Short Takes, 'Free-Loading Ethics'*

**9** He is without strict doubt a Hoorah Henry, and he is generally figured as nothing but a lob as far as doing anything useful in this world is concerned.
*Short Takes, 'Tight Shoes'*

**10** These citizens are always willing to bet that what Nicely-Nicely dies of will be over-feeding and never anything small like pneumonia, for Nicely-Nicely is known far and wide as a character who dearly loves to commit eating.
*Take it Easy, 'Lonely Heart'*

**Ruskin, John** (1819–1900) British art critic and writer on sociology and economics. His books include *Modern Painters* (1843–60), *The Seven Lamps of Architecture* (1849), and *Munera Pulveris* (1862).

**1** No person who is not a great sculptor or painter can be an architect. If he is not a sculptor or painter, he can only be a *builder*.
*Lectures on Architecture and Painting*

**2** Life without industry is guilt, and industry without art is brutality.
*Lectures on Art, 'The Relation of Art to Morals', 23 Feb 1870*

**3** What is poetry? The suggestion, by the imagination, of noble grounds for the noble emotions.
*Modern Painters, Vol. III*

**4** Mountains are the beginning and the end of all natural scenery.
*Modern Painters, Vol. IV*

**5** If a book is worth reading, it is worth buying.
*Sesame and Lilies, 'Of Kings' Treasuries'*

**6** All books are divisible into two classes, the books of the hour, and the books of all time.
*Sesame and Lilies, 'Of Kings' Treasuries'*

**7** How long most people would look at the best book before they would give the price of a large turbot for it!
*Sesame and Lilies, 'Of Kings' Treasuries'*

**8** When we build let us think that we build for ever.
*The Seven Lamps of Architecture, 'The Lamp of Memory'*

**9** Remember that the most beautiful things in the world are the most useless, peacocks and lilies for instance.
*The Stones of Venice, Vol. I, Ch. 2*

**10** To make your children *capable of honesty* is the beginning of education.
*Time and Tide, Letter VIII*

**11** Fine art is that in which the hand, the head, and the heart of man go together.
*The Two Paths, Lecture II*

**12** Nobody cares much at heart about Titian, only there is a strange undercurrent of everlasting murmur about his name, which means the deep consent of all great men that he is greater than they.
*The Two Paths, Lecture II*

**13** No human being, however great, or powerful was ever so free as a fish.
*The Two Paths, Lecture V*

**14** Whereas it has long been known and declared that the poor have no right to the property of the rich, I wish it also to be known and declared that the rich have no right to the property of the poor.
*Unto this Last, Essay III*

**15** I have seen, and heard, much of Cockney impudence before now; but never expected to hear a coxcomb ask two hundred guineas for flinging a pot of paint in the public's face.
On Whistler's painting 'Nocturne in Black and Gold'
*Letter, 18 June 1877*

**16** What have we to say to India?
Referring to the completion of the British-Indian cable
*Attrib.*

**Russell, Bertrand Arthur William, Earl** (1872–1970) British philosopher. His many books include *Principia Mathematica* (with A. N. Whitehead; 1910) and *Our Knowledge of the External World* (1914). He was an ardent pacifist and campaigner for nuclear disarmament.

**1** Three passions, simple but overwhelmingly strong, have governed my life: the longing for love, the search for knowledge, and unbearable pity for the suffering of mankind.
*The Autobiography of Bertrand Russell, Prologue*

**2** I was told that the Chinese said they would bury me by the Western Lake and build a shrine to my memory. I have some slight regret that this did not happen, as I might have become a god, which would have been very *chic* for an atheist.
*The Autobiography of Bertrand Russell, Vol. II, Ch. 3*

**3** One of the symptoms of approaching nervous breakdown is the belief that one's work is terribly important. If I were a medical man, I should prescribe a holiday to any patient who considered his work important.
*The Autobiography of Bertrand Russell*, Vol. II, Ch. 5

**4** . . . the nuns who never take a bath without wearing a bathrobe all the time. When asked why, since no man can see them, they reply 'Oh, but you forget the good God.'
*The Basic Writings*, Pt. II, Ch. 7

**5** The megalomaniac differs from the narcissist by the fact that he wishes to be powerful rather than charming, and seeks to be feared rather than loved. To this type belong many lunatics and most of the great men of history.
*The Conquest of Happiness*

**6** There are two motives for reading a book: one, that you enjoy it, the other that you can boast about it.
*The Conquest of Happiness*

**7** Man is not a solitary animal, and so long as social life survives, self-realization cannot be the supreme principle of ethics.
*History of Western Philosophy*, 'Romanticism'

**8** The more you are talked about, the more you will wish to be talked about. The condemned murderer who is allowed to see the account of his trial in the Press is indignant if he finds a newspaper which has reported it inadequately. . . . Politicians and literary men are in the same case.
*Human Society in Ethics and Politics*

**9** Of all forms of caution, caution in love is perhaps the most fatal to true happiness.
*Marriage and Morals*

**10** Mathematics may be defined as the subject in which we never know what we are talking about, nor whether what we are saying is true.
*Mysticism and Logic*, Ch. 4

**11** Pure mathematics consists entirely of assertions to the effect that, if such and such a proposition is true of *anything*, then such and such another proposition is true of that thing. It is essential not to discuss whether the first proposition is really true, and not to mention what the anything is, of which it is supposed to be true.
*Mysticism and Logic*, Ch. 5

**12** Organic life, we are told, has developed gradually from the protozoon to the philosopher, and this development, we are assured, is indubitably an advance. Unfortunately it is the philosopher, not the protozoon, who gives us this assurance.
*Mysticism and Logic*, Ch. 6

**13** Brief and powerless is Man's life; on him and all his race the slow, sure doom falls pitiless and dark.
*Mysticism and Logic*, 'A Free Man's Worship'

**14** No one gossips about other people's secret virtues.
*On Education*

**15** Matter . . . a convenient formula for describing what happens where it isn't.
*An Outline of Philosophy*

**16** It is undesirable to believe a proposition when there is no ground whatever for supposing it true.
*Sceptical Essays*

**17** We have, in fact, two kinds of morality side by side; one which we preach but do not practise, and another which we practise but seldom preach.
*Sceptical Essays*

**18** Mathematics possesses not only truth, but supreme beauty – a beauty cold and austere, like that of sculpture.
*The Study of Mathematics*

**19** In America everybody is of the opinion that he has no social superiors, since all men are equal, but he does not admit that he has no social inferiors.
*Unpopular Essays*

**20** People don't seem to realize that it takes time and effort and preparation to think. Statesmen are far too busy making speeches to think.
*Kenneth Harris Talking To: 'Bertrand Russell'* (Kenneth Harris)

**21** There's a Bible on that shelf there. But I keep it next to Voltaire – poison and antidote.
*Kenneth Harris Talking To: 'Bertrand Russell'* (Kenneth Harris)

**22** Obscenity is what happens to shock some elderly and ignorant magistrate.
*Look* magazine

**23** The collection of prejudices which is called political philosophy is useful provided that it is not called philosophy.
*The Observer*, 'Sayings of the Year', 1962

**24** Not a gentleman; dresses too well
Referring to Anthony Eden
*Six Men* (A. Cooke)

**25** Many people would sooner die than think. In fact they do.
*Thinking About Thinking* (A. Flew)

**26** You may reasonably expect a man to walk a tightrope safely for ten minutes; it would be unreasonable to do so without accident for two hundred years.
On the subject of nuclear war between the USA and the Soviets
*The Tightrope Men* (D. Bagley)

**27** Few people can be happy unless they hate some other person, nation or creed.
Attrib.

**28** Patriots always talk of dying for their country, and never of killing for their country.
Attrib.

**29** Of course not. After all, I may be wrong.
On being asked whether he would be prepared to die for his beliefs
Attrib.

**30** Every time I talk to a savant I feel quite sure that happiness is no longer a possibility. Yet when I talk with my gardener, I'm convinced of the opposite.
Attrib.

**Russell, George William** (1867–1935) Irish poet and dramatist, writing under the pseudonym 'AE'. His works include the play *Deirdre* (1902).

**1** No, thank you, I was born intoxicated.
Refusing a drink that was offered him
*10,000 Jokes, Toasts, and Stories* (L. Copeland)

**Russell, John, Earl** (1792–1878) British statesman. He became an MP in 1813 and was appointed home secretary (1835–39) by Lord Melbourne. He was twice prime minister (1846–52; 1865–66). He resigned as prime minister after the defeat of the second parliamentary reform bill.

**1** Two mothers-in-law.
His answer when asked what he would consider a proper punishment for bigamy
*Anekdotenschatz* (H. Hoffmeister)

**2** A proverb is one man's wit and all men's wisdom.
Attrib.

**Russell, Sir William Howard** (1820–1907) British journalist. As war correspondent for *The Times* he reported the Crimean War, his dispatches being collected in *The War* (1855–56).

**1** They dashed on towards that *thin red line tipped with steel.*
Description of the Russian charge against the British at the battle of Balaclava, 1854
*The British Expedition to the Crimea*

**Rutherford, Ernest, Baron** (1871–1937) British physicist, born in New Zealand. As director of the Cavendish Laboratory at Cambridge he elucidated the nature of radioactivity, discovered the atomic nucleus, and put forward the Rutherford model of the atom.

**1** We haven't the money, so we've got to think.
Attrib.

**Ryle, Gilbert** (1900–76) British philosopher. The editor of *Mind* (1947–71), he summarized his own work in *The Concept of Mind* (1949).

**1** Philosophy is the replacement of category-habits by category-disciplines.
*The Concept of Mind,* Introduction

**2** A myth is, of course, not a fairy story. It is the presentation of facts belonging to one category in the idioms appropriate to another. To explode a myth is accordingly not to deny the facts but to re-allocate them.
*The Concept of Mind,* Introduction

**3** The dogma of the Ghost in the Machine.
*The Concept of Mind,* Ch. 1

# S

**Sackville-West, Vita** (Victoria Sackville-West; 1892–1962) British poet and novelist. She established her reputation as a poet with *The Land* (1926); her novels include *The Edwardians* (1930), *All Passion Spent* (1931), and *Grand Canyon* (1942).

**1** Among the many problems which beset the novelist, not the least weighty is the choice of the moment at which to begin his novel.
*The Edwardians,* Ch. 1

**2** The country habit has me by the heart,
For he's bewitched for ever who has seen,
Not with his eyes but with his vision, Spring
Flow down the woods and stipple leaves with sun.
*The Land,* 'Winter'

**3** Travel is the most private of pleasures. There is no greater bore than the travel bore. We do not in the least want to hear what he has seen in Hong-Kong.
*Passenger to Tehran,* Ch. 1

**4** For observe, that to hope for Paradise is to live in Paradise, a very different thing from actually getting there.
*Passenger to Tehran,* Ch. 1

**5** Those who have never dwelt in tents have no idea either of the charm or of the discomfort of a nomadic existence. The charm is purely romantic, and consequently very soon proves to be fallacious.
*Twelve Days,* Ch. 6

**Sade, Donatien Alphonse François, Marquis de** (1740–1814) French novelist, who wrote whilst in prison for sexual offences. Sadism was named after him; he died in a mental asylum.

**1** All universal moral principles are idle fancies.
*The 120 Days of Sodom*

**Sadleir, Michael** (1888–1957) British author and publisher, best-known for his novel *Fanny by Gaslight* (1940).

**1** Fanny by Gaslight.
Book title

**Sagan, Françoise** (1935– ) French writer, whose works include the novels *Bonjour Tristesse* (1954) and *La femme fardée* (1981) as well as several plays.

**1** Every little girl knows about love. It is only her capacity to suffer because of it that increases.
*Daily Express*

**Sahl, Mort** (1926– ) US political comedian popular in the early 1960s. He also appeared in a few films, such as *All the Young Men* (1960) and *Don't Make Waves* (1967).

1 Would you buy a second-hand car from this man?
Referring to President Nixon
Attrib.

**Saint-Exupéry, Antoine de** (1900–44) French novelist and aviator, whose books are based on his flying experiences. He also wrote *The Little Prince* (1943), a children's story. He failed to return from a mission during World War II.

1 It is such a secret place, the land of tears.
*The Little Prince*, Ch. 7

2 You become responsible, forever, for what you have tamed. You are responsible for your rose.
*The Little Prince*, Ch. 21

**Saint-Lambert, Jean François, Marquis de** (1716–1803) French poet and philosopher.

1 Often I am still listening when the song is over.
*Les Saisons*, 'Le Printemps'

**Saintsbury, George Edward Bateman** (1845–1933) British writer and critic. He wrote many books on the history of English literature and on wines.

1 It is the unbroken testimony of all history that alcoholic liquors have been used by the strongest, wisest, handsomest, and in every way best races of all times.
*Notes on a Cellar-Book*

**Saki** (Hector Hugh Munro; 1870–1916) British writer. He is best-known for his collections of humorous short stories, including *Reginald* (1904), *The Chronicles of Clovis* (1911), and *Beasts and Super-Beasts* (1914).

1 By insisting on having your bottle pointing to the north when the cork is being drawn, and calling the waiter Max, you may induce an impression on your guests which hours of laboured boasting might be powerless to achieve. For this purpose, however, the guests must be chosen as carefully as the wine.
*The Chaplet*

2 Addresses are given to us to conceal our whereabouts.
*Cross Currents*

3 'I believe I take precedence,' he said coldly; 'you are merely the club Bore: I am the club Liar.'
*A Defensive Diamond*

4 Waldo is one of those people who would be enormously improved by death.
Referring to Ralph Waldo Emerson
*The Feast of Nemesis*

5 Children with Hyacinth's temperament don't know better as they grow older; they merely know more.
*Hyacinth*

6 The people of Crete unfortunately make more history than they can consume locally.
*The Jesting of Arlington Stringham*

7 To say that anything was a quotation was an excellent method, in Eleanor's eyes, for withdrawing it from discussion.
*The Jesting of Arlington Stringham*

8 He's simply got the instinct for being unhappy highly developed.
*The Match-Maker*

9 All decent people live beyond their incomes nowadays, and those who aren't respectable live beyond other people's. A few gifted individuals manage to do both.
*The Match-Maker*

10 Oysters are more beautiful than any religion . . . There's nothing in Christianity or Buddhism that quite matches the sympathetic unselfishness of an oyster.
*The Match-Maker*

11 His socks compelled one's attention without losing one's respect.
*Ministers of Grace*

12 The young have aspirations that never come to pass, the old have reminiscences of what never happened.
*Reginald at the Carlton*

13 There may have been disillusionments in the lives of the medieval saints, but they would scarcely have been better pleased if they could have foreseen that their names would be associated nowadays chiefly with racehorses and the cheaper clarets.
*Reginald at the Carlton*

14 The Western custom of one wife and hardly any mistresses.
*Reginald in Russia*

15 But, good gracious, you've got to educate him first.
You can't expect a boy to be vicious till he's been to a good school.
*Reginald in Russia*

16 The cook was a good cook, as cooks go; and as cooks go she went.
*Reginald on Besetting Sins*

17 People may say what they like about the decay of Christianity; the religious system that produced green Chartreuse can never really die.
*Reginald on Christmas Presents*

18 Even the Hooligan was probably invented in China centuries before we thought of him.
*Reginald on House-Parties*

19 Every reformation must have its victims. You can't expect the fatted calf to share the enthusiasm of the angels over the prodigal's return.
*Reginald on the Academy*

20 I think she must have been very strictly brought up, she's so desperately anxious to do the wrong thing correctly.
*Reginald on Worries*

**21** I always say beauty is only sin deep.

*Reginald's Choir Treat*

**22** In baiting a mouse-trap with cheese, always leave room for the mouse.

*The Square Egg*

**23** Sherard Blaw, the dramatist who had discovered himself, and who had given so ungrudgingly of his discovery to the world.

*The Unbearable Bassington*, Ch. 13

**Salinger, J(erome) D(avid)** (1919–  ) US novelist who achieved success with *The Catcher in the Rye* (1951); later books include *Franny and Zooey* (1961) and *Seymour, An Introduction* (1963).

**1** Sex is something I really don't understand too hot. You never know *where* the hell you are. I keep making up these sex rules for myself, and then I break them right away.

*The Catcher in the Rye*, Ch. 9

**2** They didn't act like people and they didn't act like actors. It's hard to explain. They acted more like they knew they were celebrities and all. I mean they were good, but they were *too* good.

*The Catcher in the Rye*, Ch. 17

**Salisbury, Robert Arthur Talbot Gascoyne-Cecil, Marquess of** (1830–1903) British statesman; Conservative prime minister (1886–92; 1895–1900; 1900–02). He was elected an MP in 1853, later becoming Disraeli's foreign secretary (1878).

**1** Written by office boys for office boys.

Reaction to the launch of the *Daily Mail*, 1896
*Northcliffe, an Intimate Biography* (Hamilton Fyfe), Ch. 4

**2** We are part of the community of Europe and we must do our duty as such.

Speech, Caernarvon, 11 Apr 1888

**Salk, Jonas E.** (1914–  ) US virologist, who developed the first antipolio vaccine.

**1** The people – could you patent the sun?

On being asked who owned the patent on his antipolio vaccine
*Famous Men of Science* (S. Bolton)

**Sallust** (Gaius Sallustius Crispus; c. 86–c. 34 BC) Roman historian and politician. He supported Caesar against Pompey and was appointed governor of Numidia, but retired from politics after being accused of corruption. He is remembered for his *Bellum Catilinae* and *Bellum Jugurthinum*.

**1** To like and dislike the same things, that is indeed true friendship.

*Bellum Catilinae*

**Salvandy, Comte de** (1795–1856) French nobleman.

**1** We are dancing on a volcano.

A remark made before the July Revolution in 1830

**Sampson, Anthony** (1926–  ) British writer and journalist. He has written several surveys of Britain, the latest being *The Changing Anatomy of Britain* (1982).

**1** Members rise from CMG (known sometimes in Whitehall as 'Call me God') to the KCMG ('Kindly Call me God') to . . . The GCMG ('God Calls me God').

*Anatomy of Britain*, Ch. 18

**Samuel, Herbert (Louis), Viscount** (1870–1963) British Liberal statesman and philosopher. He was high commissioner for Palestine (1920–25) and home secretary (1916 and 1931). His books include *Philosophy and the Ordinary Man* (1932).

**1** It takes two to make a marriage a success and only one a failure.

*A Book of Quotations*

**2** A truism is on that account none the less true.

*A Book of Quotations*

**3** A library is thought in cold storage.

*A Book of Quotations*

**4** Hansard is history's ear, already listening.

*The Observer*, 'Sayings of the Week', 18 Dec 1949

**5** Without doubt the greatest injury . . . was done by basing morals on myth, for sooner or later myth is recognized for what it is, and disappears. Then morality loses the foundation on which it has been built.

Romanes Lecture, 1947

**6** A difficulty for every solution.

Referring to the Civil Service
Attrib.

**Sand, George** (Aurore Dupin, Baronne Dudevant; 1804–76) French novelist, whose lovers included Alfred de Musset and Chopin.

**1** One is happy as a result of one's own efforts, once one knows the necessary ingredients of happiness – simple tastes, a certain degree of courage, self denial to a point, love of work, and, above all, a clear conscience. Happiness is no vague dream, of that I now feel certain.

*Correspondence*, Vol. V

**2** Liszt said to me today that God alone deserves to be loved. It may be true, but when one has loved a man it is very different to love God.

*Intimate Journal*

**Sandburg, Carl** (1878–1967) US author and poet, who wrote mostly in free verse. His *Complete Poems* were published in 1951. He also wrote books for children and a two-volume biography of Abraham Lincoln (1926, 1939).

**1** Sometime they'll give a war and nobody will come.

*The People, Yes*

**Sanders, George** (1906–72) British film actor, who specialized in playing villains and cads. His films include *Rebecca* (1940) and *All About Eve* (1950).

**1** Dear World, I am leaving you because I am bored. I am leaving you with your worries. Good luck.

Suicide note

**Santayana, George** (1863–1952) US philosopher and poet. His books include *Realms of Being* (1927–40), *Background of my Life* (1945), several volumes of poetry, and a novel.

1 The working of great institutions is mainly the result of a vast mass of routine, petty malice, self interest, carelessness, and sheer mistake. Only a residual fraction is thought.
*The Crime of Galileo*

2 The young man who has not wept is a savage, and the old man who will not laugh is a fool.
*Dialogues in Limbo*, Ch. 3

3 The Bible is literature, not dogma.
*Introduction to the Ethics of Spinoza*

4 Happiness is the only sanction of life; where happiness fails, existence remains a mad and lamentable experiment.
*The Life of Reason*

5 Progress, far from consisting in change, depends on retentiveness. Those who cannot remember the past are condemned to repeat it.
*The Life of Reason*

6 Because there's no fourth class.
On being asked why he always travelled third class
*Living Biographies of the Great Philosophers* (H. Thomas)

7 Life is not a spectacle or a feast; it is a predicament.
*The Perpetual Pessimist* (Sagittarius and George)

8 England is the paradise of individuality, eccentricity, heresy, anomalies, hobbies, and humours.
*Soliloquies in England*, 'The British Character'

9 Trust the man who hesitates in his speech and is quick and steady in action, but beware of long arguments and long beards.
*Soliloquies in England*, 'The British Character'

10 There is no cure for birth and death save to enjoy the interval.
*Soliloquies in England*, 'War Shrines'

11 It is a great advantage for a system of philosophy to be substantially true.
*The Unknowable*

12 For an idea ever to be fashionable is ominous, since it must afterwards be always old-fashioned.
*Winds of Doctrine*, 'Modernism and Christianity'

13 If all the arts aspire to the condition of music, all the sciences aspire to the condition of mathematics.
*The Observer*, 'Sayings of the Week', 4 Mar 1928

**Sarasate (y Navascués), Pablo** (1844–1908) Spanish violinist and composer.

1 A genius! For thirty-seven years I've practiced fourteen hours a day, and now they call me a genius!
On being hailed as a genius by a critic
Attrib.

**Sargent, Epes** (1813–80) US writer and dramatist.

1 A life on the ocean wave,
A home on the rolling deep.
*A Life on the Ocean Wave*

**Sargent, John Singer** (1856–1925) US portrait painter who lived in England, but visited the US annually. As an American citizen he refused a knighthood.

1 Every time I paint a portrait I lose a friend.
Attrib.

**Sargent, Sir Malcolm** (1895–1967) British conductor. He was chief conductor of the London Promenade Concerts from 1957 to 1967.

1 Just a little more reverence, please, and not so much astonishment.
Rehearsing the female chorus in 'For Unto Us a Child is Born' from Handel's *Messiah*
*2500 Anecdotes* (E. Fuller)

**Saroyan, William** (1908–81) US dramatist and writer. His writings include the play *The Time of Your Life* (1939) and the novel *The Human Comedy* (1943).

1 Everybody has got to die, but I have always believed an exception would be made in my case. Now what?
Last words
*Time*, 16 Jan 1984

**Sartre, Jean-Paul** (1905–80) French philosopher, dramatist, and novelist. The principal exponent of existentialism, he wrote a number of books on this subject, including *Critique de la raison dialectique* (1960). His novels include the trilogy *The Roads to Freedom* (1945–49), and *The Respectable Prostitute* (1946) is the best known of his plays.

1 I hate victims who respect their executioners.
*Altona*

2 An American is either a Jew, or an anti-Semite, unless he is both at the same time.
*Altona*

3 Man is condemned to be free.
*Existentialism is a Humanism*

4 Three o'clock is always too late or too early for anything you want to do.
*Nausea*

5 Things are entirely what they appear to be and *behind them* . . . there is nothing.
*Nausea*

6 My thought is *me*: that is why I can't stop. I exist by what I think . . . and I can't prevent myself from thinking.
*Nausea*

7 I know perfectly well that I don't want to do anything; to do something is to create existence – and there's quite enough existence as it is.
*Nausea*

8 I don't think the profession of historian fits a man for psychological analysis. In our work we have to deal only with simple feelings to which we give generic names such as Ambition and Interest.
*Nausea*

9 I think they do that to pass the time, nothing more. But time is too large, it refuses to let itself be filled up.
*Nausea*

10 You get the impression that their normal condition is silence and that speech is a slight fever which attacks them now and then.
*Nausea*

11 The poor don't know that their function in life is to exercise our generosity.
*Words*

12 A kiss without a moustache, they said then, is like an egg without salt; I will add to it: and it is like Good without Evil.
*Words*

13 She believed in nothing; only her scepticism kept her from being an atheist.
*Words*

14 There is no such thing as psychological. Let us say that one can improve the biography of the person.
*The Divided Self* (R. D. Laing), Ch. 8

15 In the first days of the revolt you must kill: to shoot down a European is to kill two birds with one stone, to destroy an oppressor and the man he oppresses at the same time: there remain a dead man, and a free man.
*The Wretched of the Earth* (F. Fanon), Preface

**Sassoon, Siegfried** (1886–1967) British poet and writer. After serving in World War I he published several collections of anti-war verse, including *The Old Huntsman* (1917) and *Counter Attack* (1918). His autobiographical prose work, *Memoirs of George Sherston*, included the well-known *Memoirs of a Fox-Hunting Man* (1928).

1 If I were fierce and bald and short of breath,
I'd live with scarlet Majors at the Base,
And speed glum heroes up the line to death.
*Base Details*

2 And when the war is done and youth stone dead
I'd toddle safely home and die – in bed.
*Base Details*

3 Soldiers are citizens of death's grey land,
Drawing no dividend from time's tomorrows.
*Dreamers*

4 'Good morning; good morning!' the general said
When we met him last week on our way to the line.
Now the soldiers he smiled at are most of 'em dead,
And we're cursing his staff for incompetent swine.
*The General*

5 Man, it seemed, had been created to jab the life out of Germans.
*Memoirs of an Infantry Officer*, Pt. I, Ch. 1

6 I am making this statement as a wilful defiance of military authority because I believe that the War is being deliberately prolonged by those who have the power to end it.
*Memoirs of an Infantry Officer*, Pt. X, Ch. 3

7 Safe with his wound, a citizen of life,
He hobbled blithely through the garden gate,
And thought: 'Thank God they had to amputate!'
*The One-Legged Man*

**Sassoon, Vidal** (1928– ) British hair stylist whose clientele includes many rich and famous people.

1 The only place where success comes before work is a dictionary.
Quoting one of his teachers in a BBC radio broadcast

**Satie, Erik** (1866–1925) French composer. He composed chiefly piano works, such as *Trois Gymnopédies* (1888), *Pièces froides* (1897), and *Trois morceaux en forme de poire* (1903).

1 My doctor has always told me to smoke. He even explains himself: 'Smoke, my friend. Otherwise someone else will smoke in your place.'
*Mémoires d'un amnésique*

2 When I was young, I was told: 'You'll see, when you're fifty. I am fifty and I haven't seen a thing.
From a letter to his brother
*Erik Satie* (Pierre-Daniel Templier), Ch. 1

3 To be played with both hands in the pocket.
Direction on one of his piano pieces
*The Unimportance of Being Oscar* (O. Levant)

**Savile, George, Marquis of Halifax** (1633–95) *See* Halifax.

**Sayers, Dorothy L(eigh)** (1893–1957) British writer of detective stories, featuring Lord Peter Wimsey as the detective. She also wrote plays on religious themes.

1 I can't see that she could have found anything nastier to say if she'd thought it out with both hands for a fortnight.
*Busman's Holiday*, 'Prothalamion'

2 As I grow older and older,
And totter towards the tomb,
I find that I care less and less
Who goes to bed with whom.
*That's Why I Never Read Modern Novels*

**Scanlon, Hugh, Baron** (1913– ) British trade-union leader. He was president of the Amalgamated Union of Engineering Workers (1968–78) and a member of the TUC General Council.

1 Here we are again with both feet firmly planted in the air.
Referring to his union's attitude to the Common Market
*The Observer*, 'Sayings of the Year', 30 Dec 1973

**Scarron, Paul** (1610–60) French poet, dramatist, and satirist. He was paralysed from the age of 30.

**1** At last I am going to be well!

As he lay dying
Attrib.

**Schelling, Friedrich Wilhelm Joseph von** (1775–1854) German philosopher. His metaphysical philosophy is expounded in his *System of Transcendental Idealism* (1800).

**1** Architecture in general is frozen music.

*Philosophie der Kunst*

**Schiller, Friedrich von** (1759–1805) German dramatist and writer. His early plays included *Die Rauber* (1781) and *Don Carlos* (1787), while his later dramas included the *Wallenstein* trilogy (1798–99), *Die Jungfrau von Orleans* (1801), and *Wilhelm Tell* (1804). Beethoven used Schiller's *An die Freude* (*Ode to Joy*; 1786) in his choral symphony.

**1** Against stupidity the gods themselves struggle in vain.

*Die Jungfrau von Orleans*, III:6

**2** The sun does not set in my dominions.

Said by Philip II
*Don Carlos*, I:6

**Schlegel, Friedrich von** (1772–1829) German diplomat, writer, and critic. Many of his philosophical and literary articles appeared in the journal *Das Athenäum*, which he published with his brother. He also wrote the novel *Lucinde* (1799) and various philosophical books, such as *Philosophie des Lebens* (1828).

**1** A historian is a prophet in reverse.

*Das Athenäum*

**Schlieffen, Alfred, Graf von** (1833–1913) German general. His strategy for defeating France was adopted by Germany at the start of World War I, but was unsuccessful.

**1** When you march into France, let the last man on the right brush the Channel with his sleeve.

Referring to the Schlieffen plan
*August 1914* (Barbara Tuchman), Ch. 2

**Schliemann, Heinrich** (1822–90) German archaeologist, who excavated many cities of the Mycenaean civilization.

**1** I have looked upon the face of Agamemnon.

On discovering a gold death mask at an excavation in Mycenae
*The Story of Civilization* (W. Durant), Vol. 2

**Schnabel, Artur** (1882–1951) Austrian concert pianist, famous for his performances of Beethoven. He also composed music for the piano and for orchestra.

**1** I know two kinds of audience only – one coughing and one not coughing.

See also AGATE
*My Life and Music*, Pt. II, Ch. 10

**2** The notes I handle no better than many pianists. But the pauses between the notes – ah, that is where the art resides.

*Chicago Daily News*, 11 June 1958

**3** The sonatas of Mozart are unique; they are too easy for children, and too difficult for artists.

*An Encyclopedia of Quotations about Music* (Nat Shapiro)

**4** When a piece gets difficult make faces.

Advice given to the pianist Vladimir Horowitz
*The Unimportance of Being Oscar* (O. Levant)

**Schneckenburger, Max** (1819–49) German poet. His song *Die Wacht am Rhein* (1840), set to music by Karl Wilhelm, became a patriotic song.

**1** *Die Wacht am Rhein*
The Watch on the Rhine.

Song title

**Schopenhauer, Arthur** (1788–1860) German philosopher. His books include *Die Welt als Wille und Vorstellung* (1819) and *Die Beiden Grundprobleme der Ethik* (1841).

**1** To be alone is the fate of all great minds – a fate deplored at times, but still always chosen as the less grievous of two evils.

*Aphorismen zur Lebensweisheit*

**2** Intellect is invisible to the man who has none.

*Aphorismen zur Lebensweisheit*

**3** The fundamental fault of the female character is that it has no sense of justice.

*Gedanken über vielerlei Gegenstände*, XXVII Bemerkungen'

**4** Every parting gives a foretaste of death; every coming together again a foretaste of the resurrection.

*Gedanken über vielerlei Gegenstände*, XXVI

**5** The thing-in-itself, the will-to-live, exists whole and undivided in every being, even in the tiniest; it is present as completely as in all that ever were, are, and will be, taken together.

*Parerga and Paralipomena*

**6** To expect a man to retain everything that he has ever read is like expecting him to carry about in his body everything that he has ever eaten.

*Parerga and Paralipomena*

**7** After your death you will be what you were before your birth.

*Parerga and Paralipomena*

**8** Wealth is like sea-water; the more we drink, the thirstier we become; and the same is true of fame.

*Parerga and Paralipomena*

**Schultz, Charles M.** (1922– ) US cartoonist, who created the *Peanuts* strip cartoon.

**1** I love mankind – it's people I can't stand.

*Go Fly a Kite, Charlie Brown*

**Schumacher, E. F.** (1911–77) German born economist and conservationist.

**1** The heart of the matter, as I see it, is the stark fact that world poverty is primarily a problem of two million villages, and thus a problem of two thousand million villagers.

*Small is Beautiful, A Study of Economics as if People Mattered*, Ch. 13

**2** After all, for mankind as a whole there are no exports. We did not start developing by obtaining foreign exchange from Mars or the moon. Mankind is a closed society.

*Small is Beautiful, A Study of Economics as if People Mattered,* Ch. 14

**Schwarzenberg, Felix, Prince** (1800–52) Austrian statesman. As prime minister he successfully restricted Prussian influence over German states.

**1** Austria will astound the world with the magnitude of her ingratitude.

On being asked whether Austria was under any obligation to Russia for help received previously
*The Fall of the House of Habsburg* (E. Crankshaw)

**Schweitzer, Albert** (1875–1965) French Protestant theologian, philosopher, physician, and musician. He is remembered for his medical missionary work in Lambaréné, Gabon (1913–65), and his recordings of Bach organ music.

**1** I too had thoughts once of being an intellectual, but I found it too difficult.

Remark made to an African who refused to perform a menial task on the grounds that he was an intellectual
Attrib.

**Scott, C(harles) P(restwich)** (1846–1932) British journalist. He became editor of the *Manchester Guardian* (1872) and later its owner. He was also an MP (1895–1906).

**1** Its primary office is the gathering of news. At the peril of its soul it must see that the supply is not tainted. Neither in what it gives, nor in what it does not give, nor in the mode of presentation, must the unclouded face of truth suffer wrong. Comment is free but facts are sacred.

*Manchester Guardian,* 6 May 1926

**2** Television? No good will come of this device. The word is half Greek and half Latin.

Attrib.

**Scott, Robert Falcon, Captain** (1868–1912) British explorer. He led two expeditions to the Antarctic, the first in *Discovery* (1900–04) and the second in *Terra Nova* (1910–12), in which he was beaten to the pole by Amundsen and perished on the return journey.

**1** Great God! this is an awful place.

Referring to the South Pole
*Journal,* 17 Jan 1912

**2** Had we lived, I should have had a tale to tell of the hardihood, endurance, and courage of my companions which would have stirred the heart of every Englishman. These rough notes and our dead bodies must tell the tale.

*Message to the Public*

**Scott, Sir Walter** (1771–1832) Scottish novelist. Originally a lawyer, he turned to writing for a living after the success of his narrative poem, *The Lay of the Last Minstrel* (1805). *Waverley* (1814) was the first of many successful historical novels, including *Rob Roy* (1817), *The Heart of Midlothian* (1818), *The Bride of Lammermoor* (1818), *Ivanhoe* (1819) and *The Talisman* (1825).

**1** Look back, and smile at perils past.

*The Bridal of Triermain,* Introduction

**2** It's ill taking the breeks aff a wild Highlandman.

*The Fair Maid of Perth,* Ch. 5

**3** The Big Bow-Wow strain I can do myself like any now going; but the exquisite touch, which renders ordinary commonplace things and characters interesting, from the truth of the description and the sentiment, is denied to me.

In praise of Jane Austen
*Journal,* 14 Mar 1826

**4** For ne'er
Was flattery lost on poet's ear:
A simple race! they waste their toil
For the vain tribute of a smile.

*The Lay of the Last Minstrel,* IV

**5** True love's the gift which God has given
To man alone beneath the heaven.

*The Lay of the Last Minstrel,* V

**6** Breathes there the man, with soul so dead,
Who never to himself hath said,
This is my own, my native land!
Whose heart hath ne'er within him burn'd,
As home his footsteps he hath turn'd
From wandering on a foreign strand!

*The Lay of the Last Minstrel,* VI

**7** O Caledonia! stern and wild,
Meet nurse for a poetic child!
Land of brown heath and shaggy wood,
Land of the mountain and the flood,
Land of my sires! what mortal hand
Can e'er untie the filial band
That knits me to thy rugged strand!

*The Lay of the Last Minstrel,* VI

**8** His morning walk was beneath the elms in the churchyard; 'for death,' he said, 'had been his next-door neighbour for so many years, that he had no apology for dropping the acquaintance.'

*The Legend of Montrose,* Introduction

**9** There is a Southern proverb, – fine words butter no parsnips.

*The Legend of Montrose,* Ch. 3

**10** To that dark inn, the grave!

*The Lord of the Isles,* VI

**11** But search the land of living men,
Where wilt thou find their like agen?

*Marmion,* I

**12** O, young Lochinvar is come out of the west,
Through all the wide Border his steed was the best.

*Marmion,* V

**13** So faithful in love, and so dauntless in war,
There never was knight like the young Lochinvar.

*Marmion,* V

**14** The stubborn spear-men still made good
   Their dark impenetrable wood,
   Each stepping where his comrade stood,
     The instant that he fell.
   *Marmion*, VI

**15** Ridicule often checks what is absurd, and fully as
   often smothers that which is noble.
   *Quentin Durward*

**16** But with the morning cool repentance came.
   *Rob Roy*, Ch. 12

**17** See yon pale stripling! when a boy,
   A mother's pride, a father's joy!
   *Rokeby*, III

**18** O, Brignal banks are wild and fair,
     And Gretna woods are green,
   And you may gather garlands there
     Would grace a summer queen.
   *Rokeby*, III

**19** My heart's in the Highlands, my heart is not
   here,
   My heart's in the Highlands a-chasing the deer.
   *Waverley*, Ch. 28

**20** No, this right hand shall work it all off.
   *Refusing offers of help following his bankruptcy in 1826*
   *Century of Anecdote* (J. Timbs)

**Scott, William, Baron Stowell** (1745–1836) British
jurist. A friend of Dr Johnson, he was the highest authority on
maritime and international law. He became Advocate-General for
the Lord High Admiral.

**1** A dinner lubricates business.
   *Life of Johnson* (J. Boswell), 1791

**2** A precedent embalms a principle.
   *An opinion given while Advocate-General*
   *Attrib.*

**Searle, Ronald William Fordham** (1920– ) British
cartoonist, who worked for the *Sunday Express* and *Punch*
magazine. He created the notorious schoolgirls of St Trinian's.

**1** Though loaded firearms were strictly forbidden
   at St Trinian's to all but Sixth-Formers . . .
   one or two of them carried automatics acquired
   in the holidays, generally the gift of some indul-
   gent relative.
   *The Terror of St Trinian's*, Ch. 3

**2** In the spring . . . your lovely Chloë lightly turns
   to one mass of spots.
   *The Terror of St Trinian's*, Ch. 7

**Sears, E(dmund) H(amilton)** (1810–76) US clergyman
and hymn writer.

**1** It came upon the midnight clear,
   That glorious song of old,
   From Angels bending near the earth
   To touch their harps of gold;
   'Peace on the earth; good will to man
   From Heaven's all gracious King.'
   The world in solemn stillness lay
   To hear the angels sing.
   *That Glorious Song of Old*

**Sébastiani, Horace François, Comte** (1772–1851)
French general and diplomat.

**1** At the moment of writing, calm reigned in
   Warsaw.
   *After the defeat of the military insurrection in Warsaw*

**Secombe, Sir Harry** (1921– ) Welsh singer, actor, and
comedian. He performed in BBC radio's 'Goon Show' (1949–60)
and has made many appearances on stage and television. His films
include *Oliver!* (1968).

**1** My advice if you insist on slimming: Eat as much
   as you like – just don't swallow it.
   *Daily Herald*, 5 Oct 1962

**Sedgwick, Catharine Maria** (1789–1867) US writer.

**1** I expect no very violent transition.
   *Comparing heaven with her home-town of Stockbridge,*
   *Massachussetts*
   *Edie* (Jean Stein)

**Sedgwick, John** (1813–64) US general in the Union army
during the US Civil War.

**1** Nonsense, they couldn't hit an elephant at this
   dist –
   *His last words, in response to a suggestion that he should not*
   *show himself over the parapet during the Battle of the*
   *Wilderness*
   *Attrib.*

**Seeger, Alan** (1888–1916) US poet. He came to Europe in
1912, enlisted in the French Foreign Legion in World War I, and
was killed on active service. His collections of verse include
*Juvenilia* and *Later Poems*.

**1** I have a rendezvous with Death
   At some disputed barricade.
   *I Have a Rendezvous with Death*

**Seeger, Pete** (1919– ) US folksinger and songwriter, who
wrote 'Where Have All the Flowers Gone?' and 'Kisses Sweeter
than Wine'.

**1** Where have all the flowers gone?
   Young girls picked them every one.
   *Where Have All the Flowers Gone?*

**Seeley, Sir John Robert** (1834–95) British historian and
writer. His *Ecce Homo* (1865) and *Natural Religion* (1882) caused
considerable controversy; *The Expansion of England* (1883) and
*The Growth of British Policy* (1895) were his best-known historical
works.

**1** We the English seem, as it were, to have conquered and peopled half the world in a fit of
   absence of mind.
   *The Expansion of England*, I

**2** History is past politics, and politics present history.

Quoting the historian E. A. Freeman
*The Growth of British Policy*

**Segal, Erich** (1937– ) US writer, author of the novel upon which the film *Love Story* (1970) was based.

**1** Love means never having to say you're sorry.

*Love Story*

**Selden, John** (1584–1654) English historian, jurist, antiquary, and statesman. He wrote many erudite works but is best remembered for *Table Talk* (1689), a posthumously published collection of his sayings.

**1** A king is a thing men have made for their own sakes, for quietness' sake. Just as if in a family one man is appointed to buy the meat.

*Table Talk*

**2** Every law is a contract between the king and the people and therefore to be kept.

*Table Talk*

**3** Ignorance of the law excuses no man; not that all men know the law, but because 'tis an excuse every man will plead, and no man can tell how to confute him.

*Table Talk*

**4** Pleasure is nothing else but the intermission of pain.

*Table Talk*

**5** Preachers say, Do as I say, not as I do. But if the physician had the same disease upon him that I have, and he should bid me do one thing, and himself do quite another, could I believe him?

*Table Talk*

**6** For a priest to turn a man when he lies a-dying, is just like one that has a long time solicited a woman, and cannot obtain his end; at length makes her drunk, and so lies with her.

*Table Talk*

**7** Pleasures are all alike simply considered in themselves . . . He that takes pleasure to hear sermons enjoys himself as much as he that hears plays.

*Table Talk*

**8** 'Tis not the drinking that is to be blamed, but the excess.

*Table Talk*

**9** Marriage is nothing but a civil contract.

*Table Talk*

**Selfridge, H(arry) Gordon** (1857–1947) US-born businessman who became a British subject. He came to London in 1906 and established Selfridge's, making it one of the largest department stores in Europe.

**1** The customer is always right.

Slogan adopted at his shops

**Sellar, Walter Carruthers** (1898–1951) British humorous writer who collaborated with Robert Julius Yeatman (1897–1968).

**1** For every person wishing to teach there are thirty not wanting to be taught.

*And Now All This*

**2** To confess that you are totally Ignorant about the Horse, is social suicide: you will be despised by everybody, especially the horse.

*Horse Nonsense*

**3** 1066 And All That.

Book title

**4** The Roman Conquest was, however, a *Good Thing*, since the Britons were only natives at the time.

*1066 And All That*

**5** The Cavaliers (Wrong but Wromantic) and the Roundheads (Right but Repulsive).

*1066 And All That*

**6** Napoleon's armies used to march on their stomachs, shouting: 'Vive l'intérieur!'

*1066 And All That*

**7** America became top nation and history came to a full stop.

*1066 And All That*

**8** Do not on any account attempt to write on both sides of the paper at once.

*1066 And All That*, Test Paper 5

**Seneca** (c. 4 BC–65 AD) Roman author and statesman, author of nine tragedies, 13 philosophical treatises, and many essays. Tutor to Nero, he was later forced by the emperor to commit suicide.

**1** Live among men as if God beheld you; speak to God as if men were listening.

*Epistles*

**2** Conversation has a kind of charm about it, an insinuating and insidious something that elicits secrets from us just like love or liquor.

*Epistles*

**Servetus, Michael** (1511–53) Spanish physician and theologian, who was burnt at the stake for attacking the doctrine of the Trinity. He also made discoveries concerning the circulation of blood.

**1** I will burn, but this is a mere incident. We shall continue our discussion in eternity.

Comment to the judges of the Inquisition after being condemned to be burned at the stake as a heretic
Borges: *A Reader* (E. Monegal)

**Service, Robert William** (1874–1958) Canadian poet. His best-known ballads, including "The Shooting of Dan McGrew" (1907), were based on his experience of the Yukon gold rush.

**1** A promise made is a debt unpaid.

*The Cremation of Sam McGee*

**2** Ah! the clock is always slow;
It is later than you think.

*It is Later than You Think*

3   This is the Law of the Yukon, that only the
    strong shall thrive;
    That surely the weak shall perish, and only the
    Fit survive.
    *The Law of the Yukon*

4   When we, the Workers, all demand: 'What are
    we fighting for? . . .
    Then, then we'll end that stupid crime, that dev-
    il's madness – War.
    *Michael*

**Sévigné, Marie de Rabutin-Chantal, Marquise
de** (1626–96) French writer. She left some 1500 letters, mostly
written to her children after her husband's death.

1   The more I see of men, the more I admire dogs.
    Attrib.

**Shadwell, Thomas** (1642–92) English dramatist. His works
include comedies such as *The Virtuoso* (1676) and *Bury Fair*
(1689); his best-known opera is *The Enchanted Isle* (1674).

1   Words may be false and full of art,
    Sighs are the natural language of the heart.
    *Psyche*, III

2   'Tis the way of all flesh.
    *The Sullen Lovers*, V:2

3   Every man loves what he is good at.
    *A True Widow*, V:1

**Shaffer, Peter** (1926–    ) British dramatist who established
his reputation with the play *Five-Finger Exercise* (1958); he
subsequently wrote *The Royal Hunt of the Sun* (1964), *Equus*
(1973), and *Amadeus* (1979).

1   All my wife has ever taken from the Mediterra-
    nean –from that whole vast intuitive culture –
    are four bottles of Chianti to make into lamps,
    and two china condiment donkeys labelled Sally
    and Peppy.
    *Equus*, I:18

2   Passion, you see, can be destroyed by a doctor.
    It cannot be created.
    *Equus*, II:35

3   Rehearsing a play is making the word flesh. Pub-
    lishing a play is reversing the process.
    *Equus*, Note

**Shah, Idries** (1924–    ) British author, born in India.

1   A certain person may have, as you say, a won-
    derful presence: I do not know. What I do
    know is that he has a perfectly delightful
    absence.
    *Reflections*, 'Presence and Absence'

**Shahn, Ben** (1898–1969) US artist, born in Lithuania.

1   An amateur is an artist who supports himself
    with outside jobs which enable him to paint. A
    professional is someone whose wife works to en-
    able him to paint.
    Outlining the difference between professional and amateur
    painters
    Attrib.

**Shakespeare, William** (1564–1616) English dramatist and
poet, universally acknowledged to be the greatest English writer of
historical plays, comedies, and tragedies. His sonnets have love
and friendship as their themes.

1   Our remedies oft in ourselves do lie,
    Which we ascribe to heaven.
    *All's Well that Ends Well*, I:1

2   The web of our life is of a mingled yarn, good
    and ill together.
    *All's Well that Ends Well*, IV:3

3   Th' inaudible and noiseless foot of Time.
    *All's Well that Ends Well*, V:3

4   The triple pillar of the world transform'd
    Into a strumpet's fool.
    *Antony and Cleopatra*, I:1

5   There's beggary in the love that can be
    reckon'd.
    *Antony and Cleopatra*, I:1

6   Where's my serpent of old Nile?
    *Antony and Cleopatra*, I:5

7   My salad days,
    When I was green in judgment, cold in blood,
    To say as I said then!
    *Antony and Cleopatra*, I:5

8   The barge she sat in, like a burnish'd throne,
    Burn'd on the water. The poop was beaten gold;
    Purple the sails, and so perfumed that
    The winds were love-sick with them; the oars
    were silver,
    Which to the tune of flutes kept stroke and made
    The water which they beat to follow faster,
    As amorous of their strokes. For her own
    person,
    It beggar'd all description.
    *Antony and Cleopatra*, II:2

9   Age cannot wither her, nor custom stale
    Her infinite variety. Other women cloy
    The appetites they feed, but she makes hungry
    Where most she satisfies.
    *Antony and Cleopatra*, II:2

10  I will praise any man that will praise me.
    *Antony and Cleopatra*, II:6

11  Celerity is never more admir'd
    Than by the negligent.
    *Antony and Cleopatra*, III:7

12  To business that we love we rise betime,
    And go to't with delight.
    *Antony and Cleopatra*, IV:4

13  Unarm, Eros; the long day's task is done,
    And we must sleep.
    *Antony and Cleopatra*, IV:12

14  I am dying, Egypt, dying; only
    I here importune death awhile, until
    Of many thousand kisses the poor last
    I lay upon thy lips.
    *Antony and Cleopatra*, IV:13

15 O, wither'd is the garland of the war,
The soldier's pole is fall'n! Young boys and girls
Are level now with men. The odds is gone,
And there is nothing left remarkable
Beneath the visiting moon.
*Antony and Cleopatra*, IV:13

16 The bright day is done,
And we are for the dark.
*Antony and Cleopatra*, V:2

17 Dost thou not see my baby at my breast
That sucks the nurse asleep?
Holding the asp to her breast
*Antony and Cleopatra*, V:2

18 Well said; that was laid on with a trowel.
*As You Like It*, I:2

19 I had rather bear with you than bear you.
*As You Like It*, II:4

20 If thou rememb'rest not the slightest folly
That ever love did make thee run into,
Thou hast not lov'd.
*As You Like It*, II:4

21 Under the greenwood tree
Who loves to lie with me,
And turn his merry note
Unto the sweet bird's throat,
Come hither, come hither, come hither.
Here shall he see
No enemy
But winter and rough weather.
*As You Like It*, II:5

22 And so, from hour to hour, we ripe and ripe,
And then, from hour to hour, we rot and rot;
And thereby hangs a tale.
*As You Like It*, II:7

23 All the world's a stage,
And all the men and women merely players;
They have their exits and their entrances;
And one man in his time plays many parts,
His acts being seven ages.
*As You Like It*, II:7

24 Last scene of all,
That ends this strange eventful history,
Is second childishness and mere oblivion;
Sans teeth, sans eyes, sans taste, sans every
thing.
*As You Like It*, II:7

25 Blow, blow, thou winter wind,
Thou art not so unkind
As man's ingratitude.
*As You Like It*, II:7

26 Most friendship is feigning, most loving mere
folly.
*As You Like It*, II:7

27 He that wants money, means, and content, is
without three good friends.
*As You Like It*, III:2

28 Do you not know I am a woman? When I think, I
must speak.
*As You Like It*, III:2

29 I do desire we may be better strangers.
*As You Like It*, III:2

30 The truest poetry is the most feigning.
*As You Like It*, III:3

31 Men have died from time to time, and worms
have eaten them, but not for love.
*As You Like It*, IV:1

32 Your If is the only peace-maker; much virtue in
If.
*As You Like It*, V:4

33 If it be true that good wine needs no bush, 'tis
true that a good play needs no epilogue.
*As You Like It*, Epilogue

34 Custom calls me to't.
What custom wills, in all things should we do't,
The dust on antique time would lie unswept,
And mountainous error be too highly heap'd
For truth to o'erpeer.
*Coriolanus*, II:3

35 Like a dull actor now
I have forgot my part and I am out,
Even to a full disgrace.
*Coriolanus*, V:3

36 O, this life
Is nobler than attending for a check,
Richer than doing nothing for a bribe,
Prouder than rustling in unpaid-for silk.
*Cymbeline*, III:3

37 Society is no comfort
To one not sociable.
*Cymbeline*, IV:2

38 Fear no more the heat o' th' sun
Nor the furious winter's rages;
Thou thy worldly task hast done,
Home art gone, and ta'en thy wages.
Golden lads and girls all must,
As chimney-sweepers, come to dust.
*Cymbeline*, IV:2

39 For this relief much thanks. 'Tis bitter cold,
And I am sick at heart.
*Hamlet*, I:1

40 A little more than kin, and less than kind.
*Hamlet*, I:2

41 But I have that within which passes show –
these but the trappings and the suits of woe.
*Hamlet*, I:2

42 How weary, stale, flat, and unprofitable,
Seem to me all the uses of this world!
*Hamlet*, I:2

43 Frailty, thy name is woman!
*Hamlet*, I:2

**44** It is not, nor it cannot come to good.
*Hamlet*, I:2

**45** 'A was a man, take him for all in all,
I shall not look upon his like again.
*Hamlet*, I:2

**46** Do not, as some ungracious pastors do,
Show me the steep and thorny way to heaven,
Whiles, like a puff'd and reckless libertine,
Himself the primrose path of dalliance treads
And recks not his own rede.
*Hamlet*, I:3

**47** Costly thy habit as thy purse can buy,
But not express'd in fancy; rich, not gaudy;
For the apparel oft proclaims the man.
*Hamlet*, I:3

**48** Neither a borrower nor a lender be;
For loan oft loses both itself and friend,
And borrowing dulls the edge of husbandry.
This above all: to thine own self be true,
And it must follow, as the night the day,
Thou canst not then be false to any man.
*Hamlet*, I:3

**49** But to my mind, though I am native here
And to the manner born, it is a custom
More honour'd in the breach than the
observance.
*Hamlet*, I:4

**50** Something is rotten in the state of Denmark.
*Hamlet*, I:4

**51** Murder most foul, as in the best it is;
But this most foul, strange, and unnatural.
*Hamlet*, I:5

**52** There are more things in heaven and earth,
Horatio,
Than are dreamt of in your philosophy.
*Hamlet*, I:5

**53** Brevity is the soul of wit.
*Hamlet*, II:2

**54** To be honest, as this world goes, is to be one
man pick'd out of ten thousand.
*Hamlet*, II:2

**55** Though this be madness, yet there is method
in't.
*Hamlet*, II:2

**56** There is nothing either good or bad, but thinking
makes it so.
*Hamlet*, II:2

**57** What a piece of work is a man! How noble in
reason! how infinite in faculties! in form and
moving, how express and admirable! in action,
how like an angel! in apprehension, how like a
god! the beauty of the world! the paragon of
animals! And yet, to me, what is this quintessence of dust? Man delights not me – no, nor
woman neither.
*Hamlet*, II:2

**58** The play, I remember, pleas'd not the million;
'twas caviare to the general.
*Hamlet*, II:2

**59** Use every man after his desert, and who shall
scape whipping?
*Hamlet*, II:2

**60** The play's the thing
Wherein I'll catch the conscience of the King.
*Hamlet*, II:2

**61** To be, or not to be – that is the question;
Whether 'tis nobler in the mind to suffer
The slings and arrows of outrageous fortune,
Or to take arms against a sea of troubles,
And by opposing end them? To die, to sleep –
No more; and by a sleep to say we end
The heart-ache and the thousand natural shocks
That flesh is heir to, 'tis a consummation
Devoutly to be wish'd. To die, to sleep;
To sleep, perchance to dream. Ay, there's the
rub;
For in that sleep of death what dreams may
come,
When we have shuffled off this mortal coil,
Must give us pause.
*Hamlet*, III:1

**62** The dread of something after death –
The undiscover'd country, from whose bourn
No traveller returns.
*Hamlet*, III:1

**63** Thus conscience does make cowards of us all;
And thus the native hue of resolution
Is sicklied o'er with the pale cast of thought.
*Hamlet*, III:1

**64** Madness in great ones must not unwatch'd go.
*Hamlet*, III:1

**65** It out-herods Herod.
*Hamlet*, III:2

**66** Suit the action to the word, the word to the action; with this special observance, that you
o'erstep not the modesty of nature.
*Hamlet*, III:2

**67** The lady doth protest too much, methinks.
*Hamlet*, III:2

**68** Very like a whale.
*Hamlet*, III:2

**69** A king of shreds and patches.
*Hamlet*, III:4

**70** Some craven scruple
Of thinking too precisely on th' event.
*Hamlet*, IV:4

**71** When sorrows come, they come not single
spies,
But in battalions!
*Hamlet*, IV:5

72 There's such divinity doth hedge a king
That treason can but peep to what it would.
*Hamlet, IV:5*

73 Alas, poor Yorick! I knew him, Horatio: a fellow
of infinite jest, of most excellent fancy.
*Hamlet, V:1*

74 There's a divinity that shapes our ends,
Rough-hew them how we will.
*Hamlet, V:2*

75 If thou didst ever hold me in thy heart,
Absent thee from felicity awhile,
And in this harsh world draw thy breath in pain,
To tell my story.
*Hamlet, V:2*

76 The rest is silence.
*Hamlet, V:2*

77 If all the year were playing holidays, To sport
would be as tedious as to work.
*Henry IV, Part One, I:2*

78 Falstaff sweats to death
And lards the lean earth as he walks along.
*Henry IV, Part One, II:2*

79 I have more flesh than another man, and therefore more frailty.
*Henry IV, Part One, III:3*

80 Honour pricks me on. Yea, but how if honour
prick me off when I come on? How then? Can
honour set to a leg? No. Or an arm? No. Or take
away the grief of a wound? No. Honour hath no
skill in surgery, then? No. What is honour? A
word. What is in that word? Honour. What is
that honour? Air.
*Henry IV, Part One, V:1*

81 But thoughts, the slaves of life, and life, time's
fool,
And time, that takes survey of all the world,
Must have a stop.
*Henry IV, Part One, V:4*

82 The better part of valour is discretion; in the
which better part I have saved my life.
*Henry IV, Part One, V:4*

83 I am not only witty in myself, but the cause that
wit is in other men. I do here walk before thee
like a sow that hath overwhelm'd all her litter
but one.
*Henry IV, Part Two, I:2*

84 Well, I cannot last ever; but it was always yet
the trick of our English nation, if they have a
good thing, to make it too common.
*Henry IV, Part Two, I:2*

85 I can get no remedy against this consumption of
the purse; borrowing only lingers and lingers it
out, but the disease is incurable.
*Henry IV, Part Two, I:2*

86 He hath eaten me out of house and home.
*Henry IV, Part Two, II:1*

87 Is it not strange that desire should so many
years outlive performance?
*Henry IV, Part Two, II:4*

88 Uneasy lies the head that wears a crown.
*Henry IV, Part Two, III:1*

89 We have heard the chimes at midnight.
*Henry IV, Part Two, III:2*

90 I care not; a man can die but once; we owe
God a death.
*Henry IV, Part Two, III:2*

91 Care I for the limb, the thews, the stature,
bulk, and big assemblance of a man! Give me
the spirit.
*Henry IV, Part Two, III:2*

92 I dare not fight; but I will wink and hold out
mine iron.
*Henry V, II:1*

93 Though patience be a tired mare, yet she will
plod.
*Henry V, II:1*

94 His nose was as sharp as a pen, and 'a babbl'd
of green fields.
Referring to Falstaff on his deathbed
*Henry V, II:3*

95 Once more unto the breach, dear friends, once
more;
Or close the wall up with our English dead.
*Henry V, III:1*

96 Men of few words are the best men.
*Henry V, III:2*

97 I think the King is but a man as I am: the violet
smells to him as it doth to me.
*Henry V, IV:1*

98 Every subject's duty is the King's; but every
subject's soul is his own.
*Henry V, IV:1*

99 Old men forget; yet all shall be forgot,
But he'll remember, with advantages,
What feats he did that day.
*Henry V, IV:3*

100 There is occasions and causes why and wherefore in all things.
*Henry V, V:1*

101 Heat not a furnace for your foe so hot
That it do singe yourself. We may outrun
By violent swiftness that which we run at,
And lose by over-running.
*Henry VIII, I:1*

102 I would not be a queen
For all the world.
*Henry VIII, II:3*

**103** Farewell, a long farewell, to all my greatness!
This is the state of man: to-day he puts forth
The tender leaves of hopes: to-morrow blossoms
And bears his blushing honours thick upon him;
The third day comes a frost, a killing frost,
And when he thinks, good easy man, full surely
His greatness is a-ripening, nips his root,
And then he falls, as I do.
*Henry VIII*, III:2

**104** Had I but serv'd my God with half the zeal
I serv'd my King, he would not in mine age
Have left me naked to mine enemies.
*Henry VIII*, III:2

**105** Men's evil manners live in brass: their virtues
We write in water.
*Henry VIII*, IV:2

**106** Beware the ides of March.
*Julius Caesar*, I:2

**107** Let me have men about me that are fat;
Sleek-headed men, and such as sleep o' nights.
Yond Cassius has a lean and hungry look;
He thinks too much. Such men are dangerous.
*Julius Caesar*, I:2

**108** For mine own part, it was Greek to me.
*Julius Caesar*, I:2

**109** Cowards die many times before their deaths:
The valiant never taste of death but once.
*Julius Caesar*, II:2

**110** *Et tu, Brute?*
*Julius Caesar*, III:1

**111** Why, he that cuts off twenty years of life
Cuts off so many years of fearing death.
*Julius Caesar*, III:1

**112** O mighty Caesar! dost thou lie so low?
Are all thy conquests, glories, triumphs, spoils,
Shrunk to this little measure?
*Julius Caesar*, III:1

**113** O, pardon me, thou bleeding piece of earth,
That I am meek and gentle with these butchers!
Thou art the ruins of the noblest man
That ever lived in the tide of times.
*Julius Caesar*, III:1

**114** 'Cry 'Havoc!' and let slip the dogs of war.
*Julius Caesar*, III:1

**115** Not that I lov'd Caesar less, but that I lov'd
Rome more.
*Julius Caesar*, III:2

**116** Friends, Romans, countrymen, lend me your ears
I come to bury Caesar, not to praise him.
The evil that men do lives after them;
The good is oft interred with their bones.
*Julius Caesar*, III:2

**117** For Brutus is an honourable man;
So are they all, all honourable men.
*Julius Caesar*, III:2

**118** Ambition should be made of sterner stuff.
*Julius Caesar*, III:2

**119** If you have tears, prepare to shed them now.
*Julius Caesar*, III:2

**120** For I have neither wit, nor words, nor worth,
Action, nor utterance, nor the power of speech,
To stir men's blood; I only speak right on.
*Julius Caesar*, III:2

**121** A friend should bear his friend's infirmities,
But Brutus makes mine greater than they are.
*Julius Caesar*, IV:3

**122** There is a tide in the affairs of men
Which, taken at the flood, leads on to fortune;
Omitted, all the voyage of their life
Is bound in shallows and in miseries.
On such a full sea are we now afloat,
And we must take the current when it serves,
Or lose our ventures.
*Julius Caesar*, IV:3

**123** This was the noblest Roman of them all.
All the conspirators save only he
Did that they did in envy of great Caesar.
*Julius Caesar*, V:5

**124** His life was gentle; and the elements
So mix'd in him that Nature might stand up
And say to all the world 'This was a man!'
Referring to Brutus
*Julius Caesar*, V:5

**125** Well, whiles I am a beggar, I will rail
And say there is no sin but to be rich;
And being rich, my virtue then shall be
To say there is no vice but beggary.
*King John*, II:1

**126** Bell, book, and candle, shall not drive me back,
When gold and silver becks me to come on.
*King John*, III:3

**127** Life is as tedious as a twice-told tale
Vexing the dull ear of a drowsy man.
*King John*, III:4

**128** To gild refined gold, to paint the lily,
To throw a perfume on the violet,
To smooth the ice, or add another hue
Unto the rainbow, or with taper-light
To seek the beauteous eye of heaven to garnish,
Is wasteful and ridiculous excess.
*King John*, IV:2

**129** I beg cold comfort.
*King John*, V:7

**130** Nothing will come of nothing. Speak again.
*King Lear*, I:1

131 This is the excellent foppery of the world,
that, when we are sick in fortune, often the
surfeits of our own behaviour, we make guilty
of our disasters the sun, the moon, and stars.
*King Lear*, I:2

132 Ingratitude, thou marble-hearted fiend,
More hideous when thou show'st thee in a
child
Than the sea-monster!
*King Lear* I:4

133 O, let me not be mad, not mad, sweet heaven!
Keep me in temper; I would not be mad!
*King Lear*, I:5

134 Thou whoreson zed! thou unnecessary letter!
*King Lear*, II:2

135 Down, thou climbing sorrow,
Thy element's below.
*King Lear*, II:4

136 O, reason not the need! Our basest beggars
Are in the poorest thing superfluous.
Allow not nature more than nature needs,
Man's life is cheap as beast's.
*King Lear*, II:4

137 Blow, winds, and crack your cheeks; rage,
blow.
You cataracts and hurricanoes, spout
Till you have drench'd our steeples, drown'd
the cocks.
*King Lear*, III:2

138 Rumble thy bellyful. Spit, fire; spout rain.
Nor rain, wind, thunder, fire, are my
daughters
I tax not you, you elements, with unkindness.
*King Lear*, III:2

139 I am a man
More sinn'd against than sinning.
*King Lear*, III:2

140 Poor naked wretches, wheresoe'er you are,
That bide the pelting of this pitiless storm,
How shall your houseless heads and unfed
sides,
Your loop'd and window'd raggedness, defend
you
From seasons such as these?
*King Lear*, III:4

141 Take physic, pomp;
Expose thyself to feel what wretches feel.
*King Lear*, III:4

142 Out vile jelly!
Where is thy lustre now?
Spoken by Cornwall as he puts out Gloucester's remaining eye
*King Lear*, III:7

143 The worst is not
So long as we can say 'This is the worst'.
*King Lear*, IV:1

144 As flies to wanton boys are we to th' gods –
They kill us for their sport.
*King Lear*, IV:1

145 Ay, every inch a king.
*King Lear*, IV:6

146 The wren goes to't, and the small gilded fly
Does lecher in my sight.
*King Lear*, IV:6

147 Through tatter'd clothes small vices do appear;
Robes and furr'd gowns hide all.
*King Lear*, IV:6

148 Get thee glass eyes,
And, like a scurvy politician, seem
To see the things thou dost not.
*King Lear*, IV:6

149 When we are born, we cry that we are come
To this great stage of fools.
*King Lear*, IV:6

150 Thou art a soul in bliss; but I am bound
Upon a wheel of fire, that mine own tears
Do scald like molten lead.
*King Lear*, IV:7

151 Men must endure
Their going hence, even as their coming
hither:
Ripeness is all.
*King Lear*, V:2

152 And my poor fool is hang'd! No, no, no life!
Why should a dog, a horse, a rat have life,
And thou no breath at all? Thou'lt come no
more,
Never, never, never, never.
*King Lear*, V:3

153 At Christmas I no more desire a rose
Than wish a snow in May's newfangled shows.
*Love's Labour's Lost*, I:1

154 He hath never fed of the dainties that are bred
in a book; he hath not eat paper, as it were;
he hath not drunk ink; his intellect is not
replenished.
*Love's Labour's Lost*, IV:2

155 For where is any author in the world
Teaches such beauty as a woman's eye?
Learning is but an adjunct to oneself.
*Love's Labour's Lost*, IV:3

156 A jest's prosperity lies in the ear
Of him that hears it, never in the tongue
Of him that makes it.
*Love's Labour's Lost*, V:2

157 When icicles hang by the wall,
And Dick the shepherd blows his nail,
And Tom bears logs into the hall,
And milk comes frozen home in pail,
When blood is nipp'd, and ways be foul,
Then nightly sings the staring owl:
'Tu-who;
Tu-whit, Tu-who' – A merry note,
While greasy Joan doth keel the pot.
*Love's Labour's Lost, V:2*

158 So foul and fair a day I have not seen.
*Macbeth, I:3*

159 This supernatural soliciting
Cannot be ill; cannot be good.
*Macbeth, I:3*

160 Come what come may,
Time and the hour runs through the roughest
day.
*Macbeth, I:3*

161 Nothing in his life
Became him like the leaving it: he died
As one that had been studied in his death
To throw away the dearest thing he ow'd
As 'twere a careless trifle.
*Macbeth, I:4*

162 Yet do I fear thy nature;
It is too full o' th' milk of human kindness
To catch the nearest way.
*Macbeth, I:5*

163 If it were done when 'tis done, then 'twere
well
It were done quickly.
*Macbeth, I:7*

164 That but this blow
Might be the be-all and the end-all here –
But here upon this bank and shoal of time –
We'd jump the life to come.
*Macbeth, I:7*

165 I have no spur
To prick the sides of my intent, but only
Vaulting ambition, which o'er-leaps itself,
And falls on th' other.
*Macbeth, I:7*

166 False face must hide what the false heart doth
know.
*Macbeth, I:7*

167 Sleep that knits up the ravell'd sleave of care,
The death of each day's life, sore labour's
bath,
Balm of hurt minds, great nature's second
course,
Chief nourisher in life's feast.
*Macbeth, II:2*

168 It provokes the desire, but it takes away the
performance. Therefore much drink may be
said to be an equivocator with lechery.
*Macbeth, II:3*

169 I had else been perfect,
Whole as the marble, founded as the rock,
As broad and general as the casing air,
But now I am cabin'd, cribb'd, confin'd, bound
in
To saucy doubts and fears.
*Macbeth, II:4*

170 Nought's had, all's spent,
Where our desire is got without content.
'Tis safer to be that which we destroy,
Than by destruction dwell in doubtful joy.
*Macbeth, III:2*

171 Stand not upon the order of your going,
But go at once.
*Macbeth, III:4*

172 I am in blood
Stepp'd in so far that, should I wade no more,
Returning were as tedious as go o'er.
*Macbeth, III:4*

173 Out, damned spot! out, I say!
*Macbeth, V:1*

174 Here's the smell of the blood still. All the perfumes of Arabia will not sweeten this little
hand.
*Macbeth, V:1*

175 I have liv'd long enough.
My way of life
Is fall'n into the sear, the yellow leaf;
And that which should accompany old age,
As honour, love, obedience, troops of friends,
I must not look to have.
*Macbeth, V:3*

176 I have supp'd full with horrors.
*Macbeth, V:5*

177 Tomorrow, and tomorrow, and tomorrow,
Creeps in this petty pace from day to day
To the last syllable of recorded time,
And all our yesterdays have lighted fools
The way to dusty death. Out, out, brief
candle!
Life's but a walking shadow, a poor player,
That struts and frets his hour upon the stage,
And then is heard no more; it is a tale
Told by an idiot, full of sound and fury,
Signifying nothing.
*Macbeth, V:5*

178 I gin to be aweary of the sun,
And wish th' estate o' th' world were now
undone.
*Macbeth, V:5*

179 MACBETH. I bear a charmed life, which must
not yield
To one of woman born.
MACDUFF. Despair thy charm;
And let the angel whom thou still hast serv'd
Tell thee Macduff was from his mother's womb
Untimely ripp'd.
*Macbeth, V:8*

180 But man, proud man
 Dress'd in a little brief authority,
 Most ignorant of what he's most assur'd,
 His glassy essence, like an angry ape,
 Plays such fantastic tricks before high heaven
 As makes the angels weep.
 *Measure for Measure*, II:2

181 That in the captain's but a choleric word
 Which in the soldier is flat blasphemy.
 *Measure for Measure*, II:2

182 The miserable have no other medicine
 But only hope.
 *Measure for Measure*, III:1

183 Thou hast nor youth nor age;
 But, as it were, an after-dinner's sleep,
 Dreaming on both.
 *Measure for Measure*, III:1

184 Ay, but to die, and go we know not where;
 To lie in cold obstruction, and to rot;
 This sensible warm motion to become
 A kneaded clod; and the delighted spirit
 To bathe in fiery floods or to reside
 In thrilling region of thick-ribbed ice.
 *Measure for Measure*, III:1

185 I am a kind of burr; I shall stick.
 *Measure for Measure*, IV:3

186 Haste still pays haste, and leisure answers
 leisure;
 Like doth quit like, and Measure still for
 Measure.
 *Measure for Measure*, V:1

187 As who should say 'I am Sir Oracle,
 And when I ope my lips let no dog bark'.
 *The Merchant of Venice*, I:1

188 If to do were as easy as to know what were
 good to do, chapels had been churches, and
 poor men's cottages princes' palaces.
 *The Merchant of Venice*, I:2

189 The devil can cite Scripture for his purpose.
 *The Merchant of Venice*, I:3

190 It is a wise father that knows his own child.
 *The Merchant of Venice*, II:2

191 But love is blind, and lovers cannot see
 The pretty follies that themselves commit.
 *The Merchant of Venice*, II:6

192 The ancient saying is no heresy:
 Hanging and wiving goes by destiny.
 *The Merchant of Venice*, II:9

193 Hath not a Jew eyes? Hath not a Jew hands,
 organs, dimensions, senses, affections, passions, fed with the same food, hurt with the
 same weapons, subject to the same diseases,
 healed by the same means, warmed and
 cooled by the same winter and summer, as a
 Christian is? If you prick us, do we not
 bleed? If you tickle us, do we not laugh? If
 you poison us, do we not die? And if you
 wrong us, shall we not revenge?
 *The Merchant of Venice*, III:1

194 The quality of mercy is not strain'd;
 It droppeth as the gentle rain from heaven
 Upon the place beneath. It is twice blest;
 It blesseth him that gives and him that takes.
 *The Merchant of Venice*, IV:1

195 I am never merry when I hear sweet music.
 *The Merchant of Venice*, V:1

196 The man that hath no music in himself,
 Nor is not mov'd with concord of sweet
 sounds,
 Is fit for treasons, stratagems, and spoils.
 *The Merchant of Venice*, V:1

197 How far that little candle throws his beams!
 So shines a good deed in a naughty world.
 *The Merchant of Venice*, V:1

198 For a light wife doth make a heavy husband.
 *The Merchant of Venice*, V:1

199 Why, then the world's mine oyster,
 Which I with sword will open.
 *The Merry Wives of Windsor*, II:2

200 They say there is divinity in odd numbers, either in nativity, chance, or death.
 *The Merry Wives of Windsor*, V:1

201 For aught that I could ever read,
 Could ever hear by tale or history,
 The course of true love never did run smooth.
 *A Midsummer Night's Dream*, I:1

202 Love looks not with the eyes, but with the
 mind;
 And therefore is wing'd Cupid painted blind.
 *A Midsummer Night's Dream*, I:1

203 I am slow of study.
 *A Midsummer Night's Dream*, I:2

204 A lion among ladies is a most dreadful thing;
 for there is not a more fearful wild-fowl than
 your lion living.
 *A Midsummer Night's Dream*, III:1

205 Lord, what fools these mortals be!
 *A Midsummer Night's Dream*, III:2

206 The lunatic, the lover, and the poet,
 Are of imagination all compact.
 *A Midsummer Night's Dream*, V:1

207 The poet's eye, in a fine frenzy rolling,
Doth glance from heaven to earth, from earth
to heaven;
And as imagination bodies forth
The forms of things unknown, the poet's pen
Turns them to shapes, and gives to airy
nothing
A local habitation and a name.
*A Midsummer Night's Dream*, V:1

208 Would you have me speak after my custom, as
being a professed tyrant to their sex?
*Much Ado About Nothing*, I:1

209 Friendship is constant in all other things
Save in the office and affairs of love.
*Much Ado About Nothing*, II:1

210 Silence is the perfectest herald of joy: I were
but little happy if I could say how much.
*Much Ado About Nothing*, II:1

211 Doth not the appetite alter? A man loves the
meat in his youth that he cannot endure in
his age.
*Much Ado About Nothing*, II:3

212 To be a well-favoured man is the gift of fortune; but to write and read comes by nature.
*Much Ado About Nothing*, III:3

213 I thank God I am as honest as any man living
that is an old man and no honester than I.
*Much Ado About Nothing*, III:5

214 Comparisons are odorous.
*Much Ado About Nothing*, III:5

215 Our watch, sir, have indeed comprehended
two aspicious persons.
*Much Ado About Nothing*, III:5

216 Write down that they hope they serve God;
and write God first; for God defend but God
should go before such villains!
*Much Ado About Nothing*, IV:2

217 For there was never yet philosopher
That could endure the toothache patiently.
*Much Ado About Nothing*, V:1

218 To mourn a mischief that is past and gone
Is the next way to draw new mischief on.
*Othello*, I:3

219 Put money in thy purse.
*Othello*, I:3

220 For I am nothing if not critical.
*Othello*, II:1

221 To suckle fools and chronicle small beer.
*Othello*, II:1

222 Reputation, reputation, reputation! O, I have
lost my reputation! I have lost the immortal
part of myself, and what remains is bestial.
*Othello*, II:3

223 Good name in man and woman, dear my lord,
Is the immediate jewel of their souls:
Who steals my purse steals trash; 'tis some-
thing, nothing;
'Twas mine, 'tis his, and has been slave to
thousands;
But he that filches from me my good name
Robs me of that which not enriches him
And makes me poor indeed.
*Othello*, III:3

224 O, beware, my lord, of jealousy;
It is the green-ey'd monster which doth mock
The meat it feeds on.
*Othello*, III:3

225 O curse of marriage,
That we can call these delicate creatures ours,
And not their appetites! I had rather be a toad,
And live upon the vapour of a dungeon,
Than keep a corner in the thing I love
For others' uses.
*Othello*, III:3

226 He that is robb'd, not wanting what is stol'n,
Let him not know't, and he's not robb'd at all.
*Othello*, III:3

227 Farewell the neighing steed and the shrill
trump,
The spirit-stirring drum, th'ear piercing fife,
The royal banner, and all quality,
Pride, pomp, and circumstance, of glorious
war!
*Othello*, III:3

228 Put out the light, and then put out the light.
If I quench thee, thou flaming minister,
I can again thy former light restore,
Should I repent me; but once put out thy light,
Thou cunning'st pattern of excelling nature,
I know not where is that Promethean heat
That can thy light relume.
*Othello*, V:2

229 Then must you speak
Of one that lov'd not wisely, but too well;
Of one not easily jealous, but, being wrought,
Perplexed in the extreme; of one whose hand,
Like the base Indian, threw a pearl away
Richer than all his tribe.
*Othello*, V:2

230 Crabbed age and youth cannot live together:
Youth is full of pleasure, age is full of care;
Youth like summer morn, age like winter
weather;
Youth like summer brave, age like winter bare.
*The Passionate Pilgrim*, XII

231 Kings are earth's gods; in vice their law's their
will.
*Pericles*, I:1

232 3RD FISHERMAN. Master, I marvel how the
fishes live in the sea.
1ST FISHERMAN. Why, as men do a-land – the
great ones eat up the little ones.
*Pericles*, II:1

233 Beauty itself doth of itself persuade
The eyes of men without an orator.
*The Rape of Lucrece*, I

234 The purest treasure mortal times afford
Is spotless reputation; that away,
Men are but gilded loam or painted clay.
*Richard II*, I:1

235 Things sweet to taste prove in digestion sour.
*Richard II*, I:3

236 Teach thy necessity to reason thus:
There is no virtue like necessity.
*Richard II*, I:3

237 This royal throne of kings, this sceptred isle,
This earth of majesty, this seat of Mars,
This other Eden, demi-paradise,
This fortress built by Nature for herself
Against infection and the hand of war,
This happy breed of men, this little world,
This precious stone set in the silver sea,
Which serves it in the office of a wall,
Or as a moat defensive to a house,
Against the envy of less happier lands;
This blessed plot, this earth, this realm, this
England,
This nurse, this teeming womb of royal kings,
Fear'd by their breed, and famous by their
birth.
*Richard II*, II:1

238 Not all the water in the rough rude sea
Can wash the balm from an anointed king;
The breath of worldly men cannot depose
The deputy elected by the Lord.
*Richard II*, III:2

239 For God's sake let us sit upon the ground
And tell sad stories of the death of kings:
How some have been depos'd, some slain in
war,
Some haunted by the ghosts they have
depos'd,
Some poison'd by their wives, some sleeping
kill'd,
All murder'd – for within the hollow crown
That rounds the mortal temples of a king
Keeps Death his court.
*Richard II*, III:2

240 How sour sweet music is
When time is broke and no proportion kept!
So is it in the music of men's lives.
*Richard II*, V:5

241 Now is the winter of our discontent
Made glorious summer by this sun of York.
*Richard III*, I:1

242 O Lord, methought what pain it was to drown,
What dreadful noise of waters in my ears,
What sights of ugly death within my eyes!
*Richard III*, I:4

243 A horse! a horse ! my kingdom for a horse.
*Richard III*, V:4

244 O Romeo, Romeo! wherefore art thou Romeo?
*Romeo and Juliet*, II:2

245 What's in a name? That which we call a rose
By any other name would smell as sweet.
*Romeo and Juliet*, II:2

246 O, swear not by the moon, th' inconstant
moon,
That monthly changes in her circled orb,
Lest that thy love prove likewise variable.
*Romeo and Juliet*, II:2

247 Good night, good night! Parting is such sweet
sorrow
That I shall say good night till it be morrow.
*Romeo and Juliet*, II:2

248 Wisely and slow; they stumble that run fast.
*Romeo and Juliet*, II:3

249 Therefore love moderately: long love doth so;
Too swift arrives as tardy as too slow.
*Romeo and Juliet*, II:6

250 A plague o' both your houses!
They have made worms' meat of me.
*Romeo and Juliet*, III:1

251 Thank me no thankings, nor proud me no
prouds.
*Romeo and Juliet*, III:5

252 'Tis an ill cook that cannot lick his own fingers.
*Romeo and Juliet*, IV:2

253 From fairest creatures we desire increase,
That thereby beauty's rose might never die.
*Sonnet 1*

254 Shall I compare thee to a summer's day?
Thou art more lovely and more temperate.
Rough winds do shake the darling buds of
May,
And summer's lease hath all too short a date.
*Sonnet 18*

255 A woman's face, with Nature's own hand
painted,
Hast thou, the Master Mistress of my passion.
*Sonnet 20*

**256**  When in disgrace with fortune and men's eyes
I all alone beweep my outcast state,
And trouble deaf heaven with my bootless
cries,
And look upon myself, and curse my fate,
Wishing me like to one more rich in hope
Featur'd like him, like him with friends
possess'd,
Desiring this man's art, and that man's scope,
With what I most enjoy contented least.
*Sonnet 29*

**257**  When to the sessions of sweet silent thought
I summon up remembrance of things past,
I sigh the lack of many a thing I sought,
And with old woes new wail my dear time's
waste.
*Sonnet 30*

**258**  Not marble, nor the gilded monuments
Of princes, shall outlive this powerful rhyme.
*Sonnet 55*

**259**  Like as the waves make towards the pebbled
shore,
So do our minutes hasten to their end.
*Sonnet 60*

**260**  That time of year thou mayst in me behold
When yellow leaves, or none, or few, do hang
Upon those boughs which shake against the
cold,
Bare ruin'd choirs, where late the sweet birds
sang.
*Sonnet 73*

**261**  Farewell! thou art too dear for my possessing,
And like enough thou know'st thy estimate:
The charter of thy worth gives thee releasing;
My bonds in thee are all determinate.
*Sonnet 87*

**262**  For sweetest things turn sourest by their
deeds:
Lilies that fester smell far worse than weeds.
*Sonnet 94*

**263**  When in the chronicle of wasted time
I see descriptions of the fairest wights.
*Sonnet 106*

**264**  Let me not to the marriage of true minds
Admit impediments. Love is not love
Which alters when it alteration finds,
Or bends with the remover to remove.
O, no! it is an ever-fixed mark,
That looks on tempests and is never shaken.
*Sonnet 116*

**265**  Love alters not with his brief hours and weeks,
But bears it out even to the edge of doom.
If this be error, and upon me prov'd,
I never writ, nor no man ever lov'd.
*Sonnet 116*

**266**  Th' expense of spirit in a waste of shame
Is lust in action; and till action, lust
Is perjur'd, murd'rous, bloody, full of blame,
Savage, extreme, rude, cruel, not to trust;
Enjoy'd no sooner but despised straight.
*Sonnet 129*

**267**  My mistress' eyes are nothing like the sun;
Coral is far more red than her lips' red.
*Sonnet 130*

**268**  And yet, by heaven, I think my love as rare
As any she belied with false compare.
*Sonnet 130*

**269**  Two loves I have, of comfort and despair,
Which like two spirits do suggest me still;
The better angel is a man right fair,
The worser spirit a woman colour'd ill.
*Sonnet 144*

**270**  No profit grows where is no pleasure ta'en;
In brief, sir, study what you most affect.
*The Taming of the Shrew, I:1*

**271**  This is a way to kill a wife with kindness.
*The Taming of the Shrew, IV:1*

**272**  Our purses shall be proud, our garments poor;
For 'tis the mind that makes the body rich;
And as the sun breaks through the darkest
clouds,
So honour peereth in the meanest habit.
*The Taming of the Shrew, IV:3*

**273**  Full fathom five thy father lies;
Of his bones are coral made;
Those are pearls that were his eyes;
Nothing of him that doth fade
But doth suffer a sea-change
Into something rich and strange.
*The Tempest, I:2*

**274**  When they will not give a doit to relieve a lame
beggar, they will lay out ten to see a dead
Indian.
*The Tempest, II:2*

**275**  Misery acquaints a man with strange
bedfellows.
*The Tempest, II:2*

**276**  He that dies pays all debts.
*The Tempest, III:2*

**277**  Our revels now are ended. These our actors,
As I foretold you, were all spirits, and
Are melted into air, into thin air;
And, like the baseless fabric of this vision,
The cloud-capp'd towers, the gorgeous
palaces,
The solemn temples, the great globe itself,
Yea, all which it inherit, shall dissolve,
And, like this insubstantial pageant faded,
Leave not a rack behind. We are such stuff
As dreams are made on; and our little life
Is rounded with a sleep.
*The Tempest, IV:1*

278 I'll break my staff,
Bury it certain fathoms in the earth,
And deeper than did ever plummet sound
I'll drown my book.
*The Tempest*, V:1

279 How beauteous mankind is! O brave new world
That has such people in't!
*The Tempest*, V:1

280 That she belov'd knows nought that knows not
this:
Men prize the thing ungain'd more than it is.
*Troilus and Cressida*, I:2

281 O, when degree is shak'd,
Which is the ladder of all high designs,
The enterprise is sick!
*Troilus and Cressida*, I:3

282 To be wise and love
Exceeds man's might.
*Troilus and Cressida*, III:2

283 Time hath, my lord, a wallet at his back,
Wherein he puts alms for oblivion,
A great-siz'd monster of ingratitudes.
*Troilus and Cressida*, III:3

284 Lechery, lechery! Still wars and lechery! Nothing else holds fashion.
*Troilus and Cressida*, V:2

285 If music be the food of love, play on,
Give me excess of it, that, surfeiting,
The appetite may sicken and so die.
*Twelfth Night*, I:1

286 Is it a world to hide virtues in?
*Twelfth Night*, I:3

287 Many a good hanging prevents a bad marriage.
*Twelfth Night*, I:5

288 Not to be abed after midnight is to be up
betimes.
*Twelfth Night*, II:3

289 What is love? 'Tis not hereafter;
Present mirth hath present laughter;
What's to come is still unsure.
In delay there lies no plenty,
Then come kiss me, sweet and twenty;
Youth's a stuff will not endure.
*Twelfth Night*, II:3

290 Dost thou think, because thou art virtuous,
there shall be no more cakes and ale?
*Twelfth Night*, II:3

291 She never told her love,
But let concealment, like a worm i' th' bud,
Feed on her damask cheek. She pin'd in
thought;
And with a green and yellow melancholy
She sat like Patience on a monument,
Smiling at grief.
*Twelfth Night*, II:4

292 Some are born great, some achieve greatness,
and some have greatness thrust upon 'em.
*Twelfth Night*, II:5

293 Love sought is good, but given unsought is
better.
*Twelfth Night*, III:1

294 If this were play'd upon a stage now, I could
condemn it as an improbable fiction.
*Twelfth Night*, III:4

295 Still you keep o' th' windy side of the law.
*Twelfth Night*, III:4

296 I hate ingratitude more in a man
Than lying, vainness, babbling drunkenness,
Or any taint of vice whose strong corruption
Inhabits our frail blood.
*Twelfth Night*, III:4

297 Home-keeping youth have ever homely wits.
*The Two Gentlemen of Verona*, I:1

298 I have no other but a woman's reason:
I think him so, because I think him so.
*The Two Gentlemen of Verona*, I:2

299 Who is Silvia? What is she,
That all our swains commend her?
Holy, fair, and wise is she.
*The Two Gentlemen of Verona*, IV:2

300 What's gone and what's past help
Should be past grief.
*The Winter's Tale*, III:2

301 I would there were no age between ten and
three and twenty, or that youth would sleep
out the rest; for there is nothing in the between but getting wenches with child, wronging the ancientry, stealing, fighting.
*The Winter's Tale*, III:3

302 *Exit, pursued by a bear.*
Stage direction
*The Winter's Tale*, III:3

303 A snapper-up of unconsidered trifles.
*The Winter's Tale*, IV:2

304 Though I am not naturally honest, I am so
sometimes by chance.
*The Winter's Tale*, IV:3

305 Though authority be a stubborn bear, yet he is
oft led by the nose with gold.
*The Winter's Tale*, IV:3

**Sharpe, Tom** (1928– ) British novelist, author of such
humorous works as *Indecent Exposure* (1973), *Porterhouse Blue*
(1974), and *Blott on the Landscape* (1975).

1 The South African Police would leave no stone
unturned to see that nothing disturbed the
even terror of their lives.
*Indecent Exposure*, Ch. 1

2 Skullion had little use for contraceptives at the best of times. Unnatural, he called them, and placed them in the lower social category of things along with elastic-sided boots and made-up bow ties. Not the sort of attire for a gentleman.
*Porterhouse Blue*, Ch. 9

3 His had been an intellectual decision founded on his conviction that if a little knowledge was a dangerous thing, a lot was lethal.
*Porterhouse Blue*, Ch. 18

**Shaw, George Bernard** (1856–1950) Irish dramatist and critic. His plays, with their long prefaces, established him as the leading British playwright of his time. Included among his prose works are *The Intelligent Woman's Guide to Socialism and Capitalism* (1928) and *The Black Girl in Search of God* (1932).

1 Whether you think Jesus was God or not, you must admit that he was a first-rate political economist.
*Androcles and the Lion*, Preface, 'Jesus as Economist'

2 All great truths begin as blasphemies.
*Annajanska*

3 You are a very poor soldier: a chocolate cream soldier!
*Arms and the Man*, I

4 Silence is the most perfect expression of scorn.
*Back to Methuselah*

5 When a stupid man is doing something he is ashamed of, he always declares that it is his duty.
*Caesar and Cleopatra*, III

6 A man of great common sense and good taste, – meaning thereby a man without originality or moral courage.
Referring to Julius Caesar
*Caesar and Cleopatra*, Notes

7 The British soldier can stand up to anything except the British War Office.
*The Devil's Disciple*, II

8 I never expect a soldier to think.
*The Devil's Disciple*, III

9 With the single exception of Homer, there is no eminent writer, not even Sir Walter Scott, whom I can despise so entirely as I despise Shakespeare when I measure my mind against his . . . It would positively be a relief to me to dig him up and throw stones at him.
*Dramatic Opinions and Essays*, Vol. 2

10 Physically there is nothing to distinguish human society from the farm-yard except that children are more troublesome and costly than chickens and women are not so completely enslaved as farm stock.
*Getting Married*, Preface

11 My way of joking is to tell the truth. It's the funniest joke in the world.
*John Bull's Other Island*, II

12 Cusins is a very nice fellow, certainly: nobody would ever guess that he was born in Australia.
*Major Barbara*, I

13 Nobody can say a word against Greek: it stamps a man at once as an educated gentleman.
*Major Barbara*, I

14 Alcohol is a very necessary article . . . It enables Parliament to do things at eleven at night that no sane person would do at eleven in the morning.
*Major Barbara*, II

15 He never does a proper thing without giving an improper reason for it.
*Major Barbara*, III

16 He knows nothing; and he thinks he knows everything. That points clearly to a political career.
*Major Barbara*, III

17 CUSINS. Do you call poverty a crime?
UNDERSHAFT. The worst of all crimes. All the other crimes are virtues beside it.
*Major Barbara*, IV

18 Give women the vote, and in five years there will be a crushing tax on bachelors.
*Man and Superman*, Preface

19 A lifetime of happiness: no man alive could bear it: it would be hell on earth.
*Man and Superman*, I

20 Very nice sort of place, Oxford, I should think, for people that like that sort of place.
*Man and Superman*, II

21 It is a woman's business to get married as soon as possible, and a man's to keep unmarried as long as he can.
*Man and Superman*, II

22 There are two tragedies in life. One is to lose your heart's desire. The other is to gain it.
*Man and Superman*, IV

23 In heaven an angel is nobody in particular.
*Man and Superman*, 'Maxims for Revolutionists'

24 Beware of the man who does not return your blow: he neither forgives you nor allows you to forgive yourself.
*Man and Superman*, 'Maxims for Revolutionists'

25 Do not love your neighbour as yourself. If you are on good terms with yourself it is an impertinence; if on bad, an injury.
*Man and Superman*, 'Maxims for Revolutionists'

26 Titles distinguish the mediocre, embarrass the superior, and are disgraced by the inferior.
*Man and Superman*, 'Maxims for Revolutionists'

27 Self-denial is not a virtue; it is only the effect of prudence on rascality.
*Man and Superman*, 'Maxims for Revolutionists'

**28** If you strike a child, take care that you strike it in anger, even at the risk of maiming it for life. A blow in cold blood neither can nor should be forgiven.
*Man and Superman,* 'Maxims for Revolutionists'

**29** The golden rule is that there are no golden rules.
*Man and Superman,* 'Maxims for Revolutionists'

**30** He who can, does. He who cannot, teaches.
*Man and Superman,* 'Maxims for Revolutionists'

**31** Optimistic lies have such immense therapeutic value that a doctor who cannot tell them convincingly has mistaken his profession.
*Misalliance,* Preface

**32** Heaven, as conventionally conceived, is a place so inane, so dull, so useless, so miserable, that nobody has ever ventured to describe a whole day in heaven, though plenty of people have described a day at the seaside.
*Misalliance,* Preface

**33** The secret of being miserable is to have leisure to bother about whether you are happy or not.
*Misalliance,* Preface

**34** The English have no respect for their language, and will not teach their children to speak it . . . It is impossible for an Englishman to open his mouth, without making some other Englishman despise him.
*Pygmalion,* Preface

**35** They all thought she was dead; but my father he kept ladling gin down her throat till she came to so sudden that she bit the bowl off the spoon.
*Pygmalion,* III

**36** Gin was mother's milk to her.
*Pygmalion,* III.

**37** Assassination is the extreme form of censorship.
*The Shewing-Up of Blanco Posnet,* 'The Limits of Toleration'

**38** It is the sexless novel that should be distinguished: the sex novel is now normal.
*Table-Talk of G.B.S.*

**39** It does not follow . . . that the right to criticize Shakespeare involves the power of writing better plays. And in fact . . . I do not profess to write better plays.
*Three Plays for Puritans,* Preface

**40** We're from Madeira, but perfectly respectable, so far.
*You Never Can Tell,* I

**41** Well, sir, you never can tell. That's a principle in life with me, sir, if you'll excuse my having such a thing, sir.
*You Never Can Tell,* II

**42** I've been offered titles, but I think they get one into disreputable company.
*Gossip* (A. Barrow)

**43** The thought of two thousand people crunching celery at the same time horrified me.
Explaining why he had turned down an invitation to a vegetarian gala dinner
*The Greatest Laughs of All Time* (G. Lieberman)

**44** It's a funny thing about that bust. As time goes on it seems to get younger and younger.
Referring to a portrait bust sculpted for him by Rodin
*More Things I Wish I'd Said* (K. Edwards)

**45** The trouble, Mr Goldwyn is that you are only interested in art and I am only interested in money.
Turning down Goldwyn's offer to buy the screen rights of his plays
*The Movie Moguls* (Philip French), Ch. 4

**46** I quite agree with you, sir, but what can two do against so many?
Responding to a solitary hiss heard amongst the applause at the first performance of *Arms and the Man* in 1894
*Oxford Book of Literary Anecdotes*

**47** Certainly, there is nothing else here to enjoy.
Said at a party when his hostess asked him whether he was enjoying himself
*Pass the Port* (Oxfam)

**48** Far too good to waste on children.
Reflecting upon youth
*10,000 Jokes, Toasts, and Stories* (L. Copeland)

**49** Better never than late.
Responding to an offer by a producer to present one of Shaw's plays, having earlier rejected it
*The Unimportance of Being Oscar* (Oscar Levant)

**50** LORD NORTHCLIFFE. The trouble with you, Shaw, is that you look as if there were famine in the land.
G.B.S. The trouble with you, Northcliffe, is that you look as if you were the cause of it.
Attrib.

**51** If all economists were laid end to end, they would not reach a conclusion.
Attrib.

**Shawcross, Hartley (William), Lord** (1902– )
British Labour politician and lawyer, who was Attorney-General (1945–51).

**1** We are the masters at the moment – and not only for the moment, but for a very long time to come.
Sometimes quoted as, 'We are the masters now!'
House of Commons, 2 Apr 1946

**Sheen, J(ohn) Fulton** (1895–1979) US Roman Catholic archbishop. He was a broadcaster and prolific writer of books and pamphlets.

**1** The big print giveth and the fine print taketh away.
Referring to his contract for a televison appearance
Attrib.

**Shelley, Percy Bysshe** (1792–1822) British poet. Most of his poetry was written in Italy, including *Prometheus Unbound* (1818–19), *Adonais* (1821), and much lyrical poetry.

1  I weep for Adonais – he is dead!
O, weep for Adonais! though our tears
Thaw not the frost which binds so dear a head!
*Prompted by the death of Keats*
*Adonais*, I

2  He hath awakened from the dream of life –
'Tis we, who lost in stormy visions, keep
With phantoms an unprofitable strife,
And in mad trance, strike with our spirit's knife
Invulnerable nothings.
*Adonais*, XXXIX

3  I wield the flail of the lashing hail,
And whiten the green plains under,
And then again I dissolve it in rain,
And laugh as I pass in thunder.
*The Cloud*

4  I am the daughter of Earth and Water,
And the nursling of the Sky;
I pass through the pores of the ocean and
shores;
I change, but I cannot die,
For after the rain when with never a stain
The pavilion of Heaven is bare,
And the winds and sunbeams with their convex
gleams
Build up the blue dome of air,
I silently laugh at my own cenotaph,
And out of the caverns of rain,
Like a child from the womb, like a ghost from
the tomb,
I arise and unbuild it again.
*The Cloud*

5  Poetry is the record of the best and happiest
moments of the happiest and best minds.
*A Defence of Poetry*

6  Life may change, but it may fly not;
Hope may vanish, but can die not;
Truth be veiled, but still it burneth;
Love repulsed, – but it returneth!
*Hellas*, 1

7  Let there be light! said Liberty,
And like sunrise from the sea,
Athens arose!
*Hellas*, 1

8  London, that great sea, whose ebb and flow
At once is deaf and loud, and on the shore
Vomits its wrecks, and still howls on for more.
*Letter to Maria Gisborne*, 1

9  Have you not heard
When a man marries, dies, or turns Hindoo,
His best friends hear no more of him?
*Referring to Thomas Love Peacock, who worked for the East
India Company and had recently married*
*Letter to Maria Gisborne*, 1

10  Lift not the painted veil which those who live
Call life.
*Lift not the Painted Veil*

11  I met Murder on the way–
He had a mask like Castlereagh.
*Viscount Castlereagh (1769–1822) was British foreign secretary
(1812–22); he was highly unpopular and became identified with
such controversial events as the Peterloo massacre of 1819*
*The Mask of Anarchy*, 5

12  O Wild West Wind, thou breath of Autumn's
being,
Thou, from whose unseen presence the leaves
dead
Are driven, like ghosts from an enchanter
fleeing,
Yellow, and black, and pale, and hectic red,
Pestilence-stricken multitudes.
*Ode to the West Wind*

13  If Winter comes, can Spring be far behind?
*Ode to the West Wind*

14  I met a traveller from an antique land
Who said: Two vast and trunkless legs of stone
Stand in the desert.
*Referring to the legs of a broken statue of the Pharaoh Rameses
II (1301–1234 BC; Greek name, Ozymandias)*
*Ozymandias*

15  'My name is Ozymandias, king of kings:
Look on my works, ye Mighty, and despair!'
*Ozymandias*

16  Sometimes
The Devil is a gentleman.
*Peter Bell the Third*

17  Teas,
Where small talk dies in agonies.
*Peter Bell the Third*

18  'Twas Peter's drift
To be a kind of moral eunuch.
*Peter Bell the Third*

19  Hell is a city much like London–
A populous and smoky city.
*Peter Bell the Third*

20  Death is the veil which those who live call life:
They sleep, and it is lifted.
*Prometheus Unbound*, III

21  It is a modest creed, and yet
Pleasant if one considers it,
To own that death itself must be,
Like all the rest, a mockery.
*The Sensitive Plant*, III

22  Hail to thee, blithe Spirit!
Bird thou never wert,
That from Heaven, or near it,
Pourest thy full heart
In profuse strains of unpremeditated art.
*To a Skylark*

**23** Music, when soft voices die,
Vibrates in the memory –
Odours, when sweet violets sicken,
Live within the sense they quicken.

Rose leaves, when the rose is dead,
Are heaped for the beloved's bed;
And so thy thoughts, when thou art gone,
Love itself shall slumber on.
*To –*

**24** For she was beautiful – her beauty made
The bright world dim, and everything beside
Seemed like the fleeting image of a shade.
*The Witch of Atlas, XII*

**Shenstone, William** (1714–63) British poet. His works include *The Schoolmistress* (1737) and *Pastoral Ballad* (1755).

**1** Laws are generally found to be nets of such a texture, as the little creep through, the great break through, and the middle-sized are alone entangled in.
Similar remarks have been made by others; *see* SOLON; SWIFT
*Essays on Men, Manners, and Things*, 'On Politics'

**Sheridan, Philip H(enry)** (1831–88) US general. He commanded the Army of the Shenandoah and led a number of raids into Confederate territory.

**1** The only good Indians I ever saw were dead.
*The People's Almanac 2* (D. Wallechinsky)

**Sheridan, Richard Brinsley** (1751–1816) British dramatist. His best-known comedies are *The Rivals* (1775) and *School for Scandal* (1777). He was manager of the Drury Lane Theatre and a Whig MP (1780–1812).

**1** If it is abuse – why one is always sure to hear of it from one damned good-natured friend or other!
*The Critic, I*

**2** A progeny of learning.
*The Rivals, I*

**3** Illiterate him, I say, quite from your memory.
*The Rivals, II*

**4** It gives me the hydrostatics to such a degree.
*The Rivals, III*

**5** As headstrong as an allegory on the banks of the Nile.
*The Rivals, III*

**6** He is the very pine-apple of politeness!
*The Rivals, III*

**7** If I reprehend any thing in this world, it is the use of my oracular tongue, and a nice derangement of epitaphs!
*The Rivals, III*

**8** You had no taste when you married me.
*The School for Scandal, I*

**9** I'm called away by particular business. But I leave my character behind me.
*The School for Scandal, II*

**10** Well, then, my stomach must just digest in its waistcoat.
On being warned that his drinking would destroy the coat of his stomach
*The Fine Art of Political Wit* (L. Harris)

**11** What His Royal Highness most particularly prides himself upon, is the excellent harvest.
Lampooning George IV's habit of taking credit for everything good in England
*The Fine Art of Political Wit* (L. Harris)

**12** My dear fellow, be reasonable; the sum you ask me for is a very considerable one, whereas I only ask you for twenty-five pounds.
On being refused a further loan of £25 from a friend to whom he already owed £500
*Literary and Scientific Anecdotes* (W. Keddie)

**13** Whatsoever might be the extent of the private calamity, I hope it will not interfere with the public business of the country.
On learning, whilst in the House of Commons, that his Drury Lane Theatre was on fire
*Memoirs of Life of the R. Hon. Richard Brinsley Sheridan* (T. Moore)

**14** A man may surely be allowed to take a glass of wine by his own fireside.
As he sat in a coffeehouse watching his Drury Lane Theatre burn down
*Memoirs of the Life of the Rt. Hon. Richard Brinsley Sheridan* (T. Moore)

**15** Thank God, that's settled.
Handing one of his creditors an IOU
*Wit, Wisdom, and Foibles of the Great* (C. Shriner)

**16** Won't you come into the garden? I would like my roses to see you.
Said to a young lady
Attrib. in *The Perfect Hostess*

**17** It is not my interest to pay the principal, nor my principle to pay the interest.
To his tailor when he requested the payment of a debt, or of the interest on it at least
Attrib.

**18** The Right Honourable gentleman is indebted to his memory for his jests, and to his imagination for his facts.
Replying to a speech in the House of Commons
Attrib.

**19** Mr. Speaker, I said the honorable member was a liar it is true and I am sorry for it. The honourable member may place the punctuation where he pleases.
On being asked to apologize for calling a fellow MP a liar
Attrib.

**Sheridan, Tom** (1775–1817) Son of the playwright Richard Brinsley Sheridan; he was colonial treasurer to the Cape of Good Hope.

**1** I'm sorry to hear that, sir, you don't happen to have the shilling about you now, do you?
To his father, on learning that he was to be cut off in his will with a shilling
*The Fine Art of Political Wit* (L. Harris)

**Sherman, William Tecumseh, General** (1820–91) US general. One of the great Civil War generals, he fought in Georgia and the Carolinas (1864–65), contributing to the Confederate defeat.

1 I will not accept if nominated, and will not serve if elected.
   Replying to a request that he accept the Republican presidential nomination
   Attrib.

2 I am tired and sick of war. Its glory is all moonshine . . . War is hell.
   Attrib. in address, Michigan Military Academy, 19 June 1879

**Sherrington, Sir Charles Scott** (1857–1952) British physiologist, who shared the Nobel Prize in 1932 for his study of the nervous system.

1 If it is for mind that we are seaching the brain, then we are supposing the brain to be much more than a telephone-exchange. We are supposing it a telephone-exchange along with the subscribers as well.
   Man on his Nature

**Sherwood, Robert Emmet** (1896–1955) US writer and dramatist. He wrote Waterloo Bridge (1930), The Petrified Forest (1934), and Idiot's Delight (1936). He also wrote a novel, The Virtuous Knight (1931).

1 It is disappointing to report that George Bernard Shaw appearing as George Bernard Shaw is sadly miscast in the part. Satirists should be heard and not seen.
   Reviewing a Shaw play

**Shorter, Clement King** (1857–1926) British journalist and literary critic. He founded and edited The Sketch (1893–1900), and was editor of The Sphere (1900–26). He wrote Charlotte Brontë and her Circle (1896), Sixty Years of Victorian Literature (1897), and Napoleon's Fellow Travellers (1909).

1 The latest definition of an optimist is one who fills up his crossword puzzle in ink.
   The Observer, 'Sayings of the Week', 22 Feb 1925

**Shuter, Edward** (1728–76) British actor, who excelled in plays by Goldsmith, Sheridan, Farquhar, and others.

1 A hole is the accident of a day, while a darn is premeditated poverty.
   Explaining why he did not mend the holes in his stocking
   Dictionary of National Biography

**Sickert, Walter Richard** (1860–1942) British impressionist painter and etcher, who painted scenes of Venice and Dieppe, and subjects from music hall and domestic life.

1 Nothing links man to man like the frequent passage from hand to hand of cash.
   A Certain World (W. H. Auden)

**Sidney, Algernon** (1622–83) English statesman. A prominent Whig politician, he was beheaded for his involvement in the Rye House Plot against Charles II and James, Duke of York.

1 'Tis not necessary to light a candle to the sun.
   Discourses concerning Government, Ch. 2

**Sidney, Sir Philip** (1554–86) English poet and courtier. His works include Astrophel and Stella (1591) and the first work of English literary criticism, The Defence of Poesy (1595).

1 Biting my truant pen, beating myself for spite: 'Fool!' said my Muse to me, 'look in thy heart and write.'
   Sonnet, Astrophel and Stella

2 There have been many most excellent poets that have never versified, and now swarm many versifiers that need never answer to the name of poets.
   The Defence of Poesy

3 Thy need is yet greater than mine.
   Giving his own water bottle to a humble wounded soldier after he had himself been wounded
   Attrib.

**Sieyès, Emmanuel-Joseph, Abbé de** (1748–1836) French churchman, a major figure during the Revolution who also played a key role in the rise of Napoleon.

1 J'ai vécu.
   I survived.
   Replying to an enquiry concerning what he had done during the Terror
   Dictionnaire Encyclopédique (E. Guérard)

**Sigismund** (1368–1437) Holy Roman Emperor (1411–37), King of Hungary (1387–1437), and King of Bohemia (1419–37). He conducted two unsuccessful crusades agains the Turks.

1 Only do always in health what you have often promised to do when you are sick.
   His advice on achieving happiness
   Biographiana, Vol. I

2 I am the Roman Emperor, and am above grammar.
   Responding to criticism of his Latin
   Attrib.

**Simon, Paul** (1941– ) US singer and songwriter, who has written such successful songs as 'The Boxer', 'Bridge Over Troubled Water', and 'Sound of Silence'. For many years he collaborated with Art Garfunkel.

1 Like a bridge over troubled water,
   I will ease your mind.
   Bridge Over Troubled Water

2 Here's to you, Mrs Robinson,
   Jesus loves you more than you will know.
   Mrs Robinson

3 People talking without speaking,
   People listening without hearing,
   People writing songs that voices never shared.
   Sound of Silence

**Simpson, N(orman) F(rederick)** (1919– ) British dramatist. His work, influenced by the Theatre of the Absurd, includes the plays A Resounding Tinkle (1956) and One-Way Pendulum (1959).

1 Knocked down a doctor? With an ambulance? How could she? It's a contradiction in terms.
   One-Way Pendulum, I

**Singer, Isaac Bashevis** (1904– ) Polish-born US novelist and short-story writer. His novels are written in Yiddish; they include *Gimple the Fool* (1957), *The Slave* (1960), and *Old Love* (1979).

1 Children... have no use for psychology. They detest sociology. They still believe in God, the family, angels, devils, witches, goblins, logic, clarity, punctuation, and other such obsolete stuff... When a book is boring, they yawn openly. They don't expect their writer to redeem humanity, but leave to adults such childish illusions.

Speech on receiving the Nobel Prize for Literature
*The Observer*, 17 Dec 1978

2 We have to believe in free will. We've got no choice.

*The Times*, 21 June 1982

**Sitting Bull** (c. 1834–90) US Sioux Indian chief, who defeated General Custer at the massacre of Little Big Horn in 1876. He was killed during a later outbreak of hostilities.

1 The white man knows how to make everything, but he does not know how to distribute it.

Attrib.

**Sitwell, Dame Edith** (1887–1964) British poet and writer, sister of Osbert Sitwell. *Façade* (1923) was set to music by William Walton; her other collections include *Gold Coast Customs* (1929).

1 My poems are hymns of praise to the glory of life.

*Collected Poems*, 'Some Notes on My Poetry'

2 Who dreamed that Christ has died in vain?
He walks again on the Seas of Blood,
He comes in the terrible Rain.

*The Shadow of Cain*

3 A lady asked me why, on most occasions, I wore black. "Are you in mourning?"
"Yes."
"For whom are you in mourning?"
"For the world."

*Taken Care Of*, Ch. 1

4 A pompous woman of his acquaintance, complaining that the head-waiter of a restaurant had not shown her and her husband immediately to a table, said, "We had to tell him who we were." Gerald, interested, enquired, "And who were you?"

*Taken Care Of*, Ch. 15

5 I have often wished I had time to cultivate modesty... But I am too busy thinking about myself.

*The Observer*, 'Sayings of the Week', 30 Apr 1950

6 I enjoyed talking to her, but thought *nothing* of her writing. I considered her 'a beautiful little knitter'.

Referring to Virginia Woolf
Letter to G. Singleton

**Sitwell, Sir Osbert** (1892–1969) British writer of short stories, novels, and poetry, best-known for his nostalgic memoirs. His sister was Dame Edith Sitwell.

1 In reality, *killing time*
Is only the name for another of the multifarious ways
By which Time kills us.

*Milordo Inglese*

2 But He was never, well,
What I call
A Sportsman;
For forty days
He went out into the desert
– And never shot anything.

*Old Fashioned Sportsmen*

**Skelton, Red** (Richard Bernard Skelton; 1913– ) US actor and comedian; he made more than 45 films and was the star of a long-running TV show until his retirement in 1970.

1 It proves what they say, give the public what they want to see and they'll come out for it.

Said while attending the funeral in 1958 of Hollywood producer Harry Cohn. It has also been attributed to Samuel Goldwyn while attending Louis B. Mayer's funeral in 1957

**Skelton, Robin** (1925– ) British academic and author of many books on poetry.

1 A man does not write poems about what he knows, but about what he does not know.

*Teach Yourself Poetry*

**Skinner, B(urrhus) F(rederic)** (1904– ) US psychologist. He investigated learning ability in animals by means of carefully controlled experiments and advocated behaviourism in his books, including *The Behaviour of Organisms* (1938) and *Beyond Freedom and Dignity* (1971).

1 Indeed one of the ultimate advantages of an education is simply coming to the end of it.

*The Technology of Teaching*

2 Education is what survives when what has been learnt has been forgotten.

*New Scientist*, 21 May 1964, 'Education in 1984'

**Skinner, Cornelia Otis** (1901–79) US stage actress. She made a few films, including *The Uninvited* (1944) and *The Swimmer* (1967).

1 Woman's virtue is man's greatest invention.

Attrib.

**Slezak, Leo** (1873–1946) Czechoslovakian-born tenor, noted for his performances in Wagnerian operas. He also appeared in several films.

1 What time is the next swan?

When the mechanical swan left the stage without him during a performance of *Lohengrin*
*What Time Is the Next Swan?* (Walter Slezak)

**Slocombe, George Edward** (1894–1963) British journalist. He worked for the *Daily Herald* (1920–31), the *Evening Standard* (1932–34), and the *Sunday Express* (from 1940). He also wrote several books including *A History of Poland* (1916) and *Crisis in Europe* (1934).

1 He was the Messiah of the new age, and his crucifixion was yet to come.

Referring to Woodrow Wilson and his visit to the Versailles
conference
*Mirror to Geneva*

**Smiles, Samuel** (1812–1904) British writer. He wrote
several biographies and was a railway journalist. He is
remembered for his book *Self-Help* (1859).

1 We often discover what *will* do, by finding out
what will not do; and probably he who never
made a mistake never made a discovery.

*Self-Help*, Ch. 11

2 A place for everything, and everything in its
place.

*Thrift*, Ch. 5

**Smith, Adam** (1723–90) Scottish economist. He lectured on
logic and moral philosophy (1752–63) and wrote *An Enquiry into
the Nature and Causes of the Wealth of Nations* (1776).

1 People of the same trade seldom meet together
but the conversation ends in a conspiracy
against the public, or in some diversion to raise
prices.

*The Wealth of Nations*

2 With the great part of rich people, the chief employment of riches consists in the parade of
riches.

*The Wealth of Nations*

3 There is no art which one government sooner
learns of another than that of draining money
from the pockets of the people.

*The Wealth of Nations*

**Smith, Cyril** (1928– ) British Liberal politician, noted for his
bulk and outspoken manner. His autobiography is entitled *Big Cyril*
(1977).

1 Parliament is the longest running farce in the
West End.

*The Times*, 23 Sept 1977

**Smith, Ian (Douglas)** (1919– ) Rhodesian (Zimbabwe)
politician and prime minister (1964–79). In 1965 he made a
unilateral declaration of independence (UDI) from Britain, and was
for many years opposed to black majority rule in Zimbabwe.

1 I don't believe in black majority rule ever in Rhodesia . . . not in a thousand years.

*Speech, Mar 1976*

**Smith, Logan Pearsall** (1865–1946) US writer. He spent
most of his life in England and is best known for his collections
*Trivia* (1902) and *Afterthoughts* (1931) as well as his books on
language, such as *The English Language* (1912).

1 A best-seller is the gilded tomb of a mediocre
talent.

*Afterthoughts*, 'Art and Letters'

2 It is the wretchedness of being rich that you
have to live with rich people.

*Afterthoughts*, 'In the World'

3 People say that life is the thing, but I prefer
reading.

*Afterthoughts*, 'Myself'

4 Married women are kept women, and they are
beginning to find it out.

*Afterthoughts*, 'Other people'

5 I might give my life for my friend, but he had
better not ask me to do up a parcel.

*Trivia*

6 I am one of the unpraised, unrewarded millions
without whom Statistics would be a bankrupt
science. It is we who are born, who marry,
who die, in constant ratios.

*Trivia*

7 I cannot forgive my friends for dying: I do not
find these vanishing acts of theirs at all amusing.

*Trivia*

8 Yes there is a meaning; at least for me, there is
one thing that matters – to set a chime of
words tinkling in the minds of a few fastidious
people.

Contemplating whether life has any meaning, shortly before his
death
Attrib.

**Smith, Stevie** (Florence Margaret Smith; 1902–71) British
poet and novelist. She worked as a secretary and lived in her
aunt's home in Palmer's Green, London, all her adult life. Her
novel *Novel on Yellow Paper* (1936) was followed by her first
verse collection *A Good Time Was Had by All* (1937). Her
*Collected Poems* (1975) were published posthumously.

1 A Good Time Was Had by All.

Book title

2 Nobody heard him, the dead man,
But still he lay moaning:
I was much further out than you thought
And not waving but drowning.

*Not Waving But Drowning*

3 Private Means is dead,
God rest his soul,
Officers and fellow-rankers said.

*Private Means is Dead*

4 I do really think that death will be marvellous
. . . If there wasn't death, I think you couldn't go
on.

*The Observer*, 9 Nov 1969

**Smith, Sydney** (1771–1845) British clergyman, essayist, and
wit. He helped to found the *Edinburgh Review* (1802), and
published many of his sermons, essays, speeches, and letters.

1 Mankind are always happy for having been happy, so that if you make them happy now, you
make them happy twenty years hence by the
memory of it.

*Elementary Sketches of Moral Philosophy*

2 The moment the very name of Ireland is mentioned, the English seem to bid adieu to common feeling, common prudence, and common sense, and to act with the barbarity of tyrants, and the fatuity of idiots.
*The Letters of Peter Plymley*

3 They are written as if sin were to be taken out of man like Eve out of Adam – by putting him to sleep.
Referring to boring sermons
*Anecdotes of the Clergy* (J. Larwood)

4 Heat, madam! It was so dreadful that I found there was nothing for it but to take off my flesh and sit in my bones.
Discussing the hot weather with a lady acquaintance
*Lives of the Wits* (H. Pearson)

5 You never expected justice from a company, did you? They have neither a soul to lose nor a body to kick.
*Memoir* (Lady Holland)

6 What you don't know would make a great book.
*Memoir* (Lady Holland)

7 That knuckle-end of England – that land of Calvin, oat-cakes, and sulphur.
*Memoir* (Lady Holland)

8 How can a bishop marry? How can he flirt? The most he can say is, 'I will see you in the vestry after service.'
*Memoir* (Lady Holland)

9 You find people ready enough to do the Samaritan, without the oil and twopence.
*Memoir* (Lady Holland)

10 My definition of marriage : . . . .it resembles a pair of shears, so joined that they cannot be separated; often moving in opposite directions, yet always punishing anyone who comes between them.
*Memoir* (Lady Holland)

11 He has occasional flashes of silence, that make his conversation perfectly delightful.
Referring to Lord Macaulay
*Memoir* (Lady Holland)

12 Minorities . . . are almost always in the right.
*The Smith of Smiths* (H. Pearson), Ch. 9

13 I am just going to pray for you at St Paul's, but with no very lively hope of success.
On meeting an acquaintance
*The Smith of Smiths* (H. Pearson), Ch. 13

14 I look upon Switzerland as an inferior sort of Scotland.
Letter to Lord Holland, 1815

15 He who drinks a tumbler of London water has literally in his stomach more animated beings than there are men, women and children on the face of the globe.
Letter

16 You must not think me necessarily foolish because I am facetious, nor will I consider you necessarily wise because you are grave.
Letter to Bishop Blomfield

17 No furniture so charming as books.
Attrib.

18 He rose by gravity; I sank by levity.
Comparing his career with that of his brother, Robert Percy Smith
Attrib.

**Smith, Thorne** (1892–1934) US humorist and writer. His books include *Topper* (1926) and *The Night Life of the Gods* (1931).

1 Steven's mind was so tolerant that he could have attended a lynching every day without becoming critical.
*The Jovial Ghosts*, Ch. 11

**Smollett, Tobias George** (1721–71) British novelist and journalist. His novels include *Roderick Random* (1748) and *Peregrine Pickle* (1751). He also wrote a *Complete History of England* (1757–58).

1 I think for my part one half of the nation is mad –and the other not very sound.
Referring to the English
*The Adventures of Sir Launcelot Greaves*, Ch. 6

2 True patriotism is of no party.
*The Adventures of Sir Launcelot Greaves*

3 Hark ye, Clinker, you are a most notorious offender. You stand convicted of sickness, hunger, wretchedness, and want.
*Humphrey Clinker*, Letter to Sir Watkin Phillips, 24 May

4 Some folk are wise, and some are otherwise.
*Roderick Random*, Ch. 6

5 He was formed for the ruin of our sex.
*Roderick Random*, Ch. 22

6 That great Cham of literature, Samuel Johnson.
Letter to John Wilkes, 16 Mar 1759

**Snow, C(harles) P(ercy), Baron** (1905–80) British novelist. A scientific civil servant, he wrote the 11-novel series *Strangers and Brothers* (1940–70), which included *The Masters* (1951) and *Corridors of Power* (1964). His lecture *The Two Cultures and the Scientific Revolution* (1959) created considerable controversy.

1 'I grant you that he's not two-faced,' I said. 'But what's the use of that when the one face he has got is so peculiarly unpleasant?'
*The Affair*, Ch. 4

2 The official world, the corridors of power, the dilemmas of conscience and egotism – she disliked them all.
*Homecomings*, Ch. 22

3 Jam today, and men aren't at their most exciting: Jam tomorrow, and one often sees them at their noblest.
*The Two Cultures and the Scientific Revolution*, 4

**Snowden, Philip, 1st Viscount** (1864–1937) British politician. He became chancellor of the exchequer in the 1924 and 1929 Labour governments.

1 It would be desirable if every government, when it comes to power, should have its old speeches burned.

**Socrates** (469–399 BC) Athenian philosopher. Although he wrote nothing himself, much is known of his philosophy from the writings of his pupils, especially Plato. Charged with corrupting youth and atheism, he was condemned to death.

1 Nothing can harm a good man, either in life or after death.
*Apology* (Plato)

2 The unexamined life is not worth living.
*Apology* (Plato)

3 But already it is time to depart, for me to die, for you to go on living; which of us takes the better course, is concealed from anyone except God.
*Apology* (Plato)

4 How many things I can do without!
Examining the range of goods on sale at a market
*Lives of the Eminent Philosophers* (Diogenes Laertius), II

5 I am not an Athenian or a Greek, but a citizen of the world.
*Of Banishment* (Plutarch)

6 Crito, we owe a cock to Aesculapius; please pay it and don't let it pass.
Last words before his execution by drinking hemlock
*Phaedo* (Plato), 118

**Solon** (6th century BC) Athenian statesman who founded Athenian democracy and instituted a new constitution based on a lenient legal code.

1 Wrongdoing can only be avoided if those who are not wronged feel the same indignation at it as those who are.
*Greek Wit* (F. Paley)

2 Laws are like spider's webs: if some poor weak creature come up against them, it is caught; but a bigger one can break through and get away.
Similar remarks have been made by others; *see* SHENSTONE; SWIFT
*Lives of the Eminent Philosophers* (Diogenes Laertius), I

**Solzhenitsyn, Alexander** (1918–  ) Soviet novelist. Imprisoned for political dissent, he left the Soviet Union in 1974 and now lives in the USA. His books include *One Day in the Life of Ivan Denisovich* (1962), *Cancer Ward* (1968), and *Gulag Archipelago* (1974–78).

1 The whole of his life had prepared Podduyev for living, not for dying.
*Cancer Ward*, Pt. I, Ch. 8

2 Nowadays we don't think much of a man's love for an animal; we laugh at people who are attached to cats. But if we stop loving animals, aren't we bound to stop loving humans too?
*Cancer Ward*, Pt. I, Ch. 20

3 When truth is discovered by someone else, it loses something of its attractiveness.
*Candle in the Wind*, 3

4 You took my freedom away a long time ago and you can't give it back because you haven't got it yourself.
*The First Circle*, Ch. 17

5 You only have power over people so long as you don't take *everything* away from them. But when you've robbed a man of everything he's no longer in your power – he's free again.
*The First Circle*, Ch. 17

6 Their teacher had advised them not to read Tolstoy novels, because they were very long and would easily confuse the clear ideas which they had learned from reading critical studies of him.
*The First Circle*, Ch. 40

7 No regime has ever loved great writers, only minor ones.
*The First Circle*, Ch. 57

8 This universal, obligatory force-feeding with lies is now the most agonizing aspect of existence in our country – worse than all our material miseries, worse than any lack of civil liberties.
*Letter to Soviet Leaders*, 6

9 Forget the outside world. Life has different laws in here. This is Campland, an invisible country. It's not in the geography books, or the psychology books or the history books. This is the famous country where ninety-nine men weep while one laughs.
*The Love-Girl and the Innocent*, I:3

10 For us in Russia communism is a dead dog, while, for many people in the West, it is still a living lion.
*The Listener*, 15 Feb 1979

11 In our country the lie has become not just a moral category but a pillar of the State.
*The Observer*, 'Sayings of the Year', 29 Dec 1974

12 The salvation of mankind lies only in making everything the concern of all.
Nobel Lecture, 1970

**Somerville, E(dith) Œ(none)** (1858–1949) Irish writer. In collaboration with Martin Ross (Violet Martin; 1862–1915) she wrote *Some Experiences of an Irish R.M.* (1899), which became an international success.

1 Neither principalities nor powers should force me into the drawing-room, where sat the three unhappy women of my party, being entertained within an inch of their lives by Mrs McRory.
*Further Experiences of an Irish R.M.*, 'Sharper than a Ferret's Tooth'

**Sondheim, Stephen Joshua** (1930–  ) US composer and lyricist, noted for such musicals as *West Wide Story* (1957), *A Funny Thing Happened on the Way to the Forum* (1962), and *Sweeney Todd* (1979).

1 Everything's Coming Up Roses.
*Song title*

2 Send in the Clowns.
*Song title*

**Sontag, Susan** (1933– ) US novelist and essayist. Her writings include *Against Interpretation* (1966), *Styles of Radical Will* (1969), *On Photography* (1977), and *Illness as Metaphor* (1978).

1 Illness is the night-side of life, a more onerous citizenship. Everyone who is born holds dual citizenship, in the kingdom of the well and in the kingdom of the sick. Although we all prefer to use only the good passport, sooner or later each of us is obliged, at least for a spell, to identify ourselves as citizens of that other place.
*Illness as Metaphor*

2 A photograph is not only an image (as a painting is an image), an interpretation of the real; it is also a trace, something directly stencilled off the real, like a footprint or a death mask.
*On Photography*

**Sophocles** (c. 496–406 BC) Greek dramatist. Only 7 of his 123 plays survive; the best-known are *Electra*, *Oedipus Rex*, *Oedipus at Colonus*, and *Antigone*.

1 I depict men as they ought to be, but Euripides portrays them as they are.
*Poetics* (Aristotle)

2 Someone asked Sophocles, 'How do you feel now about sex? Are you still able to have a woman?' He replied, 'Hush, man; most gladly indeed am I rid of it all, as though I had escaped from a mad and savage master.'
*Republic* (Plato), Bk. I

**Soule, John Babsone Lane** (1815–91) US writer and editor.

1 Go West, young man, go West!
*Terre Haute* (Indiana) *Express*, 1851

**Southey, Robert** (1774–1843) British poet and writer. A friend of Wordsworth, his epics include *Thalaba* (1801) and *Madoc* (1805); shorter poems include *The Battle of Blenheim* and *The Inchcape Rock*. He also wrote a *Life of Nelson* (1813) and became poet laureate in 1813.

1 'And everybody praised the Duke,
Who this great fight did win.'
'But what good came of it at last?'
Quoth little Peterkin.
'Why that I cannot tell,' said he,
'But 'twas a famous victory.'
*The Battle of Blenheim*

2 Curses are like young chickens, they always come home to roost.
*The Curse of Kehama*, Motto

3 Live as long as you may, the first twenty years are the longest half of your life.
*The Doctor*, Ch. 130

4 You are old, Father William, the young man cried,
The few locks which are left you are grey;
You are hale, Father William, a hearty old man,
Now tell me the reason, I pray.
*See also* Lewis CARROLL
*The Old Man's Comforts, and how he Gained them*

5 In the days of my youth I remembered my God!
And He hath not forgotten my age.
*The Old Man's Comforts, and how he Gained them*

**Spaak, Paul Henri** (1899–1972) Belgian statesman. He became prime minister of Belgium (1938–39; 1947–50), secretary general of NATO (1957–61), and first president of the United Nations (1946).

1 Our agenda is now exhausted. The secretary general is exhausted. All of you are exhausted. I find it comforting that, beginning with our very first day, we find ourselves in such complete unanimity.
Concluding the first General Assembly meeting of the United Nations

**Spark, Muriel** (1918– ) British novelist, born in Edinburgh. Her popular novels include *The Prime of Miss Jean Brodie* (1961), *The Abbess of Crewe* (1974), *Territorial Rights* (1979), and *The Only Problem* (1984).

1 A short neck denotes a good mind ... You see, the messages go quicker to the brain because they've shorter to go.
*The Ballad of Peckham Rye*, Ch. 7

2 Parents learn a lot from their children about coping with life.
*The Comforters*, Ch. 6

3 Every communist has a fascist frown, every fascist a communist smile.
*The Girls of Slender Means*, Ch. 4

4 Selwyn Macgregor, the nicest boy who ever committed the sin of whisky.
*The Go-Away Bird*, 'A Sad Tale's Best for Winter'

5 Being over seventy is like being engaged in a war. All our friends are going or gone and we survive amongst the dead and the dying as on a battlefield.
*Memento Mori*, Ch. 4

6 Give me a girl at an impressionable age, and she is mine for life.
*The Prime of Miss Jean Brodie*, Ch. 1

7 One's prime is elusive. You little girls, when you grow up, must be on the alert to recognize your prime at whatever time of your life it may occur. You must then live it to the full.
*The Prime of Miss Jean Brodie*, Ch. 1

8 If you had been mine when you were seven you would have been the crème de la crème.
*The Prime of Miss Jean Brodie*, Ch. 2

9 Art and religion first; then philosophy; lastly science. That is the order of the great subjects of life, that's their order of importance.
*The Prime of Miss Jean Brodie*, Ch. 2

10 To me education is a leading out of what is already there in the pupil's soul. To Miss Mackay it is a putting in of something that is not there, and that is not what I call education, I call it intrusion. . . .
*The Prime of Miss Jean Brodie*, Ch. 2

11 But I did not remove my glasses, for I had not asked for her company in the first place, and there is a limit to what one can listen to with the naked eye.
*Voices at Play*, 'The Dark Glasses'

12 Do you think it pleases a man when he looks into a woman's eyes and sees a reflection of the British Museum Reading Room?
*The Wit of Women* (L. and M. Cowan)

**Sparrow, John Hanbury Angus** (1906–  ) British lawyer and academic. He became Warden of All Souls College, Oxford (1952–77). His books include *Controversial Essays* (1966) and *Grave Epigrams and Other Verses* (1981).

1 That indefatigable and unsavoury engine of pollution, the dog.
Letter to *The Times*, 30 Sep 1975

**Speight, Johnny** (1920–  ) British television scriptwriter, best known for his creation of the character Alf Garnett in *Till Death Do Us Part*.

1 You silly moo.
*Till Death Do Us Part*

2 If Her Majesty stood for Parliament – if the Tory Party had any sense and made Her its leader instead of that grammar school twit Heath – us Tories, mate, would win every election we went in for.
*Till Death Do Us Part*

3 Don't be daft. You don't get any pornography on there, not on the telly. Get filth, that's all. The only place you get pornography is in yer Sunday papers.
*Till Death Do Us Part*

4 Have you noticed, the last four strikes we've had, it's pissed down? It wouldn't be a bad idea to check the weather reports before they pull us out next time.
*Till Death Do Us Part*

**Spencer, Herbert** (1820–1903) British philosopher and supporter of Darwinism. His *First Principles* (1862) was the first of a multivolume treatise *System of Synthetic Philosophy* (1860–96).

1 The Republican form of Government is the highest form of government; but because of this it requires the highest type of human nature – a type nowhere at present existing.
*Essays*, 'The Americans'

2 It was remarked to me by the late Mr Charles Roupell . . . that to play billiards well was a sign of an ill-spent youth.
*Life and Letters of Spencer* (Duncan), Ch. 20

3 Survival of the fittest.
*Principles of Biology*

**Spencer, Sir Stanley** (1891–1959) British artist, noted for his paintings of scenes from World War I and of religious subjects. His best-known works include *The Resurrection: Cookham* and the series *Resurrection: Port Glasgow*.

1 I no more like people personally than I like dogs. When I meet them I am only apprehensive whether they will bite me, which is reasonable and sensible.
*Stanley Spencer, a Biography* (Maurice Collis), Ch. 17

2 Beautifully done.
Said to the nurse who had injected him, just before he died
*Stanley Spencer, a Biography* (Maurice Collis), Ch. 19

**Spender, Sir Stephen** (1909–  ) British poet, who became famous as one of the left wing poets of the 1930s. His *Selected Poems* was published in 1965.

1 Pylons, those pillars
Bare like nude giant girls that have no secret.
*The Pylons*

2 Who live under the shadow of a war,
What can I do that matters?
*Who live under the Shadow*

3 People sometimes divide others into those you laugh at and those you laugh with. The young Auden was someone you could laugh-at-with.
Address, W. H. Auden's memorial service, Oxford, 27 Oct 1973

**Spenser, Edmund** (1552–99) English poet. His *Faerie Queene*, an allegory in six volumes, was dedicated to Elizabeth I.

1 Sleep after toil, port after stormy seas,
Ease after war, death after life does greatly please.
*The Faerie Queene*, I:9

2 Sweet Thames! run softly, till I end my Song.
*Prothalamion*, 18

3 And he that strives to touch the stars,
Oft stumbles at a straw.
*The Shepherd's Calendar*, 'July'

**Spiel, Hilde** (1911–  ) Austrian writer; her works include *Kati auf der Bruche* (1933).

1 Malice is like a game of poker or tennis; you don't play it with anyone who is manifestly inferior to you.
*The Darkened Room*

**Spinoza, Benedict** (Baruch de Spinoza; 1632–77) Dutch philosopher and theologian of Jewish parents. His *Tractatus Theologico-Politicus* (1670) enraged both Jewish and Christian scholars. His *Ethics* (1677) was published posthumously.

1 Nature abhors a vacuum.
*Ethics*

**2** Man is a social animal.
*Ethics*

**3** We feel and know that we are eternal.
*Ethics*

**4** Desire is the very essence of man.
*Ethics*

**5** I have striven not to laugh at human actions, not to weep at them, nor to hate them, but to understand them.
*Tractatus Theologico-Politicus*, Ch. 1

**Spock, Dr Benjamin McLane** (1903– ) US pediatrician and psychiatrist, author of *The Commonsense Book of Baby and Child Care* (1946). Subsequently he became associated with the peace movement and was a candidate for the US presidency (1972).

**1** To win in Vietnam, we will have to exterminate a nation.
*Dr Spock on Vietnam*, Ch. 7

**Spooner, William Archibald** (1844–1930) British clergyman and academic, remembered for his 'spoonerisms', phrases in which the first letters of words are transposed.

**1** You will find as you grow older that the weight of rages will press harder and harder on the employer.
*Spooner* (Sir W. Hayter), Ch. 6

**2** I remember your name perfectly, but I just can't think of your face.
*Attrib.*

**3** Kinquering Congs their titles take.
A scrambled announcement of the hymn in New College Chapel, (probably apocryphal)

**4** Let us drink to the queer old Dean.
*Attrib.*

**5** Sir, you have tasted two whole worms; you have hissed all my mystery lectures and have been caught fighting a liar in the quad; you will leave Oxford by the town drain.
*Attrib.*

**Spring-Rice, Sir Cecil Arthur** (1859–1918) British diplomat, who became ambassador to the USA (1913–18).

**1** I am the Dean of Christ Church, Sir:
There's my wife; look well at her.
She's the Broad and I'm the High;
We are the University
*The Masque of Balliol*

**Spyri, Johanna** (1827–1901) Swiss writer, best known for her story for children *Heidi* (1880–81).

**1** Oh, I wish that God had not given me what I prayed for! It was not so good as I thought.
*Heidi*, Ch. 11

**2** Anger has overpowered him, and driven him to a revenge which was rather a stupid one, I must acknowledge, but anger makes us all stupid.
*Heidi*, Ch. 23

**Squire, Sir John Collings** (1884–1958) British journalist and dramatist, a leading member of the Georgian school of pastoral poetry.

**1** But I'm not so think as you drunk I am.
*Ballade of Soporific Absorption*

**2** But Shelley had a hyper-thyroid face.
*Ballade of the Glandular Hypothesis*

**3** It did not last: the Devil howling 'Ho!
Let Einstein be!' restored the status quo.
Answer to POPE's Epitaph for Newton
*Epigrams*, 'The Dilemma'

**Stacpoole, H(enry) de Vere** (1863–1931) Irish-born novelist and ship's doctor, best known for his romance *The Blue Lagoon* (1908).

**1** In home-sickness you must keep moving – it is the only disease that does not require rest.
*The Bourgeois*

**Stalin, Joseph** (J. Dzhugashvili; 1879–1953) Soviet statesman. A Bolshevik under Lenin, he became supreme dictator in 1929. In the 1930s he eliminated his rivals in various purges, but led the Soviet Union to victory in World War II. After the war his autocratic rule was intensified and he built up an empire of Eastern European Communist countries.

**1** The Pope! How many divisions has *he* got?
When urged by Pierre Laval to tolerate Catholicism in the USSR to appease the Pope, 13 May 1935
*The Second World War* (W. S. Churchill), Vol. I, Ch. 8

**2** The state is an instrument in the hands of the ruling class for suppressing the resistance of its class enemies.
*Stalin's Kampf* (ed. M. R. Werner)

**3** The tasks of the party are . . . to be cautious and not allow our country to be drawn into conflicts by warmongers who are accustomed to have others pull the chestnuts out of the fire for them.
Speech, 8th Congress of the Communist Party, 6 Jan 1941

**4** The party is the rallying-point for the best elements of the working class.
*Attrib.*

**Stanley, Sir Henry Morton** (1841–1904) British explorer. While working as a journalist in the USA he was sent to search for Dr Livingstone in Africa. He made several subsequent expeditions into Africa.

**1** Dr Livingstone, I presume?
On finding David Livingstone at Ujiji on Lake Tanganyika, Nov 1871
*How I found Livingstone*, Ch. 11

**Stanton, C. E.** (1859–1933) US colonel who fought in World War I.

**1** Lafayette, we are here!
The Marquis de Lafayette (1757–1834) aided the colonists in the US War of Independence
Address at Lafayette's grave, Paris, 4 July 1917

**Stanton, Elizabeth** (1815–1902) US suffragette.

1 I have been into many of the ancient cathedrals – grand, wonderful, mysterious. But I always leave them with a feeling of indignation because of the generations of human beings who have struggled in poverty to build these altars to the unknown god.

*Diary*

2 ... we still wonder at the stolid incapacity of all men to understand that woman feels the invidious distinctions of sex exactly as the black man does those of color, or the white man the more transient distinctions of wealth, family, position, place, and power; that she feels as keenly as man the injustice of disfranchisement.

*History of Woman Suffrage* (with Susan B. Anthony and Mathilda Gage), Vol. I

3 It is impossible for one class to appreciate the wrongs of another.

*History of Woman Suffrage* (with Susan B. Anthony and Mathilda Gage), Vol. I

4 The prolonged slavery of women is the darkest page in human history.

*History of Woman Suffrage* (with Susan B. Anthony and Mathilda Gage), Vol. I

5 Womanhood is the great fact in her life; wifehood and motherhood are but incidental relations.

*History of Woman Suffrage* (with Susan B. Anthony and Mathilda Gage), Vol. I

6 *Declaration of Sentiments:* ... We hold these truths to be self-evident: that all men and women are created equal ...

*History of Woman Suffrage* (with Susan B. Anthony and Mathilda Gage), Vol. I

**Stanton, Frank L(ebby)** (1857–1927) US journalist and poet. He published *Songs of a Day and Songs of the Soil* (1892) and *Up From Georgia* (1902); he has been called the poet laureate of Georgia.

1 Sweetes' li'l' feller,
Everybody knows;
Dunno what to call 'im,
But he's mighty lak' a rose!

*Sweetes' Li'l' Feller*

**Stapledon, Olaf** (1886–1950) British philosopher and science-fiction writer, whose influential novels include *Last and First Men* (1930) and *Star Maker* (1937).

1 That strange blend of the commercial traveller, the missionary, and the barbarian conqueror, which was the American abroad.

*Last and First Men*, Ch. 3

**Stark, John** (1728–1822) US general in the American War of Independence.

1 Yonder are the Hessians. They were bought for seven pounds and tenpence a man. Are you worth more? Prove it. Tonight the American flag floats from yonder hill or Molly Stark sleeps a widow!

Urging on his troops at the battle of Bennington in 1777
*The American Treasury* (C. Fadiman)

**Stead, Christina** (1902–83) Australian novelist. Her best-known novels are *The Man Who Loved Children* (1940) and *For Love Alone* (1944).

1 A self-made man is one who believes in luck and sends his son to Oxford.

*House of All Nations*, 'Credo'

**Steel, David** (1938– ) British politician. He became leader of the Liberal Party in 1976. With David Owen he headed the SDP-Liberal Alliance.

1 Go back to your constituencies and prepare for government!

Speech to party conference, 1985

2 I sense that the British electorate is now itching to break out once and for all from the discredited straight-jacket of the past.

*The Times*, 2 June 1987

**Steele, Sir Richard** (1672–1729) Dublin-born British essayist and dramatist. With Joseph Addison he founded, and wrote for, the magazines *The Tatler* and *Spectator*. He wrote a number of theatrical comedies, including *The Funeral* (1701).

1 Reading is to the mind what exercise is to the body.

*The Tatler*, 147

2 A little in drink, but at all times yr faithful husband.

Letter to his wife, 27 Sept 1708

**Steffens, (Joseph) Lincoln** (1866–1936) US journalist. His books include *The Struggle for Self-Government* (1906) and an autobiography (1931).

1 I have seen the future and it works.

Speaking to Bernard Baruch after visiting the Soviet Union, 1919
*Autobiography*, Ch. 18

**Stein, Gertrude** (1874–1946) US writer, who lived in Paris from 1903. Her books include *Tender Buttons* (1914) and *The Autobiography of Alice B. Toklas* (1933).

1 She always says she dislikes the abnormal, it is so obvious. She says the normal is so much more simply complicated and interesting.

*The Autobiography of Alice B. Toklas*

2 In the United States there is more space where nobody is than where anybody is. That is what makes America what it is.

*The Geographical History of America*

3 Rose is a rose is a rose is a rose.

*Sacred Emily*

4 Besides Shakespeare and me, who do you think there is?

Speaking to a friend she considered knew little about literature
*Charmed Circle* (J. Mellow)

5 The Jews have produced only three originative geniuses: Christ, Spinoza, and myself.
*Charmed Circle* (J. Mellow)

6 That's what you are. That's what you all are. All of you young people who served in the war. You are a lost generation.
*A Moveable Feast* (E. Hemingway)

**Steinbeck, John** (1902–68) US novelist. Many of his novels are set in the mid-West of America during the Depression; they include *Of Mice and Men* (1937), *The Grapes of Wrath* (1939), and *East of Eden* (1952).

1 Man, unlike any other thing organic or inorganic in the universe, grows beyond his work, walks up the stairs of his concepts, emerges ahead of his accomplishments.
*The Grapes of Wrath*, Ch. 14

2 Okie use' to mean you was from Oklahoma. Now it means you're scum. Don't mean nothing itself, it's the way they say it.
*The Grapes of Wrath*, Ch. 18

**Stekel, Wilhelm** (1868–1940) Viennese psychiatrist, who was a noted disciple of Freud.

1 The mark of the immature man is that he wants to die nobly for a cause, while the mark of the mature man is that he wants to live humbly for one.
*The Catcher in the Rye* (J. D. Salinger), Ch. 24

**Stendhal** (Henri Beyle; 1783–1842) French novelist and writer. He is remembered for his novels *Le Rouge et le noir* (1830) and *La Chartreuse de Parme* (1839). He also wrote several biographies and popular romances.

1 A novel is a mirror walking along a main road.
*Le Rouge et le noir*, Ch. 49

2 Romanticism is the art of presenting people with the literary works which are capable of affording them the greatest possible pleasure, in the present state of their customs and beliefs. Classicism, on the other hand, presents them with the literature that gave the greatest possible pleasure to their great-grandfathers.
*Racine et Shakespeare*, Ch. 3

**Stephens, James** (1882–1950) Irish novelist and poet. His novel *The Crock of Gold* (1912) was adapted as the musical *Finian's Rainbow*.

1 Finality is death. Perfection is finality. Nothing is perfect. There are lumps in it.
*The Crock of Gold*

2 Curiosity will conquer fear even more than bravery will.
*The Crock of Gold*

3 Men come of age at sixty, women at fifteen.
*The Observer*, 'Sayings of the Week', 1 Oct 1944

**Stern, Richard G.** (1928– ) US writer. His books include *Golk* (1960) and *In Any Case* (1962).

1 Anybody can shock a baby, or a television audience. But it's too easy, and the effect is disproportionate to the effort.
*Golk*, Ch. 4

**Sterne, Laurence** (1713–68) Irish-born British writer and clergyman. *Tristram Shandy* (1759) established his reputation and was followed by *A Sentimental Journey* (1768). He also published books of sermons.

1 He gave a deep sigh – I saw the iron enter into his soul!
*A Sentimental Journey*, 'The Captive. Paris'

2 They are a loyal, a gallant, a generous, an ingenious, and good-temper'd people as is under heaven – if they have a fault, they are too *serious*.
Referring to the French
*A Sentimental Journey*, 'The Character. Versailles'

3 I am positive I have a soul; nor can all the books with which materialists have pestered the world ever convince me of the contrary.
*A Sentimental Journey*, 'Maria, Moulines'

4 I wish either my father or my mother, or indeed both of them, as they were in duty both equally bound to it, had minded what they were about when they begot me.
*Tristram Shandy*

5 So long as a man rides his hobby-horse peaceably and quietly along the king's highway, and neither compels you or me to get up behind him, – pray, Sir, what have either you or I to do with it?
*Tristram Shandy*

6 'Tis known by the name of perseverance in a good cause, – and of obstinacy in a bad one.
*Tristram Shandy*

7 Writing, when properly managed, (as you may be sure I think mine is) is but a different name for conversation.
*Tristram Shandy*

8 Whenever a man talks loudly against religion, – always suspect that it is not his reason, but his passions which have got the better of his creed.
*Tristram Shandy*

9 A man should know something of his own country, too, before he goes abroad.
*Tristram Shandy*

10 An ounce of a man's own wit is worth a ton of other people's.
*Tristram Shandy*

**Stevenson, Adlai E(wing)** (1900–65) US statesman. Governor of Illinois (1949–53), he twice stood unsuccessfully for the presidency (1952; 1956) as Democratic candidate.

1 An editor is one who separates the wheat from the chaff and prints the chaff.
*The Stevenson Wit*

2 A politician is a statesman who approaches every question with an open mouth.
Also attrib. to Arthur Goldberg
*The Fine Art of Political Wit* (L. Harris)

3 Power corrupts, but lack of power corrupts absolutely.
*The Observer*, Jan 1963

4 Let's talk sense to the American people. Let's tell them the truth, that there are no gains without pains.
Speech, Chicago, 26 July 1952

5 There is no evil in the atom; only in men's souls.
Speech, Hartford, Connecticut, 18 Sept 1952

6 My definition of a free society is a society where it is safe to be unpopular.
Speech, Detroit, Oct 1952

7 He said that he was too old to cry, but it hurt too much to laugh.
Said after losing an election, quoting a story told by Abraham Lincoln
Speech, 5 Nov 1952

8 She would rather light candles than curse the darkness, and her glow has warmed the world.
Referring to Eleanor Roosevelt
Address, United Nations General Assembly, 9 Nov 1962

**Stevenson, Robert Louis** (1850–94) Scottish writer. His books include *Treasure Island* (1883), *Kidnapped* (1886), and *The Strange Case of Dr Jekyll and Mr Hyde* (1886).

1 If your morals make you dreary, depend upon it, they are wrong.
*Across the Plains*

2 Politics is perhaps the only profession for which no preparation is thought necessary.
*Familiar Studies of Men and Books*, 'Yoshida-Torajiro'

3 Vanity dies hard; in some obstinate cases it outlives the man.
*Prince Otto*

4 Wealth I ask not; hope nor love,
Nor a friend to know me;
All I seek, the heaven above
And the road below me.
*Songs of Travel*, 'The Vagabond'

5 For my part, I travel not to go anywhere, but to go. I travel for travel's sake. The great affair is to move.
*Travels with a Donkey*, 'Cheylard and Luc'

6 Fifteen men on the dead man's chest
Yo-ho-ho, and a bottle of rum!
Drink and the devil had done for the rest –
Yo-ho-ho, and a bottle of rum!
*Treasure Island*, Ch. 1

7 Pieces of eight!
*Treasure Island*, Ch. 10

8 Many's the long night I've dreamed of cheese – toasted, mostly.
*Treasure Island*, Ch. 15

9 Of all my verse, like not a single line;
But like my title, for it is not mine.
That title from a better man I stole;
Ah, how much better, had I stol'n the whole!
*Underwoods*, Foreword

10 Under the wide and starry sky
Dig the grave and let me lie.
Glad did I live and gladly die,
– And I laid me down with a will.
This is the verse you grave for me:
'Here he lies where he longed to be;
Home is the sailor, home from sea,
And the hunter home from the hill.'
*Underwoods*, Bk. I, 'Requiem'

11 Even if we take matrimony at its lowest, even if we regard it as no more than a sort of friendship recognized by the police.
*Virginibus Puerisque*

12 Man is a creature who lives not upon bread alone, but principally by catchwords; and the little rift between the sexes is astonishingly widened by simply teaching one set of catchwords to the girls and another to the boys.
*Virginibus Puerisque*

13 The cruellest lies are often told in silence.
*Virginibus Puerisque*

14 When the torrent sweeps a man against a boulder, you must expect him to scream, and you need not be surprised if the scream is sometimes a theory.
*Virginibus Puerisque*

15 Old and young, we are all on our last cruise.
*Virginibus Puerisque*

16 Books are good enough in their own way, but they are a mighty bloodless substitute for life.
*Virginibus Puerisque*

17 Extreme *busyness*, whether at school or college, kirk or market, is a symptom of deficient vitality.
*Virginibus Puerisque*

18 There is no duty we so much underrate as the duty of being happy.
*Virginibus Puerisque*

19 Give me the young man who has brains enough to make a fool of himself!
*Virginibus Puerisque*

20 Lastly (and this is, perhaps, the golden rule), no woman should marry a teetotaller, or a man who does not smoke.
*Virginibus Puerisque*

21 Marriage is a step so grave and decisive that it attracts light-headed, variable men by its very awfulness.
*Virginibus Puerisque*

**22** In marriage, a man becomes slack and selfish and undergoes a fatty degeneration of his moral being.
*Virginibus Puerisque*

**23** Marriage is like life in this – that it is a field of battle, and not a bed of roses.
*Virginibus Puerisque*

**24** To travel hopefully is a better thing than to arrive, and the true success is to labour.
*Virginibus Puerisque*

**25** It's deadly commonplace, but, after all, the commonplaces are the great poetic truths.
*Weir of Hermiston*, Ch. 6

**Stocks, Mary, Baroness** (1891–1975) British politician, writer, and broadcaster. She was noted for her concern with the social aspects of economic policy.

**1** It is clearly absurd that it should be possible for a woman to qualify as a saint with direct access to the Almighty while she may not qualify as a curate.
*Still More Commonplace*

**Stockwood, Mervyn (Arthur)** (1913– ) British churchman, Bishop of Southwark (1959–80). He is noted for his outspokenness on both moral and political issues.

**1** A psychiatrist is a man who goes to the Folies-Bergère and looks at the audience.
*The Observer*, 'Sayings of the Week', 15 Oct 1961

**Stoddard, Elizabeth Drew (Barstow)** (1823–1902) US novelist and poet.

**1** A woman despises a man for loving her, unless she returns his love.
*Two Men*, Ch. 32

**Stone, I(sidor) F(einstein)** (1907– ) US writer and publisher, noted for his left wing views. As publisher of *I. F. Stone's Weekly* (1953–71) he condemned McCarthyism, the war in Vietnam, and racism.

**1** If you live long enough, the venerability factor creeps in; you get accused of things you never did and praised for virtues you never had.
*Peter's Quotations* (Laurence J. Peter)

**Stone, Samuel. J.** (1839–1901) US hymn writer.

**1** The Church's one foundation
Is Jesus Christ her Lord;
She is His new creation
By water and the Word.
*Hymn*

**Stoppard, Tom** (1937– ) Czech-born British dramatist. He achieved notice with his play *Rosencrantz and Guildenstern Are Dead* (1967), subsequently building on this success with *Jumpers* (1972), *Travesties* (1975), *Night and Day* (1978), and *The Real Thing* (1982).

**1** Skill without imagination is craftsmanship and gives us many useful objects such as wickerwork picnic baskets. Imagination without skill gives us modern art.
*Artist Descending a Staircase*

**2** This is a British murder inquiry and some degree of justice must be seen to be more or less done.
*Jumpers*, II

**3** Socialists treat their servants with respect and then wonder why they vote Conservative.
*Lord Malquist and Mr Moon*, Pt. V, Ch. 1

**4** The House of Lords, an illusion to which I have never been able to subscribe – responsibility without power, the prerogative of the eunuch throughout the ages.
*See* Lord ACTON
*Lord Malquist and Mr Moon*, Pt. VI, Ch. 1

**5** He's someone who flies around from hotel to hotel and thinks the most interesting thing about any story is the fact that he has arrived to cover it.
Referring to foreign correspondents
*Night and Day*, I

**6** The media. It sounds like a convention of spiritualists.
*Night and Day*, I

**7** MILNE. No matter how imperfect things are, if you've got a free press everything is correctable, and without it everything is conceivable.
RUTH. I'm with you on the free press. It's the newspapers I can't stand.
*Night and Day*, I

**8** Eternity's a terrible thought. I mean, where's it going to end?
*Rosencrantz and Guildenstern Are Dead*, II

**9** The bad end unhappily, the good unluckily. That is what tragedy means.
*Rosencrantz and Guildenstern Are Dead*, II

**10** Life is a gamble, at terrible odds – if it was a bet, you wouldn't take it.
*Rosencrantz and Guildenstern Are Dead*, III

**11** What is an artist? For every thousand people there's nine hundred doing the work, ninety doing well, nine doing good, and one lucky bastard who's the artist.
*Travesties*, I

**12** It's better to be quotable than to be honest.
*The Guardian*

**13** I doubt that art needed Ruskin any more than a moving train needs one of its passengers to shove it.
*The Times Literary Supplement*, 3 June 1977

**Stout, Rex Todhunter** (1886–1975) US writer of detective stories, including *Death of a Doxy* and *Three Witnesses*, in which the detective was Nero Wolfe.

1 There are two kinds of statistics, the kind you look up and the kind you make up.
*Death of a Doxy*, Ch. 9

2 I like to walk around Manhattan, catching glimpses of its wild life, the pigeons and cats and girls.
*Three Witnesses*, 'When a Man Murders'

**Stowe, Harriet Beecher** (1811–96) US novelist. She achieved fame with *Uncle Tom's Cabin* (1852), which greatly helped the antislavery lobby. Her other books include *The Minister's Wooing* (1859) and *Oldtown Folks* (1864). Her article accusing Lord Byron of incest with his sister caused great controversy.

1 The bitterest tears shed over graves are for words left unsaid and deeds left undone.
*Little Foxes*, Ch. 3

2 'Do you know who made you?' 'Nobody, as I knows on,' said the child, with a short laugh . . . 'I 'spect I grow'd.'
*Uncle Tom's Cabin*, Ch. 20

3 Whipping and abuse are like laudanum: You have to double the dose as the sensibilities decline.
*Uncle Tom's Cabin*, Ch. 20

4 I did not write it. God wrote it. I merely did his dictation.
Referring to *Uncle Tom's Cabin*
Attrib.

**Stowell, William Scott, Baron** (1745–1836) *See* Scott, William.

**Strachey, (Evelyn) John St Loe** (1901–63) British politician and Labour theorist. He became minister of food in Attlee's post-war government. His books include *The Menace of Fascism* (1933) and *The Economics of Progress* (1939).

1 Becoming an Anglo-Catholic must surely be a sad business – rather like becoming an amateur conjurer.
*The Coming Struggle for Power*, Pt. III, Ch. 11

2 Fascism means war.
Slogan, 1930s

**Strachey, (Giles) Lytton** (1880–1932) British writer. A member of the Bloomsbury group, he wrote biographies of Queen Victoria, Elizabeth I, and others, as well as a perceptive volume, *Eminent Victorians* (1918).

1 Yet her conception of God was certainly not orthodox. She felt towards Him as she might have felt towards a glorified sanitary engineer; and in some of her speculations she seems hardly to distinguish between the Deity and the Drains.
*Eminent Victorians*, 'Florence Nightingale'

2 It should not merely be useful and ornamental; it should preach a high moral lesson.
Referring to Prince Albert's plans for the Great Exhibition
*Queen Victoria*, Ch. 4

3 Albert was merely a young foreigner, who suffered from having no vices, and whose only claim to distinction was that he had happened to marry the Queen of England.
*Queen Victoria*, Ch. 5

4 If this is dying, I don't think much of it.
Last words
*Lytton Strachey* (Michael Holroyd), Pt. V, Ch. 17

**Stratton, Eugene** (1861–1918) British music-hall singer.

1 I know she likes me,
'Cause she says so.
*The Lily of Laguna*

2 Little Dolly Daydream, pride of Idaho.
*Little Dolly Daydream*

**Stravinsky, Igor** (1882–1971) Russian-born US composer. His early ballet scores, commissioned by Diaghilev, include *The Firebird* (1910), *Petrushka* (1911), and *The Rite of Spring* (1913). His later work includes a piano concerto (1924), the oratorio *Oedipus Rex* (1927) and the opera *The Rake's Progress* (1951).

1 Rachmaninov's immortalizing totality was his scowl. He was a six-and-a-half-foot-tall scowl.
*Conversations with Igor Stravinsky* (Igor Stravinsky and Robert Craft)

2 He was the only pianist I have ever seen who did not grimace. That is a great deal.
Referring to Rachmaninov
*Conversations with Igor Stravinsky* (Igor Stravinsky and Robert Craft)

3 I had another dream the other day about music critics. They were small and rodent-like with padlocked ears, as if they had stepped out of a painting by Goya.
*The Evening Standard*, 29 Oct 1969

4 My music is best understood by children and animals.
*The Observer*, 'Sayings of the Week', 8 Oct 1961

5 A good composer does not imitate; he steals.
*Twentieth Century Music* (Peter Yates)

6 Hurry! I never hurry. I have no time to hurry.
Responding to his publisher's request that he hurry his completion of a composition
Attrib.

**Streatfield, Sir Geoffrey Hugh Benbow** (1897–1978) British lawyer. During World War II he became Assistant Judge Advocate-General and later a high-court judge.

1 Facts speak louder than statistics.
*The Observer*, 'Sayings of the Week', 19 Mar 1950

**Strindberg, August** (1849–1912) Swedish dramatist. His plays include *The Father* (1887), *The Dance of Death* (1900), and *The Ghost Sonata* (1907).

1 I loathe people who keep dogs. They are cowards who haven't got the guts to bite people themselves.
*A Madman's Diary*

**Strunsky, Simeon** (1879–1948) Russian-born US editor and essayist. His books include *The Patient Observer* (1911) and *No Mean City* (1917).

**1** Famous remarks are seldom quoted correctly.

*No Mean City*

**Sullivan, Annie** (1866–1936) US teacher of the handicapped; her most famous pupil was Helen Keller.

**1** It's queer how ready people always are with advice in any real or imaginary emergency, and no matter how many times experience has shown them to be wrong, they continue to set forth their opinions, as if they had received them from the Almighty!

Letter, 12 June 1887

**2** She likes stories that make her cry – I think we all do, it's so nice to feel sad when you've nothing particular to be sad about.

Referring to Helen Keller
Letter, 12 Dec 1887

**3** Language grows out of life, out of its needs and experiences . . . *Language* and *knowledge* are indissolubly connected; they are interdependent. Good work in language presupposes and depends on a real knowledge of things.

Speech, American Association to Promote the Teaching of Speech to the Deaf, July 1894

**Sully, Maximilien de Béthune, Duc de** (1560–1641) French statesman. Henry IV's chief minister, he retired after Henry's assassination.

**1** The English take their pleasures sadly after the fashion of their country.

*Memoirs*

**Svevo, Italo** (Ettore Schmitz; 1861–1928) Italian writer. His novels include *Una Vita* (1883), *Senilità* (1898), and *La Coscienza di Zeno* (1923).

**1** The really original woman is the one who first imitates a man.

*Una Vita*, Ch. 8

**Swaffer, Hannen** (1879–1962) British journalist.

**1** Freedom of the press in Britain is freedom to print such of the proprietor's prejudices as the advertisers don't object to.

Attrib.

**Swift, Jonathan** (1667–1745) Irish-born Anglican priest who became a poet and satirist in London. He is remembered for his *Journal to Stella* (1710–13) and *A Tale of A Tub* (1704), but best of all for *Gulliver's Travels* (1726), written after his return to Dublin as dean of St Patrick's.

**1** Satire is a sort of glass, wherein beholders do generally discover everybody's face but their own.

*The Battle of the Books*, 'Preface'

**2** 'Tis an old maxim in the schools,
That flattery's the food of fools;
Yet now and then your men of wit
Will condescend to take a bit.

*Cadenus and Vanessa*

**3** It is folly of too many to mistake the echo of a London coffee-house for the voice of the kingdom.

*The Conduct of the Allies*

**4** I have heard of a man who had a mind to sell his house, and therefore carried a piece of brick in his pocket, which he shewed as a pattern to encourage purchasers.

*The Drapier's Letters*, 2 (4 Aug 1724)

**5** I cannot but conclude the bulk of your natives to be the most pernicious race of little odious vermin that nature ever suffered to crawl upon the surface of the earth.

Referring to the English
*Gulliver's Travels*, 'Voyage to Brobdingnag', Ch. 6

**6** Whoever could make two ears of corn or two blades of grass to grow upon a spot of ground where only one grew before would deserve better of mankind and do more essential service to his country than the whole race of politicians put together.

*Gulliver's Travels*, 'Voyage to Brobdingnag', Ch. 7

**7** So, naturalist observe, a flea
Hath smaller fleas that on him prey,
And these have smaller fleas to bite 'em.
And so proceed *ad infinitum*.

*On Poetry*

**8** Promises and pie-crust are made to be broken.

*Polite Conversation*, Dialogue 1

**9** Bachelor's fare; bread and cheese, and kisses.

*Polite Conversation*, Dialogue 1

**10** He was a bold man that first eat an oyster.

*Polite Conversation*, Dialogue 2

**11** I never saw, heard, nor read, that the clergy were beloved in any nation where Christianity was the religion of the country. Nothing can render them popular, but some degree of persecution.

*Thoughts on Religion*

**12** When a true genius appears in the world, you may know him by this sign, that the dunces are all in confederacy against him.

*Thoughts on Various Subjects*

**13** What they do in heaven we are ignorant of; what they do *not* we are told expressly, that they neither marry, nor are given in marriage.

*Thoughts on Various Subjects*

**14** I never wonder to see men wicked, but I often wonder to see them not ashamed.

*Thoughts on Various Subjects*

15 Most sorts of diversion in men, children, and other animals, are an imitation of fighting.

*Thoughts on Various Subjects*

16 Laws are like cobwebs, which may catch small flies, but let wasps and hornets break through.

Similar remarks have been made by others; *see* SHENSTONE; SOLON
*A Tritical Essay upon the Faculties of the Mind*

17 For God's sake, madam, don't say that in England for if you do, they will surely tax it.

Responding to Lady Carteret's admiration for the quality of the air in Ireland
*Lives of the Wits* (H. Pearson)

18 I shall be like that tree; I shall die from the top.

Predicting his own mental decline on seeing a tree with a withered crown
*Lives of the Wits* (H. Pearson)

19 If Heaven had looked upon riches to be a valuable thing, it would not have given them to such a scoundrel.

Letter to Miss Vanhomrigh, 12–13 Aug 1720

20 Ah, a German and a genius! a prodigy, admit him!

Learning of the arrival of Handel: Swift's last words
Attrib.

**Swinburne, Algernon Charles** (1837–1909) British poet. He made his name with *Poems and Ballads* (1866). Later works included *A Song of Italy* (1867), *Erechteus* (1876), and *Tristram of Lyonesse* (1882).

1 When the hounds of spring are on winter's traces,
The mother of months in meadow or plain
Fills the shadows and windy places
With lisp of leaves and ripple of rain . . .

*Atlanta in Calydon*

2 Here, where the world is quiet;
Here, where all trouble seems
Dead winds' and spent waves' riot
In doubtful dreams of dreams.

*The Garden of Proserpine*

3 Glory to Man in the highest! for Man is the master of things.

*Hymn of Man*

**Symonds, John Addington** (1840–93) British art historian. His major work was the seven-volume *Renaissance in Italy* (1875–86). He also wrote poetry and literary biography.

1 These things shall be! A loftier race
Than e'er the world hath known shall rise,
With flame of freedom in their souls,
And light of knowledge in their eyes.

*Hymn*

**Symons, Arthur (William)** (1865–1945) British poet. His works include *Days and Nights* (1889), *Amoris Victima* (1897), the influential *The Symbolist Movement in Literature* (1899), and other volumes of verse and criticism.

1 As a perfume doth remain
In the folds where it hath lain,
So the thought of you, remaining
Deeply folded in my brain,
Will not leave me: all things leave me:
You remain.

*Memory*

**Synge, John Millington** (1871–1909) Anglo-Irish dramatist. His plays include *The Shadow of the Glen* (1903), *Riders to the Sea* (1904), *The Playboy of the Western World* (1907), and *Deirdre of the Sorrows* (1910).

1 I've lost the only playboy of the western world.

The closing words
*The Playboy of the Western World*, III

**Syrus, Publilius** (1st century BC) Roman dramatist. He was the author of several mime plays and an anthology of stoic maxims.

1 He gives twice who gives promptly.

Attrib.

2 Necessity knows no law.

Attrib.

**Szasz, Thomas** (1920– ) US psychiatrist and writer. His writings include *Pain and Pleasure* (1957) and *The Second Sin* (1974).

1 Men are rewarded and punished not for what they do, but rather for how their acts are defined. This is why men are more interested in better justifying themselves than in better behaving themselves.

*The Second Sin*

2 Traditionally, sex has been a very private, secretive activity. Herein perhaps lies its powerful force for uniting people in a strong bond. As we make sex less secretive, we may rob it of its power to hold men and women together.

*The Second Sin*

3 Formerly, when religion was strong and science weak, men mistook magic for medicine, now, when science is strong and religion weak, men mistake medicine for magic.

*The Second Sin*

4 A child becomes an adult when he realizes that he has a right not only to be right but also to be wrong.

*The Second Sin*

5 Happiness is an imaginary condition, formerly often attributed by the living to the dead, now usually attributed by adults to children, and by children to adults.

*The Second Sin*

6 The stupid neither forgive nor forget; the naive forgive and forget; the wise forgive but do not forget.

*The Second Sin*

7 Psychiatrists classify a person as neurotic if he suffers from his problems in living, and a psychotic if he makes others suffer.
*The Second Sin*

8 If you talk to God, you are praying; if God talks to you, you have schizophrenia. If the dead talk to you, you are a spiritualist; if God talks to you, you are a schizophrenic.
*The Second Sin*

9 Masturbation: the primary sexual activity of mankind. In the nineteenth century it was a disease; in the twentieth, it's a cure.
*The Second Sin*

**Szent-Györgyi, Albert** (1893– ) Hungarian-born US biochemist. He discovered the role of vitamin C and interpreted in biochemical terms the method by which muscles contract.

1 Discovery consists of seeing what everybody has seen and thinking what nobody has thought.
*The Scientist Speculates* (I. J. Good)

# T

**Taber, Robert** (20th century) US writer. A merchant seaman (1942–45), he was the only American among Castro's defending forces at Playa Giron.

1 The guerrilla fights the war of the flea, and his military enemy suffers the dog's disadvantages: too much to defend; too small, ubiquitous, and agile an enemy to come to grips with.
*The War of the Flea*, Ch. 2

**Tabrar, Joseph** (20th century) US songwriter.

1 Daddy wouldn't buy me a bow-wow, bow-wow.
I've got a little cat
And I'm very fond of that.
*Daddy Wouldn't Buy Me A Bow-wow* (song)

**Tacitus, Cornelius** (c. 55–c. 120 AD) Roman historian. He became governor of Asia (112–13 AD). His major works were the *Histories* and the *Annals*, surveying Roman history in the periods 69–96 AD and 14–68 AD, respectively.

1 They make a wilderness and call it peace.
*Agricola*, 30

2 It is part of human nature to hate the man you have hurt.
*Agricola*, 42

3 Love of fame is the last thing even learned men can bear to be parted from.
*Histories*, IV, 6

**Taft, William Howard** (1857–1930) US statesman. He became president (1909–13), having been a judge and the secretary of war (1904–08). After his defeat for a second term as president he became professor of law at Yale.

1 Well, I have one consolation, No candidate was ever elected ex-president by such a large majority!
Referring to his disastrous defeat in the 1912 presidential election
Attrib.

**Taine, Hippolyte Adolphe** (1828–93) French writer and philosopher. His works include *Essais de critique et d'histoire* (1855), *Idéalisme anglais* (1864), and *De l'intelligence* (1870).

1 Vice and virtues are products like sulphuric acid and sugar.
*Histoire de la littérature anglaise*, Introduction

**Talleyrand** (Charles Maurice de Talleyrand-Périgord; 1754–1838) French politician. During the French Revolution he attempted to reform the church, but was excommunicated by the pope. He was foreign minister (1797–1807) and ambassador to Britain (1830–34).

1 I found there a country with thirty-two religions and only one sauce.
Referring to America
*Autant en apportent les mots* (Pedrazzini)

2 Accidentally.
Replying, during the reign of Louis Philippe, to the query "How do you think this government will end?"
*The Wheat and the Chaff* (F. Mitterrand)

3 It is the beginning of the end.
Referring to Napoleon's defeat at Borodino, 1813
Attrib.

4 Speech was given to man to disguise his thoughts.
Attrib.

5 Not too much zeal.
Attrib.

6 War is much too serious a thing to be left to military men.
Attrib.

7 Mistrust first impulses; they are nearly always good.
Sometimes attrib. to Count Montrond
Attrib.

8 Well, you might try getting crucified and rising again on the third day.
Giving his opinion upon what action might impress the French peasantry
Attrib.

**Tarkington, Booth** (1869–1946) US novelist. His books, many of which were made into films, include *Monsieur Beaucaire* (1900), *Penrod* (1914), *The Magnificent Ambersons* (1918), and *Alice Adams* (1921).

1 There are two things that will be believed of any man whatsoever, and one of them is that he has taken to drink.
*Penrod*, Ch. 10

**Tate, Allen** (1899– ) US poet and critic. His collected poems were published in 1978, including 'Ode to the Confederate Dead' (1926). He also wrote a novel, *The Fathers* (1938).

1  Row upon row with strict impunity
   The headstones yield their names to the
   element.
   *Ode to the Confederate Dead*

**Tate, Nahum** (1652–1715) Irish-born English poet and
dramatist. His plays were mostly adaptations of Shakespeare. With
Nicholas Brady (1659–1726) he wrote the *New Version of the
Psalms of David* (1696). He was poet laureate from 1692.

1  As pants the hart for cooling streams
   When heated in the chase.
   *New Version of the Psalms, 'As Pants the Hart'*

2  Through all the changing scenes of life.
   *New Version of the Psalms, 'Through all the Changing'*

3  While shepherds watch'd their flocks by night,
   All seated on the ground,
   The Angel of the Lord came down,
   And Glory shone around.
   *Supplement to the New Version of the Psalms, 'While Shepherds
   Watched'*

**Taupin, Bernie** (1913–   ) British songwriter. His musical
partnership with Elton John began in 1967. His solo album *Taupin*
was released in 1971.

1  Goodbye Norma Jean
   Though I never knew you at all
   You had the grace to hold yourself
   While those around you crawled.
   They crawled out of the woodwork
   And they whispered into your brain
   Set you on the treadmill
   And made you change your name.
   Lyrics for a song by Elton John
   *Candle in the Wind* (song)

**Tawney, R(ichard) H(enry)** (1880–1962) British
economist and historian. His best-known books were *The
Acquisitive Society* (1921) and *Religion and the Rise of Capitalism*
(1926).

1  As long as men are men, a poor society cannot
   be too poor to find a right order of life, nor a
   rich society too rich to have need to seek it.
   *The Acquisitive Society*

**Taylor, A(lan) J(ohn) P(ercivale)** (1906–   ) British
historian. His best-known book is *The Origins of the Second World
War* (1961).

1  History gets thicker as it approaches recent
   times.
   *English History, 1914–1945*, Bibliography

2  He aspired to power instead of influence, and as
   a result forfeited both.
   Referring to Lord Northcliffe
   *English History, 1914–1945*, Ch. 1

3  Communism continued to haunt Europe as a
   spectre – a name men gave to their own fears
   and blunders. But the crusade against Communism was even more imaginary than the spectre of Communism.
   *The Origins of the Second World War*, Ch. 2

4  Lenin was the first to discover that capitalism
   'inevitably' caused war; and he discovered this
   only when the First World War was already
   being fought. Of course he was right. Since every great state was capitalist in 1914, capitalism
   obviously 'caused' the First World War; but
   just as obviously it had 'caused' the previous
   generation of Peace.
   *The Origins of the Second World War*, Ch. 6

5  A racing tipster who only reached Hitler's level
   of accuracy would not do well for his clients.
   *The Origins of the Second World War*, Ch. 7

6  He was what I often think is a dangerous thing
   for a statesman to be – a student of history;
   and like most of those who study history, he
   learned from the mistakes of the past how to
   make new ones.
   Referring to Napoleon III
   *The Listener*, 6 June 1963

7  They say that men become attached even to
   Widnes.
   *The Observer*, 15 Sept 1963

**Taylor, Bert Leston** (1866–1921) US journalist. He was a
regular columnist in the Chicago *Daily Tribune*.

1  A bore is a man who, when you ask him how he
   is, tells you.
   Attrib.

**Taylor, Elizabeth** (1912–75) British writer. Her books
include the novels *A View of the Harbour* (1949), *A Wreath of
Roses* (1950), and *The Devastating Boys* (1972).

1  It is very strange . . . that the years teach us patience; that the shorter our time, the greater
   our capacity for waiting.
   *A Wreath of Roses*, Ch. 10

**Taylor, Jane** (1783–1824) British writer, who, with her sister
Ann Taylor, wrote *Original Poems for Infant Minds* and *Rhymes
for the Nursery* (1806).

1  Twinkle, twinkle, little star,
   How I wonder what you are!
   Up above the world so high,
   Like a diamond in the sky!
   *Rhymes for the Nursery* (with Ann Taylor), 'The Star'

**Taylor, Jeremy** (1613–67) English Anglican theologian, who
became Bishop of Down and Connor at the Restoration. He wrote
*The Rule and Exercise of Holy Dying* (1651) and *The Rule of
Conscience* (1660).

1  As our life is very short, so it is very miserable,
   and
   therefore it is well it is short.
   *The Rule and Exercise of Holy Dying*, Ch. 1

2  He that loves not his wife and children, feeds a
   lioness at home and broods a nest of sorrows.
   *Sermons*, 'Married Love'

**Taylor, John** (20th century) The editor of the *Tailor and
Cutter*.

**1** The only man who really needs a tail coat is a man with a hole in his trousers.
*The Observer*, 'Shouts and Murmurs'

**Tebbitt, Norman (Beresford)** (1931– ) British Conservative politician noted for his abrasive debating style. He was secretary of state for employment (1981–83), trade and industry secretary (1983–85), and chairman of the Conservative Party (1985–87).

**1** My father did not wait around . . . he got on his bike and went out looking for work.
Speech

**2** I hope Mrs Thatcher will go until the turn of the century looking like Queen Victoria.
*The Observer*, 'Sayings of the Week', 17 May 1987

**Teilhard de Chardin, Pierre** (1881–1955) French Jesuit and palaeontologist. His books, which were suppressed by the Catholic Church during his lifetime, included *The Phenomenon of Man* (1955) and *Le Milieu divin* (1957).

**1** From an evolutionary point of view, man has stopped moving, if he ever did move.
*The Phenomenon of Man*, Postscript

**Temple, Frederick** (1821–1902) British churchman. He became headmaster of Rugby (1857–69), Bishop of London (1885–96), and Archbishop of Canterbury (1896–1902).

**1** 'My aunt was suddenly prevented from going a voyage
in a ship what went down – would you call that a case
of Providential interference?'
'Can't tell: didn't know your aunt.'
*Memoirs of Archbishop Temple* (Sandford), Vol. II

**2** There is a certain class of clergyman whose mendicity is only equalled by their mendacity.
Remark at a meeting of the Ecclesiastical Commissioners.
*Years of Endeavour* (Sir George Leveson Gower)

**Temple, William** (1881–1944) British churchman. Son of Frederick Temple, he too was a headmaster (of Repton; 1910–14), who became Archbishop of Canterbury (1942–44). He wrote *Nature, Man, and God* (1934).

**1** Christianity is the most materialistic of all great religions.
*Reading in St John's Gospel*, Vol. I, Introduction

**2** It is a mistake to assume that God is interested only, or even chiefly, in religion.
*Concise Dictionary of Religious Quotations* (W. Neil)

**3** 'Are you not,' a Rugby master had asked him in discussing one of his essays, 'a little out of your depth here?' 'Perhaps, Sir,' was the confident reply, 'but I can swim.'
*William Temple* (F. A. Iremonger)

**4** Personally, I have always looked on cricket as organized loafing.
Remark to parents when headmaster of Repton School

**5** It is not the ape, nor the tiger in man that I fear, it is the donkey.
Attrib.

**6** The Church exists for the sake of those outside it.
Attrib.

**7** I believe in the Church, One Holy, Catholic and Apostolic, and I regret that it nowhere exists.
Attrib.

**Tenniel, Sir John** (1820–1914) British illustrator and cartoonist. He is best known for his illustrations for *Alice in Wonderland* (1865). He worked on *Punch* from 1851 to 1901.

**1** Dropping the pilot.
Caption of a cartoon. The cartoon refers to Bismarck's resignation portraying him as a ship's pilot walking down the gangway of the ship while Wilhelm II watches from the deck.
*Punch*, 29 Mar 1890

**Tennyson, Alfred, Baron** (1809–92) British poet. He established his reputation with *Morte d'Arthur* (1842). Of his many other works, *In Memoriam* (1850), *The Charge of the Light Brigade* (1854), *Maud* (1855), and *The Idylls of the King* (1859) are outstanding. He became poet laureate in 1850.

**1** And the stately ships go on
To their haven under the hill;
But O for the touch of a vanish'd hand,
And the sound of a voice that is still!
*Break, Break, Break*

**2** For men may come and men may go
But I go on for ever.
*The Brook*

**3** I come from haunts of coot and hern,
I make a sudden sally
And sparkle out among the fern,
To bicker down a valley.
*The Brook*

**4** Half a league, half a league,
Half a league onward,
All in the valley of Death
Rode the six hundred.
*The Charge of the Light Brigade*

**5** 'Forward the Light Brigade!'
Was there a man dismay'd?
Not tho' the soldier knew
Some one had blunder'd:
Their's not to make reply,
Their's not to reason why,
Their's but to do and die:
Into the valley of Death
Rode the six hundred.
*The Charge of the Light Brigade*

**6** Into the jaws of Death,
Into the mouth of Hell.
*The Charge of the Light Brigade*

**7** Come not, when I am dead,
To drop thy foolish tears upon my grave,
To trample round my fallen head,
And vex the unhappy dust thou wouldst not save.
*Come Not, When I Am Dead*

8 Sunset and evening star,
And one clear call for me!
And may there be no moaning of the bar
When I put out to sea.
*Crossing the Bar*

9 God made the woman for the man,
And for the good and increase of the world.
*Edwin Morris*

10 Half light, half shade,
She stood, a sight to make an old man young.
*The Gardener's Daughter*

11 That a lie which is all a lie may be met and
fought with outright,
But a lie which is part a truth is a harder matter
to fight.
*The Grandmother*

12 Dreams are true while they last, and do we not
live in dreams?
*The Higher Pantheism*

13 His honour rooted in dishonour stood,
And faith unfaithful kept him falsely true.
*Idylls of the King*, 'Lancelot and Elaine'

14 He makes no friend who never made a foe.
*Idylls of the King*, 'Lancelot and Elaine'

15 For man is man and master of his fate.
*Idylls of the King*, 'The Marriage of Geraint'

16 An arm
Rose up from out the bosom of the lake,
Clothed in white samite, mystic, wonderful.
*Idylls of the King*, 'The Passing of Arthur'

17 Authority forgets a dying king.
*Idylls of the King*, 'The Passing of Arthur'

18 For now I see the true old times are dead,
When every morning brought a noble chance,
And every chance brought out a noble knight.
*Idylls of the King*, 'The Passing of Arthur'

19 And slowly answer'd Arthur from the barge:
'The old order changeth, yielding place to new,
And God fulfils himself in many ways.'
*Idylls of the King*, 'The Passing of Arthur'

20 If thou shouldst never see my face again,
Pray for my soul. More things are wrought by
prayer
Than this world dreams of.
*Idylls of the King*, 'The Passing of Arthur'

21 I am going a long way
With these thou seest – if indeed I go
(For all my mind is clouded with a doubt) –
To the island-valley of Avilion;
Where falls not hail, or rain, or any snow,
Nor ever wind blows loudly; but it lies
Deep-meadow'd, happy, fair with orchard lawns
And bowery hollows crown'd with summer sea,
Where I will heal me of my grievous wound.
*Idylls of the King*, 'The Passing of Arthur'

22 Our little systems have their day;
They have their day and cease to be.
*In Memoriam A.H.H.*, Prologue

23 For words, like Nature, half reveal
And half conceal the Soul within.
*In Memoriam A.H.H.*, V

24 I hold it true, whate'er befall;
I feel it, when I sorrow most;
'Tis better to have loved and lost
Than never to have loved at all.
*In Memoriam A.H.H.*, XXVII

25 And so the Word had breath, and wrought
With human hands the creed of creeds
In loveliness of perfect deeds,
More strong than all poetic thought.
*In Memoriam A.H.H.*, XXXVI

26 But what am I?
An infant crying in the night:
An infant crying for the light:
And with no language but a cry.
*In Memoriam A.H.H.*, LIV

27 Are God and Nature then at strife
That Nature lends such evil dreams?
So careful of the type she seems,
So careless of the single life.
*In Memoriam A.H.H.*, LV

28 Sleep, Death's twin-brother, knows not Death,
Nor can I dream of thee as dead.
*In Memoriam A.H.H.*, LXVIII

29 I dreamed there would be Spring no more,
That Nature's ancient power was lost.
*In Memoriam A.H.H.*, LXIX

30 So many worlds, so much to do,
So little done, such things to be.
*In Memoriam A.H.H.*, LXXIII

31 Ring out, wild bells, to the wild sky,
The flying cloud, the frosty light:
The year is dying in the night;
Ring out, wild bells, and let him die.
*In Memoriam A.H.H.*, CVI

32 'Tis held that sorrow makes us wise.
*In Memoriam A.H.H.*, CXIII

33 My regret
Becomes an April violet,
And buds and blossoms like the rest.
*In Memoriam A.H.H.*, CXV

34 One God, one law, one element,
And one far-off divine event,
To which the whole creation moves.
*In Memoriam A.H.H.*, CXXXI

35 A simple maiden in her flower
Is worth a hundred coats-of-arms.
*Lady Clara Vere de Vere*, II

36 Kind hearts are more than coronets,
And simple faith than Norman blood.
*Lady Clara Vere de Vere*, VI

37 On either side the river lie
Long fields of barley and of rye,
That clothe the wold and meet the sky;
And thro' the field the road runs by
To many-tower'd Camelot.
*The Lady of Shalott*, Pt. I

38 Willows whiten, aspens quiver,
Little breezes dusk and shiver.
*The Lady of Shalott*, Pt. I

39 Or when the moon was overhead,
Came two young lovers lately wed;
'I am half sick of shadows,' said
The Lady of Shalott.
*The Lady of Shalott*, Pt. II

40 She has heard a whisper say,
A curse is on her if she stay
To look down to Camelot.
*The Lady of Shalott*, Pt. II

41 A bow-shot from her bower-eaves,
He rode between the barley-sheaves,
The sun came dazzling thro' the leaves
And flamed upon the brazen graves
Of bold Sir Lancelot.
*The Lady of Shalott*, Pt. III

42 'The curse is come upon me,' cried
The Lady of Shalott.
*The Lady of Shalott*, Pt. III

43 But Lancelot mused a little space;
He said, 'She has a lovely face;
God in his mercy lend her grace,
The Lady of Shalott.'
*The Lady of Shalott*, Pt. IV

44 Ah God! the petty fools of rhyme
That shriek and sweat in pigmy wars.
*Literary Squabbles*

45 Nourishing a youth sublime
With the fairy tales of science, and the long result of Time.
*Locksley Hall*

46 In the Spring a young man's fancy lightly turns to thoughts of love.
*Locksley Hall*

47 Such a one do I remember, whom to look at was to love.
*Locksley Hall*

48 So I triumphed ere my passion, sweeping thro' me, left me dry,
Left me with the palsied heart, and left me with the jaundiced eye.
*Locksley Hall*

49 Not with blinded eyesight poring over miserable books.
*Locksley Hall*

50 Time driveth onward fast,
And in a little while our lips are dumb.
Let us alone. What is it that will last?
All things are taken from us, and become
Portions and parcels of the dreadful Past.
*The Lotos-Eaters, 'Choric Song'*

51 Music that gentlier on the spirit lies,
Than tir'd eyelids upon tir'd eyes.
*The Lotos-Eaters, 'Choric Song'*

52 Come into the garden, Maud,
For the black bat, night, has flown,
Come into the garden, Maud,
I am here at the gate alone.
*Maud*, I

53 The rose was awake all night for your sake,
Knowing your promise to me;
The lilies and roses were all awake,
They sighed for the dawn and thee.
*Maud*, I

54 I embrace the purpose of God and the doom assigned.
*Maud*, III

55 But the churchmen fain would kill their church,
As the churches have kill'd their Christ.
*Maud*, V

56 You must wake and call me early, call me early, mother dear;
To-morrow 'ill be the happiest time of all the glad New-year;
Of all the glad New-year, mother, the maddest merriest day;
For I'm to be Queen o' the May, mother, I'm to be Queen o' the May.
*The May Queen*

57 The splendour falls on castle walls
And snowy summits old in story.
*The Princess*, III

58 Tears, idle tears, I know not what they mean,
Tears from the depth of some divine despair.
*The Princess*, IV

59 Dear as remembered kisses after death,
And sweet as those by hopeless fancy feign'd
On lips that are for others: deep as love,
Deep as first love, and wild with all regret;
O Death in Life, the days that are no more.
*The Princess*, IV

60 O tell her, brief is life but love is long.
*The Princess*, IV

61 Man is the hunter; woman is his game:
The sleek and shining creatures of the chase,
We hunt them for the beauty of their skins.
*The Princess*, V

62 Man for the field and woman for the hearth:
Man for the sword and for the needle she:
Man with the head and woman with the heart:
Man to command and woman to obey;
All else confusion.
*The Princess, V*

63 Home they brought her warrior dead.
She nor swoon'd, nor utter'd cry:
All her maidens, watching said,
'She must weep or she will die.'
*The Princess, VI*

64 The moans of doves in immemorial elms,
And murmuring of innumerable bees.
*The Princess, VII*

65 Revolts, republics, revolutions, most
No graver than a schoolboy's barring out.
*The Princess, Conclusion*

66 And they blest him in their pain, that they were
not left to Spain,
To the thumbscrew and the stake, for the glory
of the Lord.
*The Revenge, III*

67 A day less or more
At sea or ashore,
We die – does it matter when?
*The Revenge, XI*

68 My strength is as the strength of ten,
Because my heart is pure.
*Sir Galahad*

69 How sweet are looks that ladies bend
On whom their favours fall!
*Sir Galahad*

70 Battering the gates of heaven with storms of
prayer.
*St Simeon Stylites*

71 The woods decay, the woods decay and fall,
The vapours weep their burthen to the ground,
Man comes and tills the field and lies beneath,
And after many a summer dies the swan.
*Tithonus*

72 The Gods themselves cannot recall their gifts.
*Tithonus*

73 A life that moves to gracious ends
Thro' troops of unrecording friends,
A deedful life, a silent voice.
*To – , after reading a Life and Letters*

74 God gives us love. Something to love
He lends us; but, when love is grown
To ripeness that on which it throve
Falls off, and love is left alone.
*To J.S.*

75 A still small voice spake unto me,
'Thou art so full of misery,
Were it not better not to be?'
*The Two Voices*

76 All experience is an arch wherethro'
Gleams that untravelled world, whose margin
fades
For ever and for ever when I move.
*Ulysses*

77 We are not now that strength which in old days
Moved earth and heaven; that which we are, we
are;
One equal temper of heroic hearts,
Made weak by time and fate, but strong in will
To strive, to seek, to find, and not to yield.
*Ulysses*

78 Every moment dies a man,
Every moment one is born.
For a parody, *see* BABBAGE
*The Vision of Sin*

**Terence** (Publius Terentius Afer; c. 190–159 BC) Roman poet.

1 Nothing has yet been said that's not been said
before.
*Eunuchus, Prologue*

2 I am a man, I count nothing human foreign to
me.
*Heauton Timorumenos*

3 Fortune favours the brave.
*Phormio*

4 So many men, so many opinions.
*Phormio*

**Teresa, Mother** (Agnes Gonxha Bojaxhui; 1910– )
Yugoslav-born nun of Albanian parents. She founded the Order of
the Missionaries of Charity in Calcutta, her nuns helping lepers,
cripples, and the aged throughout the world.

1 . . . the poor are our brothers and sisters. . . .
people in the world who need love, who need
care, who have to be wanted.
*Time*, 'Saints Among Us', 29 Dec 1975

2 Loneliness and the feeling of being unwanted is
the most terrible poverty.
*Time*, 'Saints Among Us', 29 Dec 1975

3 To keep a lamp burning we have to keep putting
oil in it.
*Time*, 'Saints Among Us', 29 Dec 1975

**Teresa of Ávila, St** (1515–82) Spanish mystic and nun.
She reformed the Carmelite order in Ávila and described her
mystical experiences in *The Way of Perfection* (1565) and *The
Interior Castle* (1577).

1 Alas, O Lord, to what a state dost Thou bring
those who love Thee!
*The Interior Castle, VI*

**Terry, Dame Ellen** (1847–1928) British actress. She
performed with Sir Henry Irving at the Lyceum Theatre and later
managed the Imperial Theatre.

1 Wonderful women! Have you ever thought how much we all, and women especially, owe to Shakespeare for his vindication of women in these fearless, high-spirited, resolute and intelligent heroines?
*Four Lectures on Shakespeare*, 'The Triumphant Women'

2 Imagination! imagination! I put it first years ago, when I was asked what qualities I thought necessary for success upon the stage.
*The Story of My Life*, Ch. 2

3 What is a diary as a rule? A document useful to the person who keeps it, dull to the contemporary who reads it, invaluable to the student, centuries afterwards, who treasures it!
*The Story of My Life*, Ch. 14

4 How Henry would have loved it!
Referring to Sir Henry Irving's funeral
*Yesterdays* (Robert Hitchens)

**Tertullian, Quintus Septimius Florens** (c. 160–225 AD) Carthaginian father of the church. He was converted to Christianity (190 AD) but withdrew from the church in 207 to form a Montanist group. His many works include *Apologeticus* and *De Baptismo.*

1 The blood of the martyrs is the seed of the Church.
Traditional misquotation: more accurately, 'Our numbers increase as often as you cut us down: the blood of Christians is the seed.'
*Apologeticus*, L

2 See how these Christians love one another.
*Apologeticus*, XXXIX

3 I believe because it is impossible.
The usual misquotation of 'It is certain because it is impossible.'
*De Carne Christi*, V

**Thackeray, William Makepeace** (1811–63) British novelist. He became a full-time writer after the success of *Vanity Fair* (1847). Later novels include *Pendennis* (1848), *Henry Esmond* (1852), and *The Newcomes* (1853).

1 He who meanly admires mean things is a Snob.
*The Book of Snobs*, Ch. 2

2 It is impossible, in our condition of society, not to be sometimes a Snob.
*The Book of Snobs*, Ch. 3

3 'Tis not the dying for a faith that's so hard, Master Harry – every man of every nation has done that – 'tis the living up to it that is difficult.
*Henry Esmond*, Ch. 6

4 'Tis strange what a man may do, and a woman yet think him an angel.
*Henry Esmond*, Ch. 7

5 Remember, it is as easy to marry a rich woman as a poor woman.
*Pendennis*, Ch. 28

6 The *Pall Mall Gazette* is written by gentlemen for gentlemen.
*Pendennis*, Ch. 32

7 There are some meannesses which are too mean even for man – woman, lovely woman alone, can venture to commit them.
*A Shabby-Genteel Story*, Ch. 3

8 Oh, Vanity of vanities!
How wayward the decrees of Fate are;
How very weak the very wise,
How very small the very great are!
*Vanitas Vanitatum*

9 This I set down as a positive truth. A woman with fair opportunities and without a positive hump, may marry whom she likes.
*Vanity Fair*, Ch. 4

10 Whenever he met a great man he grovelled before him, and my-lorded him as only a free-born Briton can do.
*Vanity Fair*, Ch. 13

11 If a man's character is to be abused, say what you will, there's nobody like a relation to do the business.
*Vanity Fair*, Ch. 19

12 I think I could be a good woman if I had five thousand a year.
*Vanity Fair*, Ch. 36

**Thales** (c. 624–547 BC) Greek philosopher and astronomer. He predicted the solar eclipse of 585 BC from observations made by the Babylonians.

1 Because there is no difference.
His reply when asked why he chose to carry on living after saying there was no difference between life and death
*The Story of Civilization* (W. Durant), Vol. 2

**Thatcher, Denis** (1915– ) British businessman, married to Mrs Margaret Thatcher.

1 I do, and I also wash and iron them.
Replying to the question 'Who wears the pants in this house?'
*Times* (Los Angeles), 21 Apr 1981

**Thatcher, Margaret** (1925– ) British politician, prime minister since 1979. Trained as a chemist and a barrister, she became a Conservative MP in 1959 and minister of education and science (1970–74).

1 I'm not hard – I'm frightfully soft. But I will not be hounded.
*Daily Mail*, 1972

2 Let our children grow tall, and some taller than others if they have it in them to do so.
Speech, US tour, 1975

3 Britain is no longer in the politics of the pendulum, but of the ratchet.
Speech, Institute of Public Relations, 1977

4 I love argument, I love debate. I don't expect anyone just to sit there and agree with me, that's not their job.
*The Times*, 1980

5 If a woman like Eva Peron with no ideals can get that far, think how far I can go with all the ideals that I have.
*The Sunday Times*, 1980

6 U-turn if you want to. The lady's not for turning.
Speech, Conservative Conference, 1980

7 No one would have remembered the Good Samaritan if he'd only had good intentions. He had money as well.
Television interview, 1980

8 The battle for women's rights has been largely won.
*The Guardian*, 1982

9 Pennies do not come from heaven. They have to be earned here on earth.
*Sunday Telegraph*, 1982

10 Victorian values . . . were the values when our country became great.
Television interview, 1982

11 Oh. I have got lots of human weaknesses, who hasn't?
*The Times*, 1983

12 State socialism is totally alien to the British character.
*The Times*, 1983

13 I am painted as the greatest little dictator, which is ridiculous – you always take some consultations.
*The Times*, 1983

14 We are the true peace movement.
*The Times*, 1983

15 And what a prize we have to fight for: no less than the chance to banish from our land the dark divisive clouds of Marxist socialism.
Speech, Scottish Conservative Conference, 1983

16 Young people ought not to be idle. It is very bad for them.
*The Times*, 1984

17 I love being at the centre of things.
*Reader's Digest*, 1984

18 I am certain that we will win the election with a good majority. Not that I am ever over-confident.
*Evening Standard*, 1987

19 I don't mind how much my ministers talk – as long as they do what I say.
*The Times*, 1987

20 I wasn't lucky. I deserved it.
Said after receiving school prize, aged nine
Attrib.

**Thayer, W. M.** (1820–98) US writer. He wrote a biography (1881) of James Abram Garfield, the 20th president of the USA.

1 Log-cabin to White House.
The title of his biography of James Garfield, US president

**Themistocles** (c. 528–462 BC) Athenian statesman. He built up Athenian naval power and fortifications, but was ostracized in 471 and died in Asia.

1 Athens holds sway over all Greece; I dominate Athens; my wife dominates me; our newborn son dominates her.
Explaining an earlier remark to the effect that his young son ruled all Greece
Attrib.

**Theodoric** (c. 445–526) King of the Ostrogoths and of Italy (493–526). His capital was at Ravenna.

1 If this man is not faithful to his God, how can he be faithful to me, a mere man?''
Explaining why he had had a trusted minister, who had said he would adopt his master's religion, beheaded
*Dictionnaire Encyclopédique* (E. Guérard)

**Theroux, Paul** (1941– ) US-born writer. His novels include *Girls at Play* (1969), *Saint Jack* (1973), and *The Mosquito Coast* (1981). Other books include *The Great Railway Bazaar* (1975).

1 The Japanese have perfected good manners and made them indistinguishable from rudeness.
*The Great Railway Bazaar*, Ch. 2

2 They say that if the Swiss had designed these mountains they'd be rather flatter.
Referring to the Alps
*The Great Railway Bazaar*, Ch. 28

3 The ship follows Soviet custom: it is riddled with class distinctions so subtle, it takes a trained Marxist to appreciate them.
*The Great Railway Bazaar*, Ch. 30

4 A foreign swear-word is practically inoffensive except to the person who has learnt it early in life and knows its social limits.
*Saint Jack*, Ch. 12

**Thiers, Louis Adolphe** (1797–1877) French statesman and historian. He became the first president of the Third Republic (1870–73). His books include the 10-volume *History of the French Revolution* (1823–27).

1 The king reigns, and the people govern themselves.
In an unsigned article attributed to Thiers
*Le National*, 20 Jan 1830

2 Everything must be taken seriously, nothing tragically.
Speech, French National Assembly, 24 May 1873

3 She was – but I assure you that she was a very bad cook.
Defending his social status after someone had remarked that his mother had been a cook
Attrib.

**Thomas, Brandon** (1856–1914) British actor and dramatist. His best-known play is the farce *Charley's Aunt* (1892).

1 I'm Charley's aunt from Brazil, where the nuts come from.
*Charley's Aunt*, I

**Thomas, Dylan** (1914–53) Welsh poet. His collections include *18 Poems* (1934) and *Deaths and Entrances* (1946). His radio play *Under Milk Wood* (1954) is also well known. His early death resulted from alcoholism.

1 I, born of flesh and ghost, was neither
A ghost nor man, but mortal ghost.
And I was struck down by death's feather.
*Before I knocked*

2 These poems, with all their crudities, doubts, and confusions, are written for the love of Man and in praise of God, and I'd be a damn' fool if they weren't.
*Collected Poems*, Note

3 Do not go gentle into that good night,
Old age should burn and rave at close of day;
Rage, rage, against the dying of the light.
*Do not go gentle into that good night*

4 The force that through the green fuse drives the flower
Drives my green age.
*The force that through the green fuse drives the flower*

5 The hand that signed the treaty bred a fever,
And famine grew, and locusts came;
Great is the hand that holds dominion over
Man by a scribbled name.
*The hand that signed the paper*

6 The hunchback in the park
A solitary mister
Propped between trees and water.
*The hunchback in the park*

7 And the wild boys innocent as strawberries.
*The hunchback in the park*

8 Light breaks where no sun shines;
Where no sea runs, the waters of the heart
Push in their tides.
*Light breaks where no sun shines*

9 I missed the chance of a lifetime, too. Fifty lovelies in the rude and I'd left my Bunsen burner home.
*Portrait of the Artist as a Young Dog*, 'One Warm Saturday'

10 After the first death, there is no other.
*A Refusal to Mourn the Death, by Fire, of a Child in London*

11 This bread I break was once the oat,
This wine upon a foreign tree
Plunged in its fruit;
Man in the day or wind at night
Laid the crops low, broke the grape's joy.
*This bread I break*

12 MR PRITCHARD. I must dust the blinds and then I must raise them.
MRS OGMORE-PRITCHARD. And before you let the sun in, mind it wipes its shoes.
*Under Milk Wood*

13 Gomer Owen who kissed her once by the pig-sty when she wasn't looking and never kissed her again although she was looking all the time.
*Under Milk Wood*

14 Sleeping as quiet as death, side by wrinkled side, toothless, salt and brown, like two old kippers in a box.
*Under Milk Wood*

15 The hands of the clock have stayed still at half past eleven for fifty years. It is always opening time in the Sailors Arms.
*Under Milk Wood*

16 Chasing the naughty couples down the grassgreen gooseberried double bed of the wood.
*Under Milk Wood*

17 Every night of her married life she has been late for school.
*Under Milk Wood*

18 Oh, isn't life a terrible thing, thank God?
*Under Milk Wood*

19 Oh I'm a martyr to music.
*Under Milk Wood*

20 . . . his nicotine eggyellow weeping walrus Victorian moustache worn thick and long in memory of Doctor Crippen.
*Under Milk Wood*

21 Portraits of famous bards and preachers, all fur and wool from the squint to the kneecaps.
*Under Milk Wood*

22 It is a winter's tale
That the snow blind twilight ferries over the lakes
And floating fields from the farm in the cup of the vales.
*A Winter's Tale*

23 The land of my fathers. My fathers can have it.
Referring to Wales
*Dylan Thomas* (John Ackerman)

24 Somebody's boring me, I think it's me.
Remark made after he had been talking continuously for some time
*Four Absentees* (Rayner Heppenstall)

25 Too many of the artists of Wales spend too much time about the position of the artist of Wales. There is only one position for an artist anywhere: and that is, upright.
*New Statesman*, 18 Dec 1964

**Thomas, Edward** (1878–1917) British poet. His early naturalist books, such as *The Woodland Life* (1897), were succeeded by poetry after meeting Robert Frost. Collections include *Poems* (1917), the year in which he was killed in action in World War I.

1 Yes. I remember Adlestrop –
The name, because one afternoon
Of heat the express train drew up there
Unwontedly. It was late June.
*Adlestrop*

2 The past is the only dead thing that smells sweet.
*Early One Morning*

3   There is not any book
    Or face of dearest look
    That I would not turn from now
    To go into the unknown
    I must enter, and leave, alone,
    I know not how.
    *Lights Out*

4   Now all roads lead to France
    And heavy is the tread
    Of the living; but the dead
    Returning lightly dance.
    *Roads*

5   Make me content
    With some sweetness
    From Wales
    Whose nightingales
    Have no wings.
    *Words*

**Thomas, Gwyn** (1913– ) British writer and dramatist. His novels include *The Dark Philosophers* (1946), *Now Lead Us Home* (1952), and *The Sky of Our Lives* (1972). His best-known plays are *The Keep* (1961) and *Jackie the Jumper* (1962).

1   I wanted a play that would paint the full face of sensuality, rebellion and revivalism. In South Wales these three phenomena have played second fiddle only to the Rugby Union which is a distillation of all three.
    *Jackie the Jumper* (Introduction), 'Plays and Players' 19 Jan 1963

2   My life's been a meeting, Dad, one long meeting. Even on the few committees I don't yet belong to, the agenda winks at me when I pass.
    *The Keep*, I

3   A bit like God in his last years, the Alderman.
    *The Keep*, I

4   Her first economic drive will be to replace X-ray by hearsay.
    *The Keep*, II

5   There are still parts of Wales where the only concession to gaiety is a striped shroud.
    *Punch*, 18 June 1958

**Thomas, Irene** (1920– ) British writer and broadcaster.

1   Protestant women may take the Pill. Roman Catholic women must keep taking the *Tablet*.
    Attrib.

2   It should be a very happy marriage – they are both so much in love with *him*.
    Attrib.

3   It was the kind of show where the girls are not auditioned – just measured.
    Attrib.

4   The cello is not one of my favourite instruments. It has such a lugubrious sound, like someone reading a will.
    Attrib.

**Thomas, Lewis** (1913– ) US pathologist. His books include *Notes of a Biology Watcher* (1974) and *More Notes of a Biology Watcher* (1979).

1   Worrying is the most natural and spontaneous of all human functions. It is time to acknowledge this, perhaps even to learn to do it better.
    *More Notes of a Biology Watcher*, 'The Medusa and the Snail'

**Thomas, Norman M.** (1884–1968) US politician. He was socialist candidate for the presidency (1928–1948).

1   While I'd rather be right than president, at any time I'm ready to be both.
    Referring to his lack of success in presidential campaigns
    *Come to Judgment* (A. Whitman)

**Thomas, R(onald) S(tuart)** Welsh poet and clergyman. His collections of verse include *The Stones of the Field* (1946), *Song at the Year's Turning* (1955), and *Pietà* (1966).

1   . . . an impotent people,
    Sick with inbreeding,
    Worrying the carcase of an old song.
    *Welsh Landscape*

**Thompson, E(dward) P(almer)** (1924– ) British historian. His best-known book is *The Making of the English Working Class* (1963).

1   This going into Europe will not turn out to be the thrilling mutual exchange supposed. It is more like nine middle-aged couples with failing marriages meeting in a darkened bedroom in a Brussels hotel for a Group Grope.
    On the Europe debate, *Sunday Times*, 27 Apr 1975

**Thompson, Francis** (1859–1907) British poet. An opium addict, he was befriended by Wilfred Meynell and attained a critical success with his *Poems* (1893), which included 'The Hound of Heaven'. As a Roman Catholic, much of his work had religious themes.

1   I fled Him, down the nights and down the days;
    I fled Him, down the arches of the years;
    I fled Him, down the labyrinthine ways
    Of my own mind; and in the mist of tears
    I hid from Him, and under running laughter.
    *The Hound of Heaven*

2   Shall shine the traffic of Jacob's ladder
    Pitched between Heaven and Charing Cross.
    *The Kingdom of God*

3   Spring is come home with her world-wandering feet.
    And all the things are made young with young desires.
    *The Night of Forebeing*, 'Ode to Easter'

**Thompson, William Hepworth** (1810–86) British academic who became master of Trinity College, Cambridge.

1   We are none of us infallible – not even the youngest of us.
    Referring to G. W. Balfour, who was a junior fellow of Trinity College at the time
    *Collections and Recollections* (G. W. E. Russell), Ch. 18

2 What time he can spare from the adornment of his person he devotes to the neglect of his duties.
Referring to the Cambridge Professor of Greek, Sir Richard Jebb
*With Dearest Love to All* (M. R. Bobbit), Ch. 7

**Thomson, James** (1700–48) British poet born in Scotland. His works include *The Seasons* (1730), the song 'Rule Britannia' (1740), and *The Castle of Indolence* (1748), an allegory.

1 When Britain first, at heaven's command,
Arose from out the azure main,
This was the charter of the land,
And guardian angels sung this strain:
'Rule, Britannia, rule the waves;
Britons never will be slaves.'
*Alfred: a Masque*, Act II, Scene the last

2 For life is but a dream whose shapes return,
Some frequently, some seldom, some by night
And some by day.
*The City of Dreadful Night*, I

3 I find no hint throughout the universe
Of good or ill, of blessing or of curse;
I find alone Necessity Supreme.
*The City of Dreadful Night*, XIV

4 Oh! Sophonisba! Sophonisba! oh!
*Sophonisba*, III

**Thomson, Joseph** (1858–95) Scottish explorer. A geologist, he led several expeditions to central Africa, discovered Lake Rukwa, and gained part of Sudan for Britain.

1 Crossing Piccadilly Circus.
His reply when asked by J. M. Barrie what was the most hazardous part of his expedition to Africa
*J. M. Barrie* (D. Dunbar)

**Thomson of Fleet, Roy Herbert, Baron** (1894–1976) Canadian-born British newspaper proprietor, who acquired *The Sunday Times* (1959) and *The Times* (1966).

1 It's just like having a licence to print your own money.
Speaking about commercial television
Attrib.

**Thoreau, Henry David** (1817–62) US writer. He is best known for *Walden* (1854), an account of his year spent as a recluse in the Walden woods in Massachusetts. He also wrote poetry and many essays, including one on *Civil Disobedience*.

1 Under a government which imprisons any unjustly, the true place for a just man is also a prison.
*Civil Disobedience*

2 The most attractive sentences are not perhaps the wisest, but the surest and soundest.
*Journal*, 1842

3 Whatever sentence will bear to be read twice, we may be sure was thought twice.
*Journal*, 1842

4 Some circumstantial evidence is very strong, as when you find a trout in the milk.
*Journal*, 1850

5 What men call social virtues, good fellowship, is commonly but the virtue of pigs in a litter, which lie close together to keep each other warm. It brings men together in crowds and mobs in bar-rooms and elsewhere, but it does not deserve the name of virtue.
*Journal*, 1852

6 As if you could kill time without injuring eternity.
*Walden*, 'Economy'

7 The mass of men lead lives of quiet desperation.
*Walden*, 'Economy'

8 I have lived some thirty years on this planet, and I have yet to hear the first syllable of valuable or even earnest advice from my seniors.
*Walden*, 'Economy'

9 There are now-a-days professors of philosophy but not philosophers.
*Walden*, 'Economy'

10 As for doing good, that is one of the professions which are full.
*Walden*, 'Economy'

11 Beware of all enterprises that require new clothes.
*Walden*, 'Economy'

12 I never found the companion that was so companionable as solitude.
*Walden*, 'Solitude'

13 The three-o'-clock in the morning courage, which Bonaparte thought was the rarest.
*Walden*, 'Sounds'

14 Our life is frittered away by detail . . . Simplify, simplify.
*Walden*, 'Where I Lived, and What I Lived For'

15 Time is but the stream I go a-fishing in.
*Walden*, 'Where I Lived, and What I Lived For'

16 I once had a sparrow alight upon my shoulder for a moment while I was hoeing in a village garden, and I felt that I was more distinguished by that circumstance than I should have been by any epaulet I could have worn.
*Walden*, 'Winter Visitors'

17 It takes two to speak the truth – one to speak, and another to hear.
*A Week on the Concord and Merrimack Rivers*

18 Not that the story need be long, but it will take a long while to make it short.
Letter, 16 Nov 1867

19 One world at a time.
On being asked his opinion of the hereafter
Attrib.

20 I did not know that we had ever quarrelled.
On being urged to make his peace with God
Attrib.

21 Yes – around Concord.
On being asked whether he had travelled much
Attrib.

**Thorndike, Dame Sybil** (1882–1976) British actress. She played many Shakespearean roles and the title role in Shaw's *St Joan*. She was married to the actor Sir Lewis Casson.

1 Divorce? Never. But murder often!

Replying to a query as to whether she had ever considered divorce during her long marriage to Sir Lewis Casson
Attrib.

**Thorpe, Jeremy** (1929– ) British politician and lawyer. He was leader of the Liberal Party (1967–76) until he was charged with incitement to murder a man with whom he was alleged to have had a homosexual relationship. He was acquitted of the charge.

1 Greater love hath no man than this, that he lay down his friends for his life.

After Macmillan's 1962 Cabinet reshuffle
*The Pendulum Years* (Bernard Levin), Ch. 12

**Thorpe, Rose Hartwick** (1850–1939) US poet and novelist. She is remembered for her poem *Curfew Shall Not Ring Tonight* (1866).

1 And her face so sweet and pleading, yet with sorrow pale and worn,
Touched his heart with sudden pity – lit his eye with misty light;
"Go, your lover lives!" said Cromwell; "Curfew shall not ring tonight!"

*Curfew Shall Not Ring Tonight*

**Thucydides** (c. 460–c. 400 BC) Greek historian and general. An Athenian general in the Peloponnesian War, he was banished for 20 years for his failure at Amphipolis, providing him with the opportunity to write his eight-volume *History of the Peloponnesian War*.

1 To famous men all the earth is a sepulchre.

*History of the Peloponnesian War*, Bk. II, Ch. 43

2 It is a great glory in a woman to show no more weakness than is natural to her sex, and not be talked of, either for good or evil by men.

*History of the Peloponnesian War*, Bk. II, Ch. 45

**Thurber, James** (1894–1961) US writer, humorist, and cartoonist. A contributor to the *New Yorker*, he published a number of collected writings, including *The Thurber Carnival* (1945).

1 'Joe,' I said, 'was perhaps the first great nonstop literary drinker of the American nineteenth century. He made the indulgences of Coleridge and De Quincey seem like a bit of mischief in the kitchen with the cooking sherry.'

*Alarms and Diversions*, 'The Moribundant Life . . . '

2 I was seized by the stern hand of Compulsion, that dark, unseasonable Urge that impels women to clean house in the middle of the night.

*Alarms and Diversions*, 'There's a Time for Flags'

3 It is better to have loafed and lost than never to have loafed at all.

*Fables for Our Time*, 'The Courtship of Arthur and Al'

4 You can fool too many of the people too much of the time.

*Fables for Our Time*, 'The Owl Who Was God'

5 Early to rise and early to bed makes a male healthy and wealthy and dead.

*Fables for Our Time*, 'The Shrike and the Chipmunks'

6 Old Nat Burge sat . . . He was . . . watching the moon come up lazily out of the old cemetery in which nine of his daughters were lying, and only two of them were dead.

*Let Your Mind Alone*, 'Bateman Comes Home'

7 No man . . . who has wrestled with a self-adjusting card table can ever quite be the man he once was.

*Let Your Mind Alone*, 'Sex ex Machina'

8 I suppose that the high-water mark of my youth in Columbus, Ohio, was the night the bed fell on my father.

*My Life and Hard Times*, Ch. 1

9 Her own mother lived the latter years of her life in the horrible suspicion that electricity was dripping invisibly all over the house.

*My Life and Hard Times*, Ch. 2

10 Then, with that faint fleeting smile playing about his lips, he faced the firing squad; erect and motionless, proud and disdainful, Walter Mitty, the undefeated, inscrutable to the last.

*My World and Welcome to It*, 'The Secret Life of Walter Mitty'

11 A man should not insult his wife publicly, at parties. He should insult her in the privacy of the home.

*Thurber Country*

12 The difference between our decadence and the Russians' is that while theirs is brutal, ours is apathetic.

*The Observer*, 'Sayings of the Week', 5 Feb 1961

13 The War between Men and Women.

Title of a series of cartoons

14 Well, if I called the wrong number, why did you answer the phone?

Cartoon caption

15 You wait here and I'll bring the etchings down.

Cartoon caption

16 I said the hounds of spring are on winter's traces – but let it pass, let it pass!

Cartoon caption

17 Why do you have to be a nonconformist like everybody else?

Attrib. Actually a cartoon caption by Stan Hunt in the *New Yorker*

18 Surely you don't mean by unartificial insemination!

On being accosted at a party by a drunk woman who claimed she would like to have a baby by him
Attrib.

19 It had only one fault. It was kind of lousy.

Remark made about a play
Attrib.

**20** God bless . . . God damn.

His last words
Attrib.

**Thurlow, Edward, Baron** (1731–1806) British lawyer, who became lord chancellor (1778–83). He presided at the trial of Warren Hastings, favoured coercion of the American colonies, upheld the interests of slave traders, and defended royal prerogatives.

**1** When I forget my sovereign, may God forget me!

Speech, House of Lords, 15 Dec 1778

**2** As guardian of His Majesty's conscience.

Speech, House of Lords, 1779

**Tillich, Paul** (1886–1965) German-born US theologian. A Lutheran pastor, he went to the USA when the Nazis came to power and became a university lecturer. His major work is *Systematic Theology* (1950–63).

**1** Neurosis is the way of avoiding non-being by avoiding being.

*The Courage to Be*

**Tilzer, Harry** (Albert von Tilzer; 1878–1956) British songwriter.

**1** Come, Come, Come and have a drink with me Down at the old 'Bull and Bush'.

*The Old Bull and Bush*

**Tintoretto** (Jacopo Robusti; 1518–94) Venetian painter. Many of his famous religious paintings hang in Venice.

**1** Grant me paradise in this world; I'm not so sure I'll reach it in the next.

Arguing that he be allowed to paint the *Paradiso* at the doge's palace in Venice, despite his advanced age
Attrib.

**Tocqueville, Alexis de** (1805–59) French writer, historian, and politician. He wrote *Démocratie en Amérique* (1833) after visiting the USA. Elected to the Chamber of Deputies (1839), he was briefly foreign minister (1844). When Louis Napoleon came to power he retired to write *L'Ancien Régime et la révolution* (1856).

**1** The French want no-one to be their *superior*. The English want *inferiors*. The Frenchman constantly raises his eyes above him with anxiety. The Englishman lowers his beneath him with satisfaction. On either side it is pride, but understood in a different way.

*Voyage en Angleterre et en Irlande de 1835*, 18 May

**Tolkien, J(ohn) R(onald) R(euel)** (1892–1973) British writer. While professor of English literature at Oxford he wrote *The Lord of the Rings* (1954–55). Related works include *The Hobbit* (1937) and *The Silmarillion* (1977).

**1** In a hole in the ground there lived a hobbit.

*The Hobbit*, Ch. 1

**2** One Ring to rule them all, One Ring to find them,
One Ring to bring them all and in the darkness bind them.

*The Lord of the Rings*, Pt. I: *The Fellowship of the Ring*, Ch. 2

**Tolstoy, Leo (Nikolaevich), Count** (1828–1910) Russian writer. His fame rests on his two epic novels *War and Peace* (1865–69) and *Anna Karenina* (1875–77). In 1876 he was converted to a form of Christian mysticism, about which he wrote copiously.

**1** All happy families resemble one another, each unhappy family is unhappy in its own way.

*Anna Karenina*, Pt. I, Ch. 1

**2** If you want to be happy, be.

*Kosma Prutkov*

**3** I am always with myself, and it is I who am my tormentor.

*Memoirs of a Madman*

**4** The highest wisdom has but one science – the science of the whole – the science explaining the whole creation and man's place in it.

*War and Peace*, Bk. V, Ch. 2

**5** The chief attraction of military service has consisted and will consist in this compulsory and irreproachable idleness.

*War and Peace*, Bk. VII, Ch. 1

**6** All, everything that I understand, I understand only because I love.

*War and Peace*, Bk. VII, Ch. 16

**7** Our body is a machine for living. It is organized for that, it is its nature. Let life go on in it unhindered and let it defend itself, it will do more than if you paralyse it by encumbering it with remedies.

*War and Peace*, Bk. X, Ch. 29

**8** Pure and complete sorrow is as impossible as pure and complete joy.

*War and Peace*, Bk. XV, Ch. 1

**9** Art is not a handicraft, it is the transmission of feeling the artist has experienced.

*What is Art?*, Ch. 19

**10** I sit on a man's back, choking him and making him carry me, and yet assure myself and others that I am very sorry for him and wish to ease his lot by all possible means – except by getting off his back.

*What Then Must We Do?*, Ch. 16

**11** Historians are like deaf people who go on answering questions that no one has asked them.

*A Discovery of Australia*, 'Being an Historian' (Manning Clark)

**12** Even in the valley of the shadow of death, two and two do not make six.

Refusing to reconcile himself with the Russian Orthodox Church as he lay dying
Attrib.

**Tolstoy, Sophie** (1844–1919) Russian writer. The wife of Leo Tolstoy, she kept a revealing diary of her life with him.

**1** One can't live on love alone; and I am so stupid that I can do nothing but think of him.

*A Diary of Tolstoy's Wife, 1860–1891*

2 I am a source of satisfaction to him, a nurse, a piece of furniture, a *woman* – nothing more.
*A Diary of Tolstoy's Wife, 1860–1891*

3 He would like to destroy his old diaries and to appear before his children and the public only in his patriarchal robes. His vanity is immense!
*A Diary of Tolstoy's Wife, 1860–1891*

**Tomaschek, Rudolphe** (20th century) German scientist.

1 Modern Physics is an instrument of Jewry for the destruction of Nordic science . . . True physics is the creation of the German spirit.
*The Rise and Fall of the Third Reich* (W. L. Shirer), Ch. 8

**Tooke, John Horne** (1736–1812) British clergyman, politician, and etymologist. While imprisoned for supporting the Americans in the American Revolution, he wrote a treatise on etymology.

1 With all my heart. Whose wife shall it be?
Replying to the suggestion that he take a wife
Attrib.

**Toplady, Augustus Montague** (1740–78) British hymn writer and clergyman. He was a supporter of Calvinism and opponent of Methodism.

1 Rock of ages, cleft for me,
Let me hide myself in Thee.
*Rock of Ages*

**Toscanini, Arturo** (1867–1957) Italian conductor. Originally a cellist, he became famous as a conductor of opera at the Scala, Milan, and at the Metropolitan Opera in New York. He was conductor of the NBC Symphony Orchestra (1937–57).

1 They are for prima donnas or corpses – I am neither.
Refusing a floral wreath at the end of a performance
*The Elephant that Swallowed a Nightingale* (C. Galtey)

2 It's too late to apologize.
Retort to the insult 'Nuts to you!' shouted at him by a player he had just ordered from the stage during rehearsal
*The Humor of Music* (L. Humphrey)

3 After I die, I shall return to earth as a gatekeeper of a bordello and I won't let any of you – not a one of you – enter!
Rebuking an incompetent orchestra
*The Maestro: The Life of Arturo Toscanini* (Howard Taubman)

4 Can't you read? The score demands *con amore*, and what are you doing? You are playing it like married men!
Criticizing the playing of an Austrian orchestra during rehearsal
Attrib.

5 Madame, there you sit with that magnificent instrument between your legs, and all you can do is *scratch* it!
Rebuking an incompetent woman cellist
Attrib.

**Tourneur, Cyril** (1575–1626) English dramatist. His poems include *The Transformed Metamorphosis* (1600). The *Revenger's Tragedy* (1607) and *The Atheist's Tragedy* (1611) are his best-known plays.

1 Were't not for gold and women, there would be no damnation.
*The Revenger's Tragedy*, II:1

**Toynbee, Arnold** (1889–1975) British historian. His *Study of History* (12 volumes; 1934–61) was his major work.

1 No annihilation without representation.
Urging the need for a greater British influence in the UNO, 1947

2 America is a large, friendly dog in a very small room. Every time it wags its tail it knocks over a chair.
Broadcast news summary, 14 July 1954

**Tracy, Spencer** (1900–67) US film star. After playing gangster roles he costarred with Katherine Hepburn in a number of films, including *Woman of the Year* (1942) and *Guess Who's Coming to Dinner* (1967). He also made *Inherit the Wind* (1960) and *Judgement at Nuremberg* (1961).

1 There were times my pants were so thin I could sit on a dime and tell if it was heads or tails.
Of leaner times in his life
*Spencer Tracy* (L. Swindell)

2 Days off.
Explaining what he looked for in a script
Attrib.

3 This is a movie, not a lifeboat.
Defending his demand for equal billing with Katherine Hepburn
Attrib.

**Trapp, Joseph** (1679–1747) English churchman and academic.

1 The King, observing with judicious eyes
The state of both his universities,
To Oxford sent a troop of horse, and why?
That learned body wanted loyalty;
To Cambridge books, as very well discerning
How much that loyal body wanted learning.
Written after George I donated the Bishop of Ely's library to Cambridge
*Literary Anecdotes* (Nichols), Vol. III

**Tree, Sir Herbert Beerbohm** (1853–1917) British actor and theatre manager. He managed both the Haymarket Theatre and Her Majesty's Theatre and founded RADA.

1 I was born old and get younger every day. At present I am sixty years young
*Beerbohm Tree* (Hesketh Pearson)

2 My poor fellow, why not carry a watch?
Remark made to a man carrying a grandfather clock
*Beerbohm Tree* (Hesketh Pearson)

3 He is an old bore; even the grave yawns for him.
Referring to Israel Zangwill
*Beerbohm Tree* (Hesketh Pearson)

4 The only man who wasn't spoilt by being lionized was Daniel.
*Beerbohm Tree* (Hesketh Pearson)

5 A whipper-snapper of criticism who quoted dead languages to hide his ignorance of life.
Refering to A. B. Walleley
*Beerbohm Tree* (Hesketh Pearson)

6 The national sport of England is obstacle-racing. People fill their rooms with useless and cumbersome furniture, and spend the rest of their lives in trying to dodge it.
*Beerbohm Tree* (Hesketh Pearson)

7 Oh my God! Remember you're in Egypt. The *skay* is only seen in Kensington.
To a leading lady
*Beerbohm Tree* (Hesketh Pearson)

8 When I pass my name in such large letters I blush, but at the same time instinctively raise my hat.
*Beerbohm Tree* (Hesketh Pearson)

9 Take that black box away. I can't act in front of it.
Objecting to the presence of the camera while performing in a silent film
· *Hollywood: The Pioneers* (K. Brownlow)

10 Ladies, just a little more virginity, if you don't mind.
Directing a group of sophisticated actresses
*Smart Aleck* (H. Teichmann)

**Trevelyan, George Macaulay** (1876–1962) British historian, best known for his popular *English Social History* (1942).

1 Disinterested intellectual curiosity is the life blood of real civilisation.
*English Social History*, Preface

2 Education . . . has produced a vast population able to read but unable to distinguish what is worth reading.
*English Social History*, Ch. 18

3 Nelson, born in a fortunate hour for himself and for his country, was always in his element and always on his element.
*History of England*, Bk. V, Ch. 5

**Trinder, Tommy** (1909– ) British cockney music-hall, radio, and film comedian. His best-known film was *The Foreman Went to France* (1942).

1 They're overpaid, overfed, oversexed and over here.
Referring to the G.I.s
Attrib.

**Trollope, Anthony** (1815–82) British novelist. He established his reputation with the Barsetshire series of novels, including *The Warden* (1855) and *Barchester Towers* (1857). Later books include *Phineas Finn* (1869).

1 He must have known me had he seen me as he was wont to see me, for he was in the habit of flogging me constantly. Perhaps he did not recognize me by my face.
*Autobiography*, Ch. 1

2 Three hours a day will produce as much as a man ought to write.
*Autobiography*, Ch. 15

3 No man thinks there is much ado about nothing when the ado is about himself.
*The Bertrams*, Ch. 27

4 Those who have courage to love should have courage to suffer.
*The Bertrams*, Ch. 27

5 In these days a man is nobody unless his biography is kept so far posted up that it may be ready for the national breakfast-table on the morning after his demise.
*Doctor Thorne*, Ch. 25

6 The comic almanacs give us dreadful pictures of January and February; but, in truth, the months which should be made to look gloomy in England are March and April. Let no man boast himself that he has got through the perils of winter till at least the seventh of May.
*Doctor Thorne*, Ch. 47

7 It's dogged as does it. It ain't thinking about it.
*Last Chronicle of Barset*, Ch. 61

8 With many women I doubt whether there be any more effectual way of touching their hearts than ill-using them and then confessing it. If you wish to get the sweetest fragrance from the herb at your feet, tread on it and bruise it.
*Miss Mackenzie*, Ch. 10

9 We cannot bring ourselves to believe it possible that a foreigner should in any respect be wiser than ourselves. If any such point out to us our follies, we at once claim those follies as the special evidences of our wisdom.
*Orley Farm*, Ch. 18

10 It is because we put up with bad things that hotel-keepers continue to give them to us.
*Orley Farm*, Ch. 18

11 As for conceit, what man will do any good who is not conceited? Nobody holds a good opinion of a man who has a low opinion of himself.
*Orley Farm*, Ch. 22

12 Mr Turnbull had predicted evil consequences . . . and was now doing the best in his power to bring about the verification of his own prophecies.
*Phineas Finn*, Ch. 25

13 I doubt whether any girl would be satisfied with her lover's mind if she knew the whole of it.
*The Small House at Allington*, Ch. 4

14 And, above all things, never think that you're not good enough yourself. A man should never think that. My belief is that in life people will take you very much at your own reckoning.
*The Small House at Allington*, Ch. 32

15 Those who offend us are generally punished for the offence they give; but we so frequently miss the satisfaction of knowing that we are avenged!
*The Small House at Allington*, Ch. 50

**Trotsky, Leon** (Lev Davidovich Bronstein; 1879–1940) Russian revolutionary. Originally a Menshevik, he returned from exile to become a Bolshevik and played a major role in the October (1917) Revolution. After Lenin's death he was exiled by Stalin and murdered in Mexico (possibly by a Soviet agent).

1 Revolution by its very nature is sometimes compelled to take in more territory than it is capable of holding. Retreats are possible – when there is territory to retreat from.
*Diary in Exile*, 15 Feb 1935

2 Old age is the most unexpected of all the things that happen to a man.
*Diary in Exile*, 8 May 1935

3 The 23rd of February was International Woman's Day . . . It had not occurred to anyone that it might become the first day of the revolution.
*History of the Russian Revolution*, Pt. I, Ch. 7

4 The revolution does not choose its paths: it made its first steps towards victory under the belly of a Cossack's horse.
*History of the Russian Revolution*, Pt. I, Ch. 7

5 Revolutions are always verbose.
*History of the Russian Revolution*, Pt. II, Ch. 12

6 Insurrection is an art, and like all arts it has its laws.
*History of the Russian Revolution*, Pt. III, Ch. 6

7 The fundamental premise of a revolution is that the existing social structure has become incapable of solving the urgent problems of development of the nation.
*History of the Russian Revolution*, Pt. III, Ch. 6

8 From being a patriotic myth, the Russian people have become an awful reality.
*History of the Russian Revolution*, Pt. III, Ch. 7

9 For us, the tasks of education in socialism were closely integrated with those of fighting. Ideas that enter the mind under fire remain there securely and for ever.
*My Life*, Ch. 35

10 It was the supreme expression of the mediocrity of the apparatus that Stalin himself rose to his position.
*My Life*, Ch. 40

11 Lenin's method leads to this: the party organization at first substitutes itself for the party as a whole. Then the central committee substitutes itself for the party organization, and finally a single dictator substitutes himself for the central committee.
*The Communist Parties of Western Europe* (N. McInnes), Ch. 3

12 Patriotism to the Soviet State is a revolutionary duty, whereas patriotism to a bourgeois State is treachery.
*Disputed Barricade* (Fitzroy Maclean)

13 An ally has to be watched just like an enemy.
*Expansion and Coexistence* (A. Ulam)

**Troubridge, Sir T. St Vincent** (1895–1963) British army officer.

1 There is an iron curtain across Europe.
*Sunday Empire News*, 21 Oct 1945

**Truman, Harry S.** (1884–1972) US statesman. He became president (1945–53) after the death of Roosevelt and ordered the dropping of the atom bombs on Hiroshima and Nagasaki. His administration also established NATO.

1 If you can't stand the heat, get out of the kitchen.
Perhaps proverbial in origin, possibly echoes the expression 'kitchen cabinet'
*Mr Citizen*, Ch. 15

2 If we see that Germany is winning the war we ought to help Russia, and if Russia is winning we ought to help Germany, and in that way let them kill as many as possible.
*New York Times*, 24 July 1941, when Russia was invaded by Germany

3 A politician is a man who understands government, and it takes a politician to run a government. A statesman is a politician who's been dead ten or fifteen years.
*New York World Telegram and Sun*, 12 Apr 1958

4 The President spends most of his time kissing people on the cheek in order to get them to do what they ought to do without getting kissed.
*The Observer*, 'Sayings of the Week', 6 Feb 1949

5 It's a recession when your neighbour loses his job; it's a depression when you lose your own.
*The Observer*, 'Sayings of the Week', 6 Apr 1958

6 I didn't fire him because he was a dumb son of a bitch, although he was, but that's not against the law for generals. If it was, half to three-quarters of them would be in gaol.
Referring to General MacArthur
*Plain Speaking* (Merle Miller)

7 Give me a one-handed economist! All my economists say, 'on the one hand . . . on the other.
*Presidential Anecdotes* (P. Boller)

8 The buck stops here.
Sign kept on his desk during his term as president
*Presidential Anecdotes* (P. Boller)

9 You don't set a fox to watching the chickens just because he has a lot of experience in the hen house.
Referring to Vice-President Nixon's nomination for President
Speech, 30 Oct 1960

**Tuchman, Barbara W.** (1912– ) US editor and writer. Her books include *The Lost British Policy* (1938), and *August 1914* (1962).

1 Dead battles, like dead generals, hold the military mind in their dead grip.
*August 1914*, Ch. 2

**Tucker, Sophie** (Sophia Abuza; 1884–1966) Russian-born US popular singer and vaudeville star.

**1** The Last of the Red-Hot Mamas.

Description of herself. *Dictionary of Biographical Quotation* (J. Wintle and R. Kenin)

**2** Life begins at forty.

Attrib.

**3** From birth to age eighteen, a girl needs good parents. From eighteen to thirty-five, she needs good looks. From thirty-five to fifty-five, she needs a good personality. From fifty-five on, she needs good cash.

Attrib.

**Tupper, Martin Farquhar** (1810–89) British writer. His *Proverbial Philosophy* (1838) was an international success. He also wrote ballads and a novel.

**1** A good book is the best of friends, the same today and for ever.

*Proverbial Philosophy*, 'Of Reading'

**2** It is well to lie fallow for a while.

*Proverbial Philosophy*, 'Of Recreation'

**Turenne, Henri de la Tour d'Auvergne, Vicomte de** (1611–75) French marshal, who made his name in the Thirty Years' War and commanded the French armies that invaded the Spanish Netherlands and in the war against Holland.

**1** God is always on the side of the big battalions.

Attrib.

**Turgenev, Ivan** (1818–83) Russian novelist. A critic of the Russian system in *Sportsman's Sketches* (1852), he was briefly imprisoned. The novels *Fathers and Sons* (1862) and *The Torrents of Spring* (1872) established his reputation, but he is best known for the play *A Month in the Country* (1870).

**1** I agree with no man's opinion. I have some of my own.

*Fathers and Sons*, Ch. 13

**2** The temerity to believe in nothing.

*Fathers and Sons*, Ch. 14

**3** Go and try to disprove death. Death will disprove you, and that's all!

*Fathers and Sons*, Ch. 27

**4** Whatever a man prays for, he prays for a miracle. Every prayer reduces itself to this: 'Great God grant that twice two be not four.'

*Prayer*

**Turgot, Anne-Robert-Jacques, Baron de l'Aulne** (1727–81) French economist and advocate of laissez-faire. One of the Physiocrats, he became comptroller general in 1774.

**1** He snatched the lightning shaft from heaven, and the sceptre from tyrants.

An inscription for a bust of Benjamin Franklin, alluding both to Franklin's invention of the lightning conductor and to his role in the American Revolution
*Vie de Turgot* (A. N. de Condorcet)

**Turk, Roy** (20th century) US songwriter.

**1** Walking My Baby Back Home.

Title of song

**Turnbull, Margaret** (fl. 1920s–1942) US writer and dramatist of Scottish origin.

**1** No man is responsible for his father. That is entirely his mother's affair.

*Alabaster Lamps*

**2** When a man confronts catastrophe on the road, he looks in his purse – but a woman looks in her mirror.

*The Left Lady*

**Turner, Joseph Mallord William** (1775–1851) British landscape and seascape painter, who anticipated the French impressionists.

**1** My business is to paint not what I know, but what I see.

Responding to a criticism of the fact that he had painted no portholes on the ships in a view of Plymouth
*Proust: The Early Years* (G. Painter)

**2** I've lost one of my children this week.

His customary remark following the sale of one of his paintings
*Sketches of Great Painters* (E. Chubb)

**Tusser, Thomas** (1524–80) English farmer and writer. His *Five Hundred Points of Good Husbandry* (1557), written in verse, was a source of many proverbs.

**1** February, fill the dyke
With what thou dost like.

*Five Hundred Points of Good Husbandry*, 'February's Husbandry'

**2** Sweet April showers
Do spring May flowers.

*Five Hundred Points of Good Husbandry*, 'April's Husbandry'

**3** At Christmas play and make good cheer,
For Christmas comes but once a year.

*Five Hundred Points of Good Husbandry*, 'The Farmer's Daily Diet'

**4** Seek home for rest,
For home is best.

*Five Hundred Points of Good Husbandry*, 'Instructions to Housewifery'

**Tutu, Desmond, Bishop** (1931– ) South African clergyman noted for his campaign against apartheid. He became Archbishop of Johannesburg in 1984.

**1** It seems that the British Government sees black people as expendable.

Speech, June 1986

**2** Beware when you take on the Church of God. Others have tried and have bitten the dust.

Speech, Apr 1987

**Tuwim, Julian** (1894–1954) Polish writer and poet.

**1** There are two kinds of blood, the blood that flows in the veins and the blood that flows out of them.

*We, the Polish Jews*

**Twain, Mark** (Samuel Langhorne Clemens; 1835–1910) US writer. A steamboat pilot, he wrote a novel, *The Adventures of Huckleberry Finn* (1884), which established his reputation as a writer.

1 There was things which he stretched, but mainly he told the truth.
*The Adventures of Huckleberry Finn*, Ch. 1

2 There are three kinds of lies: lies, damned lies, and statistics.
*Autobiography*

3 Soap and education are not as sudden as a massacre, but they are more deadly in the long run.
*The Facts concerning the Recent Resignation*

4 It takes your enemy and your friend, working together, to hurt you to the heart; the one to slander you and the other to get the news to you.
*Following the Equator*

5 It is by the goodness of God that in our country we have those three unspeakably precious things: freedom of speech, freedom of conscience, and the prudence never to practise either of them.
*Following the Equator*, heading of Ch. 20

6 Man is the only animal that blushes. Or needs to.
*Following the Equator*, heading of Ch. 27

7 I must have a prodigious quantity of mind; it takes me as much as a week, sometimes, to make it up.
*The Innocents Abroad*, Ch. 7

8 They spell it Vinci and pronounce it Vinchy; foreigners always spell better than they pronounce.
*The Innocents Abroad*, Ch. 19

9 The radical invents the views. When he has worn them out, the conservative adopts them.
*Notebooks*

10 Familiarity breeds contempt – and children.
*Notebooks*

11 When people do not respect us we are sharply offended; yet deep down in his heart no man much respects himself.
*Notebooks*

12 Good breeding consists in concealing how much we think of ourselves and how little we think of other persons.
*Notebooks*

13 Adam was but human – this explains it all. He did not want the apple for the apple's sake, he wanted it only because it was forbidden.
*Pudd'nhead Wilson's Calendar*, Ch. 2

14 There ain't no way to find out why a snorer can't hear himself snore.
*Tom Sawyer Abroad*, Ch. 10

15 Something that everybody wants to have read and nobody wants to read.
Definition of a classic of literature
Speech at Nineteenth Century Club, New York, 20 Nov 1900

16 Reports of my death are greatly exaggerated.
On learning that his obituary had been published
Cable to the Associated Press

17 That's right. 'Taint yours, and 'taint mine.
Agreeing with a friend's comment that the money of a particular rich industrialist was 'tainted'
Attrib.

18 Scarce, sir. Mighty scarce.
Responding to the question 'In a world without women what would men become?'
Attrib.

19 I've done it a hundred times!
Referring to giving up smoking
Attrib.

**Tynan, Kenneth** (1927–80) British theatre critic and producer. He became literary manager of the National Theatre. His books inlcude *He That Plays the King* (1950) and *Curtains* (1961).

1 A novel is a static thing that one moves through; a play is a dynamic thing that moves past one.
*Curtains*

2 William Congreve is the only sophisticated playwright England has produced; and like Shaw, Sheridan, and Wilde, his nearest rivals, he was brought up in Ireland.
*Curtains*, 'The Way of the World'

3 A good drama critic is one who perceives what is happening in the theatre of his time. A great drama critic also perceives what is not happening.
*Tynan Right and Left*, Foreword

4 A good many inconveniences attend play-going in any large city, but the greatest of them is usually the play itself.
*New York Herald Tribune*

5 A critic is a man who knows the way but can't drive the car.
*New York Times Magazine*, 9 Jan 1966

6 What, when drunk, one sees in other women, one sees in Garbo sober.
*The Sunday Times*, 25 Aug 1963

**Tyrrell, George** (1861–1909) Irish Catholic theologian. Dismissed by the Jesuits for his modernism he was later excommunicated. His books include *Christianity at the Cross-Roads* (1909) and *Immortality* (1914). He also wrote an autobiography.

1 I never quite forgave Mahaffy for getting himself suspended from preaching in the College Chapel. Ever since his sermons were discontinued, I suffer from insomnia in church.
*As I Was Going Down Sackville Street* (Oliver St John Gogarty), Ch. 25

# U

**Uccello, Paolo** (1397–1475) Italian painter. His paintings, including *A Hunt in a Forest* and *St George and the Dragon*, show his concern with the problems of perspective.

1 What a delightful thing this perspective is!
*Men of Art* (T. Craven)

**Unamuno y Jugo, Miguel de** (1864–1936) Spanish writer and philosopher. His major philosophical work is *The Tragic Sense of Life* (1913).

1 All right, my lord creator, Don Miguel, you too will die and return to the nothing whence you came. God will cease to dream you!
*Mist*

2 May God deny you peace but give you glory!
Closing words
*The Tragic Sense of Life*

3 They will conquer, but they will not convince.
Referring to the Franco rebels
Attrib.

**Updike, John** (1932– ) US novelist and writer. His novels include *Rabbit, Run* (1960), *Couples* (1968), *Marry Me* (1976), and *Rabbit is Rich* (1981).

1 A healthy male adult bore consumes each year one and a half times his own weight in other people's patience.
*Assorted Prose*, 'Confessions of a Wild Bore'

2 In general the churches, visited by me too often on weekdays . . . bore for me the same relation to God that billboards did to Coca-Cola: they promoted thirst without quenching it.
*A Month of Sundays*, Ch. 2

3 Americans have been conditioned to respect newness, whatever it costs them.
*A Month of Sundays*, Ch. 18

4 He is a man of brick. As if he was born as a baby literally of clay and decades of exposure have baked him to the colour and hardness of brick.
*Rabbit, Run*

**Ure, Mary** (1933–75) British actress. She was married to the actor Robert Shaw.

1 I have a big house – and I hide a lot.
Explaining how she coped with her large family of children
Attrib.

**Ustinov, Peter** (1921– ) British actor, director, and dramatist. His plays include *The Love of Four Colonels* (1951), *Romanoff and Juliet* (1956), and *Beethoven's Tenth* (1983). He is also a well-known impersonator and raconteur.

1 Thanks to the movies, gunfire has always sounded unreal to me, even when being fired at.
*Dear Me*, Ch. 7

2 And here is the lesson I learned in the army. If you want to do a thing badly, you have to work at it as though you want to do it well.
*Dear Me*, Ch. 8

3 I am an optimist, unrepentant and militant. After all, in order not to be a fool an optimist must know how sad a place the world can be. It is only the pessimist who finds this out anew every day.
*Dear Me*, Ch. 9

4 There are no old men any more. *Playboy* and *Penthouse* have between them made an ideal of eternal adolescence, sunburnt and saunaed, with the grey dorianed out of it.
*Dear Me*, Ch. 18

5 I believe that the Jews have made a contribution to the human condition out of all proportion to their numbers: I believe them to be an immense people. Not only have they supplied the world with two leaders of the stature of Jesus Christ and Karl Marx, but they have even indulged in the luxury of following neither one nor the other.
*Dear Me*, Ch. 19

6 This is a free country, madam. We have a right to share your privacy in a public place.
*Romanoff and Juliet*, I

7 As for being a General, well, at the age of four with paper hats and wooden swords we're all Generals. Only some of us never grow out of it.
*Romanoff and Juliet*, I

8 A diplomat these days is nothing but a head-waiter who's allowed to sit down occasionally.
*Romanoff and Juliet*, I

9 If Botticelli were alive today he'd be working for *Vogue*.
*The Observer*, 'Sayings of the Week', 21 Oct 1962

10 People at the top of the tree are those without qualifications to detain them at the bottom.
Attrib.

# V

**Vachell, Horace Annesley** (1861–1955) British writer. His novels include *Quinney's* (1914) and *Vicar's Walk* (1933). *Plus Fours* (1923) was his best-known play.

1 In nature there are no rewards or punishments; there are consequences.
*The Face of Clay*, Ch. 10

**Vail, Amanda** (Warren Miller; 1921–66) US writer, author of the novels *Love me Little* (1957) and *The Bright Young Things* (1958).

1 Sometimes I think if there was a third sex men wouldn't get so much as a glance from me.
*Love Me Little*, Ch. 6

**Valéry, Paul** (1871–1945) French poet and writer. His verse includes *La Jeune Parque* (1917) and *Aurore* (1917); *L'Âme et la danse* (1924) and *Regards sur le monde actuel* (1931) are his best-known prose books.

1 God made everything out of nothing. But the nothingness shows through.
*Mauvaises Pensées et autres*

2 The term Science should not be given to anything but the aggregate of the recipes that are always successful. All the rest is literature.
*Moralités*

3 Politics is the art of preventing people from taking part in affairs which properly concern them.
*Tel quel*

**Vanbrugh, Sir John** (1664–1726) English architect and dramatist. His plays include *The Relapse* (1696) and *The Provok'd Wife* (1697), written before his most successful work as an architect, which includes Castle Howard (begun 1699) and Blenheim Palace (begun 1705).

1 The want of a thing is perplexing enough, but the possession of it is intolerable.
*The Confederacy*, I:2

2 As if a woman of education bought things because she wanted 'em.
*The Confederacy*, II:1

3 Much of a muchness.
*The Provok'd Husband*, I:1

4 Thinking is to me the greatest fatigue in the world.
*The Relapse*, II:1

5 Once a woman has given you her heart you can never get rid of the rest of her.
*The Relapse*, II:1

6 No man worth having is true to his wife, or can be true his wife, or ever was, or ever will be so.
*The Relapse*, III:2

**Vanderbilt, William Henry** (1821–85) US railway chief. Having inherited a fortune from his father, he became president of the New York Central Railroad.

1 The public be damned. I am working for my stockholders.
Refusing to speak to a reporter, who was seeking to find out his views on behalf of the public

2 I have had no real gratification or enjoyment of any sort more than my neighbor on the next block who is worth only half a million.
*Famous Last Words* (B. Conrad)

**Van der Post, Sir Laurens** (1906– ) South African novelist resident in England. His books include *The Hunter and the Whale* (1967) and *A Story Like the Wind* (1972). *Venture to the Interior* (1952) and *The Lost World of the Kalahari* (1958) were earlier travel books.

1 'The story is like the wind', the Bushman prisoner said. 'It comes from a far off place, and we feel it.'
*A Story Like the Wind*

2 Organized religion is making Christianity political rather than making politics Christian.
*The Observer*, 'Sayings of the Week', 9 Nov 1986

**Vauvenargues, Luc de Clapiers, Marquis de** (1715–47) French soldier and writer, remembered for his *Introduction à la connaissance de l'esprit humain suivie de réflexions et de maximes* (1746).

1 Great thoughts come from the heart.
*Réflexions et maximes*

2 To achieve great things we must live as though we were never going to die.
*Réflexions et maximes*

**Veblen, Thorstein Bunde** (1857–1929) US social scientist. His books include *The Theory of the Leisure Class* (1899) and *The Higher Learning in America* (1918).

1 All business sagacity reduces itself in the last analysis to a judicious use of sabotage.
*The Nature of Peace*

2 The outcome of any serious research can only be to make two questions grow where only one grew before.
*The Place of Science in Modern Civilization*

3 Conspicuous consumption of valuable goods is a means of reputability to the gentleman of leisure.
*The Theory of the Leisure Class*

**Vega Carpio, Lope Félix de** (1562–1635) Spanish dramatist and poet. Most of his plays were based on Spanish history.

1 All right, then, I'll say it: Dante makes me sick.
On being informed he was about to die
Attrib.

**Vegetius** (Flavius Vegetius Renatus; 4th century AD) Roman writer, remembered for his military treatise *Epitoma Rei Militaris*.

1 Let him who desires peace, prepare for war.
*Epitoma Rei Militaris*, 3, 'Prologue'

**Verrall, Arthur Woollgar** (1851–1912) British classicist. He edited the works of Aeschylus and Euripides.

1 Oh, quite easy! The Septuagint minus the Apostles.
Reply to a person who thought the number 58 difficult to remember

**Vespasian** (9–79 AD) Roman emperor (69–79). He ended the civil war and was deified after his death.

1 Dear me, I believe I am becoming a god. An emperor ought at least to die on his feet.
Last words
*Lives of the Caesars* (Suetonius)

**Vicky** (Victor Weisz; 1913–66) German-born British cartoonist. His work appeared in the *Evening Standard* and *The New Statesman and Nation*.

1 Introducing Super-Mac.
Cartoon caption depicting Harold Macmillan as Superman
*Evening Standard,* 6 Nov 1958

**Victoria** (1819–1901) Queen of the United Kingdom (1837–1901). She succeeded her uncle William IV and married her cousin Prince Albert of Saxe-Coburg-Gotha. Disraeli, her close ally after Albert's death in 1861, made her Empress of India.

1 I sat between the King and Queen. We left supper soon. My health was drunk. I then danced one more quadrille with Lord Paget. . . . I was *very* much amused.
Journal, 16 June 1833

2 . . . I *too well* know its truth, from experience, that whenever any poor Gipsies are encamped anywhere and crimes and robberies &c. occur, it is invariably laid to their account, which is shocking; and if they are always looked upon as vagabonds, how *can* they become good people?
Journal, 29 Dec 1836

3 The Queen is most anxious to enlist every one who can speak or write to join in checking this mad, wicked folly of 'Woman's Rights', with all its attendant horrors, on which her poor feeble sex is bent, forgetting every sense of womanly feeling and propriety.
Letter to Sir Theodore Martin, 29 May 1870

4 The danger to the country, to Europe, to her vast Empire, which is involved in having all these great interests entrusted to the shaking hand of an old, wild, and incomprehensible man of 82½, is very great!
Reaction to Gladstone's fourth and last appointment as prime minister, 1892
Letter to Lord Lansdowne, 12 Aug 1892

5 He speaks to Me as If I was a public meeting.
Referring to Gladstone
*Collections and Recollections* (G. W. E. Russell), Ch. 14

6 A strange, horrible business, but I suppose good enough for Shakespeare's day.
Giving her opinion of *King Lear*
*Living Biographies of Famous Rulers* (H. Thomas)

7 Move Queen Anne? Most certainly not! Why it might some day be suggested that *my* statue should be moved, which I should much dislike.
Said at the time of her Diamond Jubilee (1897), when it was suggested that the statue of Queen Anne should be moved from outside St. Paul's
*Men, Women and Things* (Duke of Portland), Ch. 5

8 We are not amused!
Attrib.

**Vidal, Gore** (1925– ) US novelist. His books include *Myra Breckinridge* (1968), *Burr* (1974), and *Lincoln* (1984).

1 The novel being dead, there is no point to writing made-up stories. Look at the French who will not and the Americans who cannot.
*Myra Breckinridge,* Ch. 2

2 American writers want to be not good but great; and so are neither.
*Two Sisters*

3 The astronauts! . . . Rotarians in outer space.
*Two Sisters*

4 Never have children, only grandchildren.
*Two Sisters*

5 It is not enough to succeed. Others must fail.
*Antipanegyric for Tom Driberg* (G. Irvine)

6 Whenever a friend succeeds, a little something in me dies.
*The Sunday Times Magazine,* 16 Sept 1973

7 I'm all for bringing back the birch, but only between consenting adults.
Said when asked by David Frost in a TV interview for his views about corporal punishment

**Viera Gallo, José Antonio** (1943– ) Chilean politician.

1 Socialism can only arrive by bicycle.
*Compare* Norman TEBBIT
*Energy and Equity* (Ivan Illich)

**Vigny, Alfred de** (1797–1863) French poet, novelist, and dramatist. He established his reputation with the novel *Cinq-Mars* (1826), but the play *Chatterton* (1835) is regarded as his most important work. His poetry collections include *Destinées* (1867).

1 The true God, the mighty God, is the God of ideas.
*La Bouteille à la mer*

2 Alas, Lord, I am powerful but alone. Let me sleep the sleep of the earth.
*Moïse*

3 An army is a nation within a nation; it is one of the vices of our age.
*Servitude et grandeur militaire,* 1

**Villiers, Alan John** (1903– ) Australian naval commander and writer. His books include *Vanished Fleets* (1931) and *The Making of a Sailor* (1938).

1 Only fools and passengers drink at sea.
*The Observer,* 'Sayings of the Week', 28 Apr 1957

**Villon, François** (1431–85) French poet. He became a vagrant and criminal, for which he was banished from Paris in 1463. His works include *Le Petit Testament* (1456) and *Le Grand Testament* (1461).

1 *Mais où sont les neiges d'antan?*
But where are the snows of yesteryear?
*Ballade des dames du temps jadis*

**Virchow, Rudolph** (1821–1902) German pathologist. His book *Cellular Pathology* (1858) established the foundations of this science.

**1** Human beings, yes, but not surgeons.

Answering a query as to whether human beings could survive appendectomy, which had recently become a widespread practice
*Anekdotenschatz* (H. Hoffmeister)

**Virgil** (Publius Vergilius Maro; 70–19 BC) Roman poet. His *Eclogues* (42–37 BC) were followed by the *Georgics* (36–29 BC), works that expressed his pastoral and agricultural interests. His national epic in 12 books, the *Aeneid*, led to his veneration by subsequent generations.

**1** Anger supplies the arms.

*Aeneid*, Bk. I

**2** I sing of arms and the man who first from the shores
of Troy came destined an exile to Italy and the Lavinian beaches, much buffeted he on land and on
the deep by force of the gods because of fierce Juno's never-forgetting anger.

Referring to Aeneas
*Aeneid*, Bk. I

**3** O you who have borne even heavier things, God will grant an end to these too.

*Aeneid*, Bk. I

**4** Maybe one day we shall be glad to remember even these hardships.

*Aeneid*, Bk. I

**5** A grief too much to be told, O queen, you bid me renew.

The opening words of Aeneas' account to Dido of the fall of Troy
*Aeneid*, Bk. II

**6** *Equo ne credite, Teucri.*
*Quidquid id est timeo Danaos et dona ferentis.*
Do not trust the horse, Trojans. Whatever it is, I fear the Greeks even when they bring gifts.

*Aeneid*, Bk. II

**7** It was the time when first sleep begins for weary
mortals and by the gift of the gods creeps over them
most welcomely.

*Aeneid*, Bk. II

**8** What do you not drive human hearts into, cursed craving for gold!

*Aeneid*, Bk. III

**9** Woman is always fickle and changing.

*Aeneid*, Bk. IV

**10** The way down to Hell is easy.

*Aeneid*, Bk. VI

**11** I see wars, horrible wars, and the Tiber foaming with
much blood.

Part of the Sibyl's prophecy to Aeneas, foretelling his difficulties in winning a home in Italy.
*Aeneid*, Bk. VI

**12** Fear lent wings to his feet.

*Aeneid*, Bk. VIII

**13** Everyone is dragged on by their favourite pleasure.

*Eclogue*, Bk. II

**14** There's a snake hidden in the grass.

*Eclogue*, Bk. III

**15** Love conquers all things: let us too give in to Love.

*Eclogue*, Bk. X

**16** But meanwhile it is flying, irretrievable time is flying.

*Georgics*, Bk. III

**Vizinczey, Stephen** (1933– ) Hungarian-born British writer. His works include the novels *In Praise of Older Women* (1965) and *An Innocent Millionaire* (1983).

**1** I was told I am a true cosmopolitan. I am unhappy everywhere.

*The Guardian*, 7 Mar 1968

**Voltaire** (François-Marie Arouet; 1694–1778) French writer and philosopher. A fearless campaigner against injustice, he was imprisoned in the Bastille, exiled to England, Germany, and Switzerland, and later became a hero of French culture. His works include *Lettres philosophiques* (1734), the fable *Candide* (1759), and the *Dictionnaire philosophique* (1764).

**1** If we do not find anything pleasant, at least we shall find something new.

*Candide*, Ch. 17

**2** *Dans ce pay-ci, il est bon de tuer de temps en temps un amiral pour encourager les autres.*
In this country it is good to kill an admiral from time to time, to encourage the others.

Referring to England: Admiral Byng was executed for failing to defeat the French at Minorca (1757)
*Candide*, Ch. 23

**3** All is for the best in the best of possible worlds.

*Candide*, Ch. 30

**4** 'That is well said,' replied Candide, 'but we must cultivate our garden.'

*Candide*, Ch. 30

**5** Work banishes those three great evils, boredom, vice, and poverty.

*Candide*, Ch. 30

**6** . . . use thought only to justify their injustices, and speech only to conceal their thoughts.

Referring to men
Dialogue, 'Le Chapon et la poularde'

**7** The best is the enemy of the good.

*Dictionnaire philosophique*, 'Art dramatique'

**8** Superstition sets the whole world in flames; philosophy quenches them.

*Dictionnaire philosophique*, 'Superstition'

**9** If God did not exist, it would be necessary to invent Him.

*Épîtres*, 'À l'auteur du livre des trois Imposteurs'

**10** The secret of the arts is to correct nature.

*Épîtres*, 'À M. de Verrière'

11 This agglomeration which was called and which still calls itself the Holy Roman Empire was neither holy, nor Roman, nor an empire.
*Essai sur les moeurs et l'esprit des nations, LXX*

12 All our ancient history, as one of our wits remarked, is no more than accepted fiction.
*Jeannot et Colin*

13 All styles are good except the tiresome sort.
*L'Enfant prodigue, Preface*

14 If God made us in His image, we have certainly returned the compliment.
*Le Sottisier*

15 Indeed, history is nothing more than a tableau of crimes and misfortunes.
*L'Ingénu, Ch. 10*

16 It is one of the superstitions of the human mind to have imagined that virginity could be a virtue.
*Notebooks*

17 Governments need to have both shepherds and butchers.
*Notebooks*

18 God is on the side not of the heavy battalions, but of the best shots.
*Notebooks*

19 We owe respect to the living; to the dead we owe only truth.
*Oeuvres, 'Première lettre sur Oedipe'*

20 Faith consists in believing when it is beyond the power of reason to believe. It is not enough that a thing be possible for it to be believed.
*Questions sur l'encyclopédie*

21 Marriage is the only adventure open to the cowardly.
*Thoughts of a Philosopher*

22 Never having been able to succeed in the world, he took his revenge by speaking ill of it.
*Zadig, Ch. 4*

23 There are two things for which animals are to be envied: they know nothing of future evils, or of what people say about them.
*Letter, 1739*

24 Men will always be mad and those who think they can cure them are the maddest of all.
*Letter, 1762*

25 The great consolation in life is to say what one thinks.
*Letter, 1765*

26 Once the people begin to reason, all is lost.
*Letter to Damilaville, 1 Apr 1766*

27 I am not like a lady at the court of Versailles, who said: 'What a dreadful pity that the bother at the tower of Babel should have got language all mixed up, but for that, everyone would always have spoken French.
French was the dominant language in the educated circles of 18th-century Europe
*Letter to Catherine the Great, Empress of Russia, 26 May 1767*

28 The man who leaves money to charity in his will is only giving away what no longer belongs to him.
*Letter, 1769*

29 Men of England! You wish to kill me because I am a Frenchman. Am I not punished enough in not being born an Englishman?
Addressing an angry London mob who desired to hang him because he was a Frenchman
Attrib.

30 I think it must be so, for I have been drinking it for sixty-five years and I am not dead yet.
On learning that coffee was considered a slow poison
Attrib.

31 He was a great patriot, a humanitarian, a loyal friend — provided, of course, that he really is dead.
Giving a funeral oration
Attrib.

32 I do not think this poem will reach its destination.
Reviewing Rousseau's poem 'Ode to Posterity'
Attrib.

33 Once: a philosopher; twice: a pervert!
Turning down an invitation to an orgy, having attended one the previous night for the first time
Attrib.

34 I disapprove of what you say, but I will defend to the death your right to say it.
Attrib.

**Vorster, John** (Balthazar Johannes Vorster; 1915–83) South African politician. He became prime minister (1966–78) after Verwoerd's assassination. An extreme right winger, he retired over financial irregularities.

1 As far as criticism is concerned, we don't resent that unless it is absolutely biased, as it is in most cases.
*The Observer, 'Sayings of the Week', 9 Nov 1969*

**Voznesensky, Andrei** (1933– ) Soviet poet. His translated poetry includes *Selected Poems* (1964) and *Antiworlds* (1967).

1 The art of creation
is older than the art of killing.
*Poem with a Footnote*

**Vukovich, Bill** (1918–55) US motor-racing driver.

1 There's no secret. You just press the accelerator to the floor and steer left.
Explaining his success in the Indianapolis 500
Attrib.

**Wain, John** (1925– ) British novelist and poet. His novels include *Hurry on Down* (1953), *The Contenders* (1958), and *Young Shoulders* (1982). His verse is collected in *Poems 1949–79* (1981).

1 Poetry is to prose as dancing is to walking.
Talk, BBC radio, 13 Jan 1976

**Waley, Arthur (David)** (1889–1966) British poet and translator of Chinese and Japanese poetry.

1 Keep off your thoughts from things that are past and done;
For thinking of the past wakes regret and pain.
Translation from the Chinese of Po-Chü-I
*Resignation*

**Wall, Max** (1908– ) British comedian.

1 Wall is the name – Max Wall. My father was the Great Wall of China. He was a brick.
Opening line of one of his acts

2 To me Adler will always be Jung.
Telegram to Larry Adler on his 60th birthday

**Wallace, Edgar** (1875–1932) British thriller and detective-story writer. He became a Hollywood scriptwriter having written some 170 popular novels.

1 A writer of crook stories ought never to stop seeking new material.
Said when a candidate for Parliament
*The Long Weekend* (Alan Hodge)

2 What is a highbrow? It is a man who has found something more interesting than women.
Interview

**Wallace, Henry** (1888–1965) US economist and politician. The secretary of agriculture (1933–40), he became vice-president of the USA (1941–45). His books include *New Frontiers* (1934) and *The American Choice* (1940).*

1 The century on which we are entering – the century which will come out of this war – can be and must be the century of the common man.
Speech, 'The Price of Free World Victory', 8 May 1942

**Wallace, Lew** (1827–1905) US soldier, lawyer, and writer. He became a Federal general in the Civil War and governor of New Mexico (1878–81). His books include *The Fair God* (1873), *Ben Hur* (1880), and *The Prince of India* (1893).

1 Beauty is altogether in the eye of the beholder.
*The Prince of India*

**Wallace, William Ross** (1819–81) US poet and songwriter.

1 The hand that rocks the cradle
Is the hand that rules the world.
*John o'London's Treasure Trove*

**Wallach, Eli** (1915– ) US actor and film star. An advocate of 'the method', he has appeared in many films including *Baby Doll* (1956), *Lord Jim* (1965), and *The Salamander* (1980).

1 There's something about a crowd like that that brings a lump to my wallet.
Remarking upon the long line of people at the box office before one of his performances
Attrib.

**Walpole, Horace, 4th Earl of Orford** (1717–97) British writer and fourth son of Robert Walpole. He is remembered for his gothic novel *The Castle of Otranto* (1765) and his gothic-revival villa at Twickenham, Strawberry Hill.

1 I am, sir for the last time in my life, Your Humble Servant Horace Walpole.
Ending a letter written to an uncle with whom he had recently quarrelled
*Horace Walpole* (R. Ketton-Cremes)

2 I have led a life of business so long that I have lost my taste for reading, and now – what shall I do?
*Thraliana* (K. Balderston)

3 Our supreme governors, the mob.
Letter to Sir Horace Mann, 7 Sept 1743

4 One of the greatest geniuses that ever existed, Shakespeare, undoubtedly wanted taste.
Letter to Wren, 9 Aug 1764

5 It is charming to totter into vogue.
Letter to G. A. Selwyn, 1765

6 The world is a comedy to those who think, a tragedy to those who feel.
Letter to Sir Horace Mann, 1769

7 By the waters of Babylon we sit down and weep, when we think of thee, O America!
On the eve of the American Revolution
Letter to Mason, 12 June 1775

8 When people will not weed their own minds, they are apt to be overrun with nettles.
Letter to Lady Ailesbury, 10 July 1779

9 I do not dislike the French from the vulgar antipathy between neighbouring nations, but for their insolent and unfounded airs of superiority.
Letter to Hannah More, 14 Oct 1787

10 Come, Robert, you shall drink twice while I drink once, for I cannot permit the son in his sober senses to witness the intoxication of his father.
Explaining why he filled his son's glass twice for every glass he drank himself
Attrib.

**Walpole, Sir Robert, 1st Earl of Orford** (1676–1745) British statesman. A Whig MP, he became secretary for war (1708–10) and chancellor of the exchequer (1715). He then became Britain's first prime minister (1721–42), maintaining his power by skilful management of parliament.

1 Anything but history, for history must be false.
*Walpoliana*

**2** They now *ring* the bells, but they will soon *wring* their hands.

Said when war declared in 1739 with Spain, against Walpole's wishes
*Memoirs of Sir Robert Walpole* (W. Coxe)

**3** All those men have their price.

*Memoirs of Sir Robert Walpole* (W. Coxe)

**4** My Lord Bath, you and I are now two as insignificant men as any in England.

Said to William Pulteney, Earl of Bath, when they were promoted to the peerage (1742)
*Political & Literary Anecdotes* (W. King)

**5** The balance of power.

Speech, House of Commons

**Walton, Izaak** (1593–1683) English writer, remembered for his treatise on fishing, *The Compleat Angler* (1653).

**1** Angling may be said to be so like the mathematics, that it can never be fully learnt.

*The Compleat Angler*, Epistle to the Reader

**2** Angling is somewhat like poetry, men are to be born so.

*The Compleat Angler*, Ch. 1

**3** I remember that a wise friend of mine did usually say, 'that which is everybody's business is nobody's business'.

*The Compleat Angler*, Ch. 2

**4** We may say of angling as Dr Boteler said of strawberries, 'Doubtless God could have made a better berry, but doubtless God never did.'

*The Compleat Angler*, Ch. 5

**5** I love such mirth as does not make friends ashamed to look upon one another next morning.

*The Compleat Angler*, Ch. 5

**6** Let the blessing of St Peter's Master be . . . upon all that are lovers of virtue; and dare trust in His providence; and be quiet; and go a-Angling.

*The Compleat Angler*, Ch. 21

**7** Of this blest man, let his just praise be given, Heaven was in him, before he was in heaven.

Referring to Dr Richard Sibbes
Written in a copy of *Returning Backslider* by Richard Sibbes

**Warburton, William** (1698–1779) British churchman. He became chaplain (1754) to George II and Bishop of Gloucester (1759). He was a friend and literary executor of Alexander Pope.

**1** Orthodoxy is my doxy; heterodoxy is another man's doxy.

Said to Lord Sandwich
*Memoirs* (Priestley), Vol. I

**Ward, Artemus** (Charles Farrar Browne; 1834–67) US humorous writer. He wrote for the Cleveland *Plain Dealer* and New York *Vanity Fair*, later publishing *Artemus Ward, His Book* (1862) and *Artemus Ward, His Travels* (1865).

**1** I prefer temperance hotels – although they sell worse kinds of liquor than any other kind of hotels.

*Artemus Ward's Lecture*

**2** Why is this thus? What is the reason of this thusness?

*Artemus Ward's Lecture*

**3** I am happiest when I am idle. I could live for months without performing any kind of labour, and at the expiration of that time I should feel fresh and vigorous enough to go right on in the same way for numerous more months.

*Pyrotechny*

**4** Why care for grammar as long as we are good?

*Pyrotechny*

**5** Let us all be happy, and live within our means, even if we have to borrer the money to do it with.

*Science and Natural History*

**Ware, George** (19th century) British songwriter.

**1** The boy I love is up in the gallery,
The boy I love is looking now at me.

*The Boy in the Gallery*

**Warhol, Andy** (Andrew Warhola; 1926–87) US pop artist and film producer, who made his reputation with paintings of soup cans and film stars. His films include *Sleep* (1963) and *The Chelsea Girls* (1966).

**1** An artist is someone who produces things that people don't need to have but that he – for *some reason* – thinks it would be a good idea to give them.

*From A to B and Back Again*, 'Atmosphere'

**Warner, Susan** (1819–85) US novelist. Her successful novels include *The Wide, Wide World* (1850), *Queechy* (1852), *Daisy* (1868), and *Nobody* (1882). Some books were written in collaboration with her sister Anna Bartlett Ward (1827–1915).

**1** Jesus loves me – this I know,
For the Bible tells me so.

*The Love of Jesus*

**Warren, Earl** (1891–1971) US lawyer. Attorney general (1939–43) and governor (1943–53) of California, he became chief justice of the USA in 1953, ending racial segregation in US schools.

**1** Many people consider the things which government does for them to be social progress, but they consider the things government does for others as socialism.

*Peter's Quotations* (Laurence J. Peter)

**Washington, George** (1732–99) US statesman and first president of the USA (1789–97). Commander in chief of the American forces in the American Revolution, he presided over the Constitutional Convention (1787) and was elected president of the new republic.

1 Associate yourself with men of good quality if you esteem your own reputation; for 'tis better to be alone than in bad company.
*Rules of Civility*

2 I heard the bullets whistle, and believe me, there is something charming in the sound.
Referring to a recent skirmish in the French and Indian War
*Presidential Anecdotes* (P. Boller)

3 Father, I cannot tell a lie. I did it with my little hatchet.
Attrib.

**Watson, James Dewey** (1928– ) US geneticist. With Francis Crick he discovered the double-helical structure of the DNA molecule. His book *The Double Helix* (1968) gave a popular account of the discovery.

1 The thought could not be avoided that the best home for a feminist was in another person's lab.
*The Double Helix*, Ch. 2

2 Already for thirty-five years he had not stopped talking and almost nothing of fundamental value had emerged.
Referring to Francis Crick
*The Double Helix*, Ch. 8

**Watts, Isaac** (1674–1748) English theologian and hymn writer. His 600 hymns include 'O God, our help in ages past' and 'There is a land of pure delight'.

1 For Satan finds some mischief still
For idle hands to do.
*Divine Songs for Children*, 'Against Idleness and Mischief'

2 How doth the little busy bee
Improve each shining hour,
And gather honey all the day
From every opening flower!
*Divine Songs for Children*, 'Against Idleness and Mischief'

3 Let dogs delight to bark and bite,
For God hath made them so;
Let bears and lions growl and fight,
For 'tis their nature too.
*Divine Songs for Children*, 'Against Quarrelling'

4 Lord, I ascribe it to Thy grace,
And not to chance, as others do,
That I was born of Christian race,
And not a Heathen, or a Jew.
*Divine Songs for Children*, 'Praise for the Gospel'

5 There's no repentance in the grave.
*Divine Songs for Children*, 'Solemn Thoughts of God and Death'

6 Our God, our help in ages past,
Our hope for years to come,
Our shelter from the stormy blast,
And our eternal home.
*Our God, Our Help in Ages Past*

7 'Tis the voice of the sluggard, I heard him complain:
'You have waked me too soon, I must slumber again.'
*The Sluggard*

8 When I survey the wondrous Cross,
On which the Prince of Glory died,
My richest gain I count but loss
And pour contempt on all my pride.
*When I Survey the Wondrous Cross*

**Waugh, Evelyn** (1903–66) British novelist. He established his reputation with *Decline and Fall* (1928) and *Vile Bodies* (1930). Later books, after his conversion to Catholicism, include *Brideshead Revisited* (1945) and the war trilogy *Sword of Honour* (1952–61).

1 I expect you'll be becoming a schoolmaster sir. That's what most of the gentlemen does sir, that gets sent down for indecent behaviour.
*Decline and Fall*, Prelude

2 The sound of the English county families baying for broken glass.
*Decline and Fall*, Prelude

3 We class schools you see, into four grades: Leading School, First-rate School, Good School, and School.
*Decline and Fall*, Pt. I, Ch. 1

4 We schoolmasters must temper discretion with deceit.
*Decline and Fall*, Pt. I, Ch. 1

5 Very hard for a man with a wig to keep order.
*Decline and Fall*, Pt. I, Ch. 3

6 That's the public-school system all over. They may kick you out, but they never let you down.
*Decline and Fall*, Pt. I, Ch. 3

7 Meanwhile you will write an essay on 'self-indulgence'. There will be a prize of half a crown for the longest essay, irrespective of any possible merit.
*Decline and Fall*, Pt. I, Ch. 5

8 I can't quite explain it, but I don't believe one can ever be unhappy for long provided one does just exactly what one wants to and when one wants to.
*Decline and Fall*, Pt. I, Ch. 5

9 Nonconformity and lust stalking hand in hand through the country, wasting and ravaging.
*Decline and Fall*, Pt. I, Ch. 5

10 For generations the British bourgeoisie have spoken of themselves as gentlemen, and by that they have meant, among other things, a self-respecting scorn of irregular perquisites. It is the quality that distinguishes the gentleman from both the artist and the aristocrat.
*Decline and Fall*, Pt. I, Ch. 6

11 There aren't many left like him nowadays, what with education and whisky the price it is.
*Decline and Fall*, Pt. I, Ch. 7

**12** 'The Welsh,' said the Doctor, 'are the only nation in the world that has produced no graphic or plastic art, no architecture, no drama. They just sing,' he said with disgust, 'sing and blow down wind instruments of plated silver.'
*Decline and Fall*, Pt. I, Ch. 8

**13** We can trace almost all the disasters of English history to the influence of Wales.
*Decline and Fall*, Pt. I, Ch. 8

**14** I have noticed again and again since I have been in the Church that lay interest in ecclesiastical matters is often a prelude to insanity.
*Decline and Fall*, Pt. I, Ch. 8

**15** I have often observed in women of her type a tendency to regard all athletics as inferior forms of fox-hunting.
*Decline and Fall*, Pt. I, Ch. 10

**16** I haven't been to sleep for over a year. That's why I go to bed early. One needs more rest if one doesn't sleep.
*Decline and Fall*, Pt. II, Ch. 3

**17** There is a species of person called a 'Modern Churchman' who draws the full salary of a beneficed clergyman and need not commit himself to any religious belief.
*Decline and Fall*, Pt. II, Ch. 4

**18** I came to the conclusion many years ago that almost all crime is due to the repressed desire for aesthetic expression.
*Decline and Fall*, Pt. III, Ch. 1

**19** He stood twice for Parliament, but so diffidently that his candidature passed almost unnoticed.
*Decline and Fall*, Pt. III, Ch. 1

**20** Anyone who has been to an English public school will always feel comparatively at home in prison.
*Decline and Fall*, Pt. III, Ch. 4

**21** He was greatly pained at how little he was pained by the events of the afternoon.
*Decline and Fall*, Pt. III, Ch. 4

**22** Instead of this absurd division into sexes they ought to class people as static and dynamic.
*Decline and Fall*, Pt. III, Ch. 7

**23** We are all American at puberty; we die French.
*Diaries*, 'Irregular Notes', 18 July 1961

**24** Punctuality is the virtue of the bored.
*Diaries*, 'Irregular Notes', 26 Mar 1962

**25** Assistant masters came and went . . . . Some liked little boys too little and some too much.
*A Little Learning*

**26** You never find an Englishman among the underdogs - except in England of course.
*The Loved One*

**27** In the dying world I come from quotation is a national vice. It used to be the classics, now it's lyric verse.
*The Loved One*

**28** Enclosing every thin man, there's a fat man demanding elbow-room.
Similar sentiments have been expressed by others. *See* AMIS; CONNOLLY; ORWELL
*Officers and Gentlemen*, Interlude

**29** Feather-footed through the plashy fen passes the questing vole.
*Scoop*, Bk. I, Ch. 1

**30** 'The Beast stands for strong mutually antagonistic governments everywhere', he said. 'Self-sufficiency at home, self-assertion abroad.'
*Scoop*, Bk. I, Ch. 1

**31** Yes, cider and tinned salmon are the staple diet of the agricultural classes.
*Scoop*, Bk. I, Ch. 1

**32** Pappenhacker says that every time you are polite to a proletarian you are helping to bolster up the capitalist system.
*Scoop*, Bk. I, Ch. 5

**33** 'I will not stand for being called a woman in my own house,' she said.
*Scoop*, Bk. I, Ch. 5

**34** News is what a chap who doesn't care much about anything wants to read. And it's only news until he's read it. After that it's dead.
*Scoop*, Bk. I, Ch. 5

**35** As there was no form of government common to the peoples thus segregated, nor tie of language, history, habit, or belief, they were called a Republic.
*Scoop*, Bk. II, Ch. 1

**36** The better sort of Ishmaelites have been Christian for many centuries and will not publicly eat human flesh uncooked in Lent, without special and costly dispensation from their bishop.
*Scoop*, Bk. II, Ch. 1

**37** Other nations use 'force'; we Britons alone use 'Might'.
*Scoop*, Bk. II, Ch. 5

**38** Up to a point, Lord Copper.
A euphemism for 'No'
*Scoop*, passim

**39** Particularly against books the Home Secretary is. If we can't stamp out literature in the country, we can at least stop it being brought in from outside.
*Vile Bodies*, Ch. 2

**40** When the war broke out she took down the signed photograph of the Kaiser and, with some solemnity, hung it in the menservants' lavatory; it was her one combative action.
*Vile Bodies*, Ch. 3

**41** She had heard someone say something about an Independent Labour Party, and was furious that she had not been asked.

*Vile Bodies*, Ch. 4

**42** All this fuss about sleeping together. For physical pleasure I'd sooner go to my dentist any day.

*Vile Bodies*, Ch. 6

**43** Lady Peabury was in the morning room reading a novel; early training gave a guilty spice to this recreation, for she had been brought up to believe that to read a novel before luncheon was one of the gravest sins it was possible for a gentlewoman to commit.

*Work Suspended*, 'An Englishman's Home'

**44** I wouldn't give up writing about God at this stage, if I was you. It would be like P. G. Wodehouse dropping Jeeves half-way through the Wooster series.

Said to Grahame Greene, who proposed to write a political novel
*Evelyn Waugh* (Christopher Sykes)

**45** Simply a radio personality who outlived his prime.

Referring to Winston Churchill
*Evelyn Waugh* (Christopher Sykes)

**46** Manners are especially the need of the plain. The pretty can get away with anything.

*The Observer*, 'Sayings of the Year,' 1962

**47** No writer before the middle of the 19th century wrote about the working classes other than as grotesque or as pastoral decoration. Then when they were given the vote certain writers started to suck up to them.

Interview
*Paris Review*, 1963

**48** Nurse unupblown.

Cable sent after he had failed, while a journalist serving in Ethiopia, to substantiate a rumour that an English nurse had been blown up in an Italian air raid
*Our Marvelous Native Tongue* (R. Claiborne)

**49** A typical triumph of modern science to find the only part of Randolph that was not malignant and remove it.

Remarking upon the news that Randolph Churchill had had a non-cancerous lung removed
Attrib.

**50** Like German opera, too long and too loud.

Giving his opinions of warfare after the battle of Crete, 1941
Attrib.

**51** I put the words down and push them a bit.

Obituary, *New York Times*, 11 Apr 1966

**Wavell, Archibald Percival, Earl** (1883–1950) British field marshal. He became chief of staff in Palestine after service in World War I. In World War II he defeated the Italians in Africa. He was viceroy of India (1943–47). A poet himself, he edited an anthology.

**1** It is like a cigar. If it goes out, you can light it again but it never tastes quite the same.

Giving his opinion of love
Attrib.

**Weatherly, Frederic Edward** (1848–1929) British lawyer and songwriter. His successes include 'London Bridge', 'Danny Boy', and 'Roses of Picardy'.

**1** Where are the boys of the Old Brigade?

*The Old Brigade*

**2** Roses are flowering in Picardy,
But there's never a rose like you.

*Roses of Picardy*

**Webb, Beatrice** (1858–1943) British economist and writer. The wife of Sidney Webb, Baron Passfield, she collaborated with him on several books, including *The History of Trade Unionism* (1894) and *Industrial Democracy* (1897).

**1** Religion is love; in no case is it logic.

*My Apprenticeship*, Ch. 2

**2** If I ever felt inclined to be timid as I was going into a room full of people, I would say to myself, 'You're the cleverest member of one of the cleverest families in the cleverest class of the cleverest nation in the world, why should you be frightened?'

*Portraits from Memory* (Bertrand Russell), 'Sidney and Beatrice Webb'

**Webb, Sydney, Baron Passfield** (1859–1947) British economist. An ardent socialist, he was a founder of the Fabian Society and the London School of Economics. He was a member of the London County Council and an MP. He wrote several books, some with his wife Beatrice Webb.

**1** Old people are always absorbed in something, usually themselves; we prefer to be absorbed in the Soviet Union.

*The Webbs and Their Work* (Kingsley Martin)

**2** The inevitability of gradualness.

Presidential Address to Labour Party Conference, 1923

**Webster, Daniel** (1782–1852) US statesman. A senator and renowned orator, he became secretary of state (1841–43; 1850–52) and an unsuccessful presidential candidate.

**1** Age cannot wither her, nor custom stale her infinite virginity.

Paraphrasing a line from Shakespeare's *Antony and Cleopatra* on hearing of Andrew Jackson's steadfast maintenance that his friend Peggy Eaton did not deserve her scandalous reputation
*Presidential Anecdotes* (P. Boller)

**2** The people's government, made for the people, made by the people, and answerable to the people.

Second speech on Foote's resolution, Jan 26 1830

**3** The past, at least, is secure.

Speech, US Senate, 26 Jan 1830

**4** I was born an American; I will live an American; I shall die an American.

Speech, US Senate, 17 July 1850

**5** There is always room at the top.

When advised not to become a lawyer because the profession was overcrowded
Attrib.

**Webster, John** (1580–1625) English dramatist. His plays include *The White Devil* (1612) and *The Duchess of Malfi* (1613). He also collaborated with other dramatists, including Thomas Dekker.

**1** Other sins only speak; murder shrieks out.

*The Duchess of Malfi,* IV:2

**2** Physicians are like kings, – they brook no contradiction.

*The Duchess of Malfi,* V:2

**3** We are merely the stars' tennis-balls, struck and bandied
Which way please them.

*The Duchess of Malfi,* V:4

**4** I saw him even now going the way of all flesh, that is to say towards the kitchen.

*Westward Hoe,* II:2

**5** We think caged birds sing, when indeed they cry.

*The White Devil,* V:4

**Webster, Noah** (1758–1843) US lexicographer and writer. His *American Dictionary of the English Language* (1828) did much to standardize US spellings.

**1** No, my dear, it is *I* who am surprised; you are merely astonished.

Responding to his wife's comment that she had been surprised to find him embracing their maid
Attrib.

**Weil, Simone** (1909–43) French philosopher and religious mystic. An active socialist in the 1930s, she became a Roman Catholic in 1938. Her books include *Waiting for God* (1951) and *The Need for Roots* (1952).

**1** Culture is an instrument wielded by professors to manufacture professors, who when their turn comes will manufacture professors.

*The Need for Roots*

**2** The word "revolution" is a word for which you kill, for which you die, for which you send the labouring masses to their death, but which does not possess any content.

*Oppression and Liberty,* 'Reflections Concerning the Causes of Liberty and Social Oppression'

**3** But not even Marx is more precious to us than the truth.

*Oppression and Liberty,* 'Revolution Proletarienne'

**4** The future is made of the same stuff as the present.

*On Science, Necessity, and the Love of God* (ed. Richard Rees), 'Some Thoughts on the Love of God'

**Weiss, Peter** (1916–82) German novelist and dramatist. He left Nazi Germany for Sweden in 1939. His plays include *Marat Sade* (1964) and *The Investigation* (1965).

**1** We invented the Revolution but we don't know how to run it.

*Marat Sade,* 15

**Weissmuller, Johnny** (1904–84) US swimmer and film actor. The winner of five Olympic gold medals, he later became the first Tarzan in sound films.

**1** Me? Tarzan?

Reacting to an invitation to play Tarzan
Attrib.

**Welch, Raquel** (Raquel Tejada; 1940– ) US film star, who became a sex symbol in the 1960s. Her later films include *Myra Breckinridge* (1970) and *The Prince and the Pauper* (1977).

**1** The mind can also be an erogenous zone.

*Colombo's Hollywood* (J. R. Colombo)

**Welles, Orson** (1915–85) US film actor, director, and writer. He established his film reputation with *Citizen Kane* (1941), which he followed with *The Magnificent Ambersons* (1942). He featured, as an actor, in the title role of *The Third Man* (1949).

**1** In Italy for thirty years under the Borgias they had warfare, terror, murder, bloodshed – they produced Michelangelo, Leonardo da Vinci and the Renaissance. In Switzerland they had brotherly love, five hundred years of democracy and peace, and what did they produce . . . ? The cuckoo clock.

*The Third Man*

**2** I started at the top and worked my way down.

*The Filmgoer's Book of Quotes* (Leslie Halliwell)

**3** I would just like to mention Robert Houdin who in the eighteenth century invented the vanishing bird-cage trick and the theater matinée – may he rot and perish. Good afternoon.

Addressing the audience at the end of a matinée performance
*Great Theatrical Disasters* (G. Brandreth)

**Wellington, Arthur Wellesley, Duke of** (1769– 1852) British general and statesman. He defeated the French in the Peninsular War and Napoleon at Waterloo. Known as the 'Iron Duke', he became Tory prime minister (1828–30). Under Peel he served as foreign secretary (1834–35).

**1** It all depends upon that article there.

Indicating a passing infantryman when asked if he would be able to defeat Napoleon
*The Age of Elegance* (A. Bryant)

**2** Yes, and they went down very well too.

Replying to the observation that the French cavalry had come up very well during the Battle of Waterloo
*The Age of Elegance* (A. Bryant)

**3** In my situation as Chancellor of the University of Oxford, I have been much exposed to authors.

*Collections and Recollections* (G. W. E. Russell)

**4** Not upon a man from the colonel to the private in a regiment – both inclusive. We may pick up a marshal or two perhaps; but not worth a damn.

Said during the Waterloo campaign, when asked whether he anticipated any desertions from Napoleon's army
*Creevey Papers,* Ch. X

5 It has been a damned serious business – Blücher and I have lost 30,000 men. It has been a damned nice thing – the nearest run thing you ever saw in your life . . . By God! I don't think it would have done if I had not been there.
Referring to the Battle of Waterloo
*Creevey Papers*, Ch. X

6 I always say that, next to a battle lost, the greatest misery is a battle gained.
*Diary* (Frances, Lady Shelley)

7 I see no reason to suppose that these machines will ever force themselves into general use.
Referring to steam locomotives
*Geoffrey Madan's Notebooks* (J. Gere)

8 I hate the whole race . . . There is no believing a word they say – your professional poets, I mean – there never existed a more worthless set than Byron and his friends for example.
Lady Salisbury's diary, 26 Oct 1833

9 I used to say of him that his presence on the field made the difference of forty thousand men.
Referring to Napoleon
*Notes of Conversations with the Duke of Wellington* (Stanhope), 2 Nov 1831

10 The next greatest misfortune to losing a battle is to gain such a victory as this.
*Recollections* (S. Rogers)

11 The greatest tragedy in the world, Madam, except a defeat.
In reply to the remark, 'What a glorious thing must be a victory'
*Recollections* (S. Rogers)

12 You must build your House of Parliament upon the river: so . . . that the populace cannot exact their demands by sitting down round you.
*Words on Wellington* (Sir William Fraser)

13 I don't know what effect these men will have on the enemy, but, by God, they frighten me.
Referring to his generals
Attrib.

14 It is not the business of generals to shoot one another.
Refusing an artillery officer permission to fire upon Napoleon himself during the Battle of Waterloo, 1815
Attrib.

15 Up, Guards, and at 'em.
Order given at the battle of Waterloo, 18 June 1815
Attrib.

16 The battle of Waterloo was won on the playing fields of Eton.
Attrib.

17 Yes, about ten minutes.
Responding to a vicar's query as to whether there was anything he would like his forthcoming sermon to be about
Attrib.

18 Very well, then I shall not take off my boots.
Responding to the news, as he was going to bed, that the ship in which he was travelling seemed about to sink
Attrib.

19 Ours is composed of the scum of the earth.
Of the British army
Remark, 4 Nov 1831

20 Publish and be damned!
On being offered the chance to avoid mention in the memoirs of Harriette Wilson by giving her money
Attrib.

21 I don't care a twopenny damn what becomes of the ashes of Napoleon Bonaparte.
Attrib.

22 Don't quote Latin; say what you have to say, and then sit down.
Advice to a new Member of Parliament
Attrib.

23 A battle of giants.
Referring to the Battle of Waterloo; said to Samuel Rogers
Attrib.

24 Sparrowhawks, Ma'am.
Advice when asked by Queen Victoria how to remove sparrows from the Crystal Palace
Attrib.

**Wells, H(erbert) G(eorge)** (1866–1946) British writer. After studying science, he won a literary reputation with *The Time Machine* (1895) and *Kipps* (1905). His other books included *An Outline of History* (1920) and *The Shape of Things to Come* (1933).

1 The cat is the offspring of a cat and the dog of a dog, but butlers and lady's maids do not reproduce their kind. They have other duties.
*Bealby*, Pt I, Ch. 1

2 He was quite sure that he had been wronged. Not to be wronged is to forgo the first privilege of goodness.
*Bealby*, Pt. IV, Ch. 1

3 Miss Madeleine Philips was making it very manifest to Captain Douglas that she herself was a career; that a lover with any other career in view need not – as the advertisements say – apply.
*Bealby*, Pt. V, Ch. 5

4 He began to think the tramp a fine, brotherly, generous fellow. He was also growing accustomed to something – shall I call it an olfactory bar – that had hitherto kept them apart.
*Bealby*, Pt. VI, Ch. 3

5 The army ages men sooner than the law and philosophy; it exposes them more freely to germs, which undermine and destroy, and it shelters them more completely from thought, which stimulates and preserves.
*Bealby*, Pt. VIII, Ch. 1

6 He had one peculiar weakness; he had faced death in many forms but he had never faced a dentist. The thought of dentists gave him just the same sick horror as the thought of Socialism.
*Bealby*, Pt. VIII, Ch. 1

7 In the Country of the Blind the One-eyed Man is King.
*The Country of the Blind*

8 '*Language*, man!' roared Parsons; 'why, it's LITERATURE!'
*The History of Mr Polly*, Pt. I, Ch. 3

9 'You're a Christian?' 'Church of England,' said Mr Polly. 'Mm,' said the employer, a little checked. 'For good all round business work, I should have preferred a Baptist.'
*The History of Mr Polly*, Pt. III, Ch. 1

10 Arson, after all, is an artificial crime . . . A large number of houses deserve to be burnt.
*The History of Mr Polly*, Pt. X, Ch. 1

11 'It's giving girls names like that', said Buggins, 'that nine times out of ten makes 'em go wrong. It unsettles 'em. If ever I was to have a girl, if ever I was to have a dozen girls, I'd call 'em all Jane.'
Referring to the name Euphemia
*Kipps*, Bk. I, Ch. 4

12 It's 'aving 'ouses built by men, I believe, makes all the work and trouble.
*Kipps*, Bk. III, Ch. 1

13 Everybody hates house-agents because they have everybody at a disadvantage. All other callings have a certain amount of give and take; the house-agent simply takes.
*Kipps*, Bk. III, Ch. 1

14 We were taught as the chief subjects of instruction Latin and Greek. We were taught very badly because the men who taught us did not habitually use either of these languages.
*The New Machiavelli*, Bk. I, Ch. 3

15 Cynicism is humour in ill-health.
*Short Stories*, 'The Last Trump'

16 He doubted the existence of the Deity but accepted Carnot's cycle, and he had read Shakespeare and found him weak in chemistry.
*Short Stories*, 'The Lord of the Dynamos'

17 Bricklayers kick their wives to death, and dukes betray theirs; but it is among the small clerks and shopkeepers nowadays that it comes most often to the cutting of throats.
*Short Stories*, 'The Purple Pileus'

18 The War to End War.
Book title

19 If Max gets to Heaven he won't last long. He will be chucked out for trying to pull of a merger between Heaven and Hell . . . after having secured a controlling interest in key subsidiary companies in both places, of course.
Referring to Lord Beaverbrook
*Beaverbrook* (A. J. P. Taylor)

20 One thousand years more. That's all *Homo sapiens* has before him.
*Diary* (Harold Nicolson)

**Wesker, Arnold** (1932– ) British dramatist. His early socialist plays on Jewish themes, *Chicken Soup with Barley* (1958), *Roots* (1959), and *I'm Talking About Jerusalem* (1960), were followed by *Chips with Everything* (1962) and *The Merchant* (1978).

1 You breed babies and you eat chips with everything.
*Chips with Everything*, I:2

2 Every place I look at I work out the cubic feet, and I say it will make a good warehouse or it won't. Can't help myself. One of the best warehouses I ever see was the Vatican in Rome.
*Chips with Everything*, I:6

3 Don't you sit there and sigh gal like you was Lady Nevershit.
*Roots*, III

**Wesley, Charles** (1707–88) British religious leader, who founded Methodism with his brother John Wesley. He composed a large number of hymns.

1 Gentle Jesus, meek and mild,
Look upon a little child;
Pity my simplicity,
Suffer me to come to thee.
*Hymns and Sacred Poems*

**Wesley, John** (1703–91) British religious leader, who founded Methodism with his brother Charles Wesley.

1 I look upon all the world as my parish.
*Journal*, 11 June 1739

2 Beware you be not swallowed up in books! An ounce of love is worth a pound of knowledge.
*Life of Wesley* (R. Southey), Ch. 16

3 We should constantly use the most common, little, easy words (so they are pure and proper) which our language affords.
Advice for preaching to 'plain people'
Attrib.

**West, Mae** (1892–1980) US actress, sex symbol, and comedienne. She made her reputation in the theatre with *Diamond Lil* (1928). Her films included *She Done Him Wrong* (1933) and *I'm No Angel* (1933).

1 A man in the house is worth two in the street.
*Belle of the Nineties*, film 1934

2 –My goodness those diamonds are lovely! Goodness had nothing whatever to do with it.
Used in 1959 as the title of the first volume of her autobiography
*Diamond Lil*, film 1932

3 I have a lot of respect for that dame. There's one lady barber that made good.
Referring to Delilah
*Going to Town*, film 1934

4 Beulah, peel me a grape.
*I'm No Angel*, film 1933

5 A gold rush is what happens when a line of chorus girls spot a man with a bank roll.
*Klondike Annie*, film 1936

**6** I always did like a man in uniform. And that one fits you grand. Why don't you come up sometime and see me?

Often misquoted as 'Come up and see me some time'
*She Done Him Wrong*, film 1933

**7** You're a fine woman, Lou. One of the finest women that ever walked the streets.

*She Done Him Wrong*, film 1933

**8** You can say what you like about long dresses, but they cover a multitude of shins.

*Peel Me a Grape* (J. Weintraub)

**9** It's hard to be funny when you have to be clean.

*The Wit and Wisdom of Mae West* (ed. J. Weintraub)

**10** It is better to be looked over than overlooked.

*The Wit and Wisdom of Mae West* (ed. J. Weintraub)

**11** I used to be Snow White . . . but I drifted.

*The Wit and Wisdom of Mae West* (ed. J. Weintraub)

**12** When women go wrong, men go right after them.

*The Wit and Wisdom of Mae West* (ed. J. Weintraub)

**13** I'm glad you like my Catherine. I like her too. She ruled thirty million people and had three thousand lovers. I do the best I can in two hours.

After her performance in *Catherine the Great*
Speech from the stage

**14** Everything.

When asked what she wanted to be remembered for
Attrib.

**15** When I'm good I'm very good, but when I'm bad I'm better.

Attrib.

**16** Whenever I'm caught between two evils, I take the one I've never tried.

Attrib.

**West, Nathaniel** (Nathan Weinstein; 1903–40) US novelist and scriptwriter. His novels include *Miss Lonelyhearts* (1933) and *The Day of the Locust* (1939).

**1** Are you in trouble? Do you need advice? Write to Miss Lonelyhearts and she will help.

*Miss Lonelyhearts*

**West, Dame Rebecca** (Cicely Isabel Fairfield; 1892–1983) British novelist and journalist. Novels include *The Thinking Reed* (1936) and *The Birds Fall Down* (1966). Other books, such as *The Meaning of Treason* (1949) and *A Train of Powder*, are essays in political journalism.

**1** But there are other things than dissipation that thicken the features. Tears, for example.

*Black Lamb and Grey Falcon*, 'Serbia'

**2** . . . any authentic work of art must start an argument between the artist and his audience.

*The Court and the Castle*, Pt. I, Ch. 1

**3** The point is that nobody likes having salt rubbed into their wounds, even if it is the salt of the earth.

*The Salt of the Earth*, Ch. 2

**4** God forbid that any book should be banned. The practice is as indefensible as infanticide.

*The Strange Necessity*, 'The Tosh Horse'

**5** There is no such thing as conversation. It is an illusion. There are intersecting monologues, that is all.

*There Is No Conversation*, Ch. 1

**6** Margaret Thatcher's great strength seems to be the better people know her, the better they like her. But, of course, she has one great disadvantage – she is a daughter of the people and looks trim, as the daughters of the people desire to be. Shirley Williams has such an advantage over her because she's a member of the upper-middle class and can achieve that kitchen-sink-revolutionary look that one cannot get unless one has been to a really good school.

Said in an interview with Jilly Cooper
*The Sunday Times*, 25 July 1976

**7** My dear – the people we should have been seen dead with.

Cable sent to Noël Coward after learning they had both been on a Nazi death list
*Times Literary Supplement*, 1 Oct 1982

**8** Just how difficult it is to write biography can be reckoned by anybody who sits down and considers just how many people know the real truth about his or her love affairs.

*Vogue* magazine

**Weston, R. P.** (20th century) British songwriter.

**1** Good-bye-ee! – good-bye-ee!
Wipe the tear, baby dear, from your eye-ee.
Tho' it's hard to part, I know,
Don't cry-ee! – don't sigh-ee!
There's a silver lining in the sky-ee! – ·
Bonsoir, old thing! cheerio! chin-chin!
Nahpoo! Toodle-oo! Good-bye-ee!

*Good-bye-ee!* (with Bert Lee)

**2** Some soldiers send epistles, say they'd sooner sleep in thistles
Than the saucy, soft, short shirts for soldiers, sister Susie sews.

*Sister Susie's Sewing Shirts for Soldiers*

**Wetherell, Sir Charles** (1770–1846) British lawyer and judge.

**1** Then there is my noble and biographical friend who has added a new terror to death.

Referring to Lord Campbell
*Misrepresentations in Campbell's Lives of Lyndhurst and Brougham* (Lord St. Leonards)

**Weygand, Maxime** (1867–1965) French general. He was the chief of Foch's general staff in World War I. In World War II he was in command during the 1940 retreat and subsequently the Vichy government's commander in North Africa.

**1** In three weeks England will have her neck wrung like a chicken.

Said at the fall of France; see CHURCHILL
*Their Finest Hour* (Winston S. Churchill)

**Wharton, Edith** (1862–1937) US novelist. Her books include *The Valley of Decision* (1902), *The Age of Innocence* (1920), and *Certain People* (1930).

**1** An unalterable and unquestioned law of the musical world required that the German text of French operas sung by Swedish artists should be translated into Italian for the clearer understanding of English speaking audiences.

*The Age of Innocence*, Bk. I, Ch. 1

**2** She keeps on being Queenly in her own room with the door shut.

*The House of Mirth*, Bk. II, Ch. 1

**3** Another unsettling element in modern art is that common symptom of immaturity, the dread of doing what has been done before.

*The Writing of Fiction*, Ch. 1

**4** Mrs Ballinger is one of the ladies who pursue Culture in bands, as though it were dangerous to meet it alone.

*Xingu*, Ch. 1

**Whately, Richard** (1787–1863) British churchman, theologian, and logician. He became Archbishop of Dublin (1831–63) and wrote a number of religious books but is remembered for his *Logic* (1826) and *Rhetoric* (1828).

**1** Happiness is no laughing matter.

*Apophthegms*

**2** Honesty is the best policy; but he who is governed by that maxim is not an honest man.

*Apophthegms*

**Wheeler, Hugh** (1912– ) British-born US novelist and dramatist. His plays include *A Little Night Music* (1974), adapted from an Ingmar Bergman film, and *Sweeny Todd* (1979).

**1** To lose a lover or even a husband or two during the course of one's life can be vexing. But to lose one's teeth is a catastrophe.

*A Little Night Music*

**Whewell, William** (1794–1866) British philosopher and mathematician, who became master of Trinity College (1841–66) and vice-chancellor of Cambridge University (1843; 1856). His books include *History of the Inductive Sciences* (1837) and *Plurality of Worlds* (1853).

**1** Hence no force however great can stretch a cord however fine into an horizontal line which is accurately straight: there will always be a bending downwards.

An example of unintentional versification
*Elementary Treatise on Mechanics* (1819 edition), Ch. 4

**Whistler, James Abbott McNeill** (1834–1903) US painter. Living mostly in Europe, he established his reputation with *The Artist's Mother* and *Nocturne in Blue and Gold*. He was also the author of *The Gentle Art of Making Enemies* (1890).

**1** I am not arguing with you – I am telling you.

*The Gentle Art of Making Enemies*

**2** Nature is usually wrong.

*The Gentle Art of Making Enemies*

**3** No, no, Oscar, you forget. When you and I are together we never talk about anything except me.

Cable replying to Oscar Wilde's message: 'When you and I are together we never talk about anything except ourselves'
*The Gentle Art of Making Enemies*

**4** If silicon had been a gas I should have been a major-general.

Referring to his failure in a West Point chemistry examination
*English Wits* (L. Russell)

**5** No, I ask it for the knowledge of a lifetime.

Replying to the taunt, during the Ruskin trial, that he was asking a fee of 200 guineas for two days' painting.
*Lives of the Wits* (H. Pearson)

**6** Isn't it? I know in my case I would grow intolerably conceited.

Replying to the pointed observaton that it was as well that we do not not see ourselves as others see us
*The Man Whistler* (H. Pearson)

**7** A LADY. I only know of two painters in the world: yourself and Velasquez.
WHISTLER. Why drag in Velasquez?

*Whistler Stories* (D. Seitz)

**8** You shouldn't say it is not good. You should say you do not like it; and then, you know, you're perfectly safe.

*Whistler Stories* (D. Seitz)

**9** A LADY. This landscape reminds me of your work.
WHISTLER. Yes madam, Nature is creeping up.

*Whistler Stories* (D. Seitz)

**10** Perhaps not, but then you can't call yourself a great work of nature.

Responding to a sitter's complaint that his portrait was not a great work of art
*Whistler Stories* (D. Seitz)

**11** I cannot tell you that, madam. Heaven has granted me no offspring.

Replying to a lady who had inquired whether he thought genius hereditary
*Whistler Stories* (D. Seitz)

**12** It has none, your Highness. Its history dates from today.

Replying to a query from the Prince of Wales about the history of the Society of British Artists, which he was visiting for the first time.
*Whistler Stories* (D. Seitz)

**13** It is very simple. The artists retired. The British remained.

Explaining his resignation as president of the Royal Society of British Artists
*Whistler Stories* (D. Seitz)

**14** Well, not bad, but there are decidedly too many of them, and they are not very well arranged. I would have done it differently.

His reply when asked if he agreed that the stars were especially beautiful one night.
Attrib.

**15** You will, Oscar, you will.

Replying to Oscar Wilde's exclamation 'I wish I had said that!'
Attrib.

**16** The explanation is quite simple. I wished to be near my mother.

Explaining to a snobbish lady why he had been born in such an unfashionable place as Lowell, Massachusetts
Attrib.

**17** Listen! There never was an artistic period. There never was an Art-loving nation.

Attrib.

**White, Andrew Dickson** (1832–1918) US educationalist and diplomat. He helped to found Cornell University and was its first president (1868–85). He was also US ambassador to Germany (1897–1902).

**1** I will not permit thirty men to travel four hundred miles to agitate a bag of wind.

Refusing to allow the Cornell football team to visit Michigan to play a match
The People's Almanac (D. Wallechinsky)

**White, Elwyn Brooks** (1899– ) US journalist and humorous writer. A regular contributor to The New Yorker, he has written many books including One Man's Meat (1942) and The Second Tree from the Corner (1954).

**1** Commuter – one who spends his life
In riding to and from his wife;
A man who shaves and takes a train,
And then rides back to shave again.

The Commuter

**2** As in the sexual experience, there are never more than two persons present in the act of reading – the writer who is the impregnator, and the reader who is the respondent.

The Second Tree from the Corner

**3** To perceive Christmas through its wrapping becomes more difficult with every year.

The Second Tree from the Corner

**White, Henry Kirke** (1785–1806) British poet. He is remembered for his verse collection Clifton Grove (1803) and for several hymns.

**1** Much in sorrow, oft in woe,
Onward, Christians, onward go.

A hymn, better known in its later form, 'Oft in danger, oft in woe'

**White, Patrick** (1912– ) British-born Australian novelist. His books include The Tree of Man (1955), Voss (1957), and Netherwood (1983).

**1** But bombs *are* unbelievable until they actually fall.

Riders in the Chariot, I:4

**2** 'I dunno,' Arthur said. 'I forget what I was taught. I only remember what I've learnt.'

The Solid Mandala, Ch. 2

**3** All my novels are an accumulation of detail. I'm a bit of a bower-bird.

Southerly, 139

**4** Well, good luck to you, kid! I'm going to write the Great Australian Novel.

The Vivisector, 112

**White, T(erence) H(anbury)** (1906–64) British novelist. His best-known books are on Arthurian legend and include The Once and Future King (1958).

**1** The Victorians had not been anxious to go away for the weekend. The Edwardians, on the contrary, were nomadic.

Farewell Victoria, Ch. 4

**White, William Allen** (1868–1944) US writer. His books include In Our Town (1906), In the Heart of a Fool (1918), and The Changing West (1939). He was editor and owner of the Emporia Gazette.

**1** All dressed up, with nowhere to go.

Referring to the Progressive Party, after Theodore Roosevelt's withdrawal from the 1916 US Presidential election

**Whitehead, A(lfred) N(orth)** (1861–1947) British philosopher and mathematician. With Bertrand Russell he wrote Principia Mathematica (1910–13). Other books include The Principles of Natural Knowledge (1919) and The Concept of Nature (1920).

**1** Where are no whole truths; all truths are half-truths. It is trying to treat them as whole truths that plays the devil.

Dialogues, 16

**2** Intelligence is quickness to apprehend as distinct from ability, which is capacity to act wisely on the thing apprehended.

Dialogues, 135

**3** Art is the imposing of a pattern on experience, and our aesthetic enjoyment is recognition of the pattern.

Dialogues, 228

**4** Philosophy is the product of wonder.

Nature and Life, Ch. 1

**5** A science which hesitates to forget its founders is lost.

Attrib.

**6** The history of Western philosophy is, after all, no more than a series of footnotes to Plato's philosophy.

Attrib.

**Whitehorn, Katherine** (1926– ) British journalist and writer. She has written a column in The Observer since 1960. Her books include Only on Sundays (1966), How to Survive Children (1975), and View from a Column (1981).

**1** Hats divide generally into three classes: offensive hats, defensive hats, and shrapnel.

Shouts and Murmurs, 'Hats'

**2** And what would happen to my illusion that I am a force for order in the home if I wasn't married to the only man north of the Tiber who is even untidier than I am?

Sunday Best, 'Husband-Swapping'

3 The Life and Soul, the man who will never go home while there is one man, woman or glass of anything not yet drunk.

*Sunday Best*, 'Husband-Swapping'

4 It is a pity, as my husband says, that more politicians are not bastards by birth instead of vocation.

*The Observer*, 1964

5 Have you ever taken anything out of the clothes basket because it had become, relatively, the cleaner thing?

*The Observer*, 'On Shirts', 1964

6 The best careers advice to give to the young is 'Find out what you like doing best and get someone to pay you for doing it.'

*The Observer*, 1975

7 A good listener is not someone who has nothing to say. A good listener is a good talker with a sore throat.

Attrib.

**Whitelaw, William (Stephen Ian), Viscount**
(1918– ) British politician. He became home secretary in Mrs Thatcher's administration and subsequently lord president of the council and leader of the House of Lords.

1 I do not intend to prejudge the past.

Said on arriving in Ulster as Minister for Northern Ireland
*The Times*, 3 Dec 1973

2 I am not prepared to go about the country stirring up apathy.

Attrib.

**Whiting, William** (1825–78) British hymn writer.

1 O hear us when we cry to Thee
For those in peril on the sea.

*Eternal Father Strong to Save*

**Whitlam, Gough** (1916– ) Australian statesman. He became Labor leader in 1967 and then prime minister (1972–75). He was dismissed by the governor, Sir John Kerr, and resigned the leadership of the Labor Party in 1977.

1 I do not mind the Liberals, still less do I mind the Country Party, calling me a bastard. In some circumstances I am only doing my job if they do. But I hope you will not publicly call me a bastard, as some bastards in the Caucus have.

Speech to the Australian Labor Party, 9 June 1974

**Whitman, Walt** (1819–92) US poet. His first verse collection, *Leaves of Grass* (1855), was poorly received at first, although it went through nine editions in his lifetime. Other books include *Democratic Vistas* (1871), *November Boughs* (1888), and *Goodbye, My Fancy* (1891).

1 No one will ever get at my verses who insists upon viewing them as a literary performance.

*A Backward Glance O'er Travel'd Roads*

2 I hear it was charged against me that I sought to destroy institutions,
But really I am neither for nor against institutions.

*I Hear It was Charged against Me*

3 If anything is sacred the human body is sacred.

*I Sing the Body Electric*, 8

4 I celebrate myself, and sing myself,
And what I assume you shall assume.

*Song of Myself*, 1

5 I think I could turn and live with animals, they're so placid and self-contained,
I stand and look at them long and long.

*Song of Myself*, 32

6 Behold, I do not give lectures or a little charity,
When I give I give myself.

*Song of Myself*, 40

7 I have said that the soul is not more than the body,
And I have said that the body is not more than the soul,
And nothing, but God, is greater to one than one's self is.

*Song of Myself*, 48

8 Do I contradict myself?
Very well then I contradict myself,
(I am large, I contain multitudes).

*Song of Myself*, 51

9 Where the populace rise at once against the never-ending audacity of elected persons.

*Song of the Broad Axe*, 5

10 A great city is that which has the greatest men and women.

*Song of the Broad-Axe*, 5

11 After you have exhausted what there is in business, politics, conviviality, and so on – have found that none of these finally satisfy, or permanently wear – what remains? Nature remains.

*Specimen Days*, 'New Themes Entered Upon'

12 The earth does not argue,
Is not pathetic, has no arrangements,
Does not scream, haste, persuade, threaten, promise,
Makes no discriminations, has no conceivable failures,
Closes nothing, refuses nothing, shuts none out.

*To the sayers of words*

**Whittier, John Greenleaf** (1807–92) US poet. A Quaker and an abolitionist, his books include *Legends of New England in Prose and Verse* (1831), *Songs of Labor* (1850), *Snow-Bound* (1866), and *At Sundown* (1890). His best-known poem is 'Barbara Frietchie'.

1 Up from the meadows rich with corn,
Clear in the cool September morn,

The clustered spires of Frederick stand
Green-walled by the hills of Maryland.
*Barbara Frietchie*

2 'Shoot, if you must, this old gray head,
But spare your country's flag,' she said.

A shade of sadness, a blush of shame,
Over the face of the leader came.
*Barbara Frietchie*

**Whittington, Robert** (16th century) English writer.

1 As time requireth, a man of marvellous mirth
and pastimes, and sometimes of as sad gravity,
as who say: a man for all seasons.
Referring to Sir Thomas More; after Erasmus
*Vulgaria*, Pt. II, 'De constructione nominum'

**Whorf, Benjamin Lee** (1897–1941) US linguist. His best-known work is *Language, Thought, and Reality* (1956). He earned his living as an insurance inspector.

1 We dissect nature along lines laid down by our
native language . . . Language is not simply a
reporting device for experience but a defining
framework for it.
*New Directions in the Study of Language* (ed. Hoyer), 'Thinking in Primitive Communities'

**Wigg, George Edward Cecil, Baron** (1900–76) British politician. He was paymaster general (1964–67) and became President of the Betting Office Licensees' Association.

1 For Hon. Members opposite the deterrent is a
phallic symbol. It convinces them that they are
men.
*The Observer*, 'Sayings of the Week', 8 Mar 1964

**Wilberforce, Samuel** (1805–73) British churchman. He became Bishop of Oxford (1845) and of Winchester (1869). His books include *Agathos* (1840).

1 And, in conclusion, I would like to ask the gentleman . . . whether the ape from which he is
descended was on his grandmother's or his
grandfather's side of the family.
*See* T. H. HUXLEY
Speech, 30 June 1960

2 If I were a cassowary
On the plains of Timbuctoo,
I would eat a missionary,
Cassock, band, and hymn-book too.
Also attrib. to W. M. Thackeray
Attrib.

**Wilcox, Ella Wheeler** (1850–1919) US poet. Her verse collections include *Drops of Water* (1872), *Poems of Passion* (1873), and *The Art of Being Alive* (1914).

1 We flatter those we scarcely know,
We please the fleeting guest,
And deal full many a thoughtless blow
To those who love us best.
*Life's Scars*

2 No question is ever settled
Until it is settled right.
*Settle the Question Right*

3 Laugh, and the world laughs with you;
Weep, and you weep alone,
For the sad old earth must borrow its mirth,
But has trouble enough of its own.
*Solitude*

4 So many gods, so many creeds,
So many paths that wind and wind,
While just the art of being kind
Is all the sad world needs.
*The World's Need*

**Wilde, Oscar Fingal O'Flahertie Wills** (1856–1900) Irish-born British poet and dramatist. His comedies *Lady Windermere's Fan* (1892), *An Ideal Husband* (1895), and *The Importance of Being Earnest* (1895) made him a leading figure in London society. However he was ruined by a trial (1895) arising from his homosexual relationships, especially with Lord Alfred Douglas. During his imprisonment he wrote *De Profundis* (1905) and the *The Ballad of Reading Gaol* (1898).

1 I never saw a man who looked
With such a wistful eye
Upon that little tent of blue
Which prisoners call the sky.
*The Ballad of Reading Gaol*, I:3

2 Yet each man kills the thing he loves,
By each let this be heard,
Some do it with a bitter look,
Some with a flattering word.
The coward does it with a kiss,
The brave man with a sword!
*The Ballad of Reading Gaol*, I:7

3 The Governor was strong upon
The Regulations Act:
The Doctor said that Death was but
A scientific fact:
And twice a day the Chaplain called,
And left a little tract.
*The Ballad of Reading Gaol*, III:3

4 Something was dead in each of us,
And what was dead was Hope.
*The Ballad of Reading Gaol*, III:31

5 For he who lives more lives than one
More deaths than one must die.
*The Ballad of Reading Gaol*, III:37

6 I know not whether Laws be right,
Or whether Laws be wrong;
All that we know who lie in gaol
Is that the wall is strong;
And that each day is like a year,
A year whose days are long.
*The Ballad of Reading Gaol*, V:1

7 As long as war is regarded as wicked, it will always have its fascination. When it is looked upon as vulgar, it will cease to be popular.
*The Critic as Artist*, Pt. 2

**8** The man who sees both sides of a question is a man who sees absolutely nothing at all.
*The Critic as Artist*, Pt. 2

**9** A little sincerity is a dangerous thing, and a great deal of it is absolutely fatal.
*The Critic as Artist*, Pt. 2

**10** Ah! don't say you agree with me. When people agree with me I always feel that I must be wrong.
*The Critic as Artist*, Pt. 2

**11** There is no sin except stupidity.
*The Critic as Artist*, Pt. 2

**12** There is much to be said in favour of modern journalism. By giving us the opinions of the un-educated, it keeps us in touch with the igno-rance of the community.
*The Critic as Artist*, Pt. 2

**13** Art never expresses anything but itself.
*The Decay of Lying*

**14** To love oneself is the beginning of a lifelong romance.
*An Ideal Husband*, III

**15** Other people are quite dreadful. The only possi-ble society is oneself.
*An Ideal Husband*, III

**16** Really, if the lower orders don't set us a good example, what on earth is the use of them?
*The Importance of Being Earnest*, I

**17** I have invented an invaluable permanent invalid called Bunbury, in order that I may be able to go down into the country whenever I choose.
*The Importance of Being Earnest*, I

**18** All women become like their mothers. That is their tragedy. No man does. That's his.
*The Importance of Being Earnest*, I

**19** The amount of women in London who flirt with their own husbands is perfectly scandalous. It looks so bad. It is simply washing one's clean linen in public.
*The Importance of Being Earnest*, I

**20** The old-fashioned respect for the young is fast dying out.
*The Importance of Being Earnest*, I

**21** In married life three is company and two is none.
*The Importance of Being Earnest*, I

**22** Ignorance is like a delicate exotic fruit; touch it, and the bloom is gone.
*The Importance of Being Earnest*, I

**23** To lose one parent, Mr Worthing, may be re-garded as a misfortune; to lose both looks like carelessness.
*The Importance of Being Earnest*, I

**24** I hope you have not been leading a double life, pretending to be wicked and being really good all the time. That would be hypocrisy.
*The Importance of Being Earnest*, II

**25** On an occasion of this kind it becomes more than a moral duty to speak one's mind. It becomes a pleasure.
*The Importance of Being Earnest*, II

**26** CECILY. When I see a spade I call it a spade. GWENDOLEN. I am glad to say I have never seen a spade. It is obvious that our social spheres have been widely different.
*The Importance of Being Earnest*, II

**27** I never travel without my diary. One should al-ways have something sensational to read in the train.
*The Importance of Being Earnest*, II

**28** In matters of grave importance, style, not sincerity, is the vital thing.
*The Importance of Being Earnest*, III

**29** Three addresses always inspire confidence, even in tradesmen.
*The Importance of Being Earnest*, III

**30** Never speak disrespectfully of Society, Alger-non. Only people who can't get into it do that.
*The Importance of Being Earnest*, III

**31** No woman should ever be quite accurate about her age. It looks so calculating.
*The Importance of Being Earnest*, III

**32** This suspense is terrible. I hope it will last.
*The Importance of Being Earnest*, III

**33** It is a terrible thing for a man to find out sudden-ly that all his life he has been speaking nothing but the truth.
*The Importance of Being Earnest*, III

**34** Please do not shoot the pianist. He is doing his best.
*Impressions of America*, 'Leadville'

**35** I can resist everything except temptation.
*Lady Windermere's Fan*, I

**36** It is absurd to divide people into good and bad. People are either charming or tedious.
*Lady Windermere's Fan*, I

**37** I am the only person in the world I should like to know thoroughly.
*Lady Windermere's Fan*, II

**38** We are all in the gutter, but some of us are look-ing at the stars.
*Lady Windermere's Fan*, III

**39** There is nothing in the whole world so unbecom-ing to a woman as a Nonconformist conscience.
*Lady Windermere's Fan*, III

40 A man who knows the price of everything and the value of nothing.

A cynic
*Lady Windermere's Fan*, III

41 There is no such thing as a moral or an immoral book. Books are well written, or badly written.

*The Picture of Dorian Gray*, Preface

42 All Art is quite useless.

*The Picture of Dorian Gray*, Preface

43 There is only one thing in the world worse than being talked about, and that is not being talked about.

*The Picture of Dorian Gray*, Ch. 1

44 The only way to get rid of a temptation is to yield to it.

*The Picture of Dorian Gray*, Ch. 2

45 It is only shallow people who do not judge by appearances.

*The Picture of Dorian Gray*, Ch. 2

46 I can sympathize with everything, except suffering.

*The Picture of Dorian Gray*, Ch. 3

47 Women represent the triumph of matter over mind, just as men represent the triumph of mind over morals.

*The Picture of Dorian Gray*, Ch. 4

48 A cigarette is the perfect type of a perfect pleasure. It is exquisite, and it leaves one unsatisfied. What more can one want?

*The Picture of Dorian Gray*, Ch. 6

49 Anybody can be good in the country.

*The Picture of Dorian Gray*, Ch. 19

50 As for the virtuous poor, one can pity them, of course, but one cannot possibly admire them.

*The Soul of Man under Socialism*

51 Democracy means simply the bludgeoning of the people by the people for the people.

See LINCOLN
*The Soul of Man under Socialism*

52 Art is the most intense mode of individualism that the world has known.

*The Soul of Man Under Socialism*

53 Twenty years of romance makes a woman look like a ruin; but twenty years of marriage make her something like a public building.

*A Woman of No Importance*, I

54 MRS ALLONBY. They say, Lady Hunstanton, that when good Americans die they go to Paris.
LADY HUNSTANTON. Indeed? And when bad Americans die, where do they go to?
LORD ILLINGWORTH. Oh, they go to America.

See APPLETON, Thomas Gold
*A Woman of No Importance*, I

55 The English country gentleman galloping after a fox – the unspeakable in full pursuit of the uneatable.

*A Woman of No Importance*, I

56 One should never trust a woman who tells one her real age. A woman who would tell one that, would tell one anything.

*A Woman of No Importance*, I

57 LORD ILLINGWORTH. The Book of Life begins with a man and a woman in a garden.
MRS ALLONBY. It ends with Revelations.

*A Woman of No Importance*, I

58 Moderation is a fatal thing, Lady Hunstanton. Nothing succeeds like excess.

*A Woman of No Importance*, III

59 Ah, every day dear Herbert becomes *de plus en plus Oscarié*. It is a wonderful case of nature imitating art.

Referring to Beerbohm Tree's unconscious adoption of some of the mannerisms of a character he was playing in one of Wilde's plays
*Great Theatrical Disasters* (G. Brandreth)

60 I suppose that I shall have to die beyond my means.

When told that an operation would be expensive. He is also believed to have said 'I am dying beyond my means' on accepting a glass of champagne as he lay on his deathbed
*Life of Wilde* (Sherard)

61 One would have to have a heart of stone to read the death of Little Nell without laughing.

Lecturing upon Dickens
*Lives of the Wits* (H. Pearson)

62 A thing is not necessarily true because a man dies for it.

*Oscariana*

63 He hasn't an enemy in the world, and none of his friends like him.

Said of G. B. Shaw
*Sixteen Self Sketches* (Shaw), Ch. 17

64 With our James vulgarity begins at home, and should be allowed to stay there.

Referring to the artist James Whistler
Letter to the *World*

65 The man who can dominate a London dinner-table can dominate the world.

Attrib. by R. Aldington in his edition of Wilde

66 The gods bestowed on Max the gift of perpetual old age.

Referring to Max Beerbohm
Attrib.

67 The play was a great success, but the audience was a disaster.

Referring to a play that had recently failed
Attrib.

68 Who am I to tamper with a masterpiece?

Refusing to make alterations to one of his own plays
Attrib.

**69** It requires one to assume such indecent postures.

Explaining why he did not play cricket
Attrib.

**70** If this is the way Queen Victoria treats her prisoners, she doesn't deserve to have any.

Complaining at having to wait in the rain for transport to take him to prison
Attrib.

**71** Grief has turned her fair.

Referring to the fact that a recently-bereaved lady friend had dyed her hair blonde
Attrib.

**72** Work is the curse of the drinking classes.

Attrib.

**73** Nothing, except my genius.

Replying to a US customs official on being asked if he had anything to declare
Attrib.

**74** I should be like a lion in a cave of savage Daniels.

Explaining why he would not be attending a function at a club whose members were hostile to him
Attrib.

**75** Dear Frank, we believe you; you have dined in every house in London – *once.*

Interrupting Frank Harris's interminable account of the houses he had dined at
Attrib.

**76** Either that wall paper goes, or I do.

Last words, as he lay dying in a drab Paris bedroom
*Time,* 16 Jan 1984

**Wilder, Billy** (Samuel Wilder; 1906–  ) Austrian-born US film director. His films include *The Lost Weekend* (1945), *Some Like it Hot* (1959), and *Buddy, Buddy* (1981).

**1** I've met a lot of hardboiled eggs in my time, but you're twenty minutes.

*Ace in the Hole*

**2** France is a country where the money falls apart in your hands and you can't tear the toilet paper.

Attrib.

**3** You have Van Gogh's ear for music.

Said to Cliff Osmond
Attrib.

**Wilder, Thornton** (1897–1975) US novelist and dramatist. His works include the novel *The Bridge of San Luis Rey* (1927) and the plays *Our Town* (1938) and *The Skin of Our Teeth* (1942).

**1** A living is made, Mr Kemper, by selling something that everybody needs at least once a year. Yes, sir! And a million is made by producing something that everybody needs every day. You artists produce something that nobody needs at any time.

*The Matchmaker,* II

**2** The best part of married life is the fights. The rest is merely so-so.

*The Matchmaker,* II

**3** Never support two weaknesses at the same time. It's your combination sinners – your lecherous liars and your miserly drunkards – who dishonour the vices and bring them into bad repute.

*The Matchmaker,* III

**4** But there comes a moment in everybody's life when he must decide whether he'll live among human beings or not – a fool among fools or a fool alone.

*The Matchmaker,* IV

**5** My advice to you is not to inquire why or whither, but just enjoy your ice-cream while it's on your plate, – that's my philosophy.

*The Skin of Our Teeth,* I

**6** When you're at war you think about a better life; when you're at peace you think about a more comfortable one.

*The Skin of Our Teeth,* III

**7** Literature is the orchestration of platitudes.

*Time* magazine

**Wilhelm I** (1797–1888) King of Prussia (1861–88) and Emperor of Germany (1871–88). He led the German armies in the Franco-Prussian War and supported Bismark in strengthening Prussian control of Germany.

**1** I haven't got time to be tired.

Said during his last illness

**Wilhelm II** (1859–1941) King of Prussia and Emperor of Germany (1888–1918). After Germany's defeat in World War I (in which he was known as 'Kaiser Bill') he was forced to abdicate.

**1** You will be home before the leaves have fallen from the trees.

Said to troops leaving for the Front, Aug 1914
*August 1914* (Barbara Tuchman), Ch. 9

**2** I would have liked to go to Ireland, but my grandmother would not let me. Perhaps she thought I wanted to take the little place.

Queen Victoria was his grandmother
*Carson* (H. Montgomery Hyde), Ch. 9

**3** The Admiral of the Atlantic salutes the Admiral of the Pacific.

Telegram sent to Czar Nicholas II during a naval exercise
*The Shadow of the Winter Palace* (E. Crankshaw)

**4** It is my Royal and Imperial Command that you . . . exterminate first the treacherous English, and . . . walk over General French's contemptible little Army.

Referring to the British Expeditionary Force; veterans of this force are known as 'Old Contemptibles'
*The Times,* 1 Oct 1914

**Wilhelmina** (1880–1962) Queen of the Netherlands (1890–1948).

**1** And when we open our dykes, the waters are ten feet deep.

Replying to a boast by Wilhelm II that his guardsmen were all seven feet tall
Attrib.

**Wilkes, John** (1725–97) British politician. A member of the Hellfire Club, who had led a profligate life, he became an MP in 1757. In 1764 he was expelled from Parliament for libel, failed to stand trial, and was outlawed. He was re-elected MP in 1768 and re-expelled from the House, being finally allowed back in 1774, when he also became Lord Mayor of London.

1 LORD SANDWICH. You will die either on the gallows, or of the pox.
WILKES. That must depend on whether I embrace your lordship's principles or your mistress.
Sometimes attrib. to Samuel Foote
*Portrait of a Patriot* (Charles Chenevix-Trench), Ch. 3

2 The chapter of accidents is the longest chapter in the book.
Attrib. in *The Doctor* (Southey), Vol. IV

**Wilkinson, Ellen Cicely** (1891–1947) British feminist and politician. She was active in the Labour movement and the suffragettes, becoming an MP in 1924 and minister of education in 1945.

1 I should like to help Britain to become a Third Programme country.
*The Observer*, 'Sayings of the Week', 2 Feb 1947

**William (I) the Conqueror** (1027–87) King of England (1066–87). As Duke of Normandy, he successfully invaded England, killing Harold II at the battle of Hastings, to become the first Norman King.

1 By the splendour of God I have taken possession of my realm; the earth of England is in my two hands.
Said after falling over when coming ashore at Pevensey with his army of invasion
Attrib.

**William III** (1650–1702) King of Great Britain (1689–1702) as joint sovereign with his wife, Mary II. Known as William of Orange, he defeated James II, the former king, at the battle of the Boyne (1690).

1 There is one certain means by which I can be sure never to see my country's ruin; I will die in the last ditch.
*History of England* (Hume)

2 Every bullet has its billet.
*Journal* (John Wesley), 6 June 1765

**William of Wykeham** (1324–1404) English churchman. Appointed Bishop of Winchester in 1366, he became Lord Chancellor (1367–71; 1389–91). Between his two chancellorships he founded New College, Oxford (1379), and Winchester College (1382).

1 Manners maketh man.
Motto of Winchester College and New College, Oxford

**Williams, Harry** (1874–1924) British songwriter.

1 Good-bye Piccadilly, Farewell Leicester Square; It's a long, long way to Tipperary, but my heart's right there!
Written with Jack Judge (1878–1938)
*It's a Long Way to Tipperary*

**Williams, Kenneth** (1926– ) British comic actor who has appeared in films (notably the 'Carry On' series), on stage and TV, and in radio programmes.

1 The nicest thing about quotes is that they give us a nodding acquaintance with the originator which is often socially impressive.
*Acid Drops*

**Williams, Raymond Henry** (1921– ) British academic and writer. His books include *Culture and Society* (1958), *The Country and the City* (1973), and *Writing in Society* (1983).

1 A very large part of English middle-class education is devoted to the training of servants... In so far as it is, by definition, the training of upper servants, it includes, of course, the instilling of that kind of confidence which will enable the upper servants to supervise and direct the lower servants.
*Culture and Society*, Ch. 3

**Williams, Tennessee** (1911–83) US dramatist. He established his reputation with *The Glass Menagerie* (1945). Subsequent successes include *A Streetcar Named Desire* (1947) and *Cat on a Hot Tin Roof* (1955).

1 My suit is pale yellow. My nationality is French, and my normality has been often subject to question.
*Camino Real*, Block 4

2 You can be young without money but you can't be old without it.
*Cat on a Hot Tin Roof*, I

3 That Europe's nothin' on earth but a great big auction, that's all it is.
*Cat on a Hot Tin Roof*, I

4 I can't stand a naked light bulb, any more than I can a rude remark or a vulgar action.
*A Streetcar Named Desire*, II:3

5 I have always depended on the kindness of strangers.
*A Streetcar Named Desire*, II:3

6 If people behaved in the way nations do they would all be put in straitjackets.
BBC interview

7 He was meddling too much in my private life.
Explaining why he had given up visiting his psychoanalyst
Attrib.

**Williams, William Carlos** (1883–1963) US poet. His collections include *Collected Poems* (1934) and *Pictures from Brueghel* (1963). *Paterson* (1946–58) used various experimental techniques.

1 Minds like beds always made up,
(more stony than a shore)
unwilling or unable.
*Paterson*, I, Preface

**Wilkie, Wendell Lewis** (1892–1944) US lawyer and businessman. He became Republican nominee for the president of the USA (1940). He wrote an autobiographical book *One World* (1943).

1 The constitution does not provide for first and second class citizens.
*An American Programme*, Ch. 2

2 There exists in the world today a gigantic reservoir of good will toward us, the American people.
*One World*, Ch. 10

3 Freedom is an indivisible word. If we want to enjoy it, and fight for it, we must be prepared to extend it to everyone, whether they are rich or poor, whether they agree with us or not, no matter what their race or the colour of their skin.
*One World*, Ch. 13

**Wilson, Sir Angus** (1913– ) British novelist. His books include *Hemlock and After* (1952), *Anglo-Saxon Attitudes* (1956), and *Setting the World on Fire* (1980).

1 She was more than ever proud of the position of the bungalow, so almost in the country.
*A Bit Off the Map*, 'A Flat Country Christmas'

2 I have no concern for the common man except that he should not be so common.
*No Laughing Matter*

3 'God knows how you Protestants can be expected to have any sense of direction,' she said. 'It's different with us. I haven't been to mass for years, I've got every mortal sin on my conscience, but I know when I'm doing wrong. I'm still a Catholic.'
*The Wrong Set*, 'Significant Experience'

**Wilson, Charles Erwin** (1890–1961) US engineer. He was president of General Motors (1941) and became secretary of defense (1953–57).

1 For many years I thought what was good for our country was good for General Motors, and vice versa.
Said in testimony to the Senate Armed Services Committee, Jan 1953
Attrib.

**Wilson, Edmund** (1895–1972) US critic and writer. His books include *Axel's Castle* (1931), *The Wound and the Bow* (1941), and *The Scrolls from the Dead Sea* (1955).

1 Of all the great Victorian writers, he was probably the most antagonistic to the Victorian age itself.
Referring to Dickens
*The Wound and the Bow*, 'The Two Scrooges'

**Wilson of Rievaulx, Harold, Baron** (1916– ) British Labour statesman. He became prime minister (1964–70; 1974–76), after succeeding Gaitskell as leader of the Labour Party in 1963.

1 Hence the practised performances of latter-day politicians in the game of musical daggers: never be left holding the dagger when the music stops.
*The Governance of Britain*, Ch. 2

2 If I had the choice between smoked salmon and tinned salmon, I'd have it tinned. With vinegar.
*The Observer*, 'Sayings of the Week,' 11 Nov 1962

3 Everybody should have an equal chance – but they shouldn't have a flying start.
*The Observer*, 'Sayings of the Year', 1963

4 One man's wage rise is another man's price increase.
*The Observer*, 'Sayings of the Week', 11 Jan 1970

5 The monarchy is a labour-intensive industry.
*The Observer*, 'Sayings of the Week', 13 Feb 1977

6 All these financiers, all the little gnomes of Zürich and the other financial centres, about whom we keep on hearing.
Speech, House of Commons, 12 Nov 1956

7 There is something utterly nauseating about a system of society which pays a harlot 25 times as much as it pays its Prime Minister, 250 times as much as it pays its Members of Parliament, and 500 times as much as it pays some of its ministers of religion.
Referring to the case of Christine Keeler
Speech, House of Commons, June 1963

8 We are redefining and we are restating our socialism in terms of the scientific revolution . . . the Britain that is going to be forged in the white heat of this revolution will be no place for restrictive practices or out-dated methods on either side of industry.
Speech, Labour Party Conference, 1 Oct 1963

9 After half a century of democratic advance, the whole process has ground to a halt with a 14th Earl.
Speech, Manchester, 19 Oct 1963

10 From now, the pound is worth 14 per cent or so less in terms of other currencies. It does not mean, of course, that the pound here in Britain, in your pocket or purse or in your bank, has been devalued.
Speech after devaluation of the pound, 20 Nov 1967

11 A week is a long time in politics.
First said in 1965 or 1966, and repeated on several occasions
Attrib.

12 I believe the greatest asset a head of state can have is the ability to get a good night's sleep.
*The World Tonight*, BBC Radio, 16 Apr 1975

**Wilson, Harriette** (1789–1846) British writer and courtesan, whose *Memoirs* were widely read.

1 I shall not say why and how I became, at the age of fifteen, the mistress of the Earl of Craven.
*Memoirs*, Opening

**Wilson, (Thomas) Woodrow** (1856–1925) US statesman. He became Democratic president in 1913 and declared war on Germany in 1917. He negotiated the peace treaty in 1918, making the League of Nations a part of the treaty. For this measure he received no support in the Senate.

1 Never murder a man who is committing suicide.
*Mr Wilson's War* (John Dos Passos), Pt. II, Ch. 10

2 Once lead this people into war and they'll forget there ever was such a thing as tolerance.
*Mr Wilson's War* (John Dos Passos), Pt. III, Ch. 2

3 America . . . is the prize amateur nation of the world. Germany is the prize professional nation.
Speech, Aug 1917
*Mr Wilson's War* (John Dos Passos), Pt. III, Ch. 13

4 The war we have just been through, though it was shot through with terror, is not to be compared with the war we would have to face next time.
*Mr Wilson's War* (John Dos Passos), Pt. V, Ch. 22

5 Right is more precious than peace.
*Radio Times*, 10 Sept 1964

6 Business underlies everything in our national life, including our spiritual life. Witness the fact that in the Lord's Prayer the first petition is for daily bread. No one can worship God or love his neighbour on an empty stomach.
Speech, New York, 1912

7 No nation is fit to sit in judgement upon any other nation.
Address, Apr 1915

8 There is such a thing as a man being too proud to fight.
Address to foreign-born citizens, 10 May 1915

9 The world must be made safe for democracy.
Address to Congress, asking for a declaration of war, 2 Apr 1917

10 Sometimes people call me an idealist. Well, that is the way I know I am an American. America is the only idealistic nation in the world.
Speech, Sioux Falls, 8 Sept 1919

**Wimperis, Arthur** (1874–1953) British screenwriter and songwriter.

1 My dear fellow a unique evening! I wouldn't have left a turn unstoned.
Replying when asked his opinion of a vaudeville show
*Fifty Years of Vaudeville* (E. Short)

**Winchell, Walter** (1879–1972) US journalist and broadcaster, pioneer of modern gossip-writing.

1 I saw it at a disadvantage – the curtain was up.
Referring to a show starring Earl Carroll
*Come to Judgment* (A. Whiteman)

**Windsor, Duchess of** (Wallis Warfield Simpson; 1896–1986) The wife of the Duke of Windsor (formerly Edward VIII) who abdicated in order to marry her.

1 I don't remember any love affairs. One must keep love affairs quiet.
*Los Angeles Times*, 11 Apr 1974

2 One can never be too thin or too rich.
Attrib.

**Wittgenstein, Ludwig** (1889–1951) Austrian philosopher, who studied with Bertrand Russell and G. E. Moore at Cambridge. His major works are *Tractatus Logico-Philosophicus* (1921) and *Philosophical Investigations* (1953).

1 Philosophy, as we use the word, is a fight against the fascination which forms of expression exert upon us.
*The Blue Book*

2 In order to draw a limit to thinking, we should have to be able to think both sides of this limit.
*Tractatus Logico-Philosophicus*, Preface

3 The world is everything that is the case.
*Tractatus Logico-Philosophicus*, Ch. 1

4 Philosophy is not a theory but an activity.
*Tractatus Logico-Philosophicus*, Ch. 4

5 Logic must take care of itself.
*Tractatus Logico-Philosophicus*, Ch. 5

6 Whereof one cannot speak, thereon one must remain silent.
*Tractatus Logico-Philosophicus*, Ch. 7

7 If there were a verb meaning 'to believe falsely', it would not have any significant first person, present indicative.
*A Certain World* (W. H. Auden)

**Wodehouse, Sir P(elham) G(renville)** (1881–1975) British humorous novelist. His books feature the 1920s upper-class bachelor Bertie Wooster and his immaculate manservant Jeeves. He lived abroad, becoming a US citizen in 1955.

1 All the unhappy marriages come from the husbands having brains. What good are brains to a man? They only unsettle him.
*The Adventures of Sally*

2 It is no use telling me that there are bad aunts and good aunts. At the core they are all alike. Sooner or later, out pops the cloven hoof.
*The Code of the Woosters*

3 He spoke with a certain what-is-it in his voice, and I could see that, if not actually disgruntled, he was far from being gruntled.
*The Code of the Woosters*

4 Big chap with a small moustache and the sort of eye that can open an oyster at sixty paces.
*The Code of the Woosters*

5 Jeeves coughed one soft, low, gentle cough like a sheep with a blade of grass stuck in its throat.
*The Inimitable Jeeves*, Ch. 13

6 It was my Uncle George who discovered that alcohol was a food well in advance of modern medical thought.
*The Inimitable Jeeves*, Ch. 16

7 It is a good rule in life never to apologize. The right sort of people do not want apologies, and the wrong sort take a mean advantage of them.
*The Man Upstairs*

**8** New York is a small place when it comes to the part of it that wakes up just as the rest is going to bed.

*My Man Jeeves,* 'The Aunt and the Sluggard'

**9** His ideas of first-aid stopped short at squirting soda-water.

*My Man Jeeves,* 'Doing Clarence a Bit of Good'

**10** I don't owe a penny to a single soul – not counting tradesmen, of course.

*My Man Jeeves,* 'Jeeves and the Hard-Boiled Egg'

**11** She fitted into my biggest armchair as if it had been built round her by someone who knew they were wearing armchairs tight about the hips that season.

*My Man Jeeves,* 'Jeeves and the Unbidden Guest'

**12** I spent the afternoon musing on Life. If you come to think of it, what a queer thing Life is! So unlike anything else, don't you know, if you see what I mean.

*My Man Jeeves,* 'Rallying Round Old George'

**13** If I had had to choose between him and a cockroach as a companion for a walking-tour, the cockroach would have had it by a short head.

*My Man Jeeves,* 'The Spot of Art'

**14** There is only one cure for grey hair. It was invented by a Frenchman. It is called the guillotine.

*The Old Reliable*

**15** I can honestly say that I always look on Pauline as one of the nicest girls I was ever engaged to.

*Thank You Jeeves,* Ch. 6

**16** The Right Hon. was a tubby little chap who looked as if he had been poured into his clothes and had forgotten to say 'When!'

*Very Good Jeeves!,* 'Jeeves and the Impending Doom'

**17** The stationmaster's whiskers are of a Victorian bushiness and give the impression of having been grown under glass.

*Wodehouse at Work to the End* (Richard Usborne), Ch. 2

**18** Like so many substantial Americans, he had married young and kept on marrying, springing from blonde to blonde like the chamois of the Alps leaping from crag to crag.

*Wodehouse at Work to the End* (Richard Usborne), Ch. 2

**19** Unlike the male codfish which, suddenly finding itself the parent of three million five hundred thousand little codfish, cheerfully resolves to love them all, the British aristocracy is apt to look with a somewhat jaundiced eye on its younger sons.

*Wodehouse at Work to the End* (Richard Usborne), Ch. 5

**20** He was either a man of about a hundred and fifty who was rather young for his years or a man of about a hundred and ten who had been aged by trouble.

*Wodehouse at Work to the End* (Richard Usborne), Ch. 6

**21** It is never difficult to distinguish between a Scotsman with a grievance and a ray of sunshine.

*Wodehouse at Work to the End* (Richard Usborne), Ch. 8

**Wolfe, Charles** (1791–1823) Irish poet and churchman. He is remembered for his poem *The Burial of Sir John Moore at Corunna.*

**1** Not a drum was heard, not a funeral note,
As his corse to the rampart we hurried.

*The Burial of Sir John Moore at Corunna,* I

**2** We carved not a line, and we raised not a stone –
But we left him alone with his glory.

*The Burial of Sir John Moore at Corunna,* VIII

**Wolfe, Humbert** (1886–1940) British poet. His collections include *Lampoons* (1925), *News of the Devil* (1926), and *The Blind Rose* (1928).

**1** You cannot hope
to bribe or twist,
thank God! the
British journalist.

But, seeing what
the man will do
unbribed, there's
no occasion to.

*The Uncelestial City,* Bk. I, 'Over the Fire'

**Wolfe, James** (1727–59) British general. He fought at Dettingen and Culloden Moor; in Canada, under Amherst, he played a significant part in the capture of Louisburg from the French. In 1759 he commanded at the siege of Quebec, his forces scaling the Heights of Abraham and routing the French, completing their conquest in North America. He died in the battle.

**1** I would rather have written those lines than take Quebec.

Referring to Gray's Elegy, on the eve of the Battle of Quebec, 1759
Attrib.

**2** Now God be praised, I will die in peace.

His last words, after being mortally wounded at the Battle of Quebec, 1759
*Historical Journal of Campaigns, 1757–60* (J. Knox), Vol. II

**Wolfe, Thomas** (1900–38) US novelist. His best-known book is *Look Homeward, Angel* (1929), one of four autobiographical novels.

**1** Most of the time we think we're sick, it's all in the mind.

*Look Homeward, Angel,* Pt. I, Ch. 1

**Wolff, Charlotte** (1904– ) German-born British psychiatrist and writer. Her books include *On the Way to Myself* (1969).

**1** Women have always been the guardians of wisdom and humanity which makes them natural, but usually secret, rulers. The time has come for them to rule openly, but together with and not against men.

*Bisexuality: A Study,* Ch. 2

**Wollstonecraft, Mary** (1759–97) British writer and feminist. She is remembered for *A Vindication of the Rights of Women* (1792). The wife of William Goodwin, the social philosopher, she died giving birth to her daughter Mary, who married the poet Shelley.

1 The *divine right* of husbands, like the divine right of kings, may, it is hoped, in this enlightened age, be contested without danger.

> *A Vindication of the Rights of Woman*, Ch. 3

2 I do not wish them to have power over men; but over themselves.

> Referring to women
> *A Vindication of the Rights of Woman*, Ch. 4

**Wolsey, Thomas** (1475–1530) English churchman and statesman. Henry VIII made him Bishop of Lincoln (1514), Archbishop of York and a cardinal (1515), and Lord Chancellor (1515–29). After failing to obtain the pope's agreement to Henry's divorce from Catharine of Aragon, he fell from power and died before his trial came to court.

1 Had I but served God as diligently as I have served the king, he would not have given me over in my gray hairs.

> Remark to Sir William Kingston
> *Negotiations of Thomas Wolsey* (Cavendish)

**Wood, Mrs Henry** (1814–87) British novelist, best remembered for her novel *East Lynne* (1861).

1 Dead! and . . . never called me mother.

> *East Lynne* (dramatized version; the words do not occur in the novel)

**Woodroofe, Thomas** (1899–1978) British radio broadcaster. A naval lieutenant-commander, he broadcast on behalf of the Admiralty during World War II.

1 The Fleet's lit up. It is like fairyland; the ships are covered with fairy lights.

> Said during commentary at the Coronation Review of the Royal Navy, May 1937

**Woolf, Virginia** (1882–1941) British novelist and writer, a member of the Bloomsbury Group, with her husband Leonard Woolf, the writer and publisher. She suffered from clinical depression and eventually drowned herself. Her novels include *Mrs Dalloway* (1925), *To the Lighthouse* (1927), *Orlando* (1928), and *The Waves* (1931).

1 The poet gives us his essence, but prose takes the mould of the body and mind entire.

> *The Captain's Death Bed*, 'Reading'

2 *Middlemarch*, the magnificent book which with all its imperfections is one of the few English novels for grown up people.

> *The Common Reader*, 'George Eliot'

3 Trivial personalities decomposing in the eternity of print.

> *The Common Reader*, 'Jane Eyre'

4 Those comfortably padded lunatic asylums which are known, euphemistically, as the stately homes of England.

> *The Common Reader*, 'Lady Dorothy Nevill'

5 Fraser . . . left his children unbaptized – his wife did it secretly in the washing basin.

> *Jacob's Room*, Ch. 9

6 There is in the British Museum an enormous mind. Consider that Plato is there cheek by jowl with Aristotle; and Shakespeare with Marlowe. This great mind is hoarded beyond the power of any single mind to possess it.

> *Jacob's Room*, Ch. 9

7 If you do not tell the truth about yourself you cannot tell it about other people.

> *The Moment and Other Essays*

8 The older one grows the more one likes indecency.

> *Monday or Tuesday*

9 Women have served all these centuries as look-ing-glasses possessing the magic and delicious power of reflecting the figure of man at twice its natural size.

> *A Room of One's Own*

10 Why are women . . . so much more interesting to men than men are to women?

> *A Room of One's Own*

11 I would venture to guess that Anon, who wrote so many poems without signing them, was of-ten a woman.

> *A Room of One's Own*

12 Literature is strewn with the wreckage of men who have minded beyond reason the opinions of others.

> *A Room of One's Own*, Ch. 3

**Woollcott, Alexander** (1887–1943) US journalist and writer. The drama critic of the *New York Times* (1914–22), he also wrote *Shouts and Murmurs* (1923), *Going to Pieces* (1928), and *While Rome Burns* (1934).

1 Subjunctive to the last, he preferred to ask, 'And that, sir, would be the Hippodrome?'

> *While Rome Burns*, 'Our Mrs Parker'

2 I must get out of these wet clothes and into a dry Martini.

> *Reader's Digest*

3 Just what God would have done if he had the money.

> On being shown round Moss Hart's elegant country house and grounds
> Attrib.

4 All the things I really like to do are either im-moral, illegal, or fattening.

> Attrib.

**Wordsworth, Dorothy** (1771–1855) British diarist and sister of William Wordsworth, with whom she lived in the Lake District. Her *Journals* have been widely read.

1 But as we went along there were more and yet more and at last under the boughs of the trees, we saw that there was a long belt of them along the shore, about the breadth of a country turnpike road. I never saw daffodils so beautiful they grew among the mossy stones about and about them, some rested their heads upon these stones as on pillow for weariness and the rest tossed and reeled and danced and seemed as if they verily laughed with the wind that blew upon them over the lake.

*The Grasmere Journals*, 15 Apr 1802

**Wordsworth, Mary** (1770–1850) Wife of William Wordsworth.

1 Mr Wordsworth is never interrupted.

Rebuking John Keats for interrupting a long monologue by William Wordsworth
Attrib.

**Wordsworth, William** (1770–1850) British poet. His reputation was based on his *Lyrical Ballads* (1798), written with Samuel Taylor Coleridge. After settling in the Lake District with his wife and sister he produced *The Prelude*, a verse autobiography published posthumously, and much other verse.

1 Strongest minds
Are often those of whom the noisy world
Hears least.
*The Excursion*

2 The good die first,
And they whose hearts are dry as summer dust
Burn to the socket.
*The Excursion*

3 The wiser mind
Mourns less for what age takes away
Than what it leaves behind.
*The Fountain*

4 I travelled among unknown men
In lands beyond the sea;
Nor, England! did I know till then
What love I bore to thee.
*I Travelled among Unknown Men*

5 I wandered lonely as a cloud
That floats on high o'er vales and hills,
When all at once I saw a crowd,
A host, of golden daffodils.
*I Wandered Lonely as a Cloud*

6 For oft, when on my couch I lie
In vacant or in pensive mood,
They flash upon that inward eye
Which is the bliss of solitude.
*I Wandered Lonely as a Cloud*

7 That best portion of a good man's life,
His little, nameless, unremembered acts
Of kindness and of love.
*Lines composed a few miles above Tintern Abbey*

8 That blessed mood,
In which the burthen of the mystery,
In which the heavy and the weary weight
Of all this unintelligible world,
Is lightened.
*Lines composed a few miles above Tintern Abbey*

9 We are laid asleep
In body, and become a living soul:
While with an eye made quiet by the power
Of harmony, and the deep power of joy,
We see into the life of things.
*Lines composed a few miles above Tintern Abbey*

10 I have learned
To look on nature, not as in the hour
Of thoughtless youth; but hearing often-times
The still, sad music of humanity.
*Lines composed a few miles above Tintern Abbey*

11 Nature never did betray
The heart that loved her.
*Lines composed a few miles above Tintern Abbey*

12 Nor greetings where no kindness is, nor all
The dreary intercourse of daily life,
Shall e'er prevail against us, or disturb
Our cheerful faith, that all which we behold
Is full of blessings.
*Lines composed a few miles above Tintern Abbey*

13 A power is passing from the earth
To breathless Nature's dark abyss;
But when the great and good depart,
What is it more than this –

That Man who is from God sent forth,
Doth yet again to God return? –
Such ebb and flow must ever be,
Then wherefore should we mourn?
Referring to Charles James Fox, the hero of the liberal Whigs, who died in 1806
*Lines on the Expected Dissolution of Mr. Fox*

14 If this belief from heaven be sent,
If such be Nature's holy plan,
Have I not reason to lament
What man has made of man?
*Lines written in Early Spring*

15 The sweetest thing that ever grew
Beside a human door!
*Lucy Gray*

16 There neither is, nor can be, any *essential* difference between the language of prose and metrical composition.
*Lyrical Ballads*, Preface

17 Poetry is the spontaneous overflow of powerful feelings: it takes its origin from emotion recollected in tranquillity.
*Lyrics Ballads*, Preface

18 Every great and original writer, in proportion as he is great and original, must himself create the taste by which he is to be relished.
*Lyrical Ballads*, Preface

19 There is a comfort in the strength of love;
'Twill make a thing endurable, which else
Would overset the brain, or break the heart.

*Michael*, 448

20 Why art thou silent! Is thy love a plant
Of such weak fibre that the treacherous air
Of absence withers what was once so fair?

*Miscellaneous Sonnets*, III

21 My heart leaps up when I behold
A rainbow in the sky:
So was it when my life began;
So is it now I am a man;
So be it when I shall grow old,
Or let me die!
The Child is Father of the Man;
And I could wish my days to be
Bound each to each by natural piety.

*My Heart Leaps Up*

22 There was a time when meadow, grove, and
stream,
The earth, and every common sight,
To me did seem
Apparelled in celestial light,
The glory and the freshness of a dream.

*Ode. Intimations of Immortality*, I

23 Whither is fled the visionary gleam?
Where is it now, the glory and the dream?

Our birth is but a sleep and a forgetting:
The Soul that rises with us, our life's Star,
Hath had elsewhere its setting,
And cometh from afar;
Not in entire forgetfulness,
And not in utter nakedness,
But trailing clouds of glory do we come
From God, who is our home:
Heaven lies about us in our infancy!
Shades of the prison-house begin to close
Upon the growing boy.

*Ode. Intimations of Immortality*, IV

24 Earth fills her lap with pleasures of her own:
Yearnings she hath in her own natural kind.

*Ode. Intimations of Immortality*, VI

25 Provoke
The years to bring the inevitable yoke.

*Ode. Intimations of Immortality*, VIII

26 Hence in a season of calm weather
Though inland far we be,
Our souls have sight of that immortal sea
Which brought us hither . . .

*Ode. Intimations of Immortality*, IX

27 Though nothing can bring back the hour
Of splendour in the grass, of glory in the flower;
We will grieve not, rather find
Strength in what remains behind . . .

*Ode. Intimations of Immortality*, IX

28 Another race hath been, and other palms are
won.
Thanks to the human heart by which we live,
Thanks to its tenderness, its joys and fears,
To me the meanest flower that blows can give
Thoughts that do often lie too deep for tears.

*Ode. Intimations of Immortality*, IX

29 Those obstinate questionings
Of sense and outward things,
Fallings from us, vanishings;
Blank misgivings of a Creature
Moving about in worlds not realised,
High instincts before which our mortal nature
Did tremble like a guilty thing surprised.

*Ode. Intimations of Immortality*, IX

30 The clouds that gather round the setting sun
Do take a sober colouring from an eye
That hath kept watch o'er man's mortality.

*Ode. Intimations of Immortality*, XI

31 Me this unchartered freedom tires;
I feel the weight of chance-desires:
My hopes no more must change their name,
I long for a repose that ever is the same.

*Ode to Duty*

32 O Nightingale, thou surely art
A creature of a 'fiery heart'.

*O Nightingale*

33 Fair seed-time had my soul, and I grew up
Fostered alike by beauty and by fear.

*The Prelude*, I

34 Brothers all
In honour, as in one community,
Scholars and gentlemen.

*The Prelude*, IX

35 Bliss was it in that dawn to be alive,
But to be young was very heaven!

Referring to the French Revolution
*The Prelude*, XI

36 That which sets
. . . The budding rose above the rose full
blown.

Referring to the French Revolution
*The Prelude*, XI

37 Not in Utopia, – subterranean fields, –
Or some secreted island, Heaven knows where!
But in the very world, which is the world
Of all of us, – the place where, in the end,
We find our happiness, or not at all!

Referring to the French Revolution
*The Prelude*, XI

38 There is
One great society alone on earth:
The noble living and the noble dead.

*The Prelude*, XI

39 The pious bird with the scarlet breast,
Our little English robin.

*The Redbreast chasing the Butterfly*

40 Still glides the Stream, and shall for ever glide;
The Form remains, the Function never dies.

*The River Duddon, 'After-Thought'*

41 The good old rule
Sufficeth them, the simple plan,
That they should take, who have the power,
And they should keep who can.

*Rob Roy's Grave*

42 A youth to whom was given
So much of earth – so much of heaven,
And such impetuous blood.

*Ruth*

43 She dwelt among the untrodden ways
Beside the springs of Dove,
A maid whom there were none to praise
And very few to love . . .

*She Dwelt Among the Untrodden Ways*

44 A slumber did my spirit seal;
I had no human fears:
She seemed a thing that could not feel
The touch of earthly years.

No motion has she now, no force;
She neither hears nor sees;
Rolled round in earth's diurnal course,
With rocks, and stones, and trees.

*A Slumber did my Spirit seal*

45 Behold her, single in the field,
Yon solitary Highland lass!

*The Solitary Reaper*

46 Another year! – another deadly blow!
Another mighty empire overthrown!
And we are left, or shall be left, alone.

Napoleon defeated Prussia at the Battles of Jena and Anerstädt,
14 Oct 1806
*Sonnets, 'Another year!'*

47 Earth has not anything to show more fair:
Dull would he be of soul who could pass by
A sight so touching in its majesty:
The City now doth, like a garment, wear
The beauty of the morning; silent, bare,
Ships, towers, domes, theatres, and temples lie
Open unto the fields, and to the sky;
All bright and glittering in the smokeless air.

*Sonnets, 'Composed upon Westminster Bridge'*

48 Dear God! the very houses seem asleep;
And all that mighty heart is lying still!

*Sonnets, 'Composed upon Westminster Bridge'*

49 We must be free or die, who speak the tongue
That Shakspeare spake; the faith and morals
hold
Which Milton held.

*Sonnets, 'It is not to be thought of'*

50 Milton! thou shouldst be living at this hour:
England hath need of thee; she is a fen
Of stagnant waters: altar, sword, and pen,
Fireside, the heroic wealth of hall and bower,
Have forfeited their ancient English dower
Of inward happiness.

*Sonnets, 'Milton! thou shouldst'*

51 Thy soul was like a star, and dwelt apart.

*Sonnets, 'Milton! thou shouldst'*

52 Plain living and high thinking are no more.

*Sonnets, 'O friend! I know not'*

53 Once did she hold the gorgeous east in fee;
And was the safeguard of the west.

*Sonnets, 'Once did she hold'*

54 Venice, the eldest Child of Liberty.
She was a maiden City, bright and free.

Venice, a republic since the Middle Ages, was conquered by Napoleon in 1797 and absorbed into his Kingdom of Italy in 1805
*Sonnets, 'Once did she hold'*

55 When she took unto herself a mate,
She must espouse the everlasting sea.

*Sonnets, 'Once did she hold'*

56 Men are we, and must grieve when even the
shade
Of that which once was great is passed away.

*Sonnets, 'Once did she hold'*

57 Thou hast great allies;
Thy friends are exultations, agonies,
And love, and man's unconquerable mind.

*Sonnets, 'Toussaint, the most unhappy man'*

58 Two voices are there; one is of the sea,
One of the mountains; each a mighty voice:
In both from age to age thou didst rejoice,
They were thy chosen music, Liberty!

*Sonnets, 'Two voices are there'*

59 The world is too much with us; late and soon,
Getting and spending, we lay waste our powers:
Little we see in Nature that is ours.

*Sonnets, 'The world is too much with us'*

60 I'd rather be
A Pagan suckled in a creed outworn;
So might I, standing on this pleasant lea,
Have glimpses that would make me less forlorn;
Have sight of Proteus rising from the sea;
Or hear Old Triton blow his wreathed horn.

*Sonnets, 'The world is too much with us'*

61 Strange fits of passion have I known:
And I will dare to tell,
But in the lover's ear alone,
What once to me befell.

*Strange Fits of Passion*

62 Come forth into the light of things,
Let Nature be your Teacher.

*The Tables Turned*

63 One impulse from a vernal wood
May teach you more of man,
Of moral evil and of good,
Than all the sages can.
*The Tables Turned*

64 Three years she grew in sun and shower,
Then Nature said, 'A lovelier flower
On earth was never sown;
This child I to myself will take;
She shall be mine, and I will make
A Lady of my own.'
*Three Years she Grew*

65 'Tis said that some have died for love.
*'Tis Said that some have Died*

66 Sweet childish days, that were as long
As twenty days are now.
*To a Butterfly, I've Watched you now*

67 Small service is true service, while it lasts.
*To a Child, Written in her Album*

68 Ethereal minstrel! pilgrim of the sky!
Dost thou despise the earth where cares
abound?
*To a Skylark*

69 Thrice welcome, darling of the spring!
Even yet thou art to me
No bird, but an invisible thing,
A voice, a mystery.
*To the Cuckoo*

70 Thou unassuming common-place
Of Nature.
*To the Daisy*

71 Pleasures newly found are sweet
When they lie about our feet.
*To the Small Celandine*

72 Like an army defeated
The snow hath retreated.
*Written in March*

**Work, Henry Clay** (1832–84) US songwriter. His most popular songs were 'Come Home, Father' and 'Marching Through Georgia'.

1 Father, dear father, come home with me now,
The clock in the steeple strikes one.
A temperance song
*Come Home, Father*

2 My grandfather's clock was too large for the shelf.
So it stood ninety years on the floor.
*Grandfather's Clock*

3 But it stopped short – never to go again –
When the old man died.
*Grandfather's Clock*

4 'Hurrah! hurrah! we bring the Jubilee!
Hurrah! hurrah! the flag that makes you free!'
So we sang the chorus from Atlanta to the sea
As we were marching through Georgia.
Commemorating the march (Nov–Dec 1864) by a Union army under General Sherman through Confederate Georgia
*Marching Through Georgia*

**Wotton, Sir Henry** (1568–1639) English poet and diplomat. James I's ambassador to Venice, his poems include *On his Mistress, the Queen of Bohemia.*

1 In *Architecture* as in all other *Operative* Arts, the *end* must direct the *Operation.* The *end* is to build well. Well building hath three Conditions. *Commodity, Firmness,* and *Delight.*
*Elements of Architecture,* Pt. I

2 The itch of disputing will prove the scab of churches.
*A Panegyric to King Charles*

3 An ambassador is an honest man sent to lie abroad for the good of his country.
*Life* (Izaak Walton)

4 Take heed of thinking. *The farther you go from the church of Rome, the nearer you are to God.*
*Reliquiae Wottonianae* (Izaak Walton)

**Wren, Sir Christopher** (1632–1723) English architect. Professor of astronomy at London and Oxford, he later abandoned astronomy for architecture. His plan for rebuilding London after the Great Fire (1667) was rejected but he built 51 churches, 36 company halls, and St Paul's Cathedral. Later buildings include Greenwich Hospital (1694) and some additions to Hampton Court.

1 *Si monumentum requiris, circumspice.*
If you seek my monument, look around you.
Inscription in St Paul's Cathedral, London

**Wright, Frank Lloyd** (1869–1959) US architect. One of the most individual architects of the modern movement, he designed the Guggenheim Museum in New York.

1 The physician can bury his mistakes, but the architect can only advise his client to plant vines.
*New York Times Magazine,* 4 Oct 1953

2 Give me the luxuries of life and I will willingly do without the necessities.
Attrib.

**Wright, Orville** (1871–1948) US aviator. With his brother, Wilbur (1867–1912), he made the first powered flight in 1903, in North Carolina.

1 The airplane stays up because it doesn't have the time to fall.
Explaining the principles of powered flight
Attrib.

**Wycherley, William** (1640–1716) English dramatist. His Restoration comedies include *The Country Wife* (1675) and *The Plain Dealer* (1676).

1 A mistress should be like a little country retreat near the town, not to dwell in constantly, but only for a night and away.
*The Country Wife,* I:1

**2** Well, a widow, I see, is a kind of sinecure.

*The Plain Dealer*, V:3

**Wycliffe, John** (1329–84) English religious reformer. As an Oxford student and, later, lecturer in philosophy, he supervised the first English translation of the Bible; his followers, the Lollards, were early protestants.

**1** I believe that in the end the truth will conquer.

Said to John of Gaunt, duke of Lancaster, 1381
*Short History of the English People* (J. R. Green)

**Wynne-Tyson, Esme** (1898– ) British writer. Her works include plays, novels, and some nonfiction.

**1** Scheherazade is the classical example of a woman saving her head by using it.

*See* ARABIAN NIGHTS
Attrib.

**Wynne-Tyson, Jon** (1924– ) British humorous writer, son of Esme Wynne-Tyson.

**1** The wrong sort of people are always in power because they would not be in power if they were not the wrong sort of people.

*The Times Literary Supplement*

# XYZ

**X, Malcolm** (1925–65) US Black leader. An advocate of violent means of achieving racial equality, he was assassinated while addressing a rally of the Organization of Afro-American Unity, which he founded in 1964.

**1** It's just like when you've got some coffee that's too black, which means it's too strong. What do you do? You integrate it with cream, you make it weak . . . It used to wake you up, now it puts you to sleep.

Referring to Black Power and the Civil Rights movement
*Malcolm X Speaks*, Ch. 14

**Xenophanes** (c. 560 BC–c. 478 BC) Greek poet and philosopher; fragments of his writings, elegies, and a poem on nature survive.

**1** The Ethiopians say that their gods are snub-nosed and black, the Thracians that theirs have light blue eyes and red hair.

*Fragment 15*

**Xenophon** (430–354 BC) Greek historian and soldier. His writings include *Memorabilia*, *Apology*, and *Symosium*, as well as his best-known work *Anabasis*.

**1** The sea! the sea!

*Anabasis*, IV:7

**Xerxes** (d. 465 BC) King of Persia (486–465). He invaded Greece in 480 but was forced to retreat after defeats at Salamis (480), Plataea (479), and Mycale (479); he was subsequently assassinated.

**1** I am moved to pity, when I think of the brevity of human life, seeing that of all this host of men not one will still be alive in a hundred years' time.

On surveying his army

**Yamamoto, Isoroku** (1884–1943) Japanese admiral. He became commander in chief of the combined fleet and was killed in action in the southwest Pacific.

**1** I fear we have only awakened a sleeping giant, and his reaction will be terrible.

Said after the Japanese attack on Pearl Harbor, 1941

**Yankwich, Léon R.** US lawyer and Californian judge.

**1** There are no illegitimate children – only illegitimate parents.

Decision, State District Court, Southern District of California, June 1928, quoting columnist O. O. McIntyre

**Ybarra, Thomas Russell** (1880– ) Venezuelan-born US writer. His books include *America Faces South* (1939) and the autobiographical *Young Man of Caracas* (1941).

**1** A Christian is a man who feels
Repentance on a Sunday
For what he did on Saturday
And is going to do on Monday.

*The Christian*

**Yeatman, Robert Julian** (1897–1968) British humorous writer. *See* Sellar, Walter Carruthers.

**Yeats, W(illiam) B(utler)** (1865–1939) Irish poet and dramatist. His verse collections include *The Tower* (1928) and *The Winding Stair* (1929). With Lady Gregory, he founded the Abbey Theatre in Dublin, for which he wrote many plays.

**1** That William Blake
Who beat upon the wall
Till Truth obeyed his call.

*An Acre of Grass*

**2** O chestnut tree, great rooted blossomer,
Are you the leaf, the blossom or the bole?
O body swayed to music; O brightening glance,
How can we know the dancer from the dance?

*Among School Children*

**3** When I think of all the books I have read, and of the wise words I have heard spoken, and of the anxiety I have given to parents and grandparents, and of the hopes that I have had, all life weighed in the scales of my own life seems to me preparation for something that never happens.

*Autobiography*

**4** Now that my ladder's gone
I must lie down where all the ladders start,
In the foul rag-and-bone shop of the heart.

*The Circus Animals' Desertion*

5　Though leaves are many, the root is one;
Through all the lying days of my youth
I swayed my leaves and flowers in the sun;
Now I may wither into the truth.
*The Coming of Wisdom with Time*

6　But Love has pitched his mansion in
The place of excrement.
*Crazy Jane Talks with the Bishop*

7　Wine comes in at the mouth
And love comes in at the eye;
That's all we shall know for truth
Before we grow old and die.
*A Drinking Song*

8　All changed, changed utterly:
A terrible beauty is born
*Easter 1916*

9　Out of the quarrel with others we make rhetoric;
out of the quarrel with ourselves we make
poetry.
*Essay*

10　When I play on my fiddle in Dooney,
Folk dance like a wave of the sea.
*The Fiddler of Dooney*

11　For the good are always the merry,
Save by an evil chance,
And the merry love the fiddle,
And the merry love to dance
*The Fiddler of Dooney*

12　One that is ever kind said yesterday:
'Your well-belovèd's hair has threads of grey,
And little shadows come about her eyes.'
*The Folly of Being Comforted*

13　I have drunk ale from the Country of the Young
And weep because I know all things now.
*He Thinks of his Past Greatness*

14　Nor law, nor duty bade me fight,
Nor public men, nor cheering crowds,
A lonely impulse of delight
Drove to this tumult in the clouds;
I balanced all, brought all to mind,
The years to come seemed waste of breath,
A waste of breath the years behind
In balance with this life, this death.
*An Irish Airman Foresees his Death*

15　I will arise and go now, and go to Innisfree,
And a small cabin build there, of clay and wattles
made;
Nine bean rows will I have there, a hive for the
honey bee,
And live alone in the bee-loud glade.
*The Lake Isle of Innisfree*

16　And I shall have some peace there, for peace
comes dropping slow,
Dropping from the veils of the morning to where
the cricket sings.
*The Lake Isle of Innisfree*

17　The wind blows out of the gates of the day,
The wind blows over the lonely of heart,
And the lonely of heart is withered away.
*The Land of Heart's Desire*

18　I shudder and I sigh to think
That even Cicero
And many-minded Homer were
*Mad as the mist and snow.*
*Mad as the Mist and Snow*

19　Time drops in decay,
Like a candle burnt out.
*The Moods*

20　Never to have lived is best, ancient writers say;
Never to have drawn the breath of life,
never to have looked into the eye of day
The second best's a gay goodnight and quickly
turn away.
*Oedipus at Colonus*

21　In dreams begins responsibility.
*Old Play, Epigraph, Responsibilities*

22　Where, where but here have Pride and Truth,
That long to give themselves for wage,
To shake their wicked sides at youth
Restraining reckless middle age?
*On hearing that the Students of our New University have joined*
*the Agitation against Immoral Literature*

23　A pity beyond all telling
Is hid in the heart of love.
*The Pity of Love*

24　An intellectual hatred is the worst.
*A Prayer for My Daughter*

25　That is no country for old men. The young
In one another's arms, birds in the trees
– Those dying generations – at their song,
The salmon-falls, the mackerel-crowded seas,
Fish, flesh, or fowl, commend all summer long
Whatever is begotten, born, and dies.
*Sailing to Byzantium, I*

26　Things fall apart; the centre cannot hold;
Mere anarchy is loosed upon the world,
The blood-dimmed tide is loosed, and
everywhere
The ceremony of innocence is drowned;
The best lack all conviction, while the worst
Are full of passionate intensity.
*The Second Coming*

27　A woman of so shining loveliness
That men threshed corn at midnight by a tress,
A little stolen tress.
*The Secret Rose*

28　And pluck till time and times are done
The silver apples of the moon
The golden apples of the sun.
*The Song of Wandering Aengus*

29　But was there ever dog that praised his fleas?
*To a Poet, who would have me Praise certain Bad Poets, Imitators*
*of His and Mine*

30  Under bare Ben Bulben's head
In Drumcliff churchyard Yeats is laid . . .
On limestone quarried near the spot
By his command these words are cut:
*Cast a cold eye*
*On life, on death.*
*Horseman, pass by!*
*Under Ben Bulben, VI*

31  When you are old and gray and full of sleep,
And nodding by the fire, take down this book,
And slowly read, and dream of the soft look
Your eyes had once, and of their shadows deep
. . .
*When you are Old*

32  Love fled
And paced upon the mountains overhead
And hid his face amid a crowd of stars.
*When you are Old*

33  But I, being poor, have only my dreams;
I have spread my dreams under your feet;
Tread softly because you tread on my dreams.
*He Wishes for the Cloths of Heaven*

34  It's not a writer's business to hold opinions.
Speaking to playwright, Denis Johnston
*The Guardian,* 5 May 1977

35  He is all blood, dirt and sucked sugar stick.
Referring to Wilfred Owen
*Letters on Poetry to Dorothy Wellesley,* Letter, 21 Dec 1936

36  O'CONNOR. How are you?
W.B.Y. Not very well, I can only write prose
today.
Attrib.

**Yellen, Jack** (1892– ) US lyricist and music publisher.

1  Happy Days Are Here Again.
Used by Roosevelt as a campaign song in 1932
Song title

**Yevtushenko, Yevgeny** (1933– ) Soviet poet. His poem
*Babi Yar* (1961) made him popular both inside the Soviet Union
and abroad.

1  No Jewish blood runs among my blood,
but I am as bitterly and hardly hated
by every anti-semite
as if I were a Jew. By this
I am a Russian.
*Babi Yar*

2  The hell with it. Who never knew the price of
happiness will not be happy.
*Lies*

**York and Albany, Frederick Augustus, Duke of**
(1763–1827) The second son of George III of England. He
commanded the expedition to the Netherlands against the French
(1793–95).

1  Then the little man wears a shocking bad hat.
Referring to Horace Walpole; *compare* Wellington on House of
Commons
Attrib.

**Young, Andrew John** (1885–1971) Scottish poet and
minister of the Free Church. His *Collected Poems* appeared in
1936. The *Complete Poems* were revised in 1974.

1  For still I looked on that same star,
That fitful, fiery Lucifer,
Watching with mind as quiet as moss
Its light nailed to a burning cross.
*The Evening Star*

2  Stars lay like yellow pollen
That from a flower has fallen;
And single stars I saw
Crossing themselves in awe;
Some stars in sudden fear
Fell like a falling tear.
*The Stars*

3  There is a happy land,
Far, far away,
Where saints in glory stand,
Bright, bright as day.
*There is a Happy Land*

**Young, Edward** (1683–1765) British poet. His verse
collection *Night Thoughts* (1742–45) gave rise to the 'graveyard
poets'. His plays include *Busiris* (1719), *Revenge* (1721), and *The
Brothers* (1726).

1  Some for renown, on scraps of learning dote,
And think they grow immortal as they quote.
*Love of Fame, I*

2  Be wise with speed,
A fool at forty is a fool indeed.
*Love of Fame, II*

3  All men think all men mortal, but themselves.
*Night Thoughts*

4  By night an atheist half believes a God.
*Night Thoughts*

5  Procrastination is the thief of time.
*Night Thoughts*

6  The bell strikes one. We take no note of time
But from its loss.
*Night Thoughts*

7  Time flies, death urges, knells call, heaven
invites,
Hell threatens.
*Night Thoughts*

8  Man wants but little, nor that little long.
*Night Thoughts*

**Young, G. W.** (19th century) British writer.

1  Though in silence, with blighted affection, I pine,
Yet the lips that touch liquor must never touch
mine!
*The Lips That Touch Liquor*

**Young, Michael** (1915– ) British political writer.

1  The Rise of the Meritocracy.
Book title

**Zamoyski, Jan** (1541–1605) Grand chancellor of Poland (1575–1605). He commanded the Polish army that succeeded in defending Poland against Turks, Cossacks, and Swedes.

**1** The king reigns, but does not govern.

Speech, Polish Parliament, 1605

**Zangwill, Israel** (1864–1926) British writer and dramatist. His early books, such as *Children of the Ghetto* (1892), established his reputation. Subsequent successes include *The Melting Pot* (1908), *The Next Religion* (1912), and *The Cockpit* (1921). His poetry includes *Blind Children* (1903).

**1** No Jew was ever fool enough to turn Christian unless he was a clever man.

*Children of the Ghetto*, Ch. 1

**2** America is God's Crucible, the great Melting-Pot where all the races of Europe are melting and re-forming!

*The Melting Pot*, I

**3** The law of dislike for the unlike will always prevail. And whereas the unlike is normally situated at a safe distance, the Jews bring the unlike into the heart of *every milieu*, and must there defend a frontier line as large as the world.

*Speeches, Articles and Letters*, 'The Jewish Race'

**Zanuck, Darryl F.** (1902–79) US film producer. He cofounded 20th-Century Productions, which merged with Fox in 1935 to form 20th-Century Fox, of which he became president in 1962.

**1** If two men on the same job agree all the time, then one is useless. If they disagree all the time, then both are useless.

*The Observer*, 'Sayings of the Week', 23 Oct 1949

**Zola, Émile** (1840–1902) French novelist. His first successful novel, *Thérèse Raquin* (1867), was followed by the 20-novel series *Les Rougon-Macquart* (1871–93). *Nana* (1880) and *Germinal* (1885) were later successes. His open letter *J'accuse* (1898), supporting Dreyfus, led to his exile in England followed by a hero's return after Dreyfus was cleared.

**1** Don't go on looking at me like that, because you'll wear your eyes out.

*La Bête Humaine*, Ch. 5

**2** *J'accuse.*
I accuse.

Title of an open letter to the French President, denouncing the French army's conduct in the Dreyfus affair
*L'Aurore*, 13 Jan 1898

**3** Truth is on the march; nothing can stop it now.

Referring to the Dreyfus scandal
Attrib.

# INDEX

**adjectives** be able to tell the substantives from the a.
MADARIAGA Y ROGO, S, 2
**Adler** A. will always be Jung WALL, M, 2
**Adlestrop** I remember A. THOMAS, E, 1
**admiral** good to kill an a. VOLTAIRE, 2
The A. of the Atlantic salutes the A. of the Pacific WILHELM II, 3
**admiration** Beauty stands /In the a. . . . of weak minds
MILTON, J, 49
**admire** a greater fool to a. him BOILEAU, N, 3
Not to a. POPE, A, 36
one cannot possibly a. them WILDE, O, 50
The English instinctively a. AGATE, J, 2
**admired** Few men have been a. by their servants MONTAIGNE, M, 8
**admiring** the cure for a. the House of Lords BAGEHOT, W, 2
**ado** much a. about.nothing TROLLOPE, A, 3
the heathen make much a. PSALMS, 31
**adolescence** a man suffering from petrified a. BEVAN, A, 3
maturity is only a short break in a. FEIFFER, J, 1
**Adonais** I weep for A. SHELLEY, P, 1
**adores** he a. his maker DISRAELI, 1ST EARL OF BEACONSFIELD, 15
The ignorant man always a. LOMBROSO, C, 1
**adorned** as a bride a. for her husband BIBLE: REVELATIONS, 18
**adornment** What time he can spare from the a. of his person
THOMPSON, W, 2
**adrenal** larger cerebrums and smaller a. glands MENCKEN, H, 5
**ads** He watched the a. /And not the road. NASH, O, 6
**adult** A child becomes an a. when SZASZ, T, 4
What is an a. BEAUVOIR, S, 1
**adultery** and gods a. BYRON, 6TH BARON, 16
commit a. at one end CARY, J, 1
rather be taken in a. than in provincialism HUXLEY, A, 5
the Tasmanians, who never committed a., are now extinct
MAUGHAM, W, 1
thou shalt not commit a. BIBLE: EXODUS, 20
would have constituted a.. BENCHLEY, R, 4
**advance** if civilisation is to a. . . . it must be through . . . women
PANKHURST, E, 1
**advantage** The a. of doing one's praising BUTLER, S, 26
you have the a. of me MARX, G, 16
**advantages** Wealth is not without its a. GALBRAITH, J, 1
**adventure** extravagance, . . . thrift and a. seldom go hand in hand.
CHURCHILL, J, 2
Marriage is the only a. open to the cowardly VOLTAIRE, 21
To die will be an awfully big a. BARRIE, SIR J, 5
**adventures** A good critic . . . narrates the a. of his mind
FRANCE, A, 7
**adversity** a. doth best discover virtue
BACON, 1ST BARON VERULAM, VISCOUNT ST ALBANS, 8
the bread of a. BIBLE: ISAIAH, 24
**advertised** Wealth . . . must be a. GALBRAITH, J, 2
**advertisement** the worst a. for Socialism is its adherents
ORWELL, G, 24
**advertisers** as the a. don't object to SWAFFER, H, 1
**advice** A. is seldom welcome CHESTERFIELD, 4TH EARL OF, 8
how ready people always are with a. SULLIVAN, A, 1
intended to give you some a. HARRIS, G, 1
nothing so freely as a. ROCHEFOUCAULD, DUC DE LA, 16
to hear . . . valuable or even earnest a. from my seniors
THOREAU, H, 8
woman seldom asks a. ADDISON, J, 14
**advocaat** a., a drink made from lawyers COREN, A, 4
**advocate** the soul of a martyr with the intellect of an a.
BAGEHOT, W, 10
**Aesculapius** we owe a cock to A. SOCRATES, 6
**Aesop** prettily devised of A.
BACON, 1ST BARON VERULAM, VISCOUNT ST ALBANS, 58
**aesthetic** the degree of my a. emotion BELL, C, 2
**afar** a. and asunder BOWEN, E, 1
**affair** The great a. is to move STEVENSON, R, 5
**affairs** tide in the a. of men SHAKESPEARE, W, 122
**affectation** Universities incline wits to sophistry and a.
BACON, 1ST BARON VERULAM, VISCOUNT ST ALBANS, 65
**affections** A different taste in jokes is a . . . strain on the a.
ELIOT, G, 4
**affliction** feed him with bread of a. BIBLE: 1 KINGS, 8
the water of a. BIBLE: ISAIAH, 24
**affluent** the a. society GALBRAITH, J, 4
**afford** purest treasure mortal times a. SHAKESPEARE, W, 234
**afraid** A. of Virginia Woolf ALBEE, E, 3
be not a. to do thine office MORE, SIR T, 4
Englishman . . . is a. to feel FORSTER, E, 2

Men not a. of God, a. of me POPE, A, 10
thou shalt not be a. for any terror by night PSALMS, 57
Whenever I look inside myself I am a. JOAD, C, 1
**Afric** Where A.'s sunny fountains HEBER, R, 1
**Africa** more familiar with A. than my own body ORTON, J, 1
something new out of A. PLINY THE ELDER, 3
**after-dinner** an a.'s sleep SHAKESPEARE, W, 183
**afterlife** that the a. will be any less exasperating than this one
COWARD, SIR N, 1
**afternoon** could lose the war in an a. CHURCHILL, SIR W, 28
I could have lost the war in an a. JELLICOE, EARL, 1
Summer a. – summer a. JAMES, H, 11
**against** A. whom ADLER, A, 2
He said he was a. it COOLIDGE, C, 3
If . . . you can't tell . . . who's for you and who's a. you
JOHNSON, L, 2
neither for nor a. institutions WHITMAN, W, 2
**Agamemnon** I have looked upon the face of A. SCHLIEMANN, H, 1
Many brave men . . . before A.'s time; . . . are all, unmourned and
unknown, . . . because they lack their sacred poet HORACE, 42
**age** A. cannot wither her SHAKESPEARE, W, 9
A child blown up by a. BEAUVOIR, S, 1
an a. in which useless knowledge was . . . important JOAD, C, 2
And now in a. I bud again HERBERT, G, 4
A. . . . nor custom stale her infinite virginity WEBSTER, D, 1
a. of chivalry is gone BURKE, E, 7
A. only matters when one is ageing PICASSO, P, 5
A. shall not weary them BINYON, L, 3
A tart temper never mellows with a. IRVING, W, 2
At twenty years of a. FRANKLIN, B, 6
A. will bring all things MOLIERE, 8
A. will not be defied
BACON, 1ST BARON VERULAM, VISCOUNT ST ALBANS, 42
a woman has the right to treat . . . her a. with ambiguity
RUBINSTEIN, H, 1
Cool'd a long a. in the deep-delved earth KEATS, J, 31
Crabbed a. and youth cannot live together SHAKESPEARE, W, 230
Damn the a. I'll write for antiquity LAMB, C, 19
Do you think at your a., it is right CARROLL, L, 3
Drives my green a. THOMAS, D, 4
gift of perpetual old a. WILDE, O, 66
He hath not forgotten my a. SOUTHEY, R, 5
I summon a. /To grant youth's heritage BROWNING, R, 47
It is . . . at my a. I now begin to see things as they really are
FONTENELLE, B, 1
lady of a certain a. BYRON, 6TH BARON, 29
Lo, Hudled up, together Lye /Gray A., Grene youth, White
Infancy ANONYMOUS, 54
no a. between ten and three and twenty SHAKESPEARE, W, 301
nothing in thy youth, how canst thou find any thing in thine a.
BIBLE: ECCLESIASTICUS, 10
not of an a., but for all time JONSON, B, 9
No woman should ever be quite accurate about her a. WILDE, O, 31
Old-a., a second child CHURCHILL, C, 4
Old a. . . . gives us what we have earned BRENAN, G, 3
Old a. is the most unexpected of all . . . things TROTSKY, L, 2
Our parents' a. . . . has produced us, more worthless still
HORACE, 37
Thou has nor youth nor a. SHAKESPEARE, W, 183
what a. takes away WORDSWORTH, W, 3
When men grow virtuous in their old a. POPE, A, 54
when Mozart was my a. LEHRER, T, 1
who tells one her feel a. WILDE, O, 56
Years hence, perhaps, may dawn an a. ARNOLD, M, 18
**aged** a. diplomats . . . bored than for young men to die
AUSTIN, W, 1
a man of about a hundred and ten who had been a.
WODEHOUSE, SIR P, 20
the beauty /Of an a. face CAMPBELL, J, 1
**ageing** Age only matters when one is a. PICASSO, P, 5
Like so many a. college people NABOKOV, V, 2
**agenda** Our a. is now exhausted. . . . we find ourselves in such
complete unanimity SPAAK, P, 1
the a. winks at me THOMAS, G, 2
**agent** prime a. of all human perception COLERIDGE, S, 3
**ages** His acts being seven a. SHAKESPEARE, W, 23
Our God, our help in a. past WATTS, I, 6
Rock of a., cleft for me TOPLADY, A, 1
**aggregate** the a. of the recipes that are always successful
VALERY, P, 2

my A.! my new-found-land     DONNE, J. 10
The business of A. is business     COOLIDGE, C. 1
the greatest that we owe to the discovery of A.     HELPS, SIR A. 2
the more absolute silence of A.     LAWRENCE, D. 22
The national dish of A.     ROBINSON, R. 1
Vietnam was lost in the living rooms of A.     MCLUHAN, M. 6
what makes A. what it is     STEIN, G. 2
when we think of thee, O A.     WALPOLE, 4TH EARL OF ORFORD, 7
Why will A. not reach out . . . to Russia     DUNCAN, I. 3
woman governs A.     MADARIAGA Y ROGO, S. 1
**American** A. heiress wants to buy a man     MCCARTHY, M. 3
An A. is either a Jew, or an anti-Semite     SARTRE, J. 2
A. system of rugged individualism     HOOVER, H. 1
capitalism . . . : the process whereby A. girls turn into A. women     HAMPTON, C. 3
I am willing to love all mankind, *except an A.*     JOHNSON, S. 120
If I were an A., as I am an Englishman     PITT THE ELDER, 1ST EARL OF CHATHAM, 6
It hasn't taken Winston long to get used to A. ways     ACHESON, D. 1
I was born an A.     WEBSTER, D. 4
Let's talk sense to the A. people     STEVENSON, A. 4
the A. abroad     STAPLEDON, O. 1
the feminization of the white European and A. is already far advanced     LEWIS, W. 3
the greatest A. friend we have ever known     CHURCHILL, SIR W. 18
We are all A. at puberty     WAUGH, E. 23
**Americanism** hyphenated A.     ROOSEVELT, T. 7
McCarthyism is A.     MCCARTHY, J. 1
There can be no fifty-fifty A.     ROOSEVELT, T. 8
**Americans** A. have been conditioned to respect newness     UPDIKE, J. 3
because A. won't listen to sense     KEYNES, BARON, 9
Good A., when they die, go to Paris     APPLETON, T. 1
the matter with A.     CHESTERTON, G. 39
when good A. die they go to Paris     WILDE, O. 54
**amiable** how a. are thy dwellings     PSALMS, 50
It destroys one's nerves to be a. every day     DISRAELI, 1ST EARL OF BEACONSFIELD, 12
**amis** *Changez vos a.*     DE GAULLE, C. 6
**amiss** to mark what is done a.     PSALMS, 82
**ammunition** Praise the Lord and pass the a.     FORGY, H. 1
**amor** *A. vincit insomnia*     FRY, C. 5
**amorous** the silk stockings and white bosoms of your actresses excite my a. propensities     JOHNSON, S. 43
**amplified** I'm being a. by the mike.     CHESTERTON, G. 42
**amputate** Thank God they had to a.     SASSOON, S. 7
**am'rous** dire offence from a. causes springs     POPE, A. 46
**amused** how to be a. rather than shocked     BUCK, P. 3
I was *very* much a.     VICTORIA, 1
one has to be very old before one learns how to be a.     BUCK, P. 3
We are not a.     VICTORIA, 8
**amusing** Any a. deaths     BOWRA, SIR M. 2
**analogy** Though a. is often misleading     BUTLER, S. 17
**analysis** the profession of historian fits a man for psychological a.     SARTRE, J. 8
**anarchy** a well-bred sort of emotional a.     LAWRENCE, D. 14
**anathema** A. Maranatha     BIBLE: I CORINTHIANS, 24
**ancestor** I am my own a.     JUNOT, DUC D'ABRANTES, 1
**ancestors** a. on either side of the Battle of Hastings     LEE, H. 1
when his half-civilized a. were hunting the wild boar     BENJAMIN, J. 1
**ancestry** I can trace my a. back to a . . . globule     GILBERT, SIR W. 24
**ancient** an a. Mariner     COLERIDGE, S. 22
with the a. is wisdom     BIBLE: JOB, 7
**anecdotage** man fell into his a.     DISRAELI, 1ST EARL OF BEACONSFIELD, 6
**angel** An a. writing in a book of gold:     HUNT, L. 1
A. of Death has been abroad     BRIGHT, J. 1
A. of the Lord came down     TATE, N. 3
gave you manna . . . a.s' bread     BIBLE: II ESDRAS, 1
in action, how like an a.     SHAKESPEARE, W. 57
in comparison with which . . . I am a A.     DICKENS, C. 17
In heaven an a. is nobody in particular     SHAW, G. 23
Is man an ape or an a.     DISRAELI, 1ST EARL OF BEACONSFIELD, 25
This was the A. of History     GOEBBELS, J. 2
woman yet think him an a.     THACKERAY, W. 4
You may not be an a.     DUBIN, A. 2
**angels** A. can fly     CHESTERTON, G. 31
fools rush in where a. fear to tread     POPE, A. 27
I . . . am on the side of the a.     DISRAELI, 1ST EARL OF BEACONSFIELD, 25
Its visits, /Like those of a.     BLAIR, R. 2

man did eat a. food     PSALMS, 47
Not Angles, but a.     GREGORY I. 1
One more devils'-triumph and sorrow for a.     BROWNING, R. 30
People are not fallen a.     LAWRENCE, D. 40
Tears such as a. weep     MILTON, J. 31
the tongues of men and of a.     BIBLE: I CORINTHIANS, 18
thou madest him lower than the a.     PSALMS, 3
**anger** A. is one of the sinews of the soul     FULLER, T. 5
a. makes us all stupid     SPYRI, J. 2
A. supplies the arms     VIRGIL, 1
fierce /Juno's never-forgetting a.     VIRGIL, 2
Grief and disappointment give rise to a.     HUME, D. 7
he that is slow to a. is better than the mighty     BIBLE: PROVERBS, 9
it is . . . but angels     GREGORY I. 1
**angling** A. is somewhat like poetry     WALTON, I. 2
A. may be said to be . . . like the mathematics     WALTON, I. 1
Let the blessing . . . be . . . upon all that are lovers of virtue; . . . and go a-A.     WALTON, I. 4
We may say of a. as Dr Boteler said of strawberries     WALTON, I. 4
**Anglo-Catholic** Becoming an A. must . . . be a sad business     STRACHEY, J. 1
**Anglo-Saxon** Come in, you A. swine /And drink of my Algerian wine     BEHAN, B. 9
those are A. attitudes     CARROLL, L. 30
**angry** A. Young Man     PAUL, L. 1
The man who gets a. . . . in the right way . . . is commended     ARISTOTLE, 2
**anguish** drinking deep of that divinest a.     BRONTE, E. 4
**angular** an oblong a. figure     LEACOCK, S. 6
**animal** Are you a. – or vegetable – or mineral     CARROLL, L. 32
information vegetable, a. and mineral     GILBERT, SIR W. 37
Man is a gaming a.     LAMB, C. 5
man is and will always be a wild a.     DARWIN, C. 1
Man is an intellectual a.     HAZLITT, W. 3
Man is a noble a.     BROWNE, SIR T. 12
man is . . . a religious a.     BURKE, E. 9
Man is a social a.     SPINOZA, B. 2
Man is by nature a political a.     ARISTOTLE, 6
Man is the only a. that can remain on friendly terms with the victims . . . he eats     BUTLER, S. 20
This a. is very bad     ANONYMOUS, 100
true to your a. instincts     LAWRENCE, D. 29
Whenever you observe an a. closely     CANETTI, E. 1
**animality** its own a. either objectionable or funny.     LEWIS, C. 2
**animals** A. are such agreeable friends     ELIOT, G. 7
a. . . . know nothing . . . of what people say about them     VOLTAIRE, 23
All a. are equal     ORWELL, G. 5
all a. were created . . . for the use of man     PEACOCK, T. 4
all there is to distinguish us from other a.     BEAUMARCHAIS, P. 2
But if we stop loving a.     SOLZHENITSYN, A. 2
I could . . . live with a.     WHITMAN, W. 5
My music . . . understood by children and a.     STRAVINSKY, I. 4
paragon of a.     SHAKESPEARE, W. 57
some a. are more equal than others     ORWELL, G. 5
The a. went in one by one     ANONYMOUS, 78
There are two things for which a. are . . . envied     VOLTAIRE, 23
Wild a. never kill for sport     FROUDE, J. 1
**Anna** great A.! whom three realms obey     POPE, A. 47
short and simple a. of the poor.     GRAY, T. 2
**Anne Hathaway** accurate reproductions of A.'s cottage-     LANCASTER, O. 2
**Annie Laurie** for bonnie A.     DOUGLAS, W. 1
**annihilating** A. all that's made     MARVELL, A. 2
**annihilation** No a.     TOYNBEE, A. 1
**anno domini** A. . . . the most fatal complaint     HILTON, J. 1
**annual** A. income twenty pounds     DICKENS, C. 10
**annuity** Buy an a. cheap     DICKENS, C. 25
**anomaly** Poverty is an a. to rich people     BAGEHOT, W. 11
**anon** I would . . . guess that A. . . . was often a woman     WOOLF, V. 11
**another** A. year! – a deadly blow     WORDSWORTH, W. 46
He who would do good to a.     BLAKE, W. 14
I would have given you a.     JARRY, A. 1
Life is just one damned thing after a.     HUBBARD, E. 3
No man can . . . condemn a.     BROWNE, SIR T. 7
**answer** a. a fool according to his folly     BIBLE: PROVERBS, 15
A timid question will . . . receive a confident a.     DARLING, BARON, 2
But a. came there none     CARROLL, L. 26
give a. as need requireth     BIBLE: ECCLESIASTICUS, 4
I do not a. questions like this without being paid     HELLMAN, L. 3

more than the wisest man can a.                COLTON, C, 4
The a. . . . is blowin' in the wind             DYLAN, B, 2
There are innumerable questions to which the inquisitive mind can
  . . . receive no a.                           JOHNSON, S, 124
we are not careful to a. thee in this matter    BIBLE: DANIEL, 3
where no one asks, no one needs to a.           JUNG, C, 1
would not stay for an a.
                 BACON, 1ST BARON VERULAM, VISCOUNT ST ALBANS, 56
**antagonistic** the most a. to the Victorian age   WILSON, E, 1
**antan** les neiges d'a.                       VILLON, F, 1
**anthology** a. is like all the plums and orange peel picked out of a
  cake                                          RALEIGH, SIR W, 2
**antic** dance an a. hay                       MARLOWE, C, 7
**anticipation** the intelligent a. of facts    CURZON, MARQUESS, 3
**anti-clerical** it makes me understand a. things   BELLOC, H, 14
**anti-climax** everything afterward savours of a.   FITZGERALD, F, 5
**antidote** the a. to desire                   CONGREVE, W, 15
**antipathy** I do not dislike the French from . . . vulgar a.
                             WALPOLE, 4TH EARL OF ORFORD, 9
strong a. of good to bad                        POPE, A, 9
**antiquity** Damn the age. I'll write for a.   LAMB, C, 19
**anti-Semite** An American is either a Jew, or an a.   SARTRE, J, 2
hated /by every a. /as if I were a Jew          YEVTUSHENKO, Y, 1
**anvil** My sledge and a. lie declined         ANONYMOUS, 61
**anxious** a. to do the wrong thing correctly   SAKI, 20
**anybody** If you have to tell them who you are, you aren't a.
                                                PECK, G, 1
**anyone** a. here whom I have not insulted     BRAHMS, J, 1
**anywhere** go a. I damn well please           BEVIN, E, 2
**apathy** God could cause us . . . sheer a. and boredom   GOETHE, J, 8
to go about the country stirring up a.          WHITELAW, VISCOUNT, 2
**ape** a man has no reason to be ashamed of having an a. for his
  grandfather                                   HUXLEY, T, 11
Is man an a. or an angel   DISRAELI, 1ST EARL OF BEACONSFIELD, 25
It is not the a., nor the tiger                 TEMPLE, W, 5
the a. from which he is descended               WILBERFORCE, S, 1
The exception is a naked a.                     MORRIS, D, 2
**ape-like** The a. virtues without which       CONNOLLY, C, 3
**aphorisms** The great writers of a.           CANETTI, E, 3
The hunter for a. . . . has to fish in muddy water   BRADLEY, F, 1
**aphrodisiac** Fame is a powerful a.           GREENE, G, 10
Power is the ultimate a.                        KISSINGER, H, 2
**apologize** a good rule in life never to a.   WODEHOUSE, SIR P, 7
It's too late to a.                             TOSCANINI, A, 2
**apology** Never make a defence or a.          CHARLES I, 1
**apostates** that peculiar malignity . . . characteristic of a.
                                                MACAULAY, BARON, 7
**apostle** great a. of the Philistines, Lord Macaulay   ARNOLD, M, 19
**apostles** The Septuagint minus the A.        VERRALL, A, 1
**apparatus** Brain. n An a. with which we think   BIERCE, A, 2
**apparel** a. oft proclaims the man            SHAKESPEARE, W, 47
**appeal** The whole of art is an a. to a reality   MACCARTHY, SIR D, 3
**appealed** hast thou a. unto Caesar           BIBLE: ACTS, 19
**appear** Things are . . . what they a. to be   SARTRE, J, 1
**appearances** A. are deceptive                PROVERBS, 60
A. are not . . . a clue to the truth   COMPTON-BURNETT, DAME I, 1
Keep up a.                                      CHURCHILL, C, 5
shallow people . . . do not judge by a.         WILDE, O, 45
**appeaser** An a. is one who feeds a crocodile   CHURCHILL, SIR W, 62
**appetite** A. comes with eating               RABELAIS, F, 2
a. may sicken and so die                        SHAKESPEARE, W, 285
the desire of satisfying a voracious a.         FIELDING, H, 11
**apple** An a. a day                           PROVERBS, 48
as the a. of his eye                            BIBLE: DEUTERONOMY, 7
I raised thee up under the a. tree              BIBLE: SONG OF SOLOMON, 20
keep me as the a. of an eye                     PSALMS, 6
My a. trees will never . . . eat the cones      FROST, R, 6
want the a. for the a.'s sake                   TWAIN, M, 13
When Eve ate this particular a.                 LAWRENCE, D, 7
**apple-pie** An a. without some cheese         PROVERBS, 49
**apples** comfort me with a.                   BIBLE: SONG OF SOLOMON, 3
The silver a. of the moon                       YEATS, W, 28
**applications** only a. of science             PASTEUR, L, 1
**appreciate** I never a.                       PICASSO, P, 4
**appreciation** total dependence on the a. of others   CONNOLLY, C, 9
**apprehend** Intelligence is quickness to a.   WHITEHEAD, A, 2
**apprehensions** the impalpable elations and a. of growth
                                                MAILER, N, 1
**approve** They that a. . . . call it opinion;   HOBBES, T, 3
**April** A. is the cruellest month             ELIOT, T, 23
And after A., when May follows                  BROWNING, R, 24

months . . . look gloomy in England are March and A.
                                                TROLLOPE, A, 6
My regret /Becomes an A. violet                 TENNYSON, BARON, 33
Now that A.'s there                             BROWNING, R, 23
Sweet A. showers                                TUSSER, T, 2
**Aprille** Whan that A. with his shoures sote   CHAUCER, G, 1
**Arab** I shook hands with a friendly A.       MILLIGAN, S, 1
**Arabia** All the perfumes of A.               SHAKESPEARE, W, 174
**Arabs** The Jews and A. should . . . settle their differences
                                                AUSTIN, W, 2
**arch** All experience is an a.                TENNYSON, BARON, 76
**archaeologist** An a. is the best husband     CHRISTIE, DAME A, 5
**archbishop** the sign of an a. is a double-cross   DIX, G, 1
**arch-enemy** love . . . has one a. – and that is life   ANOUILH, J, 1
**arches** Underneath the a.                    FLANAGAN, B, 1
**architect** Each man the a. of his own fate   APPIUS CAECUS, 1
the a. can only advise                          WRIGHT, F, 1
who is not a great sculptor or painter can be an a.   RUSKIN, J, 1
**architecture** A. in general is frozen music   SCHELLING, F, 1
Fashion is an a.                                CHANEL, C, 4
What has happened to a. . . . that the only passers-by who can
  contemplate it . . . are those . . . with a white stick and a dog
                                                LEVIN, B, 3
**ardua** Per a. ad astra                       ANONYMOUS, 68
**arguing** I am not a. with you                WHISTLER, J, 1
In a. too, the parson own'd his skill           GOLDSMITH, O, 5
**argument** All a. is against it               JOHNSON, S, 117
any authentic work of art must start an a.      WEST, DAME R, 2
I have found you an a.                          JOHNSON, S, 148
I love a., I love debate                        THATCHER, M, 4
**arguments** beware of long a. and long beards   SANTAYANA, G, 9
the world can be expressed in . . . a., . . . axioms and theorems
                                                FRAYN, M, 2
**Arian** In three sips the A. frustrate        BROWNING, R, 51
**arise** shall . . . a. with healing in his wings   BIBLE: MALACHI, 1
**aristocracy** a. . . . government by the badly educated
                                                CHESTERTON, G, 40
an absentee a.             DISRAELI, 1ST EARL OF BEACONSFIELD, 19
An a. in a republic is like a chicken whose head has been cut off
                                                MITFORD, N, 1
If human beings could be propagated . . . a. would be . . . sound
                                                HALDANE, J, 3
riff-raff apply to what is respectable, . . . a. to what is decent
                                                HOPE, A, 6
Unlike the male codfish . . . the British a. is   WODEHOUSE, SIR P, 19
**aristocrat** the quality that distinguishes the gentleman from both
  the artist and the a.                         WAUGH, E, 10
**aristocratic** To be a. in Art                MOORE, G, 3
to distinguish . . . the a. class from the Philistines   ARNOLD, M, 6
**arithmetic** different branches of A.         CARROLL, L, 12
Music is the a. of sounds                       DEBUSSY, C, 1
**ark** an a. of bulrushes                      BIBLE: EXODUS, 2
into the a., two and two                        BIBLE: GENESIS, 24
**arm** An a. /Rose up from . . . the lake      TENNYSON, BARON, 16
Don't carry away that a. till I have . . . my ring
                                                RAGLAN, 1ST BARON, 1
Human on my faithless a.                        AUDEN, W, 18
**Armageddon** a place called . . . A.          BIBLE: REVELATIONS, 11
**armchair** She fitted into my biggest a.      WODEHOUSE, SIR P, 11
**arm'd** a. with more than complete steel      MARLOWE, C, 12
**Armenteers** A mademoiselle from A.           ROWLAND, S, 1
**armies** ignorant a. clash by night           ARNOLD, M, 9
not a. . . . but flocks of sheep                CERVANTES, M, 3
**armistice** a short a. with truth             BYRON, 6TH BARON, 22
**armour** Conceit is the finest a.             JEROME, J, 2
Prayer makes the Christian's a. bright          COWPER, W, 13
**arms** Anger supplies the a.                  VIRGIL, 1
For the theatre one needs long a.               BERNHARDT, S, 1
I never would lay down my a.
                       PITT THE ELDER, 1ST EARL OF CHATHAM, 6
I sing of a. and the man                        VIRGIL, 2
It is always opening time in the Sailors A.     THOMAS, D, 15
So he laid down his a.                          HOOD, T, 2
**army** An a. is a nation within a nation      VIGNY, A, 3
An a. marches on its stomach                    NAPOLEON I, 9
Chief of the A.                                 NAPOLEON I, 10
contemptible little A.                          WILHELM II, 4
If you don't want to use the a., I should like to borrow it
                                                LINCOLN, A, 5
terrible as an a. with banners   BIBLE: SONG OF SOLOMON, 15

The a. ages men sooner than the law — WELLS, H. 5
The conventional a. loses if it does not win — KISSINGER, H. 1
the little ships of England brought the A. home — GUEDALLA, P. 2
**arrest** My father didn't create you to a. me — PEEL, VISCOUNT, 1
One does not a. Voltaire — DE GAULLE, C. 7
**arrested** Christ . . . would quite likely have been a. — DE BLANK, J. 1
**arrive** To travel hopefully is . . . better . . . than to a.
— STEVENSON, R. 24
**arrow** Every a. . . . feels the attraction of earth — LONGFELLOW, H. 3
I, said the Sparrow, /With my bow and a. — NURSERY RHYMES, 73
I shot an a. into the air — LONGFELLOW, H. 1
the a. that flieth by day — PSALMS, 57
**arrows** whose teeth are spears and a. — PSALMS, 40
**arse** a politician is an a. — CUMMINGS, E. 3
Sit on your a. for fifty years — MACNEICE, L. 1
**arsenal** a. of democracy — ROOSEVELT, F. 11
**arson** A., after all, is an artificial crime — WELLS, H. 10
**art** A. and religion first; then philosophy — SPARK, M. 9
A. . . . can go on mattering once it has stopped hurting
— BOWEN, E. 2
a. constantly aspires towards . . . music — PATER, W. 2
A. for a.'s sake — COUSIN, V. 1
A. for A.'s sake — FORSTER, E. 4
A. is a jealous mistress — EMERSON, R. 2
A. is long, and Time is fleeting — LONGFELLOW, H. 8
A. is not a mirror . . . but a hammer — MAYAKOVSKY, V. 1
A. is not a special sauce — LETHABY, W. 1
a. is not a weapon — KENNEDY, J. 15
A. is ruled . . . by the imagination — CROCE, B. 1
A. is the imposing of a pattern on experience — WHITEHEAD, A. 3
A. is the most intense mode of individualism — WILDE, O. 52
A. is . . . the transmission of feeling — TOLSTOY, COUNT, 9
a. is to give life a shape — ANOUILH, J. 4
All a. deals with the absurd — MURDOCH, DAME I. 1
All A. is quite useless. — WILDE, O. 42
An a. can only be learned — BUTLER, S. 5
A. never expresses anything — WILDE, O. 13
any authentic work of a. must start an argument — WEST, DAME R. 2
a. of pleasing consists — HAZLITT, W. 22
aspires . . . to the condition of a. — CONRAD, J. 5
Bullfighting is the only a. in which the artist is in danger of death
— HEMINGWAY, E. 1
Desiring this man's a. — SHAKESPEARE, W. 256
excellence of every a. is its intensity — KEATS, J. 49
Fine a. is that in which the hand — RUSKIN, J. 11
great parables, . . . , but false a. — LAWRENCE, D. 40
half a trade and half an a. — INGE, W. 8
I doubt that . . needed Ruskin — STOPPARD, T. 13
I have discovered the a. . . . lost for two thousand years
— DUNCAN, I. 1
industry without a. is brutality — RUSKIN, J. 2
Insurrection is an a. — TROTSKY, L. 6
. . . It is a wonderful case of nature imitating a. — WILDE, O. 59
It's clever but is it a. — KIPLING, R. 4
Mr Goldwyn . . . you are only interested in a. — SHAW, G. 45
nature is the a. of God — BROWNE, SIR T. 3
Nature's handmaid, a. — DRYDEN, J. 18
Politics is not a science . . . but an a. — BISMARCK, PRINCE VON, 7
Politics is the a. of the possible — BISMARCK, PRINCE VON, 3
Rules and models destroy genius and a. — HAZLITT, W. 27
sombre enemy of good a. — CONNOLLY, C. 8
the a. of the possible — BUTLER, BARON, 1
The whole of a. is an appeal to a reality — MACCARTHY, SIR D. 3
They say princes learn no a. truly, but . . . horsemanship
— JONSON, B. 6
To be aristocratic in A. — MOORE, G. 3
True ease in writing comes from a. — POPE, A. 24
**artful** The a. Dodger — DICKENS, C. 34
**article** It all depends upon that a. there — WELLINGTON, DUKE OF, 1
**articles** to pay for a. . . . they do not want — HURST, SIR G. 1
**artificial** All things are a. — BROWNE, SIR T. 3
nothing so a. as sinning nowadays — LAWRENCE, D. 24
**artist** An amateur is an a. who supports himself with outside jobs
which enable him to paint — SHAHN, B. 1
As an a., a man has no home — NIETZSCHE, F. 6
Beware of the a. who's an intellectual — FITZGERALD, F. 9
God is really only another a. — PICASSO, P. 3
only one position for an a. anywhere — THOMAS, D. 25
Remember I'm an a. — CARY, J. 2
the quality that distinguishes the gentleman from both the a. and
the aristocrat — WAUGH, E. 10

˙What is an a. — STOPPARD, T. 11
**artistic** a. temperament . . . afflicts amateurs — CHESTERTON, G. 21
There never was an a. period — WHISTLER, J. 17
**artists** A. are not engineers of the soul — KENNEDY, J. 15
Great a. have no country — MUSSET, A. 2
. . . The a. retired. The British remained — WHISTLER, J. 13
**art-loving** an A. nation — WHISTLER, J. 17
**arts** If all the a. aspire to the condition of music — SANTAYANA, G. 13
Murder . . . one of the Fine A. — DE QUINCEY, T. 2
˙secret of the a. is to correct nature — VOLTAIRE, 10
**ashamed** few people who are not a. of having been in love
— ROCHEFOUCAULD, DUC DE LA, 8
I am a. of confessing — BURNEY, F. 1
some habit of which he is deeply a. — CRISP, Q. 1
to see them not a. — SWIFT, J. 14
We are not a. of what we have done — PANKHURST, DAME C. 2
**ashes** a. of Napoleon — WELLINGTON, DUKE OF, 21
**Asia** There is too much A. and she is too old — KIPLING, R. 16
**ask** a., and it shall be given — BIBLE: MATTHEW, 26
A. a silly question — PROVERBS, 63
A. no questions — PROVERBS, 64
To labour and not a. for any reward — LOYOLA, I. 1
**asks** where no one a., no one needs to answer — JUNG, C. 1
**asleep** The devil is a. — PEARY, R. 1
**aspect** Meet in her a. — BYRON, 6TH BARON, 37
**aspens** Willows whiten, a. quiver — TENNYSON, BARON, 38
**aspicious** two a. persons — SHAKESPEARE, W. 215
**aspirations** The young have a. — SAKI, 12
**aspires** art constantly a. towards . . . music — PATER, W. 2
a. . . . to the condition of art — CONRAD, J. 5
**aspirings** The soul hath not her generous a. implanted in her in
vain — LAMB, C. 24
**ass** a strong a. — BIBLE: GENESIS, 55
every a. thinks he may kick at him — PARR, S. 1
the law is a a. — DICKENS, C. 35
the Lord opened the mouth of the a. — BIBLE: NUMBERS, 5
with the jawbone of an a. — BIBLE: JUDGES, 8
**assassination** Absolutism tempered by a. — MUNSTER, E. 1
A. has never changed — DISRAELI, 1ST EARL OF BEACONSFIELD, 26
A. . . the extreme form of censorship — SHAW, G. 37
**assemblance** Care I for the . . . a. of a man — SHAKESPEARE, W. 91
**assemblies** Kings govern by . . . a. only when — FOX, C. 4
**assertions** Pure mathematics consists entirely of a.
— RUSSELL, EARL, 11
**asset** the greatest a. a head of state can have
— WILSON OF RIEVAULX, BARON, 12
**assigned** purpose of God and the doom a. — TENNYSON, BARON, 54
**associate** good must a. — BURKE, E. 18
I . . . like to a. with . . . priests — BELLOC, H. 14
**assure** a. him that he'd live tomorrow — RABELAIS, F. 4
**astonished** a. at my own moderation — CLIVE OF PLASSEY, BARON, 1
. . it is I who am surprised; you are merely a. — WEBSTER, N. 1
**astonishment** Dear Sir, Your a.'s odd — ANONYMOUS, 15
Just a little more reverence . . . , and not so much a.
— SARGENT, SIR M. 1
**astound** Austria will a. the world with . . . her ingratitude
— SCHWARZENBERG, PRINCE, 1
**astronauts** The a.! . . . Rotarians in outer space — VIDAL, G. 3
**astronomy** A. teaches the correct use — LEACOCK, S. 5
**asunder** afar and a. — BOWEN, E. 1
what . . . God hath joined together, let not man put a.
— BIBLE: MATTHEW, 56
**asylum** world is . . . like a lunatic a.
— LLOYD GEORGE, EARL OF DWYFOR, 14
**asylums** Those comfortably padded lunatic a. . . . the stately homes
— WOOLF, V. 4
**atheism** Every luxury . . . – a., breast-feeding, circumcision.
— ORTON, J. 4
God never wrought miracle to convince a.
— BACON, 1ST BARON VERULAM, VISCOUNT ST ALBANS, 9
**atheist** an a. half believes a God — YOUNG, E. 4
An a. is a man who has no invisible means of support
— FOSDICK, H. 1
An a. is one point — PROVERBS, 50
A pious man . . . would be an a. if the king were — LA BRUYERE, J. 1
He was an embittered a. — ORWELL, G. 10
I am an a. . . . thank God — BUNUEL, L. 1
only her scepticism kept her from being an a. — SARTRE, J. 13
very chic for an a. — RUSSELL, EARL, 2
**Athens** A. arose — SHELLEY, P. 7
A. holds sway over all Greece — THEMISTOCLES, 1

men of A. . . . ye are too superstitious BIBLE: ACTS, 12
athirst my soul is a. for God PSALMS, 30
athletic The only a. sport I ever mastered JERROLD, D, 7
athletics a. as inferior forms of fox-hunting WAUGH, E, 15
Atlantic The Admiral of the A. salutes the Admiral of the Pacific WILHELM II, 3
to have the East come to the A. GOERING, H, 1
A to B She ran . . . emotions from A. PARKER, D, 28
atom The a. bomb is a paper tiger MAO TSE-TUNG, 7
There is no evil in the a. STEVENSON, A, 5
They split the a. by firing particles at it HAY, W, 1
atomic The way to win an a. war BRADLEY, O, 1
atoms Accidental and fortuitous concurrence of a. PALMERSTON, VISCOUNT, 1
atone a. for the sins of your fathers HORACE, 36
atrophy Music begins to a. POUND, E, 1
attached men become a. even to Widnes TAYLOR, A, 7
attack A. is the best form PROVERBS, 8
don't believe in . . . true love until after the first a. ESCHENBACH, M, 2
situation excellent. I shall a. FOCH, MARSHAL, 1
attainments These are rare a. . . . but . . . can she spin JAMES I, 4
attention a. to the inside . . . contempt for the outside CHESTERFIELD, 4TH EARL OF, 10
He would take his a. away from the universe CRISP, Q, 10
Attic A. wit PLINY THE ELDER, 1
glory of the A. stage ARNOLD, M, 40
attic brain a. stocked with all the furniture that he is likely to use DOYLE, SIR A, 10
attitude the largest scope for change still lies in men's a. to women BRITTAIN, V, 1
attitudes Anglo-Saxon a. CARROLL, L, 30
attraction Every arrow . . . feels the a. of earth LONGFELLOW, H, 3
The chief a. of military service TOLSTOY, COUNT, 5
attractive if they are in the least a. CAMPBELL, R, 2
The most a. sentences are not perhaps the wisest THOREAU, H, 2
audacity a. of elected persons WHITMAN, W, 9
Auden A. was someone you could laugh-at-with SPENDER, SIR S, 3
A., a sort of gutless Kipling ORWELL, GEORGE, 26
audience I know two kinds of a. SCHNABEL, A, 1
the a. want to be surprised . . . by things that they expect BERNARD, T, 1
. . . the a. was a disaster WILDE, O, 67
auditioned kind of show where the girls are not a. THOMAS, I, 3
auld a. acquaintance be forgot BURNS, R, 2
for a. lang syne BURNS, R, 3
Edna Aunt E. is universal RATTIGAN, SIR T, 1
aunt Charley's a. from Brazil THOMAS, B, 1
aunts bad a. and good a. WODEHOUSE, SIR P, 2
Aussie a dinkum hard-swearing A. HASKELL, A, 1
Austen Jane A. SCOTT, SIR W, 3
Austerlitz There rises the sun of A. NAPOLEON I, 3
Australia guess . . . he was born in A. SHAW, G, 12
So you're going to A. MELBA, DAME N, 4
Australian you're going to write the Great A. Novel WHITE, P, 4
Austria A. is Switzerland . . . with history added MORPURGO, J, 1
A. will astound the world with . . . her ingratitude SCHWARZENBERG, PRINCE, 1
author An a. who speaks about his own books DISRAELI, 1ST EARL OF BEACONSFIELD, 27
bad novel tells us . . . about its a. CHESTERTON, G, 20
He is the richest a. that ever grazed JOHNSON, S, 57
authority a. be a stubborn bear SHAKESPEARE, W, 305
A. forgets a dying king TENNYSON, BARON, 17
man /Dress'd in a little brief a. SHAKESPEARE, W, 180
No morality can be founded on a. AYER, SIR A, 1
Nothing destroyeth a. so much BACON, 1ST BARON VERULAM, VISCOUNT ST ALBANS, 22
The defiance of established a. ARENDT, H, 1
the highest a. for believing that the meek shall inherit the Earth BIRKENHEAD, EARL OF, 1
authors A. are easy to get on with JOSEPH, M, 1
much exposed to a. WELLINGTON, DUKE OF, 3
The faults of great a. COLERIDGE, S, 18
their a. could not endure being wrong CAMUS, A, 4
The reciprocal civility of a. JOHNSON, S, 16
The trouble with our younger a. is MAUGHAM, W, 29
automobile Money differs from an a. GALBRAITH, J, 7
avarice rich beyond the dreams of a. MOORE, E, 2
avenged the satisfaction of knowing that we are a. TROLLOPE, A, 15
average Take the life-lie away from the a. man IBSEN, H, 9

aves Beadsman, after thousand a. told KEATS, J, 5
Avilion To the island-valley of A. TENNYSON, BARON, 21
avoidance The a. of taxes . . . still carries . . . reward KEYNES, BARON, 11
avoiding Reading . . . ingenious device for a. thought HELPS, SIR A, 1
Avon Sweet Swan of A. JONSON, B, 10
a-waggle You must always be a. LAWRENCE, D, 1
awake A.! for Morning in the Bowl of Night FITZGERALD, E, 2
At last a. BROWNING, R, 21
I dream when I am a. CALDERON DE LA BARCA, P, 2
Onaway! A., beloved LONGFELLOW, H, 11
The lilies and roses were all a. TENNYSON, BARON, 53
We're very wide a., /The moon and I GILBERT, SIR W, 28
away Over the hills and far a. GAY, J, 3
Take the soup a. HOFFMAN, H, 1
the big one that got a. DENNIS, N, 1
aweary I gin to be a. of the sun SHAKESPEARE, W, 53
awful Abashed the devil . . . felt how a. goodness is MILTON, J, 42
awfulness by its very a. STEVENSON, R, 21
awoke I a. one morning BYRON, 6TH BARON, 42
axe his keener eye /The a.'s edge did try MARVELL, A, 4
Lizzie Borden took an a. ANONYMOUS, 53
axioms A. in philosophy are not a. KEATS, J, 54
the world can be expressed in . . . arguments, . . . a. and theorems FRAYN, M, 2
axis a. of the earth sticks out visibly through . . . every town or city HOLMES, O, 4
aye A., and what then COLERIDGE, S, 2

## B

baa B., b., black sheep NURSERY RHYMES, 4
God ha' mercy on such as we, /B.! Yah! Bah KIPLING, R, 9
Babbitt one thing wrong with the B. house LEWIS, S, 1
babbl'd 'a b. of green fields SHAKESPEARE, W, 94
babblings vain b. BIBLE: I TIMOTHY, 4
Babel B.; because the Lord did there confound the language BIBLE: GENESIS, 31
the tower of B. should have got language all mixed up VOLTAIRE, 27
babes b. shall rule over them BIBLE: ISAIAH, 5
out of the mouth of . . . b. and sucklings PSALMS, 3
babies bit the b. in the cradles BROWNING, R, 40
Other people's b. HERBERT, SIR A, 1
putting milk into b. CHURCHILL, SIR W, 55
War will never cease until b. MENCKEN, H, 5
You breed b. and you eat chips WESKER, A, 1
baby Anybody can shock a b. STERN, R, 1
Don't throw the b. out PROVERBS, 122
Every b. born into the world DICKENS, C, 30
hanging the b. on the clothes line to dry RUNYON, D, 7
Hush-a-bye, b., on the tree top NURSERY RHYMES, 19
my b. at my breast SHAKESPEARE, W, 17
no new b. in the womb of our society LAWRENCE, D, 35
Rock-a-bye b. on the tree top BLAKE, C, 1
Walking My B. Back Home TURK, R, 1
Babylon B. the great BIBLE: REVELATIONS, 13
by the waters of B. we sat down and wept PSALMS, 83
By the waters of B. we sit down and weep WALPOLE, 4TH EARL OF ORFORD, 7
How many miles to B. NURSERY RHYMES, 17
Bach J. S. B. BEECHAM, SIR T, 3
bachelor B.'s fare SWIFT, J, 9
Never trust . . . a b. too near ROWLAND, H, 4
Now I am a b., I live by myself ANONYMOUS, 63
bachelors reasons for b. to go out ELIOT, G, 6
back any of you at the b. who do not hear me AUDEN, W, 26
But at my b. I always hear MARVELL, A, 10
Either b. us or sack us CALLAGHAN, SIR J, 2
I sit on a man's b. TOLSTOY, COUNT, 10
turn your b. upon the world LONGFELLOW, H, 7
Will ye no come b. again NAIRNE, BARONESS, 1
backs With our b. to the wall . . . each . . . must fight on to the end HAIG, EARL, 1
Bacon When their lordships asked B. BENTLEY, E, 1
bad a b. novel tells us the truth about its author CHESTERTON, G, 20
A b. penny PROVERBS, 1
a good friend, but b. acquaintance BYRON, 6TH BARON, 20
B. girls don't have the time BANKHEAD, T, 8

Round and round the garden /Like a teddy b. NURSERY RHYMES, 48
they think I shall be able to b. it best CHURCHILL, SIR W, 14
**bear-baiting** Puritan hated b. MACAULAY, BARON, 8
**beard** singed the Spanish king's b. DRAKE, SIR F, 1
There was an Old Man with a b. LEAR, E, 1
**bearded** hard to hear what a b. man is saying MANKEIWICZ, H, 3
He reaps the b. grain at a breath LONGFELLOW, H, 9
**beards** beware of long arguments and long b. SANTAYANA, G, 9
men wore their b., like they wear their neckties LAWRENCE, D, 18
**bears** And dancing dogs and b., HODGSON, R, 1
And some of the bigger b. try to pretend MILNE, A, 5
b. and lions growl and fight WATTS, I, 3
**beast** b. of the earth BIBLE: GENESIS, 5
Dialect words – those terrible marks of the b. HARDY, T, 5
Either a b. or a god ARISTOTLE, 7
for man or b. FIELDS, W, 1
hardly be a b. or a fool alone on a great mountain KILVERT, F, 2
Man's life is cheap as b.'s SHAKESPEARE, W, 136
*The B.* stands for strong mutually antagonistic governments WAUGH, E, 30
the mark . . . of the b. BIBLE: REVELATIONS, 10
**beastie** Wee, sleekit, cow'rin', tim'rous b. BURNS, R, 19
**beastly** Don't let's be b. to the Germans COWARD, SIR N, 5
**beasts** man . . . compared unto the b. that perish PSALMS, 33
wild b. of the desert shall lie there BIBLE: ISAIAH, 17
**beat** make the b. keep time with short steps ANDERSEN, H, 3
Two hearts that b. as one LOVELL, M, 1
**beaten** I was b. up by Quakers ALLEN, W, 5
public school, where . . . learning was painfully b. into him PEACOCK, T, 8
**beateth** so fight I, not as one that b. the air BIBLE: I CORINTHIANS, 13
**beautiful** Against the b. . . . one can wage a pitiless war GREENE, G, 5
b. . . . for someone who could not read. CHESTERTON, G, 45
light, shade, and perspective . . . make it b. CONSTABLE, J, 1
many men, so b. COLERIDGE, S, 30
most b. things . . . are the most useless RUSKIN, J, 9
Our love of what is b. does not lead to extravagance PERICLES, 1
Rich men's houses are seldom b. ASQUITH, M, 2
The good is the b. PLATO, 1
the most b. battlefield NAPOLEON I, 4
the most b. woman I've ever seen MARX, G, 1
the name of which was B. BUNYAN, J, 4
the work comes out more b. GAUTIER, T, 2
when a woman isn't b. CHEKHOV, A, 9
**beautifully** B. done SPENCER, SIR S, 2
**beauty** A thing of b. is a joy for ever KEATS, J, 2
B. and the lust for learning BEERBOHM, SIR M, 13
b. being the best of all we know BRIDGES, R, 1
Beauty is truth, truth b. KEATS, J, 25
better to be first with an ugly woman than the hundredth with a b. BUCK, P, 5
B. in distress BURKE, E, 5
B. in things exists in the mind which contemplates them HUME, D, 4
B. is altogether in the eye of the beholder HUNGERFORD, M, 1
B. is . . . in the eye of the beholder WALLACE, L, 1
B. is in the eye PROVERBS, 79
b. is only sin deep SAKI, 2
B. is only skin-deep PROVERBS, 80
B. is potent PROVERBS, 81
B. is truth, truth b. KEATS, J, 25
B. itself doth of itself persuade /The eyes of men SHAKESPEARE, W, 233
B. sat with me all the summer day BRIDGES, R, 2
B. stands /In the admiration . . . of weak minds MILTON, J, 49
But b.'s self she is, /When all her robes are gone ANONYMOUS, 59
Clad in the b. of a thousand stars MARLOWE, C, 3
Exuberance is B. BLAKE, W, 27
Fostered alike by b. and by fear WORDSWORTH, W, 33
her b. made /The bright world dim SHELLEY, P, 24
Love built on b. DONNE, J, 7
love permanence more than . . . b. CASSON, SIR H, 1
Mathematics possesses . . . b. RUSSELL, EARL, 18
She walks in b. BYRON, 6TH BARON, 37
Teaches such b. as a woman's eye SHAKESPEARE, W, 155
the b. /Of an aged face CAMPBELL, J, 1
the laws of poetic truth and poetic b. ARNOLD, M, 13
The pain passes, but the b. remains RENOIR, P, 1

There is no excellent b. BACON, 1ST BARON VERULAM, VISCOUNT ST ALBANS, 12
this generation . . . found England a land of b. JOAD, C, 3
What *is* b., anyway? There's no such thing PICASSO, P, 4
**beaver** And cultivate a b. HUXLEY, A, 3
**because** B. it is there MALLORY, G, 1
**Becket** Thomas B. HENRY II, 1
**become** What's b. of Waring BROWNING, R, 56
**becoming** . . . I believe I am b. a god VESPASIAN, 1
Sunburn is very b. COWARD, SIR N, 8
**bed** and die – in b. SASSOON, S, 2
And so to b. PEPYS, S, 1
B. . . . is the poor man's opera HUXLEY, A, 19
Each within our narrow b. CASWALL, E, 1
Go to b. with the lamb PROVERBS, 180
Here comes a candle to light you to b. NURSERY RHYMES, 41
Lady Capricorn, . . . was . . . keeping open b. HUXLEY, A, 7
Never go to b. mad DILLER, P, 2
nicer to stay in b. LAUDER, SIR H, 2
Now deep in my b. I turn JENNINGS, E, 1
So I took her into b. and covered up her head ANONYMOUS, 63
The b. be blest ADY, T, 1
the night the b. fell on my father THURBER, J, 8
thou art . . . about my b. PSALMS, 84
Wedlock – the . . . deep peace of the double b. after the . . . chaise-longue CAMPBELL, MRS 2
Who goes to b. with whom SAYERS, D, 2
woman who goes to b. with a man MONTAIGNE, M, 4
**bedfellows** Misery acquaints . . . strange b. SHAKESPEARE, W, 275
**bedroom** meeting in a darkened b. in a Brussels hotel THOMPSON, E, 1
**beds** let the saints . . . rejoice in their b. PSALMS, 93
Minds like b. always made up WILLIAMS, W, 1
Will there be b. for me and all who seek ROSSETTI, C, 7
**bedspring** the triumphant twang of a b. PERELMAN, S, 6
**bee** How doth the little busy b. WATTS, I, 2
Sting like a b. ALI, M, 2
**beechen** spare the b. tree CAMPBELL, T, 1
**beef** The roast b. of England FIELDING, H, 6
**beefsteak** Dr Johnson's morality was as English . . . as a b. HAWTHORNE, N, 2
**beer** chronicle small b. SHAKESPEARE, W, 221
Did you ever taste b. DICKENS, C, 32
Life isn't all b. and skittles HUGHES, T, 1
that bitter b. that tastes sweet RILKE, R, 4
**Beerbohm** Max B. WILDE, O, 66
**bees** No b., no honey PROVERBS, 309
No shade, no shine, no butterflies, no b., HOOD, T, 10
**Beethoven** B.'s Fifth Symphony is the most sublime noise FORSTER, E, 7
**beetles** inordinate fondness for b. HALDANE, J, 5
**before** I have been here b. ROSSETTI, D, 3
**beg** only the poor . . . are forbidden to b. FRANCE, A, 1
**beggar'd** b. all description SHAKESPEARE, W, 8
**beggars** B. can't be choosers PROVERBS, 82
**beggary** b. in the love that can be reckon'd SHAKESPEARE, W, 5
no vice but b. SHAKESPEARE, W, 125
**begin** Are you sitting comfortably? Then I'll b. LANG, J, 1
B. at the beginning CARROLL, L, 17
**beginning** a b., a muddle, and an end. LARKIN, P, 5
As it was in the b. BOOK OF COMMON PRAYER, 5
a whole is that which has a b., a middle, and an end ARISTOTLE, 4
Begin at the b. CARROLL, L, 17
b. of fairies BARRIE, SIR J, 3
end of the b. CHURCHILL, SIR W, 52
every man at the b. doth set forth good wine BIBLE: JOHN, 5
I like a film to have a b., a middle and an end GODARD, J, 2
in the b. God BIBLE: GENESIS, 1
in the b. was the word BIBLE: JOHN, 1
Nothing so difficult as a b. BYRON, 6TH BARON, 25
the b. of the end TALLEYRAND, 3
the fear of the Lord is the b. of wisdom PSALMS, 69
**beginnings** end to the b. of all wars ROOSEVELT, F, 15
mighty things from small b. DRYDEN, J, 18
**begins** my family b. with me IPHICRATES, 1
**begot** what they were about when they b. me STERNE, L, 4
**begotten** Whatever is b., born, and dies YEATS, W, 25
**beguine** When they begin the b. PORTER, C, 2
**begun** There is an old saying 'well b. is half done KEATS, J, 50
**behaving** men are more interested in . . . justifying themselves than in . . . b. SZASZ, T, 1

**behaviour** The quality of moral b. varies — HUXLEY, A, 18
**behind** In the dusk, with a light b. her — GILBERT, SIR W, 45
  led his regiment from b. — GILBERT, SIR W, 1
  part my hair b. — ELIOT, T, 13
**behold** all which we b. /Is full of blessings — WORDSWORTH, W, 12
  B. her, single in the field — WORDSWORTH, W, 45
  b. it was a dream — BUNYAN, J, 8
  b. the man — BIBLE: JOHN, 46
  b. with thine eyes — BIBLE: EZEKIEL, 8
**beholder** Beauty is . . . in the eye of the b. — HUNGERFORD, M, 1
  Beauty is . . . in the eye of the b. — WALLACE, L, 1
**beige** It's b.! My color — DE WOLFE, E, 1
**being** in him we live, and move, and have our b. — BIBLE: ACTS, 13
  Knowledge is proportionate to b. — HUXLEY, A, 35
  To kill a human b. — JAMES, H, 5
**belfry** bats in the b. — PHILLPOTTS, E, 1
**believe** a verb meaning 'to b. falsely — WITTGENSTEIN, L, 7
  b. in the life to come — BECKETT, S, 1
  B. it or not — RIPLEY, R, 1
  B. nothing of what you hear — PROVERBS, 83
  don't b. in . . . true love until after the first attack — ESCHENBACH, M, 2
  except I . . . thrust my hand into his side, I will not b. — BIBLE: JOHN, 56
  I b. because it is impossible — TERTULLIAN, Q, 3
  . . . I b. I am becoming a god — VESPASIAN, 1
  I b. in the Church — TEMPLE, W, 7
  I don't b. in fairies — BARRIE, SIR J, 4
  inclined to b. those whom we do not know — JOHNSON, S, 14
  Infidelity . . . consists in professing to b. — PAINE, T, 1
  it brings you luck whether you b. . . . or not — BOHR, N, 1
  They didn't b. me — ROURKE, M, 1
  undesirable to b. a proposition — RUSSELL, EARL, 16
  We can b. what we choose — NEWMAN, CARDINAL, 5
  what we b. is not necessarily true — BELL, C, 3
  you must b. in God — JOWETT, B, 1
**believes** He b., . . . that there *is* such a thing as truth — BAGEHOT, W, 10
  politician never b. what he says — DE GAULLE, C, 8
**bell** B., book, and candle — SHAKESPEARE, W, 126
  for whom the b. tolls — DONNE, J, 6
  I'll b. the cat — DOUGLAS, 5TH EARL OF ANGUS, 1
  The b. strikes one — YOUNG, E, 6
  The sexton toll'd the b. — HOOD, T, 5
  Unto the B. at Edmonton — COWPER, W, 8
  Who will b. the cat — DESCHAMPS, E, 1
**Bellamy** I could eat one of B.'s veal pies — PITT THE YOUNGER, W, 3
**belle** La b. dame sans Merci — KEATS, J, 18
  La b. dame sans mercy — KEATS, J, 8
**bellies** their b. were full — BRECHT, B, 4
**bells** Ring out, wild b., and let him die — TENNYSON, BARON, 31
  Rings on her fingers and b. on her toes — NURSERY RHYMES, 46
  The b. of hell go ting-a-ling-a-ling — ANONYMOUS, 65
  'Twould ring the b. of Heaven — HODGSON, R, 1
  With silver b. and cockle shells — NURSERY RHYMES, 34
**belly** Every man with a b. full of the classics — MILLER, H, 2
  the b. for meats — BIBLE: I CORINTHIANS, 5
  thy b. is like an heap of wheat — BIBLE: SONG OF SOLOMON, 17
  to banish hunger by rubbing the b. — DIOGENES, 2
  upon thy b. shalt thou go — BIBLE: GENESIS, 15
  victory under the b. of a Cossack's horse — TROTSKY, L, 4
**bellyful** Rumble thy b. — SHAKESPEARE, W, 138
**beloved** I am my b.'s, and his desire is toward me — BIBLE: SONG OF SOLOMON, 19
  I am my b.'s, and my b. is mine — BIBLE: SONG OF SOLOMON, 14
  let my b. come into his garden — BIBLE: SONG OF SOLOMON, 11
  Onaway! Awake, b. — LONGFELLOW, H, 11
  the voice of my b. — BIBLE: SONG OF SOLOMON, 4
  this is my b. Son — BIBLE: MATTHEW, 5
**below** Capten, art tha sleepin' there b. — NEWBOLT, SIR H, 3
  Down and away b. — ARNOLD, M, 14
  What thy errand here b. — LAMB, C, 18
**Ben Adhem** And lo! B.'s name led all the rest — HUNT, L, 3
**Ben Battle** B. was a soldier bold — HOOD, T, 2
**Ben Bolt** Oh! don't you remember sweet Alice, B. — ENGLISH, T, 1
**Ben Bulben** Under bare B.'s head — YEATS, W, 30
**bench** What do you suppose I am on the B. for — BIRKENHEAD, EARL OF, 3
**benefactors** Our gratitude to most b. is the same as . . . for dentists — CHAMFORT, N, 3
**benefits** B. make a man a slave — PROVERBS, 84

It is the nature of men to be bound by the b. they confer — MACHIAVELLI, N, 1
**benevolence** husband render unto the wife due b. — BIBLE: I CORINTHIANS, 7
**bereav'd** I am black, as if b. of light — BLAKE, W, 46
**Berkeley** A Nightingale Sang in B. Square — MASCHWITZ, E, 1
**Berliner** *Ich bin ein B.* — KENNEDY, J, 13
**berries** I come to pluck your b. — MILTON, J, 16
**berth** His death, which happen'd in his b. — HOOD, T, 5
  Things hitherto undone should be given . . . a wide b. — BEERBOHM, SIR M, 6
**Bertie** I'm Burlington B. — HARGREAVES, W, 1
**best** all that's b. of dark and bright — BYRON, 6TH BARON, 37
  as in the b. it is — SHAKESPEARE, W, 51
  beauty being the b. of all we know — BRIDGES, R, 1
  b. of life is but intoxication — BYRON, 6TH BARON, 18
  b. that is known and thought in the world — ARNOLD, M, 12
  b. words in the b. order — COLERIDGE, S, 39
  Culture, the acquainting ourselves with the b. — ARNOLD, M, 20
  For home is b. — TUSSER, T, 4
  His worst is better than any other person's b. — HAZLITT, W, 6
  It was the b. of times — DICKENS, C, 53
  letting the b. be the enemy of the good — JENKINS, R, 1
  look at the b. book . . . price of a turbot . . . — RUSKIN, J, 7
  Men of few words are the b. — SHAKESPEARE, W, 96
  Stolen sweets are b. — CIBBER, C, 2
  The b. is the enemy of the good — VOLTAIRE, 7
  The b. lack all conviction — YEATS, W, 26
  The b. of friends — PROVERBS, 378
  the b. of possible worlds — VOLTAIRE, 3
  The b. things in life — PROVERBS, 380
  the b. which has been thought and said in the world — ARNOLD, M, 1
  the shortest works are always the b. — LA FONTAINE, J, 11
  we live in the b. of all possible worlds — CABELL, J, 2
  we will do our b. — CHURCHILL, SIR W, 49
**bestial** what remains is b. — SHAKESPEARE, W, 222
**bestow** Let them b. on every airth a limb — GRAHAM, MARQUIS OF MONTROSE, 1
**best-seller** A b. . . . because it was selling well — BOORSTIN, D, 2
  A b. is the gilded tomb of a mediocre talent — SMITH, L, 1
**bet** I b. my money on the bob-tail nag — FOSTER, S, 1
**Bethlehem** O come ye to B. — OAKELEY, F, 1
  O little town of B., — BROOKS, P, 1
**betimes** to be up b. — SHAKESPEARE, W, 288
**betray** Nature never did b. — WORDSWORTH, W, 11
**betrayed** woe unto that man by whom the Son of man is b. — BIBLE: MATTHEW, 77
**betraying** if I had to choose between b. my country and b. my friend — FORSTER, E, 11
  if I had to choose between b. my country and b. my friend — FORSTER, E, 11
**betrothed** a bride's attitude towards her b. — MUIR, F, 2
**better** a far, far, b. thing — DICKENS, C, 54
  always . . . trying to get the b. — LAMB, C, 5
  b. is he . . . who hath not seen the evil work under the sun — BIBLE: ECCLESIASTES, 9
  b. strangers — SHAKESPEARE, W, 29
  B. than a play — CHARLES II, 5
  b. to have loved and lost — TENNYSON, BARON, 24
  b. to have no opinion of God — BACON, 1ST BARON VERULAM, VISCOUNT ST ALBANS, 52
  b. to marry than to burn — BIBLE: I CORINTHIANS, 8
  for b. for worse — BOOK OF COMMON PRAYER, 15
  He is no b. — AUSTIN, A, 1
  I am getting b. and b. — COUE, E, 1
  if you knows of a b. 'ole — BAIRNSFATHER, B, 1
  I've got to admit it's getting b. — LENNON, J, 5
  nae b. than he should be — BURNS, R, 6
  no b. than you should be — BEAUMONT, F, 1
  something b. than our brains to depend upon — CHESTERFIELD, 4TH EARL OF, 16
  the old is b. — BIBLE: LUKE, 15
  when I'm bad I'm b. — WEST, M, 15
  When you meet someone b. . . . turn your thoughts to becoming his equal — CONFUCIUS, 1
  You're a b. man than I am, Gunga Din! — KIPLING, R, 13
**Beulah** B., peel me a grape — WEST, M, 4
**bewailing** the sum of life's b. — LANDON, L, 3
**beware** all should cry, B.! — COLERIDGE, S, 15
  B. of the artist who's an intellectual — FITZGERALD, F, 9
  B. of the dog — PETRONIUS ARBITER, 1

springing from b. to b. like the chamois of the Alps
    WODEHOUSE, SIR P, 18
**blondes** Gentlemen always seem to remember b.    LOOS, A, 1
**blood** b. and iron    BISMARCK, PRINCE VON, 1
B. is thicker    PROVERBS, 94
b., toil, tears and sweat    CHURCHILL, SIR W, 41
critics . . . desire our b., not our pain    NIETZSCHE, F, 14
He is all b., dirt and sucked sugar stick    YEATS, W, 35
his b. be on us    BIBLE: MATTHEW, 85
humble and meek are thirsting for b.    ORTON, J, 3
I am in b. /Stepp'd in so far    SHAKESPEARE, W, 172
leeches have red b..    CUVIER, BARON, 1
my b. of the new testament    BIBLE: MATTHEW, 78
. . . rather have b. on my hands . . . Pilate    GREENE, G, 3
Seas of B.    SITWELL, DAME E, 2
shed his b. for the country    ROOSEVELT, T, 6
The b. of the martyrs is the seed of the Church    TERTULLIAN, Q, 1
the b. that she has spilt    COWPER, W, 3
the old savage England, whose last b. flows still    LAWRENCE, D, 20
There are two kinds of b.    TUWIM, J, 1
the River Tiber foaming with much b.    POWELL, E, 1
thy brother's b. crieth unto me    BIBLE: GENESIS, 18
trading on the b. of my men    LEE, R, 2
washed their robes . . . in the b. of the lamb    BIBLE: REVELATIONS, 7
without shedding of b. is no remission    BIBLE: HEBREWS, 6
You can't get b.    PROVERBS, 473
your b. of your lives will I require    BIBLE: GENESIS, 27
**bloodiness** The sink is the great symbol of the b. of family life
    MITCHELL, J, 1
**bloody** All the faces . . . seem to be b. Poms    CHARLES, P, 1
My head is b., but unbowed    HENLEY, W, 1
**bloom** It's a sort of b. on a woman    BARRIE, SIR J, 8
lilac is in b.    BROOKE, R, 2
**blossom** Love's perfect b.    PATMORE, C, 1
the desert shall . . . b. as the rose    BIBLE: ISAIAH, 25
**blot** b. me . . . out of thy book    BIBLE: EXODUS, 29
**blow** A b. in cold blood    SHAW, G, 28
Another year! – another deadly b.    WORDSWORTH, W, 46
B., b., thou winter wind    SHAKESPEARE, W, 25
Beware of the man who does not return your b.    SHAW, G, 24
B. . . . till you burst    BROWNING, R, 42
but a word and a b.    BUNYAN, J, 6
B., winds, and crack your cheeks    SHAKESPEARE, W, 137
themselves must strike the b.    BYRON, 6TH BARON, 9
this b. /Might be the be-all and the end-all here
    SHAKESPEARE, W, 164
**bloweth** the wind b. where it listeth    BIBLE: JOHN, 8
**bludgeoning** the b. of the people    WILDE, O, 51
**blue** Little Boy B., /Come blow your horn    NURSERY RHYMES, 29
that little tent of b.    WILDE, O, 1
The b. ribbon of the turf.    DISRAELI, 1ST EARL OF BEACONSFIELD, 5
The essence of any b. material    RUE, D, 1
What are those b. remembered hills    HOUSMAN, A, 13
**blues** Twentieth-Century B.    COWARD, SIR N, 18
**blue-vested** short, b. people    COREN, A, 3
**blunder** . . . poverty . . . is a b.    JEROME, J, 3
worse than a crime, it is a b.    BOULAY DE LA MEURTHE, A, 1
Youth is a b.    DISRAELI, 1ST EARL OF BEACONSFIELD, 1
**blunders** escaped making the b. that he has made    HELPS, SIR A, 3
**blush** a b. to the cheek of a young person    DICKENS, C, 36
b. to find it fame    POPE, A, 8
flower is born to b. unseen    GRAY, T, 5
**blushes** Man is the only animal that b.    TWAIN, M, 6
take away the candle and spare my b.    JAMES, H, 10
**boar** when his half-civilized ancestors were hunting the wild b.
    BENJAMIN, J, 1
**boarding-house** Any two meals at a b.    LEACOCK, S, 7
**boat** a beautiful pea-green b.    LEAR, E, 8
Do they allow tipping on the b.    MARX, G, 17
It was involuntary. They sank my b.    KENNEDY, J, 1
On a slow b. to China    LOESSER, F, 1
**boating** Jolly b. weather    CORY, W, 1
**boats** messing about in b.    GRAHAME, K, 1
we look for happiness in b. and carriage rides    HORACE, 21
**Bobby** B. Shafto's gone to sea    NURSERY RHYMES, 5
**bob-tail** I bet my money on the b. nag    FOSTER, S, 1
**bodies** many b. of the saints which slept arose    BIBLE: MATTHEW, 87
our dead b. must tell the tale    SCOTT, CAPTAIN, 2
well-developed b., fairly developed minds, and undeveloped hearts
    FORSTER, E, 3
**body** a sound mind in a sound b..    JUVENAL, 10

b. of a weak and feeble woman    ELIZABETH I, 8
company, . . . have neither a soul to lose nor a b. to kick
    SMITH, S, 5
Happiness is beneficial for the b.    PROUST, M, 18
Man has no B. distinct from his Soul    BLAKE, W, 29
mind that makes the b. rich    SHAKESPEARE, W, 272
more familiar with Africa than my own b.    ORTON, J, 1
Our b. is a machine for living    TOLSTOY, COUNT, 7
Over my dead b.    KAUFMAN, G, 1
take, eat; this is my b.    BIBLE: MATTHEW, 78
the human b. is sacred    WHITMAN, W, 3
the soul is not more than the b.    WHITMAN, W, 7
Why be given a b. if you . . . keep it shut up    MANSFIELD, K, 1
your b. is the temple of the Holy Ghost    BIBLE: I CORINTHIANS, 6
**Bognor** Bugger B.    GEORGE V, 4
**boil** b. at different degrees    EMERSON, R, 22
**boiler** The United States is like a gigantic b.    GREY, VISCOUNT, 1
**bold** He was a b. man    PROVERBS, 197
**boldness** B., and again b., and always b.    DANTON, G, 1
**bombs** b. *are* unbelievable until they . . . fall    WHITE, P, 1
Come, friendly b., and fall on Slough    BETJEMAN, SIR J, 8
drop b. . . . hit civilians    GOLDWATER, B, 3
Ears like b.    CAUSLEY, C, 1
test the Russians, not the b.    GAITSKELL, H, 1
**Bonaparte** The three-o'-clock in the morning courage, which B.
thought was the rarest    THOREAU, H, 13
**Bonar** Poor B. can't bear being called a liar
    LLOYD GEORGE, EARL OF DWYFOR, 2
**bone** b. to his b.    BIBLE: EZEKIEL, 7
The nearer the b.    PROVERBS, 402
**boneless** the b. wonder    CHURCHILL, SIR W, 37
**bones** East and west on fields forgotten /Bleach the b. of
comrades slain    HOUSMAN, A, 12
Heat, madam! . . . to take off my flesh and sit in my b.    SMITH, S, 4
Of his b. are coral made    SHAKESPEARE, W, 273
O ye dry b.    BIBLE: EZEKIEL, 6
the b. which thou hast broken    PSALMS, 35
The healthy b. of a single Pomeranian grenadier
    BISMARCK, PRINCE VON, 5
**bonhomie** Overcame his natural b.    BENTLEY, E, 5
**bonjour** B. *tristesse*    ELUARD, P, 1
**bonkers** If the British public falls for this . . . it will be . . . b.
    HAILSHAM, BARON, 2
**Bonnie** My B. lies over the ocean    ANONYMOUS, 58
Oh, bring back my B. to me    ANONYMOUS, 58
**bonnie** *By the b. milldams o' Binnorie*    ANONYMOUS, 97
**bonny** the child that is born on the Sabbath day /Is b. and
blithe, and good and gay    NURSERY RHYMES, 35
**Boojum** Snark was a B.    CARROLL, L, 19
**book** A b. may be amusing    GOLDSMITH, O, 23
A b.'s a b., although there's nothing in't    BYRON, 6TH BARON, 34
a b. . . . sealed with seven seals    BIBLE: REVELATIONS, 4
A b. that furnishes no quotations is, . . . a plaything    PEACOCK, T, 3
a b. that is a b. flowers once    LAWRENCE, D, 38
a b. to kill time    MACAULAY, DAME R, 6
A good b. is the best of friends    TUPPER, M, 1
A good b. is the precious life-blood    MILTON, J, 2
An angel writing in a b. of gold:    HUNT, 1
Another damned, thick, square b.    GLOUCESTER, DUKE OF, 1
any b. should be banned    WEST, DAME R, 4
Bell, b., and candle    SHAKESPEARE, W, 126
blot me . . . out of thy b.    BIBLE: EXODUS, 29
dainties that are bred in a b.    SHAKESPEARE, W, 154
do not throw this b. about    BELLOC, H, 1
Every b. must be chewed    PROVERBS, 131
go away and write a b. about it    BRABAZON OF TARA, BARON, 1
Go, litel b.    CHAUCER, G, 19
half a library to make one b.    JOHNSON, S, 91
he who destroys a good b., kills reason    MILTON, J, 1
If a b. is worth reading    RUSKIN, J, 1
I'll drown my b.    SHAKESPEARE, W, 278
in thy b. were all my members written    PSALMS, 81
moral or an immoral b.    WILDE, O, 41
never got around to reading the b.    MARX, G, 21
Never judge a cover by its b.    LEBOWITZ, F, 1
that everyone has in him to write one b.    MAUGHAM, W, 20
the b. of the living    PSALMS, 44
The number one b. . . . was written by a committee    MAYER, L, 1
The possession of a b.    BURGESS, A, 4
There are two motives for reading a b.    RUSSELL, EARL, 6

**bough** Loaf of Bread beneath the B.                    FITZGERALD, E, 5
**bought** b. things because she wanted 'em              VANBURGH, SIR J, 2
**bouillabaisse** B. is only good because cooked by the French
                                                         DOUGLAS, N, 2
**boulder** When the torrent sweeps a man against a b.
                                                         STEVENSON, R, 14
**Boulogne** There was an old man of B.                  ANONYMOUS, 92
**bound** Tomorrow my hands will be b.                   BAILLY, J, 1
**bountiful** Lady B.                                     FARQUHAR, G, 2
**bouquet** the b. is better than the taste              POTTER, S, 7
**bourgeois** How beastly the b. is                      LAWRENCE, D, 9
**bourgeoisie** the British b. have spoken of themselves as
 gentlemen                                               WAUGH, E, 10
**bourn** from whose b. /No traveller returns            SHAKESPEARE, W, 62
**bovine** The cow is of the b. ilk                      NASH, O, 1
**bow** at the name of Jesus every knee should b.
                                                         BIBLE: PHILIPPIANS, 1
 B., b., ye lower middle classes                         GILBERT, SIR W, 15
 I'm sure I don't know, /Says the great bell at B.
                                                         NURSERY RHYMES, 41
 I, said the Sparrow, /With my b. and arrow              NURSERY RHYMES, 73
**bowels** in the b. of Christ                           CROMWELL, O, 2
 my b. were moved for him                                BIBLE: SONG OF SOLOMON, 13
**bower-bird** I'm a bit of a b.                         WHITE, P, 3
**bowl** inverted B. we call The Sky                     FITZGERALD, E, 15
 love in a golden b.                                     BLAKE, W, 9
 They came to see me bat not to see you b.               GRACE, W, 1
**bow-wow** Daddy wouldn't buy me a b.                   TABRAR, J, 1
**box** B. about: 'twill come to my father anon          AUBREY, J, 1
 Take that black b. away                                 TREE, SIR H, 9
**boy** And said, What a good b. am I                    NURSERY RHYMES, 30
 a secret way . . . of getting at a b.                   DICKENS, C, 17
 A thing of duty is a b. for ever                        O'BRIEN, F, 1
 every b. and every gal /That's born into the world alive
                                                         GILBERT, SIR W, 19
 If . . . I were the only b.                             GROSSMITH THE YOUNGER, G, 1
 Let the b. win his spurs                                EDWARD III, 1
 Love is a b.                                            BUTLER, S, 4
 Mad about the b.                                        COWARD, SIR N, 9
 rarely . . . one can see in a little b. the promise of a man
                                                         DUMAS, FILS, 3
 Shades of the prison-house begin to close /Upon the growing b.
                                                         WORDSWORTH, W, 23
 The b. I love is up in the gallery                      WARE, G, 1
 The b. stood on the burning deck                        HEMANS, F, 1
 the little b. /Who lives down the lane                  NURSERY RHYMES, 4
 'tis little joy /To know I'm farther off from heav'n /Than when . . .
 a b.                                                    HOOD, T, 7
**boyhood** The smiles, the tears, /Of b.'s years        MOORE, T, 7
**boys** As flies to wanton b.                           SHAKESPEARE, W, 144
 B. and girls come out to play                           NURSERY RHYMES, 6
 B. are capital fellows in their own way                 LAMB, C, 7
 B. do not grow up gradually                             CONNOLLY, C, 11
 B. will be b.                                           HOPE, A, 5
 Claret is the liquor for b.                             JOHNSON, S, 125
 Where are the b. of the Old Brigade                     WEATHERLY, F, 1
 Where . . . b. plan for what . . . young girls plan for whom
                                                         GILMAN, C, 3
 Written by office b. for office b.                      SALISBURY, MARQUESS OF, 1
**bracelet** diamond and safire b. lasts forever         LOOS, A, 3
**braces** Damn b.                                       BLAKE, W, 26
**braes** Ye banks and b.                                BURNS, R, 22
**brain** a Bear of Very Little B.                       MILNE, A, 6
 b. attic stocked with all the furniture that he is likely to use
                                                         DOYLE, SIR A, 10
 B., n. An apparatus with which we think                 BIERCE, A, 2
 If it is for mind that we are seaching the b.           SHERRINGTON, SIR C, 1
 Let schoolmasters puzzle their b.                       GOLDSMITH, O, 19
 the human b. is a device to keep the ears from grating
                                                         DE VRIES, P, 1
 we are supposing the b. . . . more than a telephone-exchange
                                                         SHERRINGTON, SIR C, 1
 with no deep researches vex the b.                      CRABBE, G, 3
 You've got the b. of a four-year-old boy                MARX, G, 12
**brains** a girl with b. ought to do something else     LOOS, A, 2
 b. enough to make a fool of himself                     STEVENSON, R, 19
 I mix them with my b.                                   OPIE, J, 1
 something better than our b. to depend upon
                                                         CHESTERFIELD, 4TH EARL OF, 16
 What good are b. to a man                               WODEHOUSE, SIR P, 1
**branch** Cut is the b. that might have grown           MARLOWE, C, 6

**brandy** I am not well; pray get me . . . b.           GEORGE IV, 1
**brass** Men's evil manners live in b.                  SHAKESPEARE, W, 105
 sounding b.                                             BIBLE: I CORINTHIANS, 18
**brave** Any fool can be b. on a battle field           MITCHELL, M, 2
 b. new world . . . such people in't                     SHAKESPEARE, W, 279
 Fortune favours the b.                                  TERENCE, 3
 land of the free, and the home of the b.                KEY, F, 1
 Many b. men . . . before Agamemnon's time; . . . are
 all, unmourned and unknown, . . . because they lack their sacred
 poet.                                                   HORACE, 42
 the B. deserves the Fair                                DRYDEN, J, 14
 we could never learn to be b. . . . if there were only joy
                                                         KELLER, H, 2
**braw** a b. brecht moonlecht necht                     LAUDER, SIR H, 1
**Brazil** B., where the nuts come from                  THOMAS, B, 1
**breach** a custom more honour'd in the b.              SHAKESPEARE, W, 49
 Once more unto the b.                                   SHAKESPEARE, W, 95
**bread** b. and cheese, and kisses                      SWIFT, J, 9
 b. and circuses                                         JUVENAL, 8
 b. eaten in secret is pleasant                          BIBLE: PROVERBS, 6
 b. enough and to spare                                  BIBLE: LUKE, 28
 B. is the staff of life                                 PROVERBS, 97
 cast thy b. upon the waters                             BIBLE: ECCLESIASTES, 23
 I am the b. of life                                     BIBLE: JOHN, 16
 if his son ask b., will he give him a stone             BIBLE: MATTHEW, 27
 Jesus took b., and blessed it                           BIBLE: MATTHEW, 78
 known of them in breaking of b.                         BIBLE: LUKE, 40
 Loaf of B. beneath the Bough                            FITZGERALD, E, 5
 man shall not live by b. alone                          BIBLE: MATTHEW, 6
 that b. should be so dear                               HOOD, T, 12
 the b. of tears                                         PSALMS, 49
 Their learning is like b. in a besieged town            JOHNSON, S, 93
 the living b.                                           BIBLE: JOHN, 18
 This b. I break was once the oat                        THOMAS, D, 11
**breakfast** she must not reheat his sins for b.        DIETRICH, M, 1
**breakfast-table** ready for the national b.            TROLLOPE, A, 5
**breakfast-time** critical period in matrimony is b.    HERBERT, SIR A, 5
**breaking** known of them in b. of bread               BIBLE: LUKE, 40
**breast** charms to soothe a savage b.                  CONGREVE, W, 6
 my baby at my b.                                        SHAKESPEARE, W, 17
**breast-feeding** Every luxury . . . – atheism, b., circumcision.
                                                         ORTON, J, 4
**breastplate** the b. of righteousness                  BIBLE: EPHESIANS, 4
**breasts** they add weight to the b.                    COLETTE, S, 5
**breath** blow hot and cold with the same b.            AESOP, 7
 Can storied urn . . . /Back to its mansion call the fleeting b.
                                                         GRAY, T, 4
 He reaps the bearded grain at a b.                      LONGFELLOW, H, 9
 in this harsh world draw thy b. in pain                 SHAKESPEARE, W, 75
 The years to come seemed waste of b.                    YEATS, W, 14
 when the b. of man goeth forth                          PSALMS, 89
 wish the night /Had borne my b. away                    HOOD, T, 6
 world will hold its b.                                  HITLER, A, 8
**breathed** God . . . b. into his nostrils              BIBLE: GENESIS, 8
**brecht** a braw b. moonlecht necht                     LAUDER, SIR H, 1
**breed** happy b. of men                                SHAKESPEARE, W, 237
 Men are . . . more careful of the b. of their horses and dogs than
 of their children                                       PENN, W, 2
**breeding** Good b. consists in concealing
 who are formed by a different b.                        DISRAELI, B, 9
**breeks** taking the b. aff a wild Highlandman          SCOTT, SIR W, 2
**breeze** The fair b. blew                              COLERIDGE, S, 27
**breezes** spicy b. /Blow soft o'er Ceylon's isle       HEBER, R, 2
**brethren** the least of these my b.                    BIBLE: MATTHEW, 76
**brevity** B. is the soul of lingerie                   PARKER, D, 14
 B. is the soul of wit                                   SHAKESPEARE, W, 53
**brewery** O take me to a b. /And leave me there to die
                                                         ANONYMOUS, 43
**bribe** doing nothing for a b.                         SHAKESPEARE, W, 36
 The man who offers a b. gives away . . . his own importance
                                                         GREENE, G, 2
 You cannot hope /to b. or twist . . . the /British journalist
                                                         WOLFE, H, 1
**bribes** How many b. he had taken                      BENTLEY, E, 1
**bribing** Money is good for b. yourself                REINHARDT, G, 1
**brick** carried a . . . b. in his pocket               SWIFT, J, 4
 He is a man of b.                                       UPDIKE, J, 4
 I found it b.                                           AUGUSTUS, 1
**bricklayers** B. kick their wives to death             WELLS, H, 17
**bricks** You can't make b.                             PROVERBS, 475
**bride** a b.'s attitude towards her betrothed          MUIR, F, 2

as a b. adorned for her husband     BIBLE: REVELATIONS, 18
It helps . . . to remind your b. that you gave up a throne for her
    EDWARD VIII, 4
unravish'd b. of quietness     KEATS, J, 22
**bridegroom** behold, the b. cometh     BIBLE: MATTHEW, 70
the friend of the b. . . . rejoiceth     BIBLE: JOHN, 11
**bridge** Beautiful Railway B. of the Silv'ry Tay     MCGONAGALL, W, 2
I stood on the b. at midnight     LONGFELLOW, H, 2
Like a b. over troubled water     SIMON, P, 1
London B. is broken down     NURSERY RHYMES, 33
over the B. of Sighs into eternity     KIERKEGAARD, S, 2
They promise to build a b. even where there's no river
    KHRUSHCHEV, N, 7
**brief** I strive to be b., and I become obscure.     HORACE, 1
Out, out, 'b. candle     SHAKESPEARE, W, 177
**brigade** Where are the boys of the Old B.     WEATHERLY, F, 1
**brigands** B. demand your money     BUTLER, S, 29
**bright** her beauty made /The b. world dim     SHELLEY, P, 24
Look on the b. side     PROVERBS, 268
the creature hath a purpose and its eyes are b. with it
    KEATS, J, 64
Tiger! burning b.     BLAKE, W, 37
young lady named B.     BULLER, A, 1
**brightening** He died when his prospects seemed to be b.
    ANONYMOUS, 27
**brighter** proclaiming that women are b. than men.     LOOS, A, 5
**brightness** To pass away ere life hath lost its b.     HASTINGS, L, 1
**Brighton** Like B. pier, . . . inadequate for getting to France.
    KINNOCK, N, 7
**bright-star** Johnny-the-b.     PUDNEY, J, 2
**brilliance** No b. is needed in the law     MORTIMER, J, 2
**brilliant** a far less b. pen than mine     BEERBOHM, SIR M, 2
b. men . . . will come to a bad end     BEERBOHM, SIR M, 9
The dullard's envy of b. men     BEERBOHM, SIR M, 9
**brillig** Twas b., and the slithy toves     CARROLL, L, 20
**brimstone** b. and fire     BIBLE: GENESIS, 37
**bring** thou knowest not what a day may b. forth
    BIBLE: PROVERBS, 16
**Britain** a time when B. had a savage culture     BANDA, H, 1
battle of B. is about to begin     CHURCHILL, SIR W, 45
B. . . . Fabian Society writ large     HAMILTON, W, 2
B. fit country for heroes to live in
    LLOYD GEORGE, EARL OF DWYFOR, 6
B. is no longer in the politics of the pendulum     THATCHER, M, 3
B. is not . . . easily rocked by revolution     HAMILTON, W, 2
to help B. to become a Third Programme     WILKINSON, E, 1
When B. first, at heaven's command     THOMSON, J, 1
**Britannia** Rule, B., rule the waves; /Britons never will be slaves
    THOMSON, J, 1
**British** but we are B. – thank God
    MONTGOMERY OF ALAMEIN, VISCOUNT, 2
less known by the B. than these selfsame B. Islands BORROW, G, 1
socialism . . . alien to the B. character     THATCHER, M, 12
The artists retired. The B. remained     WHISTLER, J, 13
The B., being brought up on team games     PARKINSON, C, 3
The B. love permanence     CASSON, SIR H, 1
the magnificent fair play of the B. criminal law     DOYLE, SIR A, 8
when a B. Prime Minister sneezed     LEVIN, B, 2
**British Museum** a little room somewhere in the B. that
    PRIESTLEY, J, 4
a reflection of the B. Reading Room     SPARK, M, 12
I keep my books at the B.     BUTLER, S, 8
There is in the B. an enormous mind     WOOLF, V, 6
**Briton** as only a free-born B. can do     THACKERAY, W, 10
**Britons** B. were only natives     SELLAR, W, 4
Rule, Britannia, rule the waves; /B. never will be slaves
    THOMSON, J, 1
**broad** She is a smart old b.     RUNYON, D, 5
She's the B. and I'm the High     SPRING-RICE, SIR C, 1
**broken** A b. head in Cold Bath Fields     MACAULAY, BARON, 21
baying for b. glass     WAUGH, E, 2
I am become like a b. vessel     PSALMS, 22
Laws were made to be b.     NORTH, C, 2
Like many of the upper class /He liked the sound of b. glass
    BELLOC, H, 12
peace has b. out     BRECHT, B, 10
the bones which thou hast b.     PSALMS, 35
those that are b. in heart     PSALMS, 91
**broker** An honest b.     BISMARCK, PRINCE VON, 6
**bronchitis** nobody goes to the theatre unless he . . . has b.
    AGATE, J, 1

**bronze** executed a memorial longer lasting than b.     HORACE, 39
**brook** b. no contradiction     WEBSTER, J, 2
the b. Cherith     BIBLE: I KINGS, 5
**brothel** a sort of metaphysical b. for emotions     KOESTLER, A, 1
**brothels** b. with bricks of Religion     BLAKE, W, 18
**brother** am I my b.'s keeper     BIBLE: GENESIS, 18
I want to be the white man's b.     KING, M, 2
love God, and hateth his b.     BIBLE: I JOHN, 5
Pardon me, . . . I am my b.     JACOBI, K, 1
the same is my b.     BIBLE: MATTHEW, 43
**brotherhood** Freedom! Equality! B.     ANONYMOUS, 51
**brother-in-law** not his b.     KING, M, 2
**brotherly** let b. love continue     BIBLE: HEBREWS, 5
**brothers** All men are b.     POWELL, A, 3
all the B. were valiant     NEWCASTLE, DUCHESS OF, 1
B. all /In honour     WORDSWORTH, W, 34
the poor are our b. and sisters
**brought** b. nothing into this world     BIBLE: I TIMOTHY, 5
never b. to min     BURNS, R, 2
**Brown** John B.'s body     HALL, C, 1
**bruise** it shall b. thy head     BIBLE: GENESIS, 15
sweetest fragrance from the herb . . . tread on it and b. it
    TROLLOPE, A, 8
**bruised** it is often a comfort to . . . be b. in a new place
    IRVING, W, 3
**Brunswick** Hamelin Town's in B.     BROWNING, R, 39
**Brussels** meeting in a darkened bedroom in a B. hotel
    THOMPSON, E, 1
**brutality** industry without art is b.     RUSKIN, J, 2
Sentimentality is a superstructure covering b.     JUNG, C, 8
**brute** I never saw a b. I hated so     BROWNING, R, 14
**brutes** Exterminate all b.     CONRAD, J, 1
Thanks to words, we have been able to rise above the b.
    HUXLEY, A, 1
**Brutus** B. is an honourable man     SHAKESPEARE, W, 117
Caesar had his B. – Charles the First, his Cromwell     HENRY, P, 1
**bubble** Life is mostly froth and b.     GORDON, A, 1
**bubbles** With beaded b. winking at the brim     KEATS, J, 32
**buck** The b. stops here     TRUMAN, H, 8
**Buckingham** changing guard at B. Palace     MILNE, A, 4
**buckle** One, two, /B. my shoe     NURSERY RHYMES, 40
**buckler** his faithfulness and truth shall be thy shield and b.
    PSALMS, 57
**bucks** bet you a hundred b. he ain't in here     DILLINGHAM, C, 1
**bud** And now in age I b. again     HERBERT, G, 4
**Buddhism** nothing in Christianity or B. that quite matches     SAKI, 10
**budding** That which sets / . . . The b. rose above the rose full
blown     WORDSWORTH, W, 36
**buds** Gather the flowers, but spare the b.     MARVELL, A, 8
the darling b. of May     SHAKESPEARE, W, 254
**buffalo** give me a home where the b. roam     HIGLEY, B, 1
**bugger** B. Bognor     GEORGE V, 4
**build** let us think that we b. for ever     RUSKIN, J, 8
The end is to b. well     WOTTON, SIR H, 1
They promise to b. a bridge even where there's no river
    KHRUSHCHEV, N, 7
**building** twenty years of marriage make her . . . like a public b.
    WILDE, O, 53
**buildings** I go amongst the b. of a city     KEATS, J, 64
**built** till we have b. Jerusalem     BLAKE, W, 31
**Bulben** Under bare Ben B.'s head     YEATS, W, 30
**bull** Better send them a Papal B.     CURZON, MARQUESS, 2
Down at the old 'B. and Bush'     TILZER, H, 1
take the b. between the teeth     GOLDWYN, S, 16
When you take the b. by the horns     RIDGE, W, 1
**bullet** ballot is stronger than the b.     LINCOLN, A, 7
Each b. has got its commission     DIBDIN, C, 1
Every b. has its billet     WILLIAM III, 2
The b. that is to kill me     NAPOLEON I, 6
**bullets** I heard the b. whistle, . . . charming in the sound
    WASHINGTON, G, 2
**bullfighting** B. is the only art     HEMINGWAY, E, 1
England may as well dam . . . the Nile with b.     CHILD, L, 3
**bulrushes** an ark of b.     BIBLE: EXODUS, 2
**bump** And things that go b. in the night     ANONYMOUS, 19
**bums** art and literature are left to a lot of shabby b.     LEWIS, S, 2
**Bunbury** an invaluable permanent invalid called B.     WILDE, O, 17
**bungalow** proud of the position of the b., . . . in the country
    WILSON, SIR A, 1
**bunk** History is more or less b.     FORD, H, 1

## C

candid save me, from the c. friend — CANNING, G. 1
candidates C. should not attempt more than six — BELLOC, H. 16
candle a c. of understanding — BIBLE: II ESDRAS, 7
Bell, book, and c. — SHAKESPEARE, W. 126
blow out your c. . . . to find your way — DIDEROT, D. 1
It is burning a farthing c. at Dover, — JOHNSON, S. 65
light a c., and put it under a bushel — BIBLE: MATTHEW, 11
light a c. to the sun — SIDNEY, A. 1
Like a c. burnt out — YEATS, W. 19
little c. throws his beams — SHAKESPEARE, W. 197
My c. burns at both ends — MILLAY, E. 1
Out, out, brief c. — SHAKESPEARE, W. 177
take away the c. and spare my blushes — JAMES, H. 10
thou . . . shalt light my c. — PSALMS, 7
we shall this day light such a c. . . . as I trust shall never be put out — LATIMER, H. 2
candle-light Can I get there by c. — NURSERY RHYMES, 17
candles She would rather light c. than curse the darkness — STEVENSON, A. 8
candlestick The butcher, the baker, /The c.-maker — NURSERY RHYMES, 49
canker killing as the c. to the rose — MILTON, J. 18
cannibal Better sleep with a sober c. than a drunken Christian — MELVILLE, H. 1
cannon-ball c. took off his legs, — HOOD, T. 2
canoe every man paddle his own c. — MARRYAT, F. 3
Canossa We will not go to C. — BISMARCK, PRINCE VON, 4
cant clear your mind of c. . . . — JOHNSON, S. 143
love – all the wretched c. of it — GREER, G. 3
where the Greeks had modesty, we have c. — PEACOCK, T. 2
capability Negative C. — KEATS, J. 48
capable c. of being well set to music — ADDISON, J. 9
capital Boys are c. fellows in their own way — LAMB, C. 7
capitalism C. re-creates — RICHLER, M. 1
c. . . . : the process whereby American girls turn into American women — HAMPTON, C. 3
I am going to fight c. — PANKHURST, S. 2
imperialism is the monopoly stage of c. — LENIN, V. 1
Lenin was the first to discover that c. 'inevitably' caused war — TAYLOR, A. 4
militarism . . . is one of the chief bulwarks of c. — KELLER, H. 1
unacceptable face of c. — HEATH, E. 1
We cannot remove the evils of c. — KINNOCK, N. 4
Capitalist C. production begets . . . its own negation — MARX, K. 5
Not every problem someone has with his girlfriend is . . . due to . . . c. . . . production — MARCUSE, H. 1
capitulate I will be conquered; I will not c. — JOHNSON, S. 152
Capricorn Lady C., . . . was . . . keeping open bed — HUXLEY, A. 7
captain C. of the Pinafore — GILBERT, SIR W. 7
I am the c. of my soul — HENLEY, W. 2
captains C. of industry — CARLYLE, T. 20
capten C., art tha sleepin' there below — NEWBOLT, SIR H. 3
captive Beauty stands . . . Led c. — MILTON, J. 49
they that led us away c. required . . . a song — PSALMS, 83
captivity such as are for the c., to the c. — BIBLE: JEREMIAH, 4
turn our c., O Lord — PSALMS, 79
car The c. has become the carapace — MCLUHAN, M. 5
carapace The car has become the c. — MCLUHAN, M. 5
carbon atom c. possesses certain exceptional properties — JEANS, SIR J. 1
carbuncle Like a c. on the face of an old and valued friend — CHARLES, PRINCE, 3
cardinal unbecoming for a c. to ski badly — JOHN PAUL II, 1
cards an old age of c. — POPE, A. 42
cheat at c. — BOSWELL, J. 2
I have not learned to play at c. — JOHNSON, S. 160
card table wrestled with a self-adjusting c. — THURBER, J. 7
care age is full of c. — SHAKESPEARE, W. 230
Begone, dull c. — ANONYMOUS, 10
C. /Sat on his faded cheek — MILTON, J. 30
I c. for nobody, . . . /If no one cares for me — BICKERSTAFFE, I. 2
I don't c. for war — NAPOLEON III, 2
Our progress . . . /Is trouble and c. — LONGFELLOW, H. 12
pleasures are their only c., — COWPER, W. 18
Sleep that knits up the ravell'd sleave of c. — SHAKESPEARE, W. 167
so vain . . . c. for the opinion of those we don't c. for — ESCHENBACH, M. 3
take c. of the minutes — CHESTERFIELD, 4TH EARL OF, 7
Take c. of the pence — CHESTERFIELD, 4TH EARL OF, 6
what is past my help is past my c. — BEAUMONT, F. 2
career a lover with any other c. in view — WELLS, H. 3

having a c. of my own — BALFOUR, 1ST EARL OF, 1
Miss Madeleine Philips . . . was a c. — WELLS, H. 3
nothing which might damage his c. — BARRIE, SIR J. 10
science was the only c. worth following — JOLIOT-CURIE, I. 1
careers The best c. advice to give to the young — WHITEHORN, K. 6
careful be very c. o' vidders — DICKENS, C. 42
we are not c. to answer thee in this matter — BIBLE: DANIEL, 3
careless first fine c. rapture — BROWNING, R. 25
carelessness To lose one parent, . . . a misfortune; to lose both looks like c. — WILDE, O. 23
with a slow deliberate c. — LAWRENCE, T. 4
cares the earth where c. abound — WORDSWORTH, W. 68
careth he that is married c. . . . how he may please his wife — BIBLE: I CORINTHIANS, 10
cargo With a c. of ivory — MASEFIELD, J. 2
With a c. of Tyne coal — MASEFIELD, J. 3
caring take millions off the c. services — KINNOCK, N. 8
Carpe C. diem — HORACE, 32
carpenter Walrus and the C. — CARROLL, L. 24
carpet a Turkey c. bears to a picture — MACAULAY, BARON, 17
carpet bags Eat slowly: only men in rags . . . /Mistake themselves for c. — RALEIGH, SIR W. 7
carriage Go together like a horse and c. — CAHN, S. 1
very small second-class c. — GILBERT, SIR W. 21
carriage rides we look for happiness in boats and c. — HORACE, 21
carriages when they think they are alone in railway c. — MILLER, J. 2
carry certain we can c. nothing out — BIBLE: I TIMOTHY, 5
Carthage C. must be destroyed — CATO THE ELDER, 1
Cary Grant Old C. fine — GRANT, C. 1
case If ever there was a c. of clearer evidence — ARABIN, W. 1
in our c. we have not got — REED, H. 3
the c. is still before the courts. — HORACE, 5
the reason of the c. — POWELL, SIR J. 1
there had been a lady in the c. — BYRON, 6TH BARON, 26
The world is everything that is the c. — WITTGENSTEIN, L. 2
casements Charm'd magic c. — KEATS, J. 34
cash Nothing links man to man like . . . c. — SICKERT, W. 1
only the poor who pay c. — FRANCE, A. 10
take the C. in hand — FITZGERALD, E. 6
cashiers of the Musical Banks — BUTLER, S. 2
casino I have come to regard . . . courts . . . as a c. — INGRAMS, R. 1
cask A c. of wine — PROVERBS, 5
casket seal the hushed c. of my soul — KEATS, J. 43
Cassius C. has a lean and hungry look — SHAKESPEARE, W. 107
cassock C., band, and hymn-book too — WILBERFORCE, S. 2
cassowary If I were a c. — WILBERFORCE, S. 2
cast c. thy bread upon the waters — BIBLE: ECCLESIASTES, 23
he that is without sin . . . let him first c. a stone — BIBLE: JOHN, 19
him that cometh to me I will in no wise c. out — BIBLE: JOHN, 17
pale c. of thought — SHAKESPEARE, W. 63
The die is c. — CAESAR, J. 3
casteth perfect love c. out fear — BIBLE: I JOHN, 4
casting It is no good c. out devils — LAWRENCE, D. 34
castle A c. called Doubting C. — BUNYAN, J. 7
The house of every one is to him as his c. — COKE, SIR E. 1
Castlereagh Murder . . . had a mask like C. — SHELLEY, P. 11
castles C. in the air — IBSEN, H. 7
Pale Death kicks his way equally . . . the c. of kings — HORACE, 27
the c. I have, are built with air — JONSON, B. 3
casualty except the c. list of the World War — CAPONE, A. 1
The first c. when war comes — JOHNSON, H. 1
cat A c. has nine lives — PROVERBS, 6
A c. may look — PROVERBS, 7
a C. of such deceitfulness — ELIOT, T. 14
c. is a diagram and pattern of subtle air — LESSING, D. 6
God . . . a cosmic Cheshire c. — HUXLEY, SIR J. 2
Had Tiberius been a c. — ARNOLD, M. 31
He bought a crooked c., which caught a crooked mouse — NURSERY RHYMES, 57
he is a very fine c. — JOHNSON, S. 142
Hey diddle diddle, /The c. and the fiddle — NURSERY RHYMES, 14
I'll bell the c. — DOUGLAS, 5TH EARL OF ANGUS, 1
More ways of killing a c. — KINGSLEY, C. 9
That tossed the dog, /That worried the c. — NURSERY RHYMES, 62
The C., the Rat, and Lovell our dog — COLLINGBOURNE, W. 1
What c.'s averse to fish — GRAY, T. 11
When I play with my c. — MONTAIGNE, M. 5
When the c.'s away — PROVERBS, 461
Who will bell the c. — DESCHAMPS, E. 1
cataclysm Out of their c. but one poor Noah /Dare hope to survive. — HUXLEY, A. 16

catastrophe to lose one's teeth is a c.    WHEELER, H, 1
When a man confronts c. . . . a woman looks in her mirror
    TURNBULL, M, 2
catch Go, and c. a falling star    DONNE, J, 11
only one c. and that was Catch-22    HELLER, J, 3
Catch-22 only one catch and that was C.    HELLER, J, 3
catches it is your business, when the wall next door c. fire
    HORACE, 22
catchwords Man is a creature who lives . . . by c. STEVENSON, R, 12
categorical This imperative is C.    KANT, I, 2
cathedrals the ancient c. – grand, wonderful, mysterious
    STANTON, E, 1
Catherine I'm glad you like my C.    WEST, M, 13
Catholic I am a C. . . . . I go to Mass every day   BELLOC, H, 15
I have a C. soul, but a Lutheran stomach    ERASMUS, D, 1
I'm still a C.    WILSON, SIR A, 3
quite lawful for a C. woman to avoid pregnancy by . . .
mathematics    MENCKEN, H, 4
Catholics C. and Communists have committed great crimes
    GREENE, G, 3
they may be C. but they are not Christians   MCCARTHY, M, 6
We know these new English C.    LAWRENCE, D, 37
cats All c. are grey    PROVERBS, 32
A lotta c. copy the Mona Lisa    ARMSTRONG, L, 1
what c. most appreciate . . . is . . . entertainment value
    HOUSEHOLD, G, 1
cattle Actors should be treated like c.   HITCHCOCK, SIR A, 1
O Mary, go and call the c. home    KINGSLEY, C, 4
cause for what high c. /This darling of the Gods   MARVELL, A, 7
the name of perseverance in a good c.    STERNE, L, 6
causes Home of lost c.    ARNOLD, M, 11
they should declare the c. which impel them to . . . separation
    JEFFERSON, T, 1
caustic Too c.? To hell with cost    GOLDWYN, S, 3
cavaliero a perfect c.    BYRON, 6TH BARON, 3
Cavaliers C. (Wrong but Wromantic)    SELLAR, W, 5
cave I should be like a lion in a c. of savage Daniels WILDE, O, 74
caverns Gluts tween ten thousand C.    KEATS, J, 38
Through c. measureless to man    COLERIDGE, S, 12
caves be c. . . . in which his shadow will be shown NIETZSCHE, F, 4
sunny pleasure-dome with c. of ice    COLERIDGE, S, 13
caviare c. to the general    SHAKESPEARE, W, 58
cavity John Brown is filling his last c.    ANONYMOUS, 74
cease have their day and c. to be    TENNYSON, BARON, 22
he maketh wars to c. in all the world    PSALMS, 32
I will not c. from mental fight    BLAKE, W, 31
restless Cromwell could not c.    MARVELL, A, 3
ceases forbearance c. to be a virtue    BURKE, E, 3
cedar spread abroad like a c. in Libanus    PSALMS, 58
cedars the c. of Libanus    PSALMS, 18
celebrate I c. myself    WHITMAN, W, 4
poetry cannot c. them    AUDEN, W, 6
celebrity A c. . . . works hard . . . to become known, then wears
dark glasses    ALLEN, F, 1
The c. . . . known for his well-knownness   BOORSTIN, D, 1
celerity C. is never more admir'd    SHAKESPEARE, W, 11
celery Genuineness . . . Like c.    HUXLEY, A, 32
The thought of two thousand people crunching c. at the same
time horrified me    SHAW, G, 43
Celia Come, my C., let us prove    JONSON, B, 14
celibacy c. is . . . a muddy horse-pond    PEACOCK, T, 5
cello The c. is not one of my favourite instruments THOMAS, I, 4
cemetery old c. in which nine of his daughters were lying
    THURBER, J, 6
censor Deleted by French c.    BENNETT, J, 1
censorship Assassination . . . the extreme form of c.   SHAW, G, 37
censure All c. of a man's self    JOHNSON, S, 122
centre I love being at the c. of things    THATCHER, M, 17
the c. cannot hold    YEATS, W, 26
century The c. on which we are entering . . . must be the c. of the
common man    WALLACE, H, 1
The great man . . . walks across his c.    LEACOCK, S, 9
the twentieth c. will be . . . the c. of Fascism   MUSSOLINI, B, 4
cereal Do you *know* what breakfast c. is made of   DAHL, R, 1
cerebrums larger c. and smaller adrenal glands   MENCKEN, H, 5
certain I am c. that we will win the election with a good majority.
    THATCHER, M, 18
nothing is c. but death and taxes    FRANKLIN, B, 15
Nothing is c. but death    PROVERBS, 316
One thing is c.    FITZGERALD, E, 10

certainties begin with c.
   BACON, 1ST BARON VERULAM, VISCOUNT ST ALBANS, 2
His doubts are better than . . . c.    HARDWICKE, EARL OF, 1
cesspool London, that great c.    DOYLE, SIR A, 14
Ceylon spicy breezes /Blow soft o'er C.'s isle   HEBER, R, 2
chaff An editor . . . separates the wheat from the c.
    STEVENSON, A, 1
chain A c. is no stronger    PROVERBS, 9
the flesh to feel the c.    BRONTE, E, 3
chains c. that tie /The hidden soul of harmony   MILTON, J, 15
It's often safer to be in c.    KAFKA, F, 2
Man . . . everywhere he is in c.    ROUSSEAU, J, 1
nothing to lose but their c.    MARX, K, 2
chair Give Dayrolles a c.    CHESTERFIELD, 4TH EARL OF, 19
the nineteenth century was the age of the editorial c.
    MCLUHAN, M, 3
chairs The c. are being brought in from the garden   AUDEN, W, 16
chaise All in a c. and pair    COWPER, W, 8
chaise-longue Wedlock – the . . . deep peace of the double bed
after the . . . c.    CAMPBELL, MRS, 2
chalices In old time we had treen c. and golden priests,
    JEWEL, J, 1
Cham That great C. of literature, Samuel Johnson   SMOLLETT, T, 6
chamber rapping at my c. door    POE, E, 1
Upstairs and downstairs /And in my lady's c.   NURSERY RHYMES, 13
chambermaid a man would be as happy in the arms of a c.
    JOHNSON, S, 123
chamois springing from blonde to blonde like the c. of the Alps
    WODEHOUSE, SIR P, 18
champagne Fighting is like c.    MITCHELL, M, 2
water flowed like c.    EVARTS, W, 1
chance every c. brought out a noble knight   TENNYSON, BARON, 18
time and c. happeneth to them all   BIBLE: ECCLESIASTES, 17
chancellor C. of the Exchequer   LOWE, VISCOUNT SHERBROOKE, 1
change C. is not made without inconvenience   HOOKER, R, 1
I c., but I cannot die    SHELLEY, P, 4
If you leave a thing alone you leave it to a torrent of c.
    CHESTERTON, G, 30
Most of the c. we think we see    FROST, R, 1
Most women set out to try to c. a man   DIETRICH, M, 4
Plus ça c.    KARR, A, 1
the largest scope for c. still lies in men's attitude to women
    BRITTAIN, V, 1
The more things c.    KARR, A, 1
There is a certain relief in c.    IRVING, W, 3
The wind of c.    MACMILLAN, EARL OF STOCKTON, 4
changed All c., c. utterly    YEATS, W, 8
changeth The old order c.    TENNYSON, BARON, 19
changez C. vos amis    DE GAULLE, C, 6
changing c. scenes of life    TATE, N, 2
Woman is always fickle and c.    VIRGIL, 9
Channel dream you are crossing the C.   GILBERT, SIR W, 21
let the last man . . . brush the C. with his sleeve.
    SCHLIEFFEN, GRAF VON, 1
chaos a perfectly possible means of overcoming c.   RICHARDS, I, 1
The grotesque c. of a Labour council – a *Labour* council
    KINNOCK, N, 9
chapel Devil always builds a c. there    DEFOE, D, 5
Who lied in the c. /Now lies in the Abbey   BYRON, 6TH BARON, 36
chapels c. had been churches    SHAKESPEARE, W, 188
chaplain twice a day the C. called    WILDE, O, 3
Chaplin C. is no business man    GOLDWYN, S, 7
chaps Biography is about C.    BENTLEY, E, 2
chapter c. of accidents    CHESTERFIELD, 4TH EARL OF, 14
c. of accidents is the longest . . . in the book   WILKES, J, 2
character I had become a woman of . . . c.   DOSTOEVSKY, A, 1
I leave my c. behind    SHERIDAN, R, 9
What is c. but the determination of incident   JAMES, H, 8
characteristic typically English c.    ADCOCK, SIR F, 1
characters c. in one of my novels    FITZGERALD, F, 13
Most women have no c.    POPE, A, 39
charge Electrical force . . . causes motion of electrical c.
    EDDINGTON, SIR A, 1
charged it was c. against me    WHITMAN, W, 2
charges who goeth a warfare . . . at his own c.
    BIBLE: I CORINTHIANS, 12
Charing-Cross between Heaven and C.    THOMPSON, F, 2
I went out to C., to see Major-general Harrison hanged
    PEPYS, S, 2
the full tide of human existence is at C.    JOHNSON, S, 90
chariot a c. . . . . of fire    BIBLE: II KINGS, 1

Swing low sweet c.     ANONYMOUS, 76
the dust beneath thy c. wheel     HOPE, L, 1
Time's winged c.     MARVELL, A, 10
**chariots** some put their trust in c.     PSALMS, 11
**charity** C. begins at home     BROWNE, SIR T, 8
C. is the power of defending that which we know to be
indefensible     CHESTERTON, G, 18
c. never faileth     BIBLE: I CORINTHIANS, 18
c. suffereth long, and is kind     BIBLE: I CORINTHIANS, 18
In c. there is no excess
    BACON, 1ST BARON VERULAM, VISCOUNT ST ALBANS, 27
knowledge puffeth up, but c. edifieth     BIBLE: I CORINTHIANS, 11
lectures or a little c.     WHITMAN, W, 6
now abideth faith, hope, c.     BIBLE: I CORINTHIANS, 18
the greatest of these is c.     BIBLE: I CORINTHIANS, 18
The living need c.     ARNOLD, G, 1
The man who leaves money to c. in his will     VOLTAIRE, 28
without c. are nothing worth     BOOK OF COMMON PRAYER, 2
**Charles the First** Caesar had his Brutus – C., his Cromwell
    HENRY, P, 1
**Charles the Second** There were gentlemen and . . . seamen in the
navy of C.     MACAULAY, BARON, 9
**Charley** I'm C.'s aunt from Brazil     THOMAS, B, 1
**Charlie** C. is my darling     NAIRNE, BARONESS, 2
**charm** Conversation has a kind of c.     SENECA, 2
Oozing c. . . . He oiled his way     LERNER, A, 4
the c. . . . of a nomadic existence     SACKVILLE-WEST, V, 5
**charming** c. people have something to conceal     CONNOLLY, C, 9
I heard the bullets whistle, . . . c. in the sound     WASHINGTON, G, 2
It is c. to totter into vogue     WALPOLE, 4TH EARL OF ORFORD, 5
People are either c. or tedious.     WILDE, O, 36
**charms** Whose c. all other maids surpass     MACNALLY, L, 1
**Charon** C., seeing, may forget     LANDOR, W, 1
**chaste** godly poet must be c. himself     CATULLUS, C, 1
**chastity** Give me c. and continence     AUGUSTINE OF HIPPO, 2
**Chatterley** Put thy shimmy on, Lady C.     LAWRENCE, D, 16
**cheap** flesh and blood so c.!     HOOD, T, 12
**cheat** c. at cards     BOSWELL, J, 2
**cheating** Peace, n. . . . a period of c.     BIERCE, A, 8
**check** C. enclosed     PARKER, D, 27
dreadful is the c.     BRONTE, E, 3
**cheek** Care /Sat on his faded c.     MILTON, J, 30
the c. that doth not fade,     KEATS, J, 13
turn the other c.     HOLMES, O, 5
whosoever shall smite thee on thy right c.     BIBLE: MATTHEW, 15
**cheeks** Blow, winds, and crack your c.     SHAKESPEARE, W, 137
**cheer** cups, /That c. but not inebriate     COWPER, W, 23
Don't c., boys; the poor devils are dying     PHILIP, J, 1
**cheerful** God loveth a c. giver     BIBLE: II CORINTHIANS, 2
**cheerfulness** No warmth, no c., no healthful ease     HOOD, T, 10
**cheese** 265 kinds of c.     DE GAULLE, C, 5
bread and c., and kisses     SWIFT, J, 9
c. – toasted, mostly     STEVENSON, R, 8
when the c. is gone     BRECHT, B, 8
**Cheltenham** Here lie I . . . /Killed by drinking C. waters
    ANONYMOUS, 25
**chemical** c. barrage has been hurled against the fabric of life
    CARSON, R, 2
Shelley and Keats were . . . up to date in . . . c. knowledge
    HALDANE, J, 2
**chemistry** he had read Shakespeare and found him weak in c.
    WELLS, H, 16
**cheque** Any general statement is like a c.     POUND, E, 4
Mrs Claypool's c. will come back to you     MARX, G, 18
**chequer-board** a C. of Nights and Days     FITZGERALD, E, 13
**cherish** to love and to c.     BOOK OF COMMON PRAYER, 15
**Cherith** the brook c.     BIBLE: I KINGS, 5
**cherry** Before the c. orchard was sold     CHEKHOV, A, 3
c. ripe     ALISON, R, 1
C. ripe, ripe, ripe     HERRICK, R, 1
Loveliest of trees, the c.     HOUSMAN, A, 5
Till 'C. ripe' themselves do cry     CAMPION, T, 2
**chess** Life's too short for c.     BYRON, H, 1
the devil played at c. with me     BROWNE, SIR T, 4
**chess-board** c. is the world; the pieces . . . the phenomena of the
universe;     HUXLEY, T, 6
**chest** Fifteen men on the dead man's c.     STEVENSON, R, 6
**chestnut** O c. tree     YEATS, W, 2
Under the spreading c. tree     LONGFELLOW, H, 14
**chestnuts** warmongers who . . . have others pull the c. out of the
fire     STALIN, J, 3

**chew** he can't fart and c. gum at the same time     JOHNSON, L, 1
**chewing** c. little bits of String     BELLOC, H, 3
**chicken** a c. in his pot every Sunday     HENRI IV, 1
England will have her neck wrung like a c.     WEYGAND, M, 1
Some c.     CHURCHILL, SIR W, 51
**chickens** children are more troublesome and costly than c.
    SHAW, G, 10
count their c. ere they're hatched     BUTLER, S, 3
Don't count your c.     AESOP, 8
If I didn't start painting, I would have raised c.     GRANDMA MOSES, 2
You don't set a fox to watching the c.     TRUMAN, H, 9
**chief** C. Defect of Henry King     BELLOC, H, 3
C. of the Army     NAPOLEON I, 10
**child** A c. becomes an adult when     SZASZ, T, 4
A c. deserves the maximum respect     JUVENAL, 12
A c.'s a plaything for an hour     LAMB, M, 1
all any reasonable c. can expect     ORTON, J, 2
better . . . a poor and a wise c. than an old and foolish king
    BIBLE: ECCLESIASTES, 12
C.! do not throw this book about     BELLOC, H, 1
c. of five would understand this     MARX, G, 6
flourish in a c. of six     BELLOC, H, 2
getting wenches with c.     SHAKESPEARE, W, 301
give her the living c.     BIBLE: I KINGS, 2
Give me a c. for the first seven years     PROVERBS, 175
He who shall teach the c. to doubt     BLAKE, W, 6
I don't care if doesn't make a nickel, I just want every
man, woman, and c. in America to see it     GOLDWYN, S, 8
If you strike a c.     SHAW, G, 28
nobody's c.     CASE, P, 1
Now at last our c. is just like all children     DE GAULLE, C, 3
One stops being a c. when . . . telling one's trouble does not make
it better     PAVESE, C, 1
receive one such little c. in my name     BIBLE: MATTHEW, 53
simplicity a c.     POPE, A, 16
spoil the c.     BUTLER, S, 4
sweetest Shakespeare, Fancy's c.,     MILTON, J, 14
The C. is Father of the Man     WORDSWORTH, W, 21
unless the play is stopped, the c. cannot . . . go on     KEMBLE, J, 1
unto us a c. is born     BIBLE: ISAIAH, 13
What is the use of a new-born c.     FRANKLIN, B, 9
when I was a c., I spake as a c.     BIBLE: I CORINTHIANS, 18
wise father that knows his own c.     SHAKESPEARE, W, 190
**childbirth** Death and taxes and c.     MITCHELL, M, 3
Mountains will heave in c.     HORACE, 6
**Childe** C. Roland to the Dark Tower     BROWNING, R, 15
**childhood** The books one reads in c. . . . create in one's mind a
. . . false map     ORWELL, G, 19
**childish** I put away c. things     BIBLE: I CORINTHIANS, 18
Sweet c. days     WORDSWORTH, W, 66
**childishness** second c.     SHAKESPEARE, W, 24
**children** a Friend for little c. /Above the bright blue sky
    MIDLANE, A, 1
Anybody who hates c. and dogs     FIELDS, W, 3
Are the c. all in bed? It's past eight o'clock     NURSERY RHYMES, 69
as c. fear to go in the dark     BACON, 1ST BARON VERULAM, VISCOUNT
ST ALBANS, 18
a wicked man that comes after c.     HOFFMANN, E, 1
c. are more troublesome and costly than chickens     SHAW, G, 10
C. aren't happy with nothing to ignore     NASH, O, 8
c. are true judges of character     AUDEN, W, 21
C. have never been very good at listening     BALDWIN, J, 4
C. . . . have no use for psychology. They detest sociology
    SINGER, I, 1
c., obey your parents     BIBLE: EPHESIANS, 3
Come dear c.     ARNOLD, M, 14
C. should acquire . . . heroes and villains from fiction     AUDEN, W, 2
C. sweeten labours
    BACON, 1ST BARON VERULAM, VISCOUNT ST ALBANS, 39
C. with Hyacinth's temperament . . . merely know more     SAKI, 5
desire not a multitude of unprofitable c.     BIBLE: ECCLESIASTICUS, 7
Do you hear the c. weeping,     BROWNING, E, 2
except ye . . . become as little c.     BIBLE: MATTHEW, 52
Familiarity breeds . . . c.     TWAIN, M, 10
Far too good to waste on c.     SHAW, G, 48
He that has no c.     PROVERBS, 190
He that loves not his wife and c.     TAYLOR, J, 2
his wife is beautiful and his c. smart     MENCKEN, H, 3
I love all my c.     CARTER, L, 1
in sorrow thou shalt bring forth c.     BIBLE: GENESIS, 15
I've lost one of my c. this week     TURNER, J, 2

Let our c. grow tall     THATCHER, M, 2
like a c.'s party taken over by the elders     FITZGERALD, F, 2
little c., keep yourselves from idols     BIBLE: 1 JOHN, 6
make your c. *capable of honesty* is the beginning of education.
    RUSKIN, J, 10
Men are but c. of a larger growth     DRYDEN, J, 16
Men are . . . more careful of the breed of their horses and dogs
than of their c.     PENN, W, 2
Most of the people . . . will be c.     ANDERSEN, H, 3
My music . . . understood by c. and animals     STRAVINSKY, I, 4
Never have c.     VIDAL, G, 4
Now at last our child is just like all c.     DE GAULLE, C, 3
Parents learn a lot from their c.     SPARK, M, 2
provoke not your c.     BIBLE: COLOSSIANS, 5
She had so many c. she didn't know what to do
    NURSERY RHYMES, 59
the c. I might have had     LOWRY, M, 1
the early marriages of silly c.     MARTINEAU, H, 3
thou shalt see thy c.'s c.     PSALMS, 81
thy c. like the olive-branches     PSALMS, 80
To bear many c. is considered . . . an investment     GANDHI, I, 1
We have no c., except me     BEHAN, B, 10
when they started life as c.     AMIS, K, 2
write for c. . . . as you do for adults     GORKY, M, 1
**chill** St Agnes' Eve – Ah, bitter c. it was     KEATS, J, 4
**chime** to set a c. of words tinkling in . . . a few fastidious people
    SMITH, L, 8
**chimes** c. at midnight     SHAKESPEARE, W, 89
**chimney** sixty horses wedged in a c.     MORTON, J, 2
**chimney-sweepers** As c., come to dust     SHAKESPEARE, W, 38
**China** Even the Hooligan was probably invented in C.     SAKI, 18
On a slow boat to C.     LOESSER, F, 1
The infusion of a C. plant     ADDISON, J, 10
**Chinese** Nothing . . . can destroy the C. people     BUCK, P, 2
**chip** c. of the old block     BURKE, E, 25
**chips** You breed babies and you eat c.     WESKER, A, 1
**chirche-dore** Housbondes at c.     CHAUCER, G, 10
**chivalry** age of c. is gone     BURKE, E, 7
The age of c. is never past     KINGSLEY, C, 10
**Chi Wen Tzu** c. always thought three times before taking action
    CONFUCIUS, 2
**Chloë** In the spring . . . your lovely C.     SEARLE, R, 2
**chocolate** a c. cream soldier     SHAW, G, 3
both its national products, snow and c., melt     COREN, A, 5
Venice is like eating . . . c. liqueurs     CAPOTE, T, 1
**choir** Sweet singing in the c.     ANONYMOUS, 81
**choirs** Bare ruin'd c.     SHAKESPEARE, W, 260
**choose** We can believe what we c.     NEWMAN, CARDINAL, 5
**Chopin** to bridge the awful gap between Dorothy and C..     ADE, G, 2
**chord** of music     PROCTER, A, 1
**chorus** a dozen are only a c.     FITZGERALD, F, 7
**chose** plus c'est la même c.     KARR, A, 1
**chosen** a c. vessel     BIBLE: ACTS, 8
but few are c.     BIBLE: MATTHEW, 62
ye have not c. me, but I have c. you     BIBLE: JOHN, 37
**Christ** churches have kill'd their C.     TENNYSON, BARON, 55
C. is all, and in all     BIBLE: COLOSSIANS, 3
C. . . . would quite likely have been arrested     DE BLANK, J, 1
I beseech you, in the bowels of C.     CROMWELL, O, 2
The Jews have produced . . . C., Spinoza, and myself     STEIN, G, 5
We're more popular than Jesus C.     LENNON, J, 13
Who dreamed that C. has died in vain     SITWELL, DAME E, 2
**Christendom** wisest fool in C.     HENRI IV, 3
**Christian** A C. . . . feels /Repentance on a Sunday     YBARRA, T, 1
any man . . . who could not bear another's misfortunes . . . like a
C.     POPE, A, 55
Better sleep with a sober cannibal than a drunken C.
    MELVILLE, H, 1
How very hard . . . /To be a C.     BROWNING, R, 20
I die a C.     CHARLES I, 2
in what peace a C. can die     ADDISON, J, 17
I was born of C. race, /And not a Heathen, or a Jew     WATTS, I, 4
No Jew was ever fool enough to turn C.     ZANGWILL, I, 1
object . . . to form C. men     ARNOLD, T, 1
Onward, C. soldiers     BARING-GOULD, S, 2
several young women . . . would render the C. life intensely
difficult     LEWIS, C, 4
**Christianity** C. accepted as given a metaphysical system
    HUXLEY, A, 17
C., . . . but why journalism     BALFOUR, 1ST EARL OF, 2
C. has done a great deal for love     FRANCE, A, 6

C. has made of death a terror     OUIDA, 1
C. is part of the Common Law of England     HALE, SIR M, 1
C. is the most materialistic of all great religions     TEMPLE, W, 1
C. . . . says that they are all fools     CHESTERTON, G, 19
C. the one great curse     NIETZSCHE, F, 3
C. . . . the one immortal blemish of mankind     NIETZSCHE, F, 3
decay of C.     SAKI, 10
His C. was muscular     DISRAELI, 1ST EARL OF BEACONSFIELD, 3
local cult called C.     HARDY, T, 1
loving C. better than Truth     COLERIDGE, S, 1
nothing in C. or Buddhism that quite matches     SAKI, 10
Rock and roll or C.     LENNON, J, 13
**Christians** C. awake, salute the happy morn     BYROM, J, 1
Onward, C., onward go     WHITE, H, 1
settle their differences like good C.     AUSTIN, W, 2
these C. love one another     TERTULLIAN, Q, 1
they may be Catholics but they are not C.     MCCARTHY, M, 6
**Christian Science** C. explains all cause and effect as mental
    EDDY, M, 2
**Christ-like** C. heroes and woman-worshipping Don Juans
    LAWRENCE, D, 25
**Christmas** At C. I no more desire a rose     SHAKESPEARE, W, 153
C. comes but once a year     PROVERBS, 100
C. should fall out in the Middle of Winter     ADDISON, J, 12
Eating a C. pie     NURSERY RHYMES, 30
For C. comes but once a year     TUSSER, T, 3
I'm walking backwards till C.     MILLIGAN, S, 5
perceive C. through its wrapping     WHITE, E, 3
The first day of C., /My true love sent to me     NURSERY RHYMES, 54
'Twas the night before C.     MOORE, C, 1
**Christopher** C. Robin went down with Alice     MILNE, A, 4
**chronicle** a small beer     SHAKESPEARE, W, 221
the c. of wasted time     SHAKESPEARE, W, 263
**church** an alien C.     DISRAELI, 1ST EARL OF BEACONSFIELD, 19
Beware when you take on the C. of God     TUTU, BISHOP, 2
But get me to the c. on time!     LERNER, A, 5
he'd go to c., start a revolution – *something*     MILLER, A, 3
I believe in the C.     TEMPLE, W, 7
straying away from the c.     BRUCE, L, 1
The blood of the martyrs is the seed of the C.     TERTULLIAN, Q, 1
The C. exists     TEMPLE, W, 6
The C.'s one foundation     STONE, S, 1
*The farther you go from the c. of Rome*     WOTTON, SIR H, 4
There are many who stay away from C.     MILLER, A, 1
There is no salvation outside the c.     AUGUSTINE OF HIPPO, 3
There was I, waiting at the c.     LEIGH, F, 1
**churches** chapels had been c.     SHAKESPEARE, W, 188
c. have kill'd their Christ     TENNYSON, BARON, 55
the c. . . . bore for me the same relation to God that billboards did
to Coca-Cola     UPDIKE, J, 2
The itch of disputing will prove the scab of c.     WOTTON, SIR H, 2
**churchman** a species of person called a 'Modern C.'     WAUGH, E, 17
**Church of England** where MCC ends and the C. begins
    PRIESTLEY, J, 6
**churchyard** A piece of c. fits everybody     PROVERBS, 59
nowhere worse taste, than in a c.     JOWETT, B, 3
**Cicero** C. /And . . . Homer were /Mad as the mist and snow
    YEATS, W, 18
**cider** c. and tinned salmon     WAUGH, E, 31
**cigar** a good c. is a smoke     KIPLING, R, 2
It is like a c. . . . . it never tastes quite the same     WAVELL, EARL, 1
**cigarette** A c. is . . . a perfect pleasure     WILDE, O, 48
**Cinderella** . . . poetry, "The C. of the Arts."     MONROE, H, 1
**cinema** c. is truth twenty-four times a second     GODARD, J, 1
**circle** All things from eternity . . . come round in a c.
    MARCUS AURELIUS ANTONINUS, 4
**circumcised** our fingers are c.     PERLMAN, I, 1
When they c. Herbert Samuel     LLOYD GEORGE, EARL OF DWYFOR, 10
**circumcision** Every luxury . . . – atheism, breast-feeding, c.
    ORTON, J, 4
**circumlocution** C. Office     DICKENS, C, 19
**circumstance** Pride, pomp, and c.     SHAKESPEARE, W, 227
To a philosopher no c., . . . is too minute     GOLDSMITH, O, 3
**circumstances** to face straitened c. at home     JUVENAL, 4
**circumstantial evidence** Some c. is very strong     THOREAU, H, 4
**circuses** bread and c.     JUVENAL, 8
**cities** I have sung women in three c.     POUND, E, 7
many c. had rubbed him smooth     GREENE, G, 4
The government burns down whole c.     MAO TSE-TUNG, 8
**citizen** a c. of the world
    BACON, 1ST BARON VERULAM, VISCOUNT ST ALBANS, 28

a c. of the world — SOCRATES, 5
I am a c. of the world — DIOGENES, 3
**citizens** All free men, . . . are c. of Berlin — KENNEDY, J, 13
**city** axis of the earth sticks out visibly through . . . every town or c. — HOLMES, O, 4
first c. Cain — COWLEY, A, 1
great c. . . . has the greatest men and women — WHITMAN, W, 10
. . . hiring taxis to scuttle around a c. — KINNOCK, N, 9
I go amongst the buildings of a c. — KEATS, J, 64
It is a c. where you can see a sparrow fall — O'BRIEN, C, 1
the c. is not a concrete jungle, it is a human zoo — MORRIS, D, 1
the c. of perspiring dreams — RAPHAEL, F, 1
the holy c., new Jerusalem — BIBLE: REVELATIONS, 18
very excellent things are spoken of thee, thou c. of God — PSALMS, 53
**civilian** forget about this c. — GOLDWATER, B, 3
**civilians** drop bombs . . . hit c. — GOLDWATER, B, 3
**civilisation** Disinterested intellectual curiosity . . . life blood of . . . c. — TREVELYAN, G, 1
if c. is to advance . . . it must be through . . . women — PANKHURST, E, 1
**civility** C. costs nothing — PROVERBS, 101
The reciprocal c. of authors — JOHNSON, S, 16
**civilization** As c. advances, poetry . . . declines — MACAULAY, BARON, 13
C. is a method of living — ADDAMS, J, 3
C. is . . . equal respect for all men — ADDAMS, J, 3
How idiotic c. is — MANSFIELD, K, 1
It is so stupid of modern c. — KNOX, R, 1
little in c. to appeal to a Yeti — HILLARY, SIR E, 2
Madam, I am the c. they are fighting to defend — GARROD, H, 1
Our c. is founded on the shambles — JAMES, W, 1
The degree of a nation's c. — MAUGHAM, W, 14
the Renaissance was . . . the green end of one of c.'s hardest winters — FOWLES, J, 1
without the usual interval of c. — CLEMENCEAU, G, 1
You can't say c. don't advance — ROGERS, W, 1
**civilized** it proved that I was in a c. society — PARK, M, 1
Woman may be the last thing c. by Man — MEREDITH, G, 1
**civil war** In a c., a general must know — REED, H, 4
**clap** Don't c. too hard — OSBORNE, J, 1
**clapped** the glass to his sightless eye — NEWBOLT, SIR H, 1
**claret** C. is the liquor for boys — JOHNSON, S, 125
drink a dozen of C. on my Tomb. — KEATS, J, 60
look for the second cheapest c. . . . and say, 'Number 22' — POTTER, S, 6
said of c. — BENTLEY, R, 1
**class** an . . . young Englishman of our upper c. — ARNOLD, M, 4
a special machine for the suppression of one c. by another — LENIN, V, 3
Because there's no fourth c. — SANTAYANA, G, 6
Discussion in c., which means — NABOKOV, V, 3
Every c. is unfit to govern — ACTON, 1ST BARON, 1
for one c. to appreciate the wrongs of another — STANTON, E, 3
For this c. we have . . . the designation of Philistines — ARNOLD, M, 5
Like many of the upper c. /He liked the sound of broken glass — BELLOC, H, 12
Poets and painters . . . constitute a special c. — BRENAN, G, 6
The constitution . . . first and second c. citizens — WILLKIE, W, 1
The history of all . . . society is the history of c. struggles — MARX, K, 1
The one c. you do *not* belong to — MIKES, G, 5
the proletariat will . . . wage a c. struggle for Socialism — LENIN, V, 6
**classes** back the masses against the c. — GLADSTONE, W, 2
Hats divide generally into three c. — WHITEHORN, K, 1
I'm not interested in c. — LEWIS, J, 1
responsible and the irresponsible c. — LAWRENCE, D, 10
**classical** C. quotation is the *parole* of literary men — JOHNSON, S, 134
That's the c. mind at work — PIRSIG, R, 4
The basic difference between c. music and jazz — PREVIN, A, 1
**classicism** C. . . . presents . . . the literature that gave . . . pleasure to their great-grandfathers — STENDHAL, 2
**classics** Every man with a belly full of the c. — MILLER, H, 2
The c. are only primitive literature — LEACOCK, S, 2
**clay** absorbs a c. /After his labours — CALVERLEY, C, 2
**clean** Bath . . . once a day to be passably c. — BURGESS, A, 2
c. your plate — ROSEBERY, EARL OF, 4
hard to be funny when you have to be c. — WEST, M, 9
**clear** His right was c., his will was strong — ANONYMOUS, 102
if he could make *me* understand . . . it would be c. to all — ROOSEVELT, E, 3

**clearing-house** the C. of the World — CHAMBERLAIN, J, 1
**cleft** Rock of ages, c. for me — TOPLADY, A, 1
**Clementine** In a cavern, . . . Dwelt a miner, Forty-niner, /And his daughter, C. — MONTROSE, P, 1
**clenched** You cannot shake hands with a c. fist — GANDHI, I, 3
**Cleopatra** Had C.'s nose been shorter — PASCAL, B, 6
**clergy** c. are men — FIELDING, H, 9
I never saw . . . the c. were beloved in any nation — SWIFT, J, 11
**clergyman** c. whose mendicity is only equalled by their mendacity — TEMPLE, F, 2
good enough to be a c. — JOHNSON, S, 82
**clerk** C. ther was of Oxenford also — CHAUCER, G, 5
the smartness of an attorney's c.
**clever** Be good, sweet maid, and let who can be c.; — KINGSLEY, C, 1
c. man . . . came of . . . stupid people — CARLYLE, T, 30
It's c., but is it art — KIPLING, R, 4
To be c. enough to get . . . money, one must be stupid — CHESTERTON, G, 22
**cleverest** You're the c. member of . . . the c. nation in the world — WEBB, B, 2
**cleverness** height of c. is . . . to conceal it — ROCHEFOUCAULD, DUC DE LA, 20
**cliché** The c. is dead poetry — BRENAN, G, 4
**clichés** Let's have some new c. — GOLDWYN, S, 1
**cliffs** the chalk c. of Dover. — BALDWIN, 1ST EARL BALDWIN OF BEWDLEY, 5
**climate** common where the c.'s sultry — BYRON, 6TH BARON, 16
If it's heaven for c. — BARRIE, SIR J, 1
**climax** a story that starts with an earthquake and . . . a c. — GOLDWYN, S, 5
**climb** Fain would I c., yet fear I to fall — RALEIGH, SIR W, 2
**clime** change their c., not their frame of mind, who rush across the sea — HORACE, 21
**Clive** What I like about C. — BENTLEY, E, 3
**clock** c. in the steeple strikes one — WORK, H, 1
grandfather's c. — WORK, H, 2
Stands the Church c. at ten to three — BROOKE, R, 3
The c. struck one, /The mouse ran down — NURSERY RHYMES, 15
The mouse ran up the c. — NURSERY RHYMES, 15
**clocks** hands of c. in railway stations — CONNOLLY, C, 11
the c. were striking the hour — LONGFELLOW, H, 2
**clogs** From c. to c. — PROVERBS, 167
**cloke** knyf under the c. — CHAUCER, G, 11
**Clootie** Satan, Nick, or C. — BURNS, R, 1
**close** a breathless hush in the C. tonight — NEWBOLT, SIR H, 6
I have sometimes regretted living so c. to Marie — PROUST, M, 14
**closed society** Mankind is a c. — SCHUMACHER, E, 2
**close-up** Life is a tragedy . . . in c. — CHAPLIN, C, 4
**closing time** c. in the gardens of the West — CONNOLLY, C, 1
**clothes** After that you just take the girl's c. off — CHANDLER, R, 3
as if she were taking off all her c. — COLETTE, S, 2
bought her wedding c. — ADDISON, J, 14
enterprises that require new c. — THOREAU, H, 11
Fine c. are good — JOHNSON, S, 101
if it be our c. alone which fit us for society — ESCHENBACH, M, 4
Nothing to wear but c. — KING, B, 1
No woman so naked as . . . underneath her c. — FRAYN, M, 1
walked away with their c. — DISRAELI, 1ST EARL OF BEACONSFIELD, 20
wrapped him in swaddling c. — BIBLE: LUKE, 7
**clothes basket** Have you ever taken anything out of the c. — WHITEHORN, K, 5
**clothes line** hanging the baby on the c. to dry — RUNYON, D, 7
**cloud** a c. received him out of their sight — BIBLE: ACTS, 1
a pillar of a c. — BIBLE: EXODUS, 14
Every c. has a silver lining — PROVERBS, 132
fiend hid in a c. — BLAKE, W, 36
I wandered lonely as a c. — WORDSWORTH, W, 5
**clouds** But trailing c. of glory — WORDSWORTH, W, 23
c. that gather round the setting sun — WORDSWORTH, W, 30
**clout** Ne'er cast a c. — PROVERBS, 300
**clown** I remain . . . a c. — CHAPLIN, C, 3
**clowns** Send in the C. — SONDHEIM, S, 2
**club** I don't want to belong to any c. — MARX, G, 23
Mankind is a c. — CHESTERTON, G, 37
takes you so far from the c. house — LINKLATER, E, 4
the best c. in London — DICKENS, C, 37
the most exclusive c. there is — NASH, O, 3
**cluster** The human face is . . . a whole c. of faces — PROUST, M, 3
**Clyde** the bonny banks of C. — LAUDER, SIR H, 3
**CMG** Members rise from C. . . . — SAMPSON, A, 1

**coach** c. and six horses through the Act of Settlement
RICE, SIR S, 1
indifference and a c. and six COLMAN, THE ELDER, 1
**coal** having a live c. in his hand BIBLE: ISAIAH, 9
though the whole world turn to c., HERBERT, G, 10
**coals** heap c. of fire upon his head BIBLE: PROVERBS, 13
**coaster** Dirty British c. MASEFIELD, J, 3
**coat** a c. of many colours BIBLE: GENESIS, 46
**cobbler** Let the c. stick PROVERBS, 256
**cobwebs** Laws are like c. SWIFT, J, 16
laws were like c.
BACON, 1ST BARON VERULAM, VISCOUNT ST ALBANS, 5
**Coca-Cola** that billboards did to C. UPDIKE, J, 2
**cocaine** C. isn't habit-forming BANKHEAD, T, 4
**cock** before the c. crow, thou shalt deny me BIBLE: MATTHEW, 79
He was like a c. ELIOT, G, 3
That kept the c. that crowed in the morn NURSERY RHYMES, 62
waiting for the c. to crow HUGHES, W, 1
we owe a c. to Aesculapius SOCRATES, 6
**cockles** Crying, C. and mussels! alive, alive, O ANONYMOUS, 4
**cockroach** to choose between him and a c. as a companion
WODEHOUSE, SIR P, 13
**cocksure** as c. of anything MELBOURNE, VISCOUNT, 5
**cod** piece of c. passes all understanding LUTYENS, SIR E, 2
serve both c. and salmon LEVERSON, A, 2
the c.'s wallop is always fresh made MORLEY, R, 2
The home of the bean and the c. BOSSIDY, J, 1
**codfish** Unlike the male c. . . . the British aristocracy is
WODEHOUSE, SIR P, 19
**coffee** c. that's too black . . . | X, MALCOLM, 1
C. which makes the politician wise POPE, A, 50
measured out my life with c. spoons ELIOT, T, 11
**coffee-house** It is folly . . . to mistake the echo of a . . . c. for the
. . . kingdom SWIFT, J, 3
**coffin** the silver plate on a c. O'CONNELL, D, 1
**cogito** C., ergo sum DESCARTES, R, 1
**coil** shuffled off this mortal c. SHAKESPEARE, W, 61
**coke** Happiness is like c. HUXLEY, A, 24
**cold** a period of c. peace LIE, T, 1
blow hot and c. with the same breath AESOP, 7
C. hands, warm heart PROVERBS, 102
C. Pastoral KEATS, J, 24
I beg c. comfort SHAKESPEARE, W, 129
she should catch a c. on overexposure. BUTLER, SAMUEL, 18
The Irish, . . . are needed in this c. age CHILD, L, 2
we are . . . in the midst of a c. war BARUCH, B, 3
We called a c. a c. BENNETT, A, 1
**coldly** c. she turns from their gaze, and weeps MOORE, T, 4
**Cole** Old King C. /Was a merry old soul NURSERY RHYMES, 38
**Coliseum** While stands the C., Rome shall stand
BYRON, 6TH BARON, 12
**collapse** Russia is a c., not a revolution LAWRENCE, D, 35
**collapses** Force . . . c. through its own mass HORACE, 35
**collar** no shirt or c. ever comes back twice LEACOCK, S, 13
**collections** those mutilators of c. LAMB, C, 9
**collective** the greatest c. work of science BRONOWSKI, J, 3
**college** I am Master of this c.: /What I don't know isn't
knowledge. BEECHING, H, 1
Like so many ageing c. people NABOKOV, V, 2
**Colleges of Unreason** a liberal education at the C. BUTLER, S, 1
**colonel** The gatling's jammed and the c. dead NEWBOLT, SIR H, 7
**colonnade** whispering sound of the cool c.! COWPER, W, 17
**colour** an incurable disease – c. blindness DE BLANK, J, 2
Any c., so long as it's black FORD, H, 3
water, is unsuitable in c. HERBERT, SIR A, 7
**coloured** I'm a c., one-eyed Jew DAVIS, S, 2
**colourless** C. green ideas CHOMSKY, N, 1
**colours** a coat of many c. BIBLE: GENESIS, 46
All c. will agree in the dark
BACON, 1ST BARON VERULAM, VISCOUNT ST ALBANS, 57
**combine** When bad men c. BURKE, E, 18
**come** bigger they c. FITZSIMMONS, B, 1
Cannot c., lie follows PROUST, M, 17
I c. as a thief BIBLE: REVELATIONS, 11
mine hour is not yet c. BIBLE: JOHN, 4
Mr Watson, c. here; I want you BELL, A, 1
O c. all ye faithful OAKELEY, F, 1
that thou wouldest c. down BIBLE: ISAIAH, 35
Thou'lt c. no more SHAKESPEARE, W, 152
Whistle and she'll c. to you BEAUMONT, F, 13
. . . . Why don't you c. up sometime and see me WEST, M, 6

Will ye no c. back again NAIRNE, BARONESS, 1
Will you no c. back again HOGG, J, 1
**comedian** A c. can only last ROGERS, W, 10
**comedies** c. are ended by a marriage BYRON, 6TH BARON, 19
**comedy** All I need to make a c. CHAPLIN, C, 1
at a c. we only look HUXLEY, A, 11
C. is if I walk into an open sewer and die BROOKS, M, 2
C., like sodomy, is an unnatural act FELDMAN, M, 1
C., we may say, is society PRIESTLEY, J, 1
Farce refined becomes high c. CRAIG, SIR G, 1
Life is . . . a c. in long-shot CHAPLIN, C, 4
What a fine c. this world would be DIDEROT, D, 3
world is a c. to those who think, a tragedy to those who feel
WALPOLE, 4TH EARL OF ORFORD, 6
**comely** I am black, but c. BIBLE: SONG OF SOLOMON, 1
**comes** Everything c. to him who waits PROVERBS, 144
**cometh** he c. with clouds BIBLE: REVELATIONS, 1
him that c. to me I will in no wise cast out BIBLE: JOHN, 17
**comfort** carrion c., Despair, not feast on thee HOPKINS, G, 1
c. me with apples BIBLE: SONG OF SOLOMON, 3
c. ye, c. ye my people BIBLE: ISAIAH, 27
From ignorance our c. flows PRIOR, M, 3
I beg cold c. SHAKESPEARE, W, 129
the waters of c. PSALMS, 12
thought of suicide is a great . . . c. NIETZSCHE, F, 10
thy rod and thy staff c. me PSALMS, 12
Two loves I have, of c. and despair SHAKESPEARE, W, 269
until his friends came to c. him KIERKEGAARD, S, 1
**comfortable** to be baith grand and c. BARRIE, SIR J, 2
**comfortably** Are you sitting c.? Then I'll begin LANG, J, 1
**comforted** he refused to be c. BIBLE: GENESIS, 48
**Comforter** another C., that he may abide BIBLE: JOHN, 33
if I go not . . . the C. will not come BIBLE: JOHN, 40
**comforters** miserable c. are ye all BIBLE: JOB, 10
**comic** It is so c. to hear oneself called old JAMES, A, 1
**coming** C. through the rye BURNS, R, 4
he . . . c. after me is preferred before me BIBLE: JOHN, 2
thy going out, and thy c. in PSALMS, 77
who may abide the day of his c. BIBLE: MALACHI, 2
**command** mortals to c. success ADDISON, J, 2
one of those born neither to obey nor to c. MASEFIELD, J, 1
people c. rather badly COMPTON-BURNETT, DAME I, 3
**Commandments** Where there aren't no Ten C. KIPLING, R, 23
**commandments** fear God, and keep his c. BIBLE: ECCLESIASTES, 26
if ye love me, keep my c. BIBLE: JOHN, 33
**commend** forced to c. her highly PEPYS, S, 5
into thy hands I c. my spirit BIBLE: LUKE, 38
into thy hands I c. my spirit PSALMS, 21
**commended** The man who gets angry . . . in the right way . . . is
c. ARISTOTLE, 2
**commendeth** obliquely c. himself BROWNE, SIR T, 1
**comment** C. is free but facts are sacred SCOTT, C, 1
**commentators** rather give me c. plain CRABBE, G, 3
**commerce** Friendship is a disinterested c. between equals
GOLDSMITH, O, 12
honour sinks where c. long prevails GOLDSMITH, O, 21
**commercing** looks c. with the skies MILTON, J, 7
**commission** Each bullet has got its c. DIBDIN, C, 1
**commit** woman alone, can . . . c. them THACKERAY, W, 7
**committee** A c. is a cul-de-sac COCKS, SIR B, 1
The number one book . . . was written by a c. MAYER, L, 1
**common** good thing, to make it too c. SHAKESPEARE, W, 84
He nothing c. did or mean MARVELL, A, 4
lose the c. touch KIPLING, R, 15
seldom attribute c. sense ROCHEFOUCAULD, DUC DE LA, 24
the happiness of the c. man BEVERIDGE, BARON, 1
The trivial round, the c. task KEBLE, J, 1
'Tis education forms the c. mind POPE, A, 38
**Common Law** C. of England HERBERT, SIR A, 3
**common-looking** The Lord prefers c. people LINCOLN, A, 2
**common man** I have no concern for the c. WILSON, SIR A, 5
**commonplace** nothing so unnatural as the c. DOYLE, SIR A, 5
renders . . . c. things and characters interesting SCOTT, SIR W, 2
unassuming c. /Of Nature WORDSWORTH, W, 70
**commonplaces** c. are the great poetic truths STEVENSON, R, 25
**Commons** The C., faithful to their system MACKINTOSH, SIR J, 1
**common sense** C. is the collection of prejudices EINSTEIN, A, 6
Science is nothing but trained and organized c. HUXLEY, T, 2
**Commonwealth** a C. of Nations ROSEBERY, EARL OF, 1
turn to the wider vision of the C.
MACMILLAN, EARL OF STOCKTON, 2

communications evil c. corrupt good manners
                            BIBLE: I CORINTHIANS, 21
communism arrested under the Suppression of C. Act
                            DE BLANK, J. 1
C. continued to haunt Europe as a spectre   TAYLOR, A. 3
C. is like prohibition                      ROGERS, W. 3
C. is Soviet power plus the electrification LENIN, V. 9
C. with a human face                        DUBCEK, A. 1
For us in Russia c. is a dead dog   SOLZHENITSYN, A. 10
communist Every c. has a fascist frown      SPARK, M. 3
your grandson will . . . be a C.      KHRUSHCHEV, N. 5
communists Catholics and C. have committed great crimes
                            GREENE, G. 3
In Germany, the Nazis came for the C.    NIEMOLLER, M. 1
community journalism. . . . keeps us in touch with the ignorance of
the c.                                      WILDE, O. 12
Marriage, n. . . . a c. . . . making in all two   BIERCE, A. 6
the c. of Europe            SALISBURY, MARQUESS OF, 2
We are part of the c. of Europe          GLADSTONE, W. 3
commute the agricultural labourers round here c. from London
                            POWELL, A. 4
commuter C. . . . riding to and from his wife   WHITE, E. 1
compact the damned, c., liberal majority     IBSEN, H. 3
companion to choose between him and a cockroach as a c.
                            WODEHOUSE, SIR P. 13
companionable so c. as solitude         THOREAU, H. 12
companions Boys . . . are unwholesome c. for grown people
                            LAMB, C. 7
c. for middle age
        BACON, 1ST BARON VERULAM, VISCOUNT ST ALBANS, 34
company better to be alone than in bad c.   WASHINGTON, G. 1
c., . . . have neither a soul to lose nor a body to kick   SMITH, S. 5
Crowds without c.                           GIBBON, E. 2
I've been offered titles, . . . get one into disreputable c.
                            SHAW, G. 42
pleasure of your c.                         LAMB, C. 22
Take the tone of the c.       CHESTERFIELD, 4TH EARL OF, 4
Tell me what c. thou keepest          CERVANTES, M. 20
You never expected justice from a c.         SMITH, S. 5
comparative progress is simply a c.   CHESTERTON, G. 15
compare any she belied with false c.   SHAKESPEARE, W. 268
c. thee to a summer's day             SHAKESPEARE, W. 254
compared The war we have just been through, . . . is not to be c.
                            WILSON, W. 4
comparisons c. are odious                   DONNE, J. 8
C. are odorous                     SHAKESPEARE, W. 214
compass my heart shall be /The faithful c.   GAY, J. 12
compassion But a certain Samaritan . . . had c. on him
                            BIBLE: LUKE, 22
C. is not a sloppy, sentimental feeling for people who are
underprivileged                             KINNOCK, N. 6
complacency c. and satisfaction . . . in . . . a new-married couple
                            LAMB, C. 1
complain one hardly knows to whom to c.   FIRBANK, R. 2
complaint Anno domini . . . the most fatal c.   HILTON, J. 1
how is the old c.   DISRAELI, 1ST EARL OF BEACONSFIELD, 35
I want to register a c.                     MARX, G. 14
let thine ears consider well . . . my c.   PSALMS, 82
complete disguised as a C. Man            HUXLEY, A. 4
now I feel like a c. idiot                  HEINE, H. 3
complex Wherever an inferiority c. exists, there is . . . reason for
it                                          JUNG, C. 10
compliance by a timely c.               FIELDING, H. 8
compliment returned the c.              VOLTAIRE, 14
compose Never c. . . . unless . . . not composing . . . becomes a
positive nuisance                           HOLST, G. 1
composed When I c. that, I was . . . inspired by God
                            BEETHOVEN, L. 2
composer A good c. . . . steals          STRAVINSKY, I. 5
composition difference between . . . prose and metrical c.
                            WORDSWORTH, W. 16
comprehended c. two aspicious persons   SHAKESPEARE, W. 215
compromise All government . . . is founded on c. and barter
                            BURKE, E. 12
C. used to mean that half a loaf      CHESTERTON, G. 36
not a question that leaves much room for c.   MEIR, G. 6
compulsion seized by the stern hand of C.   THURBER, J. 2
compulsory c. and irreproachable idleness   TOLSTOY, COUNT, 5
comrade stepping where his c. stood   SCOTT, SIR W. 14
comrades East and west on fields forgotten /Bleach the bones of
c. slain                                    HOUSMAN, A. 12

walked willingly to his death . . . to . . . save his c.   ATKINSON, E. 1
conceal Addresses . . . c. our whereabouts   SAKI, 2
height of cleverness is . . . to c. it   ROCHEFOUCAULD, DUC DE LA, 20
speech only to c. their thoughts.           VOLTAIRE, 6
concealed Much truth is spoken, . . . more . . . c.
                            DARLING, BARON, 3
concealing Good breeding consists in c. how . . . we think of
ourselves                                   TWAIN, M. 12
concealment c., like a worm i' th' bud   SHAKESPEARE, W. 291
conceit C. is the finest armour             JEROME, J. 2
conceited I would grow intolerably c.   WHISTLER, J. 6
what man will do any good who is not c.   TROLLOPE, A. 11
concept If the c. of God has            BALDWIN, J. 1
conception if the dad is present at the c.   ORTON, J. 2
concepts walks up the stairs of his c.   STEINBECK, J. 1
concessions The c. of the weak are the c. of fear   BURKE, E. 11
conclusions Life is the art of drawing . . . c.   BUTLER, S. 10
concord toleration produced . . . religious c.   GIBBON, E. 4
Yes – around C.                          THOREAU, H. 21
concurrence Accidental and fortuitous c. of atoms
                            PALMERSTON, VISCOUNT, 1
condemn No man can justly censure or c. another
                            BROWNE, SIR T. 7
condemned If God were suddenly c. to live the life  DUMAS, FILS, 1
Man is c. to be free                       SARTRE, J. 3
condemning One should examine oneself . . . before . . . c. others
                            MOLIERE, 7
condition hopes for the human c.           CAMUS, A. 13
The c. of man . . . is a c. of war       HOBBES, T. 1
the c. of our sex is so deplorable that it is our duty . . . to break
the law                                 PANKHURST, E. 4
To be a poet is a c.                       GRAVES, R. 4
wearisome c. of humanity   GREVILLE, BARON BROOKE, 1
what delight we married people have to see . . . fools decoyed into
our c.                                      PEPYS, S. 8
conditioned Americans have been c. to respect newness
                            UPDIKE, J. 3
conditions my people live in such awful c.   GEORGE V, 2
conduct C. . . . to the prejudice of good order and military
discipline                              ANONYMOUS, 14
conference naked into the c. chamber        BEVAN, A. 11
confess It's easy to make a man c. . . . lies  HOUSEHOLD, G. 2
Men will c.                                COLBY, F. 1
only c. our little faults   ROCHEFOUCAULD, DUC DE LA, 22
confessing I am ashamed of c.             BURNEY, F. 1
women . . . ill-using them and then c. it   TROLLOPE, A. 8
confidence never dedicated to something you have complete c. in
                            PIRSIG, R. 1
Three addresses always inspire c.           WILDE, O. 29
confident There are two things which I am c. I can do very well
                            JOHNSON, S. 49
confin'd cabin'd, cribb'd, c., bound in   SHAKESPEARE, W. 169
conflict We are in an armed c.     EDEN, 1ST EARL OF AVON, 3
conform how to rebel and c. at the same time   CRISP, Q. 2
conformable Nature is very consonant and c.   NEWTON, SIR I. 1
confound the weak things of the world to c. the . . . mighty
                            BIBLE: I CORINTHIANS, 2
confounded mine enemies shall be c.        PSALMS, 1
confusion let me never be put to c.        PSALMS, 20
Congreve C. is the only sophisticated playwright   TYNAN, K. 2
Congs Kinquering C. their titles take    SPOONER, W. 3
connect Only c.                            FORSTER, E. 9
conquer in the end the truth will c.       WYCLIFFE, J. 1
They will c., but . . . not convince   UNAMUNO Y JUGO, M. 3
We'll fight and we'll c.                    GARRICK, D. 2
when we c. without danger                CORNEILLE, P. 2
conquered I came; I saw; God c.     JOHN III SOBIESKI, 1
I came, I saw, I c.                         CAESAR, J. 4
I will be c.; I will not capitulate.     JOHNSON, S. 152
the English seem, as it were, to have c. and peopled half the
world                                     SEELEY, SIR J. 1
conquering C. kings                        CHANDLER, J. 1
not c. but fighting well          COUBERTIN, BARON, 1
See, the c. hero comes                     MORELL, T. 1
Conquest The Roman C. was, however, a *Good Thing*
                            SELLAR, W. 4
conscience a Nonconformist c.              WILDE, O. 39
As guardian of His Majesty's c.      THURLOW, BARON, 2
c. does make cowards of us all     SHAKESPEARE, W. 63
C. is a coward                     GOLDSMITH, O. 28
C. is the inner voice                   MENCKEN, H. 2

C. is the internal perception of the rejection of a particular wish
FREUD, S, 4

dilemmas of c. and egotism SNOW, BARON, 2

freedom of speech, freedom of c., and the prudence never to
practise . . . them TWAIN, M, 5

I cannot . . . cut my c. to fit this year's fashions HELLMAN, L, 2

I'll catch the c. of the King SHAKESPEARE, W, 60

why is my liberty judged of another man's c.
BIBLE: I CORINTHIANS, 16

consent No one can make you feel inferior without your c.
ROOSEVELT, E, 1

consequence It is incident to physicians . . . to mistake
subsequence for c. JOHNSON, S, 41

consequences men never violate the laws of God without
suffering the c. CHILD, L, 1

conservatism c. . . . adherence to the old and tried LINCOLN, A, 9

c. is based upon the idea CHESTERTON, G, 30

Conservative C. government is an organized hypocrisy
DISRAELI, 1ST EARL OF BEACONSFIELD, 21

Or else a little C. GILBERT, SIR W, 19

to what is called the Tory, and which might . . . be called the
C., party CROKER, J, 2

conservative The radical invents the views. . . . , the c. adopts
them TWAIN, M, 9

which makes a man more c. KEYNES, BARON, 2

consider c. your ways BIBLE: HAGGAI, 1

let thine ears c. well . . . my complaint PSALMS, 82

When I c. how my light is spent MILTON, J, 55

considerable to appear c. in his native place JOHNSON, S, 79

considered hast thou c. my servant Job BIBLE: JOB, 1

consistency C. is contrary to nature HUXLEY, A, 12

consonant Nature is very c. and conformable NEWTON, SIR I, 1

conspiracy conversation ends in a c. SMITH, A, 1

not a Party, it is a c. BEVAN, A, 1

conspirators All the c. SHAKESPEARE, W, 123

constabulary When c. duty's to be done GILBERT, SIR W, 40

constant A c. guest PROVERBS, 10

C. dripping PROVERBS, 103

Friendship is c. in all other things SHAKESPEARE, W, 209

constitution The c. . . . first and second class citizens WILLKIE, W, 1

The principles of a free c. GIBBON, E, 5

constitutional A c. king must learn to stoop LEOPOLD II, 1

c. right LINCOLN, A, 10

definition of a c. statesman BAGEHOT, W, 9

construction Our object in the c. of the state PLATO, 2

consultations dictator . . . always take some c. THATCHER, M, 13

consulted the right to be c., . . . to encourage, . . . to warn
BAGEHOT, W, 7

consume more history than they can c. SAKI, 6

statistics, born to c. resources HORACE, 17

consumer In a c. society there are . . . two kinds of slaves
ILLICH, I, 4

consumes Man . . . c. without producing ORWELL, G, 1

consummation a c. /Devoutly to be wish'd SHAKESPEARE, W, 61

consummatum c. est BIBLE: JOHN, 51

consumption Conspicuous c. . . . is a means of reputability
VEBLEN, T, 3

this c. of the purse SHAKESPEARE, W, 85

contemplate What has happened to architecture . . . that the only
passers-by who can c. it . . . LEVIN, B, 3

contemplates Beauty in things exists in the mind which c. them
HUME, D, 4

contemplation right mindfulness, right c. BUDDHA, 2

contemporary I am no one's c. – ever MANDELSTAM, O, 1

to trade a hundred c. readers for KOESTLER, A, 5

contempt attention to the inside . . . . c. for the outside
CHESTERFIELD, 4TH EARL OF, 10

she was only an Object of C. AUSTEN, J, 9

To show pity is felt as a sign of c. NIETZSCHE, F, 17

contemptible c. little Army WILHELM II, 4

content desire is got without c. SHAKESPEARE, W, 170

Let us draw upon c. for the deficiencies of fortune
GOLDSMITH, O, 26

contented How is it . . . that no one lives c. with his lot
HORACE, 45

If you are foolish enough to be c., don't show it JEROME, J, 4

With what I most enjoy c. least SHAKESPEARE, W, 256

contentment Where wealth and freedom reign, c. fails
GOLDSMITH, O, 24

contests mighty c. rise from trivial things POPE, A, 46

continence Give me chastity and c. AUGUSTINE OF HIPPO, 2

that melancholy sexual perversion known as c. HUXLEY, A, 6

Continent On the C. people have good food MIKES, G, 1

Continental C. people have sex life MIKES, G, 3

continual c. state of inelegance AUSTEN, J, 25

continuation All diplomacy is a c. of war CHOU EN LAI, 1

War is the c. of politics CLAUSEWITZ, K, 1

contraception a terrific story about oral c. ALLEN, W, 11

contraceptive It's like having a totally efficient c. BURGESS, A, 1

contraceptives C. should be used MILLIGAN, S, 8

Skullion had little use for c. SHARPE, T, 2

contract A verbal c. isn't worth the paper GOLDWYN, S, 15

Every law is a c. SELDEN, J, 2

Marriage is . . . but a civil c. SELDEN, J, 9

contradict Do I c. myself WHITMAN, W, 8

contradiction brook no c. WEBSTER, J, 2

Man is . . . an everlasting c. to himself HAZLITT, W, 3

Woman's at best a c. POPE, A, 41

contradictory Doublethink means the power of holding two c.
beliefs ORWELL, G, 17

contrairy everythink goes c. with me DICKENS, C, 8

contraries Without C. is no progression BLAKE, W, 16

contrary Mary, Mary, quite c. NURSERY RHYMES, 34

On the c. IBSEN, H, 10

control we ought to c. our thoughts DARWIN, C, 2

controversy that c. is either superfluous or hopeless
NEWMAN, CARDINAL, 6

convenient Nobody is forgotten when it is c. to remember him
DISRAELI, 1ST EARL OF BEACONSFIELD, 33

convent C. of the Sacred Heart ELIOT, T, 20

To enter the . . . Ballet is to enter a c. PAVLOVA, A, 1

conventional The c. army loses if it does not win KISSINGER, H, 1

conventionally to fail c. KEYNES, BARON, 5

conversation a c. with the finest men DESCARTES, R, 2

And third-rate c. PLOMER, W, 2

a proper subject of c. CHESTERFIELD, 4TH EARL OF, 15

C. . . . elicits secrets from us SENECA, 2

C. has a kind of charm SENECA, 2

c. must be an exchange of thought POST, E, 1

make his c. perfectly delightful SMITH, S, 11

Questioning is not the mode of c. JOHNSON, S, 100

There is no such thing as c. WEST, DAME R, 5

Writing . . . is but a different name for c. STERNE, L, 7

Your ignorance cramps my c. HOPE, A, 7

conversationalist the c. who adds 'in other words
MORLEY, R, 1

converted difficult for a Jew to be c. HEINE, H, 4

conviction The best lack all c. YEATS, W, 26

convince They will conquer, but . . . not c. UNAMUNO Y JUGO, M, 3

cook a good c., as cooks go SAKI, 16

Any c. should be able to LENIN, V, 7

C. is a little unnerved BETJEMAN, SIR J, 3

ill c. that cannot lick his own fingers SHAKESPEARE, W, 252

she was a very bad c. THIERS, L, 3

cookery c. do MEREDITH, G, 2

cooking woman accepted c. . . . but man . . . made of it a
recreation POST, E, 2

cooks Too many c. PROVERBS, 440

Coolidge C. is a better example of evolution ROGERS, W, 6

copier c. of nature can never produce anything great
REYNOLDS, SIR J, 2

copies more c. of my works are left behind BENCHLEY, R, 3

copulation Birth, and c., and death ELIOT, T, 19

copy A lotta cats c. the Mona Lisa ARMSTRONG, L, 1

copying by defying their parents and c. one another CRISP, Q, 2

coral C. is far more red SHAKESPEARE, W, 267

Of his bones are c. made SHAKESPEARE, W, 273

cord a threefold c. is not quickly broken BIBLE: ECCLESIASTES, 11

cordial gold in phisik is a c. CHAUCER, G, 9

cordiale La c. entente LOUIS PHILIPPE, 1

corn amid the alien c. KEATS, J, 34

That ate the c. NURSERY RHYMES, 62

the meadows rich with c. WHITTIER, J, 1

two ears of c. . . . grow . . . where only one grew before
SWIFT, J, 6

corner c. in the thing I love SHAKESPEARE, W, 225

some c. of a foreign field BROOKE, R, 5

corners people standing in the c. of our rooms COREN, A, 6

Cornish men twenty thousand C. HAWKER, R, 1

Coromandel On the Coast of C. LEAR, E, 2

coronets Kind hearts are more than c. TENNYSON, BARON, 36

corpse He'd make a lovely c. DICKENS, C, 26

he makes a very handsome c. GOLDSMITH, O, 15

corpses They are for prima donnas or c. ...     TOSCANINI, A, 1
corpuscles make the c. of the blood glow     LAWRENCE, D, 12
correct Astronomy teaches the c. use     LEACOCK, S, 5
correction It is a stupidity . . . to busy oneself with the c. of the
    world     MOLIERE, 6
correctly anxious to do the wrong thing c.     SAKI, 20
corridors c. of power     SNOW, BARON, 2
corroboration c. . . . in the records of Somerset House
    BIRKENHEAD, EARL OF, 1
corrupt Among a people generally c.     BURKE, E, 20
   power is apt to c.     PITT THE ELDER, 1ST EARL OF CHATHAM, 3
   Power tends to c.     ACTON, 1ST BARON, 2
corrupted They had been c. by money     GREENE, G, 6
corruptible born again, not of c. seed     BIBLE: I PETER, 2
corruption C., the most infallible symptom of constitutional liberty
    GIBBON, E, 7
   I have said to c., thou art my father     BIBLE: JOB, 11
corrupts lack of power c. absolutely     STEVENSON, A, 3
   Power c.     STEVENSON, A, 3
corse As his c. to the rampart     WOLFE, C, 1
cosmetics In the factory we make c.     REVSON, C, 1
cosmopolitan I was told I am a true c.     VIZINCZEY, S, 1
cosmos c. is about the smallest hole     CHESTERTON, G, 27
cost To give and not to count the c.     LOYOLA, I, 1
   Too caustic? To hell with c.     GOLDWYN, S, 3
cottage Love and a c.     COLMAN, THE ELDER, 1
   poorest man may in his c. bid defiance to . . . the Crown
    PITT THE ELDER, 1ST EARL OF CHATHAM, 1
cottages Pale Death kicks his way equally into the c. of the poor
    HORACE, 27
couch the century of the psychiatrist's c.     MCLUHAN, M, 3
   time as a tool not as a c.     KENNEDY, J, 4
   when on my c. I lie     WORDSWORTH, W, 6
cough Jeeves coughed one soft, low, gentle c.     WODEHOUSE, SIR P, 5
coughing The art of acting consists in keeping people from c.
    RICHARDSON, SIR R, 1
council The grotesque chaos of a Labour c. - a *Labour* c.
    KINNOCK, N, 9
counsel C. of her country's gods     COWPER, W, 2
   sometimes c. take - and sometimes Tea     POPE, A, 47
   the c. of the ungodly     PSALMS, 1
   we took sweet c. together     PSALMS, 38
count Don't c. your chickens     AESOP, 8
   Don't c. your chickens     PROVERBS, 115
   If you can . . . c. your money you are not . . . rich man     GETTY, J, 1
   To give and not to c. the cost     LOYOLA, I, 1
countenance his c. was as the sun     BIBLE: REVELATIONS, 1
   the Lord lift up his c. upon thee     BIBLE: NUMBERS, 1
counter-democratic Proportional Representation . . . is
   fundamentally c.     KINNOCK, N, 2
counterpoint Too much c.; what is worse, Protestant c.
    BEECHAM, SIR T, 3
counties see the coloured c.     HOUSMAN, A, 8
countries preferreth all c. before his own     OVERBURY, SIR T, 1
country absolved from all duty to his c.     PEACOCK, T, 10
   a c. diversion     CONGREVE, W, 13
   A c. governed by a despot     JOHNSON, S, 119
   a c. of young men     EMERSON, R, 23
   A man should know something of his own c.     STERNE, L, 9
   an honest man sent to lie abroad for . . . his c.     WOTTON, SIR H, 3
   Anybody can be good in the c.     WILDE, O, 49
   Anyone who loves his c., follow me     GARIBALDI, G, 1
   c. from whose bourn no traveller returns     SHAKESPEARE, W, 62
   Counsel of her c.'s gods     COWPER, W, 2
   God made the c.     COWPER, W, 20
   go down into the c.     WILDE, O, 17
   good news from a far c.     BIBLE: PROVERBS, 14
   Great artists have no c.     MUSSET, A, 2
   How I leave my c.     PITT THE YOUNGER, W, 4
   I have but one life to lose for my c.     HALE, N, 1
   I love thee still, My c.     COWPER, W, 21
   In the c. of the blind     PROVERBS, 224
   I would die for my c. . . .     KINNOCK, N, 12
   loathe the c.     CONGREVE, W, 13
   My c., right or wrong     CHESTERTON, G, 5
   nothing good . . . in the c.     HAZLITT, W, 11
   Our c. is the world     GARRISON, W, 1
   our c., right or wrong     DECATUR, S, 1
   Patriots . . . talk of dying for their c.     RUSSELL, EARL, 28
   proud of the position of the bungalow, . . . in the c.
    WILSON, SIR A, 1

she is my c. still     CHURCHILL, C, 2
That is no c. for old men     YEATS, W, 25
The history of every c. begins in the heart     CATHER, W, 1
The idiot who praises . . . every c. but his own     GILBERT, SIR W, 26
The past is a foreign c.     HARTLEY, L, 1
The undiscover'd c.     SHAKESPEARE, W, 62
This c., with its institutions, belongs to the people who inhabit it
    LINCOLN, A, 10
   to leave his c. as good as he had found it     COBBETT, W, 2
   we can die but once to serve our c.!     ADDISON, J, 6
   what was good for our c.     WILSON, C, 1
   When I am in the c. I wish to vegetate     HAZLITT, W, 19
countryside a more dreadful record of sin than . . . c.
    DOYLE, SIR A, 6
county The sound of the English c. families     WAUGH, E, 2
couple A married c. are well suited     ROSTAND, J, 1
courage be strong and of a good c.     BIBLE: DEUTERONOMY, 6
   C. is the price . . . for granting peace     EARHART, A, 1
   c. to love . . . courage to suffer     TROLLOPE, A, 4
   good deal of physical c. to ride a horse     LEACOCK, S, 8
   tale . . . of . . . c. of my companions     SCOTT, CAPTAIN, 2
   The Red Badge of C.     CRANE, S, 1
   three o'clock in the morning c.     THOREAU, H, 19
   Whistling aloud to bear his c. up     BLAIR, R, 1
course c. of true love never did run smooth     SHAKESPEARE, W, 201
courteous If a man be . . . c. to strangers
    BACON, 1ST BARON VERULAM, VISCOUNT ST ALBANS, 28
courtesy C. is not dead     DUHAMEL, G, 1
courtier Here lies a noble c. /Who never kept his word
    ANONYMOUS, 28
courts I have come to regard . . . c. . . . as a casino     INGRAMS, R, 1
   my soul hath a desire and longing to enter into the c. of
    PSALMS, 50
   the case is still before the c.     HORACE, 5
   The law-c. of England are open to all men     DARLING, BARON, 6
courtship C. to marriage     CONGREVE, W, 9
covenant a c. between me and the earth     BIBLE: GENESIS, 28
   a c. with death     GARRISON, W, 2
cover I . . . will c. thee with my hand     BIBLE: EXODUS, 31
   Never judge a c. by its book     LEBOWITZ, F, 1
covet thou shalt not c.     BIBLE: EXODUS, 20
cow A c. is a very good animal in the field     JOHNSON, S, 153
   That milked the c. with the crumpled horn     NURSERY RHYMES, 62
   The c. is of the bovine ilk     NASH, O, 1
   The c. jumped over the moon     NURSERY RHYMES, 14
   The c.'s in the corn     NURSERY RHYMES, 29
   till the c. comes home     BEAUMONT, F, 12
   Truth, Sir, is a c.     JOHNSON, S, 62
   Why buy a c.     PROVERBS, 467
coward better to be the widow of a hero than the wife of a c.
    IBARRURI, D, 3
   Conscience is a c.     GOLDSMITH, O, 28
   No c. soul is mine     BRONTE, E, 1
   None but a c. . . . has never known fear     FOCH, MARSHAL, 3
   The c. does it with a kiss     WILDE, O, 2
Cowardice guilty of Noel C.     DE VRIES, P, 3
cowardly Marriage is the only adventure open to the c.
    VOLTAIRE, 21
cowards C. die many times     SHAKESPEARE, W, 109
   the future . . . makes c. of us     DIX, D, 2
   Thus conscience does make c. of us all     SHAKESPEARE, W, 63
cowboy easier to get an actor to be a c.     FORD, J, 1
coxcomb to hear a c. ask two hundred guineas     RUSKIN, J, 15
coyness This c., lady, were no crime     MARVELL, A, 9
cradle Between the c. and the grave     DYER, J, 2
   Rocked in the c. of the deep     MILLARD, E, 1
   The hand that rocks the c.     WALLACE, W, 1
cradles bit the babies in the c.     BROWNING, R, 40
craft the c. so long to lerne     CHAUCER, G, 17
   The life so short, the c. so long to learn     HIPPOCRATES, 1
craftsmanship Skill without imagination is c.     STOPPARD, T, 1
crafty too c. a woman to invent a new lie     MAUGHAM, W, 7
cranny We seek . . . In every c. but the right     COWPER, W, 19
crap Books are a load of c.     LARKIN, P, 3
Craven why and how I became . . . mistress of the Earl of C.
    WILSON, H, 1
cream You integrate it with c.     X. MALCOLM, 1
create I c. new heavens and a new earth     BIBLE: ISAIAH, 37
   My father didn't c. you to arrest me     PEEL, VISCOUNT, 1
created God c. . . . the earth     BIBLE: GENESIS, 1

man alone leaves traces of what he c.     BRONOWSKI, J, 1
Man, . . . had been c. to jab the life out of Germans     SASSOON, S, 5
Thou hast c. us for Thyself     AUGUSTINE OF HIPPO, 1
we cannot be c. for this sort of suffering     KEATS, J, 66
**creates** he c. Gods by the dozen     MONTAIGNE, M, 6
**creation** greatest week . . . since the c.     NIXON, R, 6
Had I been present at the C.     ALFONSO, 1
The art of c. /is older     VOZNESENSKY, A, 1
**creator** All right, my lord c., Don Miguel     UNAMUNO Y JUGO, M, 1
Man . . . hasn't been a c., only a destroyer     CHEKHOV, A, 7
**creature** every c. of God is good     BIBLE: I TIMOTHY, 3
No c. smarts . . . as a fool     POPE, A, 15
the c. hath a purpose and its eyes are bright with it     KEATS, J, 84
Who kills a man kills a reasonable c.     MILTON, J, 1
**creatures** call these delicate c. ours     SHAKESPEARE, W, 225
From fairest c. we desire increase     SHAKESPEARE, W, 253
**credit** The way to get things done is not to mind who gets the c.     JOWETT, B, 6
**creditors** my oldest c. would hardly know me     FOX, H, 1
not everyone who wishes makes c.     RABELAIS, F, 5
**credits** c. would still read 'Rubinstein, God, and Piatigorsky'     HEIFETZ, J, 1
**credulity** C. is . . . the child's strength     LAMB, C, 10
He combined scepticism . . . with c.     POWYS, J, 1
**creed** got the better of his c.     STERNE, L, 8
the powers of a first-rate man and the c. of a second-rate man     BAGEHOT, W, 9
wrought /. . . the c. of creeds     TENNYSON, BARON, 25
**creeds** So many gods, so many c.     WILCOX, E, 4
Vain are the thousand c.     BRONTE, E, 2
**creep** I wants to make your flesh c.     DICKENS, C, 40
Wit that can c.     POPE, A, 14
**Creepers** Jeepers C.     MERCER, J, 1
**creetur** lone lorn c.     DICKENS, C, 8
**crème** you would have been the c. de la c.     SPARK, M, 8
**Crete** The people of C. . . . make more history     SAKI, 1
**Cretians** The C. are alway liars     BIBLE: TITUS, 1
**cricket** I do love c. – it's so very English.     BERNHARDT, S, 2
I have always looked on c.     TEMPLE, W, 4
It's not in support of c.     BEERBOHM, SIR M, 17
the c. on the hearth     MILTON, J, 9
where the c. sings     YEATS, W, 16
**Cricklewood** Midland, bound for C.     BETJEMAN, SIR J, 5
**cried** I c. all the way to the bank     LIBERACE, 1
**crieth** thy brother's blood c. unto me     BIBLE: GENESIS, 18
**crime** all c. is due to the repressed desire for aesthetic expression     WAUGH, E, 18
Arson, after all, is an artificial c.     WELLS, H, 10
C., like virtue, has its degrees     RACINE, J, 4
Do you call poverty a c.     SHAW, G, 17
If poverty is the mother of c., stupidity is its father     LA BRUYERE, J, 11
man's greatest c.     CALDERON DE LA BARCA, P, 1
no . . . c. so shameful as poverty     FARQUHAR, G, 1
The atrocious c. of being a young man     PITT THE ELDER, 1ST EARL OF CHATHAM, 2
the Napoleon of c.     DOYLE, SIR A, 9
The punishment fit the c.     GILBERT, SIR W, 29
This coyness, lady, were no c.     MARVELL, A, 9
Treason was no C.     DRYDEN, J, 5
worse than a c., it is a blunder     BOULAY DE LA MEURTHE, A, 1
**crimes** Catholics and Communists have committed great c.     GREENE, G, 3
history is . . . a tableau of c. and misfortunes     VOLTAIRE, 15
how many c. committed     CAMUS, A, 4
Oh liberty! . . . What c. are committed in thy name     ROLAND, M, 1
**crippled** I don't advise any one to take it up . . . unless they . . . are c.     GRANDMA MOSES, 3
**crisp** Deep and c. and even     NEALE, J, 2
**critic** A c. is a man who     TYNAN, K, 5
A good c. . . . narrates the adventures of his mind     FRANCE, A, 7
c. spits on what is done     HOOD, T, 14
Nor in the c. let the man be lost     POPE, A, 29
the function of the c.     BELL, C, 2
**critical** c. judgement is so exquisite     FRY, C, 2
nothing if not c.     SHAKESPEARE, W, 220
**criticism** A great deal of contemporary c.     CHESTERTON, G, 1
As far as c. is concerned     VORSTER, J, 1
my own definition of c.     ARNOLD, M, 12
People ask you for c.     MAUGHAM, W, 12
The Stealthy School of C.     ROSSETTI, D, 4

**criticize** don't c. /What you can't understand     DYLAN, B, 7
**criticizing** The pleasure of c.     LA BRUYERE, J, 4
**critics** Asking a working writer . . . about c.     HAMPTON, C, 5
c. all are ready made     BYRON, 6TH BARON, 35
c. . . . desire our blood, not our pain     NIETZSCHE, F, 14
**crocodile** An appeaser is one who feeds a c.     CHURCHILL, SIR W, 62
**crocodiles** wisdom of the c.     BACON, 1ST BARON VERULAM, VISCOUNT ST ALBANS, 60
**Cromwell** Caesar had his Brutus – Charles the First, his C.     HENRY, P, 1
restless C. could not cease     MARVELL, A, 3
ruins that C. knocked about a bit     LLOYD, M, 3
Some C. guiltless     GRAY, T, 6
**crony** government by c.     ICKES, H, 1
**crook** A writer of c. stories     WALLACE, E, 1
I am not a c.     NIXON, R, 7
the symbol of a bishop is a c.     DIX, G, 1
**crooked** the c. timber of humanity     KANT, I, 4
There was a c. man, and he walked a c. mile     NURSERY RHYMES, 57
**crop** watering the last year's c.     ELIOT, G, 3
**crops** Man . . . /Laid the c. low     THOMAS, D, 11
**cross** Don't c. the bridge     PROVERBS, 116
Hot c. buns! /. . . /One a penny, two a penny     NURSERY RHYMES, 16
no c., no crown     PENN, W, 1
The orgasm has replaced the C.     MUGGERIDGE, M, 2
When I survey the wondrous C.     WATTS, I, 8
**cross-bow** With my c. /I shot     COLERIDGE, S, 25
**crossed** a girl likes to be c. in love a little now and then     AUSTEN, J, 21
**crossword puzzle** an optimist . . . fills up his c. in ink     SHORTER, C, 1
**crow** before the cock c., thou shalt deny me     BIBLE: MATTHEW, 79
sun had risen to hear him c.     ELIOT, G, 3
waiting for the cock to c.     HUGHES, W, 1
**crowd** . . . a c. like that . . . brings a lump to my wallet     WALLACH, E, 1
And hid his face amid a c. of stars     YEATS, W, 32
Far from the madding c.     GRAY, T, 7
**crowds** without company     GIBBON, E, 2
If you can talk with c. and keep your virtue     KIPLING, R, 15
It brings men together in c. and mobs in bar-rooms     THOREAU, H, 5
**crown** no cross, no c.     PENN, W, 1
poorest man may in his cottage bid defiance to . . . the C.     PITT THE ELDER, 1ST EARL OF CHATHAM, 1
the c. of life     BIBLE: JAMES, 1
The influence of the C. has increased     DUNNING, BARON ASHBURTON, 1
Uneasy lies the head that wears a c.     SHAKESPEARE, W, 88
within the hollow c.     SHAKESPEARE, W, 239
**Crucible** America is God's C.     ZANGWILL, I, 2
**crucified** preach Christ c.     BIBLE: I CORINTHIANS, 1
Where the dear Lord was c.     ALEXANDER, C, 2
you might try getting c.     TALLEYRAND, 8
**crucify** Do you want to c. the boy     GRADE, BARON, 2
**cruel** A c. story runs on wheels     OUIDA, 4
C., but composed and bland     ARNOLD, M, 31
**cruellest** April is the c. month     ELIOT, T, 23
**cruelty** Fear is the parent of c.     FROUDE, J, 3
**cruise** we are all on our last c.     STEVENSON, R, 15
**crumbs** c. which fell from the rich man's table     BIBLE: LUKE, 30
**cry** don't you c. for me     FOSTER, S, 4
I often want to c.     RHYS, J, 2
let them . . . be soon brought to shame, that c. over me, there, there     PSALMS, 45
make 'em c.     READE, C, 1
mother, do not c.!     FARMER, E, 1
She likes stories that make her c.     SULLIVAN, A, 2
the c. of him that ruleth among fools     BIBLE: ECCLESIASTES, 18
the only advantage women have over men – . . . they can c.     RHYS, J, 2
the stones would immediately c. out     BIBLE: LUKE, 34
We think caged birds sing, when indeed they c.     WEBSTER, J, 5
when we c. to Thee     WHITING, W, 1
**crying** An infant c. in the night     TENNYSON, BARON, 26
It is no use c.     PROVERBS, 229
**cubic foot** One c. less     BENCHLEY, R, 4
**cuckoo** The c. clock was invented . . . to give tourists something solid     COREN, A, 5
The c. comes in April     PROVERBS, 382
This is the weather the c. likes     HARDY: T, 8
**cucumber** A c. should be well sliced     JOHNSON, S, 158

cucumbers they are but c. after all | JOHNSON, S, 129
cul C. bono | CICERO, M, 5
cul-de-sac A committee is a c. | COCKS, SIR B, 1
cult local c. called Christianity | HARDY, T, 1
What's a c. | ALTMAN, R, 1
cultivate c. our garden | VOLTAIRE, 4
cultivated I do not want to die . . . until I have . . . c. the seed | KOLLWITZ, K, 1
culture C. being a pursuit of our total perfection | ARNOLD, M, 1
C. is an instrument wielded by professors | WEIL, S, 1
C. is the passion for sweetness and light | ARNOLD, M, 21
C., the acquainting ourselves with the best | ARNOLD, M, 20
ladies who pursue C. in bands | WHARTON, E, 4
two half-cultures do not make a c. | KOESTLER, A, 3
Whenever I hear the word 'c.' | JOHST, H, 1
When I hear anyone talk of C. | GOERING, H, 4
You can lead a whore to c. | PARKER, D, 24
cunning let my right hand forget her c. | PSALMS, 83
cup Ah, fill the C. | FITZGERALD, E, 12
Come, fill the C., and in the Fire of Spring | FITZGERALD, E, 3
my c. runneth over | PSALMS, 14
my c. shall be full | PSALMS, 12
tak a c. o' kindness yet | BURNS, R, 3
the c. of the vales | THOMAS, D, 22
cupboard But when she got there /The c. was bare | NURSERY RHYMES, 39
Cupid wing'd C. painted blind | SHAKESPEARE, W, 202
cups c., That cheer but not inebriate | COWPER, W, 23
curators The Arab who builds . . . a hut out of . . . a temple . . . is more philosophical than . . . c. of the museums | FRANCE, A, 4
cur'd C. . . . of my disease | PRIOR, M, 1
curds Eating her c. and whey | NURSERY RHYMES, 31
cure C. the disease | BACON, 1ST BARON VERULAM, VISCOUNT ST ALBANS, 25
no c. for birth and death | SANTAYANA, G, 10
Show me a sane man and I will c. him for you | JUNG, C, 9
the c. for admiring the House of Lords | BAGEHOT, W, 2
There are maladies we must not seek to c. | PROUST, M, 10
Work is the grand c. | CARLYLE, T, 29
cured Poverty of goods is easily c. | MONTAIGNE, M, 10
the only disease you don't look forward to being c. of | MANKEIWICZ, H, 1
What can't be c. | PROVERBS, 454
curfew The C. tolls the knell of parting day | GRAY, T, 1
curiosities How these c. would be quite forgot | AUBREY, J, 2
curiosity C. killed the cat | PROVERBS, 104
C. will conquer fear | STEPHENS, J, 2
Disinterested intellectual c. . . . life blood of . . . civilisation. | TREVELYAN, G, 1
I would rather be a brilliant memory than a c. | EAMES, E, 1
curious Be not c. in unnecessary matters | BIBLE: ECCLESIASTICUS, 2
I am c. to see what happens . . . to one who dies unshriven | PERUGINO, P, 1
'That was the c. incident,' remarked . . . Holmes | DOYLE, SIR A, 13
curiouser C. and c. | CARROLL, L, 2
curl There was a little girl /Who had a little c. | MILLER, M, 1
curly C. locks, C. locks, /Wilt thou be mine | NURSERY RHYMES, 8
currency I will not be a party to debasing the c. | KEYNES, BARON, 8
curse A c. is on her if she stay | TENNYSON, BARON, 40
c. God, and die | BIBLE: JOB, 3
Christianity the one great c. | NIETZSCHE, F, 3
c. not the king, no not in thy thought | BIBLE: ECCLESIASTES, 22
She would rather light candles than c. the darkness | STEVENSON, A, 8
The c. is come upon me | TENNYSON, BARON, 42
Work is the c. of the drinking classes | WILDE, O, 72
cursed thou art c. above all cattle | BIBLE: GENESIS, 15
curses C. . . . always come home to roost | SOUTHEY, R, 2
curst C. be the verse | POPE, A, 13
curtain An iron c. | CHURCHILL, SIR W, 57
I saw it at a disadvantage – the c. was up | WINCHELL, W, 1
Ring down the c. | RABELAIS, F, 8
The Iron C. | GOEBBELS, J, 1
There is an iron c. across Europe | TROUBRIDGE, SIR T, 1
cushion Like a c., he always bore | LLOYD GEORGE, EARL OF DWYFOR, 11
custodiet Quis c. ipsos | JUVENAL, 5
custom A c. loathsome to the eye, hateful to the nose | JAMES I, 1
Age . . . nor c. stale her infinite virginity | WEBSTER, D, 1
C. calls me to't | SHAKESPEARE, W, 34

c. /More honour'd in the breach than the observance | SHAKESPEARE, W, 49
c. stale /Her infinite variety | SHAKESPEARE, W, 9
customer The c. is always right | SELFRIDGE, H, 1
customers When you are skinning your c. | KHRUSHCHEV, N, 2
cut c. to the heart | BIBLE: ACTS, 5
C. your coat | PROVERBS, 105
Don't c. off your nose | PROVERBS, 117
in the evening . . . c. down | PSALMS, 55
the human pack is shuffled and c. | LODGE, D, 3
cuts he that c. off twenty years of life | SHAKESPEARE, W, 111
cutting busy driving cabs and c. hair | BURNS, G, 1
cymbal a tinkling c. | BIBLE: I CORINTHIANS, 18
cymbals praise him in the c. and dances | PSALMS, 94
Cynara faithful to thee, C. | DOWSON, E, 1
cynicism C. is an unpleasant way of saying the truth | HELLMAN, L, 1
C. is humour in ill-health | WELLS, H, 15
no literature can outdo the c. of real life | CHEKHOV, A, 10

dad if the d. is present at the conception | ORTON, J, 2
They fuck you up, your mum and d. | LARKIN, P, 4
Daddy D. wouldn't buy me a bow-wow | TABRAR, J, 1
daffodils Fair d., we weep to see | HERRICK, R, 4
host, of golden d.. | WORDSWORTH, W, 5
I never saw d. so beautiful | WORDSWORTH, W, 1
dagger never be left holding the d. | WILSON OF RIEVAULX, BARON, 1
dainties d. that are bred in a book | SHAKESPEARE, W, 154
dainty Nothing's so d. sweet | BEAUMONT, F, 7
Daisy D., give me your answer, do | DACRE, H, 1
Dalhousie Alas! Lord and Lady D. are dead | MCGONAGALL, W, 1
dalliance primrose path of d. | SHAKESPEARE, W, 46
damage nothing which might d. his career | BARRIE, SIR J, 10
dame one for the d. | NURSERY RHYMES, 4
dammed Holland . . . lies so low they're only saved by being d. | HOOD, T, 13
damn D. braces | BLAKE, W, 26
D. the age. I'll write for antiquity | LAMB, C, 19
D. with faint praise | POPE, A, 12
I don't care a twopenny d. | WELLINGTON, DUKE OF, 21
not worth a d. | WELLINGTON, DUKE OF, 4
damnation there would be no d. | TOURNEUR, C, 1
the terminal point of addiction is . . . d. | AUDEN, W, 3
damnations Twenty-nine distinct d. | BROWNING, R, 52
damn'd thou must be d. perpetually | MARLOWE, C, 4
damned a d. serious business | WELLINGTON, DUKE OF, 5
d. good-natured friend | SHERIDAN, R, 1
d. if you do – And . . . d. if you don't | DOW, L, 1
Life is just one d. thing after another | HUBBARD, E, 3
Publish and be d. | WELLINGTON, DUKE OF, 20
The public be d. I am working for my stockholders | VANDERBILT, W, 1
damp Avoid d. beds and think of me | ANONYMOUS, 5
Danaos timeo D. et dona ferentis | VIRGIL, 6
dance d. an antic hay | MARLOWE, C, 7
D., d., d. little lady | COWARD, SIR N, 4
I have discovered the d. | DUNCAN, I, 1
On with the d. | BYRON, 6TH BARON, 11
will you join the d. | CARROLL, L, 14
danced I've d. with a man | FARJEON, H, 1
dancers a perfectly ghastly season . . . for you Spanish d. | BANKHEAD, T, 6
dancing And d. dogs and bears | HODGSON, R, 1
d. on a volcano | SALVANDY, COMTE DE, 1
the morals of a whore, and the manners of a d. master | JOHNSON, S, 48
danger A nation is not in d. of financial disaster | MELLON, A, 1
d. . . . lies in acting well | CHURCHILL, C, 1
Euthanasia is a long, smooth-sounding word, and . . . conceals its d. | BUCK, P, 1
I realized there was a measure of d. | EARHART, A, 2
Oft in d., oft in woe | WHITE, H, 1
the only real d. that exists is man himself | JUNG, C, 11
when we conquer without d. | CORNEILLE, P, 2
dangerous A little learning is a d. thing | POPE, A, 21
He thinks too much. Such men are d. | SHAKESPEARE, W, 107
If a little knowledge is d., where is the man . . . out of danger | HUXLEY, T, 8
if a little knowledge was a d. thing | SHARPE, T, 3
man is a d. creature | ADAMS, A, 1

more d. the abuse                          BURKE, E, 23
**dangerously** live d.                    NIETZSCHE, F, 5
**dangers** D. by being despised           BURKE, E, 27
**Daniel** brought D., and cast him into the den   BIBLE: DANIEL, 9
**Daniels** I should be like a lion in a cave of savage D.   WILDE, O, 74
**Danny Deever** they're hangin' D. in the mornin   KIPLING, R, 5
**Dante** ... D. makes me sick             VEGA CARPIO, L, 1
**dappled** Glory be to God for d. things   HOPKINS, G, 4
**dare** d. to eat a peach                 ELIOT, T, 13
**Darien** Silent, upon a peak in D.       KEATS, J, 37
**daring** d. to excel                     CHURCHILL, C, 1
**Darjeeling** There was an old man from D.   ANONYMOUS, 91
**dark** A blind man in a d. room          BOWEN, BARON, 2
children fear ... the d.
                          BACON, 1ST BARON VERULAM, VISCOUNT ST ALBANS, 18
colours will agree in the d.
                          BACON, 1ST BARON VERULAM, VISCOUNT ST ALBANS, 57
d. sayings                                 BIBLE: PROVERBS, 1
Genuineness only thrives in the d.         HUXLEY, A, 32
great leap in the d.                       HOBBES, T, 8
never to refuse a drink after d.           MENCKEN, H, 18
O d., d., d., amid the blaze of noon       MILTON, J, 53
slow, sure doom falls pitiless and d.      RUSSELL, EARL, 13
The d. night of the soul                   JOHN OF THE CROSS, 2
they grope in the d.                       BIBLE: JOB, 8
Turn up the lights, I don't want to go home in the d.   HENRY, O, 2
we are for the d.                          SHAKESPEARE, W, 16
What in me is d. /Illumine                 MILTON, J, 26
**darken** never d. my towels again        MARX, G, 8
**darkest** The d. hour                    PROVERBS, 383
**darkling** as on a d. plain              ARNOLD, M, 9
D. I listen                                KEATS, J, 35
**darkly** through a glass, d.             BIBLE: I CORINTHIANS, 18
**darkness** Before us pass'd the door of D.   FITZGERALD, E, 17
d. and light to thee are both alike        PSALMS, 86
d. is no d. with thee                      PSALMS, 86
d. was upon the face of the deep           BIBLE: GENESIS, 1
God shall make my d. to be light           PSALMS, 7
men loved d. ... because their deeds were evil   BIBLE: JOHN, 10
outer d.                                   BIBLE: MATTHEW, 32
She would rather light candles than curse the d.   STEVENSON, A, 8
The d. falls at Thy behest                 ELLERTON, J, 1
the d. inside houses                       DELANEY, S, 1
the people that walked in d.               BIBLE: ISAIAH, 12
the pestilence that walketh in d.          PSALMS, 57
**darlin'** he's a d. man '                O'CASEY, S, 1
**darling** Charlie is my d.               NAIRNE, BARONESS, 2
... d. of the Gods was born                MARVELL, A, 7
Thrice welcome, d. of the spring           WORDSWORTH, W, 69
**darn** A hole is the accident ... a d. is ... poverty   SHUTER, E, 1
**dates** .... Its history d. from today   WHISTLER, J, 12
**daughter** as is the mother, so is her d.   BIBLE: EZEKIEL, 3
d. of Earth and Water                      SHELLEY, P, 4
Don't put your d. on the stage             COWARD, SIR N, 6
I always remember that I am Caesar's d.    JULIA, 2
In a cavern, ... Dwelt a miner, Forty-niner, /And his
d., Clementine                             MONTROSE, P, 1
skipper had taken his little d.            LONGFELLOW, H, 16
**daughters** old cemetery in which nine of his d. were lying
                                           THURBER, J, 6
Words are men's d.                         MADDEN, S, 1
**dauntless** faithful in love, ... d. in war   SCOTT, SIR W, 13
**David** D. his ten thousands             BIBLE: I SAMUEL, 6
Once in royal D.'s city                    ALEXANDER, C, 1
**Davy** Sir Humphry D. /Abominated gravy   BENTLEY, E, 4
**dawn** a grey d. breaking                MASEFIELD, J, 5
Bliss was it in that d. to be alive        WORDSWORTH, W, 35
the dappled d. doth rise                   MILTON, J, 12
They sighed for the d. and thee ,          TENNYSON, BARON, 53
**dawned** each day that has d. is your last   HORACE, 18
**day** As I was saying the other d.       LEON, L, 1
compare thee to a summer's d.              SHAKESPEARE, W, 254
Drop ... what tomorrow may bring ... count as profit every d.
that Fate allows you                       HORACE, 29
each d. is like a year                     WILDE, O, 6
each d. that has dawned is your last       HORACE, 18
every dog has his d.                       BORROW, G, 2
from this d. forward                       BOOK OF COMMON PRAYER, 15
God called the light D.                    BIBLE: GENESIS, 1
Good morning to the d.: and, next, my gold   JONSON, B, 12
If every d. in the life of a school        LEACOCK, S, 1

I look upon every d. to be lost            JOHNSON, S, 151
in the d. of judgement                     BOOK OF COMMON PRAYER, 9
It takes place every d.                    CAMUS, A, 6
It was such a lovely d. .                  MAUGHAM, W, 16
let the d. perish wherein I was born       BIBLE: JOB, 4
live murmur of a summer's d.               ARNOLD, M, 33
Live this d., as ... thy last              KEN, T, 2
long d.'s task is done                     SHAKESPEARE, W, 13
Night and d.                               PORTER, C, 4
Now the d. is over                         BARING-GOULD, S, 1
one d. in thy courts is better than a thousand   PSALMS, 51
Our little systems have their d.           TENNYSON, BARON, 22
Seize the d.                               HORACE, 32
So foul and fair a d.                      SHAKESPEARE, W, 158
spend a single d. really well              KEMPIS, T, 5
Stay, stay, /Until the hasting d. /Has run   HERRICK, R, 4
Sweet d., so cool, so calm                 HERBERT, G, 9
That fellow would vulgarize the d. of judgment   JERROLD, D, 3
the arrow that flieth by d.                PSALMS, 57
The better the d.                          PROVERBS, 381
The bright d. is done                      SHAKESPEARE, W, 16
The d. begins to droop                     BRIDGES, R, 3
the d. returns too soon                   ' BYRON, 6TH BARON, 39
the sun shall not burn thee by d.          PSALMS, 77
the twenty-four hour d.                    BEERBOHM, SIR M, 4
thou knowest not what a d. may bring forth   BIBLE: PROVERBS, 16
when the d. of Pentecost was fully come ·  BIBLE: ACTS, 2
Without all hope of d.                     MILTON, J, 53
**daylight** a rule never to drink by d.   MENCKEN, H, 18
**Dayrolles** Give D. a chair.             CHESTERFIELD, 4TH EARL OF, 19
**days** D. and moments quickly flying     CASWALL, E, 1
D. off                                     TRACY, S, 2
d. of wine and roses                       DOWSON, E, 4
Do not let us speak of darker d.           CHURCHILL, SIR W, 50
Shuts up the story of our d.               RALEIGH, SIR W, 3
Sweet childish d.                          WORDSWORTH, W, 66
the d. of man are but as grass             PSALMS, 94
the d. of our age are threescore years and ten   PSALMS, 56
Thirty d. hath November                    GRAFTON, R, 1
**dead** Add: 'provided he is really d.'   LA BRUYERE, J, 12
A master is d.                             BRAHMS, J, 2
And what was d. was Hope.                  WILDE, O, 4
A statesman is a politician who's been d.   TRUMAN, H, 3
But he's just as d. as if he'd been wrong   ANONYMOUS, 102
Come not, when I am d.                     TENNYSON, BARON, 7
D.! and ... never called me mother         WOOD, MRS, 1
d., but in the Elysian fields   DISRAELI, 1ST EARL OF BEACONSFIELD, 38
D. men tell no tales                       PROVERBS, 106
Either he's d. or my watch has stopped     MARX, G, 5
England mourns for her d. across the sea   BINYON, L, 2
Fifteen men on the d. man's chest          STEVENSON, R, 6
forgotten, as a d. man out of mind         PSALMS, 22
for those who like it better d.            MACAULAY, DAME R, 6
God is d.                                  NIETZSCHE, F, 4
great deal to be said for being d.         BENTLEY, E, 3
Here lies Fred, /Who was alive and is d.   ANONYMOUS, 30
He was a great patriot ... provided ..., that he really is d.
                                           VOLTAIRE, 31
if I am d. he would like to see me         HOLLAND, BARON, 2
If the d. talk to you, you are a spiritualist   SZASZ, T, 8
... I have been drinking it for sixty-five years and I am not d.
yet                                        VOLTAIRE, 30
I've just read that I am d.                KIPLING, R, 30
let the d. bury their d.                   BIBLE: MATTHEW, 34
more to say when I am d.                    ROBINSON, E, 1
most of 'em d.                             SASSOON, S, 4
Mother is the d. heart of the family       GREER, G, 2
move in a world of the d.                  FORSTER, E, 1
My husband is d.                           MARX, G, 7
Nobody heard him, the d. man               SMITH, S, 2
Now he is d.                               ARNOLD, M, 28
Now I'm d. in the grave with my lips moving   MANDELSTAM, O, 2
O pity the d. that are d.                  LAWRENCE, D, 8
Over my d. body                            KAUFMAN, G, 1
Queen Anne's d.                            COLMAN, THE YOUNGER, 2
she was d.; but my father kept ladling gin   SHAW, G, 35
The d. don't die                           LAWRENCE, D, 42
The d. ... look on and help                LAWRENCE, D, 42
the d. shall be raised incorruptible       BIBLE: I CORINTHIANS, 23
the d. shall hear the voice of the Son of God   BIBLE: JOHN, 14
The noble living and the noble d.          WORDSWORTH, W, 38

deceive if we say that we have no sin, we d. BIBLE: I JOHN, 1
Oh, don't d.; Oh, never leave me ANONYMOUS, 16
To d. oneself PROVERBS, 436
deceived take heed . . . that your heart be not d. BIBLE: DEUTERONOMY, 3
deceiving Propaganda . . . consists in nearly d. your friends CORNFORD, F, 2
without quite d. your enemies CORNFORD, F, 2
decent d. means poor PEACOCK, T, 1
riff-raff apply to what is respectable, . . . aristocracy to what is d. HOPE, A, 6
the only d. thing . . . is to die at once BUTLER, S, 28
decision he is going to make 'a realistic d.', . . . resolved to do something bad MCCARTHY, M, 1
if usage so choose, with whom resides the d. HORACE, 34
decisive Marriage is a step so grave and d. STEVENSON, R, 21
deck d. thyself . . . with majesty and excellency BIBLE: JOB, 19
declaim Nay, Madam, when you are declaiming, d. JOHNSON, S, 109
declaration the principles of the D. of Independence bear no relation to half of the human race MARTINEAU, H, 6
declare they should d. the causes which impel them to . . . separation JEFFERSON, T, 1
declining years pass my d. saluting strange women and grandfather clocks NASH, O, 9
decomposing d. in the eternity of print WOOLF, V, 3
decorated proverb . . . much matter d. FULLER, T, 2
decorum Dulce et d. est HORACE, 34
Let them cant about d. BURNS, R, 11
decussated Anything reticulated or d. at equal distances JOHNSON, S, 8
dedicated never d. to something you have complete confidence in PIRSIG, R, 1
Dee Across the sands of D. KINGSLEY, C, 4
deed a good d. to forget a poor joke BRACKEN, 1ST VISCOUNT, 1
good d. in a naughty world SHAKESPEARE, W, 197
right d. for the wrong reason ELIOT, T, 16
The better day, the worse d. HENRY, M, 1
deeds better d. shall be in water writ BEAUMONT, F, 8
Don't listen to their words fix your attention on their d. EINSTEIN, A, 2
The bitterest tears . . . are for words . . . unsaid and d. . . . undone STOWE, H, 1
the due reward of our d. BIBLE: LUKE, 37
deep beauty is only sin d. SAKI, 21
D. and crisp and even NEALE, J, 2
his wonders in the d. PSALMS, 66
I never went down into the d. BIBLE: II ESDRAS, 3
out of the d. have I called unto thee PSALMS, 82
Rocked in the cradle of the d. MILLARD, E, 1
what a very singularly d. young man GILBERT, SIR W, 35
deeper d. than did ever plummet sound SHAKESPEARE, W, 278
whelm'd in d. gulphs COWPER, W, 4
deeth D. is an ende of every worldly sore CHAUCER, G, 12
defeat a d. without a war CHURCHILL, SIR W, 39
d. is an orphan , KENNEDY, J, 16
D. of Germany means ROOSEVELT, F, 4
every victory turns into a d. BEAUVOIR, S, 4
In d. unbeatable CHURCHILL, SIR W, 25
The greatest tragedy . . . except a d. WELLINGTON, DUKE OF, 11
defeated Like an army d. /The snow hath retreated WORDSWORTH, W, 72
man can be destroyed . . . not d. HEMINGWAY, E, 4
defect Chief D. of Henry King BELLOC, H, 3
defence Never make a d. or apology CHARLES I, 1
The best immediate d. of the United States ROOSEVELT, F, 5
the d. of England BALDWIN, 1ST EARL BALDWIN OF BEWDLEY, 5
the Lord is thy d. upon thy right hand PSALMS, 77
The only d. is in offence BALDWIN, 1ST EARL BALDWIN OF BEWDLEY, 4
defend I disapprove of what you say, but I will d. to the death your right to say it VOLTAIRE, 34
defiance in defeat, d. CHURCHILL, SIR W, 19
poorest man may in his cottage bid d. to . . . the Crown PITT THE ELDER, 1ST EARL OF CHATHAM, 1
The d. of established authority ARENDT, H, 1
defied Age will not be d. BACON, 1ST BARON VERULAM, VISCOUNT ST ALBANS, 42
defining Language is . . . a d. framework WHORF, B, 1
definite a d. maybe GOLDWYN, S, 14
definition This d. . . . would not do for a policeman NIGHTINGALE, F, 1
defying by d. their parents and copying one another CRISP, Q, 2

degenerates everything d. in the hands of man ROUSSEAU, J, 2
degeneration fatty d. of his moral being STEVENSON, R, 22
degradation a . . . sense of intellectual d. after an interview with a doctor JAMES, A, 3
degree d. of delight BURKE, E, 4
when d. is shak'd SHAKESPEARE, W, 281
degrees Crime, like virtue, has its d. RACINE, J, 4
We boil at different d. EMERSON, R, 22
deld Gey few, and they're a' d. ANONYMOUS, 36
deities the d. so kindly RABELAIS, F, 4
deity to distinguish between the D. and the Drains STRACHEY, L, 1
deleted D. by French censor BENNETT, J, 1
deliberate with a slow d. carelessness LAWRENCE, T, 1
deliberates woman that d. is lost ADDISON, J, 4
deliberation D. is the work of many men DE GAULLE, C, 1
delicacy the talent of flattering with d. AUSTEN, J, 19
delight a degree of d. BURKE, E, 4
Energy is Eternal D. BLAKE, W, 30
go to't with d. SHAKESPEARE, W, 12
his d. is in the law of the Lord PSALMS, 1
Studies serve for d. BACON, 1ST BARON VERULAM, VISCOUNT ST ALBANS, 49
Teach us d. in simple things KIPLING, R, 3
The leaping light for your d. discovers AUDEN, W, 17
very temple of d. KEATS, J, 29
wept with d. when you gave her a smile ENGLISH, T, 1
delighted Whosoever is d. in solitude BACON, 1ST BARON VERULAM, VISCOUNT ST ALBANS, 24
You have d. us long enough AUSTEN, J, 20
delightful make his conversation perfectly d. SMITH, S, 11
What a d. thing this perspective is UCCELLO, P, 1
delights Man d. not me SHAKESPEARE, W, 57
deliver d. me from myself BROWNE, SIR T, 9
delivered thou hast d. my soul from death PSALMS, 39
delivers the Man Who D. the Goods MASON, W, 1
deluge After us the d. POMPADOUR, M, 1
déluge Après nous le d. POMPADOUR, M, 1
delusions Many people have d. of grandeur IONESCO, E, 1
delusive Decades have a d. edge MACAULAY, DAME R, 2
delved When Adam d. BALL, J, 1
demagogues the vilest specimens of human nature are . . . found among d. MACAULAY, BARON, 10
demands the populace cannot exact their d. WELLINGTON, DUKE OF, 12
democracy arsenal of d. ROOSEVELT, F, 11
D. . . . government by the uneducated CHESTERTON, G, 40
D. is only an experiment in government INGE, W, 7
D. means government by discussion ATTLEE, EARL, 1
D. passes into despotism PLATO, 5
D. resumed her reign BELLOC, H, 7
extreme or absolute oligarchy, or despotism will come ARISTOTLE, 8
In Switzerland they had brotherly love, five hundred years of d. and peace WELLES, O, 1
Man's capacity for evil makes d. necessary NIEBUHR, R, 1
world . . . made safe for d.. WILSON, W, 9
demon woman wailing for her d.-lover COLERIDGE, S, 14
demons thanks to words, we have often sunk to the level of the d. HUXLEY, A, 1
den a d. of thieves BIBLE: MATTHEW, 61
denial the highest praise of God consists in the d. of Him PROUST, M, 7
denies spirit that always d. GOETHE, J, 4
Denmark rotten in the state of D. SHAKESPEARE, W, 50
dentist fuss about sleeping together . . . sooner go to my d. WAUGH, E, 42
dentists I have let d. ride roughshod over my teeth PERELMAN, S, 1
Our gratitude to most benefactors is the same as . . . for d. CHAMFORT, N, 3
The thought of d. gave him just the same sick horror WELLS, H, 6
deny before the cock crow, thou shalt d. me thrice BIBLE: MATTHEW, 79
let him d. himself BIBLE: MATTHEW, 51
Those who d. freedom LINCOLN, A, 8
depart D., . . . and let us have done with you AMERY, L, 2
lettest thou thy servant d. in peace BIBLE: LUKE, 11
when the great and good d. WORDSWORTH, W, 13
departure the time of my d. is at hand BIBLE: II TIMOTHY, 3
depends It all d. upon that article there WELLINGTON, DUKE OF, 1
depraved No one . . . suddenly became d. JUVENAL, 2

**depth** out of your d. TEMPLE, W, 3
**derangement** a nice d. of epitaphs SHERIDAN, R, 7
**derision** Ambition, Distraction, Uglification, and D. CARROLL, L, 12
**descend** Never d. to the ways of those above you MALLABY, SIR G, 1
**description** beggar'd all d. SHAKESPEARE, W, 8
**descriptions** d. of the fairest wights SHAKESPEARE, W, 263
**desert** The sand of the d. is sodden red NEWBOLT, SIR H, 7
Use every man after his d. SHAKESPEARE, W, 59
**deserts** D. of vast eternity MARVELL, A, 10
wandered in d. . . . dens and caves BIBLE: HEBREWS, 4
**deserve** I have arthritis, and I don't d. that either BENNY, J, 1
**deserved** I wasn't lucky. I d. it THATCHER, M, 20
**deserves** At 50, everyone has the face he d. ORWELL, G, 34
the government it d. MAISTRE, J, 1
**designing** I am d. St Paul's BENTLEY, E, 6
**desire** antidote to d. CONGREVE, W, 15
a universal innate d. BUTLER, S, 11
d. is got without content SHAKESPEARE, W, 170
D. is the very essence of man SPINOZA, B, 4
d. should so many years outlive performance SHAKESPEARE, W, 87
d. to be praised twice over ROCHEFOUCAULD, DUC DE LA, 18
I am my beloved's, and his d. is toward me BIBLE: SONG OF SOLOMON, 19
It provokes the d. SHAKESPEARE, W, 168
my soul hath a d. PSALMS, 50
nothing like d. for preventing the thing one says PROUST, M, 12
The D. of Man being Infinite BLAKE, W, 48
Those who restrain D. BLAKE, W, 28
to have few things to d. BACON, 1ST BARON VERULAM, VISCOUNT ST ALBANS, 21
to lose your heart's d. SHAW, G, 22
**desired** war which . . . left nothing to be d. BRECHT, B, 7
**desires** He who d. but acts not BLAKE, W, 24
made young with young d. THOMPSON, F, 3
Man's D. are limited by his Perceptions BLAKE, W, 47
Strong enough to answer back to d., to despise distinctions HORACE, 47
than nurse unacted d. BLAKE, W, 19
**desireth** like as the hart d. the water-brooks PSALMS, 30
**desiring** pessimists end up by d. the things they fear MALLET, R, 1
**desist** to d. from the experiment in despair LAMB, C, 4
**desk** what risks you take . . . to find money in a d. BALZAC, H, 4
**desks** Stick . . . to your d. and never go to sea GILBERT, SIR W, 11
**desolate** d. and sick of an old passion DOWSON, E, 3
**despair** carrion comfort, D., not feast on thee HOPKINS, G, 1
Don't d., not even over . . . d. KAFKA, F, 1
Patience, n. A minor form of d. BIERCE, A, 7
some divine d. TENNYSON, BARON, 58
to desist from the experiment in d. LAMB, C, 4
without understanding d. LAING, R, 2
**despairs** He who d. over an event is a coward CAMUS, A, 13
**desperate** D. cuts PROVERBS, 109
**desperation** lives of quiet d. THOREAU, H, 7
**despise** I d. Shakespeare SHAW, G, 9
some other Englishman d. him SHAW, G, 34
**despised** A poor man is d. the whole world over JEROME, J, 3
I doubt if the philosopher lives, . . . who could know himself . . . d. by a street boy HUXLEY, T, 5
**despises** A woman d. a man for loving her STODDARD, E, 1
**despond** name of the slough was D. BUNYAN, J, 2
**despot** A country governed by a d. JOHNSON, S, 119
**despotism** Democracy passes into d. PLATO, 5
extreme democracy or absolute oligarchy, or d. will come ARISTOTLE, 8
France was a long d. CARLYLE, T, 12
**dessicated** A d. calculating machine BEVAN, A, 4
**destination** I do not think this poem will reach its d. VOLTAIRE, 32
**destiny** I were walking with d. CHURCHILL, SIR W, 5
Riddle of d. LAMB, C, 18
**destroy** Doth the wingèd life d. BLAKE, W, 13
He would like to d. his old diaries TOLSTOY, S, 3
sought to d. institutions WHITMAN, W, 2
they shall not hurt nor d. in all my holy mountain BIBLE: ISAIAH, 15
whom God wishes to d. EURIPIDES, 1
Whom God would d. DUPORT, J, 1
Whom the gods wish to d. CONNOLLY, C, 7
**destroy'd** a bold peasantry, . . . /When once d. GOLDSMITH, O, 4
**destroyed** man can be d. . . . not defeated HEMINGWAY, E, 4
**destroyer** Man . . . hasn't been a creator, only a d. CHEKHOV, A, 7

**destroying** simplifying something by d. nearly everything CHESTERTON, G, 2
**destroys** he who d. a good book, kills reason MILTON, J, 1
**destruction** broad is the way, that leadeth to d. BIBLE: MATTHEW, 28
It is time for the d. of error AUDEN, W, 16
one purpose . . . d. of Hitler CHURCHILL, SIR W, 6
**detail** life is frittered away by d. THOREAU, H, 14
**details** with the thoroughness of a mind that reveres d. LEWIS, S, 3
**detective novel** The d. is PRITCHETT, V, 1
**deterrent** the d. is a phallic symbol WIGG, BARON, 1
**detest** they d. at leisure BYRON, 6TH BARON, 30
**detested** D. sport COWPER, W, 29
**Deutschland** D., D. über alles HOFFMANN VON FALLERSLEBEN, H, 1
**device** A banner with the strange d., /Excelsior LONGFELLOW, H, 5
**devil** Abashed the d. . . . felt how awful goodness is MILTON, J, 42
cleft the D.'s foot DONNE, J, 11
D. always builds a chapel there DEFOE, D, 5
d. can cite Scripture SHAKESPEARE, W, 189
d.'s walking parody CHESTERTON, G, 9
given up believing in the d. KNOX, R, 1
I do not see . . . why the d. should have all the good tunes HILL, R, 1
nickname is the heaviest stone that the d. can throw HAZLITT, W, 10
Renounce the d. BOOK OF COMMON PRAYER, 12
resist the d., and he will flee BIBLE: JAMES, 7
sacrifice . . . of the d.'s leavings POPE, A, 54
Sarcasm . . . the language of the d. CARLYLE, T, 24
The d. finds work PROVERBS, 384
The D. is a gentleman SHELLEY, P, 16
The d. is not so black PROVERBS, 385
the D. knows Latin KNOX, R, 2
The d. looks after his own PROVERBS, 386
the d. played at chess with me BROWNE, SIR T, 4
the world, the flesh, and the d. MURRAY, D, 1
world, the flesh, and the d. BOOK OF COMMON PRAYER, 8
**devils** It is no good casting out d. LAWRENCE, D, 34
One more d.'-triumph and sorrow for angels BROWNING, R, 30
**devoted** No man . . . gives any other definition of . . . a nurse . . . than . . . "d. and obedient." NIGHTINGALE, F, 1
**devotion** The almighty dollar, that great object of universal d. IRVING, W, 4
**devour** he shall d. the prey BIBLE: GENESIS, 57
shed tears when they would d. BACON, 1ST BARON VERULAM, VISCOUNT ST ALBANS, 60
**dew** his body was wet with the d. of heaven BIBLE: DANIEL, 6
Just to save her from the foggy, foggy d. ANONYMOUS, 63
**dexterity** Your d. seems a happy compound DISRAELI, 1ST EARL OF BEACONSFIELD, 1
**diagram** cat is a d. and pattern of subtle air LESSING, D, 6
**dialect** a d. I understand very little PEPYS, S, 6
D. words – those terrible marks of the beast HARDY, T, 5
**diamond** D.! D. NEWTON, SIR I, 3
more of rough than polished d. CHESTERFIELD, 4TH EARL OF, 9
**diamonds** D. Are ROBIN, L, 2
My goodness those d. are lovely WEST, M, 2
to give him d. back GABOR, Z, 3
**Diana** great is D. of the Ephesians BIBLE: ACTS, 15
**diaries** He would like to destroy his old d. TOLSTOY, S, 3
Let d., therefore BACON, 1ST BARON VERULAM, VISCOUNT ST ALBANS, 55
Only good girls keep d. BANKHEAD, T, 8
**diary** I never travel without my d. WILDE, O, 27
What is a d. as a rule TERRY, DAME E, 3
Dickens D. . . . never quite took BENNETT, A, 5
D.' world is not life-like CECIL, D, 1
**dictation** I did not write it. God wrote it. I merely did his d. STOWE, H, 4
**dictator** and finally a single d. substitutes himself TROTSKY, L, 11
I am painted as the greatest little d. THATCHER, M, 13
**dictators** D. ride to and fro upon tigers CHURCHILL, SIR W, 24
**dictatorship** The d. of the proletariat MARX, K, 7
**dictionaries** To make d. is dull work JOHNSON, S, 5
**dictionary** send the reader to the d. FAULKNER, W, 2
words never seen . . . before outside of a d. LODGE, D, 5
**diddle** Hey d. d., /The cat and the fiddle NURSERY RHYMES, 14
**die** A man can d. PROVERBS, 43
better to d. on your feet than to live on your knees IBARRURI, D, 2
but to do and d. TENNYSON, BARON, 5
curse God, and d. BIBLE: JOB, 3

D., ... the last thing I shall do  PALMERSTON, VISCOUNT, 2
D. when I may, ... I have always plucked a thistle and planted a
flower  LINCOLN, A, 3
either do, or d.  BEAUMONT, F, 4
Everybody has got to d., .... Now what  SAROYAN, W, 1
expedient that one man should d. for the people  BIBLE: JOHN, 43
for me to d., for you to go on living  SOCRATES, 3
How often are we to d.  POPE, A, 59
I d. a Christian  CHARLES I, 2
I d. because I do not d.  JOHN OF THE CROSS, 1
I d. happy  FOX, C, 5
I do not want to d. ... until I have ... cultivated the seed
KOLLWITZ, K, 1
If I should d.  BROOKE, R, 5
I have been learning how to d.  LEONARDO DA VINCI, 1
in what peace a Christian can d.  ADDISON, J, 17
I shall be like that tree; I shall d. from the top  SWIFT, J, 18
It is natural to d.
BACON, 1ST BARON VERULAM, VISCOUNT ST ALBANS, 19
it is youth that must fight and d.  HOOVER, H, 2
I will d. in peace  WOLFE, J, 2
I will d. in the last ditch  WILLIAM III, 1
I would d. for my country ...  KINNOCK, N, 12
let me d. drinking in an inn  MAP, W, 1
Let us determine to d. here  BEE, B, 1
Let us do or d.  BURNS, R, 16
let us eat and drink; for tomorrow we d.  BIBLE: I CORINTHIANS, 21
live for ever or d. in the attempt  HELLER, J, 2
man can d. but once  SHAKESPEARE, W, 90
Many people would sooner d. than think  RUSSELL, EARL, 25
Never say d.  PROVERBS, 305
No young man believes he shall ever d.  HAZLITT, W, 17
one may d. without ever laughing  LA BRUYERE, J, 8
place ... to d. in  BROWNE, SIR T, 10
Rather suffer than d.  LA FONTAINE, J, 1
Ring out, wild bells, and let him d.  TENNYSON, BARON, 31
save your world you asked this man to d.  AUDEN, W, 11
The dead don't d.  LAWRENCE, D, 42
The d. is cast  CAESAR, J, 3
the only decent thing ... is to d. at once  BUTLER, S, 28
those who are about to d. salute you  ANONYMOUS, 9
To achieve great things we must live as though ... never going to
d.  VAUVENARGUES, MARQUIS DE, 2
to d., and go we know not where  SHAKESPEARE, W, 184
To d. will be an awfully big adventure  BARRIE, SIR J, 5
trains all night groan on the rail /To men that d. at morn
HOUSMAN, A, 6
we can d. but once to serve our country!  ADDISON, J, 6
We d. – does it matter when  TENNYSON, BARON, 67
when good Americans d. they go to Paris  WILDE, O, 54
died dog it was that d.  GOLDSMITH, O, 9
I d. ... of my physician  PRIOR, M, 1
Men have d. from time to time  SHAKESPEARE, W, 31
there were people who d. of dropsies  JOHNSON, S, 157
'Tis said that some have d. for love  WORDSWORTH, W, 65
diem Carpe d.  HORACE, 32
dies a young person, who ... marries or d., is sure to be kindly
spoken of  AUSTEN, J, 4
because a man d. for it  WILDE, O, 62
Every moment d. a man  BABBAGE, C, 1
he d. in pain  LA BRUYERE, J, 6
He that d. pays all debts  SHAKESPEARE, W, 276
It matters not how a man d.  JOHNSON, S, 75
king never d.  BLACKSTONE, SIR W, 2
One d. only once  MOLIERE, 4
Whatever is begotten, born, and d.  YEATS, W, 25
whom the gods favour d. young  PLAUTUS, T, 1
diet Food is an important part of a balanced d.  LEBOWITZ, F, 2
diets I feel about airplanes the way I feel about d.  KERR, J, 4
difference Because there is no d.  THALES, 1
made the d. of forty thousand men  WELLINGTON, DUKE OF, 9
more d. within the sexes than between them
COMPTON-BURNETT, DAME I, 2
the d. of sex, if there is any  ANTHONY, S, 3
differences If we cannot now end our d.  KENNEDY, J, 12
The Jews and Arabs should ... settle their d.  AUSTIN, W, 2
different rich are d.  FITZGERALD, F, 3
differently ... I would have done it d.  WHISTLER, J, 14
differeth one star d. from another ... in glory  BIBLE: I
CORINTHIANS, 22
difficult D. do you call it, Sir  JOHNSON, S, 37

It is d. to be humble  DOBREE, B, 1
It is very d. to get up resentment  NEWMAN, CARDINAL, 1
When a piece gets d.  SCHNABEL, A, 4
difficulties settle up these little local d.
MACMILLAN, EARL OF STOCKTON, 2
difficulty A d. for every solution  SAMUEL, VISCOUNT, 6
I feel ... a certain d. in continuing to exist  FONTENELLE, B, 2
digest mark, learn, and inwardly d.  BOOK OF COMMON PRAYER, 1
Well, then, my stomach must just d. in its waistcoat
SHERIDAN, R, 10
digestion Things sweet to taste prove in d. sour
SHAKESPEARE, W, 235
digestions Few radicals have good d.  BUTLER, S, 16
dignity All human beings are born free and equal in d. and rights
ANONYMOUS, 3
Official d. ... in inverse ratio to ... importance  HUXLEY, A, 8
dilemmas d. of conscience and egotism  SNOW, BARON, 2
diligently Had I ... served God as d. as I have served the king
WOLSEY, T, 1
dim my lamp burns low and d.  ADAMS, F, 2
dimensions sickness enlarges the d. of a man's self  LAMB, C, 15
diminished ought to be d.  DUNNING, BARON ASHBURTON, 1
dimmed The eyes that shone, /Now d. and gone  MOORE, T, 7
dimple A d. in the chin, a devil within  PROVERBS, 13
dine wretches hang that jury-men may d.  POPE, A, 49
dined More d. against than dining  BOWRA, SIR M, 1
when Thomas Jefferson d. alone  KENNEDY, J, 10
... you have d. in every house in London – once  WILDE, O, 75
diners-out d. from whom we guard our spoons
MACAULAY, BARON, 19
Ding D. dong, bell, /Pussy's in the well  NURSERY RHYMES, 9
dinkum a d. hard-swearing Aussie  HASKELL, A, 1
dinner A d. lubricates business  SCOTT, BARON STOWELL, 1
A man is ... better pleased when he has a good d. upon his table
JOHNSON, S, 34
Breakfast, D., Lunch and Tea  BELLOC, H, 4
people ... would ask him to d.  CARLYLE, T, 26
This was a good d. enough  JOHNSON, S, 67
dinner-table dominate a London d.  WILDE, O, 65
diplomacy All d. is a continuation of war  CHOU EN LAI, 1
diplomat A d. ... always remembers a woman's birthday
FROST, R, 10
d. these days is nothing but a head-waiter  USTINOV, P, 8
diplomats aged d. to be bored  AUSTIN, W, 1
Dirce With D. in one boat conveyed  LANDOR, W, 1
direction God knows how you Protestants ... have any sense of
d.  WILSON, SIR A, 3
directions rode madly off in all d.  LEACOCK, S, 10
director Every d. bites the hand  GOLDWYN, S, 13
Theatre d.: a person  AGATE, J, 3
dirt After the first four years the d. doesn't get any worse
CRISP, Q, 4
Throw d. enough  PROVERBS, 431
dirty Is sex d.  ALLEN, W, 1
disadvantage d. of merely counting votes  INGE, W, 7
disagree Who shall decide when doctors d.?  POPE, A, 44
disappointed I am d. by that stroke of death  JOHNSON, S, 18
disappointment Grief and d. give rise to anger  HUME, D, 7
disapprove d. of what you say, but I will defend to the death
your right to say it  VOLTAIRE, 34
disarmament precede the d. of the victors  CHURCHILL, SIR W, 4
disaster ... the audience was a d.  WILDE, O, 67
disasters the middle station had the fewest d.  DEFOE, D, 3
trace ... the d. of English history to ... Wales  WAUGH, E, 13
disbelief willing suspension of d.  COLERIDGE, S, 6
disciples d. ... mark its ways and note ... its mysteries
BRADLEY, F, 2
one of his d., whom Jesus loved  BIBLE: JOHN, 30
discomforts for which, and all the d. that will accompany my being
blind, the good God prepare me  PEPYS, S, 12
discommendeth He who d. others  BROWNE, SIR T, 1
discontent lent /To youth and age ... – d.  ARNOLD, M, 44
To be discontented with the divine d.  KINGSLEY, C, 2
winter of our d.  SHAKESPEARE, W, 241
discontented you already have a d. work force  MORGAN, E, 2
discontents the family ... source of all our d..  LEACH, SIR E, 1
discourse their d. was about hunting  PEPYS, S, 6
discoverers They are ill d. that think there is no land
BACON, 1ST BARON VERULAM, VISCOUNT ST ALBANS, 3
discovery behind the d. of America  RICHLER, M, 2

D. consists of seeing what everybody has seen
SZENT-GYORGYI, A. 1
he who never made a mistake never made a d. SMILES, S. 1
Scientific d. is a private event MEDAWAR, SIR P. 1
**discretion** better part of valour is d. SHAKESPEARE, W. 82
temper d. with deceit WAUGH, E. 4
the years of d. BOOK OF COMMON PRAYER, 11
**discrimination** sympathetic without d. FIRBANK, R. 3
**discussion** D. in class, which means NABOKOV, V. 3
**disdains** He d. all things above his reach OVERBURY, SIR T. 1
**disease** an incurable d. – colour blindness DE BLANK, J. 2
Cur'd . . . of my d. PRIOR, M. 1
Cure the d. BACON, 1ST BARON VERULAM, VISCOUNT ST ALBANS, 25
Evil comes . . . like the d.; good . . . like the doctor
CHESTERTON, G. 23
if the physician had the same d. upon him that I have SELDEN, J. 5
Life is an incurable d. COWLEY, A. 2
Only those in the last stage of d. AUDEN, W. 21
remedies . . . suggested for a d. CHEKHOV, A. 2
remedy is worse than the d.
BACON, 1ST BARON VERULAM, VISCOUNT ST ALBANS, 46
strange d. of modern life ARNOLD, M. 35
the d. of writing books MONTESQUIEU, BARON DE, 8
the incurable d. of writing JUVENAL, 7
the only d. you don't look forward to being cured of
MANKEIWICZ, H. 1
this long d., my life POPE, A. 11
**diseased** One would suppose . . . women possess but one class of
physical organs, . . . always d. LIVERMORE, M. 1
**diseases** Extreme remedies . . . for extreme d. HIPPOCRATES, 2
Hungry Joe collected lists of fatal d. HELLER, J. 6
**disfranchisement** woman . . . feels as keenly as man the injustice
of d. STANTON, E. 2
**disgrace** a d. to our family name of Wagstaff MARX, G. 11
**disgracefully** The world is d. managed FIRBANK, R. 2
**disguise** virtues are . . . vices in d. ROCHEFOUCAULD, DUC DE LA, 27
**dish** And the d. ran away with the spoon NURSERY RHYMES, 1
a side d. he hadn't ordered LARDNER, R. 1
butter in a lordly d. BIBLE: JUDGES, 3
The national d. of America ROBINSON, R. 1
**dishes** Thou shalt not wash d. NURSERY RHYMES, 8
**dishonour** honour rooted in d. TENNYSON, BARON, 13
who fears d. more than death HORACE, 43
**disillusionments** d. in the lives of the medieval saints SAKI, 13
**disinclination** d. to inflict pain upon oneself MEREDITH, G. 3
**disinterested** D. intellectual curiosity . . . life blood of . . .
civilisation. TREVELYAN, G. 1
**dislike** I d. what I fancy I feel ANONYMOUS, 90
that *my* statue should be moved, which I should much d.
VICTORIA, 7
The law of d. for the unlike ZANGWILL, I. 3
**disliked** I have always d. myself CONNOLLY, C. 10
**dismal** the D. Science CARLYLE, T. 18
**Disney** D. the most significant figure . . . since Leonardo LOW, D. 1
**disobedience** Of Man's first d. MILTON, J. 25
**disorder** A sweet d. in the dress HERRICK, R. 2
**disposes** God d. KEMPIS, T. 4
**dispute** Many a long d. among divines FRANKLIN, B. 8
**disputing** The itch of d. will prove the scab of churches
WOTTON, SIR H. 2
**disreputable** I've been offered titles, . . . get one into d. company
SHAW, G. 42
**disrespectfully** Never speak d. of Society WILDE, O. 30
**dissipated** still keep looking so d. BENCHLEY, R. 2
**dissipation** At what time does the d. of energy begin
KELVIN, 1ST BARON; 1
d. without pleasure GIBBON, E. 2
other things than d. . . . thicken the features WEST, DAME R. 1
**dissolve** Fade far away, d. KEATS, J. 33
**distance** The d. doesn't matter DEFFAND, MARQUISE DU, 1
**disthressful** She's the most d. country that iver yet was seen
ANONYMOUS, 46
**distinctions** woman feels the invidious d. of sex STANTON, E. 2
**distinguish** all there is to d. us from other animals
BEAUMARCHAIS, P. 2
**distinguished** I was more d. by that . . . than . . . by any epaulet
THOREAU, H. 16
So it has come at last, the d. thing JAMES, H. 12
When a d. but elderly scientist states CLARKE, A. 1
**Distraction** Ambition, D., Uglification, and Derision CARROLL, L. 12
**distress** All pray in their d. BLAKE, W. 41

the mean man is always full of d. CONFUCIUS, 10
**distrust** shameful to d. one's friends
ROCHEFOUCAULD, DUC DE LA, 12
stay together, but we d. one another BRADBURY, M. 3
**distrusts** him who d. himself ROCHEFOUCAULD, DUC DE LA, 11
**disturb** What isn't part of ourselves doesn't d. us HESSE, H. 1
**ditchwater** Is d. dull CHESTERTON, G. 34
**diversion** Most sorts of d. . . . are an imitation of fighting
SWIFT, J. 15
'tis a country d. CONGREVE, W. 13
**diversity** make the world safe for d. KENNEDY, J. 12
**divide** D. and rule PROVERBS, 110
**divided** in their death they were not d. BIBLE: II SAMUEL, 1
Obstinate people can be d. into ARISTOTLE, 3
Thought must be d. against itself HUXLEY, A. 13
**divine** attain to the d. perfection LONGFELLOW, H. 7
The Hand that made us is d. ADDISON, J. 13
The right d. of kings to govern wrong POPE, A. 2
To be discontented with the d. discontent KINGSLEY, C. 2
To err is human, to forgive, d. POPE, A. 26
**divines** Many a long dispute among d. FRANKLIN, B. 8
**divinity** a d. that shapes our ends SHAKESPEARE, W. 74
a piece of d. in us BROWNE, SIR T. 11
d. in odd numbers SHAKESPEARE, W. 200
There's such d. doth hedge a king SHAKESPEARE, W. 72
**divisions** How many d. has *he* got STALIN, J. 1
**divorce** D.? Never. But murder often THORNDIKE, DAME S. 1
**do** Can I d. you now KAVANAGH, T. 2
D. as you would be done by CHESTERFIELD, 4TH EARL OF, 5
d. what the mob d. DICKENS, C. 41
either d., or die BEAUMONT, F. 4
for they know not what they d. BIBLE: LUKE, 36
go, and d. thou likewise BIBLE: LUKE, 23
I am to d. what I please FREDERICK THE GREAT, 2
I don't mind if I d. KAVANAGH, T. 2
Let us d. or die BURNS, R. 16
Nature . . . hath done her part; D. thou but thine MILTON, J. 45
Now what I d. with *this* EDWARD VIII, 2
Preachers say, D. as I say, not as I d. SELDEN, J. 5
so much to d., /So little done TENNYSON, BARON, 30
they would d. you DICKENS, C. 24
to d. something is to create existence SARTRE, J. 7
**doctor** A d. . . . is a patient half-cured PROUST, M. 8
a . . . sense of intellectual degradation after an interview with a d.
JAMES, A. 3
D. Foster went to Gloucester NURSERY RHYMES, 10
Evil comes . . . like the disease; good . . . like the d.
CHESTERTON, G. 23
I do not love thee, D. Fell BROWN, T. 1
Knocked down a d.? With an ambulance SIMPSON, N. 1
Passion . . . can be destroyed by a d. SHAFFER, P. 2
The d. found, . . . /Her last disorder mortal GOLDSMITH, O. 7
**doctors** sitting in the midst of the d. BIBLE: LUKE, 12
Who shall decide when d. disagree? POPE, A. 44
**doctrine** a d. so illogical and so dull KEYNES, BARON, 3
**doctrines** What makes all d. plain BUTLER, S. 7
**Dodger** artful D. DICKENS, C. 34
**doers** be ye d. of the word BIBLE: JAMES, 3
**does** It's dogged as d. it TROLLOPE, A. 7
**dog** A door is what a d. is . . . on the wrong side of NASH, O. 2
A good d. PROVERBS, 21
America is a large, friendly d. TOYNBEE, A. 2
And every d. his day KINGSLEY, C. 6
A woman's preaching is like a d.'s walking on his hinder legs
JOHNSON, S. 66
Beware of the d. PETRONIUS ARBITER, 1
D. does not eat d. PROVERBS, 113
d. that praised his fleas YEATS, W. 29
every d. has his day BORROW, G. 2
Every d. has his day PROVERBS, 133
Every d. is allowed PROVERBS, 134
Give a d. a bad name PROVERBS, 172
I am His Highness' d. at Kew POPE, A. 60
I ope my lips let no d. bark SHAKESPEARE, W. 187
That tossed the d., /That worried the cat NURSERY RHYMES, 62
The d. it was that died GOLDSMITH, O. 9
The d., . . . /Went mad and bit the man GOLDSMITH, O. 8
The little d. laughed /To see such sport NURSERY RHYMES, 14
The world regards such a person as . . . an unmuzzled d.
HUXLEY, T. 4
those . . . with a white stick and a d. LEVIN, B. 3

When a d. bites a man                                    DANA, C, 1
whose d. are you                                        POPE, A, 60
Why keep a d.                                       PROVERBS, 468
dogged It's d. as does it                            TROLLOPE, A, 7
dogging A case of the tail d. the wag             PERELMAN, S, 5
dogma Any stigma . . . to beat a d.               GUEDALLA, P, 3
no d., no Dean      DISRAELI, 1ST EARL OF BEACONSFIELD, 32
You can't teach an old d.                            PARKER, D, 17
dogmas these d. or goals are in doubt                 PIRSIG, R, 1
dogs Anybody who hates children and d.              FIELDS, W, 3
d. delight to bark and bite                           WATTS, I, 3
D., like horses, are quadrupeds                        MUIR, F, 4
how much more d. are animated when they hunt in a pack
                                                       HUME, D, 6
I loathe people who keep d.                      STRINDBERG, A, 1
I no more like people . . . than I like d.         SPENCER, SIR S, 1
let slip the d. of war                        SHAKESPEARE, W, 114
like asking a lamp-post . . . about d.             HAMPTON, C, 5
Mad d. and Englishmen                            COWARD, SIR N, 10
Men are . . . more careful of the breed of their horses and d. than
of their children                                      PENN, W, 2
Rats . . . fought the d.                          BROWNING, R, 40
Stop . . . those d. . . . peeing on my cheapest rug  HEARST, W, 1
The more I see of men, the more I admire d.
                                          SEVIGNE, MARQUISE DE, 1
woman who is . . . kind to d.                   BEERBOHM, SIR M, 12
doing Anything that is worth d.                  BEERBOHM, SIR M, 6
D. is better than saying                           PROVERBS, 114
Find out what you like d. best and get someone to pay you for d.
it                                                WHITEHORN, K, 6
let us not be weary in well d.                 BIBLE: GALATIANS, 6
we learn by d.                                     ARISTOTLE, 1
Whatever is worth d.               CHESTERFIELD, 4TH EARL OF, 2
doings All our d. without charity        BOOK OF COMMON PRAYER, 2
doleful Knight of the D. Countenance             CERVANTES, M, 4
dollar The almighty d., that great object of universal devotion
                                                      IRVING, W, 4
dollars What's a thousand d.                         MARX, G, 3
Dolly Daydream Little D.                         STRATTON, E, 2
dominate d. the world                                WILDE, O, 65
dominions The sun does not set in my d.           SCHILLER, F, 2
dona timeo Danaos et d. ferentis                     VIRGIL, 6
done bright day is d.                           SHAKESPEARE, W, 16
Do as you would be d. by            CHESTERFIELD, 4TH EARL OF, 5
Do as you would be d. by                          PROVERBS, 112
d. those things we ought not          BOOK OF COMMON PRAYER, 4
If it were d. when 'tis d.                     SHAKESPEARE, W, 163
Justice should . . . be seen to be d.            HEWART, BARON, 1
Let justice be d.                                FERDINAND I, 1
long day's task is d.                           SHAKESPEARE, W, 13
One never notices what has been d.                   CURIE, M, 4
so little d.                                   TENNYSON, BARON, 30
the dread of doing what has been d. before        WHARTON, E, 3
The way to get things d. is not to mind who gets the credit
                                                     JOWETT, B, 6
thy worldly task hast d.                        SHAKESPEARE, W, 38
What's d. cannot be undone                        PROVERBS, 456
What you do not want d. to yourself              CONFUCIUS, 14
Dong The D. with a luminous Nose                    LEAR, E, 3
Don Juans Christ-like heroes and woman-worshipping D.
                                                  LAWRENCE, D, 25
donkeys lions led by                             HOFFMANN, M, 1
Don Miguel All right, my lord creator, D.     UNAMUNO Y JUGO, M, 1
Donne Dr D.'s verses are like the peace of God;    JAMES I, 5
Don Quixote the only absolutely original creation . . . is D.
                                                  MAUGHAM, W, 22
dons If the D. sight Devon                      NEWBOLT, SIR H, 2
It is the little d. I complain about             PRIESTLEY, J, 2
donsmanship D. . . . the art of criticizing        POTTER, S, 5
don't-knows One day the d. will get in           MILLIGAN, S, 11
Doodle Yankee D. came to town                      BANGS, E, 1
doom bears it out even to the edge of d.      SHAKESPEARE, W, 265
purpose of God and the d. assigned         TENNYSON, BARON, 54
regardless of their d.                               GRAY, T, 9
slow, sure d. falls pitiless and dark            RUSSELL, EARL, 13
door A d. is what a dog is . . . on the wrong side of
I am the d.                                     BIBLE: JOHN, 25
sweetest thing that ever grew /Beside a human d.
                                               WORDSWORTH, W, 15
the judge standeth before the d.               BIBLE: JAMES, 8
When one d. shuts                               PROVERBS, 459

world will make a beaten path to his d.        EMERSON, R, 24
Youth will come . . . beat on my d.               IBSEN, H, 6
door-keeper I had rather be a d. in the house of my God
                                                    PSALMS, 51
doors be ye lift up, ye everlasting d.             PSALMS, 16
the d. of perception were cleansed               BLAKE, W, 17
Dorchester All terrorists, . . . end up with drinks at the D.
                                                GAITSKELL, H, 2
dots those damned d.                            CHURCHILL, R, 2
double But the horrible d.-entendre             ANONYMOUS, 92
double bed down the grassgreen gooseberried d.    THOMAS, D, 16
doublethink  D. means the power of holding two contradictory
beliefs                                          ORWELL, G, 17
doubt a life of d. diversified by faith          BROWNING, R, 9
all my mind is clouded with a d.           TENNYSON, BARON, 21
Humility is only d.                              BLAKE, W, 11
new Philosophy calls all in d.                    DONNE, J, 1
No . . . shadow of d.                          GILBERT, SIR W, 2
O thou of little faith, wherefore didst thou d.  BIBLE: MATTHEW, 48
these dogmas or goals are in d.                   PIRSIG, R, 1
Through the night of d. and sorrow           BARING-GOULD, S, 3
When a man is in d. about . . . his writing       BUTLER, S, 12
When in d., win the trick                         HOYLE, E, 1
doubting castle called D. Castle                  BUNYAN, J, 7
doubts end in d.   BACON, 1ST BARON VERULAM, VISCOUNT ST ALBANS, 2
His d. are better than . . . certainties      HARDWICKE, EARL OF, 1
douche the rattling of a thousand d. bags          LOWRY, M, 1
dove and the d. came in to him                 BIBLE: GENESIS, 25
No visit to D. Cottage, Grasmere, is complete      COREN, A, 1
the Spirit of God descending like a d.         BIBLE: MATTHEW, 5
the wings of a d.                                COWPER, W, 31
wings like a d.                                  PSALMS, 37
Dover It is burning a farthing candle at D.     JOHNSON, S, 65
the chalk cliffs of D.   BALDWIN, 1ST EARL BALDWIN OF BEWDLEY, 5
Dowel D., Dobet and Dobest                     LANGLAND, W, 2
dower forfeited their ancient English d.       WORDSWORTH, W, 50
down for coming d. let me shift for myself      MORE, SIR T, 3
He that is d.                                    BUNYAN, J, 10
I started at the top and worked my way d.        WELLES, O, 2
put it d. a we                                  DICKENS, C, 49
Yes, and they went d. very well too      WELLINGTON, DUKE OF, 2
downcast causes many people to feel a little d.  MCGONAGALL, W, 1
downhearted Are we d.? No                        ANONYMOUS, 7
down-sitting thou knowest my d.                  PSALMS, 84
downstairs he had known many kicked d.           BURNET, G, 1
dozen a d. are only a chorus                   FITZGERALD, F, 7
drain you will leave Oxford by the town d.       SPOONER, W, 5
drainpipe wrong end of a municipal d.
                                    LLOYD GEORGE, EARL OF DWYFOR, 1
drains to distinguish between the Deity and the D.  STRACHEY, L, 1
Drake D. he's in his hammock                  NEWBOLT, SIR H, 3
drama critic A good d. is                        TYNAN, K, 3
dramatist Sherard Blaw, the d. who had discovered himself
                                                    SAKI, 23
draught O, for a d. of vintage                  KEATS, J, 31
draw I d. what I feel in my body              HEPWORTH, DAME B, 1
drawbacks everything has its d.                  JEROME, J, 6
One of the d. of Fame                        MELBA, DAME N, 3
drawing room the Suez Canal was flowing through my d.
                                     EDEN, COUNTESS OF AVON, 1
dread the d. of doing what has been done before  WHARTON, E, 3
dreadful d. is the check                         BRONTE, E, 2
Other people are quite d.                        WILDE, O, 15
Portions and parcels of the d. Past         TENNYSON, BARON, 50
some have called the /Mighty and d.             DONNE, J, 2
Dreadnoughts A . . . Duke costs as much . . . as two D.
                                     LLOYD GEORGE, EARL OF DWYFOR, 5
dream Abou Ben Adhem (may his tribe increase!) /Awoke one
night from a deep d. of peace                     HUNT, L, 1
All men d.: but not equally                    LAWRENCE, T, 2
A sight to d. of                               COLERIDGE, S, 8
awakened from the d. of life                    SHELLEY, P, 2
behold it was a d.                               BUNYAN, J, 8
d. of perfect bliss                              BAYLY, T, 2
For life is but a d.                            THOMSON, J, 2
God will cease to d. you                    UNAMUNO Y JUGO, M, 1
Happiness is no vague d.                         SAND, G, 1
hope is . . . the d. of those that wake          PRIOR, M, 2
I d. when I am awake               CALDERON DE LA BARCA, P, 2
I have a d.                                      KING, M, 3
The young men's vision, and the old men's d.    DRYDEN, J, 12

To sleep, perchance to d. SHAKESPEARE, W, 61
warned of God in a d. BIBLE: MATTHEW, 2
Where is it now, the glory and the d. WORDSWORTH, W, 23
you d. you are crossing the Channel GILBERT, SIR W, 21
**dreamer** that prophet, or . . . d. of dreams BIBLE: DEUTERONOMY, 4
The poet and the d. are distinct KEATS, J, 11
this d. cometh BIBLE: GENESIS, 47
**dreamers** the d. of the day are dangerous men LAWRENCE, T, 2
**dreamin'** d. . . . o' Plymouth Hoe NEWBOLT, SIR H, 3
**dreaming** after-dinner's sleep, d. on both SHAKESPEARE, W, 183
a man d. I was a butterfly CHUANG TSE, 1
City with her d. spires ARNOLD, M, 43
**dreams** D. and predictions
BACON, 1ST BARON VERULAM, VISCOUNT ST ALBANS, 41
doubtful d. of d. SWINBURNE, A, 2
do we not live in d. TENNYSON, BARON, 12
dream our d. away FLANAGAN, B, 1
Fanatics have their d. KEATS, J, 10
For one person who d. of making fifty thousand pounds
MILNE, A, 3
I, being poor, have only my d. YEATS, W, 33
In d. begins responsibility YEATS, W, 21
show life . . . as we see it in our d. CHEKHOV, A, 5
Than this world d. of TENNYSON, BARON, 20
the city of perspiring d. RAPHAEL, F, 1
We are nothing; less than nothing, and d. LAMB, C, 2
We are such stuff /As d. are made on SHAKESPEARE, W, 277
what d. may come SHAKESPEARE, W, 61
**dreamt** d. of in your philosophy SHAKESPEARE, W, 52
I d. that I was making a speech DEVONSHIRE, 8TH DUKE OF, 1
**dreary** d. intercourse of daily life WORDSWORTH, W, 12
Dying is a very dull, d. affair MAUGHAM, W, 26
If your morals make you d. STEVENSON, R, 1
Once upon a midnight d. POE, E, 1
**dress** I have no d. except the one I wear CURIE, M, 3
put on a d. of guilt MCGOUGH, R, 1
sweet disorder in the d. HERRICK, R, 2
Those who make their d. . . . themselves HAZLITT, W, 13
**dress'd** D. in a little brief authority SHAKESPEARE, W, 180
**dressed** All d. up, with nowhere to go WHITE, W, 1
Some fruit for Him that d. me HERBERT, G, 3
Today I d. to meet my father's eyes . . . JULIA, 1
**dresses** long d., . . . cover a multitude of shins WEST, M, 8
**drink** A good d. PROVERBS, 22
A little in d. STEELE, SIR R, 2
a rule never to d. by daylight MENCKEN, H, 18
A taste for d., combined with gout GILBERT, SIR W, 3
D. and the devil STEVENSON, R, 6
D. deep, or taste not the Pierian spring POPE, A, 21
D.! for you know not whence you came FITZGERALD, E, 18
d. may be said to be an equivocator with lechery
SHAKESPEARE, W, 168
D. to me only with thine eyes JONSON, B, 5
First you take a d. . . . then the d. takes you FITZGERALD, F, 12
I commended mirth . . . to eat . . . to d., and to be merry
BIBLE: ECCLESIASTES, 15
let us eat and d.; for tomorrow we . . . die BIBLE: ISAIAH, 19
never to refuse a d. after dark MENCKEN, H, 18
no one has yet found a way to d. for a living KERR, J, 3
Nor any drop to d. COLERIDGE, S, 28
that he has taken to d. TARKINGTON, B, 1
There are five reasons we should d. ALDRICH, D, 1
we d. too much tea PRIESTLEY, J, 5
willing to taste any d. once CABELL, J, 1
woe unto them that . . . follow strong d. BIBLE: ISAIAH, 7
you shall d. twice while I d. once WALPOLE, 4TH
EARL OF ORFORD, 1
**drinkers** no verse can give pleasure for long, nor last, that is
written by d. of water HORACE, 23
**drinketh** whosoever d. of this water shall thirst again
BIBLE: JOHN, 12
**drinking** D. . . . and making love BEAUMARCHAIS, P, 2
d. deep of that divinest anguish BRONTE, E, 4
. . . I have been d. it for sixty-five years and I am not dead yet
VOLTAIRE, 30
let me die d. in an inn MAP, W, 1
no d. after death FLETCHER, J, 1
resolve to give up smoking, d. and loving FREUD, C, 1
smoking cigars and . . . d. of alcohol before, after, and if need be
during all meals CHURCHILL, SIR W, 17
there's nothing like d. DIBDIN, C, 2

'Tis not the d. . . . but the excess SELDEN, J, 8
two reasons for d. PEACOCK, T, 6
Work is the curse of the d. classes WILDE, O, 72
**drinks** He who d. a little too much PROVERBS, 198
**dripping** Constant d. hollows out a stone LUCRETIUS, 2
electricity was d. invisibly THURBER, J, 9
**driver** in the d.'s seat BEAVERBROOK, BARON, 1
**driving** busy d. cabs and cutting hair BURNS, G, 1
I would spend my life in d. briskly in a post-chaise JOHNSON, S, 112
**drizzle** the blasted English d. KIPLING, R, 22
**Dr Johnson** D.'s morality was as English . . . as a beefsteak
HAWTHORNE, N, 2
**droghte** d. of Marche CHAUCER, G, 1
**dromedary** whose muse on d. trots COLERIDGE, S, 19
**droop** The day begins to d. BRIDGES, R, 3
**drop** Nor any d. to drink COLERIDGE, S, 28
there are people whom one should like very well to d.
JOHNSON, S, 133
**dropping** peace comes d. slow YEATS, W, 16
**dropsies** there were people who died of d. JOHNSON, S, 157
**dropt** Mrs Montagu has d. me JOHNSON, S, 133
**drown** I'll d. my book SHAKESPEARE, W, 278
what pain it was to d. SHAKESPEARE, W, 242
**drowning** A d. man PROVERBS, 14
Being an old maid is like death by d. FERBER, E, 1
not waving but d. SMITH, S, 2
**drudge** a harmless d. JOHNSON, S, 7
**drug** Words are . . . the most powerful d. KIPLING, R, 32
**drum** brave Music of a *distant* D.! FITZGERALD, E, 6
Not a d. was heard WOLFE, C, 1
Take my d. to England NEWBOLT, SIR H, 2
**drums** the beating of war d. KOESTLER, A, 4
**drunk** If, d. with sight of power, we loose KIPLING, R, 20
man . . . must get d. BYRON, 6TH BARON, 18
My mother, d. or sober CHESTERTON, G, 5
not so think as you d. SQUIRE, SIR J, 1
this meeting is d. DICKENS, C, 46
you won't intoxicate with one glass someone who has . . . d. . . . a
. . . barrel CHEKHOV, A, 10
**drunkards** There are more old d. PROVERBS, 405
**drunken** Better sleep with a sober cannibal than a d. Christian
MELVILLE, H, 1
d., but not with wine BIBLE: ISAIAH, 23
He uses statistics as a d. man uses lamp-posts LANG, A, 1
What shall we do with the d. sailor ANONYMOUS, 105
**drunkenness** A branch of the sin of d. JAMES I, 2
If . . . 'feeling good' could decide, d. would be . . . supremely valid
JAMES, W, 2
**dry** old man in a d. month ELIOT, T, 6
out of these wet clothes and into a d. Martini WOOLLCOTT, A, 2
O ye d. bones BIBLE: EZEKIEL, 6
the midst of the sea upon d. ground BIBLE: EXODUS, 15
**Dublin** D., though . . . much worse than London JOHNSON, S, 150
In D.'s fair city, where the girls are so pretty ANONYMOUS, 47
**duckling** The Ugly D. ANDERSEN, H, 2
**ducks** you go about the country stealing d. ARABIN, W, 3
your precious lame d. GALSWORTHY, J, 1
**due** his fruit in d. season PSALMS, 1
**duke** A . . . D. costs as much . . . as two Dreadnoughts
LLOYD GEORGE, EARL OF DWYFOR, 5
a naked D. of Windlestraw addressing a naked House of Lords
CARLYLE, T, 23
**dukes** a drawing-room full of d. AUDEN, W, 5
**dulce** et decorum est HORACE, 34
**dull** a doctrine so illogical and so d. KEYNES, BARON, 3
as d. as ditch water DICKENS, C, 38
a very d. Play CONGREVE, W, 9
Heaven . . . , is a place so inane, so d. SHAW, G, 32
He was d. in a new way JOHNSON, S, 89
Music-hall songs provide the d. with wit MAUGHAM, W, 23
not only d. in himself FOOTE, S, 2
The prospect of a lot /Of d. MPs GILBERT, SIR W, 17
To make dictionaries is d. work JOHNSON, S, 5
**dullard** The d.'s envy of brilliant men BEERBOHM, SIR M, 9
**dullness** the cause of d. in others FOOTE, S, 2
**dumplings** I am the emperor, and I want d. FERDINAND I, 1
**dunces** the d. are all in confederacy against him SWIFT, J, 12
**dupe** The d. of friendship, and the fool of love HAZLITT, W, 24
**dusk** In the d., with a light behind her GILBERT, SIR W, 45
slow d. a drawing-down of blinds OWEN, W, 1
**dusky** Midnight brought on the d. hour MILTON, J, 43

**dust** A heap of d. alone remains          POPE, A, 5
As chimney-sweepers, come to d.      SHAKESPEARE, W, 38
d. shalt thou eat                      BIBLE: GENESIS, 15
d. thou art                         BIBLE: GENESIS, 16
Excuse my d.                      PARKER, D, 29
fear in a handful of d.             ELIOT, T, 25
fly . . . said, what a d. do I raise
     BACON, 1ST BARON VERULAM, VISCOUNT ST ALBANS, 58
his enemies shall lick the d.          PSALMS, 46
pride that licks the d.            POPE, A, 14
raised a d.               BERKELEY, BISHOP, 2
The d. and silence of the upper shelf   MACAULAY, BARON, 12
the d. beneath thy chariot wheel       HOPE, L, 1
The d. of great persons' graves        DONNE, J, 13
this quintessence of d.       SHAKESPEARE, W, 57
**Dutch** my dear old D.!           CHEVALIER, A, 1
**duties** he devotes to the neglect of his d.   THOMPSON, W, 2
Property has its d.             DRUMMOND, T, 1
**duty** absolved from all d. to his country    PEACOCK, T, 10
a stupid man . . . always declares that it is his d.    SHAW, G, 5
A thing of d. is a boy for ever       O'BRIEN, F, 1
d. of an opposition           CHURCHILL, R, 1
Do your d. and leave the rest to the Gods   CORNEILLE, P, 1
England expects every man will do his d.   NELSON, VISCOUNT, 3
It is my d. to warn you that it will be used against you
                              DOYLE, SIR A, 8
more than a moral d. to speak one's mind    WILDE, O, 25
Nor law, nor d. bade me fight      YEATS, W, 14
Patriotism . . . is a revolutionary d.    TROTSKY, L, 12
right of d., . . d. of some         QUINCY, J, 1
the condition of our sex is so deplorable that it is our d. . . . to
break the law                PANKHURST, E, 4
the d. of being happy         STEVENSON, R, 18
this is the whole d. of man     BIBLE: ECCLESIASTES, 26
What's a man's first d.?          IBSEN, H, 8
when constabulary d.'s to be done    GILBERT, SIR W, 40
**dwarfs** A number of anxious d.      PRIESTLEY, J, 3
**dwell** d. among scorpions       BIBLE: EZEKIEL, 1
he that sitteth on the throne shall d. among them
                       BIBLE: REVELATIONS, 7
I will d. in the house of the Lord for ever    PSALMS, 12
Let other pens d. on guilt and misery    AUSTEN, J, 10
**dwellings** how amiable are thy d.       PSALMS, 50
**dwelt** She d. among the untrodden ways   WORDSWORTH, W, 43
**dyin'** Young man, I think you're d.    ANONYMOUS, 49
**dying** alike are the groans of love to . . . d.    LOWRY, M, 2
D. for an idea,                 LEWIS, W, 2
d. for their country          RUSSELL, EARL, 28
D. is a very dull, dreary affair     MAUGHAM, W, 26
Don't cheer, boys; the poor devils are d.    PHILIP, J, 1
For a priest to turn a man when he lies a-d.   SELDEN, J, 6
He had been, he said, a most unconscionable time   CHARLES II, 7
Here am I, d.                  POPE, A, 57
I am d., Egypt, d.         SHAKESPEARE, W, 14
I cannot forgive my friends for d.      SMITH, L, 7
If this is d.                STRACHEY, L, 4
it is not death, but d., which is terrible    FIELDING, H, 1
'Tis not the d. for a faith        THACKERAY, W, 3
Truth sits upon the lips of d. men     ARNOLD, M, 39
we survive amongst the dead and the d. as on a battlefield
                           SPARK, M, 5
**dyke** February, fill the d.         TUSSER, T, 1
**dykes** . . . our d., . . . are ten feet deep   WILHELMINA, 1
**Dylan Thomas** D.           THOMAS, D, 24
**dynamic** class people as static and d.    WAUGH, E, 2
play is a d. thing            TYNAN, K, 1

# E

**ear** a pistol let off at the e.        LAMB, C, 14
he that planted the e., shall he not hear    PSALMS, 59
jest's prosperity lies in the e.    SHAKESPEARE, W, 156
more is meant than meets the e.      MILTON, J, 10
nor e. heard          BIBLE: I CORINTHIANS, 3
the e. begins to hear          BRONTE, E, 3
**earl** As far as the 14th E. is concerned
     DOUGLAS-HOME, BARON HOME OF THE HIRSEL, 1
the whole process has ground to a halt with a 14th E.
                WILSON OF RIEVAULX, BARON, 9
**early** A useless life is an e. death     GOETHE, J, 5
E. to bed                  PROVERBS, 124

E. to rise and e. to bed         THURBER, J, 5
God shall help her, and that right e.     PSALMS, 31
good die e.                DEFOE, D, 1
nobody who does not rise e.      JOHNSON, S, 155
The e. bird              PROVERBS, 387
**earn** this is the week I e. my salary    KENNEDY, J, 3
**earned** Old age . . . gives us what we have e.   BRENAN, G, 3
**earning** learning, e. and yearning     MORLEY, C, 1
**ears** A hungry stomach has no e.    LA FONTAINE, J, 9
device to keep the e. from grating     DE VRIES, P, 1
and hear not               PSALMS, 71
e. to hear, let him hear      BIBLE: MATTHEW, 40
Romans, countrymen, lend me your e.   SHAKESPEARE, W, 116
the seven thin e.         BIBLE: GENESIS, 50
**earth** a covenant between me and the e.   BIBLE: GENESIS, 28
a new heaven and a new e.     BIBLE: REVELATIONS, 18
axis of the e. sticks out visibly through . . . every town or city
                          HOLMES, O, 4
But did thee feel the e. move?    HEMINGWAY, E, 2
Cool'd . . . in the deep-delved e.      KEATS, J, 31
E. fills her lap with pleasures     WORDSWORTH, W, 24
E. has not anything to show more fair   WORDSWORTH, W, 47
from whose face the e. and the heaven fled   BIBLE: REVELATIONS, 17
God called the dry land E.      BIBLE: GENESIS, 3
God created . . . the e.       BIBLE: GENESIS, 1
heaven and e. shall pass away    BIBLE: MATTHEW, 69
heav'n on e.               MILTON, J, 40
hell upon e. . . . in a melancholy man's heart   BURTON, R, 2
he shall turn again to his e.        PSALMS, 89
in his hand are all the corners of the e.    PSALMS, 60
I will move the e.          ARCHIMEDES, 1
lards the lean e. as he walks    SHAKESPEARE, W, 78
let all the e. keep silence before him   BIBLE: HABAKKUK, 1
mine were princes of the e.       BENJAMIN, J, 1
more things in heaven and e.    SHAKESPEARE, W, 52
passenger on the spaceship, E.      FULLER, R, 1
so much of e. . . . of heaven    WORDSWORTH, W, 42
the cool flowery lap of e.       ARNOLD, M, 25
The e. does not argue        WHITMAN, W, 12
the e. is full of the goodness of the Lord    PSALMS, 24
the e. is the Lord's, and the fulness   BIBLE: I CORINTHIANS, 15
the e. is the Lord's          PSALMS, 15
. . . the e. of England is in my two hands   WILLIAM I, 1
the e. shall melt away         PSALMS, 31
the e. where cares abound    WORDSWORTH, W, 68
The meek do not inherit the e.      LASKI, H, 1
then shall the e. bring forth her increase    PSALMS, 43
This e. of majesty      SHAKESPEARE, W, 237
When e. was nigher heaven     BROWNING, R, 44
**earthquake** a story that starts with an e.   GOLDWYN, S, 5
**ease** done with so much e.       DRYDEN, J, 2
Joys in another's loss of e.       BLAKE, W, 35
No warmth, no cheerfulness, no healthful e.    HOOD, T, 10
Prodigal of E.             DRYDEN, J, 4
True e. in writing comes from art     POPE, A, 24
**easeful Death** half in love with e.     KEATS, J, 35
**easier** E. said than done       PROVERBS, 125
it is much e. to say what it is not    JOHNSON, S, 108
**east** E. is E., and West is West     KIPLING, R, 1
E., west                PROVERBS, 126
hold the gorgeous e. in fee    WORDSWORTH, W, 53
to have the E. come to the Atlantic    GOERING, H, 1
to prevent us from going into the E.    GOERING, H, 1
wise men from the e.       BIBLE: MATTHEW, 1
**East End** Now we can look the E. in the face
            ELIZABETH THE QUEEN MOTHER, 1
**east wind** the e. made flesh      APPLETON, T, 2
**easy** E. come             PROVERBS, 127
It is e. to bear           PROVERBS, 228
It is e. to be wise          DALI, S, 1
It's either e. or impossible      COLETTE, S, 5
**eat** Don't e. too many almonds    SECOMBE, SIR H, 1
E. as much as you like        MOLIERE, 2
e. to live, not live to e.        PROVERBS, 128
E. to live          SHAKESPEARE, W, 232
great ones e. up the little ones
I commended mirth . . . to e. . . . to drink, and to be merry
              BIBLE: ECCLESIASTES, 15
I could e. one of Bellamy's veal pies   PITT THE YOUNGER, W, 3
if any would not work, neither should he e.
             BIBLE: II THESSALONIANS, 1

**emperor** An e. ought at least to die on his feet  VESPASIAN, 1
I am the e., and I want dumplings  FERDINAND I, 1
the E. has nothing on  ANDERSEN, H, 1
**emperors** e. can't do it all by themselves  BRECHT, B, 6
**empire** An e. founded by war  MONTESQUIEU, BARON DE, 1
'Can't' will be the epitaph of the British E.  MOSLEY, SIR O, 3
Great Britain has lost an E.  ACHESON, D, 4
How is the E.  GEORGE V, 3
liquidation of the British E.  CHURCHILL, SIR W, 53
the Holy Roman E. was neither holy, nor Roman, nor an e.
  VOLTAIRE, 11
to the French the e. of the land  RICHTER, J, 1
**Empires** The day of E. has come  CHAMBERLAIN, J, 2
**employed** innocently e. than in getting money  JOHNSON, S, 88
The rise in the . . . e. is governed by Parkinson's Law
  PARKINSON, C, 2
**employees** Work . . . by those e. who have not yet reached . . .
incompetence  PETER, L, 2
**employment** I will undoubtedly have to seek . . . gainful e.
  ACHESON, D, 3
**empty** Bring on the e. horses  CURTIZ, M, 1
E. vessels  PROVERBS, 129
You can't think rationally on an e. stomach  REITH, BARON, 1
**enchantment** distance lends e. to the view  CAMPBELL, T, 3
**enclose** A vacuum can only exist . . . by the things which e. it
  FITZGERALD, Z, 3
**enclosed** Check e.  PARKER, D, 27
**encourage** the right to be consulted, . . . to e., . . . to warn
  BAGEHOT, W, 7
to e. the others  VOLTAIRE, 2
**encourager** pour e. les autres  VOLTAIRE, 2
**encyclopaedia** a whole E. behind the rest of the world  LAMB, C, 6
**end** a beginning, a muddle, and an e.  LARKIN, P, 5
an e. to the beginnings of all wars  ROOSEVELT, F, 15
at their wit's e.  PSALMS, 66
a whole is that which has a beginning, a middle, and an e.
  ARISTOTLE, 4
beginning of the e.  TALLEYRAND, 3
God be at my e., /And at my departing  ANONYMOUS, 20
I like a film to have a beginning, a middle and an e.  GODARD, J, 2
I move softly towards the e.  JOHN XXIII, 1
Keep right on to the e. of the road  LAUDER, SIR H, 5
of making many books there is no e.  BIBLE: ECCLESIASTES, 25
our minutes hasten to their e.  SHAKESPEARE, W, 259
the e. is not yet  BIBLE: MATTHEW, 67
The e. is to build well  WOTTON, SIR H, 1
The e. justifies the means  PROVERBS, 388
the e. of the beginning  CHURCHILL, SIR W, 52
Walt Whitman who laid e. to e.  LODGE, D, 5
we're forbidden to know – what e. the gods have in store
  HORACE, 30
world without e.  BOOK OF COMMON PRAYER, 5
Yes, to the very e.  ROSSETTI, C, 6
**endeavour** To e. to forget anyone  LA BRUYERE, J, 14
**ended** My life with girls has an e.  HORACE, 38
The day Thou gavest, Lord, is e.  ELLERTON, J, 1
**ending** The quickest way of e. a war  ORWELL, G, 28
**endless** History is an e. repetition  DURRELL, L, 3
**ends** divinity that shapes our e.  SHAKESPEARE, W, 74
my family begins . . . yours e. with you  IPHICRATES, 1
**endurance** patient e. is godlike  LONGFELLOW, H, 4
**endure** For his mercies ay e.  MILTON, J, 50
It is flattering some men to e. them  HALIFAX, MARQUIS OF, 3
Youth's a stuff will not e.  SHAKESPEARE, W, 289
**endured** Job e. everything – until his friends came
  KIERKEGAARD, S, 1
much to be e.  JOHNSON, S, 25
**endures** When a man is in love he e. more  NIETZSCHE, F, 1
**endureth** Blessed is the man that e. temptation  BIBLE: JAMES, 1
**enemies** Better a thousand e.  PROVERBS, 87
designing mausoleums for his e.  LINKLATER, E, 1
do not have to forgive my e.  NARVAEZ, R, 1
Even a paranoid can have e.  KISSINGER, H, 4
his e. shall lick the dust  PSALMS, 46
love your e.  BIBLE: MATTHEW, 16
mine e. shall be confounded  PSALMS, 2
Mountains interposed /Make e. of nations  COWPER, W, 26
The e. of Freedom  INGE, W, 2
until I make thine e. thy footstool  PSALMS, 68
we have been mortal e. ever since  LESAGE, A, 2
**enemy** Every man is his own worst e.  PROVERBS, 139

hasn't an e. in the world  WILDE, O, 63
It takes your e. and your friend . . . , to hurt you  TWAIN, M, 4
no more sombre e. of good art  CONNOLLY, C, 8
Poverty is a great e. to human happiness  JOHNSON, S, 137
We have met the e., and they are ours  PERRY, O, 1
we must be just to our e.  CAMPBELL, T, 7
**energies** quarrel . . . e. displayed in it are fine  KEATS, J, 63
**energy** At what time does the dissipation of e. begin
  KELVIN, 1ST BARON, 1
E. is Eternal Delight  BLAKE, W, 30
**enfants** Allons, e., de la patrie  ROUGET DE LISLE, C, 1
Les e. terribles  GAVARNI, P, 1
**engaged** one of the nicest girls I was ever e. to
  WODEHOUSE, SIR P, 15
**engine** indefatigable and unsavoury e. of pollution  SPARROW, J, 1
**England** A grain, which in E. is generally given to horses
  JOHNSON, S, 9
Be E. what she will  CHURCHILL, C, 2
but the King of E. cannot enter
  PITT THE ELDER, 1ST EARL OF CHATHAM, 1
Christianity is part of the Common Law of E.  HALE, SIR M, 1
Common Law of E.  HERBERT, SIR A, 3
don't say that in E. for . . . they will surely tax it  SWIFT, J, 17
E. elects a Labour Government  ROGERS, W, 2
E. expects every man will do his duty  NELSON, VISCOUNT, 3
E. is a nation of shopkeepers  NAPOLEON I, 8
E. is a paradise for women  BURTON, R, 4
E. is the mother of parliaments  BRIGHT, J, 2
E. is the paradise of individuality  SANTAYANA, G, 8
E. is the paradise of women  FLORIO, J, 1
E. mourns for her dead across the sea  BINYON, L, 2
E.'s green and pleasant land  BLAKE, W, 31
E.'s pleasant pastures  BLAKE, W, 31
E. . . . the workshop of the world
  DISRAELI, 1ST EARL OF BEACONSFIELD, 18
E.! . . . /What love I bore to thee  WORDSWORTH, W, 4
E. will have her neck wrung like a chicken  WEYGAND, M, 1
E., with all thy faults  COWPER, W, 21
For E.'s the one land  BROOKE, R, 1
go back to thy stately homes of E.  LAWRENCE, D, 16
he bores for E.  MUGGERIDGE, M, 4
in E. people have good table manners  MIKES, G, 1
In E., pop art and fine art  MACINNES, C, 1
In E. there is only silence or scandal  MAUROIS, A, 1
It was twenty-one years ago that E. and I  MIKES, G, 4
Living in E., . . . must be like being married to a stupid . . . wife
  HALSEY, M, 3
no man in E. will take away my life  CHARLES II, 4
occurred nowhere but in E.  CONRAD, J, 9
Oh, to be in E.  BROWNING, R, 23
Old E. is lost  JOHNSON, S, 110
. . . rather hew wood than be . . . King of E.  CHARLES X, 1
should they know of E. who only E. know  KIPLING, R, 6
Speak for E.  AMERY, L, 1
Stately Homes of E.  COWARD, SIR N, 12
that is forever E.  BROOKE, R, 5
The best thing I know between France and E.  JERROLD, D, 2
the defence of E.  BALDWIN, 1ST EARL BALDWIN OF BEWDLEY, 5
. . . the earth of E. is in my two hands  WILLIAM I, 1
the Kings of E., Diamonds, Hearts, Spades and Clubs  FAROUK I, 1
The Law of E. is a very strange one  DARLING, BARON, 5
the little ships of E. brought the Army home  GUEDALLA, P, 2
The national sport of E.  TREE, SIR H, 6
the old savage E., whose last blood flows still  LAWRENCE, D, 20
There'll always be an E.  PARKER, C, 1
The roast beef of E.  FIELDING, H, 6
The stately homes of E.  HEMANS, F, 2
this generation . . . found E. a land of beauty  JOAD, C, 3
this realm, this E.  SHAKESPEARE, W, 237
we are the people of E.  CHESTERTON, G, 33
**English** Dr Johnson's morality was as E. . . . as a beefsteak
  HAWTHORNE, N, 2
E. people . . . are surely the *nicest* people in the world
  LAWRENCE, D, 2
E. soldiers fight like lions  HOFFMANN, M, 1
especially if he went among the E.  BARRIE, SIR J, 9
E., . . . the language of an imaginative race  BRENAN, G, 4
E. women are elegant  MITFORD, N, 2
exterminate . . . the treacherous E.  WILHELM II, 4
forfeited their ancient E. dower  WORDSWORTH, W, 50
I do love cricket – it's so very E.  BERNHARDT, S, 2

If the E. language had been properly organized MILNE, A, 2
If you get the E. people into the way of making kings
MELBOURNE, VISCOUNT, 3
one of the few E. novels for grown up people WOOLF, V, 2
Opera in E. MENCKEN, H, 17
our E. nation, if they have a good thing, to make it too common
SHAKESPEARE, W, 84
part of E. middle-class education is devoted to the training of
servants . . . WILLIAMS, R, 1
stones kissed by the E. dead OWEN, W, 4
The attitude of the E. . . . toward E. history HALSEY, M, 2
The baby doesn't understand E. KNOX, R, 2
the E. are . . . the least a nation of pure philosophers
BAGEHOT, W, 6
the E. have hot-water bottles MIKES, G, 3
The E. have no respect for their language SHAW, G, 34
The E. instinctively admire AGATE, J, 2
The E. (it must be owned) are rather a foul-mouthed nation
HAZLITT, W, 14
The E. may not like music BEECHAM, SIR T, 2
the E. seem, as it were, to have conquered and peopled half the
world SEELEY, SIR J, 1
The E. take their pleasures SULLY, DUC DE, 1
The French want no-one to be their *superior*. The E. want
*inferiors* TOCQUEVILLE, A, 1
This is the sort of E. CHURCHILL, SIR W, 30
To Americans E. manners are . . . frightening JARRELL, R, 2
to the E. that of the sea RICHTER, J, 1
two most beautiful words in the E. language JAMES, H, 11
typically E. characteristic ADCOCK, SIR F, 1
Englishman . . . Am I not punished enough in not being born an
E. VOLTAIRE, 29
An E. . . . forms an orderly queue of one MIKES, G, 2
an E.'s heaven-born privilege of doing as he likes ARNOLD, M, 7
An E.'s way of speaking LERNER, A, 1
An E.'s word PROVERBS, 52
E. . . . is afraid to feel FORSTER, E, 2
E. never enjoys himself except for a noble purpose HERBERT, SIR
A, 6
He was born an E. BEHAN, B, 3
If I were an American, as I am an E.
PITT THE ELDER, 1ST EARL OF CHATHAM, 6
in spite of all temptations . . . He remains an E. GILBERT, SIR W, 13
it takes a great deal to produce ennui in an E. HALSEY, M, 1
never find an E. among the underdogs WAUGH, E, 26
Remember that you are an E. RHODES, C, 2
. . . some other E. despise him SHAW, G, 34
tale . . . which would have stirred . . . E. SCOTT, CAPTAIN, 2
To be an E. NASH, O, 3
to behold the E. at his *best* FIRBANK, R, 1
You may be the most liberal Liberal E. LAWRENCE, D, 10
young E. of our upper class ARNOLD, M, 4
Englishmen Mad dogs and E. COWARD, SIR N, 10
to create Frenchmen in the image of E. CHURCHILL, SIR W, 54
to see the absurd nature of E. PEPYS, S, 3
When two E. meet, their first talk is of the weather
JOHNSON, S, 12
enigma a riddle wrapped in a mystery inside an e.
CHURCHILL, SIR W, 40
enjoy Certainly, there is nothing else here to e. SHAW, G, 47
He knew everything about literature except how to e. it
HELLER, J, 4
Since God has given us the papacy . . . e. it LEO X, 1
enjoyed little to be e. JOHNSON, S, 25
enlightened in this e. age WOLLSTONECRAFT, M, 1
ennui it takes a great deal to produce e. in an Englishman
HALSEY, M, 1
enough It comes soon e. EINSTEIN, A, 9
patriotism is not e. CAVELL, E, 1
entente La cordiale e. LOUIS PHILIPPE, 1
enter but the King of England cannot e.
PITT THE ELDER, 1ST EARL OF CHATHAM, 1
entereth he that e. in by the door is the shepherd BIBLE: JOHN, 24
enterprises e. that require new clothes THOREAU, H, 11
entertained Television . . . permits you to be e. in your living
room FROST, D, 1
three unhappy women . . . being e. within an inch of their lives
SOMERVILLE, E, 1
entertainment what cats most appreciate . . . is . . . e. value
HOUSEHOLD, G, 1

enthusiasm Nothing great was ever achieved without e.
EMERSON, R, 5
We were as nearly bored as e. would permit GOSSE, SIR E, 1
enthusiastic Latins are tenderly e. DIETRICH, M, 2
enthusiasts so few e. can be trusted BALFOUR, 1ST EARL OF, 4
entities E. should not be multiplied OKHAM, W, 1
entrance all men have one e. into life BIBLE: WISDOM, 3
entrances the e. of this world made narrow BIBLE: II ESDRAS, 5
entuned E. in hir nose CHAUCER, G, 4
envied Better be e. PROVERBS, 90
There are two things for which animals are . . . e. VOLTAIRE, 23
environment President Robbins was so well adjusted to his e.
JARRELL, R, 1
envy 2 percent moral, 48 percent indignation and 50 percent e.
DE SICA, V, 1
e. is a kind of praise GAY, J, 9
prisoners of addiction and . . . prisoners of e. ILLICH, I, 4
The dullard's e. of brilliant men BEERBOHM, SIR M, 9
the upbringing a nun would e. ORTON, J, 1
Ephesians great is Diana of the E. BIBLE: ACTS, 15
Epicurus one of E.' herd of pigs. HORACE, 18
epigram it purrs like an e. MARQUIS, D, 2
epigrams long despotism tempered by e. CARLYLE, T, 12
epilogue good play needs no e. SHAKESPEARE, W, 33
epitaph 'Can't' will be the e. of the British Empire
MOSLEY, SIR O, 3
epitaphs a nice derangement of e. SHERIDAN, R, 7
epithet *Bourgeois* . . . is an e. HOPE, A, 6
epitome all Mankind's E. DRYDEN, J, 7
epoch From today . . . there begins a new e. in the history of the
world GOETHE, J, 9
Epp E.'s statues are junk ANONYMOUS, 89
There's Gert and there's E. and there's Ein ANONYMOUS, 89
Epsom Had we but stick to E. salts ANONYMOUS, 25
Epstein If people . . . a thousand years hence . . . found E.'s
statues LESSING, D, 4
equal All animals are e. ORWELL, G, 5
all men and women are created e. STANTON, E, 6
all men are created e. and independent, JEFFERSON, T, 2
all men are created e. KING, M, 3
All shall e. be GILBERT, SIR W, 4
Everybody should have an e. chance WILSON OF RIEVAULX, BARON, 3
Inferiors revolt . . . that they may be e. ARISTOTLE, 9
some animals are more e. than others ORWELL, G, 5
That all men are e. is a proposition HUXLEY, A, 28
When you meet someone better . . . turn your thoughts to
becoming his e. CONFUCIUS, 1
equality E. may perhaps be a right, but no . . . fact BALZAC, H, 1
e. . . . with our superiors BECQUE, H, 1
Freedom! E.! Brotherhood ANONYMOUS, 51
there never will be . . . e. . . . until women . . . make laws
ANTHONY, S, 2
equally I hate everyone e. FIELDS, W, 4
It comes e. to us all DONNE, J, 13
Pale Death kicks his way e. into the cottages of the poor and the
castles of kings HORACE, 27
That all who are happy, are e. happy JOHNSON, S, 70
equanimity an e. bordering on indifference GILBERT, SIR W, 46
equipping e. us with a neck KOESTLER, A, 2
erect he faced the firing squad; e. and motionless THURBER, J, 10
ergo Cogito, e. sum DESCARTES, R, 1
erogenous The mind can also be an e. zone WELCH, R, 1
Eros Unarm, E. SHAKESPEARE, W, 13
err The Most may e. as grosly DRYDEN, J, 10
those /Who e. each other must respect PATMORE, C, 1
To e. is human PROVERBS, 437
To e. is human, to forgive, divine POPE, A, 26
errand What thy e. here below LAMB, C, 18
erred We have e., and strayed from thy ways
BOOK OF COMMON PRAYER, 3
error A new maxim is often a brilliant e. MALESHERBES, C, 1
It is time for the destruction of e. AUDEN, W, 16
show a man that he is in an e. LOCKE, J, 2
the e. of his way BIBLE: JAMES, 9
errors E., like Straws, upon the surface flow DRYDEN, J, 15
few e. they have ever avoided CHURCHILL, SIR W, 56
the e. of those who think they are strong BIDAULT, G, 1
Esau E. . . . a hairy man BIBLE: GENESIS, 42
escape Gluttony is an emotional e. DE VRIES, P, 2
Let no guilty man e. GRANT, U, 5
escaped e. from a mad and savage master SOPHOCLES, 2

escaping fortunate in e. regular education    MACDIARMID, H, 3
esprit de corps English characteristic . . . e.    ADCOCK, SIR F, 1
essay an over-ambitious e. by a second-year student
    PRIESTLEY, J, 2
essence Desire is the very e. of man    SPINOZA, B, 4
The poet gives us his e.    WOOLF, V, 1
establishment to refer to your friend's country e. as a 'cottage'
    POTTER, S, 3
estate e. o' th' world were now undone    SHAKESPEARE, W, 178
estates Three E. in Parliament    CARLYLE, T, 11
etchings I'll bring the e. down    THURBER, J, 15
eternal Hope springs e. in the human breast    POPE, A, 30
The e. not ourselves that makes for righteousness    ARNOLD, M, 22
We feel . . . we are e.    SPINOZA, B, 3
eternity All things from e. . . . come round in a circle
    MARCUS AURELIUS ANTONINUS, 4
Deserts of vast e.    MARVELL, A, 10
E. by term    DICKINSON, E, 3
E. in an hour    BLAKE, W, 7
E.'s a terrible thought    STOPPARD, T, 8
from e. spinning the thread of your being
    MARCUS AURELIUS ANTONINUS, 12
Its narrow measure spans /Tears of e., and sorrow, /Not
mine, but man's    HOUSMAN, A, 3
I will burn, but . . . continue our discussion in e.    SERVETUS, M, 1
over the Bridge of Sighs into e.    KIERKEGAARD, S, 2
without injuring e.    THOREAU, H, 6
ethereal E. minstrel    WORDSWORTH, W, 68
Ethiopians The E. say that their gods are . . . black    XENOPHANES, 1
Eton the Battle of Waterloo was won on the playing-fields of E.
    ORWELL, G, 11
the playing fields of E.    WELLINGTON, DUKE OF, 16
eunuch a kind of moral e.    SHELLEY, P, 18
eureka E.    ARCHIMEDES, 2
Euripides E. portrays them as they are    SOPHOCLES, 1
Europe another war in E.    BISMARCK, PRINCE VON, 8
Communism continued to haunt E. as a spectre    TAYLOR, A, 3
E. is the unfinished negative    MCCARTHY, M, 4
glory of E. is extinguished    BURKE, E, 7
In Western E. there are now only small countries    LEFEVRE, T, 1
lamps are going out over all E.    GREY, VISCOUNT, 2
part of the community of E.    GLADSTONE, W, 3
sick man of E.    NICHOLAS I, 1
That E.'s nothin' on earth    WILLIAMS, T, 3
the community of E.    SALISBURY, MARQUESS OF, 2
the race of men is almost extinct in E.    LAWRENCE, D, 25
There is an iron curtain across E.    TROUBRIDGE, SIR T, 1
This going into E.    THOMPSON, E, 1
United States of E.    CHURCHILL, SIR W, 58
European the feminization of the white E. and American is already
far advanced    LEWIS, W, 3
to shoot down a E. is to kill two birds with one stone
    SARTRE, J, 15
Europeanism Their E. is . . . imperialism with an inferiority
complex    HEALEY, D, 2
Europeans only really materialistic people . . . E.    MCCARTHY, M, 3
euthanasia E. is a long, smooth-sounding word, and . . . conceals
its danger    BUCK, P, 1
evacuations Wars are not won by e.    CHURCHILL, SIR W, 21
evah Well, did you e.! What a swell party    PORTER, C, 6
Eva Peron If a woman like E. with no ideals    THATCHER, M, 5
Eve E. . . . the mother of all living    BIBLE: GENESIS, 16
When E. ate this particular apple    LAWRENCE, D, 7
eve from noon to dewy e.    MILTON, J, 33
even Deep and crisp and e.    NEALE, J, 2
evening e. is spread out against the sky    ELIOT, T, 9
in the e. . . . cut down, dried up    PSALMS, 55
Now came still E. on    MILTON, J, 41
Soup of the e.    CARROLL, L, 15
the quiet-coloured end of e.    BROWNING, R, 32
thou art fairer than the e. air    MARLOWE, C, 3
event greatest e. . . . that ever happened    FOX, C, 3
hurries to the main e.    HORACE, 7
one far-off divine e.    TENNYSON, BARON, 34
thinking too precisely on th' e.    SHAKESPEARE, W, 70
eventide Abide with me; fast falls the e.    LYTE, H, 1
events all great e. and personalities in . . . history reappear
    MARX, K, 6
E. which . . . never happened    INGE, W, 1
There are only three e. in a man's life    LA BRUYERE, J, 6

When in the course of human e., it becomes necessary for one
people to dissolve . . . political bonds    JEFFERSON, T, 1
ever for e. hold his peace    BOOK OF COMMON PRAYER, 14
Everest the summit of E. was hardly the place    HILLARY, SIR E, 1
treating the mons Veneris as . . . Mount E.    HUXLEY, A, 14
everlasting God from e.    PSALMS, 54
every E. day in e. way    COUE, E, 1
God bless us, e. one    DICKENS, C, 7
everybody E. has got to die, . . . . Now what    SAROYAN, W, 1
E. is always in favour of general economy
    EDEN, 1ST EARL OF AVON, 2
E. was up to something    COWARD, SIR N, 7
everyman E., I will go with thee, and be thy guide    ANONYMOUS, 17
everyone e. against e.    HOBBES, T, 1
I hate e. equally    FIELDS, W, 4
stop e. from doing it    HERBERT, SIR A, 2
everything A place for e.    SMILES, S, 2
destroying nearly e.    CHESTERTON, G, 2
e. in its place    SMILES, S, 2
E. is funny    ROGERS, W, 4
E. is only for a day    MARCUS AURELIUS ANTONINUS, 7
E.'s got a moral    CARROLL, L, 10
e. that lives is holy    BLAKE, W, 1
God made e. out of nothing    VALERY, P, 1
making e. the concern of all    SOLZHENITSYN, A, 12
men we like are good for e.    HALIFAX, MARQUIS OF, 2
One fifth of the people are against e.    KENNEDY, R, 1
Was E. by starts    DRYDEN, J, 7
evidence If ever there was a case of clearer e.    ARABIN, W, 1
Most men . . . give e. against their own understanding
    HALIFAX, MARQUIS OF, 8
evil about the dreadful wood /Of conscious e.    AUDEN, W, 12
as gods, knowing good and e.    BIBLE: GENESIS, 13
a thing may look e. in theory, . . . in practice excellent
    BURKE, E, 26
belief in a supernatural source of e.    CONRAD, J, 7
better is he . . . who hath not seen the e. work under the sun
    BIBLE: ECCLESIASTES, 9
deliver us from e.    BIBLE: MATTHEW, 18
E., be thou my Good    MILTON, J, 39
E. be to him who e. thinks    ANONYMOUS, 39
E. comes . . . like the disease; good . . . like the doctor
    CHESTERTON, G, 23
e. communications corrupt good manners    BIBLE: I CORINTHIANS, 21
e. is wrought by want of thought    HOOD, T, 8
e. men and seducers    BIBLE: II TIMOTHY, 2
Government, . . . is but a necessary e.    PAINE, T, 3
how can ye, being e., speak good    BIBLE: MATTHEW, 42
know all the e. he does    ROCHEFOUCAULD, DUC DE LA, 21
love of money is the root of all e.    BIBLE: I TIMOTHY, 6
Man's capacity for e. makes democracy necessary    NIEBUHR, R, 1
men loved darkness . . . because their deeds were e.
    BIBLE: JOHN, 10
Men's e. manners live in brass    SHAKESPEARE, W, 105
No man is justified in doing e.    ROOSEVELT, T, 1
Only lies and e. come from letting people off    MURDOCH, DAME I, 5
Put off the e. hour    PROVERBS, 345
The e. that men do lives after them    SHAKESPEARE, W, 116
the fear of one e.    BOILEAU, N, 2
the love of money is the root of all e.    BUTLER, S, 6
There is no e. in the atom    STEVENSON, A, 5
the righteous is taken away from the e. to come    BIBLE: ISAIAH, 34
Vice itself lost half its e.    BURKE, E, 8
we are the origin of all coming e.    JUNG, C, 11
woe unto them that call e. good    BIBLE: ISAIAH, 8
evils death, . . . the least of all e.
    BACON, 1ST BARON VERULAM, VISCOUNT ST ALBANS, 6
He . . . must expect new e.
    BACON, 1ST BARON VERULAM, VISCOUNT ST ALBANS, 30
There exist some e. so terrible . . . that we dare not think of
them    LA BRUYERE, J, 10
To great e. we submit; we resent little provocations
    HAZLITT, W, 20
We cannot remove the e. of capitalism    KINNOCK, N, 4
Whenever I'm caught between two e.    WEST, M, 16
Work banishes those three great e.    VOLTAIRE, 5
evolution Coolidge is a better example of e.    ROGERS, W, 6
e. of the human race    DARWIN, C, 1
sex . . . must itself be subject . . . to e.    BLACKWELL, A, 1
ewe one little e. lamb    BIBLE: II SAMUEL, 3
exact Politics is not an e. science    BISMARCK, PRINCE VON, 2

# F

The fundamental fault of the f. character SCHOPENHAUER, A. 3
The seldom f. PITTER, R. 1
What f. heart can gold despise GRAY, T. 11
feminine Taste is the f. of genius FITZGERALD, E. 1
feminist the best home for a f. WATSON, J. 1
feminization the f. of the white European and American is already far advanced LEWIS, W. 3
fence The . . . gentleman has sat so long on the f. LLOYD GEORGE, EARL OF DWYFOR, 9
fences Good f. make good neighbours FROST, R. 6
Good f. PROVERBS, 179
ferries the snow blind twilight f. THOMAS, D. 22
fettered so f. fast we are BROWNING, R. 1
fever hand that signed the treaty bred a f. THOMAS, D. 5
Février Generals Janvier and F. NICHOLAS I, 2
few err as grosly as the F. DRYDEN, J. 10
How f. of his friends' houses JOHNSON, S. 139
so much owed by so many to so f. CHURCHILL, SIR W. 46
fi' as the gen'l'm'n said to the f. pun note DICKENS, C. 44
flat f. lux BIBLE: GENESIS, 2
fickle Woman is always f. and changing VIRGIL, 9
fiction ancient history, . . . is no more than accepted f. VOLTAIRE, 12
an improbable f. SHAKESPEARE, W. 294
Children should acquire . . . heroes and villains from f. AUDEN, W. 2
one form of continuous f. BEVAN, A. 6
Poetry is a comforting piece of f. MENCKEN, H. 12
Stranger than f. BYRON, 6TH BARON, 32
fiddle consider your puny little f. when He speaks to me BEETHOVEN, L. 2
Hey diddle diddle, /The cat and the f. NURSERY RHYMES, 14
keep it shut up . . . like a rare, rare f. MANSFIELD, K. 1
When I play on my f. in Dooney YEATS, W. 10
fiddlers he called for his f. three NURSERY RHYMES, 38
field A cow is a very good animal in the f. JOHNSON, S. 153
Behold her, single in the f. WORDSWORTH, W. 45
Man for the f. and woman for the hearth TENNYSON, BARON, 62
shepherds abiding in the f. BIBLE: LUKE, 8
some corner of a foreign f. BROOKE, R. 5
What though the f. be lost MILTON, J. 27
fields 'a babbl'd of green f. SHAKESPEARE, W. 94
East and west on f. forgotten /Bleach the bones of comrades slain HOUSMAN, A. 12
Now there are f. where Troy once was OVID, 3
We plough the f., and scatter CAMPBELL, J. 1
fiend a f. hid in a cloud BLAKE, W. 36
a frightful f. /Doth close behind him tread COLERIDGE, S. 34
fierce f. and bald and short of breath SASSOON, S. 1
fiery Nightingale, . . . /A creature of a f. heart WORDSWORTH, W. 32
fifteen F. men on the dead man's chest STEVENSON, R. 6
fifth Beethoven's F. Symphony is the most sublime noise FORSTER, E. 7
One f. of the people are against everything KENNEDY, R. 1
fifty For one person who dreams of making f. thousand pounds MILNE, A. 3
Sit on your arse for f. years MACNEICE, L. 1
You'll see, when you're f. SATIE, E. 2
fifty-fifty There can be no f. Americanism ROOSEVELT, T. 8
fig they sewed f. leaves together BIBLE: GENESIS, 13
fight a great cause to f. for PANKHURST, DAME C. 2
easier to f. for one's principles ADLER, A. 1
f., f., f., and f. again GAITSKELL, H. 3
F. fire PROVERBS, 150
f. the good f. BIBLE: I TIMOTHY, 7
F. the good f. with all thy might MONSELL, J. 1
I dare not f. SHAKESPEARE, W. 92
I have not yet begun to f. JONES, J. 1
I purpose to f. it out on this line GRANT, U. 2
I will not cease from mental f. BLAKE, W. 31
Nor law, nor duty bade me f. YEATS, W. 14
so f. I, not as one that beateth the air BIBLE: I CORINTHIANS, 13
To f. and not to heed the wounds LOYOLA, I. 1
too proud to f. WILSON, W. 8
Ulster will f. CHURCHILL, R. 3
We don't want to f., but, by jingo if we do HUNT, G. 1
We'll f. and we'll conquer GARRICK, D. 2
we shall f. on the beaches CHURCHILL, SIR W. 43
when the f. begins within BROWNING, R. 10
With our backs to the wall . . . each . . . must f. on to the end HAIG, EARL, 1
You cannot f. against the future GLADSTONE, W. 1

fighting F. is like champagne MITCHELL, M. 2
Most sorts of diversion . . . are an imitation of f. SWIFT, J. 15
not conquering but f. well COUBERTIN, BARON, 1
What are we f. for SERVICE, R. 4
fights He that f. and runs away ANONYMOUS, 38
I can't spare this man; he f. LINCOLN, A. 15
figure an oblong angular f. LEACOCK, S. 6
figures prove anything by f. CARLYLE, T. 2
film A wide screen . . . makes a bad f. twice as bad GOLDWYN, S. 9
f like a f. to have a beginning, a middle and an end GODARD, J. 2
films Why . . . pay money to see bad f. GOLDWYN, S. 2
finality F. is death. Perfection is f. STEPHENS, J. 1
find terrible thing for a man to f. out WILDE, O. 33
your sin will f. you out BIBLE: NUMBERS, 6
finders F. keepers PROVERBS, 151
fine f. feathers that make f. birds AESOP, 5
Give me books, fruit, French wine and f. weather KEATS, J. 61
In England, pop art and f. art MACINNES, C. 1
The big print giveth and the f. print taketh away SHEEN, J. 1
finer every baby . . . is a f. one DICKENS, C. 30
finest their f. hour CHURCHILL, SIR W. 44
finger Moving F. writes FITZGERALD, E. 14
The least pain in our little f. HAZLITT, W. 1
fingernails See what will happen . . . if you don't stop biting your f. ROGERS, W. 11
fingers f. of a man's hand, and wrote BIBLE: DANIEL, 7
F. were made before forks PROVERBS, 154
ill cook that cannot lick his own f. SHAKESPEARE, W. 252
our f. are circumcised PERLMAN, I. 1
thy heavens, even the works of thy f. PSALMS, 3
finger-tips An accomplished man to his f. HORACE, 46
fings F. Ain't Wot They Used T'Be NORMAN, F. 1
finished it is f. BIBLE: JOHN, 50
finite Our knowledge can only be f. POPPER, SIR K. 1
fire a chariot . . . of f. BIBLE: II KINGS, 1
All things, oh priests, are on f. BUDDHA, 1
a pillar of f. BIBLE: EXODUS, 14
Billy . . . /Fell in the f. GRAHAM, H. 2
bound /Upon a wheel of f. SHAKESPEARE, W. 150
cloven tongues like as of f. BIBLE: ACTS, 2
f. and brimstone, storm and tempest PSALMS, 5
four men . . . walking in the midst of the f. BIBLE: DANIEL, 5
French Guard, f. first HAY, C. 1
F. – without hatred RIVERA, A. 1
heap coals of f. upon his head BIBLE: PROVERBS, 13
how great a matter a little f. kindleth BIBLE: JAMES, 5
It is with our passions as it is with f. and water L'ESTRANGE, SIR R. 1
I warmed both hands before the f. of life LANDOR, W. 7
the bush burned with f. BIBLE: EXODUS, 4
The f. which in the heart resides ARNOLD, M. 27
two irons in the f. BEAUMONT, F. 3
what wind is to f. BUSSY-RABUTIN, 1
firearms Though loaded f. were strictly forbidden at St Trinian's SEARLE, R. 1
fire-folk the f. sitting in the air HOPKINS, G. 5
fireirons Saint Preux never kicked the f. CARLYLE, J. 2
fires Husbands are like f. GABOR, Z. 1
fireside A man may surely be allowed to take a glass of wine by his own f. SHERIDAN, R. 14
firing he faced the f. squad; erect and motionless THURBER, J. 10
firmness Commodity, F., and Delight WOTTON, SIR H. 1
first Because of my title, I was the f. ALENÇON, DUCHESSE D', 1
F. come PROVERBS, 155
F. impressions PROVERBS, 156
F. things f. PROVERBS, 157
If at f. you don't succeed HICKSON, W. 1
many that are f. shall be last BIBLE: MATTHEW, 59
The constitution . . . f. and second class citizens WILLKIE, W. 1
The f. day a guest PROVERBS, 393
there is no last or f. BROWNING, R. 46
which came f., the Greeks or the Romans DISRAELI, 1ST EARL OF BEACONSFIELD, 36
Who ever loved, that loved not at f. sight MARLOWE, C. 8
first-aid His ideas of f. WODEHOUSE, SIR P. 9
firstborn I . . . will smite all the f. BIBLE: EXODUS, 12
firstfruits first of the f. BIBLE: EXODUS, 23
first-rate the powers of a f. man and the creed of a second-rate man BAGEHOT, W. 9
fir trees The f. dark and high HOOD, T. 7
fish a great f. to swallow up Jonah BIBLE: JONAH, 2

F. and guests — PROVERBS, 158
F. die belly-upward and rise . . . their way of falling — GIDE, A, 2
F. fuck in it — FIELDS, W, 2
I have my own f. to fry — CERVANTES, M, 8
No human being, . . . was ever so free as a f. — RUSKIN, J, 13
Phone for the f. knives Norman — BETJEMAN, SIR J, 3
This man . . . is a poor f. — DENNIS, N, 1
What cat's averse to f. — GRAY, T, 11
**fishbone** The monument sticks like a f. — LOWELL, R, 2
**fishermen** a bite every time for f. — MORTON, J, 4
**fishers** f. of men — BIBLE: MATTHEW, 9
**fishes** five barley loaves, and two small f. — BIBLE: JOHN, 15
f. live in the sea — SHAKESPEARE, W, 232
So are the f. — CHURCHILL, SIR W, 47
**fishing** Time is but the stream I go a-f. in — THOREAU, H, 15
**fishmonger** She was a f., but sure 'twas no wonder — ANONYMOUS, 47
**fishy** something f. about the French — COWARD, SIR N, 3
**fist** You cannot shake hands with a clenched f. — GANDHI, I, 3
**fit** a pleasing f. of melancholy — MILTON, J, 5
It is not f. that you should sit here — CROMWELL, O, 4
let the punishment f. the crime — GILBERT, SIR W, 29
news that's f. to print — OCHS, A, 1
only the F. survive — SERVICE, R, 3
**fits** periodical f. of morality — MACAULAY, BARON, 16
Strange f. of passion — WORDSWORTH, W, 61
**fittest** Survival of the F. — DARWIN, C, 6
Survival of the f. — SPENCER, H, 3
**five** child of f. would understand this — MARX, G, 6
F. for the symbol at your door — ANONYMOUS, 45
F. gold rings — NURSERY RHYMES, 60
If you don't find a God by f. o'clock this afternoon — JOWETT, B, 7
Mister John Keats f. feet high — KEATS, J, 56
practise f. things — CONFUCIUS, 9
The formula 'Two and two make f.' — DOSTOEVSKY, F, 1
**five-pound** get a f. note as . . . a light for a cigarette — JAMES, H, 2
**flabbiness** The moral f. born of . . . Success — JAMES, W, 4
**flag** But spare your country's f. — WHITTIER, J, 2
keep the red f. flying here — CONNELL, J, 1
Tonight the American f. floats from yonder hill — STARK, J, 1
**flagons** stay me with f. — BIBLE: SONG OF SOLOMON, 3
**flame** like a moth, the simple maid /Still plays about the f. — GAY, J, 2
**flames** Commit it then to the f. — HUME, D, 2
Superstition sets the whole world in f. — VOLTAIRE, 8
**Flanders** In F. fields — MCCRAE, J, 1
You have sent me a F. mare — HENRY VIII, 1
**flash** the f. cut him, and he lies in the stubble — ANONYMOUS, 27
**flashing** His f. eyes, his floating hair — COLERIDGE, S, 15
**flat** Very f., Norfolk — COWARD, SIR N, 14
Vile snub-nose, f.-nosed ass — ROSTAND, E, 1
**flatter** not f. me — CROMWELL, O, 1
We f. those we scarcely know — WILCOX, E, 1
**flattered** neither feared nor f. any flesh — DOUGLAS, 4TH EARL OF MORTON, 1
**flatterer** the brave beast is no f. — JONSON, B, 6
**flatterers** f. live at the expense of those who listen — LA FONTAINE, J, 2
Self-love . . . greatest of all f. — ROCHEFOUCAULD, DUC DE LA, 1
**flattering** It is f. some men to endure them — HALIFAX, MARQUIS OF, 3
the talent of f. with delicacy — AUSTEN, J, 19
**flattery** consider whether . . . your f. is worth his having — JOHNSON, S, 28
f.'s the food of fools — SWIFT, J, 2
Imitation is the sincerest of f. — COLTON, C, 3
ne'er /Was f. lost — SCOTT, SIR W, 4
woman . . . to be gained by . . . f. — CHESTERFIELD, 4TH EARL OF, 13
**flaunt** if you've got it, f. it — BROOKS, M, 1
**flautists** f. . . . know something we don't know — JENNINGS, P, 1
**flavour** Does the Spearmint Lose Its F. — ROSE, B, 1
**flea** English literature's performing f. — O'CASEY, S, 4
man's whole frame is obvious to a f. — POPE, A, 3
The guerrilla fights the war of the f. — TABER, R, 1
the point of precedency between a louse and a f. — JOHNSON, S, 141
**fleas** dog that praised his f. — YEATS, W, 29
F. . . . upon the body of a giant — LANDOR, W, 6
Great f. have little f. upon their backs — MORGAN, A, 1
the f. in my bed were as good — CERVANTES, M, 11
The f. that tease in the high Pyrenees — BELLOC, H, 13
these have smaller f. to bite 'em — SWIFT, J, 7
**fled** I f. Him, down the nights — THOMPSON, F, 1

**flee** then would I f. away, and be at rest — PSALMS, 37
**fleet** The F.'s lit up. It is like fairyland — WOODROOFE, T, 1
**flesh** all f. is as grass — BIBLE: I PETER, 2
a thorn in the f. — BIBLE: II CORINTHIANS, 5
f. and blood so cheap! — HOOD, T, 12
f. to feel the chain — BRONTE, E, 3
Heat, madam! . . . to take off my f. and sit in my bones — SMITH, S, 4
I, born of f. and ghost — THOMAS, D, 1
I have more f. than another man — SHAKESPEARE, W, 79
Ishmaelites . . . will not publicly eat human f. uncooked in Lent — WAUGH, E, 36
I wants to make your f. creep — DICKENS, C, 40
Leave the f. to the fate it was fit for — BROWNING, R, 49
Rehearsing a play is making the word f. — SHAFFER, P, 3
that which is born of the f. is f. — BIBLE: JOHN, 7
the f. is weak — BIBLE: MATTHEW, 81
the f. lusteth against the Spirit — BIBLE: GALATIANS, 4
the lust of the f. — BIBLE: I JOHN, 2
the way of all f. — CONGREVE, W, 10
the way of all f. — SHADWELL, T, 2
the way of all f. . . . towards the kitchen — WEBSTER, J, 4
the word was made f. — BIBLE: JOHN, 1
the world, the f., and the devil — MURRAY, D, 1
unto thee shall all f. come — PSALMS, 42
we do not war after the f. — BIBLE: II CORINTHIANS, 3
world, the f., and the devil — BOOK OF COMMON PRAYER, 8
**fleshly** The F. School of Poetry — BUCHANAN, R, 2
**flies** As f. to wanton boys — SHAKESPEARE, W, 144
certain, that Life f. — FITZGERALD, E, 10
dead f. cause the ointment . . . to send forth a stinking savour — BIBLE: ECCLESIASTES, 19
Time f., death urges — YOUNG, E, 7
**flight** Above the vulgar f. of common souls — MURPHY, A, 1
**fling** I'll have a f. — BEAUMONT, F, 11
**flirt** f. with their own husbands — WILDE, O, 19
**float** rather be an opportunist and f. — BALDWIN, 1ST EARL BALDWIN OF BEWDLEY, 7
**flock** he shall feed his f. — BIBLE: ISAIAH, 28
keeping watch over their f. by night — BIBLE: LUKE, 8
**flogging** There is now less f. in our great schools — JOHNSON, S, 97
**flood** was forty days upon the earth — BIBLE: GENESIS, 24
Which, taken at the f. — SHAKESPEARE, W, 122
**floor** stood ninety years on the f. — WORK, H, 2
**flowed** water f. like champagne — EVARTS, W, 1
**flower** A lovelier f. / . . . was never sown — WORDSWORTH, W, 64
Die when I may, . . . I have always plucked a thistle and planted a f. — LINCOLN, A, 5
just miss the prizes at the f. show — BRONOWSKI, J, 5
man . . . flourisheth as a f. of the field — PSALMS, 64
many a f. is born to blush unseen — GRAY, T, 5
The F. that once has blown — FITZGERALD, E, 10
the meanest f. . . . can give /Thoughts — WORDSWORTH, W, 28
**flowers** a book that is a book f. once — LAWRENCE, D, 38
Do spring May f. — TUSSER, T, 2
Gather the f., but spare the buds — MARVELL, A, 8
Letting a hundred f. blossom — MAO TSE-TUNG, 4
No fruits, no f., no leaves, no birds — HOOD, T, 10
Say it with f. — O'KEEFE, P, 1
The f. that bloom in the spring — GILBERT, SIR W, 33
Their f. the tenderness of patient minds — OWEN, W, 1
Too late for fruit, too soon for f. — DE LA MARE, W, 3
Where have all the f. gone — SEEGER, P, 1
**flowery** A little thin, f. border — LAMB, C, 23
**flows** Everything f. and nothing stays — HERACLITUS, 1
**flung** he f. himself from the room — LEACOCK, S, 10
**fly** A f., Sir, may sting a stately horse — JOHNSON, S, 46
f. . . . said, what a dust do I raise — BACON, 1ST BARON VERULAM, VISCOUNT ST ALBANS, 58
said a spider to a f. — HOWITT, M, 1
small gilded f. /Does lecher — SHAKESPEARE, W, 146
Who saw him die? /I, said the F. — NURSERY RHYMES, 73
**flying** Days and moments quickly f. — CASWALL, E, 1
**foam** the f. /Of perilous seas — KEATS, J, 34
the white f. flew — COLERIDGE, S, 27
**foe** Heat not a furnace for your f. — SHAKESPEARE, W, 101
he is the sworn f. of our nation — CAMPBELL, T, 7
He . . . who never made a f. — TENNYSON, BARON, 14
**foeman** When the f. bares his steel — GILBERT, SIR W, 39
**foes** judge of a man by his f. — CONRAD, J, 4
**fog** a London particular . . . A f. — DICKENS, C, 2

**Folies-Bergère** A psychiatrist is a man who goes to the F.
STOCKWOOD, M, 1

**folk-dancing** except incest and f.
BAX, SIR A, 1

**folks** for de old f. at home
FOSTER, S, 3

**.follies** f. as the special evidences of our wisdom
TROLLOPE, A, 9

lovers cannot see the pretty f.
SHAKESPEARE, W, 191

the f. of the town crept slowly among us
GOLDSMITH, O, 18

The f. which a man regrets
ROWLAND, H, 2

**follow** f. thou me
BIBLE: JOHN, 60

F. up!... /Till the field ring again
BOWEN, E, 2

I have to f. them, I am their leader
LEDRU-ROLLIN, A, 1

I must f. them
LAW, B, 1

take up his cross, and f. me
BIBLE: MATTHEW, 51

**folly** brood of F. without father
MILTON, J, 6

His foe was f. and his weapon wit
HOPE, A, 9

the slightest f. /That ever love did make thee run into
SHAKESPEARE, W, 20

When lovely woman stoops to f.
GOLDSMITH, O, 27

where ignorance is bliss, /'Tis f. to be wise
GRAY, T, 10

**fond** He is very f. of making things
HOPE, A, 2

**fonder** Absence makes the heart grow f.
BAYLY, T, 1

**fondness** inordinate f. for beetles
HALDANE, J, 5

**food** f. in music
LILLO, G, 1

F. is an important part of a balanced diet
LEBOWITZ, F, 2

flattery's the f. of fools
SWIFT, J, 2

f. to one man is bitter poison to others
LUCRETIUS, 4

man did eat angels' f.
PSALMS, 47

my Uncle George... discovered that alcohol was a f.
WODEHOUSE, SIR P, 6

Nothing to eat but f.
KING, B, 1

On the Continent people have good f.
MIKES, G, 1

Spleen can subsist on any kind of f.
HAZLITT, W, 29

The perpetual struggle for room and f.
MALTHUS, T, 2

the wine was a farce and the f. a tragedy
POWELL, A, 2

**fool** a f. among fools or a f. alone
WILDER, T, 4

A f. and his money
PROVERBS, 15

A f. at forty
PROVERBS, 16

A f. bolts pleasure, then complains of... indigestion
ANTRIM, M, 2

A f. sees not the same tree
BLAKE, W, 25

a greater f. to admire him
BOILEAU, N, 3

answer a f. according to his folly
BIBLE: PROVERBS, 15

a worm at one end and a f. at the other
JOHNSON, S, 161

Better be a f. than a knave
PROVERBS, 88

brains enough to make a f. of himself
STEVENSON, R, 19

Busy old f., unruly Sun
DONNE, J, 14

f. his whole life long
LUTHER, M, 2

He who holds hopes... is a f.
CAMUS, A, 13

I have played the f.
BIBLE: I SAMUEL, 7

Love is the wisdom of the f.
JOHNSON, S, 39

more of the f. than of the wise
BACON, 1ST BARON VERULAM, VISCOUNT ST ALBANS, 13

No creature smarts... as a f.
POPE, A, 15

One f.... in every married couple
FIELDING, H, 4

Send a f. to the market
PROVERBS, 361

The dupe of friendship, and the f. of love
HAZLITT, W, 24

the greatest f. may ask more
COLTON, C, 4

the old man who will not laugh is a f.
SANTAYANA, G, 2

There's no f. like an old f.
PROVERBS, 416

The wisest f. in Christendom
HENRI IV, 3

Wise Man or a F.
BLAKE, W, 15

You can f. too many of the people
THURBER, J, 4

**foolish** A f. consistency
EMERSON, R, 13

a f. man, which built his house upon the sand
BIBLE: MATTHEW, 31

anything very f.
MELBOURNE, VISCOUNT, 6

He never said a f. thing
ROCHESTER, EARL OF, 1

If you are f. enough to be contented, don't show it
JEROME, J, 4

O f. Galatians
BIBLE: GALATIANS, 1

the f. things of the world
BIBLE: I CORINTHIANS, 2

You must not think me... f. because I am facetious
SMITH, S, 16

**foolishness** by the f. of preaching
BIBLE: I CORINTHIANS, 1

Mix a little F. with your serious plans
HORACE, 44

**fools** Christianity... says that they are all f.
CHESTERTON, G, 19

f. and passengers drink at sea
VILLIERS, A, 1

F. are in a terrible, overwhelming majority
IBSEN, H, 1

F. build houses
PROVERBS, 159

flattery's the food of f.
SWIFT, J, 2

F. live poor
PROVERBS, 160

Fortune always favours f.
GAY, J, 8

Fortune, that favours f.
JONSON, B, 1

f. rush in where angels fear to tread
POPE, A, 27

I am two f.
DONNE, J, 15

---

Is Pride, the never-failing vice of f.
POPE, A, 20

Many have been the wise speeches of f.
FULLER, T, 4

suffer f. gladly
BIBLE: II CORINTHIANS, 4

the greater part of the law is learning to tolerate f.
LESSING, D, 5

Thirty millions, mostly f.
CARLYLE, T, 34

this great stage of f.
SHAKESPEARE, W, 149

To suckle f. and chronicle
SHAKESPEARE, W, 221

what delight we married people have to see... f. decoyed into our condition
PEPYS, S, 8

what f. these mortals be
SHAKESPEARE, W, 205

world is made up... of f. and knaves BUCKINGHAM, 2ND DUKE OF, 2

**foot** he will not suffer thy f. to be moved
PSALMS, 76

noiseless f. of Time
SHAKESPEARE, W, 3

**footprints** F. on the sands of time
PROVERBS, 161

**footsteps** home his f. he hath turn'd
SCOTT, SIR W, 6

**footstool** until I make thine enemies thy f.
PSALMS, 68

**foppery** excellent f. of the world
SHAKESPEARE, W, 131

**for** neither f. nor against institutions
WHITMAN, W, 2

**forbearance** f. ceases to be a virtue
BURKE, E, 3

**forbidden** F. fruit
PROVERBS, 162

he wanted it only because it was f.
TWAIN, M, 13

we're f. to know – what end the gods have in store
HORACE, 30

**force** f. alone is but *temporary*
BURKE, E, 13

F., if unassisted by judgement, collapses
HORACE, 35

F. is not a remedy
BRIGHT, J, 3

F. that through the green fuse
THOMAS, D, 4

Hence no f. however great
WHEWELL, W, 1

May the F. be with you
LUCAS, G, 1

Who overcomes /By f.
MILTON, J, 32

**forced** f. to commend her highly
PEPYS, S, 5

**force-feeding** This universal, obligatory f. with lies
SOLZHENITSYN, A, 8

**forces** one of the f. of nature
MICHELET, J, 1

**Ford** Jerry F. is so dumb
JOHNSON, L, 1

The time of our F.
HUXLEY, A, 9

**forefathers** Think of your f.
ADAMS, J, 1

**forehead** A burning f., and a parching tongue
KEATS, J, 26

**foreign** pronounce f. names as he chooses
CHURCHILL, SIR W, 29

wandering on a f. strand
SCOTT, SIR W, 6

**foreigner** f. should... be wiser than ourselves
TROLLOPE, A, 9

**foreigners** f. speak English when our backs are turned CRISP, Q, 8

f.... spell better than they pronounce
TWAIN, M, 8

Sympathy... for being f.
BRADBURY, M, 1

**forest** On Wenlock Edge the wood's in trouble; /His f. fleece the Wrekin heaves
HOUSMAN, A, 11

Wandering in a vast f. at night
DIDEROT, D, 1

**forests** the f. of the night
BLAKE, W, 37

**foretaste** Every parting gives a f. of death
SCHOPENHAUER, A, 4

**forever** That is f. England
BROOKE, R, 5

**forewarned** F. is forearmed
PROVERBS, 163

**forget** Better by far you should f. and smile
ROSSETTI, C, 5

Fade far away, dissolve, and... f.
KEATS, J, 33

if I f. thee, O Jerusalem
PSALMS, 83

I f. what I was taught
WHITE, P, 2

I'll not f. old Ireland BLACKWOOD, COUNTESS OF DUFFERIN, 2

I never f. a face, but I'll make an exception
MARX, G, 20

Oh Lord!... if I f. thee, do not thou f. me
ASTLEY, BARON, 1

Old men f.
SHAKESPEARE, W, 99

To endeavour to f. anyone
LA BRUYÈRE, J, 14

Were it not better to f.
LANDON, L, 1

When I f. my sovereign
THURLOW, BARON, 1

**forgivable** Few books today are f.
LAING, R, 3

**forgive** do not have to f. my enemies
NARVAEZ, R, 1

F. and forget
PROVERBS, 164

Father, f. them
BIBLE: LUKE, 36

how oft shall... I f. him
BIBLE: MATTHEW, 55

Men will f. a man
CHURCHILL, SIR W, 31

To err is human, to f., divine
POPE, A, 26

**forgiven** her sins, which are many, are f.
BIBLE: LUKE, 17

Once a woman has f. her man
DIETRICH, M, 1

**forgot** auld acquaintance be f.
BURNS, R, 2

How these curiosities would be quite f.
AUBREY, J, 2

I have f. my part
SHAKESPEARE, W, 35

**forgotten** five sparrows... not one of them is f.
BIBLE: LUKE, 25

Has God then f.
LOUIS XIV, 2

I am clean f., as a dead man
PSALMS, 22

I have f. more law than you ever knew...
MAYNARD, SIR J, 1

Nobody is f. when it is convenient to remember him
DISRAELI, 1ST EARL OF BEACONSFIELD, 33

The f. man
ROOSEVELT, F, 6

what has been learnt has been f.
SKINNER, B, 2

freemasonry a kind of bitter f.  BEERBOHM, SIR M, 11
French Bouillabaisse is only good because cooked by the F.  DOUGLAS, N, 2
everyone would always have spoken F.  VOLTAIRE, 27
F. governments are more selfish than most  ECCLES, VISCOUNT, 1
F. Guard, fire first  HAY, C, 1
Give me books, fruit, F. wine and fine weather  KEATS, J, 61
I do not dislike the F. from . . . vulgar antipathy  WALPOLE, 4TH EARL OF ORFORD, 9
I hate the F.  GOLDSMITH, O, 10
Imagine the Lord talking F.  DAY, C, 1
I speak . . . Italian to women, F. to men  CHARLES V, 3
My suit is pale yellow. My nationality is F.  WILLIAMS, T, 1
something fishy about the F.  COWARD, SIR N, 3
The F. are wiser than they seem  BACON, 1ST BARON VERULAM, VISCOUNT ST ALBANS, 47
the F.  STERNE, L, 2
The F. want no-one to be their *superior*. The English want *inferiors*  TOCQUEVILLE, A, 1
The F. will only be united under the threat of danger  DE GAULLE, C, 5
the German text of F. operas  WHARTON, E, 1
There's something Vichy about the F.  NOVELLO, I, 2
to the F. the empire of the land  RICHTER, J, 1
Frenchman F. must be always talking  JOHNSON, S, 130
You must hate a F.  NELSON, VISCOUNT, 2
Frenchmen F. drink wine just like  LARDNER, R, 3
to create F. in the image of Englishmen  CHURCHILL, SIR W, 54
frenzy poet's eye, in a fine f. rolling  SHAKESPEARE, W, 207
fresh f. as is the month of May  CHAUCER, G, 3
Gentlemen know that f. air  MACAULAY, DAME R, 1
the cod's wallop is always f. made  MORLEY, R, 2
freshen a mighty storm . . . to f. us up  CHEKHOV, A, 6
fret weariness, the fever, and the f.  KEATS, J, 33
fretting a moth f. a garment  PSALMS, 27
Freud The trouble with F.  DODD, K, 1
Freudian the F., it is a very low, Central European sort of humour  GRAVES, R, 2
Friday F.'s child is loving and giving  NURSERY RHYMES, 35
I takes my man F.  DEFOE, D, 4
Worse on F.  NURSERY RHYMES, 53
friend A fav'rite has no f.  GRAY, T, 12
a F. for little children /Above the bright blue sky  MIDLANE, A, 1
A f. in need  PROVERBS, 18
A f. should bear his f.'s infirmities  SHAKESPEARE, W, 121
A good f. is my nearest relation  PROVERBS, 24
a new f. is as new wine  BIBLE: ECCLESIASTICUS, 5
A woman can become a man's f.  CHEKHOV, A, 8
damned good-natured f.  SHERIDAN, R, 1
Every time I paint a portrait I lose a f.  SARGENT, J, 1
F. . . . masterpiece of Nature  EMERSON, R, 6
forsake not an old f.  BIBLE: ECCLESIASTICUS, 5
f., wherefore art thou come  BIBLE: MATTHEW, 82
He makes no f.  TENNYSON, BARON, 14
I might give my life for my f.  SMITH, L, 5
In every f. we lose a part of ourselves  POPE, A, 59
It takes your enemy and your f. . . . , to hurt you  TWAIN, M, 4
mine own familiar f.  PSALMS, 29
no f. like a sister  ROSSETTI, C, 2
save me, from the candid f.  CANNING, G, 1
that a man lay down his wife for a f.  JOYCE, J, 5
the f. of the bridegroom . . . rejoiceth  BIBLE: JOHN, 11
trust ye not in a f.  BIBLE: MICAH, 1
Whenever a f. succeeds  VIDAL, G, 6
friendly Man is the only animal that can remain on f. terms with the victims . . . he eats  BUTLER, S, 20
so large, /So f., and so rich  AUDEN, W, 20
friends Animals are such agreeable f.  ELIOT, G, 7
better to drop thy f.  CALVERLEY, C, 3
false to his f . . . . true to the public  BERKELEY, BISHOP, 1
F., Romans, countrymen  SHAKESPEARE, W, 116
Good thoughts his only f.  CAMPION, T, 4
guessed you were f.  BRADBURY, M, 4
Have no f. not equal  CONFUCIUS, 7
His best f. hear no more  SHELLEY, P, 9
How few of his f.' houses  JOHNSON, S, 139
How to Win F.  CARNEGIE, D, 1
I cannot forgive my f. for dying  SMITH, L, 7
I don't trust him. We're f.  BRECHT, B, 5
In the misfortune of our best f.  ROCHEFOUCAULD, DUC DE LA, 14
Job endured everything – until his f. came  KIERKEGAARD, S, 1

lay down his f. for his life  THORPE, J, 1
Money can't buy f.  MILLIGAN, S, 10
none of his f. like him  WILDE, O, 63
not so much our f.' help that helps us  EPICURUS, 1
Once more unto the breach, dear f.  SHAKESPEARE, W, 95
our f. are true and our happiness  BIERCE, A, 5
shameful to distrust one's f.  ROCHEFOUCAULD, DUC DE LA, 12
that a man lay down his life for his f.  BIBLE: JOHN, 36
the best of f. must part  ANONYMOUS, 87
Thy f. are exultations, agonies, /And love  WORDSWORTH, W, 57
troops of unrecording f.  TENNYSON, BARON, 73
until his f. came to comfort him  KIERKEGAARD, S, 1
we . . . walked in the house of God as f.  PSALMS, 38
with a little help from my f.  LENNON, J, 12
without three good f.  SHAKESPEARE, W, 27
you choose your f.  DELILLE, J, 1
friendship A man, Sir, should keep his f. in constant repair  JOHNSON, S, 51
Business, . . . may bring money, . . . f. hardly ever does  AUSTEN, J, 6
f. closes its eyes  ANONYMOUS, 5
F. is a disinterested commerce between equals  GOLDSMITH, O, 12
F. is constant in all other things  SHAKESPEARE, W, 209
F. is unnecessary  LEWIS, C, 1
love . . . looks more like hatred than like f.  ROCHEFOUCAULD, DUC DE LA, 9
Most f. is feigning  SHAKESPEARE, W, 26
Society, f., and love  COWPER, W, 31
The dupe of f., and the fool of love  HAZLITT, W, 24
To like . . . the same things, that is . . . true f.  SALLUST, 1
frighten by God, they f. me  WELLINGTON, DUKE OF, 13
f. the horses  CAMPBELL, MRS, 1
frittered life is f. away by detail  THOREAU, H, 14
frivolity gay without f.  ARNOLD, M, 18
frog A f. he would a-wooing go  NURSERY RHYMES, 1
frogs F. and snails /And puppy-dogs' tails  NURSERY RHYMES, 70
front polished up the handle of the big f. door  GILBERT, SIR W, 12
frontier We stand today on the edge of a new f.  KENNEDY, J, 8
froth Life is mostly f. and bubble  GORDON, A, 1
fruit brought forth f., some an hundredfold  BIBLE: MATTHEW, 44
every good tree bringeth forth good f.  BIBLE: MATTHEW, 30
his f. in due season  PSALMS, 1
Ignorance is like a delicate exotic f.  WILDE, O, 22
she took of the f. thereof  BIBLE: GENESIS, 13
Some f. for Him that dressed me  HERBERT, G, 3
the f. /Of that forbidden tree  MILTON, J, 25
the f. of the Spirit is love, joy, peace  BIBLE: GALATIANS, 1
Too late for f., too soon for flowers  DE LA MARE, W, 3
fruitful be f. and multiply  BIBLE: GENESIS, 6
fruitfulness Season of . . . mellow f.  KEATS, J, 40
secret of reaping the greatest f. . . . from life  NIETZSCHE, F, 5
fruits by their f. ye shall know them  BIBLE: MATTHEW, 30
No f., no flowers, no leaves, no birds  HOOD, T, 10
frustrate In three sips . . . Arian f.  BROWNING, R, 51
Fry Dear Roger F. whom I love as a man  MARSH, SIR E, 1
fuck Fish f. in it  FIELDS, W, 2
They f. you up, your mum and dad  LARKIN, P, 4
fucking all this cold-hearted f.  LAWRENCE, D, 15
fugitive a f. and a vagabond  BIBLE: GENESIS, 19
full f. of new wine  BIBLE: ACTS, 3
my cup shall be f.  PSALMS, 12
Reading maketh a f. man  BACON, 1ST BARON VERULAM, VISCOUNT ST ALBANS, 51
fulness the earth is the Lord's, and the f.  BIBLE: 1 CORINTHIANS, 15
fun f. to be in the same decade  ROOSEVELT, F, 2
Most people get a fair amount of f. out of their lives  ORWELL, G, 29
People must not do things for f.  HERBERT, SIR A, 4
the most f. I ever had without laughing  ALLEN, W, 2
the people have f.  MONTESQUIEU, BARON DE, 6
Work is much more f. than f.  COWARD, SIR N, 20
you feel as if a human being sitting inside were making f. of you  CANETTI, E, 1
function f. of the critic  BELL, C, 2
funeral F. marches to the grave  LONGFELLOW, H, 8
funerals If you don't go to other men's f.  DAY, C, 2
weddings is sadder than f.  BEHAN, B, 6
funny Everything is f.  ROGERS, W, 4
F. peculiar, or f. ha-ha  HAY, I, 1
F. without being vulgar  GILBERT, SIR W, 48
hard to be f. when you have to be clean  WEST, M, 9

its own animality either objectionable or f. | LEWIS, C, 2
Kings . . . are just as f. | ROOSEVELT, T, 2
**furiously** sleep f. | CHOMSKY, N, 1
**furnace** a burning fiery f. | BIBLE: DANIEL, 2
Heat not a f. for your foe | SHAKESPEARE, W, 101
heat the f. one seven times more | BIBLE: DANIEL, 4
**furniture** brain attic stocked with all the f. that he is likely to use | DOYLE, SIR A, 10
**fury** full of sound and f. | SHAKESPEARE, W, 177
hell a f. like a woman scorned | CONGREVE, W, 7
no f. like an ex-wife searching for a new lover | CONNOLLY, C, 15
strength and f. | LA FONTAINE, J, 4
the F. of a Patient Man | DRYDEN, J, 11
**fuse** force that through the green f. | THOMAS, D, 4
**fustest** I got there f. with the mostest | FORREST, N, 1
**future** F., n. That period of time in which | BIERCE, A, 5
how pleasant . . . not to have any f. | BURGESS, A, 1
If you want a picture of the f. | ORWELL, G, 14
if you would divine the f. | CONFUCIUS, 4
I have seen the f. | STEFFENS, L, 1
I mean a F. Life | BUTLER, J, 1
I never think of the f. | EINSTEIN, A, 9
people who live in the f. | BENNETT, A, 2
pick today's fruits, not relying on the f. in the slightest | HORACE, 31
The f. is . . . black. | BALDWIN, J, 5
The f. is made of the same stuff | WEIL, S, 4
The f. is the only kind of property | CAMUS, A, 9
the f. . . . makes cowards of us | DIX, D, 2
The past was nothing . . . The f. was a mystery | CHOPIN, K, 2
Who controls the past controls the f. | ORWELL, G, 13
You cannot fight against the f. | GLADSTONE, W, 1
**Fuzzy-Wuzzy** to you, F., at your 'ome in the Soudan | KIPLING, R, 8

## G

**gabble** giggle – g. – gobble – 'n' git | HOLMES, O, 8
**gaiety** the only concession to g. | THOMAS, G, 5
**gain** never broke the Sabbath, but for G. | DRYDEN, J, 8
richest g. I count but loss | WATTS, I, 8
**gained** learning hath g. most | FULLER, T, 6
**gainful** I will undoubtedly have to seek . . . g. employment | ACHESON, D, 3
**gains** no g. without pains. | STEVENSON, A, 4
**gaiters** gas and g. | DICKENS, C, 31
**Galatians** a great text in G. | BROWNING, R, 52
O foolish G. | BIBLE: GALATIANS, 1
**Galileo** If G. had said in verse that the world moved | HARDY, T, 10
**gall** the wormwood and the g. | BIBLE: LAMENTATIONS, 1
**gallant** a loyal, a g., a generous, an ingenious, and good-temper'd people | STERNE, L, 2
Hereabouts died a very g. gentleman | ATKINSON, E, 1
He was a braw g. | ANONYMOUS, 109
**gallantry** What men call g. | BYRON, 6TH BARON, 16
**galleon** The moon was a ghostly g. | NOYES, A, 1
**gallery** The boy I love is up in the g. | WARE, G, 1
**galloped** I g., Dirck g. | BROWNING, R, 26
**gallows** You will die either on the g., or of the pox | WILKES, J, 1
**gamble** Life is a g. | STOPPARD, T, 10
**game** how you played the g. | RICE, G, 1
I don't like this g. | MILLIGAN, S, 4
It's more than a g.. It's an institution | HUGHES, T, 2
Play up! play up! and play the g. | NEWBOLT, SIR H, 7
win this g. and thrash the Spaniards | DRAKE, SIR F, 2
woman is his g. | TENNYSON, BARON, 61
**gamesmanship** G. or The Art of Winning Games | POTTER, S, 1
**gaming** Man is a g. animal | LAMB, C, 5
**gangsters** The great nations have always acted like g. | KUBRICK, S, 1
**garbage** G. in | PROVERBS, 170
**Garbo** one sees in G. sober | TYNAN, K, 6
**garden** a g. in her face | CAMPION, T, 2
A g. is a lovesome thing | BROWN, T, 2
Come into the g., Maud | TENNYSON, BARON, 52
cultivate our g. | VOLTAIRE, 4
Don't go into Mr McGregor's g. | POTTER, B, 2
God Almighty first planted a g. | BACON, 1ST BARON VERULAM, VISCOUNT ST ALBANS, 26
God the first g. made | COWLEY, A, 1
I have a g. of my own | MARVELL, A, 6
let my beloved come into his g. | BIBLE: SONG OF SOLOMON, 11
My heart shall be thy g. | MEYNELL, A, 1

nearer God's Heart in a g. | GURNEY, D, 1
The chairs are being brought in from the g. | AUDEN, W, 16
the g. of Eden | BIBLE: GENESIS, 9
There are fairies at the bottom of our g. | FYLEMAN, R, 1
There is a g. in her face | ALISON, R, 2
**gardener** Every time I talk to . . . my g., I'm convinced of the opposite | RUSSELL, EARL, 30
Nor does a . . . g. scent his roses | COCTEAU, J, 1
Oh, Adam was a g. | KIPLING, R, 10
supposing him to be the g. | BIBLE: JOHN, 54
**gardens** a fountain of g. | BIBLE: SONG OF SOLOMON, 16
closing time in the g. of the West | CONNOLLY, C, 1
**garland** wither'd is the g. of the war | SHAKESPEARE, W, 15
**garlands** gather g. there | SCOTT, SIR W, 18
**garment** a moth fretting a g. | PSALMS, 27
**Garter** I like the G. | MELBOURNE, VISCOUNT, 4
**gas** g. and gaiters | DICKENS, C, 31
If silicon had been a g. I should have been a major-general | WHISTLER, J, 4
**gaslight** Fanny by G. | SADLEIR, M, 1
**gas-masks** digging trenches and trying on g. | CHAMBERLAIN, N, 2
**gate** I am here at the g. alone | TENNYSON, BARON, 52
I said to the man who stood at the g. of the year | HASKINS, M, 1
matters not how strait the g. | HENLEY, W, 2
the g. of heaven | BIBLE: GENESIS, 44
**gatekeeper** After I die, I shall return to earth as a g. of a bordello | TOSCANINI, A, 3
**gates** Battering the g. of heaven | TENNYSON, BARON, 70
lift up your heads, O ye g. | PSALMS, 16
the g. of the day | YEATS, W, 17
the iron g. of life | MARVELL, A, 11
the twelve g. were twelve pearls | BIBLE: REVELATIONS, 20
**gather** G. the flowers . . . | MARVELL, A, 8
G. ye rosebuds while ye may | HERRICK, R, 5
the Lord doth . . . g. together the out-casts of Israel | PSALMS, 91
**gathered** two or three are g. together | BOOK OF COMMON PRAYER, 6
where two or three are g. together | BIBLE: MATTHEW, 54
**gatling** The g.'s jammed and the colonel dead | NEWBOLT, SIR H, 7
**gaudy** round, neat, not g. | LAMB, C, 23
**Gaul** G. is divided into three | CAESAR, J, 1
**Gaullist** I . . . have become a G. . . . little by little | DE GAULLE, C, 2
**gave** God . . . g. his only begotten Son | BIBLE: JOHN, 9
the Lord g., and the Lord hath taken away | BIBLE: JOB, 2
**gay** g. without frivolity | ARNOLD, M, 18
**Gaza** Eyeless in G. | MILTON, J, 52
**gazelle** never nurs'd a dear g. | MOORE, T, 6
**general** caviare to the g. | SHAKESPEARE, W, 58
In a civil war, a g. must know | REED, H, 4
**generalizations** All g. are dangerous | DUMAS, FILS, 2
**generalize** To g. is to be an idiot | BLAKE, W, 50
**General Motors** was good for G. | WILSON, C, 1
**generals** at the age of four with paper hats and wooden swords we're all G. | USTINOV, P, 7
Dead battles, like dead g. | TUCHMAN, B, 1
It is not the business of g. to shoot one another | WELLINGTON, DUKE OF, 14
that's not against the law for g. | TRUMAN, H, 6
to be left to the g. | CLEMENCEAU, G, 2
wish he would bite . . . my g. | GEORGE II, 2
**generation** Each g. imagines itself . . . more intelligent than the one . . . before | ORWELL, G, 33
You are a lost g. | STEIN, G, 6
**generations** all g. shall call me blessed | BIBLE: LUKE, 2
g. . . . have struggled in poverty to build these altars | STANTON, E, 1
g. . . . pass in a short time | LUCRETIUS, 3
No hungry g. tread thee down | KEATS, J, 34
**generosity** The poor . . . their function . . . is to exercise our g. | SARTRE, J, 11
**generous** a loyal, a gallant, a g., an ingenious, and good-temper'd people | STERNE, L, 2
**genius** a country full of g., but with absolutely no talent | LEONARD, H, 1
A g.! For thirty-seven years I've practiced . . . and now they call me a g. | SARASATE, P, 1
a German and a g. | SWIFT, J, 20
G. . . . capacity of taking trouble | CARLYLE, T, 8
G. does what it must | MEREDITH, O, 1
G. is an infinite capacity | PROVERBS, 171
G. is one per cent inspiration | EDISON, T, 1

| | |
|---|---|
| Milton, Madam, was a g. | JOHNSON, S, 147 |
| Nothing, except my g. | WILDE, O, 73 |
| Only an organizing g. | BEVAN, A, 7 |
| Rules and models destroy g. and art | HAZLITT, W, 27 |
| Since when was g. . . . respectable | BROWNING, E, 1 |
| talent instantly recognizes g. | DOYLE, SIR A, 15 |
| Taste is the feminine of g. | FITZGERALD, E, 1 |
| the difference between talent and g. | ALCOTT, L, 2 |
| true g. is a mind of large general powers | JOHNSON, S, 17 |
| True g. walks along a line | GOLDSMITH, O, 1 |
| Unless one is a g. | HOPE, A, 1 |
| When a true g. appears | SWIFT, J, 12 |
| gen'i'm'n as the g. said to the fi' pun' note | DICKENS, C, 44 |
| gent what a man is to a g. | |
| | BALDWIN, 1ST EARL BALDWIN OF BEWDLEY, 8 |
| genteel A man . . . is not g. when he gets drunk | BOSWELL, J, 2 |
| gentil verray parfit g. knight | CHAUCER, G, 2 |
| Gentiles a light to lighten the G. | BIBLE: LUKE, 11 |
| gentleman A g. need not know Latin | MATTHEWS, B, 1 |
| a g. . . . never inflicts pain | NEWMAN, CARDINAL, 2 |
| A g. . . . wouldn't hit a woman with his hat on | ALLEN, F, 3 |
| God is a g. | ORTON, J, 6 |
| g. of leisure | VEBLEN, T, 3 |
| Not a g.; dresses too well | RUSSELL, EARL, 24 |
| The Devil is a g. | SHELLEY, P, 16 |
| the g. is an *attorney*. | JOHNSON, S, 77 |
| Who was then the g. | BALL, J, 1 |
| gentlemanly secondly, g. conduct | ARNOLD, T, 2 |
| gentlemen by g. for g. | THACKERAY, W, 6 |
| extremely undignified to behave like a g. | MACKENZIE, SIR C, 1 |
| g., let us do something today | COLLINGWOOD, BARON, 1 |
| God rest you merry, g. | ANONYMOUS, 21 |
| Good-morning, g. both | ELIZABETH I, 4 |
| G. . . . remember blondes | LOOS, A, 1 |
| one of Nature's G. | LINTON, W, 1 |
| religion for g. | CHARLES II, 2 |
| Scholars and g. | WORDSWORTH, W, 34 |
| the British bourgeoisie have spoken of themselves as g. | |
| | WAUGH, E, 10 |
| There were g. and . . . seamen in the navy of Charles the Second | |
| | MACAULAY, BARON, 9 |
| the seamen were not g. | MACAULAY, BARON, 9 |
| gentlewoman gravest sins it was possible for a g. to commit | |
| | WAUGH, E, 43 |
| genuineness G. only thrives in the dark | HUXLEY, A, 32 |
| geographical India is a g. term | CHURCHILL, SIR W, 38 |
| geography G. is about Maps | BENTLEY, E, 2 |
| geometrical Population, . . . increases in a g. ratio | MALTHUS, T, 1 |
| geometricians we are g. only by chance | JOHNSON, S, 19 |
| geometry G. is not true | PIRSIG, R, 2 |
| Poetry is as exact a science as g. | FLAUBERT, G, 1 |
| There is no 'royal road' to g. | EUCLID, 2 |
| George *Death of King G. V* | BETJEMAN, SIR J, 1 |
| G. Bernard Shaw is sadly miscast | SHERWOOD, R, 1 |
| G. the Third . . . may profit by their example | HENRY, P, 1 |
| King G. will be able to read that | HANCOCK, J, 1 |
| Lloyd G. | BEAVERBROOK, BARON, 1 |
| Georgia marching through G. | WORK, H, 4 |
| Georgie G. Porgie, pudding and pie | NURSERY RHYMES, 12 |
| German a G. and a genius | SWIFT, J, 20 |
| I speak . . . G. to my horse | CHARLES V, 3 |
| Life is too short to learn G. | PORSON, R, 1 |
| the G. text of French operas | WHARTON, E, 1 |
| Germans Don't let's be beastly to the G. | COWARD, SIR N, 5 |
| How . . . thorough these G. always managed to be | HUXLEY, A, 34 |
| Man, . . . had been created to jab the life out of G. | SASSOON, S, 5 |
| The G., . . . are going to be squeezed, as a lemon | |
| | GEDDES, SIR E, 1 |
| to the G. that of the air | RICHTER, J, 1 |
| Germany Defeat of G. means | ROOSEVELT, F, 4 |
| G., before all else | HOFFMANN VON FALLERSLEBEN, H, 1 |
| G. will be . . . a world power | HITLER, A, 4 |
| If we see that G. is winning | TRUMAN, H, 2 |
| In G., the Nazis came for the Communists | NIEMOLLER, M, 1 |
| Nazi G. had become a menace to all mankind | NEVINS, A, 1 |
| Gert G.'s poems are bunk | |
| | ANONYMOUS, 89 |
| There's G. and there's Epp and there's Ein | |
| | ANONYMOUS, 89 |
| gesture g. by the individual to himself | GALBRAITH, J, 8 |
| getting a secret way . . . of g. a boy at | DICKENS, C, 17 |

| | |
|---|---|
| G. and spending | WORDSWORTH, W, 59 |
| get up I thought it was a pity to g. | MAUGHAM, W, 16 |
| ghost I, born of flesh and g. | THOMAS, D, 1 |
| oh that I had given up the g. | BIBLE: JOB, 6 |
| the G. in the Machine | RYLE, G, 1 |
| The Papacy is not other than the G. of the deceased Roman | |
| Empire | HOBBES, T, 7 |
| There is a g. /That eats handkerchiefs | MORGENSTERN, C, 1 |
| yielded up the g. | BIBLE: MATTHEW, 87 |
| ghoulies From g. and ghosties and long-leggety beasties | |
| | ANONYMOUS, 19 |
| giant Fleas . . . upon the body of a g. | LANDOR, W, 6 |
| like a g. refreshed with wine | PSALMS, 48 |
| owner whereof was G. Despair | BUNYAN, J, 7 |
| giants A battle of g. | WELLINGTON, DUKE OF, 23 |
| it is by standing on the shoulders of g. | NEWTON, SIR I, 4 |
| not g. but windmills | CERVANTES, M, 2 |
| there were g. in the earth | BIBLE: GENESIS, 22 |
| war of the g. is over | CHURCHILL, SIR W, 23 |
| Gideon Why do they put the G. Bibles | MORLEY, C, 2 |
| gift Never look a g. horse | PROVERBS, 303 |
| the timeliness of the g. | LA BRUYERE, J, 5 |
| True love's the g. which God has given /To man alone | |
| | SCOTT, SIR W, 5 |
| worth more than the g. | CORNEILLE, P, 3 |
| gifts God's g. put man's best g. | BROWNING, E, 3 |
| I fear the Greeks even when they bring g.. | VIRGIL, 6 |
| The Gods themselves cannot recall their g. | TENNYSON, BARON, 72 |
| giggle g. – gabble – gobble – 'n' git | HOLMES, O, 8 |
| glid To g. refined gold | SHAKESPEARE, W, 128 |
| gilded A best-seller is the g. tomb of a mediocre talent | SMITH, L, 1 |
| She's only a bird in a g. cage | LAMB, A, 1 |
| Gilpin And G., long live he | COWPER, W, 9 |
| John G. was a citizen | COWPER, W, 7 |
| gin G. was mother's milk | SHAW, G, 36 |
| No man is genuinely happy, married, who has to drink worse g. | |
| | MENCKEN, H, 13 |
| she was dead; but my father he kept ladling g. | SHAW, G, 35 |
| gird g. up now thy loins like a man | BIBLE: JOB, 16 |
| girded Pavilioned in splendour, and g. with praise | GRANT, SIR R, 1 |
| girl Every little g. knows about love | SAGAN, F, 1 |
| From birth to age eighteen, a g. needs good parents | TUCKER, S, 3 |
| Give me a g. at an impressionable age | SPARK, M, 6 |
| g. with brains | LOOS, A, 2 |
| If you were the only g. in the world | GROSSMITH THE YOUNGER, G, 1 |
| one can . . . see in a little g. the threat of a woman | DUMAS, FILS, 3 |
| One g. can be pretty | FITZGERALD, F, 7 |
| park, a policeman and a pretty g. | CHAPLIN, C, 1 |
| There was a little g. /Who had a little curl | MILLER, M, 1 |
| girlfriend Not every problem someone has with his g. is . . . due | |
| to . . . capitalist . . . production | MARCUSE, H, 1 |
| girls Boys and g. come out to play | NURSERY RHYMES, 6 |
| g. are so queer | ALCOTT, L, 3 |
| g. from being g. | HOPE, A, 5 |
| . . . g. . . . say No when they mean Yes | ALCOTT, L, 3 |
| g. who wear glasses | PARKER, D, 26 |
| if ever I was to have a dozen g., I'd call 'em all Jane | WELLS, H, 11 |
| My life with g. has ended | HORACE, 38 |
| one of the nicest g. I was ever engaged to | WODEHOUSE, SIR P, 15 |
| the . . . rift between the sexes is . . . widened by . . . teaching . . . | |
| to the g. | STEVENSON, R, 12 |
| Treaties are like roses and young g. | DE GAULLE, C, 9 |
| When you see what some g. marry | ROWLAND, H, 1 |
| Where . . . boys plan for what . . . young g. plan for whom | |
| | GILMAN, C, 3 |
| git giggle – gabble – gobble – 'n' g. | HOLMES, O, 8 |
| give freely ye have received, freely g. | BIBLE: MATTHEW, 37 |
| g. me liberty or g. me death | HENRY, P, 2 |
| G. me your tired, . . . /Your huddled masses | LAZARUS, E, 1 |
| like the grave, cries G., g. | ADAMS, A, 1 |
| my peace I g. unto you | BIBLE: JOHN, 34 |
| such as I have g. I thee | BIBLE: ACTS, 4 |
| To g. and not to count the cost | LOYOLA, I, 1 |
| When I g. I g. myself | WHITMAN, W, 6 |
| given I wish that God had not g. me what I prayed for | SPYRI, J, 1 |
| I would have g. you another | JARRY, A, 1 |
| oh that I had g. up the ghost | BIBLE: JOB, 6 |
| unto every one that hath shall be g. | BIBLE: MATTHEW, 73 |
| gives He g. twice who g. promptly | SYRUS, P, 1 |
| giving The manner of g. | CORNEILLE, P, 3 |
| gizzard My wife hath something in her g. | PEPYS, S, 11 |

glad g., because they are at rest    PSALMS, 67
I was g. when they said unto me    PSALMS, 78
She had /A heart . . . too soon made g.    BROWNING, R, 33
with a love like that you know you should be g.    LENNON, J, 10
. . . you would have been very g. if I had written it    PIRON, A, 1
**gladsome** Let us with a g. mind /Praise the Lord    MILTON, J, 50
**Gladstone**    BAGEHOT, W, 10
Mr G. read Homer for fun    CHURCHILL, SIR W, 11
to G.'s always having the ace of trumps    LABOUCHERE, BARON TAUNTON, 1
**Glasgow** never played the G. Empire    DODD, K, 1
**glass** baying for broken g..    WAUGH, E, 2
Like many of the upper class /He liked the sound of broken g.    BELLOC, H, 12
on the other side of the g.    BENNETT, A, 4
Satire is a sort of g.    SWIFT, J, 1
through a g., darkly    BIBLE: I CORINTHIANS, 18
you won't intoxicate with one g. someone who has . . . drunk . . . a . . . barrel    CHEKHOV, A, 10
**glasses** girls who wear g.    PARKER, D, 26
**glimpse** I . . . catch a g. of a stoat    KEATS, J, 64
Same old g. of /Paradise    LAMPTON, W, 1
**glisters** Nor all that g. gold    GRAY, T, 13
**glittering** long grey beard and g. eye    COLERIDGE, S, 22
The world continues to offer g. prizes    BIRKENHEAD, EARL OF, 4
**glitters** All that g. is not gold    PROVERBS, 39
**gloamin'** Roamin' in the g.    LAUDER, SIR H, 3
**global** my wars /Were g.    REED, H, 1
the world in the image of a g. village    MCLUHAN, M, 1
**globe** the great g. itself    SHAKESPEARE, W, 277
**globule** I can trace my ancestry back to a . . . g.    GILBERT, SIR W, 24
**gloire** Le jour de g. est arrivé    ROUGET DE LISLE, C, 1
**glorious** G. things of thee are spoken    NEWTON, J, 1
Happy and g.    CAREY, H, 1
**glory** because he gave not God the g.    BIBLE: ACTS, 11
But trailing clouds of g.    WORDSWORTH, W, 23
G. be to God for dappled things    HOPKINS, G, 4
g., jest, and riddle of the world    POPE, A, 31
g. to God in the highest    BIBLE: LUKE, 9
It is a great g. in a woman    THUCYDIDES, 2
Land of Hope and G.    BENSON, A, 1
let the saints be joyful with g.    PSALMS, 93
Mine eyes have seen the g. of the coming of the Lord:    HOWE, J, 1
paths of g. lead but to the grave    GRAY, T, 3
Popularity? . . . g.'s small change    HUGO, V, 4
the g. of Europe is extinguished for ever    BURKE, E, 7
the g. of the Lord shall be revealed    BIBLE: ISAIAH, 27
the Son of man coming . . . with power and great g.    BIBLE: MATTHEW, 68
To the greater g. of God    ANONYMOUS, 2
we left him alone with his g.    WOLFE, C, 2
Where is it now, the g. and the dream    WORDSWORTH, W, 23
who is the King of g.    PSALMS, 16
**Gloucester** Doctor Foster went to G.    NURSERY RHYMES, 10
**glow** make the corpuscles of the blood g.    LAWRENCE, D, 12
**Glum** I've examined your son's head, Mr G.    MUIR, F, 1
**glum** speed g. heroes . . . to death    SASSOON, S, 1
**gluttony** G. is an emotional escape    DE VRIES, P, 2
**gnomes** the little g. of Zürich    WILSON OF RIEVAULX, BARON, 6
**go** a good cook, as cooks g.    SAKI, 16
g., and do thou likewise    BIBLE: LUKE, 23
if I g. not . . . the Comforter will not come    BIBLE: JOHN, 40
I shall be the last to g. out    ALENÇON, DUCHESSE D', 1
Let's g.    BECKETT, S, 4
Let us g. then, you and I    ELIOT, T, 9
not to g. anywhere, but to g.    STEVENSON, R, 5
stopped short – never to g. again    WORK, H, 3
Turn up the lights, I don't want to g. home in the dark    HENRY, O, 2
whither thou goest, I will g.    BIBLE: RUTH, 1
**goal** The g. stands up    HOUSMAN, A, 10
**goat-footed** This g. bard    KEYNES, BARON, 4
**goats** as a shepherd divideth his sheep from the g.    BIBLE: MATTHEW, 74
**God** A bit like G.    THOMAS, G, 3
A G. who let us prove his existence    BONHOEFFER, D, 2
A man with G.    KNOX, J, 1
America is G.'s Crucible    ZANGWILL, I, 2
an absolute faith that all things are possible to G.    EDDY, M, 1
an atheist half believes a G.    YOUNG, E, 4
An honest G.    INGERSOLL, R, 1

Are G. and Nature then at strife    TENNYSON, BARON, 27
better to have no opinion of G.    BACON, 1ST BARON VERULAM, VISCOUNT ST ALBANS, 52
but for the grace of G. goes    BRADFORD, J, 1
charged with the grandeur of G.    HOPKINS, G, 3
concept of G. has any validity    BALDWIN, J, 1
Dr Donne's verses are like the peace of G.;    JAMES I, 5
effect Whose cause is G.    COWPER, W, 24
Even G. cannot change the past    AGATHON, 1
even G. was born /too late    LOWELL, R, 3
Every man thinks G. is on his side    ANOUILH, J, 3
final proof of G.'s omnipotence    DE VRIES, P, 6
for which, and all the discomforts that will accompany my being blind, the good G. prepare me    PEPYS, S, 12
G. alone deserves to be loved    SAND, G, 2
G. as a working hypothesis    BONHOEFFER, D, 1
G. bless . . . G. damn    THURBER, J, 20
G. bless us every one    DICKENS, C, 7
G. can stand being told    PRIESTLEY, J, 7
G. could cause us considerable embarrassment    GOETHE, J, 8
G. defend me from my friends    PROVERBS, 176
G. disposes    KEMPIS, T, 4
G. does not play dice    EINSTEIN, A, 4
G. erects a house of prayer    DEFOE, D, 5
G., even our own G.    PSALMS, 43
G. . . . first planted a garden    BACON, 1ST BARON VERULAM, VISCOUNT ST ALBANS, 26
G. from everlasting    PSALMS, 54
G. has written all the books    BUTLER, S, 13
G. helps them    PROVERBS, 177
G. is a gentleman    ORTON, J, 6
G. is always on the side of the big battalions    TURENNE, VICOMTE DE, 1
G. is always on the side    PROVERBS, 178
G. is beginning to resemble not a ruler    HUXLEY, SIR J, 2
G. is dead    NIETZSCHE, F, 4
G. is nothing more than an exalted father    FREUD, S, 5
G. is on the side not of the heavy battalions, but of the best shots    VOLTAIRE, 18
G. is really only another artist    PICASSO, P, 3
G. is subtle but he is not malicious    EINSTEIN, A, 3
G. is the immemorial refuge of the incompetent    MENCKEN, H, 9
G. made everything out of nothing    VALERY, P, 1
G. made the country    COWPER, W, 20
going back to G.    BRUCE, L, 1
Great G. grant that twice two be not four    TURGENEV, I, 4
G. said, *Let Newton be*    POPE, A, 17
G. save our gracious King    CAREY, H, 1
G.'s gifts put man's best gifts    BROWNING, E, 3
G. should go before such villains    SHAKESPEARE, W, 216
G.'s in His heaven    BROWNING, R, 43
G. the first garden made    COWLEY, A, 1
G. will cease to dream you    UNAMUNO Y JUGO, M, 1
G. will grant an end to these too    VIRGIL, 3
G. will pardon me. It is His trade    HEINE, H, 5
Had I but serv'd my G. with half the zeal /I serv'd my King    SHAKESPEARE, W, 104
Had I . . . served G. as diligently as I have served the king    WOLSEY, T, 1
Has G. then forgotten    LOUIS XIV, 2
have one G. only    CLOUGH, A, 5
her conception of G. was certainly not orthodox    STRACHEY, L, 4
Holy, holy, holy, Lord G. Almighty    HEBER, R, 3
How could G. do this to me    LOUIS XIV, 1
I am glad . . . he thanks G. for anything    JOHNSON, S, 11
I did not write it. G. wrote it. I merely did his dictation    STOWE, H, 4
If G. did not exist    VOLTAIRE, 9
If G. made us in His image    VOLTAIRE, 14
If G. were suddenly condemned to live the life    DUMAS, FILS, 1
If this man is not faithful to his G.    THEODORIC, 1
If you don't find a G. by five o'clock this afternoon    JOWETT, B, 7
If you talk to G., you are praying    SZASZ, T, 8
It takes a long while for a . . . trustful person to reconcile himself to . . . G.    MENCKEN, H, 10
I wouldn't give up writing about G.    WAUGH, E, 44
I wretch lay wrestling with . . . my G.    HOPKINS, G, 2
justify the ways of G. to men    MILTON, J, 26
Just what G. would have done if he had the money    WOOLLCOTT, A, 3
Know then thyself, presume not G. to scan    POPE, A, 32

Live among men as if G. beheld you    SENECA, 1
Many people believe that they are attracted by G.    INGE, W, 4
May G. deny you peace    UNAMUNO Y JUGO, M, 2
nature is the art of G.    BROWNE, SIR T, 3
Nearer, my G., to thee    ADAMS, S, 1
none deny there is a G.
   BACON, 1ST BARON VERULAM, VISCOUNT ST ALBANS, 10
One G., one law, one element    TENNYSON, BARON, 34
One on G.'s side is a majority    PHILLIPS, W, 2
only G. can make a tree    KILMER, A, 2
Our G., our help in ages past    WATTS, I, 6
poems . . . for the love of Man and in praise of G.    THOMAS, D, 2
proof that G. is a bore    MENCKEN, H, 7
prose for G.    GRANVILLE-BARKER, H, 3
put your hand into the hand of G.    HASKINS, M, 1
Resistance to tyranny is obedience to G.    ANTHONY, S, 4
Sickness, sin and death . . . do not originate in G.    EDDY, M, 4
Since G. has given us the papacy . . . enjoy it    LEO X, 1
speak to G. as if men were listening    SENECA, 1
that G. is interested only . . . in religion    TEMPLE, W, 2
that great Leviathan, or rather . . . that *Mortal* G.    HOBBES, T, 5
The Act of G. designation    COREN, A, 2
the dear G. who loveth us    COLERIDGE, S, 37
the electric display of G. the Father    O'NEILL, E, 1
the highest praise of G. consists in the denial of Him    PROUST, M, 7
the nearer you are to G.    WOTTON, SIR H, 4
the one G. whose worshippers . . . still trust in Him    BRADLEY, F, 2
There, but for the Grace of G., goes G.    MANKEIWICZ, H, 2
The true G., . . . G. of ideas    VIGNY, A, 1
Those who marry G. . . . can become domesticated too
   GREENE, G, 1
To understand G.'s thoughts    NIGHTINGALE, F, 2
we come /From G., who is our home    WORDSWORTH, W, 23
we owe G. a death    SHAKESPEARE, W, 90
What G. does, He does well    LA FONTAINE, J, 10
When I composed that, I was . . . inspired by G.    BEETHOVEN, L, 2
when one has loved a man it is very different to love G.
   SAND, G, 2
whom G. wishes to destroy    EURIPIDES, 1
Whom G. would destroy    DUPORT, J, 1
yearning like a G. in pain.    KEATS, J, 7
you hardly ever mention G. any more    MILLER, A, 1
you must believe in G.    JOWETT, B, 1
**god** Either a beast or a g.    ARISTOTLE, 7
either a wild beast or a g.
   BACON, 1ST BARON VERULAM, VISCOUNT ST ALBANS, 24
. . . I believe I am becoming a g.    VESPASIAN, 1
if triangles invented a g., they would make him three-sided
   MONTESQUIEU, BARON DE, 4
Kill everyone, and you are a g.    ROSTAND, J, 3
to the unknown g.    BIBLE: ACTS, 12
**Goddamm** Lhude sing G.    POUND, E, 5
**godlike** patient endurance is g.    LONGFELLOW, H, 4
**gods** Against stupidity the g. . . . struggle in vain    SCHILLER, F, 1
a great king above all g.    PSALMS, 60
by force of the g.    VIRGIL, 2
deserves the name of happy who knows how to use the g.' gifts
wisely    HORACE, 43
for what high cause /This darling of the G.    MARVELL, A, 7
g. help them    AESOP, 4
Kings are earth's g.    SHAKESPEARE, W, 231
leave the rest to the G.    CORNEILLE, P, 1
Live with the g.    MARCUS AURELIUS ANTONINUS, 10
man's ignorance of the g.    BUTLER, S, 7
no other g. before me    BIBLE: EXODUS, 20
So many g., so many creeds    WILCOX, E, 4
The Ethiopians say that their g. are . . . black    XENOPHANES, 1
The G. themselves cannot recall their gifts    TENNYSON, BARON, 72
we're forbidden to know – what end the g. have in store
   HORACE, 30
whom the g. favour dies young    PLAUTUS, T, 1
Whom the g. love    MENANDER, 1
Whom the g. love    PROVERBS, 465
Whom the g. wish to destroy    CONNOLLY, C, 7
**goe** to morowe longe I to g. to God    MORE, SIR T, 2
**Gog** G. and Magog    BIBLE: REVELATIONS, 16
**Godot** waiting for G.    BECKETT, S, 4
**going** I am just g. outside    OATES, L, 1
Men must endure /Their g. hence    SHAKESPEARE, W, 151
Stand not upon the order of your g.    SHAKESPEARE, W, 171

thy g. out, and thy coming in    PSALMS, 77
**gold** A g. rush is what happens when    WEST, M, 5
all the g. that the goose could give    AESOP, 3
An angel writing in a book of g.    HUNT, L, 1
cursed /craving for g.    VIRGIL, 8
For g. in phisik is a cordial    CHAUCER, G, 9
gild refined g.    SHAKESPEARE, W, 128
Good morning to the day: and next my g.    JONSON, B, 12
Nor all that glisters g.    GRAY, T, 13
silver and g. have I none    BIBLE: ACTS, 4
Silver threads among the g.    REXFORD, E, 1
The ring so worn . . . is yet of g.    CRABBE, G, 2
To a shower of g.    CARLYLE, T, 13
travell'd in the realms of g.    KEATS, J, 36
Were't not for g. and women    TOURNEUR, C, 1
What female heart can g. despise    GRAY, T, 11
When every . . . thing you hold /Is made of silver, or of g.
   GILBERT, SIR W, 5
**golden** G. slumbers kiss your eyes    DEKKER, T, 1
In good King Charles's g. days    ANONYMOUS, 48
In old time we had treen chalices and g. priests,    JEWELL, J, 1
Jerusalem the g.    NEALE, J, 3
perhaps, the g. rule    STEVENSON, R, 20
The g. apples of the sun    YEATS, W, 28
the G. Road to Samarkand    FLECKER, J, 1
there are no g. rules    SHAW, G, 29
**Goldwyn** Mr G. . . . you are only interested in art    SHAW, G, 45
**golf** an earnest protest against g.    BEERBOHM, SIR M, 17
G. . . . a form of moral effort    LEACOCK, S, 11
**Gomorrah** Sodom and . . . G.    BIBLE: GENESIS, 37
**gone** g. with the wind    DOWSON, E, 2
it is g.; and the place thereof shall know it no more    PSALMS, 64
**gongs** women should be struck . . . like g.    COWARD, SIR N, 16
**good** a g. friend, but bad acquaintance    BYRON, 6TH BARON, 26
A g. man fallen among Fabians.    LENIN, V, 10
A g. novel tells us the truth    CHESTERTON, G, 20
A G. Time Was Had by All    SMITH, S, 1
All g. writing    FITZGERALD, F, 14
Anybody can be g. in the country    WILDE, O, 49
as gods, knowing g. and evil    BIBLE: GENESIS, 13
Be g., sweet maid, and let who can be clever;    KINGSLEY, C, 1
being really g. all the time    WILDE, O, 24
dedicate this nation to the policy of the g. neighbor
   ROOSEVELT, F, 9
Do g. by stealth    POPE, A, 8
doing g. . . . professions which are full    THOREAU, H, 10
doing g. to base fellows    CERVANTES, M, 7
dull prospect of a distant g.    DRYDEN, J, 23
every creature of God is g.    BIBLE: I TIMOTHY, 3
every man at the beginning doth set forth g. wine    BIBLE: JOHN, 5
Every man loves what he is g. at    SHADWELL, T, 3
Evil, be thou my G.    MILTON, J, 39
Evil comes . . . like the disease; g. . . . like the doctor
   CHESTERTON, G, 23
Far too g. to waste on children    SHAW, G, 48
Four legs g.    ORWELL, G, 2
G., but not religious-good    HARDY, T, 6
General G. is the plea of the scoundrel    BLAKE, W, 14
G. isn't the word    GILBERT, SIR W, 47
God saw that it was g.    BIBLE: GENESIS, 3
greatest g.    CICERO, M, 3
g. shepherd giveth his life for the sheep    BIBLE: JOHN, 26
G. things, when short, are twice as g.    GRACIAN, B, 1
g. tidings of great joy    BIBLE: LUKE, 8
happiness makes them g.    LANDOR, W, 3
He who would do g. to another    BLAKE, W, 14
hold fast that which is g.    BIBLE: I THESSALONIANS, 3
how *can* they become g. people    VICTORIA, 2
how can ye, being evil, speak g.    BIBLE: MATTHEW, 42
How g. is man's life, the mere living    BROWNING, R, 48
If . . . 'feeling g.' could decide, drunkenness would be . . .
supremely valid    JAMES, W, 2
If to do were as easy as to know what were g.
   SHAKESPEARE, W, 188
If you can't be g.    PROVERBS, 217
I have fought a g. fight    BIBLE: II TIMOTHY, 3
it cannot come to g.    SHAKESPEARE, W, 44
It is g. to know what a man is    BRADLEY, F, 3
It is seldom . . . one parts on g. terms    PROUST, M, 16
letting the best be the enemy of the g.    JENKINS, R, 1

little of what you fancy does you g.   LLOYD, M, 2
Men have never been g.   BARTH, K, 1
never was a g. war   FRANKLIN, B, 14
no hint throughout the universe /Of g. or ill   THOMSON, J, 3
Nothing can harm a g. man   SOCRATES, 1
nothing either g. or bad   SHAKESPEARE, W, 56
nothing g. to be had in the country   HAZLITT, W, 11
on earth peace, g. will toward men   BIBLE: LUKE; 9
One man is as g. as another   JOWETT, B, 2
Only g. girls keep diaries   BANKHEAD, T, 8
our people have never had it so g.   MACMILLAN, EARL OF STOCKTON, 1
Roman Conquest . . . a G. Thing   SELLAR, W, 4
sorrier for my g. knights' loss than for . . . my fair queen   MALORY, SIR T, 3
strong antipathy of g. to bad   POPE, A, 9
suppose the people g.   ROBESPIERRE, M, 1
the g. are always the merry,   YEATS, W, 11
The g. die early   DEFOE, D, 1
The g. die first   WORDSWORTH, W, 2
The g. die young   PROVERBS, 396
The g. is oft interred with their bones   SHAKESPEARE, W, 116
The g. is the beautiful   PLATO, 1
the g. must associate   BURKE, E, 18
The g. of the people   CICERO, M, 2
The g. old times   BYRON, 6TH BARON, 1
The Japanese have perfected g.   THEROUX, P, 1
The king has been very g. to me   BOLEYN, A, 1
the name of perseverance in a g. cause   STERNE, L, 6
The only g. Indians I ever saw were dead   SHERIDAN, P, 1
There is so much g. in the worst of us   ANONYMOUS, 88
the thing which is g.   BIBLE: EPHESIANS, 2
they are . . . surprised at hearing of a g. action and never of a bad one   KEATS, J, 65
those who go about doing g.   CREIGHTON, M, 1
thou g. and faithful servant   BIBLE: MATTHEW, 72
three ingredients in the g. life   MORLEY, C, 1
to write g. prose is an affair of g. manners   MAUGHAM, W, 17
"Well done thou g. and faithful servant"   ANONYMOUS, 70
we looked for peace, but no g. came   BIBLE: JEREMIAH, 2
what g. came of it at last   SOUTHEY, R, 1
What's the g. of a home   GROSSMITH, G, 1
Whenever two g. people argue over principles   ESCHENBACH, M, 1
When I'm g. I'm very g.   WEST, M, 15
when the great and g. depart   WORDSWORTH, W, 13
Why care for grammar as long as we are g.   WARD, A, 4
You shouldn't say it is not g.   WHISTLER, J, 8
**goodbye** G. to All That   GRAVES, R, 1
Without a single kiss or a g.   PATMORE, C, 2
**good-bye-ee** G.! – g.   WESTON, R, 1
**goodness** Abashed the devil . . . felt how awful g. is   MILTON, J, 42
G. does not . . . make men happy   LANDOR, W, 3
My g. those diamonds are lovely   WEST, M, 2
Not to be wronged is to forgo . . . g.   WELLS, H, 2
surely g. and mercy shall follow me   PSALMS, 14
the earth is full of the g. of the Lord   PSALMS, 24
**goods** isn't a bad bit of g., the Queen   CERVANTES, M, 11
Poverty of g. is easily cured   MONTAIGNE, M, 10
the Man Who Delivers the G.   MASON, W, 1
**good-temper'd** a loyal, a gallant, a generous, an ingenious, and g. people   STERNE, L, 2
**goodwill** a gigantic reservoir of g.   WILLKIE, W, 2
in peace, g.   CHURCHILL, SIR W, 19
**goose** all the gold that the g. could give   AESOP, 3
**goosey** G., g. gander   NURSERY RHYMES, 13
**gored** you tossed and g. several persons   BOSWELL, J, 1
**gorgeous** hold the g. east in fee   WORDSWORTH, W, 53
**gormed** I'm G.   DICKENS, C, 15
**Gospels** We had no use for the policy of the G.   KHRUSHCHEV, N, 1
**gossips** No one g. about . . . secret virtues   RUSSELL, EARL, 14
**got** Which in our case we have not g.   REED, H, 3
**gout** A taste for drink, combined with g.   GILBERT, SIR W, 3
that old enemy the g. /Had taken him in toe!   HOOD, T, 9
**govern** Every class is unfit to g.   ACTON, 1ST BARON, 1
Grammar, which can g. even kings   MOLIERE, 9
He that would g. others   MASSINGER, P, 1
I will g. according to the common weal,   JAMES I, 3
king reigns, but does not g.   ZAMOYSKI, J, 1
Kings g. by . . . assemblies only when   FOX, C, 4
Labour is not fit to g.   CHURCHILL, SIR W, 36
No man is good enough to g. another man   LINCOLN, A, 6

Under socialism *all* will g.   LENIN, V, 5
**governed** with how little wisdom the world is g.   OXENSTIERNA, COUNT, 1
**governing** the right of g. was not property but a trust   FOX, C, 1
**government** A g. . . . big enough to give you all you want   GOLDWATER, B, 1
a g. organization could do it that quickly   CARTER, J, 1
All g. . . . is founded on compromise and barter   BURKE, E, 12
As to religion, I hold it to be the . . . duty of g. to protect all . . . professors thereof   PAINE, T, 4
Democracy is only an experiment in g.   INGE, W, 7
every g. . . . should have its old speeches burned   SNOWDEN, 1ST VISCOUNT, 1
g. by crony   ICKES, H, 1
G., . . . is but a necessary evil   PAINE, T, 3
g. of the people, by the people, and for the people   LINCOLN, A, 12
I would not give half a guinea to live under one form of g.   JOHNSON, S, 80
Monarchy is a strong g.   BAGEHOT, W, 3
no man believes, that want of g., is any new kind of g.   HOBBES, T, 6
people's g.   WEBSTER, D, 2
prepare for g.   STEEL, D, 1
The g. burns down whole cities   MAO TSE-TUNG, 8
the g. it deserves   MAISTRE, J, 1
the President is dead, but the G. lives and God Omnipotent reigns   GARFIELD, J, 1
there was no form of g. common to the peoples   WAUGH, E, 35
the things which g. does . . . social progress   WARREN, E, 1
The worst g. is the most moral   MENCKEN, H, 8
We live under a g. of men and . . . newspapers   PHILLIPS, W, 1
**governments** all G. are selfish   ECCLES, VISCOUNT, 1
G. needs to have both shepherds and butchers   VOLTAIRE, 17
*The Beast* stands for strong mutually antagonistic g.   WAUGH, E, 30
**governors** Our supreme g., the mob   WALPOLE, 4TH EARL OF ORFORD, 3
**Gower** moral G.   CHAUCER, G, 19
**grace** but for the g. of God, goes   BRADFORD, J, 1
g. a summer queen   SCOTT, SIR W, 18
God in his mercy lend her g.   TENNYSON, BARON, 43
g. of our Lord Jesus Christ be with you   BIBLE: I CORINTHIANS, 24
He had at least the g.   BENTLEY, E, 1
Lord, I ascribe it to Thy g.   WATTS, I, 4
she obtained g. and favour   BIBLE: ESTHER, 1
Such g. had kings   BROWNING, R, 45
Tuesday's child is full of g.   NURSERY RHYMES, 35
**graces** the G. do not seem . . . natives of Great Britain   CHESTERFIELD, 4TH EARL OF, 9
**gracious** A life that moves to g. ends   TENNYSON, BARON, 73
O give thanks unto the Lord, for he is g.   PSALMS, 65
**gradually** Boys do not grow up g.   CONNOLLY, C, 11
**gradualness** The inevitability of g.   WEBB, BARON PASSFIELD, 2
**Grail** What were they going to do with the G.   BEERBOHM, SIR M, 20
**grain** A g., which in England is generally given to horses   JOHNSON, S, 9
He reaps the bearded g. at a breath   LONGFELLOW, H, 9
**grammar** down to posterity talking bad g.   DISRAELI, 1ST EARL OF BEACONSFIELD, 14
G., which can govern even kings   MOLIERE, 9
I am . . . above g.   SIGISMUND, 2
Why care for g. as long as we are good   WARD, A, 4
**grammatical** I have laboured to refine our language to g. purity   JOHNSON, S, 21
**gramophones** waxworks inhabited by g.   DE LA MARE, W, 2
**grand** A 'G. Old Man'   LEACOCK, S, 12
that g. old man   NORTHCOTE, 1ST EARL OF IDDESLEIGH, 1
The g. Perhaps   BROWNING, R, 8
the g. style arises in poetry   ARNOLD, M, 30
to be baith g. and comfortable   BARRIE, SIR J, 2
**grandeur** g. is a dream   COWPER, W, 28
g. of God   HOPKINS, G, 3
Many people have delusions of g.   IONESCO, E, 1
**grandfather** a man has no reason to be ashamed of having an ape for his g.   HUXLEY, T, 11
g.'s clock   WORK, H, 2
I don't know who my g. was   LINCOLN, A, 17
pass my declining years saluting strange women and g. clocks   NASH, O, 9
**grandmother** I murdered my g. this morning   ROOSEVELT, F, 1
**grandson** I am much more concerned to know what his g. will be   LINCOLN, A, 17

your g. will . . . be a Communist    KHRUSHCHEV, N, 5
granted human beings have an . . . infinite capacity for taking things
  for g.    HUXLEY, A, 31
grape Beulah, peel me a g.    WEST, M, 4
grapes He is trampling out the vintage where the g. of wrath
   HOWE, J, 1
  I am sure the g. are sour    AESOP, 2
grapeshot A whiff of g.    CARLYLE, T, 14
grasp man's reach should exceed his g.    BROWNING, R, 2
grasping that power . . . , is ever g.    ADAMS, A, 1
grass all flesh is as g.    BIBLE: I PETER, 2
  the days of man are but as g.    PSALMS, 64
  There's a snake hidden in the g.    VIRGIL, 14
grassgreen down the g. gooseberried double bed
   THOMAS, D, 16
gratification I have had no real g. . . . more than my neighbor
   VANDERBILT, W, 2
gratifying It is quite g. to feel guilty    ARENDT, H, 2
gratuite L'acte g.    GIDE, A, 1
grave a-mouldering in the g.,    HALL, C, 1
  And digs my g. at each remove    HERBERT, G, 5
  And on his g., with shining eyes    ARNOLD, M, 28
  Between the cradle and the g.    DYER, J, 2
  Dig the g. and let me lie    STEVENSON, R, 10
  Funeral marches to the g.    LONGFELLOW, H, 8
  her heart in his g. is lying    MOORE, T, 4
  If Roosevelt were alive he'd turn in his g.    GOLDWYN, S, 19
  I may dread /The g. as little    KEN, T, 1
  I shall soon be laid in the quiet g.    KEATS, J, 67
  like the g., cries 'Give, give'    ADAMS, A, 1
  Marriage is a step so g. and decisive    STEVENSON, R, 21
  no work, nor device, nor knowledge . . . in the g.
   BIBLE: ECCLESIASTES, 16
  O g., where is thy victory    BIBLE: I CORINTHIANS, 23
  O g.! where is thy victory    POPE, A, 4
  paths of glory lead but to the g.    GRAY, T, 3
  The g.'s a fine and private place    MARVELL, A, 12
  the g. yawns for him    TREE, SIR H, 3
  To that dark inn, the g.    SCOTT, SIR W, 10
grave-digger if I were a g., or . . . a hangman,    JERROLD, D, 6
graven any g. image    BIBLE: EXODUS, 20
graves The bitterest tears shed over g.    STOWE, H, 1
  The dust of great persons' g.    DONNE, J, 13
gravity He rose by g.; I sank by levity    SMITH, S, 18
gravy Sir Humphry Davy /Abominated g.    BENTLEY, E, 4
gray When you are old and g.    YEATS, W, 31
grazed He is the richest author that ever g.    JOHNSON, S, 57
great a g. voice, as of a trumpet    BIBLE: REVELATIONS, 1
  All my shows are g.    GRADE, BARON, 1
  All things both g. and small    COLERIDGE, S, 37
  deep consent of all g. men    RUSKIN, J, 12
  Everything g. in the world is done by neurotics    PROUST, M, 19
  everything that is g. . . . done by youth
   DISRAELI, 1ST EARL OF BEACONSFIELD, 2
  fate of the g. wen    COBBETT, W, 3
  g. is Diana of the Ephesians    BIBLE: ACTS, 15
  G. men are but life-sized    BEERBOHM, SIR M, 3
  g. men have not commonly been g. scholars    HOLMES, O, 3
  G. oaks    PROVERBS, 182
  History is full of ignominious getaways by the g.    ORWELL, G, 31
  how g. a matter a little fire kindleth    BIBLE: JAMES, 5
  How very small the very g.    THACKERAY, W, 8
  If I am a g. man    LAW, B, 4
  No g. man lives in vain    CARLYLE, T, 9
  On earth there is nothing g. but man    HAMILTON, SIR W, 2
  Some are born g.    SHAKESPEARE, W, 292
  the g. break through    SHENSTONE, W, 1
  The g. man . . . walks across his century    LEACOCK, S, 9
  the g. ones eat up the little ones    SHAKESPEARE, W, 232
  then . . . many of the g. men of history are frauds    LAW, B, 4
  the shade /Of that which once was g.    WORDSWOKTH, W, 56
  To be g. is to be misunderstood    EMERSON, R, 14
  when the g. and good depart    WORDSWORTH, W, 13
  you, . . . who have made me too g. for my house.
   BACON, 1ST BARON VERULAM, VISCOUNT ST ALBANS, 66
great-aunt A person may be indebted for a nose or an eye, . . . to
  a g.    HAZLITT, W, 23
Great Britain G. could say that she supported both sides
   MACDONALD, R, 1
  G. has lost an Empire    ACHESON, D, 4
  To make a union with G.    PETAIN, H, 1
greater g. love hath no man    BIBLE: JOHN, 36

The g. the power    BURKE, E, 23
Thy need is yet g. than mine    SIDNEY, SIR P, 3
greatest great city . . . has the g. men and women    WHITMAN, W, 10
  I'm the g.    ALI, M, 1
  the g. deeds require a certain insensitiveness    LICHTENBERG, G, 3
  The g. happiness of the g. number    BENTHAM, J, 1
  the g. of these is charity    BIBLE: I CORINTHIANS, 18
great-grandfathers Classicism, . . . presents . . . the literature that
  gave . . . pleasure to their g.    STENDHAL, 2
Great-heart One G.    BUNYAN, J, 9
greatness long farewell to all my g.    SHAKESPEARE, W, 103
  Men who have g. . . . don't go in for politics    CAMUS, A, 7
  some have g. thrust upon 'em    SHAKESPEARE, W, 292
Great War A Soldier of the G.    KIPLING, R, 31
Greece Athens holds sway over all G.    THEMISTOCLES, 1
  G. might still be free    BYRON, 6TH BARON, 24
  The isles of G.    BYRON, 6TH BARON, 23
greedy be not g. to add money to money    BIBLE: TOBIT, 1
Greek I . . . impress upon you the study of G. literature
   GAISFORD, T, 1
  it was G. to me    SHAKESPEARE, W, 108
  neither Jew nor G.    BIBLE: GALATIANS, 2
  Nobody can say a word against G.    SHAW, G, 13
  small Latin and less G.    JONSON, B, 8
  the intrigue of a G. of the lower empire
   DISRAELI, 1ST EARL OF BEACONSFIELD, 30
  The word is half G. and half Latin    SCOTT, C, 2
  We were taught . . . Latin and G.    WELLS, H, 14
Greeks G. Had a Word    AKINS, Z, 1
  G. seek after wisdom    BIBLE: I CORINTHIANS, 1
  I fear the G. even when they bring gifts.    VIRGIL, 6
  The Romans and G. found everything human    LAWRENCE, D, 4
  To the G. the Muse gave native wit    HORACE, 1
  uncertainty: a state unknown to the G.    BORGES, J, 1
  where the G. had modesty, we have cant    PEACOCK, T, 2
  which came first, the G. or the Romans
   DISRAELI, 1ST EARL OF BEACONSFIELD, 36
green a g. thought in a g. shade    MARVELL, A, 2
  for the wearin' o' the G.    ANONYMOUS, 46
  G. grow the rashes O    BURNS, R, 9
  in the morning it is g.    PSALMS, 55
  I was g. in judgment    SHAKESPEARE, W, 7
  There is a g. hill far away    ALEXANDER, C, 2
  tree of life is g.    GOETHE, J, 2
  When the g. woods laugh    BLAKE, W, 45
green chartreuse religious system that produced G.    SAKI, 17
green-ey'd jealousy . . . g. monster    SHAKESPEARE, W, 224
Greenland From G.'s icy mountains    HEBER, R, 1
green-rob'd g. senators of mighty woods    KEATS, J, 16
Greensleeves G. was all my joy    ANONYMOUS, 22
greenwood Under the g. tree    SHAKESPEARE, W, 21
greetings g. where no kindness is    WORDSWORTH, W, 12
  perhaps the g. are intended for me    BEETHOVEN, L, 3
grenadier The healthy bones of a single Pomeranian g.
   BISMARCK, PRINCE VON, 5
  With a tow, . . . row for the British G.    ANONYMOUS, 73
grew Three years she g.    WORDSWORTH, W, 64
grey G. hairs are death's blossoms    PROVERBS, 183
  theory is all g.    GOETHE, J, 2
  There is only one cure for g. hair. . . . the guillotine
   WODEHOUSE, SIR P, 14
  well-beloved's hair has threads of g.    YEATS, W, 12
grief A g. too much to be told    VIRGIL, 5
  calms one's g. by recounting it    CORNEILLE, P, 5
  G. and disappointment give rise to anger    HUME, D, 7
  G. has turned her fair    WILDE, O, 71
  heart which g. hath cankered / . . . remedy – the Tankard
   CALVERLEY, C, 1
  in much wisdom is much g.    BIBLE: ECCLESIASTES, 5
  Should be past g.    SHAKESPEARE, W, 300
grievances redress of the g. of the vanquished    CHURCHILL, SIR W, 4
grieve not that I die young    HASTINGS, L, 1
  Men are we, and must g.    WORDSWORTH, W, 56
grill be careful not to look like a mixed g.    COWARD, SIR N, 8
grimace the only pianist . . . who did not g.    STRAVINSKY, I, 2
grin All Nature wears one universal g.    FIELDING, H, 14
  ending with the g., which remained some time    CARROLL, L, 5
grind g. the faces of the poor    BIBLE: ISAIAH, 6
  mills of God g. slowly    LOGAU, BARON, 1
  yet they g. exceeding small    LOGAU, BARON, 1

**grinders** Writers, like teeth, are divided into incisors and g.
BAGEHOT, W, 8
**grist** All's g. that comes to the mill PROVERBS, 37
**groan** men sit and hear each other g. KEATS, J, 33
**groans** How alike are the g. of love to those of the dying
LOWRY, M, 2
**Gromyko** the G. of the Labour party HEALEY, D, 3
**grooves** specialists . . . tend to think in g. MORGAN, E, 1
**grope** they g. in the dark BIBLE: JOB, 8
**Groucho** had Marx been G. instead of Karl. BERLIN, I, 1
No, G. is not my real name MARX, G, 24
**group** A g. of closely related persons MACAULAY, DAME R, 3
**grovelled** Whenever he met a great man he g. THACKERAY, W, 10
**groves** And seek for truth in the g. of Academe. HORACE, 24
**grow** some of us never g. out USTINOV, P, 7
They shall g. not old BINYON, L, 3
Whoever could make two ears of corn . . . g. . . . where only one
grew before SWIFT, J, 6
**grow'd** I 'spect I g.. STOWE, H, 2
**growing** G. old is like being increasingly penalized POWELL, A, 6
Say I'm g. old, but add, /Jenny kissed me HUNT, L, 4
**grown** Boys . . . are unwholesome companions for g. people
LAMB, C, 7
one of the few English novels for g. people WOOLF, V, 2
**grows** Nothing g. well in the shade BRANCUSI, C, 1
**growth** as short a Spring; /As quick a g. to meet decay
HERRICK, R, 4
G. is a greater mystery than death MAILER, N, 1
the impalpable elations and apprehensions of g. MAILER, N, 1
**grub** it is poor g., poor pay, and easy work LONDON, J, 1
**grumbling** the muttering grew to a g. BROWNING, R, 41
**gruntled** he was far from being g. WODEHOUSE, SIR P, 3
**guarantee** No one can g. success in war CHURCHILL, SIR W, 20
**guard** That g. our native seas CAMPBELL, T, 6
**guardian** As g. of His Majesty's conscience THURLOW, BARON, 2
**guards** Up, G., and at 'em WELLINGTON, DUKE OF, 15
Who is to guard the g. themselves JUVENAL, 5
**gudeman** Robin Gray, he was g. to me BARNARD, A, 1
**guerre** ce n'est pas la g. BOSQUET, P, 1
**guerrilla** The g. fights the war of the flea TABER, R, 1
The g. wins if he does not lose KISSINGER, H, 1
**guest** A free-loader is a confirmed g. RUNYON, D, 8
Earth, receive an honoured g. AUDEN, W, 15
The g. who outstays PROVERBS, 397
**guests** the g. must be chosen as carefully as the wine SAKI, 1
**guide** Everyman, I will go with thee, and be thy g. ANONYMOUS, 17
I have only a faint g. DIDEROT, D, 1
**guiding** little onward lend thy g. hand MILTON, J, 51
**guillotine** There is only one cure for grey hair. . . . the g.
WODEHOUSE, SIR P, 14
**guilt** I have no sense of g. PANKHURST, E, 3
Let other pens dwell on g. and misery AUSTEN, J, 10
Life without industry is g. RUSKIN, J, 2
put on a dress of g. MCGOUGH, R, 1
**guiltless** Whose g. heart is free CAMPION, T, 3
**guilty** g. of Noel Cowardice DE VRIES, P, 3
It is quite gratifying to feel g. ARENDT, H, 2
Let no g. man escape GRANT, U, 5
ten g. persons escape than one innocent suffer BLACKSTONE, SIR W, 5
tremble like a g. thing surprised WORDSWORTH, W, 29
**guinea** a round disc of fire somewhat like a g. BLAKE, W, 10
I would not give half a g. to live under one form of government
JOHNSON, S, 80
there go two-and-forty sixpences . . . to one g. JOHNSON, S, 31
**guineas** I have only five g. in my pocket
PETERBOROUGH, 3RD EARL OF, 1
**gulphs** whelm'd in deeper g. than he COWPER, W, 4
**gun** it is necessary to take up the g. MAO TSE-TUNG, 2
The difference between a g. and a tree POUND, E, 8
we have got /The Maxim G., and they have not BELLOC, H, 10
**gunfire** Thanks to the movies, g. has always sounded unreal
USTINOV, P, 1
**Gunga Din** You're a better man than I am, G.! KIPLING, R, 13
**gunpowder** G., Printing, and the Protestant Religion CARLYLE, T, 7
**guns** But it's 'Saviour of 'is country' when the g. KIPLING, R, 27
Elevate them g. a little lower JACKSON, A, 1
G. will make us powerful GOERING, H, 3
**gutless** W. H. Auden, a sort of g. Kipling ORWELL, G, 26
**gutter** We are all in the g. WILDE, O, 38

**gypsies** My mother said that I never should /Play with the g. in
the wood NURSERY RHYMES, 36

**habit** a h. the pleasure of which increases with practise
ADAMS, A, 2
H. is a great deadener BECKETT, S, 6
honour peereth in the meanest h. SHAKESPEARE, W, 272
some h. of which he is deeply ashamed CRISP, Q, 1
**habitation** to airy nothing /A local h. SHAKESPEARE, W, 207
**habits** Curious things, h. CHRISTIE, DAME A, 4
h. that carry them far apart CONFUCIUS, 3
Old h. die hard PROVERBS, 321
**hack** Do not h. me MONMOUTH, DUKE OF, 1
**had** you h. it in you PARKER, D, 27
**hae** Scots, wha h. BURNS, R, 15
**ha-ha** Funny peculiar, or funny h. HAY, I, 1
**hail** All h., the power of Jesus' name PERRONET, E, 1
h. and farewell CATULLUS, G, 3
the flail of the lashing h. SHELLEY, P, 3
**hair** busy driving cabs and cutting h. BURNS, G, 1
if a woman have long h. BIBLE: I CORINTHIANS, 17
part my h. behind ELIOT, T, 13
scant as h. /In leprosy BROWNING, R, 13
Take a h. of the dog PROVERBS, 373
there shall not one h. of his head fall BIBLE: I SAMUEL, 4
To Crystal, h. was the most important thing on earth O'BRIEN, E, 1
you have lovely h. CHEKHOV, A, 9
**hairy** Esau . . . a h. man BIBLE: GENESIS, 42
**half** h. a loaf is better than a whole CHESTERTON, G, 36
H. a loaf PROVERBS, 184
I am only h. there when I am ill LAWRENCE, D, 41
I have not told h. of what I saw MARCO POLO, 1
longest h. of your life SOUTHEY, R, 3
One h. . . . . cannot understand . . . the other AUSTEN, J, 1
There is an old saying 'well begun is h. done' KEATS, J, 50
**half-a-dozen** six of one and h. of the other MARRYAT, F, 2
**half-developed** the working-class which, raw and h. ARNOLD, M, 7
**half way** And when they were only h. up, /They were neither up
nor down NURSERY RHYMES, 37
**half-wits** a wit out of two h.. KINNOCK, N, 3
**halitosis** h. of the intellect ICKES, H, 2
**Hall** We met . . . Dr H. in such very deep mourning AUSTEN, J, 28
**hall** one of the sparrows . . . flew . . . through the h. BEDE, 1
**Hallelujah** Here lies my wife, / . . . /H.! ANONYMOUS, 31
**hallowed** The place of justice is a h. place
BACON, 1ST BARON VERULAM, VISCOUNT ST ALBANS, 31
**halt** the whole process has ground to a h. with a 14th Earl
WILSON OF RIEVAULX, BARON, 9
**halters** talk of h. in the hanged man's house CERVANTES, M, 10
**halves** Never do things by h. PROVERBS, 301
**Hamelin** H. Town's in Brunswick BROWNING, R, 39
**hammer** Art is not a mirror . . . but a h. MAYAKOVSKY, V, 1
**Hampden** Some village-H. GRAY, T, 6
**hand** bite the h. that fed them BURKE, E, 17
educate with the head instead of with the h. KEY, E, 3
fingers of a man's h., and wrote BIBLE: DANIEL, 7
h. that signed the treaty bred a fever THOMAS, D, 5
I . . . will cover thee with my h. BIBLE: EXODUS, 31
let my right h. forget her cunning PSALMS, 83
little onward lend thy guiding h. MILTON, J, 51
No, this right h. shall work it all off SCOTT, SIR W, 20
one of those parties which got out of h. BRUCE, L, 2
put your h. into the h. of God HASKINS, M, 1
sweeten this little h. SHAKESPEARE, W, 174
The H. that made us is divine ADDISON, J, 13
The h. that rocks the cradle PROVERBS, 398
the sheep of his h. PSALMS, 62
This h. hath offended CRANMER, T, 1
touch his weaknesses with a delicate h. GOLDSMITH, O, 13
**handbook** have used the Bible as if it was a constable's h.
KINGSLEY, C, 3
**handful** for a h. of silver he left us BROWNING, R, 29
**handicraft** Art is not a h. TOLSTOY, COUNT, 9
**handkerchiefs** There is a ghost /That eats h. MORGENSTERN, C, 1
**handle** I polished up the h. of the big front door GILBERT, SIR W, 12
touch not; taste not; h. not BIBLE: COLOSSIANS, 2
**hands** a two-edged sword in their h. PSALMS, 93
don't raise your h. because I am also nearsighted. AUDEN, W, 26
Farewell, my poor h. RACHMANINOV, S, 1

He forbade me to put off my h. FOX, G. 1
little man wears a shocking bad h. YORK AND ALBANY, DUKE OF, 1
looking for a black h. BOWEN, BARON, 2
My h. and wig will soon be here COWPER, W. 10
Where did you get that h. ROLMAZ, J. 1
**hatched** chickens before they are h. AESOP, 8
count their chickens ere they're h. BUTLER, S. 3
**hatchet** I did it with my little h. WASHINGTON, G. 3
**hate** feel no h. for him RACINE, J. 1
Few . . . can be happy unless they h. RUSSELL, EARL, 27
If you h. a person, you h. . . . yourself HESSE, H. 1
I h. a fellow . . . who does nothing . . . but sit and *growl*
JOHNSON, S. 138
I h. and love CATULLUS, G. 2
I h. everyone equally FIELDS, W. 4
I h. the whole race . . . your professional poets
WELLINGTON, DUKE OF, 8
I love or I h. PICASSO, P. 4
Let them h. ACCIUS, L. 1
not to weep at them, nor to h. them, but to understand them
SPINOZA, B. 5
scarcely h. any one that we know HAZLITT, W. 15
to h. the man you have hurt TACITUS, C. 2
You must h. a Frenchman NELSON, VISCOUNT, 2
hated h. /by every anti-semite /as if I were a Jew
YEVTUSHENKO, Y. 1
h. of all men for my name's sake BIBLE: MATTHEW, 38
I never h. a man enough GABOR, Z. 3
I never saw a brute I h. so BROWNING, R. 14
**hates** Anybody who h. children and dogs FIELDS, W. 3
Everybody h. house-agents WELLS, H. 13
Everybody h. me DE VRIES, P. 8
**hateth** love God, and h. his brother BIBLE: I JOHN, 5
**hating** patriotism which consists in h. all other nations
GASKELL, E. 3
**hatred** a deep burning h. for the Tory Party BEVAN, A. 8
An intellectual h. YEATS, W. 24
Fire – without h. RIVERA, A. 1
h. is . . . the longest pleasure BYRON, 6TH BARON, 30
love . . . looks more like h. than like friendship
ROCHEFOUCAULD, DUC DE LA, 9
**hats** H. divide generally into three classes WHITEHORN, K. 1
**Hatter** 'Not the same thing a bit!' said the H. CARROLL, L. 6
**haunted** e'er beneath a waning moon was h. COLERIDGE, S. 14
**have** To h. and to hold BOOK OF COMMON PRAYER, 15
**haven** the h. where they would be PSALMS, 67
**hay** Make h. while the sun shines PROVERBS, 278
**he** For every h. has got him a she ANONYMOUS, 13
**head** call that thing under your hat a h. HOLBERG, BARON, 1
educate with the h. instead of with the hand KEY, E. 3
God be in my h., /And in my understanding ANONYMOUS, 20
Here comes a chopper to chop off your h. NURSERY RHYMES, 41
If you can keep your h. KIPLING, R. 14
I'll hold my h. so high it'll strike the stars HORACE, 26
in politics there is no heart, only h. NAPOLEON I, 1
it shall bruise thy h. BIBLE: GENESIS, 15
John Baptist's h. in a charger BIBLE: MATTHEW, 46
Lay your sleeping h. AUDEN, W. 18
no matter which way the h. lies RALEIGH, SIR W. 6
Off with his h. CARROLL, L. 9
ought to have his h. examined GOLDWYN, S. 12
Scheherazade . . . a woman saving her h. WYNNE-TYSON, E. 1
shorter by a h. ELIZABETH I, 5
show my h. to the people DANTON, G. 2
there shall not one hair of his h. fall BIBLE: I SAMUEL, 4
the Son of man hath not where to lay his h. BIBLE: MATTHEW, 33
Uneasy lies the h. that wears a crown SHAKESPEARE, W. 88
waters flowed over mine h. BIBLE: LAMENTATIONS, 1
We had shown that anyone who slapped us . . . would get his h.
kicked off KHRUSHCHEV, N. 1
you are like a pin, but without . . . h. or . . . point JERROLD, D. 8
you incessantly stand on your h. CARROLL, L. 3
**head-in-Air** Johnny h. PUDNEY, J. 1
Little Johnny H. HOFFMAN, H. 2
**headmasters** H. have powers CHURCHILL, SIR W. 10
**head of state** the greatest asset a h. can have
WILSON OF RIEVAULX, BARON, 12
**heads** H. I win CROKER, J. 1
Two h. are better than one PROVERBS, 446
**head-waiter** A pompous woman . . . complaining that the h.
SITWELL, DAME E. 4

diplomat . . . is nothing but a h. USTINOV, P. 8
**heal** I will h. me of my grievous wound TENNYSON, BARON, 21
physician, h. thyself BIBLE: LUKE, 14
**healing** the leaves . . . were for the h. of the nations
BIBLE: REVELATIONS, 21
**health** Here's a h. unto his Majesty . . . ANONYMOUS, 35
H. is better than wealth PROVERBS, 187
in sickness and in h. BOOK OF COMMON PRAYER, 15
Only do always in h. what you have often promised to do when
you are sick SIGISMUND, 1
**healthy** h. and wealthy and dead THURBER, J. 5
Nobody is h. in London AUSTEN, J. 2
the h. type that was essentially middle-class FITZGERALD, F. 8
**hear** any of you at the back who do not h. me AUDEN, W. 26
ear begins to h. BRONTE, E. 3
ears, and h. not PSALMS, 71
ears to h., and h. not BIBLE: EZEKIEL, 2
ears to h., let him h. BIBLE: MATTHEW, 40
he that planted the ear, shall he not h. PSALMS, 59
h. with thine ears BIBLE: EZEKIEL, 8
make any man sick to h. her PEPYS, S. 5
one is always sure to h. of it SHERIDAN, R. 1
out of the deep have I called . . . Lord, h. my voice PSALMS, 82
swift to h. BIBLE: JAMES, 3
to-day if ye will h. his voice PSALMS, 62
truth which men prefer not to h. AGAR, H. 1
**heard** I have already h. it RIMSKY-KORSAKOV, N. 1
nor ear h. BIBLE: I CORINTHIANS, 3
**hearsay** to replace X-ray by h. THOMAS, G. 4
**heart** a broken and contrite h. . . . shalt thou not despise
PSALMS, 36
Absence makes the h. grow fonder BAYLY, T. 1
a man after his own h. BIBLE: I SAMUEL, 3
Because my h. is pure TENNYSON, BARON, 68
. . . by want of thought, as well as want of h. HOOD, T. 8
cold untroubled h. of stone CAMPBELL, T. 4
cut to the h. BIBLE: ACTS, 5
Death took him by the h. OWEN, W. 2
first come to pass in the h. of America EISENHOWER, D. 1
God be in my h., /And in my thinking ANONYMOUS, 20
Good-night, Dear H. ANONYMOUS, 104
Great thoughts come from the h. VAUVENARGUES, MARQUIS DE, 1
h. and stomach of a King ELIZABETH I, 8
holiness of the h.'s affections KEATS, J. 46
I am sick at h. SHAKESPEARE, W. 39
If thou didst ever hold me in thy h. SHAKESPEARE, W. 75
I love thee for a h. that's kind DAVIES, W. 4
in politics there is no h., only head NAPOLEON I, 1
let not your h. be troubled BIBLE: JOHN, 34
lonely of h. is withered away YEATS, W. 17
look in thy h. and write SIDNEY, SIR P. 1
Mary . . . pondered them in her h. BIBLE: LUKE, 10
Mother is the dead h. of the family GREER, G. 2
My h. aches KEATS, J. 30
My h. is a lonely hunter MACLEOD, F. 1
my h.'s abhorrence BROWNING, R. 50
my h. shall be /The faithful compass GAY, J. 12
My h. shall be thy garden MEYNELL, A. 1
My h.'s in the Highlands BURNS, R. 13
My h.'s in the Highlands SCOTT, SIR W. 19
Once a woman has given you her h. VANBURGH, SIR J. 5
our h. is not quiet until it rests in Thee AUGUSTINE OF HIPPO, S. 1
She had /A h. . . . too soon made glad BROWNING, R. 33
So the h. be right RALEIGH, SIR W. 6
strings . . . in the human h. DICKENS, C. 1
take heed . . . that your h. be not deceived BIBLE: DEUTERONOMY, 3
Take thy beak from out my h. POE, E. 2
that mighty h. is lying still WORDSWORTH, W. 48
The fire which in the h. resides ARNOLD, M. 27
The h. has its reasons PASCAL, B. 7
The history of every country begins in the h. CATHER, W. 1
The h. that loved her WORDSWORTH, W. 11
The intellect is always fooled by the h.
ROCHEFOUCAULD, DUC DE LA, 15
Their h.'s in the right place MAUGHAM, W. 21
them which are true of h. PSALMS, 4
There is a road from the eye to the h. CHESTERTON, G. 6
the waters of the h. /Push in their tides THOMAS, D. 8
The way to a man's h. is through his stomach FERN, F. 1
those that are broken in h. PSALMS, 91
to lose your h.'s desire SHAW, G. 22

fit country for h. to live in LLOYD GEORGE, EARL OF DWYFOR, 6
speed glum h. . . . to death SASSOON, S, 1
Unhappy the land that has no h. BRECHT, B, 2
heroic human beings are h. ORWELL, G, 6
hesitate A leader who doesn't h. . . . is not fit to be a leader
MEIR, G, 1
hesitates A science which h. to forget WHITEHEAD, A, 5
He who h. is lost PROVERBS, 199
Hesperus the schooner H. LONGFELLOW, H, 16
heterodoxy h. is another man's doxy WARBURTON, W, 1
H. or Thy-doxy CARLYLE, T, 15
hewers h. of wood BIBLE: JOSHUA, 3
Hickory H., dickory, dock NURSERY RHYMES, 15
hidden Nature is often h.
BACON, 1ST BARON VERULAM, VISCOUNT ST ALBANS, 36
hide He can run, but he can't h. LOUIS, J, 1
h. me under the shadow of thy wings PSALMS, 6
I have a big house – and I h. a lot URE, M, 1
Robes and furr'd gowns h. all SHAKESPEARE, W, 147
hideous less h. than explanations. LEWIS, D, 1
hidest a God that h. thyself BIBLE: ISAIAH, 30
hiding man who looks you . . . in the eye . . . h. something
FADIMAN, C, 2
High She's the Broad and I'm the H. SPRING-RICE, SIR C, 1
high civil fury first grew h. BUTLER, S, 1
to put off my hat to . . . h. or low FOX, G, 1
up in the h. numbers KEYNES, BARON, 10
ye'll tak' the h. road ANONYMOUS, 67
highbrow What is a h. WALLACE, E, 2
higher the rock that is h. than I PSALMS, 41
highest h. type of human nature SPENCER, H, 1
Highland Yon solitary H. lass WORDSWORTH, W, 45
Highlandman taking the breeks aff a wild H. SCOTT, SIR W, 2
Highlands My heart's in the H. BURNS, R, 13
My heart's in the H. SCOTT, SIR W, 19
Ye H. and ye Lawlands ANONYMOUS, 109
high marks I had braces on my teeth and got h. MACDONALD, B, 1
Highness His Royal H. . . . prides himself upon . . . the excellent
harvest SHERIDAN, R, 11
highwayman the h. came riding NOYES, A, 1
high-water h. mark of my youth THURBER, J, 8
hill Mahomet will go to the h.
BACON, 1ST BARON VERULAM, VISCOUNT ST ALBANS, 14
There is a green h. far away ALEXANDER, C, 2
they call you . . . from the h. ARNOLD, M, 32
thou . . . hast made my h. so strong PSALMS, 19
Tonight the American flag floats from yonder h. STARK, J, 1
hills a fine thing to be out on the h. alone KILVERT, F, 2
her foundations are upon the holy h. PSALMS, 53
I will lift up mine eyes unto the h. PSALMS, 75
Over the h. and far away GAY, J, 3
the little h. like young sheep PSALMS, 70
What are those blue remembered h. HOUSMAN, A, 13
Him he could not avoid making H. set the world in motion
PASCAL, B, 5
Himself He would kill H. DUMAS, FILS, 1
himself ever written out of reputation but by h. BENTLEY, R, 2
Every man for h., and the devil PROVERBS, 138
gesture by the individual to h. GALBRAITH, J, 8
Hind Here lies the body of Richard H. ANONYMOUS, 33
hinder men that . . . h. the reception of every work JOHNSON, S, 24
Hinky H., dinky, par-lee-voo ROWLAND, E, 1
hip he smote them h. and thigh BIBLE: JUDGES, 7
Hippocrene the blushful H. KEATS, J, 32
historian A good h. is timeless FENELON, F, 2
A h. is a prophet in reverse SCHLEGEL, F, 1
Great abilities are not requisite for an H. . . . JOHNSON, S, 58
The h. must have . . . some conception of how men . . . behave
FORSTER, E, 1
the profession of h. fits a man for psychological analysis
SARTRE, J, 8
historians H. are like deaf people TOLSTOY, COUNT, 11
h. left blanks in their writings POUND, E, 6
H. tell the story of the past GONCOURT, E, 1
history ancient h., . . . is no more than accepted fiction
VOLTAIRE, 12
Austria is Switzerland . . . with h. added MORPURGO, J, 1
deal of h. to produce . . . literature JAMES, H, 3
From today . . . there begins a new epoch in the h. of the world
GOETHE, J, 9

He was . . . a student of h. TAYLOR, A, 6
H. gets thicker TAYLOR, A, 1
h. is . . . a tableau of crimes and misfortunes VOLTAIRE, 15
H. is more or less bunk FORD, H, 1
H. is past politics SEELEY, SIR J, 2
H. is philosophy teaching by examples
DIONYSIUS OF HALICARNASSUS, 1
H. is the essence of . . . biographies CARLYLE, T, 4
H. is . . . the wrong way of living DURRELL, L, 3
H. is too serious MACLEOD, I, 1
h. must be false WALPOLE, 1ST EARL OF ORFORD, 1
h. of the human spirit ARNOLD, M, 20
H. repeats itself PROVERBS, 204
'H.', Stephen said, 'is a nightmare' JOYCE, J, 4
h. . . . the biography of great men CARLYLE, T, 9
h. . . . the register of the . . . misfortunes of mankind GIBBON, E, 6
If men could learn from h. COLERIDGE, S, 21
It is impossible to write ancient h. PEGUY, C, 1
Its h. dates from today WHISTLER, J, 12
Man is a h.-making creature AUDEN, W, 7
more h. than they can consume locally SAKI, 6
no h.; only biography EMERSON, R, 7
one of these is the h. of political power POPPER, SIR K, 3
people . . . never have learned anything from h. HEGEL, G, 1
poetry is . . . more philosophical . . . than h. ARISTOTLE, 5
Political h. is far too criminal . . . to be . . . fit . . . for the young
AUDEN, W, 2
Stratford, . . . suggests powdered h. HALSEY, M, 5
The attitude of the English . . . toward English h. HALSEY, M, 2
the greatest week in the h. of the world NIXON, R, 6
The h. of all . . . society is the h. of class struggles MARX, K, 1
The h. of every country begins in the heart CATHER, W, 1
The most persistent sound . . . through men's h. KOESTLER, A, 4
This was the Angel of H. GOEBBELS, J, 2
trace . . . the disasters of English h. to . . . Wales WAUGH, E, 13
War makes . . . good h. HARDY, T, 2
hit If you would h. the mark LONGFELLOW, H, 5
hither Come h. SHAKESPEARE, W, 21
Hitler every time H. occupies a country MUSSOLINI, B, 2
H. has carried out a revolution on our lines MUSSOLINI, B, 1
H. has missed the bus CHAMBERLAIN, N, 4
H. showed surprising loyalty to Mussolini BULLOCK, BARON, 2
H. was a nuisance. Mussolini was bloody MADARIAGA Y ROGO, S, 2
one purpose, the destruction of H. CHURCHILL, SIR W, 6
The people H. never understood BULLOCK, BARON, 1
tipster who . . . reached H.'s level of accuracy TAYLOR, A, 5
hobbit In a hole in the ground there lived a h. TOLKIEN, J, 1
hobby-horse So long as a man rides his h. STERNE, L, 5
hobgoblin h. of little minds, · EMERSON, R, 13
hog Rule all England under a h. COLLINGBOURNE, W, 1
hoist H. your sail PROVERBS, 205
hold h. fast that which is good BIBLE: 1 THESSALONIANS, 3
h. your tongue and let me love DONNE, J, 7
To have and to h. BOOK OF COMMON PRAYER, 15
When every . . . thing you h. /Is made of silver, or of gold
GILBERT, SIR W, 5
holder office sanctifies the h. ACTON, 1ST BARON, 2
holders H. of one position, wrong for years AUDEN, W, 23
hole A h. is the accident . . . a darn is . . . poverty SHUTER, E, 1
if you knows of a better h. BAIRNSFATHER, B, 1
In a h. in the ground there lived a hobbit TOLKIEN, J, 1
smallest h. . . . man can hide his head in CHESTERTON, G, 27
What happens to the h. when the cheese is gone BRECHT, B, 8
holiday steamers the little h. made an excursion to hell
PRIESTLEY, J, 8
holier h. than thou BIBLE: ISAIAH, 36
holiness put off H. BLAKE, W, 15
the h. of the heart's affections KEATS, J, 46
Holland H. . . . lies so low they're only saved by being dammed
HOOD, T, 13
hollow We are the h. men ELIOT, T, 7
within the h. crown SHAKESPEARE, W, 239
holly The h. and the ivy ANONYMOUS, 81
The h. bears the crown ANONYMOUS, 81
Hollywood In H., if you don't have happiness REED, R, 1
I should not have been invited to H. CHANDLER, R, 5
the attitude of a H. director toward love HALSEY, M, 2
holy everything that lives is h. BLAKE, W, 1
h., h., h., is the Lord of hosts BIBLE: ISAIAH, 4
H., h., h., Lord God Almighty HEBER, R, 3
the H. Roman Empire was neither h. VOLTAIRE, 11

| | |
|---|---|
| Holy Thursday 'Twas on a H. | BLAKE, W, 43 |
| home against books the H. Secretary is | WAUGH, E, 39 |
| Charity begins at h. | BROWNE, SIR T, 8 |
| Comin' for to carry me h. | ANONYMOUS, 76 |
| eaten me out of house and h. | SHAKESPEARE, W, 86 |
| entertained . . . by people you wouldn't have in your h. | FROST, D, 1 |
| Father, . . . come h. with me now | WORK, H, 1 |
| for de old folks at h. | FOSTER, S, 3 |
| For h. is best | TUSSER, T, 4 |
| For the old Kentucky H. far away | FOSTER, S, 2 |
| give me a h. where the buffalo roam | HIGLEY, B, 1 |
| h. his footsteps he hath turn'd | SCOTT, SIR W, 6 |
| H. is heaven | NASH, O, 5 |
| H. is h. | CLARKE, J, 1 |
| H. is h., though it be | PROVERBS, 206 |
| H. is the sailor, h. from sea | STEVENSON, R, 10 |
| H. is where | PROVERBS, 207 |
| H. of lost causes | ARNOLD, M, 11 |
| H. . . . where . . . they have to take you in | FROST, R, 3 |
| I can get all that at h. | COOK, P, 2 |
| Many a man who thinks to found a h. | DOUGLAS, N, 3 |
| no h. . . . save in Paris | NIETZSCHE, F, 6 |
| Pleasure never is at h. | KEATS, J, 12 |
| She's leaving h. | LENNON, J, 11 |
| The Life and Soul, the man who will never go h. | WHITEHORN, K, 3 |
| there's no place like h. | PAYNE, J, 1 |
| till the cow comes h. | BEAUMONT, F, 12 |
| we come /From God, who is our h. | WORDSWORTH, W, 23 |
| What's the good of a h. | GROSSMITH, G, 1 |
| home-keeping h. youth | SHAKESPEARE, W, 297 |
| homely A h. face . . . aided many wòmen heavenward | ANTRIM, M, 1 |
| be never so h. | CLARKE, J, 1 |
| h. wits | SHAKESPEARE, W, 297 |
| Homer Cicero /And . . . H. were /Mad as the mist and snow | YEATS, W, 18 |
| even excellent H. nods. | HORACE, 9 |
| Mr Gladstone read H. for fun | CHURCHILL, SIR W, 11 |
| Seven cities warr'd for H., being dead | HEYWOOD, T, 1 |
| The author of that poem is either H. | HUXLEY, A, 33 |
| homes go back to thy stately h. of England | LAWRENCE, D, 16 |
| the Stately H. of England | COWARD, SIR N, 11 |
| home-sickness In h. you must keep moving | STACPOOLE, H, 1 |
| homo ecce h. | BIBLE: JOHN, 47 |
| The 'h.' is the legitimate child | LEWIS, W, 4 |
| homos one of the stately h. of England | CRISP, Q, 7 |
| homosexuals h. . . . set out to win the love of a 'real' man | CRISP, Q, 9 |
| honest An h. broker | BISMARCK, PRINCE VON, 6 |
| An h. God | INGERSOLL, R, 1 |
| an h. man sent to lie abroad for . . . his country | WOTTON, SIR H, 3 |
| An h. man's word | PROVERBS, 53 |
| give me six lines . . . by the most h. man | RICHELIEU, CARDINAL DE, 1 |
| I am as h. as any man living | SHAKESPEARE, W, 213 |
| It's better to be quotable than . . . h. | STOPPARD, T, 12 |
| not an h. man | WHATELY, R, 2 |
| She was poor but she was h. | ANONYMOUS, 71 |
| Though I am not naturally h. | SHAKESPEARE, W, 304 |
| Though I be poor, I'm h. | MIDDLETON, T, 1 |
| honestly If possible h., if not, somehow, make money. | HORACE, 15 |
| honesty H. is the best policy | WHATELY, R, 2 |
| make your children capable of h. is the beginning of education. | RUSKIN, J, 10 |
| Philosophers never balance between profit and h. | HUME, D, 8 |
| honey a land flowing with milk and h. | BIBLE: EXODUS, 6 |
| a land of oil olive, and h. | BIBLE: DEUTERONOMY, 2 |
| gather h. all the day | WATTS, I, 2 |
| h. still for tea | BROOKE, R, 3 |
| They took some h., and plenty of money | LEAR, E, 8 |
| what is sweeter than h. | BIBLE: JUDGES, 6 |
| honey'd the h. middle of the night. | KEATS, J, 6 |
| honey-dew on h. hath fed | COLERIDGE, S, 15 |
| honour All is lost save h. | FRANCIS I, 1 |
| a prophet is not without h. | BIBLE: MATTHEW, 45 |
| Brothers all /In h. | WORDSWORTH, W, 34 |
| h. all men | BIBLE: I PETER, 3 |
| His h. rooted in dishonour | TENNYSON, BARON, 13 |
| H. pricks me on | SHAKESPEARE, W, 80 |
| h. sinks where commerce long prevails | GOLDSMITH, O, 21 |
| h. thy father and thy mother | BIBLE: EXODUS, 20 |

| | |
|---|---|
| if I accepted the h. . . . I would not answer | FARADAY, M, 1 |
| Let us h. if we can | AUDEN, W, 10 |
| man being in h. hath no understanding | PSALMS, 33 |
| only h. and life have been spared | FRANCIS I, 1 |
| peace I hope with h. | DISRAELI, 1ST EARL OF BEACONSFIELD, 28 |
| So h. peereth in the meanest habit | SHAKESPEARE, W, 272 |
| That chastity of h. | BURKE, E, 8 |
| There is h. among thieves | PROVERBS, 408 |
| To h. we call you | GARRICK, D, 2 |
| Wealth has never been a sufficient source of h. | GALBRAITH, J, 2 |
| we're fighting for this woman's h. | MARX, G, 9 |
| honourable His designs were strictly h. | FIELDING, H, 12 |
| honoured h. in their generations | BIBLE: ECCLESIASTICUS, 15 |
| hoof I see many h.-marks going in | AESOP, 6 |
| hook canst thou draw out leviathan with an h. | BIBLE: JOB, 20 |
| hooligan Even the H. was probably invented in China | SAKI, 18 |
| Hoorah Henry He is without strict doubt a H. | RUNYON, D, 9 |
| hoo-ray H. and up she rises | ANONYMOUS, 105 |
| hope Abandon h., all ye who enter here | DANTE, A, 1 |
| a faint h. that he will die | EMERSON, R, 1 |
| And what was dead was H. | WILDE, O, 4 |
| H. for the best | PROVERBS, 209 |
| h. is . . . the dream of those that wake | PRIOR, M, 2 |
| H. is the power of being cheerful | CHESTERTON, G, 18 |
| H. may vanish, but can die not | SHELLEY, P, 6 |
| H. springs eternal in the human breast | POPE, A, 30 |
| I do not h. to turn | ELIOT, T, 1 |
| Land of H. and Glory | BENSON, A, 1 |
| no other medicine but only h. | SHAKESPEARE, W, 182 |
| Not to h. for things to last for ever, is what the year teaches | HORACE, 41 |
| now abideth faith, h., charity | BIBLE: I CORINTHIANS, 18 |
| Our h. for years to come | WATTS, I, 6 |
| the distinction between h. and expectation | ILLICH, I, 3 |
| The triumph of h. over experience | JOHNSON, S, 78 |
| The Worldly H. men set their Hearts upon | FITZGERALD, E, 7 |
| unconquerable h. | ARNOLD, M, 36 |
| What a strange thing is memory, and h. | GRANDMA MOSES, 1 |
| While there is life, there's h. | GAY, J, 7 |
| Without all h. of day | MILTON, J, 53 |
| hopeless that controversy is either superfluous or h. | NEWMAN, CARDINAL, 6 |
| hopes enough for fifty h. and fears | BROWNING, R, 7 |
| Life's short span forbids us to enter on far-reaching h. | HORACE, 28 |
| My h. no more must change their name | WORDSWORTH, W, 29 |
| Horatius brave H. | MACAULAY, BARON, 11 |
| horde Society is now one polish'd h. | BYRON, 6TH BARON, 31 |
| horizontal we value none /But the h. one | AUDEN, W, 10 |
| Homer Little Jack H. /Sat in the corner | NURSERY RHYMES, 30 |
| Hornie Auld H., Satan, Nick | BURNS, R, 1 |
| horns When you take the bull by the h. . . . | RIDGE, W, 1 |
| Horny-handed h. sons of toil | KEARNEY, D, 1 |
| Horowitz Vladimir H. | SCHNABEL, A, 4 |
| horrible A strange, h. business, . . . good enough for Shakespeare's day | VICTORIA, 6 |
| horrid are they all h. | AUSTEN, J, 11 |
| horror I have a h. of sunsets | PROUST, M, 15 |
| mere existence is swollen to a h. | LAWRENCE, D, 21 |
| The h.! The h. | CONRAD, J, 2 |
| The thought of dentists gave him just the same sick h. | WELLS, H, 6 |
| horrors I have supp'd full with h. | SHAKESPEARE, W, 176 |
| horse A fly, Sir, may sting a stately h. | JOHNSON, S, 46 |
| a pale h. | BIBLE: REVELATIONS, 6 |
| A Protestant with a h. | BEHAN, B, 1 |
| Do not trust the h., Trojans | VIRGIL, 2 |
| good deal of physical courage to ride a h. | LEACOCK, S, 8 |
| Go together like a h. and carriage | CAHN, S, 1 |
| I feel as a h. must feel | DEGAS, E, 1 |
| I know two things about the h. | ANONYMOUS, 44 |
| like to be a h. | ELIZABETH II, 1 |
| my kingdom for a h. | SHAKESPEARE, W, 243 |
| nobody has any business to go around looking like a h. | PARKER, D, 3 |
| Ride a cock-h. to Banbury Cross | NURSERY RHYMES, 46 |
| the h. and his rider hath he thrown into the sea | BIBLE: EXODUS, 16 |
| To confess that you are totally Ignorant about the H. | SELLAR, W, 2 |
| victory under the belly of a Cossack's h. | TROTSKY, L, 4 |
| You can lead a h. to water | PROVERBS, 470 |
| You may have my husband, but not my h. | LAWRENCE, D, 23 |

**idling** It is impossible to enjoy i. JEROME, J. 5
**idol** one-eyed yellow i. to the north of Khatmandu HAYES, J. 1
**Idolatry** There is no i. in the Mass. JOHNSON, S. 74
**idols** little children, keep yourselves from i. BIBLE: 1 JOHN, 6
their i. are silver and gold PSALMS, 71
**If** I. you can keep your head KIPLING, R. 14
much virtue in I. SHAKESPEARE, W. 32
**ifs** If i. and ans PROVERBS, 214
**Ignominious** History is full of i. getaways by the great
ORWELL, G. 31
**Ignorance** From i. our comfort flows PRIOR, M. 3
I. is like a delicate exotic fruit WILDE, O. 22
I. is Strength ORWELL, G. 16
I., madam, pure i. JOHNSON, S. 50
I. of the law excuses SELDEN, J. 3
journalism. . . . keeps us in touch with the i. of the community
WILDE, O. 12
Lawyers are the only persons in whom i. . . . is not punished
BENTHAM, J. 2
man's i. of the gods BUTLER, S. 7
no sin but i. MARLOWE, C. 9
than keeping women in a state of i. KNOX, V. 1
where i. is bliss GRAY, T. 10
Your i. cramps my conversation HOPE, A. 7
**Ignorant** Let no one i. of mathematics enter here PLATO, 6
The i. man always adores LOMBROSO, C. 1
the opinionated, the i., and the boorish ARISTOTLE, 3
To confess that you are totally I. about the Horse SELLAR, W. 2
what may follow it, or what preceded it, we are absolutely i.
BEDE, 1
**Ill** Cannot be i.; cannot be good SHAKESPEARE, W. 159
I am only half there when I am i. LAWRENCE, D. 41
If . . . someone is speaking i. of you EPICTETUS, 1
no hint throughout the universe /Of good or i. THOMSON, J. 3
woman colour'd i. SHAKESPEARE, W. 269
**Illegal** collect legal taxes from i. money CAPONE, A. 3
the things I really like . . . are either immoral, i., or fattening
WOOLLCOTT, A. 4
**Illegitimate** There are no i. children YANKWICH, L. 1
**Ill-health** Cynicism is humour in i. WELLS, H. 15
**Illiteracy** The ratio of literacy to i. MORAVIA, A. 1
**Illiterate** I. him . . . from your memory SHERIDAN, R. 3
**Illness** I. is the night-side of life SONTAG, S. 1
**Illogical** Faith . . . an i. belief in . . . the improbable MENCKEN, H. 14
**Ills** sharp remedy . . . for all i. RALEIGH, SIR W. 5
**Ill-spent** sign of an i. youth SPENCER, H. 2
**Illumine** What in me is dark /I. MILTON, J. 26
**Illusion** it can contain nothing but sophistry and i. HUME, D. 2
Religion is an i. FREUD, S. 3
The House of Lords, an i. STOPPARD, T. 4
visible universe was an i. BORGES, J. 2
**Illusions** It's life's i. I recall MITCHELL, J. 1
**Image** any graven i. BIBLE: EXODUS, 20
A photograph is not only an i. SONTAG, S. 2
fall down and worship the golden i. BIBLE: DANIEL, 2
If God made us in His i. VOLTAIRE, 14
make man in our own i. BIBLE: GENESIS, 6
Why should I consent to the perpetuation of the i. of this i.
PLOTINUS, 1
**Imaginary** Happiness is an i. condition SZASZ, T. 5
**Imagination** A lady's i. is very rapid AUSTEN, J. 17
Art is ruled . . . by the i. CROCE, B. 1
I.! . . . I put it first years ago TERRY, DAME E. 2
indebted to his . . . i. for his facts SHERIDAN, R. 18
I. without skill gives us modern art STOPPARD, T. 1
not an ideal of reason but of i. KANT, I. 3
of i. all compact SHAKESPEARE, W. 206
The primary i. COLERIDGE, S. 3
truth of i. KEATS, J. 46
**Imagine** never so happy . . . as we i. ROCHEFOUCAULD, DUC DE LA, 6
**Imagined** What is now proved was . . . i. BLAKE, W. 22
**Imagining** How reconcile this world . . . with . . . my i. KELLER, H. 3
**Imitate** An original writer is . . . one whom nobody can i.
CHATEAUBRIAND, F. 1
I i. the Saviour HUXLEY, A. 3
never failed to i. BALDWIN, J. 4
obliged to i. himself, and to repeat REYNOLDS, SIR J. 3
people . . . usually i. each other HOFFER, E. 1
**Imitates** Photography can never grow up if it i. ABBOTT, B. 1
**Imitation** I. is the sincerest of flattery COLTON, C. 3
Man . . . is an i. OUSPENSKY, P. 1

**Immaculate Conception** the I. was spontaneous combustion
PARKER, D. 18
**Immanuel** call his name I. BIBLE: ISAIAH, 10
**immature** the i. man . . . wants to die nobly for a cause
STEKEL, W. 1
**Immaturity** common symptom of i. WHARTON, E. 3
the executive expression of human i. BRITTAIN, V. 3
**immoral** moral or an i. book WILDE, O. 41
the things I really like . . . are either i., illegal, or fattening
WOOLLCOTT, A. 4
worse than i. ACHESON, D. 2
**Immorality** the most rigid code of i. BRADBURY, M. 2
**Immortal** I have lost the i. part SHAKESPEARE, W. 222
make me i. with a kiss MARLOWE, C. 2
Our souls have sight of that i. sea WORDSWORTH, W. 26
Why are you weeping? Did you imagine that I was i. LOUIS XIV. 7
**Immortality** I . . . want to achieve i. . . . through not dying
ALLEN, W. 10
just ourselves /And I. DICKINSON, E. 1
**Immutable** Few things are as i. GALBRAITH, J. 3
**Impediment** cause, or just i. BOOK OF COMMON PRAYER, 13
**Imperative** This i. is Categorical KANT, I. 2
**Imperfection** i. itself may have its . . . perfect state DE QUINCEY, T. 3
**Imperial** be yourself, i., plain and true BROWNING, R. 5
**Imperialism** i. is the monopoly stage of capitalism LENIN, V. 1
Their Europeanism is . . . i. with an inferiority complex
HEALEY, D. 2
**impersonal** In the philosopher there is nothing whatever i.
NIETZSCHE, F. 13
**impertinent** ask an i. question BRONOWSKI, J. 2
**impetuous** such i. blood WORDSWORTH, W. 42
**importance** Official dignity . . . in inverse ratio to . . . i.
HUXLEY, A. 8
**important** I. Person Play POTTER, S. 4
One doesn't recognize . . . the really i. moments
CHRISTIE, DAME A. 1
the little things are infinitely the most i. DOYLE, SIR A. 4
**Imposed** wish to be i. on, and then are COWPER, W. 18
**Impossibility** a physical and metaphysical i. CARLYLE, T. 1
**Impossible** complete sorrow is as i. TOLSTOY, COUNT, 8
I believe because it is i. TERTULLIAN, Q. 3
It's either easy or i. DALI, S. 1
something is i., he is . . . wrong CLARKE, A. 1
when you have excluded the i. DOYLE, SIR A. 1
**Impotent** an i. people THOMAS, R. 1
**impregnator** the writer . . . is the i. WHITE, E. 2
**Impression** knowledge and wonder . . . is an i. of pleasure
BACON, 1ST BARON VERULAM, VISCOUNT ST ALBANS, 1
**Impressionable** Give me a girl at an i. age SPARK, M. 6
**Impressions** i. . . . lasting as . . . an oar upon the water
CHOPIN, K. 3
**Improbable** an i. fiction SHAKESPEARE, W. 294
Faith . . . an illogical belief in . . . the i. MENCKEN, H. 14
whatever remains, however i., must be the truth DOYLE, SIR A. 1
**improper** I only hope it is not i. GASKELL, E. 2
**Impropriety** I. is the soul of wit MAUGHAM, W. 9
**Improved** enormously i. by death SAKI, 4
**improvement** most schemes of political i. are very laughable
JOHNSON, S. 73
**Impulse** the i. of the moment AUSTEN, J. 19
the need to talk is a primary i. CERVANTES, M. 12
**Impulses** Mistrust first i. TALLEYRAND, 7
**impure** To the Puritan all things are i. LAWRENCE, D. 3
in you had it i. you PARKER, D. 23
**Inactivity** wise and masterly i. MACKINTOSH, SIR J. 1
**Inadequate** Like Brighton pier, . . . i. for getting to France.
KINNOCK, N. 7
**Inartistic** He was unperfect, unfinished, i. JAMES, H. 4
**Inbreeding** an impotent people, /Sick with i. THOMAS, R. 1
**Incest** except i. and folk-dancing BAX, SIR A. 1
**inch** every i. a king SHAKESPEARE, W. 145
Give him an i. PROVERBS, 174
three unhappy women . . . being entertained within an i. of their
lives SOMERVILLE, E. 1
**Inches** They that die by famine die by i. HENRY, M. 2
**Incident** What is i. but the illustration of character JAMES, H. 8
**incisors** Writers, like teeth, are divided into i. and grinders
BAGEHOT, W. 8
**Inclination** A man ought to read just as i. leads him JOHNSON, S. 60
**incoherent** I'm not i. ROSS, H. 2

**irreproachable** compulsory and i. idleness TOLSTOY, COUNT, 5
**irresponsible** better to be i. and right CHURCHILL, SIR W, 59
**Isaac** the God of I. BIBLE: EXODUS, 5
**Iser** of I., rolling rapidly CAMPBELL, T, 2
**Ishmaelites** I. ... will not publicly eat human flesh uncooked in Lent WAUGH, E, 36
**Islam** I. unashamedly came with a sword RUNCIMAN, SIR S, 1
**Island** No man is an I. DONNE, J, 5
**Islands** less known by the British than these selfsame British I. BORROW, G, 1
**isle** this sceptred i. SHAKESPEARE, W, 237
**Isle of Man** Kelly from the I. MURPHY, C, 1
**Isles** The i. of Greece BYRON, 6TH BARON, 23
**Israel** peace upon I. PSALMS, 81
When I. was in Egypt land, /Let my people go ANONYMOUS, 107
**Italian** as sensible as baseball in I. MENCKEN, H, 17
I speak ... I. to women, French to men CHARLES V, 3
**Italians** The I. will laugh at me MUSSOLINI, B, 2
**Italy** A man who has not been in I. JOHNSON, S, 107
I. a paradise for horses BURTON, R, 4
**itch** The i. of disputing will prove the scab of churches WOTTON, SIR H, 2
the i. of literature LOVER, S, 1
**iteration** i. of nuptials CONGREVE, W, 14
**itself** Love seeketh not i. to please BLAKE, W, 34
**ivy** The holly and the i. ANONYMOUS, 81

## J

**jab** Man, ... had been created to j. the life out of Germans. SASSOON, S, 5
**Jack** J. and Jill went up the hill NURSERY RHYMES, 25
J. of all trades PROVERBS, 239
J. Sprat could eat no fat NURSERY RHYMES, 26
Little J. Horner NURSERY RHYMES, 30
the house that J. built NURSERY RHYMES, 62
**jackals** J. piss at their foot FLAUBERT, G, 2
**Jackson** J. standing like a stone wall BEE, B, 1
**Jacob** Talk to him of J.'s ladder JERROLD, D, 4
the God of J. BIBLE: EXODUS, 5
the traffic of J.'s ladder THOMPSON, F, 2
**Jael** J. the wife of Heber BIBLE: JUDGES, 3
**jail** being in a ship is being in a j. JOHNSON, S, 53
**jam** I. today, and men aren't at their most exciting SNOW, BARON, 3
The rule is, j. tomorrow and j. yesterday CARROLL, L, 27
**Jane** if ever I was to have a dozen girls, I'd call 'em all J. WELLS, H, 11
Time's up for Sir John, an' for little Lady J. LAWRENCE, D, 16
**January** dreadful pictures of J. and February; TROLLOPE, A, 6
**Janvier** Generals J. and Février NICHOLAS I, 2
**Japan** There was a young man of J. ANONYMOUS, 94
**Japanese** The J. have perfected good manners THEROUX, P, 1
**jaundiced** with the j. eye TENNYSON, BARON, 48
**jawbone** with the j. of an ass BIBLE: JUDGES, 8
**jaw-jaw** To j. is better than to war-war CHURCHILL, SIR W, 60
**jazz** The basic difference between classical music and j. PREVIN, A, 1
the J. Age ... became less and less an affair of youth FITZGERALD, F, 2
**jealous** a j. God BIBLE: EXODUS, 20
Art is a j. mistress EMERSON, R, 2
**jealousy** j. ... is the green-ey'd monster SHAKESPEARE, W, 224
the ear of j. heareth all things BIBLE: WISDOM, 1
**Jeepers** J. Creepers MERCER, J, 1
**jeering** laughing and j. at everything ... strange PEPYS, S, 3
**jeers** j. at Fate ADAMS, F, 1
**Jeeves** J. coughed one soft, low, gentle cough WODEHOUSE, SIR P, 5
like P. G. Wodehouse dropping J. WAUGH, E, 44
**Jefferson** when Thomas J. dined alone KENNEDY, J, 10
**jelly** Out vile j. SHAKESPEARE, W, 142
**Jenny** J. kissed me when we met HUNT, L, 4
**Jericho** by faith the walls of J. fell down BIBLE: HEBREWS, 3
**Jerusalem** if I forget thee, O J. PSALMS, 83
J. the golden NEALE, J, 3
J. ... the mother of us all BIBLE: GALATIANS, 3
that great city, the holy J. BIBLE: REVELATIONS, 19
the holy city, new J. BIBLE: REVELATIONS, 18
the Lord doth build up J. PSALMS, 91
Till we have built J. BLAKE, W, 31
**jest** a fellow of infinite j. SHAKESPEARE, W, 73
A j.'s prosperity lies in the ear SHAKESPEARE, W, 156

glory, j., and riddle of the world POPE, A, 31
Life is a j. GAY, J, 10
**jesting** j. Pilate BACON, 1ST BARON VERULAM, VISCOUNT ST ALBANS, 56
Gentle J. WESLEY, C, 1
How sweet the name of J. sounds NEWTON, J, 2
If J. Christ were to come to-day CARLYLE, T, 26
J. loves me – this I know WARNER, S, 1
J. was ... a first-rate political economist. SHAW, G, 1
when J. was born in Bethlehem of Judaea BIBLE: MATTHEW, 1
**jeunesse** Si j. savait ESTIENNE, H, 1
**Jew** An American is either a J., or an anti-Semite SARTRE, J, 2
difficult for a J. to be converted HEINE, H, 4
Einstein – the greatest J. since Jesus HALDANE, J, 1
hated ... as if I were a J. YEVTUSHENKO, Y, 1
Hath not a J. eyes SHAKESPEARE, W, 193
I'm a coloured, one-eyed J. DAVIS, S, 2
I'm not really a J.; just J.-ish MILLER, J, 1
I was born of Christian race, And not ... a J. WATTS, I, 4
neither J. nor Greek BIBLE: GALATIANS, 2
no intellectual society can flourish where a J. feels ... uneasy JOHNSON, P, 1
No J. was ever fool enough to turn Christian ZANGWILL, I, 1
Pessimism is a luxury that a J. never can allow himself MEIR, G, 4
**Jewellery** Don't ever wear artistic j. COLETTE, S, 4
j. ... wrecks a woman's reputation COLETTE, S, 4
**jewelry** she did not remember . , . her j. LOOS, A, 4
**jewels** a capital bosom to hang j. upon DICKENS, C, 21
**Jewish** A J. man with parents alive ROTH, P, 2
best that is in the J. blood LAWRENCE, D, 12
a *total solution* of the J. question GOERING, H, 2
**Jew-ish** I'm not really a Jew; just J. MILLER, J, 1
**Jewry** Modern Physics is an instrument of J. TOMASCHEK, R, 1
**Jews** J. require a sign BIBLE: 1 CORINTHIANS, 1
King of the J. BIBLE: MATTHEW, 1
not enough prisons ... in Palestine to hold all the J. MEIR, G, 7
The Irish and the J. have a psychosis BEHAN, B, 7
The J. and Arabs should ... settle their differences AUSTIN, W, 2
the J. bring the unlike into the heart of *every milieu* ZANGWILL, I, 3
the J. have made a contribution to the human condition USTINOV, P, 5
The J. have produced ... Christ, Spinoza, and myself STEIN, G, 5
To choose /The J. EWER, W, 1
**Jezebel** J. ... painted her face BIBLE: II KINGS, 2
**Jill** Jack and J. went up the hill /To fetch a pail of water NURSERY RHYMES, 25
**Jim** Lucky J. AMIS, K, 3
**Jingo** We don't want to fight, but, by j. if we do HUNT, G, 1
**jo** John Anderson my j. BURNS, R, 10
**Joan** greasy J. doth keel the pot SHAKESPEARE, W, 157
**Job** hast thou considered my servant J. BIBLE: J., 1
J. endured everything – until his friends came KIERKEGAARD, S, 1
the Lord answered J. out of the whirlwind BIBLE: J., 16
the Lord blessed the latter end of J. BIBLE: J., 21
**job** Being a husband is a whole-time j. BENNETT, A, 5
If two men on the same j. agree ZANUCK, D, 1
We have finished the j. HAILE SELASSIE, 1
we will finish the j. CHURCHILL, SIR W, 48
**jockey** the ... cup is given to the j. DEGAS, E, 1
**Joe** Poor old J. FOSTER, S, 5
**John** J. Anderson my jo BURNS, R, 10
J. Brown's body HALL, C, 1
Matthew, Mark, Luke and J. ADY, T, 1
Time's up for Sir J., an' for little Lady Jane LAWRENCE, D, 16
**John Brown** Beneath this slab /J. is stowed NASH, O, 6
**Johnny** J. head-in-air PUDNEY, J, 1
J.-the-bright-star PUDNEY, J, 2
J. underground PUDNEY, J, 1
Little J. Head-in-Air HOFFMAN, H, 2
**John Peel** D'ye ken J. GRAVES, J, 1
**Johnson** Dr J.'s sayings PEMBROKE, 10TH EARL OF, 1
That great Cham of literature, Samuel J. SMOLLETT, T, 6
There is no arguing with J. GOLDSMITH, O, 29
**join** He's gone to j. the majority PETRONIUS ARBITER, 2
will you j. the dance CARROLL, L, 14
**joined** what ... God hath j. together, let not man put asunder BIBLE: MATTHEW, 56
**joke** A j.'s a very serious thing CHURCHILL, C, 3
a j. with a double meaning BARKER, R, 1
A rich man's j. is always funny BROWN, T, 1
good deed to forget a poor j. BRACKEN, 1ST VISCOUNT, 1

**kick** every ass thinks he may k. at him    PARR, S. 1
  if I were under water I would scarcely k.    KEATS, J. 55
  k. you out, but . . . never let you down    WAUGH, E. 6
  to k. against the pricks    BIBLE: ACTS, 6
**kicked** anyone who slapped us . . . would get his head k. off
   KHRUSHCHEV, N. 1
  he had known many k. downstairs,    BURNET, G. 1
  he had known many k. down stairs    HALIFAX, MARQUIS OF, 9
  Saint Preux never k. the fireirons    CARLYLE, J. 2
**kid** a k. in his mother's milk    BIBLE: EXODUS, 23
  Here's looking at you, k.    BOGART, H. 1
**kiddies** k. have crumpled the serviettes    BETJEMAN, SIR J. 3
**kidnapped** my parents finally realize that I'm k.    ALLEN, W. 9
**kids** Cleaning your house while your k. are still growing
   DILLER, P. 1
**kill** a man can't step up and k. a woman    BENCHLEY, R. 1
  churchmen fain would k. their church    TENNYSON, BARON, 55
  good to k. an admiral    VOLTAIRE, 2
  He would k. Himself    DUMAS, FILS, 1
  it's a sin to k. a mockingbird    LEE, H. 2
  K. a man, and you are a murderer    ROSTAND, J. 3
  k. a wife with kindness    SHAKESPEARE, W. 271
  K. everyone, and you are a god    ROSTAND, J. 3
  K. not the goose    PROVERBS, 243
  k. the patient    BACON, 1ST BARON VERULAM, VISCOUNT ST ALBANS, 25
  k. us for their sport    SHAKESPEARE, W. 144
  Next week . . . I'll k. myself    RHYS, J. 1
  only k. you once    CARLYLE, T. 28
  The bullet that is to k. me    NAPOLEON I, 6
  The word "revolution" is a word for which you k.    WEIL, S. 2
  they k. you a new way    ROGERS, W. 1
  thou shalt not k.    BIBLE: EXODUS, 20
  To k. a human being    JAMES, H. 5
  When you have to k. a man    CHURCHILL, SIR W. 7
**killed** He must have k. a lot of men    MOLIERE, 5
  I don't mind your being k.    KITCHENER, EARL, 1
**killing** k. for their country    RUSSELL, EARL, 28
  K. /Is the ultimate    MACDIARMID, H. 1
  More ways of k. a cat    KINGSLEY, C. 9
  no difference between . . . k. and making decisions that . . . kill
   MEIR, G. 3
  The man is k. time    LOWELL, R. 1
  To save a man's life against his will is . . . k. him    HORACE, 12
**kills** Time is a great teacher, but . . . k. all its pupils    BERLIOZ, H. 1
  time quietly k. them    BOUCICAULT, D. 1
  Who k. a man k. a reasonable creature    MILTON, J. 3
  Yet each man k. the thing he loves    WILDE, O. 2
**kin** more than k., and less than kind    SHAKESPEARE, W. 40
**kind** a k. parent . . . or a merciless step-mother    PLINY THE ELDER, 2
  being k. /Is all the sad world needs    WILCOX, E. 4
  charity suffereth long, and is k.    BIBLE: I CORINTHIANS, 18
  He was a vicious man, but very k.    JOHNSON, S. 42
  I love thee for a heart that's k.    DAVIES, W. 4
  more than kin, and less than k.    SHAKESPEARE, W. 40
**kindle** the sole purpose of human existence is to k. a light
   JUNG, C. 4
**kindly** sure to be k. spoken of    AUSTEN, J. 4
  the deities so k.    RABELAIS, F. 4
**kindness** a cup o' k. yet    BURNS, R. 3
  full o' th' milk of human k.    SHAKESPEARE, W. 162
  greetings where no k. is    WORDSWORTH, W. 12
  kill a wife with k.    SHAKESPEARE, W. 271
  recompense k. with k.    CONFUCIUS, 5
  set a high value on spontaneous k.    JOHNSON, S. 136
  the k. of strangers    WILLIAMS, T. 5
  unremembered acts /Of k. and of love    WORDSWORTH, W. 7
  Woman Killed with K.    HEYWOOD, T. 2
**kindred** Like k. drops, been mingled    COWPER, W. 26
**king** A constitutional k. must learn to stoop    LEOPOLD II, 1
  a dainty dish, /To set before the k.    NURSERY RHYMES, 52
  a great k. above all gods    PSALMS, 60
  A k. is a thing    SELDEN, J. 1
  a k. may make a nobleman    BURKE, E. 22
  A k. of shreds and patches    SHAKESPEARE, W. 69
  All the k.'s horses    NURSERY RHYMES, 18
  a new k. over Egypt    BIBLE: EXODUS, 1
  A pious man . . . would be an atheist if the k. were
   LA BRUYERE, J. 1
  Authority forgets a dying k.    TENNYSON, BARON, 17
  A worse k. never left a realm undone    BYRON, 6TH BARON, 40

better . . . a poor and a wise child than an old and foolish k.
   BIBLE: ECCLESIASTES, 12
  but the K. of England cannot enter
   PITT THE ELDER, 1ST EARL OF CHATHAM, 1
  curse not the k., no not in thy thought    BIBLE: ECCLESIASTES, 22
  every inch a k.    SHAKESPEARE, W. 145
  Every subject's duty is the K.'s    SHAKESPEARE, W. 98
  God save our Gracious K.    CAREY, H. 1
  half the zeal I serv'd my K.    SHAKESPEARE, W. 104
  heart and stomach of a K.    ELIZABETH I, 8
  He played the K. as though . . . someone else was about to play
  the ace    FIELD, E. 1
  Here lies our sovereign lord the K.    ROCHESTER, EARL OF, 1
  if I were not k., I should lose my temper    LOUIS XIV, 6
  I'm the k. of the castle    NURSERY RHYMES, 23
  I think the K. is but a man    SHAKESPEARE, W. 97
  k. reigns, but does not govern    ZAMOYSKI, J. 1
  Old K. Cole    NURSERY RHYMES, 38
  . . . rather hew wood than be . . . K. of England    CHARLES X, 1
  such divinity doth hedge a k.    SHAKESPEARE, W. 72
  That whatsoever K. shall reign, /I'll be the Vicar of Bray, Sir
   ANONYMOUS, 48
  the k. can do no wrong    BLACKSTONE, SIR W. 4
  The k. has been very good to me    BOLEYN, A. 1
  The k. never dies    BLACKSTONE, SIR W. 2
  The K. of Spain's daughter    NURSERY RHYMES, 20
  The K. over the Water    ANONYMOUS, 82
  The k. reigns, and the people govern themselves    THIERS, L, 1
  The k. sits in Dunfermline town    ANONYMOUS, 83
  The k. was in his counting-house    NURSERY RHYMES, 52
  The present life of men on earth, O k.    BEDE, 1
  this house will in no circumstances fight for its K. and country
   ANONYMOUS, 77
  wash the balm from an anointed k.    SHAKESPEARE, W. 238
  who is the K. of glory    PSALMS, 16
  would rather hew wood than be a k.    CHARLES X, 1
**kingdom** It is folly . . . to mistake the echo of a . . . coffee-house
  for the . . . k.    SWIFT, J. 3
  my k. for a horse    SHAKESPEARE, W. 243
  No k. has . . . had as many . . . wars as the k. of Christ
   MONTESQUIEU, BARON DE, 5
  remember me when thou comest into thy k.    BIBLE: LUKE, 37
  repent: for the k. of heaven is at hand    BIBLE: MATTHEW, 8
  the k. of God is not in word, but in power    BIBLE: I CORINTHIANS, 4
  the k. of God is within you    BIBLE: LUKE, 31
**kings** Conquering k. their titles take    CHANDLER, J. 1
  Grammar, which can govern even k.    MOLIERE, 9
  If you get the English people into the way of making k.
   MELBOURNE, VISCOUNT, 3
  K. are earth's gods    SHAKESPEARE, W. 231
  K. . . . are just as funny    ROOSEVELT, T. 2
  K. are naturally lovers of low company    BURKE, E. 15
  K. govern by . . . assemblies only when    FOX, C. 4
  Or walk with K.    KIPLING, R. 15
  Pale Death kicks his way . . . into . . . the castles of k.    HORACE, 27
  sad stories of the death of k.    SHAKESPEARE, W. 239
  Such grace had k.    BROWNING, R. 45
  teeming womb of royal k.    SHAKESPEARE, W. 237
  the K. of England, Diamonds, Hearts, Spades and Clubs
   FAROUK I, 1
  This royal throne of k.    SHAKESPEARE, W. 237
  till philosophers become k.    PLATO, 4
  'Twixt k. and tyrants there's this difference    HERRICK, R. 3
**Kinquering** K. Congs their titles take    SPOONER, W. 3
**Kipling** W. H. Auden, a sort of gutless K.    ORWELL, G. 26
   THOMAS, D. 14
**kippers** like two old k. in a box    BIBLE: I SAMUEL, 2
**Kish** that is come into the son of K.    BIBLE: I SAMUEL, 2
**kiss** A k. is just a k.    HUPFELD, H. 1
  a k. without a moustache    CAWEIN, M. 1
  A k. without a moustache    SARTRE, J. 12
  come let us k. and part    DRAYTON, M. 2
  K. me, Hardy    NELSON, VISCOUNT, 4
  make me immortal with a k.    MARLOWE, C. 2
  The coward does it with a k.    WILDE, O. 2
  The k. of sun for pardon    GURNEY, D. 1
  Then come k. me, sweet and twenty    SHAKESPEARE, W. 289
  Without a single k. or a good-bye    PATMORE, C. 2
  you must not k. and tell    CONGREVE, W. 4
**kissed** Being k. by a man who didn't wax his moustache
   KIPLING, R. 24
  hail, master; and k. him    BIBLE: MATTHEW, 82

I k. her little sister    MONTROSE, P, 2
Jenny k. me when we met    HUNT, L, 4
k. her once by the pig-sty    THOMAS, D, 13
K. the girls and made them cry    NURSERY RHYMES, 12
Wherever one wants to be k.    CHANEL, C, 3
**kisses** bread and cheese, and k.    SWIFT, J, 9
remembered k. after death    TENNYSON, BARON, 59
Stolen k. much completer    HUNT, L, 5
**kissing** K. don't last    MEREDITH, G, 2
The President spends most of his time k.    TRUMAN, H, 4
when the k. had to stop    BROWNING, R, 55
**kit-bag** pack up your troubles in your old k.    ASAF, G, 1
**kitchen** can't stand the heat, get out of the k.    TRUMAN, H, 1
the way of all flesh . . . towards the k.    WEBSTER, J, 4
**Kitchener** If K. was not a great man, he was . . . a great poster    ASQUITH, M, 3
**K-K-Katy** K., beautiful Katy    O'HARA, G, 1
**knackery** end up in the Tory k.    KINNOCK, N, 10
**Knave** The K. of Hearts /He stole the tarts    NURSERY RHYMES, 56
**knaves** world is made up . . . of fools and k.    BUCKINGHAM, 2ND DUKE OF, 2
**knee** at the name of Jesus every k. should bow    BIBLE: PHILIPPIANS, 1
**knee-cap** The soul started at the k.    LEWIS, W, 1
**knew** I k. him, Horatio    SHAKESPEARE, W, 73
much righter than one k. at say 17 or 23    POUND, E, 2
**knife** I had a k. and two forks left    RIDGE, W, 2
it keeps them on the k.    ANONYMOUS, 41
last twist of the k.    ELIOT, T, 18
War even to the k.    BYRON, 6TH BARON, 8
**knight** a verray parfit gentil k.    CHAUCER, G, 2
every chance brought out a noble k.    TENNYSON, BARON, 18
K. of the Doleful Countenance    CERVANTES, M, 4
Poor K.! he really had two periods    NABOKOV, V, 4
There came a k. to be their wooer    ANONYMOUS, 97
the shortest k. of the year    RICHARDS, SIR G, 1
what can ail thee, k. at arms    KEATS, J, 17
**knitter** a beautiful little k.    SITWELL, DAME E, 6
**knock** k., and it shall be opened unto you    BIBLE: MATTHEW, 26
K. as you please    POPE, A, 7
k. him down first, and pity him afterwards    JOHNSON, S, 102
Three, four, /K. at the door    NURSERY RHYMES, 40
**knocked** K. 'em in the Old Kent Road    CHEVALIER, A, 2
**know** all /Ye k. on earth    KEATS, J, 25
A really intelligent man feels what other men . . . k.    MONTESQUIEU, BARON DE, 2
be still then, and k. that I am God    PSALMS, 32
Children with Hyacinth's temperament . . . merely k. more    SAKI, 5
for they k. not what they do    BIBLE: LUKE, 36
I do not k. myself    GOETHE, J, 1
I k. myself    FITZGERALD, F, 10
I k. that my redeemer liveth    BIBLE: JOB, 12
I k. what I like    BEERBOHM, SIR M, 16
Jesus I k., and Paul I k.    BIBLE: ACTS, 14
K. then thyself, presume not God to scan    POPE, A, 32
K. thyself    PROVERBS, 246
Mad, bad, and dangerous to k.    LAMB, C, 1
scarcely hate any one that we k.    HAZLITT, W, 15
the only person . . . I should like to k.    WILDE, O, 37
To k. how to say what others only . . . think    CHARLES, E, 1
we k. not where they have laid him    BIBLE: JOHN, 53
What we k. of the past    INGE, W, 1
What you don't k.    PROVERBS, 457
What you don't k. would make a great book    SMITH, S, 6
You k. . . . what you are    HUXLEY, A, 35
**knowed** The clever men at Oxford /Know all that there is to be k.    GRAHAME, K, 2
**knowest** not a word in my tongue, but thou . . . k. it    PSALMS, 84
thou k. all things    BIBLE: JOHN, 59
**knowing** A woman, especially if she have the misfortune of k. anything    AUSTEN, J, 13
**knowledge** a k. of nothing    DICKENS, C, 82
all k. to be my province    BACON, 1ST BARON VERULAM, VISCOUNT ST ALBANS, 67
all our k. is, ourselves to know    POPE, A, 34
an age in which useless k. was . . . important    JOAD, C, 2
an intimate k. of its ugly side    BALDWIN, J, 3
he giveth . . . k. to them that know understanding    BIBLE: DANIEL, 1
I am Master of this college: /What I don't know isn't k.    BEECHING, H, 1

If a little k. is dangerous, where is the man . . . out of danger    HUXLEY, T, 8
if a little k. was a dangerous thing    SHARPE, T, 3
if education is . . . a mere transmission of k.    MONTESSORI, M, 1
Integrity without k. is weak    JOHNSON, S, 27
K. advances by steps    MACAULAY, BARON, 3
k. and wonder . . . is an impression of pleasure    BACON, 1ST BARON VERULAM, VISCOUNT ST ALBANS, 1
K. dwells /In heads replete    COWPER, W, 30
K. is of two kinds    JOHNSON, S, 94
K. is power    PROVERBS, 244
K. is proportionate to being    HUXLEY, A, 35
K. is the mother    PROVERBS, 245
K. itself is power    BACON, 1ST BARON VERULAM, VISCOUNT ST ALBANS, 64
k. puffeth up    BIBLE: I CORINTHIANS, 11
lawyers . . . have taken away the key of k.    BIBLE: LUKE, 24
light of k. in their eyes    SYMONDS, J, 1
never has a man turned so little k. to such great account    ELIOT, T, 2
No, I ask it for the k. of a lifetime    WHISTLER, J, 5
Our k. can only be finite    POPPER, SIR K, 1
Out-topping k.    ARNOLD, M, 38
province of k. to speak    HOLMES, O, 6
such k. is too wonderful . . . for me    PSALMS, 85
the river of k. has too often turned back on itself    JEANS, SIR J, 2
the search for k.    RUSSELL, EARL, 1
the tree of the k. of good and evil    BIBLE: GENESIS, 8
worth a pound of k.    WESLEY, J, 2
**known** apart from the k. and the unknown    PINTER, H, 2
**knows** a woman who k. all . . . that can be taught    CHANEL, C, 1
He that k. little    PROVERBS, 193
He that k. nothing    PROVERBS, 194
he thinks he k. everything    SHAW, G, 16
He who k. only his own side . . . k. little    MILL, J, 2
Only the nose k. . . .    ALI, M, 3
**knuckle-end** k. of England    SMITH, S, 7
**knyf** The smyler with the k.    CHAUCER, G, 11
**Kodak** painted . . . by the great artist K.    MILLIGAN, S, 2
**Kubla** In Xanadu did K. Khan    COLERIDGE, S, 12
**Kurtz** Mistah K. - he dead    CONRAD, J, 3

## L

**Labour** an Independent L. Party    WAUGH, E, 41
England elects a L. Government    ROGERS, W, 2
L. is not fit to govern    CHURCHILL, SIR W, 36
. . . model L. voter . . .    KINNOCK, N, 11
the Gromyko of the L. party    HEALEY, D, 3
**labour** all ye that l. and are heavy laden    BIBLE: MATTHEW, 41
A mountain in l. shouted so loud    LA FONTAINE, J, 6
little effect after much l.    AUSTEN, J, 29
l. of love    BIBLE: I THESSALONIANS, 1
Man . . . can only find relaxation from one . . . l. by taking up another    FRANCE, A, 3
To l. and not ask for any reward    LOYOLA, L, 1
**labourer** the l. is worthy of his hire    BIBLE: LUKE, 19
**labours** absorbs a clay /After his l.    CALVERLEY, C, 2
Children sweeten l.    BACON, 1ST BARON VERULAM, VISCOUNT ST ALBANS, 39
**labyrinthine** I fled Him, down the l. ways    THOMPSON, F, 1
**Lacedaemonians** Go, stranger, and tell the L. that here we lie    LEONIDAS, 1
**lack** l. of power corrupts absolutely    STEVENSON, A, 3
own up to a l. of humour    COLBY, F, 1
therefore can I l. nothing    PSALMS, 12
**lad** many a lightfoot l.    HOUSMAN, A, 14
A ladder behold a l. set up on earth    BIBLE: GENESIS, 43
Now that my l.'s gone    YEATS, W, 4
Talk to him of Jacob's l.    JERROLD, D, 4
the traffic of Jacob's l.    THOMPSON, F, 2
We make ourselves a l. out of our vices    AUGUSTINE OF HIPPO, 5
**ladies** How sweet are looks that l. bend    TENNYSON, BARON, 69
lion among l.    SHAKESPEARE, W, 204
several other old l. of both sexes    DICKENS, C, 20
**lady** Dance, dance, dance little l.    COWARD, SIR N, 4
L. Bountiful    FARQUHAR, G, 2
l. doth protest too much    SHAKESPEARE, W, 67
l. of a certain age    BYRON, 6TH BARON, 29
My fair l.    NURSERY RHYMES, 33

O lang will his L. /Look owre the Castle Downe ANONYMOUS, 109
Put thy shimmy on, L. Chatterley LAWRENCE, D. 16
the L. Is a Tramp HART, L. 2
The l.'s not for turning THATCHER, M. 6
there had been a l. in the case BYRON, 6TH BARON, 26
There is a l. sweet and kind ANONYMOUS, 86
young l. named Bright BULLER, A. 1
lady barber one l. that made good WEST, M. 3
ladybird L., l., /Fly away home NURSERY RHYMES, 27
Lady Nevershit like you was L. WESKER, A. 3
ladyship When your l.'s faith has removed them CHESTERFIELD, 4TH EARL OF, 18
Lafayette L., we are here STANTON, C. 1
laid all the young ladies who attended the Yale promenade dance were l. end to end PARKER, D. 13
l. on with a trowel SHAKESPEARE, W. 18
we know not where they have l. him BIBLE: JOHN, 53
laissez L. faire, l. passer GOURNAY, J. 1
lake An arm /Rose up from . . . the l. TENNYSON, BARON, 16
Marriage may often be a stormy l. PEACOCK, T. 5
sedge is wither'd from the l. KEATS, J. 17
lamb l. as it had been slain BIBLE: REVELATIONS, 4
as a l. to the slaughter BIBLE: ISAIAH, 33
Did he who made the L. make thee BLAKE, W. 38
Little L., who made thee BLAKE, W. 44
l. . . . without blemish BIBLE: EXODUS, 11
Mary had a little l. HALE, S. 1
one little ewe l. BIBLE: II SAMUEL, 3
Pipe a song about a L. BLAKE, W. 40
the l. is the light thereof BIBLE: REVELATIONS, 20
the L. of God BIBLE: JOHN, 3
to make the lion lie down with the l. LAWRENCE, D. 30
washed . . . in the blood of the l. BIBLE: REVELATIONS, 7
worthy is the l. that was slain BIBLE: REVELATIONS, 5
Lambeth doin' the L. walk FURBER, D. 1
lambs feed my l. BIBLE: JOHN, 58
send you forth as l. among wolves BIBLE: LUKE, 19
We're poor little l. KIPLING, R. 9
lament reason to l. /What man has made of man WORDSWORTH, W. 14
lamp my l. burns low and dim ADAMS, F. 2
To keep a l. burning TERESA, 3
lampada vitai l. LUCRETIUS, 3
lamp-post I'm leaning on a l. FORMBY, G. 1
like asking a l. . . . about dogs HAMPTON, C. 5
share a quick pee over a common l. CONNOLLY, C. 12
lamp-posts He uses statistics as a drunken man uses l. LANG, A. 1
lamps l. are going out all over Europe GREY, VISCOUNT , 2
new l. for old ones ARABIAN NIGHTS, 1
the people are forbidden to light l. MAO TSE-TUNG, 8
trimmed their l. BIBLE: MATTHEW, 70
Ye living l. MARVELL, A. 5
Lancelot bold Sir L. TENNYSON, BARON, 41
land a l. flowing with milk and honey BIBLE: EXODUS, 6
a stranger in a strange l. BIBLE: EXODUS, 4
England's green and pleasant l. BLAKE, W. 31
For England's the one l. BROOKE, R. 1
his hands prepared the dry l. PSALMS, 60
I perish through great grief in a strange l. BIBLE: I MACCABEES, 1
L. of Hope and Glory BENSON, A. 1
My native L. BYRON, 6TH BARON, 7
the fat of the l. BIBLE: GENESIS, 52
the l. grows poorer and uglier every day CHEKHOV, A. 7
The l. of my fathers THOMAS, D. 23
There is a happy l. YOUNG, A. 3
They are ill discoverers that think there is no l. BACON, 1ST BARON VERULAM, VISCOUNT ST ALBANS, 3
they have the l. and we have the Bibles GEORGE, D. 1
to the French the empire of the l. RICHTER, J. 1
Unhappy the l. that has no heroes BRECHT, B. 2
We are as near to heaven by sea as by l. GILBERT, SIR H. 1
landlady The l. . . . is a parallelogram LEACOCK, S. 6
landlord Come l., fill the flowing bowl ANONYMOUS, 12
the l. does not intend to repair ADAMS, J. 2
lands in faery l. forlorn KEATS, J. 34
l. where the Jumblies live LEAR, E. 5
landscape half the l. is . . . covered by useless water DOUGLAS, N. 1
When will the l. tire the view DYER, J. 1
lane the little boy /Who lives down the l. NURSERY RHYMES, 4

language Babel; because the Lord did there confound the l. BIBLE: GENESIS, 31
I have laboured to refine our l. to grammatical purity JOHNSON, S. 21
L. grows out of life SULLIVAN, A. 3
L. is not simply a reporting device for experience WHORF, B. 1
L. is only the instrument of science JOHNSON, S. 3
Literature is simply l. charged with meaning POUND, E. 9
The English have no respect for their l. SHAW, G. 34
the theoreticians, whose l. was mathematics BUCK, P. 4
the tower of Babel should have got l. all mixed up VOLTAIRE, 27
the whole earth was of one l. BIBLE: GENESIS, 30
what l. an opera is sung in APPLETON, SIR E. 1
when his l. performs what is required of it without shyness CONNOLLY, C. 5
with l. profane and obscene COWARD, SIR N. 17
with no l. but a cry TENNYSON, BARON, 26
languages l. are the pedigree of nations JOHNSON, S. 156
speaks eighteen l. And she can't say 'No' in any of them PARKER, D. 25
the man who can be silent in several l. HARBORD, J. 1
lap the cool flowery l. of earth ARNOLD, M. 25
lap-dogs when l. breathe their last POPE, A. 48
lards And l. the lean earth as he walks SHAKESPEARE, W. 78
lapidary In l. inscriptions a man is not upon oath JOHNSON, S. 96
large But time is too l. SARTRE, J. 9
lark No l. more blithe than he BICKERSTAFFE, I. 1
To hear the l. . . . singing . . . MILTON, J. 12
larks Four L. and a Wren LEAR, E. 1
lascivious Poetry . . . set to more or less l. music MENCKEN, H. 12
lash rum, sodomy, and the l. CHURCHILL, SIR W. 27
lass On Richmond Hill there lives a l. MACNALLY, L. 1
lasses Come l. and lads, get leave of your dads ANONYMOUS, 13
lassie I love a l. LAUDER, SIR H. 4
last as if it were the l. MARCUS AURELIUS ANTONINUS, 2
Die, . . . the l. thing I shall do PALMERSTON, VISCOUNT, 2
Don't wait for the L. Judgement CAMUS, A. 6
each day that has dawned is your l. HORACE, 18
for the l. time in my life, Your Humble Servant WALPOLE, 4TH EARL OF ORFORD, 1
hoping that it will eat him l. CHURCHILL, SIR W. 62
I hope it will l. WILDE, O. 32
in the l. days . . . the Lord's house shall be established BIBLE: ISAIAH, 34
I shall be the l. to go out ALENÇON, DUCHESSE D', 1
l. day but one LEACOCK, S. 1
L. of the Mohicans COOPER, J. 1
Nice guys finish l. DUROCHER, L. 1
the feeling that I could l. for ever CONRAD, J. 8
the l. shall be first BIBLE: MATTHEW, 59
The l. straw PROVERBS, 399
the l. time that I will take part as an amateur. AUBER, D. 1
there is no l. or first BROWNING, R. 46
we are all on our l. cruise STEVENSON, R. 15
What is it that will l. TENNYSON, BARON, 50
last act l. crowns the play QUARLES, F. 2
Last Judgment 'Tis the L.'s fire BROWNING, R. 12
last words L. . . . name of – Michael Angelo REYNOLDS, SIR J, 4
late Better l. than never PROVERBS, 92
Better never than l. SHAW, G. 49
Never too l. to learn PROVERBS, 307
One doesn't recognize . . . the really important moments . . . until it's too l. CHRISTIE, DAME A. 1
So l. into the night BYRON, 6TH BARON, 38
We have met too l. You are too old . . . JOYCE, J. 10
later It is l. than you think SERVICE, R. 2
Latin A gentleman need not know L. MATTHEWS, B. 1
A silly remark can be made in L. CERVANTES, M. 1
Don't quote L. WELLINGTON, DUKE OF, 22
small L., and less Greek JONSON, B. 8
the Devil knows L. KNOX, R. 2
The word is half Greek and half L. SCOTT, C. 2
We were taught . . . L. and Greek WELLS, H. 14
Latins L. are tenderly enthusiastic DIETRICH, M. 2
laudanum Whipping and abuse are like l. STOWE, H. 3
laugh I make myself l. at everything BEAUMARCHAIS, P. 1
L. and grow fat PROVERBS, 247
L., and the world laughs with you WILCOX, E. 3
L. before breakfast PROVERBS, 248
l. before one is happy LA BRUYERE, J. 8
Make 'em l. READE, C. 1

not to l. at human actions — SPINOZA, B, 5
old man who will not l. — SANTAYANA, G, 2
The Italians will l. at me — MUSSOLINI, B, 2
**laughable** most schemes of political improvement are very l. — JOHNSON, S, 73
**laugh-at-with** Auden was someone you could l. — SPENDER, SIR S, 3
**laughed** Few women care to be l. at — AYCKBOURN, A, 1
No man who has once . . . l. — CARLYLE, T, 21
on which one has not l. — CHAMFORT, N, 2
When the first baby l. — BARRIE, SIR J, 3
**laughing** Happiness is no l. matter — WHATELY, R, 1
l. and jeering at everything . . . strange — PEPYS, S, 3
One cannot be always l. at a man — AUSTEN, J, 22
one may die without ever l. — LA BRUYERE, J, 8
the most fun I ever had without l. — ALLEN, W, 2
. . . to read the death of Little Nell without l. — WILDE, O, 61
**laughter** I said of l., it is mad — BIBLE: ECCLESIASTES, 6
L. is pleasant — PEACOCK, T, 9
L. is the best medicine — PROVERBS, 249
present l. — SHAKESPEARE, W, 289
**Launcelot** Sir L. saw her visage, but he wept not greatly — MALORY, SIR T, 4
**laundries** Land of L. — BETJEMAN, SIR J, 5
**laundry** Give me a l.-list — ROSSINI, G, 2
The general idea, . . . in any first-class l. — LEACOCK, S, 13
**laurel** Caesar's l. crown — BLAKE, W, 2
**laurel-bough** burned is Apollo's l. — MARLOWE, C, 6
**laurels** once more, O ye l. — MILTON, J, 16
The l. all are cut — HOUSMAN, A, 1
**law** Born under one l. — GREVILLE, BARON BROOKE, 1
Every l. is a contract — SELDEN, J, 2
his delight is in the l. of the Lord — PSALMS, 1
Ignorance of the l. — SELDEN, J, 3
I have forgotten more l. than you ever knew . . . — MAYNARD, SIR J, 1
lest the moral l. become . . . separated — ADDAMS, J, 2
No brilliance is needed in the l. — MORTIMER, J, 2
Nor l., nor duty bade me fight — YEATS, W, 14
nothing is l. that is not reason. — POWELL, SIR J, 1
Order is heaven's first l. — POPE, A, 35
Or lesser breeds without the L. — KIPLING, R, 20
our duty . . . to break the l. — PANKHURST, E, 4
Prisons are built with stones of L. — BLAKE, W, 18
rich men rule the l. — GOLDSMITH, O, 22
The army ages men sooner than the l. — WELLS, H, 5
the greater part of the l. is learning to tolerate fools — LESSING, D, 5
The l. does not concern itself — PROVERBS, 400
the l. is a ass — DICKENS, C, 35
The L. is the true embodiment — GILBERT, SIR W, 18
The l. of dislike for the unlike — ZANGWILL, I, 3
The L. of England is a very strange one — DARLING, BARON, 5
the L. of the Yukon — SERVICE, R, 3
the magnificent fair play of the British criminal l. — DOYLE, SIR A, 8
The majestic egalitarianism of the l. — FRANCE, A, 9
There is no universal l. — LAWRENCE, D, 31
There's one l. for the rich — PROVERBS, 420
th' windy side of the l. — SHAKESPEARE, W, 295
**laws** I know not whether L. be right — WILDE, O, 6
L. are generally found to be nets — SHENSTONE, W, 1
L. are like cobwebs — SWIFT, J, 16
L. are like spider's webs — SOLON, 2
L. grind the poor — GOLDSMITH, O, 22
l. were like cobwebs — BACON, 1ST BARON VERULAM, VISCOUNT ST ALBANS, 5
L. were made to be broken — NORTH, C, 2
Nature's l. lay hid in night — POPE, A, 17
rules of the game are what we call the l. of Nature — HUXLEY, T, 6
the individual subject . . . has nothing to do with the l. but to obey them — HORSLEY, B, 1
the l. of poetic truth and poetic beauty — ARNOLD, M, 13
there never will be . . . equality until women . . . make l. — ANTHONY, S, 2
the repeal of bad or obnoxious l. — GRANT, U, 4
Where l. end, tyranny begins — PITT THE ELDER, 1ST EARL OF CHATHAM, 4
you do not make the l. but . . . are the wives . . . of those who do — GRIMKE, A, 1
**lawyer** A client is fain to hire a l. to keep from . . . other lawyers — BUTLER, S, 22
A l. has no business with . . . justice or injustice — JOHNSON, S, 154
A l. never goes — PROVERBS, 28

A L.'s opinion — PROVERBS, 29
He that is his own l. — PROVERBS, 192
No poet ever interpreted nature . . . as a l. interprets truth — GIRAUDOUX, J, 2
**lawyers** L. are the only persons in whom ignorance . . . is not punished — BENTHAM, J, 2
woe unto you, l. — BIBLE: LUKE, 24
**laxative** sweet l. of Georgian strains — CAMPBELL, R, 1
**lay** I never would l. down my arms — PITT THE ELDER, 1ST EARL OF CHATHAM, 6
L. your sleeping head — AUDEN, W, 18
l. it on with a trowel — CONGREVE, W, 1
**Lazarus** L. . . . laid at his gate, full of sores — BIBLE: LUKE, 30
**lazy** be efficient if you're going to be l. — CONRAN, S, 2
There are no ugly women, only l. ones — RUBINSTEIN, H, 2
**lead** L., kindly Light — NEWMAN, CARDINAL, 3
**leader** A l. who doesn't hesitate . . . is not fit to be a l. — MEIR, G, 1
I have to follow them, I am their l. — LEDRU-ROLLIN, A, 1
**leadership** men do not approach to l. — BEVERIDGE, BARON, 2
**leadeth** he l. me beside the still waters — PSALMS, 13
**leaf** his l. also shall not wither — PSALMS, 1
**leap** a great l. in the dark — HOBBES, T, 8
A l. over the hedge — CERVANTES, M, 6
And twenty-nine in each l. year — NURSERY RHYMES, 61
I shall l. over the wall — PSALMS, 7
one giant l. for mankind — ARMSTRONG, N, 1
**leapt** Into the dangerous world I l. — BLAKE, W, 36
**learn** The life so short, the craft so long to l. — HIPPOCRATES, 1
we could never l. to be brave . . . if there were only joy — KELLER, H, 2
What we have to l. to do — ARISTOTLE, 1
**learned** He was naturally l. — DRYDEN, J, 21
I am . . . of the opinion with the l. — CONGREVE, W, 3
people . . . never have l. anything from history — HEGEL, G, 1
the l. roast an egg — POPE, A, 51
**learning** A little l. is a dangerous thing — POPE, A, 21
A progeny of l. — SHERIDAN, R, 2
beauty and the lust for l. — BEERBOHM, SIR M, 13
I have been l. how to die — LEONARDO DA VINCI, 1
I thought that I was l. how to live — LEONARDO DA VINCI, 1
l., earning and yearning — MORLEY, C, 1
L. hath gained most — FULLER, T, 6
L. is a treasure — PROVERBS, 250
L. is but an adjunct — SHAKESPEARE, W, 155
L. without thought is labour lost — CONFUCIUS, 5
public school, where . . . l. was painfully beaten into him — PEACOCK, T, 8
Their l. is like bread in a besieged town — JOHNSON, S, 93
**learnt** I only remember what I've l. — WHITE, P, 2
Soon l. — PROVERBS, 365
what has been l. has been forgotten — SKINNER, B, 2
**least** death . . . the l. of all evils — BACON, 1ST BARON VERULAM, VISCOUNT ST ALBANS, 6
L. said soonest mended — PROVERBS, 251
Strongest minds / . . . the noisy world /Hears l. — WORDSWORTH, W, 1
the l. of these my brethren — BIBLE: MATTHEW, 76
**leave** Fare thee well, for I must l. thee — ANONYMOUS, 87
How I l. my country — PITT THE YOUNGER, W, 4
If you l. a thing alone you l. it to a torrent of change — CHESTERTON, G, 30
L. well alone — PROVERBS, 252
to l. his country as good as he had found it — COBBETT, W, 2
**leaves** before the l. have fallen — WILHELM II, 1
If poetry comes not . . . as l. to a tree — KEATS, J, 52
No fruits, no flowers, no l., no birds — HOOD, T, 10
the l. . . . were for the healing of the nations — BIBLE: REVELATIONS, 21
Though l. are many, the root is one — YEATS, W, 5
With vine l. in his hair — IBSEN, H, 6
Words are like l. — POPE, A, 28
**leaving** became him like the l. it — SHAKESPEARE, W, 161
She's l. home — LENNON, J, 11
**leavings** sacrifice . . . of the devil's l. — POPE, A, 54
**lecher** small gilded fly does l. — SHAKESPEARE, W, 146
**lechery** drink . . . an equivocator with l. — SHAKESPEARE, W, 168
Still wars and l. — SHAKESPEARE, W, 284
**lectures** l. or a little charity — WHITMAN, W, 6
**led** l. by the nose with gold — SHAKESPEARE, W, 305
**leeches** l. have red blood. — CUVIER, BARON, 1
**left** a handful of silver he l. us — BROWNING, R, 29
And we are l., or shall be l., alone — WORDSWORTH, W, 46

believe in the l. to come BECKETT, S, 1
Books are . . . a mighty bloodless substitute for l. STEVENSON, R, 16
brief is l. but love is long TENNYSON, BARON, 60
chemical barrage has been hurled against the fabric of l.
CARSON, R, 2
death after l. does greatly please SPENSER, E, 1
doctrine of the strenuous l. ROOSEVELT, T, 4
dreary intercourse of daily l. WORDSWORTH, W, 12
For l. is but a dream THOMSON, J, 2
good shepherd giveth his l. for the sheep BIBLE: JOHN, 26
half of them prefer hiring their servants for l. CARLYLE, T, 32
hymns of praise to the glory of l. SITWELL, DAME E, 1
I am the bread of l. BIBLE: JOHN, 16
I am the resurrection, and the l. BIBLE: JOHN, 27
I am the way, the truth, and the l. BIBLE: JOHN, 32
I have but one l. to lose for my country HALE, N, 1
I have measured out my l. ELIOT, T, 11
Illness is the night-side of l. SONTAG, S, 1
I might give my l. for my friend SMITH, L, 5
in his pleasure is l. PSALMS, 19
Is l. a boon GILBERT, SIR W, 42
Is not l. . . . too short . . . to bore ourselves NIETZSCHE, F, 12
isn't l. a terrible thing THOMAS, D, 18
Is there another l. KEATS, J, 66
It's as large as l. CARROLL, L, 31
Its private l. is a disgrace ANONYMOUS, 84
I've had a happy l. HAZLITT, W, 30
I've looked at l. from both sides now MITCHELL, J, 1
I warmed both hands before the fire of l. LANDOR, W, 7
lay down his friends for his l. THORPE, J, 1
L. begins at forty PROVERBS, 257
L. begins at forty TUCKER, S, 2
l. . . . effort to prevent . . . thinking HUXLEY, A, 22
L. exists in the universe JEANS, SIR J, 1
L. flies FITZGERALD, E, 10
L. . . . happens . . . while you're busy making other plans
LENNON, J, 1
like runners hand on the torch of l. LUCRETIUS, 3
L. is a gamble STOPPARD, T, 10
L. is a jest GAY, J, 10
L. is a maze in which we take the wrong turning CONNOLLY, C, 13
L. is an incurable disease COWLEY, A, 2
L. . . . is a predicament SANTAYANA, G, 7
L. is as tedious as a twice-told tale SHAKESPEARE, W, 127
L. is a tragedy . . . in close-up CHAPLIN, C, 4
L. is just a bowl PROVERBS, 258
L. is just one damned thing after another HUBBARD, E, 3
L. is mostly froth and bubble GORDON, A, 1
L. is not all beer PROVERBS, 259
L. is not a spectacle or a feast SANTAYANA, G, 7
L. isn't all beer and skittles HUGHES, T, 1
L. is one long process BUTLER, S, 9
L. is sweet PROVERBS, 260
L. is the art of drawing sufficient conclusions BUTLER, S, 10
l. is the thing SMITH, L, 3
L. is too short to do anything for oneself MAUGHAM, W, 19
L. is too short to learn German PORSON, R, 1
L., liberty, and the pursuit of happiness JEFFERSON, T, 3
l. . . . much to be endured JOHNSON, S, 25
longest half of your l. SOUTHEY, R, 3
lot of trouble in his l. CHURCHILL, SIR W, 22
love . . . has one arch-enemy – and that is l. ANOUILH, J, 1
L.'s but a walking shadow SHAKESPEARE, W, 177
l. . . . seems to me preparation for something that never happens
YEATS, W, 3
L.'s Little Ironies HARDY, T, 4
L.'s short span forbids us to enter on far-reaching hopes.
HORACE, 28
L.'s too short for chess BYRON, H, 1
L. without industry is guilt RUSKIN, J, 2
L. would be tolerable LEWIS, SIR G, 1
meddling with any practical part of l. ADDISON, J, 8
moment's insight . . . worth a l.'s experience. HOLMES, O, 7
money has something to do with l. LARKIN, P, 1
my experience of l. has been drawn BEERBOHM, SIR M, 14
My wife . . . is troubled with her lonely l. PEPYS, S, 4
no man loses any other l. than . . . he now lives
MARCUS AURELIUS ANTONINUS, 3
Nothing in his l. /Became him like the leaving SHAKESPEARE, W, 161
only honour and l. have been spared FRANCIS I, 1
our l. is what our thoughts make it MARCUS AURELIUS ANTONINUS, 5

passion and the l. . . . within COLERIDGE, S, 9
secret of reaping the greatest fruitfulness . . . from l.
NIETZSCHE, F, 5
she is mine for l. SPARK, M, 6
show l. neither as it is nor as it ought to be CHEKHOV, A, 5
so long as you have your l. JAMES, H, 1
strange disease of modern l. ARNOLD, M, 35
Superstition is the poetry of l. GOETHE, J, 6
take my l. FARQUHAR, G, 3
Than to ever let a woman in my l. LERNER, A, 3
that a man lay down his l. for his friends BIBLE: JOHN, 36
The Book of L. begins WILDE, O, 57
the child should be allowed to meet the real experiences of l.
KEY, E, 2
the crown of l. BIBLE: JAMES, 1
The essential thing in l. COUBERTIN, BARON, 1
The first rule in opera is the first rule in l. MELBA, DAME N, 1
The L. and Soul, the man who will never go home
WHITEHORN, K, 3
The Leaves of L. keep falling FITZGERALD, E, 4
the l. of man, solitary, poor, nasty, brutish, and short
HOBBES, T, 4
The love of l. is necessary to . . . any undertaking JOHNSON, S, 22
the l.-sentence which fate carries LAWRENCE, T, 1
The l. so short, the craft so long to learn HIPPOCRATES, 1
the painted veil which those who live /Call l. SHELLEY, P, 10
The present l. of men on earth, O king BEDE, 1
the pride of l. BIBLE: I JOHN, 2
There are only three events in a man's l. LA BRUYERE, J, 6
therefore choose l. BIBLE: DEUTERONOMY, 5
the stuff l. is made of FRANKLIN, B, 7
the tree of l. BIBLE: GENESIS, 8
The vanity of human l. is like a river POPE, A, 56
the veil which those who live call l. SHELLEY, P, 20
The Wine of L. keeps oozing FITZGERALD, E, 4
they get about ten percent out of l. DUNCAN, I, 2
this l. /Is nobler SHAKESPEARE, W, 36
this long disease, my l. POPE, A, 11
Three passions . . . have governed my l. RUSSELL, EARL, 1
To save a man's l. against his will is . . . killing him HORACE, 12
total of such moments is my l. CONNOLLY, C, 10
We'd jump the l. to come SHAKESPEARE, W, 164
what a queer thing L. is WODEHOUSE, SIR P, 12
when religion is allowed to invade . . . private l.
MELBOURNE, VISCOUNT, 9
While there is l., there's hope GAY, J, 7
While there's l. PROVERBS, 464
who is there . . . would go into the temple to save his l.
BIBLE: NEHEMIAH, 1
Who saw l. steadily ARNOLD, M, 40
with an eye made quiet . . . /We see into the l. of things
WORDSWORTH, W, 9

life-blood A good book is the precious l. MILTON, J, 2
lifeboat This is a movie, not a l. TRACY, S, 3
life-insurance I detest l. agents LEACOCK, S, 3
life-lie Take the l. away from the average man IBSEN, H, 9
life-sized Great men are but l. BEERBOHM, SIR M, 3
lifetime No, I ask it for the knowledge of a l. WHISTLER, J, 5
lift I will l. up mine eyes unto the hills PSALMS, 75
l. up your heads, O ye gates PSALMS, 16
light a l. to lighten the Gentiles BIBLE: LUKE, 1
By the L. of the moon BYRON, 6TH BARON, 39
Culture is the passion for sweetness and l. ARNOLD, M, 21
darkness and l. to thee are both alike PSALMS, 86
Fond Memory brings the l. /Of other days MOORE, T, 7
Give me a l. that I may tread safely into the unknown
HASKINS, M, 1
God shall make my darkness to be l. PSALMS, 7
I am the l. of the world BIBLE: JOHN, 21
I have only a faint l. to guide me DIDEROT, D, 1
l. a candle of understanding BIBLE: II ESDRAS, 7
L. breaks where no sun shines THOMAS, D, 1
l. dwelleth with him BIBLE: DANIEL, 1
Lead, kindly L. NEWMAN, CARDINAL, 1
let there be l. BIBLE: GENESIS, 1
let your l. so shine before men BIBLE: MATTHEW, 11
Lolita, l. of my life NABOKOV, V, 1
one might get a five-pound note as one got a l. for a cigarette
JAMES, H, 2
Put out the l. SHAKESPEARE, W, 228
speed was far faster than l. BULLER, A, 1

the lamb is the l. thereof — BIBLE: REVELATIONS, 20
The leaping l. for your delight discovers — AUDEN, W, 17
the l. fantastic toe — MILTON, J, 11
the l. of the living — PSALMS, 39
the l. shineth in darkness — BIBLE: JOHN, 1
The L. that Failed — KIPLING, R, 17
the l. that led astray — BURNS, R, 21
the true l., which lighteth every man — BIBLE: JOHN, 1
thou . . . shalt l. my candle — PSALMS, 7
we shall this day l. such a candle — LATIMER, H, 2
When I consider how my l. is spent — MILTON, J, 55
wisdom excelleth folly, as . . . l. excelleth darkness
— BIBLE: ECCLESIASTES, 7
**Light Brigade** Forward the L.! — TENNYSON, BARON, 5
**light bulb** I can't stand a naked l. — WILLIAMS, T, 4
**lightened** brooding tragedy and its dark shadows can be l.
— GANDHI, I, 4
**lightfoot** many a l. lad — HOUSMAN, A, 14
**light-headed** l., variable men — STEVENSON, R, 21
**lighthouse** sitivation at the l. — DICKENS, C, 51
**lightly** Angels . . . take themselves l. — CHESTERTON, G, 31
**lightning** beheld Satan as l. fall from heaven — BIBLE: LUKE, 20
Here lies a man who was killed by l. — ANONYMOUS, 27
reading Shakespeare by flashes of l. — COLERIDGE, S, 43
snatched the l. shaft from heaven — TURGOT, BARON DE L'AULNE, 1
**lights** God made two great l. — BIBLE: GENESIS, 4
the Father of l. — BIBLE: JAMES, 2
Turn up the l., I don't want to go home in the dark — HENRY, O, 2
**like** I know what I l. — BEERBOHM, SIR M, 16
I shall not look upon his l. — SHAKESPEARE, W, 45
L. breeds l. — PROVERBS, 261
L. doth quit l. — SHAKESPEARE, W, 186
men we l. are good for everything — HALIFAX, MARQUIS OF, 2
People who l. this sort of thing — LINCOLN, A, 14
To L . . . the same things, that is . . . true friendship — SALLUST, 1
Where wilt thou find their l. agen — SCOTT, SIR W, 11
**liked** He's l., but he's not well l. — MILLER, A, 2
I'm so universally l. — DE VRIES, P, 8
**likes** I know she l. me — STRATTON, E, 1
**liking** it saves me the trouble of l. them — AUSTEN, J, 27
this l. for war — BENNETT, A, 2
you expect other people to be . . . to your l. — KEMPIS, T, 3
**lilac** the l. is in bloom — BROOKE, R, 2
**lilacs** L. out of the dead land — ELIOT, T, 23
**lilies** consider the l. of the field — BIBLE: MATTHEW, 21
he feedeth among the l. — BIBLE: SONG OF SOLOMON, 7
L. that fester — SHAKESPEARE, W, 262
The l. and roses were all awake, — TENNYSON, BARON, 53
**lily** paint the l. — SHAKESPEARE, W, 128
**limb** Let them bestow on every airth a l.
— GRAHAM, MARQUIS OF MONTROSE, 1
perils . . . of wind and l. — BUTLER, S, 5
**limericks** Whose l. never would scan — ANONYMOUS, 94
**limit** In order to draw a l. to thinking — WITTGENSTEIN, L, 2
No one who cannot l. himself — BOILEAU, N, 1
**limited** Liberty too must be l. — BURKE, E, 19
**limousine** One perfect l. — PARKER, D, 7
**Linden** On L., when the sun was low — CAMPBELL, T, 2
**line** cancel half a L. — FITZGERALD, E, 14
carved not a l. — WOLFE, C, 2
I purpose to fight it out on this l. — GRANT, U, 2
l. upon l. — BIBLE: ISAIAH, 22
*thin red l. tipped with steel* — RUSSELL, SIR W, 1
True genius walks along a l. — GOLDSMITH, O, 1
**linen** not l. you're wearing out, /But human creatures' lives
— HOOD, T, 11
washing one's clean l. in public — WILDE, O, 19
**lines** give me six l . . . by the most honest man
— RICHELIEU, CARDINAL DE, 1
Pray to God and say the l. — DAVIS, B, 3
**lingerie** Brevity is the soul of l. — PARKER, D, 14
**lingering** Something l . . . . I fancy — GILBERT, SIR W, 32
**linguistics** Essay in Sociological L. — ROSS, A, 1
**links** Nothing l. man to man like . . . cash — SICKERT, W, 1
**lion** A l. among ladies — SHAKESPEARE, W, 204
I hear the l. roar — COWPER, W, 14
I should be like a l. in a cave of savage Daniels — WILDE, O, 74
Now that the old l. is dead — PARR, S, 1
The l. and the unicorn — NURSERY RHYMES, 55
The nation had the l.'s heart — CHURCHILL, SIR W, 63
to make the l. lie down with the lamb — LAWRENCE, D, 30

**lioness** feeds a l. at home — TAYLOR, J, 2
**lionized** wasn't spoilt by being l. — TREE, SIR H, 4
**lions** bears and l. growl and fight — WATTS, I, 3
English soldiers fight like l. — HOFFMANN, M, 1
l. led by donkeys — HOFFMANN, M, 1
my soul is among l. — PSALMS, 40
**lip** He bit his l. in a manner — PERELMAN, S, 1
stiff upper l. — CARY, P, 1
**lips** l. that touch liquor must never touch mine — YOUNG, G, 1
My l. are sealed — BALDWIN, 1ST EARL BALDWIN OF BEWDLEY, 6
Red l. are not so red — OWEN, W, 4
**liquefaction** That l. of her clothes — HERRICK, R, 7
**liquidation** the l. of the British Empire — CHURCHILL, SIR W, 53
**liquor** If . . . Orientals . . . drank a l. which . . . made them vomit
— LA BRUYERE, J, 13
lips that touch l. must never touch mine — YOUNG, G, 1
**liquors** alcoholic l. have been used by the . . . best races
— SAINTSBURY, G, 1
**list** I've got a little l. — GILBERT, SIR W, 25
**listen** a limit to what one can l. to with the naked eye
— SPARK, M, 11
privilege of wisdom to l. — HOLMES, O, 6
they will l. today, they will l. tomorrow — KHRUSHCHEV, N, 8
**listener** A good l. is a good talker with a sore throat
— WHITEHORN, K, 7
**listeners** L. never hear good — PROVERBS, 263
**listening** if you ain't talking about him, ain't l. — BRANDO, M, 1
**literacy** The ratio of l. to illiteracy — MORAVIA, A, 1
**literary** Classical quotation is the *parole* of l. men — JOHNSON, S, 134
Joe, . . . the first great nonstop l. drinker — THURBER, J, 1
L. men are . . . a perpetual priesthood — CARLYLE, T, 6
**literature** All that is l. seeks to communicate power
— DE QUINCEY, T, 1
All the rest is l. — VALERY, P, 2
American professors like their l. . . . dead — LEWIS, S, 4
great deal of history to produce a little l. — JAMES, H, 3
He knew everything about l. except how to enjoy it — HELLER, J, 4
If we can't stamp out l. — WAUGH, E, 39
itch of l. — LOVER, S, 1
L. and butterflies are the two sweetest passions — NABOKOV, V, 7
*Language*, man! . . . it's L. — WELLS, H, 8
L. flourishes best — INGE, W, 8
L. is mostly about having sex — LODGE, D, 1
L. is news — POUND, E, 3
L. is simply language charged with meaning — POUND, E, 9
L. is strewn with the wreckage of men — WOOLF, V, 12
L. is the orchestration of platitudes — WILDER, T, 7
L . . . poisoned by its own secretions — BRENAN, G, 4
L . . . something that will be read twice — CONNOLLY, C, 4
no l. can outdo the cynicism of real life — CHEKHOV, A, 10
That great Cham of l., Samuel Johnson — SMOLLETT, T, 6
The Bible is l. — SANTAYANA, G, 3
**litter** social virtues . . . the virtue of pigs in a l. — THOREAU, H, 5
**little** Every l. helps — PROVERBS, 136
He who knows only his own side . . . knows l. — MILL, J, 2
it was a very l. one — MARRYAT, F, 1
L. things affect l. minds — DISRAELI, 1ST EARL OF BEACONSFIELD, 10
Man wants but l. — GOLDSMITH, O, 6
Man wants but l. — YOUNG, E, 8
So l. done, so much to do — RHODES, C, 4
the l. things are infinitely the most important — DOYLE, SIR A, 4
**little girls** L . . . slamming doors — BELLOC, H, 5
**Little Nell** . . . to read the death of L. without laughing
— WILDE, O, 61
**littleness** the l. of those that should carry them out — BRECHT, B, 6
**liv'd** And they that L. and Lov'd Either — ANONYMOUS, 54
**live** anything but l. for it — COLTON, C, 1
better to die on your feet than to l. on your knees — IBARRURI, D, 2
Come l. with me, and be my love — MARLOWE, C, 3
Come l. with me — DONNE, J, 2
Do you want to l. for ever — DALY, D, 1
eat to l. — MOLIERE, 2
he forgets to l. — LA BRUYERE, J, 6
Houses are built to l. in
— BACON, 1ST BARON VERULAM, VISCOUNT ST ALBANS, 15
If God were suddenly condemned to l. the life — DUMAS, FILS, 1
If you l. long enough, the venerability factor creeps in — STONE, I, 1
I have learned to l. each day as it comes — DIX, D, 2
in him we l., and move, and have our being — BIBLE: ACTS, 13
in Rome, l. as the Romans — AMBROSE, 1
I thought that I was learning how to l. — LEONARDO DA VINCI, 1

**Lords** a naked Duke of Windlestraw addressing a naked House of
  L.                                             CARLYLE, T, 23
the cure for admiring the House of L.     BAGEHOT, W, 2
**lords** Great l. have their pleasures    MONTESQUIEU, BARON DE, 6
**lordships** good enough for their l. on a hot summer afternoon
                                             ANONYMOUS, 101
**lorn** a lone l. creetur           DICKENS, C, 8
**lose** A man who does not l. his reason   LESSING, G, 1
In every friend we l. a part of ourselves   POPE, A, 59
I shall l. no time in reading it
       DISRAELI, 1ST EARL OF BEACONSFIELD, 16
l. the substance                 AESOP, 1
nothing to l. but their chains      MARX, K, 2
tails you l.                  CROKER, J, 1
We Don't Want To L. You      RUBENS, P, 1
What you l. on the swings       PROVERBS, 458
**losers** In war . . . all are l.    CHAMBERLAIN, N, 1
**loses** no man l. any other life than . . . he now lives
                MARCUS AURELIUS ANTONINUS, 3
The conventional army l. if it does not win   KISSINGER, H, 1
**loss** richest gain I count but l.     WATTS, I, 8
To suffer the l. they were afraid of   AUDEN, W, 23
**lost** All is l. save honour      FRANCIS I, 1
All is not l.              MILTON, J, 27
better to have fought and l.    CLOUGH, A, 7
better to have loved and l.   TENNYSON, BARON, 24
he was l., and is found      BIBLE: LUKE, 29
Home of l. causes         ARNOLD, M, 11
I can't say I was ever l.      BOONE, D, 1
I have discovered the art . . . l. for two thousand years
                    DUNCAN, I, 1
I look upon every day to be l.    JOHNSON, S, 151
It is better to have loafed and l.   THURBER, J, 3
I've l. one of my children this week   TURNER, J, 2
l. and gone for ever        MONTROSE, P, 1
never to have l. at all       BUTLER, S, 27
What though the field be l.    MILTON, J, 27
woman that deliberates is l.    ADDISON, J, 4
You are a l. generation      STEIN, G, 6
**Lot** remember L.'s wife     BIBLE: LUKE, 32
**lot** and the l. fell upon Jonah   BIBLE: JONAH, 1
policeman's l. is not a happy one  GILBERT, SIR W, 40
**lots** they parted his raiment, and cast l.   BIBLE: LUKE, 36
**loud** A l. noise at one end     KNOX, R, 3
Like German opera, too long and too l.   WAUGH, E, 50
the l. cymbals           PSALMS, 94
**Louis** Son of Saint L.      FIRMONT, E, 1
**louse** the point of precedency between a l. and a flea.
                    JOHNSON, S, 141
**lousy** only one fault. It was kind of l.   THURBER, J, 19
**lov'd** I never writ, nor no man ever l.  SHAKESPEARE, W, 265
Of one that l. not wisely, but too well  SHAKESPEARE, W, 229
**love** Absence is to l.      BUSSY-RABUTIN, 1
a comfort in the strength of l.   WORDSWORTH, W, 19
a girl likes to be crossed in l. a little  AUSTEN, J, 21
Alcohol is like l.         CHANDLER, R, 3
alike are the groans of l. to . . . dying  LOWRY, M, 2
All mankind l. a lover     EMERSON, R, 8
all's fair in l. and war      FORREST, N, 2
all the world and l. were young  RALEIGH, SIR W, 1
And l. to all men        KIPLING, R, 3
An ounce of l.          WESLEY, J, 2
ashamed of having been in l.  ROCHEFOUCAULD, DUC DE LA, 8
Because women can do nothing except l.  MAUGHAM, W, 10
brief is the l. is long     TENNYSON, BARON, 60
But L. has pitched his mansion   YEATS, W, 6
Christianity has done a great deal for l.  FRANCE, A, 6
Come live with me, and be my l.  MARLOWE, C, 13
corner in the thing I l.   SHAKESPEARE, W, 225
courage to l. . . . courage to suffer.  TROLLOPE, A, 4
Dear Roger Fry whom I l. as a man  MARSH, SIR E, 1
Deep as first l.      TENNYSON, BARON, 59
Do not l. your neighbour as yourself  SHAW, G, 25
don't believe in . . . true l. until after the first attack
                   ESCHENBACH, M, 2
Drinking . . . and making l.   BEAUMARCHAIS, P, 2
England! . . . /What I l. bore to thee  WORDSWORTH, W, 4
Every little girl knows about l.   SAGAN, F, 1
folly . . . l. did make thee run into  SHAKESPEARE, W, 20
God is l.           BIBLE: I JOHN, 3
greater l. hath no man     BIBLE: JOHN, 36

He fell in l. with himself     POWELL, A, 1
help . . . of the woman I l.    EDWARD VIII, 1
he told men to l. their neighbour   BRECHT, B, 4
how did you l. my picture    GOLDWYN, S, 23
how difficult it is to write biography . . . many people know the
. . . truth about his or her l. affairs   WEST, DAME R, 8
how fair . . . art thou, O l., for delights
                BIBLE: SONG OF SOLOMON, 18
husbands, l. your wives    BIBLE: COLOSSIANS, 4
I do not l. thee, Doctor Fell    BROWN, T, 1
I do not l. thee         NORTON, C, 1
if men and women marry those whom they do not l.
                MARTINEAU, H, 5
If music be the food of l.    SHAKESPEARE, W, 285
I hate and l.         CATULLUS, G, 2
I l. or I hate          PICASSO, P, 4
I'm tired of L.          BELLOC, H, 9
In l. . . . the amateur status    GRAVES, R, 3
In Switzerland they had brotherly l.  WELLES, O, 1
I rather suspect her of being in l.  CHURCHILL, J, 1
I shall but l. thee better after death  BROWNING, E, 4
Is thy l. a plant /Of such weak fibre  WORDSWORTH, W, 20
I think my l. as rare    SHAKESPEARE, W, 268
it jumps from admiration to l.   AUSTEN, J, 17
I understand only because I l.  TOLSTOY, COUNT, 6
I want to l. first, and live incidentally  FITZGERALD, Z, 1
know the l. of Christ, which passeth knowledge
                BIBLE: EPHESIANS, 1
labour of l.    BIBLE: I THESSALONIANS, 1
l. – all the wretched cant of it   GREER, G, 3
L. and all his pleasures    CAMPION, T, 5
l. and marriage        CAHN, S, 1
l. and murder will out    CONGREVE, W, 2
l., an . . . intercourse between tyrants and slaves  GOLDSMITH, O, 12
l. a place the less for having suffered  AUSTEN, J, 14
L. bade me welcome     HERBERT, G, 6
L. built on beauty      DONNE, J, 7
L. ceases to be a pleasure    BEHN, A, 1
L. conquers all       PROVERBS, 269
L. conquers all things     VIRGIL, 15
let brotherly l. continue   BIBLE: HEBREWS, 5
Let's Fall in L.       PORTER, C, 9
let us prove . . . the sports of l.   JONSON, B, 14
let us too give in to L.     VIRGIL, 15
L. fled            YEATS, W, 32
L. God, and hateth his brother  BIBLE: I JOHN, 5
l. . . . has one arch-enemy – and that is life  ANOUILH, J, 1
lightly turns to thoughts of l.  TENNYSON, BARON, 46
L.? I make it constantly but I never talk about it  PROUST, M, 6
l. in a golden bowl       BLAKE, W, 9
L. in a hut          KEATS, J, 19
L. is a boy          BUTLER, S, 4
L. is a sickness       DANIEL, S, 1
L. is blind        ANONYMOUS, 55
L. is blind        PROVERBS, 270
l. is blind      SHAKESPEARE, W, 191
L. is like the measles     JEROME, J, 1
L. is moral even without . . . marriage  KEY, E, 5
L. is my religion       KEATS, J, 62
L. is not l. /Which alters   SHAKESPEARE, W, 264
L. is the wisdom of the fool   JOHNSON, S, 39
live with me, and be my l.    DONNE, J, 2
L. laughs at locksmiths    PROVERBS, 271
l. . . . looks more like hatred than like friendship
         ROCHEFOUCAULD, DUC DE LA, 9
L. looks not with the eyes  SHAKESPEARE, W, 202
L. makes the world     PROVERBS, 272
L. means never having to say   SEGAL, E, 1
L. means the pre-cognitive flow  LAWRENCE, D, 43
L. me, l. my dog       PROVERBS, 273
L. of justice in most men  ROCHEFOUCAULD, DUC DE LA, 10
l. of liberty is the l. of others   HAZLITT, W, 28
l. of money is the root of all evil  BIBLE: I TIMOTHY, 6
l. of power is the l. of ourselves  HAZLITT, W, 28
longing for l.       RUSSELL, EARL, 1
l. robs those who have it of their wit  DIDEROT, D, 2
L. seeketh not itself to please   BLAKE, W, 34
L. seeketh only Self to please   BLAKE, W, 35
L.'s like the measles     JERROLD, D, 5
L. sought is good    SHAKESPEARE, W, 293
l. that loves a scarlet coat    HOOD, T, 4

lunatic l., the lover, and the poet   SHAKESPEARE, W, 206
Those comfortably padded l. asylums . . . the stately homes
  WOOLF, V, 4
luncheon to read a novel before l. was one of the gravest sins
  WAUGH, E, 49
lungs don't keep using your l.   LEACOCK, S, 4
lured down which ideas are l. and . . . strangled   COCKS, SIR B, 1
lust l. in action   SHAKESPEARE, W, 266
Nonconformity and l. stalking hand in hand   WAUGH, E, 9
the l. of the flesh   BIBLE: 1 JOHN, 2
lusteth the flesh l. against the Spirit   BIBLE: GALATIANS, 4
lute l., and instrument of ten strings   PSALMS, 23
Lutheran I have a Catholic soul, but a L. stomach   ERASMUS, D, 1
lux fiat l.   BIBLE: GENESIS, 2
luxuries Give me the l. of life   WRIGHT, F, 2
Give us the l. of life   MOTLEY, J, 1
luxury Blesses his stars, and thinks it l.   ADDISON, J, 3
Every l. . . . – atheism, breast-feeding, circumcision.   ORTON, J, 4
lyf That l. so short   CHAUCER, G, 17
lying One of you is l.   PARKER, D, 10
the air of someone who is l. . . . to a policeman   PHILIPPE, C, 1
lynching he could have attended a l. every day   SMITH, T, 1
lyre on this wall will hang my weapons and my l.   HORACE, 38
lyric poets . . . if you include me among the l., I'll hold my head
. . . high . . .   HORACE, 26

## M

macaroni And called it M..   BANGS, E, 1
Macaulay great apostle of the Philistines, Lord M.   ARNOLD, M, 19
Lord M.   SMITH, S, 11
Macavity there's no one like M.   ELIOT, T, 14
MacDonald Ramsay M.   MAXTON, J, 1
machine a taxing m.   LOWE, VISCOUNT SHERBROOKE, 1
One m. can do the work of fifty ordinary men   HUBBARD, E, 1
Our body is a m. for living   TOLSTOY, COUNT, 7
the Ghost in the M.   RYLE, G, 3
The m. threatens   RILKE, R, 2
machine-gun a m. riddling her hostess   HUXLEY, A, 21
machines I see no reason to suppose that these m. will ever
force themselves into general use   WELLINGTON, DUKE OF, 7
mackerel M. sky and mares' tails   PROVERBS, 277
Macmillan M. seemed . . . to embody the national decay
  MUGGERIDGE, M, 3
mad escaped from a m. and savage master   SOPHOCLES, 2
half of the nation is m.   SMOLLETT, T, 1
he ceased to be m. he became merely stupid   PROUST, M, 10
he first makes m.   EURIPIDES, 1
He first sends m.   DUPORT, J, 1
I said of laughter, it is m.   BIBLE: ECCLESIASTES, 6
let me not be m.   SHAKESPEARE, W, 133
M. about the boy   COWARD, SIR N, 9
M., bad, and dangerous to know   LAMB, C, 1
Men will always be m.   VOLTAIRE, 24
Never go to bed m.   DILLER, P, 2
The dog, . . . /Went m. and bit the man   GOLDSMITH, O, 8
We all are born m.   BECKETT, S, 5
who turns m. for a reason   CERVANTES, M, 9
madam M. I may not call you   ELIZABETH I, 2
madame Call me m.   PERKINS, F, 1
maddest those who think they can cure them are the m.
  VOLTAIRE, 24
made Annihilating all that's m.   MARVELL, A, 2
Don't you think I was m. for you   FITZGERALD, Z, 2
Do you know who m. you   STOWE, H, 2
Little Lamb, who m. thee   BLAKE, W, 44
we're all m. the same   COWARD, SIR N, 2
Madeira We're from M.   SHAW, G, 40
madeleine The taste was that of the little crumb of m.
  PROUST, M, 1
mademoiselle A m. from Armenteers   ROWLAND, E, 1
Madison How were the receipts today in M. Square Garden
  BARNUM, P, 2
madman If a m. were to come into this room   JOHNSON, S, 102
The m. . . . has lost everything except his reason
  CHESTERTON, G, 26
The m. is not the m. who has lost his reason   CHESTERTON, G, 26
Thou call'st me m.   BLAKE, W, 49
madness devil's m. – War   SERVICE, R, 4
Great Wits . . . to M. near alli'd   DRYDEN, J, 3
M. in great ones   SHAKESPEARE, W, 64

M. need not be all breakdown   LAING, R, 5
Now Ireland has her m.   AUDEN, W, 14
maestro Music, M., Please   MAGIDSON, H, 1
maggot how to create a m.   MONTAIGNE, M, 6
magic That old black m.   MERCER, J, 2
when religion was strong and science weak, men mistook m. for
medicine   SZASZ, T, 3
magicians if the way had not been prepared by m.   NIETZSCHE, F, 9
magistrate Obscenity . . . happens to shock some elderly . . . m.
  RUSSELL, EARL, 22
suppose . . . the m. corruptible   ROBESPIERRE, M, 1
Magna Charta M. is such a fellow   COKE, SIR E, 2
magnanimity in victory, m.   CHURCHILL, SIR W, 19
magnificent more than m. – . . . mediocre   GOLDWYN, S, 20
some m. myth   PLATO, 3
there you sit with that m. instrument between your legs
  TOSCANINI, A, 5
magnifique c'est m., mais   BOSQUET, P, 1
magnify my soul doth m. the Lord   BIBLE: LUKE, 2
Magog Gog and M.   BIBLE: REVELATIONS, 16
Mahomet If the hill will not come to M., M. will go to the hill
  BACON, 1ST BARON VERULAM, VISCOUNT ST ALBANS, 14
maid Being an old m. is like death by drowning   FERBER, E, 1
like a moth, the simple m. /Still plays about the flame   GAY, J, 2
The m. was in the garden, /Hanging out the clothes
  NURSERY RHYMES, 52
Where are you going to, my pretty m.   NURSERY RHYMES, 72
maiden A simple m. in her flower   TENNYSON, BARON, 35
How could you use a poor m. so   ANONYMOUS, 16
I've a neater, sweeter m.   KIPLING, R, 22
many a rose-lipt m.   HOUSMAN, A, 14
That kissed the m. all forlorn   NURSERY RHYMES, 62
maids And pretty m. all in a row   NURSERY RHYMES, 34
Three little m. from school   GILBERT, SIR W, 27
majesty A sight so touching in its m.:   WORDSWORTH, W, 47
deck thyself . . . with m. and excellency   BIBLE: JOB, 19
Her M. is not a subject   DISRAELI, 1ST EARL OF BEACONSFIELD, 34
her M. . . . must not . . . look upon me as a source of income
  KEMBLE, C, 1
Her M.'s Opposition   BAGEHOT, W, 4
How can I . . . dislike a sex to which Your M. belongs
  RHODES, C, 3
Ride on! ride on in m.   MILMAN, H, 1
This earth of m.   SHAKESPEARE, W, 237
major-general very model of a modern M.   GILBERT, SIR W, 37
majority A m. is always the best repartee
  DISRAELI, 1ST EARL OF BEACONSFIELD, 11
Fools are in a terrible . . . m.   IBSEN, H, 1
He's gone to join the m.   PETRONIUS ARBITER, 2
I am certain that we will win the election with a good m..
  THATCHER, M, 18
No candidate . . . elected ex-president by such a large m.
  TAFT, W, 1
One on God's side is a m.   PHILLIPS, W, 2
the damned, compact, liberal m.   IBSEN, H, 3
the great silent m.   NIXON, R, 5
The m. has the might   IBSEN, H, 2
majors scarlet M.   SASSOON, S, 1
make a Scotsman on the m.   BARRIE, SIR J, 11
Love? I m. it constantly but I never talk about it   PROUST, M, 6
The white man knows how to m. everything, but he does not
know how to distribute it   SITTING BULL, 1
maker he adores his m.   BRIGHT, J, 4
he adores his m.   DISRAELI, 1ST EARL OF BEACONSFIELD, 15
making He is very fond of m. things   HOPE, A, 2
If you get the English people into the way of m. kings
  MELBOURNE, VISCOUNT, 3
maladies all the m. and miseries   CARLYLE, T, 29
Medical men . . . call all sorts of m. . . . by one name   CARLYLE, J, 4
There are m. we must not seek to cure   PROUST, M, 10
male especially the m. of the species   LAWRENCE, D, 9
In the sex-war thoughtlessness is the weapon of the m.
  CONNOLLY, C, 14
m. and female created he them   BIBLE: GENESIS, 6
preserve one last m. thing   LAWRENCE, D, 23
the female of the species is more deadly than the m.   KIPLING, R, 7
the peculiar situation of the human m.   BEAUVOIR, S, 2
malice M. is like a game of poker   SPIEL, H, 1
malicious God is subtle but he is not m.   EINSTEIN, A, 3
malign rather m. oneself   ROCHEFOUCAULD, DUC DE LA, 17
malignant the only part of Randolph that was not m.   WAUGH, E, 49

**malignity** that peculiar m. . . . characteristic of apostates
MACAULAY, BARON, 7
**malingering** Neurosis has an absolute genius for m. PROUST, M, 9
**malt** M. does more than Milton HOUSMAN, A, 15
**Mamas** The Last of the Red-Hot M. TUCKER, S, 1
**mammon** M. wins his way where Seraphs might despair
BYRON, 6TH BARON, 5
ye cannot serve God and m. BIBLE: MATTHEW, 20
**man** A 'Grand Old M.' LEACOCK, S, 12
all animals were created . . . for the use of m. PEACOCK, T, 4
a m. after his own heart BIBLE: 1 SAMUEL, 3
a m. can die but once SHAKESPEARE, W, 90
a m. has no reason to be ashamed of having an ape for his
grandfather HUXLEY, T, 11
A m. in the house is worth two WEST, M, 1
a m. is always seeking for happiness DIX, D, 3
A m. is as old as he feels PROVERBS, 44
A m. is only as old as the woman MARX, G, 26
A m. . . . is *so* in the way GASKELL, E, 1
A m. must serve his time to every trade BYRON, 6TH BARON, 35
A m. of straw PROVERBS, 45
A m.'s a m. for a' that BURNS, R, 8
A m. should never put on his best trousers IBSEN, H, 4
A m. should . . . own he has been in the wrong POPE, A, 52
A m. with God KNOX, J, 1
an old m. in a dry month ELIOT, T, 6
apparel oft proclaims the m. SHAKESPEARE, W, 47
'A was a m., take him for all in all SHAKESPEARE, W, 45
behold the m. BIBLE: JOHN, 46
big m. has no time FITZGERALD, F, 11
Brutus is an honourable m. SHAKESPEARE, W, 117
condition of m. is a condition of war HOBBES, T, 1
disguised as a complete M. HUXLEY, A, 4
England expects every m. will do his duty NELSON, VISCOUNT, 3
every m. did that which was right in his own eyes
BIBLE: JUDGES, 9
Every m. is as Heaven made him CERVANTES, M, 13
Every m. is wanted EMERSON, R, 10
Every m. meets his Waterloo PHILLIPS, W, 3
every prospect pleases, /And only m. is vile HEBER, R, 2
for m. or beast FIELDS, W, 1
Glory to M. in the highest SWINBURNE, A, 3
God made the woman for the m. TENNYSON, BARON, 9
Go West, young m. GREELEY, H, 1
hate ingratitude more in a m. SHAKESPEARE, W, 296
He is a m. of brick UPDIKE, J, 4
he owes not any m. LONGFELLOW, H, 15
I care not whether a m. is Good BLAKE, W, 15
I don't care if doesn't make a nickel, I just want every
m., woman, and child in America to see it GOLDWYN, S, 8
If a m. be gracious and courteous
BACON, 1ST BARON VERULAM, VISCOUNT ST ALBANS, 28
If a m. stays away from his wife DARLING, BARON, 1
I love not M. the less BYRON, 6TH BARON, 13
I myself also am a m. BIBLE: ACTS, 9
In wit a m. POPE, A, 16
I said to the m. who stood at the gate of the year HASKINS, M, 1
I see a m. hurrying along – to what KEATS, J, 64
I sing of arms and the m. VIRGIL, 2
It is good to know what a m. is BRADLEY, F, 3
Its narrow measure spans /Tears of eternity, and sorrow, /Not
mine, but m.'s HOUSMAN, A, 3
It's that m. again KAVANAGH, T, 3
It takes . . . twenty years to make a m. ROWLAND, H, 3
King is but a m. SHAKESPEARE, W, 97
little m. wears a shocking bad hat YORK AND ALBANY, DUKE OF, 1
make m. in our own image BIBLE: GENESIS, 6
m. alone leaves traces of what he created BRONOWSKI, J, 1
M.'s inhumanity to m. BURNS, R, 12
M.'s love is of m.'s life a thing apart BYRON, 6TH BARON, 17
m. being in honour hath no understanding PSALMS, 33
M., being reasonable, must get drunk BYRON, 6TH BARON, 18
M. . . . can neither repeat his past nor leave it behind AUDEN, W, 7
M. . . . can only find relaxation from one . . . labour by taking up
another FRANCE, A, 3
M. . . . consumes without producing ORWELL, G, 1
M. delights not me SHAKESPEARE, W, 57
m. did eat angels' food PSALMS, 47
mean m. is always full of distress CONFUCIUS, 10
m. fell into his anecdotage DISRAELI, 1ST EARL OF BEACONSFIELD, 6
m. . . . flourisheth as a flower of the field PSALMS, 64

M. for the field and woman for the hearth TENNYSON, BARON, 62
M., . . . grows beyond his work STEINBECK, J, 1
M. has his will HOLMES, O, 1
m. has stopped moving TEILHARD DE CHARDIN, P, 1
m. hath penance done COLERIDGE, S, 33
m. is a dangerous creature ADAMS, A, 1
M. is a history-making creature AUDEN, W, 7
M. is . . . an everlasting contradiction to himself HAZLITT, W, 3
M. is an intellectual animal HAZLITT, W, 3
M. is a noble animal BROWNE, SIR T, 12
M. is . . . a political animal ARISTOTLE, 6
m. is . . . a religious animal BURKE, E, 9
M. is a social animal SPINOZA, B, 2
m. is as old as he's feeling COLLINS, M, 1
M. is a tool-making animal FRANKLIN, B, 10
m. is . . . a wild animal DARWIN, C, 1
m. is like a thing of nought PSALMS, 88
M. is not a solitary animal RUSSELL, EARL, 7
M. is something that is to be surpassed NIETZSCHE, F, 16
M. is the hunter TENNYSON, BARON, 61
M. is the master of things SWINBURNE, A, 3
M. is the only animal that can remain on friendly terms with the
victims . . . he eats BUTLER, S, 20
M. . . . /Laid the crops low THOMAS, D, 11
m. made the town COWPER, W, 20
M. proposes KEMPIS, T, 4
m. right fair SHAKESPEARE, W, 269
m.'s greatest crime CALDERON DE LA BARCA, P, 1
M.'s inhumanity to m. BURNS, R, 12
M.'s life is cheap as beast's SHAKESPEARE, W, 136
M.'s love is of m.'s life a thing apart BYRON, 6TH BARON, 17
m. so various DRYDEN, J, 7
m.'s worth something BROWNING, R, 10
m. that hath no music in himself SHAKESPEARE, W, 196
m. that hath not walked in the counsel of the ungodly PSALMS, 1
m. that is born of a woman BIBLE: JOB, 9
m. that is young in years
BACON, 1ST BARON VERULAM, VISCOUNT ST ALBANS, 61
M. to command and woman to obey TENNYSON, BARON, 62
M. wants but little GOLDSMITH, O, 6
M. was born free ROUSSEAU, J, 1
m. who . . . had the largest . . . soul DRYDEN, J, 20
m. who's untrue to his wife AUDEN, W, 19
m. with all his noble qualities DARWIN, C, 1
M. with the head and woman with the heart TENNYSON, BARON, 62
no m. . . . hath lived better than I MALORY, SIR T, 1
No m. is a hypocrite in his pleasures CAMUS, A, 5
No m. is an Island DONNE, J, 5
No m. is good enough to govern another LINCOLN, A, 6
Nor in the critic let the m. be lost POPE, A, 29
Nothing happens to any m. MARCUS AURELIUS ANTONINUS, 9
Nothing links m. to m. like . . . cash SICKERT, W, 1
No young m. believes he shall ever die HAZLITT, W, 17
Of M.'s first disobedience MILTON, J, 25
On earth there is nothing great but m. HAMILTON, SIR W, 2
One cannot be always laughing at a m. AUSTEN, J, 22
one m. pick'd out of ten thousand SHAKESPEARE, W, 54
One m. shall have one vote CARTWRIGHT, J, 1
one small step for m. ARMSTRONG, N, 1
only place where a m. can feel . . . secure GREER, G, 1
rarely . . . one can see in a little boy the promise of a m.
DUMAS, FILS, 3
reason to lament /What m. has made of m. WORDSWORTH, W, 14
say to all the world 'This was a m.!' SHAKESPEARE, W, 124
single sentence . . . for modern m. CAMUS, A, 3
some meannesses . . . too mean even for m. THACKERAY, W, 7
Style is the m. himself BUFFON, COMTE DE, 1
superior m. is distressed by his want of ability CONFUCIUS, 13
superior m. is satisfied CONFUCIUS, 10
that grand old m. NORTHCOTE, 1ST EARL OF IDDESLEIGH, 1
That married the m. all tattered and torn NURSERY RHYMES, 62
The atrocious crime of being a young m.
PITT THE ELDER, 1ST EARL OF CHATHAM, 2
the century of the common m. WALLACE, H, 1
The Child is Father of the M. WORDSWORTH, W, 21
the field of the stars is so vast, but . . . m. has measured it
FRANCE, A, 5
the honest m. who married GOLDSMITH, O, 25
the M. Who Delivers the Goods MASON, W, 1
The m. who makes no mistakes PHELPS, E, 1
the m. whose second thoughts are good BARRIE, SIR J, 12

MCC where M. ends and the Church of England begins
PRIESTLEY, J, 6
McCarthyism M. is Americanism MCCARTHY, J, 1
McGregor Don't go into Mr M.'s garden POTTER, B, 2
me Besides Shakespeare and m., who do you think there is
STEIN, G, 4
between m. and the sun DIOGENES, 1
My thought is m. SARTRE, J, 6
on m. PARKER, D, 19
. . . we never talk about anything except m. WHISTLER, J, 3
meal A m. without flesh PROVERBS, 46
meals Any two m. at a boarding-house LEACOCK, S, 7
mean Down these m. streets CHANDLER, R, 4
He nothing common did or m. MARVELL, A, 4
He who meanly admires m. things is a Snob THACKERAY, W, 1
it means just what I choose it to m. CARROLL, L, 29
She was a woman of m. understanding AUSTEN, J, 16
'. . . you should say what you m.,' the March Hare went on
CARROLL, L, 6
meaner A patronizing disposition . . . has its m. side ELIOT, G, 1
motives m. than your own BARRIE, SIR J, 13
meanest the m. . . . deeds require spirit and talent
LICHTENBERG, G, 3
the m. of his creatures /Boasts two soul-sides BROWNING, R, 38
meaning Even when poetry has a m. HOUSMAN, A, 4
Literature is simply language charged with m. POUND, E, 9
Nature has never put the fatal question as to the m. of their lives
JUNG, C, 1
The least of things with a m. is worth more . . . than the greatest
JUNG, C, 7
meannesses some m. . . . too mean even for man THACKERAY, W, 7
means I shall have to die beyond my m., WILDE, O, 60
Let us all be happy, and live within our m. WARD, A, 5
m. just what I choose it to mean CARROLL, L, 29
We are living beyond our m. MEAD, M, 1
measles Love is like the m. JEROME, J, 1
Love's like the m. JERROLD, D, 5
measure M. still for Measure SHAKESPEARE, W, 186
Shrunk to this little m. SHAKESPEARE, W, 112
measured the field of the stars is so vast, but . . . man has m. it
FRANCE, A, 5
measureless caverns m. to man COLERIDGE, S, 12
meat man loves the m. in his youth SHAKESPEARE, W, 211
one man is appointed to buy the m. SELDEN, J, 1
One man's m. PROVERBS, 329
out of the eater came forth m. BIBLE: JUDGES, 5
Some hae m., and canna eat BURNS, R, 17
The public buys its opinions as it buys its m. BUTLER, S, 15
meats m. for the belly BIBLE: I CORINTHIANS, 5
meddling He was m. too much in my private life WILLIAMS, T, 7
media The m. . . . a convention of spiritualists STOPPARD, T, 6
medicine miserable have no other m. SHAKESPEARE, W, 182
when religion was strong and science weak, men mistook magic
for m. SZASZ, T, 3
medieval disillusionments in the lives of the m. saints SAKI, 13
mediocre A best-seller is the gilded tomb of a m. talent
SMITH, L, 1
more than magnificent – . . . m. GOLDWYN, S, 20
Some men are born m. HELLER, J, 5
Titles distinguish the m. SHAW, G, 26
Women want m. men MEAD, M, 2
mediocrity M. knows nothing higher DOYLE, SIR A, 15
supreme expression of the m. TROTSKY, L, 10
Mediterranean All my wife has ever taken from the M.
SHAFFER, P, 1
medium The m. is the message MCLUHAN, M, 4
meek humble and m. are thirsting for blood ORTON, J, 3
m. and lowly in heart BIBLE: MATTHEW, 41
m. and mild WESLEY, C, 1
Moses was very m. BIBLE: NUMBERS, 2
the highest authority for believing that the m. shall inherit the
Earth BIRKENHEAD, EARL OF, 1
The m. do not inherit the earth LASKI, H, 1
Wisdom has taught us to be calm and m. HOLMES, O, 3
meet M. on the stairs PROVERBS, 291
never the twain shall m. KIPLING, R, 1
The only way for writers to m. CONNOLLY, C, 12
Two may talk . . . yet never really m. CATHERWOOD, M, 1
We only part to m. again GAY, J, 12
meeting as If I was a public m. VICTORIA, 5
My life's been a m., Dad THOMAS, G, 2

this m. is drunk DICKENS, C, 46
megalomaniac m. . . . seeks to be feared RUSSELL, EARL, 5
melancholy a pleasing fit of m. MILTON, J, 5
hell upon earth . . . in a m. man's heart BURTON, R, 2
M. has her sovran shrine KEATS, J, 29
Most musical, most m. MILTON, J, 8
so sweet as M. BURTON, R, 1
Melba Dame Nellie M. HASKELL, A, 1
mellows A tart temper never m. with age IRVING, W, 2
melodies Heard m. are sweet KEATS, J, 23
melody m. imposes continuity upon the disjointed MENUHIN, SIR Y, 1
melting the races of Europe are m. ZANGWILL, I, 2
melting-pot America is . . . the great M. ZANGWILL, I, 2
member the tongue is a little m. BIBLE: JAMES, 5
members in thy book were all my m. written PSALMS, 87
même plus c'est la m. chose KARR, A, 1
memorandum A m. is written ACHESON, D, 5
memorial executed a m. longer lasting than bronze. HORACE, 39
some there be, which have no m. BIBLE: ECCLESIASTICUS, 15
memories M. are hunting horns APOLLINAIRE, G, 1
memory Everyone complains of his m.
ROCHEFOUCAULD, DUC DE LA, 13
Fond M. brings the light /Of other days MOORE, T, 7
For my name and m., I leave it to . . . the next ages
BACON, 1ST BARON VERULAM, VISCOUNT ST ALBANS, 68
good m. is needed after one has lied CORNEILLE, P, 4
His m. is going JOHNSON, S, 140
How sweet their m. still COWPER, W, 12
Illiterate him . . . from your m. SHERIDAN, R, 3
I would rather be a brilliant m. than a curiosity EAMES, E, 1
m. is a painter GRANDMA MOSES, 1
Music . . . /Vibrates in the m. SHELLEY, P, 23
O m., hope, love of finished years ROSSETTI, C, 1
Time whereof the m. of man BLACKSTONE, SIR W, 3
Unless a man feels he has a good enough m. MONTAIGNE, M, 3
What a strange thing is m., and hope GRANDMA MOSES, 1
men all m. are created equal JEFFERSON, T, 3
all m. are liars PSALMS, 73
all m. have one entrance into life BIBLE: WISDOM, 3
all m. would be tyrants DEFOE, D, 2
depict m. as they ought to be SOPHOCLES, 1
England . . . purgatory of m. FLORIO, J, 1
fishers of m. BIBLE: MATTHEW, 9
give place to better m. CROMWELL, O, 4
great city . . . has the greatest m. and women WHITMAN, W, 10
Great m. are almost always bad m. . . . ACTON, 1ST BARON, 2
great m. have not commonly been great scholars HOLMES, O, 3
happy breed of m. SHAKESPEARE, W, 237
honour all m. BIBLE: I PETER, 3
If m. knew how women pass the time HENRY, O, 1
It brings m. together in crowds and mobs in bar-rooms
THOREAU, H, 5
m. about me that are fat SHAKESPEARE, W, 107
m. and sea interpenetrate CONRAD, J, 8
Many m. would take the death-sentence LAWRENCE, T, 1
M. are but children of a larger growth DRYDEN, J, 16
M. are . . . more careful of the breed of their horses PENN, W, 2
M. are not hanged for stealing horses HALIFAX, MARQUIS OF, 1
M. are we, and must grieve WORDSWORTH, W, 56
m. . . . capable of every wickedness CONRAD, J, 7
M. come of age at sixty STEPHENS, J, 3
m. devote the greater part of their lives LA BRUYÈRE, J, 2
m. everywhere could be free LINCOLN, A, 4
M. fear death BACON, 1ST BARON VERULAM, VISCOUNT ST ALBANS, 18
M. have never been good BARTH, K, 1
M. of few words are the best m. SHAKESPEARE, W, 96
Most m. admire /Virtue MILTON, J, 48
m. represent . . . mind over morals WILDE, O, 47
M.'s natures are alike CONFUCIUS, 3
m. think all m. mortal YOUNG, E, 3
M. will always be mad VOLTAIRE, 24
M. will confess COLBY, F, 1
O! m. with sisters dear HOOD, T, 11
power over m. WOLLSTONECRAFT, M, 2
proclaiming that women are brighter than m. LOOS, A, 5
rich m. rule the law GOLDSMITH, O, 22
schemes o' mice an' m. BURNS, R, 20
So many m., so many opinions TERENCE, 4
Such m. are dangerous SHAKESPEARE, W, 107
That all m. are equal HUXLEY, A, 28

Wives are young men's m.
BACON, 1ST BARON VERULAM, VISCOUNT ST ALBANS, 34
**mistrust** M. first impulses TALLEYRAND, 7
**mistrusted** If the white man *says* he does, he is instantly . . . m.
MACINNES, C, 3
**mists** Season of m. KEATS, J, 40
**misunderstood** To be great is to be m. EMERSON, R, 14
**Mitty** Walter M., the undefeated THURBER, J, 10
**mix** I m. them with my brains OPIE, J, 1
**mixed** a m. infant BEHAN, B, 4
not to look like a m. grill COWARD, SIR N, 8
**mob** do what the m. do DICKENS, C, 41
Our supreme governors, the m. WALPOLE, 4TH EARL OF ORFORD, 3
**mobs** It brings men together in crowds and m. in bar-rooms
THOREAU, H, 5
**mock** Let not Ambition m. GRAY, T, 2
M. on, m. on, Voltaire, Rousseau BLAKE, W, 32
**mockery** death itself must be . . . a m. SHELLEY, P, 21
**mockingbird** it's a sin to kill a m. LEE, H, 2
**mode** Fancy is . . . a m. of memory COLERIDGE, S, 4
**model** The idea that there is a m. Labour voter, . . . is patronizing
KINNOCK, N, 11
very m. of a modern Major-General GILBERT, SIR W, 37
**models** Rules and m. destroy genius and art HAZLITT, W, 27
**moderation** astonished at my own m. CLIVE OF PLASSEY, BARON, 1
M. in all things PROVERBS, 293
m. in the pursuit of justice is no virtue GOLDWATER, B, 2
**modern** a m. poet's fate HOOD, T, 14
Imagination without skill gives us m. art STOPPARD, T, 1
It is so stupid of m. civilization KNOX, R, 1
The m. pantheist not only LAWRENCE, D, 19
**modest** and is m. about it AGATE, J, 2
Be m.! It is the kind of pride least likely to offend RENARD, J, 1
**modester** People ought to be m. CARLYLE, T, 31
**modesty** a woman . . . ought to lay aside . . . m. with her skirt
MONTAIGNE, M, 4
Enough for m. BUCHANAN, R, 1
I have often wished I had time to cultivate m. SITWELL, DAME E, 5
There is false m., but there is no false pride RENARD, J, 3
where the Greeks had m., we have cant PEACOCK, T, 2
**Mohammed** If the mountain will not come to M.
BACON, 1ST BARON VERULAM, VISCOUNT ST ALBANS, 14
**Mohicans** The Last of the M. COOPER, J, 1
**moi** *L'Etat c'est m.* LOUIS XIV, 4
**mole** Death is still working like a m. HERBERT, G, 5
**Molly** Tonight the American flag floats from yonder hill or M.
Stark sleeps a widow STARK, J, 1
**moment** a m. of time ELIZABETH I, 9
A m. of time may make us unhappy for ever GAY, J, 1
Every m. one is born TENNYSON, BARON, 78
in a m. of time BIBLE: LUKE, 13
**Mona** A lotta cats copy the M. Lisa ARMSTRONG, L, 1
I have . . . . . . several original M. Lisas MILLIGAN, S, 2
**monarch** of all I survey COWPER, W, 32
**monarchy** M. is a strong government BAGEHOT, W, 3
The m. is a labour-intensive industry WILSON OF RIEVAULX, BARON, 5
The Sovereign has, under a constitutional m. . . . three rights
BAGEHOT, W, 7
tourists . . . take in the M. . . . with . . . the pigeons
HAMILTON, W, 1
**Monday** is going to do on M. YBARRA, T, 1
M.'s child is fair of face NURSERY RHYMES, 35
M.'s child PROVERBS, 294
Solomon Grundy,/Born on a M. NURSERY RHYMES, 53
**money** a bank that would lend m. to such a poor risk
BENCHLEY, R, 5
a licence to print your own m. THOMSON OF FLEET, BARON, 1
always try to rub up against m. RUNYON, D, 2
art . . . of draining m. SMITH, A, 3
be not greedy to add m. to m. BIBLE: TOBIT, 1
Brigands demand your m. or your life BUTLER, S, 29
Business, . . . may bring m., . . . friendship hardly ever does
AUSTEN, J, 6
collect legal taxes from illegal m. CAPONE, A, 3
descriptions of m. changing hands DENNIS, N, 2
except for large sums of m. AYCKBOURN, A, 1
France is a country where the m. falls apart WILDER, B, 2
Give him the m. PICKLES, W, 1
Good Samaritan . . . had m. as well THATCHER, M, 7
He that wants m., means, and content SHAKESPEARE, W, 27
If possible honestly, if not, somehow, make m. HORACE, 15

If you can . . . count your m. you are not . . . rich man GETTY, J, 1
innocently employed than in getting m. JOHNSON, S, 88
Just what God would have done if he had the m. WOOLLCOTT, A, 3
killed a lot of men to have made so much m. MOLIERE, 5
love of m. is the root of all evil BIBLE: 1 TIMOTHY, 6
m. answereth all things BIBLE: ECCLESIASTES, 21
M. can't buy friends MILLIGAN, S, 10
m. can't buy me love LENNON, J, 2
M. gives me pleasure BELLOC, H, 9
m. has something to do with life LARKIN, P, 1
M. is good for bribing yourself REINHARDT, G, 1
M. is like a sixth sense MAUGHAM, W, 13
M. is like muck BACON, 1ST BARON VERULAM, VISCOUNT ST ALBANS, 45
M., it turned out, was exactly like sex BALDWIN, J, 2
M. . . . . source of anxiety GALBRAITH, J, 7
pleasant it is to have m. CLOUGH, A, 3
Put m. in thy purse SHAKESPEARE, W, 219
the love of m. is the root of all evil BUTLER, S, 6
The man who leaves m. to charity in his will VOLTAIRE, 28
the poor person . . . thinks m. would help KERR, J, 2
The profession of letters . . . in which one can make no m.
without being ridiculous RENARD, J, 2
They had been corrupted by m. GREENE, G, 6
they have more m. FITZGERALD, F, 3
time is m. FRANKLIN, B, 1
To be clever enough to get . . . m., one must be stupid
CHESTERTON, G, 22
to waste my time making m. AGASSIZ, J, 1
We all know how the size of sums of m. appears to vary
HUXLEY, SIR J, 1
We haven't the m., so we've got to think RUTHERFORD, BARON, 1
We've got the ships, we've got the men, we've got the m. too
HUNT, G, 1
what risks you take . . . to find m. in a desk BALZAC, H, 4
what the Lord God thinks of m. BARING, M, 1
Where large sums of m. are concerned, . . . trust nobody
CHRISTIE, DAME A, 2
with m. . . . . they have not got HURST, SIR G, 1
You can be young without m. WILLIAMS, T, 2
**monkey** no reason to attack the m. when the organ-grinder is
present BEVAN, A, 10
the biggest asset the m. possesses ROGERS, W, 6
**monopoly** imperialism is the m. stage of capitalism LENIN, V, 1
**Monroe** Marilyn M.'s MILLER, A, 6
**monster** jealousy . . . green-ey'd m. SHAKESPEARE, W, 224
**Montagu** Mrs M. has dropt me JOHNSON, S, 133
**Monte Carlo** M. BRADLEY, F, 2
the man who broke the Bank at M. GILBERT, F, 1
**month** April is the cruellest m. ELIOT, T, 23
**months** two m. of every year BYRON, 6TH BARON, 4
**monument** If you seek my m., look around you WREN, SIR C, 1
like Patience on a m. SHAKESPEARE, W, 291
sonnet is a moment's m. ROSSETTI, D, 1
The m. sticks like a fishbone LOWELL, R, 2
**monuments** Not marble, nor the gilded m. SHAKESPEARE, W, 258
**monumentum** *Si m. requiris, circumspice* WREN, SIR C, 1
**moo** You silly m. SPEIGHT, J, 1
**moon** By the light of the m. BYRON, 6TH BARON, 39
If they had said the sun and the m. was gone CARLYLE, J, 3
I saw the new m. late yestreen ANONYMOUS, 83
I see the m., /And the m. sees me NURSERY RHYMES, 24
moving M. went up the sky COLERIDGE, S, 33
neither the m. by night PSALMS, 77
nothing left remarkable beneath the . . . m. SHAKESPEARE, W, 15
shine on, shine on, harvest m. NORWORTH, J, 1
The m. doth shine as bright as day NURSERY RHYMES, 6
the m.'s /a balloon CUMMINGS, E, 1
The m. was a ghostly galleon NOYES, A, 1
They danced by the light of the m. LEAR, E, 9
th' inconstant m. SHAKESPEARE, W, 246
We're very wide awake, /The m. and I GILBERT, SIR W, 28
**moonlecht** a braw brecht m. necht LAUDER, SIR H, 1
**moonlight** Look for me by m. NOYES, A, 2
**moons** So sicken waning m. too near the sun DRYDEN, J, 17
**moral** 2 percent m., 48 percent indignation and 50 percent envy
DE SICA, V, 1
All universal m. principles are idle fancies SADE, MARQUIS DE, 1
each man must struggle, lest the m. law become . . . separated
ADDAMS, J, 2
Everything's got a m. CARROLL, L, 10
it should preach a high m. lesson STRACHEY, L, 2

Let us be m.     DICKENS, C. 23
Love is m. even without . . . marriage     KEY, E. 5
m. attribute of a Scotsman     BARRIE, SIR J. 10
M. indignation is in most cases     DE SICA, V. 1
m. or an immoral book     WILDE, O. 41
more than a m. duty to speak one's mind     WILDE, O. 25
one is unhappy one becomes m.     PROUST, M. 5
The highest possible stage in m. culture     DARWIN, C. 2
the m. law     KANT, I. 1
The worst government is the most m.     MENCKEN, H. 8
moralist A Scotsman must be a very sturdy m.     JOHNSON, S. 15
no sterner m. than Pleasure     BYRON, 6TH BARON, 21
morality Dr Johnson's m. was as English . . . as a beefsteak     HAWTHORNE, N. 2
M. . . . is herd-morality     NIETZSCHE, F. 11
M.'s a gesture. . . . learnt from books     BOLT, R. 1
M.'s not practical     BOLT, R. 1
M. which is based on ideas     LAWRENCE, D. 6
No m. can be founded on authority     AYER, SIR A. 1
periodical fits of m.     MACAULAY, BARON, 16
This imperative may be called that of M.     KANT, I. 2
two kinds of m. . . . ; one which we preach but do not practise     RUSSELL, EARL, 17
morals basing m. on myth     SAMUEL, VISCOUNT, 5
If your m. make you dreary     STEVENSON, R. 1
men represent . . . mind over m.     WILDE, O. 47
the faith and m. hold /Which Milton held     WORDSWORTH, W. 49
the m. of a whore, and the manners of a dancing master     JOHNSON, S. 48
mordre M. wol out     CHAUCER, G. 15
More Sir Thomas M.     WHITTINGTON, R. 1
more As I know m. of mankind     JOHNSON, S. 144
M. than somewhat     RUNYON, D. 3
Oliver Twist has asked for m.     DICKENS, C. 33
Specialist – A man who knows m. and m. about less and less     MAYO, W. 1
The m. the merrier     PROVERBS, 401
morn From m. to night, my friend     ROSSETTI, C. 6
From m. /To noon he fell     MILTON, J. 33
He rose the morrow m.     COLERIDGE, S. 38
the opening eye-lids of the m.     MILTON, J. 17
mornin' nice to get up in the m.     LAUDER, SIR H. 2
morning Early one m., just as the sun was rising     ANONYMOUS, 16
I awoke one m.     BYRON, 6TH BARON, 42
I'm getting married in the m.     LERNER, A. 5
in the m. it is green     PSALMS, 55
joy cometh in the m.     PSALMS, 19
M. in the Bowl of Night     FITZGERALD, E. 2
Oh, what a beautiful m.     HAMMERSTEIN, O. 3
she has lived . . . the space of one m.     MALHERBE, F. 1
that . . . turneth the shadow of death into the m.     BIBLE: AMOS, 1
the m. cometh, and also the night     BIBLE: ISAIAH, 18
'Tis always m. somewhere     HORNE, R. 1
morrow take . . . no thought for the m.     BIBLE: MATTHEW, 22
mortal All men are m.     PROVERBS, 35
I was not unaware that I had begotten a m.     GOETHE, J. 10
men think all men m.     YOUNG, E. 3
The doctor found, . . . /Her last disorder m.     GOLDSMITH, O. 7
we have been m. enemies ever since     LESAGE, A. 2
mortality kept watch o'er man's m.     WORDSWORTH, W. 30
M., behold and fear     BEAUMONT, F. 9
mortals A novelist is, like all m.     NABOKOV, V. 6
We m. cross the ocean     BROWNING, R. 6
what fools these m. be     SHAKESPEARE, W. 205
Moscow don't march on M.     MONTGOMERY OF ALAMEIN, VISCOUNT, 1
Moses he saw his role as being that of M.     JAY, P. 1
M. was very meek     BIBLE: NUMBERS, 1
there arose not a prophet . . . like unto M.     BIBLE: DEUTERONOMY, 9
most The M. may err as grosly     DRYDEN, J. 10
mostest I got there fustest with the m.     FORREST, N. 1
mote the m. that is in thy brother's eye     BIBLE: MATTHEW, 24
moth a m. fretting a garment     PSALMS, 27
like a m., the simple maid /Still plays about the flame     GAY, J. 2
The desire of the m. for the star     JOYCE, J. 8
mother And Her M. Came Too     NOVELLO, I. 1
as is the m., so is her daughter     BIBLE: EZEKIEL, 3
because my m. needed a fourth at meals     LILLIE, B. 1
behold thy m.     BIBLE: JOHN, 49
Dead! and . . . never called me m.     WOOD, MRS. 1
Eve . . . the m. of all living     BIBLE: GENESIS, 16
I am old enough to be – in fact am – your m.     MILNE, A. 1

If poverty is the m. of crime, stupidity is its father     LA BRUYERE, J. 11
I wished to be near my m.     WHISTLER, J. 16
Jerusalem . . . the m. of us all     BIBLE: GALATIANS, 3
May you be the m. of a bishop     BEHAN, B. 11
M. is the dead heart of the family     GREER, G. 2
M. of the Free     BENSON, A. 1
My m., drunk or sober     CHESTERTON, G. 5
the m. of parliaments     BRIGHT, J. 2
the titles of wife and m. . . . are transitory and accidental     LIVERMORE, M. 2
this war, . . . which did not justify the sacrifice of a single m.'s son     PANKHURST, S. 1
motherhood wifehood and m. are but incidental relations     STANTON, E. 5
mother-in-law as the man said when his m. died     JEROME, J. 6
What a marvellous place to drop one's m.     FOCH, MARSHAL, 2
mothers Come m. and fathers /Throughout the land     DYLAN, B. 7
O! men with m. and wives!     HOOD, T. 11
women become like their m.     WILDE, O. 18
mothers-in-law Two m.     RUSSELL, EARL, 1
motives m. meaner than your own     BARRIE, SIR J. 13
mould If you cannot m. yourself     KEMPIS, T. 3
Nature made him, and then broke the m.     ARIOSTO, L. 1
mountain A m. in labour shouted so loud     LA FONTAINE, J. 6
hardly be a beast or a fool alone on a great m.     KILVERT, F. 2
If the m. will not come to Mohammed     BACON, 1ST BARON VERULAM, VISCOUNT ST ALBANS, 14
Land of the m. and the flood     SCOTT, SIR W. 7
never see another m.     LAMB, C. 22
mountains all faith, so that I could remove m.     BIBLE: I CORINTHIANS, 18
England's m. green     BLAKE, W. 31
highest intellects, like the tops of m.     MACAULAY, BARON, 6
how beautiful upon the m. are the feet     BIBLE: ISAIAH, 32
if the Swiss had designed these m.     THEROUX, P. 2
M. interposed /Make enemies of nations     COWPER, W. 26
m. look on Marathon     BYRON, 6TH BARON, 24
M. . . . the beginning and the end of all natural scenery.     RUSKIN, J. 4
M. will heave in childbirth     HORACE, 6
the m. skipped like rams     PSALMS, 70
Two voices . . . one is of the sea, /One of the m.     WORDSWORTH, W. 58
when men and m. meet     BLAKE, W. 12
mourn countless thousands m.     BURNS, R. 12
it is chiefly our own deaths that we m. for     BRENAN, G. 1
To m. a mischief that is past     SHAKESPEARE, W. 218
mourning I'm in m. for my life     CHEKHOV, A. 4
in m. . . . for the world     SITWELL, DAME E. 3
tedium is the very basis of m.     HUGO, V. 3
We met . . . Dr Hall in such very deep m.     AUSTEN, J. 28
What we call m. for our dead     MANN, T. 1
with my m. . . . and new periwig     PEPYS, S. 10
mouse a silly little m. will be born     HORACE, 6
He bought a crooked cat, which caught a crooked m.     NURSERY RHYMES, 57
leave room for the m.     SAKI, 22
she brought forth a m.     LA FONTAINE, J. 6
The m. ran up the clock     NURSERY RHYMES, 15
mouse-trap If a man make a better m.     EMERSON, R. 24
moustache a kiss without a m.     CAWEIN, M. 1
A kiss without a m.     SARTRE, J. 12
a man outside with a big black m.     MARX, G. 10
Being kissed by a man who didn't wax his m.     KIPLING, R. 24
his nicotine eggyellow weeping walrus Victorian m.     THOMAS, D. 20
mouth A politician is a statesman . . . with an open m.     STEVENSON, A. 2
butter wouldn't melt in her m.     LANCHESTER, E. 1
God be in my m., /And in my speaking     ANONYMOUS, 20
Keep your m. shut and your eyes open     PROVERBS, 241
out of the m. of . . . babes and sucklings     PSALMS, 3
out of thine own m. will I judge thee     BIBLE: LUKE, 33
the praises of God be in their m.     PSALMS, 93
mouth-brothels Great restaurants are . . . nothing but m.     RAPHAEL, F. 4
mouths m., and speak not     PSALMS, 71
move But did thee feel the earth m.?     HEMINGWAY, E. 2
in him we live, and m., and have our being     BIBLE: ACTS, 13
I will m. the earth     ARCHIMEDES, 1
The great affair is to m.     STEVENSON, R. 5

## N

The weariest n. . . . must . . . end ORCZY, BARONESS, 2
They shorten tedious n. CAMPION, T, 5
nihilist a part-time n. CAMUS, A, 10
Nile England may as well dam . . . the N. with bulrushes
CHILD, L, 3
my serpent of old N. SHAKESPEARE, W, 6
Nimrod N. the mighty hunter BIBLE: GENESIS, 29
nine N. drummers drumming NURSERY RHYMES, 60
N. for the n. bright shiners ANONYMOUS, 45
ninepence I have but n. in ready money ADDISON, J, 16
ninety stood n. years on the floor WORK, H, 2
Nineveh Quinquireme of N. MASEFIELD, J, 2
nip I'll n. him in the bud ROCHE, SIR B, 2
Nixon standing between N. and the White House KENNEDY, J, 7
You won't have N. to kick around NIXON, R, 3
no girls . . . say N. when they mean Yes ALCOTT, L, 3
rebel . . . man who says n. CAMUS, A, 11
Noah Out of their cataclysm but one poor N. /Dare hope to
survive. HUXLEY, A, 16
nobility N. has its own obligations LEVIS, DUC DE, 1
noble a n. nature, . . . treats . . . a serious subject ARNOLD, M, 30
Englishman never enjoys himself except for a n. purpose
HERBERT, SIR A, 6
n. grounds for the n. emotions RUSKIN, J, 3
Ridicule . . . smothers that which is n. SCOTT, SIR W, 15
The n. living and the n. dead WORDSWORTH, W, 38
nobleman a king may make a n. BURKE, E, 22
nobleness perfect plainness of speech . . . perfect n. ARNOLD, M, 29
noblest n. man /That ever lived in the tide of times
SHAKESPEARE, W, 113
n. Roman of them all SHAKESPEARE, W, 123
nobly the immature man . . . wants to die n. for a cause
STEKEL, W, 1
nobody a man is n. unless his biography TROLLOPE, A, 5
I care for n. . . . /If no one cares for me BICKERSTAFFE, I, 2
N. asked you, sir, she said NURSERY RHYMES, 71
whom n. loves CORNFORD, F, 1
Nod the land of N. BIBLE: GENESIS, 20
nod A n. is as good as a wink PROVERBS, 55
nods even excellent Homer n. HORACE, 9
no go It's n. the picture palace MACNEICE, L, 1
noise A loud n. at one end KNOX, R, 3
dreadful n. of waters in my ears SHAKESPEARE, W, 242
the less they have . . . the more n. they make POPE, A, 53
the n. of the shout of joy BIBLE: EZRA, 1
they . . . love the n. it makes BEECHAM, SIR T, 2
Those people . . . are making such a n. I can't hear a word you're
saying PARKER, H, 1
noises Like n. in a swound COLERIDGE, S, 24
noisome the n. pestilence PSALMS, 57
noisy Strongest minds / . . . the n. world /Hears least
WORDSWORTH, W, 1
The people would be just as n. CROMWELL, O, 6
noli n. me tangere BIBLE: JOHN, 55
nomadic the charm . . . of a n. existence SACKVILLE-WEST, V, 5
No Man's Land why Absurdist plays take place in N. ADAMOV, A, 1
nominated I will not accept if n., and will not serve if elected
SHERMAN, GENERAL, 1
No-more I am also called N. ROSSETTI, D, 2
non-being Neurosis is the way of avoiding n. TILLICH, P, 1
non-combatant War hath no fury like a n. MONTAGUE, C, 1
nonconformist a N. conscience WILDE, O, 39
man must be a n. EMERSON, R, 12
Why do you have to be a n. THURBER, J, 17
nonconformity N. and lust stalking hand in hand WAUGH, E, 9
none N. but the Brave DRYDEN, J, 14
nonsense you intend to talk n. KEYNES, BARON, 9
Non-U U and N. ROSS, A, 1
non-violence to disagree . . . about . . . n. without wanting to kick
HAMPTON, C, 4
noon From morn /To n. he fell MILTON, J, 33
from n. to dewy eve MILTON, J, 53
O dark, dark, dark, amid the blaze of n. MILTON, J, 53
noon-day the sickness that destroyeth in the n. PSALMS, 57
no one become accustomed to n. governing LENIN, V, 5
Norfolk bear him up the N. sky BETJEMAN, SIR J, 1
Very flat, N. COWARD, SIR N, 14
Norgay Tenzing N. HILLARY, SIR E, 1
Norma Goodbye N. Jean TAUPIN, B, 1
normal the n. is so . . . interesting STEIN, G, 1
Normans The Saxon is not like us N. KIPLING, R, 18

north The n. wind does blow PROVERBS, 403
nose A custom loathsome to the eye, hateful to the n. JAMES I, 1
A person may be indebted for a n. or an eye, . . . to a great-aunt
HAZLITT, W, 23
Dong with a luminous N. LEAR, E, 3
Entuned in hir n. ful semely CHAUCER, G, 4
Had Cleopatra's n. been shorter PASCAL, B, 6
led by the n. with gold SHAKESPEARE, W, 305
My n. is huge ROSTAND, E, 1
Only the n. knows ALI, M, 3
This fellow did not see further than his . . . n. LA FONTAINE, J, 5
will it come without warning /Just as I'm picking my n.
AUDEN, W, 24
noses n. . . . and smell not PSALMS, 71
nostrils God . . . breathed into his n. BIBLE: GENESIS, 8
not Believe it or n. RIPLEY, R, 1
how n. to do it DICKENS, C, 19
note make a n. of DICKENS, C, 16
The world will little n., nor long remember LINCOLN, A, 12
notes the pauses between the n. SCHNABEL, A, 2
nothin' You ain't heard n. yet JOLSON, A, 1
nothing Blessed is the man who expects n. POPE, A, 58
Certainly, there is n. else here to enjoy SHAW, G, 47
certain we can carry n. out BIBLE: I TIMOTHY, 5
Children aren't happy with n. to ignore NASH, O, 8
doing n. for each other CROSBY, B, 1
from n. to a state of extreme poverty MARX, G, 13
God made everything out of n. VALERY, P, 1
have n. whatever to do with it MAUGHAM, W, 26
N. can be created out of n. LUCRETIUS, 1
n. can bring back the hour WORDSWORTH, W, 27
n. either good or bad SHAKESPEARE, W, 56
N., except my genius WILDE, O, 73
N. happens BECKETT, S, 2
n. if not critical SHAKESPEARE, W, 220
n. is certain but death and taxes FRANKLIN, B, 15
n., . . . is greater . . . than one's self WHITMAN, W, 7
n. is had for n. CLOUGH, A, 2
n. is law that is not reason. POWELL, SIR J, 1
N. long DRYDEN, J, 7
N. matters very much BALFOUR, 1ST EARL OF, 5
N. to do but work KING, B, 1
n. to do with the case GILBERT, SIR W, 33
N. will come of n. SHAKESPEARE, W, 130
one would almost feel disposed to bury for n. DICKENS, C, 27
opened it only to find – n. AESOP, 1
Signifying n. SHAKESPEARE, W, 177
sooner read a time-table . . . than n. MAUGHAM, W, 28
take more than n. CARROLL, L, 8
The House of Peers, throughout the war, /Did n. in particular
GILBERT, SIR W, 20
The temerity to believe in n. TURGENEV, I, 2
those who were up to n. COWARD, SIR N, 7
To marvel at n. is just about the one and only thing HORACE, 19
We are n.; less than n., and dreams LAMB, C, 2
When you have n. to say, say n. COLTON, C, 2
Where some people are very wealthy and others have n.
ARISTOTLE, 8
nothingness the n. shows through VALERY, P, 1
notice The State, in choosing men . . . takes no n. of their opinions
CROMWELL, O, 7
notices One never n. what has been done CURIE, M, 4
nought man is like a thing of n. PSALMS, 88
N.'s had, all's spent SHAKESPEARE, W, 170
nourisher a n. of thine old age BIBLE: RUTH, 1
Chief n. in life's feast SHAKESPEARE, W, 167
novel Among the many problems . . . the choice of the moment . . .
to begin his n. SACKVILLE-WEST, V, 1
A n. is a mirror STENDHAL, 1
A n. is a static thing TYNAN, K, 1
because a n.'s invented, it isn't true POWELL, A, 7
good n. tells us the truth CHESTERTON, G, 20
I'm going to write the Great Australian N. WHITE, P, 4
not a n. to be tossed aside lightly PARKER, D, 15
scrofulous French n. BROWNING, R, 53
the last fashionable n. on the tables of young ladies
MACAULAY, BARON, 20
The n. being dead VIDAL, G, 1
the n. tells a story FORSTER, E, 5
The only obligation to which . . . we may hold a n. JAMES, H, 6

to read a n. before luncheon was one of the gravest sins
WAUGH, E, 43
When I want to read a n.   DISRAELI, 1ST EARL OF BEACONSFIELD, 37
**novelist** A n. is, like all mortals   NABOKOV, V, 6
**novelists** n. the story of the present   GONCOURT, E, 1
There are many reasons why n. write   FOWLES, J, 3
**novels** characters in one of my n.   FITZGERALD, F, 13
one of the few English n. for grown up people   WOOLF, V, 2
**novelty** N., n., n.   HOOD, T, 15
**November** N.!   HOOD, T, 10
Please to remember the Fifth of N.   ANONYMOUS, 69
Thirty days hath N.   GRAFTON, R, 1
**now** We are all Socialists n.   HARCOURT, SIR W, 1
**nowhere** All dressed up, with n. to go   WHITE, W, 1
He's a real N. Man   LENNON, J, 8
**noxious** the most n. is a tourist   KILVERT, F, 1
**nude** To keep one from going n.   KING, B, 1
**nuisance** exchange of one n. for another n.   ELLIS, H, 1
Inflation in the Sixties was a n.   LEVIN, B, 1
Never compose . . . unless . . . not composing . . . becomes a
positive n.   HOLST, G, 1
**nuisances** a change of n. is as good as a vacation
LLOYD GEORGE, EARL OF DWYFOR, 12
**number** a very interesting n.   RAMANUJAN, S, 1
Does it contain any abstract reasoning concerning quantity or n.?
HUME, D, 2
Look after n. one   PROVERBS, 266
**numbers** divinity in odd n.   SHAKESPEARE, W, 200
Round n.   JOHNSON, S, 116
the greatest happiness for the greatest n.   HUTCHESON, F, 1
up in the high n.   KEYNES, BARON, 10
**numble** We live in a n. abode   DICKENS, C, 11
**numbness** drowsy n. pains /My sense   KEATS, J, 30
**nun** the upbringing a n. would envy   ORTON, J, 1
**nuns** the n. who never take a bath   RUSSELL, EARL, 4
**nuptials** prone to any iteration of n.   CONGREVE, W, 14
**nurse** No *man* . . . gives any other definition of . . . a n. . . . than
. . . "devoted and obedient."   NIGHTINGALE, F, 1
N. unupblown   WAUGH, E, 48
**nurseries** n. of all vice   FIELDING, H, 7
**nurses** old men's n.
BACON, 1ST BARON VERULAM, VISCOUNT ST ALBANS, 34
**nut** I had a little n. tree, /Nothing would it bear
NURSERY RHYMES, 20
**nut-brown** the spicy ,n. ale   MILTON, J, 13
**nutmeg** But a silver n.   NURSERY RHYMES, 20

# O

**oak** Absalom hanged in an o.   BIBLE: II SAMUEL, 5
Heart of o. are our ships   GARRICK, D, 2
To win the palm, the o., or bays   MARVELL, A, 1
**oar** impressions . . . lasting as . . . an o. upon the water
CHOPIN, K, 3
**oat** This bread I break was once the o.   THOMAS, D, 11
**oat-cakes** land of Calvin, o., and sulphur   SMITH, S, 7
**oath** In lapidary inscriptions a man is not upon o.   JOHNSON, S, 96
**oaths** O. are but words   BUTLER, S, 6
**obedience** Resistance to tyranny is o. to God   ANTHONY, S, 4
The reluctant o. of distant provinces   MACAULAY, BARON, 5
**obedient** definition of . . . a nurse . . . "devoted and o."
NIGHTINGALE, F, 1
o. unto death   BIBLE: PHILIPPIANS, 1
**obey** born to o.   COMPTON-BURNETT, DAME I, 3
children, o. your parents   BIBLE: EPHESIANS, 3
one of those born neither to o. nor to command   MASEFIELD, J, 1
safer to o. than to rule   KEMPIS, T, 2
**obeyed** Nature, . . . must be o.
BACON, 1ST BARON VERULAM, VISCOUNT ST ALBANS, 62
She-who-must-be-o.   HAGGARD, SIR H, 1
**object** o. will be, if possible to form Christian men   ARNOLD, T, 1
**objectionable** its own animality either o. or funny.   LEWIS, C, 2
**obligation** The only o. to which . . . we may hold a novel
JAMES, H, 6
To the University of Oxford I acknowledge no o.   GIBBON, E, 1
**oblige** One should o. everyone to . . . one's ability   LA FONTAINE, J, 3
**oblivion** alms for o.   SHAKESPEARE, W, 283
that ineluctable o. which awaits the uncreative mind   HALDANE, J, 1
**oblong** an o. angular figure   LEACOCK, S, 6
**obscene** would not say that our Press is o.   LONGFORD, EARL OF, 2

**obscenity** O. . . . happens to shock some elderly . . . magistrate
RUSSELL, EARL, 22
**obscure** I strive to be brief, and I become o.   HORACE, 2
**observance** More honour'd in the breach than the o.
SHAKESPEARE, W, 49
the o. of trifles   DOYLE, SIR A, 2
**observations** To o. which ourselves we make   POPE, A, 37
**observe** Whenever you o. an animal closely   CANETTI, E, 1
**obstinacy** the name of . . : o. in a bad one   STERNE, L, 6
**obstinate** O. people can be divided into   ARISTOTLE, 3
**obtain** so run, that ye may o.   BIBLE: I CORINTHIANS, 13
**occupation** for ever apologizing for his o.   MENCKEN, H, 15
**occur** Accidents will o.   DICKENS, C, 14
**ocean** A life on the o. wave   SARGENT, E, 1
on the o. of life we pass   LONGFELLOW, H, 13
the great o. of truth lay all undiscovered before me
NEWTON, SIR I, 2
We mortals cross the o.   BROWNING, R, 6
**o'clock** Three o. is always too late or too early   SARTRE, J, 4
**odd** How o. /Of God   EWER, W, 1
This world is very o. we see   CLOUGH, A, 4
**odds** The o. is gone   SHAKESPEARE, W, 15
**odious** comparisons are o.   DONNE, J, 8
little o. vermin   SWIFT, J, 5
One is not superior . . . because one sees the world in an o. light
CHATEAUBRIAND, F, 2
**odium** He lived in the o.   BENTLEY, E, 4
**odorous** Comparisons are o.   SHAKESPEARE, W, 214
**odours** O. . . . /Live within the sense they quicken   SHELLEY, P, 23
**Oedipuses** a tense and peculiar family, the O.   BEERBOHM, SIR M, 19
**o'er** Returning were as tedious as go o.   SHAKESPEARE, W, 172
**o'er-leaps** Vaulting ambition, which o. itself   SHAKESPEARE, W, 165
**off** Days o.   TRACY, S, 2
O. with his head   CARROLL, L, 9
**offence** dire o. from am'rous causes springs   POPE, A, 46
greatest o. against virtue   HAZLITT, W, 12
It is a public scandal that gives o.   MOLIERE, 1
rock of o.   BIBLE: ISAIAH, 11
The only defence is in o.
BALDWIN, 1ST EARL BALDWIN OF BEWDLEY, 4
**offend** Be modest! It is the kind of pride least likely to o.
RENARD, J, 1
Those who o. us are generally punished   TROLLOPE, A, 15
**offended** This hand hath o.   CRANMER, T, 1
This hath not o. the king   MORE, SIR T, 5
When people do not respect us we are sharply o.   TWAIN, M, 11
**offender** a most notorious o.   SMOLLETT, T, 3
**offensive** extremely o., young man   BIRKENHEAD, EARL OF, 2
**office** not describe holding public o.   ACHESON, D, 3
o. sanctifies the holder   ACTON, 1ST BARON, 2
Written by o. boys for o. boys   SALISBURY, MARQUESS OF, 1
**officer** unbecoming the character of an o.   ANONYMOUS, 6
**official** O. dignity . . . in inverse ratio to . . . importance
HUXLEY, A, 8
**offspring** Heaven has granted me no o.   WHISTLER, J, 1
**often** Do you come here o.   MILLIGAN, S, 3
**oiled** Oozing charm . . . He o. his way   LERNER, A, 4
**oil** olive a land of o., and honey   BIBLE: DEUTERONOMY, 2
**ointment** a good name is better than precious o.
BIBLE: ECCLESIASTES, 14
dead flies cause the o. . . . to send forth a stinking savour
BIBLE: ECCLESIASTES, 19
**Okie** O. use' to mean you was from Oklahoma   STEINBECK, J, 2
**Oklahoma** Okie use' to mean you was from O.   STEINBECK, J, 2
**old** a nourisher of thine o. age   BIBLE: RUTH, 2
an o., wild, and incomprehensible man   VICTORIA, 4
a sight to make an o. man young   TENNYSON, BARON, 10
Before we grow o. and die   YEATS, W, 7
being o. is having lighted rooms   LARKIN, P, 2
Better be an o. man's darling   PROVERBS, 89
first sign of o. age: . . . how young the policemen look
HICKS, SIR S, 1
for de o. folks at home   FOSTER, S, 3
gift of perpetual o. age   WILDE, O, 66
He cannot bear o. men's jokes   FRISCH, M, 1
I am o. enough to be – in fact am – your mother   MILNE, A, 1
I grow o . . . I grow o.   ELIOT, T, 12
I have been young, and now am o.   PSALMS, 26
I love everything that's o.   GOLDSMITH, O, 17
inclination . . . to suppose an o. man decayed in his intellects
JOHNSON, S, 140

I prefer o. age to the alternative CHEVALIER, M. 2
It is so comic to hear oneself called o. JAMES, A. 1
I was born o. TREE, SIR H. 1
I will never be an o. man BARUCH, B. 2
man . . . as o. as the woman he feels MARX, G. 26
new book is published, read an o. one ROGERS, S. 2
no more work for poor o. Ned FOSTER, S. 6
o. age a regret DISRAELI, 1ST EARL OF BEACONSFIELD, 1
O. age brings . . . the comfort that you will soon be out of it
EMERSON, R. 19
o. age is . . . older than I am BARUCH, B. 2
o., and well stricken in age BIBLE: GENESIS, 41
O. men forget SHAKESPEARE, W. 99
one has to be very o. before one learns how to be amused
BUCK, P. 3
O. people are always absorbed WEBB, BARON PASSFIELD, 1
O. sins PROVERBS, 322
Poor o. Joe FOSTER, S. 5
redress the balance of the O. CANNING, G. 3
Tell me the o., o. story HANKEY, K. 1
that grand o. man NORTHCOTE, 1ST EARL OF IDDESLEIGH, 1
That is no country for o. men YEATS, W. 25
that o. serpent BIBLE: REVELATIONS, 9
the o. have reminiscences SAKI, 12
the o. have rubbed it into the young that they are wiser
MAUGHAM, W. 3
the o. is better BIBLE: LUKE, 15
The o. man has his death PROVERBS, 404
There are no o. men any more USTINOV, P. 4
There is too much Asia and she is too o. KIPLING, R. 16
They shall grow not o. BINYON, L. 3
they think he is growing o. IRVING, W. 1
too o. to go again to my travels CHARLES II, 1
When you are o. and gray YEATS, W. 31
Where are the boys of the O. Brigade WEATHERLY, F. 1
You are o., Father William CARROLL, L. 3
older make way for an o. man MAUDLING, R. 1
O. men declare war HOOVER, H. 2
o. than the rocks among which she sits PATER, W. 1
The o. one grows the more one likes indecency WOOLF, V. 8
to go on getting o. ADENAUER, K. 1
old-fashioned o. respect for the young WILDE, O. 20
O. ways which no longer apply to changed conditions ADDAMS, J. 1
olfactory an o. bar WELLS, H. 4
oligarchy extreme democracy or absolute o., or despotism will
come ARISTOTLE, 8
olive an o. leaf pluckt off BIBLE: GENESIS, 25
thy children like the o.-branches PSALMS, 80
Oliver Goldsmith To O. JOHNSON, S. 111
Oliver Twist O. has asked for more DICKENS, C. 33
Olympic Games The most important thing in the O.
COUBERTIN, BARON, 1
Omega Alpha and O. BIBLE: REVELATIONS, 1
omelette You can't make an o. PROVERBS, 474
ominous an idea . . . to be fashionable is o. SANTAYANA, G. 12
omnibuses if he had only ridden more in o. HELPS, SIR A. 3
omnipotence final proof of God's o. DE VRIES, P. 6
on O. with the dance BYRON, 6TH BARON, 11
Onan O. knew that the seed should not be his BIBLE: GENESIS, 49
Onaway O.! Awake, beloved LONGFELLOW, H. 11
once For Christmas comes but o. a year TUSSER, T. 3
O. more unto the breach, dear friends SHAKESPEARE, W. 95
One dies only o. MOLIÈRE, 4
. . . you have dined in every house in London – o. WILDE, O. 75
you shall drink twice while I drink o.
WALPOLE, 4TH EARL OF ORFORD, 10
one All for o., and o. for all DUMAS, PERE, 1
have we not all o. father BIBLE: MALACHI, 1
if we knew o., we knew two EDDINGTON, SIR A. 2
o. and o. are two EDDINGTON, SIR A. 2
O. is o. and all alone ANONYMOUS, 45
The number o. book . . . was written by a committee MAYER, L. 1
one-eyed o. yellow idol to the north of Khatmandu HAYES, J. 1
the O. Man is King WELLS, H. 7
One Great Scorer when the O. comes RICE, G. 1
one-handed Give me a o. economist TRUMAN, H. 7
oneself It is a stupidity . . . to busy o. with the correction of the
world MOLIÈRE, 6
One should examine o. . . . before . . . condemning others
MOLIÈRE, 7
only possible society is o. WILDE, O. 15

one up How to be o. POTTER, S. 2
onions carry their own o. when cycling abroad COREN, A. 3
onward little o. lend thy guiding hand MILTON, J. 51
O., Christian soldiers BARING-GOULD, S. 2
O., Christians, o. go WHITE, H. 1
open I declare this thing o. – whatever it is
PHILIP, DUKE OF EDINBURGH, 4
O. Sesame ARABIAN NIGHTS, 2
opened the eyes of the blind shall be o. BIBLE: ISAIAH, 26
opening time It is always o. in the Sailors Arms THOMAS, D. 15
opera an o. without an interval, or an interval without an o.
NEWMAN, E. 1
Bed . . . is the poor man's o. HUXLEY, A. 19
Like German o., too long and too loud WAUGH, E. 50
O. in English MENCKEN, H. 17
The first rule in o. is the first rule in life MELBA, DAME N. 1
what language an o. is sung in APPLETON, SIR E. 1
operas the German text of French o. WHARTON, E. 1
opinion A man . . . must have a very good o. of himself
AUSTEN, J. 3
better to have no o. of God
BACON, 1ST BARON VERULAM, VISCOUNT ST ALBANS, 52
give him my o. DICKENS, C. 4
he is . . . /Now but a climate of o. AUDEN, W. 13
heresy signifies no more than private o. HOBBES, T. 3
I agree with no man's o. TURGENEV, I. 1
I am . . . of the o. with the learned CONGREVE, W. 3
Nobody holds a good o. of a man who has a low o. of himself
TROLLOPE, A. 11
nothing to admire except his o. FRY, C. 2
of his own o. still BUTLER, S. 8
so vain . . . care for the o. of those we don't care for
ESCHENBACH, M. 3
the English think of an o. as something . . . to hide HALSEY, M. 4
The superiority of one man's o. over another's JAMES, H. 9
They that approve . . . call it o. HOBBES, T. 3
opinionated the o., the ignorant, and the boorish ARISTOTLE, 3
opinions a decent respect to the o. of mankind JEFFERSON, T. 1
New o. are always suspected LOCKE, J. 1
not a writer's business to hold o. YEATS, W. 34
So many men, so many o. TERENCE, 4
the proper o. for the time of year AUDEN, W. 25
The public buys its o. as it buys its meat BUTLER, S. 15
The State, in choosing men . . . takes no notice of their o.
CROMWELL, O. 5
The wish to spread those o. that we hold BUTLER, S. 4
opium an o.-dose for keeping beasts of burden KINGSLEY, C. 3
Religion . . . is the o. of the people MARX, K. 4
opponent Never ascribe to an o. motives meaner than your own
BARRIE, SIR J. 13
opportunist rather be an o. and float
BALDWIN, 1ST EARL BALDWIN OF BEWDLEY, 7
opportunities A wise man will make more o.
BACON, 1ST BARON VERULAM, VISCOUNT ST ALBANS, 16
opportunity follies . . . he didn't commit when he had the o.
ROWLAND, H. 2
O. seldom knocks twice PROVERBS, 331
oppose duty . . . to o. CHURCHILL, R. 1
opposition Her Majesty's O. BAGEHOT, W. 4
I have spent many years . . . in o. ROOSEVELT, E. 4
The duty of an o. CHURCHILL, R. 1
oppression when fanatics are on top there is no limit to o.
MENCKEN, H. 8
Where rumour of o. and deceit COWPER, W. 25
optimism Pessimism, . . . is just as agreeable as o. BENNETT, A. 3
optimist an o. . . . fills up his crossword puzzle in ink SHORTER, C. 1
I am an o., unrepentant and militant USTINOV, P. 3
The o. proclaims CABELL, J. 2
optimistic O. lies SHAW, G. 31
Oracle I am Sir O. SHAKESPEARE, W. 187
oracular the use of my o. tongue SHERIDAN, R. 7
oral a terrific story about o. contraception ALLEN, W. 11
orange Oh that I were an o.-tree HERBERT, G. 3
oranges O. and lemons, /Say the bell of St Clement's
NURSERY RHYMES, 41
orangutang an o. trying to play the violin BALZAC, H. 3
oratorium Laboratorium est o. NEEDHAM, J. 1
orchard Before the cherry o. was sold CHEKHOV, A. 3
orchestration Literature is the o. of platitudes WILDER, T. 7
order done decently and in o. BIBLE: I CORINTHIANS, 19
O. is heaven's first law POPE, A. 35

The old o. changeth                                         TENNYSON, BARON, 19
upon the o. of your going                                 SHAKESPEARE, W, 171
wisdom . . . sweetly doth . . . o. all things              BIBLE: WISDOM, 5
words in the best o.                                        COLERIDGE, S, 39
**ordered** a side dish he hadn't o.                            LARDNER, R, 1
**ordering** the better o. of the universe                     ALFONSO, 1
**ordinary** One machine can do the work of fifty o. men
                                                             HUBBARD, E, 1
**organ** my second favourite o.                                ALLEN, W, 6
Seated . . . at the o.                                         PROCTER, A, 1
**organ-grinder** no reason to attack the monkey when the o. is
present                                                        BEVAN, A, 10
**organic** O. life . . . has developed . . . from the protozoon to the
philosopher                                               RUSSELL, EARL, 12
**organization** a government o. could do it that quickly   CARTER, J, 1
**organized** War is an o. bore                          |HOLMES, O, JR., 1
**organs** he'd have given us all more o.                     BRADBURY, M, 7
**orgasm** The o. has replaced the Cross                   MUGGERIDGE, M, 2
**orgies** o. are vile                                          NASH, O, 5
**orgy** An o. looks particularly alluring                 MUGGERIDGE, M, 1
you need an o., once in a while                                NASH, O, 5
**Orientals** If . . . O. . . . drank a liquor which . . . made them vomit
                                                           LA BRUYERE, J, 13
**origin** the indelible stamp of his lowly o.               DARWIN, C, 3
**original** An o. writer is . . . one whom nobody can imitate
                                                       CHATEAUBRIAND, F, 1
Mona did researches in o. sin                              PLOMER, W, 3
o. is unfaithful to the translation                         BORGES, J, 3
The more intelligence . . . the more . . . one finds o.     PASCAL, B, 3
the only absolutely o. creation . . . is Don Quixote   MAUGHAM, W, 22
thought is often o.                                         HOLMES, O, 2
**originality** absence of inverted commas guarantees . . . o.
                                                            FADIMAN, C, 1
All good things . . . are the fruits of o.                    MILL, J, 3
without o. or moral courage                                  SHAW, G, 6
**originator** quotes . . . give us a nodding acquaintance with the o.
                                                           WILLIAMS, K, 1
**Orion** canst thou . . . loose the bands of O.             BIBLE: JOB, 18
**Ormus** Outshone the wealth of O. and of Ind             MILTON, J, 34
**ornamental** not merely . . . useful and o.              STRACHEY, L, 2
**orphan** defeat is an o.                                   KENNEDY, J, 16
**orthodoxy** O. is my doxy                                WARBURTON, W, 1
O. or My-doxy                                              CARLYLE, T, 15
**ostrich** the wings of an o.                            MACAULAY, BARON, 2
**other** O. people are quite dreadful.                       WILDE, O, 15
you expect o. people to be . . . to your liking             KEMPIS, T, 3
**others** By persuading o. we convince ourselves            JUNIUS, 2
delight in . . . misfortunes . . . of o.                    BURKE, E, 4
some more than o.                                         COWARD, SIR N, 2
tell the o. by their hunted expression                       LEWIS, C, 6
to encourage the o.                                        VOLTAIRE, 2
**otherwise** Some folk . . . are o.                         SMOLLETT, T,|4
**Otis** Miss O. regrets                                      PORTER, C, 5
**ounce** An o. of a man's own wit                          STERNE, L, 10
**ours** We have met the enemy, and they are o.               PERRY, O, 1
**ourselves** all our knowledge is, o. to know               POPE, A, 34
By persuading others we convince o.                         JUNIUS, 2
In every friend we lose a part of o.                         POPE, A, 59
remedies oft in o. do lie                                 SHAKESPEARE, W, 1
we but praise o. in other men                              POPE, A, 25
What isn't part of o. doesn't disturb us                     HESSE, H, 1
**out** Mordre wol o.                                       CHAUCER, G, 15
O., damned spot                                          SHAKESPEARE, W, 173
once o., what you've said can't be stopped                 HORACE, 11
**outlive** o. this powerful rhyme                        SHAKESPEARE, W, 258
**outlook** religious o. on life                             JUNG, C, 6
**out-of-doors** God having given us indoors and o.
                                                         MACAULAY, DAME R, 1
**outrun** We may o. / . . . And lose by over-running
                                                         SHAKESPEARE, W, 101
**outside** I am just going o.                               OATES, L, 1
I support it from the o.                               MELBOURNE, VISCOUNT, 8
**outward** I may not hope from o. forms                    COLERIDGE, S, 9
over Now the day is o.                                   BARING-GOULD, S, 1
**overcome** I have o. the world                           BIBLE: JOHN, 42
**overcomes** Who o. /By force                             MILTON, J, 32
**over-confident** Not that I am ever o.                   THATCHER, M, 18
**over-educated** I've o. myself in all the things         COWARD, SIR N, 19
**overexposure** she should catch a cold on o.              BUTLER, S, 18
**overfed** They're overpaid, o., oversexed and over here
                                                           TRINDER, T, 1

**over-feeding** what Nicely-Nicely dies of will be o.       RUNYON, D, 10
**overlooked** better to be looked over than o.              WEST, M, 10
**overpaid** They're o., overfed, oversexed and over here
                                                           TRINDER, T, 1
**overpaying** o. him but he's worth it                   GOLDWYN, S, 4
**overrated** matrimony, . . . a highly o. performance     DUNCAN, I, 4
**overrun** apt to be o. with nettles     WALPOLE, 4TH EARL OF ORFORD, 8
**over-running** and lose by o.                          SHAKESPEARE, W, 101
**oversexed** They're overpaid, overfed, o. and over here
                                                           TRINDER, T, 1
**overtakers** It is the o. who                              PITTS, W, 1
**overthrown** Another mighty empire o.                  WORDSWORTH, W, 46
**overtures** I tried to resist his o.                      PERELMAN, S, 3
**owe** I don't o. a penny to a single soul              WODEHOUSE, SIR P, 10
**owed** so much o. by so many to so few                  CHURCHILL, SIR W, 46
**owes** A nation is not in danger . . . because it o. itself money
                                                           MELLON, A, 1
he o. not any man                                        LONGFELLOW, H, 15
**owl** The O. and the Pussy-Cat went to sea                LEAR, E, 8
**owls** Two O. and a Hen                                   LEAR, E, 1
**own** mine o. Executioner                                 DONNE, J, 4
**ownership** its source of power: o.                       KINNOCK, N, 4
transform this society without . . . extension of public o.
                                                           KINNOCK, N, 1
**ox** When he stands like an o. in the furrow              KIPLING, R, 18
**Oxenford** Clerk . . . of O.                              CHAUCER, G, 5
**Oxford** a secret in the O. sense                         FRANKS, BARON, 1
It is O. that has made me insufferable                   BEERBOHM, SIR M, 7
nice sort of place, O.                                      SHAW, G, 20
O. is on the whole more attractive than Cambridge
                                                           BAEDEKER, K, 1
The clever men at O. /Know all that there is to be knowed
                                                           GRAHAME, K, 2
To O. sent a troop of horse                                 TRAPP, J, 1
To the University of O. I acknowledge no obligation       GIBBON, E, 1
You will hear more good things on . . . a stagecoach from London
to O.                                                      HAZLITT, W, 8
you will leave O. by the town drain                        SPOONER, W, 5
**oyster** bold man that first eat an o.                     SWIFT, J, 10
sympathetic unselfishness of an o.                          SAKI, 10
the sort of eye that can open an o. at sixty paces
                                                         WODEHOUSE, SIR P, 4
world's mine o.                                          SHAKESPEARE, W, 199
**oysters** Poverty and o.                                  DICKENS, C, 3

# P

**pace** this petty p. from day to day                    SHAKESPEARE, W, 177
**Pacific** The Admiral of the Atlantic salutes the Admiral of the P.
                                                           WILHELM II, 3
**pack** how much more dogs are animated when they hunt in a p.
                                                           HUME, D, 6
the human p. is shuffled and cut                           LODGE, D, 3
**paddle** every man p. his own canoe                      MARRYAT, F, 3
**padlocked** music critics. . . . small and rodent-like with p. ears
                                                         STRAVINSKY, I, 3
**Pagan** A P. suckled in a creed outworn                WORDSWORTH, W, 60
**pageant** insubstantial p. faded                       SHAKESPEARE, W, 277
**paid** I do not answer questions like this without being p.
                                                           HELLMAN, L, 3
**pain** a gentleman . . . never inflicts p.            NEWMAN, CARDINAL, 2
Although p. isn't real                                     ANONYMOUS, 90
critics . . . desire our blood, not our p.                NIETZSCHE, F, 14
disinclination to inflict p. upon oneself                 MEREDITH, G, 3
I feel no p., dear mother, now                             ANONYMOUS, 43
I have no p., dear mother, now                             FARMER, E, 1
momentary intoxication with p.                           BRONOWSKI, J, 4
Neither shame nor physical p. have any . . . effect         KEY, E, 4
owes its pleasures to another's p.                         COWPER, W, 29
Pleasure is . . . intermission of p.                       SELDEN, J, 4
The least p. in our little finger                          HAZLITT, W, 1
The p. passes, but the beauty remains                      RENOIR, P, 1
they blest him in their p.                              TENNYSON, BARON, 66
what p. it was to drown                                  SHAKESPEARE, W, 242
yearning like a God in p.                                  KEATS, J, 7
**pained** greatly p. at how little he was p.               WAUGH, E, 21
**pains** no gains without p.                            STEVENSON, A, 4
the p. of hell gat hold upon me                            PSALMS, 72
**paint** A professional is someone whose wife works to enable him
to p.                                                       SHAHN, B, 1
flinging a pot of p. in the public's face                  RUSKIN, J, 16

My business is to p. . . . what I see — TURNER, J. 1
to p. the lily — SHAKESPEARE, W. 128
**painted** As idle as a p. ship — COLERIDGE, S. 26
I am p. as the greatest little dictator — THATCHER, M. 13
Most women are not so young as they are p. — BEERBOHM, SIR M. 5
p. . . . , by the great artist Kodak — MILLIGAN, S. 2
**painter** I am married to Beatrice Salkeld, a p. — BEHAN, B. 10
I could have become a real p. — HOKUSAI, 1
memory is a p. — GRANDMA MOSES, 1
who is not a great sculptor or p. can be an architect — RUSKIN, J. 1
**painters** Good p. imitate nature — CERVANTES, M. 21
P. and poets . . . licence to dare anything — HORACE, 1
Poets and p. are outside the class system — BRENAN, G. 6
**painting** a great difference between p. a face — FULLER, T. 1
If I didn't start p., I would have raised chickens — GRANDMA MOSES, 2
If people only knew . . . about p. — LANDSEER, SIR E, 1
I just keep p. till I feel like pinching. Then I know it's right — RENOIR, P. 2
P. is a blind man's profession — PICASSO, P. 2
**pajamas** I shot an elephant in my p. — MARX, G. 2
**palace** Love in a p. — KEATS, J. 19
**palaces** Mid pleasures and p. though we may roam — PAYNE, J. 1
**pale** a p. horse — BIBLE: REVELATIONS, 6
**Palestine** not enough prisons . . . in P. to hold all the Jews — MEIR, G. 7
**pall** The pallor of girls' brows shall be their p. — OWEN, W. 1
**Palladium** Liberty of the press is the P. of . . . rights — JUNIUS, 1
**pallor** The p. of girls' brows shall be their pall — OWEN, W. 1
**palm** happy state of getting the victor's p. without the dust of racing — HORACE, 14
To win the p., the oak, or bays — MARVELL, A. 1
**palms** p. before my feet — CHESTERTON, G. 10
they found no more of her than . . . the p. of her hands — BIBLE: II KINGS, 3
**palm-tree** the righteous shall flourish like a p. — PSALMS, 58
**palsied** with the p. heart — TENNYSON, BARON, 48
**pan** Put on the p.; /Says Greedy Nan — NURSERY RHYMES, 7
**Pandora** open that P.'s Box . . . Trojan 'orses will jump out — BEVIN, E. 1
**Panjandrum** the grand P. — FOOTE, S. 1
**pantheist** The modern p. not only — LAWRENCE, D. 19
**pants** There were times my p. were so thin — TRACY, S. 1
Your eyes shine like the p. — MARX, G. 4
**papacy** Since God has given us the p. . . . enjoy it — LEO X, 1
The P. is not other than the Ghost of the deceased Roman Empire — HOBBES, T. 7
**paper** reactionaries are p. tigers — MAO TSE-TUNG, 3
The atom bomb is a p. tiger — MAO TSE-TUNG, 7
This p. will no doubt be found interesting — DALTON, J. 1
Where were you fellows when the p. was blank — ALLEN, F. 2
**papers** fornicated and read the p. — CAMUS, A. 3
only two posh p. on a Sunday — OSBORNE, J. 2
**parables** great p., . . . , but false art — LAWRENCE, D. 40
**parade** the chief employment of riches consists in the p. of riches — SMITH, A. 2
**paradise** A p. for a sect — KEATS, J. 10
drunk the milk of P. — COLERIDGE, S. 15
England is a p. for women — BURTON, R. 4
England is the p. of individuality — SANTAYANA, G. 8
England is the p. of women — FLORIO, J. 1
Grant me p. in this world — TINTORETTO, 1
If a man could pass through P. — COLERIDGE, S. 2
Same old glimpse of /P. — LAMPTON, W. 1
to hope for P. is to live in P. — SACKVILLE-WEST, V. 4
Wilderness is P. enow — FITZGERALD, E, 5
**paragon** the p. of animals — SHAKESPEARE, W. 57
**parallel** We never remark any passion . . . in others, of which, . . . we may not find a p. — HUME, D. 5
**parallelogram** The landlady . . . is a p. — LEACOCK, S. 6
**paralyse** p. it by encumbering it with remedies — TOLSTOY, COUNT, 7
**paranoid** Even a p. can have enemies. — KISSINGER, H, 4
**parcels** Portions and p. of the dreadful Past — TENNYSON, BARON, 50
**pardon** God may p. you, but I never can — ELIZABETH I, 3
God will p. me. It is His trade — HEINE, H, 5
the government that should ask me for a p. — DEBS, E, 1
**pardoned** The women p. all — BYRON, 6TH BARON, 27
**parent** a kind p. . . . or a merciless step-mother — PLINY THE ELDER, 2
To lose one p., . . . a misfortune; to lose both looks like carelessness. — WILDE, O, 23
**parents** A Jewish man with p. alive — ROTH, P. 2

by defying their p. and copying one another — CRISP, Q. 2
children, obey your p. — BIBLE: EPHESIANS, 3
From birth to age eighteen, a girl needs good p. — TUCKER, S, 3
joys of p. are secret — BACON, 1ST BARON VERULAM, VISCOUNT ST ALBANS, 38
P. learn a lot from their children — SPARK, M. 2
what p. were created for — NASH, O, 8
**Paris** delivered of a city bigger than P. — LA FONTAINE, J. 6
Good Americans, when they die, go to P. — APPLETON, T. 1
I love P. — PORTER, C, 3
Is P. burning — HITLER, A, 9
no home . . . save in P. — NIETZSCHE, F, 6
P. is worth a mass — HENRI IV, 2
when good Americans die they go to P. — WILDE, O, 54
**parish** all the world as my p. — WESLEY, J. 1
born, bred, and hanged, all in the same p. — ANONYMOUS, 34
**park** The hunchback in the p. — THOMAS, D, 6
**Parkinson's Law** The rise in the . . . employed is governed by P. — PARKINSON, C. 2
**par-lee-voo** Hinky, dinky, p. — ROWLAND, E, 1
**Parliament** build your House of P. upon the river — WELLINGTON, DUKE OF, 12
He stood twice for P. — WAUGH, E, 19
If Her Majesty stood for P. — SPEIGHT, J, 2
no reference to fun in any Act of P. — HERBERT, SIR A, 4
P. is the longest running farce — SMITH, C, 1
Three Estates in P. — CARLYLE, T, 11
**parliaments** England . . . mother of p. — BRIGHT, J, 1
**parlour** Will you walk into my p.? — HOWITT, M. 1
**parochial** worse than provincial – he was p. — JAMES, H, 4
**parody** devil's walking p. — CHESTERTON, G, 9
**parrot** to sell the family p. — ROGERS, W, 12
**parsnips** fine words butter no p. — SCOTT, SIR W, 9
**parson** If P. lost his senses — HODGSON, R, 1
In arguing too, the p. own'd his skill — GOLDSMITH, O, 5
Once a p. — PROVERBS, 324
**part** I have forgot my p. — SHAKESPEARE, W. 5
In every friend we lose a p. of ourselves — POPE, A, 59
it is a little flesh and breath, and the ruling p. — MARCUS AURELIUS ANTONINUS, 1
let us kiss and p. — DRAYTON, M, 2
read p. of it all the way — GOLDWYN, S, 18
till death us do p. — BOOK OF COMMON PRAYER, 15
We only p. to meet again — GAY, J, 12
**particular** a London p. . . . A fog — DICKENS, C, 2
did nothing in p. — GILBERT, SIR W, 20
**particulars**| Minute P. — BLAKE, W, 14
**parties** it is always like that at p. — PROUST, M, 13
one of those p. which got out of hand — BRUCE, L, 2
**parting** Every p. gives a foretaste of death — SCHOPENHAUER, A, 4
P. is all we know of heaven — DICKINSON, E, 2
P. is such sweet sorrow — SHAKESPEARE, W, 247
**partisanship** P. is our great curse — ROBINSON, J, 1
**partly** Man p. is — BROWNING, R, 19
**partridge** A p. in a pear tree — NURSERY RHYMES, 54
well-shot woodcock, p., snipe — BETJEMAN, SIR J, 1
**parts** It is seldom . . . one p. on good terms — PROUST, M, 16
one man in his time plays many p. — SHAKESPEARE, W, 23
Today we have naming of p. — REED, H, 2
truth in the inward p. — PSALMS, 35
**part-time** p. nihilist — CAMUS, A, 10
**party** A great p. is not to be brought\ down — HAILSHAM, BARON, 1
Heard there was a p. Came — LILLIE, B, 2
I always voted at my p.'s call — GILBERT, SIR W, 10
The p. is the rallying-point for the . . . working class — STALIN, J, 4
The sooner every p. breaks up the better — AUSTEN, J, 5
Well, did you evah! What a swell p. — PORTER, C, 6
**pass** but let it p., let it p. — THURBER, J, 16
Horseman, p. by — YEATS, W, 30
ideas simply p. through him — BRADLEY, F, 6
I shall not p. this way again — GRELLET, S, 1
p. for forty-three — GILBERT, SIR W, 45
Praise the Lord and p. the ammunition — FORGY, H, 1
They shall not p.! — IBARRURI, D, 1
They shall not p. — PETAIN, H, 2
To p. away ere life hath lost its brightness — HASTINGS, L, 1
**passage** calm p. . . . across many a bad night — NIETZSCHE, F, 10
Patience and p. of time — LA FONTAINE, J, 4
**passageways** smell of steaks in p. — ELIOT, T, 17
**passed** p. by on the other side — BIBLE: LUKE, 21
p. from death unto life — BIBLE: JOHN, 14

We wanted p. on earth — MCCARTNEY, P, 1
When there was p., he was for p. — AUDEN, W, 25
**peach** dare to eat a p. — ELIOT, T, 13
Fan vaulting . . . belongs to the Last-supper-carved-on-a-p.-stone — LANCASTER, O, 1
**peaches** poetry in p. — GRANVILLE-BARKER, H, 1
with p. and women, it's . . . the side next the sun that's tempting — OUIDA, 2
**peak** One sees . . . only small things from the p. — CHESTERTON, G, 12
Silent, upon a p. in Darien — KEATS, J, 37
**pear** And a golden p. — NURSERY RHYMES, 20
**pearl** base Indian, threw a p. away — SHAKESPEARE, W, 229
**pearls** He who would search for P. — DRYDEN, J, 15
p. before swine — BIBLE: MATTHEW, 25
p. that were his eyes — SHAKESPEARE, W, 273
the twelve gates were twelve p. — BIBLE: REVELATIONS, 20
**peas** I always eat p. with honey — ANONYMOUS, 41
**peasantry** a bold p., . . . /When once destroy'd — GOLDSMITH, O, 4
**peck** Peter Piper picked a p. of pickled pepper — NURSERY RHYMES, 43
**peculiar** . . . a tense and p. family, the Oedipuses, . . . — BEERBOHM, SIR M, 19
Funny p., or funny ha-ha — HAY, I, 1
the p. situation of the human male — BEAUVOIR, S, 2
**pedestal** at fourteen every boy should be in love with some ideal woman . . . on a p. — NORMAN, B, 1
**pedigree** languages are the p. of nations — JOHNSON, S, 156
**pee** share a quick p. over a common lamp-post — CONNOLLY, C, 12
**Peel** P.'s smile — O'CONNELL, D, 1
Sir Robert P. — BAGEHOT, W, 9
**peerage** When I want a p., I shall buy one — NORTHCLIFFE, VISCOUNT, 2
**peers** Fears, prejudices, misconceptions – those are the p. — LLOYD GEORGE, EARL OF DWYFOR, 7
**pen** how much more cruel the p. — BURTON, R, 3
less brilliant p. than mine — BEERBOHM, SIR M, 2
nothing can cure it but the scratching of a p. — LOVER, S, 1
p. is mightier than the sword — BULWER-LYTTON, 1ST BARON LYTTON, 1
**penance** The man hath p. done — COLERIDGE, S, 33
**pence** Take care of the p. — CHESTERFIELD, 4TH EARL OF, 6
**pendulum** politics of the p., but of the ratchet — THATCHER, M, 3
The p. of the mind oscillates between sense and nonsense — JUNG, C, 2
**penetrable** most things are p. — CARLYLE, T, 13
**pennies** P. do not come from heaven — THATCHER, M, 9
P. from Heaven — BURKE, J, 1
**penny** A p. saved — PROVERBS, 58
Hot cross buns! / . . . /One a p., two a p. — NURSERY RHYMES, 16
I don't owe a p. to a single soul — WODEHOUSE, SIR P, 10
In for a p. — PROVERBS, 223
Not a p. off the pay — COOK, A, 1
P. wise — PROVERBS, 335
**pens** Let other p. dwell on guilt and misery — AUSTEN, J, 10
**Pentecost** when the day of P. was fully come — BIBLE: ACTS, 2
**people** a loyal, a gallant . . . and good-temper'd p — STERNE, L, 2
always been interested in p. — MAUGHAM, W, 28
Be nice to p. on your way up — MIZNER, W, 1
Boys . . . are unwholesome companions for grown p. — LAMB, C, 7
good of the p. — CICERO, M, 2
government of the p., by the p., and for the p. — LINCOLN, A, 12
How do p. go to sleep — PARKER, D, 4
I am for p. — CHAPLIN, C, 2
If p. behaved in the way nations do — WILLIAMS, T, 6
if the p. . . . can be reached with the truth — ROOSEVELT, E, 2
indictment against an whole p. — BURKE, E, 14
I no more like p. . . . than I like dogs — SPENCER, SIR S, 1
It is with . . . p. as with . . . bottles — POPE, A, 53
Most of the p. . . . will be children — ANDERSEN, H, 3
my p. live in such awful conditions — GEORGE V, 2
Once the p. begin to reason — VOLTAIRE, 26
p. . . . are attracted by God — INGE, W, 4
P. are either charming or tedious. — WILDE, O, 36
P. are not fallen angels — LAWRENCE, D, 40
p. are the masters — BURKE, E, 16
p. may be made to follow a course of action — CONFUCIUS, 11
P. must help one another — LA FONTAINE, J, 8
p.'s government — WEBSTER, D, 2
p. standing in the corners of our rooms — COREN, A, 6
p. under suspicion are better moving — KAFKA, F, 3
p. . . . usually imitate each other — HOFFER, E, 1
P. who like this sort of thing — LINCOLN, A, 14
P. who need p. are the luckiest — MERRILL, B, 1

p. whose company is coveted — MACCARTHY, SIR D, 1
p. who stay in the middle of the road — BEVAN, A, 5
P. will cross the road . . . to say 'We saw you on the telly' — CRISP, Q, 1
Religion . . . is the opium of the p. — MARX, K, 4
show my head to the p. — DANTON, G, 2
the bludgeoning of the p. — WILDE, O, 51
The Lord prefers common-looking p. — LINCOLN, A, 2
the p. are forbidden to light lamps — MAO TSE-TUNG, 8
The p. – could you patent the sun — SALK, J, 1
the p. of his pasture — PSALMS, 62
The p.'s flag is deepest red; — CONNELL, J, 1
. . . the p. we should have been seen dead with — WEST, DAME R, 7
The p. would be just as noisy — CROMWELL, O, 6
The right p. are rude — MAUGHAM, W, 15
The Swiss . . . are not a p. so much as a . . . business — FAULKNER, W, 1
They didn't act like p. — SALINGER, J, 2
This country . . . belongs to the p. who inhabit it — LINCOLN, A, 10
thy p. shall be my p. — BIBLE: RUTH, 1
two p. with one pulse. — MACNEICE, L, 2
When . . . it becomes necessary for one p. to dissolve . . . political bonds — JEFFERSON, T, 1
When the P. contend for their Liberty — HALIFAX, MARQUIS OF, 6
You can fool too many of the p. — THURBER, J, 4
**Pepper** Sergeant P.'s Lonely Hearts Club Band — LENNON, J, 9
**pepper** Peter Piper picked a peck of pickled p. — NURSERY RHYMES, 43
**perception** any truth but from a clear p. — KEATS, J, 58
doors of p. were cleansed — BLAKE, W, 17
prime agent of all human p. — COLERIDGE, S, 3
**perceptions** Man's Desires are limited by his P. — BLAKE, W, 47
**perfect** A cigarette is . . . a p. pleasure — WILDE, O, 48
be ye therefore p. — BIBLE: MATTHEW, 17
p. in a short time — BIBLE: WISDOM, 2
p. love casteth out fear — BIBLE: I JOHN, 4
**perfection** attain to the divine p. — LONGFELLOW, H, 7
Culture being a pursuit of our total p. — ARNOLD, M, 1
Finality is death. P. is finality — STEPHENS, J, 1
The pursuit of p. — ARNOLD, M, 3
**performance** desire should . . . outlive p. — SHAKESPEARE, W, 87
it takes away the p. — SHAKESPEARE, W, 168
verses . . . as a literary p. — WHITMAN, W, 1
**performing** English literature's p. flea — O'CASEY, S, 4
**perfume** As a p. doth remain — SYMONS, A, 1
perfumes All the p. of Arabia — SHAKESPEARE, W, 174
**perhaps** I am going in search of a great p. — RABELAIS, F, 9
The grand P. — BROWNING, R, 8
**peril** For those in p. on the sea — WHITING, W, 1
**perils** all p. and dangers of this night — BOOK OF COMMON PRAYER, 7
smile at p. past — SCOTT, SIR W, 1
**periods** Decades . . . are not . . . really p. at all — MACAULAY, DAME R, 2
**perish** man . . . compared unto the beasts that p. — PSALMS, 33
P. the Universe — CYRANO DE BERGERAC, S, 1
then all his thoughts p. — PSALMS, 89
they that take the sword shall p. with the sword — BIBLE: MATTHEW, 83
though the world p. — FERDINAND I, 1
weak shall p. — SERVICE, R, 3
**periwig** with my mourning . . . and new p. — PEPYS, S, 10
**perjury** P. . . . is truth that is shamefaced — DARLING, BARON, 4
**permanence** love p. more than . . . beauty — CASSON, SIR H, 1
**pernicious** the most p. race — SWIFT, J, 5
**Perón** If I had not been born P. — PERÓN, J, 1
**perpetual** gift of p. old age — WILDE, O, 66
Literary men are . . . a p. priesthood — CARLYLE, T, 6
**perpetuation** Why should I consent to the p. of the image of this image — PLOTINUS, 1
**persecutest** Saul, why p. thou me — BIBLE: ACTS, 6
**perseverance** the name of p. in a good cause — STERNE, L, 6
**persistent** The most p. sound . . . through men's history — KOESTLER, A, 4
**person** A p. may be indebted for a nose or an eye, . . . to a great-aunt — HAZLITT, W, 23
My idea of an agreeable p. — DISRAELI, 1ST EARL OF BEACONSFIELD, 8
the only p. . . . I should like to know — WILDE, O, 37
the only thing that can exist is an uninterested p. — CHESTERTON, G, 14
The world regards such a p. as . . . an unmuzzled dog — HUXLEY, T, 4
to the cheek of a young p. — DICKENS, C, 36

p. bird with the scarlet breast WORDSWORTH, W, 39
p. frauds of friendship FIELDING, H, 12
**pipe** Blow your p. there BROWNING, R, 42
He called for his p. NURSERY RHYMES, 38
praise him upon the strings and p. PSALMS, 94
**piped** their fountains p. an answer LAWRENCE, D, 4
**Piper** Peter P. picked a peck of pickled pepper NURSERY RHYMES, 43
**pipers** Wi' a hundred p. an' a', an' a NAIRNE, BARONESS, 3
**piping** Helpless, naked, p. loud BLAKE, W, 36
P. down the valleys wild BLAKE, W, 39
**pips** squeezed – until the p. squeak GEDDES, SIR E, 1
**piss** I can p. the old boy LIEBERMANN, M, 1
**pissed** the last four strikes we've had, it's p. down SPEIGHT, J, 4
**pissing** inside my tent p. out JOHNSON, L, 4
**pistol** a p. let off at the ear LAMB, C, 14
**pitchfork** drive out nature with a p. HORACE, 20
**pith** all the p. is in the postscript HAZLITT, W, 4
**pitied** one has . . . ceased to be an object of *fear* as soon as one is
p. NIETZSCHE, F, 17
**pitiless** slow, sure doom falls p. and dark RUSSELL, EARL, 13
**Pitt** P. is to Addington CANNING, G, 2
**pity** A p. beyond all telling YEATS, W, 23
knock him down first, and p. him afterwards JOHNSON, S, 102
My subject is War, and the p. of War OWEN, W, 5
P. a human face BLAKE, W, 42
p. for the suffering of mankind RUSSELL, EARL, 1
The Poetry is in the p. OWEN, W, 5
'Tis P. She's a whore FORD, J, 3
To marry a man out of p. is folly ASQUITH, M, 1
To show p. is felt as a sign of contempt NIETZSCHE, F, 17
**place** A p. for everything SMILES, S, 2
everything in its p. SMILES, S, 2
firm p. to stand ARCHIMEDES, 1
give p. to better men CROMWELL, O, 4
Home is the p. where FROST, R, 3
I go to prepare a p. for you BIBLE: JOHN, 31
Never the time and the p. BROWNING, R, 34
running . . . to keep in the same p. CARROLL, L, 21
there's no p. like home PAYNE, J, 1
the summit of Everest was hardly the p. HILLARY, SIR E, 1
this is an awful p. SCOTT, CAPTAIN, 1
Upon the p. beneath SHAKESPEARE, W, 194
**plague** A p. o' both your houses SHAKESPEARE, W, 250
**plagues** of all p. with which mankind are curst DEFOE, D, 6
**plain** be yourself, imperial, p. and true BROWNING, R, 5
making things p. to uninstructed people HUXLEY, T, 7
Manners are . . . the need of the p. WAUGH, E, 46
**plainness** perfect p. of speech . . . perfect nobleness ARNOLD, M, 29
**planet** I have lived some thirty years on this p. THOREAU, H, 8
it fell on the wrong p. BRAUN, W, 1
When a new p. swims into his ken KEATS, J, 37
**plans** Life . . . happens . . . while you're busy making other p.
LENNON, J, 1
The finest p. have always been spoiled BRECHT, B, 6
what a man still p. . . . shows the . . . injustice in his death
CANETTI, E, 2
**plant** Is thy love a p. /Of such weak fibre WORDSWORTH, W, 20
The infusion of a China p. ADDISON, J, 10
**planted** like a tree p. by the water-side PSALMS, 1
**plants** bottinney means a knowledge of p. DICKENS, C, 29
p. left over from the Edwardian Wilderness OSBORNE, J, 6
**plashy** p. fen passes the questing vole WAUGH, E, 29
**plate** clean your p. ROSEBERY, EARL OF, 4
the silver p. on a coffin O'CONNELL, D, 1
**platitude** A longitude with no p. FRY, C, 4
A p. is simply a truth repeated
BALDWIN, 1ST EARL BALDWIN OF BEWDLEY, 10
To stroke a p. until it purrs MARQUIS, D, 2
**platitudes** Literature is the orchestration of p. WILDER, T, 7
**Plato** P. is dear to me ARISTOTLE, 10
Western philosophy is, . . . a series of footnotes to P.'s philosophy
WHITEHEAD, A, 6
**play** a good p. needs no epilogue SHAKESPEARE, W, 33
a p. is a dynamic thing TYNAN, K, 1
behold the Englishman . . . p. tip-and-run FIRBANK, R, 1
Better than a p. CHARLES II, 5
If you p. with fire PROVERBS, 219
Judge not the p. DAVIES, W, 1
Judge not the p. QUARLES, F, 2
p., I remember, pleas'd not the million SHAKESPEARE, W, 58
p.'s the thing SHAKESPEARE, W, 60

P. up! p. up! and p. the game NEWBOLT, SIR H, 7
Rehearsing a p. is making the word flesh SHAFFER, P, 3
The little victims p. GRAY, T, 9
this may be p. to you, 'tis death to us L'ESTRANGE, SIR R, 2
unless the p. is stopped, the child cannot . . . go on KEMBLE, J, 1
**playboy** p. of the western world SYNGE, J, 1
**played** I have p. the fool BIBLE: I SAMUEL, 7
**player** poor p., /That struts and frets his hour SHAKESPEARE, W, 177
**players** men and women merely p. SHAKESPEARE, W, 23
to conceal the fact that the p. cannot act AGATE, J, 3
**play-going** A good many inconveniences attend p. TYNAN, K, 4
**plays** p. about rape, sodomy and drug addiction COOK, P, 2
**plaything** A book that furnishes no quotations is, . . . a p.
PEACOCK, T, 3
A child's p. for an hour LAMB, M, 1
**pleasant** If we do not find anything p. VOLTAIRE, 1
lovely and p. in their lives BIBLE: II SAMUEL, 1
p. it is to have money CLOUGH, A, 3
**please** go anywhere I damn well p. BEVIN, E, 2
he that is married careth . . . how he may p. his wife
BIBLE: I CORINTHIANS, 10
I . . . do what I p. FREDERICK THE GREAT, 2
Music, Maestro, P. MAGIDSON, H, 1
Natural to p. DRYDEN, J, 2
Nothing can permanently p. COLERIDGE, S, 5
They . . . say what they p. FREDERICK THE GREAT, 2
You can't p. everyone PROVERBS, 476
**pleases** every prospect p. HEBER, R, 2
one makes lovers as fast as one p. CONGREVE, W, 12
**pleasing** The art of p. consists in HAZLITT, W, 22
the surest method . . . of p. CHESTERFIELD, 4TH EARL OF, 5
**pleasure** A fool bolts p. ANTRIM, M, 2
a p. in the pathless woods BYRON, 6TH BARON, 13
as much p. in the reading QUARLES, F, 1
Debauchee, n. One who has . . . pursued p. BIERCE, A, 3
did p. me in his top-boots MARLBOROUGH, DUCHESS OF, 1
dissipation without p. GIBBON, E, 4
Everyone is dragged on by their favourite p. VIRGIL, 13
gave p. to the spectators MACAULAY, BARON, 8
greatest p. . . . to do a good action LAMB, C, 16
hatred is by far the longest p. BYRON, 6TH BARON, 30
He that takes p. to hear sermons SELDEN, J, 7
I make poetry and give . . . because of you HORACE, 40
in his p. is life PSALMS, 19
knowledge and wonder . . . is an impression of p.
BACON, 1ST BARON VERULAM, VISCOUNT ST ALBANS, 1
Love ceases to be a p. BEHN, A, 1
Money gives me p. BELLOC, H, 9
No p. without pain PROVERBS, 315
no sterner moralist than P. BYRON, 6TH BARON, 21
P. after all is a safer guide BUTLER, S, 25
P. is . . . intermission of pain SELDEN, J, 4
P. is . . . seldom found where it is sought JOHNSON, S, 13
P. never is at home. KEATS, J, 12
p. of your company LAMB, C, 22
The only sensual p. without vice JOHNSON, S, 36
The p. of criticizing LA BRUYERE, J, 4
the p. of offering my seat to three ladies CHESTERTON, G, 38
The sight . . . gave me infinite p. PARK, M, 1
The ugliest of trades have their moments of p. JERROLD, D, 6
understanding will . . . extinguish p. HOUSMAN, A, 4
what p. . . . they have in taking their roguish tobacco JONSON, B, 4
Youth is full of p. SHAKESPEARE, W, 230
**pleasure-dome** A stately P. decree COLERIDGE, S, 12
sunny p. with caves of ice COLERIDGE, S, 13
**pleasures** Earth fills her lap with p. WORDSWORTH, W, 24
Love and all his p. CAMPION, T, 5
Mid p. and palaces though we may roam PAYNE, J, 1
No man is a hypocrite in his p. CAMUS, A, 5
No man is a hypocrite in his p. JOHNSON, S, 149
One half . . . cannot understand the p. AUSTEN, J, 1
One of the p. of middle age POUND, E, 2
P. are all alike SELDEN, J, 7
p. are their only care, COWPER, W, 18
P. newly found are sweet WORDSWORTH, W, 71
purest of human p.
BACON, 1ST BARON VERULAM, VISCOUNT ST ALBANS, 26
The English take their p. SULLY, DUC DE, 1
the paucity of human p. JOHNSON, S, 32
**Pleiades** canst thou bind the sweet influences of P. BIBLE: JOB, 18
**plenteousness** p. of tears to drink PSALMS, 49

**plenty** but just had p. BURNS, R, 5
that p. should attain the poor BYRON, 6TH BARON, 2
**plods** plowman homeward p. his weary way GRAY, T, 1
**plot** p. hath many changes QUARLES, F, 2
the p. thickens BUCKINGHAM, 2ND DUKE OF, 1
**plough** To get it ready for the p. BETJEMAN, SIR J, 6
We p. the fields, and scatter CAMPBELL, J, 1
**ploughing** Is my team p. HOUSMAN, A, 9
**plowed** p. with my heifer BIBLE: JUDGES, 6
**plowman** The p. homeward plods his weary way GRAY, T, 1
**plowshares** beat their swords into p. BIBLE: ISAIAH, 4
**pluck** if thy right eye offend thee, p. it out BIBLE: MATTHEW, 14
p. till time and times are done YEATS, W, 28
**plural** in the p. and they bounce LUTYENS, SIR E, 1
**plus** *P. ça change* KARR, A, 1
**Plymouth** dreamin'. . . o' P. Hoe NEWBOLT, SIR H, 3
**poacher** a p. a keeper turned inside out KINGSLEY, C, 8
**pocket** carried a . . . brick in his p. SWIFT, J, 4
smile I could feel in my hip p. CHANDLER, R, 2
To be played with both hands in the p. SATIE, E, 3
**pockets** the p. of the people SMITH, A, 3
**Podduyev** life had prepared P. for living SOLZHENITSYN, A, 1
**poem** A long p. is a test of invention KEATS, J, 45
A p. lovely as a tree KILMER, A, 1
I do not think this p. will reach its destination VOLTAIRE, 32
P. me no poems MACAULAY, DAME R, 4
**poems** A man does not write p. SKELTON, R, 1
My p. are hymns of praise SITWELL, DAME E, 1
p. . . . for the love of Man and in praise of God THOMAS, D, 2
that Anon, who wrote so many p. WOOLF, V, 11
The few bad p. . . . created during abstinence REICH, W, 1
We all write p. FOWLES, J, 2
**poet** A true p. does not bother to be poetical COCTEAU, J, 1
godly p. must be chaste himself CATULLUS, G, 1
lunatic, the lover, and the p. SHAKESPEARE, W, 206
Many brave men . . . lack their sacred p. HORACE, 42
no person can be a p. . . . without . . . unsoundness of mind MACAULAY, BARON, 14
No p. . . . has his complete meaning alone ELIOT, T, 21
p.'s eye, in a fine frenzy SHAKESPEARE, W, 207
p. without love CARLYLE, T, 1
The p. and the dreamer are distinct KEATS, J, 11
The p. gives us his essence WOOLF, V, 1
To be a p. is a condition GRAVES, R, 4
**poetic** the laws of p. truth and p. beauty ARNOLD, M, 13
**poetical** A true poet does not bother to be p. COCTEAU, J, 1
that werges on the p. DICKENS, C, 47
**poetry** Angling is somewhat like p. WALTON, I, 2
As civilization advances, p. . . . declines MACAULAY, BARON, 13
Even when p. has a meaning HOUSMAN, A, 4
If p. comes not . . . as leaves to a tree KEATS, J, 52
I make p. and give pleasure . . . because of you HORACE, 40
Mr Shaw . . . has never written any p. CHESTERTON, G, 29
no man ever talked p. DICKENS, C, 45
no person can . . . enjoy p. without . . . unsoundness of mind MACAULAY, BARON, 14
P. is a comforting piece of fiction MENCKEN, H, 12
P. is as exact a science as geometry FLAUBERT, G, 1
P. is baroque MAUGHAM, W, 17
p. is . . . more philosophical . . . than history ARISTOTLE, 5
P. is not a turning loose of emotion ELIOT, T, 22
P. is opposed to science, . . . prose to metre COLERIDGE, S, 16
P. is the record of the best and happiest moments SHELLEY, P, 5
P. is the spontaneous overflow of powerful feelings WORDSWORTH, W, 17
P. is to prose WAIN, J, 1
P. is what gets lost in translation FROST, R, 11
p. makes nothing happen AUDEN, W, 14
p. reminds him of the richness KENNEDY, J, 14
P. . . . set to more or less lascivious music MENCKEN, H, 12
P. should be great and unobtrusive KEATS, J, 51
p. sinks and swoons under . . . prose LANDOR, W, 2
P.'s unnatural DICKENS, C, 45
p. = the best words in the best order COLERIDGE, S, 39
. . . p., 'The Cinderella of the Arts.' MONROE, H, 1
read a little p. sometimes HOPE, A, 7
Superstition is the p. of life GOETHE, J, 6
that is p. CAGE, J, 1
The difference between genuine p. ARNOLD, M, 42
the grand style arises in p. ARNOLD, M, 30
The one . . . p. . . . continually flowing is slang CHESTERTON, G, 7

The P. is in the pity OWEN, W, 5
there is p. in peaches GRANVILLE-BARKER, H, 1
to resuscitate the dead art /Of p. POUND, E, 10
truest p. is the most feigning SHAKESPEARE, W, 30
What is p.? RUSKIN, J, 3
**poets** among the English P. after my death KEATS, J, 57
excellent p. that have never versified SIDNEY, SIR P, 2
I hate the whole race . . . your professional p. WELLINGTON, DUKE OF, 8
nor even booksellers have put up with p.' being second-rate. HORACE, 10
Painters and p. . . . licence to dare anything HORACE, 1
P. and painters are outside the class system BRENAN, G, 6
p. are the ones who write in words FOWLES, J, 2
Souls of p. dead and gone KEATS, J, 21
**point** Up to a p., Lord Copper WAUGH, E, 38
you are like a pin, but without . . . head or . . . p. JERROLD, D, 8
**poison** food to one man is bitter p. to others LUCRETIUS, 4
strongest p. ever known BLAKE, W, 2
**poker** Malice is like a game of p. SPIEL, H, 1
**pokers** Wreathe iron p. into true-love knots COLERIDGE, S, 19
**pole** And see all sights from p. to p. ARNOLD, M, 41
Beloved from p. to p. COLERIDGE, S, 32
One step beyond the p. PEARY, R, 2
**Poles** few virtues . . . the P. do not possess CHURCHILL, SIR W, 56
**police** Reading isn't an occupation . . . among p. officers ORTON, J, 5
**policeman** A p.'s lot is not a happy one GILBERT, SIR W, 40
park, a p. and a pretty girl CHAPLIN, C, 1
the air of someone who is lying . . . to a p. PHILIPPE, C, 1
The terrorist and the p. CONRAD, J, 6
This definition . . . would not do for a p. NIGHTINGALE, F, 1
**policemen** first sign of old age: . . . how young the p. look HICKS, SIR S, 1
P. are numbered MILLIGAN, S, 9
repressed sadists . . . become p. or butchers CONNOLLY, C, 6
**polished** Satire should, like a p. razor keen MONTAGU, M, 1
whole man in himself, p. and well-rounded HORACE, 47
**polite** it costs nothing to be p. CHURCHILL, SIR W, 7
p. by telling lies BRADBURY, M, 6
time to be p. MONTESQUIEU, BARON DE, 7
**politeness** pine-apple of p. SHERIDAN, R, 6
Punctuality is the p. of kings LOUIS XVIII, 1
**political** addiction of p. groups to ideas GALBRAITH, J, 3
After all, we are not p. whores MUSSOLINI, B, 3
Every intellectual attitude is latently p. MANN, T, 2
Jesus was . . . a first-rate p. economist SHAW, G, 1
most schemes of p. improvement are very laughable JOHNSON, S, 73
one of these is the history of p. power POPPER, SIR K, 3
p. speech and writing . . . the defence of the indefensible ORWELL, G, 18
That points clearly to a p. career SHAW, G, 16
the formation of the p. will of the nation HITLER, A, 6
When . . . necessary for one people to dissolve . . . p. bonds JEFFERSON, T, 1
**politician** a p. is an arse CUMMINGS, E, 3
A p. is a statesman . . . with an open mouth STEVENSON, A, 2
A statesman is a p. who POMPIDOU, G, 1
A statesman is a p. who's been dead TRUMAN, H, 3
at home you're just a p. MACMILLAN, EARL OF STOCKTON, 3
Coffee which makes the p. wise POPE, A, 50
like a scurvy p. SHAKESPEARE, W, 148
p. never believes what he says DE GAULLE, C, 8
the p. poses as the servant DE GAULLE, C, 10
**politicians** It is a pity . . . that more p. are not bastards WHITEHORN, K, 4
P. are the same all over KHRUSHCHEV, N, 7
P. neither love nor hate DRYDEN, J, 5
politics are too serious . . . to be left to the p. DE GAULLE, C, 11
**politics** A week is a long time in p. WILSON OF RIEVAULX, BARON, 11
Britain is no longer in the p. of the pendulum THATCHER, M, 3
History is past p. SEELEY, SIR J, 2
in p. there is no heart, only head NAPOLEON I, 1
making p. Christian VAN DER POST, SIR L, 2
Men who have greatness . . . don't go in for p. CAMUS, A, 7
P. are now nothing more than JOHNSON, S, 95
p. are too serious . . . to be left to the politicians DE GAULLE, C, 11
P. is not an exact science BISMARCK, PRINCE VON, 7
P. is not a science . . . but an art BISMARCK, PRINCE VON, 7
P. is the art of preventing people from taking part VALERY, P, 3
P. is the art of the possible BISMARCK, PRINCE VON, 3

P. is . . . the only profession STEVENSON, R, 2
that men enter local p. PARKINSON, C, 4
The more you read about p. ROGERS, W, 9
they can at least pretend that p. is a game PARKINSON, C, 3
War is the continuation of p. CLAUSEWITZ, K, 1
War is the continuation of p. MAO TSE-TUNG, 1
pollution indefatigable and unsavoury engine of p. SPARROW, J, 1
Polly P. put the kettle on NURSERY RHYMES, 44
polygamy P. was made a Sin DRYDEN, J, 1
Pomeranian The healthy bones of a single P. grenadier
BISMARCK, PRINCE VON, 5
pomp In lowly p. ride on to die MILMAN, H, 1
Pride, p., and circumstance SHAKESPEARE, W, 227
Take physic, p. SHAKESPEARE, W, 141
pompous A p. woman . . . complaining that the head-waiter
SITWELL, DAME E, 4
p. in the grave BROWNE, SIR T, 12
Poms All the faces . . . seem to be bloody P. CHARLES, PRINCE, 1
pondered Mary . . . p. them in her heart BIBLE: LUKE, 10
ponies And wretched, blind, pit p. HODGSON, R, 1
pony I had a little p., /His name was Dapple Grey
NURSERY RHYMES, 21
poodle Mr Balfour's P. LLOYD GEORGE, EARL OF DWYFOR, 4
Pooh-Bah P. (Lord High Everything Else) GILBERT, SIR W, 22
poor A p. man is despised the whole world over JEROME, J, 3
a p. society cannot be too p. TAWNEY, R, 1
as for me, I am p. and needy PSALMS, 28
decent means p. PEACOCK, T, 1
Few, save the p., feel for the p. LANDON, L, 2
give to the p. BIBLE: MATTHEW, 57
great men have their p. relations DICKENS, C, 5
grind the faces of the p. BIBLE: ISAIAH, 6
Hard to train to accept being p. HORACE, 25
I, being p., have only my dreams; YEATS, W, 33
I can dare to be p. GAY, J, 11
I have nothing; the rest I leave to the p. RABELAIS, F, 7
inconvenient to be p. COWPER, W, 5
it is p. grub, p. pay, and easy work LONDON, J, 1
It's the p. wot gets the blame ANONYMOUS, 71
Laws grind the p. GOLDSMITH, O, 22
only the p. . . . are forbidden to beg FRANCE, A, 1
only the p. who pay cash FRANCE, A, 10
Pale Death kicks his way . . . into the cottages of the p.
HORACE, 27
p. have no right to the property of the rich RUSKIN, J, 14
P. Little Rich Girl COWARD, SIR N, 13
P. old Joe FOSTER, S, 5
p. relation LAMB, C, 13
Resolve not to be p. JOHNSON, S, 137
She was p. but she was honest ANONYMOUS, 71
short and simple annals of the p. GRAY, T, 2
that plenty should attain the p. BYRON, 6TH BARON, 2
the p. are our brothers and sisters TERESA, 1
the p. . . . need love, . . . need care TERESA, 1
the p. person . . . thinks money would help KERR, J, 2
The p. . . . their function . . . is to exercise our generosity
SARTRE, J, 11
Though I be p., I'm honest MIDDLETON, T, 1
To be p. and independent COBBETT, W, 1
What fun it would be to be p. ANOUILH, J, 5
poorer for richer for p. BOOK OF COMMON PRAYER, 15
poorest p. man may . . . bid defiance to . . . the Crown
PITT THE ELDER, 1ST EARL OF CHATHAM, 1
pop art In England, p. and fine art MACINNES, C, 1
poplars The p. are felled COWPER, W, 17
poppies the p. blow MCCRAE, J, 1
populace society distributes itself into Barbarians, Philistines, and
P. ARNOLD, M, 2
the p. cannot exact their demands WELLINGTON, DUKE OF, 12
this vast residuum we may . . . give the name of P. ARNOLD, M, 7
popular Nothing can render them p. SWIFT, J, 11
The worse I do, the more p. I get KENNEDY, J, 6
We're more p. than Jesus Christ LENNON, J, 13
popularity P.? . . . glory's small change HUGO, V, 4
P. is a crime HALIFAX, MARQUIS OF, 5
population a starving p. DISRAELI, 1ST EARL OF BEACONSFIELD, 19
P., . . . increases in a geometrical ratio MALTHUS, T, 1
populi vox p., vox dei ALCUIN, 1
porcupines I shall throw two p. under you KHRUSHCHEV, N, 4
Porlock by a person on business from P. COLERIDGE, S, 11
pornography P. is the attempt to insult sex LAWRENCE, D, 33

p. of war RAE, J, 1
You don't get any p. . . . on the telly SPEIGHT, J, 3
port Any p. in a storm PROVERBS, 56
it would be p. if it could BENTLEY, R, 1
porter Oh, mister p., what shall I do LLOYD, M, 1
portion best p. of a good man's life WORDSWORTH, W, 7
portions P. and parcels of the dreadful Past TENNYSON, BARON, 50
portrait Every man's work . . . is always a p. of himself
BUTLER, S, 23
Every time I paint a p. I lose a friend SARGENT, J, 1
portraits P. of famous bards and preachers THOMAS, D, 21
posh only two p. papers on a Sunday OSBORNE, J, 2
posies a thousand fragrant p. MARLOWE, C, 14
position only one p. for an artist THOMAS, D, 25
possessing too dear for my p. SHAKESPEARE, W, 261
possession P. is nine points PROVERBS, 337
The p. of a book BURGESS, A, 4
the p. of it is intolerable VANBURGH, SIR J, 1
possessions Not the owner of many p. will you . . . call happy
HORACE, 43
p. for a moment of time ELIZABETH I, 9
possibility too much of a sceptic to deny the p. of anything
HUXLEY, T, 10
possible Politics is the art of the p. BISMARCK, PRINCE VON, 3
something is p., he is . . . right CLARKE, A, 1
the art of the p. BUTLER, BARON, 1
post p. of honour is a private station ADDISON, J, 5
post-chaise I would spend my life in driving briskly in a p.
JOHNSON, S, 112
posterity doing something for p. ADDISON, J, 15
The nations which have put mankind and p. most in their debt
INGE, W, 12
Think of your p. ADAMS, J, 1
Thy p. shall sway COWPER, W, 1
What has p. done for us ROCHE, SIR B, 1
postgraduate The British p. student is a lonely forlorn soul
LODGE, D, 3
postscript all the pith is in the p. HAZLITT, W, 4
that which was most material in the p.
BACON, 1ST BARON VERULAM, VISCOUNT ST ALBANS, 17
postures It requires one to assume such indecent p. WILDE, O, 69
pot greasy Joan doth keel the p. SHAKESPEARE, W, 157
potent how p. cheap music is COWARD, SIR N, 15
Potter Who is the P. FITZGERALD, E, 16
poultry A p. matter MARX, G, 3
pound the p. . . . in your pocket WILSON OF RIEVAULX, BARON, 10
pounds My dear fellow, . . . I only ask you for twenty-five p.
SHERIDAN, R, 12
the p. will take care of themselves CHESTERFIELD, 4TH EARL OF, 6
two hundred p. a year BUTLER, S, 7
pouvait si vieillesse p. ESTIENNE, H, 1
poverty a darn is . . . p. SHUTER, E, 1
crime so shameful as p. FARQUHAR, G, 1
Do you call p. a crime SHAW, G, 17
easy enough to say that p. is no crime JEROME, J, 3
from nothing to a state of extreme p. MARX, G, 13
generations . . . have struggled in p. to build these altars
STANTON, E, 1
If p. is the mother of crime LA BRUYERE, J, 11
Loneliness . . . is the most terrible p. TERESA, 2
Notwithstanding the p. of my . . . experience JAMES, A, 2
P. and oysters DICKENS, C, 43
. . . p. . . . is a blunder JEROME, J, 3
P. is a great enemy to human happiness JOHNSON, S, 137
P. is an anomaly to rich people BAGEHOT, W, 11
P. is not a crime PROVERBS, 338
P. of goods is easily cured MONTAIGNE, M, 10
p. of soul, impossible MONTAIGNE, M, 10
The misfortunes of p. JUVENAL, 3
three great evils, boredom, vice, and p. VOLTAIRE, 5
world p. is primarily a problem of two million villages,
SCHUMACHER, E, 1
powder keep your p. dry BLACKER, V, 1
She burst while drinking a seidlitz p. ANONYMOUS, 32
when your p.'s runnin' low NEWBOLT, SIR H, 2
powdered Stratford, . . . suggests p. history HALSEY, M, 1
power according to the p. that worketh in us BIBLE: EPHESIANS, 1
As we make sex less secretive, we may rob it of its p.
SZASZ, T, 2
corridors of p. SNOW, BARON, 2
Germany will be . . . a world p. HITLER, A, 4

**races** human species ... composed of two distinct r.    LAMB, C, 8
the r. of Europe are melting    ZANGWILL, I, 2
**Rachmaninov** R.'s immortalizing totality was his scowl
   STRAVINSKY, I, 1
**racially** those who are not r. pure    HITLER, A, 1
**racing** happy state of getting the victor's palm without the dust of
r.    HORACE, 14
**rack** Leave not a r. behind    SHAKESPEARE, W, 277
**radical** A r. is a man    ROOSEVELT, F, 10
The r. invents the views. . . . , the conservative adopts them
   TWAIN, M, 9
**radicals** Few r. have good digestions    BUTLER, S, 16
**radio** I had the r. on    MONROE, M, 1
Simply a r. personality    WAUGH, E, 45
**rage** all Heaven in a r.    BLAKE, W, 8
R., r., against the dying of the light    THOMAS, D, 3
**rages** the weight of r.    SPOONER, W, 1
**rags** Eat slowly: only men in r. . . . /Mistake themselves for carpet
bags    RALEIGH, SIR W, 7
no scandal like r.    FARQUHAR, G, 1
**railing** R. at life, and yet afraid of death    CHURCHILL, C, 4
**railway** when they think they are alone in r. carriages    MILLER, J, 2
**raiment** they parted his r., and cast lots    BIBLE: LUKE, 36
**rain** A Hard R.'s A-Gonna Fall    DYLAN, B, 9
drop of r. maketh a hole in the stone    LATIMER, H, 1
droppeth as the gentle r.    SHAKESPEARE, W, 194
falls not hail, or r., or any snow    TENNYSON, BARON, 21
hath the r. a father    BIBLE: JOB, 17
He comes in the terrible R.    SITWELL, DAME E, 2
R. before seven    PROVERBS, 346
R., r., go away    PROVERBS, 347
singing in the r.    FREED, A, 1
**rainbow** A r. in the morning    PROVERBS, 62
A r. in the sky    WORDSWORTH, W, 21
Somewhere over the r.    HARBURG, E, 2
the R. gave thee birth    DAVIES, W, 1
**raineth** it r. on the just    BOWEN, BARON, 1
**rains** It never r. but it pours    PROVERBS, 230
**rainy** Keep something for a r. day    PROVERBS, 240
when it is not r.    BYRON, 6TH BARON, 4
**raise** My God shall r. me up    RALEIGH, SIR W, 3
Now he will r. me to be a martyr.    BOLEYN, A, 1
**rake** every woman is at heart a r.    POPE, A, 40
lene . . . as is a r.    CHAUCER, G, 6
**rallying-point** The party is the r. for the . . . working class
   STALIN, J, 4
**Ralph** R. wept for the end of innocence    GOLDING, W, 2
**ram** a r. caught in a thicket    BIBLE: GENESIS, 40
**rams** the mountains skipped like r.    PSALMS, 70
**Randolph** the only part of R. that was not malignant    WAUGH, E, 49
**rapidly** but not so r.    BECKETT, S, 3
**rapping** r. at my chamber door    POE, E, 1
**rapture** a r. on the lonely shore    BYRON, 6TH BARON, 13
The first fine careless r.    BROWNING, R, 25
**rare** as r. things will, it vanished    BROWNING, R, 37
keep it shut up . . . like a r., r. fiddle    MANSFIELD, K, 1
O r. Ben Jonson    JONSON, B, 15
**rascal** Get down you dirty r.    NURSERY RHYMES, 23
**rascals** R., would you live for ever    FREDERICK THE GREAT, 1
**rat** Mr Speaker, I smell a r.    ROCHE, SIR B, 2
That killed the r.    NURSERY RHYMES, 62
**ratchet** politics of the pendulum, but of the r.    THATCHER, M, 3
**rationalized** Happiness . . . should never be r.    CHESTERTON, G, 17
**rats** R.! /They fought the dogs    BROWNING, R, 40
**ravages** What do the r. of time not injure    HORACE, 37
**raven** Quoth the R., 'Nevermore'    POE, E, 2
**ravens** I have commanded the r. to feed thee there
   BIBLE: I KINGS, 5
There were three r. sat on a tree    ANONYMOUS, 96
**ravished** He . . . r. this fair creature    FIELDING, H, 8
**raw** the working-class which, r. and half-developed    ARNOLD, M, 7
**razor** Satire should, like a polished r. keen    MONTAGU, M, 1
**razors** R. pain you    PARKER, D, 1
**reach** a man's r. should exceed his grasp    BROWNING, R, 2
**reactionaries** r. are paper tigers    MAO TSE-TUNG, 3
**read** A lonesome man . . . who does not know how to r.
   FRANKLIN, B, 11
A man ought to r. just as inclination leads him    JOHNSON, S, 60
beautiful . . . for someone who could not r.    CHESTERTON, G, 45
books. . . . criticized and r. by people who don't understand them
   LICHTENBERG, G, 2

do *you* r. books *through*    JOHNSON, S, 84
Education . . . has produced a vast population able to r.
   TREVELYAN, G, 2
everybody wants to have r.    TWAIN, M, 15
He writes as fast as they can r.    HAZLITT, W, 5
His books were r.    BELLOC, H, 8
In my early years I r. very hard    JOHNSON, S, 40
I've just r. that I am dead . . .    KIPLING, R, 30
King George will be able to r. that    HANCOCK, J, 1
R., mark, learn and inwardly digest    BOOK OF COMMON PRAYER, 1
sooner r. a time-table . . . than nothing    MAUGHAM, W, 18
When I want to r. a novel    DISRAELI, 1ST EARL OF BEACONSFIELD, 37
will bear to be r. twice, . . . was thought twice    THOREAU, H, 3
**reader** A r. seldom peruses a book with pleasure    ADDISON, J, 7
memo . . . not to inform the r.    ACHESON, D, 5
send the r. to the dictionary    FAULKNER, W, 2
the writer . . . is the impregnator, . . . the r. . . . is the respondent
   WHITE, E, 2
**readers** his r. are proud to live in it    CONNOLLY, C, 2
The human race, . . . many of my r.    CHESTERTON, G, 25
to trade a hundred contemporary r. for    KOESTLER, A, 5
Was there ever yet anything written . . . that was wished longer
by its r.    JOHNSON, S, 33
**reading** as much pleasure in the r.    QUARLES, F, 1
a substitute for r. it    BURGESS, A, 4
a tragedy and therefore not worth r.    AUSTEN, J, 8
but I prefer r.    SMITH, L, 3
If a book is worth r.    RUSKIN, J, 5
**reading** as much pleasure in the r.    QUARLES, F, 1
a substitute for r. it    BURGESS, A, 4
a tragedy and therefore not worth r.    AUSTEN, J, 8
but I prefer r.    SMITH, L, 3
If a book is worth r.    RUSKIN, J, 5
I have led a life of business so long that I have lost my taste for
r., and now – what shall I do    WALPOLE, 4TH EARL OF ORFORD, 2
I loitered my life away, r. books    HAZLITT, W, 7
I shall lose no time in r. it    DISRAELI, 1ST EARL OF BEACONSFIELD, 16
Peace is poor r.    HARDY, T, 2
R. . . . ingenious device for avoiding thought    HELPS, SIR A, 1
R. isn't an occupation we encourage among police officers
   ORTON, J, 5
R. is to the mind    STEELE, SIR R, 1
R. maketh a full man
   BACON, 1ST BARON VERULAM, VISCOUNT ST ALBANS, 51
There are two motives for r. a book    RUSSELL, EARL, 6
The r. of all good books    DESCARTES, R, 2
When I am not walking, I am r.    LAMB, C, 11
**ready** I have but ninepence in r. money    ADDISON, J, 16
**ready made** critics all are r.    BYRON, 6TH BARON, 35
Why not 'r.'    CHURCHILL, SIR W, 3
**real** I could have become a r. painter    HOKUSAI, 1
Nothing ever becomes r. till it is experienced    KEATS, J, 59
whether Zelda and I are r.    FITZGERALD, F, 13
**realistic** he is going to make 'a r. decision', . . . resolved to do
something bad    MCCARTHY, M, 1
**reality** art . . . r. which is . . . in our minds    MACCARTHY, SIR D, 3
As far as the laws of mathematics refer to r.    EINSTEIN, A, 8
by r. I mean shops like Selfridges    LAWRENCE, T, 3
Cannot bear very much r.    ELIOT, T, 5
statesmen of the world who boast and threaten that they have
Doomsday weapons are far more dangerous, and far more
estranged from r.    LAING, R, 1
The whole of art is an appeal to a r.    MACCARTHY, SIR D, 3
**realize** I saw it, but I did not r.    PEABODY, E, 1
**realm** A worse king never left a r. undone    BYRON, 6TH BARON, 40
**realms** travell'd in the r. of gold    KEATS, J, 36
**reap** sow . . . in righteousness, r. in mercy    BIBLE: HOSEA, 2
sown the wind . . . r. the whirlwind    BIBLE: HOSEA, 1
they that sow in tears shall r. in joy    PSALMS, 79
whatsoever a man soweth, that shall he also r.
   BIBLE: GALATIANS, 6
**reaper** a R. whose name is Death    LONGFELLOW, H, 9
**reaping** No, r.    BOTTOMLEY, H, 1
**reappear** all great events and personalities in . . . history r.
   MARX, K, 6
**reason** A man who does not lose his r.    LESSING, G, 1
Faith consists in believing when it is beyond the power of r. to
believe    VOLTAIRE, 20
happiness is not an ideal of r.    KANT, I, 3
He never does a proper thing without . . . an improper r.
   SHAW, G, 15

he who destroys a good book, kills r.     MILTON, J, 1
Human r. won. Mankind won     KHRUSHCHEV, N, 3
it was neither rhyme nor r.     MORE, SIR T, 1
man . . . is R.'s slave     CONNOLLY, C, 18
nothing is law that is not r.     POWELL, SIR J, 1
not to r. why     TENNYSON, BARON, 5
Once the people begin to r.     VOLTAIRE, 26
Only r. can convince us     BELL, C, 3
right deed for the wrong r.     ELIOT, T, 16
R. is itself a matter of faith     CHESTERTON, G, 28
r. not the need     SHAKESPEARE, W, 136
The madman . . . has lost everything except his r.     CHESTERTON, G, 26
the r. of the case     POWELL, SIR J, 1
The ruling passion conquers r. still     POPE, A, 43
who turns mad for a r.     CERVANTES, M, 9
woman's r.     SHAKESPEARE, W, 298
**reasonable** something which no r. man could have expected     HERBERT, SIR A, 8
figure of 'The R.'     HERBERT, SIR A, 3
Who kills a man kills a r. creature     MILTON, J, 1
**reasoners** most plausible r.     HAZLITT, W, 26
**reasons** Metaphysics is the finding of bad r.     BRADLEY, F, 5
never give your r.     MANSFIELD, EARL OF, 1
r. for not printing any list of subscribers     JOHNSON, S, 135
The heart has its r.     PASCAL, B, 7
two r. for drinking     PEACOCK, T, 6
**rebel** how to r. and conform at the same time     CRISP, Q, 2
What is a r.     CAMUS, A, 11
**rebellion** A little r. now and then     JEFFERSON, T, 4
**recall** The Gods themselves cannot r. their gifts     TENNYSON, BARON, 72
**receipts** How were the r. today in Madison Square Garden     BARNUM, P, 2
**receive** whoso shall r. one such little child     BIBLE: MATTHEW, 53
**received** a cloud r. him out of their sight     BIBLE: ACTS, 1
freely ye have r., freely give     BIBLE: MATTHEW, 37
**receiver** your wife . . . is a r. of stolen goods     JOHNSON, S, 131
**reception** men that . . . hinder the r. of every work     JOHNSON, S, 24
**recession** It's a r. when your neighbour     TRUMAN, H, 5
**reckon'd** beggary in the love that can be r.     SHAKESPEARE, W, 5
**reckoning** take you . . . at your own r.     TROLLOPE, A, 14
**recognize** did not r. me by my face     TROLLOPE, A, 1
**recoils** Revenge . . . back on itself r.     MILTON, J, 46
**recompense** R. injury with justice     CONFUCIUS, 12
**reconcile** How r. this world . . . with . . . my imagining     KELLER, H, 3
It takes a long while for a . . . trustful person to r. himself to . . . God     MENCKEN, H, 10
**recounting** calms one's grief by r. it     CORNEILLE, P, 5
**recreation** woman accepted cooking . . . but man . . . made of it a r.     POST, E, 2
**red** Coral is far more r.     SHAKESPEARE, W, 267
his eyes shall be r. with wine     BIBLE: GENESIS, 54
it's not even r. brick, but white tile     OSBORNE, J, 4
. . . leeches have r. blood     CUVIER, BARON, 1
R. Badge of Courage     CRANE, S, 1
R. lips are not so r.     OWEN, W, 4
R. sky at night     PROVERBS, 348
The people's flag is deepest r.     CONNELL, J, 1
The sand of the desert is sodden r.     NEWBOLT, SIR H, 7
thin r. line tipped with steel     RUSSELL, SIR W, 1
**redeemed** he hath visited and r. his people     BIBLE: LUKE, 4
**redeemer** I know that my r. liveth     BIBLE: JOB, 12
O Lord, my strength, and my r.     PSALMS, 10
**redemption** married past r.     DRYDEN, J, 26
**red-hot** The Last of the R. Mamas     TUCKER, S, 1
**redundancy** handing out r. notices to its own workers.     KINNOCK, N, 9
**reel** they r. to and fro     PSALMS, 66
**references** Always verify your r.     ROUTH, M, 1
**reflection** a r. of the British Museum Reading Room     SPARK, M, 12
**reform** All r. . . . will prove unavailing     CARLYLE, T, 3
Any attempt to r. the university     ILLICH, I, 1
**reformation** Every r. must have its victims     SAKI, 19
**refreshed** like a giant r. with wine     PSALMS, 48
The tree of liberty must be r.     JEFFERSON, T, 5
**refuge** God is the immemorial r. of the incompetent     MENCKEN, H, 9
Idleness . . . the r. of weak minds     CHESTERFIELD, 4TH EARL OF, 11
Lord . . . our r. from one generation to another     PSALMS, 54
Patriotism is the last r.     JOHNSON, S, 92
the God of Jacob is our r.     PSALMS, 32

**refuse** To r. praise     ROCHEFOUCAULD, DUC DE LA, 18
**refused** She r. to begin the 'Beguine'     COWARD, SIR N, 17
**refute** I r. it *thus*     JOHNSON, S, 68
**regardless** r. of their doom     GRAY, T, 9
**regime** No r. has ever loved great writers     SOLZHENITSYN, A, 7
**regiment** led his r. from behind     GILBERT, SIR W, 1
**register** history; . . . is; . . . the r. of the . . . misfortunes of mankind     GIBBON, E, 6
I want to r. a complaint     MARX, G, 14
**regret** My r. /Becomes an April violet     TENNYSON, BARON, 33
remember and r.     LANDON, L, 1
wild with all r.     TENNYSON, BARON, 59
**regrets** the Cup that clears /to-day of past R.     FITZGERALD, E, 9
The follies which a man r.     ROWLAND, H, 2
**rehearsing** R. a play is making the word flesh     SHAFFER, P, 3
**reign** Better to r. in Hell     MILTON, J, 29
**reigned** I have r. with your loves     ELIZABETH I, 1
**reigns** king r., but does not govern     ZAMOYSKI, J, 1
**reject** If you r. me on account of my religion     BELLOC, H, 15
**rejoice** let the saints . . . r. in their beds     PSALMS, 93
let us heartily r. in the strength of our salvation     PSALMS, 60
new sights of Nature made me r.     CURIE, M, 2
r. in the Lord alway     BIBLE: PHILIPPIANS, 2
r. with joy unspeakable     BIBLE: I PETER, 1
the bones which thou hast broken may r.     PSALMS, 35
**rejoiced** my spirit hath r. in God my Saviour     BIBLE: LUKE, 2
**related** A group of closely r. persons     MACAULAY, DAME R, 3
**relation** If a man's character is to be abused . . . there's nobody like a r. to do the business     THACKERAY, W, 11
**relations** Fate chooses your r.     DELILLE, J, 1
great men have their poor r.     DICKENS, C, 5
**relaxation** Man . . . can only find r. from one . . . labour by taking up another     FRANCE, A, 3
**relaxes** Bless r.     BLAKE, W, 26
**relief** For this r. much thanks     SHAKESPEARE, W, 39
There is a certain r. in change     IRVING, W, 3
thou wilt give thyself r.     MARCUS AURELIUS ANTONINUS, 2
**religion** a feeling of inward tranquillity which r. is powerless to bestow     FORBES, C, 1
Art and r. first; then philosophy     SPARK, M, 9
As to r., I hold it to be the . . . duty of government to protect all . . . professors thereof     PAINE, T, 4
brothels with bricks of R.     BLAKE, W, 18
Fascism is a r.     MUSSOLINI, B, 4
If you reject me on account of my r.     BELLOC, H, 15
Love is my r.     KEATS, J, 62
Men will wrangle for r.     COLTON, C, 1
no reason to bring r. into it     O'CASEY, S, 3
Not a r. for gentlemen     CHARLES II, 2
Nothing is so fatal to r. as indifference,     BURKE, E, 21
One r. is as true as another     BURTON, R, 5
One's r. . . . yours is Success     BARRIE, SIR J, 7
R. /Has made an honest woman of the supernatural     FRY, C, 3
R. is an illusion     FREUD, S, 3
R. is by no means a proper subject     CHESTERFIELD, 4TH EARL OF, 15
R. is love     WEBB, B, 1
R. . . . is the opium of the people     MARX, K, 4
r. of feeble minds     BURKE, E, 10
r. of Socialism     BEVAN, A, 2
R.'s in the heart     JERROLD, D, 1
Science without r. is lame     EINSTEIN, A, 1
Sensible men are all of the same r.     DISRAELI, 1ST EARL OF BEACONSFIELD, 4
talks loudly against r.     STERNE, L, 8
that God is interested only . . . in r.     TEMPLE, W, 2
To become a popular r.     INGE, W, 5
when r. is allowed to invade . . . private life     MELBOURNE, VISCOUNT, 9
when r. was strong and science weak, men mistook magic for medicine     SZASZ, T, 3
**religions** a country with thirty-two r. and only one sauce     TALLEYRAND, 1
sixty different r., and only one sauce     CARACCIOLO, MARQUIS, 1
The r. we call false were once true     EMERSON, R, 4
**religious** a r. animal     BURKE, E, 9
first, r. and moral principles     ARNOLD, T, 2
not r.-good     HARDY, T, 6
r. outlook on life     JUNG, C, 6
skilled appeals to r. prejudice     HUXLEY, T, 11
To be at all is to be r.     BUTLER, S, 21
**relished** the taste by which he is . . . r.     WORDSWORTH, W, 18

reluctant The r. obedience of distant provinces
MACAULAY, BARON, 5
remarkable nothing left r. /Beneath the visiting moon
SHAKESPEARE, W, 15
remedies Extreme r. . . . for extreme diseases HIPPOCRATES, 2
He that will not apply new r.
BACON, 1ST BARON VERULAM, VISCOUNT ST ALBANS, 30
Our r. oft in ourselves do lie SHAKESPEARE, W, 1
paralyse it by encumbering it with r. TOLSTOY, COUNT, 7
r. . . . suggested for a disease CHEKHOV, A, 2
remedy a r. for everything except death CERVANTES, M, 15
Force is not a r. BRIGHT, J, 3
r. is worse than the disease
BACON, 1ST BARON VERULAM, VISCOUNT ST ALBANS, 46
Tis a sharp r., but a sure one RALEIGH, SIR W, 5
remember I only r. what I've learnt WHITE, P, 2
I r., I r. HOOD, T, 6
Oh! don't you r. sweet Alice, Ben Bolt ENGLISH, T, 1
r. and regret LANDON, L, 1
r. Lot's wife BIBLE: LUKE, 32
R. me when I am gone away ROSSETTI, C, 4
r. me when thou comest into thy kingdom BIBLE: LUKE, 37
she did not r. . . . her jewelry LOOS, A, 4
The world will little note, nor long r. LINCOLN, A, 12
we shall be glad to r. even these hardships VIRGIL, 4
We will r. them BINYON, L, 3
When I meet a man whose name I can't r.
DISRAELI, 1ST EARL OF BEACONSFIELD, 35
remembered By this may I r. be ANONYMOUS, 106
I r. my God SOUTHEY, R, 5
remembrance r. of things past SHAKESPEARE, W, 257
there is no r. of former things BIBLE: ECCLESIASTES, 3
reminiscences the old have r. SAKI, 12
remorse r. for what you have thought about your wife
ROSTAND, J, 2
remove all faith, so that I could r. mountains
BIBLE: I CORINTHIANS, 18
Renaissance the R. was . . . the green end of one of civilization's
hardest winters FOWLES, J, 1
render husband r. unto the wife due benevolence
BIBLE: I CORINTHIANS, 7
r. . . . unto Caesar BIBLE: MATTHEW, 63
rendezvous a r. with Death SEEGER, A, 1
renegades Political r. always start their career of treachery
KINNOCK, N, 10
renew r. a right spirit within me PSALMS, 35
renewal urban r. in New York City ILLICH, I, 1
rent they r. out my room ALLEN, W, 9
repair the landlord does not intend to r. ADAMS, J, 2
repartee A majority is always the best r.
DISRAELI, 1ST EARL OF BEACONSFIELD, 1
repast A new r., or an untasted spring ADDISON, J, 3
repay whatsoever thou spendest more . . . I will r. BIBLE: LUKE, 22
repeal the r. of bad or obnoxious laws GRANT, U, 4
repeat obliged to imitate himself, and to r. REYNOLDS, SIR J, 3
repeated A platitude is simply a truth r.
BALDWIN, 1ST EARL BALDWIN OF BEWDLEY, 10
repent Do you . . . Never, my Love, r. PATMORE, C, 2
r. at leisure CONGREVE, W, 8
r.: for the kingdom of heaven is at hand BIBLE: MATTHEW, 8
repentance A Christian . . . feels /R. on a Sunday YBARRA, T, 1
There's no r. in the grave WATTS, I, 5
with the morning cool r. SCOTT, SIR W, 16
repented it r. the Lord that he had made man BIBLE: GENESIS, 23
repenteth joy . . . over one sinner that r. BIBLE: LUKE, 27
repetition constant r. will finally succeed in imprinting an idea
HITLER, A, 2
History is an endless r. DURRELL, L, 3
replenished His intellect is not r. SHAKESPEARE, W, 154
replied And I r., 'My Lord' HERBERT, G, 2
reporter A r. is a man who has renounced everything MURRAY, D, 1
I am a r. GREENE, G, 9
reporting Language is not simply a r. device for experience
WHORF, B, 1
reprehend If I r. any thing SHERIDAN, R, 7
representation Proportional R. . . . is fundamentally counter-
democratic. KINNOCK, N, 2
Taxation without r. OTIS, J, 1
reproductions accurate r. of Anne Hathaway's cottage
LANCASTER, O, 2
I've seen colour r. ROSS, H, 1

republic An aristocracy in a r. is like a chicken whose head has
been cut off MITFORD, N, 1
the r. of letters ADDISON, J, 1
Republican The R. form of Government SPENCER, H, 1
Republicans Please assure me that you are all R. REAGAN, R, 1
republics Revolts, r., revolutions TENNYSON, BARON, 65
repulsive Roundheads (Right but R.) SELLAR, W, 5
reputability Conspicuous consumption . . . is a means of r.
VEBLEN, T, 3
reputation ever written out of r. but by himself BENTLEY, R, 2
it is better for the r. KEYNES, BARON, 5
it wrecks a woman's r. COLETTE, S, 4
O, I have lost my r. SHAKESPEARE, W, 222
spotless r. SHAKESPEARE, W, 234
Until you've lost your r., you never realize . . . what freedom
really is MITCHELL, M, 1
requests thou wilt grant their r. BOOK OF COMMON PRAYER, 6
requires all the Human Frame r. BELLOC, H, 4
research R.! A mere excuse for idleness JOWETT, B, 5
The outcome of any serious r. VEBLEN, T, 2
resent To great evils we submit; we r. little provocations
HAZLITT, W, 20
resentment It is very difficult to get up r. NEWMAN, CARDINAL, 1
reservoir a gigantic r. of good will WILLKIE, W, 2
residuum this vast r. we may . . . give the name of Populace
ARNOLD, M, 7
resign'd R. unto the Heavenly will ANONYMOUS, 11
resist r. everything except temptation WILDE, O, 35
r. the devil, and he will flee BIBLE: JAMES, 7
there is almost nothing to r. at all LAWRENCE, D, 2
resistance R. to tyranny is obedience to God ANTHONY, S, 4
resisting fond of r. temptation BECKFORD, W, 1
resolution In war, r. CHURCHILL, SIR W, 19
native hue of r. SHAKESPEARE, W, 63
resources statistics, born to consume r. HORACE, 17
respect A child deserves the maximum r. JUVENAL, 12
Civilization is . . . equal r. for all men ADDAMS, J, 3
old-fashioned r. for the young WILDE, O, 20
The English have no r. for their language SHAW, G, 34
those /Who err each other must r. PATMORE, C, 1
We must r. the other fellow's religion MENCKEN, H, 3
We owe r. to the living VOLTAIRE, 19
When people do not r. us we are sharply offended TWAIN, M, 11
respectable riff-raff apply to what is r. HOPE, A, 6
R. means rich PEACOCK, T, 1
r., middle-class, . . . lady RATTIGAN, SIR T, 1
respecter God is no r. of persons BIBLE: ACTS, 10
respects no man much r. himself TWAIN, M, 11
respondent the writer . . . is the impregnator, . . . the reader . . . is
the r. WHITE, E, 2
responsibility he wanted to be an actor. He had . . . a total lack of
r. HOPPER, H, 1
In dreams begins r. YEATS, W, 21
no sense of r. at the other KNOX, R, 3
No sex without r. LONGFORD, EARL OF, 1
power without r. BALDWIN, 1ST EARL BALDWIN OF BEWDLEY, 3
Power without r. KIPLING, R, 33
responsible An idea isn't r. for the people MARQUIS, D, 1
every man is r. for his face CAMUS, A, 1
No man is r. for his father TURNBULL, M, 1
r. and the irresponsible classes LAWRENCE, D, 10
You are r. for your rose SAINT-EXUPERY, A, 2
rest All the r. have thirty-one NURSERY RHYMES, 61
get rid of the r. of her VANBURGH, SIR J, 5
glad, because they are at r. PSALMS, 67
I have nothing; the r. I leave to the poor RABELAIS, F, 7
leave the r. to the Gods CORNEILLE, P, 1
Mary Ann has gone to r. ANONYMOUS, 56
Seek home for r. TUSSER, T, 4
then would I flee away, and be at r. PSALMS, 37
The r. is silence SHAKESPEARE, W, 76
To toil and not to seek for r. LOYOLA, I, 1
restaurants Great r. are . . . nothing but mouth-brothels
RAPHAEL, F, 4
rested God . . . r. on the seventh day BIBLE: GENESIS, 7
restore Time may r. us ARNOLD, M, 26
rests our heart is not quiet until it r. in Thee
AUGUSTINE OF HIPPO, 1
result the long r. of Time TENNYSON, BARON, 45
resurrection I am the r., and the life BIBLE: JOHN, 27

**retain** To expect a man to r. everything that he has ever read
SCHOPENHAUER, A. 6
**reticulated** Anything r. or decussated at equal distances
JOHNSON, S. 8
**retire** can't put off being young until you r. LARKIN, P. 1
**retreat** A mistress should be like a . . . r. WYCHERLEY, W. 1
**retrograde** All that is human must r. GIBBON, E. 8
**return** I shall r. MACARTHUR, D. 1
r., r., O Shulamite BIBLE: SONG OF SOLOMON. 16
**returning** R. were as tedious as go o'er SHAKESPEARE, W. 172
**reveal** words . . . half r. and half conceal TENNYSON, BARON, 23
**revealeth** he r. the deep and secret things BIBLE: DANIEL, 1
**Revelations** It ends with R. WILDE, O. 57
**revelry** a sound of r. by night BYRON, 6TH BARON, 10
**revels** Our r. now are ended SHAKESPEARE, W. 277
**revenge** A man that studieth r.
BACON, 1ST BARON VERULAM, VISCOUNT ST ALBANS, 44
he took his r. by speaking ill VOLTAIRE, 22
if you wrong us, shall we not r. SHAKESPEARE, W. 193
R., at first though sweet MILTON, J. 46
R. . . . back on itself recoils MILTON, J. 46
R. is a dish PROVERBS, 349
R. is a . . . wild justice
BACON, 1ST BARON VERULAM, VISCOUNT ST ALBANS, 43
R. is sweet PROVERBS, 350
**revenue** name a virtue that brings in as much r. NAPOLEON III, 1
**reverence** Just a little more r. . . . , and not so much astonishment
SARGENT, SIR M, 1
**reviewers** R. . . . would have been poets COLERIDGE, S, 17
**reviewing** Prolonged . . . r. of books involves constantly *inventing*
reactions ORWELL, G, 9
**revolts** R., republics, revolutions TENNYSON, BARON, 65
**revolution** Britain . . . is going to be forged in the white heat of
this r. WILSON OF RIEVAULX, BARON, 8
Britain is not . . . easily rocked by r. HAMILTON, W, 2
fundamental premise of a r. TROTSKY, L, 7
he'd go to church, start a r. – *something* MILLER, A, 3
Hitler has carried out a r. on our lines MUSSOLINI, B, 1
R. by its very nature TROTSKY, L, 1
restating our socialism in terms of the scientific r.
WILSON OF RIEVAULX, BARON, 8
Russia is a collapse, not a r. LAWRENCE, D, 35
The r. eats RICHLER, M, 1
We invented the R. WEISS, P, 1
**revolutionary** fierce and r. in a bathroom LINKLATER, E, 3
If you feed people just with r. slogans KHRUSHCHEV, N, 8
I would be a r. myself GEORGE V, 2
Patriotism . . . is a r. duty TROTSKY, L, 12
r. right LINCOLN, A, 10
The r. simpleton LEWIS, W, 6
**revolutions** All modern r. have ended CAMUS, A, 12
R. are always verbose TROTSKY, L, 5
Revolts, republics, r. TENNYSON, BARON, 65
state of mind which creates r. ARISTOTLE, 9
**revolver** I reach for my r. GOERING, H, 4
**reward** my r. is with me BIBLE: REVELATIONS, 22
The avoidance of taxes . . . still carries . . . r. KEYNES, BARON, 11
the due r. of our deeds BIBLE: LUKE, 37
The r. of a thing well done EMERSON, R, 9
To labour and not ask for any r. LOYOLA, I, 1
Vice is its own r. CRISP, Q, 6
**rewarded** Men are r. and punished not for what they do
SZASZ, T, 1
**rewards** In nature there are neither r. nor punishments
INGERSOLL, R, 2
In nature there are no r. VACHELL, H, 1
**Reynolds** When Sir Joshua R. died BLAKE, W, 33
**rhetoric** Out of the quarrel . . . we make r. YEATS, W, 9
**Rhine** The Watch on the R. SCHNECKENBURGER, M, 1
You think of the R. BALDWIN, 1ST EARL BALDWIN OF BEWDLEY, 5
**rhyme** it was neither r. nor reason MORE, SIR T, 1
outlive this powerful r. SHAKESPEARE, W, 258
R. being no necessary adjunct or true ornament MILTON, J, 23
the petty fools of r. TENNYSON, BARON, 44
**rhyming** troublesome . . . bondage of R. MILTON, J, 24
**rhythm** r. imposes unanimity upon the divergent MENUHIN, SIR Y, 1
**rib** the r. . . . made he a woman BIBLE: GENESIS, 11
**ribbon** The road was a r. of moonlight NOYES, A, 1
**rich** a r. man shall hardly enter into . . . heaven BIBLE: MATTHEW, 58
A r. man's joke is always funny BROWN, T E, 1
as easy to marry a r. woman as a poor woman THACKERAY, W, 5

as well off as if he were r. ASTOR, J, 1
If you can . . . count your money you are not . . . r. man
GETTY, J, 1
It's the r. wot gets the gravy ANONYMOUS, 71
nor a r. society too r. TAWNEY, R, 1
no sin but to be r. SHAKESPEARE, W, 125
poor have no right to the property of the r. RUSKIN, J, 14
Poor Little R. Girl COWARD, SIR N, 13
r. are different from us FITZGERALD, F, 3
r. beyond the dreams of avarice MOORE, E, 2
Respectable means r. PEACOCK, T, 1
R. men's houses are seldom beautiful ASQUITH, M, 2
so large, /So friendly, and so r. AUDEN, W, 20
The r. and powerful know ANOUILH, J, 3
The r. are the scum of the earth CHESTERTON, G, 11
the r. he hath sent empty away BIBLE: LUKE, 3
The r. man has his motor car ADAMS, F, 1
the wretchedness of being r. SMITH, L, 2
Victim of a r. man's game ANONYMOUS, 71
whether to be r. in things ILLICH, I, 2
you have to live with r. people SMITH, L, 2
**richer** for r. for poorer BOOK OF COMMON PRAYER, 15
R. than all his tribe SHAKESPEARE, W, 229
**riches** Infinite r. in a little room MARLOWE, C, 10
R. are for spending
BACON, 1ST BARON VERULAM, VISCOUNT ST ALBANS, 23
R. have wings COWPER, W, 28
r. to be a valuable thing SWIFT, J, 19
the chief employment of r. consists in the parade of r. SMITH, A, 2
**richesses** *l'embarras des r.* ALLAINVAL, L, 1
**richest** He is the r. author that ever grazed JOHNSON, S, 57
**Richmond Hill** On R. there lives a lass MACNALLY, L, 1
**rid** gladly . . . am I r. of it all SOPHOCLES, 2
glad to get r. of it MARX, G, 12
**riddle** a r. wrapped in a mystery inside an enigma
CHURCHILL, SIR W, 40
glory, jest, and r. of the world POPE, A, 31
R. of destiny LAMB, C, 18
**ride on** In lowly pomp r. to die MILMAN, H, 1
**rides** He who r. a tiger PROVERBS, 202
**ridicule** R. often checks what is absurd SCOTT, SIR W, 15
R. . . . smothers that which is noble SCOTT, SIR W, 15
**ridiculous** a fine sense of the r. ALBEE, E, 1
a step from the sublime to the r. NAPOLEON I, 5
no spectacle so r. MACAULAY, BARON, 16
The profession of letters . . . in which one can make no money
without being r. RENARD, J, 1
The sublime and the r. PAINE, T, 2
**riding** Commuter . . . r. to and from his wife WHITE, E, 1
the highwayman came r. NOYES, A, 1
**riff-raff** r. apply to what is respectable, . . . aristocracy to what is
decent HOPE, A, 6
**rift** the . . . r. between the sexes is . . . widened by . . . teaching
. . . to the girls STEVENSON, R, 12
**Riga** There was a young lady of R. ANONYMOUS, 93
**right** All's r. with the world BROWNING, R, 43
better to be irresponsible and r. CHURCHILL, SIR W, 59
every man did that which was r. in his own eyes BIBLE: JUDGES, 9
Every man has a r. to utter what he thinks truth JOHNSON, S, 128
I am not and never have been, a man of the r. MOSLEY, SIR O, 2
I disapprove of what you say, but I will defend to the death your
r. to say it VOLTAIRE, 34
I'd rather be r. than president THOMAS, N, 1
I . . . may not always be r., but I am never wrong GOLDWYN, S, 6
It will all come r. in the wash PROVERBS, 237
Keep r. on to the end of the road LAUDER, SIR H, 5
Liberty is the r. to do everything MONTESQUIEU, BARON DE, 3
Minorities . . . are almost always in the r. SMITH, S, 12
no r. to strike against public safety COOLIDGE, C, 2
No, this r. hand shall work it all off SCOTT, SIR W, 20
One of the pleasures of middle age is to *find out* that one WAS r.
POUND, E, 2
'orthodoxy' . . . no longer means being r. CHESTERTON, G, 13
our country, r. or wrong DECATUR, S, 1
publish, r. or wrong BYRON, 6TH BARON, 33
rather be r. than be President CLAY, H, 1
R. is more precious WILSON, W, 5
r. mindfulness, r. contemplation BUDDHA, 2
r. of all, . . . duty of some QUINCY, J, 1
settled r. WILCOX, E, 2
something is possible, he is . . . r. CLARKE, A, 1

The customer is always r.      SELFRIDGE, H, 1
The *divine r.* of husbands      WOLLSTONECRAFT, M, 1
The man who gets angry . . . in the r. way . . . is commended
     ARISTOTLE, 2
The minority is always r.      IBSEN, H, 2
The r. divine of kings to govern wrong      POPE, A, 2
The r. people are rude      MAUGHAM, W, 15
the r. to be consulted, . . . to encourage, . . . to warn
     BAGEHOT, W, 7
the r. to criticize Shakespeare      SHAW, G, 39
Those who believe that they are exclusively in the r.
     HUXLEY, A, 29
Ulster will be r.      CHURCHILL, R, 3
Women would rather be r. than reasonable      NASH, O, 4
**righteous** leave r. ways behind      BUDDHA, 3
let them . . . not be written among the r.      PSALMS, 44
the r. perisheth, and no man layeth it to heart      BIBLE: ISAIAH, 34
the r. shall flourish like a palm-tree      PSALMS, 58
to slay the r. with the wicked      BIBLE: GENESIS, 36
yet saw I never the r. forsaken      PSALMS, 26
**righteousness** He made r. readable      BONE, J, 1
in r. he doth judge and make war      BIBLE: REVELATIONS, 14
r. and peace have kissed each other      PSALMS, 52
r. hath looked down from heaven      PSALMS, 52
the breastplate of r.      BIBLE: EPHESIANS, 4
The eternal *not ourselves* that makes for r.      ARNOLD, M, 22
the paths of r.      PSALMS, 12
the r. of the scribes and Pharisees      BIBLE: MATTHEW, 13
**righter** much r. than one knew at say 17 or 23      POUND, E, 2
**right hand** sit thou on my r.      PSALMS, 68
**rights** All human beings are born free and equal in dignity and r.
     ANONYMOUS, 3
Men their r. and nothing more      ANTHONY, S, 1
The battle for women's r.      THATCHER, M, 8
The Sovereign has, under a constitutional monarchy . . . three r.
     BAGEHOT, W, 7
We are here to claim our r. as women      PANKHURST, DAME C, 3
women their r. and nothing less      ANTHONY, S, 1
**ring** Don't carry away that arm till I have . . . my r.
     RAGLAN, 1ST BARON, 1
One R. to rule them all      TOLKIEN, J, 2
R. down the curtain      RABELAIS, F, 8
r. is worn away by use      OVID, 2
The r. so worn . . . is yet of gold      CRABBE, G, 2
**rings** R. on her fingers and bells on her toes      NURSERY RHYMES, 46
**riot** A r. is at bottom      KING, M, 1
**ripe** cherry r.      ALISON, R, 1
Cherry r.      HERRICK, R, 1
we r. and r.      SHAKESPEARE, W, 22
**ripeness** R. is all      SHAKESPEARE, W, 151
**ripp'd** mother's womb untimely r.      SHAKESPEARE, W, 179
**rise** Early to r. and early to bed      THURBER, J, 5
Fish die belly-upward and r. . . . their way of falling      GIDE, A, 2
in the name of Jesus . . . r. up and walk      BIBLE: ACTS, 4
nobody who does not r. early      JOHNSON, S, 155
Thanks to words, we have been able to r. above the brutes
     HUXLEY, A, 1
**risen** the Lord is r. indeed      BIBLE: LUKE, 40
we are r., and stand upright      PSALMS, 11
**risk** a bank that would lend money to such a poor r.
     BENCHLEY, R, 5
**risks** what r. you take . . . to find money in a desk      BALZAC, H, 4
**Ritz** like the R. hotel      MATHEW, SIR J, 1
**river** a pure r. of water of life      BIBLE: REVELATIONS, 21
build your House of Parliament upon the r.
     WELLINGTON, DUKE OF, 12
can't step into the same r. twice      HERACLITUS, 2
Fame is like a r.
     BACON, 1ST BARON VERULAM, VISCOUNT ST ALBANS, 40
Ol' man r.      HAMMERSTEIN, O, 4
On either side the r. lie      TENNYSON, BARON, 37
On the breast of the r. of Time      ARNOLD, M, 16
the r. of knowledge has too often turned back on itself
     JEANS, SIR J, 2
the R. Tiber foaming with much blood      POWELL, E, 1
The vanity of human life is like a r.      POPE, A, 56
They promise to build a bridge even where there's no r.
     KHRUSHCHEV, N, 7
**rivers** turn our captivity . . . as the r. in the south      PSALMS, 79
**road** All I seek . . . the r. below me      STEVENSON, R, 4
a r. . . . that does not go through the intellect      CHESTERTON, G, 6

Does the r. wind up-hill      ROSSETTI, C, 6
free as the r.      HERBERT, G, 1
He watched the ads /And not the r.      NASH, O, 6
Keep right on to the end of the r.      LAUDER, SIR H, 5
On the r. to Mandalay      KIPLING, R, 21
tell us of the R.      FITZGERALD, E, 17
the Golden R. to Samarkand      FLECKER, J, 1
There is a r. from the eye to the heart      CHESTERTON, G, 6
the rolling English r.      CHESTERTON, G, 32
The r. was a ribbon of moonlight      NOYES, A, 1
They shut the r. through the woods      KIPLING, R, 28
**roads** all r. lead to France      THOMAS, E, 4
All r. lead to Rome      PROVERBS, 36
How many r. must a man walk down      DYLAN, B, 1
New r.: new ruts      CHESTERTON, G, 47
Two r. diverged      FROST, R, 7
**roam** Mid pleasures and palaces though we may r.      PAYNE, J, 1
**roamin'** R. in the gloamin'      LAUDER, SIR H, 3
**roar** luck to give the r.      CHURCHILL, SIR W, 63
**roast** the learned r. an egg      POPE, A, 51
**rob** Why r. one to feed the other      JUANG-ZU, 1
**robb'd** He that is r., not wanting what is stol'n
     SHAKESPEARE, W, 226
**robbed** We was r.      JACOBS, J, 1
when you've r. a man of everything      SOLZHENITSYN, A, 5
**robber** now Barabbas was a r.      BIBLE: JOHN, 45
**Robbins** President R. was so well adjusted to his environment
     JARRELL, R, 1
**Robert Browning** R., you writer of plays      BROWNING, R, 28
**Robes** R. and furr'd gowns hide all      SHAKESPEARE, W, 147
**robin** A r. redbreast in a cage      BLAKE, W, 8
Our little English r.      WORDSWORTH, W, 39
Who killed Cock R.      NURSERY RHYMES, 73
**Robin Gray** R., he was gudeman to me      BARNARD, A, 1
**Robinson** Here's to you, Mrs R.      SIMON, P, 2
**robot** the modern conception of a r.      CHURCHILL, SIR W, 16
**rock** a wise man, which built his house upon a r.
     BIBLE: MATTHEW, 31
he smote the r. twice      BIBLE: NUMBERS, 4
R. of ages, cleft for me      TOPLADY, A, 1
r. of offence      BIBLE: ISAIAH, 11
the r. that is higher than I      PSALMS, 41
upon this r. I will build my church      BIBLE: MATTHEW, 50
With my little stick of Blackpool r.      FORMBY, G, 2
**rock and roll** R. or Christianity      LENNON, J, 13
**rocked** R. in the cradle of the deep      MILLARD, E, 1
**rocks** older than the r. among which she sits      PATER, W, 1
The hand that r. the cradle      WALLACE, W, 1
**rod** Aaron's r.      BIBLE: EXODUS, 14
he that spareth his r. hateth his son      BIBLE: PROVERBS, 7
rule them with a r. of iron      BIBLE: REVELATIONS, 2
spare the r.      BUTLER, S, 4
thy r. and thy staff comfort me      PSALMS, 12
**rode** and r. madly off in all directions      LEACOCK, S, 10
**rodent-like** music critics. . . . small and r. with padlocked ears
     STRAVINSKY, I, 3
**Roland** Childe R. to the Dark Tower came      BROWNING, R, 15
**role** he saw his r. as being that of Moses      JAY, P, 1
**roll** our soul /Had *felt* him like the thunder's r.      ARNOLD, M, 24
R. up that map      PITT THE YOUNGER, W, 2
**rolled** bottoms of my trousers r.      ELIOT, T, 12
**rolling** Like a r. stone      DYLAN, B, 4
The r. English drunkard      CHESTERTON, G, 32
**Rolls** She has a R. body and a Balham mind      MORTON, J, 1
**Roman** noblest R. of them all      SHAKESPEARE, W, 123
the Holy R. Empire was neither holy, nor R., nor an empire
     VOLTAIRE, 11
The Papacy is not other than the Ghost of the deceased R.
Empire      HOBBES, T, 7
the R. people had but one neck      CALIGULA, 1
**romance** The r. of *Tom Jones*      GIBBON, E, 3
Twenty years of r. makes a woman look like a ruin      WILDE, O, 53
**Romans** Friends, R., countrymen, lend me your ears
     SHAKESPEARE, W, 116
The R. and Greeks found everything human      LAWRENCE, D, 4
which came first, the Greeks or the R.
     DISRAELI, 1ST EARL OF BEACONSFIELD, 36
**Romanticism** R. is . . . presenting people with the literary works
. . . affording . . . the greatest . . . pleasure      STENDHAL, 2
**Rome** I lov'd R. more      SHAKESPEARE, W, 115
R. has spoken; the case is concluded      AUGUSTINE OF HIPPO, 4

# S

being kind /Is all the s. world needs WILCOX, E. 4
when thou art absent I am s. NORTON, C. 1
**sadder** A s. and a wiser man COLERIDGE, S. 38
**sadists** repressed s. . . . become policemen or butchers
CONNOLLY, C. 6
**sadness** Good day s. ELUARD, P. 1
**safe** Better be s. than sorry PROVERBS, 91
make the world s. for diversity KENNEDY, J. 12
thou shalt be s. under his feathers PSALMS, 57
**safeguard** the s. of the west WORDSWORTH, W. 53
**safer** s. to obey than to rule KEMPIS, T. 2
**safest** Just when we are s. BROWNING, R. 7
**safety** Safe though all s.'s lost BROOKE, R. 4
s. is in our speed EMERSON, R. 11
There is s. in numbers PROVERBS, 411
**sage** without hardness will be s. ARNOLD, M. 18
**said** a great deal to be s. /For being dead BENTLEY, E. 3
I was glad when they s. unto me PSALMS, 78
Nothing has yet been s. that's not been s. before TERENCE, 1
the best which has been thought and s. in the world ARNOLD, M. 1
they do not know what they have s. CHURCHILL, SIR W. 34
'Tis s. that some have died for love WORDSWORTH, W. 65
**sailor** No man will be a s. JOHNSON, S. 53
Tinker, /Tailor, /Soldier, /S. NURSERY RHYMES, 65
**sailors** It is always opening time in the S. Arms THOMAS, D. 15
S. have a port PROVERBS, 352
**saint** before we *know* he is a s., there will have to be miracles
GREENE, G. 8
I consider myself superior to the s., the scientist LAWRENCE, D. 36
never a s. took pity on /My soul COLERIDGE, S. 29
possible for a woman to qualify as a s. STOCKS, BARONESS, 1
**saints** All are not s. PROVERBS, 31
let the s. be joyful with glory PSALMS, 93
many bodies of the s. which slept arose BIBLE: MATTHEW, 87
**sake** Art for art's s. COUSIN, V. 1
**sakes** king . . . men have made for their own s. SELDEN, J. 1
**salad** My s. days SHAKESPEARE, W. 7
**salary** The s. of the chief executive GALBRAITH, J. 8
this is the week I earn my s. KENNEDY, J. 3
**Salkeld** I am married to Beatrice S., a painter BEHAN, B. 10
**Sally** There's none like pretty S. CAREY, H. 3
**sally** a sudden s. TENNYSON, BARON, 3
**salmon** cider and tinned s. WAUGH, E. 31
serve both cod and s. LEVERSON, A. 2
the choice between smoked s. and tinned s.
WILSON OF RIEVAULX, BARON, 1
**salt** a pillar of s. BIBLE: GENESIS, 38
like an egg without s. CAWEIN, M. 1
nobody likes having s. rubbed into their wounds WEST, DAME R. 3
speech . . . seasoned with s. BIBLE: COLOSSIANS, 6
S. water and absence PROVERBS, 353
the s. of the earth BIBLE: MATTHEW, 11
**salvation** let us heartily rejoice in the strength of our s.
PSALMS, 60
the helmet of s. BIBLE: EPHESIANS, 1
the Lord is my light, and my s. PSALMS, 17
There is no s. outside the church AUGUSTINE OF HIPPO, 3
The s. of mankind SOLZHENITSYN, A, 12
water out of the wells of s. BIBLE: ISAIAH, 16
**Sam** Play it, S. BOGART, H. 2
**Samaritan** But a certain S. . . . had compassion on him
BIBLE: LUKE, 22
No one would have remembered the Good S. THATCHER, M. 7
ready enough to do the S. SMITH, S. 9
**Samarkand** the Golden Road to S. FLECKER, J. 1
**same** he is much the s. AUSTIN, A. 1
It will be all the s. PROVERBS, 238
it would be all the s. a hundred years hénce DICKENS, C. 22
principle seems the s. CHURCHILL, SIR W. 1
the s. is my brother BIBLE: MATTHEW, 43
we must all say *the s.* MELBOURNE, VISCOUNT, 1
we're all made the s. COWARD, SIR N. 2
**samite** Clothed in white s. TENNYSON, BARON, 16
**Samuel** When they circumcised Herbert S.
LLOYD GEORGE, EARL OF DWYFOR, 10
**sanction** Happiness is the only s. of life SANTAYANA, G. 4
**sand** a foolish man, which built his house upon the s.
BIBLE: MATTHEW, 31
and throws . . . s. in their eyes HOFFMANN, E. 1
The s. of the desert is sodden red NEWBOLT, SIR H. 7

They wept like anything to see /Such quantities of s.
CARROLL, L. 24
throw the s. against the wind BLAKE, W. 32
World in a grain of s. BLAKE, W. 7
**sane** Show me a s. man and I will cure him for you JUNG, C. 9
**sans** S. teeth, s. eyes, s. taste, s. every thing SHAKESPEARE, W, 24
**Sappho** Where burning S. loved BYRON, 6TH BARON, 23
**Sarah** and S. shall have a son BIBLE: GENESIS, 35
**sarcasm** petulance is not s. DISRAELI, 1ST EARL OF BEACONSFIELD, 23
S. . . . the language of the devil CARLYLE, T, 24
**sardines** Life is . . . like a tin of s. BENNETT, A. 1
sat by the waters of Babylon we s. down and wept PSALMS, 83
The . . . gentleman has s. so long on the fence
LLOYD GEORGE, EARL OF DWYFOR, 9
**Satan** And S. trembles COWPER, W. 13
beheld S. as lightning fall from heaven BIBLE: LUKE, 20
S. exalted sat, by merit raised MILTON, J. 34
S. finds . . . mischief . . . /For idle hands WATTS, I. 1
S., Nick, or Clootie BURNS, R. 1
**satire** hard not to write s. JUVENAL, 1
S. is a sort of glass SWIFT, J. 1
S. should, like a polished razor keen MONTAGU, M. 1
**satirists** S. should be heard and not seen SHERWOOD, R. 1
**satisfaction** complacency and s. . . . in . . . a new-married couple
LAMB, C. 1
the s. of knowing that we are avenged TROLLOPE, A. 15
**satisfied** his soul is s. with what is assigned to him
MARCUS AURELIUS ANTONINUS, 10
The superior man is s. CONFUCIUS, 10
**Saturday** betwixt /A S. and Monday CAREY, H. 2
Died on S. NURSERY RHYMES, 53
S.'s child works hard for his living NURSERY RHYMES, 35
what he did on S. YBARRA, T, 1
**satyr** man is . . . either a stoic or a s. PINERO, SIR A, 1
**sauce** a country with thirty-two religions and only one s.
TALLEYRAND, 1
Art is not a special s. LETHABY, W. 1
sixty different religions, and only one s. CARACCIOLO, MARQUIS, 1
The best s. in the world CERVANTES, M. 14
**Saul** S. hath slain his thousands BIBLE: I SAMUEL, 6
**savage** a time when Britain had a s. culture BANDA, H. 1
soothe a s. breast CONGREVE, W. 6
s. place! as holy and enchanted COLERIDGE, S. 14
The young man who has not wept is a s. SANTAYANA, G. 2
**savaged** s. by a dead sheep HEALEY, D. 1
**savait** *Si jeunesse s.* ESTIENNE, H. 1
**save** Christ Jesus came into the world to s. sinners
BIBLE: I TIMOTHY, 1
S. your breath PROVERBS, 354
To s. a man's life against his will is . . . killing him HORACE, 12
**saved** he that endureth to the end shall be s. BIBLE: MATTHEW, 38
they only s. the world BELLOC, H. 6
thy faith hath s. thee BIBLE: LUKE, 18
**saviour** I imitate the S. HUXLEY, A. 3
**saw** I came; I s.; God conquered JOHN III SOBIESKI, 1
I came, I s., I conquered CAESAR, J. 4
I s. it, but I did not realize it PEABODY, E. 1
**Saxon** The S. is not like us Normans KIPLING, R. 18
**say** cannot s. what you have to s. in twenty minutes
BRABAZON OF TARA, BARON, 1
Do as I s. PROVERBS, 111
if we s. that we have no sin, we deceive BIBLE: I JOHN, 1
I have nothing to s., I am saying it CAGE, J. 1
Preachers s., Do as I s., not as I do SELDEN, J. 5
say what you have to s., and then sit down
WELLINGTON, DUKE OF, 22
S. it with flowers O'KEEFE, P, 1
The great consolation . . . is to s. what one thinks VOLTAIRE, 25
They are to s. what they please FREDERICK THE GREAT, 2
they do not know what they are going to s. CHURCHILL, SIR W. 34
What have we to s. to India RUSKIN, J. 10
When you have nothing to s. COLTON, C. 2
**saying** S. is one thing PROVERBS, 355
when . . . speaking, they do not know what they are s.
CHURCHILL, SIR W. 34
**sayings** Dr Johnson's s. PEMBROKE, 10TH EARL OF, 1
His s. are generally like women's letters HAZLITT, W. 4
**scab** The itch of disputing will prove the s. of churches
WOTTON, SIR H, 2
**scaffold** no middle course between the throne and the s.
CHARLES X, 2

Two voices . . . one is of the s., /One of the mountains
WORDSWORTH, W, 58
We are as near to heaven by s. as by land GILBERT, SIR H, 1
when they can see nothing but s.
BACON, 1ST BARON VERULAM, VISCOUNT ST ALBANS, 3
why the s. is boiling hot CARROLL, L, 25
**sea-change** doth suffer a s. SHAKESPEARE, W, 273
**seagreen** The s. Incorruptible CARLYLE, T, 16
**sealed** My lips are s. BALDWIN, 1ST EARL BALDWIN OF BEWDLEY, 6
**sea-life** When men come to like a s. JOHNSON, S, 98
**seals** sealed with seven s. BIBLE: REVELATIONS, 3
**seam** And sew a fine s. NURSERY RHYMES, 8
**seamen** There were gentlemen and . . . s. in the navy of Charles
the Second MACAULAY, BARON, 9
the s. were not gentlemen MACAULAY, BARON, 9
**search** in s. of a great perhaps RABELAIS, F, 9
s. for knowledge RUSSELL, EARL, 1
s. the land of living men SCOTT, SIR W, 11
**searched** O Lord, thou hast s. me out PSALMS, 84
**seas** I must down to the s. again MASEFIELD, J, 5
That guard our native s. CAMPBELL, T, 6
the waters called the S. BIBLE: GENESIS, 3
**seaside** Beside the S. GLOVER-KIND, J, 1
the drawback of all s. places DOUGLAS, N, 1
**season** a perfectly ghastly s. . . . for you Spanish dancers.
BANKHEAD, T, 6
Only in the mating s. MILLIGAN, S, 3
to every thing there is a s. BIBLE: ECCLESIASTES, 8
**seasoned** speech . . . s. with salt BIBLE: COLOSSIANS, 6
**seasons** a man for all s. WHITTINGTON, R, 1
**seat** the pleasure of offering my s. to three ladies
CHESTERTON, G, 38
**seated** S. . . . at the organ PROCTER, A, 1
**sea-water** Wealth is like s. SCHOPENHAUER, A, 8
**second** The constitution . . . first and s. class citizens WILLKIE, W, 1
**second-hand** Would you buy a s. car SAHL, M, 1
**second-rate** an infallible sign of the s. LEVERSON, A, 1
nor even booksellers have put up with poets' being s. HORACE, 10
the powers of a first-rate man and the creed of a s. man
BAGEHOT, W, 9
**secret** a s. in the Oxford sense FRANKS, BARON, 1
bread eaten in s. is pleasant BIBLE: PROVERBS, 6
I know that's a s. CONGREVE, W, 5
it is no sin to sin in s. MOLIERE, 10
joys of parents are s.
BACON, 1ST BARON VERULAM, VISCOUNT ST ALBANS, 38
Learn the s. of the sea LONGFELLOW, H, 10
not to give way to it in s. CRISP, Q, 1
s. of reaping the greatest fruitfulness . . . from life NIETZSCHE, F, 5
Three may keep a s. FRANKLIN, B, 5
when it ceases to be a s. BEHN, A, 1
**secreted** Not in Utopia, . . . – /Or some s. island
WORDSWORTH, W, 37
**secretive** As we make sex less s., we may rob it of its power
SZASZ, T, 2
sex has been a very private, s. activity SZASZ, T, 2
**secrets** Conversation . . . elicits s. from us SENECA, 2
the family, with its narrow privacy and tawdry s. LEACH, SIR E, 1
**sect** paradise for a s. KEATS, J, 10
sedate, sober, silent, serious, sad-coloured s. HOOD, T, 1
**secure** only place where a man can feel . . . s. GREER, G, 1
The past, at least, is s. WEBSTER, D, 3
**security** only freedom can make s. secure POPPER, SIR K, 4
**sedan chair** in a flood of tears and a S. DICKENS, C, 50
**sedge** s. has wither'd from the lake KEATS, J, 17
**seducers** evil men and s. BIBLE: II TIMOTHY, 2
**see** change we think we s. FROST, R, 1
complain we cannot s. BERKELEY, BISHOP, 2
eyes . . . and s. not PSALMS, 71
eyes to s., and s. not BIBLE: EZEKIEL, 2
he that made the eye, shall he not s. PSALMS, 59
I s. none coming out AESOP, 6
It is . . . at my age I now begin to s. things as they really are
FONTENELLE, B, 1
My business is to paint . . . what I s. TURNER, J, 1
seem to s. things thou dost not SHAKESPEARE, W, 148
s. . . . into a hypocrite CHESTERTON, G, 16
there shall no man s. me, and live BIBLE: EXODUS, 30
these men s. the works of the Lord PSALMS, 66
thou shalt s. thy children's children PSALMS, 81
whereas I was blind, now I s. BIBLE: JOHN, 23

. . . . Why don't you come up sometime and s. me WEST, M, 6
**seed** I do not want to die . . . until I have . . . cultivated the s.
KOLLWITZ, K, 1
Onan knew that the s. should not be his BIBLE: GENESIS, 49
**seedtime** Fair s. had my soul WORDSWORTH, W, 33
In s. learn, in harvest teach BLAKE, W, 209
s. and harvest BIBLE: GENESIS, 26
**seeing** S. is believing PROVERBS, 358
**seek** I will undoubtedly have to s. . . . gainful employment
ACHESON, D, 3
s., and ye shall find BIBLE: MATTHEW, 26
To toil and not to s. for rest LOYOLA, I, 1
We s. him here, we s. him there ORCZY, BARONESS, 1
We s. . . . In every cranny but the right COWPER, W, 19
why s. ye the living among the dead BIBLE: LUKE, 39
**seem** Things are not always what they s. PROVERBS, 429
**seen** blessed are they that have not s., and yet have believed
BIBLE: JOHN, 57
eye hath not s. BIBLE: I CORINTHIANS, 3
Who has s. the wind ROSSETTI, C, 9
**sees** fool s. not the same tree BLAKE, W, 25
What, when drunk, one s. in other women TYNAN, K, 6
**Seine** Today I spat in the S. PATTON, G, 1
**seize** S. the day HORACE, 32
**seldom** s. attribute common sense ROCHEFOUCAULD, DUC DE LA, 24
**selection** Natural S. DARWIN, C, 4
**self** All censure of a man's s. JOHNSON, S, 122
nothing, . . . is greater . . . than one's s. WHITMAN, W, 7
sickness enlarges the dimensions of a man's s. LAMB, C, 15
to thine own s. be true SHAKESPEARE, W, 48
**self-adjusting** No man . . . who has wrestled with a s. card table
THURBER, J, 7
**self-denial** S. is not a virtue SHAW, G, 27
**self-employed** I'm s. PHILIP, DUKE OF EDINBURGH, 3
**self-indulgence** her favourite form of s. MAUGHAM, W, 5
**self-interest** S. speaks all sorts of tongues
ROCHEFOUCAULD, DUC DE LA, 5
**selfish** all Governments are s. ECCLES, VISCOUNT, 1
a man becomes slack and s. STEVENSON, R, 22
French governments are more s. than most ECCLES, VISCOUNT, 1
I have been a s. being all my life AUSTEN, J, 24
**self-love** S. is the greatest of all flatterers
ROCHEFOUCAULD, DUC DE LA, 7
S. seems so often unrequited POWELL, A, 1
true s. and social are the same POPE, A, 34
**self-made** A s. man . . . believes in luck STEAD, C, 1
a s. man who owed his lack of success to nobody HELLER, J, 1
**self-praise** S. is no recommendation PROVERBS, 360
**Selfridges** by reality I mean shops like S. LAWRENCE, T, 3
**self-sufficiency** S. at home, self-assertion abroad WAUGH, E, 30
**self-sufficient** know how to be s. MONTAIGNE, M, 1
**selling** A best-seller . . . because it was s. well DOORSTIN, D, 2
A living is made . . . by s. something that everybody needs
WILDER, T, 1
**semed** he s. bisier than he was CHAUCER, G, 8
**senators** Do you pray for the s., Dr Hale HALE, E, 1
green-rob'd s. of mighty woods KEATS, J, 16
**senile** a sign that they now consider him s. COLLINGWOOD, R, 1
**seniors** to hear . . . valuable or even earnest advice from my s.
THOREAU, H, 8
**sensations** life of s. rather than of thoughts KEATS, J, 47
**sense** because Americans won't listen to s. KEYNES, BARON, 9
between a man of s. and his books. CHESTERFIELD, 4TH EARL OF, 10
drowsy numbness pains my s. KEATS, J, 30
Let's talk s. to the American people STEVENSON, A, 4
Money is like a sixth s. MAUGHAM, W, 13
seldom attribute common s. ROCHEFOUCAULD, DUC DE LA, 24
Take care of the s. CARROLL, L, 24
The sound must seem an echo to the s. POPE, A, 24
**senses** If Parson lost his s. HODGSON, R, 1
**sensitive** more s. one is to great art BEERBOHM, SIR M, 8
**sensual** The only s. pleasure without vice JOHNSON, S, 36
**sent** If this belief from heaven be s. WORDSWORTH, W, 14
**sentence** structure of the . . . British s. CHURCHILL, SIR W, 9
**sentences** The most attractive s. are not perhaps the wisest
THOREAU, H, 2
**sentimentality** S. is a superstructure covering brutality JUNG, C, 8
S. is only sentiment MAUGHAM, W, 25
s. . . . rubs you up the wrong way MAUGHAM, W, 25
**sentiments** Declaration of S. STANTON, E, 6
high s. always win in the end ORWELL, G, 6

**sentinels** men . . . who stand as s. in the avenues of fame
JOHNSON, S. 24
**separation** prepare for a s. QUINCY, J. 1
they should declare the causes which impel them to . . . s.
JEFFERSON, T. 1
**September** Clear in the cool S. morn WHITTIER, J. 1
Thirty days hath S., /April, June, and November
NURSERY RHYMES, 61
**Septuagint** The S. minus the Apostles VERRALL, A. 1
**sepulchre** a new s., wherein was never man yet laid
BIBLE: JOHN, 52
no man knoweth of his s. BIBLE: DEUTERONOMY, 8
the stone taken away from the s. BIBLE: JOHN, 53
To famous men all the earth is a s. THUCYDIDES, 1
**sepulchres** whited s. BIBLE: MATTHEW, 65
**seraphims** the s.: each one had six wings BIBLE: ISAIAH, 9
**Seraphs** Mammon wins his way where S. might despair
BYRON, 6TH BARON, 5
**Sergeant** S. Pepper's Lonely Hearts Club Band LENNON, J, 9
**serious** a damned s. business WELLINGTON, DUKE OF, 5
A joke's a very s. thing CHURCHILL, C, 3
a noble nature, . . . treats . . . a s. subject ARNOLD, M, 30
Mix a little foolishness with your s. plans HORACE, 44
War is much too s. . . . to be left to military men TALLEYRAND, 6
**seriously** Everything must be taken s., nothing tragically
THIERS, L, 2
**sermons** Ever since his s. were discontinued TYRRELL, G, 1
He that takes pleasure to hear s. SELDEN, J, 7
**serpent** my s. of old Nile SHAKESPEARE, W, 6
sharper than a s.'s tooth DICKENS, C, 38
that old s. BIBLE: REVELATIONS, 9
the s. beguiled me BIBLE: GENESIS, 15
the s. was more subtil BIBLE: GENESIS, 12
**servant** for the last time in my life, Your Humble S.
WALPOLE, 4TH EARL OF ORFORD, 1
speak, Lord; for thy s. heareth BIBLE: I SAMUEL, 1
The cracked looking glass of a s. JOYCE, J, 7
the politician poses as the s. DE GAULLE, C, 10
thou good and faithful s. BIBLE: MATTHEW, 72
**servants** Few men have been admired by their s. MONTAIGNE, M, 8
good s., but bad masters L'ESTRANGE, SIR R, 1
half of them prefer hiring their s. for life CARLYLE, T, 32
part of English middle-class education is devoted to the training of
s . . . WILLIAMS, R, 1
Socialists treat their s. with respect STOPPARD, T, 3
We teachers can only help . . . as s. MONTESSORI, M, 2
**serve** if thou . . . s. the Lord, prepare . . . for temptation
BIBLE: ECCLESIASTICUS, 1
They also s. who only stand and wait MILTON, J, 56
**served** I must have things daintily s. BETJEMAN, SIR J, 3
Youth will be s. BORROW, G, 2
**service** I will see you in the vestry after s. SMITH, S, 8
Small s. is true s. WORDSWORTH, W, 67
**serviettes** kiddies have crumpled the s. BETJEMAN, SIR J, 3
**Sesame** Open S. THE ARABIAN NIGHTS, 2
**sessions** s. of sweet silent thought SHAKESPEARE, W, 257
**set** all, except their sun, is s. BYRON, 6TH BARON, 23
best plain s. BACON, 1ST BARON VERULAM, VISCOUNT ST ALBANS, 11
s. thine house in order BIBLE: II KINGS, 4
**sets** on which the sun never s. NORTH, C, 1
**setting** clouds that gather round the s. sun WORDSWORTH, W, 30
**settled** No question is ever s. /Until WILCOX, E, 2
Thank God, that's s. SHERIDAN, R, 15
**Settlement** coach and six horses through the Act of S.
RICE, SIR S, 1
**seven** his acts being s. ages SHAKESPEARE, W, 23
sealed with s. seals BIBLE: REVELATIONS, 3
S. for the s. stars in the sky ANONYMOUS, 45
S. swans a-swimming NURSERY RHYMES, 60
wisdom . . . hath hewn out her s. pillars BIBLE: PROVERBS, 5
**seventh** God . . . rested on the s. day BIBLE: GENESIS, 7
**seventy** Being over s. is like being engaged in a war SPARK, M. 5
Being s. is not a sin MEIR, G, 5
Oh, to be s. again HOLMES, O, JR., 3
**sever** a tie that only death can s. MAUGHAM, W, 6
**severity** Summer has set in with its usual s. COLERIDGE, S, 44
**sex** As we make s. less secretive, we may rob it of its power
SZASZ, T, 2
Continental people have s. life MIKES, G, 3
farmyard world of s. GRANVILLE-BARKER, H, 2

How can I . . . dislike a s. to which Your Majesty belongs
RHODES, C, 3
if there was a third s. VAIL, A, 1
In the s.-war thoughtlessness is the weapon of the male
CONNOLLY, C, 14
Is s. dirty ALLEN, W, 1
it's s. with someone you love ALLEN, W, 3
Literature is mostly about having s. LODGE, D, 1
meant us to have group s. BRADBURY, M, 7
Money, it turned out, was exactly like s. BALDWIN, J, 2
much more fundamental than s. DENNIS, N, 2
no more weakness than is natural to her s. THUCYDIDES, 2
No s. without responsibility. LONGFORD, EARL OF, 1
Pornography is the attempt to insult s. LAWRENCE, D, 33
professed tyrant to their s. SHAKESPEARE, W, 208
s. has been a very private, secretive activity SZASZ, T, 2
S. is one of the nine reasons for reincarnation MILLER, H, 1
S. is something I really don't understand SALINGER, J, 1
s. . . . must itself be subject . . . to evolution BLACKWELL, A, 1
the condition of our s. is so deplorable that it is our duty . . . to
break the law PANKHURST, E, 4
the difference of s., if there is any ANTHONY, S, 3
the schoolroom . . . does the difference of s. . . . need to be
forgotten ANTHONY, S, 3
the s. novel is now normal SHAW, G, 38
woman feels the invidious distinctions of s. STANTON, E, 2
**sexes** husbands and wives . . . belong to different s. DIX, D, 4
more difference within the s. than between them
COMPTON-BURNETT, DAME I, 2
several other old ladies of both s. DICKENS, C, 20
the . . . rift between the s. is . . . widened by . . . teaching . . . to
the girls STEVENSON, R, 12
**sexton** went and told the s. HOOD, T, 5
**sexual** Industrial relations are like s. relations FEATHER, BARON, 1
Masturbation: the primary s. activity SZASZ, T, 9
music throatily . . . s. HUXLEY, A, 2
**shabby** For tamed and s. tigers HODGSON, R, 1
**shade** a green thought in a green s. MARVELL, A, 2
inviolable s. ARNOLD, M, 36
No s., no shine, no butterflies, no bees HOOD, T, 10
Nothing grows well in the s. BRANCUSI, C, 1
the s. /Of that which once was great WORDSWORTH, W, 56
**shadow** be caves . . . in which his s. will be shown NIETZSCHE, F, 4
hide me under the s. of thy wings PSALMS, 6
lose the substance by grasping at the s. AESOP, 1
My S. ROSE, B, 2
the valley of the s. of death PSALMS, 12
unhappy s. CAMPION, T, 1
Who live under the s. of a war SPENDER, SIR S, 2
Your s. at morning ELIOT, T, 25
**shadows** brooding tragedy and its dark s. can be lightened
GANDHI, I, 4
half sick of s. TENNYSON, BARON, 39
**shak'd** when degree is s. SHAKESPEARE, W, 281
**Shakespeare** after S. and Milton are forgotten PORSON, R, 2
A strange, horrible business, . . . good enough for S.'s day
VICTORIA, 6
Besides S. and me, who do you think there is STEIN, G, 4
he had read S. and found him weak in chemistry WELLS, H, 16
I despise S. SHAW, G, 9
myriad-minded S. COLERIDGE, S, 7
reading S. by flashes of lightning COLERIDGE, S, 43
S. ARNOLD, M, 38
S., I come DREISER, T, 1
S. is . . . really very good GRAVES, R, 5
S. never had six lines together without a fault JOHNSON, S, 72
S. – the nearest thing OLIVIER, BARON, 1
S., undoubtedly wanted taste WALPOLE, 4TH EARL OF ORFORD, 4
sweetest S., Fancy's child MILTON, J, 14
the making up of a S. or a Milton COLERIDGE, S, 45
the right to criticize S. SHAW, G, 39
tried lately to read S. DARWIN, C, 1
We can say of S. ELIOT, T, 2
When I read S. I am struck LAWRENCE, D, 28
who speak the tongue /That S. spake WORDSWORTH, W, 49
Wonderful women! . . . how much we . . . owe to S.
TERRY, DAME E, 1
**shaking** After s. hands with a Greek PROVERBS, 20
all these great interests entrusted to the s. hand VICTORIA, 1
**Shalimar** Pale hands I loved beside the S. HOPE, L, 2
**shambles** Our civilization is founded on the s. JAMES, W, 1

**shame** expense of spirit in a waste of s.    SHAKESPEARE, W, 266
Neither s. nor physical pain have any . . . effect    KEY, E, 4
put to s. suddenly    PSALMS, 2
**shamefaced** Perjury . . . is truth that is s.    DARLING, BARON, 4
**shapely** it's . . . more important for a theory to be s., than . . . true    HAMPTON, C, 1
**shapen** I was s. in wickedness    PSALMS, 35
**share** s. in the good fortunes of the mighty    BRECHT, B, 1
**Sharon** the rose of S.    BIBLE: SONG OF SOLOMON, 2
**sharp** those who have stout hearts and s. swords    BIRKENHEAD, EARL OF, 4
**sharper** the word of God is . . . s. than any two-edged sword    BIBLE: HEBREWS, 2
**shaves** man who s. and takes a train    WHITE, E, 1
**Shaw** Bernard S.    LENIN, V, 10
G. B. S.    WILDE, Θ, 63
Mr S. . . . has never written any poetry    CHESTERTON, G, 29
S.    SHERWOOD, R, 1
**she** s. is my country still    CHURCHILL, C, 2
S.-who-must-be-obeyed    HAGGARD, SIR H, 1
**shears** marriage . . . resembles a pair of s.    SMITH, S, 10
**sheaves** shall . . . bring his s. with him    PSALMS, 79
**Sheba** the queen of S.    BIBLE: 1 KINGS, 3
**shed** s. . . . for the remission of sins    BIBLE: MATTHEW, 78
**shedding** without s. of blood is no remission    BIBLE: HEBREWS, 6
**sheep** as a shepherd divideth his s. from the goats    BIBLE: MATTHEW, 74
A s. in s.'s clothing    GOSSE, SIR E, 2
Baa, baa, black s.    NURSERY RHYMES, 4
feed my s.    BIBLE: JOHN, 59
good shepherd giveth his life for the s.    BIBLE: JOHN, 26
hungry s. look up, and are not fed    MILTON, J, 21
I have found my s. which was lost    BIBLE: LUKE, 27
like lost s.    BOOK OF COMMON PRAYER, 3
make a man by standing a s.    BEERBOHM, SIR M, 15
not armies . . . but flocks of s.    CERVANTES, M, 3
savaged by a dead s.    HEALEY, D, 1
s.'s clothing    BIBLE: MATTHEW, 29
the little hills like young s.    PSALMS, 70
The mountain s. are sweeter, /But the valley s. are fatter    PEACOCK, T, 7
the s. . . . know his voice    BIBLE: JOHN, 24
the s. of his hand    PSALMS, 62
The s.'s in the meadow    NURSERY RHYMES, 29
the wolf in the s.'s clothing    AESOP, 10
useless for the s. to pass resolutions in favour of vegetarianism    INGE, W, 6
**shelf** The dust and silence of the upper s.    MACAULAY, BARON, 12
**Shelley** S. and Keats were . . . up to date in . . . chemical knowledge    HALDANE, J, 2
S. had a hyper-thyroid face    SQUIRE, SIR J, 2
the right sphere for S.'s genius    ARNOLD, M, 23
**shells** With silver bells and cockle s.    NURSERY RHYMES, 34
**shelter** Our s. from the stormy blast    WATTS, I, 6
**Shenandoah** O, S., I long to hear you    ANONYMOUS, 66
**shepherd** Go, for they call you, S., from the hill    ARNOLD, M, 32
he that entereth in by the door is the s.    BIBLE: JOHN, 24
I am the good s.    BIBLE: JOHN, 26
The King of love my S. is    BAKER, SIR H, 1
the Lord is my s.    PSALMS, 12
This is the weather the s. shuns    HARDY, T, 9
**shepherds** Governments needs to have both s. and butchers    VOLTAIRE, 17
s. abiding in the field    BIBLE: LUKE, 8
s. watch'd their flocks    TATE, N, 3
**Sherard Blaw** S., the dramatist who had discovered himself    SAKI, 23
**sherry** With first-rate s. flowing into second-rate whores    PLOMER, W, 2
**shield** his faithfulness and truth shall be thy s. and buckler    PSALMS, 57
the s. of faith    BIBLE: EPHESIANS, 4
**shift** for coming down let me s. for myself    MORE, SIR T, 3
**shilling** you don't happen to have the s. about you now, do you    SHERIDAN, T, 1
**Shiloh** until S. come    BIBLE: GENESIS, 53
**shimmy** Put thy s. on, Lady Chatterley    LAWRENCE, D, 16
**shine** s. on, s. on, harvest moon    NORWORTH, J, 1
**shining** A woman of so s. loveliness    YEATS, W, 27
**shins** long dresses, . . . cover a multitude of s.    WEST, M, 8
**ship** A whale s. was my Yale College    MELVILLE, H, 2

being in a s. is being in a jail    JOHNSON, S, 53
Don't give up the s.    LAWRENCE, J, 1
S. me somewhere east of Suez    KIPLING, R, 23
The s. follows Soviet custom    THEROUX, P, 3
**ships** Heart of oak are our s.    GARRICK, D, 2
I spied three s. come sailing by    ANONYMOUS, 8
something wrong with our bloody s.    BEATTY, 1ST EARL, 1
stately s. go on    TENNYSON, BARON, 1
S. that pass in the night    LONGFELLOW, H, 13
the face that launch'd a thousand s.    MARLOWE, C, 2
the little s. of England brought the Army home    GUEDALLA, P, 2
they that go down to the sea in s.    PSALMS, 66
We've got the s., we've got the men, we've got the money too    HUNT, G, 1
**shipwreck** husbands and wives make s. of their lives    DIX, D, 3
**shirt** no s. or collar ever comes back twice    LEACOCK, S, 13
**shit** the sun shining ten days a year and s. in the streets    KENEALLY, T, 1
when you s.? Singing, it's the same thing    CARUSO, E, 1
**shock** Anybody can s. a baby    STERN, R, 1
**shocked** how to be amused rather than s.    BUCK, P, 3
**shock-headed** S. Peter    HOFFMAN, H, 4
**shocking** 'little man wears a s. bad hat    YORK AND ALBANY, DUKE OF, 1
**shocks** s. /That flesh is heir to    SHAKESPEARE, W, 61
**shoemaker** I take my shoes from the s.    GOLDSMITH, O, 30
The s.'s son    PROVERBS, 424
**shoes** before you let the sun in, mind it wipes its s.    THOMAS, D, 12
I take my s. from the shoemaker    GOLDSMITH, O, 30
s. and ships and sealing wax    CARROLL, L, 25
**shoot** do not s. the pianist    WILDE, O, 34
except to s. rabbits and hit his father on the jaw    MASEFIELD, J, 1
It is not the business of generals to s. one another    WELLINGTON, DUKE OF, 14
S., if you must, this old gray head    WHITTIER, J, 2
the ungodly . . . privily s. at them which are true of heart    PSALMS, 4
they could s. me in my absence    BEHAN, B, 2
**shooting** war minus the s.    ORWELL, G, 30
**shop** A man must keep a little back s.    MONTAIGNE, M, 2
**shopkeepers** A nation of s.    ADAMS, S, 1
England is a nation of s.    NAPOLEON I, 8
**shopping** Today you're unhappy? . . . Go s.    MILLER, A, 3
**shore** adieu! my native s.    BYRON, 6TH BARON, 6
waves make towards the pebbled s.    SHAKESPEARE, W, 259
**Shoreditch** When I grow rich, /Say the bells of S.    NURSERY RHYMES, 41
**shores** eternal whisperings around Desolate s.    KEATS, J, 38
**short** Good things, when s., are twice as good    GRACIAN, B, 1
Is not life . . . too s. . . . to bore ourselves    NIETZSCHE, F, 12
it will take a long while to make it s.    THOREAU, H, 18
Life is too s. to do anything for oneself    MAUGHAM, W, 19
Life is too s. to do anything . . . one can pay others to do    MAUGHAM, W, 19
Life's s. span forbids us . . . far-reaching hopes    HORACE, 28
make the beat keep time with s. steps    ANDERSEN, H, 2
s. and simple annals of the poor.    GRAY, T, 2
the life of man, solitary, poor, nasty, brutish, and s.    HOBBES, T, 4
We have s. time to stay, as you    HERRICK, R, 4
**shortage** a s. of coal and fish . . . at the same time    BEVAN, A, 7
**shorter** not had the time to make it s.    PASCAL, B, 1
s. by a head    ELIZABETH I, 5
**shortest** I never realized that I'd end up being the s. knight of the year    RICHARDS, SIR G, 1
the s. works are always the best    LA FONTAINE, J, 11
**shot** had them all s.    NARVAEZ, R, 1
he once s. a bookseller.    CAMPBELL, T, 7
**shots** God is on the side not of the heavy battalions, but of the best s.    VOLTAIRE, 18
They really are bad s.    DE GAULLE, C, 4
**should** nae better than he s. be    BURNS, R, 6
no better than you s. be    BEAUMONT, F, 1
**shoulder-blade** I have a left s.    GILBERT, SIR W, 31
**shoulders** it is by standing on the s. of giants    NEWTON, SIR I, 4
**shout** S. with the largest    DICKENS, C, 41
**show** I have that within which passes s.    SHAKESPEARE, W, 41
I often wish they would s. off a little more    MACCARTHY, SIR D, 1
**showers** Sweet April s.    TUSSER, T, 2
**shows** All my s. are great    GRADE, BARON, 1
**shreds** A thing of s. and patches    GILBERT, SIR W, 23

Shrewsbury They hang us now in S. jail: /The whistles blow
forlorn — HOUSMAN, A. 6
shriek That s. and sweat in pigmy wars — TENNYSON, BARON, 44
shrine Melancholy has her . . . s. — KEATS, J. 29
shrink all the boards did s. — COLERIDGE, S. 28
shuffled s. off this mortal coil — SHAKESPEARE, W. 61
the human pack is s. and cut — LODGE, D. 3
Shulamite return, return, O S. — BIBLE: SONG OF SOLOMON, 1
shut when I was there it seemed to be s. — FREUD, C. 2
shy Why so s., my pretty Thomasina — FRY, C. 1
sick A person seldom falls s. — EMERSON, R. 1
Dante makes me s. — VEGA CARPIO, L. 1
I am s. at heart — SHAKESPEARE, W. 39
Let me remind you what the wary fox said . . . to the s. lion
— HORACE, 16
make any man s. to hear her — PEPYS, S. 5
The prayer that . . . heals the s. — EDDY, M. 1
We have on our hands a s. man — NICHOLAS I, 1
sickness convicted of s., hunger, wretchedness, and want
— SMOLLETT, T. 3
in s. and in health — BOOK OF COMMON PRAYER, 15
Love is a s. — DANIEL, S. 1
s. enlarges the dimensions of a man's self — LAMB, C. 15
S., sin and death . . . do not originate in God — EDDY, M. 4
the s. that destroyeth in the noon-day — PSALMS, 57
Sidcup If only I could get down to S. — PINTER, H. 1
side A door is what a dog is . . . on the wrong s. of — NASH, O. 2
a s. dish he hadn't ordered — LARDNER, R. 1
He who knows only his own s. . . . knows little — MILL, J. 2
passed by on the other s. — BIBLE: LUKE, 21
Time is on our s. — GLADSTONE, W. 1
sides Do not . . . write on both s. of the paper — SELLAR, W. 8
said on both s. — ADDISON, J. 11
We . . . assume that everything has two s. — ROBINSON, J. 1
sieve They went to sea in a s. — LEAR, E. 4
sighed They s. for the dawn and thee — TENNYSON, BARON, 53
sighs over the Bridge of S. into eternity — KIERKEGAARD, S. 2
S. are the natural language of the heart — SHADWELL, T. 1
sight a s. to make an old man young — TENNYSON, BARON, 10
Out of s. — PROVERBS, 333
we walk by faith, not by s. — BIBLE: II CORINTHIANS, 1
sightless clapped the glass to his s. eye — NEWBOLT, SIR H. 1
sights And see all s. from pole to pole — ARNOLD, M. 41
few more impressive s. in the world — BARRIE, SIR J. 11
sign Jews require a s. — BIBLE: I CORINTHIANS, 1
Never s. a wallentine — DICKENS, C. 48
s. documents which they do not read — HURST, SIR G. 1
s. of an ill-spent youth — SPENCER, H. 2
writing a letter and forgetting to s. his name — BEECHER, H. 1
significant s. form — BELL, C. 1
signifying S. nothing — SHAKESPEARE, W. 177
signing I am s. my death warrant — COLLINS, M. 1
silence Come to me in the s. of the night — ROSSETTI, C. 1
foster-child of s. and slow time — KEATS, J. 22
In England there is only s. or scandal — MAUROIS, A. 1
let all the earth keep s. before him — BIBLE: HABAKKUK, 1
Make him a bishop, and you will s. him
— CHESTERFIELD, 4TH EARL OF, 17
occasional flashes of s. — SMITH, S. 11
S. is as full of potential wisdom — HUXLEY, A. 26
S. is become his mother tongue — GOLDSMITH, O. 16
S. is golden — PROVERBS, 362
S. is the best tactic — ROCHEFOUCAULD, DUC DE LA, 11
S. is the perfectest herald of joy — SHAKESPEARE, W. 210
S. is the . . . perfect expression of scorn — SHAW, G. 4
Sorrow and s. are strong — LONGFELLOW, H. 4
s. sank /Like music — COLERIDGE, S. 35
That man's s. is wonderful to listen to — HARDY, T. 7
The cruellest lies are . . . told in s. — STEVENSON, R. 13
The dust and s. of the upper shelf — MACAULAY, BARON, 12
the impression that their normal condition is s. — SARTRE, J. 10
the more absolute s. of America — LAWRENCE, D. 22
the rest is s. — SHAKESPEARE, W. 76
With s. and tears — BYRON, 6TH BARON, 41
silent burst /Into that s. sea — COLERIDGE, S. 27
the great s. majority — NIXON, R. 5
the man who can be s. in several languages — HARBORD, J. 1
thereon one must remain s. — WITTGENSTEIN, L. 6
silicon If s. had been a gas I should have been a major-general
— WHISTLER, J. 4
silk rustling in unpaid-for s. — SHAKESPEARE, W. 36

s., too often hides eczema — CAMUS, A. 2
the s. stockings and white bosoms of your actresses
— JOHNSON, S. 43
silks Whenas in s. my Julia goes — HERRICK, R. 7
silly A s. remark can be made in Latin — CERVANTES, M. 1
it's lovely to be s. at the right moment — HORACE, 44
some damned s. thing in the Balkans — BISMARCK, PRINCE VON, 8
You s. twisted boy — MILLIGAN, S. 7
silver for a handful of s. — BROWNING, R. 29
s. and gold have I none — BIBLE: ACTS, 4
S. buckles on his knee — NURSERY RHYMES, 5
Selling the family s.. — MACMILLAN, EARL OF STOCKTON, 6
S. threads among the gold — REXFORD, E. 1
The s. apples of the moon — YEATS, W. 28
thirty pieces of s. — BIBLE: MATTHEW, 84
When every . . . thing you hold /Is made of s., or of gold
— GILBERT, SIR W. 5
silvery the s. adamant walls of life's exclusive city — LAWRENCE, D. 8
Silvia Who is S.? What is she — SHAKESPEARE, W. 299
Simon Simple S. met a pieman — NURSERY RHYMES, 51
simple A s. race — SCOTT, SIR W. 4
short and s. annals of the poor. — GRAY, T. 2
Teach us delight in s. things — KIPLING, R. 3
simpleton The revolutionary s. — LEWIS, W. 6
simplicity O holy s.! — HUSS, J. 1
s. a child — POPE, A. 16
simplify S., s. — THOREAU, H. 14
simplifying s. something by destroying nearly everything
— CHESTERTON, G. 2
sin A branch of the s. of drunkenness, — JAMES I, 2
All s. tends to be addictive — AUDEN, W. 3
a more dreadful record of s. than . . . countryside — DOYLE, SIR A. 6
A private s. is not so prejudicial — CERVANTES, M. 19
beauty is only s. deep — SAKI, 21
Being seventy is not a s. — MEIR, G. 5
go, and s. no more — BIBLE: JOHN, 20
he that is without s. . . . let him first cast a stone — BIBLE: JOHN, 19
if we say that we have no s., we deceive — BIBLE: I JOHN, 1
it is no s. to s. in secret — MOLIERE, 10
it's a s. to kill a mockingbird — LEE, H. 2
my s. is ever before me — PSALMS, 34
nicest boy who ever committed the s. of whisky — SPARK, M. 4
no s. but to be rich — SHAKESPEARE, W. 125
no s. except stupidity. — WILDE, O. 11
S. brought death — EDDY, M. 3
Sickness, sin and death . . . do not originate in God — EDDY, M. 4
s. no more, lest a worse thing come unto thee — BIBLE: JOHN, 13
than that one soul . . . should commit one single venial s.
— NEWMAN, CARDINAL, 4
The physicists have known s. — OPPENHEIMER, J. 2
They are written as if s. were to be taken out . . . by . . . sleep
— SMITH, S. 3
which taketh away the s. of the world — BIBLE: JOHN, 3
your s. will find you out — BIBLE: NUMBERS, 6
Sinai S. was . . . on a smoke — BIBLE: EXODUS, 19
sincerest Imitation . . . s. of flattery — COLTON, C. 3
sincerity A little s. is a dangerous thing — WILDE, O. 9
style, not s., is the vital thing — WILDE, O. 28
sinecure a widow . . . is a kind of s. — WYCHERLEY, W. 2
sinews Anger is one of the s. of the soul — FULLER, T. 5
sing Did certain persons die before they s. — COLERIDGE, S. 10
I will s. of the sun — POUND, E. 7
O come, let us s. unto the Lord — PSALMS, 60
s. unto the Lord a new song — PSALMS, 23
s. us one of the songs of Sion — PSALMS, 83
The Welsh . . . just s. — WAUGH, E. 12
we s. no more — BRAHMS, J. 2
singed s. the Spanish king's beard — DRAKE, SIR F. 1
singing nightingales are s. near — ELIOT, T. 20
s. in the rain — FREED, A. 1
To hear the lark . . . s. . . . /From his watch-tower in the skies
— MILTON, J. 12
when you shit? S., it's the same thing — CARUSO, E. 1
single a s. man in possession of a good fortune must be in want
of a wife — AUSTEN, J. 15
Behold her, s. in the field — WORDSWORTH, W. 45
sink The s. is the great symbol of the bloodiness of family life
— MITCHELL, J. 1
sinn'd More s. against than sinning — SHAKESPEARE, W. 139
sinned father, I have s. against heaven — BIBLE: LUKE, 28
sinner one s. that repenteth — BIBLE: LUKE, 27

**sinners** At such an hour the s. are still in bed     RUNYON, D, 6
Christ Jesus came into the world to save s.     BIBLE: I TIMOTHY, 1
It's your combination s. . . . who dishonour the vices
    WILDER, T, 3
the way of s.     PSALMS, 1
**sinning** nothing so artificial as s. nowadays     LAWRENCE, D, 24
**sins** atone for the s. of your fathers.     HORACE, 36
from Expensive S. refrain     DRYDEN, J, 8
gravest s. it was possible for a gentlewoman to commit
    WAUGH, E, 43
her s., which are many, are forgiven     BIBLE: LUKE, 17
hide a multitude of s.     BIBLE: JAMES, 9
His s. were scarlet     BELLOC, H, 8
One of the unpardonable s., . . . , is . . . to go about unlabelled
    HUXLEY, T, 4
shed . . . for the remission of s.     BIBLE: MATTHEW, 78
she must not reheat his s. for breakfast     DIETRICH, M, 1
though your s. be as scarlet     BIBLE: ISAIAH, 1
to read a novel before luncheon was one of the gravest s.
    WAUGH, E, 43
**Sion** sing us one of the songs of S.     PSALMS, 83
the Lord loveth the gates of S.     PSALMS, 53
thou, O God, art praised in S.     PSALMS, 42
**Sir** I am S. Oracle     SHAKESPEARE, W, 187
**Sirens** Blest pair of S.     MILTON, J, 4
**Sisera** the stars . . . fought against S.     BIBLE: JUDGES, 2
**sister** I kissed her little s.     MONTROSE, P, 2
no friend like a s.     ROSSETTI, C, 2
**sisters** all the S. virtuous     NEWCASTLE, DUCHESS OF, 1
And so do his s.     GILBERT, SIR W, 9
little s. to all the world     DIX, D, 1
O! men with s. dear     HOOD, T, 11
**sit** I will s. down now     DISRAELI, 1ST EARL OF BEACONSFIELD, 17
men s. and hear each other groan     KEATS, J, 33
nobody can tell you when to s. down     EISENHOWER, D, 2
say what you have to say, and then s. down
    WELLINGTON, DUKE OF, 22
So I did s. and eat     HERBERT, G, 7
s. thou on my right hand     PSALMS, 68
**sitting** Are you s. comfortably? Then I'll begin     LANG, J, 1
by s. down round you     WELLINGTON, DUKE OF, 12
I do most of my work s. down     BENCHLEY, R, 6
**situation** s. excellent. I shall attack     FOCH, MARSHAL, 1
**six** Candidates should not attempt more than s.     BELLOC, H, 16
S. for the s. proud walkers     ANONYMOUS, 45
S. geese a-laying     NURSERY RHYMES, 60
s. of one and half-a-dozen of the other     MARRYAT, F, 2
two and two do not make s.     TOLSTOY, COUNT, 12
**sixpence** He found a crooked s. against a crooked stile
    NURSERY RHYMES, 57
I love s., jolly little s.     NURSERY RHYMES, 22
Sing a song of s.     NURSERY RHYMES, 52
**sixpences** there go two-and-forty s. . . . to one guinea
    JOHNSON, S, 31
**sixth** Money is like a s. sense     MAUGHAM, W, 13
**sixty** at the rate of s. minutes an hour     LEWIS, C, 5
close-up of a woman past s.     ASTOR, VISCOUNTESS, 2
Men come of age at s.     STEPHENS, J, 3
s. horses wedged in a chimney     MORTON, J, 2
**sixty-five** . . . I have been drinking it for s. years and I am not
dead yet     VOLTAIRE, 30
**size** I am not this s., really     CHESTERTON, G, 42
**skating** s. over thin ice     EMERSON, R, 11
**skeleton** Every family has a s. in the cupboard     PROVERBS, 135
**ski** unbecoming for a cardinal to s. badly     JOHN PAUL II, 1
**skies** looks commercing with the s.     MILTON, J, 7
look up at the s.!     HOPKINS, G, 5
**skill** In arguing too, the parson own'd his s.     GOLDSMITH, O, 5
S. without imagination is craftsmanship     STOPPARD, T, 1
**skin** I've Got You Under My S.     PORTER, C, 2
never . . . sell the bear's s.     LA FONTAINE, J, 7
There is more than one way to s. a cat     PROVERBS, 409
**skinning** When you are s. your customers     KHRUSHCHEV, N, 2
**skins** beauty of their s.     TENNYSON, BARON, 61
**skipped** the mountains s. like rams     PSALMS, 70
**skipper** s. had taken his little daughter     LONGFELLOW, H, 16
**skirt** a woman . . . ought to lay aside . . . modesty with her s.
    MONTAIGNE, M, 4
**skittles** Life isn't all beer and s.     HUGHES, T, 1
**sky** a Friend for little children /Above the bright blue s.
    MIDLANE, A, 1

inverted Bowl we call The S.     FITZGERALD, E, 15
Which prisoners call the s.     WILDE, O, 1
**Skye** Over the sea to S.     BOULTON, SIR H, 1
**slack** a man becomes s. and selfish     STEVENSON, R, 22
**slain** a lamb as it had been s.     BIBLE: REVELATIONS, 4
Saul hath s. his thousands     BIBLE: I SAMUEL, 6
**slamming** little girls . . . s. doors     BELLOC, H, 5
**slander** it is always said of s. that something always sticks
    BACON, 1ST BARON VERULAM, VISCOUNT ST ALBANS, 4
**slang** All s. is metaphor     CHESTERTON, G, 8
The one . . . poetry . . . continually flowing is s.     CHESTERTON, G, 7
**slapped** We had shown that anyone who s. us . . . would get his
head kicked off     KHRUSHCHEV, N, 1
**slaughter** as a lamb to the s.     BIBLE: ISAIAH, 33
**slave** Be not the s. of Words     CARLYLE, T, 22
man . . . is Reason's s.     CONNOLLY, C, 18
s. for livelihood     ADAMS, F, 2
**slavery** Freedom is S.     ORWELL, G, 16
The prolonged s. of women     STANTON, E, 4
**slaves** In a consumer society there are . . . two kinds of s.
    ILLICH, I, 4
love, an . . . intercourse between tyrants and s.     GOLDSMITH, O, 12
Practical men, . . . are usually the s. of some defunct economist
    KEYNES, BARON, 7
S. cannot breathe in England     COWPER, W, 27
that the masters willingly concede to s.     CAMUS, A, 9
**slay** to s. the righteous with the wicked     BIBLE: GENESIS, 36
**slaying** the s. of a beautiful hypothesis by an ugly fact.
    HUXLEY, T, 1
**slays** moves, and mates, and s.     FITZGERALD, E, 13
**sleave** ravell'd s. of care     SHAKESPEARE, W, 167
**sleep** A professor is one who talks in someone else's s.
    AUDEN, W, 27
Better s. with a sober cannibal than a drunken Christian
    MELVILLE, H, 1
haven't been to s. for over a year     WAUGH, E, 16
he that keepeth thee will not s.     PSALMS, 76
How do people go to s.     PARKER, D, 4
Let me s. the s. of the earth     VIGNY, A, 2
Now I lay me down to s.     ANONYMOUS, 64
Our birth is but a s.     WORDSWORTH, W, 23
our little life /Is rounded with a s.     SHAKESPEARE, W, 277
s. a perpetual s.     BIBLE: JEREMIAH, 5
s. begins for weary /mortals . . . creeps over them /most
welcomely     VIRGIL, 7
S. is good, death is better     HEINE, H, 4
s.! it is a gentle thing     COLERIDGE, S, 32
S. . . . knows not Death     TENNYSON, BARON, 28
S. that knits up the ravell'd sleave     SHAKESPEARE, W, 167
The past was a s.     BROWNING, R, 54
they are even as a s.     PSALMS, 55
They are written as if sin were to be taken out . . . by . . . s.
    SMITH, S, 3
To s., perchance to dream     SHAKESPEARE, W, 61
we must s.     SHAKESPEARE, W, 13
youth would s. out the rest     SHAKESPEARE, W, 301
**sleepin'** Capten, art tha s. there below     NEWBOLT, SIR H, 3
**sleeping** fuss about s. together . . . sooner go to my dentist
    WAUGH, E, 42
Let s. dogs lie     PROVERBS, 255
S. as quiet as death     THOMAS, D, 14
There will be s. enough     PROVERBS, 422
we have only awakened a s. giant     YAMAMOTO, I, 1
**sleeps** eats, s. and watches the television     GREER, G, 2
**sleepwalker** that Providence dictates with the assurance of a s.
    HITLER, A, 7
**sleepy** Come, let's to bed /Says S.-head     NURSERY RHYMES, 7
**sleeve** let the last man . . . brush the Channel with his s..
    SCHLIEFFEN, GRAF VON, 1
**slept** David s. with his fathers     BIBLE: I KINGS, 1
**slick** I have three phobias which . . . would make my life as s. as a
sonnet     BANKHEAD, T, 1
**slimy** thousand thousand s. things     COLERIDGE, S, 30
**sling** his s. was in his hand     BIBLE: I SAMUEL, 5
**slings** s. and arrows of outrageous fortune     SHAKESPEARE, W, 61
**slip** he gave us all the s.     BROWNING, R, 56
There's many a s.     PROVERBS, 415
**slippers** Same old s.     LAMPTON, W, 1
**slipping** Time is s. underneath     FITZGERALD, E, 12
**slogans** If you feed people just with revolutionary s.
    KHRUSHCHEV, N, 8

**Slough** Come, friendly bombs, and fall on S.     BETJEMAN, SIR J, 6
**slough** the s. was Despond     BUNYAN, J, 2
**slow** I am s. of study     SHAKESPEARE, W, 203
On a s. boat to China     LOESSER, F, 1
S. and steady wins the race     LLOYD, R, 1
S. but sure     PROVERBS, 363
s. of speech     BIBLE: EXODUS, 8
Tarry a while, says S.     NURSERY RHYMES, 7
too swift arrives as tardy as too s.     SHAKESPEARE, W, 249
with a s. deliberate carelessness     LAWRENCE, T, 4
**slug-horn** the s. to my lips I set     BROWNING, R, 15
**slum** if you've seen one city s.     AGNEW, S, 1
**slumber** A s. did my spirit seal     WORDSWORTH, W, 44
Oft in the stilly night, /Ere S.'s chain     MOORE, T, 7
**slumbers** Golden s. kiss your eyes     DEKKER, T, 1
**slush** pure as the driven s.     BANKHEAD, T, 7
**smack** much more indecent... than a good s.     LAWRENCE, D, 5
**small** Errors look so very ugly in persons of s. means     ELIOT, G, 5
From s. beginnings     PROVERBS, 168
In Western Europe there are now only s. countries     LEFEVRE, T, 1
It's a s. world     PROVERBS, 232
Microbe is so very s.     BELLOC, H, 11
Popularity?... glory's s. change     HUGO, V, 4
S. is beautiful     PROVERBS, 364
The best things come in s. parcels     PROVERBS, 379
virtue's still far too s.     COLETTE, S, 3
**smaller** accepts a s. as a favour     CARLYLE, J, 1
someone s. than oneself     LA FONTAINE, J, 3
these have s. fleas to bite 'em     SWIFT, J, 7
**small-talking** Where in this s. world     FRY, C, 4
**smartness** is that of an attorney's clerk     DISRAELI, 1ST EARL OF BEACONSFIELD, 30
**smarts** No creature s.... as a fool     POPE, A, 15
**smattering** A s. of everything     DICKENS, C, 52
**smell** noses... and s. not     PSALMS, 71
rose... would s. as sweet     SHAKESPEARE, W, 245
Sweet S. of Success     LEHMAN, E, 1
**smells** the only dead thing that s. sweet     THOMAS, E, 2
**smile** a s. I could feel in my hip pocket     CHANDLER, R, 2
Oh, good gigantic s.     BROWNING, R, 27
s. at perils past     SCOTT, SIR W, 1
S. at us, pay us, pass us     CHESTERTON, G, 33
s., s., s.     ASAF, G, 1
the vain tribute of a s.     SCOTT, SIR W, 4
**smiled** the soldiers he s. at     SASSOON, S, 4
**smiles** She is Venus when she s.     JONSON, B, 11
s., /Wan as primroses     KEATS, J, 3
The s., the tears, /Of boyhood's years     MOORE, T, 7
**smite** whosoever shall s. thee on thy right cheek     BIBLE: MATTHEW, 15
**Smith** Chuck it, S.!     CHESTERTON, G, 3
**smith** The s., a mighty man is he     LONGFELLOW, H, 14
**smoke** no woman should marry... a man who does not s.     STEVENSON, R, 20
resembling the horrible Stygian s. of the pit     JAMES I, 1
Sinai was... on a s.     BIBLE: EXODUS, 19
S., my friend     SATIE, E, 1
There's no s. without fire     PROVERBS, 418
**smoking** resolve to give up s., drinking and loving     FREUD, C, 1
s. at such a rate     LAMB, C, 20
s. cigars and... drinking of alcohol before, after, and... during all meals     CHURCHILL, SIR W, 17
What a blessing this s. is     HELPS, SIR A, 2
**smooth** course of true love never did run s.     SHAKESPEARE, W, 201
many cities had rubbed him s.     GREENE, G, 4
**smote** he s. them hip and thigh     BIBLE: JUDGES, 7
they s. the city with the edge of the sword     BIBLE: JUDGES, 1
**smyler** The s. with the knyf     CHAUCER, G, 11
**snail** said a whiting to a s.     CARROLL, L, 13
s.'s on the thorn     BROWNING, R, 43
**snails** Frogs and s. /And puppy-dogs' tails     NURSERY RHYMES, 70
**snake** A s. came to my water-trough     LAWRENCE, D, 26
There's a s. hidden in the grass     VIRGIL, 14
**snapper-up** s. of unconsidered trifles     SHAKESPEARE, W, 303
**snare** a s. in which the feet of women have always become readily entangled     ADDAMS, J, 1
the s. of the hunter     PSALMS, 57
**snares** the s. of death compassed me round     PSALMS, 52
**Snark** For the S. was a Boojum     CARROLL, L, 19
**sneezed** Not to be s. at     COLMAN, THE YOUNGER, 3
when a British Prime Minister s.     LEVIN, B, 2

**snipe** well-shot woodcock, partridge, s.     BETJEMAN, SIR J, 1
**snob** He who meanly admires... is a S.     THACKERAY, W, 1
impossible, in our condition of society, not to be sometimes a S.     THACKERAY, W, 2
**snobbish** Don't be s., we seek to abolish     LOGUE, C, 1
**snobs** His hatred of s.     PROUST, M, 11
**snore** snorer can't hear himself s.     TWAIN, M, 14
**snotgreen** The s. sea     JOYCE, J, 6
**snow** both its national products, s. and chocolate, melt     COREN, A, 5
Like an army defeated /The s. hath retreated     WORDSWORTH, W, 72
S. had fallen, s. on s.     ROSSETTI, C, 3
the s. blind twilight ferries     THOMAS, D, 22
wish a s. in May     SHAKESPEARE, W, 153
**snows** the s. of yesteryear     VILLON, F, 1
**Snow White** I used to be S.     WEST, M, 11
**snub** Vile s.-nose, flat-nosed ass     ROSTAND, E, 1
**snuff** time for me to enjoy another pinch of s.     BAILLY, J, 1
**snug** s. /As a bug /In a rug     FRANKLIN, B, 12
**so** It is s.. It is not s.     FRANKLIN, B, 8
**soap** S. and education... are more deadly     TWAIN, M, 3
**soar** to run, though not to s.     MACAULAY, BARON, 2
**sober** a s. colouring from an eye     WORDSWORTH, W, 30
as s. as a Judge     FIELDING, H, 5
Better sleep with a s. cannibal than a drunken Christian     MELVILLE, H, 1
England should be compulsorily s.     MAGEE, W, 1
he that will go to bed s.     FLETCHER, J, 2
How do you look when I'm s.     LARDNER, R, 2
My mother, drunk or s.     CHESTERTON, G, 5
one sees in Garbo s.     TYNAN, K, 6
sedate, s., silent, serious, sad-coloured sect.     HOOD, T, 1
Tomorrow we'll be s.     ANONYMOUS, 12
**sociable** I am a s. worker     BEHAN, B, 5
Society is no comfort to one not s.     SHAKESPEARE, W, 37
**social** Man is a s. animal     SPINOZA, B, 1
our s. spheres have been widely different     WILDE, O, 26
the things which government does... s. progress     WARREN, E, 1
the... world was stumbling... in s. blindness     KELLER, H, 3
true self-love and s. are the same     POPE, A, 34
**socialism** religion of S.     BEVAN, A, 2
restating our s. in terms of the scientific revolution     WILSON OF RIEVAULX, BARON, 8
s.... alien to the British character     THATCHER, M, 12
S. can only arrive by bicycle     VIERA GALLO, J, 1
the proletariat will... wage a class struggle for S.     LENIN, V, 6
the worst advertisement for S. is its adherents     ORWELL, G, 24
to banish... the dark divisive clouds of Marxist s.     THATCHER, M, 15
To the ordinary working man, ... S.     ORWELL, G, 25
Under s. all will govern     LENIN, V, 5
**socialists** S. treat their servants with respect     STOPPARD, T, 3
We are all S. now     HARCOURT, SIR W, 1
**societies** range of human s. in time, the other in space     LEVI-STRAUSS, C, 1
**society** a poor s. cannot be too poor     TAWNEY, R, 1
A s.... of individuals... capable of original thought would probably be unendurable     MENCKEN, H, 11
Comedy, we may say, is s.     PRIESTLEY, J, 1
if it be our clothes alone which fit us for s.     ESCHENBACH, M, 4
impossible, in our condition of s., not to be sometimes a Snob.     THACKERAY, W, 2
In a consumer s. there are... two kinds of slaves     ILLICH, I, 4
it proved that I was in a civilized s.     PARK, M, 1
Man was formed for s.     BLACKSTONE, SIR W, 1
Never speak disrespectfully of S.     WILDE, O, 30
no intellectual s. can flourish where a Jew feels... uneasy     JOHNSON, P, 1
no new baby in the womb of our s.     LAWRENCE, D, 35
only possible s. is oneself     WILDE, O, 15
S., friendship, and love     COWPER, W, 31
S. goes on and on and on     MACDONALD, R, 2
S. is no comfort /To one not sociable     SHAKESPEARE, W, 37
S. is now one polish'd horde     BYRON, 6TH BARON, 31
so famous, that it would permit me... to break wind in s.     BALZAC, H, 5
s.... pays a harlot 25 times as much as it pays its Prime Minister     WILSON OF RIEVAULX, BARON, 7
s., where none intrudes     BYRON, 6TH BARON, 13
The history of all... s. is the history of class struggles     MARX, K, 1

transform this s. without a major extension of public ownership KINNOCK, N, 1
**sociology** Children . . . have no use for psychology. They detest s. SINGER, I, 1
**socks** His s. compelled one's attention SAKI, 11
**sodium** Of having discovered S. BENTLEY, E, 4
**Sodom** S. and . . . Gomorrah BIBLE: GENESIS, 37
the men of S. were wicked BIBLE: GENESIS, 33
**sodomy** Comedy, like s., is an unnatural act FELDMAN, M, 1
rum, s., and the lash CHURCHILL, SIR W, 27
**sofa** rather lie on a s. than sweep beneath it CONRAN, S, 2
**soft** I'm not hard – I'm frightfully s. THATCHER, M, 1
our love . . . of the mind does not make us s. PERICLES, 1
**solar** the whole s. and stellar systems CARLYLE, T, 28
**soldier** a chocolate cream s. SHAW, G, 3
A S. of the Great War KIPLING, R, 31
Ben Battle was a s. bold HOOD, T, 2
I never expect a s. to think SHAW, G, 8
in the s. is flat blasphemy SHAKESPEARE, W, 181
The summer s. and the sunshine patriot PAINE, T, 5
Tinker, /Tailor, /S., /Sailor NURSERY RHYMES, 65
**soldiers** English s. fight like lions HOFFMANN, M, 1
Old s. never die PROVERBS, 323
S. are citizens of death's grey land SASSOON, S, 3
saucy, soft, short shirts for s., sister Susie sews WESTON, R, 2
**soliciting** supernatural s. SHAKESPEARE, W, 159
**solitary** Man is not a s. animal RUSSELL, EARL, 7
**solitude** In s. alone can he know true freedom MONTAIGNE, M, 2
In s. /What happiness MILTON, J, 44
so companionable as s. THOREAU, H, 12
s.! where are the charms COWPER, W, 32
the bliss of s.. WORDSWORTH, W, 6
Whosoever is delighted in s. BACON, 1ST BARON VERULAM, VISCOUNT ST ALBANS, 24
**Solomon** S. Grundy, /Born on a Monday NURSERY RHYMES, 53
S. loved many strange women BIBLE: 1 KINGS, 4
the song of songs, which is S.'s BIBLE: SONG OF SOLOMON, 1
**solution** A difficulty for every s. SAMUEL, VISCOUNT, 6
total s. of the Jewish question GOERING, H, 2
**some** I . . . may be s. time OATES, L, 1
s. more than others COWARD, SIR N, 2
You can fool s. of the people all the time LINCOLN, A, 13
**somebody** s. may be looking MENCKEN, H, 2
**someone** I wouldn't be . . . talking to s. like you CARTLAND, B, 1
like sleeping with s. else's wife BRADBURY, M, 5
**somer** In a s. season LANGLAND, W, 1
**Somerset** corroboration . . . in the records of S. House BIRKENHEAD, EARL OF, 1
**something** Everybody was up to s. COWARD, SIR N, 7
S. must be done EDWARD VIII, 3
S. nasty in the woodshed GIBBONS, S, 1
Time for a little s. MILNE, A, 7
**sometime** Why don't you come up s. and see me WEST, M, 6
**somewhat** More than s. RUNYON, D, 3
**somewhere** 'Tis always morning s. HORNE, R, 1
**Son** the form of the fourth is like the S. of God BIBLE: DANIEL, 5
the S. of man coming . . . with power BIBLE: MATTHEW, 68
the S. of man hath not where to lay his head BIBLE: MATTHEW, 33
**son** and Sarah shall have a s. BIBLE: GENESIS, 35
An only s., sir, might expect more indulgence GOLDSMITH, O, 14
I've examined your s.'s head, Mr Glum MUIR, F, 1
O Absalom, my s. BIBLE: II SAMUEL, 6
the s. of peace BIBLE: LUKE, 19
woman, behold thy s. BIBLE: JOHN, 49
**sonatas** The s. of Mozart are unique SCHNABEL, A, 3
**song** I have a s. to sing O GILBERT, SIR W, 43
listening when the s. is over SAINT-LAMBERT, MARQUIS DE, 1
sing unto the Lord a new s. PSALMS, 23
the s. of songs, which is Solomon's BIBLE: SONG OF SOLOMON, 1
the s. that is sung in our hearts OUIDA, 3
they shall not drink wine with a s. BIBLE: ISAIAH, 20
they that led us away captive required . . . a s. PSALMS, 83
Who loves not wine, woman and s. LUTHER, M, 2
**songs** Sing no sad s. ROSSETTI, C, 8
Where are the s. of Spring KEATS, J, 41
**sonne** when soft was the s. LANGLAND, W, 1
**sonnet** I have three phobias which . . . would make my life as slick as a s. BANKHEAD, T, 1
s. is a moment's monument ROSSETTI, D, 1
**son-of-a-bitch** The poor s. PARKER, D, 12
**sons** I have a wife, I have s. LUCAN, 1

Now we are all s. of bitches BAINBRIDGE, K, 1
S. of Belial had a Glorious Time DRYDEN, J, 9
**soon** day returns too s. BYRON, 6TH BARON, 39
**sophistry** Commit it then to the flames: for it can contain nothing but s. and illusion HUME, D, 2
Universities incline wits to s. and affectation BACON, 1ST BARON VERULAM, VISCOUNT ST ALBANS, 65
**Sophonisba** Oh! S. THOMSON, J, 4
**sores** Lazarus . . . laid at his gate, full of s. BIBLE: LUKE, 30
**sorrow** Down, thou climbing s. SHAKESPEARE, W, 135
in s. thou shalt bring forth children BIBLE: GENESIS, 15
Its narrow measure spans /Tears of eternity, and s., /Not mine, but man's HOUSMAN, A, 3
Much in s., oft in woe WHITE, H, 1
One for s. PROVERBS, 325
Parting is such sweet s. SHAKESPEARE, W, 247
Pure and complete s. is as impossible TOLSTOY, COUNT, 8
S. and silence are strong LONGFELLOW, H, 4
S. is tranquility remembered in emotion PARKER, D, 8
s. makes us wise TENNYSON, BARON, 32
the Lord . . . give thee joy for this thy s. BIBLE: TOBIT, 2
There is no greater s. DANTE, A, 2
Through the night of doubt and s. BARING-GOULD, S, 3
**sorrows** When s. come, they come not single spies SHAKESPEARE, W, 71
**sort** that like that s. of place SHAW, G, 20
**Soudan** to you, Fuzzy-Wuzzy, at your 'ome in the S. KIPLING, R, 8
**sought** by night on my bed I s. him whom my soul loveth BIBLE: SONG OF SOLOMON, 8
Love s. is good SHAKESPEARE, W, 293
Pleasure is . . . seldom found where it is s. JOHNSON, S, 13
**soul** And never once possess our s. ARNOLD, M, 41
Anger is one of the sinews of the s. FULLER, T, 5
Artists are not engineers of the s. KENNEDY, J, 15
a . . . s. like season'd timber HERBERT, G, 10
become a living s. WORDSWORTH, W, 9
company, . . . have neither a s. to lose nor a body to kick SMITH, S, 5
education is a leading out of what is . . . in the pupil's s. SPARK, M, 10
Education is . . . the s. of a society CHESTERTON, G, 41
Fair seed-time had my s. WORDSWORTH, W, 33
he shall convert my s. PSALMS, 12
His s. is marching on HALL, C, 1
his s. is satisfied with what is assigned to him MARCUS AURELIUS ANTONINUS, 10
I am positive I have a s. STERNE, L, 3
I am the captain of my s. HENLEY, W, 2
Impropriety is the s. of wit MAUGHAM, W, 9
In mystery our s. abides ARNOLD, M, 27
I pray the Lord my s. to keep ANONYMOUS, 64
Man has no Body distinct from his S. BLAKE, W, 29
my s. doth magnify the Lord BIBLE: LUKE, 2
my s. hath a desire PSALMS, 50
My s. in agony COLERIDGE, S, 29
my s. is among lions PSALMS, 40
my s. is athirst for God PSALMS, 30
my s. is exceeding sorrowful BIBLE: MATTHEW, 80
my s. is white BLAKE, W, 46
my s. . . . should flee as a bird PSALMS, 4
Never mind about my s. . . . get my tie right JOYCE, J, 9
No coward s. is mine BRONTE, E, 1
passion in the human s. LILLO, G, 1
poverty of s., impossible MONTAIGNE, M, 10
Raises from Hell a human s. BLAKE, W, 3
real dark night of the s. FITZGERALD, F, 1
seal the hushed casket of my s. KEATS, J, 43
than that one s. . . . should commit one single venial sin NEWMAN, CARDINAL, 4
The British postgraduate student is a lonely forlorn s. LODGE, D, 3
The dark night of the s. JOHN OF THE CROSS, 2
the . . . essence of a human s. CARLYLE, T, 25
the eyes are the windows of the s. BEERBOHM, SIR M, 10
the iron enter into his s. STERNE, L, 1
the iron has entered his s. LLOYD GEORGE, EARL OF DWYFOR, 1
their s. melteth away because of the trouble PSALMS, 66
the largest and most comprehensive s. DRYDEN, J, 20
The Life and S., the man who will never go home WHITEHORN, K, 3
The s. hath not her generous aspirings implanted in her in vain LAMB, C, 24

the s. is not more than the body WHITMAN, W, 7
the s. of a martyr with the intellect of an advocate BAGEHOT, W, 10
The s. started at the knee-cap LEWIS, W, 1
The S. that rises with us, our life's Star WORDSWORTH, W, 23
The voice of the sea speaks to the s. CHOPIN, K, 1
thou hast delivered my s. from death PSALMS, 73
Thy rapt s. sitting in thine eyes MILTON, J, 7
Thy s. was like a star, and dwelt apart WORDSWORTH, W, 51
souls Above the vulgar flight of common s. MURPHY, A, 1
damp s. of the housemaids ELIOT, T, 15
Our s. have sight of that immortal sea WORDSWORTH, W, 26
S. of poets dead and gone KEATS, J, 21
the s. of five hundred . . . Newtons COLERIDGE, S, 45
The s. of women are so small BUTLER, S, 9
Two s. dwell, alas! in my breast GOETHE, J, 3
Two s. with but a single thought LOVELL, M, 1
soul-sides the meanest of his creatures /Boasts two s.
BROWNING, R, 38
sound full of s. and fury SHAKESPEARE, W, 177
s. of a great Amen. PROCTER, A, 1
The hills are alive with the s. of music HAMMERSTEIN, O, 5
The most persistent s. . . . through men's history KOESTLER, A, 4
The s. must seem an echo to the sense POPE, A, 24
the s. of many waters BIBLE: REVELATIONS, 1
The s. of the English county families WAUGH, E, 2
the trumpet shall s. BIBLE: I CORINTHIANS, 23
whispering s. of the cool colonnade! COWPER, W, 17
sounding s. brass BIBLE: I CORINTHIANS, 18
sounds Music is the arithmetic of s. DEBUSSY, C, 1
the s. will take care of themselves CARROLL, L, 11
soup concludes that it will . . . make better s. MENCKEN, H, 16
S. of the evening, beautiful S. CARROLL, L, 15
Take the s. away HOFFMAN, H, 1
sour How s. sweet music is SHAKESPEARE, W, 240
I am sure the grapes are s. AESOP, 2
source her Majesty . . . must not . . . look upon me as a s. of
income KEMBLE, C, 1
sourest sweetest things turn s. SHAKESPEARE, W, 262
south beaker full of the warm S. KEATS, J, 32
go s. in the winter ELIOT, T, 24
hardly be a town in the S. of England ORWELL, G, 23
southern mother bore me in the s. wild BLAKE, W, 46
sovereign he will have no s. COKE, SIR E, 2
The S. has, under a constitutional monarchy . . . three rights
BAGEHOT, W, 1
When I forget my s. THURLOW, BARON, 1
Soviet Communism is S. power plus the electrification LENIN, V, 9
The ship follows S. custom. THEROUX, P, 3
sow Ireland is the old s. JOYCE, J, 2
like a s. that hath overwhelm'd all her litter SHAKESPEARE, W, 83
s. . . . in righteousness, reap in mercy BIBLE: HOSEA, 2
they that s. in tears shall reap in joy PSALMS, 79
soweth whatsoever a man s., that shall he also reap
BIBLE: GALATIANS, 6
sown A lovelier flower / . . . was never s. WORDSWORTH, W, 64
space annihilate but s. and time POPE, A, 1
In the United States there is more s. STEIN, G, 2
range of human societies in time, the other in s.
LEVI-STRAUSS, C, 1
spaceship passenger on the s., Earth FULLER, R, 1
spade When I see a s. I call it a s. WILDE, O, 26
Spain Farewell and adieu to you, Ladies of S. ANONYMOUS, 18
not left to S. TENNYSON, BARON, 66
spam he wanted steak and they offered s. MALAMUD, B, 1
Spaniards the S. seem wiser than they are
BACON, 1ST BARON VERULAM, VISCOUNT ST ALBANS, 47
time to win this game, and to thrash the S. DRAKE, SIR F, 2
Spanish I speak S. to God CHARLES V, 3
singed the S. king's beard DRAKE, SIR F, 1
spare bread enough and to s. BIBLE: LUKE, 28
I can't s. this man; he fights LINCOLN, A, 15
S. all I have FARQUHAR, G, 3
s. the rod BUTLER, S, 4
S. the rod PROVERBS, 366
Woodman, s. that tree MORRIS, G, 1
spareth he that s. his rod hateth his son BIBLE: PROVERBS, 7
sparrow a s. alight upon my shoulder THOREAU, H, 16
I, said the S., /With my bow and arrow NURSERY RHYMES, 73
It is a city where you can see a s. fall O'BRIEN, C, 1
the s. hath found her an house PSALMS, 50
sparrowhawks S., Ma'am WELLINGTON, DUKE OF, 24

sparrows five s. . . . not one of them is forgotten BIBLE: LUKE, 25
one of the s. . . . flew . . . through the hall BEDE, 1
spasm individual existence goes out in a lonely s. of helpless
agony JAMES, W, 1
spat So he stood up and s. on the ceiling ANONYMOUS, 91
Today I s. in the Seine PATTON, G, 1
speak I only s. right on SHAKESPEARE, W, 120
Let him now s. BOOK OF COMMON PRAYER, 14
more than a moral duty to s. one's mind WILDE, O, 25
mouths, and s. not PSALMS, 71
neither s. they through their throat PSALMS, 71
Never s. ill of the dead PROVERBS, 306
province of knowledge to s. HOLMES, O, 6
s., Lord; for thy servant heareth BIBLE: I SAMUEL, 1
some . . . s. . . . before they think LA BRUYERE, J, 3
S. softly and carry a big stick ROOSEVELT, T, 5
s. to God as if men were listening SENECA, 1
S. when you are spoken to PROVERBS, 367
time to think before I s. DARWIN, E, 1
When I think, I must s. SHAKESPEARE, W, 28
Whereof one cannot s. WITTGENSTEIN, L, 6
speaking An Englishman's way of s. LERNER, A, 1
People talking without s. SIMON, P, 3
when . . . s., they do not know what they are saying
CHURCHILL, SIR W, 34
speak up I didn't s. NIEMOLLER, M, 1
spearmint Does the S. Lose Its Flavour ROSE, B, 1
specialist S. – A man who knows more and more about less and
less MAYO, W, 1
specialists s. . . . tend to think in grooves MORGAN, E, 1
species the idea of its death as a s. KOESTLER, A, 6
the one s. I wouldn't mind seeing vanish BENNETT, A, 3
spectacle Life is not a s. SANTAYANA, G, 7
spectator a S. of mankind ADDISON, J, 8
spectre Communism continued to haunt Europe as a s.
TAYLOR, A, 3
speculation If the world were good for . . . s. HAZLITT, W, 2
speech freedom of s. and expression ROOSEVELT, F, 12
freedom of s., freedom of conscience TWAIN, M, 5
I dreamt that I was making a s. DEVONSHIRE, 8TH DUKE OF, 1
let thy s. be short BIBLE: ECCLESIASTICUS, 12
perfect plainness of s. . . . perfect nobleness ARNOLD, M, 29
S. is silver PROVERBS, 368
s. only to conceal their thoughts. VOLTAIRE, 6
s. . . . seasoned with salt BIBLE: COLOSSIANS, 6
S. was given to man to disguise his thoughts TALLEYRAND, 4
The most precious things in s. RICHARDSON, SIR R, 3
The true use of s. GOLDSMITH, O, 11
the whole earth was . . . of one s. BIBLE: GENESIS, 30
True and False are attributes of s., not of things HOBBES, T, 2
speeches every government . . . should have its old s. burned
SNOWDEN, 1ST VISCOUNT, 1
Many have been the wise s. of fools FULLER, T, 4
solved by s. and majority votes BISMARCK, PRINCE VON, 1
Statesmen are far too busy making s. RUSSELL, EARL, 20
speechless The Times is s. CHURCHILL, SIR W, 33
speed safety is in our s. EMERSON, R, 11
s. was faster than light BULLER, A, 1
spell s. it Vinci and pronounce it Vinchy TWAIN, M, 8
spend s. a single day really well KEMPIS, T, 5
spendest whatsoever thou s. more . . . I will repay BIBLE: LUKE, 22
spending Getting and s. WORDSWORTH, W, 59
Riches are for s.
BACON, 1ST BARON VERULAM, VISCOUNT ST ALBANS, 23
Spens Before they see Sir Patrick S. /Come sailing to the strand
ANONYMOUS, 83
spent Nought's had, all's s. SHAKESPEARE, W, 170
When I consider how my light is s. MILTON, J, 55
spermatozoa million million s., /All of them alive HUXLEY, A, 16
spheres our social s. have been widely different WILDE, O, 26
spice gathered my myrrh with my s. BIBLE: SONG OF SOLOMON, 12
Sugar and s. /And all that's nice NURSERY RHYMES, 70
Variety's the very s. of life COWPER, W, 22
spices a young hart upon the mountains of s.
BIBLE: SONG OF SOLOMON, 21
spider said a s. to a fly: HOWITT, M, 1
spies sorrows . . . come not single s. SHAKESPEARE, W, 71
spilt the blood that she has s. COWPER, W, 3
spin These are rare attainments . . . but . . . can she s. JAMES I, 4
spinning from eternity s. the thread of your being
MARCUS AURELIUS ANTONINUS, 12

**Spinoza** The Jews have produced . . . Christ, S., and myself
STEIN, G, 5
**spires** City with her dreaming s. ARNOLD, M, 43
**spirit** and an haughty s. before a fall BIBLE: PROVERBS, 8
bound in the s. BIBLE: ACTS, 16
Give me the s. SHAKESPEARE, W, 91
Hail to thee, blithe S.! SHELLEY, P, 22
history of the human s. ARNOLD, M, 20
into thy hands I commend my s. BIBLE: LUKE, 38
into thy hands I commend my s. PSALMS, 21
Music that gentlier on the s. lies TENNYSON, BARON, 51
my s. found outlet in the air JOHNSON, A, 1
my s. hath rejoiced in God my Saviour BIBLE: LUKE, 2
renew a right s. within me PSALMS, 35
s. . . . of a sound mind BIBLE: II TIMOTHY, 1
that which is born of the S. is s. BIBLE: JOHN, 7
the flesh lusteth against the S. BIBLE: GALATIANS, 4
the fruit of the S. is love, joy, peace BIBLE: GALATIANS, 5
the meanest . . . deeds require s. and talent LICHTENBERG, G, 3
the sacrifice of God is a troubled s. PSALMS, 36
The s. burning but unbent BYRON, 6TH BARON, 14
the s. . . . is willing BIBLE: MATTHEW, 81
the S. of God descending like a dove BIBLE: MATTHEW, 5
the S. of God moved upon . . . the waters BIBLE: GENESIS, 1
the S. of truth BIBLE: JOHN, 33
the s. that always denies GOETHE, J, 4
the sword of the S. BIBLE: EPHESIANS, 4
Th' expense of s. in a waste of shame SHAKESPEARE, W, 266
waxed strong in s. BIBLE: LUKE, 5
**spiritualist** If the dead talk to you, you are a s. SZASZ, T, 8
**spiritualists** The media . . . a convention of s. STOPPARD, T, 6
**spiteful** I like to write when I feel s. LAWRENCE, D, 39
**spits** Who s. against the wind PROVERBS, 466
**spleen** S. can subsist on any kind of food HAZLITT, W, 29
**splendour** Pavilioned in s., and girded with praise GRANT, SIR R, 1
s. falls on castle walls TENNYSON, BARON, 57
**splinters** teeth like s. CAUSLEY, C, 1
**split** They s. the atom by firing particles at it HAY, W, 1
when I s. an infinitive . . . it stays s. CHANDLER, R, 6
**spoil** Don't s. the ship PROVERBS, 120
s. the child BUTLER, S, 4
**spoke** s. among your wheels BEAUMONT, F, 5
**spoken** Speak when you're s. to CARROLL, L, 33
very excellent things are s. of thee PSALMS, 53
**spontaneous** set a high value on s. kindness JOHNSON, S, 136
the Immaculate Conception was s. combustion. PARKER, D, 18
Worrying is the most natural and s. of . . . functions THOMAS, L, 1
**spoof** even the weather forecast seemed to be some kind of s. LODGE, D, 4
**spoon** And the dish ran away with the s. NURSERY RHYMES, 14
S. feeding . . . teaches us nothing but the shape of the s. FORSTER, E, 12
**spoons** diners-out from whom we guard our s. MACAULAY, BARON, 19
let us count our s. JOHNSON, S, 61
the faster we counted our s. EMERSON, R, 3
**sport** In love as in s., the amateur status GRAVES, R, 3
kill us for their s. SHAKESPEARE, W, 144
Serious s. has nothing to do with fair play ORWELL, G, 30
s. would be as tedious as to work SHAKESPEARE, W, 77
The national s. of England TREE, SIR H, 6
The only athletic s. I ever mastered JERROLD, D, 7
to make s. for our neighbours AUSTEN, J, 23
**sportsman** But He was never . . . /A S. SITWELL, SIR O, 2
**spot** Out, damned s. SHAKESPEARE, W, 173
thou art all fair . . . there is no s. in thee BIBLE: SONG OF SOLOMON, 9
**spotless** s. reputation SHAKESPEARE, W, 234
**spots** or the leopard his s. BIBLE: JEREMIAH, 3
**sprang** I s. to the stirrup BROWNING, R, 26
**sprat** Throw out a s. PROVERBS, 432
**spreading** Under the s. chestnut tree LONGFELLOW, H, 14
**spring** A new repast, or an untasted s. ADDISON, J, 3
as short a S.; /As quick a growth to meet decay HERRICK, R, 4
By chilly finger'd s. KEATS, J, 3
can S. be far behind SHELLEY, P, 13
Drink deep, or taste not the Pierian s. POPE, A, 21
flowers that bloom in the s. GILBERT, SIR W, 33
In the S. a young man's fancy TENNYSON, BARON, 46
In the s. . . . your lovely Chloë SEARLE, R, 2
I said the hounds of s. THURBER, J, 16

lived light in the s. ARNOLD, M, 10
S. and summer did happen in Cambridge NABOKOV, V, 5
S. /Flow down the woods SACKVILLE-WEST, V, 2
S. has returned RILKE, R, 1
S. is come home THOMPSON, F, 3
s. now, comes unheralded by the return of the birds CARSON, R, 3
there would be S. no more TENNYSON, BARON, 29
They call it easing the S. REED, H, 3
The year's at the s. BROWNING, R, 43
Thrice welcome, darling of the s. WORDSWORTH, W, 69
Where are the songs of S. KEATS, J, 41
**spur** A s. in the head PROVERBS, 65
Fame is the s. MILTON, J, 20
**spurs** Let the boy win his s. EDWARD III, 1
**spurts** They move forward in s. CONNOLLY, C, 11
**square** Shed his blood . . . given a s. deal ROOSEVELT, T, 6
you broke a Bitish s.! KIPLING, R, 8
**squares** walk on the lines or the s. MILNE, A, 5
**squeezed** The Germans, . . . are going to be s., as a lemon GEDDES, SIR E, 1
**squire** Bless the s. and his relations DICKENS, C, 6
**stable** It's too late to shut the s. door PROVERBS, 233
**staff** I'll break my s. SHAKESPEARE, W, 278
the stay and the s. BIBLE: ISAIAH, 5
**stage** All the world's a s. SHAKESPEARE, W, 23
Don't put your daughter on the s. COWARD, SIR N, 6
If this were play'd upon a s. SHAKESPEARE, W, 294
no man dies for love, but on the s. DRYDEN, J, 27
qualities . . . necessary for success upon the s. TERRY, DAME E, 2
the Attic s. ARNOLD, M, 40
this great s. of fools SHAKESPEARE, W, 149
we go quite off this s. POPE, A, 59
**stagecoach** You will hear more good things on . . . a s. from London to Oxford HAZLITT, W, 8
**stagger** they . . . s. like a drunken man PSALMS, 66
**St Agnes** S.' Eve – Ah, bitter chill it was KEATS, J, 4
**stair** As I was going up the s. MEARNS, H, 1
**stairs** he had known many kicked down s. HALIFAX, MARQUIS OF, 9
walks up the s. of his concepts STEINBECK, J, 1
**stake** To the thumbscrew and the s. TENNYSON, BARON, 66
**Stalin** If Mr S. dies EDEN, 1ST EARL OF AVON, 1
S. hates the guts of ROOSEVELT, F, 3
**stammer** You persisted . . . like a s. LEWIS, W, 5
**stamp** If we can't s. out literature WAUGH, E, 39
the indelible s. of his lowly origin DARWIN, C, 3
to order a new s. . . . with my face on it CHARLES FRANCIS JOSEPH, 1
**stand** a firm place to s. ARCHIMEDES, 1
no time to s. and stare DAVIES, W, 2
s. not upon the order of . . . going SHAKESPEARE, W, 171
S. your ground . . . if they mean to have a war, let it begin here PARKER, J, 1
They also serve who only s. and wait MILTON, J, 56
we are risen, and s. upright PSALMS, 11
We s. today on the edge of a new frontier KENNEDY, J, 8
**stands** S. the Church clock BROOKE, R, 3
**star** a s. or two beside COLERIDGE, S, 31
Being a s. has made it possible DAVIS, S, 1
Bright s., would I were steadfast KEATS, J, 1
Go, and catch a falling s. DONNE, J, 11
Hitch your wagon to a s. EMERSON, R, 21
one s. differeth from another . . . in glory BIBLE: I CORINTHIANS, 22
Someday I'll wish upon a s. HARBURG, E, 1
Sunset and evening s. TENNYSON, BARON, 8
that same s., /That fitful, fiery Lucifer YOUNG, A, 1
The desire of the moth for the s. JOYCE, J, 8
The Soul that rises with us, our life's S. WORDSWORTH, W, 23
Thy soul was like a s., and dwelt apart WORDSWORTH, W, 51
Twinkle, twinkle, little s. TAYLOR, J, 1
we have seen his s. in the east BIBLE: MATTHEW, 1
we no time to stand and s. DAVIES, W, 2
**Starkie** There was a young woman called S. ANONYMOUS, 95
**starry** Under the wide and s. sky STEVENSON, R, 10
**starry heaven** the s. above me KANT, I, 1
**stars** Clad in the beauty of a thousand s. MARLOWE, C, 3
Hard and high to the s. ANONYMOUS, 68
he made the s. also BIBLE: GENESIS, 4
he telleth the number of the s. PSALMS, 91
I'll hold my head so high it'll strike the s. HORACE, 26
Look at the s. HOPKINS, G, 5
One sees the mud, and one the s. LANGBRIDGE, F, 1

some of us are looking at the s.     WILDE, O, 38
Some s. . . . Fell like a falling tear     YOUNG, A, 2
strives to touch the s.     SPENSER, E, 3
Tempt not the s.     FORD, J, 1
the field of the s. is so vast, but . . . man has measured it     FRANCE, A, 5
The s. grew bright in the winter sky     MASEFIELD, J, 4
the s. in their courses     BIBLE: JUDGES, 2
the Stone that puts the S. to Flight     FITZGERALD, E, 2
The Syrian s. look down     ARNOLD, M, 28
We are merely the s.' tennis-balls     WEBSTER, J, 3
what is the s.     O'CASEY, S, 1
**star-spangled** 'Tis the s. banner     KEY, F, 1
**start** Wrong from the s.     POUND, E, 10
**starts** make certain it never s.     BRADLEY, O, 1
**starve** Let not poor Nelly s.     CHARLES II, 6
**starving** all around you people are s.     PANKHURST, S, 2
**state** a s. in the proper sense of the word     LENIN, V, 3
attacking an ex-secretary of s.!     ACHESON, D, 1
I am the S.     LOUIS XIV, 4
In a free society the s. . . . administers justice among men     LIPPMAN, W, 1
O Lord, to what a s. . . . those who love Thee     TERESA OF AVILA, 1
Our object in the construction of the s.     PLATO, 2
reinforcement of the power of the S.     CAMUS, A, 12
So long as the s. exists there is no freedom     LENIN, V, 4
S. socialism is totally alien     THATCHER, M, 12
the lie has become . . . a pillar of the S.     SOLZHENITSYN, A, 11
The S., in choosing men . . . takes no notice of their opinions     CROMWELL, O, 5
The s. is an instrument . . . of the ruling class     STALIN, J, 2
the s. . . . Man is in     NIETZSCHE, F, 4
The worth of a S.     MILL, J, 5
**stately** go back to thy s. homes of England     LAWRENCE, D, 16
S. Homes of England ope their doors     CAMPBELL, R, 1
the S. Homes of England     COWARD, SIR N, 11
The S. Homes of England     COWARD, SIR N, 12
The s. homes of England     HEMANS, F, 2
Those comfortably padded lunatic asylums . . . the s. homes     WOOLF, V, 4
**statement** Any general s. is like a cheque     POUND, E, 4
**states** S., like men, have their growth, . . . , their decay     LANDOR, W, 4
**statesman** abroad you're a s.     MACMILLAN, EARL OF STOCKTON, 3
A politician is a s. . . . with an open mouth     STEVENSON, A, 2
A s. is a politician who     POMPIDOU, G, 1
A s. is a politician who's been dead     TRUMAN, H, 3
definition of a constitutional s.     BAGEHOT, W, 9
**statesmen** S. are far too busy making speeches     RUSSELL, EARL, 20
s. . . . estranged from reality     LAING, R, 1
**static** class people as s. and dynamic     WAUGH, E, 22
novel is a s. thing     TYNAN, K, 1
**station** honour is a private s.     ADDISON, J, 5
**stationmaster** The s.'s whiskers are of a Victorian bushiness     WODEHOUSE, SIR P, 17
**stations** always know our proper s.     DICKENS, C, 6
**statistics** Facts speak louder than s.     STREATFIELD, SIR G, 1
He uses s. as a drunken man uses lamp-posts     LANG, A, 1
lies, damned lies and s.     DISRAELI, 1ST EARL OF BEACONSFIELD, 13
lies, damned lies, and s.     TWAIN, M, 2
s., born to consume resources     HORACE, 17
There are two kinds of s.     STOUT, R, 1
unrewarded millions without whom S. would be a bankrupt science     SMITH, L, 6
we must study s.     NIGHTINGALE, F, 2
You cannot feed the hungry on s..     LLOYD GEORGE, EARL OF DWYFOR, 3
**statue** that *my* s. should be moved, which I should much dislike     VICTORIA, 7
there's a s. inside every block of stone     ORWELL, G, 7
**statues** worth a million s.     CUMMINGS, E, 2
**status** restored the s. quo     SQUIRE, SIR J, 3
**stay** s. me with flagons     BIBLE: SONG OF SOLOMON, 3
S., s., /Until the hasting day /Has run     HERRICK, R, 4
the s. and the staff     BIBLE: ISAIAH, 5
**stay-at-home** Sweet S.     DAVIES, W, 3
**steak** he wanted s. and they offered spam     MALAMUD, B, 1
**steaks** smell of s. in passageways     ELIOT, T, 17
**steal** A man who will s. *for* me will s. *from* me     ROOSEVELT, T, 3
thou shalt not s.     BIBLE: EXODUS, 20

**stealing** hanged for s. horses     HALIFAX, MARQUIS OF, 1
**steals** A good composer . . . s.     STRAVINSKY, I, 5
what can plead that man's excuse /Who s. a common from a goose     ANONYMOUS, 80
Who s. my purse s. trash     SHAKESPEARE, W, 223
**stealth** Do good by s.     POPE, A, 8
greatest pleasure I know, is to do a good action by s.     LAMB, C, 16
**stealthy** The S. School of Criticism     ROSSETTI, D, 4
**steamer** tossing about in a s. from Harwich     GILBERT, SIR W, 21
**steel** arm'd with more than complete s.     MARLOWE, C, 12
the cold s.     ARMINSTEAD, L, 1
When the foeman bares his s.     GILBERT, SIR W, 39
**steep** When things are s., remember to stay level-headed.     HORACE, 33
**steeple** clock in the s. strikes one     WORK, H, 1
**steeples** Talk about the pews and s.     CHESTERTON, G, 3
Till you have drench'd our s.     SHAKESPEARE, W, 137
**steer** press the accelerator to the floor and s. left     VUKOVICH, B, 1
**Stein** There's a wonderful family called S.     ANONYMOUS, 89
**stellar** the whole solar and s. systems     CARLYLE, T, 28
**stem** a rod out of the s. of Jesse     BIBLE: ISAIAH, 14
**step** a s. from the sublime to the ridiculous     NAPOLEON I, 5
One s. forward, two steps back     LENIN, V, 2
one small s. for man     ARMSTRONG, N, 1
only the first s. . . . is difficult     DEFFAND, MARQUISE DU, 1
The first s.     PROVERBS, 394
**step-mother** a kind parent . . . or a merciless s.     PLINY THE ELDER, 2
**Stepney** When will that be? /Say the bells of S.     NURSERY RHYMES, 41
**stepp'd** in blood s. in so far     SHAKESPEARE, W, 172
**stick** if we praise ourselves fearlessly, something will always s.     BACON, 1ST BARON VERULAM, VISCOUNT ST ALBANS, 4
kind of burr; I shall s.     SHAKESPEARE, W, 185
meant us to s. it out     KOESTLER, A, 2
Speak softly and carry a big s.     ROOSEVELT, T, 5
**sticks** it is always said of slander that something always s.     BACON, 1ST BARON VERULAM, VISCOUNT ST ALBANS, 4
S. and stones     PROVERBS, 369
**stiff** a s. upper lip     CARY, J, 1
**stiffnecked** a s. people     BIBLE: EXODUS, 27
**stigma** Any s. . . . to beat a dogma     GUEDALLA, P, 3
**stile** He found a crooked sixpence against a crooked s.     NURSERY RHYMES, 57
I'm sitting on the s., Mary     BLACKWOOD, COUNTESS OF DUFFERIN, 1
**still** And if she's not gone /She lives there s.     NURSERY RHYMES, 58
a s. small voice     BIBLE: I KINGS, 7
A s. small voice     TENNYSON, BARON, 75
A s. tongue     PROVERBS, 67
be s. then, and know that I am God     PSALMS, 32
of his own opinion s.     BUTLER, S, 8
S. waters run deep     PROVERBS, 370
**stilly** Oft in the s. night, /Ere Slumber's chain     MOORE, T, 7
**sting** O death, where is thy s.     BIBLE: I CORINTHIANS, 23
O death! where is thy s.     POPE, A, 4
**stings** stroke a nettle, /And it s. you for your pains     HILL, A, 1
**stirrup** Betwixt the s. and the ground     CAMDEN, W, 1
I sprang to the s.     BROWNING, R, 26
**stitch** A s. in time     PROVERBS, 68
**St Ives** As I was going to S.     NURSERY RHYMES, 3
**stoat** I . . . catch a glimpse of a s.     KEATS, J, 64
**stock** the public s. of harmless pleasure     JOHNSON, S, 18
**stockholders** The public be damned. I am working for my s.     VANDERBILT, W, 1
**stockings** the silk s. and white bosoms of your actresses excite my amorous propensities     JOHNSON, S, 43
**stoic** man is . . . either a s. or a satyr     PINERO, SIR A, 1
**stole** That title from a better man I s.     STEVENSON, R, 9
**stolen** not wanting what is s.     SHAKESPEARE, W, 226
S. sweets are best     CIBBER, C, 2
S. sweets are always sweeter     HUNT, L, 5
s. waters are sweet     BIBLE: PROVERBS, 6
your wife . . . is a receiver of s. goods     JOHNSON, S, 131
**stomach** A hungry s. has no ears     LA FONTAINE, J, 9
An army marches on its s.     NAPOLEON I, 9
a proud look and a high s.     PSALMS, 63
No one can worship God . . . on an empty s.     WILSON, W, 6
The way to a man's heart is through his s.     FERN, F, 1
use a little wine for thy s.'s sake     BIBLE: I TIMOTHY, 4
Well, then, my s. must just digest in its waistcoat     SHERIDAN, R, 10
**stomachs** Napoleon's armies used to march on their s.     SELLAR, W, 6

struts player that s. and frets SHAKESPEARE, W, 177
St Trinian Though loaded firearms were strictly forbidden at S.'s
SEARLE, R, 1
stubborn s. spear-men SCOTT, SIR W, 14
student an over-ambitious essay by a second-year s.
PRIESTLEY, J, 2
a s. to the end of my days CHEKHOV, A, 1
He was . . . – a s. of history TAYLOR, A, 6
studies S. serve for delight
BACON, 1ST BARON VERULAM, VISCOUNT ST ALBANS, 49
study I am slow of s. SHAKESPEARE, W, 203
much s. is a weariness of the flesh BIBLE: ECCLESIASTES, 25
s. what you most affect SHAKESPEARE, W, 270
The proper s. of Mankind is Man POPE, A, 32
the result of previous s. AUSTEN, J, 19
studying By s. the masters ABEL, N, 1
stuff Ambition should be made of sterner s. SHAKESPEARE, W, 118
such s. as dreams are made on SHAKESPEARE, W, 277
The future is made of the same s. WEIL, S, 4
to s. a mushroom CONRAN, S, 1
stuffed We are the s. men ELIOT, T, 7
stumble they s. that run fast SHAKESPEARE, W, 248
stumbling the . . . world was s. . . . in social blindness KELLER, H, 3
stupid anger makes us all s. SPYRI, J, 2
clever man . . . came of . . . s. people CARLYLE, T, 30
he ceased to be mad he became merely s. PROUST, M, 10
Living in England, . . . must be like being married to a s. . . . wife
HALSEY, M, 3
The s. neither forgive SZASZ, T, 6
To be clever enough to get . . . money, one must be s.
CHESTERTON, G, 22
stupidity Against s. the gods . . . struggle in vain SCHILLER, F, 1
Human S. consists in having lots of ideas, but stupid ones
MONTHERLANT, H, 2
If poverty is the mother of crime, s. is its father LA BRUYERE, J, 11
It is a s. . . . to busy oneself with the correction of the world
MOLIERE, 6
no sin except s.. WILDE, O, 11
Stygian resembling the horrible S. smoke of the pit JAMES I, 1
ye S. set LANDOR, W, 1
style s. is the man himself BUFFON, COMTE DE, 1
s., not sincerity, is the vital thing WILDE, O, 28
s. . . . often hides eczema CAMUS, A, 2
the grand s. arises in poetry ARNOLD, M, 30
The s. is the man PROVERBS, 426
styles All s. are good except the tiresome sort VOLTAIRE, 13
subject a noble nature, . . . treats . . . a serious s. ARNOLD, M, 30
Every s.'s duty is the King's SHAKESPEARE, W, 98
Her Majesty is not a s. DISRAELI, 1ST EARL OF BEACONSFIELD, 34
the individual s. . . . has nothing to do with the laws but to obey
them HORSLEY, B, 1
subjects Although there exist many thousand s. PROVERBS, 42
subjunctive To the last, he preferred WOOLLCOTT, A, 1
sublime a step from the s. to the ridiculous NAPOLEON I, 5
Beethoven's Fifth Symphony is the most s. noise FORSTER, E, 7
From the s. to the ridiculous PROVERBS, 169
how s. . . . /To suffer and be strong LONGFELLOW, H, 6
The s. and the ridiculous PAINE, T, 2
submit To great evils we s.; we resent little provocations
HAZLITT, W, 20
subscribers reasons for not printing any list of s. JOHNSON, S, 135
subsequence It is incident to physicians . . . to mistake s. for
consequence. JOHNSON, S, 41
substance faith is the s. of things hoped for BIBLE: HEBREWS, 7
lose the s. by grasping at the shadow AESOP, 1
substantial he that chiefly owes himself . . . is the s. Man
BROWNE, SIR T, 2
substantives be able to tell the s. from the adjectives
MADARIAGA Y ROGO, S, 2
substitute a s. for reading it BURGESS, A, 4
no s. for talent HUXLEY, A, 25
substitutes and finally a single dictator s. himself TROTSKY, L, 11
subtil the serpent was more s. BIBLE: GENESIS, 12
subtle Time, the s. thief of youth MILTON, J, 54
suburbia I come from s. RAPHAEL, F, 3
subverts whoever is moved by faith to assent to it, is conscious of
a continued miracle in his own person, which s. all the principles
of his understanding HUME, D, 3
succeed If at first you don't s. HICKSON, W, 1
If at first you don't s. PROVERBS, 213
If they s., they fail CRISP, Q, 9

I'm . . . ugly enough to s. on my own ALLEN, W, 4
It is not enough to s. VIDAL, G, 5
Never having been able to s. in the world VOLTAIRE, 22
those who ne'er s. DICKINSON, E, 4
to s. unconventionally KEYNES, BARON, 5
succeeds Nothing s. PROVERBS, 318
Whenever a friend s. VIDAL, G, 6
success a self-made man who owed his lack of s. to nobody
HELLER, J, 1
I thought that s. spelled happiness PAVLOVA, A, 3
I was never affected by the question of the s. MEIR, G, 2
no s. like failure DYLAN, B, 5
not in mortals to command s. ADDISON, J, 2
no very lively hope of s. SMITH, S, 13
only place where s. comes before work SASSOON, V, 1
religion . . . yours is S. BARRIE, SIR J, 7
s. and miscarriage are empty sounds JOHNSON, S, 4
s. . . . by dint of hard work PAVLOVA, A, 2
s. depends . . . upon individual initiative and exertion PAVLOVA, A, 2
S. is counted sweetest DICKINSON, E, 4
Sweet Smell of S. LEHMAN, E, 1
The moral flabbiness born of . . . S. JAMES, W, 4
two to make a marriage a s. SAMUEL, VISCOUNT, 1
successful It was very s. BRAUN, W, 1
we do everything we can to appear s.
ROCHEFOUCAULD, DUC DE LA, 7
sucker a s. born every minute BARNUM, P, 1
suckle To s. fools SHAKESPEARE, W, 221
sucklings out of the mouth of . . . babes and s. PSALMS, 3
sucks s. the nurse asleep SHAKESPEARE, W, 17
suddenly No one . . . s. became depraved JUVENAL, 2
sued publish and be s. INGRAMS, R, 2
Suez Ship me somewheres east of S. KIPLING, R, 23
the S. Canal was flowing through my drawing room
EDEN, COUNTESS OF AVON, 1
suffer courage to love . . . courage to s.. TROLLOPE, A, 4
how sublime . . . /To s. and be strong LONGFELLOW, H, 6
If s. we must, let's s. on the heights HUGO, V, 1
Rather s. than die LA FONTAINE, J, 1
s. fools gladly BIBLE: II CORINTHIANS, 4
suffered love a place the less for having s. AUSTEN, J, 14
suffering A man who fears s. MONTAIGNE, M, 11
pity for the s. of mankind RUSSELL, EARL, 1
sympathize with everything, except s. WILDE, O, 46
we cannot be created for this sort of s. KEATS, J, 66
sufficient s. unto the day is the evil thereof BIBLE: MATTHEW, 22
suffragettes we s. aspire to be . . . ambassadors of freedom to
women PANKHURST, DAME C, 4
sugar like sulphuric acid and s. TAINE, H, 1
S. and spice /And all that's nice NURSERY RHYMES, 70
suicide Never murder a man who is committing s. WILSON, W, 1
thought of s. is a great . . . comfort NIETZSCHE, F, 10
suit in a light so dim he would not have chosen a s. by it
CHEVALIER, M, 1
My s. is pale yellow. My nationality is French WILLIAMS, T, 1
suitable no s. material to work on COMPTON-BURNETT, DAME I, 3
Sukey S. take it off again NURSERY RHYMES, 44
sulphur and of Calvin, oat-cakes, and s. SMITH, S, 7
Puffed its s. to the sunset BETJEMAN, SIR J, 5
sulphuric like s. acid and sugar TAINE, H, 1
sultry common where the climate's s. BYRON, 6TH BARON, 16
sum Cogito, ergo s. DESCARTES, R, 1
sumer S. is icumen in ANONYMOUS, 75
summer after many a s. dies the swan TENNYSON, BARON, 71
All on a s. day CARROLL, L, 16
Beauty sat with me all the s. day BRIDGES, R, 2
Before the war . . . it was s. all the year round ORWELL, G, 8
Made glorious s. SHAKESPEARE, W, 241
Now the peak of s.'s past DAY LEWIS, C, 1
S. afternoon – s. afternoon JAMES, H, 11
S. has set in with its usual severity COLERIDGE, S, 44
Spring and s. did happen in Cambridge NABOKOV, V, 5
the last rose of s. MOORE, T, 5
Warm s. sun shine kindly here ANONYMOUS, 104
summit the s. of Everest was hardly the place HILLARY, SIR E, 1
summits snowy s. old in story TENNYSON, BARON, 57
summons when Fate s. DRYDEN, J, 24
sun all, except their s. is set BYRON, 6TH BARON, 23
aweary of the s. SHAKESPEARE, W, 178
before you let the s. in, mind it wipes its shoes. THOMAS, D, 12

swift s. to hear | BIBLE: JAMES, 3
Too s. arrives as tardy as too slow | SHAKESPEARE, W, 249
swimming s. under water | FITZGERALD, F, 14
swine a s. to show you where the truffles are | ALBEE, E, 2
Come in, you Anglo-Saxon s. | BEHAN, B, 9
pearls before s. | BIBLE: MATTHEW, 25
the husks that the s. did eat | BIBLE: LUKE, 28
swing S., s. together | CORY, W, 1
swings we pulls up on the s. | CHALMERS, P, 1
Swiss if the S. had designed these mountains | THEROUX, P, 2
The S. . . . are not a people so much as a . . . business | FAULKNER, W, 1
Swithin St. S.'s Day, if thou dost rain | PROVERBS, 372
Switzerland Austria is S. . . . with history added | MORPURGO, J, 1
In S. they had brotherly love, five hundred years of democracy and peace | WELLES, O, 1
S. . . . an inferior sort of Scotland | SMITH, S, 14
swollen mere existence is s. to a horror | LAWRENCE, D, 21
sword his sore and great and strong s. | BIBLE: ISAIAH, 21
Islam unashamedly came with a s. | RUNCIMAN, SIR S, 1
more cruel . . . the pen than the s. | BURTON, R, 3
nation shall not lift up s. against nation | BIBLE: ISAIAH, 4
not to send peace, but a s. | BIBLE: MATTHEW, 39
pen is mightier than the s. | BULWER-LYTTON, 1ST BARON LYTTON, 1
s. sleep in my hand | BLAKE, W, 31
the bank was mightier than the s. | PLOMER, W, 1
the praises of God be in their mouth, and a two-edged s. in | PSALMS, 93
the s. of the Spirit | BIBLE: EPHESIANS, 4
the word of God is . . . sharper than any two-edged s. | BIBLE: HEBREWS, 2
they smote the city with the edge of the s. | BIBLE: JUDGES, 1
they that take the s. shall perish with the s. | BIBLE: MATTHEW, 83

## T

table a good dinner upon his t. | JOHNSON, S, 34
crumbs which fell from the rich man's t. | BIBLE: LUKE, 30
patient etherized upon a t. | ELIOT, T, 9
put them at a t. together | CHURCHILL, SIR W, 26
tableau history is . . . a t. of crimes and misfortunes | VOLTAIRE, 15
tables It is not your trade to make t. | JOHNSON, S, 56
t. of stone, and a law | BIBLE: EXODUS, 24
tact T. consists in knowing | COCTEAU, J, 2
tactic Silence is the best t. | ROCHEFOUCAULD, DUC DE LA, 11
tae Here's t. us wha's like us | ANONYMOUS, 36
tail A case of the t. dogging the wag | PERELMAN, S, 5
The only man who really needs a t. coat | TAYLOR, J, 1
tailor I go to a better t. than any of you | DARROW, C, 1
Tinker, /T., /Soldier, /Sailor | NURSERY RHYMES, 65
tails t. you lose | CROKER, J, 1
tainted the supply is not t. | SCOTT, C, 1
take T. care of the sense | CARROLL, L, 11
They have to t. you in | FROST, R, 3
they . . . t., who have the power | WORDSWORTH, W, 41
T. things as they come | PROVERBS, 375
You can't t. it with you | PROVERBS, 477
taken from him that hath not shall be t. away | BIBLE: MATTHEW, 73
the Lord gave, and the Lord hath t. away | BIBLE: JOB, 2
takes It t. all sorts | PROVERBS, 234
taking not winning but t. part | COUBERTIN, BARON, 1
tale A t. never loses | PROVERBS, 69
a t. that is told | PSALMS, 56
a t. /Told by an idiot | SHAKESPEARE, W, 177
Life is as tedious as a twice-told t. | SHAKESPEARE, W, 127
thereby hangs a t. | SHAKESPEARE, W, 22
t. to tell of the hardihood, . . . of my companions | SCOTT, CAPTAIN, 2
talent A best-seller is the gilded tomb of a mediocre t. | SMITH, L, 1
a country . . . with absolutely no t. | LEONARD, H, 1
any man who has no t. | AGATE, J, 2
T. alone cannot make a writer | EMERSON, R, 16
T. develops in quiet places | GOETHE, J, 7
T. does what it can | MEREDITH, O, 1
the difference between t. and genius | ALCOTT, L, 2
the meanest . . . deeds require spirit and t. | LICHTENBERG, G, 3
the most extraordinary collection of t. | KENNEDY, J, 10
There is no substitute for t. | HUXLEY, A, 25
There is no such thing as a great t. without great will-power | BALZAC, H, 2
the t. of flattering with delicacy | AUSTEN, J, 19
t. instantly recognizes genius | DOYLE, SIR A, 15

talents If you have great t., industry will improve them | REYNOLDS, SIR J, 1
the difference between our t. and our expectations | BONO, E, 1
talk If you can t. with crowds and keep your virtue | KIPLING, R, 15
my ministers t. - as long as they do what I say | THATCHER, M, 19
Teas, /Where small t. dies | SHELLEY, P, 17
the need to t. is a primary impulse | CERVANTES, M, 12
think too little . . . t. too much | DRYDEN, J, 6
T. of the devil | PROVERBS, 376
Two may t. . . . yet never really meet | CATHERWOOD, M, 1
we never t. about anything except me | WHISTLER, J, 3
when I hear anyone t. of Culture | GOERING, H, 4
When two Englishmen meet, their first t. is of the weather. | JOHNSON, S, 12
women should t. an hour | BEAUMONT, F, 10
you wished him to t. on for ever | HAZLITT, W, 9
talked He t. on for ever | HAZLITT, W, 9
The more you are t. about | RUSSELL, EARL, 8
There is only one thing . . . worse than being t. about | WILDE, O, 43
talker A good listener is a good t. with a sore throat | WHITEHORN, K, 7
a non-stop t. to whom someone has given a typewriter | BRENAN, G, 5
Nothing is more despicable than a professional t. | FENELON, F, 1
talkers fluent t. | HAZLITT, W, 26
talking for thirty-five years he had not stopped t. | WATSON; J, 2
Frenchman must be always t. | JOHNSON, S, 130
good newspaper, . . . is a nation t. to itself | MILLER, A, 5
if you ain't t. about him, ain't listening | BRANDO, M, 1
I wouldn't be . . . t. to someone like you | CARTLAND, B, 1
People t. without speaking | SIMON, P, 3
T. and eloquence are not the same | JONSON, B, 7
T. of Michelangelo | ELIOT, T, 10
While we're t., time will have meanly run on | HORACE, 31
tall Let our children grow t. | THATCHER, M, 2
tambourine Hey! Mr T. Man | DYLAN, B, 6
tame the tongue can no man t. | BIBLE: JAMES, 6
tamper Who am I to t. with a masterpiece | WILDE, O, 68
tangere noli me t. | BIBLE: JOHN, 55
tangerine t. trees and marmalade skies | LENNON, J, 7
tankard heart which grief hath cankered / . . . remedy - the T. | CALVERLEY, C, 1
tanned getting more t. and more tired | PEGLER, W, 1
tapeworm as fitted to survive - . . . as a t. | GOLDING, W, 1
Tara through T.'s halls | MOORE, T, 2
tarnished neither t. nor afraid | CHANDLER, R, 4
tarry having lost . . . your prime, /You may for ever t. | HERRICK, R, 6
tarrying make no long t., O my God | PSALMS, 28
Tartar Scratch the Russian and . . . find the T. | MAISTRE, J, 2
tarts He's lost us the t.' vote | DEVONSHIRE, 10TH DUKE OF, 1
she made some t. | CARROLL, L, 16 -
The Queen of Hearts /She made some t. | NURSERY RHYMES, 56
Tarzan Me T. | BURROUGHS, E, 1
Me? T. | WEISSMULLER, J, 1
task No t. is a long one | BAUDELAIRE, C, 1
Tasmanians the T., who never committed adultery, are now extinct | MAUGHAM, W, 1
taste A different t. in jokes | ELIOT, G, 4
bad t. is better than no t. | BENNETT, A, 7
Drink deep, or t. not the Pierian spring | POPE, A, 21
Every one to his t. | PROVERBS, 142
great common sense and good t. | SHAW, G, 6
I suspect his t. in higher matters | LAMB, C, 3
no t. when you married me | SHERIDAN, R, 8
nowhere worse t., than in a churchyard | JOWETT, B, 3
Shakespeare, undoubtedly wanted t. | WALPOLE, 4TH EARL OF ORFORD, 4
the bouquet is better than the t. | POTTER, S, 7
the t. by which he is . . . relished | WORDSWORTH, W, 18
The t. was that of the little crumb of madeleine | PROUST, M, 1
Things sweet to t. prove . . . sour | SHAKESPEARE, W, 235
T. is the feminine of genius | FITZGERALD, E, 1
willing to t. any drink once | CABELL, J, 1
tasted Sir, you have t. two whole worms | SPOONER, W, 5
Some books are to be t. | BACON, 1ST BARON VERULAM, VISCOUNT ST ALBANS, 50
tastes It is like a cigar. . . . it never t. quite the same | WAVELL, EARL, 1
Our t. greatly alter | JOHNSON, S, 71
There is no accounting for t. | PROVERBS, 410

What is there to make so much of in the T.
QUEENSBERRY, 4TH DUKE OF, 1
**thank** Don't bother to t. me BANKHEAD, T. 6
T. me no thankings SHAKESPEARE, W, 251
**thankful** I am . . . t. for not having married MARTINEAU, H, 1
it becometh well the just to be t. PSALMS, 23
**thanks** For this relief much t. SHAKESPEARE, W, 39
I am glad . . . he t. God for anything JOHNSON, S, 11
O give t. unto the Lord, for he is gracious PSALMS, 65
T. For the Memory ROBIN, L, 1
**thanksgiving** come before his presence with t. PSALMS, 60
With proud t. BINYON, L, 2
**that** 1066 And All T. SELLAR, W, 3
Goodbye to All T. GRAVES, R, 1
**Thatcher** Blimpish patriotism in the mode of Margaret T.
KINNOCK, N, 8
**thcream** I'll t., an' t., . . . till I'm thick CROMPTON, R, 1
**theatre** Farce is the essential t. CRAIG, SIR G, 1
For the t. one needs long arms BERNHARDT, S, 1
nobody goes to the t. unless he . . . has bronchitis AGATE, J, 1
T. director: a person AGATE, J, 3
**theatrical** one may fail to find happiness in t. life PAVLOVA, A, 1
**theft** Property is t. PROUDHON, P, 1
**themselves** power . . . over t. WOLLSTONECRAFT, M, 2
**theologian** This stranger is a t. DIDEROT, D, 1
**theorems** About binomial t. GILBERT, SIR W, 38
the world can be expressed in . . . t. FRAYN, M, 2
**theory** A t. can be proved by experiment EINSTEIN, A, 7
a thing may look evil in t. BURKE, E, 26
it's . . . more important for a t. to be shapely HAMPTON, C, 1
no path leads from experiment to . . . t. EINSTEIN, A, 7
Philosophy is not a t. WITTGENSTEIN, L, 4
the scream is sometimes a t. STEVENSON, R, 14
t. is all grey GOETHE, J, 2
**therapeutic** have such immense t. value SHAW, G, 31
**there** soon brought to shame, that cry over me, t., t. PSALMS, 45
**thick** Through t. and thin BUTLER, S, 5
**thicken** other things . . . t. the features WEST, DAME R, 1
**thickens** plot t. BUCKINGHAM, 2ND DUKE OF, 1
**thief** as a t. in the night BIBLE: I THESSALONIANS, 2
I come as a t. BIBLE: REVELATIONS, 11
Time, the subtle t. of youth MILTON, J, 54
**thieves** a den of t. BIBLE: MATTHEW, 61
fell among t. BIBLE: LUKE, 21
**thigh** he smote them hip and t. BIBLE: JUDGES, 7
**thighs** thy t. are like jewels BIBLE: SONG OF SOLOMON, 17.
**thin** Enclosing every t. man, there's a fat man WAUGH, E, 28
in every fat man a t. one CONNOLLY, C, 16
One can never be too t. WINDSOR, DUCHESS OF, 2
there's a t. man inside every fat man ORWELL, G, 7
There were times my pants were so t. TRACY, S, 1
Through thick and t. BUTLER, S, 5
**thing** call that t. under your hat a head HOLBERG, BARON, 1
good t., to make it too common SHAKESPEARE, W, 84
It is a far, far, better t. that I do DICKENS, C, 54
something between a t. and a thought PALMER, S, 1
The play's the t. SHAKESPEARE, W, 60
the t. which is good BIBLE: EPHESIANS, 2
**thing-in-itself** The t. . . . , exists . . . in every being
SCHOPENHAUER, A, 5
**things** all t. were made by him BIBLE: JOHN, 1
Glorious t. of thee are spoken NEWTON, J, 1
T. are entirely what they appear to be SARTRE, J, 5
To talk of many t. CARROLL, L, 25
**think** apparatus with which we t. BIERCE, A, 2
I cannot sit and t. LAMB, C, 11
I exist by what I t. SARTRE, J, 6
I never t. of the future EINSTEIN, A, 9
I t. him so SHAKESPEARE, W, 298
I t. therefore I am DESCARTES, R, 1
Many people would sooner die than t. RUSSELL, EARL, 25
not so t. as you drunk SQUIRE, SIR J, 1
some evils so terrible . . . that we dare not t. of them
LA BRUYERE, A, 5
some . . . speak . . . before they t. LA BRUYERE, J, 3
time to t. before I speak DARWIN, E, 2
T. of your posterity ADAMS, J, 1
To know how to say what others only . . . t. CHARLES, E, 1
t. only this of thee BROOKE, R, 5
t. too little . . . talk too much DRYDEN, J, 6
We haven't the money, so we've got to t. RUTHERFORD, BARON, 1

When I t. of all the books I have read YEATS, W, 3
You can't t. rationally on an empty stomach REITH, BARON, 1
**thinkers** not always the justest t. HAZLITT, W, 26
**thinking** In order to draw a limit to t. WITTGENSTEIN, L, 2
It ain't t. about it TROLLOPE, A, 7
one prolonged effort to prevent oneself t. HUXLEY, A, 22
Plain living and high t. are no more WORDSWORTH, W, 52
T. is to me the greatest fatigue in the world VANBRUGH, SIR J, 4
t. makes it so SHAKESPEARE, W, 56
try t. of love FRY, C, 5
We are t. beings JAMES, W, 3
**thinks** He t. too much . . . dangerous SHAKESPEARE, W, 107
never t. of me ANONYMOUS, 87
The great consolation . . . is to say what one t. VOLTAIRE, 25
**third** if there was a t. sex VAIL, A, 1
to help Britain to become a T. Programme WILKINSON, E, 1
T. time lucky PROVERBS, 430
**third-rate** And t. conversation PLOMER, W, 2
**thirst** the t. to come RABELAIS, F, 1
whosoever drinketh of this water shall t. again BIBLE: JOHN, 12
**thirsty** t., and ye gave me drink BIBLE: MATTHEW, 75
**thirty** T. days hath November GRAFTON, R, 1
T. days hath September ANONYMOUS, 99
T. days hath September NURSERY RHYMES, 61
T. millions, mostly fools CARLYLE, T, 34
t. pieces of silver BIBLE: MATTHEW, 84
**thirty-five** for t. years he had not stopped talking WATSON, J, 2
**this** All t. and heaven too HENRY, M, 3
**thistle** I have always plucked a t. and planted a flower
LINCOLN, A, 3
**Thomasina** Why so shy, my pretty T. FRY, C, 1
**thorn** A rose without a t. MACNALLY, L, 1
a t. in the flesh BIBLE: II CORINTHIANS, 5
**thorough** How . . . t. these Germans always managed to be
HUXLEY, A, 34
**thoroughness** with the t. of a mind that reveres details LEWIS, S, 3
**thou** Book of Verse – and T. FITZGERALD, E, 5
**thought** a green t. in a green shade MARVELL, A, 2
A library is t. in cold storage SAMUEL, VISCOUNT, 3
A society . . . of individuals . . . capable of original t.
MENCKEN, H, 11
A t. is often original HOLMES, O, 2
conversation must be an exchange of t. POST, E, 1
evil is wrought by want of t. HOOD, T, 8
Learning without t. is labour lost CONFUCIUS, 5
My t. is me SARTRE, J, 6
Only a residual fraction is t. SANTAYANA, G, 1
pale cast of t. SHAKESPEARE, W, 63
Reading . . . ingenious device for avoiding t. HELPS, SIR A, 1
sessions of sweet silent t. SHAKESPEARE, W, 257
silent form, dost tease us out of t. KEATS, J, 24
something between a thing and a t. PALMER, S, 1
the best which has been t. and said in the world ARNOLD, M, 1
T. must be divided against itself HUXLEY, A, 13
t. only to justify their injustices VOLTAIRE, 6
t. without learning is perilous CONFUCIUS, 5
Two souls with but a single t. LOVELL, M, 1
will bear to be read twice, . . . was t. twice THOREAU, H, 3
**thoughtlessness** In the sex-war t. is the weapon of the male
CONNOLLY, C, 14
**thoughts** Great t. come from the heart
VAUVENARGUES, MARQUIS DE, 1
Keep off your t. from things that are past WALEY, A, 1
man whose second t. are good BARRIE, SIR J, 12
our life is what our t. make it MARCUS AURELIUS ANTONINUS, 5
sensations rather than of t. KEATS, J, 47
speech only to conceal their t. VOLTAIRE, 6
Speech . . . to disguise . . . t. TALLEYRAND, 4
Suspicions amongst t.
BACON, 1ST BARON VERULAM, VISCOUNT ST ALBANS, 53
the meanest flower . . . can give /T. WORDSWORTH, W, 28
then all his t. perish PSALMS, 89
thou understandest my t. long before PSALMS, 84
To understand God's t. NIGHTINGALE, F, 2
we ought to control our t. DARWIN, C, 2
**thousand** a t. shall fall beside thee PSALMS, 57
a t. years . . . are but as yesterday PSALMS, 55
I can draw for a t. pounds ADDISON, J, 16
I could be a good woman if I had five t. THACKERAY, W, 12
if I were a t. years old BAUDELAIRE, C, 2
one day in thy courts is better than a t. PSALMS, 51

One t. years more. That's all *Homo sapiens* has before him
WELLS, H, 20
the face that launch'd a t. ships MARLOWE, C, 2
The thought of two t. people crunching celery SHAW, G, 43
Victory has a t. fathers KENNEDY, J, 16
What's a t. dollars MARX, G, 3
thousands Why only twelve? . . . get t. GOLDWYN, S, 21
thread from eternity spinning the t. of your being
MARCUS AURELIUS ANTONINUS, 12
threads well-beloved's hair has t. of grey YEATS, W, 12
threat one can . . . see in a little girl the t. of a woman
DUMAS, FILS, 3
three Chi Wen Tzu always thought t. times before taking action
CONFUCIUS, 2
T. Estates in Parliament CARLYLE, T, 11
T. for the rivals ANONYMOUS, 45
T. French hens NURSERY RHYMES, 60
t. fundamental truths BELL, C, 3
There are only t. events in a man's life LA BRUYERE, J, 6
there are only t. things to see ROSS, H, 1
t. in the morning courage THOREAU, H, 13
T. little maids from school GILBERT, SIR W, 27
T. o'clock is always too late or too early SARTRE, J, 4
t. things . . . the public will always clamour for HOOD, T, 15
T. years she grew WORDSWORTH, W, 64
we galloped all t. BROWNING, R, 26
who sneaked into my room at t. o'clock this morning MARX, G, 14
threefold a t. cord is not quickly broken BIBLE: ECCLESIASTES, 11
three-pipe a t. problem DOYLE, SIR A, 11
threescore the days of our age are t. years and ten PSALMS, 56
three-sided if triangles invented a god, they would make him t.
MONTESQUIEU, BARON DE, 4
thrice before the cock crow, thou shalt deny me t.
BIBLE: MATTHEW, 79
thrift extravagance, . . . t. and adventure seldom go hand in hand
CHURCHILL, J, 2
thrive strong shall t. SERVICE, R, 3
throat A good listener is a good talker with a sore t.
WHITEHORN, K, 7
neither speak they through their t. PSALMS, 71
throats cutting each other's t. CARLYLE, T, 32
throne A man may build . . . a t. of bayonets INGE, W, 11
A tavern chair is the t. JOHNSON, S, 35
barge . . . like a burnished t. SHAKESPEARE, W, 8
he that sitteth on the t. shall dwell among them
BIBLE: REVELATIONS, 7
High on a t. of royal state MILTON, J, 34
It helps . . . to remind your bride that you gave up a t. for her
EDWARD VIII, 4
no middle course between the t. and the scaffold. CHARLES X, 2
royal t. of kings SHAKESPEARE, W, 237
something behind the t. PITT THE ELDER, 1ST EARL OF CHATHAM, 5
through part of it all the way t. GOLDWYN, S, 18
throve that on which it t. /Falls off TENNYSON, BARON, 74
throw t. an egg into an electric fan HERFORD, O, 1
t. away the dearest thing he ow'd SHAKESPEARE, W, 161
thrush That's the wise t. BROWNING, R, 25
Thucydides the historical works of T. COBDEN, R, 1
thumbscrew To the t. and the stake TENNYSON, BARON, 66
Thummim Urim and . . . T. BIBLE: EXODUS, 25
thunder laugh as I pass in t. SHELLEY, P, 3
our soul /Had *felt* like the t.'s roll ARNOLD, M, 24
Thurlow No man . . . so wise as T. looked FOX, C, 2
Thursday Took ill on T. NURSERY RHYMES, 53
T.'s child has far to go NURSERY RHYMES, 35
thusness What is the reason of this t. WARD, A, 2
thyself Be so true to t.
BACON, 1ST BARON VERULAM, VISCOUNT ST ALBANS, 59
Know then t., presume not God to scan POPE, A, 32
Resolve to be t. ARNOLD, M, 37
Tiber married to the only man north of the T. . . . untidier than I
am WHITEHORN, K, 2
the T. foaming with /much blood VIRGIL, 11
Tiberius Had T. been a cat ARNOLD, M, 31
tickle a feather to t. the intellect LAMB, C, 14
ticky-tacky They're all made out of t. REYNOLDS, M, 1
tide a t. in the affairs of men SHAKESPEARE, W, 122
a t. in the affairs of women BYRON, 6TH BARON, 28
ever lived in the t. of times SHAKESPEARE, W, 113
the full t. of human existence JOHNSON, S, 90
The t. is full ARNOLD, M, 8

The western t. crept up KINGSLEY, C, 5
tides the waters of the heart /Push in their t. THOMAS, D, 8
tidings good t. of great joy BIBLE: LUKE, 8
tie Never mind about my soul . . . get my t. right JOYCE, J, 9
tiger It is not the ape, nor the t. TEMPLE, W, 5
The atom bomb is a paper t. MAO TSE-TUNG, 7
T.! T.! burning bright BLAKE, W, 37
tigers Dictators ride to and fro upon t. CHURCHILL, SIR W, 24
reactionaries are paper t. MAO TSE-TUNG, 3
tightrope You may reasonably expect a man to walk a t. safely
RUSSELL, EARL, 26
tile it's not even red brick, but white t. OSBORNE, J, 4
tiller a t. of the ground BIBLE: GENESIS, 17
timber a . . . soul like season'd t. HERBERT, G, 10
Timbuctoo On the plains of T. WILBERFORCE, S, 2
time a book to kill t. MACAULAY, BARON, 6
Aging . . . the only . . . way to live a long t. AUBER, D, 2
A Good T. Was Had by All SMITH, S, 1
And t., that takes survey of all the world SHAKESPEARE, W, 81
annihilate but space and t. POPE, A, 1
Art is long, and T. is fleeting LONGFELLOW, H, 8
As if you could kill t. THOREAU, H, 6
As T. Goes By BOGART, H, 2
As t. goes by HUPFELD, H, 1
a t. to be born, and a t. to die BIBLE: ECCLESIASTES, 8
big man has no t. FITZGERALD, F, 11
But get me to the church on t.! LERNER, A, 5
But t. is too large SARTRE, J, 9
chronicle of wasted t. SHAKESPEARE, W, 263
do not squander t. FRANKLIN, B, 7
Even such is T. RALEIGH, SIR W, 3
For technological man it is t. MCLUHAN, M, 2
Had we but world enough, and t. MARVELL, A, 9
He hath shook hands with t. FORD, J, 2
his t. passeth away like a shadow PSALMS, 88
I have no t. to hurry STRAVINSKY, I, 6
I haven't got t. to be tired WILHELM I, 1
I . . . may be some t. OATES, L, 1
in a moment of t. BIBLE: LUKE, 13
inaudible and noiseless foot of T. SHAKESPEARE, W, 3
irretrievable t. is flying VIRGIL, 16
I shall lose no t. in reading it
DISRAELI, 1ST EARL OF BEACONSFIELD, 16
it's for such a long t.! MOLIERE, 1
*killing t.* /Is only . . . another of the multifarious ways SITWELL, SIR
O, 1
make the beat keep t. with short steps ANDERSEN, H, 3
Men talk of killing t. BOUCICAULT, D, 1
moment of t. ELIZABETH I, 9
My t. has not yet come NIETZSCHE, F, 7
Never before have we had so little t. ROOSEVELT, F, 13
Never the t. and the place BROWNING, R, 34
not had the t. to make it shorter PASCAL, B, 1
No t. like the present PROVERBS, 320
not of an age, but for all t. JONSON, B, 9
no t. to stand and stare DAVIES, W, 2
O aching t. KEATS, J, 15
On the breast of the river of T. ARNOLD, M, 16
peace for our t. CHAMBERLAIN, N, 3
peace in our t., O Lord BOOK OF COMMON PRAYER, 10
pluck till t. and times are done YEATS, W, 28
range of human societies in t. LEVI-STRAUSS, C, 1
Redeem thy mis-spent t. KEN, T, 2
t. and chance happeneth to them all BIBLE: ECCLESIASTES, 17
T. and the hour runs through SHAKESPEARE, W, 160
T. and tide PROVERBS, 433
t. as a tool not as a couch KENNEDY, J, 4
T. driveth onward fast TENNYSON, BARON, 50
T. drops in decay YEATS, W, 19
T. flies, death urges YOUNG, E, 7
T. for a little something MILNE, A, 7
T. hath, my lord, a wallet at his back SHAKESPEARE, W, 283
That passed the t. BECKETT, S, 2
The Bird of T. . . . little way /To fly FITZGERALD, E, 3
the long result of T. TENNYSON, BARON, 45
the original good t. that was had by all DAVIS, B, 2
There is a t. and place PROVERBS, 407
'The t. has come,' the Walrus said CARROLL, L, 25
the t. of my departure is at hand BIBLE: II TIMOTHY, 3
the t. will come when you will hear me
DISRAELI, 1ST EARL OF BEACONSFIELD, 17

| | |
|---|---|
| sunset t. | BROWNING, R. 7 |
| t. me not | BIBLE: JOHN, 54 |
| t. of a vanish'd hand | TENNYSON, BARON, 1 |
| Wound with a t. | MONTAGU, M. 1 |
| **tourist** the most vulgar, . . . is the British t. | KILVERT, F. 1 |
| **tourists** t. . . . take in the Monarchy . . . with . . . the pigeons | |
| | HAMILTON, W. 1 |
| **toves** slithy t. did gyre | CARROLL, L. 20 |
| **towels** never darken my t. again | MARX, G. 8 |
| **tower** Childe Roland to the Dark T. | BROWNING, R. 15 |
| **towering** the height of his own t. style | CHESTERTON, G. 35 |
| **towers** The cloud-capp'd t. | SHAKESPEARE, W. 277 |
| **town** axis of the earth sticks out visibly through . . . every t. | |
| | HOLMES, O. 4 |
| man made the t. | COWPER, W. 20 |
| **toy** but a childish t. | MARLOWE, C. 9 |
| **trade** Every man to his t. | PROVERBS, 140 |
| God will pardon me. It is His t. | HEINE, H. 5 |
| half a t. and half an art | INGE, W. 8 |
| It is not your t. to make tables | JOHNSON, S. 56 |
| man must serve his time to every t. | BYRON, 6TH BARON, 35 |
| no nation was ever ruined by t. | FRANKLIN, B. 2 |
| Two of a t. can ne'er agree | GAY, J. 6 |
| **trades** The ugliest of t. have their moments of pleasure | |
| | JERROLD, D. 6 |
| **trading** t. on the blood of my men | LEE, R. 2 |
| **tradition** It's t. We don't want t. | FORD, H. 1 |
| **traffic** the t. of Jacob's ladder | THOMPSON, F. 2 |
| **tragedie** go litel myn t. | CHAUCER, G. 19 |
| T. is to seyn a certeyn storie | CHAUCER, G. 13 |
| **tragedies** t. are finish'd by a death | BYRON, 6TH BARON, 19 |
| There are two t. in life | SHAW, G. 22 |
| **tragedy** a t. and therefore not worth reading | AUSTEN, J. 8 |
| brooding t. and its dark shadows can be lightened | GANDHI, I. 4 |
| farce brutalized becomes t. | CRAIG, SIR G. 4 |
| great t. of Science | HUXLEY, T. 1 |
| That is their t. | WILDE, O. 18 |
| The greatest t. . . . except a defeat | WELLINGTON, DUKE OF. 11 |
| the wine was a farce and the food a t. | POWELL, A. 2 |
| T. is if I cut my finger | BROOKS, M. 2 |
| We participate in a t. | HUXLEY, A. 11 |
| what t. means | STOPPARD, T. 9 |
| world is . . . a t. to those who feel | |
| | WALPOLE, 4TH EARL OF ORFORD, 6 |
| You *may* abuse a t. | JOHNSON, S. 56 |
| You're a bloody t. | MAXTON, J. 1 |
| **tragically** Everything must be taken seriously, nothing t. | |
| | THIERS, L. 2 |
| **train** man who shaves and takes a t. | WHITE, E. 1 |
| The only way . . . of catching a t. | CHESTERTON, G. 44 |
| **trained** Science is nothing but t. and organized common sense | |
| | HUXLEY, T. 2 |
| **trains** t. all night groan on the rail | HOUSMAN, A. 6 |
| **tramp** He began to think the t. a fine . . . fellow | WELLS, H. 4 |
| the Lady Is a T. | HART, L. 2 |
| the t. of the twenty-two men | BOWEN, E. 2 |
| **trampling** He is t. out the vintage where the grapes of wrath | |
| | HOWE, J. 1 |
| **tranquillity** Sorrow is t. remembered in emotion | PARKER, D. 8 |
| **transform** t. this society without . . . extension of public ownership | |
| | KINNOCK, N. 1 |
| **transformation** The universe is t. | MARCUS AURELIUS ANTONINUS, 5 |
| **transit** Sic t. *gloria mundi* | KEMPIS, T. 1 |
| **transition** I expect no very violent t. | SEDGWICK, C. 1 |
| **transitory** the titles of wife and mother . . . are t. and accidental | |
| | LIVERMORE, M. 2 |
| **translation** original is unfaithful to the t. | BORGES, J. 3 |
| Poetry is what gets lost in t. | FROST, R. 11 |
| **translations** T. (like wives) are seldom faithful | CAMPBELL, R. 2 |
| **transplanted** Many ideas grow better when t. into another mind | |
| | HOLMES, O. JR., 2 |
| **trapeze** daring young man on the flying t. | LEYBOURNE, G. 1 |
| **trappings** the t. and the suits of woe | SHAKESPEARE, W. 41 |
| **trash** Who steals my purse steals t. | SHAKESPEARE, W. 223 |
| **travel** T. broadens the mind | PROVERBS, 441 |
| t. for t.'s sake | STEVENSON, R. 5 |
| T., in the younger sort | |
| | BACON, 1ST BARON VERULAM, VISCOUNT ST ALBANS, 54 |
| T. is the most private of pleasures | SACKVILLE-WEST, V. 3 |
| T. light | JUVENAL, 9 |
| To t. hopefully is . . . better . . . than to arrive | STEVENSON, R. 24 |

| | |
|---|---|
| wherever the wind takes me I t. as a visitor | HORACE, 13 |
| **travelled** I t. among unknown men | WORDSWORTH, W. 4 |
| **traveller** a t. from an antique land | SHELLEY, P. 14 |
| from whose bourn no t. returns | SHAKESPEARE, W. 62 |
| **travelling** The grand object of t. | JOHNSON, S. 107 |
| T. is . . . like talking with men of other centuries | DESCARTES, R. 3 |
| **travels** A man t. the world over | MOORE, G. 1 |
| He t. fastest | PROVERBS, 196 |
| too old to go again to my t. | CHARLES II, 1 |
| **treachery** Political renegades always start their career of t. | |
| | KINNOCK, N. 10 |
| **tread** fools rush in where angels fear to t. | POPE, A. 27 |
| frightful fiend . . . behind him t. | COLERIDGE, S. 34 |
| Where'er you t. | POPE, A. 45 |
| **treason** If *this* be t., make the most of it | HENRY, P. 1 |
| T. doth never prosper | HARINGTON, SIR J. 1 |
| T. was no Crime | DRYDEN, J. 9 |
| **treasure** Preserve it as your chiefest t. | BELLOC, H. 1 |
| purest t. mortal times afford | SHAKESPEARE, W. 234 |
| **treasures** greater riches than the t. in Egypt | BIBLE: HEBREWS, 9 |
| lay not up . . . t. upon earth | BIBLE: MATTHEW, 19 |
| **Treasury** the Vatican, the T. and the miners | |
| | BALDWIN, 1ST EARL BALDWIN OF BEWDLEY, 9 |
| **treated** Actors should be t. like cattle | HITCHCOCK, SIR A. 1 |
| **treaties** T. are like roses and young girls | DE GAULLE, C. 9 |
| **treaty** hand that signed the t. bred a fever | THOMAS, D. 5 |
| **tree** A billboard lovely as a t. | NASH, O. 10 |
| A poem lovely as a t. | KILMER, A. 1 |
| as the twig is bent, the t.'s inclined | POPE, A. 38 |
| If poetry comes not . . . as leaves to a t. | KEATS, J. 52 |
| if the t. fall . . . there it shall be | BIBLE: ECCLESIASTES, 24 |
| I shall be like that t. | SWIFT, J. 18 |
| like a t. planted by the water-side | PSALMS, 1 |
| only God can make a t. | KILMER, A. 2 |
| Rock-a-bye baby on the t. top | BLAKE, C. 1 |
| same t. that a wise man sees | BLAKE, W. 25 |
| spare the beechen t. | CAMPBELL, T. 1 |
| The difference between a gun and a t. | POUND, E. 8 |
| the fruit /Of that forbidden t. | MILTON, J. 25 |
| The t. of liberty must be refreshed | JEFFERSON, T. 5 |
| the t. of life | BIBLE: GENESIS, 8 |
| the t. of the knowledge of good and evil | BIBLE: GENESIS, 8 |
| t. of life is green | GOETHE, J. 2 |
| **treen** In old time we had t. chalices and golden priests, | JEWEL, J. 1 |
| **trees** Loveliest of t., the cherry | HOUSMAN, A. 5 |
| the t. . . . said . . . make war against the sea | BIBLE: II ESDRAS, 4 |
| **Trelawny** shall T. die | HAWKER, R. 1 |
| **tremble** t. like a guilty thing surprised | WORDSWORTH, W. 29 |
| **trembled** And t. with fear at your frown | ENGLISH, T. 1 |
| **trembles** And Satan t. | COWPER, W. 13 |
| **trenches** digging t. and trying on gas-masks | CHAMBERLAIN, N, 2 |
| **trial** T. by jury . . . a delusion | DENMAN, BARON, 1 |
| **triangles** if t. invented a god, they would make him three-sided | |
| | MONTESQUIEU, BARON DE, 4 |
| **tribe** Abou Ben Adhem (may his t. increase!) | HUNT, L. 1 |
| Mankind is not a t. | CHESTERTON, G. 37 |
| Richer than all his t. | SHAKESPEARE, W. 229 |
| **tribute** the vain t. of a smile | SCOTT, SIR W. 4 |
| **trick** When in doubt, win the t. | HOYLE, E. 1 |
| **trifle** Is t. sufficient for sweet | BETJEMAN, SIR J. 4 |
| **trifles** observance of t. | DOYLE, SIR A. 2 |
| snapper-up of unconsidered t. | SHAKESPEARE, W. 303 |
| **trigger** Whose Finger do you want on the T. | ANONYMOUS, 108 |
| **Trinity** I the T. illustrate | BROWNING, R. 51 |
| **Triton** Old T. blow his wreathed horn | WORDSWORTH, W. 60 |
| **triumph** One more devils'-t. and sorrow for angels | BROWNING, R. 30 |
| We t. without glory | CORNEILLE, P. 2 |
| **triumphed** So I t. ere my passion | TENNYSON, BARON, 48 |
| **trivial** mighty contests rise from t. things | POPE, A. 46 |
| The t. round, the common task, | KEBLE, J. 1 |
| **triviality** you're deluded by t. | IONESCO, E. 1 |
| **Trojan** T. 'orses will jump out | BEVIN, E. 1 |
| **Trojans** Do not trust the horse, T. | VIRGIL, 6 |
| **troops** t. of unrecording friends | TENNYSON, BARON, 59 |
| **trot** I don't t. it out and about | COLETTE, S. 3 |
| **trouble** a lot of t. in his life | CHURCHILL, SIR W. 22 |
| A t. shared | PROVERBS, 70 |
| a woman is on a . . . hunt for t. | DIX, D. 3 |
| it saves me the t. of liking them | AUSTEN, J. 27 |
| man . . . is . . . full of t. | BIBLE: JOB, 9 |
| Our progress . . . /Is t. and care | LONGFELLOW, H. 12 |

Prostitution . . . keeps her out of t.      HELLER, J, 7
telling one's t. does not make it better      PAVESE, C, 1
their soul melteth away because of the t.      PSALMS, 66
**troubled** let not your heart be t.      BIBLE: JOHN, 34
**troubles** Don't meet t. half-way      PROVERBS, 118
I have had t. enough      BROWNING, R, 36
pack up your t. in your old kit-bag      ASAF, G, 1
take arms against a sea of t.      SHAKESPEARE, W, 61
**troublesome** t. . . . bondage of Rhyming      MILTON, J, 24
**trousers** bottoms of my t. rolled      ELIOT, T, 12
I shall wear white flannel t.      ELIOT, T, 13
man should never put on his best t.      IBSEN, H, 4
**trout** as when you find a t. in the milk.      THOREAU, H, 4
**trowel** laid on with a t.      SHAKESPEARE, W, 18
lays it on with a t.      CONGREVE, W, 1
**Troy** from the shores /of T. came destined an exile      VIRGIL, 2
Now there are fields where T. once was      OVID, 3
**true** a great advantage for . . . philosophy to be . . . t.      SANTAYANA, G, 11
All one's inventions are t.      FLAUBERT, G, 1
A thing is not necessarily t.      WILDE, O, 62
because a novel's invented, it isn't t.      POWELL, A, 7
Be so t. to thyself      BACON, 1ST BARON VERULAM, VISCOUNT ST ALBANS, 59
be yourself, imperial, plain and t.      BROWNING, R, 5
false to his friends . . . t. to the public      BERKELEY, BISHOP, 1
Geometry is not t.      PIRSIG, R, 2
He said t. things      BROWNING, R, 11
if they keep on saying it . . . it will be t.      BENNETT, A, 6
I said the honorable member was a liar it is t.      SHERIDAN, R, 19
it's . . . more important for a theory to be shapely, than . . . t.      HAMPTON, C, 1
Journalists say a thing that they know isn't t.      BENNETT, A, 6
Many a t. word      PROVERBS, 282
No man worth having is t. to his wife      VANBURGH, SIR J, 6
One religion is as t. as another      BURTON, R, 5
Small service is t. service      WORDSWORTH, W, 67
T. and False are attributes of speech, not of things      HOBBES, T, 2
them which are t. of heart      PSALMS, 4
The religions we call false were once t.      EMERSON, R, 4
T. love never grows old      PROVERBS, 442
to thine own self be t.      SHAKESPEARE, W, 48
truism is . . . none the less t.      SAMUEL, VISCOUNT, 2
t. to you, darlin', in my fashion      PORTER, C, 8
whatsoever things are t.      BIBLE: PHILIPPIANS, 4
**truffles** a swine to show you where the t. are      ALBEE, E, 2
**truism** A t. is on that account none the less true      SAMUEL, VISCOUNT, 2
**truly** A t. great man      PROVERBS, 71
**trumpet** the t. shall sound      BIBLE: 1 CORINTHIANS, 23
**trunkless** Two vast and t. legs of stone      SHELLEY, P, 14
**trust** I don't t. him. We're friends      BRECHT, B, 5
in thee, O Lord, have I put my t.      PSALMS, 20
my t. shall be under the covering of thy wings      PSALMS, 41
Never t. a husband too far      ROWLAND, H, 4
never t. a woman      WILDE, O, 56
Never t. the man who . . . hath injured you      FIELDING, H, 7
put not your t. in princes      PSALMS, 89
some put their t. in chariots      PSALMS, 11
the one God whose worshippers . . . still t. in Him      BRADLEY, F, 2
the right of governing was not property but a t.      FOX, C, 1
t. ye not in a friend      BIBLE: MICAH, 1
Where large sums of money are concerned, . . . t. nobody      CHRISTIE, DAME A, 2
**trusted** familiar friend, whom I t.      PSALMS, 29
**trustful** for a long while for a . . . t. person to reconcile himself to . . . God      MENCKEN, H, 10
**trusting** it never extended to t. him      BULLOCK, BARON, 2
**truth** And seek for t. in the groves of Academe.      HORACE, 24
any t. but from a clear perception      KEATS, J, 58
A platitude is simply a t. repeated      BALDWIN, 1ST EARL BALDWINNBOF BEWDLEY, 10
Appearances are not . . . a clue to the t.      COMPTON-BURNETT, DAME I, 1
a short armistice with t.      BYRON, 6TH BARON, 22
A t. that's told with bad intent      BLAKE, W, 4
a t. universally acknowledged      AUSTEN, J, 15
Beauty is t.; t. beauty      KEATS, J, 25
before the t. has got its boots on      CALLAGHAN, SIR J, 1
cheated into passion, but . . . reasoned into t.      DRYDEN, J, 28
cinema is t. twenty-four times a second      GODARD, J, 1

Cynicism is an unpleasant way of saying the t.      HELLMAN, L, 1
dearer still is t.      ARISTOTLE, 10
economical with the t.      ARMSTRONG, SIR R, 1
Every man has a right to utter what he thinks t.      JOHNSON, S, 128
few enthusiasts . . . speak the t.      BALFOUR, 1ST EARL OF, 4
for thy t.'s sake      PSALMS, 95
He believes, . . . that there is such a thing as t.      BAGEHOT, W, 10
his faithfulness and t. shall be thy shield and buckler      PSALMS, 57
I am the way, the t., and the life      BIBLE: JOHN, 32
if the people . . . can be reached with the t.      ROOSEVELT, E, 2
If you do not tell the t. about yourself      WOOLF, V, 7
in the end the t. will conquer      WYCLIFFE, J, 1
it cannot compel anyone to tell the t.      DARLING, BARON, 5
It takes two to speak the t.      THOREAU, H, 17
Let us begin by committing ourselves to the t.      NIXON, R, 4
loving Christianity better than T.      COLERIDGE, S, 1
mainly he told the t.      TWAIN, M, 1
mercy and t. are met together      PSALMS, 52
Much t. is spoken, . . . more . . . concealed.      DARLING, BARON, 3
My way of joking is to tell the t.      SHAW, G, 11
Nobody speaks the t. when      BOWEN, E, 3
No poet ever interpreted nature . . . as a lawyer interprets t.      GIRAUDOUX, J, 2
not even Marx is more precious . . . than the t.      WEIL, S, 3
Now I may wither into the t.      YEATS, W, 5
Perjury . . . is t. that is shamefaced      DARLING, BARON, 4
Photography is t.      GODARD, J, 1
polite by telling the t.      BRADBURY, M, 6
Pride and T. . . . shake their . . . sides at youth      YEATS, W, 22
put him in possession of t.      LOCKE, J, 2
Some men have t. so much      BUTLER, S, 18
speaking nothing but the t.      WILDE, O, 33
T. be veiled      SHELLEY, P, 6
T. comes out in wine      PLINY THE ELDER, 4
T. fears no trial      PROVERBS, 443
the laws of poetic t. and poetic beauty      ARNOLD, M, 13
the Spirit of t.      BIBLE: JOHN, 30
the t. is not in us      BIBLE: 1 JOHN, 1
the t. of imagination      KEATS, J, 46
the t. shall make you free      BIBLE: JOHN, 22
the unclouded face of t. suffer wrong      SCOTT, C, 1
The worst enemy of t. and freedom      IBSEN, H, 3
those who live . . . believe . . . to be the t.      HAMPTON, C, 2
t. in the inward parts      PSALMS, 35
t. is always strange      BYRON, 6TH BARON, 32
T. is on the march      ZOLA, E, 3
T. is stranger      PROVERBS, 444
T., like a torch      HAMILTON, SIR W, 1
to the dead we owe only t.      VOLTAIRE, 19
t. shall flourish out of the earth      PSALMS, 52
T.; Sir, is a cow      JOHNSON, S, 62
T. sits upon the lips of dying men      ARNOLD, M, 39
t. that makes men free      AGAR, H, 1
T. will out      PROVERBS, 445
Two half-truths do not make a t.      KOESTLER, A, 3
whatever remains, however improbable, must be the t.      DOYLE, SIR A, 1
What is t.      BACON, 1ST BARON VERULAM, VISCOUNT ST ALBANS, 56
what is t.      BIBLE: JOHN, 44
When t. is discovered by someone else      SOLZHENITSYN, A, 3
whilst the great ocean of t. lay all undiscovered before me      NEWTON, SIR I, 2
who ever knew T. put to the worse      MILTON, J, 3
You can only find t. with logic      CHESTERTON, G, 24
**truths** All great t. begin as blasphemies      SHAW, G, 2
all t. are half-t.      WHITEHEAD, A, 1
commonplaces are the great poetic t.      STEVENSON, R, 25
He was a man of two t.      MURDOCH, DAME I, 4
new t. . . . begin as heresies      HUXLEY, T, 3
t. being in and out of favour      FROST, R, 1
There are no new t.      MCCARTHY, M, 2
those three fundamental t.      BELL, C, 3
We hold these t. to be sacred and undeniable      JEFFERSON, T, 2
**try** t. everything once      BAX, SIR A, 1
T., t. again      HICKSON, W, 1
**trying** I am t. to be, and you can't help it      BIRKENHEAD, EARL OF, 2
**tu** Et t., Brute      CAESAR, J, 5
Et t., Brute      SHAKESPEARE, W, 110
**tub** Rub-a-dub-dub, /Three men in a t.      NURSERY RHYMES, 49
**tubby** a t. little chap      WODEHOUSE, SIR P, 16
**Tuesday** Christened on T.      NURSERY RHYMES, 53

## U

a good u. have all they that do thereafter PSALMS, 69
a man of u. BIBLE: PROVERBS, 1
man being in honour hath no u. PSALMS, 33
Most men . . . give evidence against their own u.
HALIFAX, MARQUIS OF, 8
piece of cod passes all u. LUTYENS, SIR E, 2
the peace of God, which passeth all u. BIBLE: PHILIPPIANS, 3
u. will . . . extinguish pleasure HOUSMAN, A, 4
We need more u. of human nature JUNG, C, 11
**understood** Only one man ever u. me HEGEL, G, 2
**undertakers** I have nothing against u. personally MITFORD, J, 1
**undertaking** The love of life is necessary to . . . any u.
JOHNSON, S, 22
**under water** if I were u. I would scarcely kick KEATS, J, 55
**undiscovered** whilst the great ocean of truth lay all u. before me
NEWTON, SIR I, 2
**undone** estate o' th' world were now u. SHAKESPEARE, W, 178
left u. those things BOOK OF COMMON PRAYER, 4
Things hitherto u. should be given . . . a wide berth
BEERBOHM, SIR M, 6
**uneasy** U. lies the head that wears a crown SHAKESPEARE, W, 88
**uneatable** the unspeakable in full pursuit of the u. WILDE, O, 55
**uneducated** Democracy . . . government by the u.
CHESTERTON, G, 40
**unendurable** A society . . . of individuals . . . capable of original
thought would probably be u. MENCKEN, H, 11
**unequal** Men are made by nature u. FROUDE, J, 2
**unexamined** The u. life SOCRATES, 2
**unexpected** Old age is the most u. of all . . . things TROTSKY, L, 2
**unfaithful** original is u. to the translation BORGES, J, 3
**unfortunates** one of those u. to whom death is LEWIS, D, 1
**ungain'd** Men prize the thing u. more SHAKESPEARE, W, 280
**ungodliness** the tents of u. PSALMS, 51
**ungodly** the u. . . . privily shoot at them which are true of heart
PSALMS, 4
the way of the u., he turneth it upside down PSALMS, 90
**unhappily** The bad end u. STOPPARD, T, 9
**unhappy** A moment of time may make us u. for ever GAY, J, 1
don't believe one can ever be u. for long WAUGH, E, 8
each u. family is u. in its own way TOLSTOY, COUNT, 1
It is better that some should be u. JOHNSON, S, 106
making their remaining years u. LA BRUYERE, J, 2
most u. kind of misfortune BOETHIUS, A, 1
one is u. one becomes moral PROUST, M, 5
the instinct for being u. SAKI, 8
Today you're u.? . . . Go shopping MILLER, A, 3
U. the land that has no heroes BRECHT, B, 2
**unheralded** spring now comes u. by the return of the birds
CARSON, R, 3
**unicorn** The lion and the u. NURSERY RHYMES, 55
**uniform** love that loves a scarlet coat /Should be more u.
HOOD, T, 4
The u. 'e wore KIPLING, R, 11
**uniformity** let use be preferred before u.
BACON, 1ST BARON VERULAM, VISCOUNT ST ALBANS, 15
**uninstructed** making things plain to u. people was . . . best means
of clearing . . . one's own mind HUXLEY, T, 7
**uninteresting** no . . . u. subject CHESTERTON, G, 14
**union** To make a u. with Great Britain PETAIN, H, 1
U. is strength PROVERBS, 448
**unite** Workers of the world, u. MARX, K, 2
**united** States of Europe CHURCHILL, SIR W, 58
U. we stand PROVERBS, 449
**United States** In the U. there is more space STEIN, G, 2
so near to the U. DIAZ, P, 1
The best immediate defence of the U. ROOSEVELT, F, 5
The U., . . . are twenty years in advance of this country
HOBSON, SIR H, 1
The U. has to move very fast KENNEDY, J, 5
The U. is like a gigantic boiler GREY, VISCOUNT , 1
The U. . . . six hours behind . . . HOBSON, SIR H, 1
**universal** Aunt Edna is u. RATTIGAN, SIR T, 1
There is no u. law LAWRENCE, D, 31
**universe** chess-board is the world; the pieces . . . the phenomena
of the u. HUXLEY, T, 6
He would take his attention away from the u. CRISP, Q, 10
I accept the u. CARLYLE, T, 33
I don't pretend to understand the U. CARLYLE, T, 31
Life exists in the u. JEANS, SIR J, 1
no hint throughout the u. /Of good or ill THOMSON, J, 3
Perish the U. CYRANO DE BERGERAC, S, 1

the better ordering of the u. ALFONSO, 1
the u. and all that surrounds it COOK, P, 1
the u. is expanding and contracting DE VRIES, P, 5
The u. is not hostile HOLMES, J, 1
the u. is . . . queerer than we *can* suppose HALDANE, J, 4
The u. is transformation MARCUS AURELIUS ANTONINUS, 5
The u. ought to be presumed too vast PEIRCE, C, 1
The visible u. was an illusion BORGES, J, 2
**universities** mortifying fate of most English u. LODGE, D, 2
The King, observing . . . the state of both his u. TRAPP, J, 1
U. incline wits to sophistry and affectation.
BACON, 1ST BARON VERULAM, VISCOUNT ST ALBANS, 65
**university** Any attempt to reform the u. ILLICH, I, 1
it is necessary to go to a u.'. . . to become a successful writer
BRITTAIN, V, 2
u., where it was carefully taken out PEACOCK, T, 8
**unjust** he that is u., let him be u. still BIBLE: REVELATIONS, 22
The u. steals the just's umbrella BOWEN, BARON, 1
**unkind** Thou art not so u. SHAKESPEARE, W, 25
**unkindness** I tax not you, you elements, with u.
SHAKESPEARE, W, 138
**unknown** apart from the known and the u. PINTER, H, 2
Give me a light that I may tread safely into the u. HASKINS, M, 1
I travelled among u. men WORDSWORTH, W, 4
Many brave men . . . before Agamemnon's time; . . . are
all, unmourned and u., . . . because they lack their sacred poet.
HORACE, 42
the U. Prime Minister ASQUITH, 1ST EARL OF OXFORD AND ASQUITH, 2
To go into the u. THOMAS, E, 3
to the u. god BIBLE: ACTS, 12
**unlabelled** One of the unpardonable sins, . . . , is . . . to go about
u. HUXLEY, T, 4
**unlike** the Jews bring the u. into the heart of *every milieu*
ZANGWILL, I, 3
The law of dislike for the u. ZANGWILL, I, 3
**unluckily** the good u. STOPPARD, T, 9
**unmarried** to keep u. SHAW, G, 21
**unmotivated** The u. action GIDE, A, 1
**unmuzzled** The world regards such a person as . . . an u. dog
HUXLEY, T, 4
**unnatural** so u. as the commonplace DOYLE, SIR A, 5
**unobtrusive** Poetry should be great and u. KEATS, J, 51
**unpaid** A promise made is a debt u. SERVICE, R, 1
**unpardonable** One of the u. sins, . . . , is . . . to go about
unlabelled HUXLEY, T, 4
**unperfect** He was u., unfinished, inartistic JAMES, H, 1
**unpleasant** Cynicism is an u. way of saying the truth
HELLMAN, L, 1
without mentioning a single book, or *in fact anything u.* REED, H, 6
**unpopular** a free society . . . where it is safe to be u.
STEVENSON, A, 6
**unprofitable** How weary, stale, flat, and u. SHAKESPEARE, W, 42
**unrecording** troops of u. friends TENNYSON, BARON, 73
**unremembered** u. acts /Of kindness and of love WORDSWORTH, W, 7
**unremitting** That u. humanity BENNETT, A, 5
**unrequited** Self-love seems so often u. POWELL, A, 1
**unsaid** The bitterest tears . . . are for words . . . u. and deeds . . .
undone STOWE, H, 1
**unsatisfied** It is exquisite, and it leaves one u. WILDE, O, 48
**unsavoury** indefatigable and u. engine of pollution SPARROW, J, 1
**unsealed** my lips are not yet u.
BALDWIN, 1ST EARL BALDWIN OF BEWDLEY, 6
**unseemly** an u. exposure of the mind, HAZLITT, W, 16
**unseen** to deny the existence of an u. kingdom is bad BUTLER, S, 3
We keep passing u. PIRSIG, R, 4
**unshriven** I am curious to see what happens . . . to one who dies
u. PERUGINO, P, 1
**unsoundness** no person can be a poet . . . without . . . u. of mind
MACAULAY, BARON, 14
no person can . . . enjoy poetry, without . . . u. of mind
MACAULAY, BARON, 14
**unspeakable** the psychopathologist the u. MAUGHAM, W, 8
the u. in full pursuit of the uneatable WILDE, O, 55
**unstoned** I wouldn't have left a turn u. WIMPERIS, A, 1
**untidier** married to the only man north of the Tiber . . . u. than I
am WHITEHORN, K, 2
**untravelled** Gleams that u. world TENNYSON, BARON, 76
**untruth** The camera . . . an accessory to u. EVANS, H, 1
**unupblown** Nurse u. WAUGH, E, 48
**unused** left over from last year u. HARRIS, G, 1
**unwashed** The great U. BROUGHAM, BARON, 1

unwholesome Boys . . . are u. companions for grown people
  LAMB, C, 7
up I saw it at a disadvantage – the curtain was u. WINCHELL, W, 1
  u. with which I will not put CHURCHILL, SIR W, 30
upbringing the u. a nun would envy ORTON, J, 1
upper Like many of the u. class /He liked the sound of broken
  glass BELLOC, H, 12
  the person that . . . has the u. hand will inevitably give place to
  another MAUGHAM, W, 24
  the u. classes /Have still the u. hand COWARD, SIR N, 12
upper-middle class Shirley Williams . . . a member of the u.
  WEST, DAME R, 6
upright man of life u. CAMPION, T, 3
up-rising thou knowest . . . mine u. PSALMS, 84
upside the way of the ungodly, he turneth it u. down PSALMS, 90
upstairs U. and downstairs /And in my lady's chamber
  NURSERY RHYMES, 13
Uriah U., . . . made a ghastly writhe DICKENS, C, 13
Urim U. and . . . Thummim BIBLE: EXODUS, 25
urn Can storied u. . . . /Back to its mansion call the fleeting breath
  GRAY, T, 4
usage if u. so choose, with whom resides the decision HORACE, 4
use I see no reason to suppose that these machines will ever
  force themselves into general u. WELLINGTON, DUKE OF, 7
  let u. be preferred before uniformity
  BACON, 1ST BARON VERULAM, VISCOUNT ST ALBANS, 15
  what is the u. of a book CARROLL, L, 1
  What is the u. of a new-born child FRANKLIN, B, 9
useful not merely . . . u. and ornamental STRACHEY, L, 2
  the most u. thing about a principle . . . sacrificed to expediency
  MAUGHAM, W, 4
useless All Art is quite u. WILDE, O, 42
  A u. life is an early death GOETHE, J, 5
  most beautiful things . . . are the most u. RUSKIN, J, 9
uses all the u. of this world SHAKESPEARE, W, 42
usual Business as u. CHURCHILL, SIR W, 35
Utopia Not in U., . . . – /Or some secreted island
  WORDSWORTH, W, 37
U-turn U. if you want to THATCHER, M, 6

# V

vacant In v. or in pensive mood WORDSWORTH, W, 6
vacation a change of nuisances is as good as a v.
  LLOYD GEORGE, EARL OF DWYFOR, 12
vacuum A v. can only exist . . . by the things which enclose it
  FITZGERALD, Z, 3
  Nature abhors a v. SPINOZA, B, 1
vadis quo v. BIBLE: JOHN, 39
vagabond a fugitive and a v. BIBLE: GENESIS, 19
vaguery For V. in the Field OSBORNE, J, 3
vain The soul hath not her generous aspirings implanted in her in
  v. LAMB, C, 24
  thou shalt not take the name of . . . God in v. BIBLE: EXODUS, 20
  V. are the thousand creeds BRONTE, E, 2
  v. babblings BIBLE: 1 TIMOTHY, 8
  V. wisdom all, and false philosophy MILTON, J, 36
vales the cup of the v. THOMAS, D, 22
valet No man is a hero to his v. CORNUEL, A, 1
valiant all the Brothers were v. NEWCASTLE, DUCHESS OF, 1
  v. never taste of death but once SHAKESPEARE, W, 109
valid If . . . 'feeling good' could decide, drunkenness would be . . .
  supremely v. JAMES, W, 2
valley One sees great things from the v. CHESTERTON, G, 12
  the v. of the shadow of death PSALMS, 12
valleys Piping down the v. wild BLAKE, W, 39
valour The better part of v. is discretion SHAKESPEARE, W, 82
  thou mighty man of v. BIBLE: JUDGES, 4
valuable riches to be a v. thing SWIFT, J, 19
value Friendship . . . has no survival v. LEWIS, C, 1
  the price of everything and the v. of nothing WILDE, O, 40
values ideas are of more importance than v. BRENAN, G, 2
  Victorian v. . . . were the v. when our country THATCHER, M, 10
Vanbrugh Dead Sir John V.'s house of clay EVANS, A, 1
Van Gogh V.'s ear for music WILDER, B, 3
vanished as rare things will, it v. BROWNING, R, 37
vanity all is v. and vexation of spirit BIBLE: ECCLESIASTES, 4
  The v. of human life is like a river POPE, A, 56
  v. and love . . . universal characteristics
  CHESTERFIELD, 4TH EARL OF, 12
  V. dies hard STEVENSON, R, 3

v. of vanities BIBLE: ECCLESIASTES, 1
V. of vanities THACKERAY, W, 8
Vanity Fair name of V. F. BUNYAN, J, 5
vanquished redress of the grievances of the v. CHURCHILL, SIR W, 4
variable light-headed, v. men STEVENSON, R, 21
varies quality of moral behaviour v. HUXLEY, A, 18
variety a sad v. of woe POPE, A, 6
  custom stale her infinite v. SHAKESPEARE, W, 9
  V.'s the very spice of life COWPER, W, 22
various man so v., that he seem'd to be DRYDEN, J, 7
vary money appears to v. HUXLEY, SIR J, 1
vast The universe ought to be presumed too v. PEIRCE, C, 1
Vatican One of the best warehouses I ever see was the V.
  WESKER, A, 2
  the V., the Treasury and the miners
  BALDWIN, 1ST EARL BALDWIN OF BEWDLEY, 9
vaulting Fan v. . . . belongs to the 'Last-supper-carved-on-a-peach-
  stone' LANCASTER, O, 1
veal I could eat one of Bellamy's v. pies PITT THE YOUNGER, W, 3
vegetable animal or v. or mineral CARROLL, L, 32
vegetarianism useless for the sheep to pass resolutions in favour
  of v. INGE, W, 6
Vegetarians V. have wicked, shifty eyes MORTON, J, 3
vegetate When I am in the country I wish to v. HAZLITT, W, 19
veil Death is the v. SHELLEY, P, 20
  the painted v. which those who live /Call life SHELLEY, P, 10
  the v. of the temple was rent in twain BIBLE: MATTHEW, 87
veils v. of the morning YEATS, W, 16
Velasquez Why drag in V.? WHISTLER, J, 7
venerability If you live long enough, the v. factor creeps in
  STONE, I, 1
vengeance No one delights more in v. than a woman. JUVENAL, 11
venial than that one soul . . . should commit one single v. sin
  NEWMAN, CARDINAL, 4
Venice V. is like eating . . . chocolate liqueurs CAPOTE, T, 1
  V., the eldest Child of Liberty WORDSWORTH, W, 54
venite v., exultemus PSALMS, 61
ventured Nothing v. PROVERBS, 319
Venus She is V. when she smiles JONSON, B, 11
verb a v. meaning 'to believe falsely' WITTGENSTEIN, L, 7
verbal v. contract isn't worth the paper GOLDWYN, S, 15
verbose Revolutions are always v. TROTSKY, L, 5
verbosity inebriated with . . . his own v.
  DISRAELI, 1ST EARL OF BEACONSFIELD, 29
Verdi strains of V. will come back to you tonight MARX, G, 18
verdict Sentence first – v. afterwards CARROLL, L, 18
verification bring about the v. of his own prophecies
  TROLLOPE, A, 12
verify Always v. your references ROUTH, M, 1
veritas In vino v. PLINY THE ELDER, 4
vermin lower than v. BEVAN, A, 9
vernal One impulse from a v. wood WORDSWORTH, W, 63
Versailles a lady at the court of V. VOLTAIRE, 27
verse Curst be the v. POPE, A, 13
  If Galileo had said in v. that the world moved HARDY, T, 10
  no v. can give pleasure for long, nor last, that is written by
  drinkers of water HORACE, 23
  Writing free v. FROST, R, 9
verses V. . . . as a literary performance WHITMAN, W, 1
versified excellent poets that have never v. SIDNEY, SIR P, 2
versifiers now swarm many v. SIDNEY, SIR P, 2
vertical The v. man AUDEN, W, 10
vessel a chosen v. BIBLE: ACTS, 8
  the weaker v. BIBLE: 1 PETER, 4
vestry I will see you in the v. after service SMITH, S, 8
vex they die to v. me MELBOURNE, VISCOUNT, 7
  with no deep researches v. the brain CRABBE, G, 3
vexation all is vanity and v. of spirit BIBLE: ECCLESIASTES, 4
viable I'm v. from ten o'clock till five BETJEMAN, SIR J, 2
vice extremism in the defence of liberty is no v. GOLDWATER, B, 2
  Hypocrisy is the most . . . nerve-racking v. MAUGHAM, W, 2
  Is Pride, the never-failing v. of fools POPE, A, 20
  no v. but beggary SHAKESPEARE, W, 125
  Prosperity doth best discover v.
  BACON, 1ST BARON VERULAM, VISCOUNT ST ALBANS, 8
  Public schools are the nurseries of all v. FIELDING, H, 10
  quotation is a national v. WAUGH, E, 27
  That v. pays homage to virtue BUTLER, S, 24
  The only sensual pleasure without v. JOHNSON, S, 36
  there is no distinction between virtue and v. JOHNSON, S, 61

This v. brings in one hundred million francs . . . every year
NAPOLEON III, 1
three great evils, boredom, v., and poverty VOLTAIRE, 5
V. and virtues are products TAINE, H, 1
V. is its own reward CRISP, Q, 6
V. is often clothed PROVERBS, 450
V. itself lost half its evil BURKE, E, 6
When v. prevails ADDISON, J, 5
vices It's your combination sinners . . . who dishonour the v.
WILDER, T, 3
most v. may be committed very genteelly BOSWELL, J, 2
one of the v. of our age VIGNY, A, 3
small v. do appear SHAKESPEARE, W, 147
virtues and v. couple with one another HALIFAX, MARQUIS OF, 4
virtues are . . . v. in disguise ROCHEFOUCAULD, DUC DE LA, 27
We make ourselves a ladder out of our v.
AUGUSTINE OF HIPPO, 5
Vichy There's something V. about the French NOVELLO, I, 2
vicious can't expect a boy to be v. SAKI, 15
He was a v. man, but very kind JOHNSON, S, 42
victim more easily fall v. to a big lie HITLER, A, 3
v. must be found /I've got a little list GILBERT, SIR W, 25
victims Every reformation must have its v. SAKI, 19
Man is the only animal that can remain on friendly terms with the
v. . . . he eats BUTLER, S, 20
The little v. play GRAY, T, 9
v. who respect their executioners SARTRE, J, 1
victor happy state of getting the v.'s palm without the dust of
racing HORACE, 14
Victoria take a ticket at V. Station BEVIN, E, 2
Victorian the most antagonistic to the V. age WILSON, E, 1
V. values . . . were the values when our country THATCHER, M, 10
Victorians The V. had not been anxious to go away WHITE, T, 1
victorious Peace hath her v. MILTON, J, 58
victorious Send him v. CAREY, H, 1
victory Before Alamein we never had a v. CHURCHILL, SIR W, 8
death is swallowed up in v. BIBLE: I CORINTHIANS, 23
every v. turns into a defeat BEAUVOIR, S, 4
in v. unbearable CHURCHILL, SIR W, 25
In . . . war it is not right that matters, but v. HITLER, A, 5
O grave! where is thy v. POPE, A, 4
Such another v. and we are ruined PYRRHUS, 1
to gain such a v. as this WELLINGTON, DUKE OF, 10
'twas a famous v. SOUTHEY, R, 1
V. at all costs CHURCHILL, SIR W, 42
V. has a thousand fathers KENNEDY, J, 16
v. under the belly of a Cossack's horse TROTSKY, L, 4
without v. there is no survival CHURCHILL, SIR W, 42
vidders be very careful o' v. DICKENS, C, 42
vieillesse si v. pouvait ESTIENNE, H, 1
Vietnam To win in V. SPOCK, B. 1
V. was lost in the living rooms of America MCLUHAN, M, 6
vigilance eternal v. CURRAN, J, 1
vile every prospect pleases, /And only man is v. HEBER, R, 2
orgies are v. NASH, O, 5
vilest the v. specimens of human nature are . . . found among
demagogues MACAULAY, BARON, 10
village the world in the image of a global v. MCLUHAN, M, 1
villages world poverty is primarily a problem of two million v.
SCHUMACHER, E, 1
villains Children should acquire . . . heroes and v. from fiction
AUDEN, W, 2
God should go before such v. SHAKESPEARE, W, 216
vine I am the true v. BIBLE: JOHN, 35
thy wife shall be as the fruitful v. PSALMS, 80
With v. leaves in his hair IBSEN, H, 5
vines the little foxes, that spoil the v. BIBLE: SONG OF SOLOMON, 6
vino In v. veritas PLINY THE ELDER, 4
vintage He is trampling out the v. where the grapes of wrath
HOWE, J, 1
O, for a draught of v. KEATS, J, 31
violate men never v. the laws of God without suffering the
consequences CHILD, L, 1
violence v. masquerading as love LAING, R, 4
violent I expect no very v. transition SEDGWICK, C. 1
virtue in ambition is v.
BACON, 1ST BARON VERULAM, VISCOUNT ST ALBANS, 29
violet My regret /Becomes an April v. TENNYSON, BARON, 33
violets Good God, I forgot the v. LANDOR, W, 6
violin an orangutang trying to play the v. BALZAC, H, 3
If the Almighty himself played the v. HEIFETZ, J, 1

vipers O generation of v. BIBLE: MATTHEW, 4
virgin a v. shall conceive BIBLE: ISAIAH, 10
v. territory for whorehouses CAPONE, A, 2
Virginia Woolf Afraid of V. ALBEE, E, 3
V. SITWELL, DAME E, 6
virginity Age . . . nor custom stale her infinite v. WEBSTER, D, 1
a little more v., if you don't mind TREE, SIR H, 10
that v. could be a virtue VOLTAIRE, 16
virgins those v. arose, and trimmed their lamps
BIBLE: MATTHEW, 70
virtue adversity doth best discover v.
BACON, 1ST BARON VERULAM, VISCOUNT ST ALBANS, 8
as some men toil after v. LAMB, C, 20
Crime, like v., has its degrees RACINE, J, 4
Fine words . . . seldom associated with v. CONFUCIUS, 6
forbearance ceases to be a v. BURKE, E, 3
greatest offence against v. HAZLITT, W, 12
Let the blessing . . . be . . . upon all that are lovers of v.; . . . and
go a-Angling WALTON, I, 6
moderation in the pursuit of justice is no v. GOLDWATER, B, 2
Most men admire /V. MILTON, J, 48
much v. in If SHAKESPEARE, W, 32
My v.'s still far too small COLETTE, S, 3
name a v. that brings in as much revenue NAPOLEON III, 1
no v. like necessity SHAKESPEARE, W, 236
Self-denial is not a v. SHAW, G, 27
That vice pays homage to v. BUTLER, S, 24
there is no distinction between v. and vice JOHNSON, S, 61
to practise five things . . . constitutes perfect v. CONFUCIUS, 9
v. in ambition is violent
BACON, 1ST BARON VERULAM, VISCOUNT ST ALBANS, 29
V. is like a rich stone
BACON, 1ST BARON VERULAM, VISCOUNT ST ALBANS, 11
Woman's v. is man's greatest invention. SKINNER, C, 1
virtues ape-like v. without which CONNOLLY, C, 3
few v. . . . the Poles do not possess CHURCHILL, SIR W, 56
greater v. to sustain good fortune ROCHEFOUCAULD, DUC DE LA, 3
No one gossips about . . . secret v. RUSSELL, B, 14
v. and vices couple with one another HALIFAX, MARQUIS OF, 4
v. are . . . vices in disguise ROCHEFOUCAULD, DUC DE LA, 27
Vice and v. are products TAINE, H, 1
v. /We write in water SHAKESPEARE, W, 105
What men call social v., . . . is . . . but the virtue of pigs in a litter
THOREAU, H, 5
world to hide v. in SHAKESPEARE, W, 286
virtuous all the Sisters v. NEWCASTLE, DUCHESS OF, 1
the v. poor WILDE, O, 50
When men grow v. in their old age POPE, A, 54
who can find a v. woman BIBLE: PROVERBS, 17
visage Sir Launcelot saw her v., but he wept not greatly
MALORY, SIR T, 1
vision The young men's v., and the old men's dream DRYDEN, J, 12
turn to the wider v. of the Commonwealth
MACMILLAN, EARL OF STOCKTON, 2
visionary Whither is fled the v. gleam WORDSWORTH, W, 23
visited he hath v. and redeemed his people BIBLE: LUKE, 4
visits Its v., /Like those of angels BLAIR, R, 2
vital v. lampada LUCRETIUS, 3
vitality a symptom of deficient v. STEVENSON, R, 17
The lower one's v. BEERBOHM, SIR M, 8
vivify quarrels which v. its barrenness GREER, G, 3
vogue It is charming to totter into v.
WALPOLE, 4TH EARL OF ORFORD, 5
voice a bird of the air shall carry the v. BIBLE: ECCLESIASTES, 22
a great v., as of a trumpet BIBLE: REVELATIONS, 1
a still small v. BIBLE: I KINGS, 7
A still small v. TENNYSON, BARON, 75
Conscience is the inner v. MENCKEN, H, 2
his v. as the sound of many waters BIBLE: REVELATIONS, 1
the dead shall hear the v. of the Son of God BIBLE: JOHN, 14
The higher the v. NEWMAN, E, 2
The melting v. through mazes running MILTON, J, 15
the sheep . . . know his v. BIBLE: JOHN, 24
the v. of my beloved BIBLE: SONG OF SOLOMON, 4
The v. of the intellect is a soft one FREUD, S, 1
the v. of the Lord breaketh the cedar-trees PSALMS, 18
the v. of the turtle is heard BIBLE: SONG OF SOLOMON, 5
to-day if ye will hear his v. PSALMS, 62
v. of the people is the v. of God ALCUIN, 1
voices Two v. . . . one is of the sea, /One of the mountains
WORDSWORTH, W, 58

# W

though hell should bar the w. NOYES, A, 2
Through Eden took their solitary w. MILTON, J, 47
w. of all flesh CONGREVE, W, 10
w. of all flesh SHADWELL, T, 2
woman has her w. HOLMES, O, 1
**Wayne** John W. is dead ANONYMOUS, 50
**ways** consider your w. BIBLE: HAGGAI, 1
She dwelt among the untrodden w. WORDSWORTH, W, 43
thou . . . spiest out all my w. PSALMS, 84
**we** put it down a w. DICKENS, C, 49
**weak** Beauty stands /In the admiration . . . of w. minds
MILTON, J, 49
concessions of the w. BURKE, E, 11
disarm the strong and arm the w. FRANCE, A, 2
Idleness . . . the refuge of w. minds CHESTERFIELD, 4TH EARL OF, 11
I inhabit a w., frail, decayed tenement ADAMS, J, 2
Is thy love a plant /Of such w. fibre WORDSWORTH, W, 20
Like all w. men . . . an exaggerated stress MAUGHAM, W, 11
surely the w. shall perish SERVICE, R, 3
The w. have one weapon BIDAULT, G, 1
**weaker** the w. vessel BIBLE: I PETER, 4
**weakest** The w. goes to the wall PROVERBS, 428
**weakness** no more w. than is natural to her sex THUCYDIDES, 2
**weaknesses** I have got lots of human w. THATCHER, M, 11
Never support two w. WILDER, T, 3
touch his w. with a delicate hand GOLDSMITH, O, 13
**weal** I will govern according to the common w. JAMES I, 3
**wealth** His w. a well-spent age CAMPION, T, 4
Outshone the w. of Ormus and of Ind MILTON, J, 34
the insolence of w. JOHNSON, S, 121
W. has never been a sufficient source of honour GALBRAITH, J, 2
Where w. and freedom reign, contentment fails GOLDSMITH, O, 21
W. I ask not STEVENSON, R, 4
W. is like sea-water SCHOPENHAUER, A, 8
W. is not without its advantages GALBRAITH, J, 1
**wealthy** Where some people are very w. and others have nothing
ARISTOTLE, 8
**weaned** w. on a pickle LONGWORTH, A, 1
**weapon** art is not a w. KENNEDY, J, 15
In the sex-war thoughtlessness is the w. of the male
CONNOLLY, C, 14
The weak have one w. BIDAULT, G, 1
tinned food is a deadlier w. ORWELL, G, 22
**weapons** books are w. ROOSEVELT, F, 14
on this wall will hang my w. and my lyre, discharged from the war HORACE, 38
**wear** I . . . chose my wife . . . for . . . such qualities as would w. well GOLDSMITH, O, 24
I want you to w. me FITZGERALD, Z, 2
you'll w. your eyes out ZOLA, E, 1
**weariest** The w. nights . . . must . . . end ORCZY, BARONESS, 2
**weariness** much study is a w. of the flesh BIBLE: ECCLESIASTES, 25
The w., the fever, and the fret KEATS, J, 33
**weary** Art thou w. NEALE, J, 1
let us not be w. in well doing BIBLE: GALATIANS, 6
**weather** even the w. forecast seemed to be some kind of spoof LODGE, D, 4
I like the w. BYRON, 6TH BARON, 4
This is the w. the cuckoo likes HARDY, T, 8
This is the w. the shepherd shuns HARDY, T, 9
When two Englishmen meet, their first talk is of the w.
JOHNSON, S, 12
**weather-eye** Keep your w. open PROVERBS, 242
**weather-wise** Some are w. FRANKLIN, B, 4
**web** The w. of our life is of a mingled yarn SHAKESPEARE, W, 2
**webs** Laws are like spider's w. SOLON, 2
**weddings** w. is sadder than funerals BEHAN, B, 6
**Wednesday** Married on W. NURSERY RHYMES, 53
W.'s child is full of woe NURSERY RHYMES, 35
**wee** W., . . . tim'rous beastie BURNS, R, 19
**weed** that tawney w. tobacco JONSON, B, 2
What is a w.? EMERSON, R, 15
**weeds** Lilies that fester smell far worse than w.
SHAKESPEARE, W, 262
nature runs either to herbs, or to w.
BACON, 1ST BARON VERULAM, VISCOUNT ST ALBANS, 37
Worthless as wither'd w. BRONTE, E, 2
**week** A w. is a long time in politics WILSON OF RIEVAULX, BARON, 11
greatest w. . . . since the creation NIXON, R, 6
Of all the days that's in the w. CAREY, H, 2
the greatest w. in the history of the world NIXON, R, 6

**weekendmanship** that basic w. should contain some reference to Important Person Play POTTER, S, 4
**weep** By the waters of Babylon we sit down and w.
WALPOLE, 4TH EARL OF ORFORD, 7
Fair daffodils, we w. to see HERRICK, R, 4
For men must work, and women must w. KINGSLEY, C, 7
not to w. at them, nor to hate them, but to understand them
SPINOZA, B, 5
She must w. or she will die TENNYSON, BARON, 63
so that I do not w. BEAUMARCHAIS, P, 1
Tears such as angels w. MILTON, J, 31
w. for her sins at the other CARY, J, 1
W. no more, my lady FOSTER, S, 2
**weeping** Do you hear the children w. BROWNING, E, 2
Why are you w.? Did you imagine that I was immortal
LOUIS XIV, 7
**weigh** my innocence begins to w. me down RACINE, J, 2
**weighed** thou art w. in the balances, and art found wanting
BIBLE: DANIEL, 8
**weight** the w. of rages CARLYLE, T, 5
**welcome** Advice is seldom w. CHESTERFIELD, 4TH EARL OF, 8
Love bade me w. HERBERT, G, 6
Thrice w., darling of the spring WORDSWORTH, W, 69
**well** as rare as a w.-spent one CARLYLE, T, 5
At last I am going to be w. SCARRON, P, 1
A w.-written Life CARLYLE, T, 5
do not speak w. of yourself PASCAL, B, 4
I am not w.; pray get me . . . brandy GEORGE IV, 1
lov'd not wisely, but too w. SHAKESPEARE, W, 229
nothing . . . and did it very w. GILBERT, SIR W, 20
reward of a thing w. done EMERSON, R, 9
The celebrity . . . known for his w.-knownness BOORSTIN, D, 1
There are two things which I am confident I can do very w.
JOHNSON, S, 49
the world's work, . . . is done by men who do not feel . . . w.
GALBRAITH, J, 6
the w.-tuned cymbals PSALMS, 94
W. building hath three Conditions WOTTON, SIR H, 1
We never do anything w. HAZLITT, W, 25
worth doing w. CHESTERFIELD, 4TH EARL OF, 2
**well-bred** a w. sort of emotional anarchy LAWRENCE, D, 14
**well-dressed** The sense of being w. FORBES, C, 1
**well off** as w. as if he were rich ASTOR, J, 1
**Welsh** but he wouldn't put up with the W. MORTIMER, J, 1
The W. . . . just sing WAUGH, E, 12
**Wembley** W., adj. Suffering from a vague *malaise* JENNINGS, P, 2
**wen** the fate of the great w. COBBETT, W, 3
**Wenceslas** Good King W. looked out NEALE, J, 2
**wench** beside the w. is dead MARLOWE, C, 11
**Wenlock Edge** On W. the wood's in trouble; /His forest fleece the Wrekin heaves HOUSMAN, A, 11
**went** as cooks go she w. SAKI, 16
**wept** by the waters of Babylon we . . . w. PSALMS, 83
Jesus w. BIBLE: JOHN, 28
They w. like anything to see CARROLL, L, 24
young man who has not w. SANTAYANA, G, 2
**west** closing time in the gardens of the W. CONNOLLY, C, 1
East is East, and W. is W. KIPLING, R, 1
Go W., young man GREELEY, H, 1
Go W., young man SOULE, J, 1
the safeguard of the w. WORDSWORTH, W, 53
**western** W. philosophy is, . . . a series of footnotes to Plato's philosophy WHITEHEAD, A, 6
**wet** -joly whistle wel y-w. CHAUCER, G, 16
out of these w. clothes and into a dry Martini WOOLLCOTT, A, 2
**whale** A w. ship was my Yale College MELVILLE, H, 2
Very like a w. SHAKESPEARE, W, 68
**what** Aye, and w. then COLERIDGE, S, 2
W. is truth BACON, 1ST BARON VERULAM, VISCOUNT ST ALBANS, 56
**wheat** An editor . . . separates the w. from the chaff
STEVENSON, A, 1
**wheel** bound upon a w. of fire SHAKESPEARE, W, 150
**wheels** A cruel story runs on w. OUIDA, 4
spoke among your w. BEAUMONT, F, 5
**when** have they fixed the where and w.? HAWKER, R, 1
w. a man should marry
BACON, 1ST BARON VERULAM, VISCOUNT ST ALBANS, 35
**where** have they fixed the w. and when? HAWKER, R, 2
to die, and go we know not w. SHAKESPEARE, W, 184
W. are you now HOPE, L, 2
W. were you fellows when the paper was blank ALLEN, F, 2

When a man is in doubt about . . . his w. BUTLER, S, 12
W. . . . is but a different name for conversation STERNE, L, 7
W. is like getting married MURDOCH, DAME I, 2
**writings** historians left blanks in their w. POUND, E, 6
**written** Books are well w., or badly w. WILDE, O, 41
books . . . w. by people who don't understand them LICHTENBERG, G, 2
in thy book were all my members w. PSALMS, 87
what I have w. I have w. BIBLE: JOHN, 48
. . . you would have been very glad if I had w. it PIRON, A, 1
**wromantic** Cavaliers (Wrong but W.) SELLAR, W, 5
**wrong** A door is what a dog is . . . on the w. side of NASH, O, 2
A man should . . . own he has been in the w. POPE, A, 52
anxious to do the w. thing correctly SAKI, 20
History is . . . the w. way of living DURRELL, L, 3
Holders of one position, w. for years AUDEN, W, 23
If anything can go w. PROVERBS, 212
I . . . may not always be right, but I am never w. GOLDWYN, S, 6
I was w. to have *thought* that I was w. DULLES, J, 1
Of course not . . . I may be w. RUSSELL, EARL, 29
orthodoxy . . . practically means being w. CHESTERTON, G, 13
our country, right or w. DECATUR, S, 1
right deed for the w. reason ELIOT, T, 16
sentimentality . . . rubs you up the w. way MAUGHAM, W, 25
something is impossible, he is . . . w. CLARKE, A, 1
something w. with our bloody ships BEATTY, 1ST EARL, 1
support me when I am . . . w. MELBOURNE, VISCOUNT, 2
their authors could not endure being w. CAMUS, A, 4
The multitude is always in the w. ROSCOMMON, EARL OF, 2
The right divine of kings to govern w. POPE, A, 2
the unclouded face of truth suffer w. SCOTT, C, 1
The w. sort of people are always in power WYNNE-TYSON, J, 1
The w. war, at the w. place BRADLEY, O, 2
W. from the start POUND, E, 10
When women go w. WEST, M, 12
**wrongdoing** W. can only be avoided if SOLON, 1
**wronged** Not to be w. is to forgo . . . goodness WELLS, H, 2
**wrongs** for one class to appreciate the w. of another STANTON, E, 3
Two w. do not make a right PROVERBS, 447

## XYZ

**Xanadu** In X. did Kubla Khan COLERIDGE, S, 12
**X-ray** to replace X. by hearsay THOMAS, G, 4
**yacht** I had to sink my y. to make my guests go home FITZGERALD, F, 4
**Yale** all the young ladies who attended the Y. promenade dance PARKER, D, 13
A whale ship was my Y. College MELVILLE, H, 2
**Yankee** Y. Doodle came to town BANGS, E, 1
Y. Doodle came to town NURSERY RHYMES, 74
**yard** a y. . . . 3.37 inches longer than other people's COREN, A, 3
**yarn** web of our life is of a mingled y. SHAKESPEARE, W, 2
**yawn** When a book is boring, they y. openly SINGER, I, 1
**yawns** grave y. for him TREE, SIR H, 3
**year** all the y. were playing holidays SHAKESPEARE, W, 77
Another y.! – another deadly blow WORDSWORTH, W, 46
each day is like a y. WILDE, O, 6
I said to the man who stood at the gate of the y. HASKINS, M, 1
Let it be kept till the ninth y. HORACE, 11
Not to hope for things to last for ever, is what the y. teaches HORACE, 41
That time of y. thou mayst in me behold SHAKESPEARE, W, 260
two months of every y. BYRON, 6TH BARON, 4
y.'s at the spring BROWNING, R, 43
**yearning** learning, earning and y. MORLEY, C, 1
**years** After long y. BYRON, 6TH BARON, 41
a thousand y. . . . are but as yesterday PSALMS, 55
he that cuts off twenty y. of life SHAKESPEARE, W, 111
how many y. can some people exist DYLAN, B, 2
I have been talking prose for over forty y. MOLIÈRE, 3
It will keep for y. LEACOCK, S, 4
One thousand y. more. That's all *Homo sapiens* has before him WELLS, H, 20
world must be made safe for . . . fifty y. CHURCHILL, SIR W, 2
Y. hence, perhaps, may dawn an age ARNOLD, M, 18
y. of discretion BOOK OF COMMON PRAYER, 11
**Yeats** In Drumcliff churchyard Y. is laid YEATS, W, 30
**yes** . . . girls . . . say No when they mean Y. ALCOTT, L, 2
**yesterday** a thousand years . . . are but as y. PSALMS, 55
wiser to-day than . . . y. POPE, A, 52

**yesterdays** And all our y. SHAKESPEARE, W, 177
**yesteryear** snows of y. VILLON, F, 1
**yet** A young man not y. A young man not y. BACON, 1ST BARON VERULAM, VISCOUNT ST ALBANS, 35
but not y. AUGUSTINE OF HIPPO, 2
My time has not y. come NIETZSCHE, F, 7
**Yeti** little in civilization to appeal to a Y. HILLARY, SIR E, 2
**yld** put the id back in y. ROTH, P, 1
**yield** To strive, to seek . . . and not to y. TENNYSON, BARON, 77
**yo-ho-ho** Y., and a bottle of rum STEVENSON, R, 6
**yoke** good . . . that he bear the y. in his youth BIBLE: LAMENTATIONS, 2
Rome's gross y. /Drops off BROWNING, R, 16
the inevitable y. WORDSWORTH, W, 25
**Yorick** Alas, poor Y. SHAKESPEARE, W, 73
**York** Oh! the grand old Duke of Y. NURSERY RHYMES, 37
**you** For y. but not for me ANONYMOUS, 65
For y. but not for me ANONYMOUS, 65
Y. also OVID, 4
**young** aged diplomats . . . bored than for y. men to die AUSTIN, W, 1
ale from the Country of the Y. YEATS, W, 13
a man of about a hundred and fifty who was rather y. WODEHOUSE, SIR P, 20
A man that is y. in years BACON, 1ST BARON VERULAM, VISCOUNT ST ALBANS, 61
a sight to make an old man y. TENNYSON, BARON, 10
can't put off being y. until you retire LARKIN, P, 1
country of y. men EMERSON, R, 23
first sign of old age: . . . how y. the policemen look HICKS, SIR S, 1
Grieve not that I die y. HASTINGS, F, 1
I am sixty years y. TREE, SIR H, 1
I have been y., and now am old PSALMS, 26
look y. till forty DRYDEN, J, 25
made y. with y. desires THOMPSON, F, 3
man's friends begin to compliment him about looking y. IRVING, W, 1
Most women are not so y. as they are painted BEERBOHM, SIR M, 5
old-fashioned respect for the y. WILDE, O, 20
Political history is far too criminal . . . to be . . . fit . . . for the y. AUDEN, W, 2
The atrocious crime of being a y. man PITT THE ELDER, 1ST EARL OF CHATHAM, 2
The best careers advice to give to the y. WHITEHORN, K, 6
the old have rubbed it into the y. that they are wiser MAUGHAM, W, 3
The y. always have the same problem CRISP, Q, 2
The y. Cambridge group LAWRENCE, D, 14
The y. have aspirations SAKI, 12
to be y. was very heaven WORDSWORTH, W, 35
to make me y. again ADENAUER, K, 1
to make me y. again ADENAUER, K, 1
When all the world is y., lad KINGSLEY, C, 6
You can be y. without money WILLIAMS, T, 2
Y. men make great mistakes in life JOWETT, B, 4
Y. people ought not to be idle THATCHER, M, 16
**younger** I . . . get y. every day TREE, SIR H, 1
**youngest** not even the y. of us THOMPSON, W, 1
**yourself** Better to write for y. CONNOLLY, C, 17
If you do not tell the truth about y. WOOLF, V, 7
If you hate a person, you hate . . . y. HESSE, H, 1
no friends not equal to y. CONFUCIUS, 7
What you do not want done to y. CONFUCIUS, 14
**youth** age and y. cannot live together SHAKESPEARE, W, 230
A y. to whom was given /So much WORDSWORTH, W, 42
everything that is great . . . done by y. DISRAELI, 1ST EARL OF BEACONSFIELD, 2
good . . . that he bear the yoke in his y. BIBLE: LAMENTATIONS, 2
Here rests . . . /A y. to fortune and to fame unknown GRAY, T, 8
high-water mark of my y. THURBER, J, 8
Home-keeping y. SHAKESPEARE, W, 297
if thou has gathered nothing in thy y. BIBLE: ECCLESIASTICUS, 10
I summon age /To grant y.'s heritage BROWNING, R, 47
it is y. that must fight and die HOOVER, H, 2
Lo, Hudled up, together Lye /Grave Age, Grene y., White Infancy ANONYMOUS, 54
man loves the mean in his y. SHAKESPEARE, W, 211
Pride and Truth . . . shake their . . . sides at y. YEATS, W, 22
sign of an ill-spent y. SPENCER, H, 2
the Jazz Age . . . became less and less an affair of y. FITZGERALD, F, 2

the world hath lost his y.      BIBLE: II ESDRAS, 6

Thou hast nor y. nor age      SHAKESPEARE, W, 183

Time, the subtle thief of y.      MILTON, J, 54

y. would sleep out the rest      SHAKESPEARE, W, 301

Y. is a blunder      DISRAELI, 1ST EARL OF BEACONSFIELD, 1

Y. is something very new      CHANEL, C, 2

Y.'s a stuff will not endure      SHAKESPEARE, W, 289

Y. will be served      BORROW, G, 2

Y. will come . . . beat on my door      IBSEN, H, 6

**youthe** Withouten other companye in y.      CHAUCER, G, 10

**Yukon** Law of the Y.      SERVICE, R, 3

**zeal** Not too much z.      TALLEYRAND, 5

stir up the z. of women      MILL, J, 6

**zed** whoreson z.      SHAKESPEARE, W, 134

**zero** My scribbling pays me z. francs per line – not including the

white spaces      ROCHEFORT, MARQUIS DE ROCHEFORT-LUÇAY, 1

**Zion** Beneath this stone, in hope of Z.      ANONYMOUS, 11

**Zürich** the little gnomes of Z.      WILSON OF RIEVAULX, BARON, 6